广东统计年鉴

GUANGDONG STATISTICAL YEARBOOK

2018

（总第34期 No.34）

广　东　省　统　计　局
国家统计局广东调查总队　编

Compiled by
Statistics Bureau of Guangdong Province
Guangdong Survey Office of National Bureau of Statistics

中国统计出版社
China Statistics Press

图书在版编目（C I P）数据

广东统计年鉴. 2018 : 汉英对照 / 广东省统计局, 国家统计局广东调查总队编.
-- 北京 : 中国统计出版社, 2018.8
ISBN 978-7-5037-8528-3

Ⅰ. ①广…
Ⅱ. ①广… ②国…
Ⅲ. ①统计资料－广东－2018－年鉴－汉、英
Ⅳ. ①C832.65-54

中国版本图书馆CIP数据核字(2018)第155060号

广东统计年鉴-2018

作　　者/ 广东省统计局　国家统计局广东调查总队
责任编辑/ 钟钰
责任校对/ 彭惜君　马彦君　国剑敏
装帧设计/ 广州九禾教育信息咨询有限公司
出版发行/ 中国统计出版社
地　　址/ 北京市丰台区西三环南路甲6号
邮政编码/ 100073
电　　话/ 邮购（010）63376909　书店（010）68783171
网　　址/ http://www.zgtjcbs.com
印　　刷/ 广州星河印刷有限公司
经　　销/ 新华书店
开　　本/ 890mm×1240mm　1/16
字　　数/ 1500千字
印　　张/ 46
版　　别/ 2018年8月第1版
版　　次/ 2018年8月第1次印刷
定　　价/ 460.00元　Price:460.00(RMB)

本书附同版本CD-ROM一张，光盘内容以书面文字为准。
如有印装差错，由本社发行部调换。

2018

编者说明

一、《广东统计年鉴－2018》(下简称《年鉴》)系统收录了全省及各市、县（区）2017年经济、社会各方面的统计数据，以及1978年以来各个主要时期全省主要统计数据，是一部全面反映广东国民经济和社会发展情况的资料性年刊。

二、本《年鉴》正文内容分为22个篇章，即：1.综合；2.国民经济核算；3.人口；4.就业和工资；5.固定资产投资；6.对外经济；7.能源、资源和环境；8.财政、银行和保险；9.价格；10.人民生活；11.农业；12.工业；13.建筑业；14.规模以上服务业；15.运输和邮电；16.批发零售业；17.住宿餐饮业和旅游；18.教育和科技；19.文化和体育；20.卫生、社会福利、社会保障和其他；21.区域经济主要指标；22.县（市、区）主要经济指标。同时，附录有4个篇章：1.全国31个省(市)主要统计指标；2.中国香港特别行政区和中国澳门特别行政区主要统计资料；3.中国台湾省主要统计指标；4.部分国家和地区主要统计资料。为方便读者使用，各篇章前设有《简要说明》，对本篇章的主要内容、资料来源、统计范围、统计方法以及历史变动情况予以简要概述，篇末附有《主要统计指标解释》。

三、本《年鉴》资料主要来自政府各级统计局、国家统计局调查总队的各种定期统计报表和抽样调查资料；部分资料来自中央部属单位和省直有关部门。附录资料根据国家统计局有关资料整理。

四、本年鉴涉及珠江三角洲、东翼、西翼和山区的具体划分为：

珠江三角洲包括：广州、深圳、珠海、佛山、江门、东莞、中山、惠州和肇庆。

东翼指汕头、汕　、潮州和揭阳。

西翼指湛江、茂名和阳江。

山区指韶关、河源、梅州、清远和云浮。

五、资料中所使用的度量衡单位，除灌溉、播种面积照顾我国使用习惯继续用“亩”为单位外，其余均采用国际统一标准计量单位。

六、本年鉴中涉及到的历史数据，均以最新出版的本年鉴数据为准;本年鉴中部分数据合计数或相对数由于单位取舍不同而产生的计算误差，均未做机械调整。

七、本《年鉴》统计表中的符号使用说明：

“…”表示数据不足本表最小单位数；

“#”表示其中主要项；

“空格”表示该项统计指标数据不详或无该项数据；

“①”表示本表下有注解。

八、与2017年版《广东统计年鉴》相比较，本《年鉴》在内容上主要做了如下修订：“综合”增加国民经济和社会发展比例和效益指标数据；“核算”根据新的研发支出核算方法对历史数据进行调整以反映地区生产总值包含研发投入情况；“人口”增加常住人口年龄结构和抚养比、按城镇和性别分常住人口历史年份数据；“进出口”增加按人民币计价的历史年份进出口数据；“人民生活”增加按五等分分组的常住居民耐用消费品拥有量和分市人均可支配收入来源等数据；“农业”增加反映农业生产条件表和历史年份畜产品和水产品情况数据；“教育和科技”增加规模以上工业企业研发活动情况和研发经费支出结构等数据；根据新的部门报表制度对个别专业内容及相关统计指标进行了调整。

本《年鉴》在整理编辑过程中，得到省直有关部门和单位的大力支持，在此表示感谢!

EDITOR' S NOTES

Ⅰ. Guangdong Statistical Yearbook 2018 (hereinafter referred to as the Yearbook) is an annual statistical publication, which reflects comprehensively the economic and social development of Guangdong Province. It covers data for 2017 and key statistical data in some historically important years since 1978 at the provincial level and the local levels of city, county and district.

Ⅱ. The Yearbook contains twenty-two chapters: 1. General Survey; 2. National Accounts; 3. Population; 4. Employment and Wages; 5. Investment in Fixed Assets; 6. Foreign Trade and Economic Cooperation ; 7. Energy, Resources and Environment ; 8. Government Finance, Banking and Insurance; 9. Prices; 10. People's Living Conditions; 11. Agriculture; 12. Industry; 13. Service Enterprises Above Designated Size; 14.Construction; 15. Transport, Postal and Telecommunication Services; 16. Wholesale , Retail Trades and Tourism; 17. Hotels, Catering Services and Tourism; 18. Education, Science and Technology; 19 Culture and Sports. 20.Public Health, Social Welfare, Social Insurance and Others; 21. Main Economic Indicators of Economic Regions; 22. Main Economic Indicators of Counties (County-level Cities) and Districts. Meanwhile, four chapters are listed as appendices: 1. Main Statistical Indicators of 31 Provinces and Municipalities; 2. Main Statistics of Hong Kong and Macao Special Administrative Regions; 3. Main Statistical Indicators of Taiwan Province; 4. Main Statistics of Some Countries and Territories. To facilitate readers, the Brief Introduction at the beginning of each chapter provides a summary of the main contents of the chapter, data sources, statistical scope, statistical methods and historical changes. At the end of each chapter, Explanatory Notes on Main Statistical Indicators are included.

Ⅲ. The data in the Yearbook are mainly obtained from regular statistical reports and sample surveys conducted by the statistical bureaus of all levels of government and the Survey Office of the National Bureau of Statistics in Guangdong. Some data are collected from the departments of the central government and the provincial government. Data in the appendices are compiled from statistical publications published by the National Bureau of Statistics and other sources.

Ⅳ. The pearl river delta, east wing, west wing and mountainous areas in the Yearbook are divided as following:

The pearl river delta include Guangzhou, Shenzhen, Zhuhai, Foshan, Jiangmen, Dongguan, Zhongshan, Huizhou and Zhaoqing.

The east wing includes Shantou, Shanwei, Chaozhou and Jieyang.

The west wing includes Zhanjiang, Maoming and Yangjiang.

The mountainous areas include Shaoguan, Heyuan, Meizhou, Qingyuan and Yunfu.

Ⅴ. The units of measurement used in the Yearbook are internationally standard measurement units, except that the unit of cultivated land and sown areas uses "mu" with regard to the Chinese tradition.

Ⅵ. Please refer to the newly published version of the Yearbook for updated historical data.Statistical discrepancies on totals and relative figures due to rounding are not adjusted in the Yearbook.

Ⅶ. Notations used in the Yearbook:

" … " indicates that the figure is not large enough to be measured with the smallest unit in the table;

" # " indicates a major breakdown of the total;

" blank space " indicates that the data are unknown or are not available;

" ① " indicates footnotes at the end of the table.

Ⅷ. In comparison with Guangdong Statistical Yearbook 2017, following revisions have been made in this new version in terms of the statistical contents and in editing: Of the chapter of " General Survey" , data of indicators on national economic and social development are added. Of the chapter of " National Economic Account" , historical data of GDP has been revised according to the new accounting methodology of expenditure for research and development. Of the chapter of " Population" , data of age composition and dependency ratio of permanent population, and data of composition of permanent population are added. Of the chapter of " People's Living Condition" , data of grouped by five equal shares of number of major durable consumer goods income and expenditure owned per100 rural and urban permanent households at year-end, and data of per capita disposable income of permanent households by sources and city are added. Of the chapter of " Education and Technology" , data of R&D expenditure by above designated industry and its composition are added. Of the chapter of " Agriculture" , data of agriculture production basic conditions and historical data of output of aquatic products and livestock products are added. Of the chapter of " Foreign trade and Economic Cooperation" , indicators of export and import of goods in RMB are added. According to the new departmental reporting system, some professional contents and indicators have been adjusted.

Acknowledgements: our gratitude goes to relevant departments and units under the provincial government, from which we have received tremendous support when compiling the Yearbook.

《广东统计年鉴—2018》编委会和编辑出版人员

编委会

主　任：杨新洪　赵云城

副主任：朱遂文　杨骁婷　刘智华　梁　彦　杨少浪　熊德国

黄碧玲　邓远军　夏泽宽　田秀华　黄　丹

编　委（以姓氏笔画为序）：

王丽莹　王　彪　刘广荣　孙华标　李良胜
李珠桥　李新娇　杨　凡　邱国祥　张汉杰
张锦平　郑祖辉　徐　谦　黄日何　黄俊彪
彭黄磊　蓝品良

编辑工作人员

编辑部主任：王丽莹　彭黄磊

责 任 编 辑：彭惜君　马彦君　国剑敏

编辑人员（以姓氏笔画为序）：

马　佳　王学良　王　晴　王慧艳　叶卫红
叶　田　田志峰　汤　良　严　洁　李金晶
李昭曼　李奕思　李　晶　杨际昌　杨　健
吴　娱　余少玲　邹　聪　张作丹　张建梅
陈东清　陈仕燕　陈丽芬　陈　颖　国剑敏
周媛媛　徐　可　黄平光　黄海燕　黄　楠
曹文群　谢洪芳　赖晓燕　翟　丰

英文翻译：廖卓希

出版发行人员：严继发

光盘责任编辑：熊　威

Guangdong Statistical Yearbook – 2018
EDITORIAL BOARD AND STAFF

目 录
CONTENTS

一、综合
General Survey

简要说明 …… (2)
Brief Introduction

1-1 行政区划 (2017 年) …… (3)
Divisions of Administrative Areas (2017)

1-2 国民经济和社会发展总量与速度指标 …… (4)
Principal Aggregate Indicators on National Economic and Social Development and Growth Rates

1-3 国民经济和社会发展结构指标 …… (12)
Composition Indicators of National Economic and Social Development

1-4 国民经济和社会发展比例和效益指标 …… (16)
Indicators on National Economic and Social Development

1-5 国民经济和社会发展主要指标占全国比重 …… (18)
Percentage of National Total of Main Indicators of Economic and Social Development of Guangdong

1-6 各部门机构数 …… (20)
Grassroots Units in Various Sectors

1-7 法人和产业活动单位数 …… (21)
Number of Corporate Units and Industrial Establishments

1-8 各市法人和产业活动单位数 …… (22)
Number of Corporate Units and Industrial Establishments by City

1-9 按行业和登记注册类型分组的法人单位数 (2017 年) …… (23)
Number of Corporate Units by Sector and by Status of Registration (2017)

1-10 各市按机构类型分法人单位数 (2017 年) …… (27)
Number of Corporate Units by Type by City (2017)

1-11 各市按行业分法人单位数 (2017 年) …… (28)
Number of Corporate Units by Sector by City (2017)

1-12 各市按注册类型分法人单位数 (2017 年) …… (32)
Number of Corporate Units by Status of Registration by City (2017)

1-13 民营经济主要指标 …… (36)
Main Indicators on Private Economy

1-14 全省商品、服务类电子商务交易情况 …… (37)
E-commerce transactions in commodities and services of Guangdong

主要统计指标解释 …… (38)
Explanatory Notes on Main Statistical Indicators

二、国民经济核算
National Economic Accounts

简要说明 …… (46)
Brief Introduction

2-1 国民经济核算主要指标 …… (47)
Main Indicators of Gross Domestic Product

2-2 地区生产总值 …… (48)
Gross Domestic Product

2-3 地区生产总值指数 …… (49)
Indices of Gross Domestic Product

2-4 地区生产总值指数 …… (50)
Indices of Gross Domestic Product

2-5 地区生产总值产业构成 …… (51)
Composition of Gross Domestic Product by Industry

2-6 三次产业贡献率 …… (52)
Share of the Contributions of the Three Strata of Industry

2-7 三次产业对地区生产总值增长的拉动 …… (53)
Contribution of the Three Strata of Industry to GDP Growth

2-8 地区生产总值项目结构 …… (54)
Components of Gross Domestic Product

2-9 各行业收入法增加值构成项目 (2017 年) …… (55)
Components of Value Added by Sector (2017)

2-10 支出法地区生产总值 …… (56)
Gross Domestic Product by Expenditure Approach

2-11 资本形成总额及构成 …… (57)
Gross Capital Formation and Its Composition

2-12 最终消费及构成 …… (58)
Final Consumption Expenditure and Its Composition

2-13 三大需求对地区生产总值增长的贡献率和拉动 …… (59)
Contribution Share and Contribution of the Three Components of GDP to GDP Growth

2-14 人均地区生产总值及人均消费水平 …… (60)
Per Capita Gross Domestic Product and Consumption

2-15 人均地区生产总值及人均消费水平指数 …… (61)
Indices of Per Capita Gross Domestic Product and Consumption

2-16 各市地区生产总值 …… (62)
Gross Domestic Product by City

2-17 各市地区生产总值指数 …… (64)
Indices of Gross Domestic Product by City

2-18 各市第一产业增加值 …… (66)
Value-added of the Tertiary Industry by City
2-19 各市第二产业增加值 …… (67)
Value-added of the Tertiary Industry by City
2-20 各市第三产业增加值 …… (68)
Value-added of the Tertiary Industry by City
2-21 各市第一产业增加值指数 …… (69)
Indices of Value-added of the Tertiary Industry by City
2-22 各市第二产业增加值指数 …… (70)
Indices of Value-added of the Tertiary Industry by City
2-23 各市第三产业增加值指数 …… (71)
Indices of Value-added of the Tertiary Industry by City
2-24 各市地区生产总值 (2017 年) …… (72)
Gross Domestic Product by City (2017)
2-25 各市地区生产总值指数 (2017 年) …… (74)
Growth Index of Gross Domestic Product by City (2017)
2-26 各市地区生产总值产业构成 (2017 年) …… (76)
Composition of Gross Domestic Product by Industry by City (2017)
2-27 各市支出法地区生产总值 (2017 年) …… (77)
Gross Domestic Product by Expenditure Approach by City (2017)
2-28 各市资本形成总额及构成 (2017 年) …… (78)
Gross Capital Formation and Its Composition by City (2017)
2-29 各市最终消费及构成 (2017 年) …… (79)
Final Consumption Expenditure and Its Composition by City (2017)
2-30 各市人均地区生产总值 …… (80)
Per Capita Gross Domestic Product by City
2-31 各市人均地区生产总值指数 …… (82)
Indices of Per Capita Gross Domestic Product by City
2-32 各市人均地区生产总值指数 …… (84)
Indices of Per Capita Gross Domestic Product by City
2-33 全省生产性服务业增加值 …… (86)
Value-added of Productive Service Industry
主要统计指标解释 …… (87)
Explanatory Notes on Main Statistical Indicators

三、人口
Population

简要说明 …… (92)
Brief Introduction
3-1 人口主要指标 …… (93)
Main Population Indicators

3-2 人口自然变动情况 …… (94)
Status of Natural Population Changes
3-3 常住人口构成 …… (95)
Composition of Permanent Population
3-4 常住人口年龄结构和抚养比 …… (96)
Age Composition and Dependency Ratio of Permanent Population
3-5 年末户籍总人口 …… (97)
Total Population with Residence Registration at Year-end
3-6 户籍人口迁移变动情况 …… (98)
Status of Migrant Changes
3-7 各市年末常住人口数 …… (99)
Permanent Population at Year-end by City
3-8 各市城镇人口占常住人口的比例 …… (100)
Proportion of Urban Population to Permanent Population by City
3-9 各市年末户籍人口数 (2017 年) …… (101)
Total Population with Residence Registration at Year-end by City (2017)
3-10 各市年末户籍迁移人口数 (2017 年) …… (102)
Number of Migrant Population at the Year-end by City (2017)
主要统计指标解释 …… (103)
Explanatory Notes on Main Statistical Indicators

四、就业和工资
Employment and Wages

简要说明 …… (106)
Brief Introduction
4-1 就业人员主要指标 …… (107)
Main Indicators of Employed Persons
4-2 就业人员年末人数 …… (108)
Number of Employed Persons at the Year-end
4-3 按三次产业分就业人员年末人数 …… (109)
Number of Employed Persons at Year-end by Three strata of Industry
4-4 按各种分组的就业人员年末人数 …… (110)
Number of Employed Persons at the Year-end by Grouping
4-5 各市就业人员年末人数 …… (111)
Number of Employed Persons at the Year-end by City
4-6 各市按三次产业分就业人员年末人数 …… (112)
Number of Employed Persons at the Year-end by Strata of Industry by City
4-7 城镇单位就业人员和在岗职工年末人数 (2017 年) …… (113)
Number of Employed Persons and Fully Employed Staff and Workers in Urban Units at the Year-end (2017)
4-8 各市城镇单位就业人员和在岗职工 (2017 年) …… (115)
Number of Employed Persons and of Fully Employed Staff and Workers in Urban Units by City (2017)

4-9 各市城镇单位各行业在岗职工年末人数 (2017 年) …… (116)
Number of Fully Employed Staff and Workers in Urban Units at the Year-end by Sector and by City (2017)
4-10 城镇单位女性就业人员年末人数 (2017 年) …… (119)
Number of Females Employed in Urban Units at the Year-end (2017)
4-11 城镇单位职工工资总额与年平均工资 …… (120)
Total Wages Bill and Average Wage of Staff and Workers in Urban Units
4-12 各市城镇单位就业人员工资总额和在岗职工年平均工资 (2017 年) …… (121)
Earnings of Employed Persons and Wages of Fully Employed Staff and Workers in Urban Units by City (2017)
4-13 城镇单位就业人员工资总额 (2017 年) …… (122)
Earnings of Employed Persons in Urban Units (2017)
4-14 城镇单位在岗职工工资总额 (2017 年) …… (123)
Total Wages Bill of Fully Employed Staff and Workers in Urban Units (2017)
4-15 城镇单位就业人员年平均工资 (2017 年) …… (124)
Average Earning of Employed Persons in Urban Units (2017)
4-16 城镇单位在岗职工年平均工资 (2017 年) …… (125)
Annual Average Wage of Fully Employed Staff and Workers in Urban Units (2017)
4-17 各市年末城镇登记失业人数 …… (126)
Number of Registered Unemployed Persons in Urban Area at the Year-end by City
主要统计指标解释 …… (127)
Explanatory Notes on Main Statistical Indicators

五、固定资产投资
Investment in Fixed Assets

简要说明 …… (130)
Brief Introduction
5-1 固定资产投资主要指标 …… (131)
Main Indicators of Investment in Fixed Assets
5-2 固定资产投资总额 …… (132)
Investment in Fixed Assets
5-3 按资金来源和构成分固定资产投资 …… (133)
Investment in Fixed Assets by Source of Funds and Structure of Investment
5-4 按构成分固定资产投资 …… (134)
Investment in Fixed Assets by Structure
5-5 各市固定资产投资额 …… (135)
Investment in Fixed Assets by City
5-6 各市按项目和房地产开发分固定资产投资 …… (136)
Investment in Fixed Assets By Project and Real Estate Development and by City
5-7 各市按登记注册类型分固定资产投资 (2017 年) …… (137)
Investment in Fixed Assets by Status of Registration and City (2017)
5-8 各市按主要行业分固定资产投资 (2017 年) …… (139)
Investment in Fixed Assets by Sector and by City (2017)

5-9 国有经济固定资产投资主要指标 …… (142)
Main Indicators of Investment in Fixed Assets of State-owned Economy
5-10 基础产业和基础设施完成投资额 …… (143)
Completed Investment in Basic Industries and Infrastructure
5-11 按行业分固定资产投资主要指标 (2017 年) …… (144)
Main Indicators of Investment by Sector (2017)
5-12 各行业财务拨贷款资金来源主要指标 (2017 年) …… (147)
Main Indicators on Sources of Funds and Loans for Investment by Sector (2017)
5-13 各市财务拨贷款资金来源主要指标 (2017 年) …… (150)
Main Indicators on Sources of Funds and Loans for Investment by City (2017)
5-14 各市按构成和建设性质分固定资产投资 (2017 年) …… (151)
Investment in Fixed Assets in Urban Area by Composition of Funds,Type of Construction and City (2017)
5-15 各市农业、能源、原材料、运输邮电业投资和比重 (2017 年) …… (152)
Volume and Proportion of Investment in Capital Construction of Agriculture, Energy, Raw Materials, Transport, Post and Telecommunications (2017)
5-16 各市工业投资和比重 (2017 年) …… (153)
Investment in Industry and Proportion by City (2017)
5-17 投资效益指标 …… (154)
Indicators on Investment Efficiency
5-18 新增主要生产能力或效益 …… (155)
Newly Increased Production Capacity or Efficiency
5-19 各市施工和竣工面积 (2017 年) …… (156)
Floor Space Under Construction and Floor Space Completed(2017)
5-20 房地产开发主要指标 …… (157)
Main Indicators on Real Estate Development
5-21 房地产开发投资情况 …… (158)
Investment in Real Estate Development
5-22 房地产开发房屋建筑面积及价值 (2017 年) …… (158)
Floor Space and Value of Buildings in Real Estate Development (2017)
5-23 各市房地产开发投资情况 (2017 年) …… (159)
Investment in Real Estate Development by City (2017)
5-24 各市房地产开发房屋建筑面积及价值 (2017 年) …… (160)
Floor Space and Value of Buildings in Real Estate Development by City (2017)
5-25 按用途分商品房屋销售面积 (2017 年) …… (161)
Floor Space of Commercialized Buildings Sold by Use(2017)
5-26 按用途分商品房屋销售额 (2017 年) …… (161)
Sales Volume of Commercialized Buildings Sold by Use(2017)
5-27 各市商品房屋销售情况 (2017 年) …… (162)
Sales of Commercial Buildings by City (2017)
主要统计指标解释 …… (163)
Explanatory Notes on Main Statistical Indicators

六、对外经济
Foreign Economy

简要说明 …… (168)
Brief Introduction

6-1 对外经济主要指标 …… (169)
Main Indicators of Foreign Trade and Economic Cooperation

6-2 人民币对主要外币汇率(年平均价) …… (170)
Reference Exchange Rate of Renminbi (Period Average)

6-3 进出口总额 …… (171)
Total Value of Imports and Exports

6-4 按贸易方式和经济类型分的进出口额(人民币) …… (172)
Total Value of Imports and Exports by Customs Regime and Ownership Type

6-5 按贸易方式和经济类型分的进出口额(美元) …… (172)
Total Value of Imports and Exports by Customs Regime and Ownership Type

6-6 按产品类型分的进出口额 …… (173)
Total Value of Imports and Exports by Product Type

6-7 广东同主要国家(地区)进出口额 (2017 年) …… (174)
Total Value of Imports and Exports with Main Countries and Regions(2017)

6-8 进出口商品分类金额 (2017 年) …… (175)
Total Value of Imports and Exports by Category of Commodities (2017)

6-9 出口主要商品数量和金额 (2017 年) …… (178)
Main Export Commodities in Volume and Value (2017)

6-10 进口主要商品数量和金额 (2017 年) …… (180)
Volume and Value of Main Import Commodities (2017)

6-11 各市出口总额 …… (182)
Total Value of Exports by City

6-12 各市进口总额 …… (183)
Total Value of Imports by City

6-13 各市外商投资企业出口总额 …… (184)
Total Value of Exports of Enterprises with Foreign Investment by City

6-14 各市外商投资企业进口总额 …… (185)
Total Value of Imports of Enterprises with Foreign Investment by City

6-15 外商投资企业进出口主要指标 (2017 年) …… (186)
Main Indicators on Imports and Exports of Enterprises with Foreign Investment(2017)

6-16 外商投资企业出口主要商品数量和金额 (2017 年) …… (187)
Volume and Value of Main Export Commodities of Enterprises with Foreign Investment (2017)

6-17 外商投资企业进口主要商品数量和金额 (2017 年) …… (189)
Volume and Value of Main Import Commodities by Enterprises with Foreign Investment (2017)

6-18 私营企业进出口主要指标 (2017 年) …… (191)
Main Indicators on Imports and Exports of Private Enterprises (2017)

6-19 利用外资情况 …… (192)
Utilization of Foreign Capital

6-20 分方式利用外资 (2017 年) …… (193)
Utilization of Foreign Capital by Type (2017)
6-21 分行业外商直接投资 (2017 年) …… (193)
Foreign Direct Investment by Sector (2017)
6-22 分国别(地区)外商直接投资 …… (194)
Foreign Direct Investment by Country (Region)
6-23 各市外商直接投资 …… (197)
Foreign Direct Investment by City
6-24 对外经济技术合作情况 …… (198)
Economic and Technical Cooperation with Foreign Countries and Regions
6-25 分行业外商投资企业工商注册登记情况 (2017 年末) …… (199)
Registration Status of Enterprises with Foreign Investment by Sector (Year-end of 2017)
6-26 各市外商投资企业工商注册登记情况 (2017 年末) …… (200)
Registration Status of Enterprises with Foreign Investment by City(Year-end of 2017)
6-27 一类口岸开放使用情况 (2017 年末) …… (201)
Opening and Operating Status of Category-1 Ports (Year-end of 2017)
6-28 分国别(地区)对外直接投资 …… (202)
Foreign Direct Investment by Country (Region)
6-29 分行业对外直接投资 …… (203)
Overseas Direct Investment by Sector
主要统计指标解释 …… (204)
Explanatory Notes on Main Statistical Indicators

七、能源、资源和环境

Energy, Resources and Environment

简要说明 …… (208)
Brief Introduction
7-1 能源主要指标 …… (210)
Main Indicators of Energy
7-2 能源生产总量及构成 …… (211)
Total Production of Energy and its Composition
7-3 能源消费总量及构成 …… (211)
Total Consumption of Energy and Its Composition
7-4 综合能源平衡表 …… (212)
Overall Energy Balance Sheet
7-5 分行业能源消费总量和原煤、电力消费量 (2017 年) …… (213)
Consumption of Total Energy, Coal and Electricity by Sector (2017)
7-6 各市电力消费量 …… (214)
Electricity Consumption by City
7-7 各市单位 GDP 能耗增长速度 …… (215)
Energy Consumption per Unit of GDP by City

7-8 各市单位 GDP 电耗增长速度 …… (216)
Growth Rate of Electricity Consumption per Unit of GDP by City
7-9 各市单位工业增加值能耗增长速度 …… (217)
Growth Rate of Energy Consumption per Unit of Industrial Value-added by City
7-10 平均每天各种能源消费量 …… (218)
Average Daily Energy Consumption by Variety
7-11 平均每人年生活用能源 …… (218)
Annual per Capita Energy Consumption of Households
7-12 分品种生活能源年消费总量 …… (219)
Annual Total Energy Consumption of Households by Variety
7-13 能源加工转换效率 …… (219)
Efficiency of Energy Conversion
7-14 能源生产弹性系数 …… (220)
Elasticity Ratio of Energy Production
7-15 能源消费弹性系数 …… (221)
Elasticity Ratio of Energy Consumption
7-16 自然资源 (2017 年) …… (222)
Natural Resources (2017)
7-17 各地区年平均气温 …… (223)
Average Temperature by Region
7-18 各地区年降雨量 …… (224)
Annual Precipitation by Region
7-19 各地区年日照时数 …… (225)
Annual Sunshine Hours by Region
7-20 各市土地面积和人口密度 …… (226)
Land Area and Population Density by City
7-21 环境保护基本情况 …… (227)
Basic Conditions of Environmental Protection
7-22 各市“三废”排放情况 (2017 年) …… (230)
Statistics on Discharge of Waste Water, Waste Gas and Solid Wastes by City (2017)
7-23 各市城市建设基本情况 …… (231)
Basic Statistics on Urban Sanitation by City
主要统计指标解释 …… (233)
Explanatory Notes on Main Statistical Indicators

八、财政、银行和保险
Government Finance, Banking and Insurance
简要说明 …… (240)
Brief Introduction
8-1 地方一般公共预算收支和增长速度 …… (241)
Local Government General Public Budget Revenue and Expenditure and Their Growth Rates

8-2 地方一般公共预算收支基本情况 …… (242)
Basic Items of General Public Budget Revenue and Expenditure
8-3 各市地方一般公共预算收支 …… (243)
Local Government General Budgetary Revenue and Expenditure by City
8-4 各市人均地方一般公共预算收入 …… (245)
Per Capita Local Government General Public Budget Revenue by City
8-5 各市财政收支 (2017 年) …… (246)
Basic Conditions of Local Government General Public Budget Revenue and Expenditure by City(2017)
8-6 历年金融机构存贷款 …… (250)
Deposits and Loans in All Financial Institutions
8-7 金融机构本外币存贷款余额 …… (251)
Deposits and Loans in Renminbi and Foreign Currencies in All Financial Institutions
8-8 金融机构人民币存贷款余额 …… (252)
Deposits and Loans in Renminbi in All Financial Institutions
8-9 各市中资金融机构基本情况 …… (253)
Basic Conditions of Chinese-funded Financial Institutions by City
8-10 各市金融机构本外币存贷款 …… (255)
Deposits and Loans in Renminbi and Foreign Currencies in All Financial Institutions by City
8-11 各市金融机构住户存款 …… (257)
Savings Deposit by Household in All Financial Institutions by City
8-12 财产保险公司主要指标 …… (259)
Main Indicators of Property Insurance Companies
8-13 人身保险公司主要指标 …… (260)
Main Indicators of Life Insurance Companies
8-14 保险业务主要指标 …… (261)
Main Indicators of Insurance Business
8-15 分市原保险保费收入和赔付支出情况 (2017 年) …… (262)
Premium of Primary Insurance and Payment by City (2017)
主要统计指标解释 …… (263)
Explanatory Notes on Main Statistical Indicators

九、价格
Price
简要说明 …… (266)
Brief Introduction
9-1 各种价格指数 …… (267)
Price Indices
9-2 各种价格定基指数 …… (268)
Fixed-base Price Indices
9-3 居民消费价格分类指数 (2017 年) …… (269)
Consumer Price Indices by Category (2017)

9-4 商品零售价格分类指数 (2017 年) …… (271)
Retail Price Indices by Category (2017)
9-5 各市居民消费价格分类指数 (2017 年) …… (273)
Consumer Price Indices by Category and by City (2017)
9-6 各市服务项目价格分类指数 (2017 年) …… (275)
Service Price Indices by Category and by City (2017)
9-7 工业生产者出厂价格指数 …… (276)
Producer Price Indices for Manufactured Goods
9-8 各市工业生产者出厂价格指数 …… (277)
Producer Price Indices for Manufactured Goods by City
9-9 分行业工业生产者出厂价格指数 …… (278)
Producer Price Indices for Manufactured Goods by Sector
9-10 工业生产者购进价格指数 …… (279)
Producer Price Indices for Purchased Goods
9-11 固定资产投资价格指数 …… (279)
Price Indices for Investment in Fixed Assets
9-12 农业生产资料价格分类指数 (2017) …… (280)
Price Indices for Means of Agricultural Production by Category
9-13 农产品生产者价格指数 …… (281)
Producer Price Indices for Agricultural Products
主要统计指标解释 …… (282)
Explanatory Notes on Main Statistical Indicators

十、人民生活
People's Living Conditions
简要说明 …… (286)
Brief Introduction
10-1 全省常住居民家庭基本情况 …… (287)
Basic Conditions of All Permanent Households in the Province
10-2 按收入五等份分组的全体常住居民人均可支配收入 …… (288)
Per Capita Disposable Income of Provincewide Households by Income Quintile
10-3 全省常住居民人均主要食品消费量 …… (288)
Per Capita Consumption of Major Foods Provincewide
10-4 全省常住居民家庭平均每百户年末主要耐用消费品拥有量 …… (289)
Number of Major Durable Consumer Goods Owned per 100 Permanent Households
10-5 按收入五等份分组的全体常住居民家庭平均每百户主要耐用消费品年末拥有量 (2017) …… (289)
Grouped by Five Equal Shares of Number of Major Durable Consumer Goods Owned per100 Rural and Urban Permanent Households at Year-end (2017)
10-6 全省常住居民家庭年末住房情况 …… (290)
Housing Condition of All Permanent Households in the Provinceat the Year-end

10-7 各市全体常住居民人均可支配收入 …………………………………………………………………… (291)
Per Capita Disposable Income of Urban Permanent Households by City
10-8 各市全体常住居民人均可支配收入来源 (2017 年) ……………………………………………………… (292)
Per Capita Disposable Income of Permanent Households by Sources and City (2017)
10-9 各市全体常住居民人均消费支出 ……………………………………………………………………… (293)
Per Capita Consumption Expenditure of Urban Permanent Households by City
10-10 城镇常住居民家庭基本情况 ………………………………………………………………………… (294)
Basic Conditions of Urban Permanent Households
10-11 历年城镇常住居民人均可支配收入及生活消费支出 (1978-2012) …………………………………… (295)
Per Capita Disposable Income and Consumption Expenditure of Urban Permanent Households (1978-2012)
10-12 按收入五等份分组的城镇常住居民家庭平均每人收支及构成 (2017) ……………………………… (296)
Per Capita of Disposal Income and Expenditure and Composition of Urban Permanent Households by Income Quintile(2017)
10-13 全省城镇常住居民人均主要食品消费量 …………………………………………………………… (297)
Per Capita Consumption of Major Foods Urban Househoulds
10-14 城镇常住居民平均每百户主要耐用品年末拥有量 ………………………………………………… (298)
Number of Major Durable Consumer Goods Owned per 100 Rural and Urban Permanent Households at the Year-end
10-15 按收入五等份分组的城镇常住居民家庭平均每百户主要耐用消费品年末拥有量 (2017) … (298)
Grouped by Five Equal Shares of Number of Major Durable Consumer Goods Owned per100 Rural and Urban Permanent Households at Year-end (2017)
10-16 城镇常住居民家庭年末住房情况 ……………………………………………………………………… (299)
Housing Condition of the Urban Permanent Households at the Year-end
10-17 各市城镇常住居民人均可支配收入 ………………………………………………………………… (300)
Per Capita Disposable Income of Urban Permanent Households by City
10-18 各市城镇常住居民人均可支配收入来源 (2017 年) ………………………………………………… (301)
Per Capita Disposable Income of Urban Permanent Households by Sources and City (2017)
10-19 各市城镇常住居民人均消费支出 ……………………………………………………………………… (302)
Per Capita Consumption Expenditure of Urban Permanent Households by City
10-20 农村常住居民家庭基本情况 ………………………………………………………………………… (303)
Basic Conditions of Rural Permanent Households
10-21 历年农村常住居民人均收入及生活消费支出 (1978-2012) ………………………………………… (304)
Per Capita Income and Consumption Expenditure of Rural Households (1978-2012)
10-22 按收入五等份分组的农村常住居民家庭平均每人收支及构成 (2017) ……………………………… (305)
Per Capita of Disposal Income and Expenditure and Composition of Rural Permanent Households by Income Quintile (2017)
10-23 全省农村常住居民人均主要食品消费量 …………………………………………………………… (306)
Per Capita Consumption of Major Foods Rural Househoulds
10-24 农村常住居民平均每百户主要耐用品年末拥有量 ………………………………………………… (307)
Number of Major Durable Consumer Goods Owned per 100 Rural and Urban Permanent Households at the Year-end

10-25 按收入五等份分组的农村常住居民家庭平均每百户主要耐用消费品年末拥有量 (2017) ··· (307)
Grouped by Five Equal Shares of Number of Major Durable Consumer Goods Owned per100 Rural and Urban Permanent Households at Year-end (2017)
10-26 农村常住居民家庭年末住房情况 ······ (308)
Housing Condition of the Rural Permanent Households at the Year-end
10-27 各市农村常住居民人均可支配收入 ······ (309)
Per Capita Disposal Income of Rural Permanent Households by City
10-28 各市农村常住居民人均可支配收入来源 (2017 年) ······ (310)
Per Capita Disposable Income of Rural Permanent Households by Sources and City (2017)
10-29 各市农村常住居民人均消费支出 ······ (311)
Per Capita Consumption Expenditure of Rural Permanent Households by City
10-30 常住居民人均可支配收入及生活消费支出 (2013-2017) ······ (312)
Per Capita Disposable Income and Consumption Expenditure of Househoulds (2013-2017)
主要统计指标解释 ······ (313)
Explanatory Notes on Main Statistical Indicators

十一、农业
Agriculture
简要说明 ······ (318)
Brief Introduction
11-1 农业主要指标 ······ (319)
Main Indicators of Agriculture
11-2 各市农村基层组织情况 (2017 年) ······ (320)
Basic Conditions of Rural Grassroots Units by City (2017)
11-3 农业生产条件 ······ (321)
Agricultural Production Basic Conditions
11-4 农业自然灾害情况 ······ (321)
Statistics on Agriculture Covered and Affected by Natural Disasters
11-5 农林牧渔业总产值 ······ (322)
Gross Output Value of Farming, Forestry, Animal Husbandry and Fishery
11-6 农林牧渔业总产值指数 (1978 年=100) ······ (323)
Indices of Gross Output Value of Farming, Forestry, Animal Husbandry and Fishery (year of 1978=100)
11-7 农林牧渔业总产值指数 (上年=100) ······ (324)
Indices of Gross Output Value of Farming, Forestry, Animal Husbandry and Fishery (preceding year=100)
11-8 各市农林牧渔业总产值 (2017 年) ······ (325)
Gross Output Value of Farming, Forestry, Animal Husbandry and Fishery by City (2017)
11-9 各市农林牧渔业总产值指数 (2017 年) ······ (326)
Indices of Gross Output Value of Farming, Forestry, Animal Husbandry and Fishery by City (2017)
11-10 农作物播种面积 ······ (327)
Total Sown Area of Farm Crops

11-11 主要农产品产量 …… (329)
Output of Major Farm Products
11-12 主要畜产品和水产品产量 …… (330)
Output of Major Farm Products
11-13 主要农作物播种面积、亩产及总产量 …… (331)
Sown Area, Yield per Mu and Total Output of Major Farm Crops
11-14 各市主要农作物播种面积、亩产及总产量 (2017 年) …… (332)
Sown Area, Yield per Mu and Total Output of Major Farm Crops by City (2017)
11-15 造林面积及主要林产品产量 …… (336)
Area of Afforestation and Output of Major Forest Products
11-16 水产养殖面积和水产品产量 …… (336)
Area of Cultivation and Output of Aquatic Products
11-17 牲畜头数及肉类产量 …… (337)
Number of Livestock and Output of Meat
11-18 各市造林面积、水产品产量、牲畜头数及猪肉产量 (2017 年) …… (338)
Area of Afforestation, Output of Aquatic Products, Number of Livestock and Output of Pork by City (2017)
11-19 茶叶、桑、水果面积及产量 …… (339)
Planted Area and Output of Tea, Mulberry and Fruits
11-20 各市水果面积及产量 (2017 年) …… (340)
Planted Area and Output of Fruits by City (2017)
11-21 主要农产品产量与最高年份比较 (2017 年) …… (342)
Output of Major Farm Products in Comparison with Peak Year (2017)
主要统计指标解释 …… (343)
Explanatory Notes on Main Statistical Indicators

十二、工业
Industry
简要说明 …… (346)
Brief Introduction
12-1 工业主要指标 …… (347)
Main Indicators of Industry
12-2 规模以上工业企业增加值和指数 …… (348)
Value-added of Industrial Enterprises above Designated Size and Their Indices
12-3 历年规模以上工业增加值增长速度 …… (349)
Growth Rates of Industrial Enterprises above Designated Size
12-4 规模以上分行业工业增加值和增长速度 …… (350)
Value-added and Growth Rates of Industry above Designated Size by Sector
12-5 规模以上工业企业单位数和产值 …… (351)
Number of Industrial Enterprises above Designated Size and Their Gross Output Values
12-6 全部工业总产值和指数 …… (352)
Gross Industrial Output Value of All Industrial Enterprises and Theirs Indices

12-7 规模以上工业总产值和指数 …………………………………………………………… (353)
Gross Output Value of Industrial Enterprises above Designated Size and Their Indices
12-8 规模以上工业产品产量 ……………………………………………………………… (354)
Output of Industrial Products of Enterprises above Designated Size
12-9 各市规模以上工业企业单位数和工业总产值 ………………………………………… (356)
Number and Gross Output Value of Industrial Enterprises above Designated Size by City
12-10 各市规模以上工业增加值和指数 …………………………………………………… (358)
Value-added and Indices of Industry above Designated Size by City
12-11 各市规模以上工业企业单位数 (2017 年) …………………………………………… (360)
Number of Industrial Enterprises above Designated Size by City (2017)
12-12 各市规模以上工业总产值 (2017 年) ………………………………………………… (364)
Gross Output Value of Industry above Designated Size by City (2017)
12-13 各市规模以上工业增加值 (2017 年) ………………………………………………… (368)
Value-added of Industry above Designated Size by City (2017)
12-14 规模以上工业企业主要经济指标 …………………………………………………… (372)
Main Indicators of Industrial Enterprises above Designated Size
12-15 规模以上国有控股工业企业主要经济指标 ………………………………………… (373)
Main Indicators of State-owned and State-holding Industrial Enterprises above Designated Size
12-16 规模以上工业企业主要经济指标 (2017 年) ………………………………………… (374)
Main Economic Indicators of Industrial Enterprises above Designated Size (2017)
12-17 规模以上国有控股工业企业主要经济指标 (2017 年) ……………………………… (376)
Main Economic Indicators of State-holding Industrial Enterprises above Designated Size (2017)
12-18 规模以上集体工业企业主要经济指标 (2017 年) …………………………………… (378)
Main Economic Indicators of Collective-owned Industrial Enterprises above Designated Size (2017)
12-19 规模以上股份合作工业企业主要经济指标 (2017 年) ……………………………… (380)
Main Economic Indicators of Share-holding Cooperative Industrial Enterprises above Designated Size (2017)
12-20 规模以上股份制工业企业主要经济指标 (2017 年) ………………………………… (382)
Main Economic Indicators of Share-holding Industrial Enterprises above Designated Size (2017)
12-21 规模以上"三资"工业企业主要经济指标 (2017 年) ……………………………… (384)
Main Economic Indicators of Foreign-funded Industrial Enterprises above Designated Size (2017)
12-22 规模以上私营工业企业主要经济指标 (2017 年) …………………………………… (386)
Main Economic Indicators of Private Industrial Enterprises above Designated Size (2017)
12-23 规模以上大中型工业企业主要经济指标 (2017 年) ………………………………… (388)
Main Economic Indicators of Large and Medium-sized Industrial Enterprises above Designated Size (2017)
12-24 规模以上高技术制造业主要经济指标 (2017 年) …………………………………… (390)
Main Indicators on High-tech Manufacturingl Enterprises above Designated Size (2017)
12-25 规模以上先进制造业主要经济指标 (2017 年) ……………………………………… (392)
Main Indicators on Advanced Manufacturing Enterprises above Designated Size (2017)
12-26 规模以上工业企业主要经济效益指标 (2017 年) …………………………………… (394)
Main Indicators on Economic Benefit of Industrial Enterprises above Designated Size (2017)

12-27 规模以上制造业工业企业主要经济指标 …… (396)
Main Economic Indicators of Manufacturing Enterprises above Designated Size
12-28 各市规模以上工业企业主要经济指标 (2017 年) …… (397)
Main Economic Indicators of Industrial Enterprises above Designated Size by City (2017)
12-29 各市私营工业企业主要经济指标 (2017 年) …… (398)
Main Economic Indicators of Private Industrial Enterprises by City (2017)
12-30 各市工业企业主要经济效益指标 (2017 年) …… (399)
Main Indicators on Economic Benefit of Industrial Enterprises by City (2017)
12-31 各市规模以上国有控股工业企业主要经济效益指标 (2017 年) …… (401)
Main Indicators on Economic Benefit of State-holding Industrial Enterprises above Designated Size by City (2017)
12-32 各市按经济类型分的工业企业资产 (2017 年) …… (402)
Total Assets of Industrial Enterprises by Ownership and by City (2017)
12-33 各市规模以上大中型工业企业产值资产 (2017 年) …… (403)
Gross Output Value and Total Assets of Large and Medium-sized Industrial Enterprises above Designated Size by City (2017)
12-34 各市现代产业增加值及比重 (2017 年) …… (404)
Value Added and Ratio of Modern Industries by City (2017)
12-35 全省工业总产值最大的 50 家工业企业 (2017 年) …… (405)
Top 50 Industrial Enterprises of the Province in Terms of Gross Industrial Output Value (2017)
12-36 全省主营业务收入最大的 50 家工业企业 (2017 年) …… (406)
Top 50 Industrial Enterprises of the Province in Terms of Principal Business Revenue (2017)
12-37 全省固定资产合计最大的 50 家工业企业 (2017 年) …… (407)
Top 50 Industrial Enterprises of the Province in Terms of Net Value of Fixed Assets (2017)
主要统计指标解释 …… (408)
Explanatory Notes on Main Statistical Indicators

十三、建筑业
Construction
简要说明 …… (418)
Brief Introduction
13-1 建筑业企业生产情况 …… (419)
Production Conditions of Construction Enterprises
13-2 建筑业企业主要指标 …… (420)
Main Indicators on Construction Enterprises
13-3 各市建筑业企业个数 …… (421)
Number of Construction Enterprises by City
13-4 各市建筑业企业总产值 …… (422)
Gross Output Value of Construction Enterprises by City
13-5 各市建筑业企业利税总额 …… (423)
Total Pre-tax Profits of Construction Enterprises by City

13-6 各市建筑业企业利润总额 …………………………………………………………………… (424)
Total Profits of Construction Enterprises by City
13-7 各市建筑业企业房屋建筑施工面积 ………………………………………………………… (425)
Floor Space of Buildings under Construction by Construction Enterprises by City
13-8 各市建筑业企业房屋建筑施工新开工面积 …………………………………………………… (426)
Floor Space of Buildings Started This Year by Construction Enterprises by City
13-9 各市建筑业企业期末就业人员 ……………………………………………………………… (427)
Number of Employed Persons of Construction Enterprises at the Year-end by City
13-10 各市建筑业企业劳动生产率 ………………………………………………………………… (428)
Labor Productivity of Construction Enterprises by City
主要统计指标解释 …………………………………………………………………………… (429)
Explanatory Notes on Main Statistical Indicators

十四、规模以上服务业
Service Enterprises Above Designated Size

简要说明 ……………………………………………………………………………………… (434)
Brief Introduction
14-1 规模以上服务业企业财务指标 ……………………………………………………………… (435)
Main Financial Indicators of Service Enterprises above Designated Size
14-2 规模以上服务业企业分行业主要指标 (2017 年) …………………………………………… (436)
Main Indicators of Service Enterprises above Designated Size by Sector(2017)
14-3 各市规模以上服务业企业主要指标 (2017 年) ……………………………………………… (444)
Main Indicators of Service Enterprises above Designated Size by City (2017)
主要统计指标解释 …………………………………………………………………………… (448)
Explanatory Notes on Main Statistical Indicators

十五、运输和邮电
Transportation, Postal and Telecommunication Services

简要说明 ……………………………………………………………………………………… (450)
Brief Introduction
15-1 运输邮电主要指标 ………………………………………………………………………… (452)
Main Indicators on Transport, Postal and Telecommunication Services
15-2 全社会旅客运输量 ………………………………………………………………………… (453)
Total Passenger Traffic
15-3 旅客运输量指数 …………………………………………………………………………… (454)
Indices of Passenger Traffic
15-4 各市客运量 ………………………………………………………………………………… (455)
Passenger Traffic by City
15-5 各市旅客周转量 …………………………………………………………………………… (456)
Passenger-kilometers by City
15-6 全社会货物运输量 ………………………………………………………………………… (457)
Total Freight Traffic

15-7 货物运输量指数 …… (458)
Indices of Freight Traffic
15-8 各市货运量 …… (459)
Freight Traffic by City
15-9 各市货物周转量 …… (460)
Freight Ton-kilometers by City
15-10 运输工具和线路拥有量 …… (461)
Number of Means of Transport and Length of Transport Routes
15-11 各市民用汽车拥有量 (2017 年) …… (462)
Possession of Civil Vehicles by City (2017)
15-12 各市私人汽车拥有量 (2017 年) …… (464)
Possession of Private Vehicles by City (2017)
15-13 各市公路基本情况 (2017 年) …… (465)
Basic Conditions of Highways by City (2017)
15-14 公路通车里程和桥梁数 …… (466)
Length of Highways and Number of Bridges
15-15 输油(气)管道长度和运输量 …… (466)
Length and Traffic of Petroleum and Gas Pipelines
15-16 民航航站吞吐量 …… (467)
Throughput of Civil Aviation Airports
15-17 港口泊位及吞吐量 …… (468)
Berth and Throughput of Coastal Ports
15-18 各市港口货物吞吐量 …… (469)
Freight Throughput of Ports by City
15-19 各市城市公共交通情况 (2017 年) …… (470)
Basic Statistics on Public Transportation in Cities by City (2017)
15-20 邮电业务总量和指数 …… (472)
Business Volume of Postal and Telecommunication Services and Their Indices
15-21 各市邮电业务总量 …… (473)
Business Volume of Postal and Telecommunication Services by City
15-22 各市邮电业务情况 (2017 年) …… (474)
Conditions of Postal and Telecommunication Services by City (2017)
15-23 邮政通信业基本情况 …… (475)
Basic Conditions of Postal and Telecommunication Services
主要统计指标解释 …… (476)
Explanatory Notes on Main Statistical Indicators

十六、批发零售业
Wholesale and Retail Trades
简要说明 …… (484)
Brief Introduction

16-1 批发零售业主要指标 …………………………………………………………………… (485)
Main Indicators on Domestic Trade
16-2 按行业及城乡分社会消费品零售总额 ………………………………………………… (486)
Total Retail Sales of Consumer Goods by Sector and by Urban and Rural Area
16-3 各市社会消费品零售总额(2017年) ……………………………………………………… (487)
Total Retail Sales of Consumer Goods by City (2017)
16-4 各市社会消费品零售总额 ………………………………………………………………… (488)
Total Retail Sales of Consumer Goods by City
16-5 批发零售业商品销售总额 ………………………………………………………………… (489)
Total Sales of Commodities in Wholesale and Retail Trades
16-6 批发零售业商品批发额 …………………………………………………………………… (490)
Total Wholesale Value of Commodities in Wholesale and Retail Trades
16-7 批发零售业商品零售额 …………………………………………………………………… (491)
Total Retail Value of Commodities in Wholesale and Retail Trades
16-8 各市批发零售业商品销售总额 …………………………………………………………… (492)
Total Sales of Enterprises in Wholesale and Retail Trades by City
16-9 限额以上批发企业商品购、销、存总额(2017年) ………………………………………… (493)
Total Purchases, Sales and Inventory of Enterprises above Designated Size in Wholesale Trade (2017)
16-10 限额以上零售企业商品购、销、存总额(2017年) ………………………………………… (495)
Total Purchases, Sales and Inventory of Enterprises above Designated Size in Retail Trade (2017)
16-11 各市限额以上批发零售企业商品购、销、存总额(2017年) ………………………………… (497)
Total Purchases, Sales and Inventory of Enterprises above Designated Size in Wholesale and Retail Trades by City (2017)
16-12 限额以上批发零售业个体户商品购、销、存总额(2017年) ………………………………… (498)
Total Purchases, Sales and Inventory of Enterprises above Designated Size in Wholesale and Retail Trade Individuals(2017)
16-13 限额以上连锁批发零售业经营情况(2017年) …………………………………………… (500)
Business of Chain Stores above Designated Size in Wholesale and Retail Trade (2017)
16-14 亿元以上商品交易市场成交额 …………………………………………………………… (502)
Turnover of Commodity Exchange Markets with Transaction Value over 100 Million Yuan
16-15 限额以上批发零售企业财务状况(2017年) ……………………………………………… (503)
Financial Indicators of Enterprises above Designated Size in Wholesale and Retail Trades Services(2017)
16-16 限额以上批发企业财务状况(2017年) …………………………………………………… (504)
Financial Indicators of Enterprises above Designated Size in Wholesale Trade (2017)
16-17 限额以上零售企业财务状况(2017年) …………………………………………………… (508)
Financial Indicators of Enterprises above Designated Size in Retail Trade (2017)
16-18 各市限额以上批发零售企业财务状况(2017年) ………………………………………… (512)
Financial Indicators of Enterprises above Designated Size in Wholesale and Retail Trades by City (2017)
主要统计指标解释 ……………………………………………………………………………… (516)
Explanatory Notes on Main Statistical Indicators

十七、住宿餐饮业和旅游
Hotels, Catering Services and Tourism

简要说明 …… (520)
Brief Introduction
17-1 住宿、餐饮业、旅游主要指标 …… (521)
Main Indicators on Hotels, Catering Services and Tourism
17-2 限额以上住宿业经营情况 (2017 年) …… (522)
Business of Hotels above Designated Size (2017)
17-3 限额以上餐饮业经营情况 (2017 年) …… (523)
Business of Catering Services Enterprises above Designated Size (2017)
17-4 各市限额以上住宿餐饮业经营情况 (2017 年) …… (524)
Business of Enterprises above Designated Size of Hotels and Catering Services by City (2017)
17-5 限额以上连锁住宿餐饮业经营情况 (2017 年) …… (525)
Business of Chain Stores above Designated Size in Hotels and Catering Services (2017)
17-6 限额以上住宿餐饮企业财务状况 (2017 年) …… (527)
Financial Indicators of Enterprises above Designated Size in Hotels and Catering Services (2017)
17-7 限额以上住宿企业财务状况 (2017 年) …… (528)
Financial Indicators of Hotels above Designated Size (2017)
17-8 限额以上餐饮企业财务状况 (2017 年) …… (532)
Financial Indicators of Catering Services Enterprises above Designated Size (2017)
17-9 各市限额以上住宿和餐饮企业财务状况 (2017 年) …… (536)
Financial Indicators of Enterprises above Designated Size of Hotels and Catering Services by City (2017)
17-10 各市住宿餐饮业营业收入 …… (540)
Business of Enterprises above Designated Size of Hotels and Catering Services by City
17-11 旅游部门基本情况 …… (541)
Basic Statistics on Tourism-related Agencies
17-12 城市接待外国游客人数 …… (541)
Number of Foreign Visitors Received by Cities
17-13 各市旅游宾馆(酒店)住宿设施 (2017 年) …… (542)
Lodging Facilities of Tourist Hotels by City (2017)
17-14 各市接待过夜旅游者人数 …… (543)
Number of Overnight Tourists by City
17-15 各市旅行社组团出境游人数 (2017 年) …… (544)
Number of Outbound Visitors in Group Tours by City (2017)
17-16 各市旅游业收入 …… (545)
Tourism Earnings by City
17-17 国际旅游外汇收入 …… (546)
Foreign Exchange Earnings from International Tourism
17-18 各市国际旅游外汇收入 …… (547)
Foreign Exchange Earnings from International Tourism by City
主要统计指标解释 …… (548)
Explanatory Notes on Main Statistical Indicators

十八、教育和科技

Education and Technology

简要说明 …………………………………………………………………………………… (550)
Brief Introduction

18-1 教育、科技主要指标 …………………………………………………………………… (551)
Main Indicators on Education, Science and Technology

18-2 各级各类学校在校学生数 ……………………………………………………………… (552)
Number of Total Enrollment by Level and Type of School

18-3 各级各类学校情况 ……………………………………………………………………… (553)
Statistics on Various Levels and Types of Schools

18-4 研究生教育情况 ………………………………………………………………………… (555)
Statistics on Postgraduate Education

18-5 各级各类成人教育在校学生数 ………………………………………………………… (555)
Number of Total Enrollment by Level and Type of Adult School

18-6 高等学校情况 (2017 年) ……………………………………………………………… (556)
Statistics on Institutions of Higher Education (2017)

18-7 中等学校情况 (2017 年) ……………………………………………………………… (556)
Statistics on Secondary Schools (2017)

18-8 各市普通中学情况 (2017 年) ………………………………………………………… (557)
Statistics on Regular Secondary Schools by City (2017)

18-9 各市中等职业教育基本情况 (2017 年) ……………………………………………… (559)
Basic Statistics on Vocational Secondary Education by City (2017)

18-10 各市小学情况 (2017 年) ……………………………………………………………… (560)
Statistics on Primary Schools by City (2017)

18-11 各市学龄儿童入学情况 ………………………………………………………………… (561)
Statistics on School-age Children Enrolled in Schools by City

18-12 研究与试验发展(R&D)基本情况 ……………………………………………………… (562)
Basic Statistics on Research and Development (R&D)

18-13 公有经济企业、事业单位专业技术人员年末人数 …………………………………… (563)
Number of Professional and Technical Personnel in State-owned Enterprises and Institutions at the Year-end

18-14 高层次人才情况 ………………………………………………………………………… (564)
Statistics on High-level Talents

18-15 各类技术合同签订情况 ………………………………………………………………… (564)
Statistics on Technical Contracts Signed by Type

18-16 科技成果项数 …………………………………………………………………………… (565)
Number of Achievements for Scientific and Technological Research

18-17 县级政府部门属研究与开发机构基本情况 …………………………………………… (565)
Basic Statistics on Research and Development Institutions under Government Departments at County Level

18-18 县级以上政府部门属研究与开发机构基本情况 …… (566)
Basic Statistics on Research and Development Institutions under Government Departments at and above County Level
18-19 各市县级及以上政府部门属研究与开发机构基本情况 …… (567)
Basic Statistics on Research and Development Institutions under Government Departments at and above County Level by City
18-20 三种专利申请量与授权量 …… (569)
Three Types of Patent Application and Granted
18-21 分市全社会研究与试验发展经费 (2017 年) …… (570)
Researoh and Developmant Expenditure by City (2017)
18-22 规模以上工业企业的科技活动基本情况 …… (571)
Basic Statistics on Science and Technology Activities of Industrial Enterprises above Designated size
18-23 规上工业企业研究与发展经费内部支出 …… (572)
Internal Expenditures of Industrial Enterprises Above Designated Size
18-24 分市规模以上工业企业 R&D 活动人员和经费 …… (574)
R&D Personnel and Expenditure of Industrial Enterprises by City
18-25 分市规模以上工业企业新产品产出情况 …… (575)
Production of New Products by Industrial Enterprises by City
18-26 科协机构及活动情况 …… (576)
Statistics on Associations for Science and Technology and Their Activities
主要统计指标解释 …… (577)
Explanatory Notes on Main Statistical Indicators

十九、文化与体育
Culture and Sports
简要说明 …… (582)
Brief Introduction
19-1 文化、体育主要指标 …… (583)
Main Indicators on Culture and Education
19-2 文化艺术、文物事业机构数 …… (584)
Number of Institutions of Culture, Arts and Cultural Relics
19-3 文化部门艺术表演团体演出基本情况 (2017 年) …… (585)
Basic Statistics on Performances of Art Troupes under(of) Cultural Departments (2017)
19-4 文化、文物机构及人员数 (2017 年) …… (586)
Number of Institutions and Personnel in Culture and Cultural Relics (2017)
19-5 公共图书馆、群众文化事业机构及人员数 (2017 年) …… (586)
Number of Institutions and Personnel in Public Libraries and Mass Culture (2017)
19-6 各市文化、文物事业机构数 (2017 年) …… (587)
Number of Institutions in Culture and Cultural Relics by City (2017)
19-7 各市文化、文物事业机构的人员数 (2017 年) …… (588)
Number of Personnel in Culture and Cultural Relics by City (2017)

19-8 图书、杂志、报纸出版数量 …… (589)
Number of Books, Magazines and Newspapers Published
19-9 图书出版情况 (2017 年) …… (589)
Statistics on Books Published (2017)
19-10 杂志出版情况 (2017 年) …… (590)
Statistics on Magazines Published (2017)
19-11 报纸出版情况 (2017 年) …… (590)
Statistics on Newspapers Published (2017)
19-12 广播、电视事业发展情况 …… (591)
Statistics on Radio and Television Stations
19-13 广播电台宣传基本情况 (2017 年) …… (591)
Basic Statistics on Radio Stations (2017)
19-14 电视台宣传基本情况 (2017 年) …… (592)
Basic Statistics on Television Stations (2017)
19-15 各市广播、电视事业机构数 (2017 年) …… (592)
Number of Institutions of Radio and Television by City (2017)
19-16 体育事业情况 …… (593)
Statistics on Sports
主要统计指标解释 …… (594)
Explanatory Notes on Main Statistical Indicators

二十、卫生、社会福利、社会保障和其他
Public Health, Social Welfare, Social Insurance and Others

简要说明 …… (596)
Brief Introduction
20-1 卫生、社会福利和其他主要指标 …… (597)
Main Indicators of Sports, Public Health, Social Welfare, Environmental Protection and Others
20-2 医疗卫生机构、床位及人员数 …… (598)
Number of Health Care Institutions, Beds and Personnel
20-3 医疗卫生机构、床位和人员数 (2017 年) …… (599)
Number of Health Care Institutions, Beds and Personnel (2017)
20-4 各市医疗卫生机构、床位和人员数 (2017 年) …… (600)
Number of Health Care Institutions, Beds and Personnel by City (2017)
20-5 各类医疗卫生机构、床位和人员数 …… (601)
Number of Health Institutions, Beds and Personnel by Type
20-6 各市社会保险基金征缴收入(2017 年) …… (602)
Amount Collected of Security Insurance (2017)
20-7 各市社会保险参保人数 (2017 年) …… (603)
Number of Persons Participating in Social Insurance by City (2017)
20-8 优抚、社会救济和福利事业情况 …… (604)
Statistics on Preferential Treatment and Resettlement, Social Relief and Welfare

20-9 婚姻登记情况 …… (606)
Statistics on Marriage Registration
20-10 律师、公证、基层司法基本情况 …… (607)
Basic Statistics on Lawyers, Notarization, Grassroots Judicial Work
20-11 交通事故发生情况 (2017 年) …… (608)
Statistics on Traffic Accidents (2017)
20-12 火灾事故发生情况 (2017 年) …… (608)
Statistics on Fire Accidents (2017)
20-13 各市亿元生产总值生产安全事故死亡率 …… (609)
Rate of Death from Work Safety Accidents per 100 Million Yuan of Gross Domestic Product by City
主要统计指标解释 …… (610)
Explanatory Notes on Main Statistical Indicators

二十一、区域主要经济指标

Major Economic Regions

简要说明 …… (612)
Brief Introduction
21-1 区域主要经济指标 …… (613)
Main Indicators on Regional Economies
21-2 区域主要经济指标占全省比重 …… (615)
Percentage of Main Regional Economic Indicators to the Provincial Total
21-3 珠江三角洲主要经济指标 …… (617)
Main Economic Indicators of the Pearl River Delta Economic Zone
21-4 珠江三角洲工业企业主要指标 (2017 年) …… (620)
Main Indicators of Industrial Enterprises of the Pearl River Delta (2017)
21-5 广州、深圳主要经济指标 (2017 年) …… (624)
Main Economic Indicators of Guangzhou and Shenzhen (2017)
21-6 粤东西北主要经济指标 …… (625)
Main Economic Indicators of the East and West and Mountainous Area
21-7 东翼主要经济指标 …… (628)
Main Economic Indicators of the East Wing
21-8 西翼主要经济指标 …… (629)
Main Economic Indicators of the West Wing
21-9 山区主要经济指标 …… (630)
Main Economic Indicators of Mountainous Areas
21-10 山区县(市、区)主要经济指标 …… (631)
Main Economic Indicators of Counties (County-level Cities and Districts) in Mountainous Areas
21-11 少数民族县主要经济指标 (2017 年) …… (632)
Main Economic Indicators of Minority Counties (2017)

二十二、县（市、区）主要经济指标
Counties and Districts Under City Administration

简要说明 …… (634)
Brief Introduction

22-1 各县(市、区)地区生产总值 …… (635)
Gross Domestic Product by County (County-level City and District)

22-2 各县(市、区)三次产业地区生产总值 …… (638)
Gross Domestic Product by County (County-level City and District)

22-3 各县(市、区)三次产业地区生产总值指数 …… (641)
Gross Domestic Product by County (County-level City and District)

22-4 各县(市、区)人均地区生产总值及指数 …… (644)
Per Capita Gross Domestic Product and Growth Rates by County (County-level City and District)

22-5 各县(市、区)工、农业总产值 …… (647)
Gross Output Value of Industry and Agriculture by County (County-level City and District)

22-6 各县(市、区)粮食产量 …… (650)
Output of Grain by County (County-level City and District)

22-7 各县(市、区)糖蔗、水果和蔬菜产量 …… (653)
Output of Sugarcane,Fruits and Vegetable by County (County-level City and District)

22-8 各县(市、区)猪肉产量、禽肉产量和水产品产量 …… (656)
Output of Pork ,Output of Meat of Poultry and Output of Aquatic Products by County (County-level City and District)

22-9 各县(市、区)固定资产投资 …… (659)
Investment in Fixed Assets by County (County-level City and District)

22-10 各县(市、区)社会消费品零售总额 …… (662)
Total Retail Sales of Consumer Goods by County (County-level City and District)

22-11 各县(市、区)年末就业人员和城镇单位就业人员 …… (665)
Number of Fully Employed Staff and Workers by County (County-Level City and District)

22-12 各县(市、区)城镇单位就业人员工资总额及平均工资 …… (668)
Total Wages and Average Wage of Fully Employed Staff and Workers by County (County-level City and District)

22-13 各县(市、区)财政收支 …… (671)
Local Government Budgetary Revenue and Expenditure by County (County-level City and District)

附录
Appendix

简要说明 …… (676)
Brief Introduction

附录 A-1 人口及地区生产总值 (2017 年) …… (678)
Population and Gross Domestic Product (2017)

附录 A-2 固定资产投资完成额 (2017 年) …… (679)
Investment in Fixed Assets (2017 年)

附录 A-3　居民人均收入与支出(2017 年) ………………………………………………………… (680)
Per Capita Income and Expenditure (2017)
附录 A-4　居民消费价格指数(2017 年) ……………………………………………………………… (681)
Consumer Price Indices (2017)
附录 A-5　农林牧渔业总产值和增速 (2017 年) ………………………………………………… (682)
Gross Output Value of Farming,Forestry,Animal Husbandry and Fishery and Growth Rate (2017)
附录 A-6　主要农产品产量 (2017 年) ……………………………………………………………… (683)
Output of Major Agricultural Products (2017)
附录 A-7　规模以上工业企业主要经济指标 (2017 年) ………………………………………… (684)
Main Economic Indicators of Industrial Enterprises above Designated Size (2017)
附录 A-8　主要工业产品产量(2017 年) …………………………………………………………… (685)
Output of Major Industrial Products (2017)
附录 A-9　建筑业主要指标 (2017 年) ……………………………………………………………… (686)
Indicators of Construction Industry (2017)
附录 A-10　客运量和旅客周转量 (2017 年) ……………………………………………………… (687)
Passenger Traffic and Passenger-kilometers (2017)
附录 A-11　货运量和货物周转量(2017 年) ………………………………………………………… (688)
Freight Traffic and Freight Ton_Kilometers (2017)
附录 A-12　国内外贸易(2017 年) …………………………………………………………………… (689)
Retail Trades and Foreign Trades (2017)
附录 B-1　中国香港特别行政区主要社会经济指标 ……………………………………………… (690)
Main Statistical Indicators of Hong Kong Special Administrative Region
附录 B-2　中国澳门特别行政区主要社会经济指标 ……………………………………………… (691)
Main Statistical Indicators of Macao Special Administrative Region
附录 C　中国台湾省主要社会经济指标 …………………………………………………………… (692)
Main Statistical Indicators of Taiwan Province
附录 D-1　部分国家和地区主要经济指标 (2016 年) …………………………………………… (693)
Main Economic Indicators of Some Countries and Territories (2016)
附录 D-2　部分国家和地区国内生产总值 ………………………………………………………… (695)
Gross Domestic Product of Some Countries and Territories
附录 D-3　部分国家和地区国内生产总值增长率 ………………………………………………… (696)
Growth Rates of GDP of Some Countries and Territories
附录 D-4　部分国家和地区人均国民总收入 ……………………………………………………… (697)
Per Capita Gross National Income of Some Countries and Territories
附录 D-5　部分国家和地区人均国内生产总值增长率 …………………………………………… (698)
Growth Rates of Per Capita GDP of Some Countries and Territories
主要统计指标解释 …………………………………………………………………………………… (699)
Explanatory Notes on Main Statistical Indicators

一、综合

GENERAL SURVEY

一　综合

简要说明

一、本篇资料反映广东行政区划、国民经济和社会发展综合资料，并收录了基本单位统计情况。

二、本篇资料分别由省民政厅、省统计局各专业处、综合处、政法处、普查中心和国家统计局广东调查总队整理提供。

三、综合统计资料是根据广东省统计局各专业统计年报资料以及国家统计局、广东省有关部门提供的统计资料加工整理而成。

四、基本单位资料中的产业活动单位按“在地”原则，国民经济行业分类标准（GB/T 4754-2011)汇总。

1 General Survey

Brief Introduction

Ⅰ.The summary data in this chapter reflect the divisions of administrative areas, summary data on the national economy and social development, and related indications on.

Ⅱ.The data are prepared and provided by the Civil Affairs Department of Guangdong Province., the Division of Professional Statistics, the Division of Comprehensive Statistics, the Division of Law, the Census Center of Statistics Bureau of Guangdong Province, and the Survey Office in Guangdong of National Bureau of Statistics respectively.

Ⅲ.The summary data are processed and prepared on the basis of the annual reports of various specialized fields provided by Statistics Bureau of Guangdong Province and the statistics provided by the National Bureau of Statistics and some related departments of Guangdong Province.

Ⅳ. The data on “Units of Industrial Establishments” of the basic industrial units are prepared on the principle of location and the standard of Industrial Classification of the National Economy(GB/T 4754-2011).

1-1 行政区划（2017年）

Divisions of Administrative Areas (2017)

单位：个 (unit)

市 别	City	地级市 Number of Cities at Prefecture Level	县级市 Number of Cities at County Level	县 Number of Counties	自治县 Number of Autonomous Counties	市辖区 Number of Districts under the Jurisdiction of Cities	市辖镇 Number of Towns under the Jurisdiction of Cities	乡 Number of Townships	#民族乡 Ethnic Townships	街道 Number of Street Communities
全省合计	**Provincial Total**	**21**	**20**	**34**	**3**	**64**	**1124**	**11**	**7**	**466**
广 州	Guangzhou	1				11	34			136
深 圳	Shenzhen	1				8				74
珠 海	Zhuhai	1				3	15			9
汕 头	Shantou	1		1		6	32			37
佛 山	Foshan	1				5	21			11
韶 关	Shaoguan	1	2	4	1	3	93	1	1	10
河 源	Heyuan	1		5		1	94	1	1	6
梅 州	Meizhou	1	1	5		2	104			6
惠 州	Huizhou	1		3		2	48	1	1	22
汕 尾	Shanwei	1	1	2		1	44			10
东 莞	Dongguan	1					28			4
中 山	Zhongshan	1					18			6
江 门	Jiangmen	1	4			3	61			12
阳 江	Yangjiang	1	1	1		2	38			10
湛 江	Zhanjiang	1	3	2		4	82	2		37
茂 名	Maoming	1	3			2	87			22
肇 庆	Zhaoqing	1	1	4		3	91	1	1	12
清 远	Qingyuan	1	2	2	2	2	77	3	3	5
潮 州	Chaozhou	1		1		2	41			9
揭 阳	Jieyang	1	1	2		2	61	2		20
云 浮	Yunfu	1	1	2		2	55			8

注：本行政区划截止2017年底。

Note: The divisions of administrative areas reflect the status at the end of 2017.

1–2 国民经济和社会发展总量与速度指标

指　标	Item	1978	1990	2000
人口与就业	**Population and Employment**			
人口　（万人）	**Population　(10000 persons)**			
年末户籍总人口	Population with Residence Registration at the Year-end	5064.15	6246.32	7498.54
年末常住人口	Permanent Population at the Year-end	5064.15	6347.19	8650.03
男性人口	Male	2586.68	3249.76	4402.87
女性人口	Female	2477.47	3097.43	4247.16
城镇人口	Urban Population		2335.77	4757.52
乡村人口	Rural Population		4011.42	3892.51
就业　（万人）	**Employment　(10000 persons)**			
年末就业人员人数	Employed Persons at the Year-end	2275.95	3118.10	3989.32
城镇登记失业人数	Number of Registered Unemployed Persons in Urban Areas			
宏观经济	**Macro Economy**			
国民经济核算　（亿元）	**National Accounting　(100 million yuan)**			
地区生产总值	Gross Domestic Product	185.85	1559.03	10810.21
第一产业	Primary Industry	55.31	384.59	986.32
第二产业	Secondary Industry	86.62	615.86	5055.71
第三产业	Tertiary Industry	43.92	558.58	4768.18
人均地区生产总值　（元）	Per Capita Gross Domestic Product　(yuan)	370	2484	12817
支出法地区生产总值（亿元）	Gross Domestic Product by Expenditure Approach(100 million yuan)	194.14	1541.99	10810.21
最终消费支出	Final Consumption Expenditures	130.02	938.48	5717.11
居民消费	Household Consumption Expenditures	111.46	807.84	4474.11
政府消费	Government Consumption Expenditures	18.56	130.64	1243.00
资本形成总额	Gross Capital Formation	54.79	502.90	3917.11
固定资本形成总额	Gross Fixed Capital Formation	37.93	336.61	3160.12
存货增加	Changes in Inventories	16.86	166.29	756.99
货物和服务净流出	Net Exports of Goods and Services	9.33	100.61	1175.99
固定资产投资　（亿元）	**Investment in Fixed Assets　(100 million yuan)**			
固定资产投资总额	Investment in Fixed Assets	27.23	381.47	3233.70
#房地产开发	Real Estate Development		32.70	858.61
施工房屋建筑面积(万平方米)	Floor Space of Buildings under Construction　(10 000 sq.m)			23520.91
竣工房屋建筑面积(万平方米)	Floor Space of Buildings Completed　(10 000 sq.m)			13492.94
消费　（亿元）	**Domestic Trade　(100 million yuan)**			
社会消费品零售总额	Total Retail Sales of Consumer Goods	79.86	667.36	4379.81
对外贸易　（亿美元）	**Foreign Trade　(USD 100 million)**			
货物进出口总额	Total Exports and Imports		418.98	1701.06
进口额	Imports		196.77	781.87
出口额	Exports		222.21	919.19
利用外资　（亿美元）	**Foreign Capital Utilized　(USD 100 million)**			
实际利用外商直接投资	Foreign Direct Investment Actually Utilized		14.60	122.37
财政　（亿元）	**Government Finance　(100 million yuan)**			
地方一般公共预算收入	Local Public Budgetary Revenue	41.82	131.02	910.56
地方一般公共预算支出	Local Public Budgetary Expenditure	28.70	150.69	1069.86
价格指数　（上年=100）	**Price Indices　(preceding year=100)**			
商品零售价格指数	Retail Price Index	100.4	95.6	99.9
居民消费价格指数	Consumer Price Index		97.5	101.4
工业生产者出厂价格指数	Producer Price Index for Manufactured Goods			103.4
固定资产投资价格指数	Investment in Fixed Assets Price Indices			
能源生产与消费　（万吨标准煤）	**Production and Consumption of Energy　(10000 tons of SCE)**			
能源生产总量	Total Energy Production		1006.24	3711.69
能源消费总量	Total Energy Consumption		4044.28	9447.70

Principal Aggregate Indicators on National Economic and Social Development and Growth Rates

2010	2016	2017	速度指标(%) Indices and Growth Rates (%)								
			指数(2017为以下各年) Index (2017 as percentage of the following years)					平均增长速度 Average Annual Growth Rate			
			1978	1990	2000	2010	2016	1979–2017	1991–2017	2001–2017	2011–2017
8521.55	9164.90	9316.91	184.0	149.2	124.2	109.3	101.7	1.6	1.5	1.3	1.3
10440.94	10999.00	11169.00	220.6	176.0	129.1	107.0	101.5	2.0	2.1	1.5	1.0
5444.95	5763.48	5862.61	226.6	180.4	133.2	107.7	101.7	2.1	2.2	1.7	1.1
4995.99	5235.52	5306.39	214.2	171.3	124.9	106.2	101.4	2.0	2.0	1.3	0.9
6908.77	7611.31	7801.55		334.0	164.0	112.9	102.5		4.6	3.0	1.8
3532.17	3387.69	3367.45		83.9	86.5	95.3	99.4		-0.6	-0.8	-0.7
5870.48	6279.22	6340.79	278.6	203.4	158.9	108.0	101.0	2.7	2.7	2.8	1.1
39.23	37.99	37.13				94.6	97.7				-0.8
46544.63	80666.72	89705.23	10242.7	2429.5	586.8	174.2	107.5	12.6	12.5	11.0	8.2
2254.49	3500.49	3611.44	689.1	278.5	185.4	126.7	103.6	5.1	3.9	3.7	3.4
23296.73	35109.66	38008.06	20155.2	3957.1	660.3	166.5	106.5	14.5	14.6	11.7	7.6
20993.41	42056.57	48085.73	13500.0	2287.7	590.0	187.2	108.7	13.4	12.3	11.0	9.4
45252	73844	80932	4645.0	1375.5	446.5	161.6	106.0	10.3	10.2	9.2	7.1
46544.63	80666.72	89705.23									
22501.78	40885.91	45128.95									
17702.35	31127.58	34097.05									
4799.43	9758.33	11031.90									
18226.60	34647.09	39657.52									
17035.10	33279.65	38390.85									
1191.50	1367.44	1266.67									
5816.25	5133.72	4918.76									
16113.19	33008.86	37477.96	137634.8	9824.6	1159.0	232.6	113.5	20.4	18.5	15.5	15.2
3659.69	10307.80	12075.69		36928.7	1406.4	330.0	117.2		24.5	16.8	18.6
57221.79	84623.21	92203.09			392.0	161.1	109.0			8.4	7.1
20420.60	14042.25	14680.63			108.8	71.9	104.5			0.5	-4.6
17458.44	34739.00	38200.07	47833.8	5724.1	872.2	218.8	110.0	17.1	16.2	13.6	11.8
7848.96	9552.86	10066.80		2402.7	591.8	128.3	105.4		12.5	11.0	3.6
3317.05	3567.21	3838.05		1950.5	490.9	115.7	107.6		11.6	9.8	2.1
4531.91	5985.64	6228.73		2803.1	677.6	137.4	104.1		13.1	11.9	4.6
202.61	233.49	229.07		1569.0	187.2	113.1	98.1		10.7	3.8	1.8
4517.04	10390.35	11320.35	27069.2	8640.2	1243.2	250.6	109.0		18.0	16.0	14.0
5421.54	13446.09	15037.48	52395.4	9979.1	1405.6	277.4	111.8		18.6	16.8	15.7
103.3	100.8	101.6									
103.1	102.3	101.5									
103.2	99.4	103.3									
103.0	100.3	105.3									
4858.07	7137.95	7037.37		699.4	189.6	144.9	98.6		7.5	3.8	5.4
25445.22	31240.75	32341.66		799.7	342.3	127.1	103.5		8.0	7.5	3.5

1-2 续表 1

指 标	Item	1978	1990	2000
产业	**Industry**			
农业	**Agriculture**			
农林牧渔业总产值 (亿元)	Gross Output Value of Farming, Forestry, Animal Husbandry and Fishery (100 million yuan)	85.94	600.71	1701.18
主要农产品产量 (万吨)	Output of Major Farm Products (10000 tons)			
粮食	Grain	1509.51	1896.29	1822.33
油料	Oil-bearing Crops	36.04	58.93	78.78
糖蔗	Sugarcane	835.42	2093.46	1137.59
茶叶	Tea	0.90	2.59	4.21
水果	Fruits	29.40	328.58	643.52
肉类	Meat	48.45	202.45	324.48
水产品	Aquatic Products	65.50	207.66	593.19
工业	**Industry**			
主要工业产品产量	Output of Major Industrial Products			
布 (亿米)	Cloth (100 million m)	2.27	4.59	16.99
机制纸及纸板 (万吨)	Machine-made Paper and Paperboard (10000 tons)	27.47	104.13	260.30
成品糖 (万吨)	Sugar (10000 tons)	96.15	184.50	91.30
家用电冰箱 (万台)	Household Refrigerators (10000 sets)		105.75	320.70
家用洗衣机 (万台)	Household Washing Machines (10000 sets)		143.01	244.18
彩色电视机 (万台)	Color Television Sets (10000 sets)		262.37	1531.53
照相机 (万架)	Cameras (10000 sets)		99.30	3545.88
原油 (万吨)	Crude Oil (10000 tons)	10.22	49.05	1393.17
发电量 (亿千瓦时)	Electricity (100 million kwh)	92.32	343.98	1292.69
粗钢 (万吨)	Raw Steel (10000 tons)	35.84	116.96	286.99
钢材 (万吨)	Steel Products (10000 tons)	43.67	133.74	406.28
水泥 (万吨)	Cement (10000 tons)	369.08	2070.91	5872.00
汽车 (万辆)	Motor Vehicles (10000 units)			3.94
规模以上工业企业主要指标	Main Indicators of Industrial Enterprises above Designated Size			
工业增加值 (亿元)	Value-added of Industry (101 million yuan)			3422.60
资产总计 (亿元)	Total Assets (100 million yuan)			14370.57
主营业务收入 (亿元)	Main Business Revenue (100 million yuan)		1287.91	12380.65
利税总额 (亿元)	Pre-tax Profits (100 million yuan)	32.91	121.50	1042.77
建筑业	**Construction**			
建筑业企业年末就业人员 (万人)	Number of Employed Persons in Construction Enterprises at the Year-end (10000 persons)	14.78	67.22	141.46
建筑业总产值(当年价) (亿元)	Gross Output Value (at current prices) (100 million yuan)	5.47	113.40	944.61
交通运输业	**Transportation**			
客运量 (万人)	Passenger Traffic (10000 persons)	15906	78046	164791
铁路	Railways	2410	4467	12165
公路	Highways	10897	70681	148945
水运	Waterways	2546	2428	2363
民航	Civil Aviation	53	470	1318
货运量 (万吨)	Freight Traffic (10000 tons)	15204	85809	119216
铁路	Railways	3206	4803	15172
公路	Highways	3967	63709	75365
水运	Waterways	7887	16198	25696
管道	Pipelines	143	1091	2952
民航	Civil Aviation	1	8	31
港口货物吞吐量 (万吨)	Volume of Freight Handled at Ports (10000 tons)	7133	11904	31649

1-2 1 continued

2010	2016	2017	速度指标(%) Indices and Growth Rates (%)								
			指数(2017为以下各年) Index (2017 as Percentage of the Following Years)					平均增长速度 Average Annual Growth Rate			
			1978	1990	2000	2010	2016	1979–2017	1991–2017	2001–2017	2011–2017
3697.18	5817.55	5969.87	730.8	319.2	187.7	124.5	103.3	5.2	4.4	3.8	3.2
1249.15	1204.22	1208.56	80.1	63.7	66.3	96.8	100.4	-0.6	-1.7	-2.4	-0.5
83.34	99.35	101.28	281.0	171.9	128.6	121.5	102.0	2.7	2.0	1.5	2.8
1064.09	1096.56	1144.14	137.0	54.7	100.6	107.5	104.3	0.8	-2.2	0.0	1.0
5.38	8.92	9.29	1032.1	358.6	220.6	172.5	104.1	6.2	4.8	4.8	8.1
1049.21	1331.99	1421.23	4834.1	432.5	220.9	135.5	106.7	10.5	5.6	4.8	4.4
454.86	448.70	444.08	916.6	219.4	136.9	97.6	99.0	5.8	3.0	1.9	-0.3
729.03	818.29	833.54	1272.6	401.4	140.5	114.3	101.9	6.7	5.3	2.0	1.9
28.27	27.10	27.01	1189.8	588.4	159.0	95.54	107.0	6.6	6.8	2.8	-0.7
1434.68	2127.52	2177.74	7927.7	2091.4	836.6	151.79	102.9	11.9	11.9	13.3	6.1
91.66	116.12	82.27	85.6	44.6	90.1	89.76	97.3	-0.4	-2.9	-0.6	-1.5
1457.76	2135.51	1556.37		1471.7	485.3	106.76	110.7		10.5	9.7	0.9
467.83	762.32	749.62		524.2	307.0	160.23	123.0		6.3	6.8	7.0
4494.78	8106.36	8399.88		3201.5	548.5	186.88	104.1		13.7	10.5	9.3
3798.93	641.94	656.59		661.2	18.5	17.28	107.7		7.2	-9.4	-22.2
1287.15	1556.29	1435.20				111.50	92.2				1.6
3101.28	4081.97	4407.30				142.10	108.0				5.1
1239.34	2283.19	2890.71	8065.6	2471.5	1007.2	233.25	124.7	11.9	12.6	14.6	12.9
2918.89	4113.34	4213.69	9648.9	3150.7	1037.1	144.36	105.9	12.4	13.6	14.8	5.4
11536.67	15078.64	15752.98	4268.2	760.7	268.3	136.55	107.7	10.1	7.8	6.0	4.6
156.29	280.25	321.06			8148.6	205.42	113.4			29.5	10.8
20338.34	31330.24	31349.47			1044.6	176.3	107.2			14.8	8.4
62626.90	105604.17	115201.19			789.6	189.9	109.7			12.9	9.6
84114.85	129151.31	133924.37			1137.7	182.6	111.5			15.4	9.0
9418.42	13150.85	13769.27			1542.9	197.8	113.0			17.5	10.2
196.32	246.17	289.97	1961.9	431.4	205.0	147.7	117.8	7.9	5.6	4.3	5.7
4742.09	9805.00	11571.33	211541.6	10204.0	1225.0	244.0	118.0	21.7	18.7	15.9	13.6
467049	144262	148549	931.1	693.1	335.8	179.0	105.6	5.9	7.4	7.4	8.7
14956	28954	28476	1266.6	701.9	371.1	217.0	112.1	6.7	7.5	8.0	11.7
442224	102094	105919	1133.7	692.5	328.6	173.1	103.7	6.4	7.4	7.2	8.2
2241	2648	2733	32.3	146.8	150.8	131.6	103.2	-2.9	1.4	2.4	4.0
7628	10566	11420	21612.6	2429.3	866.3	149.7	108.1	14.8	12.5	13.5	5.9
205034	377645	400601	1438.6	615.1	468.4	194.2	106.9	7.1	7.0	9.5	9.9
12170	10135	7254	303.1	177.7	98.9	84.4	101.3	2.9	2.2	-0.1	-2.4
142389	272826	288904	1293.8	697.0	589.2	201.7	105.9	6.8	7.5	11.0	10.5
43092	85633	94871	883.3	604.1	380.8	208.8	110.8	5.7	6.9	8.2	11.1
7267	8891	9407	6315.4	827.8	305.9	129.4	105.8	11.2	8.1	6.8	3.8
116	160	166	17085.0	2073.4	535.1	143.4	103.7	14.1	11.9	10.4	5.3
122258	179924	198015	2776.0	1663.4	625.7	162.0	110.1	8.9	11.0	11.4	7.1

1-2 续表 2

指　　标	Item	1978	1990	2000
邮电通信业	**Postal and Telecommunication Services**			
邮电业务总量 （亿元）	Total Business Volume (100 million yuan)	0.90	26.30	757.22
函件 （亿件）	Number of Letters Delivered (100 million pieces)		4.72	10.66
报刊累计数 （亿份）	Accumulated Number of Newspapers and Magazines Distributed (100 million copies)		11.63	10.78
本地电话用户 （万户）	Number of Subscribers of Local Telephones (10000 accounts)		113.00	1414.94
移动电话用户 （万户）	Number of Subscribers of Mobile Telephones (10000 accounts)		1.11	1357.26
互联网宽带接入用户（万户）	Broadband Subscribers of Internet (10000 accounts)			216.41
国际旅游	**International Tourism**			
国际旅游外汇收入（亿美元）	Foreign Exchange Earnings from International Tourism (USD 100 million)		7.17	41.12
金融保险	**Banking and Insurance**			
金融机构存款余额 （亿元）	Deposits of Financial Institutions (100 million yuan)			19083.64
金融机构贷款余额 （亿元）	Loans in in Financial Institutions (100 million yuan)			13227.62
保费收入 （亿元）	Premium Income (100 million yuan)		18.05	191.88
教育、科技、文化	**Education, Science and Technology and Culture**			
教育	**Education**			
专任教师数 （万人）	Full-time Teachers (10000 persons)			
普通高等学校	Institutions of Higher Education	0.90	1.57	2.04
中等学校	Secondary Schools	15.93	16.33	27.24
小学	Primary Schools	26.09	27.73	36.41
在校学生数 （万人）	Students Enrollment (10000 persons)			
普通高等学校	Institutions of Higher Education	3.07	9.59	29.95
中等学校	Secondary Schools	316.96	284.52	541.72
小学	Primary Schools	743.02	747.29	929.93
财政教育支出 （亿元）	Government Expenditures on Education (100 million yuan)		21.34	144.39
科技	**Science and Technology**			
研究与试验发展(R&D)活动人员 （万人）	Number of R&D Personnel (10000 persons)			
研究与试验发展(R&D)经费内部支出 （亿元）	Internal Expenditure on R&D (100 million yuan)			
研究与试验发展(R&D)活动课题(项目)数 （个）	Number of R&D Programs/Projects (item)			
文化	**Culture**			
出版数量	Number of Publications			
图书 （亿册）	Number of Books Published (100 million copies)	1.72	2.81	2.70
杂志 （万册）	Number of Magazines Issued (10000 copies)	1519	11325	26299
报纸 （亿份）	Number of Newspapers Issued (100 million copies)	3.19	13.81	34.63

1-2 2 continued

2010	2016	2017	速度指标(%) Indices and Growth Rates (%)								
			指数(2017为以下各年) Index (2017 as percentage of the following years)					平均增长速度 Average Annual Growth Rate			
			1978	1990	2000	2010	2016	1979–2017	1991–2017	2001–2017	2011–2017
4832.94	6892.41	6107 19	2671391.4	135961.8	4722.3	587.8	158.0	29.9	30.6	25.5	28.8
7.62	7.04	6 66		141.1	62.5	87.4	94.6		1.3	-2.7	-1.9
8.79	8.34	7 91		68.0	73.4	90.0	94.8		-1.4	-1.8	-1.5
3169.14	2609.71	2406.09		2129.3	170.0	75.9	92.2		12.0	3.2	-3.9
9710.09	14348.96	14798.85		1333229.7	1090.3	152.4	103.1		42.2	15.1	6.2
1523.22	2850.60	3288.15			1519.4	215.9	115.3			17.4	11.6
124.32	185.77	196.63		2742.4	478.2	158.2	105.8		13.0	9.6	6.8
82019.40	179829.19	194535.75			1019.4	237.2	108.2			14.6	13.1
51799.30	110928.41	126031.95			952.8	243.3	113.6			14.2	13.5
1421.68	3820.51	4304.60		23848.2	2243.4	302.8	112.7		22.5	20.1	17.1
7.86	10.12	10.44	1160.0	665.0	511.8	132.8	103.2	6.5	7.3	10.1	4.1
45.48	49.38	49.91	313.3	305.6	183.2	109.7	101.1	3.0	4.2	3.6	1.3
43.07	48.66	50.78	194.6	183.1	139.5	117.9	104.4	1.7	2.3	2.0	2.4
142.66	189.29	192.58	6273.0	2008.1	643.0	135.0	101.7	11.2	11.8	11.6	4.4
939.39	705.05	700.14	220.9	246.1	129.2	74.5	99.3	2.1	3.4	1.5	-4.1
848.55	905.22	941.96	126.8	126.1	101.3	111.0	104.1	0.6	0.9	0.1	1.5
921.48	2318.47	2575.52		12069.0	1783.7	279.5	111.1		19.4	18.5	15.8
44.66	73.52	87.99				197.0	119.7				10.2
808.75	2035.14	2343.63				289.8	115.2				16.4
72747	135652	170214				234.0	125.5				12.9
2.31	3.12	3.02	175.6	107.5	111.9	130.7	96.8	1.5	0.3	0.7	3.9
21201	12270	11428	752.3	100.9	43.5	53.9	93.1	5.3	0.0	-4.8	-8.4
45.59	29.88	27.47	861.2	198.9	79.3	60.3	91.9	5.7	2.6	-1.4	-7.0

1-2 续表 3

指　　标	Item	1978	1990	2000
家庭、生活、环境	**Family, People's Livelihood and Environment**			
家庭	**Family**			
城镇常住居民平均每户家庭人口（人）	Average Permanent Household Size in Urban Areas (person)	4.84	3.85	3.57
农村常住居民平均每户家庭人口（人）	Average Permanent Household Size in Rural Areas (person)	5.99	5.65	5.15
婚姻	**Marriages and Divorces**			
结婚登记总数（万对）	Registered Number of Marriages (10000 couples)		50.66	56.21
离婚数（万对）	Number of Divorces (10000 couples)		2.58	4.75
居住	**Residence**			
城镇常住居民人均住房建筑面积(平方米)	Per Capita Floor Space of Urban Permanent Residents (sq.m)	5.47	15.77	24.60
农村常住居民人均住房建筑面积(平方米)	Per Capita Floor Space of Rural Permanent Residents (sq.m)	8.73	17.39	22.42
生活	**People's Livelihood**			
全体常住居民人均可支配收入（元）	Per Capita Disposable Income of Permanent Residents (yuan)			
城镇常住居民人均可支配收入（元）	Per Capita Disposable Income of Urban Permanent Residents(yuan)	412.13	2303.15	9761.57
农村常住居民人均可支配收入（元）	Per Capita Disposable Income of Rural Permanent Residents(yuan)	193.25	1043.03	3654.48
人民币住户存款（亿元）	Savings Deposits by Househoulds in Renminbi (100 million yuan)	17.56	752.16	8667.29
工资	**Wages**			
城镇单位就业人员工资总额（亿元）	Earnings of Employed Persons in Urban Areas (100 million yuan)	30.59	223.29	1057.57
城镇单位就业人员平均工资（元）	Average Earnings of Employed Persons in Urban Areas (yuan)	615	2929	13859
卫生	**Health Care**			
医院、卫生院（个）	Number of Hospitals (unit)	1968	1885	2426
执业(助理)医师（万人）	Number of Doctors (10000 persons)	4.79	8.11	11.12
医院、卫生院床位数（万张）	Number of Hospital Beds (10000 units)	8.41	11.41	15.72
环境、灾害	**Environment and Disaster**			
废水中化学需氧量排放量（万吨）	Volume of COD Discharged from Waste Water (10000 tuns)			95.10
废气中二氧化硫排放总量（万吨）	Total Volume of Industrial Sulfur Dioxide Emission (1000 tuns)			90.5
火灾发生数（起）	Number of Fire Disasters (time)		1725	8622
火灾损失（万元）	Fire Loss (10000 yuan)		9102	10065
交通事故发生数（起）	Number of Traffic Accidents (time)		25909	66072
交通事故损失（万元）	Loss of Traffic Accidents (10000 yuan)		5044	27526

注：1. 2006—2009年年末常住人口根据2010年第六次全国人口普查快速汇总数据进行平滑调整。
2. 2003年起，职工改为单位从业人员，2000年数据作了相应调整。
3. 农业、工业总产值绝对数按当年价格计算，增长速度按可比价计算。
4. 工业指标统计范围为规模以上工业企业(即年主营业务收入500万元以上的法人工业企业，2000—2006年为全部国有工业企业及年主营业务收入500万元以上的非国有工业企业，2011年起，调整为年主营业务收入2000万元及以上的法人工业企业)。
5. 2000年起，粮食产量为抽样调查数据。
6. 1994年起，财政收入按税改新口径统计(即不含中央返还部分)。
7. 邮电业务总量2000年以前按1990年不变价计算，2000年至2010年按2000年不变价计算,2011年起按2010年不变价计算。
8. 1986年以前中等学校不含成人中专数据。
9. 城镇居民人均住房建筑面积1995、2000年为使用面积， 2005年以后为建筑面积。
10. 2011年起，固定资产投资项目统计起点由50万元提高至500万元，且不包含农村农户投资；2010年以前为全社会固定资产投资。
11. 自2015年起，地方公共财政预算收入和地方公共财政预算支出统一更名为地方一般公共预算收入和地方一般公共预算支出。
12. 2013年起，居民人均可支配收入为城乡一体化住户收支与生活状况调查数据，与此前分城镇和农村住户调查的统计口径不可比，2013年以前农村居民收入为纯收入。

1-2 3 continued

2010	2016	2017	速度指标(%) Indices and Growth Rates (%)								
			指数(2017为以下各年) Index (2017 as Percentage of the Following Years)					平均增长速度 Average Annual Growth Rate			
			1978	1990	2000	2010	2016	1979–2017	1991–2017	2001–2017	2011–2017
3.21	2.83	2.87	59.3	74.5	80.4	89.4	101.4	-1.3	-1.1	-1.3	-1.6
4.95	3.69	3.65	60.9	64.6	70.9	73.7	98.9	-1.3	-1.6	-2.0	-4.3
85.71	78.61	75.81		149.6	134.9	88.4	96.4		1.5	1.8	-1.7
12.70	21.19	22.03		854.0	463.9	173.4	104.0		8.3	9.4	8.2
34.13	32.74	33.09	604.9	209.8	134.5	97.0	101.1	4.7	2.8	1.8	-0.4
29.23	43.92	45.27	518.6	260.3	201.9	154.9	103.1	4.3	3.6	4.2	6.4
	30295.80	33003.29					108.9				10.3
23897.80	37684.25	40975.14					108.7				9.8
7890.25	14512.15	15779.74					108.7				11.2
36318.66	58618.89	61890.08	352449.2	8228.3	714.1	170.4	105.6	23.3	17.7	12.3	7.9
4484.29	14156.81	15511.55	50707.9	6946.8	1466.7	345.9	109.6	17.3	17.0	17.1	19.4
40432	72326	79183	12875.3	2703.4	571.3	195.8	109.5	13.3	13.0	10.8	10.1
2444	2581	2666	135.5	141.4	109.9	109.1	103.3	0.8	1.3	0.6	1.2
16.85	24.41	25.89	540.5	319.2	232.8	153.6	106.0	4.4	4.4	5.1	6.3
27.71	42.84	49.21	585.2	431.3	313.0	177.6	114.9	4.6	5.6	6.9	8.6
85.84	96.40										
105.5	35.4										
6065	16923	16501		956.6	191.4	272.1	97.5		8.7	3.9	15.4
17500	40838	28017		307.8	278.4	160.1	68.6		4.3	6.2	7.0
30480	24876	24138		93.2	36.5	79.2	97.0		-0.3	-5.8	-3.3
8051	7414	10553		209.2	38.3	131.1	142.3		2.8	-5.5	3.9

Notes: a) Figures of permanent population at the year-end from 2006 to 2009 have been adjusted in accordance with the flash sums of the 6th National Population Cencus in 2010.

b)The number of staff and workers has been recoded as employed persons in units since 2003.The data of 2000 have been adjusted accordingly.

c)Figures in value terms on gross output value of agriculture and industry are calculated at current prices, whereas their growth rates are calculated at constant prices.

d)The statistical coverage of the industrial indicators refers to the industrial enterprises above designated size, i.e.legal person industrial enterprises with annual main business revenue over 5 million yuan.The industrial indicators from 2000 to 2006 covered all state-owned industrial enterprises and non-state-owned industrial enterprises with annual main business revenue over 5 million yuan. Since 2011, it refers to legal person industrial enterprises with annual principal business revenue of over 20 million yuan.

e) Figures of output of grain have been obtained from sample surveys since 2000.

f) Figures of government revenues since 1994 are calculated according to new standards stipulated in the tax reform (excluding revenues refunded by the central government).

g)The total business volume of postal and telecommunication services are at 1990 constant prices before 2000 and at 2000 constant prices from 2000 to 2010,and at 2010 constant price since 2010.

h) Before 1986, the figures of secondary schools excluded those of specialized secondary schools for adults.

i) The per capital floor space of urban residents of 1995 and 2000 are useable area, and that since 2005 are building area.

j) Since 2011, the cut-off point of investment statistics is changed from a minimum of 500,000 yuan to a minimum of 5,000,000 yuan, and the data do not include the investment made by rural households. Data before 2010 refer to total investment in fixed assets.

k) From 2015, the name of local government budgetary revenue and local government budgetary expenditure have been changed to local public budgetary revenue and local public budgetary expenditure.

l) The NBS started and integrated households income and expenditure survey in 2013,including both urban and rural households. The coverage, methodology and definitions used in the survey are different from those used for the separate urban and rural household surveys prior ot 2013.

1-3 国民经济和社会发展结构指标

Composition Indicators of National Economic and Social Development

单位：% (%)

指　　标	Item	2000	2010	2015	2016	2017
人口与就业	**Population and Employment**					
人口	**Population**					
城乡结构(常住人口)	Urban and Rural Composition(by permanent population)					
城镇	Urban	55.0	66.2	68.7	69.2	69.9
乡村	Rural	45.0	33.8	31.3	30.8	30.2
性别结构(户籍人口)	Sexual Composition(by residential population)					
男	Male	51.6	51.5	51.5	51.5	51.4
女	Female	48.4	48.5	48.5	48.5	48.6
就业	**Employment**					
产业结构	Industrial Structure					
第一产业	Primary Industry	40.0	24.4	22.1	21.7	21.4
第二产业	Secondary Industry	27.9	42.4	41.0	40.5	40.1
第三产业	Tertiary Industry	32.1	33.2	36.9	37.8	38.5
按登记注册类型分组	Grouped by Status of Registration					
国有单位	State-owned Units	11.8	6.7	6.3	6.2	6.1
集体单位	Collective-owned Units	59.4	31.6	25.3	24.9	24.5
股份合作单位	Share-holding Cooperative Units	0.3	0.4	0.4	0.4	0.4
联营单位	Joint Ownership Units	0.2	0.3	0.1	0.1	0.1
有限责任公司	Limited Liability Corporations	1.0	5.2	9.5	9.8	10.2
股份有限公司	Share-holding Corporations Ltd.	0.7	1.5	2.7	3.0	3.0
外商投资单位	Units with Foreign Investment	1.1	4.9	5.5	5.0	4.8
港澳台商投资单位	Units with Investment from Hong Kong，Macao and Taiwan	2.6	12.5	9.9	9.8	9.6
私营企业	Private Enterprises	5.5	17.7	20.8	21.2	21.6
个体经济	Individual Economy	7.7	17.8	18.1	18.2	18.4
宏观经济	**Macro Economy**					
国民经济核算	**National Accounts**					
地区生产总值产业结构	Industrial Structure of Gross Domestic Product					
第一产业	Primary Industry	9.1	4.8	4.3	4.4	4.0
第二产业	Secondary Industry	46.8	50.1	45.5	43.5	42.4
第三产业	Tertiary Industry	44.1	45.1	50.2	52.1	53.6
支出法地区生产总值结构	Domestic Expenditure Structure					
最终消费	Final Consumption	52.9	48.3	50.4	50.7	50.3
居民消费	Household Consumption	41.4	38.0	38.5	38.6	38.0
农村居民	Rural Households	28.9	33.2	32.3	32.4	32.0
城镇居民	Urban Households	12.5	4.9	6.2	6.2	6.0
政府消费	Government Consumption	11.5	10.3	11.9	12.1	12.3
资本形成总额	Gross Capital Formation	36.2	39.2	42.8	43.0	44.2
固定资本形成总额	Gross Fixed Capital Formation	29.2	36.6	41.3	41.3	42.8
存货增加	Changes in Inventories	7.0	2.6	1.5	1.7	1.4
净流出	Net Exports	10.9	12.5	6.9	6.4	5.5
固定资产投资	**Investment**					
按登记注册类型分	Grouped by Status of Registration					
内资	Domestic-funded	82.8	85.4	88.4	87.8	89.1
国有	State-owned	37.7	32.0	21.2	18.7	19.6
集体	Collective-owned	12.2	4.6	4.3	3.0	2.6
股份合作	Cooperative	0.6	0.3	0.4	0.2	0.1
联营	Joint ownership	1.5	0.1	…	0.1	0.1
其他有限责任公司	Limited Liability	11.3	21.1	30.7	34.5	35.5
股份有限公司	Share-holding	4.7	5.4	4.2	3.1	3.0
私营	Private	6.4	13.7	22.6	23.3	23.2
个体	Induvidual	7.7	5.6	1.1	1.3	0.9
其他	Others	0.7	2.6	3.9	3.6	4.1
港澳台商投资	Investment from Hong Kong, Macao & Taiwan	12.9	9.2	6.9	7.5	6.5
外商投资	Foreign investment	4.3	5.4	4.7	4.7	4.4

1-3 续表 1 continued

单位：% (%)

指 标	Item	2000	2010	2015	2016	2017
资金来源结构	Structure of Sources of Funds					
国家预算资金	State Budgetary Appropriation	1.7	2.2	4.9	4.8	5.7
国内贷款	Domestic Loans	17.2	16.8	12.5	12.6	16.1
利用外资	Foreign Investment	10.5	3.3	0.6	0.7	0.6
自筹投资	Fundraising	42.9	56.6	57.9	52.6	51.3
其他投资	Others	27.7	21.1	24.2	29.3	26.2
对外贸易（美元）	**Foreign Trade （USD）**					
出口按贸易方式分	Exports by Customs Regime					
一般贸易	Ordinary Trade	19.0	32.9	42.9	43.6	45.7
加工贸易	Processing Trade	78.1	60.8	43.7	39.9	38.3
其他	Others	2.9	6.3	13.4	16.5	16.0
进口按贸易方式分	Imports by Customs Regime					
一般贸易	Ordinary Trade	26.7	36.0	40.9	43.6	46.7
加工贸易	Processing Trade	63.1	51.4	41.9	37.0	35.1
其他	Others	10.2	12.6	17.2	19.5	18.2
利用外资	**Utilization of Foreign Capital**					
实际利用外资结构	Structure of Foreign Capital Actually Utilized					
外商直接投资	Foreign Direct Investment	84.0	96.4	99.4	99.8	99.8
外商其他投资	Other Foreign Investment	11.2	3.6	0.6	0.2	0.2
国内贸易	**Domestic Trade**					
社会消费品零售总额结构	Structure of Total Retail Sales of Consumer Goods					
城镇	Urban Areas	75.1	85.3	87.6	87.6	87.5
乡村	Rural Areas	24.9	14.7	12.4	12.4	12.5
能源生产与消费	**Production and Consumption of Energy**					
能源生产总量结构	Structure of Total Energy Production					
原煤	Coal	8.0				
原油	Crude Oil	53.6	37.8	32.8	30.7	31.6
电力	Electricity	27.1	40.7	48.5	54.5	51.5
天然气	Natural Gas	11.3	21.5	18.7	14.8	16.9
一次能源消费总量结构	Structure of Total Primary Energy Consumption					
原煤	Coal	52.2	45.2	42.3	39.7	39.5
原油	Crude Oil	35.0	29.0	27.3	26.6	25.9
电力	Electricity	12.6	20.1	24.0	25.6	26.2
天然气	Natural Gas	0.2	5.7	6.4	8.1	8.4
其他	Others					
农业	**Agriculture**					
农林牧渔业产值结构	Structure of Gross Output Value of Farming, Forestry, Animal Husbandry and Fishery					
农业	Farming	47.5	45.1	47.0	47.5	48.4
林业	Forestry	3.5	4.9	5.8	5.7	6.0
牧业	Animal Husbandry	26.5	26.5	22.6	22.7	20.1
渔业	Fishery	22.5	19.9	20.8	20.3	21.4
农林牧渔服务业	Services for Farming, Forestry, Animal Husbandry and Fishery	…	3.6	3.9	3.9	4.1
工业(规模以上)	**Industry(aboved designated size)**					
按轻重工业分	Grouped by Light and Heavy Industry					
轻工业	Light Industry	52.9	38.3	38.2	37.6	35.2
重工业	Heavy Industry	47.1	61.7	61.8	62.4	64.8
按经济类型分	Grouped by Ownership					
国有工业	State-owned Industry	11.6	5.4	0.5	0.5	0.6
集体工业	Collective-owned Industry	9.6	0.9	0.4	0.3	0.2
股份合作工业	Share-holding Cooperative Industry	0.9	0.2	0.1	0.1	0.1
股份制工业	Share-holding Industry	14.3	35.7	53.8	56.6	59.4
外商投资工业	Industry with Foreign Investment	20.2	25.4	20.8	19.4	17.8
港澳台商投资工业	Industry with Investment from Hong Kong, Macao and Taiwan	38.0	27.6	22.3	21.1	20.3
按企业规模分	Grouped by Size of Enterprise					
大型企业	Large	36.2	33.0	44.4	45.0	46.9
中型企业	Medium-sized	11.4	33.3	26.6	25.8	23.8
小微型企业	Small and Micro	52.3	33.7	29.0	29.2	29.3

1−3 续表 2 continued

单位：% (%)

指　　标	Item	2000	2010	2015	2016	2017
建筑业	**Construction**					
按登记注册类型分	Grouped by Status of Registration					
内资	Domestic-funded	97.6	96.5	97.4	97.5	97.7
国有	State-owned	38.8	20.3	9.8	7.9	7.9
集体	Collective-owned	33.2	6.2	4.5	4.3	3.8
股份合作	Cooperative	0.8	0.3	0.1	0.1	0.1
联营	Joint ownership	1.2	0.4	0.1	0.1	0.1
有限责任公司	Limited Liability	13.9	42.0	53.7	54.3	54.5
股份有限公司	Share-holding	5.2	7.3	9.7	10.3	10.7
私营	Private	4.4	18.6	19.6	20.5	20.6
其他	Others	...	1.0	...	...	...
港澳台商投资	Investment from Hong Kong, Macao & Taiwan	1.6	1.5	0.8	0.9	0.9
外商投资	Foreign investment	0.8	2.0	1.7	1.6	1.4
交通运输和旅游	**Transportation and Tourism**					
客运量结构	Structure of Passenger Traffic					
铁路	Railways	7.4	3.2	12.8	20.1	19.2
公路	Highways	90.4	94.6	81.0	70.8	71.3
水运	Waterways	1.4	0.5	1.3	1.8	1.8
民用航空	Civil Aviation	0.8	1.6	4.8	7.3	7.7
货运量结构	Structure of Freight Traffic					
铁路	Railways	12.7	5.9	2.7	2.7	1.8
公路	Highways	63.2	69.4	74.4	72.2	72.1
水运	Waterways	21.6	21.0	20.7	22.7	23.7
民用航空	Civil Aviation	...	0.1	...	...	0.0
管道输油(气)	Pipelines	2.5	3.5	2.2	2.4	2.3
接待过夜旅游者人数	Composition of Tourists Staying Overnight					
入境旅游者	Overseas Visitor Arrivals Inbound Tourists	15.6	14.8	9.5	8.9	8.2
国内旅游者	Domestic Tourists	84.4	85.2	90.5	91.1	91.8
教育与科技	**Education and Technology**					
教育	**Education**					
在校学生结构	Structure of Enrolled Students					
大学生	Colleges and Universities	2.1	8.4	11.5	11.5	11.5
中学生	Regular Secondary Schools	32.4	41.7	34.7	33.3	32.5
小学生	Primary Schools	65.5	49.9	53.8	55.2	56.1
专任教师结构	Structure of Full-time Teachers					
大学	Colleges and Universities	3.3	8.7	10.0	10.0	10.0
中学	Secondary Schools	37.3	43.5	42.9	42.1	41.3
小学	Primary Schools	59.4	47.8	47.1	47.9	48.7

1-3　续表 3　continued

单位：%　　　　(%)

指　　标	Item	2000	2010	2015	2016	2017
科技	**Science and Technology**					
研究与试验发展(R&D)经费内部支出机构	Structure of Internal Expenditure on R&D					
科学研究与技术开发机构	Scientific Research and Technological Development Institutions		2.6	3.6	1.4	0.9
全日制普通高等学校	Full-time Regular Institutions of Higher Education		3.5	3.5	7.8	5.9
工业企业	Industrial Enterprises		87.0	84.6	82.7	85.9
其他	Others		6.8	8.4	8.1	7.4
研究与试验发展(R&D)经费内部支出	R&D Expenditure Internal Expernditure					
#基础研究	Basic Research		2.1	3.0	4.2	4.7
应用研究	Applied Research		4.6	9.2	8.1	9.2
试验发展	Experimental Development		93.3	87.8	87.7	86.1
生活、卫生、环境	**People's Livelihood，Health Care and Environment**					
生活	**People's Livelihood**					
城镇居民消费结构	Composition of Consumption Expenditure					
食品烟酒	Food,Tobacco and Liquor	38.6	36.5	33.2	32.9	32.2
衣着	Clothing	4.6	6.7	5.7	5.5	5.3
居住	Living	13.7	10.4	22.3	22.4	23.5
生活用品及服务	Daily Necessities and Services	7.5	6.5	5.9	6.0	5.9
交通通信	Transportation and Telecommunication	13.4	18.5	15.2	14.7	14.2
教育文化娱乐	Education,Culture and Entertainment	11.5	12.9	10.4	10.9	10.9
医疗保健	Health Service	4.3	5.0	4.3	4.6	5.0
其他用品和服务	Other Necessities and Services	6.4	3.5	3.0	3.0	3.0
农村居民消费结构	Composition of Consumption Expenditure					
食品烟酒	Food,Tobacco and Liquor	49.8	47.7	40.6	40.4	40.2
衣着	Clothing	3.9	3.9	3.3	3.3	3.5
居住	Living	14.3	17.9	22.5	22.2	22.0
生活用品及服务	Daily Necessities and Services	4.7	4.3	5.9	5.8	5.5
交通通信	Transportation and Telecommunication	7.8	11.6	10.5	11.0	10.8
教育文化娱乐	Education,Culture and Entertainment	11.8	5.9	8.6	8.5	9.0
医疗保健	Health Service	3.9	5.6	6.5	6.5	6.9
其他用品和服务	Other Necessities and Services	3.8	3.1	2.2	2.3	2.1
卫生	**Health Care**					
卫生技术人员结构	Structure of Medical Technical Personnel					
#医生	Doctors	42.0	37.7	36.4	36.6	36.5
注册护士	Nurses	31.4	37.1	41.3	42.6	43.4
床位结构	Structure of Hospital Beds					
#医院	Hospitals	71.4	74.7	79.2	79.9	80.0
环境、灾害	**Environment and Disaster**					
工业污染源治理投资结构	Investment Structure of Treatment of Industrial Pollution Sources					
治理废水	Treatment of Waste Water		56.8	31.9	21.4	
治理废气	Treatment of Waste Gas		20.5	39.3	63.7	
治理固体废物	Treatment of Waste Solid Wastes		1.7	11.3	2.9	
治理噪声	Treatment of Noise		0.1	4.2	1.6	
治理其它	Treatment of Others		20.9	13.3	10.4	
火灾事故损失额结构	Structure of Fire Losses Converted into Cash					
特大或重大	Extraordinarily Serious Fires					
较大	Serious Fires		0.2	0.8	0.4	0.05
一般	Ordinary Fires		99.8	99.2	99.6	99.95
交通事故损失额结构	Structure of Losses from Traffic Accidents Converted into Cash					
机动车道	Roads for Motored Vehicles		81.5	83.9	85.5	89.0
非机动车道	Roads for Nonmotored Vehicles		1.4	1.4	0.9	0.8
混合道	Mixed Roads		12.8	11.8	10.8	7.7
其他道	Others		4.3	3.0	3.0	2.7

注：1. 由于数据计算进位的原因，部分结构总和不等于100。
2. 2014年起工业污染源治理投资结构进行了调整，治理其他包括绿化和生态环保投资。

Note: a) Owing to the rounding-off of figures, some totals in this table are not equal to 100.
b) The investment structure of treatment of industrial pollution sources in 2007 has been modified. Treatment of others include greening and inverstment in environmental protection.

1-4 国民经济和社会发展比例和效益指标
Indicators on National Economic and Social Development

指　标	Item	2000	2015	2016	2017
人口与就业	**Population and Employment**				
总抚养比 (%)	Gross Dependency Ratio (%)	43.31	34.87	34.72	34.84
少儿抚养比 (%)	Children Dependency Ratio (%)	34.64	23.43	23.21	23.21
老年抚养比 (%)	Old Dependency Ratio (%)	8.67	11.44	11.52	11.62
城镇登记失业率 (%)	Registered Unemployment Rate in Urban Areas (%)	2.50	2.45	2.47	2.47
国民经济核算	**National Accounts**				
人均地区生产总值 (元)	Per Capita GDP (yuan)	12817	68490	73844	80932
人均地区生产总值 (美元)	Per Capita GDP (USD)	1548	10996	11117	11986.7
服务业增加值占地区生产总值比重 (%)	Proportion of Service Industry Value-added in GDP(%)	44.1	50.2	52.1	53.6
生产性服务业增加值占地区生产总值比重 (%)	Proportion of M anufacture-related service Industry Value-added in GDP (%)		26.5	26.9	27.5
全社会劳动生产率 (万元/人)	Gross labour productivity (million yuan/person)	2.78	11.91	12.91	14.22
人民生活	**People's Living Conditions**				
全体常住居民恩格尔系数 (%)	Engel coefficient for all permanent residents (%)		34.5	34.2	33.5
城镇常住居民恩格尔系数 (%)	Engel coefficient of permanent urban residents (%)	38.6	33.2	32.9	32.2
农村常住居民恩格尔系数 (%)	Engel coefficient of permanent rural residents (%)	49.8	40.6	40.4	40.2
城乡收入比 (农村居民收入为1)	Urban and Rural Income ratio (Rural Income as 1)	2.7	2.6	2.6	2.6
财政	**Government Finance**				
一般公共预算收入与地区生产总值之比(%)	Propotion of Government Revenue to GDP (%)	8.4	12.7	12.9	12.6
一般公共预算支出与地区生产总值之比(%)	Propotion of Government Expenditure to GDP (%)	9.9	17.4	16.7	16.8
能源	**Energy**				
能源生产弹性系数	Elasticity Ratio of Energy Production	0.50	2.84	0.53	
电力生产弹性系数	Elasticity Ratio of Electricity Production	1.63	0.06	0.76	0.85
能源消费弹性系数	Elasticity Ratio of Energy Consumption	0.71	0.24	0.48	0.47
电力消费弹性系数	Elasticity Ratio of Electricity Consumption	1.99	0.18	0.75	0.83
能源加工转换总效率 (%)	Total Effficiency of Energy Conversion (%)	66.63	69.01	69.98	68.27
资源环境	**Resources and Environment**				
万元地区生产总值用水量 (立方米/万元)	Water Use Per 10000 Yuan GDP (cu.m)		61	55	48
万元工业增加值用水量 (立方米/万元)	Water Use Per 10000 Yuan of Industrial Added Value (cu.m)		37	34	30
环境污染治理投资与国内生产总值之比(%)	Proportion of Total Investment in the Treatment of Environmental Pollution to GDP (%)		0.08	0.09	0.10
固定资产投资	**Investment in Fixed Assets**				
固定资产交付使用率 (%)	Rate of Projects of Rixed Assets Completed and Put into Use (%)	87.1	61.5	51.0	50.5
项目建成投产率 (%)	Rate of Projects Completed and Put into Use (%)	49.3	70.8	71.8	70.8
房地产开发企业房屋建筑面积竣工率 (%)	Rate of Floor Space of Buildings Completed (%)	31.9	10.4	10.3	11.3
对外贸易 (按美元计价)	**Foreign Trade (calculated by USD)**				
进出口总额相当于地区生产总值比重 (%)	Proportion of Total Value of Imports & Exports to GDP (%)		86.0	78.2	76.0
高新技术产品出口额占出口总额的比重(%)	Proportion of High and New-tech Products to Total Exports (%)	18.5	36.1	22.4	21.4
一般贸易进出口总额占进出口总额的比重 (%)	Proportion of Ordinary Trade to Total Value of Imports and Exports (%)	22.5	42.2	43.6	46.1
加工贸易进出口总额占进出口总额的比重 (%)	Proportion of Processing Trade to Total Value of Imports and Exports (%)	71.2	43.1	38.8	37.1

1－4 续表 continued

指 标	Item	2000	2015	2016	2017
农业	**Agriculture**				
每公顷播种面积农产品产量（公斤）	Output of Farm Crops per Hectare of Sown Area (kg)				
粮食	Grain	5879	5524	5530	5570
糖料	Sugar Crops	70380	77619	78157	79421
油料	Oil-bearing Crops	2295	2963	3015	3052
工业	**Industry**				
高技术制造业增加值占规模以上工业比重 (%)	Ratio of Value Added of Advanced Manufacturing Industry to the Industry above designated sized (%)		25.6	27.1	30.3
先进制造业增加值占规模以上工业比重 (%)	Ratio of Value Added of High-tech Industry to the Industry above designated sized (%)		47.9	48.7	55
总资产贡献率 (%)	Ratio of Total Assets to Industrial Output Value (%)	8.9	13.6	13.0	12.5
资产负债率 (%)	Assets-Liability Ratio (%)	57.6	57.4	56.2	56.1
成本费用利润率 (%)	Ratio of Profits to Industrial Costs (%)	4.8	6.9	6.9	7.0
产品销售率 (%)	Proportion of Products Sold (%)	97.4	97.1	97.1	98.0
每百元主营业务收入中的成本（元）	Cost per Every 100 Yuan Revenue in Principal Businesses(yuan)		84.2	84.1	83.8
建筑业	**Construction**				
建筑业劳动生产率 （元／人）（按增加值计算）	Overall Labor Productivity (yuan/person) (in terms of value-added per employee)	39831	103972	104427	97732
交通运输业	**Transport**				
铁路网密度 （公里／万平方公里）	Railway Density (km/10000sq.km)	108.07	214.75	237.34	239.68
公路网密度 （公里／万平方公里）	Highway Density (km/10000sq.km)	5710	12021	12136	12219.3
邮电通信业	**Postal and Telecommunication Services**				
电话普及率(含移动电话)(部/百人)	Popularization Rate of Telephone (set/100 persons)	39.5	164.2	154.2	154.0
移动电话普及率 （部/百人）	Popularization Rate of Mobile Telephone (set/100 persons)	15.7	138.4	130.5	132.5
金融业	**Financial Intermediation**				
金融机构存款与地区生产总值之比 (%)	Porportion of Deposits of Financial Institutions to GDP (%)	176.5	217.1	222.9	216.9
金融机构贷款与地区生产总值之比 (%)	Porportion of Loans of Financial Institutions to GDP (%)	122.4	129.5	137.5	140.5
金融机构年末人民币贷、存款余额比例 (%)	Porportion of Loans to Deposits of Financial Institutions in RMB at the year-end (%)	69.7	58.1	60.6	64.4
科技	**Science and Technology**				
研究与试验发展经费内部支出相当于地区生产总值之比 (%)	Porportion of R&D Expenditure to GDP (%)	0.99	2.43	2.52	2.61
每万人口发明专利拥有量 （件/万人）	Number of patents per 10 000 persons (patents/10 000 persons)		12.80	15.32	18.96
教育	**Education**				
学龄儿童入学率 (%)	Percentage of School-age Children Enrolled (%)	99.70	99.98	100.00	99.99
小学毕业生升学率 (%)	Percentage of Graduates of Primary School Entering Junior Secondary School (%)	96.15	95.90	95.90	96.04
高中毛入学率 (%)	Gross Enrollment Rate of Senior Secondary Schools (%) Senior Secondary Schools (%)	38.70	95.70	96.00	96.48
高等教育毛入学率 (%)	Gross Enrollment Rate of High Education (%)	11.35	33.00	35.10	38.71
卫生	**Public Health**				
每千人口执业(助理)医师数 （人）	Number of Licensed(Assistant) Doctors per 10000 Population (person)	1.29	2.11	2.22	2.32
每千人口医疗卫生机构床位数（张）	Number of Beds of Hospitals and Health Centers per 1000 Population (bed)	1.94	4.02	4.23	4.41
医疗卫生机构病床使用率 (%)	Beds Utilization Rate of Medical Organizations (%)		83.5	83.9	84.0
城市市政建设	**Municipal Works**				
人均公园绿地面积 （平方米）	Per Capita Public Green Area (Sq.m)		17.40	17.87	18.24

1-5 国民经济和社会发展主要指标占全国比重

Percentage of National Total of Main Indicators of Economic and Social Development of Guangdong

指标	Item	2016 广东 Guang-dong	2016 全国 National Total	2016 广东占全国(%) As Percentage of National Total	2017 广东 Guang-dong	2017 全国 National Total	2017 广东占全国(%) As Percentage of National Total
人口	**Population**						
年末常住人口数 (万人)	Permanent Population at the Year-end (10000 persons)	10999	138271	8.0	11169	139008	8.0
土地面积 (万平方公里)	**Land Area (10000 sp.km)**	**17.97**	**960**	**1.9**	**17.97**	**960**	**1.9**
国内(地区)生产总值(亿元)	**Gross Domestic Product (100 million yuan)**	**80666.72**	**743585.5**	**10.3**	**89705.23**	**827121.7**	**10.6**
第一产业	Primary Industry	3500.49	63672.8	5.5	3611.44	65467.6	5.8
第二产业	Secondary Industry	35109.66	296547.7	10.5	38008.06	334622.6	10.7
第三产业	Tertiary Industry	42056.57	383365.0	11.0	48085.73	427031.5	11.2
人均国内(地区)生产总值 (元)	**Per Capita Gross Domestic Product (yuan)**	**73844**	**53935**		**80932**	**59660**	
主要工农业产品产量	**Output of Major Farm Products and Industrial Products**						
粮食 (万吨)	Grain (10000 tons)	1204.22	61625.0	2.0	1208.56	61793.0	2.0
油料 (万吨)	Oil-bearing Crops (10000 tons)	99.35	3629.5	2.7	101.28		
肉类 (万吨)	Meat (10000 tons)	448.70	8537.8	5.3	444.08	8588.1	5.2
水产品 (万吨)	Aquatic Products (10000 tons)	818.29	6901.3	11.9	833.54	6953.0	12.0
水果 (万吨)	Fruits (10000 tons)	1331.99	28351.1	4.7	1421.23		
茶叶 (万吨)	Tea (10000 tons)	8.92	240.5	3.7	9.29		
农用化肥 (万吨)	Chemical Fertilizer (10000 tons)	68.62	6629.6	1.0	77.06	6184.3	1.2
发电量 (亿千瓦时)	Electricity (100 million kwh)	4081.97	61331.6	6.7	4407.20	64951.4	6.8
水泥 (万吨)	Cement (10000 tons)	15078.64	241031.0	6.3	15752.98	233679.1	6.7
布 (亿米)	Cloth (100 million m)	27.10	906.8	3.0	27.01	868.1	3.1
机制纸及纸板 (万吨)	Machine-made Paper and Paperboard (10000 tons)	2127.52	12319.2	17.3	2177.74	12542.0	17.4
成品钢材 (万吨)	Steel (10000 tons)	4113.34	104813.5	3.9	4213.69	104958.8	4.0
成品糖 (万吨)	Sugar (10000 tons)	116.12	1443.3	8.0	82.27	1470.6	5.6
平板玻璃 (万重量箱)	Flat Glass (10000 wt.cases)	9048.44	80408.5	11.3	9146.24	79023.5	11.6
家用电冰箱 (万台)	Household Refrigerators(10000 units)	2135.51	8481.6	25.2	1556.37	8548.4	18.2
家用洗衣机 (万台)	Household Washing Machines (10000 units)	762.32	7620.9	10.0	749.62	7500.9	10.0
彩电电视机 (万台)	Color Television Sets (10000 sets)	8106.36	15769.6	51.4	8399.88	15932.6	52.7
家用房间空气调节器 (万台)	Room Air Conditioners (10000 sets)	5641.96	14342.4	39.3	5374.97	17861.5	30.1
汽车 (万辆)	Vehicles	280.25	2811.9	9.9	321.06	2901.8	11.1
微型计算机设备 (万台)	Microcomputers (10000 units)	3344.93	29008.5	11.5	4338.56	30678.4	14.1
固定资产投资	**Investment in Fixed Assets**						
固定资产投资额 (亿元)	Investment in Fixed Assets (100 million yuan)	33008.86	596500.8	5.5	37477.96	631684.0	5.9
#房地产开发	Real Estate Development	10307.80	102580.6	10.0	12075.69	109798.5	11.0

1-5 续表 continued

指 标	Item	2016 广东 Guang-dong	2016 全国 National Total	2016 广东占全国(%) As Percentage of National Total	2017 广东 Guang-dong	2017 全国 National Total	2017 广东占全国(%) As Percentage of National Total
运输、邮电	**Transport, Postal and Telecommunication Services**						
货物周转量 (亿吨公里)	Freight Traffic (100 million ton-kilometers)	22032.27	186629	12.2	28192.23	197372	14.3
旅客周转量 (亿人公里)	Passenger Traffic (100 million personkilometers)	3842.58	31258	12.3	4140.29	32813	12.6
港口货物吞吐量 (万吨)	Volume of Freight Handled at Major Coastal Ports (10000 tons)	179924	1320100	13.6	198015	1400700	14.1
邮电业务总量 (亿元)	Total Business Volume of Postal and Telecommunication Services (100 million yuan)	6892.41	43345.5	15.9	6107.19	37320	16.4
财政金融	**Government Finance and Banking**						
地方一般公共预算收入 (亿元)	Local Public Budgetary Revenue (100 million yuan)	10390.35	87239.4	11.9	11320.35	91447.5	12.4
地方一般公共预算支出 (亿元)	Local Public Budgetary Expenditure (100 million yuan)	13446.09	160351.4	8.4	15037.48	173471.1	8.7
人民币住户存款 (亿元)	Savings Deposits by Residents in Renminbi (100 million yuan)	58618.89	597751.0	9.8	60645.23	643768.0	9.4
外经旅游	**Foreign Trade and International Tourism**						
进口总额 (亿美元)	Total Imports (USD 100 million)	3567.21	15879.3	22.5	3838.06	18409.8	20.8
出口总额 (亿美元)	Total Exports (USD 100 million)	5985.64	20976.3	28.5	6228.73	22635.2	27.5
实际外商直接投资(亿美元)	Foreign Direct Investment(USD 100 million)	233.49	1260.0	18.5	229.07	1310.4	17.5
国际旅游外汇收入(亿美元)	Total Foreign Exchange Earnings from International Tourism (USD 100 million)	185.77	1200.0	15.5	196.63	1234.0	15.9
国内贸易和物价	**Domestic Trade and Prices**						
社会消费品零售总额 (亿元)	Total Amount of Retail Sales of Consumer Goods (100 million yuan)	34739.00	332316.3	10.5	38200.07	366261.6	10.4
居民消费价格指数 (%)	General Consumer Price Index (%)	102.3	102.0		101.5	101.6	
商品零售价格指数 (%)	General Retail Price Index (%)	100.8	100.7		101.6	101.1	
人民生活	**People's Livelihood**						
城镇单位就业人员工资总额 (亿元)	Earnings of Urban Employed Persons (100 million yuan)	14156.81	120074.8	11.8	15511.55	129889.1	11.9
全体常住居民人均可支配收入 (元)	Per Capita Disposable Incom Permanent Households (yuan)	30295.80	23821.0		33003.29	25973.8	
城镇常住居民人均可支配收入 (元)	Per Capita Disposable Income of Permanent Urban Households (yuan)	37684.25	33616.2		40975.14	36396.2	
农村常住居民人均可支配收入 (元)	Per Capita Net Income of Permanent Rural Households (yuan)	14512.15	12363.4		15779.74	13432.4	
教育、科技、卫生	**Education, Science and Technology and Health Care**						
普通本专科学校在校学生数 (万人)	Students Enrolled in Colleges and Universities (10000 persons)	189.28	2695.8	7.0	192.58	2753.6	7.0
研究与试验发展(R&D)经费内部支出 (亿元)	Internal Expenditure on R&D (100 million yuan)	2035.14	15677	13.1	2343.63	17500	13.4
医疗卫生机构床位数(万张)	Number of Hospital Beds (10000 units)	46.52	741.0	6.3	49.21	794.0	6.2
专业卫生技术人员 (万人)	Number of Medical Technical Personnel (10000 persons)	66.75	845.4	7.9	70.99	897.8	7.9

注：1．本表水果产量含瓜果产量。
2．全国2017年数为快报数并来自中国统计摘要。

Note: a) The output of fruits includes melons in this table.
b) The 2017 data of the whole nation are based on flash reports and from China Statistical Abstract.

1–6 各部门机构数

Grassroots Units in Various Sectors

部　　门		Sector		2010	2015	2016	2017
农村基层组织	**（个）**	**Rural Grassroots Units**	**(unit)**				
镇政府		Town Governments		1134	1128	1128	1124
乡政府		Township Governments		11	11	11	10
村民委员会		Villagers' Committees		22140	19632	19731	19785
工业企业	**（个）**	**Industrial Enterprises**	**(unit)**	**250853**	**379804**	**455545**	**505550**
规模以上工业		Industrial Enterprises above Designated Size		53418	42134	42709	47224
#国有工业		State-owned		567	200	201	140
集体工业		Collective-owned		872	212	185	160
建筑业企业	**（个）**	**Construction Enterprises**	**(unit)**	**20195**	**36124**	**47290**	**63398**
#国有企业		State-owned		648	482	483	472
批发零售和住宿餐饮企业法人单位数	**（万个）**	**Number of Corporate Units in Wholesale and Retail Trades, Accommodations and Catering Services**	**(10000 units)**	**22.18**	**41.58**	**52.39**	**63.99**
医疗卫生机构数	（个）	**Health Care**	**(unit)**	**16541**	**21189**	49124	49926
#医院、卫生院		Hospitals and Health Centers		2444	2539	2581	2666
提供住宿的社会服务机构		Social Welfare Institutions		2514	1588	1643	1734
教育事业		**Education**					
普通高等学校	（所）	Regular Institutions of Higher Education	(unit)	131	143	149	151
中等学校	（所）	Secondary Schools	(unit)	5146	5078	5144	5187
#普通中学		Regular Secondary Schools		4334	4434	4510	4566
小学	（万所）	Primary Schools	(10000 units)	1.68	1.01	1.02	1.03
幼儿园	（所）	Kindergartens	(unit)	11161	16368	17288	18048
艺术表演团体	（个）	Art Performance Troupes	(unit)	133	72	72	74
文化事业	（个）	Cultural Institutions	(unit)	2384	2275	2283	2289
文物事业	（个）	Cultural Relic Establishments	(unit)	208	260	258	264
广播电视	**（座）**	**Radio and Television**	**(unit)**				
广播电台		Radio Stations		22	22	22	22
电视台		Television Stations		24	24	24	24
县、市广播电视台		Radio and Television Stations in Counties and County-level Cities		79	79	79	79
研究机构数	**（个）**	**Number of R&D Institutions**	**(units)**	**4452**	**8164**	**14311**	**23318**
科学研究与技术开发机构		Scientific Research and Technological Development Institutions		186	189	202	199
全日制普通高等学校		Full-time Regular Institutions of Higher Education		450	850	1123	1369
工业企业		Industrial Enterprises		3309	6553	11834	20030
其他		Others		507	572	1152	1720

1-7 法人和产业活动单位数
Number of Corporate Units and Industrial Establishments

单位：个 (unit)

项 目	Item	2016 法人单位数 Corporate Units	2016 产业单位数 Industrial Establishments	2017 法人单位数 Corporate Units	2017 产业单位数 Industrial Establishments
总 计	**Total**	**1671255**	**1890136**	**1955088**	**2206419**
按行业分	By Sector				
农、林、牧、渔业	Farming,Forestry,Anima lHusbandry and Fishery	42163	43690	47531	49133
采矿业	Mining	4096	4301	4116	4339
制造业	Manufacture	440630	448291	490284	498834
电力、燃气及水的生产和供应业	Production and Supply of Electric Power, Gas and Water	10819	13694	11150	14088
建筑业	Construction	47290	54246	63398	73151
批发和零售业	Wholesale and Retail Trades	495492	559646	607193	679281
交通运输、仓储和邮政业	Transport, Storage and Postal Services	41597	54377	49663	64235
住宿和餐饮业	Hotels and Catering Services	28393	35768	32729	40888
信息传输、软件和信息技术服务业	Information Transmission, Computer Services and Software	47640	55112	63782	73459
金融业	Finance	11234	32819	12751	38800
房地产业	Real Estate	60511	73918	70369	86389
租赁和商务服务业	Leasing and Business Services	187062	203367	221659	243155
科学研究和技术服务业	Scientific Research, Technical Services	63521	69152	75646	83801
水利、环境和公共设施管理业	Management of Water Conservancy, Environment and Public Facilities	7983	9271	8942	10411
居民服务、修理和其他服务业	Services to Households,Repair and Other Services	27018	30168	32250	35964
教育	Education	42387	51688	45293	54706
卫生和社会工作	Health and Social Service	11847	24572	12472	25207
文化、体育和娱乐业	Culture, Sports and Entertainment	21645	24591	25782	29013
公共管理、社会保障和社会组织	Public Administration,Social Security and Social Organizations	79927	101465	80078	101565
按注册类型分	By Status of Registration				
内资	Domestic-funded	1608963	1811244	1889179	2118990
国有	State-owned	65937	116313	65911	116290
集体	Collective-owned	30819	45401	30983	45665
股份合作企业	Share-holding Cooperative Enterprises	8759	13284	8569	13143
联营企业	Joint-operation Enterprises	5387	6849	5097	6574
有限责任公司	Limited Liability Corporations	425356	461405	441258	484222
股份有限公司	Share-holding Corporations Ltd.	18451	35738	19450	39635
私营企业	Private Enterprises	870459	925934	1122317	1193626
其他	Other	183795	206320	195594	219835
港、澳、台商投资企业	Enterprises with Investment from Hong Kong,Macao and Taiwan	43370	51610	46465	56906
合资经营企业(港或澳、台资)	Joint Ventures	5102	6969	5321	7441
合作经营企业(港或澳、台资)	Cooperative Enterprises	1828	2231	2007	2433
港、澳、台商独资经营企业	Sole Investment Enterprises	34092	39476	36750	43921
港、澳、台商投资股份有限公司	Share-holding Corporations Ltd.	1051	1444	1067	1536
其他港、澳、台商投资	Other Enterprises	1297	1490	1320	1575
外商投资企业	Enterprises with Foreign Investment	18922	27282	19444	30523
中外合资经营企业	Sino-foreign Joint Ventures	3401	5658	3519	6002
中外合作经营企业	Sino-foreign Cooperative Enterprises	714	1081	718	1103
外资企业	Foreign-funded Enterprises	12005	17067	12677	19681
外商投资股份有限公司	Share-holding Corporations Ltd.	1657	2059	1363	2236
其他外商投资	Other Enterprises	1145	1417	1167	1501

注：产业单位数包含法人单位数。
Note:The number of the industrial establishments include the number of the coporate units.

1–8 各市法人和产业活动单位数

Number of Corporate Units and Industrial Establishments by City

单位：个 (unit)

市 别	City	2016		2017	
		法人单位数 Corporate Units	产业单位数 Industrial Establishments	法人单位数 Corporate Units	产业单位数 Industrial Establishments
总 计	**Total**	**1671255**	**1890136**	**1955088**	**2206419**
广 州	Guangzhou	309786	345347	338264	387483
深 圳	Shenzhen	317980	354981	442146	492577
珠 海	Zhuhai	65727	72788	75007	82889
汕 头	Shantou	47089	53874	49345	56137
佛 山	Foshan	164406	179133	181642	196540
韶 关	Shaoguan	25296	32663	26505	33936
河 源	Heyuan	24438	30859	25657	32056
梅 州	Meizhou	34315	44759	38552	49282
惠 州	Huizhou	71888	83106	95068	107883
汕 尾	Shanwei	10527	12685	11159	13389
东 莞	Dongguan	210871	226892	243583	259526
中 山	Zhongshan	93845	103078	104610	114203
江 门	Jiangmen	60516	66845	70530	77705
阳 江	Yangjiang	23180	28476	25333	31110
湛 江	Zhanjiang	50295	61000	58120	69315
茂 名	Maoming	39897	45516	41342	46985
肇 庆	Zhaoqing	31520	39070	32846	40385
清 远	Qingyuan	28852	37879	30935	40108
潮 州	Chaozhou	20756	22813	21894	24046
揭 阳	Jieyang	23201	26834	25115	28753
云 浮	Yunfu	16870	21538	17435	22111
按经济区域分	By Region				
珠 三 角	Pearl River Delta	1326539	1471240	1583696	1759191
东 翼	Eastern Region	101573	116206	107513	122325
西 翼	Western Region	113372	134992	124795	147410
山 区	Mountainous Region	129771	167698	139084	177493

1-9 按行业和登记注册类型分组的法人单位数（2017年）

Number of Corporate Units by Sector and by Status of Registration (2017)

单位：个 (unit)

项 目	Item	总 计 Total	内资 Domestic-funded	国有 State-owned	集体 Collective-owned	股份合作企业 Share-holding Cooperative Enterprises
总 计	**Total**	**1955088**	**1889179**	**65911**	**30983**	**8569**
农、林、牧、渔业	Farming,Forestry,Anima lHusbandry and Fishery	47531	46974	822	715	97
采矿业	Mining	4116	4066	41	83	39
制造业	Manufacture	490284	453081	990	2642	1737
电力、燃气及水的生产和供应业	Production and Supply of Electric Power, Gas and Water	11150	10842	546	1235	125
建筑业	Construction	63398	62990	472	716	176
批发和零售业	Wholesale and Retail Trades	607193	595105	3025	4688	2695
交通运输、仓储和邮政业	Transport, Storage and Postal Services	49663	48051	1160	541	208
住宿和餐饮业	Hotels and Catering Services	32729	31458	429	354	338
信息传输、软件和信息技术服务业	Information Transmission, Computer Services and Software	63782	61799	415	76	145
金融业	Finance	12751	12105	311	76	173
房地产业	Real Estate	70369	67680	1228	2406	786
租赁和商务服务业	Leasing and Business Services	221659	217461	3137	11424	1096
科学研究和技术服务业	Scientific Research, Technical Services	75646	73741	3507	632	236
水利、环境和公共设施管理业	Management of Water Conservancy, Environment and Public Facilities	8942	8812	2252	282	27
居民服务、修理和其他服务业	Services to Households,Repair and Other Services	32250	31901	511	410	328
教育	Education	45293	45186	16045	1517	139
卫生和社会工作	Health and Social Service	12472	12424	3897	1083	45
文化、体育和娱乐业	Culture, Sports and Entertainment	25782	25478	1919	266	153
公共管理、社会保障和社会组织	Public Administration,Social Security and Social Organizations	80078	80025	25204	1837	26

1-9 续表 1　continued

单位：个　(unit)

项　　目	Item	联营企业 Joint-operation Enterprises	有限责任公司 Limited Liability Corpor-ations	股份有限公司 Share-holding Corpor-ations Ltd.	私营企业 Private Enter-prises	其他 Other
总　计	**Total**	**5097**	**441258**	**19450**	**1122317**	**195594**
农、林、牧、渔业	Farming,Forestry,Anima lHusbandry and Fishery	118	4036	318	11428	29440
采矿业	Mining	17	795	93	2685	313
制造业	Manufacture	1090	122613	4944	303721	15344
电力、燃气及水的生产和供应业	Production and Supply of Electric Power, Gas and Water	116	1744	170	6089	817
建筑业	Construction	127	17368	681	41735	1715
批发和零售业	Wholesale and Retail Trades	1649	154867	5148	398139	24894
交通运输、仓储和邮政业	Transport, Storage and Postal Services	167	12257	585	31404	1729
住宿和餐饮业	Hotels and Catering Services	69	6217	349	22265	1437
信息传输、软件和信息技术服务业	Information Transmission, Computer Services and Software	140	15799	927	42483	1814
金融业	Finance	41	2884	1333	6788	499
房地产业	Real Estate	226	21931	1128	37466	2509
租赁和商务服务业	Leasing and Business Services	628	44939	2018	119819	34400
科学研究和技术服务业	Scientific Research, Technical Services	169	20580	852	43970	3795
水利、环境和公共设施管理业	Management of Water Conservancy, Environment and Public Facilities	29	1971	96	3497	658
居民服务、修理和其他服务业	Services to Households,Repair and Other Services	116	5976	289	21747	2524
教育	Education	134	1988	200	10518	14645
卫生和社会工作	Health and Social Service	59	526	40	2546	4228
文化、体育和娱乐业	Culture, Sports and Entertainment	88	4581	252	15639	2580
公共管理、社会保障和社会组织	Public Administration,Social Security and Social Organizations	114	186	27	378	52253

1-9 续表 2 continued

单位：个 (unit)

项 目	Item	港、澳、台商投资企业 Enterprises with Investment from Hong Kong, Macao and Taiwan	合资经营企业(港或澳、台资) Joint Ventures	合作经营企业(港或澳、台资) Cooperative Enterprises	港、澳、台商独资经营企业 Sole Investment Enterprises	港、澳、台商投资股份有限公司 Shareholding Corporations Ltd.	其他港、澳、台商投资 Other Enterprises
总 计	**Total**	**46465**	**5321**	**2007**	**36750**	**1067**	**1320**
农、林、牧、渔业	Farming,Forestry,Anima lHusbandry and Fishery	476	60	19	332	43	22
采矿业	Mining	35	8	4	23		
制造业	Manufacture	27649	2962	930	22849	515	393
电力、燃气及水的生产和供应业	Production and Supply of Electric Power,Gas and Water	190	94	13	76	4	3
建筑业	Construction	340	59	28	205	9	39
批发和零售业	Wholesale and Retail Trades	7841	624	116	6533	238	330
交通运输、仓储和邮政业	Transport, Storage and Postal Services	1112	170	304	571	27	40
住宿和餐饮业	Hotels and Catering Services	733	150	66	476	27	14
信息传输、软件和信息技术服务业	Information Transmission, Computer Services and Software	1295	123	40	1040	43	49
金融业	Finance	329	95	3	211	8	12
房地产业	Real Estate	2034	398	309	1241	40	46
租赁和商务服务业	Leasing and Business Services	2608	315	67	1948	65	213
科学研究和技术服务业	Scientific Research, Technical Services	1224	126	40	908	30	120
水利、环境和公共设施管理业	Management of Water Conservancy, Environment and Public Facilities	87	20	10	48	6	3
居民服务、修理和其他服务业	Services to Households,Repair and Other Services	204	28	15	140	5	16
教育	Education	58	9	7	35	1	6
卫生和社会工作	Health and Social Service	32	12	1	16		3
文化、体育和娱乐业	Culture, Sports and Entertainment	197	65	33	84	5	10
公共管理、社会保障和社会组织	Public Administration,Social Security and Social Organizations	21	3	2	14	1	1

1—9 续表 3 continued

单位：个 (unit)

项 目	Item	外商投资企业 Enterprises with Foreign Investment	中外合资经营企业 Sino-foreign Joint Ventures	中外合作经营企业 Sino-foreign Cooperative Enterprises	外资企业 Foreign-funded Enterprises	外商投资股份有限公司 Share-holding Corporations Ltd.	其他外商投资 Other Enter-prises
总 计	**Total**	**19444**	**3519**	**718**	**12677**	**1363**	**1167**
农、林、牧、渔业	Farming,Forestry,Anima lHusbandry and Fishery	81	18	6	36	10	11
采矿业	Mining	15	5	3	4	1	2
制造业	Manufacture	9554	1783	299	6825	347	300
电力、燃气及水的生产和供应业	Production and Supply of Electric Power,Gas and Water	118	53	14	32	7	12
建筑业	Construction	68	16	5	31	6	10
批发和零售业	Wholesale and Retail Trades	4247	538	49	2844	479	337
交通运输、仓储和邮政业	Transport, Storage and Postal Services	500	140	122	173	40	25
住宿和餐饮业	Hotels and Catering Services	538	92	34	252	132	28
信息传输、软件和信息技术服务业	Information Transmission, Computer Services and Software	688	126	6	466	46	44
金融业	Finance	317	117	4	116	64	16
房地产业	Real Estate	655	158	83	313	60	41
租赁和商务服务业	Leasing and Business Services	1590	221	29	986	114	240
科学研究和技术服务业	Scientific Research, Technical Services	681	168	19	428	27	39
水利、环境和公共设施管理业	Management of Water Conservancy, Environment and Public Facilities	43	6	15	19		3
居民服务、修理和其他服务业	Services to Households,Repair and Other Services	145	27	10	82	7	19
教育	Education	49	7	6	14	5	17
卫生和社会工作	Health and Social Service	16	9		3		4
文化、体育和娱乐业	Culture, Sports and Entertainment	107	29	14	36	17	11
公共管理、社会保障和社会组织	Public Administration,Social Security and Social Organizations	32	6		17	1	8

1-10 各市按机构类型分法人单位数（2017年）
Number of Corporate Units by Type by City (2017)

单位：个 (unit)

市别	city	法人单位 Corporate Units	企业 Enterprises	事业单位 Institutions	机关 Gover-nment Agencies	社会团体 Social Organi-zations	民办非企业 Non-enterprise Units Run by l NGO	其他组织机构 Other Organi-zations
总 计	**Total**	**1955088**	**1752018**	**46420**	**12147**	**24332**	**21804**	**98367**
广 州	Guangzhou	338264	313799	5427	1120	3347	2897	11674
深 圳	Shenzhen	442146	433028	1816	584	2346	2753	1619
珠 海	Zhuhai	75007	70944	987	420	870	836	950
汕 头	Shantou	49345	41148	2236	560	1347	1165	2889
佛 山	Foshan	181642	170170	1969	456	1537	1761	5749
韶 关	Shaoguan	26505	16235	1894	770	3657	614	3335
河 源	Heyuan	25657	17792	2238	533	477	611	4006
梅 州	Meizhou	38552	28814	2290	769	898	651	5130
惠 州	Huizhou	95068	79669	2281	589	843	1089	10597
汕 尾	Shanwei	11159	7095	1471	474	304	276	1539
东 莞	Dongguan	243583	234200	1710	395	857	2093	4328
中 山	Zhongshan	104610	99123	981	179	523	1325	2479
江 门	Jiangmen	70530	59524	2072	649	1808	920	5557
阳 江	Yangjiang	25333	20554	1460	432	525	492	1870
湛 江	Zhanjiang	58120	37525	4059	873	615	982	14066
茂 名	Maoming	41342	29028	4056	658	1413	754	5433
肇 庆	Zhaoqing	32846	22748	2255	734	784	686	5639
清 远	Qingyuan	30935	22682	1650	652	764	665	4522
潮 州	Chaozhou	21894	17149	1758	307	478	423	1779
揭 阳	Jieyang	25115	18050	2319	548	457	517	3224
云 浮	Yunfu	17435	12741	1491	445	482	294	1982
按经济区域分	By Region							
珠三角	Pearl River Delta	1583696	1483205	19498	5126	12915	14360	48592
东 翼	Eastern Region	107513	83442	7784	1889	2586	2381	9431
西 翼	Western Region	124795	87107	9575	1963	2553	2228	21369
山 区	Mountainous Region	139084	98264	9563	3169	6278	2835	18975

1-11 各市按行业分法人单位数（2017年）

Number of Corporate Units by Sector by City (2017)

单位：个 (unit)

市别	city	总计 Total	农、林、牧、渔业 Farming, Forestry, Animal Husbandry and Fishery	采矿业 Mining	制造业 Manufacture	电力、燃气及水的生产和供应业 Production and Supply of Electric Power, Gas and Water
全　省	**Provincial Total**	**1955088**	**47531**	**4116**	**490284**	**11150**
广　州	Guangzhou	338264	1786	39	51115	372
深　圳	Shenzhen	442146	252	34	90814	221
珠　海	Zhuhai	75007	594	17	8307	89
汕　头	Shantou	49345	999	54	14755	132
佛　山	Foshan	181642	1015	34	62170	267
韶　关	Shaoguan	26505	2348	308	2470	1227
河　源	Heyuan	25657	3563	467	2788	870
梅　州	Meizhou	38552	5995	538	4370	1601
惠　州	Huizhou	95068	2756	211	20162	476
汕　尾	Shanwei	11159	1001	23	1737	246
东　莞	Dongguan	243583	417	20	111270	325
中　山	Zhongshan	104610	867	8	48114	129
江　门	Jiangmen	70530	1915	141	23692	333
阳　江	Yangjiang	25333	1647	203	5240	544
湛　江	Zhanjiang	58120	12184	243	6366	259
茂　名	Maoming	41342	1105	509	5446	799
肇　庆	Zhaoqing	32846	1633	392	6235	777
清　远	Qingyuan	30935	4653	663	3671	1526
潮　州	Chaozhou	21894	1269	30	9651	269
揭　阳	Jieyang	25115	785	46	8027	277
云　浮	Yunfu	17435	747	136	3884	411
按经济区域分	By Region					
珠三角	Pearl River Delta	1583696	11235	896	421879	2989
东　翼	Eastern Region	107513	4054	153	34170	924
西　翼	Western Region	124795	14936	955	17052	1602
山　区	Mountainous Region	139084	17306	2112	17183	5635

1-11 续表 1 continued

单位：个 (unit)

市别	city	建筑业 Construction	批发和零售业 Wholesale and Retail Trades	交通运输、仓储和邮政业 Transport, Storage and Postal Services	住宿和餐饮业 Hotels and Catering Services	信息传输、软件和信息技术服务业 Information Transmission, Computer Services and Software
全 省	**Provincial Total**	**63398**	**607193**	**49663**	**32729**	**63782**
广 州	Guangzhou	11870	113081	10849	7498	18102
深 圳	Shenzhen	7980	186756	15504	5681	23485
珠 海	Zhuhai	5171	25185	1920	1686	3913
汕 头	Shantou	1083	13649	1424	915	1131
佛 山	Foshan	4147	60535	3734	3363	3238
韶 关	Shaoguan	643	5311	482	512	336
河 源	Heyuan	1118	4995	409	469	432
梅 州	Meizhou	2044	8315	620	586	848
惠 州	Huizhou	7137	22287	1649	1629	2071
汕 尾	Shanwei	317	1938	218	326	171
东 莞	Dongguan	8618	67093	4583	3037	3253
中 山	Zhongshan	4276	23635	1779	2118	1747
江 门	Jiangmen	2327	15954	1335	1162	1138
阳 江	Yangjiang	942	6376	492	552	519
湛 江	Zhanjiang	1661	14480	1398	977	1042
茂 名	Maoming	1013	12470	735	580	599
肇 庆	Zhaoqing	1011	6192	670	457	523
清 远	Qingyuan	904	5909	756	355	516
潮 州	Chaozhou	314	3125	385	311	234
揭 阳	Jieyang	409	5615	375	294	254
云 浮	Yunfu	413	4292	346	221	230
按经济区域分	By Region					
珠 三 角	Pearl River Delta	52537	520718	42023	26631	57470
东 翼	Eastern Region	2123	24327	2402	1846	1790
西 翼	Western Region	3616	33326	2625	2109	2160
山 区	Mountainous Region	5122	28822	2613	2143	2362

1−11 续表 2 continued

单位：个 (unit)

市 别	city	金融业 Finance	房地产业 Real Estate	租赁和商务服务业 Leasing and Business Services	科学研究和技术服务业 Scientific Research, Technical Services and Geological Prospecting	水利、环境和公共设施管理业 Management of Water Conservancy, Environment and Public Facilities
全 省	**Provincial Total**	**12751**	**70369**	**221659**	**75646**	**8942**
广 州	Guangzhou	2008	15882	51888	23620	1320
深 圳	Shenzhen	5131	10333	53535	19371	833
珠 海	Zhuhai	805	3876	11344	4467	385
汕 头	Shantou	380	1399	3641	1063	247
佛 山	Foshan	616	5600	16560	7375	779
韶 关	Shaoguan	160	984	2096	681	306
河 源	Heyuan	229	1202	1785	729	259
梅 州	Meizhou	197	1166	3177	801	449
惠 州	Huizhou	430	8315	16388	1911	631
汕 尾	Shanwei	81	444	646	195	122
东 莞	Dongguan	605	5575	20443	5366	652
中 山	Zhongshan	277	3322	9050	1549	300
江 门	Jiangmen	444	2875	8106	1858	581
阳 江	Yangjiang	114	1247	2114	815	217
湛 江	Zhanjiang	306	1978	5095	1648	337
茂 名	Maoming	214	1261	5319	1064	311
肇 庆	Zhaoqing	191	1664	3604	936	371
清 远	Qingyuan	149	1888	2959	911	361
潮 州	Chaozhou	118	303	896	422	171
揭 阳	Jieyang	183	395	1800	333	143
云 浮	Yunfu	113	660	1213	531	167
按经济区域分	By Region					
珠 三 角	Pearl River Delta	10507	57442	190918	66453	5852
东 翼	Eastern Region	762	2541	6983	2013	683
西 翼	Western Region	634	4486	12528	3527	865
山 区	Mountainous Region	848	5900	11230	3653	1542

1-11 续表 3 continued

单位：个 (unit)

市 别	city	居民服务、修理和其他服务业 Services to Households and Other Services	教育 Education	卫生和社会工作 Health Care, Social Security and Social Welfare	文化、体育和娱乐业 Culture, Sports and Recreation	公共管理、社会保障和社会组织 Public Administration and Social Organizations
全 省	**Provincial Total**	**32250**	**45293**	**12472**	**25782**	**80078**
广 州	Guangzhou	6368	5457	2031	6001	8977
深 圳	Shenzhen	7317	5321	1237	3812	4529
珠 海	Zhuhai	1648	1323	569	1736	1972
汕 头	Shantou	992	2301	486	791	3903
佛 山	Foshan	3082	2649	902	2034	3542
韶 关	Shaoguan	334	1029	426	440	6412
河 源	Heyuan	388	1754	334	388	3478
梅 州	Meizhou	467	1177	696	585	4920
惠 州	Huizhou	1480	2176	495	1196	3668
汕 尾	Shanwei	140	1101	161	240	2052
东 莞	Dongguan	3452	2624	1070	2583	2597
中 山	Zhongshan	2442	1902	459	1317	1319
江 门	Jiangmen	897	1629	547	859	4737
阳 江	Yangjiang	424	1157	230	360	2140
湛 江	Zhanjiang	815	3523	643	954	4211
茂 名	Maoming	490	3239	752	549	4887
肇 庆	Zhaoqing	408	1533	380	489	5380
清 远	Qingyuan	394	1251	333	511	3225
潮 州	Chaozhou	234	1210	215	400	2337
揭 阳	Jieyang	236	2074	261	275	3333
云 浮	Yunfu	242	863	245	262	2459
按经济区域分	By Region					
珠 三 角	Pearl River Delta	27094	24614	7690	20027	36721
东 翼	Eastern Region	1602	6686	1123	1706	11625
西 翼	Western Region	1729	7919	1625	1863	11238
山 区	Mountainous Region	1825	6074	2034	2186	20494

1-12 各市按注册类型分法人单位数（2017年）

Number of Corporate Units by Status of Registration by City (2017)

单位：个 (unit)

市别	city	总计 Total	内资 Domestic-funded	国有 State-owned	集体 Collective-owned	股份合作企业 Share-holding Cooperative Enterprises
全省	**Provincial Total**	**1955088**	**1889179**	**65911**	**30983**	**8569**
广州	Guangzhou	338264	326899	8553	8307	2806
深圳	Shenzhen	442146	425495	2890	434	1622
珠海	Zhuhai	75007	71101	1875	888	223
汕头	Shantou	49345	48488	3767	1910	687
佛山	Foshan	181642	177612	2052	2066	761
韶关	Shaoguan	26505	26036	3199	1442	146
河源	Heyuan	25657	25010	3125	462	99
梅州	Meizhou	38552	37548	3366	656	233
惠州	Huizhou	95068	90795	3476	1497	154
汕尾	Shanwei	11159	10883	2203	429	64
东莞	Dongguan	243583	230794	1799	2440	660
中山	Zhongshan	104610	101517	899	2207	101
江门	Jiangmen	70530	67763	2712	1849	173
阳江	Yangjiang	25333	24984	2094	308	15
湛江	Zhanjiang	58120	57744	5574	1355	101
茂名	Maoming	41342	40946	5122	1562	244
肇庆	Zhaoqing	32846	31972	3342	985	101
清远	Qingyuan	30935	30257	2460	486	142
潮州	Chaozhou	21894	21407	2231	574	152
揭阳	Jieyang	25115	24740	3074	628	44
云浮	Yunfu	17435	17188	2098	498	41
按经济区域分	By Region					
珠三角	Pearl River Delta	1583696	1523948	27598	20673	6601
东翼	Eastern Region	107513	105518	11275	3541	947
西翼	Western Region	124795	123674	12790	3225	360
山区	Mountainous Region	139084	136039	14248	3544	661

1−12 续表 1 continued

单位：个 (unit)

市 别	city	联营企业 Joint-operation Enterprises	有限责任公司 Limited Liability Corporations	股份有限公司 Share-holding Corporations Ltd.	私营企业 Private Enterprises	其他 Other
全 省	**Provincial Total**	**5097**	**441258**	**19450**	**1122317**	**195594**
广 州	Guangzhou	629	53289	3088	231432	18795
深 圳	Shenzhen	1707	48608	3988	346375	19871
珠 海	Zhuhai	181	45566	645	16693	5030
汕 头	Shantou	153	15416	853	18639	7063
佛 山	Foshan	377	60240	1742	96865	13509
韶 关	Shaoguan	90	6421	392	6975	7371
河 源	Heyuan	89	5810	674	7419	7332
梅 州	Meizhou	131	5967	602	16901	9692
惠 州	Huizhou	161	13897	657	57399	13554
汕 尾	Shanwei	47	1227	181	4267	2465
东 莞	Dongguan	289	95907	2530	113054	14115
中 山	Zhongshan	174	26691	300	66863	4282
江 门	Jiangmen	225	15641	757	34260	12146
阳 江	Yangjiang	29	2910	144	15446	4038
湛 江	Zhanjiang	211	3578	413	29537	16975
茂 名	Maoming	173	11269	692	10867	11017
肇 庆	Zhaoqing	157	8104	439	10565	8279
清 远	Qingyuan	105	7368	560	12074	7062
潮 州	Chaozhou	50	2964	273	11233	3930
揭 阳	Jieyang	74	5842	331	9044	5703
云 浮	Yunfu	45	4543	189	6409	3365
按经济区域分	By Region					
珠 三 角	Pearl River Delta	3900	367943	14146	973506	109581
东 翼	Eastern Region	324	25449	1638	43183	19161
西 翼	Western Region	413	17757	1249	55850	32030
山 区	Mountainous Region	460	30109	2417	49778	34822

1−12 续表 2 continued

单位：个 (unit)

市别	city	港、澳、台商投资企业 Enterprises with Investment from Hong Kong, Macao and Taiwan	合资经营企业（港或澳、台资） Joint Ventures	合作经营企业（港或澳、台资） Cooperative Enterprises	港、澳、台商独资经营企业 Sole Investment Enterprises	港、澳、台商投资股份有限公司 Share-holding Corporations Ltd.	其他港、澳、台商投资 Other Enterprises
全　省	**Provincial Total**	**46465**	**5321**	**2007**	**36750**	**1067**	**1320**
广　州	Guangzhou	7018	924	470	4862	178	584
深　圳	Shenzhen	12262	1177	198	10525	179	183
珠　海	Zhuhai	2925	395	231	2144	98	57
汕　头	Shantou	599	109	65	396	17	12
佛　山	Foshan	2457	729	82	1571	46	29
韶　关	Shaoguan	378	53	29	252	28	16
河　源	Heyuan	537	50	11	356	78	42
梅　州	Meizhou	891	93	48	721	22	7
惠　州	Huizhou	3440	312	137	2898	63	30
汕　尾	Shanwei	235	26	14	183	11	1
东　莞	Dongguan	8860	437	221	7778	201	223
中　山	Zhongshan	2084	233	31	1768	32	20
江　门	Jiangmen	2062	348	83	1528	50	53
阳　江	Yangjiang	258	52	51	145	8	2
湛　江	Zhanjiang	195	54	43	89	2	7
茂　名	Maoming	320	57	19	218	10	16
肇　庆	Zhaoqing	624	107	35	450	21	11
清　远	Qingyuan	522	52	46	411	8	5
潮　州	Chaozhou	350	53	137	137	8	15
揭　阳	Jieyang	253	31	41	176	3	2
云　浮	Yunfu	195	29	15	142	4	5
按经济区域分	By Region						
珠三角	Pearl River Delta	41732	4662	1488	33524	868	1190
东　翼	Eastern Region	1437	219	257	892	39	30
西　翼	Western Region	773	163	113	452	20	25
山　区	Mountainous Region	2523	277	149	1882	140	75

1−12 续表 3 continued

单位：个 (unit)

市 别	city	外商投资企业 Enterprises with Foreign Investment	中外合资经营企业 Sino-foreign Joint Ventures	中外合作经营企业 Sino-foreign Cooperative Enterprises	外资企业 Foreign-funded Enterprises	外商投资股份有限公司 Share-holding Corporations Ltd.	其他外商投资 Other Enterprises
全 省	**Provincial Total**	**19444**	**3519**	**718**	**12677**	**1363**	**1167**
广 州	Guangzhou	4347	949	161	2791	240	206
深 圳	Shenzhen	4389	791	76	2934	115	473
珠 海	Zhuhai	981	204	38	639	61	39
汕 头	Shantou	258	66	34	117	32	9
佛 山	Foshan	1573	405	59	835	215	59
韶 关	Shaoguan	91	25	11	35	14	6
河 源	Heyuan	110	13	12	48	24	13
梅 州	Meizhou	113	34	19	38	15	7
惠 州	Huizhou	833	129	34	583	63	24
汕 尾	Shanwei	41	8	4	20	4	5
东 莞	Dongguan	3929	339	62	2983	376	169
中 山	Zhongshan	1009	164	14	710	73	48
江 门	Jiangmen	705	147	30	436	55	37
阳 江	Yangjiang	91	15	9	58	4	5
湛 江	Zhanjiang	181	45	6	119	3	8
茂 名	Maoming	76	28	4	24	9	11
肇 庆	Zhaoqing	250	63	17	142	8	20
清 远	Qingyuan	156	30	36	67	14	9
潮 州	Chaozhou	137	20	57	38	16	6
揭 阳	Jieyang	122	27	28	37	18	12
云 浮	Yunfu	52	17	7	23	4	1
按经济区域分	By Region						
珠 三 角	Pearl River Delta	18016	3191	491	12053	1206	1075
东 翼	Eastern Region	558	121	123	212	70	32
西 翼	Western Region	348	88	19	201	16	24
山 区	Mountainous Region	522	119	85	211	71	36

1-13 民营经济主要指标

Main Indicators on Private Economy

指　标	Indicator	2002	2010	2015	2016	2017	2017比2016增长(%) Growth Rate in 2017 over 2016 (%)
单位个数　（万个）	**Number of Units　(10000 units)**	**210.39**	**438.66**	**756.78**	**872.54**	**999.82**	**14.6**
#私营	Private	25.86	94.82	248.12	317.17	381.58	20.3
个体	Individual	175.31	334.63	492.99	541.17	600.96	11.0
就业人数　（万人）	**Number of Employed Persons (10000 persons)**	**1002.45**	**2616.21**	**3297.38**	**3364.50**	**3462.86**	**2.9**
#私营	Private	422.35	953.44	1279.55	1329.49	1375.65	3.5
个体	Individual	430.82	978.41	1133.39	1152.13	1167.33	1.3
地区生产总值（亿元）	**Gross Domestic Product　(100 million yuan)**	**5265.20**	**22865.32**	**38854.68**	**43059.44**	**48142.76**	**8.1**
第一产业	Primary Industry	438.48	2184.07	3288.66	3350.66	3450.97	3.5
第二产业	Secondary Industry	2129.35	10075.26	15969.96	17674.12	19718.83	9.7
工业	Industry	1857.07	9169.01	14624.76	16264.14	18062.86	9.8
建筑业	Construction	272.28	906.24	1378.11	1443.32	1690.30	9.0
第三产业	Tertiary Industry	2697.36	10605.99	19596.06	22034.66	24972.95	7.5
批发零售贸易业	Wholesale and Retail Trades	1054.80	3245.98	5724.46	6138.28	6435.47	3.2
交通运输仓储和邮政业	Transport, Storage and Postal Services	287.09	852.11	1596.94	1746.21	1998.56	12.3
住宿和餐饮业	Hotels and Catering Services	280.41	914.44	1238.52	1338.78	1413.37	3.2
金融业	Finance	36.25	629.51	1685.30	1816.17	1996.97	7.0
房地产业	Real Estate	552.50	1954.45	3633.87	4221.81	5169.07	6.5
其他服务业	Other Services	486.30	3009.51	5607.68	6653.71	7831.86	11.8
固定资产投资（亿元）	**Investment in Fixed Assets (100 million yuan)**	**1501.71**	**7325.07**	**18052.95**	**20504.39**	**23158.46**	**12.9**
进出口总额（亿美元）	**Total Value of Imports and Exports (USD 100 million)**	**85.61**	**1688.86**	**3994.22**	**4144.70**	**4641.78**	**11.8**
出口总额	Exports	41.48	1002.44	2604.42	2644.23	2930.05	10.3
进口总额	Imports	44.13	686.42	1389.80	1500.47	1711.73	14.3
运输邮电业	**Transportation, Postal and Telecommunication Services**						
营业收入　（亿元）	Business Revenue　(100 million yuan)	122.10	313.78	662.17	680.30	824.06	21.1
批发零售业　（亿元）	**Wholesale and Retail Trades　(100 million yuan)**						
批发零售业销售额	Sales Value of Wholesale and Retail Trades	8821.17	30264.58	86971.83	93806.985	103394.52	10.2
批发零售业零售额	Retail Value of Wholesale and Retail Trades	3455.13	12098.52	22704.49	25483.163	28162.82	10.5
税金　（亿元）	**Taxes　(100 million yuan)**	**535.71**	**4163.26**	**8612.13**	**9455.09**	**11263.89**	**19.1**
#私营	Private	141.72	763.64	1576.32	1563.02	2195.1	40.4
个体	Individual	139.46	418.47	768.13	826.35	950.35	15.0

注：1.民营经济统计范围调整为集体企业、股份合作企业、集体联营企业、其他联营企业、私营企业、其他企业、个体工商户，以及国有与集体联营企业、其他有限责任公司、股份有限公司、"三资"企业中的集体控股、私人控股、其他控股部分。

2.2010年就业人数、固定资产投资数据根据统计口径变化作了相应调整。

3.地区生产总值采用年报数。2016/2017年数据按照国家统计局新的核算制度修正。

Note: a)The statistical coverage of private economy in this table refers to collective enterprises,private enterprises,share-holding cooperative enterprises, other joint-operation enterprises, other corporations and individual economy.

b)The numbers of employed persons and investment in fixed assets in 2010 have been adjusted in accordance with change of statistical system. data are not comparable to the previous years.

c)Data of Gross Domestic Product are based on annual report. The data of 2016/2017 are revised according to the new Accounting Methodology.

1-14 全省商品、服务类电子商务交易情况
E-commerce transactions in commodities and services of Guangdong

单位：亿元 (100 million yuan)

指 标	Item	2017	2017年比2016年增长(%) Growth Rate in 2017 over 2016(%)
广东商品、服务类电子商务交易额	E-commerce transactions in commodities and services of Guangdong	37291.67	21.3
按交易平台分	According to the Transaction Platform		
广东在本地平台实现的电子商务交易额	E-commerce Transaction Volume of Guangdong on the Local Platform	17293.15	12.6
广东在省外平台实现的电子商务交易额	E-commerce Transaction Volume of Guangdong not on the Local Platform	19998.52	30.1
按交易对象分	According to the Transaction Object		
B2B+B2G	B2B+B2G	18453.09	11.0
B2C+C2C	B2C+C2C	18838.58	33.6
按交易内容分	According to the Transaction Content		
商品	Commodity	29883.71	19.0
服务	Service	7407.96	32.0

注：1.统计范围：辖区内规模以上工业、有资质的建筑业、限额以上批发和零售业、限额以上住宿和餐饮业、房地产开发经营业、规模以上服务业法人单位拥有的商品、服务类电子商务交易平台，辖区内规模以下法人单位拥有的且电子商务年交易额2000万元以上的商品、服务类电子商务交易平台。

2.电子商务交易额=在本地平台实现的电子商务交易额+在省外平台实现的电子商务交易额。

3.2016年起国家统计局仅反馈商品、服务类电子商务交易分地区数据，合约类电子商务交易数据不分地区反馈。

Note: a)Statistical scope: within the jurisdiction of the industrial enterprises above Designated Size, qualified construction enterprises, the enterprises above designated size in wholesale and retail industry, enterprises above designated size of hotels and catering services,real estate enterprises, the services enterprises above designated size have e-commerce trading platform,within the jurisdiction of the enterprises below the designated size have e-commerce trading platform with e-commerce transaction volume of more than 2000 million yuan.

b)E-commerce transaction volume=E-commerce transaction volume of Guangdong on the local platform+E-commerce transaction volume not on the local platform.

c)since 2016, the National Bureau of statistics only feedback the data of commodity and service e-commerce transactions regard of region, but the data of contract e-commerce transaction data regardless of region.

主要统计指标解释

行政区划 指国家对行政区域的划分。根据有关法规规定，我国的行政区域划分如下: (1)全国分为省、自治区、直辖市;(2)省、自治区分为自治州、县、自治县、市; (3)自治州分为县、自治县、市; (4)县、自治县分为乡、民族乡、镇; (5)直辖市和较大的市分为区、县; (6)国家在必要时设立的特别行政区。

发展速度 用以反映社会经济发展程度的相对指标，根据两个不同时期发展水平的对比而得。由于比较的标准时期不同，发展速度可分为定期发展速度和环比发展速度两种。

增长速度 发展速度－1（或100%）就是增长速度。即增长速度＝发展速度－1（或100%）。

平均每年增长速度 我国计算平均增长速度有两种方法，一种是习惯上经常使用的“水平法”，又称几何平均法，是以间隔最后一年的水平同基期水平对比来计算平均每年增长（或下降）的速度；另一种是“累计法”又称代数平均法或方程法，是以间隔年内各年水平的总和同基期水平对比来计算平均每年增长（或下降）的速度。具体计算方法，可参照中国财经出版社出版的《平均增长速度查对表》。

在一般正常情况下，两种方法计算的平均每年增长速度比较接近，但在经济发展不平衡出现大起大落时，两种方法计算的结果差别较大。

本《年鉴》内所列的平均每年增长速度都是用水平法计算的。从某年到某年平均增长速度的年份，均不包基期年在内。如1981－2010年平均每年增长速度，是以1980年为基期，2010年为报告期，年份从1981年算起，共30年。

当年价格 是报告期的实际价格，如工厂的出厂价格、农产品的收购价格、商品的零售价格等。按当年价格计算，是指一些以货币表现的物量指标，如工业总产值、国内生产总值等，按照当年的实际价格来计算总量。按当年价格计算的价值指标，在不同年份之间进行对比时，因为包含有各年间价格变动的因素，不能确切地反映实物量的增减变动。因此，在计算增长速度时都使用按可比价格计算的数字。

国民经济行业分类 自2012年定期报表开始使用新的《国民经济行业分类》（GB/T4754-2011）。该分类是由国家统计局组织修订，国家质量监督检验检疫总局和中国国家标准化管理委员会于2011年4月29日发布。这次修订是在2002年分类标准的基础上，参照联合国《全部经济活动的国际标准产业分类》（ISIC/Rev.4）进行的。修订后的《国民经济行业分类》（GB/T4754-2012）共有门类20个，大类96个，中类432个，小类1094个。

企业(单位)登记注册类型 是以在工商行政管理机关登记注册的各类企业为划分对象，以工商行政管理部门对企业登记注册的类型为依据，将企业登记注册类型分为内资企业、港澳台商投资企业和外商投资企业三大类。内资企业包括国有企业、集体企业、股份合作企业、联营企业、有限责任公司、股份有限公司、私营企业和其他企业；港澳台商投资企业和外商投资企业分别包括合资经营企业、合作经营企业、独资经营企业和股份有限公司等。对不在工商行政管理部门进行登记注册的行政机关、事业单位和社会团体，主要按其经费来源和管理方式进行划分。

国有企业 指企业全部资产归国家所有，并按《中华人民共和国企业法人登记管理条例》规定登记注册的非公司制的经济组织。不包括有限责任公司中的国有独资公司。

集体企业 指企业资产归集体所有，并按《中华人民共和国企业法人登记管理条例》规定登记注册的经济组织。

股份合作企业 指以合作制为基础，由企业职工共同出资入股，吸收一定比例的社会资产投资组建，实行自主经营，自负盈亏，共同劳动，民主管理，按劳分配与按股分红相结合的一种集体经济组织。

联营企业　指两个及两个以上相同或不同所有制性质的企业法人或事业单位法人，按自愿、平等、互利的原则，共同投资组成的经济组织。联营企业包括国有联营企业、集体联营企业、国有与集体联营企业和其他联营企业。

有限责任公司　指根据《中华人民共和国公司登记管理条例》规定登记注册，由两个以上、五十个以下的股东共同出资，每个股东以其所认缴的出资额对公司承担有限责任，公司以其全部资产对其债务承担责任的经济组织。有限责任公司包括国有独资公司以及其他有限责任公司。

股份有限公司　指根据《中华人民共和国公司登记管理条例》规定登记注册，其全部注册资本由等额股份构成并通过发行股票筹集资本，股东以其认购的股份对公司承担有限责任，公司以其全部资产对其债务承担责任的经济组织。

私营企业　指由自然人投资设立或由自然人控股，以雇佣劳动为基础的营利性经济组织。包括按照《公司法》、《合伙企业法》、《私营企业暂行条例》规定登记注册的私营有限责任公司、私营股份有限公司、私营合伙企业和私营独资企业。

其他企业　指上述企业之外的其他内资经济组织。

合资经营企业（港或澳、台资）　指港澳台地区投资者与内地企业依照《中华人民共和国中外合资经营企业法》及有关法律的规定，按合同规定的比例投资设立、分享利润和分担风险的企业。

合作经营企业（港或澳、台资）指港澳台地区投资者与内地企业依照《中华人民共和国中外合作经营企业法》及有关法律的规定，依照合作合同的约定进行投资或提供条件设立、分配利润和分担风险的企业。

港澳台商独资经营企业　指依照《中华人民共和国外资企业法》及有关法律的规定，在内地由港澳台地区投资者全额投资设立的企业。

港澳台商投资股份有限公司　指根据国家有关规定，经原外经贸部依法批准设立，其中港、澳、台商的股本占公司注册资本的比例达 25%以上的股份有限公司。凡其中港、澳、台商的股本占公司注册资本的比例小于 25%的，属于内资企业中的股份有限公司。

其他港澳台商投资企业　指在中国境内参照《外国企业或个人在中国境内设立合伙企业管理办法》和《外商投资合伙企业登记管理规定》，依法设立的港、澳、台商投资合伙企业等。

中外合资经营企业　指外国企业或外国人与中国内地企业依照《中华人民共和国中外合资经营企业法》及有关法律的规定，按合同规定的比例投资设立、分享利润和分担风险的企业。

中外合作经营企业　指外国企业或外国人与中国内地企业依照《中华人民共和国中外合作经营企业法》及有关法律的规定，依照合作合同的约定进行投资或提供条件设立、分配利润和分担风险的企业。

外资企业　指依照《中华人民共和国外资企业法》及有关法律的规定，在中国内地由外国投资者全额投资设立的企业。

外商投资股份有限公司　指根据国家有关规定，经原外经贸部依法批准设立，其中外资的股本占公司注册资本的比例达 25% 以上的股份有限公司。凡其中外资股本占公司注册资本的比例小于 25%的，属于内资企业中的股份有限公司。

其他外商投资企业　指在中国境内依照《外国企业或个人在中国境内设立合伙企业管理办法》和《外商投资合伙企业登记管理规定》，依法设立的外商投资合伙企业等。

行政机关、事业单位和社会团体　参照企业登记注册类型，主要按其经费来源和管理方式划分。具体规定如下：

⑴行政机关：包括国家机关和政党机关，原则上均列为“国有”。但有特殊规定的，如供销社等，则列为“集体”。

⑵事业单位：包括经国家机构编制部门和有关业务主管部门批准成立的各类事业单位，不包括实行企业化管理的事业单位。事业单位的划分办法如下：

①由国家财政预算拨款或列入财政预算外资金管理以及经费主要来源于国有主管部门或国有上级单位的事业单位，列为“国有”。

②经费主要来源于集体单位的事业单位，列为“集体”。

③公民个人(或个人合伙)开办的事业单位，列为“私营”。

④上述以外的其他事业单位，如果其经费来源不明确，按管理方式进行归类。

⑶社会团体：包括经民政部门批准成立以及未纳入社会团体管理条例范围的工会、妇联等各类社会团体。社会团体的划分办法如下：

①未纳入民政部社会团体管理条例范围的工会、妇联、共青团、青联、工商联、科协、侨联等社会团体，国家拨款设立的基金会或基金管理组织以及经费主要来源于国有业务主管部门或国有上级单位的社会团体，列为“国有”。

②经费主要来源于集体单位的社会团体，列为“集体”。

③公民个人(或个人合伙)开办的社会团体，划为“私营”。

④上述以外的其他社会团体，如果其经费来源不明确，改按管理方式进行归类。

电子商务交易平台　指在电子商务活动中为交易双方或多方提供交易撮合及相关服务的信息网络系统总合。

Explanatory Notes on Main Statistical Indicators

Divisions of Administrative Areas refer to the divisions of administrative areas by the state. Relevant laws of the People' s Republic of China stipulate the following principles for the divisions of administrative areas: 1)The whole country is divided into provinces, autonomous regions and municipalities directly under the central government; 2) Provinces and autonomous regions are divided into autonomous prefectures, counties, autonomous counties and cities; 3) Autonomous prefectures are divided into counties, autonomous counties and cities; 4) Counties and autonomous counties are divided into townships, ethnic townships and towns, 5) Municipalities under the central government and large cities are divided into districts and counties; 6) The state will, when necessary, establish special administrative regions.

Development Rate is a relative indicator of the degree of social and economic development calculated through the comparison of two different periods in the degree of development. Development rate can take the form of either fixed-base development rate or chain base development rate.

Growth Rate is equal to development rate minus one (or 100%), i.e. growth rate = development rate −1 (or 100%)

Average Annual Growth Rate Two methods for calculating average annual growth rate are applied in China, one is the more commonly-used "level approach" or the method of calculating geometric average, which is derived by comparing the level of the last year of the interval to that of the base year; the other is called "accumulative approach" or algebraic average or equation method, which is derived by comparing the summation of the actual figure of each year in the interval to the figure in the base year. The detailed calculating methods can be found by reference to the Check Table of Average Growth Rate published by China Financial Publishing House.

Under normal conditions the results calculated by the two methods are fairly close, but they differed sharply when uneven economic development occurred with striking fluctuations in growth.

The average annual growth rates listed in this statistical yearbook are calculated by level approach. The base years are not included when the years are listed for average annual growth rates. For instance, the average annual growth rate of 30 years since 1981 is listed as average annual growth rate of 1981-2010, among which 1980 is the base year and 2010 is the reference year.

Current Price refers to the actual price in the reference period, such as ex-factory price, purchasing price of agricultural products, retail price of commodities, etc. Total values of some quantum indicators in value terms at current prices, such as gross industrial output value and gross domestic product, are calculated in accordance with actual prices of the current year. When comparing indicators of value over time at current prices, they cannot accurately reflect the changes in real term due to price fluctuations of each year. That is why growth rates are calculated at constant prices.

Industrial Classification of the National Economy The new Industrial Classification of the National Economy (GB/T 4754-2011) is introduced starting from the compilation of 2012 annual statistics. The revision, based on the 2002 classification, was organized by the National Bureau of Statistics taking into consideration of the International Standards of the Industrial Classification of All Economic Activities (ISIC/Rev.4) of the United Nations. The new Classification was promulgated by the National Administration of Quality Supervision, Inspection and Quarantine and the Standardization Administration of the People's Republic of China on April 29, 2011. The revised version of the Industrial Classification of the National Economy (GB/T 4754-2012) is composed of 20 sections, 96 divisions, 432 groups and 1094 classes.

Registration Status of Enterprises (Units) Enterprises are classified into 3 categories, namely domestic-funded enterprises, enterprises with investment from Hong Kong, Macao and Taiwan, and enterprises with foreign investment, according to the registration status of an enterprise in industrial and commercial administration agencies. Domestic-funded enterprises include State-owned enterprises, collective-owned enterprises, cooperative enterprises, joint ownership enterprises, limited liability corporations, share-holding corporations Ltd., private enterprises and other enterprises. Included in the enterprises with investment from Hong Kong, Macao and Taiwan and enterprises with foreign investment are joint-venture enterprises, cooperative enterprises, sole investment enterprises and share-holding corporations Ltd. For government agencies, institutions and social organizations which are not registered in industrial and commercial administration agencies, they are classified mainly by their sources of funding and manner of management.

State-owned Enterprises refer to non-corporation economic units where the entire assets are owned by the State and which have been registered in accordance with the Regulation of the People's Republic of China on the Management of Registration of Corporate Enterprises. Not included from this category are solely State-funded corporations in the limited liability corporations.

Collective-owned Enterprises refer to economic units where the assets are owned collectively and which have been registered in accordance with the Regulation of the People's Republic of China on the Management of Registration of Corporate Enterprises.

Cooperative Enterprises refer to a form of collective economic units (enterprises) where capitals come mainly from employees as their shares, with certain proportion of capital from the outside, where production is organized on the basis of independent operation, independent accounting for profits and losses, joint work, democratic management, and a distribution system that integrates remuneration according to work with dividend according to capital share.

Joint Ownership Enterprises refer to economic units established by two or more corporate enterprises or corporate institutions of the same or different ownership, through joint investment on the basis of voluntary participation, equality, and mutual benefits. They include State joint ownership enterprises; collective joint ownership enterprises; joint State-collective enterprises; and other joint ownership enterprises.

Limited Liability Corporations refer to economic units established with investment from 2-50 investors and registered in accordance with the Regulation of the People's Republic of China on the Management of Registration of Corporations, each investor bearing limited liability to the corporation depending on its share of investment, and the corporation bearing liability to its debt to the maximum of its total assets. Limited liability corporations include solely State-funded limited liability corporations and other limited liability corporations.

Share-holding Corporations Ltd. refer to economic units registered in accordance with the Regulation of the People's Republic of China on the Management of Registration of Corporations, with total registered capital divided into equal shares and raised through issuing stocks. Each investor bears limited liability to the corporation depending on the holding of shares, and the corporation bears liability to its debt to the maximum of its total assets.

Private Enterprises refer to profit-making economic units invested and established by natural persons, or controlled by natural persons using employed labour. Included in this category are private limited liability corporations, private share-holding corporations Ltd., private partnership enterprises and private-funded enterprises registered in accordance with the Company Law, the Law on Partnership Business and Interim Regulations on Private Enterprises.

Other Domestic-funded Enterprises refer to domestic-funded economic units other than those mentioned above.

Joint Venture Enterprises(Funds are from Hong Kong, Macao or Taiwan.) are enterprises established by investors from Hong Kong, Macao and Taiwan with enterprises in the mainland of China in accordance with the Law of the People's Republic of China on Sino-foreign Equity Joint Ventures and other relevant laws, where the establishment of the investment and the sharing of profits and risks are stipulated under joint venture contracts.

Cooperative Enterprises(Funds are from Hong Kong, Macao or Taiwan.) established by investors from Hong Kong, Macao and Taiwan with enterprises in the mainland of China in accordance with the Law of the People's Republic of China on Sino-foreign Contractual Joint Venture and other relevant laws, where the investment or provision of facilities and the sharing of profits and risks are stipulated under cooperative contracts.

Enterprises with Sole (exclusive) Investment from Hong Kong, Macao and Taiwan refer to enterprises established in the mainland of China with exclusive investment from investors from Hong Kong, Macao and Taiwan in accordance with the Law of the People's Republic of China on Wholly Foreign-owned Enterprises and other relevant laws.

Share-holding Corporations Ltd. with Investment from Hong Kong, Macao and Taiwan refer to share-holding corporations Ltd. established with the approval from the former Ministry of Foreign Trade and Economic Relations in line with relevant State regulations, where the share of investment from Hong Kong, Macao or Taiwan businessmen exceeds 25% of the total registered capital of the corporation. In case the share of investment from Hong Kong, Macao or Taiwan is less than 25% of the total registered capital, the enterprise is to be classified as domestic-funded share-holding corporation Ltd.

Other Enterprises with Funds From Hong Kong, Macao and Taiwan refer to partnership enterprises with investments from Hong Kong, Macao and Taiwan established within the territory of China in accordance with Administrative Measures on the Establishment of Partnership Enterprises in China by Foreign Enterprises or Foreign Individuals and Regulations for the Administration of the Registration of Foreign-invested Partnership Enterprises.

Joint Venture Enterprises with Foreign Investment refer to enterprises jointly established by foreign enterprises or foreigners with enterprises in the mainland of China in accordance with the Law of the People's Republic of China on Sino-foreign Equity Joint Venturesand other relevant laws, where the sharing of investment, profits and risks is stipulated under contract.

Cooperative Enterprises with Foreign Investment refer to enterprises jointly established by foreign enterprises or foreigners with enterprises in the mainland of China in accordance with the *Law of the People's Republic of China on Sino-foreign Contractual Joint Venture*and other relevant laws, where the investment or provision of facilities and the sharing of profits and risks are stipulated under cooperative contracts.

Enterprises with Sole (exclusive) Foreign Investment refer to enterprises established in the mainland of China with exclusive investment from foreign investors in accordance with the Law of the People's Republic of China on Wholly Foreign-owned Enterprises and other relevant laws.

Share-holding Corporations Ltd. with Foreign Investment refer to share-holding corporations Ltd. established with the approval from the former Ministry of Foreign Trade and Economic Relations in line with relevant State regulations, where the share of investment from foreign investors exceeds 25% of the total registered capital of the corporation. In case the share of foreign investment is less than 25% of the total registered capital, the enterprise is to be classified as domestic-funded share-holding corporation Ltd.

Other Enterprises with Foreign Funds refer to partnership enterprises established within the territory of China in accordance with Administrative Measures on the Establishment of Partnership Enterprises in China by Foreign Enterprises or Foreign Individuals and Regulations for the Administration of the Registration of Foreign-invested Partnership Enterprises.

Government Agencies, Institutions and Social Organizations are classified into the following categories by source of funds and manner of management taking reference of the registration status of enterprises:

(1) Government agencies: include State and party agencies, classified in principle as State-owned. There are exceptions, such as supply and marketing cooperatives which are classified as collective-owned.

(2) Institutions: include institutions of various types established with the approval by organization and staffing departments of the government, but exclude institutions where enterprise management system is introduced. Institutions are further classified as follows:

(a) Institutions for which their main budgets are from government budget appropriations or extra-budget funds, or allocated from the budget of their competent government agencies. Such institutions are classified as state-owned.

(b) Institutions for which their budget mainly come from collective units. Such institutions are classified as collective-owned.

(c) Social institutions established by individual or a group of citizens, which are classified as private.

(d) Institutions other than those mentioned above for which their sources of budget are not clear. Such institutions are classified by the manner of management.

(3) Social organizations: include social organizations established with the approval from the Ministry of Civil Affairs, and organizations that are not covered by social organization management regulations such as trade unions, women's federations etc.. Social organizations are further classified as follows:

(a) Social organizations that are not covered by social organization management regulations of the Ministry of Civil Affairs such as trade unions, women federations, communist youth leagues, youth associations, industrial and commerce associations, scientist associations, overseas Chinese associations, etc., foundations and fund management organizations established with funds from the state, and social organizations whose funds mainly come from the budget of their competent government agencies. Such institutions are classified as State-owned.

(b) Social organizations for which their budget mainly come from collective units. Such institutions are classified as collective-owned.

(c) Social organizations established by individual or a group of citizens, which are classified as private.

(d) Social organizations other than those mentioned above for which their sources of budget are not clear. Such organizations are classified by the manner of management.

E-commerce Trading Platform refers to the total information network system which provide the dealmaking and related service for the transaction parties in e-commerce activities.

二、国民经济核算

NATIONAL ECONOMIC ACCOUNTS

二 国民经济核算

简要说明

一、本篇资料反映广东国民经济核算情况。

二、国民经济核算资料主要包括地区生产总值及其有关资料。地区生产总值是根据不同产业部门、不同支出构成的特点和资料来源情况而采用不同方法计算的。

三、本年鉴公布的国民经济核算资料为最终核实数。如果在开展全国经济普查，发现对地区生产总值数据有较大影响的新的基础资料，或核算方法及分类标准发生变化后，也要对年度地区生产总值历史数据进行修订。2016 年，国家统计局改革地区研发支出的核算方法，将能够为所有者带来经济利益的研发支出不再作为中间消耗，而是作为固定资本形成处理。根据新的核算方法，修订了 1995-2016 年全省地区生产总值数据。2018 年根据第三次农业普查，修订了 2006-2017 年全省地区生产数据。本年鉴数据是修订后的数据。

四、国民经济核算数据绝对数按当年价格计算，速度和指数按不变价格计算。

五、分市的国民经济核算数据由各市统计局提供，由于采取分级核算，各市数据相加不等于全省总计。

六、本篇资料由广东省统计局国民经济核算处整理提供。

2 National Economic Accounts

Brief Introduction

Ⅰ.The data in this chapter reflect the national accounts of Guangdong Province.

Ⅱ. The data on national accounts mainly include gross domestic product (GDP) and related data. Data on GDP are calculated with various approaches in accordance with the features of various industrial sectors, various expenditure structures and the data resources.

Ⅲ. The national economic accounting data published in this yearbook is the final verification number. During the national economic census, It is also necessary to revise the historical data of annual gross domestic product (GDP) after the discovery of new basic data, or changes in accounting methods and classification standards, which have a greater impact on the regional gross domestic product data.In 2016, National Bureau of Statistics reforms the Methodology of Expenditure for Research and Development, which that will bring economic benefit for the owners is not treated as Intermediate Consumption, and is treated as fixed assets formation. According to the new Accounting Methodology, Statistics Bureau of Guangdong Province revised historical data of GDP from 1995 to 2016. In 2018, According to the Third Agriculture Census, Statistics Bureau of Guangdong Province revised historical data of GDP from 2006 to 2017. Data published in this yearbook are adjusted data.

Ⅳ. The data on national accounts are calculated at current prices, and the growth rates and the index are calculated at constant prices.

Ⅴ. The data on national accounts by city are provided by the statistical bureaus of various cities. The sum of the city data is not equal to the provincial total due to the decentralized accounting approach.

Ⅵ. The data in this chapter are prepared and provided by the Division of National Accounts of Statistics Bureau of Guangdong Province.

2-1 国民经济核算主要指标

Main Indicators of Gross Domestic Product

指标	Item	2000	2015	2016	2017
地区生产总值 (亿元)	Gross Domestic Product (100 million yuan)	10810.21	73876.37	80666.72	89705.23
第一产业	Primary Industry	986.32	3189.76	3500.49	3611.44
第二产业	Secondary Industry	5055.71	33642.00	35109.66	38008.06
第三产业	Tertiary Industry	4768.18	37044.61	42056.57	48085.73
地区生产总值指数 (上年=100)	Indices of Gross Domestic Product (preceding year=100)	111.7	108.0	107.5	107.5
第一产业	Primary Industry	102.3	103.4	103.1	103.6
第二产业	Secondary Industry	112.3	106.9	106.1	106.5
第三产业	Tertiary Industry	113.4	109.5	109.2	108.7
地区生产总值构成 (%)	Composition of Grosss Domestic Product (%)	100.0	100.0	100.0	100.0
第一产业	Primary Industry	9.1	4.3	4.4	4.0
第二产业	Secondary Industry	46.8	45.5	43.5	42.4
第三产业	Tertiary Industry	44.1	50.2	52.1	53.6
地区生产总值贡献率 (%)	Share of the Contribution of the Three Strata of Industry	100.0	100.0	100.0	100.0
第一产业	Primary Industry	1.9	1.6	1.8	2.0
第二产业	Secondary Industry	60.2	42.8	36.8	39.0
第三产业	Tertiary Industry	37.9	55.5	61.4	59.1
地区生产总值拉动率 (%)	Contribution of the Three Strata of Industry to GDP Growth	11.7	8.0	7.5	7.5
第一产业	Primary Industry	0.2	0.1	0.1	0.1
第二产业	Secondary Industry	7.1	3.4	2.8	2.9
第三产业	Tertiary Industry	4.4	4.4	4.6	4.5
人均地区生产总值 (元)	Per Capita Gross Domestic Product (yuan)	12817	68490	73844	80932
人均地区生产总值指数 (上年=100)	Indices of Per Capita Gross Domestic Product (preceding year=100)	107.3	107.0	106.2	106.0
支出法地区生产总值 (亿元)	Gross Domestic Product by Expenditure Approach (100 million yuan)	10810.21	73876.37	80666.72	89705.23
最终消费支出	Final Consumption Expenditures	5717.11	37198.29	40885.91	45128.95
资本形成总额	Gross Capital Formation	3917.11	31602.03	34647.09	39657.52
货物和服务净流出	Net Exports of Goods and Services	1175.99	5076.05	5133.72	4918.76
支出法地区生产总值构成 (%)	Composition of Gross Domestic Product by Expenditure Approach (%)	100.0	100.0	100.0	100.0
最终消费支出	Final Consumption Expenditures	52.9	50.4	50.7	50.3
资本形成总额	Gross Capital Formation	36.2	42.8	43.0	44.2
货物和服务净流出	Net Exports of Goods and Services	10.9	6.9	6.4	5.5
支出法地区生产总值贡献率(%)	Share of the Contribution of Gross Domestic Product by Expenditure Approach (%)	100.0	100.0	100.0	100.0
最终消费支出	Final Consumption Expenditures	33.0	47.6	49.6	48.6
资本形成总额	Gross Capital Formation	27.3	48.8	48.8	44.9
货物和服务净流出	Net Exports of Goods and Services	39.7	3.6	1.6	6.5
生产性服务业增加值 (亿元)	Value-added of Productive Service Industry(100 million yuan)		19551.98	21719.60	24665.14

2-2 地区生产总值

Gross Domestic Product

单位：亿元 (100 million yuan)

年份 Year	地区生产总值 Gross Domestic Product	第一产业 Primary Industry	第二产业 Secondary Industry	第三产业 Tertiary Industry	#工业 Industry	#建筑业 Construction	#批发和零售业 Wholesale and Retail Trades	#交通运输、仓储和邮政业 Transport, Storage, and Post	#金融业 Financial Intermediation	#房地产业 Real Estate
1978	185.85	55.31	86.62	43.92	76.12	10.49	19.39	10.05	4.53	1.42
1979	209.34	66.62	91.65	51.06	82.36	9.29	23.52	11.26	4.74	1.62
1980	249.65	82.97	102.53	64.14	89.87	12.66	29.53	13.72	6.10	2.13
1981	290.36	94.30	120.34	75.71	103.60	16.74	33.57	16.71	6.76	2.79
1982	339.92	118.17	135.37	86.39	113.13	22.24	38.07	18.34	7.98	3.39
1983	368.75	121.24	152.27	95.24	125.82	26.45	41.42	19.47	8.94	4.09
1984	458.74	145.25	187.55	125.93	154.33	33.22	54.41	25.68	11.76	5.09
1985	577.38	171.87	229.82	175.69	185.81	44.01	79.86	35.91	12.74	6.16
1986	667.53	188.37	255.88	223.28	208.46	47.42	89.78	40.18	20.84	11.69
1987	846.69	232.14	330.35	284.20	273.77	56.58	104.17	53.20	34.25	16.44
1988	1155.37	306.50	460.17	388.70	386.35	73.82	145.89	65.22	46.80	22.84
1989	1381.39	351.73	554.13	475.53	464.06	90.07	136.65	79.02	72.70	41.36
1990	1559.03	384.59	615.86	558.58	523.42	92.45	152.90	101.61	82.46	42.87
1991	1893.30	416.00	782.67	694.63	675.55	107.12	185.77	138.54	94.83	54.09
1992	2447.54	465.83	1100.32	881.39	899.28	201.04	236.59	174.28	122.79	81.74
1993	3469.28	558.70	1704.88	1205.70	1386.83	318.05	340.49	233.15	149.29	126.25
1994	4619.02	692.25	2253.25	1673.52	1865.44	387.80	486.46	336.95	199.84	171.11
1995	5940.34	864.49	2906.27	2169.58	2454.87	451.40	647.77	433.10	229.27	230.75
1996	6848.23	935.24	3318.51	2594.48	2853.85	464.66	798.55	505.91	264.86	283.92
1997	7792.97	978.32	3719.69	3094.96	3250.72	468.97	944.61	642.37	302.87	342.54
1998	8555.33	994.55	4087.41	3473.37	3584.54	502.87	1073.36	705.98	306.39	419.76
1999	9289.64	1009.01	4391.33	3889.30	3864.77	526.56	1174.76	766.84	331.10	505.74
2000	10810.21	986.32	5055.71	4768.18	4518.65	537.06	1371.49	938.90	443.69	626.10
2001	12126.59	988.84	5577.91	5559.84	5012.16	565.75	1543.83	1114.31	450.81	696.41
2002	13601.89	1015.08	6224.73	6362.08	5628.70	596.03	1761.27	1206.35	454.65	808.16
2003	15959.25	1072.91	7687.81	7198.53	6980.97	706.84	2009.33	1263.54	534.28	955.66
2004	19005.61	1248.59	9398.61	8358.41	8602.59	796.02	1989.53	859.88	602.68	1103.75
2005	22723.29	1428.27	11497.85	9797.17	10630.06	867.79	2250.66	1032.06	661.81	1430.37
2006	26800.32	1532.17	13655.80	11612.35	12703.78	952.02	2606.79	1208.94	899.91	1722.07
2007	32063.91	1705.69	16252.47	14105.75	15190.14	1062.33	2912.30	1418.66	1705.08	2029.77
2008	37138.85	1969.46	18813.11	16356.28	17615.09	1198.02	3476.44	1634.54	1972.40	2057.45
2009	39923.24	1996.38	19718.72	18208.14	18386.25	1332.47	3953.35	1581.72	2335.08	2453.64
2010	46544.63	2254.49	23296.73	20993.41	21740.56	1556.17	4760.11	1793.89	2780.73	2775.38
2011	53908.59	2614.59	26733.70	24560.30	24931.69	1802.01	5881.51	2036.47	3119.08	3253.27
2012	57924.76	2778.48	27981.32	27164.96	26086.03	1895.29	6622.92	2286.37	3469.67	3544.67
2013	63357.92	2876.42	29837.46	30644.04	27735.26	2165.29	7323.55	2451.52	4122.81	4207.46
2014	68777.25	3038.71	32357.19	33381.35	30079.24	2345.38	7778.82	2741.77	4447.43	4486.92
2015	73876.37	3189.76	33642.00	37044.61	31290.75	2441.85	7625.98	2929.90	5757.08	5117.95
2016	80666.72	3500.49	35109.66	42056.57	32650.89	2551.82	8382.48	3209.72	6127.05	6229.50
2017	89705.23	3611.44	38008.06	48085.73	35291.83	2818.82	8976.59	3580.94	6853.01	7635.96

注：1. 2004年及以前年份第一产业不包括农林牧渔服务业，交通运输仓储和邮政业包括电信业，但不包括城市公共交通业，批发与零售业包括餐饮业（以下相关表同）。

2. 2013年起，三次产业分类依据国家统计局2012年制定的《三次产业划分规定》执行(以下相关表同)。

Notes: a)In 2004 and prior to it, the primary industry did not include service activities for farming, forestry, animal husbandry and fishery;transport, storage,and postal services included telecommunication services,but excluded urban public transport; and wholesale and retail trades included catering services. The same applies to the following tables.

b)Since 2013, three industry classification are divided according to the deputy of three industry classification which is developed by NBS in 2012(the same applied to the following table).

2–3 地区生产总值指数

Indices of Gross Domestic Product

上年=100 (preceding year=100)

年份 Year	地区生产总值 Gross Domestic Product	第一产业 Primary Industry	第二产业 Secondary Industry	第三产业 Tertiary Industry	#工业 Industry	#建筑业 Construction	#批发和零售业 Wholesale and Retail Trades	#交通运输、仓储和邮政业 Transport, Storage, and Post	#金融业 Financial Interme-diation	#房地产业 Real Estate
1978	101.0	104.3	97.1	101.2						
1979	108.5	106.1	104.3	117.6	107.6	89.5	123.1	112.7	103.1	115.2
1980	116.6	112.7	116.9	122.1	113.2	136.6	119.6	119.5	126.4	136.0
1981	109.0	105.1	112.9	110.0	110.8	122.0	106.8	107.5	106.4	129.5
1982	112.0	111.9	111.5	112.5	108.1	124.9	108.0	117.4	110.0	121.0
1983	107.3	103.6	110.1	108.9	109.6	111.6	106.9	105.0	110.0	117.9
1984	115.6	112.5	118.8	115.7	120.5	113.0	116.6	105.7	116.8	109.3
1985	118.0	106.2	120.7	128.7	120.9	120.1	127.6	123.1	130.0	148.3
1986	112.7	105.6	108.1	124.7	108.8	105.4	117.9	120.9	130.2	161.1
1987	119.6	109.6	127.5	120.6	131.6	112.1	116.5	122.2	140.3	132.2
1988	115.8	106.6	124.9	113.7	128.0	111.4	108.3	121.8	115.0	127.6
1989	107.2	107.2	108.6	105.7	110.8	97.1	80.1	118.2	133.0	141.4
1990	111.6	107.3	112.7	113.4	114.4	102.7	112.2	106.8	117.3	97.6
1991	117.7	105.4	123.6	119.4	123.0	127.5	119.6	128.3	107.2	114.3
1992	122.1	105.6	133.4	119.0	130.8	149.8	119.4	120.9	121.2	146.2
1993	123.0	102.5	136.3	116.7	139.8	117.0	122.0	124.9	102.5	129.0
1994	119.7	103.1	125.7	118.4	127.2	116.2	119.4	127.6	107.4	127.4
1995	115.7	105.4	118.9	114.7	119.8	112.8	115.9	117.3	101.8	122.1
1996	111.3	104.9	112.7	111.5	114.1	102.6	114.2	109.4	107.5	115.8
1997	111.2	104.7	112.9	110.7	114.5	100.0	113.6	109.1	109.6	111.6
1998	110.9	103.8	112.5	110.4	113.0	107.6	115.0	106.7	103.1	110.6
1999	110.3	103.9	110.8	111.3	111.1	107.5	110.4	105.7	110.8	119.3
2000	111.7	102.3	112.3	113.4	113.6	99.2	109.4	117.3	122.7	115.4
2001	110.5	102.2	110.7	112.0	111.3	106.1	111.6	113.9	101.7	108.7
2002	112.4	104.3	113.7	112.5	114.8	103.5	113.3	106.3	100.6	111.9
2003	114.8	102.2	120.2	111.3	120.9	113.1	111.6	106.1	110.6	115.3
2004	114.7	104.1	118.6	112.0	120.1	102.9	109.8	113.9	106.9	108.2
2005	114.2	104.9	115.3	114.2	116.0	106.6	111.1	118.8	107.7	121.2
2006	114.9	104.2	117.2	113.7	117.9	108.9	113.0	116.3	124.7	112.8
2007	115.0	103.2	117.3	113.7	118.1	107.5	108.0	111.0	141.8	113.1
2008	110.5	103.9	111.6	109.8	112.4	100.5	112.6	108.3	109.0	93.5
2009	109.9	105.1	109.1	111.5	108.6	115.7	117.0	105.5	117.9	120.5
2010	112.5	104.5	114.6	110.8	114.7	111.9	114.9	111.4	113.4	104.4
2011	110.2	104.4	110.5	110.4	110.7	107.2	113.8	112.0	105.6	105.5
2012	108.3	103.9	107.3	109.8	107.6	103.2	110.1	112.8	110.0	108.6
2013	108.5	102.4	107.6	110.0	107.9	103.9	110.2	108.7	115.7	113.0
2014	107.8	103.3	107.9	108.0	108.0	106.2	107.2	110.8	108.3	102.6
2015	108.0	103.4	106.9	109.5	107.0	105.8	106.6	105.5	119.0	109.1
2016	107.5	103.1	106.1	109.2	106.2	104.1	107.0	109.5	106.3	110.2
2017	107.5	103.6	106.5	108.7	106.8	102.9	105.4	109.5	108.8	107.2

2-4 地区生产总值指数

Indices of Gross Domestic Product

1978年=100　　(1978=100)

年份 Year	地区生产总值 Gross Domestic Product	第一产业 Primary Industry	第二产业 Secondary Industry	第三产业 Tertiary Industry	#工业 Industry	#建筑业 Construction	#批发和零售业 Wholesale and Retail Trades	#交通运输、仓储和邮政业 Transport, Storage, and Post	#金融业 Financial Intermediation	#房地产业 Real Estate
1978	100.0	100.0	100.0	100.0	100.0	100.0	100.0	100.0	100.0	100.0
1979	108.5	106.1	104.3	117.6	107.6	89.5	123.1	112.7	103.1	115.2
1980	126.5	119.6	121.9	143.5	121.8	122.2	147.3	134.6	130.4	156.6
1981	137.9	125.8	137.6	157.8	135.0	149.1	157.2	144.8	138.6	202.8
1982	154.4	140.8	153.4	177.5	145.9	186.4	169.7	170.0	152.6	245.3
1983	165.6	145.9	168.8	193.3	159.9	208.0	181.5	178.6	167.8	289.1
1984	191.4	164.1	200.6	223.7	192.7	235.1	211.7	188.8	196.0	316.0
1985	225.7	174.2	242.1	287.9	233.0	282.4	270.1	232.5	254.7	468.8
1986	254.5	184.0	261.6	359.0	253.4	297.5	318.5	281.0	331.7	755.1
1987	304.5	201.7	333.4	433.0	333.4	333.5	370.9	343.4	465.3	998.5
1988	352.6	215.0	416.5	492.6	426.7	371.4	401.6	418.2	535.1	1273.9
1989	377.9	230.6	452.1	520.5	472.8	360.6	321.8	494.3	711.7	1801.5
1990	421.6	247.4	509.3	590.1	540.9	370.4	361.1	527.8	834.5	1758.4
1991	496.1	260.9	629.7	704.6	665.4	472.2	431.9	677.2	894.5	2009.4
1992	605.8	275.4	840.2	838.6	870.4	707.4	515.7	818.6	1084.5	2938.0
1993	745.1	282.4	1145.2	979.1	1217.2	827.9	629.1	1022.1	1111.4	3788.9
1994	891.9	291.2	1439.6	1159.6	1547.9	962.4	751.2	1304.3	1193.3	4828.9
1995	1031.9	306.9	1712.2	1330.2	1854.5	1085.2	870.7	1529.5	1214.2	5898.4
1996	1149.0	321.9	1929.8	1483.4	2115.1	1113.5	994.7	1673.6	1305.2	6832.4
1997	1278.1	336.9	2179.7	1642.1	2421.6	1113.7	1129.7	1826.4	1429.8	7621.6
1998	1416.9	349.6	2452.0	1813.2	2736.4	1198.7	1299.0	1948.7	1474.6	8430.9
1999	1562.5	363.3	2717.2	2018.3	3041.5	1288.3	1434.7	2060.5	1634.4	10060.9
2000	1745.5	371.7	3052.5	2288.0	3455.1	1278.5	1570.1	2416.6	2004.6	11611.0
2001	1929.3	379.9	3380.5	2563.0	3845.5	1356.4	1751.8	2753.6	2039.4	12625.6
2002	2167.9	396.3	3843.3	2883.6	4416.4	1404.0	1984.9	2927.1	2052.4	14124.2
2003	2488.8	405.1	4618.8	3209.5	5339.4	1587.9	2215.3	3105.8	2269.9	16289.3
2004	2855.3	421.7	5478.9	3595.0	6413.9	1633.8	2433.5	3538.7	2427.3	17628.9
2005	3259.9	442.5	6315.8	4106.9	7439.2	1741.3	2704.2	4203.0	2614.1	21371.9
2006	3744.8	461.0	7401.0	4670.7	8767.5	1897.0	3055.7	4887.6	3260.9	24097.3
2007	4306.0	476.0	8682.2	5312.5	10350.1	2039.3	3301.6	5423.5	4625.2	27255.8
2008	4756.8	494.6	9690.5	5835.1	11631.1	2049.7	3718.0	5876.3	5043.4	25489.1
2009	5227.2	520.0	10567.5	6506.1	12636.1	2372.1	4349.6	6197.1	5945.2	30719.0
2010	5881.1	543.7	12106.1	7210.6	14497.9	2654.5	4997.5	6905.9	6740.3	32078.2
2011	6479.0	567.4	13378.0	7961.2	16055.1	2846.2	5689.6	7737.5	7120.9	33856.2
2012	7015.2	589.5	14355.9	8740.8	17274.3	2937.7	6265.6	8729.7	7829.9	36759.4
2013	7610.9	603.8	15452.3	9613.2	18638.6	3051.3	6904.9	9486.0	9057.2	41539.8
2014	8202.6	623.8	16678.2	10381.8	20137.6	3240.3	7401.6	10514.6	9809.3	42639.1
2015	8858.7	644.9	17835.7	11367.8	21555.2	3428.1	7888.3	11097.3	11677.3	46534.6
2016	9524.2	665.0	18917.6	12414.2	22895.1	3568.3	8441.8	12154.2	12417.8	51279.7
2017	10242.7	689.1	20155.2	13500.0	24459.0	3670.0	8898.4	13305.5	13510.4	54984.2

2-5 地区生产总值产业构成

Composition of Gross Domestic Product by Industry

单位：% (%)

年份 Year	地区生产总值 Gross Dcmestic Product	第一产业 Primary Industry	第二产业 Secondary Industry	第三产业 Tertiary Industry	#工 业 Industry
1978	100.0	29.8	46.6	23.6	41.0
1979	100.0	31.8	43.8	24.4	39.3
1980	100.0	33.2	41.1	25.7	36.0
1981	100.0	32.5	41.4	26.1	35.7
1982	100.0	34.8	39.8	25.4	33.3
1983	100.0	32.9	41.3	25.8	34.1
1984	100.0	31.7	40.9	27.4	33.6
1985	100.0	29.8	39.8	30.4	32.2
1986	100.0	28.2	38.3	33.5	31.2
1987	100.0	27.4	39.0	33.6	32.3
1988	100.0	26.5	39.8	33.7	33.4
1989	100.0	25.5	40.1	34.4	33.6
1990	100.0	24.7	39.5	35.8	33.6
1991	100.0	22.0	41.3	36.7	35.7
1992	100.0	19.0	45.0	36.0	36.7
1993	100.0	16.1	49.1	34.8	40.0
1994	100.0	15.0	48.8	36.2	40.4
1995	100.0	14.6	48.9	36.5	41.3
1996	100.0	13.6	48.5	37.9	41.7
1997	100.0	12.6	47.7	39.7	41.7
1998	100.0	11.6	47.8	40.6	41.9
1999	100.0	10.8	47.3	41.9	41.6
2000	100.0	9.1	46.8	44.1	41.8
2001	100.0	8.2	46.0	45.8	41.3
2002	100.0	7.4	45.8	46.8	41.4
2003	100.0	6.7	48.2	45.1	43.7
2004	100.0	6.6	49.4	44.0	45.3
2005	100.0	6.3	50.6	43.1	46.8
2006	100.0	5.7	51.0	43.3	47.4
2007	100.0	5.3	50.7	44.0	47.4
2008	100.0	5.3	50.7	44.0	47.4
2009	100.0	5.0	49.4	45.6	46.1
2010	100.0	4.8	50.1	45.1	46.7
2011	100.0	4.8	49.6	45.6	46.2
2012	100.0	4.8	48.3	46.9	45.0
2013	100.0	4.5	47.1	48.4	43.8
2014	100.1	4.4	47.1	48.5	43.7
2015	100.1	4.3	45.5	50.2	42.4
2016	100.1	4.4	43.5	52.1	40.5
2017	100.0	4.0	42.4	53.6	39.3

2-6 三次产业贡献率

Share of the Contributions of the Three Strata of Industry

单位：% (%)

年份 Year	地区生产总值 Gross Domestic Product	第一产业 Primary Industry	第二产业 Secondary Industry	第三产业 Tertiary Industry	#工 业 Industry
1979	100.0	30.0	16.6	53.4	24.2
1980	100.0	31.0	32.1	36.9	21.0
1981	100.0	22.4	45.4	32.2	31.0
1982	100.0	37.8	31.5	30.7	17.8
1983	100.0	18.7	45.1	36.2	33.4
1984	100.0	29.2	40.5	30.3	34.1
1985	100.0	12.2	39.8	48.0	31.4
1986	100.0	14.1	22.3	63.6	19.1
1987	100.0	14.7	47.3	38.0	42.9
1988	100.0	11.4	56.8	31.8	52.0
1989	100.0	25.5	46.2	28.3	48.8
1990	100.0	16.0	43.1	40.9	41.7
1991	100.0	7.5	53.1	39.4	44.8
1992	100.0	5.5	63.1	31.4	50.1
1993	100.0	2.1	72.0	25.9	66.8
1994	100.0	2.5	65.9	31.6	60.4
1995	100.0	4.7	64.0	31.3	58.7
1996	100.0	5.3	61.1	33.6	59.6
1997	100.0	4.8	63.6	31.6	63.6
1998	100.0	3.8	64.5	31.7	60.8
1999	100.0	3.9	59.9	36.2	56.2
2000	100.0	1.9	60.2	37.9	60.6
2001	100.0	1.9	47.7	50.4	44.9
2002	100.0	2.9	51.9	45.2	50.5
2003	100.0	1.2	64.6	34.2	60.8
2004	100.0	2.0	62.8	35.3	61.9
2005	100.0	2.2	55.3	42.4	53.5
2006	100.0	1.8	58.4	39.8	56.1
2007	100.0	1.2	59.6	39.1	57.8
2008	100.0	1.9	58.4	39.7	58.2
2009	100.0	2.5	48.7	48.8	43.8
2010	100.0	1.7	61.5	36.9	58.4
2011	100.0	2.1	51.7	46.2	49.4
2012	100.0	2.2	44.3	53.5	43.1
2013	100.0	1.2	44.7	54.1	43.4
2014	100.0	1.7	50.3	48.0	48.0
2015	100.0	1.6	42.8	55.5	40.9
2016	100.0	1.8	36.8	61.4	35.0
2017	100.0	2.0	39.0	59.1	37.9

注：三次产业贡献率指各产业增加值增量与GDP增量之比。
Notes: Industrial contribution rate refers to the proportion of the increment of every industrial value added to the increment of GDP.

2-7 三次产业对地区生产总值增长的拉动
Contribution of the Three Strata of Industry to GDP Growth

单位：百分点 (percentage points)

年份 Year	地区生产总值 Gross Dcmestic Product	第一产业 Primary Industry	第二产业 Secondary Industry	第三产业 Tertiary Industry	#工 业 Industry
1979	8.5	2.6	1.4	4.5	2.0
1980	16.6	5.2	5.3	6.1	3.5
1981	9.0	2.0	4.1	2.9	2.8
1982	12.0	4.5	3.8	3.7	2.1
1983	7.3	1.4	3.3	2.6	2.4
1984	15.6	4.6	6.3	4.7	5.3
1985	18.0	2.2	7.2	8.6	5.6
1986	12.7	1.8	2.8	8.1	2.4
1987	19.6	2.9	9.3	7.4	8.4
1988	15.8	1.8	9.0	5.0	8.2
1989	7.2	1.8	3.3	2.1	3.5
1990	11.6	1.9	5.0	4.7	4.8
1991	17.7	1.3	9.4	7.0	7.9
1992	22.1	1.2	14.0	6.9	11.1
1993	23.0	0.5	16.5	6.0	15.3
1994	19.7	0.5	13.0	6.2	11.9
1995	15.7	0.7	10.0	4.9	9.2
1996	11.3	0.6	6.9	3.8	6.8
1997	11.2	0.5	7.2	3.5	7.1
1998	10.9	0.4	7.0	3.4	6.6
1999	10.3	0.4	6.2	3.7	5.8
2000	11.7	0.2	7.1	4.4	7.1
2001	10.5	0.2	5.0	5.3	4.7
2002	12.4	0.4	6.4	5.6	6.2
2003	14.8	0.2	9.6	5.1	9.0
2004	14.7	0.3	9.2	5.2	9.1
2005	14.2	0.3	7.8	6.0	7.6
2006	14.9	0.3	8.7	5.9	8.4
2007	15.0	0.2	8.9	5.9	8.7
2008	10.5	0.2	6.1	4.2	6.1
2009	9.9	0.2	4.8	4.8	4.3
2010	12.5	0.2	7.7	4.6	7.3
2011	10.2	0.2	5.3	4.7	5.0
2012	8.3	0.2	3.7	4.4	3.6
2013	8.5	0.1	3.8	4.6	3.7
2014	7.8	0.1	3.9	3.7	3.7
2015	8.0	0.1	3.4	4.4	3.3
2016	7.5	0.1	2.8	4.6	2.6
2017	7.5	0.1	2.9	4.5	2.9

注：三次产业拉动指GDP增长速度与各产业贡献率之乘积。
Notes: Industrial pulling rate is the growth rate of GDP multiplying industrial contribution rate.

2−8 地区生产总值项目结构

Components of Gross Domestic Product

单位：亿元 (100 million yuan)

年份 Year	地区生产总值 Gross Domestic Product	劳动者报酬 Compens-ation of Employees	生产税净额 Net Taxes on Production	固定资产折旧 Depreciation of Fixed Assets	营业盈余 Operating Surplus	构成(地区生产总值=100) Composition(GDP=100) 劳动者报酬 Compens-ation of Employees	生产税净额 Net Taxes on Production	固定资产折旧 Depreciation of Fixed Assets	营业盈余 Operating Surplus
1978	185.85	112.58	25.13	21.07	27.07	60.6	13.5	11.3	14.6
1979	209.34	126.64	28.07	23.67	30.96	60.5	13.4	11.3	14.8
1980	249.65	151.09	32.62	28.25	37.69	60.5	13.1	11.3	15.1
1981	290.36	175.16	38.66	33.28	43.26	60.3	13.3	11.5	14.9
1982	339.92	207.09	43.58	38.11	51.14	60.9	12.8	11.2	15.0
1983	368.75	222.02	48.33	41.82	56.58	60.2	13.1	11.3	15.3
1984	458.74	274.33	59.74	52.06	72.61	59.8	13.0	11.3	15.8
1985	577.38	343.38	74.24	65.66	94.10	59.5	12.9	11.4	16.3
1986	667.53	393.11	84.86	77.99	111.57	58.9	12.7	11.7	16.7
1987	846.69	486.39	108.63	99.73	151.94	57.4	12.8	11.8	17.9
1988	1155.37	662.14	149.93	135.89	207.41	57.3	13.0	11.8	18.0
1989	1381.39	769.17	176.84	169.99	265.39	55.7	12.8	12.3	19.2
1990	1559.03	864.69	197.92	192.05	304.37	55.5	12.7	12.3	19.5
1991	1893.30	1031.46	248.47	240.20	373.17	54.5	13.1	12.7	19.7
1992	2447.54	1287.81	352.00	328.48	479.25	52.6	14.4	13.4	19.6
1993	3469.28	1822.72	478.22	450.06	718.29	52.5	13.8	13.0	20.7
1994	4619.02	2451.06	630.43	635.37	902.15	53.1	13.6	13.8	19.5
1995	5940.34	3077.86	827.17	907.53	1127.78	51.8	13.9	15.3	19.0
1996	6848.23	3584.34	985.78	1082.01	1196.10	52.3	14.4	15.8	17.5
1997	7792.97	4053.33	1111.15	1217.75	1410.74	52.0	14.3	15.6	18.1
1998	8555.33	4858.94	1268.93	1380.21	1047.25	56.8	14.8	16.1	12.2
1999	9289.64	5109.07	1375.14	1609.72	1195.71	55.0	14.8	17.3	12.9
2000	10810.21	5600.63	1759.12	1884.83	1565.63	51.8	16.3	17.4	14.5
2001	12126.59	6104.83	1939.52	2027.83	2054.41	50.3	16.0	16.7	16.9
2002	13601.89	7116.01	1988.13	2207.47	2290.28	52.3	14.6	16.2	16.8
2003	15959.25	7941.03	2303.35	2523.76	3191.11	49.8	14.4	15.8	20.0
2004	19005.61	9016.48	2659.30	2907.85	4421.98	47.4	14.0	15.3	23.3
2005	22723.29	10618.90	3177.03	3697.93	5229.43	46.7	14.0	16.3	23.0
2006	26800.32	12075.99	4038.50	4371.93	6313.90	45.1	15.1	16.3	23.6
2007	32063.91	14222.96	4947.40	4865.88	8027.67	44.4	15.4	15.2	25.0
2008	37138.85	16654.79	5796.13	5387.75	9300.18	44.8	15.6	14.5	25.0
2009	39923.24	17880.58	5996.57	5702.10	10343.99	44.8	15.0	14.3	25.9
2010	46544.63	20440.39	6769.63	6318.81	13015.80	43.9	14.5	13.6	28.0
2011	53908.59	24282.29	8453.19	7201.71	13971.40	45.0	15.7	13.4	25.9
2012	57924.76	27227.32	8860.93	7805.73	14030.78	47.0	15.3	13.5	24.2
2013	63357.92	29712.08	9623.38	8274.16	15748.30	46.9	15.2	13.1	24.9
2014	68777.25	32237.37	10669.94	9555.15	16314.79	46.9	15.5	13.9	23.7
2015	73876.37	35624.52	10204.88	10377.28	17669.69	48.2	13.8	14.0	23.9
2016	80666.72	38928.21	10977.35	11220.03	19541.13	48.3	13.6	13.9	24.2
2017	89705.23	43620.15	12130.58	11989.32	21965.18	48.6	13.5	13.4	24.5

2-9 各行业收入法增加值构成项目（2017年）
Components of Value Added by Sector (2017)

单位：亿元 (100 million yuan)

行业	Sector	地区生产总值 Gross Domestic Product	劳动者报酬 Compensation of Employees	生产税净额 Net Taxes on Production	固定资产折旧 Depreciation of Fixed Assets	营业盈余 Operating Surplus
地区生产总值	**Gross Domestic Product**	89705.23	43620.15	12130.58	11989.32	21965.18
农、林、牧、渔业	Farming, Forestry, Animal Husbandry and Fishery	3712.71	3675.35	1.38	35.98	
工业	Industry	35291.83	15354.47	5469.06	5074.85	9393.45
建筑业	Construction	2818.82	1637.93	447.35	124.73	608.81
批发和零售业	Wholesale and Retail Trade	8976.59	4343.10	2422.17	246.32	1965.00
交通运输、仓储和邮政业	Transport, Storage and Postal Services	3580.94	1822.78	252.00	871.87	634.29
住宿和餐饮业	Hotels and Catering Services	1646.85	1190.57	119.60	165.99	170.69
信息传输、软件和信息技术服务业	Information Transmission, Computer Services and Software	3817.23	1374.36	317.65	534.19	1591.03
金融业	Finance	6853.01	1891.76	786.37	92.92	4081.96
房地产业	Real Estate	7635.96	1134.41	1610.24	2879.99	2011.32
租赁和商务服务业	Leasing and Business Services	3351.15	1803.34	353.57	719.18	475.06
科学研究和技术服务业	Scientific Research and Technical Services	1506.19	841.20	134.81	171.25	358.93
水利、环境和公共设施管理业	Water Conservancy, Environment and Public Facilities Management	605.14	242.56	42.56	211.48	108.54
居民服务、修理和其他服务业	Resident Services and Other Services	1525.00	1270.50	67.24	54.65	132.61
教育	Education	3009.02	2511.89	27.06	333.19	136.88
卫生和社会工作	Health Care and Social Work	1885.32	1464.30	21.57	128.00	271.45
文化、体育和娱乐业	Culture, Sports and Recreation	438.25	264.48	45.14	104.28	24.35
公共管理、社会保障和社会组织	Public Administration and Social Organizations	3051.22	2797.15	12.81	240.45	0.81
第一产业	Primary Industry	3611.44	3575.06	1.38	35.00	
第二产业	Secondary Industry	38008.06	16931.99	5909.54	5189.53	9977.00
第三产业	Tertiary Industry	48085.73	23113.10	6219.66	6764.79	11988.18

2-10 支出法地区生产总值

Gross Domestic Product by Expenditure Approach

年份 Year	支出法地区生产总值(亿元) Gross Domestic Product by Expenditure Approach (100 million yuan)	最终消费支出 Final Consumption Expenditure	资本形成总额 Gross Capital Formation	货物和服务净流出 Net Exports of Goods and Services	最终消费率(消费率)(%) Final Consumption Rate (%)	资本形成率(投资率)(%) Capital Formation Rate (%)
1978	194.14	130.02	54.79	9.33	67.0	28.2
1979	215.43	147.11	55.86	12.46	68.3	25.9
1980	259.32	180.93	71.37	7.02	69.8	27.5
1981	305.22	201.43	96.74	7.05	66.0	31.7
1982	349.13	233.21	112.35	3.57	66.8	32.2
1983	367.36	252.07	113.49	1.80	68.6	30.9
1984	446.06	288.26	150.07	7.72	64.6	33.6
1985	568.98	347.18	238.58	-16.78	61.0	41.9
1986	650.99	415.91	256.75	-21.67	63.9	39.4
1987	815.05	516.02	312.33	-13.29	63.3	38.3
1988	1129.64	667.03	462.07	0.54	59.0	40.9
1989	1348.54	857.33	472.75	18.46	63.6	35.1
1990	1541.99	938.48	502.90	100.61	60.9	32.6
1991	1847.99	1081.39	610.18	156.42	58.5	33.0
1992	2440.58	1359.08	987.96	93.54	55.7	40.5
1993	3465.31	1852.06	1554.46	58.79	53.4	44.9
1994	4618.25	2598.57	1930.86	88.82	56.3	41.8
1995	5940.34	3363.65	2401.80	174.89	56.6	40.4
1996	6848.23	3859.84	2795.64	192.75	56.4	40.8
1997	7792.97	4245.89	2992.18	554.90	54.5	38.4
1998	8555.33	4583.10	3354.63	617.60	53.6	39.2
1999	9289.64	5085.11	3548.75	655.78	54.7	38.2
2000	10810.21	5717.11	3917.11	1175.99	52.9	36.2
2001	12126.59	6259.29	4476.48	1390.82	51.6	36.9
2002	13601.89	7290.47	4858.53	1452.89	53.6	35.7
2003	15959.25	8647.86	6022.16	1289.23	54.2	37.7
2004	19005.61	10167.48	7350.24	1487.89	53.5	38.7
2005	22723.29	11457.36	8399.25	2866.68	50.4	37.0
2006	26800.32	12643.78	9512.26	4644.28	47.2	35.5
2007	32063.91	14853.52	10967.58	6242.81	46.3	34.2
2008	37138.85	17215.48	12590.33	7333.04	46.4	33.9
2009	39923.24	19196.56	15378.86	5347.82	48.1	38.5
2010	46544.63	22501.78	18226.60	5816.25	48.3	39.2
2011	53908.59	26102.28	21689.12	6117.19	48.4	40.2
2012	57924.76	29283.03	23698.87	4942.86	50.6	40.9
2013	63357.92	30449.07	27019.94	5888.91	48.1	42.6
2014	68777.25	33921.86	29850.09	5005.30	49.3	43.4
2015	73876.37	37198.29	31602.03	5076.05	50.4	42.8
2016	80666.72	40885.91	34647.09	5133.72	50.7	43.0
2017	89705.23	45128.95	39657.52	4918.76	50.3	44.2

注：2013年起，国家统计局推行城乡住户调查一体化改革，支出法地区生产总值数据与以前年份不可比(以下相关表同)。

Notes: Since 2013,the data of gross domestic product by expenditure approach are not comparable to year before 2013 due to the integrated household reform conducted by the NBS(the same applied to the related table).

2-11 资本形成总额及构成

Gross Capital Formation and Its Composition

年份 Year	资本形成总额 (亿元) Gross Capital Formation (100 million yuan)	固定资本形成总额 Gross Fixed Capital Formation	存货变动 Change in Inventories	比重(资本形成总额=100) Proportion (gross capital formation=100) 固定资本形成总额 Gross Fixed Capital Formation	存货变动 Change in Inventories
1978	54.79	37.93	16.86	69.2	30.8
1979	55.86	41.81	14.05	74.8	25.2
1980	71.37	57.15	14.23	80.1	19.9
1981	96.74	73.39	23.34	75.9	24.1
1982	112.35	94.64	17.71	84.2	15.8
1983	113.49	96.80	16.69	85.3	14.7
1984	150.07	133.04	17.03	88.7	11.3
1985	238.58	163.84	74.74	68.7	31.3
1986	256.75	182.15	74.59	70.9	29.1
1987	312.33	197.01	115.32	63.1	36.9
1988	462.07	286.00	176.07	61.9	38.1
1989	472.75	266.68	206.07	56.4	43.6
1990	502.90	336.61	166.29	66.9	33.1
1991	610.18	396.49	213.70	65.0	35.0
1992	987.96	683.66	304.30	69.2	30.8
1993	1554.46	1110.69	443.77	71.5	28.5
1994	1930.86	1375.09	555.76	71.2	28.8
1995	2401.80	1826.18	575.62	76.0	24.0
1996	2795.64	1932.16	863.48	69.1	30.9
1997	2992.18	2096.88	895.30	70.1	29.9
1998	3354.63	2497.33	857.30	74.4	25.6
1999	3548.75	2907.86	640.89	81.9	18.1
2000	3917.11	3160.12	756.99	80.7	19.3
2001	4476.48	3531.49	944.99	78.9	21.1
2002	4858.53	4119.36	739.17	84.8	15.2
2003	6022.16	5096.72	925.44	84.6	15.4
2004	7350.24	6093.41	1256.83	82.9	17.1
2005	8399.25	7577.75	821.50	90.2	9.8
2006	9512.26	8694.07	818.19	91.4	8.6
2007	10967.58	10230.11	737.47	93.3	6.7
2008	12590.33	11803.75	786.58	93.8	6.2
2009	15378.86	14452.53	926.33	94.0	6.0
2010	18226.60	17035.10	1191.50	93.5	6.5
2011	21689.12	20118.29	1570.83	92.8	7.2
2012	23698.87	22860.84	838.03	96.5	3.5
2013	27019.94	25966.92	1053.02	96.1	3.9
2014	29850.09	29021.09	829.00	97.2	2.8
2015	31602.03	30478.30	1123.73	96.4	3.6
2016	34647.09	33279.65	1367.44	96.1	3.9
2017	39657.52	38390.85	1266.67	96.8	3.2

2-12 最终消费及构成
Final Consumption Expenditure and Its Composition

年份 Year	最终消费支出(亿元) Final Consumption Expenditure (100 million yuan)	居民消费支出 Household Consumption	城镇居民 Urban Households	农村居民 Rural Households	政府消费支出 Government Consumption	比重 Proportion 最终消费支出=100 Final Consumption Expenditure=100 居民消费支出 Household Consumption	政府消费支出 Government Consumption	居民消费支出=100 Household Consumption=100 城镇居民 Urban Households	农村居民 Rural Households
1978	130.02	111.46	40.12	71.34	18.56	85.7	14.3	36.0	64.0
1979	147.11	128.48	46.57	81.91	18.63	87.3	12.7	36.2	63.8
1980	180.93	156.51	60.55	95.95	24.42	86.5	13.5	38.7	61.3
1981	201.43	175.12	64.50	110.62	26.31	86.9	13.1	36.8	63.2
1982	233.21	202.70	74.76	127.93	30.51	86.9	13.1	36.9	63.1
1983	252.07	220.14	85.69	134.45	31.93	87.3	12.7	38.9	61.1
1984	288.26	250.92	105.87	145.05	37.34	87.0	13.0	42.2	57.8
1985	347.18	298.00	137.84	160.16	49.17	85.8	14.2	46.3	53.7
1986	415.91	349.52	164.49	185.03	66.39	84.0	16.0	47.1	52.9
1987	516.02	442.20	223.51	218.69	73.82	85.7	14.3	50.5	49.5
1988	667.03	566.25	283.39	282.86	100.77	84.9	15.1	50.0	50.0
1989	857.33	743.90	377.08	366.82	113.42	86.8	13.2	50.7	49.3
1990	938.48	807.84	406.22	401.62	130.64	86.1	13.9	50.3	49.7
1991	1081.39	923.37	511.00	412.36	158.02	85.4	14.6	55.3	44.7
1992	1359.08	1118.52	648.51	470.01	240.55	82.3	17.7	58.0	42.0
1993	1852.06	1574.61	957.16	617.45	277.45	85.0	15.0	60.8	39.2
1994	2598.57	2287.69	1442.66	845.03	310.88	88.0	12.0	63.1	36.9
1995	3363.65	2912.58	1890.75	1021.83	451.07	86.6	13.4	64.9	35.1
1996	3859.84	3343.00	2154.56	1188.44	516.84	86.6	13.4	64.4	35.6
1997	4245.89	3539.63	2317.15	1222.48	706.26	83.4	16.6	65.5	34.5
1998	4583.10	3781.21	2499.29	1281.92	801.89	82.5	17.5	66.1	33.9
1999	5085.11	4072.05	2774.14	1297.91	1013.06	80.1	19.9	68.1	31.9
2000	5717.11	4474.11	3125.44	1348.67	1243.00	78.3	21.7	69.9	30.1
2001	6259.29	4733.53	3318.28	1415.25	1525.76	75.6	24.4	70.1	29.9
2002	7290.47	5449.58	4025.54	1424.04	1840.89	74.7	25.3	73.9	26.1
2003	8647.86	6537.53	5273.69	1263.84	2110.33	75.6	24.4	80.7	19.3
2004	10167.48	7953.60	6729.38	1224.22	2213.88	78.2	21.8	84.6	15.4
2005	11457.36	8968.54	7560.24	1408.30	2488.82	78.3	21.7	84.3	15.7
2006	12643.78	9895.13	8470.02	1425.11	2748.65	78.3	21.7	85.6	14.4
2007	14853.52	11781.66	10229.41	1552.25	3071.86	79.3	20.7	86.8	13.2
2008	17215.48	13599.73	11812.60	1787.13	3615.75	79.0	21.0	86.9	13.1
2009	19196.56	15261.29	13233.01	2028.28	3935.27	79.5	20.5	86.7	13.3
2010	22501.78	17702.35	15438.42	2263.93	4799.43	78.7	21.3	87.2	12.8
2011	26102.28	20504.11	17735.53	2768.58	5598.17	78.6	21.4	86.5	13.5
2012	29283.03	23022.47	19898.98	3123.49	6260.56	78.6	21.4	86.4	13.6
2013	30449.07	23449.85	19691.73	3758.12	6999.22	77.0	23.0	84.0	16.0
2014	33921.86	26263.14	21913.85	4349.29	7658.72	77.4	22.6	83.4	16.6
2015	37198.29	28438.58	23884.12	4554.46	8759.71	76.5	23.5	84.0	16.0
2016	40885.91	31127.58	26113.94	5013.64	9758.33	76.1	23.9	83.9	16.1
2017	45128.95	34097.05	28712.16	5384.89	11031.90	75.6	24.4	84.2	15.8

2-13 三大需求对地区生产总值增长的贡献率和拉动

Contribution Share and Contribution of the Three Components of GDP to GDP Growth

年份 Year	最终消费支出 Final Consumption Expenditure		资本形成总额 Gross Capital Formation		货物和服务净流出 Net Exports of Goods and Services	
	贡献率(%) Contribution Share (%)	拉动(百分点) Contribution (percentage points)	贡献率(%) Contribution Share (%)	拉动(百分点) Contribution (percentage points)	贡献率(%) Contribution Share (%)	拉动(百分点) Contribution (percentage points)
1979	95.7	5.3	-13.8	-0.8	18.2	1.0
1980	71.3	13.0	33.5	6.1	-4.8	-0.9
1981	50.5	6.3	56.4	7.1	-6.9	-0.9
1982	72.7	8.3	40.6	4.6	-13.2	-1.5
1983	124.4	5.6	-12.9	-0.6	-11.5	-0.5
1984	56.5	8.5	42.2	6.3	1.3	0.2
1985	32.0	6.9	80.6	17.4	-12.6	-2.7
1986	83.6	8.8	15.5	1.6	0.8	0.1
1987	38.6	4.9	34.9	4.4	26.4	3.3
1988	-2.8	-0.3	60.1	7.4	42.8	5.2
1989	110.8	9.4	-35.6	-3.0	24.8	2.1
1990	60.9	7.2	9.5	1.1	29.6	3.5
1991	39.9	7.1	35.1	6.3	25.0	4.5
1992	56.0	12.4	65.2	14.5	-21.1	-4.7
1993	50.2	11.6	60.1	13.9	-10.3	-2.4
1994	53.8	10.4	36.1	7.0	10.1	1.9
1995	49.8	7.8	40.7	6.4	9.5	1.5
1996	45.0	5.1	52.3	5.9	2.7	0.3
1997	21.7	2.4	7.5	0.8	70.8	8.0
1998	39.5	4.3	44.1	4.8	16.4	1.8
1999	54.7	5.6	22.5	2.3	22.8	2.3
2000	33.0	3.9	27.3	3.2	39.7	4.7
2001	45.8	4.8	49.0	5.2	5.3	0.6
2002	68.0	8.4	23.3	2.9	8.7	1.1
2003	63.4	9.4	50.4	7.5	-13.8	-2.0
2004	50.4	7.4	37.4	5.5	12.2	1.8
2005	42.7	6.1	30.7	4.4	26.5	3.8
2006	31.2	4.6	29.3	4.4	39.5	5.9
2007	44.8	6.7	23.9	3.6	31.2	4.7
2008	45.4	4.8	35.2	3.7	19.4	2.0
2009	62.8	6.2	80.3	7.9	-43.1	-4.3
2010	52.7	6.6	47.0	5.9	0.3	0.0
2011	47.9	4.9	50.1	5.1	2.0	0.2
2012	52.7	4.4	45.1	3.7	2.2	0.2
2013	43.4	3.7	69.9	5.9	-13.3	-1.1
2014	49.4	3.8	50.2	3.9	0.3	0.0
2015	47.6	3.8	48.8	3.9	3.6	0.3
2016	49.6	3.7	48.8	3.7	1.6	0.1
2017	48.6	3.7	44.9	3.4	6.5	0.5

注：1．三大需求指支出法地区生产总值的三大构成项目，即最终消费支出、资本形成总额、货物和服务净流出；
2．贡献率指三大需求增量与地区支出法生产总值增量之比。
3．拉动指地区生产总值增长速度与三大需求贡献率的乘积。

Notes: a) Three major demands refer to three major components of gross domestic product by expenditure approach,i.e.final consumption expenditure, gross capital formation, and net exports of goods and services.
b) Contribution rate refers to the proportion of the increment of three major demands to the increment of gross domestic product by expenditure approach.
c) Pulling rate is the growth rate of gross regional product multiplying the contribution rates of three major demands.

2-14 人均地区生产总值及人均消费水平

Per Capita Gross Domestic Product and Consumption

年份 Year	人均地区生产总值 Per Capita Gross Domestic Product		人均消费水平 Per Capita Consumption					
			全体居民 Households		城镇居民 Urban Households		农村居民 Rural Households	
	绝对数(元) Absolute Figure (yuan)	增长速度(%) Growth Rate (%)	绝对数(元) Absolute Figure (yuan)	增长速度(%) Growth Rate (%)	绝对数(元) Absolute Figure (yuan)	增长速度(%) Growth Rate (%)	绝对数(元) Absolute Figure (yuan)	增长速度(%) Growth Rate (%)
1978	370		222		466		171	
1979	410	6.9	252	8.3	507	2.6	196	9.8
1980	481	14.8	302	14.9	620	12.7	228	14.1
1981	550	7.1	332	7.9	627	-1.9	260	13.3
1982	633	10.0	377	10.3	696	8.3	298	10.4
1983	675	5.6	403	7.2	764	8.5	310	5.1
1984	827	13.8	453	10.3	878	9.7	334	7.8
1985	1026	16.2	529	5.7	1038	10.2	372	-2.6
1986	1164	10.6	609	9.5	1146	8.4	430	6.3
1987	1443	17.0	754	6.4	1382	1.1	515	4.9
1988	1926	13.2	944	-3.5	1716	-6.8	651	0.5
1989	2251	4.8	1212	19.7	2188	15.0	831	23.1
1990	2484	9.1	1287	9.3	2263	4.7	896	12.9
1991	2941	14.7	1434	8.3	2712	14.8	906	0.2
1992	3699	18.8	1690	14.7	3210	15.7	1023	9.7
1993	5085	19.3	2308	20.5	4280	17.0	1347	17.6
1994	6530	15.5	3234	17.8	5870	15.7	1831	14.3
1995	8139	12.1	3991	10.1	7091	7.6	2206	8.4
1996	9157	8.7	4470	6.9	7660	2.3	2547	11.6
1997	10154	8.4	4612	-2.1	7807	-4.8	2597	-0.4
1998	10850	7.9	4796	4.2	8054	2.2	2681	5.8
1999	11463	7.3	5025	4.5	8598	5.9	2661	0.8
2000	12817	7.3	5305	0.2	9189	0.2	2680	-1.3
2001	13952	7.3	5445	1.9	9312	0.3	2759	3.0
2002	15478	11.1	6199	13.2	10358	10.2	2904	5.7
2003	17927	13.3	7342	17.0	11136	6.4	3032	3.4
2004	21032	13.0	8800	15.9	12409	7.9	3386	8.2
2005	24828	12.7	9799	10.0	13609	8.5	3915	13.2
2006	28762	12.8	10619	7.4	14695	6.9	4009	2.2
2007	33572	12.2	12336	12.9	16982	12.6	4401	5.0
2008	37988	7.9	13911	7.1	19101	7.1	4975	5.6
2009	39876	7.3	15243	10.9	20852	11.3	5533	6.9
2010	45252	9.5	17211	9.3	23159	7.5	6255	9.4
2011	51474	8.2	19578	7.9	25527	5.3	7854	14.1
2012	54908	7.5	21823	8.3	28269	7.9	8898	7.7
2013	59665	7.8	22083	6.4	27531	5.5	10841	8.0
2014	64374	7.1	24582	8.3	30216	6.9	12674	13.4
2015	68490	7.0	26365	6.8	32393	6.2	13344	7.5
2016	73844	6.2	28495	5.7	34667	4.9	14784	7.0
2017	80932	6.0	30762	5.2	37257	4.3	15943	7.6

注：2006—2009年根据2010年全国人口普查快速汇总数据进行平滑调整，本表人均地区生产总值是人口平滑后的数据，以下相关表同。

Note: Figures of permanent population at the year-end from 2006 to 2009 have been adjusted in accordance with the flash sums of the 6th National Population Cescus in 2010. Per capita gross domestic product in this table are caculated with the adjustments of population. The same applied to the following tables.

2-15 人均地区生产总值及人均消费水平指数

Indices of Per Capita Gross Domestic Product and Consumption

年份 Year	人均地区生产总值 Per Capita Gross Domestic Product		人均消费水平 Per Capita Consumption					
			全体居民 Households		城镇居民 Urban Households		农村居民 Rural Households	
	绝对数（元） Absolute Figure (yuan)	1978年为100（%） 1978=100 (%)	绝对数（元） Absolute Figure (yuan)	1978年为100（%） 1978=100 (%)	绝对数（元） Absolute Figure (yuan)	1978年为100（%） 1978=100 (%)	绝对数（元） Absolute Figure (yuan)	1978年为100（%） 1978=100 (%)
1978	370	100.0	222	100.0	466	100.0	171	100.0
1979	410	106.9	252	108.3	507	102.6	196	109.8
1980	481	122.6	302	124.4	620	115.6	228	125.2
1981	550	131.3	332	134.2	627	113.4	260	141.9
1982	633	144.4	377	148.1	696	122.8	298	156.7
1983	675	152.5	403	158.7	764	133.3	310	164.8
1984	827	173.5	453	175.0	878	146.3	334	177.6
1985	1026	201.6	529	184.9	1038	161.2	372	172.9
1986	1164	223.1	609	202.5	1146	174.7	430	183.7
1987	1443	260.9	754	215.6	1382	176.6	515	192.6
1988	1926	295.4	944	208.1	1716	164.6	651	193.6
1989	2251	309.6	1212	249.0	2188	189.3	831	238.2
1990	2484	337.7	1287	272.1	2263	198.2	896	269.0
1991	2941	387.5	1434	294.7	2712	227.5	906	269.5
1992	3699	460.3	1690	338.1	3210	263.2	1023	295.7
1993	5085	549.0	2308	407.5	4280	308.1	1347	347.8
1994	6530	633.9	3234	480.2	5870	356.5	1831	397.6
1995	8139	710.7	3991	528.9	7091	383.5	2206	430.8
1996	9157	772.3	4470	565.4	7660	392.3	2547	480.6
1997	10154	837.1	4612	553.4	7807	373.5	2597	478.6
1998	10850	903.2	4796	576.9	8054	381.6	2681	506.5
1999	11463	969.2	5025	602.6	8598	404.2	2661	510.6
2000	12817	1040.2	5305	603.5	9189	405.0	2680	503.8
2001	13952	1115.7	5445	615.2	9312	406.3	2759	519.0
2002	15478	1240.1	6199	696.1	10358	447.6	2904	548.8
2003	17927	1405.2	7342	814.5	11136	476.2	3032	567.2
2004	21032	1588.2	8800	944.4	12409	513.8	3386	613.6
2005	24828	1790.3	9799	1039.1	13609	557.5	3915	694.6
2006	28762	2020.1	10619	1116.3	14695	596.2	4009	710.0
2007	33572	2266.2	12336	1260.1	16982	671.2	4401	745.3
2008	37938	2445.7	13911	1349.9	19101	718.9	4975	787.2
2009	39876	2624.3	15243	1496.7	20852	800.0	5533	841.4
2010	45252	2874.1	17211	1636.2	23159	860.0	6255	920.6
2011	51474	3109.6	19578	1765.5	25527	905.6	7854	1050.4
2012	54908	3342.5	21823	1911.4	28269	977.1	8898	1131.6
2013	59665	3602.6	22083	2034.4	27531	1030.9	10841	1222.2
2014	64374	3859.1	24582	2204.1	30216	1102.4	12674	1385.6
2015	68490	4128.2	26365	2353.9	32393	1170.7	13344	1489.5
2016	73844	4382.4	28495	2488.1	34667	1228.1	14784	1593.8
2017	80932	4645.0	30762	2617.5	37257	1280.9	15943	1714.9

2-16 各市地区生产总值

Gross Domestic Product by City

单位：亿元 (100 million yuan)

市 别	City	2000	2005	2006	2007	2008	2009	2010
广 州	Guangzhou	2505.58	5187.85	6124.20	7202.95	8366.02	9240.58	10859.29
深 圳	Shenzhen	2219.20	5035.77	5920.66	6925.23	7941.43	8485.82	10002.22
珠 海	Zhuhai	335.92	640.53	753.63	902.45	1006.62	1049.04	1225.88
汕 头	Shantou	450.16	637.68	720.33	832.33	954.65	1024.73	1135.10
佛 山	Foshan	1050.38	2450.67	3020.83	3696.35	4419.04	4852.88	5685.36
韶 关	Shaoguan	192.72	337.03	404.60	480.43	557.89	579.84	642.98
河 源	Heyuan	87.22	204.81	258.08	329.49	395.37	405.47	453.65
梅 州	Meizhou	180.64	315.17	350.03	411.71	478.62	516.50	605.19
惠 州	Huizhou	439.19	805.11	930.93	1121.71	1309.51	1421.45	1741.93
汕 尾	Shanwei	128.49	205.75	239.78	288.41	345.86	384.06	452.98
东 莞	Dongguan	821.14	2188.19	2635.62	3169.26	3715.68	3811.01	4308.92
中 山	Zhongshan	345.44	894.59	1064.31	1283.88	1473.84	1587.55	1877.87
江 门	Jiangmen	504.66	801.70	943.79	1098.82	1272.33	1341.82	1581.52
阳 江	Yangjiang	160.20	294.55	345.78	403.61	478.28	521.60	630.90
湛 江	Zhanjiang	373.81	682.67	808.50	928.48	1101.20	1160.74	1399.77
茂 名	Maoming	417.36	739.13	873.67	998.78	1181.24	1225.69	1477.93
肇 庆	Zhaoqing	249.78	435.95	507.04	621.25	762.64	866.46	1094.06
清 远	Qingyuan	157.92	323.60	431.11	557.86	653.56	718.46	875.49
潮 州	Chaozhou	177.87	283.44	321.83	374.87	439.85	482.28	561.87
揭 阳	Jieyang	311.09	414.00	480.22	584.87	721.98	813.12	999.64
云 浮	Yunfu	137.70	202.46	230.97	274.81	322.26	341.08	396.01
按经济区域分	By Region							
珠 三 角	Pearl River Delta	8471.28	18440.37	21901.00	26021.88	30267.12	32656.62	38377.06
东 翼	Eastern Region	1067.61	1540.87	1762.16	2080.48	2462.34	2704.20	3149.59
西 翼	Western Region	951.37	1716.35	2027.94	2330.87	2760.72	2908.04	3508.60
山 区	Mountainous Region	756.20	1383.07	1674.79	2054.29	2407.70	2561.35	2973.33

2—16 续表 continued

单位：亿元 (100 million yuan)

市 别	City	2011	2012	2013	2014	2015	2016	2017
广 州	Guangzhou	12562.12	13697.91	15663.48	16896.62	18313.80	19782.19	21503.15
深 圳	Shenzhen	11807.23	13319.68	14979.45	16449.48	18014.07	20079.70	22490.06
珠 海	Zhuhai	1430.95	1536.74	1709.63	1901.42	2066.35	2267.02	2675.18
汕 头	Shantou	1283.87	1436.13	1579.27	1721.14	1872.60	2086.35	2350.97
佛 山	Foshan	6259.68	6677.17	7117.48	7561.37	8133.66	8757.72	9398.52
韶 关	Shaoguan	751.16	861.78	947.94	1027.64	1066.63	1134.51	1245.26
河 源	Heyuan	532.76	608.93	689.74	754.09	782.83	853.61	946.16
梅 州	Meizhou	691.50	744.13	797.25	874.36	945.14	1027.18	1075.43
惠 州	Huizhou	2116.10	2407.01	2738.80	3035.25	3178.68	3453.14	3830.58
汕 尾	Shanwei	537.01	607.70	670.60	715.74	760.70	826.50	850.91
东 莞	Dongguan	4815.32	5095.96	5590.57	5968.38	6374.29	6937.08	7582.09
中 山	Zhongshan	2226.56	2482.58	2692.96	2865.19	3052.79	3248.68	3430.31
江 门	Jiangmen	1846.20	1899.14	2020.13	2104.80	2264.19	2444.09	2690.25
阳 江	Yangjiang	760.54	880.25	1040.04	1156.96	1235.16	1255.98	1311.45
湛 江	Zhanjiang	1713.42	1865.54	2059.87	2245.35	2363.31	2560.69	2806.88
茂 名	Maoming	1730.15	1928.37	2184.02	2363.56	2462.76	2657.71	2904.07
肇 庆	Zhaoqing	1337.38	1477.78	1685.15	1857.61	1984.02	2100.64	2110.01
清 远	Qingyuan	1014.18	1040.38	1111.66	1205.11	1285.63	1397.28	1469.34
潮 州	Chaozhou	651.70	710.90	787.90	853.64	912.60	979.44	1012.76
揭 阳	Jieyang	1216.49	1383.22	1592.91	1765.86	1871.30	1981.54	1987.89
云 浮	Yunfu	472.95	522.87	597.07	650.09	696.44	759.67	803.56
按经济区域分	By Region							
珠 三 角	Pearl River Delta	44401.55	48593.96	54197.64	58640.12	63381.85	69070.26	75710.14
东 翼	Eastern Region	3689.06	4137.95	4630.69	5056.38	5417.20	5873.83	6202.54
西 翼	Western Region	4204.12	4674.16	5283.94	5765.87	6061.23	6474.39	7022.40
山 区	Mountainous Region	3462.55	3778.10	4143.66	4511.29	4776.67	5172.26	5539.75

注：2017年起，深圳市地区生产总值数据包含深汕合作区。
Notes: Since 2017,GDPof Shenshεn Special Cooperation Zone is included in that of Shenzhen city.

2–17 各市地区生产总值指数
Indices of Gross Domestic Product by City

上年=100 (preceding year=100)

市 别	City	2000	2005	2006	2007	2008	2009	2010
广 州	Guangzhou	113.4	113.0	115.0	115.5	112.6	111.9	113.2
深 圳	Shenzhen	116.3	115.3	116.7	114.8	112.3	111.3	112.2
珠 海	Zhuhai	112.0	113.2	116.3	116.8	109.4	106.6	113.2
汕 头	Shantou	107.0	111.3	111.5	113.0	110.6	109.0	110.5
佛 山	Foshan	112.5	119.3	119.6	118.8	115.3	113.1	114.3
韶 关	Shaoguan	111.3	110.1	115.3	114.9	112.2	109.7	112.8
河 源	Heyuan	110.7	122.9	127.9	122.6	110.3	110.1	112.7
梅 州	Meizhou	108.1	107.9	109.7	112.4	110.2	109.8	114.2
惠 州	Huizhou	111.3	116.1	116.8	117.7	111.7	113.3	118.3
汕 尾	Shanwei	111.5	116.0	115.7	118.5	115.9	115.0	117.0
东 莞	Dongguan	119.7	119.5	119.3	118.3	114.0	105.7	110.4
中 山	Zhongshan	112.4	121.1	117.3	116.8	111.1	110.4	114.2
江 门	Jiangmen	110.2	112.6	115.2	115.0	110.8	109.7	114.5
阳 江	Yangjiang	109.6	113.9	116.3	113.7	111.7	112.1	116.5
湛 江	Zhanjiang	107.1	113.6	113.7	113.0	111.6	110.8	114.3
茂 名	Maoming	111.2	114.1	113.9	113.0	109.8	110.4	114.1
肇 庆	Zhaoqing	110.6	115.8	116.3	117.5	116.1	113.8	117.2
清 远	Qingyuan	108.3	127.7	129.4	124.9	109.9	112.8	113.0
潮 州	Chaozhou	105.6	111.5	112.4	114.5	112.2	112.3	114.1
揭 阳	Jieyang	105.4	111.3	114.9	118.1	116.1	116.0	119.6
云 浮	Yunfu	105.3	113.3	114.3	115.8	110.7	110.5	113.9
按经济区域分	By Region							
珠 三 角	Pearl River Delta	113.9	115.7	116.9	116.3	112.9	109.7	112.2
东 翼	Eastern Region	106.7	112.0	113.1	115.4	113.2	111.4	114.2
西 翼	Western Region	109.4	113.8	114.2	113.1	110.8	110.5	114.1
山 区	Mountainous Region	108.7	115.7	119.1	118.3	110.7	110.3	113.1

注：2009年—2014年区域生产总值增速由广东省统计局统一调整核算，其它年份增速由分市汇总计算。
Note: The GDP growth rates of 2009 are calculated by Statistics Bureau of Guangdong Province, and those of the previous years are calculated by each city.

2-17 续表 continued

上年=100 (preceding year=100)

市别	City	2011	2012	2013	2014	2015	2016	2017
广州	Guangzhou	111.4	110.4	111.7	108.6	108.4	108.2	107.0
深圳	Shenzhen	110.0	110.2	110.6	108.8	108.9	109.1	108.8
珠海	Zhuhai	111.6	107.6	110.8	110.4	110.0	108.3	110.8
汕头	Shantou	110.2	109.5	109.9	109.0	108.4	108.8	109.2
佛山	Foshan	111.5	108.2	109.8	108.3	108.3	108.1	108.3
韶关	Shaoguan	110.7	111.8	110.4	107.9	106.2	106.6	106.8
河源	Heyuan	112.9	111.8	112.1	108.5	106.1	106.6	105.1
梅州	Meizhou	113.8	110.0	111.1	108.5	108.6	107.5	106.8
惠州	Huizhou	115.2	112.8	113.8	109.9	109.2	108.1	107.6
汕尾	Shanwei	114.1	113.4	112.3	109.0	108.1	107.0	108.1
东莞	Dongguan	108.1	106.3	109.9	107.9	108.0	108.0	108.1
中山	Zhongshan	113.4	111.3	110.0	107.9	108.3	107.6	106.6
江门	Jiangmen	113.2	108.1	109.7	107.9	108.4	107.4	108.1
阳江	Yangjiang	115.1	112.9	115.4	110.6	108.4	106.7	106.2
湛江	Zhanjiang	112.8	109.6	112.0	110.0	108.5	107.6	106.8
茂名	Maoming	110.9	110.8	113.1	110.4	108.0	107.1	107.5
肇庆	Zhaoqing	114.8	111.1	111.5	110.0	108.2	105.1	105.2
清远	Qingyuan	108.5	105.2	108.2	107.8	108.1	107.8	104.2
潮州	Chaozhou	113.2	110.6	111.1	108.2	108.2	107.1	106.8
揭阳	Jieyang	114.8	111.3	114.6	110.7	108.1	106.3	105.0
云浮	Yunfu	114.3	113.1	113.5	110.4	108.5	108.0	105.3
按经济区域分	By Region							
珠三角	Pearl River Delta	110.1	108.2	109.3	107.8	108.6	108.3	107.9
东翼	Eastern Region	111.8	110.2	111.2	109.3	108.2	107.4	107.2
西翼	Western Region	111.2	110.1	111.9	110.0	108.3	107.2	107.0
山区	Mountainous Region	110.3	109.1	108.2	108.2	107.5	107.3	105.6

注：2009—2014年区域生产总值增速由广东省统计局统一调整核算，其它年份增速由分市汇总计算。

Note: The GDP growth rates of 2009-2014 are calculated by Statistics Bureau of Guangdong Province, and those of the previous years are calculated by each city.

2−18 各市第一产业增加值

Value-added of the Tertiary Industry by City

单位：亿元 (100 million yuan)

市别	City	2000	2005	2010	2011	2012	2013	2014	2015	2016	2017
广州	Guangzhou	94.37	130.22	181.31	194.03	200.27	196.13	200.81	206.52	216.03	220.45
深圳	Shenzhen	15.57	9.74	6.84	6.95	6.82	6.35	5.76	7.21	8.28	19.57
珠海	Zhuhai	15.27	22.69	32.48	36.70	39.46	42.21	44.36	48.30	45.15	48.82
汕头	Shantou	39.38	44.52	63.66	72.15	78.43	81.96	87.55	91.39	100.35	103.39
佛山	Foshan	61.74	75.76	102.87	114.73	124.88	122.74	126.19	127.29	135.21	133.65
韶关	Shaoguan	44.01	55.47	88.76	104.54	111.14	117.09	123.04	131.73	143.75	148.59
河源	Heyuan	30.36	42.42	59.62	71.11	76.71	80.67	86.75	93.34	99.13	102.46
梅州	Meizhou	56.02	72.73	120.03	137.65	148.84	155.02	161.87	172.97	187.74	187.76
惠州	Huizhou	62.23	75.10	100.88	114.06	121.55	130.11	136.54	146.13	164.21	166.57
汕尾	Shanwei	46.71	46.12	75.44	87.02	95.41	99.36	105.24	112.97	123.41	124.42
东莞	Dongguan	25.91	20.55	15.94	16.97	17.80	18.43	19.16	19.92	22.76	22.85
中山	Zhongshan	23.51	30.71	48.80	55.07	58.62	59.98	61.54	59.56	60.93	55.64
江门	Jiangmen	69.83	72.47	117.71	138.29	149.01	154.13	165.30	170.46	183.68	187.35
阳江	Yangjiang	62.95	80.38	133.80	151.43	164.60	172.55	179.87	190.04	203.79	211.46
湛江	Zhanjiang	105.06	160.50	284.52	336.27	373.93	385.50	408.18	429.39	465.86	491.17
茂名	Maoming	125.91	167.04	277.84	324.62	350.20	363.61	372.75	398.05	449.63	470.23
肇庆	Zhaoqing	91.75	120.72	191.11	227.75	240.16	253.94	270.41	288.50	317.67	326.62
清远	Qingyuan	61.43	71.54	120.86	141.29	155.28	164.19	175.61	192.30	214.16	218.90
潮州	Chaozhou	28.76	32.64	39.96	45.53	48.84	50.66	59.65	62.64	68.28	70.56
揭阳	Jieyang	71.06	65.20	102.86	117.41	125.55	129.78	134.99	141.33	154.64	156.99
云浮	Yunfu	54.81	63.42	93.89	109.69	113.44	116.49	123.18	129.44	135.09	142.65
按经济区域分	By Region										
珠三角	Pearl River Delta	460.17	557.96	797.94	904.55	958.57	984.03	1030.07	1073.87	1153.92	1181.53
东翼	Eastern Region	185.92	188.48	281.92	322.11	348.22	361.75	387.43	408.34	446.68	455.36
西翼	Western Region	293.92	407.92	696.16	812.31	888.74	921.67	960.80	1017.49	1119.28	1172.86
山区	Mountainous Region	246.64	305.58	483.16	564.28	605.40	633.47	670.46	719.77	779.88	800.36

2–19　各市第二产业增加值

Value-added of the Tertiary Industry by City

单位：亿元　　(100 million yuan)

市　别	City	2000	2005	2010	2011	2012	2013	2014	2015	2016	2017
广　州	Guangzhou	1029.94	2067.00	4078.90	4673.65	4828.67	5377.98	5725.53	5873.54	5912.94	6011.01
深　圳	Shenzhen	1108.76	2709.69	4737.98	5612.86	6055.91	6657.99	7224.25	7678.10	8310.65	9318.10
珠　海	Zhuhai	176.30	344.14	676.60	784.36	798.67	869.76	966.30	1037.97	1114.54	1287.19
汕　头	Shantou	217.39	328.07	603.02	658.59	742.94	831.85	910.67	969.52	1060.10	1182.68
佛　山	Foshan	553.61	1494.20	3576.49	3920.18	4167.27	4360.96	4727.69	4975.83	5279.33	5424.65
韶　关	Shaoguan	75.71	143.51	249.00	279.67	337.12	365.57	383.44	367.91	386.22	420.98
河　源	Heyuan	20.99	80.46	218.35	251.98	281.40	321.36	349.05	344.97	349.45	376.52
梅　州	Meizhou	63.30	129.80	250.52	276.24	280.00	299.20	332.41	353.29	370.87	358.29
惠　州	Huizhou	255.26	456.79	1027.09	1236.25	1392.31	1565.34	1733.99	1768.08	1885.11	2017.20
汕　尾	Shanwei	37.31	83.10	203.22	248.75	286.44	319.00	336.53	352.38	373.00	383.59
东　莞	Dongguan	451.47	1232.14	2218.61	2455.46	2496.68	2688.94	2874.10	3007.87	3268.30	3663.23
中　山	Zhongshan	180.83	548.21	1101.28	1259.92	1395.79	1514.54	1607.54	1680.96	1729.85	1724.97
江　门	Jiangmen	235.11	425.57	882.34	1012.43	979.51	1026.46	1044.73	1110.76	1178.13	1324.96
阳　江	Yangjiang	47.03	110.83	266.86	330.21	394.24	491.39	566.65	569.03	526.48	484.50
湛　江	Zhanjiang	135.52	298.80	570.04	695.19	702.97	817.03	898.49	913.07	989.62	1058.97
茂　名	Maoming	147.72	260.23	583.77	683.64	770.38	873.31	982.11	1008.33	1068.15	1131.24
肇　庆	Zhaoqing	53.10	114.87	462.28	596.06	680.36	842.29	935.05	1002.89	1013.95	771.53
清　远	Qingyuan	40.72	127.21	399.15	451.54	421.22	441.19	497.38	489.04	511.94	501.15
潮　州	Chaozhou	86.52	151.68	311.49	356.52	392.24	424.74	470.46	488.00	507.13	505.55
揭　阳	Jieyang	141.91	202.13	576.29	729.07	848.93	1003.28	1105.44	1133.77	1126.76	1043.84
云　浮	Yunfu	39.98	73.69	163.60	199.76	213.79	258.35	294.94	305.25	323.89	316.44
按经济区域分	By Region										
珠三角	Pearl River Delta	4044.38	9392.60	18761.56	21551.16	22795.18	24904.27	26839.16	28135.99	29692.80	31542.82
东　翼	Eastern Region	483.13	764.98	1694.02	1992.93	2270.54	2578.87	2823.09	2943.66	3066.98	3115.66
西　翼	Western Region	330.27	669.87	1420.67	1709.03	1867.59	2181.74	2447.25	2490.43	2584.25	2674.70
山　区	Mountainous Region	240.70	554.68	1280.62	1459.19	1533.53	1685.67	1857.22	1860.46	1942.37	1973.38

2−20 各市第三产业增加值
Value-added of the Tertiary Industry by City

单位：亿元 (100 million yuan)

市别	City	2000	2005	2010	2011	2012	2013	2014	2015	2016	2017
广州	Guangzhou	1381.27	2990.63	6599.09	7694.45	8668.96	10089.37	10970.28	12233.74	13653.21	15271.69
深圳	Shenzhen	1094.87	2316.34	5257.40	6187.43	7256.95	8315.11	9219.47	10328.76	11760.77	13152.39
珠海	Zhuhai	144.35	273.71	516.80	609.89	698.61	797.66	890.76	980.08	1107.32	1339.17
汕头	Shantou	193.39	265.10	468.43	553.13	614.77	665.47	722.92	811.69	925.90	1064.91
佛山	Foshan	435.03	880.70	2006.00	2224.77	2385.02	2633.77	2707.50	3030.55	3343.18	3840.22
韶关	Shaoguan	73.00	138.05	305.23	366.94	413.52	465.27	521.16	567.00	604.54	675.69
河源	Heyuan	35.87	81.93	175.68	209.67	250.82	287.70	318.29	344.51	405.03	467.18
梅州	Meizhou	61.32	112.64	234.63	277.61	315.30	343.03	380.08	418.88	468.56	529.38
惠州	Huizhou	121.70	273.22	613.96	765.79	893.15	1043.35	1164.73	1264.48	1403.82	1646.81
汕尾	Shanwei	44.48	76.53	174.32	201.25	225.86	252.24	273.97	295.35	330.09	342.89
东莞	Dongguan	343.76	935.50	2074.36	2342.88	2581.48	2883.20	3075.12	3346.51	3646.02	3896.01
中山	Zhongshan	141.09	315.67	727.80	911.57	1028.16	1118.44	1196.11	1312.27	1457.91	1649.71
江门	Jiangmen	199.72	303.66	581.47	695.48	770.61	839.54	894.77	982.97	1082.28	1177.94
阳江	Yangjiang	50.21	103.33	230.24	278.90	321.41	376.10	410.43	476.09	525.71	615.50
湛江	Zhanjiang	133.24	223.37	545.21	681.97	788.64	857.34	938.69	1020.86	1105.21	1256.74
茂名	Maoming	143.73	311.87	616.31	721.90	807.79	947.09	1008.70	1056.38	1139.93	1302.60
肇庆	Zhaoqing	104.93	200.37	440.67	513.57	557.27	588.91	652.15	692.64	769.02	1011.86
清远	Qingyuan	55.77	124.85	355.48	421.35	463.89	506.28	532.12	604.29	671.18	749.29
潮州	Chaozhou	62.59	99.12	210.42	249.64	269.82	312.50	323.53	361.96	404.03	436.66
揭阳	Jieyang	98.11	146.66	320.49	370.01	408.74	459.85	525.43	596.20	700.14	787.07
云浮	Yunfu	42.90	65.34	138.52	163.50	195.64	222.23	231.97	261.76	300.69	344.48
按经济区域分	By Region										
珠三角	Pearl River Delta	3966.73	8489.80	18817.56	21945.84	24840.21	28309.35	30770.89	34171.99	38223.54	42985.80
东翼	Eastern Region	398.57	587.41	1173.65	1374.03	1519.19	1690.07	1845.86	2065.20	2360.17	2631.53
西翼	Western Region	327.18	638.56	1391.77	1682.78	1917.84	2180.54	2357.82	2553.32	2770.85	3174.84
山区	Mountainous Region	268.86	522.80	1209.54	1439.08	1639.17	1824.52	1983.61	2196.43	2450.01	2766.01

2-21 各市第一产业增加值指数

Indices of Value-added of the Tertiary Industry by City

上年=100 (preceding year=100)

市别	City	2000	2005	2010	2011	2012	2013	2014	2015	2016	2017
广州	Guangzhou	101.7	105.6	103.2	103.1	103.2	98.7	101.8	102.4	100.6	102.2
深圳	Shenzhen	103.1	79.6	90.8	93.8	102.7	74.6	90.4	104.2	99.6	127.0
珠海	Zhuhai	108.5	105.2	105.1	101.3	105.1	103.3	103.1	100.3	93.2	108.7
汕头	Shantou	105.2	104.6	105.0	103.9	104.6	103.5	103.8	103.0	102.6	104.0
佛山	Foshan	107.2	102.0	104.4	103.8	102.1	101.0	102.5	101.5	102.2	102.0
韶关	Shaoguan	103.6	102.6	105.7	105.0	105.1	104.0	103.9	103.8	103.5	104.4
河源	Heyuan	106.5	102.6	103.4	105.1	104.8	104.4	104.7	103.8	102.3	104.1
梅州	Meizhou	102.8	103.0	106.6	104.0	105.0	103.2	102.8	103.4	102.9	102.8
惠州	Huizhou	106.1	105.6	104.0	103.9	102.9	103.3	104.6	104.3	104.7	104.5
汕尾	Shanwei	106.1	102.5	106.1	105.6	105.9	103.1	103.8	104.5	102.4	105.6
东莞	Dongguan	99.8	102.3	101.4	100.8	99.9	100.1	103.1	102.6	106.0	102.1
中山	Zhongshan	101.9	101.9	103.2	102.4	102.5	101.1	100.2	99.6	98.8	93.6
江门	Jiangmen	104.9	100.9	104.9	104.5	104.2	102.7	103.1	103.2	103.2	102.6
阳江	Yangjiang	106.4	95.5	105.9	103.9	103.8	104.5	102.8	103.9	101.1	102.3
湛江	Zhanjiang	104.0	108.4	104.2	105.0	106.0	102.3	103.5	102.9	102.7	103.0
茂名	Maoming	108.5	104.0	104.1	104.0	103.5	100.2	103.3	104.0	103.7	103.7
肇庆	Zhaoqing	105.0	105.8	105.4	105.8	104.0	103.4	104.0	103.8	103.5	103.6
清远	Qingyuan	102.7	104.0	106.7	104.6	106.1	104.2	104.4	104.4	104.0	104.7
潮州	Chaozhou	101.0	102.1	104.5	105.1	105.0	102.8	105.2	102.9	103.6	105.3
揭阳	Jieyang	104.0	102.9	105.0	104.5	104.4	101.3	103.7	103.6	103.9	104.0
云浮	Yunfu	106.0	106.4	104.6	104.1	104.4	103.0	103.8	103.0	102.3	105.4
按经济区域分	By Region										
珠三角	Pearl River Delta	104.3	103.5	104.2	103.9	103.3	101.8	102.9	102.8	102.2	103.1
东翼	Eastern Region	104.3	103.0	105.3	105.0	105.3	111.3	104.7	103.6	103.2	104.8
西翼	Western Region	106.6	103.7	104.5	104.4	104.6	103.2	103.3	103.5	102.8	103.2
山区	Mountainous Region	104.1	104.0	105.6	104.5	105.1	103.6	103.9	103.7	103.1	104.3

2-22 各市第二产业增加值指数

Indices of Value-added of the Tertiary Industry by City

上年=100 (preceding year=100)

市 别	City	2000	2005	2010	2011	2012	2013	2014	2015	2016	2017
广 州	Guangzhou	111.9	113.0	113.0	111.9	108.5	111.3	107.5	106.8	105.5	104.6
深 圳	Shenzhen	118.5	117.9	113.8	111.7	107.7	109.7	107.8	107.5	108.1	109.2
珠 海	Zhuhai	114.7	116.9	118.2	112.0	103.3	111.9	112.1	110.1	107.8	110.9
汕 头	Shantou	107.2	113.5	110.2	108.1	111.7	112.6	109.7	107.4	109.1	108.8
佛 山	Foshan	112.4	125.2	115.1	112.3	109.3	110.7	109.0	107.2	107.2	108.2
韶 关	Shaoguan	115.6	109.7	113.6	110.3	116.2	110.0	106.9	102.9	102.8	104.3
河 源	Heyuan	113.1	145.6	114.4	115.2	114.6	114.9	110.4	104.3	103.8	100.6
梅 州	Meizhou	109.2	108.0	118.4	117.5	112.5	115.8	110.7	108.6	107.2	104.4
惠 州	Huizhou	113.1	117.4	124.2	115.4	114.5	121.7	111.7	109.8	108.1	102.5
汕 尾	Shanwei	115.7	123.8	122.7	121.6	119.3	117.7	110.2	107.1	106.3	108.2
东 莞	Dongguan	120.7	120.0	117.1	107.7	106.6	111.7	109.3	106.0	108.6	110.7
中 山	Zhongshan	115.3	119.6	116.1	114.1	114.1	111.0	108.2	107.4	106.2	104.8
江 门	Jiangmen	111.1	122.3	117.0	116.6	106.1	110.8	109.1	108.6	106.8	109.2
阳 江	Yangjiang	111.7	125.2	121.6	122.3	117.8	122.9	115.6	110.4	105.3	104.3
湛 江	Zhanjiang	106.2	111.4	117.0	112.3	109.7	112.5	115.3	109.9	107.0	107.6
茂 名	Maoming	110.8	114.3	114.1	113.1	116.4	115.1	114.3	108.6	107.6	105.5
肇 庆	Zhaoqing	114.2	120.6	131.0	121.7	118.7	119.2	111.6	109.6	103.8	102.3
清 远	Qingyuan	104.6	162.1	111.1	105.9	103.7	109.2	112.4	106.3	107.1	99.6
潮 州	Chaozhou	105.5	115.1	115.6	113.8	110.9	114.0	108.7	106.6	106.1	105.5
揭 阳	Jieyang	104.9	114.3	126.3	120.0	115.1	118.2	111.0	107.1	102.4	102.8
云 浮	Yunfu	105.2	128.3	120.5	122.7	115.7	121.8	114.2	106.9	107.3	99.0
按经济区域分	By Region										
珠 三 角	Pearl River Delta	114.6	118.3	114.2	110.5	106.8	107.6	107.6	107.5	107.1	107.4
东 翼	Eastern Region	106.8	115.1	117.0	113.5	112.5	113.3	109.9	107.1	105.7	105.9
西 翼	Western Region	109.2	114.8	115.9	112.8	112.6	114.0	114.5	109.5	106.9	106.0
山 区	Mountainous Region	109.5	125.9	115.2	111.0	110.0	108.5	110.1	105.9	105.7	101.5

2-23 各市第三产业增加值指数

Indices of Value-added of the Tertiary Industry by City

上年=100 (preceding year=100)

市别	City	2000	2005	2010	2011	2012	2013	2014	2015	2016	2017
广州	Guangzhou	116.3	113.3	113.5	111.3	111.9	112.1	109.5	109.5	109.6	108.2
深圳	Shenzhen	113.8	112.3	110.5	108.6	112.4	111.5	109.7	110.1	109.9	108.4
珠海	Zhuhai	108.9	109.2	107.2	111.8	113.4	109.8	108.8	110.2	109.7	110.8
汕头	Shantou	106.9	109.9	111.5	113.7	107.4	107.3	108.6	110.5	109.1	110.2
佛山	Foshan	113.6	112.2	113.2	110.3	106.4	108.6	107.3	110.7	109.8	108.5
韶关	Shaoguan	110.9	114.0	113.8	112.6	110.1	112.5	109.7	109.3	109.9	108.8
河源	Heyuan	112.4	117.1	113.6	112.8	110.5	110.9	106.9	109.2	110.5	109.6
梅州	Meizhou	112.6	110.9	113.2	114.9	109.7	109.4	108.2	110.6	109.7	110.3
惠州	Huizhou	108.6	117.3	110.6	116.8	111.5	113.3	107.5	108.6	108.6	115.0
汕尾	Shanwei	112.0	119.7	114.3	109.2	109.0	108.2	109.0	110.8	109.7	108.7
东莞	Dongguan	120.0	119.4	103.7	108.7	106.1	108.0	106.3	110.3	107.6	105.7
中山	Zhongshan	110.0	126.0	112.0	113.0	107.6	109.0	107.9	110.3	109.8	109.3
江门	Jiangmen	110.2	104.0	111.9	109.9	112.2	109.4	106.9	108.9	108.7	107.9
阳江	Yangjiang	111.1	120.5	116.9	113.3	111.6	111.0	106.8	107.4	110.7	109.9
湛江	Zhanjiang	110.4	119.4	116.0	117.3	111.3	115.8	107.4	109.2	110.1	107.7
茂名	Maoming	114.4	120.5	117.5	111.8	108.4	116.2	108.9	108.7	107.8	110.8
肇庆	Zhaoqing	112.2	120.2	110.5	111.4	105.2	104.7	110.2	107.8	107.5	109.9
清远	Qingyuan	120.0	118.2	117.6	112.7	106.4	109.2	104.1	111.2	109.7	107.6
潮州	Chaozhou	107.8	109.6	114.0	113.7	111.0	108.1	107.9	111.5	109.0	108.8
揭阳	Jieyang	107.2	112.0	113.0	108.9	105.7	110.8	112.0	111.3	114.4	109.0
云浮	Yunfu	104.7	107.5	112.1	111.3	115.2	108.1	108.4	113.7	111.7	112.2
按经济区域分	By Region										
珠三角	Pearl River Delta	114.0	113.7	110.4	109.8	109.7	111.3	108.2	109.8	109.4	108.4
东翼	Eastern Region	107.7	111.6	112.1	110.9	107.8	108.0	109.4	110.9	110.7	109.4
西翼	Western Region	112.3	120.1	116.6	112.9	110.0	113.6	107.9	108.7	109.3	109.4
山区	Mountainous Region	111.9	113.9	113.7	111.9	109.5	109.5	107.4	110.6	110.1	109.3

2-24 各市地区生产总值（2017年）
Gross Domestic Product by City (2017)

单位：亿元　　(100 million yuan)

市别	City	地区生产总值 Gross Domestic Product	第一产业 Primary Industry	第二产业 Secondary Industry	第三产业 Tertiary Industry	#农、林、牧、渔业 Farming, Forestry, Animal Husbandry and Fishery	#工业 Industry
广州	Guangzhou	21503.15	220.45	6011.01	15271.69	242.33	5459.69
深圳	Shenzhen	22490.06	19.57	9318.10	13152.39	20.35	8739.14
珠海	Zhuhai	2675.18	48.82	1287.19	1339.17	52.51	1133.21
汕头	Shantou	2350.97	103.39	1182.68	1064.91	107.11	1073.30
佛山	Foshan	9398.52	133.65	5424.65	3840.22	141.43	5230.53
韶关	Shaoguan	1245.26	148.59	420.98	675.69	149.84	360.31
河源	Heyuan	946.16	102.46	376.52	467.18	103.51	329.40
梅州	Meizhou	1075.43	187.76	358.29	529.38	190.33	283.58
惠州	Huizhou	3830.58	166.57	2017.20	1646.81	168.18	1898.16
汕尾	Shanwei	850.91	124.42	383.59	342.89	128.48	353.01
东莞	Dongguan	7582.09	22.85	3663.23	3896.01	23.38	3568.24
中山	Zhongshan	3430.31	55.64	1724.97	1649.71	56.61	1648.43
江门	Jiangmen	2690.25	187.35	1324.96	1177.94	191.99	1253.48
阳江	Yangjiang	1311.45	211.46	484.50	615.50	215.17	445.70
湛江	Zhanjiang	2806.88	491.17	1058.97	1256.74	502.59	926.87
茂名	Maoming	2904.07	470.23	1131.24	1302.60	478.96	1006.70
肇庆	Zhaoqing	2110.01	326.62	771.53	1011.86	330.25	706.78
清远	Qingyuan	1469.34	218.90	501.15	749.29	227.65	454.42
潮州	Chaozhou	1012.76	70.56	505.55	436.66	73.12	472.10
揭阳	Jieyang	1987.89	156.99	1043.84	787.07	161.73	968.16
云浮	Yunfu	803.56	142.65	316.44	344.48	145.86	272.59
按经济区域分	By Region						
珠三角	Pearl River Delta	75710.14	1181.53	31542.82	42985.80	1227.01	29637.65
东翼	Eastern Region	6202.54	455.36	3115.66	2631.53	470.44	2866.57
西翼	Western Region	7022.40	1172.86	2674.70	3174.84	1196.72	2379.27
山区	Mountainous Region	5539.75	800.36	1973.38	2766.01	817.19	1700.30

2–24 续表 continued

单位：亿元 (100 million yuan)

市 别	City	#建筑业 Construction	#批发和零售业 Wholesale and Retail Trades	#交通运输、仓储和邮政业 Transport, Storage and Post	#住宿和餐饮业 Hotels and Catering Services	#金融业 Financial Intermediation	#房地产业 Real Estate
广 州	Guangzhou	588.98	3155.81	1499.45	433.05	1955.12	1833.78
深 圳	Shenzhen	594.07	2367.43	701.29	394.10	2924.26	1894.32
珠 海	Zhuhai	164.20	257.39	54.96	56.53	194.83	197.40
汕 头	Shantou	110.26	338.14	76.17	46.92	90.78	136.68
佛 山	Foshan	196.35	641.06	401.20	74.89	407.81	838.19
韶 关	Shaoguan	61.56	134.16	94.24	35.09	55.63	67.18
河 源	Heyuan	47.36	101.24	28.91	29.11	48.74	91.09
梅 州	Meizhou	75.87	111.43	29.56	22.25	53.13	76.26
惠 州	Huizhou	120.03	393.96	85.88	92.40	189.54	321.68
汕 尾	Shanwei	31.91	69.70	26.57	10.68	31.15	63.83
东 莞	Dongguan	100.94	868.25	262.26	141.02	457.63	662.10
中 山	Zhongshan	77.32	335.05	79.46	38.80	197.58	263.92
江 门	Jiangmen	71.89	199.91	99.51	38.09	135.79	163.78
阳 江	Yangjiang	39.11	132.42	109.12	26.08	40.21	97.86
湛 江	Zhanjiang	137.89	245.06	158.63	44.56	87.02	164.43
茂 名	Maoming	125.67	298.13	81.75	32.35	74.61	201.46
肇 庆	Zhaoqing	66.07	205.95	97.03	60.06	74.85	128.05
清 远	Qingyuan	48.07	129.01	113.20	19.75	69.77	117.70
潮 州	Chaozhou	34.74	109.59	27.81	12.81	45.51	76.37
揭 阳	Jieyang	79.92	392.66	30.41	28.62	37.22	56.95
云 浮	Yunfu	44.17	63.77	39.08	10.27	37.35	46.88
按经济区域分	By Region						
珠 三 角	Pearl River Delta	1979.86	8424.82	3281.04	1328.95	6537.38	6303.22
东 翼	Eastern Region	256.83	910.09	160.96	99.03	204.66	333.84
西 翼	Western Region	302.66	675.61	349.50	102.99	201.84	463.74
山 区	Mountainous Region	277.03	539.61	304.98	116.47	264.63	399.10

2-25 各市地区生产总值指数（2017年）

Growth Index of Gross Domestic Product by City (2017)

单位：% (%)

市别	City	地区生产总值 Gross Domestic Product	第一产业 Primary Industry	第二产业 Secondary Industry	第三产业 Tertiary Industry	#农、林、牧、渔业 Farming, Forestry, Animal Husbandry and Fishery	#工业 Industry
广州	Guangzhou	107.0	102.2	104.6	108.2	101.7	105.2
深圳	Shenzhen	108.8	127.0	109.2	108.4	125.2	109.4
珠海	Zhuhai	110.8	108.7	110.9	110.8	108.3	109.7
汕头	Shantou	109.2	104.0	108.8	110.2	103.9	108.9
佛山	Foshan	108.3	102.0	108.2	108.5	102.0	108.4
韶关	Shaoguan	106.8	104.4	104.3	108.8	104.4	105.9
河源	Heyuan	105.1	104.1	100.6	109.6	104.2	99.4
梅州	Meizhou	106.8	102.8	104.4	110.3	102.8	105.0
惠州	Huizhou	107.6	104.5	102.5	115.0	104.5	102.3
汕尾	Shanwei	108.1	105.6	108.2	108.7	105.7	108.5
东莞	Dongguan	108.1	102.1	110.7	105.7	102.0	110.8
中山	Zhongshan	106.6	93.6	104.8	109.3	93.7	104.9
江门	Jiangmen	108.1	102.6	109.2	107.9	102.9	109.6
阳江	Yangjiang	106.2	102.3	104.3	109.9	102.3	104.1
湛江	Zhanjiang	106.8	103.0	107.6	107.7	103.1	108.7
茂名	Maoming	107.5	103.7	105.5	110.8	103.8	105.5
肇庆	Zhaoqing	105.2	103.6	102.3	109.9	103.7	102.2
清远	Qingyuan	104.2	104.7	99.6	107.6	104.8	99.3
潮州	Chaozhou	106.8	105.3	105.5	108.8	106.4	105.8
揭阳	Jieyang	105.0	104.0	102.8	109.0	104.2	102.9
云浮	Yunfu	105.3	105.4	99.0	112.2	105.4	97.1
按经济区域分	By Region						
珠三角	Pearl River Delta	107.9	103.1	107.4	108.4	103.0	107.6
东翼	Eastern Region	107.2	104.8	105.9	109.4	104.9	106.0
西翼	Western Region	107.0	103.2	106.0	109.4	103.2	106.3
山区	Mountainous Region	105.6	104.3	101.5	109.3	104.3	101.2

2-25 续表 continued

单位：% (%)

市 别	City	#建筑业 Construction	#批发和零售业 Wholesale and Retail Trades	#交通运输、仓储和邮政业 Transport, Storage and Post	#住宿和餐饮业 Hotels and Catering Services	#金融业 Financial Interme-diation	#房地产业 Real Estate
广 州	Guangzhou	99.2	105.4	111.1	100.8	107.2	99.1
深 圳	Shenzhen	105.1	105.8	121.5	105.9	102.0	103.4
珠 海	Zhuhai	121.3	110.8	107.5	116.0	113.8	90.6
汕 头	Shantou	107.6	106.7	118.1	102.2	104.9	121.2
佛 山	Foshan	102.4	105.4	109.2	103.0	105.6	107.7
韶 关	Shaoguan	95.8	109.1	105.8	105.0	104.0	107.8
河 源	Heyuan	109.3	105.8	105.5	102.7	100.5	117.9
梅 州	Meizhou	101.9	107.7	106.4	104.8	108.2	115.7
惠 州	Huizhou	106.5	108.2	108.0	102.2	119.6	131.6
汕 尾	Shanwei	105.3	91.4	113.8	94.5	128.1	124.5
东 莞	Dongguan	103.0	100.5	105.0	90.4	105.9	124.7
中 山	Zhongshan	103.9	109.3	101.4	86.0	106.0	116.7
江 门	Jiangmen	101.4	104.3	109.5	106.7	101.8	99.7
阳 江	Yangjiang	107.4	108.8	107.9	106.4	105.8	109.1
湛 江	Zhanjiang	100.7	110.6	111.0	102.4	115.4	112.2
茂 名	Maoming	105.8	103.8	109.0	102.6	107.9	117.2
肇 庆	Zhaoqing	102.9	95.7	104.6	98.8	100.6	118.6
清 远	Qingyuan	102.9	113.0	113.8	88.1	104.0	103.6
潮 州	Chaozhou	100.4	105.2	108.9	102.3	104.2	110.5
揭 阳	Jieyang	102.0	105.2	118.5	105.4	108.8	107.3
云 浮	Yunfu	112.2	107.2	126.3	104.8	100.9	109.3
按经济区域分	By Region						
珠 三 角	Pearl River Delta	103.8	105.2	112.0	101.5	104.9	106.0
东 翼	Eastern Region	104.5	104.5	115.2	101.9	108.8	117.4
西 翼	Western Region	103.7	107.3	109.5	103.5	110.6	113.8
山 区	Mountainous Region	103.5	108.9	110.9	101.1	103.7	110.3

2–26 各市地区生产总值产业构成（2017年）

Composition of Gross Domestic Product by Industry by City (2017)

单位：%　　(%)

市别	City	地区生产总值 Gross Domestic Product	第一产业 Primary Industry	第二产业 Secondary Industry	第三产业 Tertiary Industry	# 工业 Industry
广州	Guangzhou	100.0	1.0	28.0	71.0	25.4
深圳	Shenzhen	100.0	0.1	41.4	58.5	38.9
珠海	Zhuhai	100.0	1.8	48.1	50.1	42.4
汕头	Shantou	100.0	4.4	50.3	45.3	45.7
佛山	Foshan	100.0	1.4	57.7	40.9	55.7
韶关	Shaoguan	100.0	11.9	33.8	54.3	28.9
河源	Heyuan	100.0	10.8	39.8	49.4	34.8
梅州	Meizhou	100.0	17.5	33.3	49.2	26.4
惠州	Huizhou	100.0	4.3	52.7	43.0	49.6
汕尾	Shanwei	100.0	14.6	45.1	40.3	41.5
东莞	Dongguan	100.0	0.3	48.3	51.4	47.1
中山	Zhongshan	100.0	1.6	50.3	48.1	48.1
江门	Jiangmen	100.0	7.0	49.2	43.8	46.6
阳江	Yangjiang	100.0	16.1	37.0	46.9	34.0
湛江	Zhanjiang	100.0	17.5	37.7	44.8	33.0
茂名	Maoming	100.0	16.2	38.9	44.9	34.7
肇庆	Zhaoqing	100.0	15.5	36.6	47.9	33.5
清远	Qingyuan	100.0	14.9	34.1	51.0	30.9
潮州	Chaozhou	100.0	7.0	49.9	43.1	46.6
揭阳	Jieyang	100.0	7.9	52.5	39.6	48.7
云浮	Yunfu	100.0	17.7	39.4	42.9	33.9
按经济区域分	By Region					
珠三角	Pearl River Delta	100.0	1.5	41.7	56.8	39.1
东翼	Eastern Region	100.0	7.4	50.2	42.4	46.2
西翼	Western Region	100.0	16.7	38.1	45.2	33.9
山区	Mountainous Region	100.0	14.5	35.6	49.9	30.7

2-27 各市支出法地区生产总值（2017年）

Gross Domestic Product by Expenditure Approach by City (2017)

市 别	City	支出法地区生产总值（亿元）Gross Domestic Product by Expenditure Approach (100 million yuan)	最终消费支出 Final Consumption Expenditure	资本形成总额 Gross Capital Formation	货物和服务净流出 Net Export of Goods and Services	最终消费率（消费率）(%) Final Consumption Rate (%)	资本形成率（投资率）(%) Capital Formation Rate (%)
广 州	Guangzhou	21503.15	10989.04	8045.41	2468.70	51.1	37.4
深 圳	Shenzhen	22490.06	9262.78	7807.09	5420.19	41.2	34.7
珠 海	Zhuhai	2675.18	1065.86	2017.72	-408.40	39.8	75.4
汕 头	Shantou	2350.97	1410.72	889.12	51.14	60.0	37.8
佛 山	Foshan	9398.52	3843.88	3980.43	1574.21	40.9	42.4
韶 关	Shaoguan	1245.26	820.63	620.25	-195.62	65.9	49.8
河 源	Heyuan	946.16	694.70	821.81	-570.35	73.4	86.9
梅 州	Meizhou	1075.43	824.79	499.27	-248.64	76.7	46.4
惠 州	Huizhou	3830.58	1922.76	2016.46	-108.64	50.2	52.6
汕 尾	Shanwei	850.91	538.54	567.18	-254.81	63.3	66.7
东 莞	Dongguan	7582.09	4133.56	2718.75	729.79	54.5	35.9
中 山	Zhongshan	3430.31	1635.96	1395.23	399.12	47.7	40.7
江 门	Jiangmen	2690.25	1305.15	1291.56	93.53	48.5	48.0
阳 江	Yangjiang	1311.45	587.15	723.04	1.25	44.8	55.1
湛 江	Zhanjiang	2806.88	1759.22	1314.70	-267.04	62.7	46.8
茂 名	Maoming	2904.07	1336.36	1032.31	535.40	46.0	35.5
肇 庆	Zhaoqing	2110.01	1030.06	996.20	83.75	48.8	47.2
清 远	Qingyuan	1469.34	982.49	740.06	-253.22	66.9	50.4
潮 州	Chaozhou	1012.77	664.91	333.99	13.87	65.7	33.0
揭 阳	Jieyang	1987.89	1091.42	831.18	65.29	54.9	41.8
云 浮	Yunfu	803.56	529.51	493.53	-219.48	65.9	61.4
按经济区域分	By Region						
珠 三 角	Pearl River Delta	75710.14	35189.04	30268.87	10252.24	46.5	40.0
东 翼	Eastern Region	6202.54	3705.58	2621.47	-124.52	59.7	42.3
西 翼	Western Region	7022.40	3682.74	3070.05	269.62	52.4	43.7
山 区	Mountainous Region	5539.75	3852.13	3174.93	-1487.31	69.5	57.3

2–28 各市资本形成总额及构成（2017年）

Gross Capital Formation and Its Composition by City (2017)

市别	City	资本形成总额（亿元）Gross Capital Formation (100 million yuan)	固定资本形成总额 Gross Fixed Capital Formation	存货变动 Change in Inventories	比重（资本形成总额=100）Proportion (gross capital formation=100) 固定资本形成总额 Gross Fixed Capital Formation	存货变动 Change in Inventories
广州	Guangzhou	8045.41	7660.96	384.46	95.2	4.8
深圳	Shenzhen	7807.09	7549.33	257.76	96.7	3.3
珠海	Zhuhai	2017.72	1856.38	161.34	92.0	8.0
汕头	Shantou	889.12	836.89	52.23	94.1	5.9
佛山	Foshan	3980.43	3755.23	225.21	94.3	5.7
韶关	Shaoguan	620.25	601.91	18.34	97.0	3.0
河源	Heyuan	821.81	797.95	23.86	97.1	2.9
梅州	Meizhou	499.27	485.00	14.27	97.1	2.9
惠州	Huizhou	2016.46	1893.92	122.55	93.9	6.1
汕尾	Shanwei	567.18	556.03	11.15	98.0	2.0
东莞	Dongguan	2718.75	2392.03	326.72	88.0	12.0
中山	Zhongshan	1395.23	1316.45	78.78	94.4	5.6
江门	Jiangmen	1291.56	1174.71	116.85	91.0	9.0
阳江	Yangjiang	723.04	695.73	27.31	96.2	3.8
湛江	Zhanjiang	1314.70	1269.33	45.37	96.5	3.5
茂名	Maoming	1032.31	818.57	213.74	79.3	20.7
肇庆	Zhaoqing	996.20	936.44	59.77	94.0	6.0
清远	Qingyuan	740.06	724.59	15.47	97.9	2.1
潮州	Chaozhou	333.99	319.29	14.70	95.6	4.4
揭阳	Jieyang	831.18	755.23	75.95	90.9	9.1
云浮	Yunfu	493.53	497.74	-4.20	100.9	-0.9
按经济区域分	By Region					
珠三角	Pearl River Delta	30268.87	28535.44	1733.43	94.3	5.7
东翼	Eastern Region	2621.47	2467.44	154.04	94.1	5.9
西翼	Western Region	3070.05	2783.63	286.42	90.7	9.3
山区	Mountainous Region	3174.93	3107.19	67.74	97.9	2.1

2-29 各市最终消费及构成（2017年）

Final Consumption Expenditure and Its Composition by City (2017)

市别	City	最终消费（亿元） Final Consumption Expenditure (100 million yuan)	居民消费 Household Consumption	城镇居民 Urban Households	农村居民 Rural Households	政府消费 Government Consumption	比重 Proportion 最终消费=100 Final Consumption Expenditure=100 居民消费 Household Consumption	政府消费 Government Consumption	居民消费=100 Household Consumption=100 城镇居民 Urban Households	农村居民 Rural Households
广州	Guangzhou	10989.04	8169.57	7506.80	662.76	2819.47	74.3	25.7	91.9	8.1
深圳	Shenzhen	9262.78	7114.73	7108.08	6.65	2148.05	76.8	23.2	99.9	0.1
珠海	Zhuhai	1065.86	765.06	710.86	54.20	300.80	71.8	28.2	92.9	7.1
汕头	Shantou	1410.72	1188.60	1033.44	155.16	222.12	84.3	15.7	86.9	13.1
佛山	Foshan	3843.88	3005.37	2890.02	115.35	838.51	78.2	21.8	96.2	3.8
韶关	Shaoguan	820.63	572.62	425.99	146.63	248.00	69.8	30.2	74.4	25.6
河源	Heyuan	694.70	494.00	269.74	224.27	200.70	71.1	28.9	54.6	45.4
梅州	Meizhou	824.79	609.01	370.39	238.62	215.78	73.8	26.2	60.8	39.2
惠州	Huizhou	1922.76	1446.78	1158.97	287.81	475.98	75.2	24.8	80.1	19.9
汕尾	Shanwei	538.54	446.84	296.33	150.50	91.71	83.0	17.0	66.3	33.7
东莞	Dongguan	4133.56	3429.11	3102.16	326.95	704.44	83.0	17.0	90.5	9.5
中山	Zhongshan	1635.96	1403.86	1310.93	92.93	232.10	85.8	14.2	93.4	6.6
江门	Jiangmen	1305.15	1066.21	846.98	219.23	238.94	81.7	18.3	79.4	20.6
阳江	Yangjiang	587.15	424.13	273.95	150.18	163.03	72.2	27.8	64.6	35.4
湛江	Zhanjiang	1759.22	1398.18	814.27	583.91	361.04	79.5	20.5	58.2	41.8
茂名	Maoming	1336.36	982.12	640.94	341.18	354.24	73.5	26.5	65.3	34.7
肇庆	Zhaoqing	1030.06	738.56	478.58	259.97	291.50	71.7	28.3	64.8	35.2
清远	Qingyuan	982.49	776.12	529.19	246.93	206.37	79.0	21.0	68.2	31.8
潮州	Chaozhou	664.91	564.43	446.02	118.41	100.47	84.9	15.1	79.0	21.0
揭阳	Jieyang	1091.42	925.85	612.80	313.05	165.56	84.8	15.2	66.2	33.8
云浮	Yunfu	529.51	394.34	261.20	133.14	135.17	74.5	25.5	66.2	33.8
按经济区域分	By Region									
珠三角	Pearl River Delta	35189.04	27139.25	25113.39	2025.86	8049.79	77.1	22.9	92.5	7.5
东翼	Eastern Region	3705.58	3125.73	2388.60	737.12	579.86	84.4	15.6	76.4	23.6
西翼	Western Region	3682.74	2804.43	1729.16	1075.26	878.31	76.2	23.8	61.7	38.3
山区	Mountainous Region	3852.13	2846.11	1856.51	989.60	1006.02	73.9	26.1	65.2	34.8

2-30 各市人均地区生产总值

Per Capita Gross Domestic Product by City

单位：元 (yuan)

市 别	City	2000	2005	2006	2007	2008	2009	2010
广 州	Guangzhou	25758	54160	62930	70284	77165	80272	88361
深 圳	Shenzhen	33276	61844	69702	77660	85088	87066	98437
珠 海	Zhuhai	28068	45682	52690	61826	67432	68722	79002
汕 头	Shantou	9741	12919	14491	16540	18690	19767	21384
佛 山	Foshan	20231	42434	51018	59915	68667	72167	80794
韶 关	Shaoguan	7028	11608	13875	16583	19398	20283	22638
河 源	Heyuan	3826	7483	9222	11843	14109	14163	15564
梅 州	Meizhou	4731	7684	8485	9942	11515	12386	14372
惠 州	Huizhou	13877	21942	24556	28384	31881	33300	38917
汕 尾	Shanwei	5262	7419	8489	10051	11913	13131	15433
东 莞	Dongguan	13563	33363	39287	45189	50635	49601	53575
中 山	Zhongshan	15077	36800	42716	49046	53533	54887	61691
江 门	Jiangmen	12844	19546	22858	26262	29944	31021	35873
阳 江	Yangjiang	7377	12724	14829	17170	20246	22021	26303
湛 江	Zhanjiang	6231	10269	11937	13514	15964	16767	20085
茂 名	Maoming	7981	12743	14816	16742	19831	20753	25254
肇 庆	Zhaoqing	7422	11915	13646	16483	20098	22671	28198
清 远	Qingyuan	5003	9088	11947	15328	17853	19569	23724
潮 州	Chaozhou	7444	11256	12725	14682	17028	18461	21206
揭 阳	Jieyang	6001	7417	8552	10321	12626	14107	17126
云 浮	Yunfu	6399	8690	9857	11745	13791	14594	16862
按经济区域分	By Region							
珠 三 角	Pearl River Delta	20398	40691	47187	53841	60118	62202	69916
东 翼	Eastern Region	7294	9747	11031	12850	15042	16370	18814
西 翼	Western Region	7099	11626	13518	15348	18142	19135	23053
山 区	Mountainous Region	5345	8847	10606	13002	15208	16109	18578

注：2009—2014年区域人均生产总值增速由广东省统计局统一调整核算，其他年份增速由分市汇总计算。
Note: The growth rates of per capital GDP from 2009 to 2014 are calculated by Statistics Bureau of Guangdong Province, and those of the previous years are calculated by each city.

2−30 续表 continued

单位：元 (yuan)

市 别	City	2011	2012	2013	2014	2015	2016	2017
广 州	Guangzhou	98677	107055	121584	129938	137793	143638	150678
深 圳	Shenzhen	113316	126765	141474	153677	162599	172453	183544
珠 海	Zhuhai	91458	97565	107765	118672	127227	137005	155502
汕 头	Shantou	23746	26435	28905	31285	33814	37486	42029
佛 山	Foshan	86759	92145	97784	103253	110054	117606	124324
韶 关	Shaoguan	26448	30139	32906	35426	36526	38539	41961
河 源	Heyuan	17938	20325	22810	24721	25513	27739	30659
梅 州	Meizhou	16246	17382	18538	20262	21817	23609	24623
惠 州	Huizhou	45829	51721	58434	64398	67046	72465	80205
汕 尾	Shanwei	18222	20517	22522	23887	25238	27285	28628
东 莞	Dongguan	58440	61593	67320	71651	76812	84007	91329
中 山	Zhongshan	71079	78846	85101	90007	95365	100897	105711
江 门	Jiangmen	41412	42447	44990	46727	50143	53932	59089
阳 江	Yangjiang	31232	35820	42025	46472	49301	49845	51720
湛 江	Zhanjiang	24351	26315	28857	31230	32702	35285	38508
茂 名	Maoming	29553	32546	36461	39192	40607	43555	47116
肇 庆	Zhaoqing	33971	37253	42106	46106	49016	51586	51464
清 远	Qingyuan	27256	27729	29420	31671	33595	36385	38135
潮 州	Chaozhou	24336	26409	29117	31428	34047	37054	38241
揭 阳	Jieyang	20621	23304	26658	29357	30945	32610	32642
云 浮	Yunfu	19947	21806	24647	26681	28397	30748	32232
按经济区域分	By Region							
珠 三 角	Pearl River Delta	78846	85793	95110	102173	108929	116351	124564
东 翼	Eastern Region	21789	24309	27044	29348	31350	33924	35844
西 翼	Western Regicn	27431	30211	33865	36702	38369	40773	43922
山 区	Mountainous Region	21429	23198	25257	27328	28775	31004	33039

注：2009−2014年区域人均生产总值增速由广东省统计局统一调整核算，其他年份增速由分市汇总计算。

Note: The growth rates of per capital GDP from 2009 to 2014 are calculated by Statistics Bureau of Guangdong Province, and those of the previous years are calculated by each city.

2-31 各市人均地区生产总值指数

Indices of Per Capita Gross Domestic Product by City

上年=100 (preceding year=100)

市别	City	2000	2005	2006	2007	2008	2009	2010
广州	Guangzhou	108.4	114.3	113.2	109.7	106.5	105.4	106.0
深圳	Shenzhen	105.8	111.8	111.9	109.4	107.3	106.6	107.7
珠海	Zhuhai	104.9	110.5	114.0	114.5	106.9	104.2	111.3
汕头	Shantou	104.5	110.4	110.7	111.6	109.0	107.4	107.9
佛山	Foshan	106.3	117.6	116.6	114.1	110.5	108.3	109.2
韶关	Shaoguan	111.8	108.7	114.8	115.6	113.0	110.4	113.5
河源	Heyuan	111.9	118.3	125.1	123.3	109.5	107.8	110.7
梅州	Meizhou	108.9	106.5	109.1	112.0	109.8	109.4	113.1
惠州	Huizhou	107.7	113.2	113.1	112.9	107.5	109.0	112.8
汕尾	Shanwei	110.2	113.3	113.6	116.7	114.5	114.1	116.6
东莞	Dongguan	105.1	119.5	116.6	113.1	109.0	100.9	105.4
中山	Zhongshan	105.4	120.7	114.5	111.2	105.6	105.1	108.5
江门	Jiangmen	108.7	112.1	114.5	113.5	109.1	107.8	112.4
阳江	Yangjiang	109.6	112.7	115.5	112.8	111.2	111.8	115.1
湛江	Zhanjiang	106.0	111.6	111.6	111.4	111.2	110.4	113.6
茂名	Maoming	110.5	111.9	112.1	111.7	109.9	111.3	115.1
肇庆	Zhaoqing	109.9	114.2	114.5	115.8	115.3	113.0	115.5
清远	Qingyuan	108.9	124.7	127.7	123.8	109.3	112.4	112.4
潮州	Chaozhou	104.3	110.8	111.9	113.4	110.9	111.0	112.5
揭阳	Jieyang	103.0	110.2	114.2	117.0	115.1	115.1	118.1
云浮	Yunfu	105.1	111.8	113.7	116.0	110.8	110.5	113.4
按经济区域分	By Region							
珠三角	Pearl River Delta	107.4	114.7	114.1	111.7	108.4	105.2	107.3
东翼	Eastern Region	104.7	110.7	112.0	113.9	111.9	110.1	112.5
西翼	Western Region	108.6	111.9	112.4	111.7	110.6	110.7	114.0
山区	Mountainous Region	109.2	113.4	117.9	118.2	110.4	109.8	112.4

2-31 续表 continued

上年=100 (preceding year=100)

市 别	City	2011	2012	2013	2014	2015	2016	2017
广 州	Guangzhou	107.6	109.9	110.9	107.6	106.1	104.4	103.2
深 圳	Shenzhen	107.3	109.2	109.8	107.6	105.2	103.8	103.9
珠 海	Zhuhai	110.7	106.9	110.0	109.3	108.5	106.3	106.6
汕 头	Shantou	108.2	109.0	109.3	108.2	107.7	108.2	108.6
佛 山	Foshan	108.7	107.7	109.4	107.7	107.3	107.3	106.6
韶 关	Shaoguan	110.7	111.1	109.6	107.2	105.5	105.8	105.9
河 源	Heyuan	110.8	110.8	111.1	107.5	105.5	106.3	104.8
梅 州	Meizhou	112.6	109.4	110.6	108.1	108.2	107.0	106.3
惠 州	Huizhou	111.7	112.0	113.0	109.3	108.5	107.6	107.4
汕 尾	Shanwei	113.7	112.8	111.7	108.3	107.4	106.5	107.6
东 莞	Dongguan	105.6	105.9	109.5	107.6	108.5	108.6	107.5
中 山	Zhongshan	110.2	110.8	109.5	107.3	107.7	107.0	105.8
江 门	Jiangmen	112.0	107.8	109.3	107.6	108.1	107.0	107.6
阳 江	Yangjiang	113.4	111.9	114.6	109.9	107.7	106.1	105.6
湛 江	Zhanjiang	111.7	108.8	111.2	109.2	108.0	107.1	106.4
茂 名	Maoming	110.8	109.4	111.9	109.6	107.4	106.4	106.4
肇 庆	Zhaoqing	113.1	110.2	110.5	109.3	107.7	104.4	104.5
清 远	Qingyuan	107.6	104.3	107.4	107.1	107.5	107.5	103.8
潮 州	Chaozhou	112.0	110.0	110.5	107.8	109.7	108.6	106.6
揭 阳	Jieyang	113.6	110.6	113.8	110.0	107.5	105.8	104.8
云 浮	Yunfu	113.2	111.8	112.4	109.7	107.8	107.2	104.3
按经济区域分	By Region							
珠 三 角	Pearl River Delta	107.3	107.5	108.7	107.1	107.1	106.1	105.4
东 翼	Eastern Region	110.4	109.5	109.9	108.5	107.9	107.2	107.3
西 翼	Western Region	110.4	109.0	111.0	109.3	107.7	106.6	106.3
山 区	Mountainous Region	109.3	108.2	107.4	107.5	106.9	106.8	105.0

2-32 各市人均地区生产总值指数

Indices of Per Capita Gross Domestic Product by City

2000年=100 (2000=100)

市别	City	2000	2005	2006	2007	2008	2009	2010
广州	Guangzhou	100.0	194.3	219.9	241.2	256.8	270.5	286.8
深圳	Shenzhen	100.0	175.2	196.1	214.5	230.1	245.3	264.2
珠海	Zhuhai	100.0	162.6	185.4	212.2	227.0	236.6	263.4
汕头	Shantou	100.0	130.9	144.9	161.7	176.2	189.3	204.2
佛山	Foshan	100.0	193.2	225.3	257.1	284.1	307.6	335.9
韶关	Shaoguan	100.0	155.9	179.0	206.9	233.9	258.2	293.0
河源	Heyuan	100.0	179.4	224.4	276.7	302.9	326.6	361.5
梅州	Meizhou	100.0	148.1	161.6	180.9	198.7	217.3	245.8
惠州	Huizhou	100.0	157.0	177.6	200.5	215.5	234.9	265.0
汕尾	Shanwei	100.0	157.8	179.3	209.3	239.6	273.4	318.8
东莞	Dongguan	100.0	232.8	271.4	307.0	334.6	337.6	355.9
中山	Zhongshan	100.0	230.7	264.1	293.7	310.2	326.0	353.7
江门	Jiangmen	100.0	153.5	175.8	199.5	217.7	234.7	263.8
阳江	Yangjiang	100.0	163.6	189.0	213.2	237.0	265.0	305.0
湛江	Zhanjiang	100.0	153.2	170.9	190.4	211.8	233.8	265.6
茂名	Maoming	100.0	159.2	178.4	199.3	219.1	243.8	280.6
肇庆	Zhaoqing	100.0	160.7	184.0	213.0	245.6	277.5	320.6
清远	Qingyuan	100.0	181.4	231.6	286.7	313.4	352.3	396.0
潮州	Chaozhou	100.0	152.2	170.3	193.1	214.1	237.7	267.4
揭阳	Jieyang	100.0	123.7	141.2	165.3	190.2	218.9	258.6
云浮	Yunfu	100.0	139.7	158.8	184.2	204.1	225.5	255.8
按经济区域分	By Region							
珠三角	Pearl River Delta	100.0	188.2	214.7	239.9	259.9	273.3	293.4
东翼	Eastern Region	100.0	135.2	151.4	172.3	192.9	212.3	238.9
西翼	Western Region	100.0	157.4	177.0	197.8	218.8	242.1	275.9
山区	Mountainous Region	100.0	158.5	186.9	220.9	243.9	267.8	301.0

2-32 续表 continued

2000年=100 (2000=100)

市 别	City	2011	2012	2013	2014	2015	2016	2017
广 州	Guangzhou	308.5	339.0	375.9	404.6	429.2	448.1	462.7
深 圳	Shenzhen	283.5	309.6	339.9	365.8	384.8	399.4	415.0
珠 海	Zhuhai	291.6	311.5	342.6	374.6	406.4	432.1	460.5
汕 头	Shantou	220.9	240.7	263.1	284.9	306.9	332.1	360.7
佛 山	Foshan	365.2	393.3	430.3	463.4	497.2	533.5	568.9
韶 关	Shaoguan	324.4	360.4	395.0	423.4	446.7	472.6	500.5
河 源	Heyuan	400.6	443.8	493.1	530.1	559.2	594.5	623.0
梅 州	Meizhou	276.8	302.8	334.9	362.0	391.7	419.1	445.7
惠 州	Huizhou	296.0	331.5	374.6	409.5	444.3	478.0	513.3
汕 尾	Shanwei	362.4	408.8	456.7	494.6	531.2	565.7	608.8
东 莞	Dongguan	375.8	398.0	435.8	468.9	508.7	552.5	593.9
中 山	Zhongshan	389.8	431.9	472.9	507.4	546.5	584.8	618.4
江 门	Jiangmen	295.4	318.5	348.1	374.5	404.9	433.2	466.3
阳 江	Yangjiang	345.9	387.1	443.6	487.5	525.0	557.1	588.1
湛 江	Zhanjiang	296.6	322.7	358.9	391.9	423.3	453.3	482.2
茂 名	Maoming	310.9	340.2	380.6	417.2	448.1	476.7	507.4
肇 庆	Zhaoqing	362.6	399.5	441.5	482.5	519.7	542.6	566.8
清 远	Qingyuan	426.1	444.4	477.3	511.1	549.5	590.7	613.4
潮 州	Chaozhou	299.5	329.4	364.0	392.4	430.5	467.5	498.4
揭 阳	Jieyang	293.7	324.9	369.7	406.7	437.2	462.5	484.7
云 浮	Yunfu	289.5	323.7	363.8	399.1	430.3	461.2	481.2
按经济区域分	By Region							
珠 三 角	Pearl River Delta	314.7	338.4	367.7	393.7	421.6	447.5	471.5
东 翼	Eastern Region	263.9	289.0	317.6	344.8	372.0	398.7	427.6
西 翼	Western Region	304.7	332.1	368.7	402.9	433.9	462.7	491.7
山 区	Mountainous Region	328.9	355.9	382.3	410.9	439.3	469.2	492.8

2-33 全省生产性服务业增加值

Value-added of Productive Service Industry

单位：亿元 (100 million yuan)

分行业	By Sector	增加值 Value-added				指数(上年=100) Indices(Preceding Year=100)			
		2014	2015	2016	2017	2014	2015	2016	2017
合　计	**Total**	**17621.58**	**19551.98**	**21719.60**	**24665.14**	**109.0**	**110.1**	**106.5**	**108.6**
研发设计与其他技术服务	Scientific Research Services	894.20	1052.63	1105.97	1391.62	114.4	116.9	103.9	106.1
货物运输、仓储和邮政快递服务	Transport, Storage and Postal Services	1890.52	2058.44	2162.35	2509.19	111.5	105.3	105.0	113.3
信息服务	Information Services	1968.84	2289.07	2871.41	3821.01	108.3	109.8	119.4	121.2
金融服务	Finance Services	3046.39	4556.38	4772.26	5170.49	108.9	124.5	95.9	105.4
节能与环保服务	Energy Conservation and Environment Protection Services	319.86	392.67	413.95	409.28	107.4	123.7	103.1	94.1
生产性租赁服务	Productive Leasing Services	118.85	136.78	155.55	179.32	107.1	112.0	106.5	112.3
商务服务	Business Services	2217.67	2182.59	2487.18	2746.32	111.5	107.6	110.0	106.0
人力资源管理与培训服务	Human Resource Services	647.93	767.23	913.06	1159.45	108.5	117.7	115.8	119.4
批发经纪代理服务	Wholesale Services	4345.85	3798.43	4225.13	4510.50	107.4	101.8	106.8	105.1
生产性支持服务	Productive Support Services	2171.47	2317.75	2612.75	2767.96	107.2	106.6	111.1	104.1

注：考虑到可操作性，表中数据计算范围相对宽泛，生产性服务业所涉及的国民经济行业小类除货币银行服务外，其他全部计入生产性服务业。

Note: In consideration of operability, the data scope in this table are relatively broad. All of the small class of national economic industry classification relative to productive service industry are Included in the calculation excluding the industry of money and banking.

主要统计指标解释

国内（地区）生产总值 指按市场价格计算的一个国家（或地区）所有常住单位在一定时期内生产活动的最终成果。国内（地区）生产总值有三种计算方法，即生产法、收入法和支出法。三种方法分别从不同的方面反映国内生产总值及其构成。

三次产业 三次产业的划分是世界上较为常用的产业结构分类，但各国的划分不尽一致。根据《国民经济行业分类》（GB/T 4754—2011），我国的三产产业划分是：

第一产业是指农、林、牧、渔业（不含农、林、牧、渔服务业）。

第二产业是指采矿业（不含开采辅助活动），制造业（不含金属制品、机械和设备修理业），电力、热力、燃气及水生产和供应业，建筑业。

第三产业即服务业，是指除第一产业、第二产业以外的其他行业。

劳动者报酬 指劳动者从事生产活动所获得的全部报酬。包括劳动者获得的各种形式的工资、奖金和津贴，既有货币形式的，也有实物形式的，还包括劳动者所享受的公费医疗和医药卫生费、上下班交通补贴、单位支出的社会保险费、住房公积金等。

生产税净额 指生产税减生产补贴后的余额。生产税指政府对生产单位从事生产、销售和经营活动以及因从事生产活动使用某些生产要素（如固定资产、土地、劳动力）所征收的各种税、附加费和规费。生产补贴与生产税相反，指政府对生产单位的单方面转移支付，因此视为负生产税，包括政策性亏损补贴、价格补贴等。

固定资产折旧 指一定时期内为弥补固定资产损耗按照规定的固定资产折旧率提取的固定资产折旧，或按国民经济核算统一规定的折旧率虚拟计算的固定资产折旧。它反映了固定资产在当期生产中的转移价值。各类企业和企业化管理的事业单位的固定资产折旧是指实际计提的折旧费；不计提折旧的政府机关、非企业化管理的事业单位和居民住房的固定资产折旧是按照统一规定的折旧率和固定资产原值计算的虚拟折旧。原则上，固定资产折旧应按固定资产的重置价值计算，但是目前我国尚不具备对全社会固定资产进行重估价的基础，所以暂时还不能采用上述办法。

营业盈余 指常住单位创造的增加值扣除劳动者报酬、生产税净额和固定资产折旧后的余额。它相当于企业的营业利润加上生产税补贴，但要扣除从利润中开支的工资和福利等。

支出法国内（地区）生产总值 是从最终使用的角度反映一个国家（或地区）一定时期内生产活动最终成果的一种方法，包括最终消费支出、资本形成总额及货物和服务净出口三部分。计算公式为：

支出法国内（地区）生产总值=最终消费支出+资本形成总额+货物和服务净出口

最终消费支出 指常住单位为满足物质、文化和精神生活的需要，从本国经济领土和国外购买的货物和服务的支出。不包括非常住单位在本国经济领土内的消费支出。最终消费支出分为居民消费支出和政府消费支出。

居民消费支出 指常住住户在一定时期内对于货物和服务的全部最终消费支出。居民消费支出除了直接以货币形式购买的货物和服务的消费之外，还包括以其他方式获得的货物和服务的消费，即所谓的虚拟消费支出。居民虚拟消费支出包括如下几种类型：单位以实物报酬及实物转移的形式提供给劳动者的货物和服务；住户生产并由本住户消费发的货物和服务，其中的服务仅指住户的自有住房服务和付酬的家庭雇员提供的家庭和个人服务；金融机构提供的金融媒介服务等。

政府消费支出 指政府部门为全社会提供公共服务的消费支出和免费或以较低价格向住户提供的货物和服务的净支出。前者等于政府服务的产出价值减去政府单位所获得的经营收入后的价值，后者等于政府部门免费或以较低价格向住户提供的货物和服务的市场价值减去向住户收取的价值。

资本形成总额 指常住单位在一定时期内获得的减去处置的固定资产和存货的净额，包括固定资本形成总额和存货变动两部分。

固定资本形成总额 指生产者在一定时期内获得的固定资产减处置的固定资产的价值总额。固定资产是通过生产活动生产出来的，且其使用年限在一年以上、单位价值在规定标准以上的资产，不包括自然资产。可分为有形固定资本形成总额和无形固定资本形成总额。有形固定资本形成总额包括一定时期内完成的建筑工程、安装工程、设备工器具购置（减处置）价值，以及土地改良、新增役、种、奶、毛、娱乐用牲畜和新增经济林木价值。无形固定资本形成总额包括矿藏的勘探、计算机软件等获得减处置的价值。

存货变动 指常住单位存货实物量变动的市场价值，即期末价值减期初价值的差额，再扣除当期由于价格变动而产生的持有收益。存货增加可以是正值，也可以是负值；正值表示存货上升，负值表示存货下降。存货包括生产单位购进的原材料、燃料和储备物资等存货，以及生产单位生产的产成品、在制品和半成品等存货。

货物和服务净流出 指货物和服务流出减货物和服务流入的差额。流出包括常住单位向非常住单位出售或无偿转让的各种货物和服务的价值；流入包括常住单位从非常住单位购买或无偿得到的各种货物和服务价值。由于服务活动的提供与使用同时发生，一般把常住单位从非常住单位得到的服务作为流入，非常住单位从常住单位得到的服务作为流出。货物的流出和流入都按离岸价格计算。

生产性服务业 是指为生产活动提供的研发设计与其他技术服务、货物运输仓储和邮政快递服务、信息服务、金融服务、节能与环保服务、生产性租赁服务、商务服务、人力资源管理与培训服务、批发经纪代理服务、生产性支持服务。分类执行国家统计局《生产性服务业分类（2015）》标准。

Explanatory Notes on Main Statistical Indicators

Gross Domestic (Regional) Product refers to the final products at market prices produced by all resident units in a country (or a region) during a certain period of time. It is calculated with three approaches, i.e. production approach, income approach and expenditure approach, which reflect gross domestic product and its composition from different aspects.

Three Strata of Industry Classification of economic activities into three strata of industry is a common practice in the world, although the grouping varies to some extent from country to country. In China, according to Industrial classification for National Economic Activities (GB/T 4754—2011), economic activities are categorized into the following three strata of industry:Primary industry refers to agriculture, forestry, animal husbandry and fishery and services in support of these industries.

Secondary industry refers to mining and quarrying(not including support activities for mining), manufacturing(not including repair service of metal products, machinery and equipment), production and supply of electricity, heat, gas and water, and construction.

Tertiary industry refers to all other economic activities not included in the primary or secondary industries.

Compensation of Employees refers to the total payment of various forms to employees for the productive activities they are engaged in. It includes wages, bonuses and allowances, which the employees earn in cash or in kind. It also includes the free medical services provided to the employees and the medicine expenses, transport subsidies and social insurance, and housing fund paid by the employers.

Net Taxes on Production refers to the residual of the taxes on production minus the subsidies on production. The taxes on production refers to the various taxes, extra charges and fees levied on the production units on their production, sale and business activities as well as on some factors of production, such as fixed assets, land and labor force, used in the production activities they are engaged in. In contrast to the taxes on production, the subsidies on production refer to the unilateral transfer of part of the government’s revenue to the production units and are therefore regarded as negative taxes on production. They include subsidies on the loss due to implementation of government policies and price subsidies, etc.

Depreciation of Fixed Assets refers to the depreciation of fixed assets of a given period, drawn in accordance with the stipulated depreciation rate for the purpose of compensating the wear loss of the fixed assets or the depreciation of fixed assets calculated in a fictitious way in accordance with the stipulated unified depreciation rate in the national economic accounting system. It reflects the value of transfer of the fixed assets in the production of the current period. The depreciation of fixed assets in various enterprises and institutions managed as enterprises refers to the depreciation expenses actually drawn and calculated as part of the cost. In government agencies and institutions not managed as enterprises which do not draw the depreciation expenses, as well as for the houses of residents, the depreciation of fixed assets is the imputed depreciation, which is calculated in accordance with the stipulated unified depreciation rate and the original value of the fixed assets. In principle, the depreciation of fixed assets should be calculated on the basis of the repurchase value of the fixed assets. However, there is no actual condition to reevaluate all the fixed assets in China. Therefore, the above-mentioned methods are temporarily adopted at present.

Operating Surplus refers to the balance of the value-added created by the resident units deducting the laborers’ remuneration, net taxes on production and the depreciation of fixed assets. It is equivalent to the business profit of the enterprises plus subsidies on production, but the wages and welfare expenses paid from the profits should be deducted.

Gross Domestic (Regional) Product Calculated by Expenditure Approach refers to the method of measuring the final results of production activities of a country (region) during a given period from the perspective of final uses. It includes final consumption expenditure, gross capital formation and net export of goods and services. The formula for computation is:

GDP by expenditure approach = final consumption expenditure + gross capital formation + net export of goods and services

Final Consumption Expenditure refers to the total expenditure of resident units for purchases of goods and services from both the domestic economic territory and abroad to meet the needs of material, cultural and spiritual life. It does not include the expenditure of non-resident units on consumption in the economic territory of the country. The final consumption expenditure is broken down into household consumption expenditure and government consumption expenditure.

Household Consumption Expenditure refers to the total expenditure of resident households on the final consumption of goods and services. In addition to the consumption of goods and services bought by the households directly with money, the household consumption expenditure also includes expenditure on goods and services obtained by the households in other ways, i.e. the so-called imputed consumption expenditure, which includes the following: (a) the goods and services provided to households by employers in the form of payment in kind and transfer in kind; (b) goods and services produced and consumed by the households themselves, in which the services refer to the owner-occupied housing and services offered by paid family employees; (c) financial intermediate services provided by financial institution.

Government Consumption Expenditure refers to the consumption expenditure spent for the provision of public services provided by the government to the whole country and the net expenditure on the goods and services provided by the government to households free of charge or at reduced prices. The former equals to the output value of the government services minus the value of operating income obtained by the government departments. The latter equals to the market value of the goods and services provided by the government free of charge or at reduced prices to the households minus the value received by the government from the households.

Gross Capital Formation refers to the fixed assets acquired less disposals and the net value of inventory, thus including gross fixed capital formation and changes in inventories.

Gross Fixed Capital Formation refers to the value of acquisitions less those disposals of fixed assets during a given period. Fixed assets are the assets produced through production activities with unit value above a specified amount and which could be used for over one year. Natural assets are not included. Gross fixed capital formation can be categorized into total tangible fixed capital formation and total intangible fixed capital formation. Total tangible fixed capital formation includes the value of the construction projects and installation projects completed and the equipment, apparatus and instruments purchased (less those disposed) as well as the value of land improved, the value of draught animals, breeding stock and animals for milk, for wool and for recreational purposes and the newly increased forest with economic value. Total intangible fixed capital formation includes the prospecting of minerals and the acquisition of computer software minus the disposal of them.

Changes in Inventories refers to the market value of the change in the physical volume of inventory of resident units during a given period, i.e. the difference between the values at the beginning and at the end of the period minus the gains due to the change in prices. The changes in inventories can have a positive or a negative value. A positive value indicates an increase in inventory while a negative value indicates a decrease in inventory. The inventory includes raw materials, fuels and reserve materials purchased by the production units as well as theinventory of finished products, semi-finished products and work-in-progress.

Net Export of Goods and Services refers to the exports of goods and services subtracting the imports of goods and services. Exports include the value of various goods and services sold or gratuitously transferred by resident units to non-resident units. Imports include the value of various goods and services purchased or gratuitously acquired resident units from non-resident units. Because the provision of services and the use of them happen simultaneously, the acquisition of services by resident units from abroad is usually treated as import while the acquisition of services by non-resident units in this country is usually treated as export. The exports and imports of goods are calculated at FOB.

Productive Service Industry refers to the production activities to provide R&D design and other technical services, transport, storage and postal services, information services, financial services, energy saving and environmental protection services, production of leasing services, business services, human resource management and training services, wholesale brokerage services, production support services. The classification implemented the Production Service Industry Classification (2015) developed by NBS.

三、人口

POPULATION

三　人口

简要说明

一、本篇资料反映广东人口发展变化基本情况，主要内容包括：

1. 年末常住人口、性别比例、年龄比例、城镇人口比例以及人口出生率、人口死亡率和人口自然增长率。数据由广东省统计局根据人口普查、1%人口抽样调查或年度人口变动情况抽样调查推算所得。

2. 1990-2009 年年末常住人口数、出生率、死亡率以及自然增长率，除人口普查和 1%人口抽样调查年份直接推算外，其余年份数据均已按人口普查和 1%人口抽样调查结果作平滑调整。

3. 户籍总人口、按性别分以及迁移人口等，数据来源于广东省公安厅人口统计年报。

二、本资料由广东省统计局人口和就业统计处整理提供。

3 Population

Brief Introduction

Ⅰ. The data in this chapter show the basic conditions of development and changes of population in Guangdong, including mainly:

（1）Permanent population at the year-end, proportion of population by sex, proportion of population by age, proportion of urban population, birth rate, death rate and natural growth rate of population. The data are estimated by Guangdong Provincial Bureau of Statistics on the basis of population censuses, the one percent sample survey on population， or annual sample surveys on population changes.

（2）Permanent population at the year-end, birth rate, death rate and natural growth rate of population from 1990 to 2009 result from smooth adjustment on population census and national one-percent sample survey on population with the exceptions of 1990 and 2000 data, which are direct estimates from the result of population censuses.

（3）The total population with residence registration, population by sex, by agricultural and non-agricultural population, and migrant population are obtained from the annual reports of population of Guangdong Provincial Department of Public Security.

Ⅱ. The date in this chapter are prepared and provided by the Division of Population and Employment Statistics of Statistics Bureau of Guangdong Province.

3-1 人口主要指标
Main Population Indicators

项 目	Item	2000	2010	2014	2015	2016	2017
年末常住人口 （万人）	**Permanent Population at the Year-end (10000 persons)**	**8650.03**	**10440.94**	**10724.00**	**10849.00**	**10999.00**	**11169.00**
男性比例 (%)	Proportion of Male Population (%)	50.90	52.15	52.93	52.29	52.40	52.49
女性比例 (%)	Proportion of Female Population (%)	49.10	47.85	47.07	47.71	47.60	47.51
0-14岁人口比例 (%)	Proportion of Population Aged 0-14 (%)	24.17	16.90	15.38	17.37	17.23	17.21
15-64岁人口比例 (%)	Proportion of Population Aged 15-64 (%)	69.78	76.30	76.35	74.15	74.22	74.17
65岁及以上人口比例(%)	Proportion of Population Aged 65 And Over (%)	6.05	6.80	8.27	8.48	8.55	8.62
城镇人口比例 (%)	Proportion of Urban Population (%)	55.00	66.17	68.00	68.71	69.20	69.85
人口密度（人/平方公里）	Population Density (person/sq.km.)	486	581	597	604	612	621
户籍人口	**Population with Residence Registration**						
年末总户数 （万户）	Total Households at the Year-end (10000 households)	1901.91	2296.61	2388.47	2415.90	2452.26	2468.29
年末总人口 （万人）	Total Population at the Year-end(10000 persons)	7498.54	8521.55	8886.88	9008.38	9164.90	9316.91
性别比 （女=100）	Sex Ratio (female=100)	106.70	106.20	106.20	106.08	106.06	105.75
人口变动情况 （‰）	**Status of Population Changes (‰)**						
出生率	Birth Rate	12.91	11.18	10.80	11.12	11.85	13.68
死亡率	Death Rate	4.77	4.21	4.70	4.32	4.41	4.52
自然增长率	Natural Growth Rate	8.14	6.97	6.10	6.80	7.44	9.16
迁入率	Immigration Rate	16.59	12.07	10.60	8.34	9.72	14.40
迁出率	Emigration Rate	12.94	8.35	7.74	7.45	8.13	9.30
总迁移率	Total Migration Rate	29.53	20.42	18.34	15.79	17.84	23.70
净迁移率	Net Migration Rate	3.65	3.72	2.85	0.89	1.59	5.11
跨省净迁移率	Net Cross-Provincial Migration Rate	1.01	2.52	2.12	0.80	2.14	4.69

3-2 人口自然变动情况
Status of Natural Population Changes

单位：万人、‰ (10000 persons, ‰)

年 份 Year	常住人口 Permanent Population	出生 Birth 出生人数 Number of Birth	出生率 Birth Rate	死亡 Death 死亡人数 Number of Death	死亡率 Death Rate	自然增长 Natural Growth 自然增长人数 Number of Natural Growth	自然增长率 Rate of Natural Growth	人口密度 (人/平方公里) Population Density (person/sq.km.)
1978	5064.15	111.23	22.14	27.35	5.44	83.88	16.70	285
1980	5230.00	118.31	22.82	28.40	5.48	89.91	17.34	294
1982	5419.35	123.98	23.09	31.79	5.92	92.19	17.17	304
1983	5501.85	114.55	21.00	34.47	6.32	80.08	14.68	309
1984	5585.61	114.86	20.75	34.37	6.21	80.49	14.54	313
1985	5670.65	115.70	20.60	35.53	6.33	80.17	14.27	318
1986	5799.75	126.23	22.15	32.48	5.70	93.75	16.45	323
1987	5931.79	128.00	22.12	32.98	5.70	95.02	16.42	328
1988	6066.84	122.90	20.90	29.81	5.07	93.09	15.83	333
1989	6204.96	121.15	20.27	34.25	5.73	86.90	14.54	338
1990	6347.19	140.11	22.26	36.25	5.76	103.86	16.50	353
1991	6527.01	131.31	20.40	38.04	5.91	93.27	14.49	363
1992	6706.45	125.17	18.92	40.00	6.05	85.17	12.87	373
1993	6936.69	120.00	17.59	38.00	5.57	82.00	12.02	386
1994	7209.58	121.00	17.11	38.00	5.37	83.00	11.74	401
1995	7387.49	123.54	16.93	38.91	5.33	84.63	11.60	411
1996	7569.78	124.80	16.69	42.11	5.63	82.69	11.06	421
1997	7779.69	118.40	15.43	37.83	4.93	80.57	10.50	433
1998	7990.03	117.00	14.84	40.00	5.07	77.00	9.77	444
1999	8217.91	110.00	13.57	39.00	4.81	71.00	8.76	457
2000	8650.03	108.85	12.91	40.21	4.77	68.64	8.14	486
2001	8733.18	107.99	12.42	39.63	4.56	68.36	7.86	486
2002	8842.08	103.94	11.82	39.73	4.52	64.21	7.30	492
2003	8962.69	108.00	12.13	41.98	4.71	66.02	7.42	499
2004	9110.66	106.73	11.81	41.62	4.60	65.11	7.21	507
2005	9194.00	107.11	11.70	42.24	4.68	64.87	7.02	511
2006	9442.07	108.96	11.69	41.53	4.46	67.43	7.24	525
2007	9659.52	112.00	11.73	44.00	4.61	68.00	7.12	537
2008	9893.48	112.00	11.46	43.00	4.40	69.00	7.06	550
2009	10130.19	113.00	11.29	43.00	4.29	70.00	6.99	563
2010	10440.94	115.00	11.18	43.27	4.21	71.73	6.97	581
2011	10505.00	109.44	10.45	45.56	4.35	63.88	6.10	584
2012	10594.00	122.37	11.60	49.06	4.65	73.31	6.95	590
2013	10644.00	113.73	10.71	49.80	4.69	63.93	6.02	592
2014	10724.00	115.39	10.80	50.21	4.70	65.18	6.10	597
2015	10849.00	119.95	11.12	46.60	4.32	73.35	6.80	604
2016	10999.00	129.45	11.85	48.17	4.41	81.28	7.44	612
2017	11169.00	151.63	13.68	50.10	4.52	101.53	9.16	621

注：2006—2009年年末常住人口根据2010年第六次全国人口普查快速汇总数据进行平滑调整，出生率、死亡率、自然增长率也作了相应的调整。

Note: Figures of permanent population at the year-end from 2006 to 2009 have been adjusted in accordance with the flash sums of the 6th National Population Census in 2010. Figures of birth rate, death rate, natural growth rate have been adjusted accordingly.

3-3 常住人口构成
Composition of Permanent Population

单位：万人、% (10000 persons, %)

年 份 Year	按性别分 By Sex				按城乡分 By Residence			
	男 Male		女 Female		城镇 Urban		农村 Rural	
	人口数 Population	比重 Proportion	人口数 Population	比重 Proportion	人口数 Population	比重 Proportion	人口数 Population	比重 Proportion
1982	2774.17	51.19	2645.18	48.81	972.23	17.94	4447.12	82.06
1990	3249.76	51.20	3097.43	48.80	2335.77	36.80	4011.42	63.20
2000	4402.87	50.90	4247.16	49.10	4757.52	55.00	3892.51	45.00
2005	4655.84	50.64	4538.16	49.36	5578.92	60.68	3615.08	39.32
2006	4787.13	50.70	4654.94	49.30	5948.50	63.00	3493.57	37.00
2007	4926.36	51.00	4733.16	49.00	6099.02	63.14	3560.50	36.86
2008	5065.46	51.20	4828.02	48.80	6269.50	63.37	3623.98	36.63
2009	5166.40	51.00	4963.79	49.00	6422.54	63.40	3707.65	36.60
2010	5444.95	52.15	4995.99	47.85	6908.77	66.17	3532.17	33.83
2011	5557.15	52.90	4947.86	47.10	6985.83	66.50	3519.18	33.50
2012	5572.44	52.60	5021.56	47.40	7140.36	67.40	3453.64	32.60
2013	5545.52	52.10	5098.48	47.90	7212.37	67.76	3431.63	32.24
2014	5676.21	52.93	5047.79	47.07	7292.32	68.00	3431.68	32.00
2015	5672.94	52.29	5176.06	47.71	7454.35	68.71	3394.65	31.29
2016	5763.48	52.40	5235.52	47.60	7611.31	69.20	3387.69	30.80
2017	5862.61	52.49	5306.39	47.51	7801.55	69.85	3367.45	30.15

注：2006—2009年年末常住人口根据2010年第六次全国人口普查快速汇总数据进行平滑调整。

Note: Figures of Permanent population at the year-end from 2006 to 2009 have been adjusted with flash sums from the 6th National Population Census in 2010.

3-4 常住人口年龄结构和抚养比

Age Composition and Dependency Ratio of Permanent Population

单位：万人、%　　　　(10000 persons, %)

年份 Year	0—14岁 Aged 0-14		15—64岁 Aged 15-64		65岁及以上 Aged 65 and Over		少年儿童抚养比 Children Dependency Ratio	老年人口抚养比 Old Dependency Ratio	总抚养比 Gross Dependency Ratio
	人数 Population	比重 Proportion	人数 Population	比重 Proportion	人数 Population	比重 Proportion			
1982	1802.68	33.61	3267.68	60.93	292.83	5.46	55.16	8.96	64.12
1990	1879.73	29.92	4030.66	64.15	372.58	5.93	46.64	9.24	55.88
2000	2088.56	24.17	6029.96	69.78	523.65	6.05	34.64	8.67	43.31
2005	1960.16	21.32	6552.56	71.27	681.28	7.41	29.91	10.40	40.31
2006	1935.62	20.50	6807.73	72.10	698.71	7.40	28.43	10.26	38.70
2007	1941.56	20.10	6983.83	72.30	734.12	7.60	27.80	10.51	38.31
2008	1949.02	19.70	7162.88	72.40	781.58	7.90	27.21	10.91	38.12
2009	1955.13	19.30	7364.65	72.70	810.42	8.00	26.55	11.00	37.55
2010	1760.40	16.87	7963.03	76.33	708.62	6.79	22.15	8.91	31.06
2011	1775.00	16.90	8016.00	76.30	714.00	6.80	22.14	8.91	31.05
2012	1695.04	16.00	8157.38	77.00	741.58	7.00	20.78	9.09	29.87
2013	1558.28	14.64	8216.10	77.19	869.62	8.17	18.97	10.58	29.55
2014	1649.19	15.38	8187.91	76.35	886.90	8.27	20.14	10.83	30.97
2015	1884.67	17.37	8044.05	74.15	920.28	8.48	23.43	11.44	34.87
2016	1894.67	17.23	8164.05	74.22	940.28	8.55	23.21	11.52	34.72
2017	1922.48	17.21	8283.89	74.17	962.63	8.62	23.21	11.62	34.83

注：1982、1990、2000、2010年常住人口年龄结构使用普查数据，因此合计数据与表3-2不一致。

Note: Age composition of permanent population for the years 1982, 1990, 2000 and 2010 are census year estimates.

3-5 年末户籍总人口

Total Population with Residence Registration at Year-end

单位：万人、%　　(10000 persons，%)

年份 Year	总人口 Total Population	按性别分 By Sex			
		男 Male		女 Female	
		人口数 Total Population	比例 Proportion	人口数 Total Population	比例 Proportion
1978	5064.15	2586.68	51.08	2477.47	48.92
1980	5227.67	2671.28	51.10	2556.39	48.90
1982	5415.35	2771.86	51.19	2643.49	48.81
1983	5494.12	2818.92	51.31	2675.20	48.69
1984	5576.62	2865.90	51.39	2710.72	48.61
1985	5655.60	2909.52	51.44	2746.08	48.56
1986	5740.70	2955.68	51.49	2785.02	48.51
1987	5832.15	3003.09	51.49	2829.06	48.51
1988	5928.31	3053.50	51.51	2874.81	48.49
1989	6024.98	3106.37	51.56	2918.61	48.44
1990	6246.32	3213.20	51.44	3033.12	48.56
1991	6348.95	3266.26	51.45	3082.69	48.55
1992	6463.17	3327.67	51.49	3135.50	48.51
1993	6581.60	3390.37	51.51	3191.23	48.49
1994	6691.46	3450.68	51.57	3240.78	48.43
1995	6788.74	3501.19	51.57	3287.55	48.43
1996	6896.77	3559.54	51.61	3337.23	48.39
1997	7013.73	3620.32	51.62	3393.41	48.38
1998	7115.65	3676.95	51.67	3438.70	48.33
1999	7298.88	3769.70	51.65	3529.18	48.35
2000	7498.54	3871.13	51.63	3627.41	48.37
2001	7565.33	3905.28	51.62	3660.05	48.38
2002	7649.29	3948.25	51.62	3701.04	48.38
2003	7723.42	3989.24	51.65	3734.18	48.35
2004	7804.75	4025.87	51.58	3778.88	48.42
2005	7899.64	4080.74	51.66	3818.90	48.34
2006	8048.71	4154.03	51.61	3894.68	48.39
2007	8156.05	4204.47	51.55	3951.58	48.45
2008	8267.09	4263.24	51.57	4003.85	48.43
2009	8365.98	4309.11	51.51	4056.87	48.49
2010	8521.55	4388.61	51.50	4132.94	48.50
2011	8637.19	4445.48	51.47	4191.71	48.53
2012	8635.89	4448.45	51.51	4187.44	48.49
2013	8759.46	4513.51	51.53	4245.95	48.47
2014	8886.88	4577.10	51.50	4309.78	48.50
2015	9008.38	4637.13	51.48	4371.25	48.52
2016	9164.90	4717.29	51.47	4447.61	48.50
2017	9316.91	4788.55	51.40	4528.36	48.60

注：1．人口密度数为常住人口。
2．2006—2009年年末常住人口根据2010年第六次全国人口普查快速汇总数据进行平滑调整，人口密度也作相应调整。

Note: a) The population density refers to that of the permant population.
b) Figures of permanent population at the year-end from 2006 to 2009 have been adjusted in accordance with the flash sums of the 6th National Population Cescus in 2010. Figures of population density have been adjusted accordingly.

3-6 户籍人口迁移变动情况

Status of Migrant Changes

单位：万人、‰ (10000 persons, ‰)

年份 Year	迁入 Immigration		迁出 Emigration		总迁移 Total Migration		净迁移 Net Migration	
	迁入人数 Number of Immigration	迁入率 Immigration Rate	迁出人数 Number of Emigration	迁出率 Emigration Rate	总迁入数 Total Number of Migration	总迁移率 Total Migration Rate	净迁移人数 Net Number of Migration	净迁移率 Net Migration Rate
1978	81.83	16.29	75.58	15.04	157.41	31.33	6.25	1.25
1980	91.45	17.64	82.09	15.83	173.54	33.47	9.36	1.81
1982	71.63	13.34	65.06	12.11	136.69	25.45	6.57	1.23
1983	66.26	12.14	59.35	10.88	125.61	23.02	6.91	1.26
1984	92.30	16.67	83.31	15.05	175.61	31.72	8.99	1.62
1985	100.10	17.82	84.90	15.12	185.00	32.94	15.20	2.70
1986	85.61	15.02	70.83	12.43	156.44	27.45	14.78	2.59
1987	92.89	16.05	73.26	12.66	166.15	28.71	19.63	3.39
1988	93.82	15.96	73.46	12.49	167.28	28.45	20.36	3.47
1989	95.26	15.94	73.87	12.36	169.13	28.30	21.39	3.58
1990	94.39	15.38	77.07	12.56	171.46	27.94	17.32	2.82
1991	97.23	15.44	83.74	13.30	180.97	28.74	13.49	2.14
1992	135.89	21.21	108.39	16.92	244.28	38.13	27.50	4.29
1993	158.20	24.25	128.06	19.63	286.26	43.88	30.14	4.62
1994	140.93	21.24	115.72	17.44	256.65	38.68	25.21	3.80
1995	108.09	16.04	89.74	13.31	197.83	29.35	18.35	2.73
1996	113.47	16.58	88.88	12.99	202.35	29.57	24.59	3.59
1997	130.94	18.83	98.90	14.22	229.84	33.05	32.04	4.61
1998	117.93	16.69	94.18	13.33	212.11	30.02	23.75	3.36
1999	107.68	14.94	89.13	12.37	196.81	27.31	18.55	2.57
2000	122.72	16.59	95.76	12.94	218.48	29.53	26.96	3.65
2001	109.88	14.59	92.34	12.26	202.22	26.85	17.54	2.33
2002	102.26	13.44	81.95	10.77	184.21	24.21	20.31	2.67
2003	105.27	13.70	83.22	10.83	188.49	24.53	22.05	2.87
2004	133.91	17.25	104.26	13.43	238.17	30.68	29.65	3.82
2005	107.21	13.65	70.45	8.97	177.66	22.62	36.76	4.68
2006	145.49	18.25	80.56	10.10	226.05	28.35	64.93	8.14
2007	119.95	14.80	71.67	8.85	191.62	23.65	48.28	5.96
2008	110.56	13.46	79.47	9.68	190.03	23.14	31.09	3.79
2009	96.80	11.64	64.93	7.81	161.73	19.45	31.87	3.83
2010	101.90	12.07	70.48	8.35	172.38	20.42	31.43	3.72
2011	94.47	11.01	65.37	7.62	159.84	18.63	29.10	3.39
2012	97.91	11.34	112.62	13.04	210.53	24.38	-14.70	-1.70
2013	97.86	11.25	77.72	8.94	175.58	20.19	20.14	2.32
2014	93.48	10.60	68.29	7.74	161.78	18.34	25.19	2.85
2015	74.65	8.34	66.67	7.45	141.32	15.79	7.98	0.89
2016	88.31	9.72	73.84	8.13	162.15	17.84	14.47	1.59
2017	133.09	14.40	85.91	9.30	219.00	23.70	47.18	5.11

3-7 各市年末常住人口数

Permanent Population at Year-end by City

单位：万人 (10000 persons)

市 别	City	2000	2005	2010	2012	2013	2014	2015	2016	2017
全 省	**Provincial Total**	**8650.03**	**9194.00**	**10440.94**	**10594.00**	**10644.00**	**10724.00**	**10849.00**	**10999.00**	**11169.00**
广 州	Guangzhou	994.80	949.68	1270.96	1283.89	1292.68	1308.05	1350.11	1404.35	1449.84
深 圳	Shenzhen	701.24	827.75	1037.20	1054.74	1062.89	1077.89	1137.87	1190.84	1252.83
珠 海	Zhuhai	123.65	141.57	156.16	158.26	159.03	161.42	163.41	167.53	176.54
汕 头	Shantou	467.78	494.45	539.62	544.81	547.91	552.37	555.21	557.92	560.82
佛 山	Foshan	534.05	580.03	719.91	726.18	729.57	735.06	743.06	746.27	765.67
韶 关	Shaoguan	273.65	292.26	283.02	286.87	289.27	290.89	293.15	295.61	297.92
河 源	Heyuan	226.78	278.24	295.82	301.01	303.76	306.32	307.35	308.10	309.11
梅 州	Meizhou	380.52	411.84	424.46	429.41	430.70	432.33	434.08	436.08	437.43
惠 州	Huizhou	321.80	370.69	460.11	467.40	470.00	472.66	475.55	477.50	477.70
汕 尾	Shanwei	245.71	279.87	293.90	296.90	298.62	300.66	302.16	303.66	297.76
东 莞	Dongguan	644.84	656.07	822.48	829.23	831.66	834.31	825.41	826.14	834.25
中 山	Zhongshan	236.47	243.46	312.27	315.50	317.39	319.27	320.96	323.00	326.00
江 门	Jiangmen	395.24	410.29	445.08	448.27	449.76	451.14	451.95	454.40	456.17
阳 江	Yangjiang	217.20	232.14	242.53	247.00	247.96	249.95	251.12	252.84	254.29
湛 江	Zhanjiang	603.43	668.95	700.38	710.92	716.71	721.24	724.14	727.30	730.50
茂 名	Maoming	524.82	584.04	582.64	596.76	601.25	604.90	608.08	612.32	620.41
肇 庆	Zhaoqing	337.69	367.60	392.22	398.23	402.21	403.58	405.96	408.46	411.54
清 远	Qingyuan	314.98	359.37	370.38	376.60	379.11	381.91	383.45	384.60	386.00
潮 州	Chaozhou	240.44	252.01	267.21	270.00	271.21	272.04	264.05	264.60	265.08
揭 阳	Jieyang	524.61	559.69	588.30	595.59	599.47	603.54	605.89	609.40	608.60
云 浮	Yunfu	215.49	233.99	236.29	241.65	242.84	244.46	246.05	248.08	250.54
按经济区域分	By Region									
珠 三 角	Pearl River Delta	4289.78	4547.14	5616.39	5689.64	5715.19	5763.38	5874.27	5998.49	6150.54
东 翼	Eastern Region	1478.54	1586.02	1689.03	1709.69	1717.21	1728.61	1727.31	1735.58	1732.26
西 翼	Western Region	1345.45	1485.13	1525.55	1556.85	1565.92	1576.09	1583.35	1592.46	1605.20
山 区	Mountainous Region	1411.42	1575.7	1609.97	1637.82	1645.68	1655.91	1664.07	1672.47	1681.00

注：1.2000年全省数据含根据普查误差率推算的漏登人口。
2.2006—2009年年末常住人口根据2010年第六次全国人口普查快速汇总数据进行平滑调整。
3.2012年各市年末常住人口与全省差额14.78万人，为难以确定的常住地人口。
4.2017年，深圳市包含深汕合作区常住人口。

Note: 1. Data for the permanent population of 2000 has been adjusted to account for the unregistered population, per the Population Census Error Rate
2. Data for the permanent population from 2006 to 2009 have been adjusted with flash sums from the 6th National Population Census in 2010
3. In the data for 2012, there is a population difference of 147,800 between the permenant population of cities and provinces. This difference is a result of difficulties defining the permenant residence of a portion of the population
4. Data for the 2017 permanent population of Shenzhen includes the permanent population of the Shenshan Special Cooperation Zone

3-8 各市城镇人口占常住人口的比例

Proportion of Urban Population to Permanent Population by City

单位：%　　(%)

市　别	City	2000	2005	2010	2012	2013	2014	2015	2016	2017
全　省	**Provincial Total**	**55.00**	**60.68**	**66.17**	**67.40**	**67.76**	**68.00**	**68.71**	**69.20**	**69.85**
广　州	Guangzhou	83.79	91.51	83.78	85.02	85.27	85.43	85.53	86.06	86.14
深　圳	Shenzhen	92.46	100.00	100.00	100.00	100.00	100.00	100.00	100.00	99.74
珠　海	Zhuhai	85.48	87.90	87.65	87.82	87.85	87.87	88.07	88.80	89.37
汕　头	Shantou	67.00	72.34	68.46	69.50	69.79	69.85	70.22	70.30	70.39
佛　山	Foshan	75.06	78.39	94.09	94.87	94.88	94.89	94.94	94.95	94.96
韶　关	Shaoguan	51.13	49.76	52.53	53.30	53.73	53.80	54.29	54.79	55.49
河　源	Heyuan	26.53	32.47	40.04	40.46	40.65	41.26	42.15	43.04	43.94
梅　州	Meizhou	37.21	41.63	43.01	43.57	46.00	46.90	47.79	48.59	49.49
惠　州	Huizhou	51.66	55.01	61.84	63.90	66.00	67.00	68.15	69.05	69.55
汕　尾	Shanwei	52.58	51.88	54.18	54.60	54.70	54.70	55.03	55.08	55.06
东　莞	Dongguan	60.04	73.02	88.46	88.67	88.75	88.81	88.82	89.14	89.86
中　山	Zhongshan	60.67	74.29	87.82	87.92	88.00	88.07	88.12	88.20	88.28
江　门	Jiangmen	47.08	56.78	62.30	63.20	64.10	64.20	64.84	65.06	65.81
阳　江	Yangjiang	41.92	44.09	46.81	48.00	48.80	49.05	49.91	50.81	51.61
湛　江	Zhanjiang	38.47	39.71	36.68	38.30	39.10	39.81	40.74	41.44	42.09
茂　名	Maoming	37.45	39.30	35.06	37.43	38.33	39.01	40.02	40.80	41.90
肇　庆	Zhaoqing	32.52	38.99	42.39	42.62	43.82	44.01	45.16	46.08	46.78
清　远	Qingyuan	32.60	38.46	47.54	47.93	48.00	48.30	49.07	50.00	50.70
潮　州	Chaozhou	43.41	53.62	62.75	63.15	63.15	63.41	63.80	64.00	64.50
揭　阳	Jieyang	37.91	41.15	47.31	49.00	50.03	50.53	50.89	51.00	51.08
云　浮	Yunfu	35.86	37.26	36.96	39.10	39.34	39.47	40.23	40.95	41.20
按经济区域分	By Region									
珠三角	Pearl River Delta	71.59	77.32	82.72	83.84	84.03	84.12	84.59	84.85	85.29
东　翼	Eastern Region	50.45	54.75	57.71	59.05	59.38	59.55	59.93	60.02	60.07
西　翼	Western Region	38.64	40.23	37.67	39.72	40.45	41.03	42.01	42.68	43.52
山　区	Mountainous Region	36.96	40.16	44.29	45.30	45.98	46.37	47.17	47.85	48.58

注：1．本表2000年、2005年数据按国家统计局1999年发布的《关于统计上划分城乡的规定(试行)》计算；2006年起数据按国家统计局2006年颁布的《关于统计上划分城乡的暂行规定》计算。
2．2006–2009年年末常住人口根据2010年第六次全国人口普查快速汇总数据进行平滑调整，城镇人口占常住人口比重也作相应调整。
3．深圳市包含深汕合作区人口数。

Note: a) The 2000 and 2005 data in this table are calculated according to Interim Regulations on Statistical Classification of Urban and Rural Populationissued by National Bureau of Statistics in 1999. The 2006 data are calculated according to Provisional Regulations on Statistical Classification of Urban and Rural Population issued by National Bureau of Statistics in 2006.
b) Figures of permanent population at the year-end from 2006 to 2009 have been adjusted in accordance with the flash sums of the 6th National Population Cescus in 2010 and the proportion of urban population to permanent population is also adjusted.
c) In 2017,figures of permanent population of Shenzhen include the data of the Shenshan Special Cooperation Zone.

3-9 各市年末户籍人口数（2017年）

Total Population with Residence Registration at Year-end by City (2017)

单位：万人、% (10000 persons，%)

市别	City	总人口 Total Population	按性别分 By Sex 男 Male 人口数 Total Population	男 Male 比例 Proportion	女 Female 人口数 Total Population	女 Female 比例 Proportion
全省	**Provincial Total**	**9316.91**	**4788.55**	**51.40**	**4528.36**	**48.60**
广州	Guangzhou	897.87	449.39	50.05	448.48	49.95
深圳	Shenzhen	445.74	225.90	50.68	219.84	49.32
珠海	Zhuhai	118.87	59.88	50.37	59.00	49.63
汕头	Shantou	565.44	284.14	50.25	281.30	49.75
佛山	Foshan	419.59	206.90	49.31	212.69	50.69
韶关	Shaoguan	335.29	172.95	51.58	162.34	48.42
河源	Heyuan	372.95	190.78	51.15	182.17	48.85
梅州	Meizhou	550.11	283.29	51.50	266.82	48.50
惠州	Huizhou	369.24	186.35	50.47	182.89	49.53
汕尾	Shanwei	362.82	189.14	52.13	173.68	47.87
东莞	Dongguan	211.31	106.30	50.30	105.01	49.70
中山	Zhongshan	170.47	83.93	49.24	86.54	50.76
江门	Jiangmen	396.37	199.26	50.27	197.10	49.73
阳江	Yangjiang	297.08	157.65	53.07	139.43	46.93
湛江	Zhanjiang	838.94	446.31	53.20	392.63	46.80
茂名	Maoming	803.83	429.67	53.45	374.16	46.55
肇庆	Zhaoqing	445.65	231.39	51.92	214.26	48.08
清远	Qingyuan	436.84	226.62	51.88	210.23	48.12
潮州	Chaozhou	275.50	139.64	50.68	135.86	49.32
揭阳	Jieyang	703.23	361.45	51.40	341.78	48.60
云浮	Yunfu	299.78	157.63	52.58	142.15	47.42
按经济区域分	By Region					
珠三角	Pearl River Delta	3475.10	1749.29	50.34	1725.81	49.66
东翼	Eastern Region	1906.99	974.37	51.09	932.62	48.91
西翼	Western Region	1939.84	1033.63	53.28	906.22	46.72
山区	Mountainous Region	1994.98	1031.26	51.69	963.71	48.31

3-10 各市年末户籍迁移人口数（2017年）

Number of Migrant Population at the Year-end by City (2017)

单位：人 (person)

市别	City	迁入 Immigration		迁出 Emigration		净迁移 Net Migration	
		省内迁入 Within Guangdong	省外迁入 Outside Guangdong	迁往省内 Within Guangdong	迁往省外 Outside Guangdong	省内 Within Guangdong	省外 Outside Guangdong
全　省	**Provincial Total**	**708635**	**622269**	**670612**	**188517**	**38023**	**433752**
广　州	Guangzhou	87233	93352	22166	24948	65067	68404
深　圳	Shenzhen	118192	235515	5806	19473	112386	216042
珠　海	Zhuhai	16370	23460	4804	9518	11566	13942
汕　头	Shantou	9553	5174	29641	4692	-20088	482
佛　山	Foshan	71364	64883	6944	6583	64420	58300
韶　关	Shaoguan	11747	6018	32337	6451	-20590	-433
河　源	Heyuan	10745	4262	35802	11312	-25057	-7050
梅　州	Meizhou	23986	6284	66687	6630	-42701	-346
惠　州	Huizhou	47612	24869	44327	7516	3285	17353
汕　尾	Shanwei	14573	5271	33646	8696	-19073	-3425
东　莞	Dongguan	25225	46643	3575	3619	21650	43024
中　山	Zhongshan	30101	37201	2265	3026	27836	34175
江　门	Jiangmen	56597	12001	60510	9688	-3913	2313
阳　江	Yangjiang	4805	2836	14279	1864	-9474	972
湛　江	Zhanjiang	13594	7499	43563	17430	-29969	-9931
茂　名	Maoming	40237	12192	72332	17956	-32095	-5764
肇　庆	Zhaoqing	31603	9082	40778	5742	-9175	3340
清　远	Qingyuan	30935	12435	31329	4519	-394	7916
潮　州	Chaozhou	3602	2032	15424	2151	-11822	-119
揭　阳	Jieyang	46996	7401	83947	11813	-36951	-4412
云　浮	Yunfu	13565	3859	20450	4890	-6885	-1031
按经济区域分	By Region						
珠三角	Pearl River Delta	484297	547006	191175	90113	293122	456893
东　翼	Eastern Region	74724	19878	162658	27352	-87934	-7474
西　翼	Western Region	58636	22527	130174	37250	-71538	-14723
山　区	Mountainous Region	90978	32858	186605	33802	-95627	-944

主要统计指标解释

总人口 指一定时点、一定地区范围内有生命的个人的总和。按不同的统计范围可分为常住人口和户籍人口；统计时点通常为每年 12 月 31 日 24 时。

0-14 岁人口比例 （少年儿童人口系数或少年儿童人口比例） 指 0-14 岁的少年儿童人口与同期总人口之比，反映人口的年龄结构特征。通常以百分比表示。

15-64 岁人口比例 （成年人口系数或成年人口比例） 指 15-64 岁的成年人口与同期总人口之比，反映人口的年龄结构特征。通常以百分比表示。

65 岁及以上人口比例 （老年人口系数或老年人口比例） 指 65 岁及以上的老年人口与同期总人口之比，反映人口的老龄化程度。通常以百分比表示。

城镇人口比例 指城镇人口与同期总人口之比，反映该区域人口的城镇化水平。通常以百分比表示。

人口密度 指某一时点单位土地面积上居住的人口数。通常以每平方公里常住的人口数表示。

性别比 总人口（或分年龄人口）中男性人数与女性人数之比。通常以每 100 个女性人口相应有多少男性人口表示。

其计算公式为：性别比=男性人口数/女性人口数×100

出生率(也称粗出生率) 指某一人口在一定时期（通常为一年）内活产婴儿数与同期总人口的生存人口数（或同期平均总人口、年中人口数）之比。通常以千分比表示。

死亡率(也称粗死亡率) 指一定时期（通常为一年）内全部死亡人数与同期平均总人口之比，反映该时期人口的死亡强度。通常以千分比表示。

自然增长率 指一定时期（通常为一年）内人口自然增加数（出生人口减死亡人口）与同期平均总人口之比。通常以千分比表示。

迁入率（迁出率） 指一定时期（通常为一年）内迁入（迁出）人数与同期平均总人口之比。通常以千分比表示。

总迁移率 指一定时期（通常为一年）内人口迁移总量（迁入人口加迁出人口）与同期平均总人口之比。通常以千分比表示。

净迁移率 指一定时期（通常为一年）内人口迁入迁出相抵后（迁入人口减迁出人口）与同期平均总人口之比。通常以千分比表示。

跨省净迁移率 指一定时期（通常为一年）内省外迁入人口和迁往省外（含出国）人口之差与同期平均总人口之比。通常以千分比表示。

总抚养比 总抚养比也称总负担系数，是指人口总体中非劳动年龄人口数（0-14 岁人口+65 岁及以上人口）与劳动年龄人口数（15-64 岁人口）之比，通常用百分比表示。

少年儿童抚养比 少年儿童抚养比也称少年儿童抚养系数，是指某一人口中少年儿童人口数（0-14 岁人口）与劳动年龄人口数（15-64 岁人口）之比，通常用百分比表示。

老年人口抚养比 老年人口抚养比也称老年人口抚养系数，是指某一人口中老年人口数（65 岁及以上人口）与劳动年龄人口数（15-64 岁人口）之比，通常用百分比表示。

Explanatory Notes on Main Statistical Indicators

Total Population refers to the total number of people alive within a given area at a certain point of time. It can be divided into the permanent population and the population with residence registration according to different statistical coverage. The reference time of the statistics on total population is usually taken at midnight of December 31.

Proportion of Population Aged 0-14 (coefficient of child population or proportion of child population) refers to the proportion of population aged 0-14 in the total population during the same period of time. It is an indicator of age structure, usually expressed in percentage.

Proportion of Population Aged 15-64 (coefficient of adult population or proportion of adult population) refers to the proportion of population aged 15-64 in the total population during the same period of time. It is an indicator of age structure, usually expressed in percentage.

Proportion of Population Aged 65 and Over (coefficient of aged population or proportion of aged population) refers to the proportion of population aged 65 and over in the total population during the same period of time. It is an indicator of population ageing, usually expressed in percentage.

Proportion of Urban Population refers to the proportion of urban population in the total population during the same period of time. It is an indicator of population urbanization in a certain region, usually expressed in percentage.

Population Density refers to the number of people located in a given land area at a certain point of time, usually expressed in the number of permanent population per square kilometer.

Sex Ratio refers to the ratio of the male population to the female population among the total population (or population grouped by age), usually expressed in the number of males per 100 females.

The following formula is used:

Sex Ration = Number of Male Population / Number of Female Population ×100

Birth Rate (or Crude Birth Rate) refers to the ratio of live births to the total number of population alive (or average population, mid-year population) during a certain period of time (usually one year), expressed in ‰.

Death Rate (or Crude Death Rate) refers to the ratio of deaths to the average population during a certain period of time (usually one year), expressed in ‰. Death rate reflects the death intensity of the population during the same period of time.

Natural Growth Rate refers to the ratio of natural increase in population (number of births minus number of deaths) during a certain period of time (usually one year) to the average population of the same period, expressed in ‰.

Immigration Rate (Emigration Rate) refers to the ratio of the number of immigration (emigration) to the average population during a certain period of time (usually one year), expressed in ‰.

Total Migration Rate refers to the ratio of the total number of migration (number of immigration plus number of emigration) to the average population during a certain period of time (usually one year),expressed in ‰.

Net Migration Rate refers to the ratio of the net number of migration (number of immigration minus number of emigration) to the average population during a certain period of time (usually one year), expressed in ‰

Net Migration Rate across Province refers to the ratio of the number of immigration from outside the province minus the number of emigration to outside the province (including those going abroad) to the average population during a certain period of time (usually one year), expressed in ‰.

Gross Dependency Ratio also called gross dependency coefficient, refers to the ratio of the non-working-age population to the working-age population, expressed in %.

Children Dependency Ratio also called children dependency coefficient, refers to the ratio of the children population to the working-age population, expressed in %.

Old Dependency Ratio also called old dependency coefficient, refers to the ratio of the elderly population to the working-age population, expressed in %.

四、就业和工资

EMPLOYMENT AND WAGES

四　就业和工资

简要说明

一、本篇资料反映广东劳动就业与工资的基本情况。主要内容包括全社会就业人员数、城镇单位在岗职工人数、城镇私营企业和个体工商业就业人数、在岗职工工资总额、平均工资和城镇登记失业率等。

二、本篇资料由广东省统计局人口和就业处整理提供。

三、本篇资料主要根据国家统计调查制度搜集汇总，部分由省人力资源和社会保障厅提供并加工整理。

四、本篇资料中的城镇单位就业人员、在岗职工及其工资统计范围只包括城镇国有、集体及其他经济类型单位，不包括私营企业和个体劳动者。根据国家劳动统计报表制度的统一规定，从 2013 年年报起，将原属于乡镇企业且符合城镇非私营单位条件的“四上”企业（即规模以上工业企业、有资质的建筑业及全部房地产开发经营企业、限额以上批发和零售业、限额以上住宿和餐饮业、部分规模以上服务业企业）纳入城镇单位就业人员及工资统计的范围。本篇“城镇单位”均指“城镇非私营单位”。

五、1998 年，劳动统计年报中对全部调查单位改按企业登记注册类型分组。即国有单位中不再包括国有联营和有限责任公司中的国有独资公司；城镇集体单位中不再包括集体联营和股份合作企业；其他单位则包括国有联营和有限责任公司中的国有独资公司，集体联营和股份合作企业。

4 Employment and Wages

Brief Introduction

Ⅰ. The data in this chapter show the basic conditions of labor employment and wages of Guangdong Province, mainly including the number of all employed persons, number of fully employed staff and workers in units in urban areas, number of the persons employed in urban private enterprises and self-employed persons in industry and commerce, total wages and average wage of fully employed staff and workers and registered urban unemployment rate, etc.

Ⅱ. The data in this chapter are prepared and provided by the Division of Population and Employment Statistics of Statistics Bureau of Guangdong Province.

Ⅲ. The data in this chapter are collected and tabulated mainly in accordance with the statistical survey scheme of the National Bureau of Statistics, part of which are processed and prepared from figures provided by Guangdong Provincial Department of Human Resources and Social Security.

Ⅳ. The statistical coverage of urban unit employed persons, fully employed staff and workers, staff and workers and wages in this chapter only includes state-owned units, collective-owned units and other types of ownership in urban areas, but excludes private enterprises and self-employed individuals. According to the The National Reporting Form System on Labour Wage Statistics, from the 2013 annual report.,the four enterprises original part of township enterprise and urban corporate unit excluding private units those are industrial enterprises above designated size,quality of the construction industry and real estate development enterprises,wholesale and retail trade enterprises above designated size, hotels and catering service enterprises above designated size and part of the service industry above designated size, are brought into the scope of statistics on employed person in urban areas and total wage bills. In this chapter, urban corporate units refers to urban corporate unit excluding private units.

Ⅴ. In annual labor reports since 1998, survey units are categorized by registration status. As a result, exclusively state-invested companies in state-owned joint ownership units and limited liability companies are no longer entered as state-owned units, and collective-owned joint ownership units and cooperative units are no longer entered as urban collective-owned units. These units excluded from the categories of state-owned joint ownership units and urban collective-owned units are now categorized as units of other types of ownership.

4-1 就业人员主要指标
Main Indicators of Employed Persons

指 标	Item	2000	2010	2014	2015	2016	2017
就业人员人数 （万人）	**Number of Employed Persons (10000 persons)**	**3989.32**	**5870.48**	**6183.23**	**6219.31**	**6279.22**	**6340.79**
第一产业	Primary Industry	1593.68	1435.17	1382.41	1375.15	1365.43	1359.12
第二产业	Secondary Industry	1114.86	2487.25	2560.65	2546.57	2543.07	2541.82
第三产业	Tertiary Industry	1280.78	1948.06	2240.16	2297.58	2370.72	2439.85
#城镇单位就业人员	Urban Employed Persons	759.21	1118.52	1973.28	1948.04	1957.57	1963.10
国有单位	State-owned Units	425.52	400.65	396.20	388.81	387.75	384.09
城镇集体单位	Urban Collective-owned Units	105.97	57.66	56.69	50.34	47.83	45.46
其他各种单位	Units of Other Types of Ownership	227.73	660.21	1520.39	1508.89	1521.99	1533.56
#城镇私营企业就业人员	Employed Persons in Urban Private Enterprises	161.73	896.69	1112.98	1161.03	1178.64	1255.09
#城镇个体就业人员	Self-employed Individuals in Urban Areas	278.40	429.99	734.53	751.05	756.92	770.97
城镇登记失业率 (%)	Registered Unemployment Rate in Urban Area (%)	2.50	2.52	2.44	2.45	2.47	2.47
城镇单位就业人员工资总额 （亿元）	**Earnings of Urban Employed Persons (100 million yuan)**	**1057.57**	**4484.29**	**11764.82**	**12918.81**	**14156.81**	**15511.55**
国有单位	State-owned Units	612.17	1951.16	2714.28	2975.96	3314.72	3742.62
城镇集体单位	Urban Collective-owned Units	93.04	129.01	229.52	227.71	234.59	249.68
其他各种单位	Units of Other Types of Ownership	352.37	2404.12	8821.02	9715.14	10607.49	11519.25
城镇单位就业人员平均工资 （元）	**Average Labor Remuneration of Urban Employed Persons (yuan)**	**13859**	**40432**	**59481**	**65788**	**72326**	**79183**
国有单位	State-owned Units	14296	49027	68803	76870	86159	98074
城镇集体单位	Urban Collective-owned Units	8605	22453	40509	45027	49357	55013
其他各种单位	Units of Other Types of Ownership	15538	36779	57777	63664	69552	75193

注：2003年起城镇职工改为城镇就业人员，2000年的数据作了相应调整。2006—2010年就业人员人数，根据“全省第六次人口普查”资料作了相应调整。2014—2015年根据第三次经济普查结果对城镇个体就业人员数据进行推算。

Note: Since 2003, the urban staff and workers have been referred to as the urban employed persons. The figures in 2000 are adjusted correspondingly. Figures of "Number of Employed Persons" from 2006 to 2010 have been adjusted in accordance with the results of the 6th population census. The data on self-employed individuals from 2014 to 2015 have been adjusted in accordance with the result of the third national economic census.

4-2 就业人员年末人数

Number of Employed Persons at the Year-end

单位：万人 (10000 persons)

年份 Year	就业人员年末人数 Number of Employed Persons at the Year-end	#城镇单位就业人员 Urban Employed Persons	国有单位 State-owned Units	城镇集体单位 Urban Collective-owned Units	其他单位 Units of Other Types of Ownership	#城镇私营企业从业人员年末人数 Employed Persons in Urban Private Enterprises	#城镇个体就业人员年末人数 Self-employed Individuals in Urban Areas
1978	2275.95	515.85	369.04	146.81			
1979	2304.95	535.37	378.57	156.80			
1980	2367.78	563.62	400.19	163.43			
1981	2423.79	587.34	422.03	165.31			
1982	2521.38	608.12	443.43	164.69			
1983	2569.70	612.65	446.51	166.14			
1984	2637.49	631.77	429.65	197.89	4.23		
1985	2731.11	660.82	449.40	203.32	8.10		
1986	2811.92	686.20	465.59	208.85	11.76		
1987	2910.99	720.34	485.59	216.16	18.59		
1988	2994.72	747.67	503.20	216.96	27.51		
1989	3041.27	762.61	511.88	212.50	38.23		
1990	3118.10	785.49	528.13	207.62	49.74		
1991	3259.20	827.58	544.55	216.86	66.17	19.58	121.63
1992	3367.21	858.12	559.71	216.57	81.84	26.21	146.75
1993	3433.91	877.16	563.63	199.99	113.54	39.51	191.30
1994	3493.15	901.57	568.80	202.86	129.91	58.22	209.90
1995	3551.20	931.58	565.48	204.12	161.98	76.00	168.90
1996	3641.30	920.55	565.68	193.24	161.63	89.40	241.76
1997	3701.90	912.74	556.56	181.44	174.74	105.80	250.71
1998	3783.87	897.98	521.34	161.50	215.13	126.42	265.08
1999	3796.32	793.54	449.87	122.70	220.97	132.95	268.00
2000	3989.32	759.21	425.52	105.97	227.73	161.73	278.40
2001	4058.63	737.12	400.12	91.33	245.67	182.09	280.71
2002	4134.37	751.23	382.91	82.81	285.51	303.07	295.68
2003	4395.93	781.14	376.56	78.47	326.11	443.70	346.56
2004	4681.89	830.72	374.34	72.28	384.10	541.21	365.38
2005	5022.97	904.27	380.19	68.70	455.38	660.05	369.17
2006	5177.02	954.44	384.78	67.25	502.41	666.04	324.98
2007	5341.50	1001.46	381.00	65.49	554.97	733.14	371.53
2008	5471.72	1007.87	385.14	60.64	562.09	761.43	375.79
2009	5688.62	1055.03	389.17	58.33	607.53	834.06	433.40
2010	5870.48	1118.52	400.65	57.66	660.21	896.69	429.99
2011	5960.74	1238.22	423.88	62.83	751.51	899.46	433.18
2012	5965.95	1303.98	430.33	55.28	818.38	907.42	441.15
2013	6117.68	1966.98	402.75	58.52	1505.71	935.31	493.06
2014	6183.23	1973.28	396.20	56.69	1520.39	1112.98	734.53
2015	6219.31	1948.04	388.81	50.34	1508.89	1161.03	751.05
2016	6279.22	1957.57	387.75	47.83	1521.99	1178.64	756.92
2017	6340.79	1963.10	384.09	45.46	1533.56	1255.09	770.97

注：2006—2010年就业人员人数，根据全省第六次人口普查资料作了相应调整。2014—2015年根据第三次经济普查结果对城镇个体就业人员数据进行推算。1993年及以前城镇单位就业人员为城镇单位职工人数。

Note: Figures of Number of Employed Persons from 2006 to 2010 have been adjusted in accordance with the results of the 6th population census. The data on self-employed individuals from 2014 to 2015 have been adjusted in accordance with the result of the third national economic census. Data of urban employed persons before 1993 are data of urban employed staff and workers.

4–3 按三次产业分就业人员年末人数

Number of Employed Persons at Year-end by Three strata of Industry

年 份 Year	就业人数（万人） Total Emplcyed Persons (10000 persons)	第一产业 Primary Industry	第二产业 Secondary Industry	第三产业 Tertiary Industry	构成（%）Composition in Percentage(%) 第一产业 Primary Industry	第二产业 Secondary Industry	第三产业 Tertiary Industry
1978	2275.95	1677.01	312.94	286.00	73.7	13.7	12.6
1979	2304.95	1659.01	381.11	264.83	72.0	16.5	11.5
1980	2367.78	1673.57	404.80	289.41	70.7	17.1	12.2
1981	2423.79	1699.85	409.93	314.01	70.1	16.9	13.0
1982	2521.38	1723.46	447.18	350.74	68.4	17.7	13.9
1983	2569.70	1729.47	458.80	381.43	67.3	17.9	14.8
1984	2637.49	1679.46	498.09	459.94	63.7	18.9	17.4
1985	2731.11	1646.82	614.52	469.77	60.3	22.5	17.2
1986	2811.92	1624.15	637.76	550.01	57.8	22.6	19.6
1987	2910.99	1605.10	704.24	601.65	55.1	24.2	20.7
1988	2994.72	1607.11	743.91	643.70	53.7	24.8	21.5
1989	3041.27	1632.36	747.78	661.13	53.7	24.6	21.7
1990	3118.10	1651.71	848.37	618.02	53.0	27.2	19.8
1991	3259.20	1645.25	932.76	681.19	50.5	28.6	20.9
1992	3367.21	1594.32	1024.98	747.91	47.3	30.5	22.2
1993	3433.91	1512.88	1115.42	805.61	44.1	32.4	23.5
1994	3493.15	1478.37	1172.84	841.94	42.3	33.6	24.1
1995	3551.20	1473.60	1199.00	878.60	41.5	33.8	24.7
1996	3641.30	1481.40	1218.00	941.90	40.7	33.4	25.9
1997	3701.90	1511.38	1217.25	973.27	40.8	32.9	26.3
1998	3783.87	1554.33	1214.96	1014.58	41.1	32.1	26.8
1999	3796.32	1574.25	1181.58	1040.49	41.5	31.1	27.4
2000	3989.32	1593.68	1114.86	1280.78	40.0	27.9	32.1
2001	4058.63	1587.48	1131.96	1339.19	39.1	27.9	33.0
2002	4134.37	1572.92	1202.92	1358.53	38.0	29.1	32.9
2003	4395.93	1617.69	1557.19	1221.05	36.8	35.4	27.8
2004	4681.89	1622.50	1727.86	1331.53	34.7	36.9	28.4
2005	5022.97	1609.89	1916.16	1496.92	32.1	38.1	29.8
2006	5177.02	1562.17	2015.88	1598.97	30.2	38.9	30.9
2007	5341.50	1562.19	2102.28	1677.04	29.2	39.4	31.4
2008	5471.72	1526.66	2172.93	1772.13	27.9	39.7	32.4
2009	5688.62	1514.04	2292.05	1882.53	26.6	40.3	33.1
2010	5870.48	1435.17	2487.25	1948.06	24.4	42.4	33.2
2011	5960.74	1427.34	2526.48	2006.92	23.9	42.4	33.7
2012	5965.95	1418.38	2509.69	2037.88	23.8	42.0	34.2
2013	6117.68	1405.06	2563.50	2149.12	23.0	41.9	35.1
2014	6183.23	1382.41	2560.65	2240.16	22.4	41.4	36.2
2015	6219.31	1375.15	2546.57	2297.58	22.1	41.0	36.9
2016	6279.22	1365.43	2543.07	2370.72	21.7	40.5	37.8
2017	6340.79	1359.12	2541.82	2439.85	21.4	40.1	38.5

4-4 按各种分组的就业人员年末人数

Number of Employed Persons at the Year-end by Grouping

单位：万人 (10000 persons)

项　目	Item	2005	2010	2015	2016	2017
就业人员总数	**Total Number of Employed Persons**	**5022.97**	**5870.48**	**6219.31**	**6279.22**	**6340.79**
按登记注册类型分组	Grouped by Status of Registration					
#国有单位	State-owned Units	380.19	392.84	393.12	391.26	388.59
集体单位	Collective-owned Units	2037.35	1856.34	1572.62	1565.95	1550.34
股份合作单位	Cooperative Units	20.19	25.51	22.36	22.59	23.30
联营单位	Joint Ownership	16.53	15.99	8.95	9.04	8.62
有限责任公司	Limited Liability Corporations	205.69	307.64	593.00	615.02	644.78
股份有限公司	Share-holding Corporations Ltd.	52.33	87.29	168.18	186.28	190.91
外商投资单位	Foreign Funded Units	216.68	289.61	340.58	311.61	307.15
港、澳、台商投资单位	Units Funded by Entrepreneurs from Hong Kong, Macao and Taiwan	602.72	732.06	613.39	615.29	605.95
私营企业	Private Enterprises	666.20	1039.69	1291.43	1329.03	1369.37
个体经济	Individuals	732.92	1044.11	1126.47	1144.78	1166.02
按国民经济行业分组	Grouped by Economic Sector					
农、林、牧、渔业	Farming, Forestry, Animal Husbandry and Fishery	1609.89	1435.17	1376.37	1367.94	1361.61
采矿业	Mining and Quarrying	15.92	12.48	13.30	13.65	13.36
制造业	Manufacture	1666.23	2214.67	2236.33	2230.35	2220.03
电力、热力、燃气及水生产和供应业	Production and Supply of Electric Power,Gas and Water	24.27	31.94	32.97	33.93	34.60
建筑业	Construction	209.74	228.17	265.74	269.41	277.99
批发和零售业	Wholesale and Retail Trade	562.18	763.92	819.69	844.28	851.25
交通运输、仓储和邮政业	Transport, Storage and Postal Services	117.65	160.53	184.87	186.80	192.31
住宿和餐饮业	Hotels and Catering Services	166.67	201.71	227.92	235.30	237.98
信息传输、软件和信息技术服务业	Information Transmission, Computer Services and Software	36.72	53.94	86.62	94.96	99.92
金融业	Finance	29.83	55.28	55.40	58.12	58.66
房地产业	Real Estate	44.31	69.58	104.47	108.28	130.22
租赁和商务服务业	Leasing and Business Services	61.11	90.21	158.26	164.31	171.64
科学研究、技术服务业	Scientific Research and Technical Services	16.35	26.41	55.16	58.35	62.95
水利、环境和公共设施管理业	Water Conservancy, Environment and Public Facilities Management	15.42	19.88	25.93	26.32	27.07
居民服务、修理和其他服务业	Household's Services,Repair and Other Services	179.84	159.15	172.88	175.17	178.93
教育	Education	113.18	131.55	157.92	161.31	164.68
卫生和社会工作	Health Care and Social Work	44.01	57.57	70.69	73.06	75.21
文化、体育和娱乐业	Culture, Sports and Recreation	17.03	25.63	28.76	29.95	30.86
公共管理、社会保障和社会组织	Public Administration and Social Security and Social Organizations	92.61	132.71	146.03	147.73	151.53

注：2006—2010年就业人员人数，根据“全省第六次普查”资料作了相应调整。
Note: Figures of “Number of Employed Persons” from 2006 to 2010 have been adjusted in accordance with the results of the 6th population census.

4-5 各市就业人员年末人数

Number of Employed Persons at the Year-end by City

单位：万人　　　　(10000 persons)

市　别	City	2010	2011	2012	2013	2014	2015	2016	2017
全　省	**Provincial Total**	**5870.48**	**5960.74**	**5965.95**	**6117.68**	**6183.23**	**6219.31**	**6279.22**	**6340.79**
广　州	Guangzhou	711.07	743.18	751.30	759.93	784.84	810.99	835.26	862.33
深　圳	Shenzhen	758.14	764.54	771.20	899.20	899.66	906.14	926.38	943.29
珠　海	Zhuhai	103.02	104.09	104.93	106.32	108.79	108.92	109.55	112.37
汕　头	Shantou	237.91	238.55	239.05	239.67	238.26	238.50	239.24	239.76
佛　山	Foshan	443.46	445.13	437.25	437.29	438.09	438.41	438.81	435.51
韶　关	Shaoguan	142.51	142.65	143.10	143.78	144.13	144.17	144.48	144.67
河　源	Heyuan	133.15	135.47	136.59	135.19	134.63	136.52	138.42	141.02
梅　州	Meizhou	208.07	209.48	211.00	211.93	213.01	213.52	214.34	216.55
惠　州	Huizhou	260.14	267.94	270.04	277.27	280.62	281.51	285.57	289.10
汕　尾	Shanwei	119.15	119.23	119.45	119.68	119.36	119.86	121.10	120.21
东　莞	Dongguan	626.25	628.54	631.40	633.25	660.46	653.41	653.97	660.39
中　山	Zhongshan	207.34	208.64	208.84	210.30	211.76	210.51	213.01	212.18
江　门	Jiangmen	249.55	253.03	248.34	244.30	243.24	242.92	244.07	244.94
阳　江	Yangjiang	131.34	137.87	131.98	128.97	128.35	128.79	129.02	129.22
湛　江	Zhanjiang	319.78	329.13	331.64	336.37	340.76	340.85	343.75	344.51
茂　名	Maoming	273.18	275.58	278.30	280.54	281.00	281.78	282.52	284.06
肇　庆	Zhaoqing	213.05	215.13	215.55	216.22	217.79	218.44	220.31	221.31
清　远	Qingyuan	196.07	197.49	197.68	200.14	203.98	210.67	205.75	205.42
潮　州	Chaozhou	138.48	138.80	134.98	131.02	127.68	124.94	124.55	124.71
揭　阳	Jieyang	270.26	273.55	271.94	273.64	274.16	275.07	274.97	274.94
云　浮	Yunfu	128.57	132.73	131.41	132.66	132.67	133.37	134.15	134.31
按经济区域分	By Region								
珠三角	Pearl River Delta	3572.01	3630.21	3638.83	3784.09	3845.25	3871.26	3926.93	3981.41
东　翼	Eastern Region	765.79	770.13	765.42	764.01	759.46	758.37	759.87	759.62
西　翼	Western Region	724.30	742.58	741.92	745.88	750.10	751.42	755.29	757.79
山　区	Mountainous Region	808.37	817.81	819.78	823.70	828.42	838.26	837.13	841.96

注：2010年就业人员人数，根据“六普”资料作了相应调整。

Note: Figures of “ Number of Employed Persons ” of 2010 have been adjusted in accordance with the results of the 6th population census.

4–6 各市按三次产业分就业人员年末人数

Number of Employed Persons at the Year-end by Strata of Industry by City

单位：万人 (10000 persons)

市别	City	2016 合计 Total	2016 第一产业 Primary Industry	2016 第二产业 Secondary Industry	2016 第三产业 Tertiary Industry	2017 合计 Total	2017 第一产业 Primary Industry	2017 第二产业 Secondary Industry	2017 第三产业 Tertiary Industry
全　省	**Provincial Total**	**6279.22**	**1365.43**	**2543.07**	**2370.72**	**6340.79**	**1359.12**	**2541.82**	**2439.85**
广　州	Guangzhou	835.26	62.09	288.09	485.09	862.33	62.00	286.61	513.72
深　圳	Shenzhen	926.38	0.11	418.45	507.82	943.29	1.64	419.29	522.36
珠　海	Zhuhai	109.55	6.15	54.71	48.69	112.37	6.16	54.79	51.41
汕　头	Shantou	239.24	62.71	109.25	67.29	239.76	62.28	108.48	69.00
佛　山	Foshan	438.81	22.06	252.06	164.70	435.51	21.37	247.04	167.10
韶　关	Shaoguan	144.48	58.67	32.14	53.67	144.67	59.02	31.86	53.79
河　源	Heyuan	138.42	71.07	27.18	40.17	141.02	70.74	27.78	42.50
梅　州	Meizhou	214.34	78.16	63.33	72.84	216.55	79.33	63.44	73.77
惠　州	Huizhou	285.57	49.37	142.71	93.48	289.10	49.02	143.97	96.11
汕　尾	Shanwei	121.10	51.93	33.94	35.23	120.21	50.59	34.23	35.38
东　莞	Dongguan	653.97	5.89	446.32	201.76	660.39	5.79	450.78	203.82
中　山	Zhongshan	213.01	10.00	140.76	62.26	212.18	9.98	138.11	64.09
江　门	Jiangmen	244.07	79.41	95.95	68.71	244.94	78.89	97.13	68.93
阳　江	Yangjiang	129.02	47.25	42.89	38.88	129.22	47.15	42.88	39.19
湛　江	Zhanjiang	343.75	204.82	51.82	87.11	344.51	205.12	52.35	87.04
茂　名	Maoming	282.52	141.54	62.30	78.69	284.06	139.92	63.62	80.52
肇　庆	Zhaoqing	220.31	106.48	56.82	57.00	221.31	106.63	57.03	57.65
清　远	Qingyuan	205.75	103.21	41.91	60.63	205.42	101.38	40.40	63.64
潮　州	Chaozhou	124.55	39.22	56.47	28.87	124.71	38.47	56.82	29.41
揭　阳	Jieyang	274.97	88.46	96.14	90.38	274.94	87.31	95.79	91.84
云　浮	Yunfu	134.15	76.83	29.84	27.48	134.31	76.31	29.42	28.59
按经济区域分	By Region								
珠三角	Pearl River Delta	3926.93	341.56	1895.86	1689.50	3981.41	341.49	1894.75	1745.17
东　翼	Eastern Region	759.87	242.32	295.80	221.76	759.62	238.66	295.32	225.64
西　翼	Western Region	755.29	393.61	157.01	204.68	757.79	392.20	158.84	206.75
山　区	Mountainous Region	837.13	387.94	194.40	254.79	841.96	386.78	192.90	262.29

4-7 城镇单位就业人员和在岗职工年末人数（2017年）

Employed Persons and Fully Employed Staff and Workers in Urban Units at the Year-

单位：万人 (10000 persons)

项目	Item	就业人员 Employed Persons	国有单位 State-owned Units	城镇集体单位 Urban Collectiveowned Units	其他单位 Other Types of Ownership
合计	**Total**	**1963.10**	**384.09**	**45.46**	**1533.56**
按企业、事业和机关分	Grouped by Enterprises,Institutions and Agencies				
企业	Enterprises	1637.38	74.80	39.36	1523.23
事业	Institutions	211.41	203.89	5.07	2.45
机关	Organ	103.69	103.62	0.03	0.03
民营非盈利组织	Private Non-profit Organizations	3.59	0.12	0.12	3.36
其他	Others	7.03	1.66	0.88	4.49
按国民经济行业分	Grouped by Economic Sector				
农、林、牧、渔业	Farming, Forestry, Animal Husbandry and Fishery	4.59	4.40	0.03	0.17
采矿业	Mining and Quarrying	2.45	0.44	0.02	1.99
制造业	Manufacture	929.36	3.81	6.18	919.37
电力、热力、燃气及水生产和供应业	Production and Supply of Electric Power, Gas and Water	29.92	7.34	0.86	21.72
建筑业	Construction	154.21	13.93	15.96	124.32
批发和零售业	Wholesale and Retail Trade	102.65	3.90	2.58	96.17
交通运输、仓储和邮政业	Transport, Storage and Postal Services	83.33	11.66	0.78	70.89
住宿和餐饮业	Hotels and Catering Services	36.52	2.12	0.57	33.83
信息传输、软件和信息技术服务业	Information Transmission, Computer Services and Software	49.86	2.74	0.26	46.86
金融业	Finance	48.89	9.55	4.08	35.26
房地产业	Real Estate	66.31	2.57	1.39	62.36
租赁和商务服务业	Leasing and Business Services	76.11	12.61	6.18	57.31
科学研究、技术服务业	Scientific Research and Technical Services	33.86	9.17	0.31	24.39
水利、环境和公共设施管理业	Water Conservancy, Environment and Public Facilities Management	17.24	10.75	1.13	5.36
居民服务、修理和其他服务业	Household's Services,Repair and Other Services	8.96	1.84	0.22	6.90
教育	Education	127.46	109.26	2.65	15.55
卫生和社会工作	Health Care and Social Work	65.82	58.14	2.11	5.58
文化、体育和娱乐业	Culture, Sports and Recreation	11.45	6.03	0.14	5.28
公共管理、社会保障和社会组织	Public Administration and Social Security and Social Organizations	114.09	113.82	0.01	0.26
按产业分	Grouped by Industry				
第一产业	Primary Industry	4.59	4.40	0.03	0.17
第二产业	Secondary Industry	1115.94	25.52	23.02	1067.39
第三产业	Tertiary Industry	842.56	354.16	22.41	465.99

4-7 续表 continued

单位：万人 (10000 persons)

项 目	Item	在岗职工 Fully Employed Staff and Workers	国有单位 State-owned Units	城镇集体单位 Urban Collecti-veowned Units	其他单位 Other Types of Ownership
合 计	**Total**	**1892.85**	**371.66**	**43.01**	**1478.18**
按企业、事业和机关分	Grouped by Enterprises,Institutions and Agencies				
企业	Enterprises	1575.83	70.33	37.16	1468.34
事业	Institutions	205.22	197.99	4.87	2.37
机关	Organ	101.67	101.61	0.03	0.03
民营非盈利组织	Private Non-profit Organizations	3.38	0.12	0.11	3.15
其他	Others	6.74	1.61	0.83	4.30
按国民经济行业分	Grouped by Economic Sector				
农、林、牧、渔业	Farming, Forestry, Animal Husbandry and Fishery	4.50	4.31	0.03	0.16
采矿业	Mining and Quarrying	2.38	0.44	0.02	1.92
制造业	Manufacture	920.05	3.72	6.01	910.32
电力、热力、燃气及水生产和供应业	Production and Supply of Electric Power, Gas and Water	29.75	7.27	0.85	21.62
建筑业	Construction	132.13	12.29	14.60	105.24
批发和零售业	Wholesale and Retail Trade	98.37	3.71	2.48	92.17
交通运输、仓储和邮政业	Transport, Storage and Postal Services	79.60	11.15	0.71	67.74
住宿和餐饮业	Hotels and Catering Services	33.49	2.04	0.56	30.89
信息传输、软件和信息技术服务业	Information Transmission, Computer Services and Software	48.63	2.65	0.26	45.71
金融业	Finance	38.03	8.15	4.04	25.85
房地产业	Real Estate	64.46	2.42	1.25	60.80
租赁和商务服务业	Leasing and Business Services	73.39	12.45	5.89	55.05
科学研究、技术服务业	Scientific Research and Technical Services	32.96	8.87	0.30	23.79
水利、环境和公共设施管理业	Water Conservancy, Environment and Public Facilities Management	16.31	10.16	0.99	5.16
居民服务、修理和其他服务业	Household's Services,Repair and Other Services	8.66	1.78	0.21	6.67
教育	Education	123.89	106.48	2.62	14.79
卫生和社会工作	Health Care and Social Work	64.04	56.48	2.06	5.49
文化、体育和娱乐业	Culture, Sports and Recreation	10.48	5.78	0.12	4.59
公共管理、社会保障和社会组织	Public Administration and Social Security and Social Organizations	111.75	111.51	0.01	0.23
按产业分	Grouped by Industry				
第一产业	Primary Industry	4.50	4.31	0.03	0.16
第二产业	Secondary Industry	1084.30	23.72	21.49	1039.09
第三产业	Tertiary Industry	804.05	343.63	21.49	438.93

4－8 各市城镇单位就业人员和在岗职工（2017年）

Number of Employed Persons and of Fully Employed Staff and Workers in Urban Units by City (2017)

单位：万人 (10000 persons)

市别	City	就业人员 Employed Persons 合计 Total	国有单位 State-owned Units	城镇集体单位 Urban Collective-owned Units	其他单位 Other Types of Ownership	在岗职工 Fully Employed Staff and Workers 合计 Total	国有单位 State-owned Units	城镇集体单位 Urban Collective-owned Units	其他单位 Other Types of Ownership
年末人数	**Year-end Number**								
全省	**Provincial Total**	**1963.10**	**384.09**	**45.46**	**1533.56**	**1892.85**	**371.66**	**43.01**	**1478.18**
广州	Guangzhou	329.17	72.56	7.25	249.35	316.42	70.66	6.74	239.02
深圳	Shenzhen	463.79	42.44	2.86	418.49	447.32	41.92	2.84	402.55
珠海	Zhuhai	76.20	9.83	0.67	65.70	72.59	9.65	0.63	62.30
汕头	Shantou	59.62	18.77	4.78	36.07	57.15	17.82	4.57	34.76
佛山	Foshan	165.16	19.68	3.24	142.24	162.33	19.27	3.19	139.87
韶关	Shaoguan	32.00	13.65	2.01	16.34	30.73	13.06	1.91	15.75
河源	Heyuan	28.10	11.01	0.93	16.17	27.47	10.93	0.90	15.64
梅州	Meizhou	29.13	15.85	1.24	12.04	28.16	15.61	1.21	11.34
惠州	Huizhou	98.76	18.23	0.99	79.54	94.97	17.67	0.95	76.36
汕尾	Shanwei	20.40	8.14	1.65	10.61	19.76	7.86	1.44	10.46
东莞	Dongguan	242.40	14.52	3.46	224.42	237.16	14.26	3.34	219.56
中山	Zhongshan	77.90	7.77	1.12	69.01	75.21	7.45	1.12	66.64
江门	Jiangmen	56.71	14.04	1.52	41.15	53.63	12.99	1.30	39.33
阳江	Yangjiang	23.74	10.41	1.87	11.46	22.60	10.16	1.81	10.63
湛江	Zhanjiang	50.87	27.78	2.12	20.97	47.08	26.23	2.06	18.79
茂名	Maoming	49.36	20.54	2.86	25.97	46.62	20.07	2.78	23.77
肇庆	Zhaoqing	39.29	14.85	1.46	22.98	37.87	13.91	1.42	22.53
清远	Qingyuan	32.90	13.23	0.54	19.14	31.39	12.40	0.47	18.52
潮州	Chaozhou	19.68	7.78	1.43	10.47	18.54	7.28	0.99	10.27
揭阳	Jieyang	37.86	14.50	2.84	20.53	37.03	14.18	2.69	20.17
云浮	Yunfu	19.43	8.49	0.63	10.31	18.20	8.30	0.63	9.27
年平均人数	**Annual Aver-age Number**								
全省	**Provincial Total**	**1958.95**	**381.61**	**45.39**	**1531.96**	**1888.37**	**369.17**	**42.69**	**1476.51**
广州	Guangzhou	327.97	72.18	7.27	248.51	314.69	70.27	6.76	237.66
深圳	Shenzhen	462.43	41.98	2.98	417.46	446.20	41.43	2.97	401.80
珠海	Zhuhai	75.49	9.80	0.66	65.04	71.93	9.61	0.62	61.70
汕头	Shantou	58.55	18.54	4.30	35.71	56.06	17.59	4.15	34.32
佛山	Foshan	165.09	19.66	3.28	142.15	162.12	19.24	3.23	139.65
韶关	Shaoguan	31.85	13.43	1.89	16.54	30.63	12.85	1.80	15.98
河源	Heyuan	27.66	10.96	0.81	15.88	27.00	10.87	0.78	15.34
梅州	Meizhou	28.96	15.76	1.21	12.00	28.01	15.52	1.17	11.31
惠州	Huizhou	98.16	18.05	0.98	79.13	94.28	17.44	0.93	75.91
汕尾	Shanwei	20.37	8.15	1.86	10.37	19.57	7.86	1.49	10.22
东莞	Dongguan	246.09	14.40	3.55	228.14	240.91	14.13	3.43	223.36
中山	Zhongshan	78.31	7.72	1.17	69.42	75.82	7.41	1.17	67.25
江门	Jiangmen	56.48	14.03	1.48	40.98	53.46	12.98	1.29	39.19
阳江	Yangjiang	23.26	10.40	1.94	10.92	22.16	10.15	1.82	10.20
湛江	Zhanjiang	49.87	27.61	2.12	20.14	46.25	26.24	2.06	17.95
茂名	Maoming	48.70	20.28	2.75	25.66	45.95	19.77	2.68	23.50
肇庆	Zhaoqing	39.27	14.85	1.45	22.98	37.83	13.89	1.42	22.53
清远	Qingyuan	32.76	13.13	0.51	19.12	31.21	12.26	0.47	18.48
潮州	Chaozhou	19.84	7.77	1.76	10.31	18.61	7.32	1.17	10.11
揭阳	Jieyang	37.91	14.47	2.82	20.62	37.08	14.15	2.68	20.25
云浮	Yunfu	19.32	8.43	0.60	10.28	18.01	8.20	0.60	9.21

4-9 各市城镇单位各行业在岗职工年末人数（2017年）
Number of Fully Employed Staff and Workers in Urban Units at the Year-end by Sector and by City (2017)

单位：万人 (10000 persons)

市别	City	合计 Total	农、林、牧、渔业 Farming, Forestry, Animal Husbandry and Fishery	采矿业 Mining and Quarrying	制造业 Manufacture	电力、热力、燃气及水的生产和供应业 Production and Supply of Electric Power,Gas and Water	建筑业 Construction	批发和零售业 Wholesale and Retail Trade
全　省	**Provincial Total**	**1892.85**	**4.50**	**2.38**	**920.05**	**29.75**	**132.13**	**98.37**
广　州	Guangzhou	316.42	0.17		76.18	3.65	24.43	27.12
深　圳	Shenzhen	447.32	0.05	0.36	229.71	2.10	25.99	26.51
珠　海	Zhuhai	72.59	0.64	0.03	37.61	0.58	4.59	3.56
汕　头	Shantou	57.15	0.05	0.07	19.76	0.46	13.34	3.06
佛　山	Foshan	162.33	0.02	0.04	109.45	1.42	4.43	6.32
韶　关	Shaoguan	30.73	0.15	0.39	8.18	0.84	5.33	1.24
河　源	Heyuan	27.47	0.08	0.07	11.29	0.31	1.71	0.80
梅　州	Meizhou	28.16	0.04	0.10	5.92	0.89	3.63	1.10
惠　州	Huizhou	94.97	0.11	0.02	65.97	0.92	1.54	2.42
汕　尾	Shanwei	19.76	0.12	0.03	9.74	0.27	0.58	0.58
东　莞	Dongguan	237.16	0.03	…	186.46	0.80	5.50	7.05
中　山	Zhongshan	75.21			52.97	0.92	2.29	3.32
江　门	Jiangmen	53.63	0.06	0.01	26.88	0.82	3.62	2.79
阳　江	Yangjiang	22.60	0.38	0.01	5.74	0.65	3.63	1.02
湛　江	Zhanjiang	47.08	1.44	0.65	6.58	0.72	8.96	2.34
茂　名	Maoming	46.62	0.71	0.18	7.60	0.87	12.97	2.40
肇　庆	Zhaoqing	37.87	0.08	0.13	16.35	1.01	1.72	1.92
清　远	Qingyuan	31.39	0.14	0.04	11.98	0.62	2.53	1.13
潮　州	Chaozhou	18.54	0.01	…	8.64	0.84	0.96	0.55
揭　阳	Jieyang	37.03	0.18		16.27	0.58	3.29	2.29
云　浮	Yunfu	18.20	0.04	0.24	6.25	0.38	1.08	0.86
按经济区域分	By Region							
珠三角	Pearl River Delta	1508.11	1.15	0.60	802.09	22.32	74.11	81.01
东　翼	Eastern Region	132.49	0.37	0.10	54.41	2.14	18.17	6.48
西　翼	Western Region	116.30	2.53	0.85	19.92	2.25	25.56	5.76
山　区	Mountainous Region	135.94	0.45	0.83	43.62	3.04	14.28	5.12

4-9 续表 1 continued

单位：万人 (10000 persons)

市 别	City	交通运输、仓储和邮政业 Transport, Storage and Postal Services	住宿和餐饮业 Hotels and Catering Services	信息传输、软件和信息技术服务业 Information Transmi-ssion, Computer Services and Software	金融业 Finance	房地产业 Real Estate	租赁和商务服务业 Leasing and Business Services	科学研究、技术服务业 Scientific Research and Technical Services
全 省	**Provincial Total**	**79.60**	**33.49**	**48.63**	**38.03**	**64.46**	**73.39**	**32.96**
广 州	Guangzhou	29.45	9.10	16.39	7.22	19.02	23.09	13.41
深 圳	Shenzhen	24.50	9.32	18.53	9.52	21.75	30.34	10.09
珠 海	Zhuhai	2.51	2.37	2.74	1.38	3.36	2.78	1.18
汕 头	Shantou	1.47	0.65	0.64	1.21	1.02	1.75	0.42
佛 山	Foshan	4.11	1.92	1.44	2.32	4.23	2.84	1.81
韶 关	Shaoguan	0.79	0.45	0.28	0.76	0.75	0.45	0.33
河 源	Heyuan	0.75	0.33	0.31	0.60	0.78	0.58	0.19
梅 州	Meizhou	0.73	0.24	0.44	0.86	0.32	0.16	0.32
惠 州	Huizhou	1.88	0.89	0.71	1.40	2.12	0.70	0.62
汕 尾	Shanwei	0.44	0.21	0.38	0.37	0.13	0.26	0.07
东 莞	Dongguan	2.79	2.67	2.47	2.61	3.00	5.06	1.60
中 山	Zhongshan	1.31	1.20	0.61	1.34	2.00	1.35	0.40
江 门	Jiangmen	1.65	0.94	0.59	1.76	1.13	0.96	0.39
阳 江	Yangjiang	0.78	0.25	0.25	0.64	0.39	0.26	0.21
湛 江	Zhanjiang	2.39	0.75	0.71	1.18	1.01	1.23	0.60
茂 名	Maoming	1.24	0.44	0.44	1.09	0.88	0.56	0.42
肇 庆	Zhaoqing	0.99	0.46	0.38	1.12	0.73	0.33	0.28
清 远	Qingyuan	0.63	0.60	0.34	0.85	0.93	0.18	0.23
潮 州	Chaozhou	0.31	0.13	0.26	0.53	0.26	0.15	0.15
揭 阳	Jieyang	0.54	0.31	0.51	0.82	0.34	0.23	0.14
云 浮	Yunfu	0.34	0.27	0.22	0.49	0.31	0.14	0.10
按经济区域分	By Region							
珠 三 角	Pearl River Delta	69.19	28.86	43.87	28.66	57.34	67.45	29.78
东 翼	Eastern Region	2.75	1.31	1.78	2.92	1.74	2.38	0.78
西 翼	Western Region	4.41	1.44	1.40	2.91	2.28	2.05	1.22
山 区	Mountainous Region	3.25	1.89	1.58	3.54	3.10	1.51	1.17

4-9 续表 2 continued

单位：万人 (10000 persons)

市别	City	水利、环境和公共设施管理业 Management of Water Conservancy, Environment and Public Facilities	居民服务、修理和其他服务业 Household's Services, Repair and Other Services	教育 Education	卫生和社会工作 Health and Social Service	文化、体育和娱乐业 Culture, Sports and Entertainment	公共管理、社会保障和社会组织 Public Management, Social Security and Social Organizations
全　省	**Provincial Total**	**16.31**	**8.66**	**123.89**	**64.04**	**10.48**	**111.75**
广　州	Guangzhou	5.05	3.08	23.82	12.87	3.66	18.73
深　圳	Shenzhen	1.31	2.37	10.80	6.60	2.44	15.03
珠　海	Zhuhai	0.79	0.26	2.72	1.59	0.30	3.60
汕　头	Shantou	0.53	0.04	6.16	2.50	0.30	3.73
佛　山	Foshan	1.38	0.48	8.53	4.60	0.42	6.56
韶　关	Shaoguan	0.48	0.21	3.77	2.00	0.17	4.17
河　源	Heyuan	0.27	0.14	3.80	1.54	0.20	3.71
梅　州	Meizhou	0.78	0.03	5.45	2.29	0.18	4.68
惠　州	Huizhou	0.69	0.09	5.21	2.89	0.36	6.43
汕　尾	Shanwei	0.14	0.02	3.04	0.94	0.12	2.32
东　莞	Dongguan	0.42	1.28	4.18	4.94	0.62	5.68
中　山	Zhongshan	0.28	0.06	2.47	2.03	0.22	2.45
江　门	Jiangmen	0.55	0.17	3.93	2.66	0.18	4.55
阳　江	Yangjiang	0.43	0.03	3.05	1.42	0.11	3.34
湛　江	Zhanjiang	1.18	0.11	8.63	3.53	0.27	4.80
茂　名	Maoming	0.51	0.04	8.68	2.98	0.22	4.40
肇　庆	Zhaoqing	0.49	0.05	4.61	2.65	0.19	4.39
清　远	Qingyuan	0.31	0.10	3.78	1.97	0.16	4.88
潮　州	Chaozhou	0.25	0.02	2.65	1.01	0.14	1.71
揭　阳	Jieyang	0.30	0.06	5.89	1.70	0.16	3.42
云　浮	Yunfu	0.17	0.01	2.73	1.33	0.08	3.17
按经济区域分	By Region						
珠 三 角	Pearl River Delta	10.96	7.85	66.26	40.83	8.39	67.41
东　翼	Eastern Region	1.22	0.14	17.73	6.15	0.72	11.19
西　翼	Western Region	2.11	0.18	20.37	7.93	0.59	12.55
山　区	Mountainous Region	2.02	0.49	19.53	9.13	0.78	20.61

4-10 城镇单位女性就业人员年末人数（2017年）

Number of Females Employed in Urban Units at the Year-end (2017)

单位：万人 (10000 persons)

行业	Sector	合计 Total	国有单位 State-owned Units	城镇集体单位 Urban Collective-owned Units	其他单位 Other Types of Ownership
合计	**Total**	**805.87**	**171.26**	**15.67**	**618.95**
农、林、牧、渔业	Farming, Forestry, Animal Husbandry and Fishery	1.59	1.52	0.01	0.06
采矿业	Mining and Quarrying	0.47	0.08	...	0.39
制造业	Manufacture	406.35	1.16	3.91	401.28
电力、热力、燃气及水生产和供应业	Production and Supply of Electric Power, Gas and Water	6.96	1.87	0.23	4.86
建筑业	Construction	18.68	1.71	2.01	14.95
批发和零售业	Wholesale and Retail Trade	50.88	1.30	0.99	48.59
交通运输、仓储和邮政业	Transport, Storage and Postal Services	22.17	3.72	0.20	18.25
住宿和餐饮业	Hotels and Catering Services	19.51	1.09	0.34	18.09
信息传输、软件和信息技术服务业	Information Transmission, Computer Services and Software	18.95	0.91	0.09	17.95
金融业	Finance	25.62	4.84	1.68	19.10
房地产业	Real Estate	23.58	0.91	0.40	22.27
租赁和商务服务业	Leasing and Business Services	27.10	2.51	1.42	23.17
科学研究、技术服务业	Scientific Research and Technical Services	10.97	2.99	0.10	7.88
水利、环境和公共设施管理业	Management of Water Conservancy, Environment and Public Facilities	7.14	4.26	0.47	2.41
居民服务、修理和其他服务业	Household's Services,Repair and Other Services	4.05	0.70	0.08	3.27
教育	Education	76.85	64.38	2.28	10.19
卫生和社会工作	Health Care and Social Service	43.79	38.64	1.40	3.75
文化、体育和娱乐业	Culture, Sports and Entertainment	4.99	2.57	0.06	2.35
公共管理、社会保障和社会组织	Public Administration and Social Security and Social Organizations	36.25	36.11	...	0.13

4-11 城镇单位职工工资总额与年平均工资

Total Wages Bill and Average Wage of Staff and Workers in Urban Units

年份 Year	工资总额（亿元） Total Wages Bill (100 million yuan)				平均工资（元） Average Wage (yuan)			
	合计 Total	国有单位 State-owned Units	城镇集体单位 Urban Collective-owned Units	其他单位 Other Types of Ownership	合计 Total	国有单位 State-owned Units	城镇集体单位 Urban Collective-owned Units	其他单位 Other Types of Ownership
1978	30.59	22.67	7.92		615	638	558	
1979	35.56	26.37	9.19		685	718	605	
1980	42.83	32.00	10.83		789	828	691	
1981	49.40	37.01	12.39		873	912	774	
1982	56.69	43.03	13.66		961	1000	856	
1983	60.85	46.25	14.60		1021	1061	907	
1984	72.82	52.66	19.59	0.57	1187	1261	1017	1697
1985	88.91	63.42	23.85	1.64	1393	1458	1216	2209
1986	102.13	73.10	26.69	2.34	1541	1619	1330	2198
1987	121.10	84.99	31.99	4.12	1743	1805	1544	2469
1988	162.76	113.60	41.23	7.93	2250	2320	1979	3134
1989	200.39	139.38	47.74	13.27	2678	2763	2302	3641
1990	223.29	154.96	50.06	18.27	2929	3000	2508	3972
1991	268.19	179.81	60.15	28.23	3358	3383	2931	4558
1992	334.61	222.27	72.06	40.28	4027	4059	3510	5157
1993	455.33	300.91	83.79	70.63	5327	5431	4388	6435
1994	612.73	401.80	107.03	103.90	7117	7410	5565	8216
1995	734.14	458.86	124.32	150.96	8250	8540	6395	9546
1996	803.50	512.22	124.35	166.93	9127	9494	6799	10569
1997	858.35	539.95	120.36	198.04	9698	10032	6814	11635
1998	899.68	530.11	105.59	263.98	10233	10432	6671	12410
1999	970.70	567.54	101.72	301.44	11309	11579	7025	13492
2000	1038.38	604.59	91.81	341.98	13823	14387	8615	15240
2001	1146.11	663.85	82.67	399.59	15682	16779	9040	16392
2002	1306.32	737.63	80.26	488.43	17814	19696	9881	17597
2003	1515.58	841.02	83.52	591.05	19986	22944	10836	18782
2004	1771.05	942.39	84.73	743.94	22116	25979	11937	20267
2005	2085.64	1058.97	88.63	938.04	23959	28835	13240	21500
2006	2413.63	1165.88	94.91	1152.84	26186	31352	14520	23794
2007	2854.99	1343.92	104.01	1407.06	29443	36396	16328	26215
2008	3294.17	1520.88	110.28	1663.02	33110	40775	18461	29580
2009	3698.34	1687.96	114.71	1895.66	36355	44964	20347	32377
2010	4363.82	1913.19	125.99	2324.64	40358	49610	22470	36347
2011	5444.34	2235.58	149.68	3059.08	45152	54739	25679	41390
2012	6397.01	2508.29	165.71	3723.02	50577	60116	31219	46860
2013	10213.35	2434.53	196.96	7581.85	53611	63390	35812	51717
2014	11471.24	2667.14	221.64	8582.47	59827	69694	40850	57972
2015	12596.61	2927.11	220.22	9449.28	66296	78058	45436	63994
2016	13790.07	3255.53	223.74	10310.80	72848	87482	50159	69844
2017	15110.67	3684.67	238.28	11187.73	80020	99809	55813	75772

注：从2000年起统计口径为在岗职工。

Note: Since 2000, statistical coverage refers to the fully employed staff and workers.

4-12 各市城镇单位就业人员工资总额和在岗职工年平均工资（2017年）

Earnings of Employed Persons and Wages of Fully Employed Staff and Workers in Urban Units by City (2017)

市别	City	就业人员工资 Earnings of Employed Persons				在岗职工工资 Wages of Fully Employed Staff and Workers			
		合计 Total	国有单位 State-owned Units	城镇集体单位 Urban Collective-owned Units	其他单位 Other Types of Ownership	合计 Total	国有单位 State-owned Units	城镇集体单位 Urban Collective-owned Units	其他单位 Other Types of Ownership
总额（亿元）	**Total(100 million yuan)**								
全　省	**Provincial Total**	**15511.55**	**3742.62**	**249.68**	**11519.25**	**15110.67**	**3684.67**	**238.28**	**11187.73**
广　州	Guangzhou	3198.39	883.00	34.71	2280.68	3103.28	870.42	32.71	2200.15
深　圳	Shenzhen	4584.48	628.60	21.28	3934.60	4469.76	623.28	21.20	3825.28
珠　海	Zhuhai	606.43	107.05	6.04	493.35	582.71	106.22	5.88	470.61
汕　头	Shantou	356.57	147.35	15.97	193.26	346.80	142.99	15.45	188.36
佛　山	Foshan	1193.69	188.56	28.76	976.37	1178.78	185.49	28.61	964.69
韶　关	Shaoguan	205.39	109.39	8.97	87.03	201.33	107.49	8.70	85.15
河　源	Heyuan	168.20	83.60	3.87	80.73	166.22	83.37	3.71	79.13
梅　州	Meizhou	191.31	126.88	5.20	59.23	188.16	126.10	5.08	56.98
惠　州	Huizhou	690.24	176.69	4.77	508.79	668.32	173.65	4.54	490.14
汕　尾	Shanwei	115.43	48.17	9.68	57.59	111.20	47.40	6.96	56.84
东　莞	Dongguan	1510.32	165.45	30.89	1313.98	1484.47	164.36	30.41	1289.70
中　山	Zhongshan	530.40	94.87	6.39	429.14	515.87	93.67	6.38	415.82
江　门	Jiangmen	366.81	122.95	9.47	234.39	353.38	117.80	8.74	226.85
阳　江	Yangjiang	136.07	68.33	7.55	60.19	131.98	67.45	7.11	57.41
湛　江	Zhanjiang	303.28	183.41	8.19	111.68	287.16	177.26	8.07	101.82
茂　名	Maoming	292.05	144.79	15.36	131.91	282.31	143.45	15.08	123.79
肇　庆	Zhaoqing	252.29	123.81	7.64	120.85	246.79	120.53	7.56	118.70
清　远	Qingyuan	235.06	131.20	4.25	99.60	228.81	128.39	4.06	96.36
潮　州	Chaozhou	114.98	56.16	7.49	51.34	110.78	54.91	5.27	50.61
揭　阳	Jieyang	190.57	84.67	9.98	95.92	187.61	83.50	9.56	94.55
云　浮	Yunfu	120.86	67.71	3.23	49.92	116.22	66.93	3.21	46.09
平均工资（元）	**Average Wage (yuan)**								
全　省	**Provincial Total**	**79183**	**98074**	**55013**	**75193**	**80020**	**99809**	**55813**	**75772**
广　州	Guangzhou	97522	122325	47731	91775	98612	123863	48364	92576
深　圳	Shenzhen	99139	149729	71322	94250	100173	150444	71380	95203
珠　海	Zhuhai	80329	109281	91240	75857	81014	110560	94109	76280
汕　头	Shantou	60901	79470	37110	54125	61868	81288	37243	54890
佛　山	Foshan	72307	95911	87740	68686	72712	96429	88520	69079
韶　关	Shaoguan	64479	81474	47487	52623	65739	83681	48229	53290
河　源	Heyuan	60815	76280	47557	50823	61561	76669	47481	51571
梅　州	Meizhou	66055	80505	43129	49375	67186	81239	43310	50378
惠　州	Huizhou	70317	97869	48789	64297	70890	99570	48769	64571
汕　尾	Shanwei	56674	59136	52137	55552	56810	60292	46579	55627
东　莞	Dongguan	61373	114873	87136	57595	61619	116358	88696	57742
中　山	Zhongshan	67728	122871	54534	61818	68034	126477	54623	61831
江　门	Jiangmen	64941	87631	64093	57202	66107	90764	67739	57888
阳　江	Yangjiang	58491	65693	38815	55132	59559	66476	39187	56304
湛　江	Zhanjiang	60819	66441	38689	55441	62094	67556	39191	56738
茂　名	Maoming	59974	71393	55773	51401	61442	72554	56286	52679
肇　庆	Zhaoqing	64238	83376	52754	52594	65227	86772	53393	52687
清　远	Qingyuan	71745	99889	83310	52101	73323	104693	87074	52154
潮　州	Chaozhou	57942	72227	42629	49780	59540	75009	44917	50039
揭　阳	Jieyang	50273	58520	35446	46513	50598	59007	35709	46690
云　浮	Yunfu	62570	80295	53405	48569	64527	81629	53529	50023

4-13 城镇单位就业人员工资总额（2017年）

Earnings of Employed Persons in Urban Units (2017)

单位：亿元 (100 million yuan)

项　目	Item	合计 Total	国有单位 State-owned Units	城镇集体单位 Urban Collectiveo-wned Units	其他单位 Other Types of Ownership
合　计	**Total**	**15511.55**	**3742.62**	**249.68**	**11519.25**
按企业、事业和机关分	Grouped by Enterprises, Institutions and Organ				
企业	Enterprises	12295.72	638.57	201.94	11455.22
事业	Institutions	2077.42	2015.74	41.92	19.75
机关	Organ	1072.41	1071.98	0.14	0.28
民营非盈利组织	Private Non-profit Organizations	19.29	0.90	0.56	17.83
其他	Others	46.71	15.43	5.13	26.16
按国民经济行业分	Grouped by Economic Sector				
农、林、牧、渔业	Farming, Forestry, Animal Husbandry and Fishery	19.01	17.90	0.15	0.96
采矿业	Mining and Quarrying	26.08	4.42	0.08	21.58
制造业	Manufacture	6267.68	29.94	31.19	6206.55
电力、热力、燃气及水生产和供应业	Production and Supply of Electric Power, Gas and Water	354.23	73.40	6.82	274.01
建筑业	Construction	843.05	82.8	60.08	700.17
批发和零售业	Wholesale and Retail Trade	727.97	26.12	7.99	693.86
交通运输、仓储和邮政业	Transport, Storage and Postal Services	754.82	100.68	3.43	650.71
住宿和餐饮业	Hotels and Catering Services	170.68	12.49	2.96	155.23
信息传输、软件和信息技术服务业	Information Transmission, Computer Services and Software	726.15	27.50	3.60	695.05
金融业	Finance	741.50	134.92	43.91	562.67
房地产业	Real Estate	524.74	17.5	6.88	500.36
租赁和商务服务业	Leasing and Business Services	581.84	77.76	30.95	473.12
科学研究、技术服务业	Scientific Research and Technical Services	420.06	116.20	2.57	301.28
水利、环境和公共设施管理业	Management of Water Conservancy, Environment and Public Facilities	102.27	65.48	5.35	31.44
居民服务、修理和其他服务业	Household's Services,Repair and Other Services	46.96	12.50	1.02	33.44
教育	Education	1209.06	1072.81	24.00	112.25
卫生和社会工作	Health Care and Social Service	698.98	634.15	17.73	47.1
文化、体育和娱乐业	Culture, Sports and Entertainment	120.48	61.29	0.93	58.26
公共管理、社会保障和社会组织	Public Administration and Social Security and Social Organizations	1176.01	1174.74	0.05	1.21
按产业分	Grouped by Industry				
第一产业	Primary Industry	19.01	17.90	0.15	0.96
第二产业	Secondary Industry	7491.04	190.56	98.17	7202.31
第三产业	Tertiary Industry	8001.52	3534.14	151.37	4315.98

4-14 城镇单位在岗职工工资总额（2017年）

Total Wages Bill of Fully Employed Staff and Workers in Urban Units (2017)

单位：亿元 (100 million yuan)

项目	Item	合计 Total	国有单位 State-owned Units	城镇集体单位 Urban Collectiveo-wned Units	其他单位 Other Types of Ownership
合计	**Total**	**15110.67**	**3684.67**	**238.28**	**11187.73**
按企业、事业和机关分	Grouped by Enterprises, Institutions and Organ				
企业	Enterprises	11934.78	617.13	191.84	11125.81
事业	Institutions	2047.66	1987.62	40.87	19.17
机关	Organ	1064.29	1063.88	0.14	0.27
民营非盈利组织	Private Non-profit Organizations	18.60	0.89	0.55	17.17
其他	Others	45.34	15.15	4.88	25.31
按国民经济行业分	Grouped by Economic Sector				
农、林、牧、渔业	Farming, Forestry, Animal Husbandry and Fishery	18.77	17.70	0.15	0.92
采矿业	Mining and Quarrying	25.61	4.42	0.08	21.11
制造业	Manufacture	6189.74	29.63	28.75	6131.36
电力、热力、燃气及水生产和供应业	Production and Supply of Electric Power, Gas and Water	353.33	73.26	6.80	273.27
建筑业	Construction	724.2	74.73	54.53	594.93
批发和零售业	Wholesale and Retail Trade	710.67	25.41	7.75	677.51
交通运输、仓储和邮政业	Transport, Storage and Postal Services	731.45	97.43	3.20	630.83
住宿和餐饮业	Hotels and Catering Services	163.78	12.07	2.94	148.77
信息传输、软件和信息技术服务业	Information Transmission, Computer Services and Software	718.00	27.10	3.59	687.32
金融业	Finance	686.24	129.51	43.70	513.03
房地产业	Real Estate	515.63	16.94	6.38	492.31
租赁和商务服务业	Leasing and Business Services	568.55	77.19	30.06	461.29
科学研究、技术服务业	Scientific Research and Technical Services	411.21	114.02	2.53	294.65
水利、环境和公共设施管理业	Management of Water Conservancy, Environment and Public Facilities	98.38	63.58	4.56	30.24
居民服务、修理和其他服务业	Household's Services,Repair and Other Services	45.69	12.14	0.98	32.58
教育	Education	1189.74	1059.19	23.88	106.67
卫生和社会工作	Health Care and Social Service	688.74	624.76	17.48	46.5
文化、体育和娱乐业	Culture, Sports and Entertainment	104.30	60.07	0.87	43.36
公共管理、社会保障和社会组织	Public Administration and Social Security and Social Organizations	1166.63	1165.51	0.05	1.06
按产业分	Grouped by Industry				
第一产业	Primary Industry	18.77	17.70	0.15	0.92
第二产业	Secondary Industry	7292.88	182.04	90.16	7020.67
第三产业	Tertiary Industry	7799.01	3484.92	147.97	4166.12

4-15 城镇单位就业人员年平均工资（2017年）
Average Earning of Employed Persons in Urban Units (2017)

单位：元 (yuan)

项　目	Item	合计 Total	国有单位 State-owned Units	城镇集体单位 Urban Collectiveowned Units	其他单位 Other Types of Ownership
合　计	**Total**	**79183**	**98074**	**55013**	**75193**
按企业、事业和机关分	Grouped by Enterprises, Institutions and Organ				
企业	Enterprises	75197	86275	51333	75276
事业	Institutions	98820	99424	83194	80926
机关	Organ	103963	103982	49943	89902
民营非盈利组织	Private Non-profit Organizations	55421	73268	48594	54989
其他	Others	67008	94280	59255	58527
按国民经济行业分	Grouped by Economic Sector				
农、林、牧、渔业	Farming, Forestry, Animal Husbandry and Fishery	40926	40295	52730	55050
采矿业	Mining and Quarrying	104687	99172	39766	106558
制造业	Manufacture	66823	78284	46716	66921
电力、热力、燃气及水生产和供应业	Production and Supply of Electric Power, Gas and Water	119094	100907	79667	126777
建筑业	Construction	57839	62947	39152	59711
批发和零售业	Wholesale and Retail Trade	71209	66452	30990	72488
交通运输、仓储和邮政业	Transport, Storage and Postal Services	91022	85387	44122	92484
住宿和餐饮业	Hotels and Catering Services	46454	57789	51475	45649
信息传输、软件和信息技术服务业	Information Transmission, Computer Services and Software	147039	99935	137899	149886
金融业	Finance	149936	140340	107703	157331
房地产业	Real Estate	79479	69070	49266	80582
租赁和商务服务业	Leasing and Business Services	77407	62407	49171	83872
科学研究、技术服务业	Scientific Research and Technical Services	125634	127605	84775	125403
水利、环境和公共设施管理业	Management of Water Conservancy, Environment and Public Facilities	58945	60613	47581	57979
居民服务、修理和其他服务业	Household's Services,Repair and Other Services	53418	68688	45906	49546
教育	Education	95136	98460	90648	72507
卫生和社会工作	Health Care and Social Service	107710	110546	85702	86258
文化、体育和娱乐业	Culture, Sports and Entertainment	104446	101738	73246	108207
公共管理、社会保障和社会组织	Public Administration and Social Security and Social Organizations	103752	103823	64807	63702
按产业分	Grouped by Industry				
第一产业	Primary Industry	40926	40295	52730	55050
第二产业	Secondary Industry	67128	77155	42872	67416
第三产业	Tertiary Industry	95442	100268	67393	93130

4-16 城镇单位在岗职工年平均工资（2017年）

Annual Average Wage of Fully Employed Staff and Workers in Urban Units (2017)

单位：元 (yuan)

项 目	Item	合计 Total	国有单位 State-owned Units	城镇集体单位 Urban Collectiveo-wned Units	其他单位 Other Types of Ownership
合 计	**Total**	**80020**	**99809**	**55813**	**75772**
按企业、事业和机关分	Grouped by Enterprises, Institutions and Organ				
企业	Enterprises	75858	88701	51987	75849
事业	Institutions	100377	100998	84450	81250
机关	Organ	105226	105245	49943	92245
民营非盈利组织	Private Non-profit Organizations	56808	74214	48682	56424
其他	Others	68164	95073	60215	59587
按国民经济行业分	Grouped by Economic Sector				
农、林、牧、渔业	Farming, Forestry, Animal Husbandry and Fishery	41285	40578	55500	58505
采矿业	Mining and Quarrying	106311	99516	39766	108563
制造业	Manufacture	66716	79407	45272	66812
电力、热力、燃气及水生产和供应业	Production and Supply of Electric Power, Gas and Water	119475	101650	80066	127000
建筑业	Construction	57986	63890	39255	59911
批发和零售业	Wholesale and Retail Trade	72448	68061	31316	73734
交通运输、仓储和邮政业	Transport, Storage and Postal Services	92382	86605	44930	93852
住宿和餐饮业	Hotels and Catering Services	48783	58566	51926	48074
信息传输、软件和信息技术服务业	Information Transmission, Computer Services and Software	148885	101786	139744	151704
金融业	Finance	181153	158852	108426	199633
房地产业	Real Estate	80390	71061	50769	81373
租赁和商务服务业	Leasing and Business Services	78349	62761	50098	85007
科学研究、技术服务业	Scientific Research and Technical Services	126555	129583	85821	125930
水利、环境和公共设施管理业	Water Conservancy, Environment and Public Facilities Management	60014	62374	46176	58021
居民服务、修理和其他服务业	Household's Services,Repair and Other Services	53646	68683	46184	49823
教育	Education	96411	99819	91284	72684
卫生和社会工作	Health Care and Social Work	109053	112058	86392	86436
文化、体育和娱乐业	Culture, Sports and Recreation	98731	104616	76106	92104
公共管理、社会保障和社会组织	Public Administration and Social Security and Social Organizations	105115	105170	69091	67747
按产业分	Grouped by Industry				
第一产业	Primary Industry	41285	40578	55500	58505
第二产业	Secondary Industry	67237	78875	42706	67476
第三产业	Tertiary Industry	97589	101979	68652	95578

4-17 各市年末城镇登记失业人数

Number of Registered Unemployed Persons in Urban Area at the Year-end by City

单位：人 (person)

市 别	City	2005	2010	2014	2015	2016	2017
合 计	**Total**	**344904**	**392274**	**368318**	**369667**	**379866**	**371337**
广 州	Guangzhou	54162	76485	57597	53090	53602	44013
深 圳	Shenzhen	26746	35302	38752	41697	42583	41370
珠 海	Zhuhai	11453	12501	11077	11095	11188	10972
汕 头	Shantou	17731	16127	15475	14778	17816	18369
佛 山	Foshan	26062	19628	21917	22389	22926	23127
韶 关	Shaoguan	18831	16928	13641	13031	13098	13800
河 源	Heyuan	14096	13951	8992	9504	9251	9135
梅 州	Meizhou	14510	14200	13955	14013	14029	14062
惠 州	Huizhou	14001	15696	18772	19705	21468	23125
汕 尾	Shanwei	9436	11314	12281	12621	12856	13196
东 莞	Dongguan	4437	8655	12026	12893	13822	13687
中 山	Zhongshan	6593	9246	9444	9276	10672	10562
江 门	Jiangmen	19639	21380	24833	24972	24839	24874
阳 江	Yangjiang	14608	15012	12302	12506	12832	12930
湛 江	Zhanjiang	22835	23882	20700	20885	21185	21434
茂 名	Maoming	22203	30504	26396	27832	28164	27879
肇 庆	Zhaoqing	10668	11662	12585	12543	12440	12248
清 远	Qingyuan	9796	14257	13550	13621	13773	13894
潮 州	Chaozhou	8142	8362	9246	8483	8555	8034
揭 阳	Jieyang	10350	11357	9173	9008	8968	8845
云 浮	Yunfu	8605	5825	5604	5725	5799	5781
按经济区域分	By Region						
珠 三 角	Pearl River Delta	173761	210555	207003	207660	213540	203978
东 翼	Eastern Region	45659	47160	46175	44890	48195	48444
西 翼	Western Region	59646	69398	59398	61223	62181	62243
山 区	Mountainous Region	65838	65161	55742	55894	55950	56672

主要统计指标解释

就业人员 指在16周岁及以上，从事一定社会劳动并取得劳动报酬或经营收入的人员。这一指标反映了一定时期内全部劳动力资源的实际利用情况，是研究我国基本国情国力的重要指标。

单位就业人员 指报告期末最后一日24时在本单位中工作，并取得工资或其他形式劳动报酬的人员数。该指标为时点指标，不包括最后一日当天及以前已经与单位解除劳动合同关系的人员，是在岗职工、劳务派遣人员及其他就业人员之和。就业人员不包括：

(1)离开本单位仍保留劳动关系，并定期领取生活费的人员；

(2)在本单位实习的各类在校学生；

(3)本单位因劳务外包而使用的人员。

城镇私营和个体就业人员 城镇私营就业人员指在工商管理部门注册登记，其经营地址设在县城关镇(含县城关镇)以上的私营企业就业人员，包括私营企业投资者和雇工。城镇个体就业人员指在工商管理部门注册登记，并持有城镇户口或在城镇长期居住，经批准从事个体工商经营的就业人员，包括个体经营者和在个体工商户劳动的家庭帮工和雇工。

在岗职工 指在本单位工作且与本单位签订劳动合同，并由单位支付各项工资和社会保险、住房公积金的人员，以及上述人员中由于学习、病伤、产假等原因暂未工作仍由单位支付工资的人员。在岗职工还包括：

(1)应订立劳动合同而未订立劳动合同人员(如使用的农村户籍人员)；

(2)处于试用期人员；

(3)编制外招用的人员；

(4)派往外单位工作，但工资仍由本单位发放的人员(如挂职锻炼、外派工作等情况)。

工资总额 指根据《关于工资总额组成的规定》(1990年1月1日国家统计局发布的一号令)进行修订，在报告期内(季度或年度)直接支付给本单位全部就业人员的劳动报酬总额。包括计时工资、计件工资、奖金、津贴和补贴、加班加点工资、特殊情况下支付的工资，是在岗职工工资总额、劳务派遣人员工资总额和其他就业人员工资总额之和。

工资总额是税前工资，包括单位从个人工资中直接为其代扣或代缴的房费、水费、电费、住房公积金和社会保险基金个人缴纳部分等。

工资总额不论是计入成本的还是不计入成本的，不论是以货币形式支付的还是以实物形式支付的，均应列入工资总额的计算范围。

平均工资 是指在报告期内单位发放工资的人均水平。计算公式为：

$$\text{平均工资} = \frac{\text{报告期工资总额}}{\text{报告期平均人数}}$$

城镇登记失业人员 指有非农业户口，在一定的劳动年龄内(16周岁至退休年龄)，有劳动能力，无业而要求就业，并在当地劳动保障部门进行失业登记的人员。

Explanatory Notes on Main Statistical Indicators

Employed Persons refer to persons aged 16 and over who are engaged in gainful employment and thus receive remuneration payment or earn business income. This indicator reflects the actual utilization of total labour force during a certain period of time and is often used for the research on China's economic situation and national power.

Persons Employed in Various Units refer to the total number of employees who work at his unit and obtain wages or other forms of payment at the end of the reporting period. This indicator is a kind of time point index and it equals to the sum of the number of employed staff and workers, labor dispatch personnel and other employed persons. Employed persons do not include:

1)persons who have left their working units while keeping their labour contract (employment relation) unchanged and receiving regular alimony;

2) all kinds of enrolled students who do internship in various units;

3)persons employed due to labor outsourcing;

4)persons who dissolve labor contracts with their units on the last day of reporting period or before.

Persons Employed in Private Enterprises and Self-Employed Individuals in Urban Areas Persons employed in private enterprises refer to the persons employed in the private enterprises which have been registered at the departments of industrial and commercial administration for which the business operation are situated at a county town (i.e. a town where the county government is located), or at urban areas with administrative hierarchy higher than a county town. The self-employed individuals in urban areas refer to persons who hold the certificates of residence in urban areas or have resided in the urban areas for a long time and have been registered at the departments of industrial and commercial administration and approved to be engaged in individual industrial or commercial business, including self-employed persons as well as helpers and hired laborers who work in individual households.

Employed Staff and Workers refer to persons who signed labor contracts with working units and working units would pay wages, social insurance and housing funds for them. Persons who have their work posts but are temporarily absent from work for reasons of study or on sick, injury or maternal leave and still receive wages from their working units are also included. Employed staff and workers also include:

1)Persons who should have signed the labor contracts but not (like people with rural household registration);

2)Employees on probation;

3)Employees beyond the staffing quota;

4)Employees who are sent to other working units but still obtain wages from their original units (situations like on-the-job placement, expatriated assignment, etc.)

Total Wage Bill It is revised according to the "Provision of Composition of Total Wages" (Order No.1 by National Bureau of Statistics on January, 1st, ,1990), total wage bill refers to the total remuneration payment to all employed persons in various units during the reporting period (by quarter or by year), including hourly-paid wages, piece-rate wages, bonuses, allowance and subsidies, overtime wages and wages paid under special circumstances. It equals to the sum of total wages of employed staff and workers, dispatch labors and other employed persons.

Total wage bill is pre-tax wages, including the room charges, utility bills, housing funds and social insurance paid or withheld by employee's units.

Total wage bill, whether or not included in cost, whether or not paid in money or in kind, shall be included in the calculation of total wage.

Average Wage refers to the average per capita wage in money terms during a certain period of time for employed persons. It shows the general level of wage income of staff and worker during a certain period of time, one major indicator to reflect the wage level. It is calculated as follows:

$$\text{Average Wage} = \frac{\text{Total Wage Bill of Employed Persons at Reference Time}}{\text{Average Number of Persons Employed at Reference Time}}$$

Registered Unemployed Persons in Urban Areas refer to the persons with non-agricultural household registration at certain working ages (16 years old to retirement age), who are capable of working, unemployed and willing to work, and have been registered at the local employment service agencies to apply for a job.

五、固定资产投资

INVESTMENT IN FIXED ASSETS

五　固定资产投资

简要说明

一、本篇资料反映广东省固定资产投资的基本情况，主要包括：固定资产投资，房地产开发、国有单位固定资产投资情况以及各市固定资产投资的主要指标数据。

二、本篇资料由广东省统计局固定资产投资统计处整理提供。

三、固定资产投资统计的资料来源主要为全面统计报表。按照现行的固定资产投资统计报表制度，固定资产投资按登记注册类型可分为：国有、集体、股份合作、联营、其他有限责任公司、股份有限公司、私营、个体、其他、港澳台商投资、外商投资。

四、2011 年起，固定资产投资项目统计起点由 50 万元提高到 500 万元，且不包含农户投资；2010 年以前为全社会固定资产投资。

五、2011 年报起，原国家预算内资金改为国家预算资金。

六、2014 年定报起，固定资产投资取消城乡分组。

5　Investment in Fixed Assets

Brief Introduction

Ⅰ.The data in this chapter reflect the basic conditions of investment in fixed assets of Guangdong Province, mainly including investment in fixed assets in the whole province, investment in fixed assets in the real estate development, and main indicators on investment in fixed assets by city.

Ⅱ.The data in this chapter are prepared and provided by the Division of Investment and Construction Statistics of Statistics Bureau of Guangdong Province.

Ⅲ.The data sources for the statistics of investment in fixed assets mainly come from complete statistical report forms. According to the present regulations on the statistics of investment in fixed assets, the investment in fixed assets is classified by the following status of registration: state-owned units, collective-owned units, Cooperative Units joint ownership units, other Limited liability units, share-holding corporations, units with funds from Hong Kong, Macao and Taiwan, foreign-funded units, private, self-employed individuals and others.

Ⅳ.Since 2011, the cut-off point of investment statistics is changed from a minimum of 500,000 yuan to a minimum of 5,000,000 yuan, and the data do not include the investment made by rural households. Data before 2010 refer to total investment in fixed assets.

Ⅴ.Since 2011, state budget is changed to state and local budget.

VI.Since 2014, investment by urban is canceled.

5-1 固定资产投资主要指标

Main Indicators of Investment in Fixed Assets

项目	Item	2000	2010	2014	2015	2016	2017
投资完成额 （亿元）	**Investment (100 million yuan)**	**3233.70**	**16113.19**	**25928.09**	**30031.20**	**33008.86**	**37477.96**
#房地产开发	Real Estate Development	858.61	3659.69	7638.45	8538.47	10307.80	12075.69
按登记注册类型分	Grouped by Status of Registration						
内资	Domestic	2676.65	13759.62	22782.88	26552.22	28971.90	33387.76
国有	State-owned	1219.19	5152.60	5824.56	6363.86	6181.63	7341.39
集体	Collective-owned	393.23	735.49	1105.34	1281.87	984.79	952.67
股份合作	Cooperative	19.43	49.91	128.09	108.25	70.28	54.21
联营	Joint	47.78	15.05	18.99	14.99	35.34	27.60
有限责任公司	Limited Liability	366.63	3393.58	7510.90	9228.26	11394.03	13316.28
股份有限公司	Share-holding	153.58	869.46	1239.60	1261.28	1017.75	1122.15
私营	Private	207.67	2212.44	5764.43	6772.59	7700.36	8708.22
个体	Self-employed Individual	248.51	909.02	271.85	344.79	415.89	342.69
其他	Others	20.63	422.07	919.11	1176.33	1171.84	1522.55
港澳台商投资	Funds from Hong Kong, Macao and Taiwan	416.34	1489.78	1819.51	2080.99	2470.68	2442.51
外商投资	Foreign Funded	140.71	863.78	1325.70	1398.00	1566.28	1647.69
按构成分	Grouped by Use of Funds						
建筑安装工程	Construction and Installation	2103.78	10396.22	17486.27	20083.47	21463.77	23943.51
设备工具器具购置	Purchase of Equipments and Instruments	597.29	2966.13	4265.61	5336.57	5806.33	6443.34
其他费用	Others	532.63	2750.84	4176.21	4611.16	5738.75	7091.11
按三次产业分	Grouped by Three Strata of Industry						
第一产业	Primary Industry	23.40	181.83	275.70	420.38	445.11	395.19
第二产业	Secondary Industry	768.82	5241.53	8428.21	10184.51	11088.49	12128.94
第三产业	Tertiary Industry	2441.48	10689.83	17224.18	19426.31	21475.25	24953.84
按财务拨贷款合计	**Grouped by Source of Funds**	**3396.79**	**18864.04**	**30138.60**	**36352.25**	**39510.62**	**42444.60**
国家预算资金	State and Local Budget	56.80	411.16	1418.73	1764.42	1911.77	2432.86
国内贷款	Domestic Loans	584.34	3171.76	4350.88	4546.87	4993.53	6853.86
利用外资	Foreign Investment	357.05	630.48	405.01	204.11	263.73	259.69
自筹资金	Self-raising Funds	1456.24	10668.57	17696.16	21056.20	20769.67	21767.71
其他资金	Others	942.35	3982.07	6267.82	8780.65	11571.92	11130.48
房屋建筑面积（万平方米）	**Floor Space of Buildings (10000 sq.m)**						
施工面积	Floor Space under Construction	23520.91	57221.79	81692.25	84133.98	84623.21	92203.09
竣工面积	Floor Space Completed	13492.94	20420.60	17294.71	15303.96	14042.25	14680.63
#住宅	Residential Buildings	8888.66	12267.54	6304.28	4998.12	5091.61	5954.07
商品房屋销售面积 （万平方米）	**Floor Space of Commercial Buildings (10000 sq.m)**	**2259.95**	**7321.76**	**9315.76**	**11681.01**	**14611.60**	**15958.81**
#住宅	Residential Buildings	2009.34	6552.81	8163.56	10497.62	13021.97	13522.51

注：1. 2011年起固定资产投资项目统计起点由50万元提高至500万元，且不包含农村农户投资；2010年以前为全社会固定资产投资，下表同。

2. 2011年报起，原国家预算内资金改为国家预算资金，下表同。

Note: a)Since 2011,the cut-off point of investment statistics is changed from a minimum of 500,000 yuan to a minimum of 5,000,000 yuan, and the data do not include the investment made by rural households. Data before 2010 refer to total investment in fixed assets. The same applies to all tables following.

b) Since 2011, state budget is changed to state and local budget.The same applies to all tables following.

5-2 固定资产投资总额

Investment in Fixed Assets

单位：亿元 (100 million yuan)

年份 Year	投资总额 Total Investment	#房地产开发 Real Estate Development	按产业分 Grouped by Three Strata of Industry 第一产业 Primary Industry	第二产业 Secondary Industry	第三产业 Tertiary Industry
1978	27.23		5.52	9.71	12.00
1979	28.29		3.29	16.98	8.02
1980	38.29		3.29	22.64	12.36
1981	60.40		3.66	27.46	29.28
1982	84.73		4.05	36.76	43.92
1983	88.71		3.52	37.22	47.97
1984	130.37		3.68	50.16	76.53
1985	184.59		4.90	95.99	83.70
1986	216.50	10.00	4.49	142.10	69.91
1987	251.01	16.29	4.19	168.28	78.54
1988	353.59	21.96	4.72	240.34	108.53
1989	347.34	48.15	4.99	127.90	214.45
1990	381.47	32.70	5.66	160.02	215.79
1991	478.20	49.75	9.11	174.64	294.45
1992	921.75	125.57	7.49	273.75	640.51
1993	1629.87	316.53	9.43	524.69	1095.75
1994	2141.15	404.13	10.63	714.97	1415.55
1995	2327.22	563.89	14.27	682.40	1630.55
1996	2327.64	528.85	19.41	665.68	1642.55
1997	2298.14	528.31	16.45	603.94	1677.75
1998	2668.13	602.72	19.46	660.64	1988.03
1999	3027.56	710.20	21.05	734.14	2272.37
2000	3233.70	858.61	23.40	768.82	2441.48
2001	3536.41	972.34	23.38	891.87	2621.16
2002	3970.69	1115.25	24.09	1217.29	2729.31
2003	5030.57	1233.52	14.56	1366.10	3649.91
2004	6025.53	1355.84	24.49	2153.67	3847.37
2005	7164.11	1591.90	28.72	2868.45	4266.94
2006	8132.37	1843.51	49.19	3247.29	4835.89
2007	9596.95	2519.13	69.92	3512.12	6014.91
2008	11165.06	2932.34	109.54	3936.80	7118.72
2009	13353.15	2961.32	130.25	4458.17	8764.73
2010	16113.19	3659.69	181.83	5241.53	10689.83
2011	16843.83	4809.91	213.58	5561.01	11069.23
2012	19307.53	5352.79	274.28	6544.31	12488.93
2013	22828.65	6489.59	354.13	7423.12	15051.40
2014	25928.09	7638.45	275.70	8428.21	17224.18
2015	30031.20	8538.47	420.38	10184.51	19426.31
2016	33008.86	10307.80	445.11	11088.49	21475.25
2017	37477.96	12075.69	395.19	12128.94	24953.84

注：1993年以前房地产开发投资主要是商品房建设投资。
Notes: Prior to 1993, investment in real estate development focused mainly on the construction of commercial buildings.

 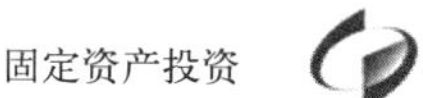

5-3 按资金来源和构成分固定资产投资
Investment in Fixed Assets by Source of Funds and Structure of Investment

年 份 Year	按财务拨贷款资金来源分 By Source of Funds				按构成分 By Structure of Investment		
	国家预算资金 State Budget Funds	国内贷款 Domestic Loans	利用外资 Foreign Investment	自筹和其他资金 Fundraising and Others	建筑安装工程 Construction and Installation	设备工具器具购置 Purchase of Equipment and Instruments	其他费用 Others
投资额(亿元) Investment (100 million yuan)							
1985	15.02	45.70	19.00	104.87	138.31	32.71	13.57
1990	12.92	73.92	61.07	261.60	246.56	103.97	30.94
1995	26.98	376.11	465.13	1641.16	1507.92	464.75	354.55
1996	22.52	347.75	494.70	1573.54	1507.04	498.79	321.81
1997	21.75	296.54	477.70	1605.60	1511.58	464.55	322.01
1998	46.53	414.58	394.44	1971.60	1688.14	546.06	433.93
1999	60.95	549.97	323.63	2167.05	1960.22	588.35	478.99
2000	56.80	584.34	357.05	2398.59	2103.78	597.29	532.63
2001	58.10	592.65	361.09	2680.24	2293.93	698.49	543.99
2002	73.58	749.21	439.31	3040.07	2548.91	783.70	638.08
2003	90.23	950.98	568.95	3996.32	3201.16	977.70	851.71
2004	72.39	1132.08	655.75	4864.42	3784.12	1247.82	993.59
2005	69.13	1366.09	786.05	5726.75	4520.62	1593.83	1049.67
2006	105.55	1659.26	865.58	6662.41	5221.87	1796.20	1114.29
2007	179.42	1755.86	984.01	8494.11	6088.11	1979.44	1529.39
2008	253.16	1877.90	779.48	9293.86	7140.54	2264.31	1760.21
2009	379.74	2695.36	682.36	12131.70	8800.83	2467.73	2084.60
2010	411.16	3171.76	630.48	14650.64	10396.22	2966.13	2750.84
2011	412.55	2827.15	574.03	15797.27	11019.16	3022.94	2801.72
2012	1002.17	3255.23	599.17	17799.55	12794.53	3366.14	3146.85
2013	1173.87	4147.42	683.35	21557.09	15262.61	3982.71	3583.33
2014	1418.73	4350.88	405.01	23963.98	17486.27	4265.61	4176.21
2015	1764.42	4546.87	204.11	29836.85	20083.47	5336.57	4611.16
2016	1911.77	4993.53	263.73	32341.59	21463.77	5806.33	5738.75
2017	2432.86	6853.86	259.69	32898.19	23943.51	6443.34	7091.11
构成(%) Percentage (%)							
1985	8.1	24.8	10.3	56.8	74.9	17.7	7.4
1990	3.2	18.1	14.9	63.9	64.6	27.3	8.1
1995	1.1	15.0	18.5	65.4	64.8	20.0	15.2
1996	0.9	14.3	20.3	64.5	64.7	21.4	13.8
1997	0.9	12.3	19.9	66.9	65.8	20.2	14.0
1998	1.6	14.7	14.0	69.7	63.3	20.5	16.3
1999	2.0	17.7	10.4	69.9	64.7	19.4	15.8
2000	1.7	17.2	10.5	70.6	65.1	18.5	16.5
2001	1.6	16.1	9.8	72.6	64.9	19.8	15.4
2002	1.7	17.4	10.2	70.7	64.2	19.7	16.1
2003	1.6	17.0	10.1	71.3	63.6	19.4	16.9
2004	1.1	16.8	9.8	72.3	62.8	20.7	16.5
2005	0.9	17.2	9.9	72.1	63.1	22.2	14.7
2006	1.1	17.9	9.3	71.7	64.2	22.1	13.7
2007	1.6	15.4	8.6	74.4	63.4	20.6	15.9
2008	2.1	15.4	6.4	76.1	64.0	20.3	15.7
2009	2.4	16.9	4.3	76.4	65.9	18.5	15.6
2010	2.2	16.8	3.3	77.7	64.5	18.4	17.1
2011	2.1	14.4	2.9	80.6	65.4	17.9	16.6
2012	4.4	14.4	2.6	78.6	66.3	17.4	16.3
2013	4.3	15.0	2.5	78.2	66.9	17.4	15.7
2014	4.7	14.4	1.3	79.5	67.4	16.5	16.1
2015	4.9	12.5	0.6	82.1	66.9	17.8	15.4
2016	4.8	12.6	0.7	81.9	65.0	17.6	17.4
2017	5.7	16.1	0.6	77.5	63.9	17.2	18.9

注： 1986年及以后的资金来源为财务拨贷款数，各项相加不等于投资总额。
Note: The source of funds since 1986 refers to financial appropriations, which do not add up to total investment.

5-4 按构成分固定资产投资

Investment in Fixed Assets by Structure

项目	Item	2016 合计 Total	2016 项目投资 Project	2016 房地产开发 Real Estate Devel-opmewt	2017 合计 Total	2017 项目投资 Project	2017 房地产开发 Real Estate Devel-opmewt
建设项目个数（个）	**Number of Projects (unit)**	**44652**	**44652**		**51117**	**51117**	
其中：本年新开工	Newly-commenced Projects	32059	32059		34351	34351	
全部建成投产项目	Projects Completed and Put into Use	31493	31493		36204	36204	
计划总投资（亿元）	**Total Planned Investment (100 million yuan)**	**126902.21**	**69281.77**	**57620.45**	**152892.15**	**84453.74**	**68438.40**
自开始建设累计完成投资	Investment Completed Since the Beginning of Construction	85181.36	40936.97	44244.39	102621.02	49000.02	53621.00
本年投资总额（亿元）	**Total Investment in this year (100 million yuan)**	**33008.86**	**22701.07**	**10307.80**	**37477.96**	**25402.26**	**12075.69**
#住宅	Residential Buildings	7147.15	169.49	6977.66	8232.53	131.60	8100.93
按隶属关系分	Investment by Jurisdiction of Management						
中央	Central Investment	1762.59	1557.12	205.47	1976.25	1731.83	244.42
地方	Local Invesement	31246.27	21143.95	10102.32	35501.71	23670.43	11831.28
按构成分	Grouped by Structure						
建筑安装工程	Construction and Installation	21463.77	14138.97	7324.80	23943.51	15614.64	8328.87
设备工具器具购置	Purchase of Equipment and Instruments	5806.33	5707.21	99.12	6443.34	6322.88	120.46
其他费用	Others	5738.75	2854.88	2883.87	7091.11	3464.74	3626.36
财务拨贷款合计（亿元）	**Total Financial Appropriations (100 million yuan)**	**39510.62**	**21844.58**	**17666.05**	**42444.60**	**23288.91**	**19155.68**
国家预算资金	State and Local Budget	1911.77	1911.77		2432.86	2432.86	
国内贷款	Domestic Loans	4993.53	2434.39	2559.13	6853.86	2770.39	4083.46
利用外资	Foreign Investment	263.73	233.50	30.23	259.69	207.03	52.66
自筹资金	Self-raising Funds	20769.67	15925.67	4844.00	21767.71	16426.13	5341.58
其他资金	Others	11571.92	1339.24	10232.68	11130.48	1452.50	9677.98
新增固定资产（亿元）	**Newly Increased Fixed Assets (100 million yuan)**	**16834.10**	**13620.84**	**3213.26**	**18936.58**	**15517.50**	**3419.07**
房屋建筑面积（万平方米）	**Floor Space of Buildings (10000 sq.m)**						
施工面积	Floor Space under Construction	84623.21	20389.41	64233.80	92203.09	19710.99	72492.10
竣工面积	Floor Space Completed	14042.25	7448.51	6593.75	14680.63	6484.29	8196.34
#住宅	Residential Buildings	5091.61	318.58	4773.04	5954.07	170.06	5784.01

注：施工项目个数不含房地产开发。
Note: The total number projects under construction excludes the projects of real estate development.

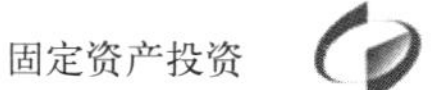

5-5 各市固定资产投资额

Investment in Fixed Assets by City

单位：亿元 (100 million yuan)

市　别	City	2000	2005	2010	2012	2013	2014	2015	2016	2017
全省总计	**Provincial Total**	**3233.70**	**7164.11**	**16113.19**	**19307.53**	**22828.65**	**25928.09**	**30031.20**	**33008.86**	**37477.96**
广　州	Guangzhou	923.67	1514.01	3263.57	3758.39	4447.30	4889.50	5405.95	5703.59	5919.83
深　圳	Shenzhen	677.12	1182.32	1944.70	2314.43	2490.20	2717.42	3298.31	4078.16	5147.32
珠　海	Zhuhai	95.08	218.23	501.55	787.62	960.89	1135.05	1305.14	1389.75	1662.02
汕　头	Shantou	112.48	154.14	361.68	611.92	780.90	1002.73	1274.32	1579.53	2006.40
佛　山	Foshan	198.96	741.43	1719.63	2128.33	2375.60	2612.45	3035.52	3512.04	4265.79
韶　关	Shaoguan	56.82	139.75	433.73	548.48	664.52	746.74	701.67	702.09	692.82
河　源	Heyuan	26.54	111.10	242.74	278.59	342.73	453.29	564.14	652.29	778.47
梅　州	Meizhou	44.45	97.66	195.52	230.14	280.50	407.51	568.06	650.36	806.77
惠　州	Huizhou	77.41	352.37	894.02	1208.68	1401.30	1606.71	1863.93	2039.71	2234.88
汕　尾	Shanwei	36.21	101.86	366.99	391.56	462.09	500.97	585.20	652.45	669.33
东　莞	Dongguan	102.89	592.20	1114.98	1180.35	1383.94	1427.11	1446.52	1557.46	1712.83
中　山	Zhongshan	109.95	320.92	660.37	893.43	962.93	903.66	1055.41	1149.01	1248.48
江　门	Jiangmen	104.34	228.87	631.77	850.41	1000.84	1111.65	1307.87	1517.77	1774.83
阳　江	Yangjiang	33.23	82.25	329.20	483.67	598.66	662.01	691.13	503.92	540.21
湛　江	Zhanjiang	68.94	168.00	526.57	572.28	795.58	1020.76	1313.69	1531.60	1641.53
茂　名	Maoming	73.57	147.72	244.54	427.37	660.53	850.55	1115.50	1262.76	1415.73
肇　庆	Zhaoqing	75.29	178.01	625.21	852.60	1007.78	1138.73	1330.03	1373.74	1497.55
清　远	Qingyuan	48.37	222.42	996.92	437.95	505.97	596.35	620.63	620.95	666.31
潮　州	Chaozhou	30.70	97.59	182.78	224.16	253.63	313.01	391.95	454.62	501.05
揭　阳	Jieyang	68.43	115.16	564.07	663.51	829.39	1093.80	1362.10	1485.54	1667.31
云　浮	Yunfu	32.98	103.44	312.66	463.66	623.38	738.09	794.15	591.51	628.50
按经济区域分	By Region									
珠三角	Pearl River Delta	2364.71	5328.37	11355.80	13974.24	16030.78	17542.28	20048.69	22321.24	25463.54
东　翼	Eastern Region	247.82	468.75	1475.51	1891.15	2326.01	2910.51	3613.56	4172.14	4844.08
西　翼	Western Region	175.74	397.97	1100.32	1483.32	2054.77	2533.33	3120.31	3298.27	3597.47
山　区	Mountainous Region	209.16	674.38	2181.56	1958.82	2417.10	2941.98	3248.64	3217.21	3572.87

注：2008年前全省总计中含不分区部分。

Note: Provincial total prior to 2008 includes investment unclassified by region.

5-6 各市按项目和房地产开发分固定资产投资

Investment in Fixed Assets By Project and Real Estate Development and by City

单位：亿元 (100 million yuan)

市别	City	2016 投资 Total	2016 项目投资 Project	2016 房地产开发 Real Estate Development	2017 投资 Total	2017 项目投资 Project	2017 房地产开发 Real Estate Development
全省总计	**Provincial Total**	**33008.86**	**22701.07**	**10307.80**	**37477.96**	**25402.26**	**12075.69**
广州	Guangzhou	5703.59	3162.73	2540.85	5919.83	3216.94	2702.89
深圳	Shenzhen	4078.16	2321.64	1756.52	5147.32	3011.46	2135.86
珠海	Zhuhai	1389.75	748.72	641.03	1662.02	995.90	666.12
汕头	Shantou	1579.53	1273.14	306.38	2006.40	1645.43	360.97
佛山	Foshan	3512.04	2282.07	1229.97	4265.79	2811.80	1453.99
韶关	Shaoguan	702.09	555.26	146.84	692.82	503.09	189.73
河源	Heyuan	652.29	476.57	175.72	778.47	554.54	223.93
梅州	Meizhou	650.36	477.83	172.53	806.77	588.73	218.04
惠州	Huizhou	2039.71	1292.07	747.63	2234.88	1350.69	884.19
汕尾	Shanwei	652.45	595.68	56.77	669.33	582.91	86.42
东莞	Dongguan	1557.46	914.70	642.76	1712.83	1010.68	702.15
中山	Zhongshan	1149.01	605.43	543.59	1248.48	624.51	623.97
江门	Jiangmen	1517.77	1164.16	353.62	1774.83	1324.27	450.56
阳江	Yangjiang	503.92	402.53	101.38	540.21	395.35	144.86
湛江	Zhanjiang	1531.60	1308.39	223.21	1641.53	1323.84	317.69
茂名	Maoming	1262.76	1152.92	109.84	1415.73	1247.51	168.22
肇庆	Zhaoqing	1373.74	1228.55	145.20	1497.55	1289.51	208.04
清远	Qingyuan	620.95	393.43	227.52	666.31	389.99	276.32
潮州	Chaozhou	454.62	392.88	61.75	501.05	434.24	66.81
揭阳	Jieyang	1485.54	1432.04	53.51	1667.31	1558.02	109.29
云浮	Yunfu	591.51	520.33	71.18	628.50	542.87	85.63
按经济区域分	By Region						
珠三角	Pearl River Delta	22321.24	13720.07	8601.16	25463.54	15635.76	9827.78
东翼	Eastern Region	4172.14	3693.74	478.40	4844.08	4220.60	623.49
西翼	Western Region	3298.27	2863.84	434.43	3597.47	2966.71	630.77
山区	Mountainous Region	3217.21	2423.41	793.80	3572.87	2579.20	993.66

5-7 各市按登记注册类型分固定资产投资（2017年）

Investment in Fixed Assets by Status of Registration and City (2017)

单位：亿元 (100 million yuan)

市别	City	总计 Total	内资 Domestic	国有 State-owned	集体 Collective-owned	股份合作 Cooperative	联营 Joint
全省总计	**Provincial Total**	**37477.96**	**33387.76**	**7341.39**	**952.67**	**54.21**	**27.60**
广州	Guangzhou	5919.83	4904.37	1355.98	81.79	1.40	0.06
深圳	Shenzhen	5147.32	4464.60	1355.83	7.00	12.16	10.67
珠海	Zhuhai	1662.02	1418.15	434.82	2.42	2.51	
汕头	Shantou	2006.40	1964.15	231.19	206.92	3.92	0.29
佛山	Foshan	4265.79	3674.09	529.76	89.74	8.61	0.52
韶关	Shaoguan	692.82	637.90	227.80	7.45	0.52	
河源	Heyuan	778.47	727.52	159.69	6.72		2.01
梅州	Meizhou	806.77	791.69	218.51	1.09	0.01	0.54
惠州	Huizhou	2234.88	2024.28	419.80	31.28	1.78	0.58
汕尾	Shanwei	669.33	619.32	84.62	17.51	0.12	
东莞	Dongguan	1712.83	1398.53	193.39	56.97	0.77	5.62
中山	Zhongshan	1248.48	1081.02	135.11	24.96	0.12	0.24
江门	Jiangmen	1774.83	1566.95	304.03	51.35	3.66	0.92
阳江	Yangjiang	540.21	518.47	94.40	1.14		
湛江	Zhanjiang	1641.53	1496.17	270.02	130.56	1.73	0.02
茂名	Maoming	1415.73	1392.10	274.31	57.83	1.82	0.55
肇庆	Zhaoqing	1497.55	1366.50	478.14	39.85	0.71	0.15
清远	Qingyuan	666.31	621.57	174.33	6.10	0.86	0.24
潮州	Chaozhou	501.05	491.01	135.18	6.94	0.57	
揭阳	Jieyang	1667.31	1620.99	157.44	118.27	9.71	5.19
云浮	Yunfu	628.50	608.39	107.07	6.80	3.23	
按经济区域分	By Region						
珠三角	Pearl River Delta	25463.54	21898.48	5206.85	385.34	31.71	18.75
东翼	Eastern Region	4844.08	4695.46	608.42	349.64	14.33	5.48
西翼	Western Region	3597.47	3406.75	638.73	189.53	3.54	0.57
山区	Mountainous Region	3572.87	3387.07	887.39	28.15	4.63	2.79

5−7 续表 Continued

单位：亿元 (100 million yuan)

市 别	City	有限责任公司 Limited Liability	股份有限公司 Share-holding	私营 Private	个体 Self-employed Indicuvual	其他 Others	港、澳台商投资 Funds from Hong Kong Macao and Twaiwan	外商投资 Foreign Funded
全省总计	**Provincial Total**	**13316.28**	**1122.15**	**8708.22**	**342.69**	**1522.55**	**2442.51**	**1647.69**
广 州	Guangzhou	2195.43	325.56	862.59	0.28	81.28	390.60	624.86
深 圳	Shenzhen	1682.47	209.69	1150.99	0.07	35.72	513.45	169.27
珠 海	Zhuhai	737.86	43.12	173.40	0.10	23.92	158.45	85.42
汕 头	Shantou	1134.36	30.22	311.39	8.60	37.26	23.08	19.17
佛 山	Foshan	1658.62	127.14	1082.90	7.66	169.13	348.45	243.25
韶 关	Shaoguan	259.00	16.41	114.64	3.10	8.98	24.63	30.28
河 源	Heyuan	272.13	26.18	201.08	0.18	59.54	41.99	8.95
梅 州	Meizhou	260.92	59.03	242.24	0.23	9.11	11.50	3.58
惠 州	Huizhou	629.67	39.03	752.12	10.98	139.06	146.32	64.28
汕 尾	Shanwei	143.75	1.35	74.20	61.74	236.03	46.42	3.58
东 莞	Dongguan	611.99	33.63	476.92	1.16	18.09	193.11	121.18
中 山	Zhongshan	444.36	19.62	406.46	27.22	22.94	94.41	73.05
江 门	Jiangmen	596.60	30.67	516.18	15.96	47.59	142.21	65.68
阳 江	Yangjiang	233.99	12.52	165.17	3.25	8.00	19.04	2.70
湛 江	Zhanjiang	425.16	36.90	450.81	18.81	162.17	92.10	53.26
茂 名	Maoming	517.28	29.61	426.51	47.56	36.63	21.50	2.13
肇 庆	Zhaoqing	341.05	25.33	386.31	8.64	86.31	86.10	44.95
清 远	Qingyuan	299.97	7.40	131.37	0.09	1.22	38.98	5.76
潮 州	Chaozhou	128.30	12.45	174.98	0.38	32.21	5.28	4.76
揭 阳	Jieyang	414.78	25.87	472.51	121.12	296.10	28.64	17.68
云 浮	Yunfu	328.59	10.43	135.46	5.56	11.26	16.21	3.90
按经济区域分	By Region							
珠 三 角	Pearl River Delta	8898.05	853.80	5807.87	72.06	624.04	2073.12	1491.93
东 翼	Eastern Region	1821.19	69.88	1033.07	191.84	601.61	103.43	45.20
西 翼	Western Region	1176.43	79.03	1042.49	69.63	206.79	132.64	58.09
山 区	Mountainous Region	1420.62	119.45	824.78	9.16	90.11	133.32	52.48

5-8 各市按主要行业分固定资产投资（2017年）

Investment in Fixed Assets by Sector and by City (2017)

单位：亿元 (100 million yuan)

市别	City	合计 Total	农、林、牧、渔业 Agriculture, Forestry, Animal Husbandry and Fishery	采矿业 Mining	制造业 Manufacturing	电力热力燃气及水的生产和供应业 Production and Supply of Electricity, Gas and Water	建筑业 Construction	批发和零售业 Wholesale and Retail Trades
全省总计	**Provincial Total**	**37477.96**	**477.21**	**145.34**	**10311.22**	**1653.88**	**33.88**	**708.77**
广　州	Guangzhou	5919.83	10.57		578.87	157.39	16.38	111.48
深　圳	Shenzhen	5147.32	0.21		795.94	119.95		30.66
珠　海	Zhuhai	1662.02	2.18	0.82	295.29	40.66		6.30
汕　头	Shantou	2006.40	14.07	1.17	1017.00	47.23	4.85	60.24
佛　山	Foshan	4265.79	19.40	0.34	1616.66	73.71	0.64	32.64
韶　关	Shaoguan	692.82	29.76	4.83	109.96	77.56		12.12
河　源	Heyuan	778.47	31.03	4.85	242.67	22.02		4.38
梅　州	Meizhou	806.77	3.05	1.87	200.92	39.40		14.12
惠　州	Huizhou	2234.88	24.14	2.65	667.26	114.54		29.26
汕　尾	Shanwei	669.33	22.36		174.94	95.83	1.24	35.89
东　莞	Dongguan	1712.83	0.45		555.33	91.76	0.16	19.31
中　山	Zhongshan	1248.48	0.25		285.36	42.36	0.41	33.14
江　门	Jiangmen	1774.83	20.88	4.84	657.54	122.14	0.49	23.74
阳　江	Yangjiang	540.21	9.80	2.43	173.58	99.61		3.06
湛　江	Zhanjiang	1641.53	121.03	67.60	386.26	173.40	1.18	50.03
茂　名	Maoming	1415.73	46.95	32.81	616.07	86.32	3.03	76.24
肇　庆	Zhaoqing	1497.55	52.07	7.23	549.74	71.99	3.29	29.18
清　远	Qingyuan	666.31	6.44	5.12	110.72	45.96		1.61
潮　州	Chaozhou	501.05	12.41	0.09	175.88	47.45		10.38
揭　阳	Jieyang	1667.31	30.98	1.59	777.77	62.29	2.01	97.17
云　浮	Yunfu	628.50	19.16	7.10	323.48	22.33	0.20	27.83
按经济区域分	By Region							
珠三角	Pearl River Delta	25463.54	130.16	15.88	6001.99	834.49	21.38	315.71
东　翼	Eastern Region	4844.08	79.83	2.85	2145.58	252.80	8.10	203.68
西　翼	Western Region	3597.47	177.78	102.84	1175.90	359.33	4.20	129.33
山　区	Mountainous Region	3572.87	89.45	23.77	987.74	207.27	0.20	60.05

5-8 续表 1 Continued 1

单位：亿元 (100 million yuan)

市 别	City	交通运输、仓储和邮政业 Transport, Storage and Post	住宿和餐饮业 Hotels and Catering Services	信息传输、软件和信息技术服务业 Information Transmission, Software and Information Technology Services	金融业 Financial Interme-diation	房地产业 Real Estate	租赁和商务服务业 Leasing and Business Services	科学研究和技术服务 Scientific Research, Technical Service
全省总计	**Provincial Total**	**3796.63**	**311.65**	**541.92**	**70.04**	**13623.59**	**610.94**	**266.82**
广 州	Guangzhou	906.71	31.85	217.59	5.17	2871.47	224.65	50.30
深 圳	Shenzhen	508.75	7.83	91.83	57.18	2602.40	135.49	83.39
珠 海	Zhuhai	266.41	7.62	8.34		744.74	49.96	14.68
汕 头	Shantou	94.21	17.02	16.62	0.64	426.87	18.71	10.87
佛 山	Foshan	321.62	13.99	34.09	0.49	1562.88	50.57	7.30
韶 关	Shaoguan	108.10	21.82	6.81		204.64	6.01	0.88
河 源	Heyuan	122.39	2.32	4.62		239.10	10.82	0.25
梅 州	Meizhou	133.23	16.74	7.16		250.30	8.10	0.29
惠 州	Huizhou	149.06	30.72	16.02		963.43	11.77	1.28
汕 尾	Shanwei	8.77	17.26	5.08		176.88	4.76	1.63
东 莞	Dongguan	127.31	3.01	20.53	1.90	767.22	6.12	20.82
中 山	Zhongshan	77.83	5.69	18.87	0.44	685.08	8.95	4.21
江 门	Jiangmen	162.69	23.32	23.63	0.49	492.29	35.16	45.76
阳 江	Yangjiang	59.26	6.33	3.97		145.25	4.06	0.66
湛 江	Zhanjiang	148.29	27.44	15.06	1.41	346.12	4.06	4.01
茂 名	Maoming	144.64	25.44	10.69	0.77	174.77	6.07	2.95
肇 庆	Zhaoqing	186.13	14.42	13.71	0.69	230.68	10.63	7.97
清 远	Qingyuan	100.67	4.94	6.29	0.14	283.84	3.61	1.74
潮 州	Chaozhou	82.67	6.33	7.53	0.34	77.46	3.54	1.81
揭 阳	Jieyang	52.69	25.14	6.62	0.37	277.29	4.77	3.02
云 浮	Yunfu	35.21	2.43	6.86		100.88	3.12	3.00
按经济区域分	By Region							
珠 三 角	Pearl River Delta	2706.51	138.45	444.61	66.37	10920.20	533.30	235.71
东 翼	Eastern Region	238.34	65.74	35.86	1.35	958.50	31.78	17.34
西 翼	Western Region	352.19	59.22	29.72	2.18	666.14	14.19	7.62
山 区	Mountainous Region	499.60	48.24	31.73	0.14	1078.75	31.67	6.15

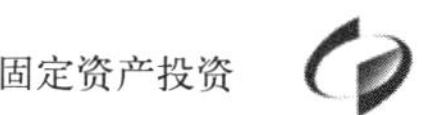

5-8 续表 2 Continued 2

单位：亿元 (100 million yuan)

市别	City	水利、环境和公共设施管理业 Management of Water Conservancy, Environment and Public Facilities	居民、修理服务和其他服务业 Household's Services, Repair and Other Services	教育 Education	卫生和社会工作 Health and Social Service	文化、体育和娱乐业 Culture, Sports and Entert-ainment	公共管理、社会保障和社会组织 Public Management, Social Security and Social Organization
全省总计	**Provincial Total**	**3548.85**	**47.23**	**528.55**	**333.57**	**304.05**	**163.82**
广　州	Guangzhou	537.66	0.47	67.23	80.47	37.18	14.40
深　圳	Shenzhen	513.09	2.93	91.51	56.63	21.47	28.02
珠　海	Zhuhai	152.03	0.94	25.42	6.36	18.15	22.12
汕　头	Shantou	217.29	11.82	15.12	7.86	22.23	2.58
佛　山	Foshan	429.98	3.75	45.32	22.95	23.94	5.53
韶　关	Shaoguan	81.07		11.27	4.33	4.67	8.98
河　源	Heyuan	67.35	0.51	11.66	6.81	5.59	2.11
梅　州	Meizhou	89.70		16.11	10.04	14.35	1.40
惠　州	Huizhou	167.09	3.76	25.76	13.50	10.96	3.68
汕　尾	Shanwei	86.15	1.85	15.89	10.16	8.35	2.28
东　莞	Dongguan	69.10	1.02	17.41	7.59	1.25	2.55
中　山	Zhongshan	69.27	0.68	3.99	8.71	2.87	0.37
江　门	Jiangmen	118.75	2.51	14.73	11.87	8.74	5.25
阳　江	Yangjiang	23.90	1.33	2.84	2.48	0.63	1.05
湛　江	Zhanjiang	176.95	0.71	53.91	27.92	26.18	9.96
茂　名	Maoming	122.63	6.62	25.86	11.93	9.96	11.98
肇　庆	Zhaoqing	248.66	3.03	23.96	9.75	23.94	10.50
清　远	Qingyuan	69.78	0.56	6.71	8.06	7.52	2.61
潮　州	Chaozhou	53.75	0.31	5.83	4.68	6.15	4.45
揭　阳	Jieyang	204.65	2.63	35.63	13.06	47.54	22.09
云　浮	Yunfu	50.01	1.80	12.40	8.41	2.37	1.93
按经济区域分	By Region						
珠三角	Pearl River Delta	2305.63	19.09	315.32	217.83	148.51	92.41
东　翼	Eastern Region	561.84	16.61	72.47	35.76	84.27	31.39
西　翼	Western Region	323.48	8.67	82.61	42.34	36.77	22.99
山　区	Mountainous Region	357.91	2.87	58.14	37.64	34.50	17.03

5-9 国有经济固定资产投资主要指标

Main Indicators of Investment in Fixed Assets of State-owned Economy

项　目	Item	2000	2010	2014	2015	2016	2017
建设项目个数　（个）	**Number of Projects　(unit)**						
施工项目	Projects under Construction	8934	8669	9219	9997	10267	11596
全部建成投产项目	Projects Completed and Put into Use	4070	4659	5220	5863	5360	5856
投资总额　（亿元）	**Total Investment　(100 million yuan)**	**1286.91**	**5152.60**	**5824.56**	**6363.86**	**6181.63**	**7341.39**
#住宅	Residential Buildings	185.38	171.36	181.56	184.86	126.35	154.17
按构成分	Grouped by Structure of Investment						
建筑安装工程	Construction and Installation	835.63	3558.70	4343.61	4747.02	4589.08	5429.88
设备工具器具购置	Purchase of Equipment and Instruments	222.31	741.84	700.78	777.93	643.88	583.75
其他费用	Others	228.97	852.06	780.16	838.91	948.67	1327.77
按建设性质分	Grouped by Type of Construction						
#新建	New Construction	635.88	3291.99	4283.19	4588.39	4833.83	6021.16
扩建	Expansion	280.76	684.71	644.90	865.39	634.87	525.23
改建	Reconstruction	128.62	844.39	683.52	718.42	529.53	651.43
按资金来源分	Grouped by Source of Funds						
国家预算资金	State and Local Budget	48.77	366.85	1213.39	1591.75	1658.74	2129.71
国内贷款	Domestic Loans	275.53	1111.67	1048.29	906.61	1129.78	1382.33
利用外资	Foreign Investment	55.08	35.97	24.64	1.62	11.30	43.23
自筹资金	Self-raising Funds	743.32	3303.88	3176.16	3576.48	2438.12	2558.56
其他资金	Others	164.21	533.65	432.73	668.40	630.22	606.35
新增固定资产　（亿元）	**Newly Increased Fixed Assets (100 million yuan)**	**1022.34**	**3305.85**	**4551.30**	**3901.13**	**2530.71**	**3106.39**
房屋建筑面积（万平方米）	**Floor Space of Buildings　(10000 sq.m)**						
施工面积	Floor Space under Construction	5010.21	5043.04	5946.25	5241.35	4098.01	4452.94
竣工面积	Floor Space Completed	2062.14	1261.43	1158.37	1078.40	842.23	542.67
#住宅	Residential Buildings	1024.44	231.48	226.66	139.32	145.18	101.36

注：建设项目个数、投资总额按建设性质分不含房地产开发部分。

Note: Number of projects and total investment by type of construction exclude real estate development.

5-10 基础产业和基础设施完成投资额
Completed Investment in Basic Industries and Infrastructure

单位：亿元 (100 million yuan)

年份 Year	基础产业 Basic Industries	基础设施 Infrastructure	电力、燃气及水的生产和供应业 Production and Supply of Electric Power, Gas and Water	交通运输和邮政业 Transport and Postal Services	信息传输、互联网和相关服务业 Information Transmission, Internet and Related Services	水利、环境和公共设施管理业 Management of Water Conservancy, Environment and Public Facilities
1990	139.95	132.62	24.73	46.77	28.75	32.37
1995	779.53	738.70	137.77	260.49	160.13	180.31
2000	1159.40	1098.68	204.91	387.43	238.16	268.18
2001	1187.24	1049.32	225.93	340.61	247.38	235.40
2002	1237.56	1127.94	300.13	348.87	242.34	236.60
2003	1655.29	1426.24	338.85	473.57	264.35	349.47
2004	2221.66	1858.46	548.32	627.93	267.91	414.30
2005	2612.47	2154.45	691.16	675.40	241.07	546.82
2006	2800.36	2392.07	714.76	820.49	218.37	638.45
2007	2989.95	2462.09	636.07	891.56	214.35	720.11
2008	3559.61	2935.03	749.57	1106.76	242.05	836.65
2009	5151.98	4488.32	1222.37	1664.65	278.46	1322.84
2010	5981.47	5394.68	1332.84	1908.64	239.17	1914.02
2011	5314.74	4544.10	934.31	1657.06	343.39	1609.34
2012	5642.85	4693.66	1063.32	1700.77	298.32	1631.25
2013	6578.24	5477.03	1133.46	2243.47	268.04	1832.06
2014	7392.42	5984.42	1099.42	2528.29	330.82	2025.89
2015	8558.98	6976.83	1206.47	2929.05	397.89	2443.42
2016	8904.91	7376.79	1294.06	2883.31	366.82	2832.61
2017	10506.02	9168.79	1653.88	3600.72	365.33	3548.85

5-11 按行业分固定资产投资主要指标（2017年）

Main Indicators of Investment by Sector (2017)

行业	Sector	投资额（亿元） Investment (100 million yuan)	施工项目个数（个） Number of Projects under Construction (unit)	全部建成投产项目个数（个） Number of Projects Completed and Put into Use (unit)	新增固定资产（亿元） Newly Increased Fixed Assets (100 million yuan)
全省总计	**Provincial Total**	**37477.96**	**51117**	**34351**	**18936.58**
农、林、牧、渔业	**Farming, Forestry, Animal Husbandry and Fishery**	**477.21**	**1880**	**1390**	**387.65**
农业	Farming	214.40	833	609	169.87
林业	Forestry	30.90	129	99	22.60
畜牧业	Animal Husbandry	88.33	325	232	73.24
渔业	Fishery	61.56	248	189	53.78
农、林、牧、渔服务业	Service Activities for Farming, Forestry, Animal Husbandry and Fishery	82.03	345	261	68.15
采矿业	**Mining**	**145.34**	**262**	**183**	**71.67**
煤炭开采和洗选业	Mining and Washing of Coal				
石油和天然气开采业	Extraction of Petroleum and Natural Gas	63.94	5	2	1.92
黑色金属矿采选业	Mining and Dressing of Ferrous Metal Ores	2.96	12	7	3.88
有色金属矿采选业	Mining and Dressing of Non-Ferrous Metal Ores	13.91	32	15	8.11
非金属矿采选业	Mining and Dressing of Nonmetal Ores	63.50	206	157	56.43
开采辅助活动	Auxiliary Minning Operations	0.66	3	1	0.69
其他采矿业	Mining of Other Ores	0.37	4	1	0.65
制造业	**Manufacture**	**10311.22**	**24153**	**17265**	**8154.01**
农副食品加工业	Processing of Farm and Sideline Food	284.17	779	547	227.25
食品制造业	Manufacture of Food	239.93	691	464	179.08
酒、饮料和精制茶制造业	Manufacture of Wine, Beverage and Refined Tea	106.50	245	166	81.24
烟草制品业	Tobacco Products	4.13	14	3	1.99
纺织业	Textile Industry	449.17	1316	1136	405.90
纺织服装、服饰业	Manufacture of Textile Garments, Apparel	447.86	1388	1149	411.12
皮革、毛皮、羽毛及其制品和制鞋业	Leather, Fur, Feather and Related Products, and Footwear	220.38	746	592	212.54
木材加工及木、竹、藤、棕、草制品业	Timber Processing, Bamboo, Cane, Palm Fiber & Straw Products	133.77	410	304	125.70
家具制造业	Manufacture of Furniture	276.21	648	396	200.67
造纸和纸制品业	Papermaking and Paper Products	220.95	461	329	197.06
印刷业和记录媒介复制业	Printing and Record Medium Reproduction	167.91	499	411	139.22
文教、工美、体育和娱乐用品制造业	Manufacture of Culture, Arts, Sports and Entertainment Articles	342.13	936	761	265.19
石油加工、炼焦及核燃料加工业	Petroleum Refining, Coking and Nuclear Fuel Processing	242.86	222	149	524.14
化学原料及化学制品制造业	Manufacture of Raw Chemical Materials and Chemical Products	455.98	1233	870	384.78
医药制造业	Manufacture of Medicines	161.56	420	237	100.04
化学纤维制造业	Manufacture of Chemical Fibers	11.66	25	16	9.77
橡胶和塑料制品业	Manufacture of Rubber and Plastic Products	509.04	1426	1091	410.39
非金属矿物制品业	Nonmetal Mineral Products	903.88	2449	1830	738.07
黑色金属冶炼及压延加工业	Smelting and Pressing of Ferrous Metals	104.55	200	132	67.34
有色金属冶炼及压延加工业	Smelting and Pressing of Nonferrous Metals	114.78	279	183	83.31
金属制品业	Metal Products	788.55	2217	1583	676.01
通用设备制造业	Manufacture of General-purpose Machinery	405.66	1020	700	278.42
专用设备制造业	Manufacture of Special-purpose Machinery	555.27	1339	880	399.63
汽车制造业	Manufacture of Automobile	449.14	541	319	268.71

注：施工项目个数不含房地产开发。

Note: The number of projects under construction does not include those of real estate development.

5-11 续表 1 continued 1

行业	Sector	投资额(亿元) Investment (100 million yuan)	施工项目个数(个) Number of Projects under Construction (unit)	全部建成投产项目个数(个) Number of Projects Completed and Put into Use (unit)	新增固定资产(亿元) Newly Increased Fixed Assets (100 million yuan)
铁路、船舶、航空航天和其他运输设备制造业	Manufacture of Railway, Slip, Aeronautics and Other Transport Equipment	143.07	192	124	78.11
电气机械及器材制造业	Manufacture of Electrical Machinery and Equipment	759.55	1942	1220	622.31
计算机、通信和其他电子设备制造业	Manufacture of Computers, Communication Equipment and Other Electronic Equipment	1560.76	1894	1243	883.50
仪器仪表制造业	Manufacture of Instrments and Meters	120.59	228	134	70.43
其他制造业	Other Manufactures	53.41	184	137	44.29
废弃资源综合利用业	Comprehensive Utilization of Waste	63.09	167	133	59.59
金属制品、机械和设备修理业	Manufacture of Metal Products, Machinery and Equipment Maintenance	14.72	42	26	8.21
电力、热力、燃气及水生产和供应业	**Production and Supply of Electric Power, Heat Power, Gas and Water**	**1653.88**	**2801**	**1666**	**907.51**
电力、热力生产和供应业	Production and Supply of Electric Power and Heat Power	1193.21	1694	1007	655.43
燃气生产和供应业	Production and Supply of Gas	77.38	131	57	42.75
水的生产和供应业	Production and Supply of Water	383.29	976	602	209.33
建筑业	**Construction**	**33.88**	**70**	**55**	**25.07**
房屋建筑业	Housing Construciton	2.68	11	8	5.17
土木工程建筑业	Civil Engineering Construction	19.59	21	17	9.70
建筑安装业	Construction and Installation	1.90	9	6	2.02
建筑装饰和其他建筑业	Architectural Decoration and Other Construction	9.71	29	24	8.18
批发和零售业	**Wholesale and Retail Trades**	**708.77**	**2020**	**1392**	**475.88**
批发业	Wholesale	284.02	834	611	197.08
零售业	Retail Trade	424.75	1186	781	278.80
交通运输、仓储和邮政业	**Transport, Storage and Postal Services**	**3796.63**	**2161**	**1118**	**1117.67**
铁路运输业	Railway Transport	479.43	54	11	6.95
道路运输业	Road Transport	2489.18	1579	882	630.40
水上运输业	Waterway Transport	207.14	143	45	121.49
航空运输业	Air Transport	357.92	18	5	225.54
管道运输业	Pipeline Transport	2.79	8	4	1.40
装卸搬运和运输代理业	Transportation and Handling	48.98	78	45	23.15
仓储业	Storage	195.91	245	103	99.27
邮政业	Postal Services	15.28	36	23	9.47
住宿和餐饮业	**Hotels and Catering Services**	**311.65**	**842**	**583**	**228.83**
住宿业	Hotels	233.59	519	343	161.16
餐饮业	Catering Services	78.06	323	240	67.66
信息传输、软件和信息技术服务业	**Information Transmission, Software and Information Technology Services**	**541.92**	**842**	**550**	**343.68**
电信、广播电视和卫星传输服务	Telecommunications, Broadcasting Television and Satellite Transmission Services	305.92	584	397	271.76
互联网和相关服务	Internet and Related Services	59.41	101	71	28.40
软件和信息技术服务业	Software and Information Technology Services	176.59	157	82	43.52
金融业	**Finance**	**70.04**	**53**	**18**	**11.22**
货币金融服务	Monetary and Financial Services	9.64	25	10	3.89

5-11 续表 2 continued 2

行　　业	Sector	投资额（亿元）Investment (100 million yuan)	施工项目个数（个）Number of Projects under Construction	全部建成投产项目个数（个）Number of Projects Completed and Put into Use	新增固定资产（亿元）Newly Increased Fixed Assets (100 million yuan)
资本市场服务	Capital Market Services	20.59	16	5	1.58
保险业	Insurance	32.24	7	2	0.09
其他金融活动	Other Financial Activities	7.57	5	1	5.66
房地产业	**Real Estate**	**13623.59**	**2463**	**1655**	**4055.80**
房地产业	Real Estate	13623.59	2463	1655	4055.80
租赁和商务服务业	**Leasing and Business Services**	**610.94**	**391**	**248**	**265.20**
租赁业	Leasing	166.97	30	22	143.77
商务服务业	Business Services	443.96	361	226	121.43
科学研究、技术服务业	**Scientific Research, Technological Services**	**266.82**	**432**	**238**	**94.73**
研究与试验发展	Research and Experimental Development	127.63	120	41	28.51
专业技术服务业	Professional Technical Services	46.10	171	108	27.34
科技推广和应用服务业	Science and Technology Popularization and Application Services	93.09	141	89	38.89
水利、环境和公共设施管理业	**Management of Water Conservancy, Environment and Public Facilities**	**3548.85**	**9132**	**5729**	**1912.25**
水利管理业	Management of Water Conservancy	403.21	1323	736	218.26
生态保护和环境治理业	Ecological Protection and Environmental Treatment	97.19	265	144	68.49
公共设施管理业	Management of Public Facilities	3048.46	7544	4849	1625.50
居民服务、修理和其他服务业	**Households' service, Repair and Other Services**	**47.23**	**189**	**145**	**41.33**
居民服务业	Services to Households	22.28	90	63	18.08
机动车、电子产品和日用产品修理业	Motor Vehicle, Electronic Products and Consumer Products Repair	19.70	76	61	18.43
其他服务业	Other Services	5.26	23	21	4.83
教育	**Education**	**528.55**	**1363**	**807**	**317.67**
教育	Education	528.55	1363	807	317.67
卫生和社会工作	**Health and Social Work**	**333.57**	**745**	**461**	**176.89**
卫生	Health	298.47	625	384	158.11
社会工作	Social Work	35.10	120	77	18.79
文化、体育和娱乐业	**Culture, Sports and Recreation**	**304.05**	**816**	**549**	**225.82**
新闻出版业	Publication	3.76	8	2	1.82
广播、电视、电影和影视录音制作业	Production of Radio, Television, Film and Video Recording	20.86	45	26	7.10
文化艺术业	Culture and Arts	137.13	386	260	91.16
体育	Sports	97.56	258	172	99.38
娱乐业	Recreation	44.73	119	89	26.36
公共管理、社会保障和社会组织	**Public Administration, Social Security and Social Organizations**	**163.82**	**502**	**299**	**123.67**
中国共产党机关	Organs of Communist Party of China	1.44	7	3	0.97
国家机构	Government Agencies	107.15	298	154	75.56
人民政协、民主党派	Chinese Peoples Political Consultative Conference, Democratic Parties	0.47	1	1	0.47
社会保障	Social Security	0.66	7	5	0.99
群众社团、社会团体和其他成员组织	Mass Organizations, Social Organizations and Other Member Organizations	35.73	98	60	28.43
基层群众自治组织	Self-governing Mass Organizations at the Grass-roots Level	18.38	91	76	17.24

5-12 各行业财务拨贷款资金来源主要指标(2017年)
Main Indicators on Sources of Funds and Loans for Investment by Sector (2017)

单位：亿元 (100 million yuan)

项目	Item	本年资金来源合计 Sources of Funds	国家预算资金 State and Local Budget	国内贷款 Domestic Loans	利用外资 Foreign Investment	自筹资金 Self-raising Fund	其他资金 Others
全省总计	**Provincial Total**	**42444.60**	**2432.86**	**6853.86**	**259.69**	**21767.71**	**11130.48**
农、林、牧、渔业	**Farming, Forestry, Animal Husbandry and Fishery**	**468.47**	**39.67**	**6.48**	**2.73**	**381.91**	**37.68**
农业	Farming	210.69	16.00	1.88	1.40	178.93	12.48
林业	Forestry	30.58	4.97	0.22	0.30	20.19	4.89
畜牧业	Animal Husbandry	87.19	1.33	4.11	0.13	76.74	4.88
渔业	Fishery	61.17	0.23	0.16	0.90	54.98	4.90
农、林、牧、渔服务业	Service Activities for Farming, Forestry, Animal Husbandry and Fishery	78.84	17.13	0.11		51.06	10.54
采矿业	**Mining**	**165.74**	**0.76**	**0.89**		**161.13**	**2.96**
煤炭开采和洗选业	Mining and Washing of Coal						
石油和天然气开采业	Extraction of Petroleum and Natural Gas	87.19				87.19	
黑色金属矿采选业	Mining and Dressing of Ferrous Metal Ores	2.97	0.03			2.94	
有色金属矿采选业	Mining and Dressing of Non-Ferrous Metal Ores	12.21				11.70	0.51
非金属矿采选业	Mining and Dressing of Nonmetal Ores	62.33	0.72	0.89		58.27	2.45
开采辅助活动	Auxiliary Minning Operations	0.66				0.66	
其他采矿业	Mining of Other Ores	0.37				0.37	
制造业	**Manufacture**	**9634.67**	**26.46**	**441.42**	**111.15**	**8698.82**	**356.82**
农副食品加工业	Processing of Farm and Sideline Food	274.61	0.94	9.91		248.92	14.84
食品制造业	Manufacture of Food	234.35	0.23	8.53	0.26	213.71	11.62
酒、饮料和精制茶制造业	Manufacture of Wine,Beverage and refined tea	107.67	0.06	3.61		101.34	2.66
烟草制品业	Tobacco Products	3.76				3.76	
纺织业	Textile Industry	436.46		3.72	5.61	419.95	7.18
纺织服装、服饰业	Manufacture of Textile Garments, Apparel	440.75		2.75	1.63	429.69	6.68
皮革、毛皮、羽毛及其制品和制鞋业	Leather, Fur, Feather and Related Products, and Footwear	213.96		4.36	1.28	184.68	23.64
木材加工及木、竹、藤、棕、草制品业	Timber Processing, Bamboo, Cane, Palm Fiber & Straw Products	130.71	0.07	3.61	0.48	123.39	3.16
家具制造业	Manufacture of Furniture	262.47	1.22	7.25	0.76	242.28	10.96
造纸和纸制品业	Papermaking and Paper Products	183.22		15.19	4.63	153.14	10.25
印刷业和记录媒介复制业	Printing and Record Medium Reproduction	165.08		7.51	0.86	148.52	8.19
文教、工美、体育和娱乐用品制造业	Manufacture of Culture, Arts, Sports and Entertainment Articles	329.79		5.58	3.52	311.77	8.93
石油加工、炼焦及核燃料加工业	Petroleum Refining, Coking and Nuclear Fuel Processing	203.73		51.22		150.80	1.71
化学原料及化学制品制造业	Manufacture of Raw Chemical Materials and Chemical Products	438.18	0.73	15.70	2.12	407.40	12.22
医药制造业	Manufacture of Medicines	156.40	1.42	8.86	1.31	139.67	5.15
化学纤维制造业	Manufacture of Chemical Fibers	11.38		0.05	0.48	8.52	2.34
橡胶和塑料制品业	Manufacture of Rubber and Plastic Products	492.47	0.10	19.75	4.67	446.76	21.19
非金属矿物制品业	Nonmetal Mineral Products	861.19	1.34	30.15	0.45	805.33	23.92
黑色金属冶炼及压延加工业	Smelting and Pressing of Ferrous Metals	99.77	0.10	14.10	1.11	79.94	4.51
有色金属冶炼及压延加工业	Smelting and Pressing of Nonferrous Metals	105.91		7.36	2.67	92.89	3.00
金属制品业	Metal Products	759.63	0.53	25.03	7.77	706.02	20.29
通用设备制造业	Manufacture of General-purpose Machinery	374.36	2.74	15.32	6.16	338.64	11.50
专用设备制造业	Manufacture of Special-purpose Machinery	503.38	5.86	14.48	9.17	446.06	27.81
汽车制造业	Manufacture of Automobile	353.80	6.29	9.37	5.05	323.73	9.36

5-12 续表 1 Contunued 1

单位：亿元 (100 million yuan)

项　目	Item	本年资金来源合计 Sources of Funds	国家预算内资金 State Budget	国内贷款 Domestic Loans	利用外资 Foreign Investment	自筹资金 Self-raising Fund	其他资金 Others
铁路、船舶、航空航天和其他运输设备制造业	Manufacture of Railway, Slip, Aeronautics and Other Transport Equipment	140.52	0.03	22.29	0.01	104.87	13.31
电气机械及器材制造业	Manufacture of Electrical Machinery and Equipment	705.54	0.78	20.02	7.28	666.64	10.82
计算机、通信和其他电子设备制造业	Manufacture of Computers, Communication Equipment and Other Electronic Equipment	1399.03	3.16	68.73	42.40	1208.45	76.28
仪器仪表制造业	Manufacture of Instrments and Meters	116.86	0.06	28.94	1.20	85.86	0.79
其他制造业	Other Manufactures	52.12	0.07	1.20	0.12	48.38	2.34
废弃资源综合利用业	Comprehensive Utilization of Waste	61.17	0.21	15.05	0.15	43.68	2.08
金属制品、机械和设备修理业	Manufacture of Metal Products, Machinery and Equipment Maintenance	16.42	0.52	1.80		14.02	0.07
电力、热力、燃气及水生产和供应业	**Production and Supply of Electric Power, Heat Power, Gas and Water**	**1570.75**	**96.95**	**418.94**	**13.05**	**926.37**	**115.43**
电力、热力生产和供应业	Production and Supply of Electric Power and Heat Power	1138.22	29.78	386.20	13.05	654.02	55.17
燃气生产和供应业	Production and Supply of Gas	68.47	3.92	13.27	…	38.60	12.68
水的生产和供应业	Production and Supply of Water	364.05	63.25	19.48		233.75	47.57
建筑业	**Construction**	**33.07**		**1.79**		**30.08**	**1.20**
房屋建筑业	Housing Construciton	2.68				2.38	0.29
土木工程建筑业	Civil Engineering Construction	19.01		1.58		17.43	
建筑安装业	Construction and Installation	1.90				1.80	0.10
建筑装饰和其他建筑业	Architectural Decoration and Other Construction	9.48		0.21		8.46	0.80
批发和零售业	**Wholesale and Retail Trades**	**683.09**	**9.61**	**54.32**	**3.10**	**566.23**	**49.83**
批发业	Wholesale	280.83	4.23	15.86	0.34	248.22	12.19
零售业	Retail Trade	402.26	5.38	38.46	2.76	318.02	37.64
交通运输、仓储和邮政业	**Transport, Storage and Postal Services**	**3374.10**	**717.40**	**1299.57**	**45.10**	**1109.90**	**202.14**
铁路运输业	Railway Transport	388.82	62.70	135.14		153.62	37.37
道路运输业	Road Transport	2222.93	593.06	837.15	39.42	625.43	127.88
水上运输业	Waterway Transport	172.20	34.34	16.79		93.34	27.73
航空运输业	Air Transport	352.58	9.07	281.73		61.75	0.04
管道运输业	Pipeline Transport	3.63	2.35			1.28	
装卸搬运和运输代理业	Transportation and Handling	41.20	0.55	5.02	0.21	35.04	0.38
仓储业	Storage	180.99	15.34	23.60	5.47	128.75	7.83
邮政业	Postal Services	11.75		0.14		10.70	0.91
住宿和餐饮业	**Hotels and Catering Services**	**296.54**	**0.73**	**14.17**	**7.36**	**248.68**	**25.60**
住宿业	Hotels	219.87	0.18	13.82	3.33	183.18	19.35
餐饮业	Catering Services	76.67	0.55	0.34	4.04	65.50	6.25
信息传输、软件和信息技术服务业	**Information Transmission, Software and Information Technology Services**	**306.84**	**13.41**	**15.51**	**0.28**	**265.60**	**12.05**
电信、广播电视和卫星传输服务	Telecommunications, Broadcasting Television and Satellite Transmission Services	89.56	4.42	1.62		80.27	3.24
互联网和相关服务	Internet and Related Services	43.72	7.59	0.75	0.27	32.79	2.31
软件和信息技术服务业	Software and Information Technology Services	173.57	1.41	13.13	0.01	152.53	6.50
金融业	**Finance**	**55.93**	**1.71**	**0.60**		**52.73**	**0.89**
货币金融服务	Monetary and Financial Services	10.83	0.71			9.97	0.15

5-12 续表 2 Continued 2

单位：亿元 (100 million yuan)

项　目	Item	本年资金来源合计 Sources of Funds	国家预算内资金 State Budget	国内货款 Domestic loans	利用外资 Foreign Inives-tment	自筹资金 Self-raising Fund	其他资金 Others
资本市场服务	Capital Market Services	18.78	1.00	0.60		16.45	0.73
保险业	Insurance	18.75				18.75	
其他金融活动	Other Financial Activities	7.57				7.56	0.01
房地产业	**Real Estate**	**20642.97**	**228.20**	**4249.89**	**61.46**	**6351.12**	**9752.29**
房地产业	Real Estate	20642.97	228.20	4249.89	61.46	6351.12	9752.29
租赁和商务服务业	**Leasing and Business Services**	**621.28**	**55.65**	**104.21**	**0.91**	**435.25**	**25.26**
租赁业	Leasing	180.36		68.31	0.91	110.04	1.11
商务服务业	Business Services	440.91	55.65	35.90		325.22	24.15
科学研究、技术服务业	**Scientific Research, Technological Services**	**256.06**	**19.59**	**24.65**	**0.23**	**201.68**	**9.91**
研究与试验发展	Research and Experimental Development	133.52	4.54	12.77	0.08	111.37	4.78
专业技术服务业	Professional Technical Services	44.07	11.46	0.31	0.15	27.86	4.28
科技推广和应用服务业	Science and Technology Popularization and Application Services	78.47	3.60	11.58		62.45	0.85
水利、环境和公共设施	**Management of Water Conservancy,**	**3057.43**	**877.40**	**166.95**	**2.52**	**1617.12**	**393.44**
管理业	**Environment and Public Facilities**	**391.68**	**184.77**	**21.00**	**0.39**	**125.13**	**60.39**
水利管理业	Management of Water Conservancy	88.46	29.42	2.85	0.60	47.28	8.32
生态保护和环境治理业	Ecological Protection and Environmental Treatment	2577.29	663.21	143.10	1.54	1444.71	324.73
公共设施管理业	Management of Public Facilities						
居民服务、修理和其他服务业	**Households'service,Repair and Other Services**	**44.41**	**2.25**	**0.06**	**0.62**	**38.54**	**2.94**
居民服务业	Services to Households	21.06	2.15	0.06	0.15	16.90	1.80
机动车、电子产品和日用产品修理业	Motor Vehicle, Electronic Products and Consumer Products repair	18.09	0.10		0.10	17.49	0.41
其他服务业	Other Services	5.26			0.37	4.15	0.73
教育	**Education**	**485.80**	**166.57**	**21.91**	**1.00**	**254.74**	**41.60**
教育	Education	485.80	166.57	21.91	1.00	254.74	41.60
卫生和社会工作	**Health and Social Work**	**307.24**	**98.24**	**6.45**	**0.32**	**167.68**	**34.55**
卫生	Health	273.97	91.44	6.15	0.32	146.42	29.64
社会工作	Social Work	33.28	6.81	0.30		21.26	4.90
文化、体育和娱乐业	**Culture, Sports and Recreation**	**291.35**	**28.20**	**24.30**	**9.69**	**183.40**	**45.77**
新闻出版业	Publication	3.81	0.10			3.46	0.25
广播、电视、电影和影视录音制作业	Production of Radio, Television, Film and Video Recording	19.81	0.03	6.40	0.69	12.08	0.61
文化艺术业	Culture and Arts	122.28	17.80	3.97	0.30	82.62	17.60
体育	Sports	102.61	9.61	12.82	8.30	51.31	20.57
娱乐业	Recreation	42.85	0.66	1.11	0.40	33.94	6.74
公共管理、社会保障和社会组织	**Public Administration, Social Security and Social Organizations**	**148.86**	**50.07**	**1.73**	**0.18**	**76.75**	**20.13**
中国共产党机关	Organs of Communist Party of China	1.08	0.51			0.38	0.18
国家机构	Government Agencies	95.90	47.34	0.87		39.18	8.51
人民政协、民主党派	Chinese Peoples Political Consultative Conference, Democratic Parties	0.47				0.42	0.05
社会保障	Social Security	0.66	0.01			0.65	
群众社团、社会团体和其他成员组织	Mass Organizations, Social Organizations and Other Member Organizations	32.44		0.74	0.18	24.51	7.01
基层群众自治组织	Self-governing Mass Organizations at the Grass-roots Level	18.32	2.21	0.12		11.61	4.38

5-13 各市财务拨贷款资金来源主要指标（2017年）

Main Indicators on Sources of Funds and Loans for Investment by City (2017)

单位：亿元 (100 million yuan)

市别	City	本年资金来源合计 Sources of Funds	国家预算资金 State and Local Budget	国内贷款 Domestic Loans	利用外资 Foreign Investment	自筹资金 Self-raising Fund	其他资金 Others
全省总计	**Provincial Total**	**42444.60**	**2432.86**	**6853.86**	**259.69**	**21767.71**	**11130.48**
广　州	Guangzhou	6715.08	537.47	1414.82	31.65	2722.35	2008.79
深　圳	Shenzhen	5860.05	783.88	1589.52	21.17	2127.00	1338.49
珠　海	Zhuhai	2258.96	74.15	627.49	67.62	914.74	574.97
汕　头	Shantou	1948.84	61.58	116.55	3.26	1578.85	188.60
佛　山	Foshan	4745.22	73.07	732.33	32.99	2561.55	1345.27
韶　关	Shaoguan	725.55	35.15	108.74	0.70	387.26	193.70
河　源	Heyuan	729.56	81.80	88.77	2.68	405.37	150.95
梅　州	Meizhou	748.90	63.87	84.92	0.11	414.20	185.79
惠　州	Huizhou	2659.45	68.17	269.71	29.00	1306.53	986.06
汕　尾	Shanwei	645.70	12.84	22.23	1.57	498.75	110.31
东　莞	Dongguan	2447.97	39.07	340.96	41.07	1003.72	1023.16
中　山	Zhongshan	1709.28	58.96	177.29	8.41	934.97	529.65
江　门	Jiangmen	1878.30	53.19	311.73	3.76	1025.07	484.55
阳　江	Yangjiang	607.19	18.93	98.76	0.32	337.92	151.26
湛　江	Zhanjiang	1716.09	78.26	168.75	1.92	987.92	479.25
茂　名	Maoming	1500.92	123.74	134.27	0.09	1008.33	234.50
肇　庆	Zhaoqing	1642.08	102.81	230.97	4.85	958.71	344.73
清　远	Qingyuan	1110.20	79.38	197.03	3.97	375.04	454.78
潮　州	Chaozhou	484.74	42.76	45.03	0.30	334.45	62.20
揭　阳	Jieyang	1648.92	19.70	37.38	3.94	1424.86	163.05
云　浮	Yunfu	661.59	24.10	56.61	0.33	460.13	120.43
按经济区域分	By Region						
珠三角	Pearl River Delta	29916.39	1790.77	5694.82	240.51	13554.64	8635.66
东　翼	Eastern Region	4728.20	136.87	221.19	9.07	3836.91	524.16
西　翼	Western Region	3824.21	220.92	401.78	2.33	2334.16	865.01
山　区	Mountainous Region	3975.80	284.30	536.07	7.78	2042.00	1105.65

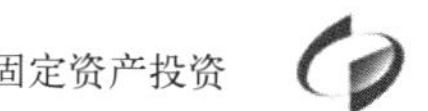

5-14 各市按构成和建设性质分固定资产投资（2017年）
Investment in Fixed Assets in Urban Area by Composition of Funds,Type of Construction and City (2017)

单位：亿元 (100 million yuan)

市别	City	投资额 Total Investment	按构成分 By Composition of Funds			按建设性质分 By Type of Construction		
			建筑安装工程 Construction and Installion	设备、工具器具购置 Purchase of Equipment and Instruments	其他费用 Others	#新建 New Construction	#扩建 Expansion	#改建和技术改造 Reconstruction and Technological Transformation
全省总计	**Provincial Total**	**37477.96**	**23943.51**	**6443.34**	**7091.11**	**29078.93**	**3308.90**	**3749.26**
广州	Guangzhou	5919.83	3197.03	894.75	1828.05	4881.53	146.62	459.59
深圳	Shenzhen	5147.32	3000.08	656.19	1491.05	4598.94	141.29	293.25
珠海	Zhuhai	1662.02	1030.57	158.65	472.80	1449.89	36.48	120.15
汕头	Shantou	2006.40	912.73	773.30	320.37	845.11	1012.73	101.87
佛山	Foshan	4265.79	3004.34	648.40	613.05	3322.52	300.92	556.31
韶关	Shaoguan	692.82	515.74	106.75	70.33	550.63	59.39	78.36
河源	Heyuan	778.47	553.51	131.67	93.29	651.09	19.58	85.02
梅州	Meizhou	806.77	635.73	91.49	79.55	699.92	18.16	78.40
惠州	Huizhou	2234.88	1658.01	359.91	216.96	1758.40	157.38	197.57
汕尾	Shanwei	669.33	458.28	93.93	117.12	417.19	130.11	107.93
东莞	Dongguan	1712.83	994.72	390.34	327.78	1259.69	73.72	254.67
中山	Zhongshan	1248.48	852.18	136.47	259.82	949.47	76.16	172.28
江门	Jiangmen	1774.83	1154.04	329.51	291.29	1334.78	170.66	216.40
阳江	Yangjiang	540.21	368.20	121.25	50.76	450.98	35.04	46.76
湛江	Zhanjiang	1641.53	1271.44	242.45	127.65	1199.98	258.45	144.89
茂名	Maoming	1415.73	905.90	371.17	138.66	1088.65	132.13	189.82
肇庆	Zhaoqing	1497.55	911.05	369.07	217.44	966.62	216.52	207.33
清远	Qingyuan	666.31	490.93	78.06	97.33	574.44	34.72	51.95
潮州	Chaozhou	501.05	353.80	74.99	72.26	381.63	32.66	69.90
揭阳	Jieyang	1667.31	1208.30	286.13	172.88	1236.98	218.00	205.57
云浮	Yunfu	628.50	466.95	128.87	32.68	460.48	38.19	111.24
按经济区域分	By Region							
珠三角	Pearl River Delta	25463.54	15802.01	3943.29	5718.24	20521.86	1319.74	2477.56
东翼	Eastern Region	4844.08	2933.11	1228.34	682.63	2880.92	1393.50	485.26
西翼	Western Region	3597.47	2545.54	734.87	317.06	2739.60	425.62	381.47
山区	Mountainous Region	3572.87	2662.85	536.85	373.17	2936.57	170.05	404.96

5-15 各市农业、能源、原材料、运输邮电业投资和比重（2017年）

Volume and Proportion of Investment in Capital Construction of Agriculture, Energy, Raw Materials, Transport, Post and Telecommunications (2017)

市 别	City	投资额(亿元) Volume of Investment (100 million yuan)				比重(以投资总额为100) Proportion (total investment=100)			
		农、林、牧、渔业 Farming, Forestry, Animal Husbandry and Fishery	能 源 Energy	原材料 Raw Materials	交通运输、仓储和邮政业 Transport, Storage and Postal Services	农、林、牧、渔业 Farming, Forestry, Animal Husbandry and Fishery	能 源 Energy	原材料 Raw Materials	交通运输、仓储和邮政业 Transport, Storage and Postal Services
全省总计	**Provincial Total**	**477.21**	**1577.39**	**1580.19**	**3796.63**	**1.3**	**4.2**	**4.2**	**10.1**
广 州	Guangzhou	10.57	89.54	19.76	906.71	0.2	1.5	0.3	15.3
深 圳	Shenzhen	0.21	99.93	25.03	508.75	…	1.9	0.5	9.9
珠 海	Zhuhai	2.18	74.12	29.06	266.41	0.1	4.5	1.7	16.0
汕 头	Shantou	14.07	28.16	80.04	94.21	0.7	1.4	4.0	4.7
佛 山	Foshan	19.40	46.06	281.11	321.62	0.5	1.1	6.6	7.5
韶 关	Shaoguan	29.76	67.06	54.28	108.10	4.3	9.7	7.8	15.6
河 源	Heyuan	31.03	17.72	55.69	122.39	4.0	2.3	7.2	15.7
梅 州	Meizhou	3.05	18.77	28.67	133.23	0.4	2.3	3.6	16.5
惠 州	Huizhou	24.14	148.47	69.35	149.06	1.1	6.6	3.1	6.7
汕 尾	Shanwei	22.36	88.79	10.25	8.77	3.3	13.3	1.5	1.3
东 莞	Dongguan	0.45	82.56	20.27	127.31	…	4.8	1.2	7.4
中 山	Zhongshan	0.25	36.31	16.22	77.83	…	2.9	1.3	6.2
江 门	Jiangmen	20.88	114.98	86.91	162.69	1.2	6.5	4.9	9.2
阳 江	Yangjiang	9.80	98.36	30.75	59.26	1.8	18.2	5.7	11.0
湛 江	Zhanjiang	121.03	255.04	90.84	148.29	7.4	15.5	5.5	9.0
茂 名	Maoming	46.95	124.93	188.47	144.64	3.3	8.8	13.3	10.2
肇 庆	Zhaoqing	52.07	53.55	144.64	186.13	3.5	3.6	9.7	12.4
清 远	Qingyuan	6.44	39.07	51.80	100.67	1.0	5.9	7.8	15.1
潮 州	Chaozhou	12.41	39.32	9.78	82.67	2.5	7.8	2.0	16.5
揭 阳	Jieyang	30.98	40.09	121.11	52.69	1.9	2.4	7.3	3.2
云 浮	Yunfu	19.16	14.58	166.17	35.21	3.0	2.3	26.4	5.6
按经济区域分	By Region								
珠 三 角	Pearl River Delta	130.16	745.51	692.34	2706.51	0.5	2.9	2.7	10.6
东 翼	Eastern Region	79.83	196.36	221.17	238.34	1.6	4.1	4.6	4.9
西 翼	Western Region	177.78	478.33	310.06	352.19	4.9	13.3	8.6	9.8
山 区	Mountainous Region	89.45	157.19	356.61	499.60	2.5	4.4	10.0	14.0

 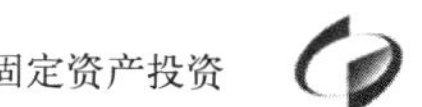

5-16 各市工业投资和比重（2017年）

Investment in Industry and Proportion by City (2017)

市别	City	投资额（亿元） Volume of Investment (100 million yuan) 工业合计 Total	采矿业 Mining	制造业 Manufacturing	电力热力燃气及水的生产和供应业 Production and Supply of Electricity,Gas and Water	比重（以投资总额为100） Proportion (total investment=100) 合计 Total	采矿业 Mining	制造业 Manufacturing	电力、燃气及水的生产和供应业 Production and Supply of Electricity,Gas and Water
全省总计	**Provincial Total**	**12110.44**	**145.34**	**10311.22**	**1653.88**	**32.3**	**0.4**	**27.5**	**4.4**
广　州	Guangzhou	736.26		578.87	157.39	12.4		9.8	2.7
深　圳	Shenzhen	915.89		795.94	119.95	17.8		15.5	2.3
珠　海	Zhuhai	336.78	0.82	295.29	40.66	20.3	…	17.8	2.4
汕　头	Shantou	1065.40	1.17	1017.00	47.23	53.1	0.1	50.7	2.4
佛　山	Foshan	1690.71	0.34	1616.66	73.71	39.6	…	37.9	1.7
韶　关	Shaoguan	192.35	4.83	109.96	77.56	27.8	0.7	15.9	11.2
河　源	Heyuan	269.53	4.85	242.67	22.02	34.6	0.6	31.2	2.8
梅　州	Meizhou	242.19	1.87	200.92	39.40	30.0	0.2	24.9	4.9
惠　州	Huizhou	784.45	2.65	667.26	114.54	35.1	0.1	29.9	5.1
汕　尾	Shanwei	270.77		174.94	95.83	40.5		26.1	14.3
东　莞	Dongguan	647.09		555.33	91.76	37.8		32.4	5.4
中　山	Zhongshan	327.71		285.36	42.36	26.2		22.9	3.4
江　门	Jiangmen	784.52	4.84	657.54	122.14	44.2	0.3	37.0	6.9
阳　江	Yangjiang	275.61	2.43	173.58	99.61	51.0	0.4	32.1	18.4
湛　江	Zhanjiang	627.26	67.60	386.26	173.40	38.2	4.1	23.5	10.6
茂　名	Maoming	735.20	32.81	616.07	86.32	51.9	2.3	43.5	6.1
肇　庆	Zhaoqing	628.95	7.23	549.74	71.99	42.0	0.5	36.7	4.8
清　远	Qingyuan	161.81	5.12	110.72	45.96	24.3	0.8	16.6	6.9
潮　州	Chaozhou	223.41	0.09	175.88	47.45	44.6	…	35.1	9.5
揭　阳	Jieyang	841.65	1.59	777.77	62.29	50.5	0.1	46.6	3.7
云　浮	Yunfu	352.91	7.10	323.48	22.33	56.2	1.1	51.5	3.6
按经济区域分	By Region								
珠三角	Pearl River Delta	6852.36	15.88	6001.99	834.49	26.9	0.1	23.6	3.3
东　翼	Eastern Region	2401.23	2.85	2145.58	252.80	49.6	0.1	44.3	5.2
西　翼	Western Region	1638.07	102.84	1175.90	359.33	45.5	2.9	32.7	10.0
山　区	Mountainous Region	1218.78	23.77	987.74	207.27	34.1	0.7	27.6	5.8

5-17 投资效益指标

Indicators on Investment Efficiency

项　　目	Item	2005	2010	2014	2015	2016	2017
固定资产及交付使用率	**Fixed Assets Rate of Put into Use**						
本年完成投资　(亿元)	Investment Completed in Current Year (100 million yuan)	7164.11	16113.19	25928.09	30031.20	33008.86	37477.96
本年新增固定资产 (亿元)	Newly Increased Fixed Assets in Current Year (100 million yuan)	4668.97	10744.63	18090.89	18466.39	16834.10	18936.58
固定资产交付使用率 (%)	Rate of Fixed Assets Put into Use (%)	65.2	66.7	69.8	61.5	51.0	50.5
建成项目及投产率	**Projects Completed Rate of Projects Completed and Put into Use**						
本年施工项目　(个)	Number of Projects under Construction (unit)	23472	50626	33416	38740	44652	51117
本年建成投产项目(个)	Projects Completed and Put into Use (unit)	10680	36926	22767	27410	32059	36204
建成项目投产率　(%)	Rate of Projects Completed and Put into Use(%)	45.5	72.9	68.1	70.8	71.8	70.8
房屋建筑面积	**Floor Space of Buildings Completed**						
本年房屋施工面积 (万平方米)	Floor Space of Buildings under Construction (10000 sq.m)	38351.76	57221.79	81692.25	84133.98	84623.21	92203.09
本年房屋竣工面积 (万平方米)	Floor Space of Buildings Completed (10000 sq.m)	17053.80	20420.60	17294.71	15303.96	14042.25	14680.63
房屋面积竣工率　(%)	Rate of Floor Space of Buildings Completed(%)	44.5	35.7	21.2	18.2	16.6	15.9
建设周期	**Period to Complete Total Planned Investment**						
计划总投资　(亿元)	Total Planned Investment (100 million yuan)	26335.04	62193.20	101000.17	110176.52	126902.21	152892.15
本年完成投资　(亿元)	Investment Completed in Current Year (100 million yuan)	7164.11	16113.19	25928.09	30031.20	33008.86	37477.96
建设周期　(年/月)	Period to Complete Total Planned Investment (year/month)	3/8	3/10	3/11	3/8	3/10	4/1

5-18 新增主要生产能力或效益

Newly Increased Production Capacity or Efficiency

指　　标	Item	2005	2010	2015	2016	2017
石油加工：	Petroleum Refining:					
蒸馏设备能力　(处理万吨/年)	Distillation Equipment Capacity　(10000 tons/year)	300		20	5	1000
裂化设备能力　(处理万吨/年)	Cracking Equipment Capacity　(10000 tons/year)	10	102	17	10	70
加氢精制设备能力　(处理万吨/年)	Hydro-refining Equipment Capacity　(10000 tons/year)	120	200			
钢材：	Steels:			512.85	561.20	267.60
热轧钢材　(万吨/年)	Hot-roll　(10000 tons/year)	280.35	103.60			
冷轧(拔)钢材　(万吨/年)	Non-hot-roll　(10000 tons/year)	377.55	75.45			
铜冶炼　(吨/年)	Copper Smelting　(tons/year)	25477	155000	3200		
铝加工材　(吨/年)	Aluminum Processing　(tons/year)	119780	184230	397572	83589	149222
铜加工材　(吨/年)	Copper Material　(tons/year)			15030	2000	
发电机组装机容量　(万千瓦)	Capacity of Generating Sets　(10000 kw)	526.93	763.96	770.20	382.27	309.67
#水力发电　(万千瓦)	Hydropower　(10000 kw)	37.32	108.39	7.26	20.84	9.49
火力发电　(万千瓦)	Thermal Power　(10000 kw)	433.57	580.00	559.20	181.50	69.70
输电线路(11万伏及以上)　(公里)	Transmission Lines(≥110000kv)　(km)	4066.05	6996.95	3171.11	2252.35	2239.82
水泥　(万吨/年)	Cement　(10000 tons/year)	1792	1751	638	450	400
塑料树脂及共聚物　(吨/年)	Plastic Resin and Copolymer　(ton/year)	32999	340713	204103	267409	331509
内燃机　(台/年)	Internal Combustion Engine　(set/year)				120000	
(万千瓦/年)	(10000 kw/year)				1152	
轿车制造　(万辆/年)	Manufacture of Car　(10000 units/year)			28	51	
电视机　(万部/年)	Television　(10000 units/year)				150	
新建公路　(公里)	Newly Constructed Highways　(km)	1860.61	3028.90	2441.95	1658.79	1171.55
#高速公路　(公里)	Express Highways　(km)	187.86	508.70	751.01	532.01	612.00
改建公路　(公里)	Reconstructed Highways　(km)	5379.79	4253.65	2664.16	2160.70	1461.21
#一级公路　(公里)	First Class Highways　(km)	309.70	237.85	197.76	366.80	230.71
新建独立公路桥梁　(延长米)	Length of Newly Constructed Highway Bridges　(m)	13032	22739	14080	9914	18382
(座)	Number of Newly Constructed Highway Bridges(unit)	118	48	22	12	10
新(扩)建港口码头　(年吞吐量：万吨)	Annual Handling Capacity of Newly Constructed or Expanded Ports　(10000 tons)	3158	3516	704	1227	9840
(泊位：个)	Number of Berths in Newly Constructed or Expanded Ports　(unit)	13	28	14	5	8
新(扩)建客、货运站　(个)	Number of Newly Constructed or Expanded Passenger and Freight Stations　(unit)	29	22	10	5	5
(平方米)	Area of Newly Constructed or Expanded Passenger and Freight Stations　(sq.m)	90564	221957	107349	30145	11165
程控交换机(指安装能力)(万线/年)	Program-controlled Switchboards　(10 000 lines/year)	82				
飞机购置　(架)	Aircraft Purchase　(unit)			33	36	56
城市自来水供水能力　(万吨/日)	Capacity of City Tap Water Supply　(10000 tons/day)	359.41	62.77	0.50	30.15	38.00
城市污水处理能力　(万吨/日)	Disposal Capacity of City Sewage　(10000 tons/day)	124.46	506.88	17.68	29.65	60.70

5-19 各市施工和竣工面积(2017年)

Floor Space Under Construction and Floor Space Completed(2017)

市 别	City	施工建筑面积(万平方米) Floor Space under Construction (10000 sq.m)	#住宅 Residential Buildings	竣工建筑面积(万平方米) Floor Space Completed (10000 sq.m)	#住宅 Residential Buildings
总 计	**Provincial Total**	**92203.09**	**50260.79**	**14680.63**	**5954.07**
广 州	Guangzhou	12044.84	6427.97	1496.38	832.80
深 圳	Shenzhen	7560.49	3076.68	351.23	183.89
珠 海	Zhuhai	3706.41	1921.69	454.09	281.06
汕 头	Shantou	3654.40	1756.00	685.80	241.35
佛 山	Foshan	11160.87	5880.58	1360.26	500.46
韶 关	Shaoguan	2085.24	1390.98	280.23	125.73
河 源	Heyuan	1665.14	1163.92	479.80	372.65
梅 州	Meizhou	1994.75	1355.42	310.09	211.74
惠 州	Huizhou	9160.92	5966.15	1742.73	847.26
汕 尾	Shanwei	954.01	561.69	100.13	14.02
东 莞	Dongguan	5617.97	3258.42	611.53	369.23
中 山	Zhongshan	6466.26	3780.01	1087.13	528.06
江 门	Jiangmen	4475.61	2219.08	946.41	339.42
阳 江	Yangjiang	1979.34	1331.58	208.39	93.48
湛 江	Zhanjiang	3144.35	1880.52	314.08	69.42
茂 名	Maoming	2756.88	1590.95	495.39	122.19
肇 庆	Zhaoqing	3037.39	1834.69	394.25	220.28
清 远	Qingyuan	3852.18	2801.50	447.02	288.01
潮 州	Chaozhou	879.24	546.12	249.48	129.90
揭 阳	Jieyang	4503.45	651.54	2542.37	121.21
云 浮	Yunfu	1503.37	865.32	123.85	61.90

5-20 房地产开发主要指标
Main Indicators on Real Estate Development

项　目	Item	2000	2010	2015	2016	2017
土地开发及购置（万平方米）	**Land Development and Purchases (10000 sq.m)**					
本年土地购置面积	Land Space Purchased in Current Year	1942.30	1726.31	1478.80	1750.32	1841.19
本年完成投资额（亿元）	**Investment Completed in Current Year (100 million yuan)**	**858.61**	**3659.69**	**8538.47**	**10307.80**	**12075.69**
#住宅	Residential Buildings	593.74	2539.03	5890.51	6977.66	8100.93
本年实际到位资金（亿元）	**Total Actual Funds in Place This Year (100 million yuan)**	**1064.51**	**7426.13**	**14164.30**	**17666.05**	**19155.68**
#国内贷款	Domestic Loans	228.53	1256.11	2577.81	2559.13	4083.46
利用外资	Foreign Investment	39.16	90.85	26.65	30.23	52.66
自筹资金	Self-raising Funds	287.71	1582.94	3933.40	4844.00	5341.58
定金及预收款	Deposit and Advances Received	423.32	1537.64	4656.66	5586.91	5988.25
个人按揭贷款	Personal Mortgage Loan		974.17	2322.61	3569.32	2974.61
其他到位资金	Others	85.79	1984.42	647.17	1076.46	715.12
房屋建筑面积（万平方米）	**Floor Space of Buildings (10000 sq.m)**					
施工面积	Floor Space under Construction	9922.12	29301.36	57941.86	64233.80	72492.10
#住宅	Residential Buildings	7400.38	22253.76	40388.82	44171.00	49450.82
竣工面积	Floor Space Completed	3161.39	5659.10	6044.43	6593.75	8196.34
#住宅	Residential Buildings	2598.52	4589.22	4435.40	4773.04	5784.01
竣工房屋价值（亿元）	**Value of Buildings Completed(100 million yuan)**	**511.46**	**1587.46**	**2256.69**	**2493.40**	**2871.97**
#住宅	Residential Buildings	415.94	1276.09	1639.45	1776.33	1980.80
商品房屋销售额（亿元）	**Total Sales (100 million yuan)**	**729.50**	**5480.77**	**11442.80**	**16214.61**	**18792.76**
#住宅	Residential Buildings	597.36	4589.82	9967.32	14240.33	15437.89
商品房屋销售面积（万平方米）	**Floor Space of Commerdal Buildings Sold (10000 sq.m)**	**2259.95**	**7321.76**	**11681.01**	**14611.60**	**15958.81**
#住宅	Residential Buildings	2009.34	6552.81	10497.62	13021.97	13522.51

注：2000年其他到位在资金包括个人按揭贷款。
Note:Others funds in place in 2000 include personal mortgage loan.

5-21 房地产开发投资情况
Investment in Real Estate Development

单位：亿元 (100 million yuan)

按登记注册类型分组	By Registration Status	2016 完成投资额 Investment Completed	2016 #住宅 Residential Buildings	2017 完成投资额 Investment Completed	2017 #住宅 Residential Buildings
全省总计	**Provincial Total**	**10307.80**	**6977.66**	**12075.69**	**8100.93**
内资	Domestic	8868.10	6085.04	10696.77	7289.99
国有	State-owned	166.95	92.61	252.25	123.85
集体	Collective-owned	63.85	48.34	50.32	40.92
股份合作	Cooperative	24.02	20.11	3.77	3.05
联营	Joint	0.26	0.14		
其他有限责任公司	Other Limited Liability	5497.62	3784.69	6626.80	4545.08
股份有限公司	Share-holding	233.21	168.62	222.29	163.67
私营	Private	2856.60	1954.42	3507.33	2391.01
其他	Others	25.59	16.11	34.01	22.42
港、澳、台商投资	Funds from Hong Kong, Macao and Taiwan	1002.20	613.44	975.02	518.71
外商投资	Foreign Funded	437.49	279.18	403.90	292.23

5-22 房地产开发房屋建筑面积及价值（2017年）
Floor Space and Value of Buildings in Real Estate Development (2017)

按登记注册类型分组	By Registration Status	房屋建筑面积(万平方米) Floor Space of Buildings(10000 sq.m) 施工面积 Floor Space of Buildings under Construction	竣工面积 Floor Space of Buildings Completed	#住宅 Residential Buildings	竣工房屋价值（亿元）Value of Buildings Completed (100 million yuan)	#住宅 Residential Buildings
全省总计	**Provincial Total**	**72492.10**	**8196.34**	**5784.01**	**2871.97**	**1980.80**
内资	Domestic-funded Economy	64063.86	7375.11	5215.36	2573.90	1778.79
国有	State-owned	1387.95	110.12	74.96	50.38	36.17
集体	Collective-owned	395.07	128.61	98.24	40.47	33.74
股份合作	Cooperative	52.65	7.97	5.63	2.79	1.97
联营	Joint					
有限责任公司	Limited Liability	39818.02	4400.70	3073.17	1516.44	1024.06
股份有限公司	Share-holding	1629.99	346.30	244.21	160.47	113.18
私营	Private	20692.83	2377.00	1714.75	802.75	569.07
其他	Others	87.36	4.40	4.40	0.60	0.60
港、澳、台商投资	Funds from Hong Kong, Macao and Taiwan	6036.62	581.49	394.93	210.07	136.81
外商投资	Foreign Funded	2391.62	239.73	173.72	87.99	65.21

5-23 各市房地产开发投资情况（2017年）
Investment in Real Estate Development by City (2017)

单位：亿元 (100 million yuan)

市别	City	完成投资额 Investment Completed	按用途分 By use #住宅 Residential Buildings	#别墅、高档公寓 Villas,High-grade Apartments	办公楼 Office Buildings	商业营业用房 Houses for Business Use	其他 Others
全省总计	**Provincial Total**	**12075.69**	**8100.93**	**515.34**	**1173.67**	**1445.15**	**1355.95**
广　州	Guangzhou	2702.89	1769.49	160.58	330.23	298.50	304.67
深　圳	Shenzhen	2135.86	1014.05	65.91	535.82	340.06	245.92
珠　海	Zhuhai	666.12	425.22	40.18	89.70	72.10	79.09
汕　头	Shantou	360.97	219.93	7.69	17.57	31.26	92.21
佛　山	Foshan	1453.99	1017.42	34.51	68.23	188.83	179.51
韶　关	Shaoguan	189.73	147.89	3.20	1.08	25.37	15.39
河　源	Heyuan	223.93	179.28	1.22	7.18	22.85	14.62
梅　州	Meizhou	218.04	171.18	5.86	0.71	26.51	19.64
惠　州	Huizhou	884.19	725.21	49.58	9.91	78.33	70.75
汕　尾	Shanwei	86.42	60.37	4.06	0.10	9.34	16.61
东　莞	Dongguan	702.15	512.44	63.99	64.90	67.05	57.76
中　山	Zhongshan	623.97	444.74	7.93	16.52	83.70	79.01
江　门	Jiangmen	450.56	344.12	23.32	1.89	46.95	57.60
阳　江	Yangjiang	144.86	112.80	8.79	2.18	18.00	11.88
湛　江	Zhanjiang	317.69	241.58	8.96	8.78	33.35	33.98
茂　名	Maoming	168.22	144.31	3.96	2.63	11.93	9.34
肇　庆	Zhaoqing	208.04	146.86	9.72	11.72	28.89	20.57
清　远	Qingyuan	276.32	214.35	13.39	2.47	38.98	20.52
潮　州	Chaozhou	66.81	49.49		1.39	4.85	11.08
揭　阳	Jieyang	109.29	92.34	0.31	0.39	6.48	10.09
云　浮	Yunfu	85.63	67.86	2.18	0.27	11.82	5.68
按经济区域分	By Region						
珠三角	Pearl River Delta	9827.78	6399.56	455.71	1128.91	1204.42	1094.89
东　翼	Eastern Region	623.49	422.12	12.07	19.45	51.92	129.99
西　翼	Western Region	630.77	498.69	21.71	13.59	63.28	55.20
山　区	Mountainous Region	993.66	780.56	25.85	11.71	125.53	75.87

5-24 各市房地产开发房屋建筑面积及价值（2017年）

Floor Space and Value of Buildings in Real Estate Development by City (2017)

市别	City	房屋建筑面积(万平方米) Floor Spaceof Buildings(10000 sq.m)			竣工房屋价值(亿元) Value of Buildings Completed (100 million yuan)	
		施工面积 Floor Space of Buildings under Construction	竣工面积 Floor Space of Buildings Completed	#住宅 Residential Buildings		#住宅 Residential Buildings
全省总计	**Provincial Total**	**72492.10**	**8196.34**	**5784.01**	**2871.97**	**1980.80**
广州	Guangzhou	10658.49	1320.66	831.83	487.57	305.82
深圳	Shenzhen	5709.34	285.06	183.79	278.46	170.72
珠海	Zhuhai	3253.98	422.80	280.07	160.03	102.76
汕头	Shantou	2663.64	325.95	229.68	109.14	79.13
佛山	Foshan	9102.96	784.54	500.46	354.87	223.52
韶关	Shaoguan	1804.42	202.76	124.75	45.89	27.26
河源	Heyuan	1409.90	437.30	371.80	104.92	86.88
梅州	Meizhou	1730.15	267.33	210.86	60.52	48.88
惠州	Huizhou	7604.45	1039.86	824.64	301.44	248.80
汕尾	Shanwei	606.03	17.77	11.72	2.30	1.81
东莞	Dongguan	4553.68	471.02	363.39	218.70	185.57
中山	Zhongshan	5331.97	810.20	526.89	263.53	158.04
江门	Jiangmen	3161.66	463.83	336.02	127.82	80.49
阳江	Yangjiang	1788.38	105.87	91.50	24.18	21.66
湛江	Zhanjiang	2584.73	155.84	68.24	47.22	20.96
茂名	Maoming	2002.00	116.15	93.97	28.78	23.96
肇庆	Zhaoqing	2483.61	260.55	207.94	71.97	55.64
清远	Qingyuan	3595.95	386.63	282.77	108.93	80.10
潮州	Chaozhou	699.90	154.71	128.43	36.61	29.43
揭阳	Jieyang	582.66	57.25	53.35	16.49	15.36
云浮	Yunfu	1164.21	110.26	61.90	22.60	13.99
按经济区域分	By Region					
珠三角	Pearl River Delta	51860.12	5858.52	4055.02	2264.38	1531.37
东翼	Eastern Region	4552.24	555.69	423.18	164.54	125.73
西翼	Western Region	6375.11	377.86	253.71	100.18	66.58
山区	Mountainous Region	9704.63	1404.27	1052.09	342.87	257.12

5-25 按用途分商品房屋销售面积(2017年)

Floor Space of Commercialized Buildings Sold by Use(2017)

单位：万平方米 (10 000 sq.m)

按登记注册类型分组	By Registration Status	商品房销售面积合计 Floor Space of Commercialized Buildings Sold	按用途分 By use 住宅 Residential Buildings	#别墅、高档公寓 Villas, Highgrade Apartments	办公楼 Office Buildings	商业营业用房 Houses for Business Use	其他 Others
全省总计	**Provincial Total**	**15958.81**	**13522.51**	**543.25**	**659.40**	**885.74**	**891.15**
内资	Domestic-funded Economy	14385.92	12289.18	461.58	562.59	803.08	731.07
国有	State-owned	203.11	167.30	4.88	18.30	12.12	5.39
集体	Collective-owned	122.67	107.65	0.63	2.44	5.44	7.14
股份合作	Cooperative	13.47	12.88			0.59	
联营	Joint						
有限责任公司	Limited Liability	9046.46	7605.93	318.97	388.06	523.29	529.17
股份有限公司	Share-holding	366.89	333.27	5.87	10.14	15.33	8.14
私营	Private	4603.89	4041.11	130.24	135.34	246.22	181.22
其他	Others	29.43	21.04	1.00	8.31	0.08	
港、澳、台商投资	Funds from Hong Kong, Macao and Taiwan	1075.76	863.17	58.01	67.48	52.08	93.04
外商投资	Foreign Funded	497.12	370.16	23.66	29.34	30.58	67.04

5-26 按用途分商品房屋销售额(2017年)

Sales Volume of Commercialized Buildings Sold by Use(2017)

单位：亿元 (100 million yuan)

按登记注册类型分组	By Registration Status	商品房销售额合计 Floor Space of Commercialized Buildings Sold	按用途分 By use 住宅 Residential Buildings	#别墅、高档公寓 Villas, Highgrade Apartments	办公楼 Office Buildings	商业营业用房 Houses for Business Use	其他 Others
全省总计	**Provincial Total**	**18792.76**	**15437.89**	**900.33**	**1394.74**	**1286.90**	**673.23**
内资	Domestic-funded Economy	16460.36	13651.05	762.15	1163.45	1100.87	544.99
国有	State-owned	293.41	225.79	11.80	32.23	23.32	12.07
集体	Collective-owned	136.69	122.59	0.52	2.64	7.65	3.80
股份合作	Cooperative	9.61	8.96			0.64	
联营	Joint						
有限责任公司	Limited Liability	10602.64	8735.44	563.51	788.65	701.11	377.43
股份有限公司	Share-holding	466.53	427.20	7.44	10.40	18.35	10.58
私营	Private	4901.54	4104.50	177.06	306.29	349.65	141.11
其他	Others	49.95	26.57	1.82	23.23	0.15	
港、澳、台商投资	Funds from Hong Kong, Macao and Taiwan	1600.84	1230.80	94.71	166.75	115.37	87.93
外商投资	Foreign Funded	731.56	556.05	43.47	64.54	70.66	40.31

5-27 各市商品房屋销售情况（2017年）
Sales of Commercial Buildings by City (2017)

市 别	City	商品房销售面积（万平方米）Floor Space of Buildings Commerdal Actually Sold (10000 sq.m)	#住宅 Residential Buildings	商品房销售额（亿元）Sales Volume of Buildings Commerdal Actually Sold (100 million yuan)	#住宅 Residential Buildings
全省总计	**Provincial Total**	**15958.81**	**13522.51**	**18792.76**	**15437.89**
广 州	Guangzhou	1757.75	1367.48	3099.52	2418.36
深 圳	Shenzhen	671.03	520.97	3216.65	2533.04
珠 海	Zhuhai	509.65	420.28	1093.42	881.39
汕 头	Shantou	639.58	594.16	629.73	554.65
佛 山	Foshan	2800.17	2076.51	3073.04	2362.10
韶 关	Shaoguan	449.09	426.72	235.44	215.15
河 源	Heyuan	536.15	507.09	269.19	251.52
梅 州	Meizhou	498.79	463.15	286.35	258.36
惠 州	Huizhou	1645.65	1543.40	1628.81	1537.12
汕 尾	Shanwei	231.32	183.82	141.41	99.02
东 莞	Dongguan	799.46	588.81	1349.22	1016.96
中 山	Zhongshan	874.81	650.07	884.65	705.45
江 门	Jiangmen	788.16	710.99	572.40	514.39
阳 江	Yangjiang	452.07	424.75	247.91	223.67
湛 江	Zhanjiang	589.40	554.57	425.93	393.30
茂 名	Maoming	516.08	500.86	317.17	302.97
肇 庆	Zhaoqing	598.01	542.08	365.61	322.75
清 远	Qingyuan	900.58	808.74	585.11	517.47
潮 州	Chaozhou	145.72	135.15	85.54	77.91
揭 阳	Jieyang	220.71	211.87	122.29	113.07
云 浮	Yunfu	334.62	291.04	163.38	139.26
按经济区域分	By Region				
珠 三 角	Pearl River Delta	10444.70	8420.58	15283.32	12291.55
东 翼	Eastern Region	1237.33	1125.00	978.97	844.64
西 翼	Western Region	1557.56	1480.18	991.00	919.94
山 区	Mountainous Region	2719.22	2496.75	1539.47	1381.76

主要统计指标解释

固定资产投资额 是以货币形式表现的在一定时期内建造和购置固定资产的工作量以及与此有关的费用的总称。它是反映固定资产投资规模、结构和发展速度的综合性指标，又是观察工程进度和考核投资效果的重要依据。

房地产开发投资 各种登记注册类型的房地产开发公司 、商品房建设公司及其他房地产开发单位统一开发的包括统代建、拆迁还建的住宅、厂房、仓库、饭店、宾馆、度假村、写字楼、办公楼等房屋建筑物和配套的服务设施、土地开发工程，如道路、给水、排水、供电 、供热、通讯、平整场地等基础设施工程的投资。包括实际从事房地产开发或经营活动的附营房地产开发单位。不包括单纯的土地交易活动。

固定资产投资的资金来源 根据固定资产投资的资金来源不同，分为国家预算资金、国内贷款、债券、利用外资、自筹资金和其他资金来源。

(1)国家预算资金 自 2011 年起，按照全国人大和国务院的要求，各级财政的所有资金，包括税收和非税收入，均必须纳入预算管理，我国已不存在预算外资金的概念，因此各级政府用于固定资产投资的财政资金均为预算资金。由于已经没有预算外资金，因此名称改为国家预算资金，包括中央预算资金和地方预算资金，旧的国家预算内资金的内容和现中央预算资金的内容基本一致。

国家预算包括一般预算、政府性基金预算、国有资本经营预算和社保基金预算。各类预算中用于固定资产投资的资金全部作为国家预算资金填报，其中一般预算中用于固定资产投资的部分包括基建投资、车购税、灾后恢复重建基金和其他财政投资。各级政府债券也应归入国家预算资金。

(2)国内贷款 指报告期固定资产投资单位向银行及非银行金融机构借入的用于固定资产投资的各种国内借款，包括银行利用自有资金及吸收存款发放的贷款、上级主管部门拨入的国内贷款、国家专项贷款（包括煤代油贷款、劳改煤矿专项贷款等），地方财政专项资金安排的贷款、国内储备贷款、周转贷款等。

(3)债券 是企业（公司）或金融机构通过发行各种债券筹集到的用于固定资产投资的资金，包括由银行代理发行的重点企业债券和重点建设债券。

(4)利用外资 指报告期内收到的用于固定资产建造和购置的国外资金（包括设备、材料、技术）。包括对外借款、外商直接投资、外商其他投资。不包括我国自有外汇资金。

(5)自筹资金 指固定资产投资单位报告期内收到的，由各地区、各部门及企事业单位筹集用于固定资产投资的预算外资金，包括中央各部门、各级地方和企事业单位的自筹资金。

(6)其他资金来源 指报告期收到的除以上各种资金之外其他用于固定资产投资的资金。包括集资、个人资金、无偿捐赠的资金及其他单位拨入的资金。

新增生产能力（或工程效益） 指通过固定资产投资活动而增加的设计能力（或工程效益），是以实物形态表示的固定资产投资成果的指标，也是考核投资经济效果的重要依据之一。

房屋建筑面积 是房屋建筑物勒脚以上外墙外围的水平截面面积，包括房屋建筑物的有效面积和结构面积。房屋建筑面积统计指标是建设规模和建设成果的重要指标之一，也是检查工程形象进度、计算工程造价、分析投资效果、研究施工任务和建筑材料之间平衡情况的重要依据。

住宅 指供人们居住的房屋，包括职工家属宿舍、集体宿舍（包括职工单身宿舍和学生宿舍）及供居住的各种公寓等。住宅建筑面积中不包括作为人防用、不住人的地下室面积和供办公用的公寓。

房屋施工面积 指在报告期内施工的全部房屋建筑面积。包括本期新开工的面积和上期开工跨入本期继续施工的面积，以及上期已停建在本期恢复施工的房屋面积。本期竣工和本期施工后又停缓建的房屋，其建筑面积仍计入本期房屋施工面积中。

房屋竣工面积 指在报告期内房屋建筑按照设计要求已经全部完工，达到住人和使用条件，经验收鉴定合格（或达到竣工验收标准），正式移交使用的各栋房屋建筑面积的总和。

房屋建筑面积竣工率 是指一定时期内房屋竣工面积与施工面积的比率。它是从房屋建筑施工速度的角度反映投资效果的指标。

新增固定资产 指已经完成建造和购置过程，并已交付生产或使用单位的固定资产的价值。它是表示固定资产投资成果的价值指标，也是反映建设进度，计算固定资产投资效果的重要依据。

固定资产交付使用率 指一定时期新增固定资产与同期完成投资额的比率。它是反映各个时期固定资产动用速度，衡量建设过程中投资效果的一个综合性指标。

建设项目投产率 是建设周期的逆指标，是指一定时期内全部建成投产项目个数与同期施工项目个数的比率。它是从建设速度的角度反映投资效果的指标。

基础设施 基础设施投资指在电力、热水的生产和供应业，燃气生产和供应业，水的生产和供应业，铁路运输业，道路运输业，水上运输业，航空运输业，管道运输业，装卸搬运和运输代理业，邮政业，电信、广播电视和卫星传输服务，互联网和相关服务，水利管理业，生态保护和环境治理业和公共设施管理业等行业方面的固定资产投资。

Explanatory Notes on Main Statistical Indicators

Amount of Investment in Fixed Assets refers to the sum in monetary terms of the volume of activities in the construction and purchase of fixed assets as well as related expenses. It is not only a comprehensive indicator of the size, proportional relations and developmental pace of investment in fixed assets, but also an important basis to follow the progress of projects and check the result of investment on. By status of registration, investment in fixed assets consists state-owned, collectively-owned, cooperative, joint, limited-liability, share-holding,, private, self-employed individual, funds from Hong Kong, Macao and Taiwan, foreign funded, and others.

Investment in Real Estate Development refers to investment by real estate development companies, commercialized buildings construction companies and other real estate development units of various types of ownership in the construction of buildings, such as residential buildings, factory buildings, warehouses, hotels, guesthouses, holiday villages, office buildings, and the complementary service facilities and land development projects, such as roads, water supply, water drainage, power supply, heating supply, telecommunications, land leveling and other infrastructural projects. It does not include activities in pure land transactions.

Sources of Funds for Investment in Fixed Assets are categorized as funds from the State budget, domestic loans, foreign investment, self-raised funds, and others, depending on the sources of investment.

(1)State Budgetary Funds Since 2011, in accordance with the requirements of the National People's Congress and the State Council, budgetary funds at all levels, including tax and non-tax revenues, must be included into budgetary management. As a result, the concept of "extra-budgetary funds" no longer exist. Therefore, all the fiscal funds used in fixed asset investment by governments at all levels are state budgetary funds. Without extra-budgetary funds, the name is changed into State Budgetary Funds. It includes central budgetary funds and local budgetary funds. The contents of the previously named "Fund from the State budget" is basically the same as the content of the central budgetary funds.

State budget includes general budget, government fund budget, state-owned capital operation budget and social insurance fund budget. Of all the budgets, the funds used in fixed asset investment are recorded as state budgetary funds. In general budget, the funds used in fixed asset investment include investment in infrastructure, vehicle purchase tax, post-disaster reconstruction fund and other fiscal investments. Government bonds at all levels shall also be included in state budgetary funds.

(2) Domestic loans refer to loans of various forms borrowed by investing units from banks and non-bank financial institutions during the reference period for the purpose of investment in fixed assets, including loans issued by banks from their self-owned funds and deposit, loans appropriated by higher authorities, special loans by government, loans arranged by local government from special funds, domestic reserve loan, and working loan.

(3) Bonds refer to funds raised by enterprises (companies) and financial institutions through issuing various bonds for the purpose of investment in fixed assets, including key enterprise bonds and key construction bonds issued through the agency of banks.

(4) Foreign investment refers to foreign funds received during the reference period for the purpose of construction and purchase of fixed assets (including equipment, materials and technologies). It includes foreign loans, foreign direct investment and other foreign investment, but excludes self-owned foreign exchanges of China.

(5) Fundraising refers to extra-budgetary funds received and raised by enterprises and institutions at all levels during the reference period for the purpose of investment in fixed assets, including funds raised by various departments under the central government, government departments of various levels, enterprises and institutions.

(6) Other funds refer to funds received during the reference period for the purpose of investment in fixed assets which are not included in the above-mentioned sources, including mass financing, individual funds, donations and funds from other units.

Newly Increased Production Capacity (or Project Efficiency) refers to the increase of designed capacity or project efficiency through investment in fixed assets, which is not only an indicator of the accomplishment in kind of investment in fixed assets but also an important basis to check the economic result of investment on..

Floor Space of Buildings refers to level cross-section floor space in each story of buildings calculated from the cutside line of building walls above the plinth, including the effective space and structural space occupied by constructions. It is one of the important indicators of construction size and results, as well as an important foundation for checking the progress of projects, calculating the value of project, analyzing the investment result and studying the balance between building materials.

Residential Buildings refer to buildings used as residence by people, including dormitories for families of staff and workers, mass dormitories like those for single workers and students, and various apartments. The floor space of residential buildings excludes the floor space of basement used for air-raid shelters and other purposes than residence and apartments used as offices.

Floor Space under Construction refers to total floor space of all buildings under construction during the reference period, including floor space of newly started buildings during the reference period, floor space of construction extended from the previous period to the current period, and floor space of construction suspended during the previous period but resumed in the current period. Floor space of construction completed in the current period and floor space of construction started and then suspended in the current period are also included in floor space under construction.

Floor Space of Buildings Completed refers to total floor space of all buildings completed in the reference period, which have come up to the designed standards with proper conditions of residence and use, and have been examined and accepted (or met the standards for completion), and put into use.

Completion Rate of Floor Space of Buildings refers to the ratio of the floor space of buildings completed in a certain period of time to the floor space of buildings under construction in the same period, which reflects the investment result of the construction industry from the perspective of the speed of project construction.

Newly Increased Fixed Assets refer to the value of fixed assets which have been completed and transferred to production units or users. It is a value indicator of the achievements of investment in fixed assets as well as an important basis to evaluate the result of investment in fixed assets on.

Rate of Projects of Fixed Assets Completed and Put into Use refers to the ratio of newly increased fixed assets to total investment made in the same period. It is a comprehensive indicator of the speed of the deployment of fixed assets and investment efficiency.

Rate of Construction Projects Completed and Put into Use is the inverse indicator of construction period, referring to the ratio of the number of construction projects completed and put into use in certain period of time to the number of projects under construction in the same period. This reflects the investment efficiency from the perspective of the speed of project construction.

Infrastructure Investment Infrastructure investment refers to the fixed assets investments in the industry of electric power, hot water production and supply industry, gas production and supply industry, water production and supply industry, railway transport, road transport, water transport, air transport industry, pipeline transportation, handling and transportation agent industry, postal services, telecommunications, radio, television and satellite transmission service, Internet and related services, water management industry, ecological protection and environmental governance industry and public facilities management.

六、对外经济

FOREIGN ECONOMY

六 对外经济

简要说明

一、本篇资料综合反映广东对外贸易、利用外资、对外承包工程和劳务合作以及“三资”企业工商登记等历年概况和近年发展的详细情况。

二、本篇资料由广东省统计局贸易外经处负责整理、编辑。

三、资料来源和统计范围：

1．人民币对美元、日元、港元的年平均汇价资料来源于外汇管理部门，是根据当年国家外汇管理局提供的每日汇价进行加权平均计算而得出的。

2．进出口贸易规模、结构情况资料，来源于海关总署广东分署，统计范围为在广东境内经海关报关注册登记的经营单位（包括有进出口经营权和无进出口经营权的经营单位）。进出口商品价值，出口按离岸价（FOB）、进口按到岸价（CIF）统计；进出口商品分类按海关合作理事会（世界海关组织 WCO）制定的《商品名称及编码协调制度》（HS）目录进行分类统计。

3. 利用外资规模、结构、对外直接投资和广东对外承包工程和劳务合作状况资料来源于广东省商务厅。

4. 外商投资企业注册登记情况资料来源于广东省工商行政管理局。

5. 对外开放使用口岸分布状况资料来源于广东省商务厅。

6 Foreign Economy

Brief Introduction

Ⅰ. The data in this chapter show the development of Guangdong's foreign trade, utilization of foreign capital, contracted projects and labor services cooperation with foreign countries or regions, and registration status of enterprises with foreign investment over the years.

Ⅱ. The data in this chapter are prepared and edited by the Division of Trade and External Economic Relations Statistics of Statistics Bureau of Guangdong Province.

Ⅲ. Data sources and statistical coverage:

(1) The data on the average exchange rates of RMB yuan to US dollar, Japanese yen and Hong Kong dollar over the years come from the State Administration of Foreign Exchange. The annual average exchange rate is calculated as the weighted mean of the daily exchange rates provided by the State Administration of Foreign Exchange in current year.

(2) The data on the size and composition of Guangdong's imports and exports come from Guangdong Customs Office. The statistics cover the operating units (with or without the right to handle imports and exports) which have a declaration and register at customs within the boundary of Guangdong. The values of export commodities are calculated on an FOB basis, while the values of import commodities are calculated on a CIF basis. The Harmonized Commodity Description and Coding System (HS) stipulated by the Customs Cooperation Council（World Customs Organization）is used in the classification of import and export commodities.

(3) The data on the scale and composition of the utilization of foreign capital,overseas direct invest ment and the conditions of contracted projects and labor cooperation with foreign countries or territories in Guangdong come from the Department of Commerce of Guangdong Province.

(4) The data on registration status of enterprises with foreign investment come from the Administration of Industry and Commerce of Guangdong Province.

(5) The data on the distribution of ports opening to the outside world come from the Department of Commerce of Guangdong Province.

6-1 对外经济主要指标
Main Indicators of Foreign Trade and Economic Cooperation

指　　标	Item	2013	2014	2015	2016	2017
进出口总额　　(亿元)	Total Value of Imports and Exports (100 million)	67806.10	66137.28	63559.70	63099.68	68168.86
出口总额	Total Exports	39513.95	39693.38	39983.10	39520.54	42192.86
进口总额	Total Imports	28292.14	26443.90	23567.60	23579.14	25976.00
进出口总额　　(亿美元)	Total Value of Imports and Exports (USD 100 million)	10918.22	10765.84	10227.96	9552.86	10066.80
出口总额	Total Exports	6363.64	6460.87	6434.68	5985.64	6228.73
#农产品	Farm Produce	81.31	84.32	86.45	91.99	94.79
机电产品	Machanical and Electrical Products	4395.69	4285.59	4380.34	4064.84	4201.31
高新技术产品	High and New-tech Products	2564.07	2310.17	2325.47	2135.92	2157.98
进口总额	Total Imports	4554.58	4304.97	3793.28	3567.21	3838.06
#农产品	Farm Produce	148.82	168.19	178.48	176.61	181.27
机电产品	Machanical and Electrical Products	2836.64	2543.12	2489.04	2411.23	2571.39
高新技术产品	High and New-tech Products	2186.64	1932.83	1932.84	1897.10	2025.79
签订利用外资协议(合同)项目　　(个)	Number of Projects with Contracted Foreign Capital (unit)	5740	6175	7033	8078	15599
#外商直接投资	Foreign Direct Investment	5520	6016	7029	8078	15599
签订利用外资协议(合同)金额　　(亿美元)	Amount of Contracted Foreign Capital (USD 100 million)	366.63	433.94	561.46	867.34	730.97
#外商直接投资	Foreign Direct Investment	363.13	430.59	561.10	866.75	730.87
实际利用外资额(亿美元)	Amount of Foreign Capital Actually Utilized (USD 100 million)	253.27	272.78	270.25	234.07	229.48
#外商直接投资	Foreign Direct Investment	249.52	268.71	268.75	233.49	229.07
外商投资企业年底工商登记数　　(户)	Number of Registered Enterprises with Foreign Investment at the Year-end (unit)	100639	104555	111169	119688	135869
投资总额　　(亿美元)	Total Investment (USD 100 million)	5126.40	5620.63	6443.10	7815.71	17622.27
注册资本　　(亿美元)	Registered Capital (USD 100 million)	3037.15	3377.37	3906.14	5085.88	6431.86
对外承包工程合同数(份)	Number of Contracted Projects with Foreign Countries and Territories (unit)	617	1139	1937	1503	1151
合同金额　　(亿美元)	Contracted Value (USD 100 million)	236.65	152.49	207.24	219.87	221.83
完成营业额　(亿美元)	Value of Turnover Fulfilled(USD 100 million)	228.65	124.11	198.78	181.64	180.96
对外劳务人员合同工资总额　　(亿美元)	Contracted Value (USD 100 million)	5.39	13.88	13.97	6.55	7.28
对外劳务人员实际工资总额　　(亿美元)	Value of Turnover Fulfilled(USD 100 million)	4.47	6.62	11.78	8.92	8.67

6-2 人民币对主要外币汇率(年平均价)
Reference Exchange Rate of Renminbi (Period Average)

单位：人民币，元 (RMB/yuan)

年份 Year	100美元 100 US Dollars	100日元 100 Japanese Yen	100港元 100 Hong Kong Dollars	100欧元 100 Euros
1987	372.21	2.5799	47.74	
1988	372.21	2.9082	47.70	
1989	376.51	2.7360	48.28	
1990	478.32	3.3233	61.39	
1991	532.33	3.9602	68.45	
1992	551.46	4.3608	71.24	
1993	576.20	5.2020	74.41	
1994	861.87	8.4370	111.53	
1995	835.10	8.9225	107.96	
1996	831.42	7.6352	107.51	
1997	828.98	6.8600	107.09	
1998	827.91	6.3488	106.88	
1999	827.83	7.2932	106.66	
2000	827.84	7.6864	106.18	
2001	827.70	6.8075	106.08	
2002	827.70	6.6237	106.07	800.58
2003	827.70	7.1466	106.24	936.13
2004	827.68	7.6552	106.23	1029.00
2005	819.17	7.4484	105.30	1019.53
2006	797.18	6.8570	102.62	1001.90
2007	760.40	6.4632	97.46	1041.75
2008	694.51	6.7427	89.19	1022.27
2009	683.10	7.2986	88.12	952.70
2010	676.95	7.7279	87.13	897.25
2011	645.88	8.1050	82.97	900.11
2012	631.25	7.9037	81.38	810.78
2013	619.36	6.3323	79.85	822.19
2014	614.28	5.8196	79.22	816.51
2015	622.84	5.1543	80.34	691.41
2016	664.23	6.1243	85.58	734.26
2017	675.18	6.0244	86.64	763.03

6-3 进出口总额

Total Value of Imports and Exports

年份 Year	亿元人民币 RMB 100 million				亿美元 USD 100 million			
	进出口总额 Total Imports and Exports	出口 Exports	进口 Imports	差额 Balance	进出口总额 Total Imports and Exports	出口 Exports	进口 Imports	差额 Balance
1987					210.37	101.40	108.97	-7.57
1988					310.19	148.17	162.02	-13.85
1989					355.78	181.13	174.65	6.48
1990					418.98	222.21	196.77	25.44
1991					525.21	270.73	254.48	16.25
1992					657.48	334.58	322.90	11.68
1993					783.44	373.94	409.50	-35.56
1994					966.63	502.11	464.52	37.59
1995					1039.72	565.92	473.80	92.12
1996					1099.60	593.46	506.14	87.32
1997					1301.20	745.64	555.56	190.08
1998					1297.98	756.18	541.80	214.38
1999					1403.68	777.05	626.63	150.42
2000					1701.06	919.19	781.87	137.32
2001					1764.87	954.21	810.66	143.55
2002					2210.92	1184.58	1026.34	158.24
2003					2835.22	1528.48	1306.74	221.74
2004					3571.29	1915.69	1655.60	260.09
2005	35121.80	19542.06	15579.74	3962.32	4280.02	2381.71	1898.31	483.40
2006	42114.53	24119.13	17995.40	6123.73	5272.07	3019.48	2252.59	766.89
2007	48445.43	28210.96	20234.46	7976.50	6340.35	3692.39	2647.96	1044.43
2008	47869.07	28342.66	19526.41	8816.25	6834.92	4041.88	2793.04	1248.83
2009	41736.14	24517.40	17218.74	7298.66	6111.18	3589.56	2521.62	1067.93
2010	53203.22	30718.98	22484.24	8234.74	7848.96	4531.91	3317.05	1214.86
2011	59276.15	34519.93	24756.22	9763.71	9133.34	5317.93	3815.41	1502.52
2012	62123.46	36242.50	25880.96	10361.54	9839.47	5740.59	4098.88	1641.71
2013	67806.10	39513.95	28292.14	11221.81	10918.22	6363.64	4554.58	1809.06
2014	66137.28	39693.38	26443.90	13249.48	10765.84	6460.87	4304.97	2155.90
2015	63559.70	39983.10	23567.60	16415.50	10227.96	6434.68	3793.28	2641.41
2016	63099.68	39520.54	23579.14	15941.40	9552.86	5985.64	3567.21	2418.43
2017	68168.86	42192.86	25976.00	16216.86	10066.80	6228.73	3838.06	2390.67

注：进出口差额负数为入超。
Note: A negative balance indicates trade deficit. That is, imports surpassing exports.

6-4 按贸易方式和经济类型分的进出口额（人民币）

Total Value of Imports and Exports by Customs Regime and Ownership Type

单位：亿元人民币 (RMB 100 million)

项　目	Item	2015 出口 Exports	2015 进口 Imports	2016 出口 Exports	2016 进口 Imports	2017 出口 Exports	2017 进口 Imports
总　计	**Total**	**39983.10**	**23576.60**	**39520.54**	**23579.14**	**42192.86**	**25976.00**
按贸易方式分	By Customs Regime						
一般贸易	Ordinary Trade	17146.42	9633.41	17212.53	10268.70	19301.25	12120.83
来料加工	Processing and Assembling with Customer's Materials	1939.42	1437.67	1639.71	1194.09	1637.29	1186.61
补偿贸易	Compensation Trade						
进料加工	Processing and Assembling with Import Materials	15533.43	8449.25	14119.43	7522.50	14502.12	7937.80
加工设备	Processing Equipments		18.72		16.04		29.61
外资设备	Foreign-funded Equipments		45.97		65.22		41.46
保税仓库	Bonded Warehouse	1659.04	1452.87	1606.60	2209.19	1672.93	2386.23
捐赠	Donation	1.39	0.20	1.03	0.04	2.00	0.01
其他	Others	3703.40	2603.20	4941.24	2303.36	5077.27	2273.44
按经济类型分	By Type of Ownership						
国有经济	State-owned Economy	3080.25	1892.14	2895.45	1660.21	2867.65	1843.51
集体经济	Collective-owned Economy	1152.26	321.39	1155.76	406.56	1138.45	419.22
私营经济	Private Economy	15010.99	8323.40	16361.16	9493.12	18689.69	11157.06
外商投资经济	Foreign-funded Economy	20686.69	13030.17	19050.56	11994.32	19466.95	12456.14
其他经济	Others	52.89	9.49	57.61	24.93	30.11	99.89

6-5 按贸易方式和经济类型分的进出口额（美元）

Total Value of Imports and Exports by Customs Regime and Ownership Type

单位：亿美元 (USD 100 million)

项　目	Item	2015 出口 Exports	2015 进口 Imports	2016 出口 Exports	2016 进口 Imports	2017 出口 Exports	2017 进口 Imports
总　计	**Total**	**6434.68**	**3793.28**	**5985.64**	**3567.21**	**6228.73**	**3838.06**
按贸易方式分	By Customs Regime						
一般贸易	Ordinary Trade	2760.71	1550.87	2608.58	1554.23	2851.83	1789.99
来料加工	Processing and Assembling with Customer's Materials	312.29	231.39	248.32	180.79	241.76	175.24
补偿贸易	Compensation Trade						
进料加工	Processing and Assembling with Import Materials	2499.81	1359.82	2138.69	1138.01	2141.84	1173.00
加工设备	Processing Equipments		3.03		2.43		4.38
外资设备	Foreign-funded Equipments		7.45		9.91		6.10
保税仓库	Bonded Warehouse	266.92	233.31	243.23	333.51	247.16	352.56
捐赠	Donation	0.23	0.03	0.15	0.01	0.30	
其他	Others	594.73	407.39	746.67	348.33	745.84	336.80
按经济类型分	By Type of Ownership						
国有经济	State-owned Economy	496.31	302.58	439.13	251.36	422.69	272.05
集体经济	Collective-owned Economy	185.48	51.53	175.26	61.51	168.22	61.68
私营经济	Private Economy	2181.77	1336.91	2476.45	1435.48	2759.32	1650.26
外商投资经济	Foreign-funded Economy	3329.59	2097.16	2886.80	1815.63	2874.06	1839.53
其他经济	Others	241.54	5.09	8.00	3.23	4.44	14.55

6-6 按产品类型分的进出口额

Total Value of Imports and Exports by Product Type

项目	Item	亿元人民币 RMB 100 million			亿美元 USD 100 million		
		2015	2016	2017	2015	2016	2017
出口总额	**Total Exports**	**39983.10**	**39520.54**	**42192.86**	**6434.68**	**5985.64**	**6228.73**
#农产品	Farm Produce	537.51	607.27	641.62	86.45	91.99	94.79
机电产品	Machanical and Electrical Products	27223.40	26830.86	28449.74	4380.34	4064.84	4201.31
金属制品	Metal Products	1358.89	1292.84	1607.87	218.97	195.76	237.16
机械及设备	Machinery and Equipments	5840.47	5828.64	6136.03	940.56	883.76	905.28
电器及电子产品	Electric and Electronic Products	15598.00	15368.06	16184.89	2508.05	2327.88	2391.88
运输工具	Transport Equipments	991.91	953.62	1077.44	160.07	144.57	158.87
仪器仪表	Instruments and Meters	1559.05	1557.26	1638.76	251.05	235.89	241.93
其他	Others	1875.09	1830.44	1804.76	301.65	276.98	266.19
高新技术产品	High and New-tech Products	14467.10	14103.12	14602.17	2325.47	2135.92	2157.98
生物技术	Biotechnology	1.72	1.70	1.68	0.28	0.26	0.25
生命科学技术	Life Sciences Technology	132.31	150.23	178.24	21.30	22.74	26.32
光电技术	Photoelectric Technology	835.00	821.79	845.35	134.47	124.50	124.82
计算机与通信技术	Computer and Communication Technology	11147.87	10760.52	11194.24	1792.00	1629.49	1654.74
电子技术	Electronic Technology	1995.17	1994.14	1947.57	320.19	302.16	287.62
计算机集成制造技术	Computer Integrated Manufacturing Technology	178.71	197.75	224.15	28.81	29.97	33.06
材料技术	Material Technology	69.27	62.36	72.68	11.17	9.45	10.73
航空航天技术	Aerospace Technology	100.99	106.88	129.40	16.28	16.19	19.14
其他	Others	6.05	7.75	8.85	0.97	1.17	1.31
进口总额	**Total Imports**	**23576.60**	**23579.14**	**25976.00**	**3793.28**	**3567.21**	**3838.06**
#农产品	Farm Produce	1108.14	11662.29	1227.27	178.48	176.61	181.27
机电产品	Machinery and Electrical Products	15474.75	159333.53	17397.14	2489.04	2411.23	2571.39
金属制品	Metal Products	186.02	1699.61	188.20	30.00	25.71	27.82
机械及设备	Machinery and Equipments	2359.56	23410.42	2536.82	379.90	354.46	374.79
电器及电子产品	Electric and Electronic Products	10619.03	113159.28	12363.85	1706.94	1712.49	1827.69
运输工具	Transport Equipments	462.03	3573.42	469.87	74.52	53.90	69.55
仪器仪表	Instruments and Meters	1719.98	16327.65	1696.77	277.07	247.08	250.62
其他	Others	128.13	1163.15	141.63	20.62	17.59	20.93
高新技术产品	High and New-tech Products	12018.33	125361.72	13705.37	1932.84	1897.10	2025.79
生物技术	Biotechnology	4.76	46.03	11.78	0.77	0.69	1.72
生命科学技术	Life Sciences Technology	172.50	1948.36	228.66	27.79	29.46	33.79
光电技术	Photoelectric Technology	1127.91	10410.20	1020.09	181.80	157.59	150.57
计算机与通信技术	Computer and Communication Technology	3181.54	31017.04	3411.90	511.68	469.27	505.18
电子技术	Electronic Technology	6717.65	74770.82	8172.71	1079.60	1131.61	1207.46
计算机集成制造技术	Computer Integrated Manufacturing Technology	367.12	3823.24	444.83	59.07	57.99	65.58
材料技术	Material Technology	107.38	922.05	90.24	17.32	13.96	13.32
航空航天技术	Aerospace Technology	336.79	2372.31	308.13	54.39	35.76	45.68
其他	Others	2.68	44.22	17.02	0.43	0.67	2.50

6-7 广东同主要国家(地区)进出口额(2017年)

Total Value of Imports and Exports with Main Countries and Regions(2017)

国别（地区）	Country (Region)	亿元人民币 RMB 100 million			亿美元 USD 100 million		
		进出口 Total	出口 Exports	进口 Imports	进出口 Total	出口 Exports	进口 Imports
合计	**Total**	**68168.86**	**42192.86**	**25976.00**	**10066.80**	**6228.73**	**3838.06**
亚洲	**Asia**	**43845.07**	**23290.71**	**20554.35**	**6476.10**	**3438.97**	**3037.13**
#香港	Hong Kong, China	11632.25	11348.21	284.04	1719.48	1677.58	41.90
韩国	Republic of Korea	4522.14	1504.56	3017.59	667.18	221.79	445.39
台湾省	Taiwan, China	4412.01	512.90	3899.12	651.96	75.72	576.25
日本	Japan	4261.00	1682.28	2578.72	629.09	248.33	380.76
越南	Vietnam	1867.42	820.75	1046.67	276.93	121.12	155.81
马来西亚	Malaysia	1826.68	821.38	1005.30	269.54	121.23	148.31
泰国	Thailand	1518.85	607.56	911.29	224.21	89.63	134.58
印度	India	1428.74	1271.27	157.47	210.56	187.33	23.23
新加坡	Singapore	1357.45	813.75	543.69	200.36	120.09	80.27
菲律宾	Philippines	981.57	482.81	498.76	144.94	71.24	73.71
印度尼西亚	Indonesia	907.52	561.58	345.94	133.97	82.86	51.11
阿联酋	United Arab Emirates	666.66	523.84	142.82	98.31	77.17	21.14
沙特阿拉伯	Saudi Arabia	542.92	423.78	119.13	79.89	62.28	17.62
东盟	Association of Southeast Asian Nations	8677.23	4294.24	4382.98	1282.13	633.72	648.42
非洲	**Africa**	**2493.91**	**1728.90**	**765.00**	**367.81**	**254.78**	**113.03**
#南非	South Africa	830.13	232.64	597.48	122.68	34.37	88.31
尼日利亚	Nigeria	337.81	305.20	32.61	49.80	44.98	4.82
欧洲	**Europe**	**8628.32**	**6598.87**	**2029.45**	**1273.99**	**973.95**	**300.04**
#德国	Germany	1651.54	1072.57	578.96	243.95	158.33	85.62
英国	United Kingdom	1223.24	1093.65	129.59	180.53	161.40	19.14
荷兰	Netherlands	982.84	854.66	128.18	145.11	126.19	18.92
法国	France	778.42	484.19	294.23	114.99	71.43	43.56
意大利	Italy	667.26	471.37	195.89	98.55	69.54	29.01
俄罗斯	Russia	497.85	468.42	29.43	73.54	69.20	4.34
西班牙	Spain	448.60	384.76	63.83	66.18	56.75	9.44
波兰	Poland	325.87	309.79	16.08	48.15	45.77	2.38
比利时	Belgium	300.53	238.40	62.13	44.30	35.14	9.16
瑞士	Switzerland	247.65	56.37	191.28	36.57	8.32	28.25
匈牙利	Hungary	223.65	200.45	23.20	32.99	29.56	3.43
瑞典	Sweden	154.72	118.88	35.84	22.82	17.53	5.29
捷克	Czech	139.49	121.64	17.85	20.59	17.95	2.64
欧盟	European Union	7695.85	5924.63	1771.22	1136.27	874.37	261.90
拉丁美洲	**Latin America**	**2564.90**	**1966.33**	**598.57**	**378.62**	**290.31**	**88.31**
#墨西哥	Mexico	785.66	642.32	143.34	115.99	94.83	21.16
巴西	Brazil	612.88	384.00	228.88	90.48	56.71	33.77
智利	Chile	294.83	181.32	113.51	43.44	26.74	16.70
阿根廷	Argentina	167.92	141.01	26.91	24.82	20.84	3.98
北美洲	**North America**	**9319.56**	**7858.20**	**1461.36**	**1375.87**	**1160.02**	**215.85**
#美国	United States of America	8625.13	7320.78	1304.35	1273.38	1080.69	192.68
加拿大	Canada	686.63	529.62	157.01	101.36	78.19	23.17
大洋洲及其他	**Oceania and others**	**1317.10**	**749.84**	**567.25**	**194.40**	**110.71**	**83.69**
#澳大利亚	Australia	1105.70	634.47	471.23	163.23	93.70	69.53
新西兰	New Zealand	159.65	78.15	81.50	23.55	11.54	12.02

注：本表数字按产销国别原则统计。
Note: The data in the table are calculated on the basis of production and consumption courtries.

6-8 进出口商品分类金额（2017年）
Total Value of Imports and Exports by Category of Commodities (2017)

商品类别	Category of Commodities	万元人民币 RMB10 000		万美元 USD 10 000	
		出口 Exports	进口 Imports	出口 Exports	进口 Imports
总　计	**Total Value**	**421928621**	**259759982**	**62287338**	**38380631**
第一类 活动物；动物产品	**Live Animals and Animal Products**	**1497759**	**2651084**	**221244**	**391910**
活动物	Live Animals	132309	4071	19510	601
肉及食用杂碎	Meat and Edible Haslets	237139	1604145	35035	237352
水产品	Aquatic Products	1041252	550716	153860	81446
乳品、蛋品、天然蜂蜜、其他食用动物产品	Dairy Products, Eggs, Natural Honey and Other Edible Animal Products	46834	448917	6915	66141
其他动物产品	Other Animal Products	40224	43235	5924	6370
第二类 植物产品	**Plant Products**	**780770**	**5116870**	**115288**	**754356**
树苗及花草	Saplings, Flowers and Herbs	37063	20060	5459	2970
蔬菜	Edible Vegetables	214674	26795	31665	3974
水果及坚果	Fruits and Nuts	120463	1763329	17908	259242
咖啡、茶叶及调味香料	Coffee, Tea and Spices	162930	63819	23987	9369
谷物	Cereals	3828	1386983	561	204366
制粉工业产品	Flour, Starch and Related Products	64352	112148	9501	16561
植物油籽及果实、种子、药材及饲料	Oil Seeds and Kernels, Seeds, Medical Materials and Forage	99080	1689057	14648	249804
虫胶、树胶、树脂	Shellac, Gum, Resin	39844	26630	5878	3934
编结植物材料、其他植物产品	Stuff of Knitting Plant, Other Plants and Related Products	38536	28048	5681	4137
第三类 动、植物油脂及蜡	**Animal Fat, Vegetable Oil and Wax**	**168670**	**650632**	**25008**	**96217**
动、植物油脂及蜡	Animal Fat, Vegetable Oil and Wax	168670	650632	25008	96217
第四类 食品、烟草及制品	**Food, Tobacco and Related Products**	**3867815**	**3546350**	**571383**	**524736**
动物产品制品	Animal Products	1285743	20677	189910	3065
糖及糖食	Sugar and Sugar Products	440225	172366	64983	25429
可可及可可制品	Cocoa and Cocoa Products	89880	79034	13354	11785
粮食及乳制品、糕饼点心	Foodstuff, Dairy Products and Pastry Products	382647	1212569	56544	179613
蔬菜、水果等植物制品	Products of Vegetables and Fruits	327622	160576	48423	23789
杂项制品	Miscellaneous Edible Products	360364	380650	53209	56266
饮料、酒及醋	Beverages, Liquor and Vinegar	847896	1047587	125239	155028
食品的残渣、动物饲料	Dreg of Food, Animal Forage	90250	378150	13344	55776
烟草及烟草制品	Tobacco and Related Products	43189	94741	6379	13985
第五类 矿产品	**Minerals**	**3536031**	**12715778**	**522661**	**1877321**
盐、硫磺、建筑材料	Salt, Sulphur, Building Materials	523296	391401	77349	57858
矿砂、矿渣及矿灰	Ore, Slag and Mortar	55721	2593425	8150	382428
矿物燃料、矿物油及产品	Mineral Fuels, Mineral Oils and Related Products	2957015	9730953	437161	1437034
第六类 化工产品	**Chemicals**	**6259774**	**9987911**	**924590**	**1475387**
无机化学品	Inorganic Chemicals	870064	614827	128617	90762
有机化学品	Organic Chemicals	1062335	2681953	156696	396091
药品	Medicinal and Pharmaceutical Products	521319	1756157	77060	259149
肥料	Fertilizer	82020	72411	12078	10596
鞣料、染料浸膏、染料、颜料、油漆、油墨	Tanning Materials, Dyeing Extracts, Dyestuff, Colourant, Paint and Printing Ink	493028	708559	72838	104680

6-8 续表 1 continued

商品类别	Category of Commodities	万元人民币 RMB10 000		万美元 USD 10 000	
		出口 Exports	进口 Imports	出口 Exports	进口 Imports
化妆品及其原料、芳香料制品	Cosmetics and Cosmetic Raw Materials, Perfume Products	1142384	678286	168840	100558
洗涤用品	Detergents	464817	510221	68643	75419
蛋白类物质、改性淀粉、胶、酶	Protein Materials, Modified Starch, Gum and Enzyme	387069	700330	57139	103522
炸药、烟火制品、易燃材料制品	Explosive, Pyrotechnic Products, Inflammable Material Products	34489	265	5089	39
照相及电影用品	Photographic and Film Products	130157	418989	19191	61823
杂项化学产品	Miscellaneous Chemical Products	1072091	1845913	158398	272746
第七类 塑料、橡胶及其制品	**Plastics, Rubber and Related Products**	**13125090**	**14735904**	**1936460**	**2175548**
塑料及其制品	Plastics and Related Products	12137309	13622664	1790695	2011213
橡胶及其制品	Rubber and Related Products	987781	1113240	145764	164335
第八类 皮革、毛皮及其制品、旅行用品、手提包	**Leather, Furs and Related Products, Travel Articles, Handbags**	**8205037**	**1444398**	**1209322**	**213098**
生皮及皮革	Raw Hides and Leather	179619	1193207	26453	176015
皮革制品、旅行用品及手提包	Leather Products, Travel Articles and Handbags	7939775	165831	1170203	24486
毛皮、人造毛皮及制品	Furs, Artificial Furs and Related Products	85643	85359	12666	12596
第九类 木及木制品、草柳编结品	**Wood and Wooden Products, Straw and Wicker Knitting Products**	**1306718**	**2728727**	**192991**	**403238**
木及木制品、木炭	Wood and Wooden Products, Charcoal	1090040	2724645	161103	402632
软木及软木制品	Cork and Related Products	1884	741	278	110
草柳编结品	Straw and Wicker Knitting Products	214793	3340	31610	497
第十类 木浆、纸、纸板及制品	**Wood Pulp, Paper, Paperboard and Related Products**	**4969230**	**3663297**	**733255**	**540663**
木浆及其他纤维素浆、废碎纸板	Wood Pulp and Cellulose Pulp, Waste Paper and Paperboard	555	2357224	82	347414
纸及纸板、纸浆、纸制品	Paper, Paperboard, Paper Pulp, Paper Products	3433231	966831	506465	143100
书籍、印刷品、设计图纸	Books, Printed Matter, Design Blueprint	1535444	339241	226708	50149
第十一类 纺织原料及纺织制品	**Textile Materials and Products**	**32237707**	**4125738**	**4750333**	**608968**
蚕丝	Natural Silk	65057	13308	9618	1965
羊毛、动物毛、毛纱线及制品	Wool, Animal Hair, Woolen Yarn and Woven Fabrics	67521	132460	9963	19496
棉花	Cotton	1504041	1251832	221833	184634
其他纺织纤维、纸纱线及机织物	Other Textile Fibers, Yarn and Related Woven Fabrics	50602	82565	7524	12228
化学纤维长丝	Chemical Fiber, Continuous Filament	528596	598360	77726	88351
化学纤维短丝	Chemical Fiber, Staple Fiber	254813	298380	37581	44009
絮胎、毡尼及无纺物、特种纱线、线绳索缆	Wadding, Felt and Adhesive-bond Fabrics, Special Yarn, Threads, Ropes, Cables	501407	252941	73988	37352
地毯及纺织铺地制品	Carpets and Related Woven Products	135721	8239	19973	1215
特种机织物、纺织装饰品、刺绣品	Special Woven Fabrics, Woven Ornaments, Embroidery	717143	129995	105848	19172
浸渍、涂布、包覆或层压的纺织物	Impregnated, Coated, Covered or Laminated Textile Products	672271	334259	99182	49359
针织物及钩编织物	Knit Wear and Crocheted Fabrics	2399725	463564	353994	68415
针织或钩编的服装及衣着附件	Knitted or Crocheted Garments and Clothing Accessories	9976163	246086	1471938	36395
非针织或非钩编的服装及衣着附件	Garments Not Knitted or Not Crocheted and Clothing Accessories	13758755	253799	2024379	37538
其他纺织制成品、成套物品	Other Textile Products	1605892	59949	236786	8840
第十二类 鞋帽伞杖、加工羽毛、人造花、人发制品	**Footwear, Headgear, Umbrellas, Canes, Processed Feather, Artificial Flowers, Wigs**	**11627119**	**298371**	**1712170**	**44092**
鞋类及零件	Footwear and Accessories	9931143	276654	1462066	40890
帽类及零件	Headgear and Accessories	534551	10599	78828	1567

6-8 续表 2 continued

商品类别	Category of Commodities	万元人民币 RMB10 000		万美元 USD 10 000	
		出口 Exports	进口 Imports	出口 Exports	进口 Imports
伞、杖、鞭及零件	Umbrellas, Canes, Whips and Accessories	203959	3061	30029	450
加工羽毛、羽绒及制品、人造花、人发制品	Processed Feathers, Down and Related Products, Artificial Flowers, Wigs	957465	8056	141247	1185
第十三类 石材制品、陶瓷产品、玻璃及其制品	**Stone Products, Ceramics, Glass and Glassware**	**9907319**	**2302625**	**1462276**	**340334**
矿物材料的制品	Stone and Related Products	1632802	257328	241252	38025
陶瓷产品	Ceramics	5710509	83968	842791	12460
玻璃及其制品	Glass and Glassware	2564008	1961328	378234	289849
第十四类 珠宝首饰、硬币	**Jewellery, Coins**	**7962216**	**4223959**	**1176561**	**623830**
珠宝首饰	Jewellery	7962216	4223959	1176561	623830
第十五类 贱金属及其制品	**Base Metals and Related Products**	**21381026**	**12881863**	**3153473**	**1902166**
钢铁	Iron and Steel	2134207	2949639	314350	435098
钢铁制品	Iron and Steel Products	7690111	922788	1134502	136270
铜及其制品	Copper and Related Products	645174	5315846	95192	785030
镍及其制品	Nickel and Related Products	5888	304624	869	44979
铝及其制品	Aluminum and Related Products	3435316	2047066	507039	302331
铅及其制品	Lead and Related Products	2595	4804	382	712
锌及其制品	Zinc and Related Products	48364	233540	7146	34507
锡及其制品	Tin and Related Products	13952	57136	2057	8435
其他贱金属金属陶瓷及其制品	Other Base Metals, Metallic Ceramics and Related Products	471458	429901	69468	63548
贱金属工具器具利口器餐具及零件	Base Metal Tools, Utensils, Sharp Tools, Dinner-sets and Accessories	2525226	389471	372662	57691
贱金属杂项制品	Miscellaneous Base Metal Products	4408736	227048	649806	33565
第十六类 机械、电气设备、电视机及音响设备	**Machinery, Electric Equipment, TV Sets, Sound Appliances**	**223209138**	**149006658**	**32971603**	**22024789**
核反应堆、锅炉、机械设备及零件	Nuclear Reactor, Boilers, Mechanic Equipment and Accessories	61360250	25368165	9052819	3747905
机电、电气设备、电视机及音响设备	Machinery, Electric Equipment, TV Sets and Sound Appliances	161848888	123638493	23918784	18276885
第十七类 车辆、航空器、船舶及有关运输设备	**Vehicles, Aircraft, Ships and Related Transport Equipment**	**10774364**	**4698699**	**1588683**	**695481**
铁道及电车机车、车辆及零件	Rail Locomotives, Tramcars and Accessories	1115411	18852	165191	2793
车辆及零附件	Vehicles and Related Parts and Accessories	7001042	2662161	1032365	393306
航空器、航天器及零件	Aircraft, Spacecraft and Related Parts and Accessories	1064691	1906383	156263	282910
船舶及浮动结构体	Ships and Related Products	1593220	111303	234864	16472
第十八类 仪器、医疗器械、钟表及乐器	**Instruments, Medical Instruments and Equipment,Clocks and Watches, Musical Instruments**	**18914714**	**17922006**	**2792507**	**2647236**
光学、照相电影、计量检验、医疗仪器设备	Optical, Photographic, Film, Measuring and Checking, Medical Instruments and Equipment	16387631	16967746	2419326	2506216
钟表及零件	Clocks, Watches and Parts	2178623	920061	321681	135952
乐器及零附件	Musical Instruments and Parts	348460	34198	51500	5068
第十九类杂项制品	**Miscellaneous Manufactured Articles**	**40846162**	**1377670**	**6027507**	**203753**
家具、床上用品、照明装置、发光标志	Furniture, Bed Articles, Lighting Apparatus, Radiate Marks	24377642	370374	3594243	54806
玩具、游戏、运动用品及零附件	Toys, Game Goods, Sports Articles and Related Parts and Accessories	14377547	524433	2124688	77464
杂项制品	Miscellaneous Manufactured Articles	2090973	482863	308576	71483
第二十类 艺术品、收藏品及古物	**Works of Art, Collection Pieces and Antiques**	**24754**	**4374**	**3656**	**647**
第二十一类 特殊交易品及未分类商品	**Special Trading Goods and Unclassified Goods**	**1327208**	**5677071**	**196367**	**836860**

6-9 出口主要商品数量和金额（2017年）

Main Export Commodities in Volume and Value (2017)

商品名称		Item		数量 Volume	金额 Value 万元人民币 RMB 10 000	万美元 USD 10 000
活猪	(吨)	Live Hogs	(ton)	63524	114212	16840
活家禽	(吨)	Live Poultry	(ton)	580	1424	207
鲜、冻猪肉	(吨)	Fresh and Frozen Pork	(ton)	10986	34778	5124
冻鸡	(吨)	Frozen Chicken	(ton)	3224	6224	920
水产品	(吨)	Aquatic Products	(ton)	558425	2177567	321744
#活鱼	(吨)	Live Fish	(ton)	46798	128642	18986
鲜冻对虾	(吨)	Fresh and Frozen Prawn	(ton)	4507	31553	4684
谷物	(吨)	Cereals	(ton)	99967	35630	5255
#大米	(吨)	Rice	(ton)	12609	3825	561
蔬菜	(吨)	Vegetables	(ton)	676247	274122	40464
#鲜蔬菜	(吨)	Fresh Vegetables	(ton)	618637	169395	24973
鲜、干果类	(吨)	Fresh and Dried Fruit	(ton)	148884	118261	17583
#柑桔橙	(吨)	Mandarins and Oranges	(ton)	28336	22643	3395
食用油籽	(吨)	Edible Oil Seeds	(ton)	2518	1902	283
食用植物油	(吨)	Edible Vegetable Oil	(ton)	93867	69232	10288
食糖	(吨)	Sugar	(ton)	36427	19041	2805
茶叶	(吨)	Tea	(ton)	6353	71369	10509
猪肉罐头	(吨)	Canned Pork	(ton)	101	223	33
蘑菇罐头	(吨)	Canned Mushroom	(ton)	4826	6229	915
羽毛、羽绒	(吨)	Feather and Down	(ton)	3471	25796	3807
药材	(吨)	Medicinal Materials	(ton)	25134	108189	15988
纸烟		Cigarettes			13351	1981
生丝	(吨)	Raw Silk	(ton)	594	22407	3316
成品油	(吨)	Finished Petroleum Products	(ton)	3550661	1065907	157728
合成有机染料	(吨)	Synthetic Organic Dyestuff	(ton)	8740	17215	2540
医药品	(吨)	Medicinal and Pharmaceutical Products	(ton)	80138	846238	125031
#抗菌素	(吨)	Antibiotics	(ton)	15547	281853	41619
烟花爆竹	(吨)	Fireworks and Firecrackers	(ton)	20623	31429	4637
松香、树脂	(吨)	Rosin, Resin	(ton)	15926	18760	2753
轮胎		Rubber Tire			358781	52918
纸及纸板	(吨)	Paper and Paperboard	(ton)	852443	789965	116291
纺织品		Textiles			8474739	1249870
#棉纱线	(吨)	Cotton Yarn	(ton)	51998	184349	27118
丝绸		Silk			62576	9205
棉布		Cotton Cloth			1368945	201979
麻纺布	(万米)	Linen Cloth	(10000 m)	1932	33318	4968
混纺布	(万米)	Blended Cloth	(10000 m)	4142	35710	5277
玻璃制品		Glass Products			890910	131414
家用陶瓷		Porcelain and Pottery Wares for Household Use			3019573	445671
家用或装饰用木制品	(吨)	Wood Articles for Household or Decoration Use	(ton)	92398	260980	38576
珍珠、宝石		Pearls and Precious Stones			545387	80527

6-9 续表 continued

商品名称	Item	数量 Volume	金额 Value 万元人民币 RMB 10 000	金额 Value 万美元 USD 10 000
贵金属及首饰	Precious Metal and Jewelry		6735070	995508
钢材 (吨)	Steel Products (ton)	3617587	2590492	381527
铝材 (吨)	Aluminum Products (ton)	667135	1339471	197775
铜材 (吨)	Copper Products (ton)	101144	501076	73928
工具	Tools		1102320	162898
微波炉 (万个)	Microwave Ovens (10000 units)	4972	1415335	208783
电扇 (万台)	Electric Fans (10000 sets)	40866	2263538	332538
普通缝纫机 (万台)	Sewing Machines (10000 sets)	231	38203	5637
金属加工机床 (台)	Machine Tools (set)	342003	319747	47235
电子计算器 (万台)	Electric Calculators (10000 sets)	9355	162486	23932
数据处理设备 (万台)	Data Processing Equipment (10000 sets)	77343	24696775	3647395
电动、发电机 (万台)	Electric Motors and Generators (10000 sets)	167994	2446487	360922
静止式变流器 (万个)	Static Converters (10000 units)	247730	7193237	1061758
原电池 (万个)	Primary Cells and Batteries (10000 units)	1522251	589166	86990
蓄电池 (万个)	Electric Accumulators (10000 units)	132109	3397985	502546
有线电话 (万台)	Landline Telephone Sets (10000 sets)	6372	682408	100755
手持或车载无线电话(万台)	Hand-held or Vehicle-mounted Cordless Telephone (10000 sets)	64966	30459028	4509813
扬声器 (万个)	Loudspeakers (10000 units)	88225	3175081	470030
收录机、组合音响 (万台)	Radio Recorders and Audio Systems(10000 sets)	16299	2169709	320143
彩电(整套散件) (万台)	Colour TV Sets (Complete Sets of Spare Parts) (10000 sets)	5098	5431402	802906
集成电路、微电子件(万个)	Integrated Circuit and Parts of Electronic Compoments (10000 units)	3680937	6577904	971788
集装箱 (个)	Containers (unit)	468892	1098805	162734
自行车 (万辆)	Bicycles (10000 units)	616	323707	47681
船舶	Ships		1562740	230375
照相机 (万架)	Cameras (10000 sets)	2185	1038231	154064
手表 (万只)	Wrist Watches (10000 units)	39662	1251908	184830
#电子手表 (万只)	Electronic Watches (10000 units)	38789	1175328	173546
日用钟 (万只)	Clocks (10000 units)	5978	161944	23880
家具	Furniture		13406693	1977385
床垫、卧具用品	Mattress and Bedding Articles		737304	108831
灯具、照明用品	Lights and Lighting Apparatus		9902116	1459058
箱包、旅行用品	Boxes and Bags, Travel Goods		7455911	1098771
服装、衣着附件	Garments and Clothing Accessories		24873065	3664287
#织物服装	Textile Garments		21778885	3207927
皮革服装 (万件)	Leather Garments (10000 pcs)	137	42833	6362
皮革手套	Leather Gloves		191398	28241
帽类 (万个)	Headgear (10000 units)	107979	509782	75186
鞋	Footwear		9288628	1367265
#橡胶、塑料鞋	Rubber and Plastic Shoes		4155512	611008
皮鞋	Leather Shoes		2482878	365684
塑料制品	Plastic Articles		8205200	1210440
玩具	Toys		8825212	1304331
体育用品及设备	Sports Articles and Facilities		1862459	274731

6-10 进口主要商品数量和金额（2017年）

Volume and Value of Main Import Commodities (2017)

商品名称		Item		数量 Volume	金额 Value 万元人民币 RMB 10 000	金额 Value 万美元 USD 10 000
谷物	(吨)	Cereals	(ton)	7561334	1395212	205584
#小麦	(吨)	Wheat	(ton)	749281	114510	16796
稻谷和大米	(吨)	Paddy and Rice	(ton)	2036319	634741	93562
大豆	(吨)	Soybean	(ton)	4733761	1330013	196752
鲜、干果类	(吨)	Fresh and Dried Fruit	(ton)	1188670	1740369	255827
#香蕉	(吨)	Mandarins and Oranges	(ton)	15015	7594	1122
食用植物油	(吨)	Edible Vegetable Oil	(ton)	765400	380450	56262
#棕榈油	(吨)	Palm Oil	(ton)	726530	340747	50344
食糖	(吨)	Sugar	(ton)	322110	104049	15320
饲料	(吨)	Forage	(ton)	276047	252299	37196
纸烟	(万条)	Cigarettes	(carton)		91832	13553
天然橡胶	(吨)	Natural Rubber	(ton)	106587	113681	16754
合成橡胶	(吨)	Synthetic Rubber	(ton)	240578	409998	60472
原木	(立方米)	Logs	(cu.m)	2526323	607474	89842
锯材	(立方米)	Sawn Timber	(cu.m)	5810594	1866824	275904
纸浆	(吨)	Paper Pulp	(ton)	2164557	891111	131616
羊毛	(吨)	Wool	(ton)	2584	7454	1091
原棉	(吨)	Raw Cotton	(ton)	21463	27585	4116
合成纤维	(吨)	Synthetic Fiber	(ton)	46554	69948	10346
#聚酯纤维	(吨)	Polyester Fiber	(ton)	38639	35407	5235
聚丙烯晴纤维	(吨)	Polyacrylonitrile Fibre	(ton)	3652	6178	908
人造纤维	(吨)	Artificial Fiber	(ton)	2772	4729	702
铁矿砂	(吨)	Iron Ore	(ton)	34125758	1748530	257656
氧化铝	(吨)	Aluminum Oxide	(ton)	500114	121391	17880
原油	(万吨)	Crude Oil	(10000 tons)	852	2197866	324705
成品油	(万吨)	Finished Petroleum Products	(10000 tons)	269	910566	134146
液化石油气	(万吨)	LPG	(10000 tons)	448	671848	99045
乙二醇	(吨)	Glycol	(ton)	359945	209393	31032
对苯二甲酸	(吨)	Terephthalic Acid	(ton)	194811	85983	12715
己内酰胺	(吨)	Caprolactam	(ton)	22299	28918	4279
医药品	(吨)	Medicinal and Pharmaceutical Products	(ton)	44418	1795367	264911
#抗菌素	(吨)	Antibiotics	(ton)	163	18866	2784
肥料	(吨)	Fertilizer	(ton)	418745	72538	10615
#氯化钾	(吨)	Potassium Chloride	(ton)	360819	55323	8106
合成有机染料	(吨)	Synthetic Organic Dyestuff	(ton)	6298	39611	5843
初级型状聚乙烯	(吨)	Polyethylene in Primary Form	(ton)	1356356	1122953	165958
初级型状聚丙烯	(吨)	Polypropylene in Primary Form	(ton)	1333733	1139467	168196
初级型状聚苯乙烯	(吨)	Polystyrene in Primary Form	(ton)	1620883	2020407	298451
#ABS树脂	(吨)	ABS Copolymer Resin	(ton)	1009204	1339543	197853
初级型状聚氯乙烯	(吨)	Polyvinyl Chloride in Primary Form	(ton)	418253	293007	43261
初级型状聚酯	(吨)	Polyester in Primary Form	(ton)	862752	1776805	262318
农药	(吨)	Pesticides	(ton)			
牛皮革、马皮革	(吨)	Cattlehide and Horsehide	(ton)	298132	900966	132840

6−10 续表 continued

商品名称		Item		数量 Volume	金额 Value 万元人民币 RMB 10 000	万美元 USD 10 000
胶合板	(立方米)	Plywood	(cu.m)		24511	3627
纸及纸板	(吨)	Paper and Paperboard	(ton)	1518016	831482	123120
#牛皮纸	(吨)	Kraft-paper	(ton)	327724	147053	21800
毛纱线	(吨)	Wool and Cotton Thread	(ton)	8116	98804	14533
棉纱线	(吨)	Cotton Yarn	(ton)	466608	969615	142913
合成纤维纱线	(吨)	Synthetic Fiber,Continuous Filament and Yarn	(ton)	118360	402456	59375
丝绸		Silk			12875	1900
棉布		Cotton Cloth			247322	36531
化纤布	(万米)	Chemical Fibre Cloth	(10000 m)	26067	243155	35898
钢材	(吨)	Steel Products	(ton)	4147453	2626468	387489
#钢铁板材	(吨)	Iron & Steel Plate	(ton)	3668241	2122109	313024
铜材	(吨)	Copper Products	(ton)	308500	1922223	283865
铝材	(吨)	Aluminium Products	(ton)	66027	285578	42160
制冷压缩机	(台)	Refrigeration Compressors	(set)	4185092	198251	29303
空调	(台)	Air Conditioners	(set)	3389	5317	785
制冷设备		Refrigerating Equipments			37044	5485
机械装卸设备		Mechanical Handling Equipments			314142	46439
建筑采矿设备		Building and Mining Equipments			458726	67657
食品机械		Food-processing Machinery			16779	2485
造纸、纸品机械		Paper and Pulp Mill Machinery			68998	10229
印刷机械		Printing Machinery			2400253	354141
纺织机械		Textile Machinery			399650	59084
工业缝纫机	(台)	Industrial Sewing Machines	(set)	3832	7383	1092
机床	(台)	Machine Tools	(set)	14846	732690	108318
橡、塑加工机械		Rubber and Plastic Processing Machinery			329281	48708
数据处理设备		Data Processing Equipments			7018282	1037640
电动、发电机	(万台)	Electric Motors and Generators	(10000 sets)	60659	564238	83270
发电机组、变流机	(台)	Generating Sets and Converters	(set)	1052	64827	9558
电视机	(台)	TV Sets	(set)	5351	1856	273
#彩色电视机	(台)	Colour TV Sets	(set)	5351	1856	273
半导体器件	(万个)	Parts of Semi-conductor Devices	(10000 units)	24439205	7692139	1135612
电路保护装置		Circuit Protection Devices			5304136	783564
显像管		Kinescopes				
集成电路、电子件	(万个)	Integrated Circuits and Parts of Electronic Components	(10000 units)	14424228	68385502	10104994
电线、电缆	(吨)	Electric Wires and Cables	(ton)	76842	1158712	171049
汽车及底盘	(辆)	Motor Vehicles and Chassis	(unit)	8702	299971	44495
#小轿车	(辆)	Sedan Cars	(unit)	141	8601	1280
旅行车	(辆)	Station Wagons	(unit)	3157	77960	11590
船舶	(艘)	Ships	(unit)	389	66423	9864
塑料制品		Plastic Products			689553	101901
印刷品	(吨)	Presswork	(ton)	27939	339241	50149

6-11 各市出口总额
Total Value of Exports by City

市别	City	亿元人民币 RMB100 million					亿美元 USD100 million				
		2013	2014	2015	2016	2017	2013	2014	2015	2016	2017
全省合计	**Provincial Total**	**39513.95**	**39693.38**	**39983.07**	**39520.54**	**42192.86**	**6363.64**	**6460.87**	**6434.68**	**5985.64**	**6228.73**
广　州	Guangzhou	3897.24	4467.77	5034.62	5158.77	5792.43	628.07	727.07	811.70	781.77	853.20
深　圳	Shenzhen	19000.22	17468.90	16415.38	15666.51	16542.62	3057.02	2843.62	2640.40	2373.39	2443.59
珠　海	Zhuhai	1647.12	1784.48	1794.84	1802.99	1883.07	265.81	290.15	288.11	273.29	278.89
汕　头	Shantou	409.54	427.88	419.30	423.59	453.93	66.02	69.66	67.55	64.26	67.12
佛　山	Foshan	2638.25	2869.41	2999.00	3099.48	3153.68	425.23	467.17	482.05	469.80	464.84
韶　关	Shaoguan	57.07	74.92	88.99	89.25	76.30	9.20	12.20	14.25	13.43	11.28
河　源	Heyuan	139.32	162.70	176.24	188.86	195.36	22.47	26.49	28.33	28.52	28.85
梅　州	Meizhou	95.72	115.96	141.17	139.39	114.94	15.44	18.87	22.72	21.13	16.97
惠　州	Huizhou	2067.80	2231.13	2160.94	1972.45	2233.11	333.20	363.31	347.75	298.78	329.60
汕　尾	Shanwei	120.94	112.47	97.93	91.98	88.14	19.51	18.32	15.78	13.92	13.02
东　莞	Dongguan	5636.73	5962.10	6429.54	6545.65	7024.10	908.61	970.67	1036.10	990.14	1038.12
中　山	Zhongshan	1643.20	1712.22	1738.88	1762.18	2055.54	264.75	278.78	280.07	266.61	302.78
江　门	Jiangmen	868.71	926.72	954.43	993.58	1075.56	139.99	150.87	153.72	150.31	158.62
阳　江	Yangjiang	129.84	142.58	150.48	115.01	113.49	20.92	23.21	24.04	17.40	16.75
湛　江	Zhanjiang	162.65	180.69	174.31	194.77	217.07	26.23	29.41	28.07	29.47	32.03
茂　名	Maoming	49.96	60.41	68.68	75.89	97.22	8.06	9.76	10.99	11.42	14.44
肇　庆	Zhaoqing	298.98	283.67	296.70	308.87	222.26	48.26	46.05	47.66	46.80	32.78
清　远	Qingyuan	139.65	146.84	168.75	173.84	184.94	22.50	23.91	27.09	26.32	27.27
潮　州	Chaozhou	172.70	175.07	171.55	173.52	176.18	27.83	28.50	27.64	26.31	25.99
揭　阳	Jieyang	271.88	312.15	416.45	446.20	401.85	43.80	50.81	67.04	67.80	59.20
云　浮	Yunfu	66.43	75.23	84.90	97.77	91.08	10.72	12.04	13.62	14.80	13.40
按经济区域分	By Region										
珠三角	Pearl River Delta	37698.26	37706.4	37824.33	37310.47	39982.37	6070.93	6137.68	6087.57	5650.87	5902.41
东　翼	Eastern Region	975.05	1027.56	1105.23	1135.29	1120.10	157.17	167.29	178.02	172.28	165.34
西　翼	Western Region	342.45	383.69	393.47	385.68	427.78	55.21	62.38	63.10	58.29	63.22
山　区	Mountainous Region	498.19	575.66	660.04	689.10	662.62	80.33	93.52	106.00	104.20	97.76

6-12 各市进口总额

Total Value of Imports by City

市别	City	亿元人民币 RMB100 million					亿美元 USD100 million				
		2013	2014	2015	2016	2017	2013	2014	2015	2016	2017
全省合计	**Provincial Total**	**28292.14**	**26443.90**	**23576.60**	**23579.14**	**25976.00**	**4554.58**	**4304.97**	**3793.28**	**3567.21**	**3838.06**
广　州	Guangzhou	3480.81	3555.65	3271.74	3382.26	3923.09	560.89	578.69	526.92	511.32	579.30
深　圳	Shenzhen	14415.99	12491.78	11100.98	10640.39	11481.87	2317.73	2033.79	1784.15	1610.97	1697.87
珠　海	Zhuhai	1717.31	1593.38	1167.30	951.07	1109.45	277.07	259.44	188.26	144.02	163.96
汕　头	Shantou	163.28	159.30	156.82	138.78	142.04	26.33	25.86	25.29	21.01	20.97
佛　山	Foshan	1327.68	1357.22	1088.19	1006.16	1203.90	214.17	220.91	175.07	152.04	177.77
韶　关	Shaoguan	87.06	69.55	60.01	68.08	90.53	14.02	11.34	9.65	10.29	13.33
河　源	Heyuan	61.11	80.37	74.81	72.23	65.01	9.85	13.06	11.98	10.85	9.64
梅　州	Meizhou	13.56	18.11	11.30	13.90	17.80	2.19	2.95	1.82	2.10	2.63
惠　州	Huizhou	1492.82	1417.57	1215.11	1072.66	1182.54	240.70	230.81	195.81	162.67	174.57
汕　尾	Shanwei	137.84	129.95	100.71	121.27	110.78	22.23	21.16	16.24	18.32	16.30
东　莞	Dongguan	3859.59	4018.97	3971.18	4865.00	5235.62	622.09	654.30	639.33	734.82	772.91
中　山	Zhongshan	567.69	557.81	471.44	474.32	526.39	91.48	90.81	75.94	71.88	77.77
江　门	Jiangmen	355.92	324.77	276.73	268.32	309.45	57.34	52.87	44.59	40.59	45.75
阳　江	Yangjiang	17.83	22.49	28.02	23.27	28.82	2.88	3.67	4.51	3.53	4.29
湛　江	Zhanjiang	179.51	207.28	144.70	109.63	128.63	28.90	33.75	23.39	16.57	19.00
茂　名	Maoming	25.80	24.44	33.28	29.28	38.69	4.17	3.98	5.36	4.42	5.73
肇　庆	Zhaoqing	136.12	198.12	214.67	149.12	135.65	21.91	32.25	34.42	22.58	19.99
清　远	Qingyuan	130.73	123.36	110.92	117.70	145.18	21.08	20.09	17.87	17.79	21.43
潮　州	Chaozhou	70.53	35.09	23.46	26.42	34.69	11.34	5.72	3.77	4.00	5.12
揭　阳	Jieyang	19.36	23.40	21.12	19.34	23.46	3.12	3.81	3.40	2.93	3.47
云　浮	Yunfu	31.60	35.27	34.12	29.94	42.42	5.10	5.74	5.50	4.53	6.28
按经济区域分	By Region										
珠三角	Pearl River Delta	27353.93	25515.29	22777.35	22809.29	25107.96	4403.38	4153.86	3664.49	3450.88	3709.89
东　翼	Eastern Region	391.01	347.74	302.10	305.82	310.97	63.01	56.54	48.70	46.26	45.86
西　翼	Western Region	223.13	254.21	206.00	162.18	196.13	35.95	41.39	33.26	24.52	29.01
山　区	Mountainous Region	324.07	326.66	291.15	301.86	360.93	52.24	53.18	46.83	45.56	53.31

6-13 各市外商投资企业出口总额

Total Value of Exports of Enterprises with Foreign Investment by City

市 别	City	亿元人民币 RMB100 million					亿美元 USD100 million				
		2013	2014	2015	2016	2017	2013	2014	2015	2016	2017
全省合计	**Provincial Total**	**22172.01**	**21869.32**	**20684.00**	**19050.56**	**19466.95**	**3572.93**	**3560.75**	**3329.98**	**2886.80**	**2874.06**
广 州	Guangzhou	2047.71	2114.11	2127.42	2021.29	2093.53	329.87	344.16	342.86	306.34	308.96
深 圳	Shenzhen	9049.93	8685.00	8028.75	7029.60	6918.86	1458.41	1414.10	1291.43	1065.18	1022.13
珠 海	Zhuhai	1043.74	967.99	933.04	830.76	788.04	168.36	157.64	150.19	125.74	116.39
汕 头	Shantou	143.36	125.17	94.04	88.31	85.16	23.10	20.38	15.17	13.40	12.56
佛 山	Foshan	1317.70	1338.12	1235.80	1175.10	1252.44	212.18	217.87	199.35	178.30	184.70
韶 关	Shaoguan	38.10	39.48	43.81	44.83	49.92	6.14	6.43	7.05	6.79	7.37
河 源	Heyuan	117.33	143.49	139.45	140.83	142.07	18.91	23.36	22.45	21.35	20.97
梅 州	Meizhou	41.14	42.50	44.88	41.11	37.15	6.63	6.92	7.23	6.24	5.48
惠 州	Huizhou	1897.13	2042.66	1944.24	1725.21	1975.71	305.69	332.63	312.87	261.28	291.61
汕 尾	Shanwei	91.47	88.84	79.99	76.38	71.89	14.76	14.47	12.89	11.56	10.62
东 莞	Dongguan	4241.19	4120.58	3955.09	3907.32	4006.77	683.56	670.88	636.96	591.91	591.49
中 山	Zhongshan	1089.88	1083.95	1018.25	977.26	1027.86	175.57	176.50	164.11	148.23	151.67
江 门	Jiangmen	527.16	545.32	517.64	491.48	537.32	84.95	88.79	83.45	74.54	79.27
阳 江	Yangjiang	17.34	15.12	14.73	14.02	13.33	2.79	2.46	2.37	2.13	1.96
湛 江	Zhanjiang	70.03	67.91	58.71	58.94	66.75	11.29	11.05	9.46	8.92	9.84
茂 名	Maoming	14.79	12.94	12.22	16.73	18.61	2.38	2.11	1.97	2.51	2.76
肇 庆	Zhaoqing	127.90	135.80	147.19	139.65	129.00	20.61	22.11	23.64	21.15	19.02
清 远	Qingyuan	122.77	126.86	123.51	132.66	139.99	19.79	20.66	19.89	20.11	20.65
潮 州	Chaozhou	48.35	44.72	36.74	30.74	24.04	7.79	7.28	5.92	4.67	3.54
揭 阳	Jieyang	88.59	83.43	86.86	71.17	57.45	14.27	13.58	14.00	10.82	8.47
云 浮	Yunfu	36.40	45.33	41.64	37.16	31.05	5.87	7.38	6.71	5.63	4.59
按经济区域分	By Region										
珠 三 角	Pearl River Delta	21342.35	21033.53	19907.42	18297.69	18729.54	3439.19	3424.68	3204.86	2772.68	2765.25
东 翼	Eastern Region	371.77	342.16	297.62	266.60	238.54	59.93	55.71	47.98	40.45	35.19
西 翼	Western Region	102.16	95.97	85.66	89.69	98.69	16.46	15.62	13.81	13.56	14.57
山 区	Mountainous Region	355.74	397.66	393.30	396.58	400.19	57.34	64.74	63.34	60.12	59.06

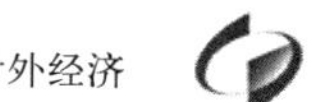

6-14 各市外商投资企业进口总额

Total Value of Imports of Enterprises with Foreign Investment by City

市别	City	亿元人民币 RMB100 million					亿美元 USD100 million				
		2013	2014	2015	2016	2017	2013	2014	2015	2016	2017
全省合计	**Provincial Total**	**14568.76**	**14297.87**	**13029.41**	**11994.32**	**12456.14**	**2347.78**	**2327.71**	**2097.49**	**1815.63**	**1839.53**
广州	Guangzhou	1951.34	2050.22	1875.25	1937.93	2048.07	314.39	333.78	301.99	293.18	302.24
深圳	Shenzhen	5858.70	5872.06	5453.49	4873.76	4767.20	944.01	955.93	877.09	737.76	704.42
珠海	Zhuhai	727.74	545.54	563.71	452.07	587.42	117.35	88.83	90.77	68.45	86.86
汕头	Shantou	60.40	52.89	52.14	49.07	48.38	9.75	8.61	8.40	7.42	7.14
佛山	Foshan	578.01	545.89	528.62	506.76	591.02	93.13	88.86	85.17	76.62	87.29
韶关	Shaoguan	11.87	10.45	10.71	10.63	11.59	1.91	1.70	1.73	1.61	1.71
河源	Heyuan	55.48	63.87	56.29	52.50	54.60	8.95	10.39	9.04	7.94	8.08
梅州	Meizhou	9.36	10.14	9.03	8.13	9.65	1.51	1.65	1.46	1.23	1.42
惠州	Huizhou	1391.94	1298.51	1076.23	941.45	1039.82	224.43	211.43	173.48	142.80	153.44
汕尾	Shanwei	112.50	109.11	86.26	110.36	100.34	18.15	17.77	13.92	16.67	14.75
东莞	Dongguan	2820.89	2730.92	2429.21	2272.42	2324.94	454.63	444.62	391.34	343.93	343.16
中山	Zhongshan	450.86	433.08	392.60	382.07	425.17	72.65	70.50	63.24	57.90	62.82
江门	Jiangmen	244.56	221.73	185.23	182.27	211.73	39.39	36.09	29.83	27.57	31.29
阳江	Yangjiang	7.89	17.85	23.10	16.33	15.95	1.28	2.91	3.74	2.48	2.38
湛江	Zhanjiang	100.51	132.83	64.35	13.29	23.01	16.17	21.63	10.41	2.01	3.39
茂名	Maoming	2.52	3.71	5.33	3.83	11.36	0.41	0.60	0.86	0.57	1.70
肇庆	Zhaoqing	74.72	89.02	113.50	90.08	78.08	12.04	14.49	18.21	13.64	11.51
清远	Qingyuan	73.35	64.23	62.34	55.42	63.75	11.82	10.46	10.05	8.39	9.41
潮州	Chaozhou	14.09	18.04	11.82	12.18	15.89	2.28	2.94	1.90	1.85	2.35
揭阳	Jieyang	7.38	6.34	6.83	6.04	5.82	1.19	1.03	1.10	0.92	0.86
云浮	Yunfu	14.65	21.43	23.37	17.74	22.34	2.36	3.49	3.77	2.69	3.31
按经济区域分	By Region										
珠三角	Pearl River Delta	14098.76	13786.97	12617.85	11638.81	12073.45	2272.02	2244.53	2031.12	1761.86	1783.03
东翼	Eastern Region	194.38	186.39	157.05	177.65	170.44	31.36	30.35	25.32	26.86	25.10
西翼	Western Region	110.92	154.40	92.77	33.45	50.32	17.85	25.14	15.01	5.06	7.47
山区	Mountainous Region	164.71	170.12	161.74	144.41	161.93	26.55	27.69	26.04	21.85	23.93

6–15 外商投资企业进出口主要指标（2017年）

Main Indicators on Imports and Exports of Enterprises with Foreign Investment(2017)

项　目	Item	亿元人民币 RMB 100 million			亿美元 USD 100 million		
		进出口总额 Total	出口 Exports	进口 Imports	进出口总额 Total	出口 Exports	进口 Imports
总　计	**Total**	**31923.09**	**19466.95**	**12456.14**	**4713.59**	**2874.06**	**1839.53**
按贸易方式分	By Customs Regime						
一般贸易	Ordinary Trade	7643.99	4281.58	3362.42	1128.29	631.93	496.36
来料加工	Processing and Assembling with Customer's Materials	1833.81	1077.26	756.55	270.94	159.14	111.80
进料加工	Processing and Assembling with Import Materials	19865.80	12877.84	6987.96	2933.32	1901.31	1032.01
加工设备	Processing Equipments	21.87		21.87	3.24		3.24
外资设备	Foreign-funded Equipments	41.46		41.46	6.10		6.10
保税仓库	Bonded Warehouse	606.37	329.27	277.10	89.50	48.61	40.89
其他	Others	5.82	1.24	4.59	0.86	0.18	0.68
按经济类型分	By Type of Ownership						
合作经营企业	Joint Ventures	358.41	309.99	48.42	52.88	45.74	7.14
合资经营企业	Cooperative Enterprises	6958.85	4241.99	2716.86	1026.94	625.99	400.95
外资(独资)企业	Enterprises with Sole Foreign Investment	24605.83	14914.97	9690.86	3633.78	2202.34	1431.44
按产品类型分	By Type of Product						
#机电产品	Machanical and Electrical Products	23058.12	14741.66	8316.46	3404.93	2176.63	1228.30
#机械及设备	Machinery and Equipments	5121.89	3735.68	1386.21	755.27	550.66	204.61
电器及电子产品	Electric and Electronic Products	13695.58	8216.21	5479.36	2023.69	1214.21	809.48
高新技术产品	High and New-tech Products	14041.35	8031.88	6009.47	2074.02	1186.50	887.52
#计算机与通信技术	Computer and Communication Technology	7395.19	5825.97	1569.22	1092.76	860.75	232.01
电子技术	Electronic Technology	4498.32	1254.15	3244.17	664.42	185.28	479.15
按主要国家(地区)分	By Main Country (Region)						
亚洲	**Asia**	**21559.69**	**11453.89**	**10105.80**	**3183.90**	**1691.48**	**1492.41**
中国香港	Hong Kong, China	7066.15	6987.10	79.06	1044.26	1032.59	11.68
中国澳门	Macao, China	41.69	39.02	2.67	6.15	5.76	0.39
中国台湾	Taiwan, China	2147.42	284.51	1862.91	317.21	42.01	275.19
日本	Japan	2890.12	1188.13	1702.00	426.61	175.38	251.22
韩国	Republic of Korea	2506.18	1083.97	1422.21	369.46	159.73	209.73
东盟	Association of Southeast Asian Nations	3173.40	1227.81	1945.59	468.90	181.23	287.66
中东十七国	The Seventeen Countries of the Middle East	594.10	375.71	218.39	87.57	55.31	32.26
非洲	**Africa**	**572.46**	**176.83**	**395.63**	**84.59**	**26.09**	**58.50**
欧洲	**Europe**	**3612.73**	**2694.24**	**918.49**	**533.28**	**397.57**	**135.71**
欧盟	European Union	3333.74	2505.71	828.03	492.13	369.76	122.37
#英国	United Kingdom	486.23	426.45	59.78	71.81	62.99	8.83
德国	Germany	813.22	518.38	294.85	120.09	76.49	43.60
法国	France	331.34	211.68	119.66	48.89	31.22	17.66
意大利	Italy	263.93	152.18	111.75	38.99	22.44	16.55
荷兰	Netherlands	498.54	436.89	61.65	73.55	64.46	9.08
芬兰	Finland	23.01	11.31	11.70	3.40	1.67	1.73
瑞士	Switzerland	97.36	31.66	65.69	14.37	4.67	9.70
俄罗斯	Russia	137.04	126.18	10.86	20.22	18.62	1.60
拉丁美洲	**Latin America**	**941.22**	**748.04**	**193.18**	**138.94**	**110.42**	**28.52**
北美洲	**North America**	**4792.44**	**4113.13**	**679.31**	**707.29**	**607.05**	**100.24**
加拿大	Canada	262.83	212.72	50.12	38.78	31.39	7.40
美国	United States of America	4529.51	3900.32	629.19	668.49	575.64	92.84
大洋洲	**Oceania**	**439.94**	**280.82**	**159.12**	**64.92**	**41.46**	**23.46**
澳大利亚	Australia	380.07	251.52	128.55	56.08	37.13	18.95
新西兰	New Zealand	53.16	24.37	28.79	7.85	3.60	4.25

6-16 外商投资企业出口主要商品数量和金额（2017年）

Volume and Value of Main Export Commodities of Enterprises with Foreign Investment (2017)

商品名称	Item	数量 Volume	金额 Value 万元人民币 RMB10 000	万美元 USD 10 000
活猪 (吨)	Live Hogs (ton)	2697	4723	697
活家禽 (吨)	Live Poultry (ton)			
冻鸡 (吨)	Frozen Chicken (ton)	152	397	59
水产品 (吨)	Aquatic Products (ton)	116717	674222	99569
#活鱼 (吨)	Live Fish (ton)	6357	14312	2110
鲜冻对虾 (吨)	Fresh and Frozen Prawn (ton)	1480	9272	1380
谷物 (吨)	Cereals (ton)	86474	30652	4523
蔬菜 (吨)	Vegetables (ton)	62878	52657	7772
#鲜蔬菜 (吨)	Fresh Vegetables (ton)	51840	17986	2647
鲜、干果类 (吨)	Fresh and Dried Fruit (ton)	8238	10731	1583
#柑桔橙 (吨)	Mandarins and Oranges (ton)	396	391	58
食用植物油 (吨)	Edible Vegetable Oil (ton)	26143	25166	3716
食糖 (吨)	Sugar (ton)	4881	1650	243
茶叶 (吨)	Tea (ton)	1382	9758	1431
烤鳗鱼 (吨)	Daked Eel (ton)			
蘑菇罐头 (吨)	Canned Mushroom (ton)	990	1303	192
羽毛、羽绒 (吨)	Feather and Down (ton)	1543	20152	2975
药材 (吨)	Medicinal Materials (ton)	4210	38409	5665
成品油 (吨)	Finished Petroleum Products (ton)	1976473	705925	104745
合成有机染料 (吨)	Synthetic Organic Dyestuff (ton)	242	899	133
医药品 (吨)	Medicinal and Pharmaceutical Products (ton)	38094	182357	26893
#抗菌素 (吨)	Antibiotics (ton)	623	15691	2301
美容护肤用品 (吨)	Cosmetic and Skin Care Products (ton)	45954	361451	53362
口腔清洁剂 (吨)	Dental Cleanser (ton)	114766	147068	21697
轮胎	Rubber Tire		230968	34048
纸及纸板 (吨)	Paper and Paperboard (ton)	329970	211403	31128
纺织品	Textiles		3633362	536108
#棉纱线 (吨)	Cotton Yarn (ton)	24023	87033	12825
丝绸	Silk		1141	169
棉布	Cotton Cloth		274128	40481
麻纺布 (万米)	Linen Cloth (10000 m)	55	1461	216
混纺布 (万米)	Blended Cloth (10000 m)	387	3057	451
玻璃制品	Glass Products		139333	20553
家用陶瓷	Porcelain and Pottery Wares for Household Use		241602	35617
家用或装饰用木制品(吨)	Wood Articles for Household or Decoration Use(ton)	29647	65704	9694
珍珠、宝石	Pearls and Gems		523666	77344
贵金属及首饰	Precious Metal and Jewelry		3981494	589158
钢材 (吨)	Steel Products (ton)	573488	538688	79200
铝材 (吨)	Aluminum Products (ton)	149428	326417	48230
铜材 (吨)	Copper Products (ton)	78075	372538	54983
工具	Tools		473953	69949
微波炉 (万个)	Microwave Ovens (10000 units)	3012	901062	132804
电扇 (万台)	Electric Fans (10000 sets)	21124	997451	146541
普通缝纫机 (万台)	Sewing Machines (10000 sets)	31	20409	3007

6-16 续表 continued

商品名称		Item		数量 Volume	金额 Value 万元人民币 RMB10 000	万美元 USD 10 000
金属加工机床	(台)	Machine Tools	(set)	138113	44045	6512
电子计算器	(万台)	Electronic Calculators	(10000 sets)	5202	125575	18491
数据处理设备	(万台)	Data Processing Equipment	(10000 sets)	32181	16083332	2370924
#显示器	(万台)	Displays	(10000 sets)	415	422962	62565
电动、发电机	(万台)	Electric Motors and Generators	(10000 sets)	107342	1542804	227641
静止式变流器	(万个)	Static Converters	(10000 units)	94456	4067712	600570
原电池	(万个)	Primary Cells and Batteries	(10000 units)	524346	264670	39040
蓄电池	(万个)	Electric Accumulators	(10000 units)	33668	710041	104849
有线电话	(万台)	Landline Telephone Sets	(10000 sets)	3837	416492	61445
手持或车载无线电话	(万台)	Hand-held or Vehicle-mounted Cordless Telephones	(10000 units)	14133	13458876	1997124
扬声器	(万个)	Loudspeakers	(10000 sets)	35408	1703033	252505
收录机、组合音响	(万台)	Radio Recorders and Audio Systems	(10000 sets)	1615	773652	114752
彩电(整套散件)	(万台)	Colour TV Sets (Complete Sets of Spare Parts)	(10000 sets)	2473	2729081	403713
电路保护装置		Circuit Protection Devices			4067322	600358
半导体器件	(万个)	Parts of Semi-conductor Devices	(10000 units)	12285451	2667524	394074
集成电路、微电子件	(万个)	Integrated Circuits and Parts of Electronic Components	(10000 units)	2781866	3538694	523558
电线、电缆		Electric Wires and Cables			2796661	412820
集装箱	(个)	Containers	(unit)	440880	1091203	161609
自行车	(万辆)	Bicycles	(10000 units)	159	134348	19778
船舶		Ships			299905	44488
照相机	(万架)	Cameras	(10000 sets)	1823	793522	117351
手表	(万只)	Wrist Watches	(10000 units)	19506	982876	145190
#电子手表	(万只)	Electronic Watches	(10000 units)	19213	935055	138123
日用钟	(万只)	Clocks	(10000 units)	2619	78893	11632
家具		Furniture			3555155	524449
床垫、卧具用品		Mattresses and Bedding Articles			273012	40286
灯具、照明用品		Lights and Lighting Apparatus			2115958	312090
箱包、旅行用品		Boxes, Bags and Travel Goods			1972260	290835
服装、衣着附件		Garments and Clothing Accessories			5789953	854326
#织物服装		Textile Garments			4487519	662325
皮革服装	(万件)	Leather Garments	(10000 units)	27	13950	2056
裘皮服装		Fur Garments			20488	3032
皮革手套		Leather Gloves			66595	9811
帽类	(万个)	Headgear	(10000 units)	45831	245461	36190
鞋		Footwear			2955732	435412
#橡胶、塑料鞋		Rubber and Plastic Shoes			740407	108941
皮鞋		Leather Shoes			1106642	163100
塑料制品		Plastic Articles			3140737	463280
圣诞用品		Articles for Christmas			331179	49068
玩具		Toys			3790370	560152
体育用品及设备		Sports Articles and Facilities			1138365	167879

6-17 外商投资企业进口主要商品数量和金额（2017年）

Volume and Value of Main Import Commodities by Enterprises with Foreign Investment (2017)

商品名称		Item		数量 Volume	金额 Value 万元人民币 RMB10 000	万美元 USD 10 000
谷物	(吨)	Cereals	(ton)	862262	154216	22625
#小麦	(吨)	Wheat	(ton)	403444	60101	8753
面粉	(吨)	Flour	(ton)	3363	1032	152
大豆	(吨)	Soya Bean	(ton)	905815	254632	37783
食用植物油	(吨)	Edible Vegetable Oil	(ton)	413937	204792	30311
#棕榈油	(吨)	Palm Oil	(ton)	381663	173590	25661
食糖	(吨)	Sugar	(ton)	32042	9916	1477
饲料	(吨)	Forage	(ton)	50132	47212	6973
天然橡胶	(吨)	Natural Rubber	(ton)	41799	52969	7795
合成橡胶	(吨)	Synthetic Rubber	(ton)	115422	232615	34301
原木	(立方米)	Logs	(cu.m)	134022	23375	3455
纸浆	(吨)	Paper Pulp	(ton)	1457239	608469	89851
羊毛	(吨)	Wool	(ton)	1505	6635	972
原棉	(吨)	Raw Cotton	(ton)	9539	12510	1849
合成纤维	(吨)	Synthetic Fiber	(ton)	17546	38198	5655
#聚酯纤维	(吨)	Polyester Fiber	(ton)	13847	13392	1976
聚丙烯睛纤维	(吨)	Polyacrylonitrile Fibre	(ton)	981	1897	280
人造纤维	(吨)	Artificial Fiber	(ton)	1783	3710	549
铁矿砂	(吨)	Iron Ore	(ton)	5874675	318218	46954
氧化铝	(吨)	Aluminium Oxide	(ton)	4851	4232	627
原油	(吨)	Crude Oil	(ton)			
成品油	(吨)	Finished Petroleum Products	(ton)	892646	337268	49860
苯乙烯	(吨)	Styrene	(ton)	111825	96262	14240
乙二醇	(吨)	Glycol	(ton)	171479	100630	14862
对苯二甲酸	(吨)	Terephthalic Acid	(ton)	180379	79640	11776
己内酰胺	(吨)	Caprolactam	(ton)	22219	28865	4271
医药品	(吨)	Medicinal and Pharmaceutical Products	(ton)	16200	1180653	174138
肥料	(吨)	Fertilizer	(ton)	409845	70320	10291
#氯化钾	(吨)	Potassium Chloride	(ton)	360819	55323	8106
复合肥料	(吨)	Compound Fertilizer	(ton)	48510	13510.7	1968.4
合成有机染料	(吨)	Synthetic Organic Dyestuff	(ton)	3881	26523	3909
初级形状聚乙烯	(吨)	Polyethylene in Primary Form	(ton)	617294	521510	76974
初级形状聚丙烯	(吨)	Polypropylene in Primary Form	(ton)	794800	694316	102499
初级形状聚苯乙烯	(吨)	Polystyrene in Primary Form	(ton)	1003677	1290850	190580
#ABS树脂	(吨)	ABS Copolymer Resin	(ton)	634989	864518	127631
初级形状聚氯乙烯	(吨)	Polyvinyl Chloride in Primary Form	(ton)	351646	241637	35676
初级形状聚酯	(吨)	Polyester in Primary Form	(ton)	623572	1323941	195380
农药	(吨)	Pesticides	(ton)	2374	14722	2173
牛皮革、马皮革	(吨)	Cattlehide and Horsehide	(ton)	140189	655192	96563
胶合板	(立方米)	Plywood	(cu.m)	13209	10391	1538
纸及纸板	(吨)	Paper and Paperboard	(ton)	1038628	554352	82065
#牛皮纸	(吨)	Kraft-paper	(ton)	196084	82984	12308

6-17 续表 continued

商品名称		Item		数量 Volume	金额 Value 万元人民币 RMB10 000	万美元 USD 10 000
毛纱线	(吨)	Wool and Cotton Thread	(ton)	6844	80802	11878
棉纱线	(吨)	Cotton Yarn	(ton)	277880	644659	95086
合成纤维纱线	(吨)	Synthetic Fiber, Continuous Filament and Yarn	(ton)	103865	365864	53973
丝绸		Silk			10765	1588
棉布		Cotton Cloth			193266	28535
化纤布	(万米)	Chemical Fibre Cloth	(10000 m)	95	3092	455
钻石	(千克拉)	Diamond	(1000 carats)	4296	1847041	272991
钢材	(吨)	Steel Products	(ton)	3634851	2225441	328282
#钢铁板材	(吨)	Iron & Steel Plate	(ton)	3291597	1846596	272344
铜材	(吨)	Copper Products	(ton)	271253	1647681	243373
铝材	(吨)	Aluminium Products	(ton)	44684	189519	27954
制冷压缩机	(台)	Refrigeration Compressors	(set)	2805120	105266	15529
空调	(台)	Air Conditioners	(set)	592	1913	283
制冷设备		Refrigeration Equipments			26600	3939
机械装卸设备		Mechanical Handling Equipments			225484	33327
建筑采矿设备		Building and Mining Equipments			54175	7967
食品机械		Food-processing Machinery			8551	1269
造纸、纸品机械		Paper and Pulp Mill Machinery			51041	7559
印刷机械		Printing Machinery			1711522	252337
纺织机械		Textile Machinery			291631	43129
工业缝纫机	(台)	Industrial Sewing Machines	(set)	1558	4978	738
机床	(台)	Machine Tools	(set)	5655	353685	52260
橡、塑加工机械		Rubber and Plastic Processing Machinery			202742	30012
数据处理设备	(万台)	Data Processing Equipment	(10000 sets)	9011	2450654	362157
电动、发电机	(万台)	Electric Motors and Generators	(10000 sets)	54253	474940	70047
发电机组、变流机	(台)	Generating Sets and Converters	(set)	189	26721	3923
电视摄像机	(万台)	Pickup Cameras	(10000 sets)	5080	346874	51526
电视机	(台)	Colour TV Sets	(set)	1668	757	112
半导体器件	(万个)	Parts of Semi-conductor Devices	(10000 units)	11692652	3898601	575292
电路保护装置		Circuit Protection Devices			3382372	499340
显像管	(万只)	Kinescopes	(10000 units)			
集成电路、电子件	(万个)	Integrated Circuits and Parts of Electronic Components	(10000 units)	6045644	24422748	3608365
电线、电缆	(吨)	Electric Wires and Cables	(ton)	62881	938936	138532
汽车及底盘	(辆)	Motor Vehicles and Chassis	(unit)	1284	43335	6477
#小轿车	(辆)	Sedan Cars	(unit)	18	2292	342
货车	(辆)	Trucks	(unit)	1	52	8
船舶	(艘)	Ships	(unit)	80	14555	2178
塑料制品	(吨)	Plastic Products	(ton)	73617	522584	77215
印刷品	(吨)	Presswork	(ton)	18489	77007	11369

6-18 私营企业进出口主要指标（2017年）

Main Indicators on Imports and Exports of Private Enterprises (2017)

项 目	Item	亿元人民币 RMB100 million			亿美元 USD 100 milliom		
		进出口总额 Total	出口 Exports	进口 Imports	进出口总额 Total	出口 Exports	进口 Imports
总 计	**Total**	**29846.76**	**18689.69**	**11157.06**	**4409.58**	**2759.32**	**1650.26**
按贸易方式分	By Customs Regime						
一般贸易	Ordinary Trade	19320.90	12523.34	6797.56	2856.13	1851.57	1004.56
来料加工	Processing and Assembling with Customer's Materials	670.53	352.41	318.12	98.93	52.00	46.93
进料加工	Processing and Assembling with Import Materials	2217.00	1355.85	861.15	328.90	200.99	127.91
加工设备	Processing Equipments	7.10		7.10	1.05		1.05
保税仓库	Bonded Warehouse	2455.59	463.13	1992.46	363.12	68.64	294.48
其他	Others	3291.45	3244.54	46.92	482.39	475.45	6.94
按产品类型分	By Type of Product						
#机电产品	Machanical and Electrical Products	21145.48	10777.80	10367.67	3125.84	1592.31	1533.53
#机械及设备	Machinery and Equipments	2550.83	1683.31	867.52	377.29	248.89	128.40
电器及电子产品	Electric and Electronic Products	12425.27	6226.04	6199.24	1837.61	920.35	917.26
高新技术产品	High and New-tech Products	11744.96	4978.06	6766.90	1737.64	736.27	1001.36
#计算机与通信技术	Computer and Communication Technology	5648.17	4017.27	1630.90	836.35	594.39	241.96
电子技术	Electronic Technology	5020.14	610.38	4409.76	742.02	90.09	651.92
按主要国家(地区)分	By Main Country (Region)						
亚洲	**Asia**	**18822.83**	**9966.66**	**8856.17**	**2781.76**	**1471.69**	**1310.07**
中国香港	Hong Kong, China	3956.74	3788.93	167.80	585.36	560.61	24.76
中国澳门	Macao, China	75.09	72.75	2.35	11.22	10.87	0.35
中国台湾	Taiwan, China	2053.97	203.69	1850.28	303.69	30.06	273.63
日本	Japan	1049.35	380.19	669.15	155.03	56.13	98.90
韩国	Republic of Korea	1761.63	344.25	1417.38	260.23	50.80	209.43
东盟	Association of Southeast Asian Nations	4583.56	2583.52	2000.04	677.70	381.26	296.45
中东十七国	The Seventeen Countries of the Middle East	1564.22	1376.67	187.55	230.51	202.73	27.78
非洲	**Africa**	**1653.59**	**1333.14**	**320.45**	**243.68**	**196.38**	**47.30**
欧洲	**Europe**	**3893.57**	**3067.54**	**826.03**	**575.25**	**452.93**	**122.32**
欧盟	European Union	3390.74	2692.91	697.83	500.91	397.57	103.35
#英国	United Kingdom	613.12	564.55	48.57	90.48	83.30	7.18
德国	Germany	652.28	435.12	217.16	96.38	64.25	32.13
法国	France	356.03	224.91	131.12	52.72	33.20	19.52
意大利	Italy	321.57	251.99	69.58	47.49	37.18	10.31
荷兰	Netherlands	382.92	344.83	38.09	56.58	50.95	5.63
俄罗斯	Russia	278.56	271.06	7.50	41.17	40.07	1.11
拉丁美洲	**Latin America**	**1264.28**	**944.02**	**320.25**	**186.59**	**139.39**	**47.20**
北美洲	**North America**	**3606.09**	**3027.16**	**578.93**	**532.71**	**447.07**	**85.64**
加拿大	Canada	335.41	250.04	85.36	49.55	36.94	12.61
美国	United States of America	3270.61	2777.04	493.57	483.15	410.12	73.03
大洋洲及其他	**Oceania and others**	**606.40**	**351.17**	**255.23**	**89.58**	**51.85**	**37.73**
澳大利亚	Australia	500.86	297.81	203.05	74.01	43.98	30.03
新西兰	New Zealand	85.15	39.90	45.25	12.56	5.89	6.67

6-19 利用外资情况

Utilization of Foreign Capital

年份 Year	签订项目（个）Number of Signed Projects (unit)	#外商直接投资 Foreign Direct Investment	合同外资额（万美元）Amount of Contracted Foreign Capital (USD 10000)	#外商直接投资 Foreign Direct Investment	实际利用外资（万美元）Amount of Foreign Capital Actually Utilized (USD 10000)	#外商直接投资 Foreign Direct Investment
1979	1642	70	22889	14616	9143	3074
1980	5048	188	138920	120046	21419	12320
1981	6803	236	167507	156206	28837	17326
1982	8171	151	155916	147698	28103	17123
1983	11318	412	72660	61552	40685	24523
1984	17452	1105	144489	116958	64379	54163
1985	13621	1640	256521	200073	91910	51529
1986	9417	774	183480	85902	142829	64392
1987	6999	1186	201750	124647	121671	59396
1988	7662	2741	382748	224196	243965	91906
1989	6636	2438	362311	243813	239915	115644
1990	7196	3042	316751	268958	202347	145984
1991	8507	4554	580152	490530	258250	182286
1992	12916	9769	1986673	1885764	486147	355150
1993	19012	16768	3489660	3314887	965225	749805
1994	11956	10558	2638753	2382441	1144664	939708
1995	9345	8177	2610480	2483244	1210037	1018028
1996	5955	4608	1744639	1554584	1389943	1162362
1997	17737	3744	964527	769202	1420519	1171083
1998	15459	4349	1237802	916180	1509945	1202005
1999	14824	3013	871592	617451	1447383	1220300
2000	16879	4245	1108598	868393	1457466	1223720
2001	13198	5317	1580386	1343463	1575526	1297240
2002	11706	6613	1890108	1617119	1658946	1311071
2003	11472	7306	2446711	2178926	1894081	1557779
2004	10530	8322	2217800	1936046	1289900	1001158
2005	11786	8384	2675695	2374365	1517358	1236391
2006	11276	8452	2838923	2456820	1780780	1451065
2007	11705	9506	3646583	3393817	1961771	1712603
2008	8980	6999	3071447	2863991	2126657	1916703
2009	5693	4346	1824109	1755834	2028688	1953460
2010	6022	5641	2516987	2460075	2102646	2026098
2011	7289	7035	3485492	3469238	2232847	2179836
2012	6263	6043	3544579	3499424	2410578	2354911
2013	5740	5520	3666273	3631343	2532719	2495210
2014	6175	6016	4339446	4305905	2727751	2687144
2015	7033	7029	5614566	5611000	2702512	2687546
2016	8078	8078	8673350	8667477	2340689	2334921
2017	15599	15599	7309658	7308672	2294813	2290668

注：1. 2002年起外商直接投资统计口径调整，企业投资总额内的境外借款只包括外方股东贷款。
2. 2004年实际利用外商直接投资统计口径作了调整，与2003年以前的年份不可比。
3. 2004年起签订项目数、合同外资额、实际利用外资不包含对外借款。

Notes:a)Since 2002, the foreign direct investment statistic has been adjusted, of which the overseas borrowings in total investment of enterprises only include loans by foreign shareholders.
b)The foreign direct investment actually utilized of 2004 is adjusted, incomparable to values of preceding years.
c)Since2004,the number of signed projects,amount of contracted foreign capital and foreign capital actually utilized exclude foreign borrowings.

6–20 分方式利用外资（2017年）

Utilization of Foreign Capital by Type (2017)

指　　标	Item	签订项目（个）Number of Signed Projects (unit)	合同利用金额（万美元）Amount of Contracted Foreign Capital (USD 10000)	实际使用金额（万美元）Amount of Foreign Capital Actually Utilized (USD 10000)
总　计	**Total**	**15599**	**7309658**	**2294813**
外商直接投资	**Foreign Direct Investment**	**15599**	**7308672**	**2290668**
合资经营企业	Joint Ventures	2122	1519662	454062
合作经营企业	Cooperative Enterprises	15	129879	25277
外资(独资)企业	Enterprises with Sole Foreign Investment	13441	5275119	1501600
外商投资股份制	Foreign Share-holding Corporations Ltd.	18	377195	303234
合作开发	Cooperative Development			
其他	Others	3	6817	6495
外商其它投资	**Other Foreign Investment**		**986**	**4145**
加工装配	Processing and Assembly		986	4145

6–21 分行业外商直接投资（2017年）

Foreign Direct Investment by Sector (2017)

指　　标	Item	签订项目（个）Number of Signed Projects (unit)	合同利用金额（万美元）Amount of Contracted Foreign Capital (USD 10000)	实际使用金额（万美元）Amount of Foreign Capital Actually Utilized (USD 10000)
总　计	**Total**	**15599**	**7308672**	**2290668**
农、林、牧、渔业	Farming, Forestry, Animal Husbandry and Fishery	301	151973	7908
采矿业	Mining	3	1083	70
制造业	Manufacture	1382	973399	621118
电力、燃气及水的生产和供应业	Production and Supply of Electric Power, Gas and Water	23	144347	75127
建筑业	Construction	368	103123	90425
交通运输、仓储和邮政业	Transport, Storage and Postal Services	209	84115	46829
信息传输、计算机服务和软件业	Information Transmission, Computer Services and Software	1615	489089	228859
批发和零售业	Wholesale and Retail Trades	6609	948803	196552
住宿和餐饮业	Hotels and Catering Services	250	68274	11281
金融业	Finance	850	1860111	155061
房地产业	Real Estate	260	371511	344634
租赁和商务服务业	Leasing and Business Services	2140	1589422	342871
科学研究、技术服务和地质勘查业	Scientific Research, Technical Servicesand Geologic Prospecting	1205	383172	86533
水利、环境和公共设施管理业	Management of Water Conservancy, Environment and Public Facilities	53	6565	1299
居民服务和其他服务业	Services to Households and Other Services	167	20571	12164
教育	Education	53	14920	6663
卫生、社会保障和社会福利业	Health, Social Security and Social Welfare	16	25254	1198
文化、体育和娱乐业	Culture, Sports and Recreation	95	72940	62076
公共管理和社会组织	Public Administration and Social Organizations			

注：本表中的行业分类仍执行2002年国民经济行业分类标准。表6–25，6–29同。
Note：Classification for national standerd of industry classification in this table are still implementing the version of 2002.

6-22 分国别(地区)外商直接投资
Foreign Direct Investment by Country (Region)

指 标	Item	1979-2017	2000	2010	2015	2016	2017
签订协议(合同)数(个)	**Number of Agreements (Contracts) Signed (unit)**	**209974**	**4245**	**5641**	**7029**	**8078**	**15599**
亚洲	**Asia**	**182095**	**3482**	**4991**	**6312**	**7239**	**14061**
#中国香港	Hong Kong, China	151313	2474	4051	4855	5365	11356
中国台湾	Taiwan, China	12982	482	326	376	385	620
中国澳门	Macao, China	10870	304	133	476	589	756
新加坡	Singapore	2761	76	72	104	117	141
日本	Japan	2503	51	108	51	37	64
韩国	Republic of Korea	2429	52	97	189	166	166
马来西亚	Malaysia	1106	14	47	57	90	123
泰国	Thailand	722	12	8	12	18	23
文莱	Brunei	641		19	3	3	2
也门	Yemen	379		9	12	82	167
伊朗	Iran	323		16	15	78	111
印度	India	321		18	27	47	92
印度尼西亚	Indonesia	239	6	4	9	11	19
非洲	**Africa**	**1787**	**14**	**120**	**147**	**230**	**353**
#塞舌尔	Seychelles			73	64	43	54
毛里求斯	Mauritius	518	12	20	6	2	3
埃及	Egypt	130	1	2	22	23	33
欧洲	**Europe**	**3577**	**81**	**115**	**190**	**212**	**381**
#英国	United Kingdom	866	18	14	31	40	68
德国	Germany	545	11	19	35	29	43
法国	France	430	7	17	18	20	38
意大利	Italy	427	8	16	32	14	25
荷兰	Netherlands	239	14	9	11	11	14
俄罗斯	Russia	175	2	5	15	19	58
西班牙	Spain	155	4	7	4	12	11
瑞士	Switzerland	150	3	5	3	7	6
瑞典	Sweden	80	2	1	5	10	8
丹麦	Denmark	76	1	4	3	5	11
比利时	Belgium	68		1	4	3	5
芬兰	Finland	46	2	2	1	3	4
奥地利	Austria	45		2	1	4	3
波兰	Poland	41		1	1	2	5
拉丁美洲	**Latin America**	**6716**	**428**	**158**	**123**	**96**	**128**
#维尔京群岛	Virgin Islands	5732	380	138	77	45	58
开曼群岛	Cayman Islands	421	26	5	16	13	20
巴拿马	Panama	97	3	1	2	3	1
伯利兹	Belize	72	9	5	3	3	2
委内瑞拉	Venezuela	66	2	2	9	3	6
巴哈马	Bahamas	61	8		1		
北美洲	**North America**	**6375**	**229**	**139**	**192**	**219**	**287**
#美国	United States of America	5255	193	110	142	164	209
加拿大	Canada	1216	32	28	48	53	77
百慕大	Bermuda	49	3	1	1	2	
大洋洲	**Oceania**	**3473**	**96**	**154**	**123**	**119**	**146**
#萨摩亚	Samoa	2281	52	114	65	62	58
澳大利亚	Australia	1067	31	30	48	48	66
新西兰	New Zealand	167	4	5	10	7	21
马绍尔群岛	Marshall Islands	33	1	3		1	
其它	**Others**	**1233**	**2**	**31**	**34**	**79**	**458**
投资性公司投资	Investment Companies	723		31	33	60	354

6-22 续表 1 continued

指　　标	Item	1979-2017	2000	2010	2015	2016	2017
协议利用外资额（万美元）	**Amount of Utilization of Foreign Capital through Signed Agreements(USD 10000)**	**75920856**	**868393**	**2460075**	**5611000**	**8667477**	**7308672**
亚洲	**Asia**	**62575147**	**548646**	**2065786**	**4938547**	**7936677**	**6410368**
#中国香港	Hong Kong, China	54022418	412219	1853437	4530090	7366508	5362192
中国澳门	Macao, China	2374868	12863	44138	171068	321186	563142
新加坡	Singapore	1758315	46516	37456	57345	75620	190529
日本	Japan	1547214	19608	37066	39835	35540	184878
中国台湾	Taiwan, China	1504010	48354	29271	81894	59789	46028
韩国	Republic of Korea	599521	8143	30011	172	26277	28472
马来西亚	Malaysia	204175	4006	3508	30110	13480	19904
泰国	Thailand	172377		7000	20342	775	946
文莱	Brunei	124326		8679		2202	
印度尼西亚	Indonesia	80242		3573	862	371	301
阿 联 酋	United Arab Emirates	53696	27	7576	163		65
伊朗	Iran	29605		191	230	25434	2158
印度	India	19923		818	1963	864	1753
非洲	**Africa**	**462957**	**4397**	**17872**	**25965**	**29760**	**52838**
#毛里求斯	Mauritius	321961	4275	10292	8676	12436	34587
塞舌尔	Seychelles	94464		7401	15722	9950	10551
埃及	Egypt	8935	6	17	667	645	2478
欧洲	**Europe**	**2174234**	**28033**	**37902**	**148081**	**228414**	**72246**
#英国	United Kingdom	636705	7158		80601	99556	21080
荷兰	Netherlands	542727	5948	7537	17332	76126	15036
法国	France	314594	5670	5187	16138	1760	10645
德国	Germany	292614	2461	4971	22321	12569	6268
瑞士	Switzerland	78131	619	244	1349	8430	168
意大利	Italy	65201	411	1315	2543	5209	387
西班牙	Spain	37057	858	3945	395	2028	183
卢森堡	Luxembourg	25584	1962	6364		5290	917
丹麦	Eire	24966	765	3646	305	3706	217
摩纳哥	Monaco	24219					
爱 尔 兰	Ireland	23553		3748	4660	257	561
比利时	Belgium	21018	187		72	4120	6729
瑞典	Sweden	20055	333	31	979	6287	570
拉丁美洲	**Latin America**	**6110088**	**208680**	**155430**	**233811**	**196319**	**237892**
#维尔京群岛	Virgin Islands	5220623	181692	137874	164486	147297	93043
开曼群岛	Cayman Islands	714022	20578	8907	53313	45773	146744
巴巴多斯	Barbados	51797					2540
巴拿马	Panama	34840	1793	921	125	643	60
巴哈马	Belize	27728	2897	8718	5420		
伯利兹	Belize	20851	1690	875	222	593	923
委内瑞拉	Venezuela	15913	15	320	10088	35	276
圣其茨-尼维斯	StKitts-Nevis	6250		360		1480	
北美洲	**North America**	**1667220**	**48580**	**34076**	**44928**	**59097**	**40442**
#美国	United States of America	1271088	44389	28995	32507	37130	33390
加拿大	Canada	225918	3126	927	13147	20186	4354
百慕大	Bermuda	169511	1039	4154		1781	2567
大洋洲	**Oceania**	**1087265**	**26715**	**72007**	**48307**	**35121**	**39250**
#萨摩亚	Samoa	859799	16151	70040	46587	29139	25879
澳大利亚	Australia	154385	7507	281	352	3382	5669
马绍尔群岛	Marshall Islands	23091	1073	1196	188	885	
新西兰	New Zealand	22388	108	284	95	112	7695
其它太平洋岛屿	Other Pacific Islands	5555		126	1085		
其它	**Others**	**1843707**	**3342**	**76972**	**171128**	**182089**	**455636**
投资性公司投资	Investment Companies	1542738		76806	172325	144778	429392

6−22 续表 2 continued

指 标	Item	1979-2017	2000	2010	2015	2016	2017
实际利用外资(万美元)	**Foreign Capital Actually Utilized (USD 10000)**	**42375631**	**1223720**	**2026098**	**2687546**	**2334921**	**2290668**
亚洲	**Asia**	**32415988**	**927071**	**1486723**	**2268764**	**1899631**	**1883742**
#中国香港	Hong Kong, China	27285488	744826	1291738	2047856	1741924	1692741
日本	Japan	1403089	30852	51044	45514	42953	42817
新加坡	Singapore	1151651	49115	46482	47343	33506	43159
中国澳门	Macao, China	874336	26137	30189	73718	64434	55994
中国台湾	Taiwan, China	870380	49746	24543	10525	6882	6854
韩国	Republic of Korea	471942	13671	20658	34770	7206	37979
文莱	Brunei	97617		8825	3133	932	1651
马来西亚	Malaysia	86889	4993	5133	4541	790	579
泰国	Thailand	64903	2895	998	822	385	1455
印度尼西亚	Indonesia	52739	3352	877	36	55	31
阿联酋	United Arab Emirates	22419	100	5370	10	6	28
菲律宾	Philippines	8719	191	91	5		
印度	India	5035	964	69	148	168	32
非洲	**Africa**	**292209**	**4272**	**16972**	**12060**	**18891**	**47234**
#毛里求斯	Mauritius	243297	4576	14738	7327	14160	42163
塞舌尔	Seychelles	39731		1772	4635	4289	4920
欧洲	**Europe**	**1587448**	**38643**	**78713**	**83864**	**94148**	**83798**
#荷兰	Netherlands	399300	7886	9646	7246	12645	45886
英国	United Kingdom	368338	8258	1859	13139	52900	15086
法国	France	280384	4551	52008	21078	7657	7977
德国	Germany	245266	10057	3657	33898	5778	3099
瑞士	Switzerland	66788	3349	2839	1191	7059	185
意大利	Italy	55231		1736	1344	411	859
西班牙	Spain	30558	44	2089	444	126	692
芬兰	Finland	23052	2302	18		2	953
卢森堡	Luxembourg	20962	90	660	860	810	99
爱 尔 兰	Ireland	20131		2010	3762		
瑞典	Sweden	18441	360	500	647	5711	382
奥地利	Austria	17379	101	1000		25	644
比利时	Belgium	16299	499	60	129	824	7099
丹麦	Denmark	13649		201	11	23	715
拉丁美洲	**Latin America**	**5043907**	**161983**	**303059**	**142932**	**151629**	**84200**
#维尔京群岛	Virgin Islands	4429217	149200	270979	123429	128386	58287
开曼群岛	Cayman Islands	467533	6694	24644	16671	16939	24939
巴哈马	Bahamas	51314	3543	1649	1019	4266	
巴巴多斯	Barbados	44120		3254	701	200	690
巴拿马	Panama	26171	1544	1953	288	84	22
北美洲	**North America**	**1138070**	**74453**	**40816**	**35221**	**24128**	**30888**
#美国	United States of America	881080	66972	25388	19049	23298	30419
百慕大	Bermuda	155570	2320	13341	15808	557	93
加拿大	Canada	99532	5161	2087	364	273	376
大洋洲	**Oceania**	**820379**	**14510**	**53171**	**57284**	**20628**	**15606**
#萨摩亚	Samoa	698282	8942	49714	54362	18804	12458
澳大利亚	Australia	86881	4697	2869	2538	227	1261
马绍尔群岛	Marshall Islands	9593	680	183	384	808	3
新西兰	New Zealand	7720	86	181		224	449
其它	**Others**	**1077385**		**46644**	**87276**	**125866**	**145200**
投资性公司投资	Investment Companies	845082		35196	87119	125866	140120
创业投资公司投资	Resuccess Investments Limited	5172			157		2995

6-23 各市外商直接投资
Foreign Direct Investment by City

市别	City	2016 签订项目(个) Number of Signed Projects (unit)	2016 合同利用金额(万美元) Amount of Contracted Foreign Capital (USD 10000)	2016 实际使用金额(万美元) Amount of Foreign Capital Actually Utilized (USD 10000)	2017 签订项目(个) Number of Signed Projects (unit)	2017 合同利用金额(万美元) Amount of Contracted Foreign Capital (USD 10000)	2017 实际使用金额(万美元) Amount of Foreign Capital Actually Utilized (USD 10000)
全省合计	**Provincial Total**	**8078**	**8667477**	**2334921**	**15599**	**7308672**	**2290668**
广州	Guangzhou	1757	990123	570121	2458	1339009	628868
深圳	Shenzhen	4132	5219268	673221	6756	3685736	740129
珠海	Zhuhai	803	905590	229465	1565	1072244	243305
汕头	Shantou	21	26937	9086	37	34515	35535
佛山	Foshan	229	222794	147166	315	158427	162347
韶关	Shaoguan	14	19635	5062	60	6739	5284
河源	Heyuan	35	36449	9500	453	68483	10405
梅州	Meizhou	37	38213	5711	889	28277	5716
惠州	Huizhou	154	213412	114251	661	166982	114351
汕尾	Shanwei	16	12916	4442	91	23714	10004
东莞	Dongguan	444	473173	392617	925	260785	171972
中山	Zhongshan	133	106269	47447	270	76873	50933
江门	Jiangmen	123	107661	47634	215	94031	51097
阳江	Yangjiang	15	28318	6990	20	164469	4661
湛江	Zhanjiang	12	27267	6133	48	16065	8095
茂名	Maoming	57	30084	7547	394	32811	7406
肇庆	Zhaoqing	42	135134	37049	132	26752	18133
清远	Qingyuan	16	31702	10717	177	32755	14395
潮州	Chaozhou	4	5319	3430	38	6967	3544
揭阳	Jieyang	10	3917	3071	63	8312	1680
云浮	Yunfu	24	33296	4261	32	4726	2808
按经济区域分	By Region						
珠三角	Pearl River Delta	7817	8373424	2258971	13297	6880839	2181135
东翼	Eastern Region	51	49089	20029	229	73508	50763
西翼	Western Region	84	85669	20670	462	213345	20162
山区	Mountainous Region	126	159295	35251	1611	140980	38608

6-24 对外经济技术合作情况

Economic and Technical Cooperation with Foreign Countries and Regions

年 份 Year	对外承包工程 Contracted Projects				对外劳务合作 Labor Services		
	签订合同数 (个) Number of Contracts Signed (unit)	合同金额 (万美元) Contracted Value (USD 10000)	营业金额 (万美元) Value of Turnover (USD 10000)	年末在外人数 (人) Number of Persons Abroad at the Year-end (person)	劳务人员合同工资总额 (万美元) Total Wages of Contract Workers (USD 10000)	劳务人员实际收入总额 (万美元) Actual Total Income of Contract Workers (USD 10000)	年末在外人数 (人) Number of Persons Abroad at the Year-end (person)
1985	28	1897	2491	305	424	433	1197
1990	23	5953	7586	688	6055	3189	8045
1995	29	19183	10924	850	20593	17775	33263
1996	37	14823	9474	1680	11784	19365	23319
1997	67	22435	10940	354	17356	14743	22857
1998	28	13331	17526	566	12925	14464	20816
1999	63	52961	21857	603	9327	13230	19128
2000	86	36555	34515	634	12941	10777	19564
2001	250	53924	26192	641	13271	11752	30695
2002	165	64827	58986	643	19114	17059	18922
2003	193	97055	86898	730	23132	21926	21738
2004	810	168338	161287	856	27392	28315	17043
2005	2061	326752	247189	606	32762	30878	20469
2006	1625	458442	344170	752	41898	37030	27024
2007	757	597733	546069	946	80824	62927	27880
2008	331	844352	686045	886	68209	58420	33691
2009	556	814859	758799	2105	45718	59469	33124
2010	605	986740	820815	4554	76575	58428	33901
2011	528	1343526	1134158	4017	46578	46445	38621
2012	517	1905053	1605342	3863	46643	38600	44301
2013	617	2366492	2286507	3243	53917	44689	54272
2014	1139	1524873	1241121	3405	138820	66218	72788
2015	1937	2072350	1987790	3633	139705	117787	81600
2016	1503	2198726	1816382	4350	65540	89185	80468
2017	1151	2218294	1809649	6293	72805	86660	79440

注：1．2009年以后，“对外承包工程”包含“对外设计咨询”。
2．2011年对外劳务合作统计口径调整。

Note: a) Since 2009, foreign design cousultation is inclued in foreign contracted projects.
b) The statistics coverage of foreign labor service has been adjusted in 2011.

6-25 分行业外商投资企业工商注册登记情况（2017年末）

Registration Status of Enterprises with Foreign Investment by Sector (Year-end of 2017)

行业	Sector	企业数（户）Number of Registered Enterprises (unit)	投资总额（亿美元）Total Investment (USD 100 million)	注册资本（亿美元）Registered Capital (USD 100 million)	#外方 Capital Invested by Foreign Partners
总　计	**Total**	**135869.00**	**17622.27**	**6431.86**	**4791.60**
农、林、牧、渔业	Farming, Forestry, Animal Husbandry and Fishery	1837.00	8071.41	56.62	50.35
采矿业	Mining	71.00	5.46	2.89	2.25
制造业	Manufacture	45091.00	3434.61	2075.05	1662.50
电力、燃气及水的生产和供应业	Production and Supply of Electric Power, Gas and Water	752.00	681.77	281.47	117.28
建筑业	Construction	1530.00	161.32	89.03	57.84
交通运输、仓储和邮政业	Transport, Storage and Postal Services	3403.00	267.52	144.46	100.02
信息传输、计算机服务和软件业	Information Transmission, Computer Services and Software	6397.00	270.67	176.93	146.20
批发和零售业	Wholesale and Retail Trades	37176.00	720.30	415.61	356.36
住宿和餐饮业	Hotels and Catering Services	5773.00	71.63	47.13	39.57
金融业	Finance	4016.00	1191.91	1170.89	699.80
房地产业	Real Estate	5137.00	1127.50	658.41	568.58
租赁和商务服务业	Leasing and Business Services	14803.00	1156.80	1003.19	727.65
科学研究、技术服务和地质勘查业	Scientific Research, Technical Services and Geological Prospecting	6675.00	290.65	194.63	164.64
水利、环境和公共设施管理业	Management of Water Conservancy, Environment and Public Facilities	225.00	19.65	11.29	9.43
居民服务和其他服务业	Households and Other Servies	1685.00	64.42	46.50	37.62
教育	Education	167.00	1.87	1.56	1.42
卫生、社会保障和社会福利业	Health Care, Social Security and Social Welfare	66.00	15.47	10.82	8.59
文化、体育和娱乐业	Culture, Sports and Recreation	973.00	66.79	43.33	40.12
其他	Others	92.00	2.52	2.04	1.38

6-26 各市外商投资企业工商注册登记情况（2017年末）
Registration Status of Enterprises with Foreign Investment by City(Year-end of 2017)

市 别	City	企业数(户) Number of Registered Enterprises(unit)	投资总额 (亿美元) Total Investment (USD 100 million)	注册资本 (亿美元) Registered Capital (USD 100 million)	#外 方 Capital Invested by Foreign Partners
全省合计	**Provincial Total**	**135869**	**17622.27**	**6431.86**	**4791.60**
广 州	Guangzhou	25194	9921.73	1068.89	783.40
深 圳	Shenzhen	50769	3606.52	2835.10	1899.60
珠 海	Zhuhai	8300	661.31	463.00	397.57
汕 头	Shantou	1419	85.28	59.54	44.49
佛 山	Foshan	6630	542.67	333.74	274.81
韶 关	Shaoguan	824	32.37	22.58	20.30
河 源	Heyuan	1504	62.04	39.99	37.43
梅 州	Meizhou	2268	42.07	26.61	24.38
惠 州	Huizhou	7952	490.97	288.51	240.12
汕 尾	Shanwei	693	43.86	30.05	29.28
东 莞	Dongguan	13417	714.28	482.54	455.92
中 山	Zhongshan	4157	250.89	150.90	132.83
江 门	Jiangmen	5206	357.67	195.74	151.44
阳 江	Yangjiang	576	227.79	70.61	36.05
湛 江	Zhanjiang	678	61.43	31.86	17.81
茂 名	Maoming	1128	31.29	22.47	19.15
肇 庆	Zhaoqing	1535	160.71	96.83	89.33
清 远	Qingyuan	1260	104.76	64.31	48.61
潮 州	Chaozhou	603	15.81	11.75	8.34
揭 阳	Jieyang	732	24.61	19.19	17.04
云 浮	Yunfu	447	27.57	14.82	12.58
局 本 部	Unclassified by Region	577	156.64	102.85	51.13

6-27 一类口岸开放使用情况（2017年末）

Opening and Operating Status of Category-1 Ports (Year-end of 2017)

市别 City	个数 Number	口岸类型 Name of Ports				
		水运	Water Transport	陆运	Land Transport	空运 Air Transport
合计 Total	**61**	**39**		**17**		**5**
广州 Guangzhou	6	广州港口岸	Guangzhou Port	广州铁路客运	Guangzhou Railway Station for Passenger Service	白云国际机场 Baiyun International Airport
		广州南沙港口岸	Nansha Port			
		广州莲花山港口岸	Lianhuashan Port			
		增城新塘港客运口岸	Xintang Port			
深圳 Shenzhen	17	蛇口码头	Shekou Port	罗湖	Luohu	深圳保安国际机场 Shenzhen International Airport
		赤湾码头	Chiwan Port	文锦渡	Wenjindu	
		梅沙旅游专用口岸	Meisha Port	沙头角	Shatoujiao	
		东角头码头	Dongjiaotou Port	皇岗	Huanggang	
		妈湾码头	Mawan Port	深圳湾	Shenzhen Bay	
		盐田码头	Yiantian Port	福田	Futian	
		大亚湾核电站专用码头	Dayawan Port	广深港高铁西九龙站	Guangzhou-Shenzhen-Hong Kong Express Rail Link West Kowloon Terminus	
		西冲旅游专用口岸	Xichong Port			
		大铲湾港区	Dachan Bay Port			
珠海 Zhuhai	10	九州港口岸	Jiuzhou Port	拱北	Gongbei	
		湾仔口岸	Wanzai Port	横琴	Hengqin	
		珠海港口岸	Zhuhai Port	珠澳跨境工业区专用口岸	The Industrial Zone Dedicated port cross-border between The Pearl River Delta and Macao	
		万山港口岸	Wanshan Port	港珠澳大桥珠海口岸	Zhuhai Port of Hong Kong Zhuhai Macao Bridge	
		斗门港口岸	Doumen Port	珠海青茂口岸	Qingmao Port	
汕头 Shantou	4	汕头港口岸	Shantou Port			
		潮阳港口岸	Chaoyang Port			
		南澳港口岸	Nanao Port			
梅州 Meizhou	1					梅县机场 Meixian Airport
惠州 Huizhou	1	惠州港口岸	Huizhou Port			
汕尾 Shanwei	1	汕尾港口岸	Shanwei Port			
东莞 Dongguan	2	虎门港口岸	Humen Port	东莞铁路客运	Dongguan Railway Stations for Passenger Service	
中山 Zhongshan	1	中山港口岸	Zhongshan Port			
江门 Jiangmen	5	江门客运港口岸	Jiangmen Port			
		开平三埠港客运口岸	Sanfu Port			
		台山广海港口岸	Guanghai Port			
		鹤山港客运口岸	Heshan Port			
		新会港口岸	Xinhui Port			
佛山 Foshan	4	顺德容奇港口岸	Shunde Port	佛山铁路客运	Foshan Railway Stations for Passenger Service	
		南海港口岸	Nanhai Port			
		高明港客运口岸	Gaoming Port			
阳江 Yangjiang	1	阳江港口岸	Yangjiang Port			
湛江 Zhanjiang	2	湛江港口岸	Zhanjiang Port			湛江机场 Zhanjiang Airport
茂名 Maoming	1	水东港口岸	Shuidong Port			
肇庆 Zhaoqing	2	肇庆港客运口岸	Zhaoqing Port	肇庆铁路客运	Zhaoqing Railway Station for Passenger Service	
潮州 Chaozhou	1	潮州港口岸	Chaozhou Port			
揭阳 Jieyang	1	揭阳港口岸	Jieyang Port			揭阳潮汕国际机场 Jieyang International Airport
河源 Heyuan	1			河源口岸	Heyuan Highway Port	

注：目前为止肇庆火车站因重建暂停使用；广深港高铁西九龙站口岸、港珠澳大桥珠海口岸、珠海青茂口岸在建未启用；东角头口岸、梅沙口岸、湾仔口岸暂停运作；西冲口岸未开通使用；南澳口岸尚未建设。

Note: To date, the Zhaoqing Station is temporarily not in use, due to ongoing reconstruction; the West Kowloon Station Port on the Guangzhou-Shenzhen-Hong Kong Express Rail Link,the Hong Kong-Zhuhai-Macao Bridge Port,and the Zhuhai Qing Mao Port are under construction and not in use yet; the Dongjiaotou Port, the Meisha Port, and the Wanzai Port are temporarily out of operation; the Xichong Port has not been opened yet; the South Macao Port has not been constructed.

6-28 分国别(地区)对外直接投资
Foreign Direct Investment by Country (Region)

国家(地区)	Country of Region	项目个数 (个) Number of Projects (unit)			对外直接投资额 (万美元) Net Overseas Direct Investment (USD10000)		
		2015	2016	2017	2015	2016	2017
合计	**Total**	**1559**	**1429**	**703**	**1064509**	**2068424**	**875025**
亚洲	**Asia**	**1253**	**1003**	**479**	**661616**	**1369876**	**534265**
中国香港	Hong Kong, China	1073	777	324	593952	1273070	503192
印度尼西亚	Indonesia	10	16	16	13491	22464	1066
泰国	Thailand	12	16	6	1192	21080	1245
阿拉伯联合酋长国	United Arab Emirates	7	15	3	253	11022	243
新加坡	Singapore	14	21	9	19203	10783	1611
日本	Japan	12	18	14	281	7885	1034
台湾省	Taiwan, China	12	16	10	8345	5963	145
马来西亚	Malaysia	8	21	12	386	4545	3948
中国澳门	Macao, China	16	12	13	7787	4092	131
越南	Vietnam	13	16	22	915	2895	1757
柬埔寨	Cambodia	10	6	7	10263	2839	10231
以色列	Israel	5	2	1	1690	1024	
老挝	Laos	3	3	3	314	681	2128
非洲	**Africa**	**28**	**32**	**29**	**7303**	**3509**	**6492**
加纳	Ghana	1	2		4217	841	1196
肯尼亚	Kenya	2	3	4	452	822	1206
塞舌尔	Seychelles	5	8	1	1539	530	300
欧洲	**Europe**	**58**	**89**	**65**	**8011**	**49093**	**24979**
法国	France	6	7	6	290	27697	318
爱尔兰	Ireland	1	2			5155	50
荷兰	Netherlands	5	3	4	1105	3629	2373
俄罗斯	Russia	3	5	5	48	3562	2
德国	Germany	20	24	21	2520	3141	8824
英国	United Kingdom	10	21	7	128	2388	2997
卢森堡	Luxembourg		3			2115	661
立陶宛	Lithuania					1000	
瑞士	Switzerland		2	1	2848	223	421
瑞典	Sweden	1	3	1		114	54
挪威	Norway			1	847	50	168
罗马尼亚	Romania		1			6	
保加利亚	Bulgaria		1			5	
匈牙利	Hungary		1			5	
拉丁美洲	**Latin America**	**41**	**28**	**10**	**33904**	**74918**	**79819**
英属维尔京群岛	Virgin Islands	18	7	2	22546	41784	63090
开曼群岛	Cayman Islands	10	12	2	10009	32703	8387
巴西	Brazil	3	1	2		297	8052
秘鲁	Peru		1		345	132	
哥伦比亚	Colombia	3	2	1		2	
智利	Chile	1	3				
北美洲	**North America**	**141**	**233**	**107**	**97108**	**201849**	**56968**
美国	United States of America	135	219	99	56478	193748	49462
加拿大	Canada	6	14	8	40630	8101	7507
大洋洲	**Oceania**	**38**	**44**	**13**	**12955**	**25416**	**14306**
新西兰	New Zealand	7	7	3	4081	16779	1831
澳大利亚	Australia	24	31	7	7929	6893	12236
萨摩亚	Samoa	2	4	1		1587	5
巴布亚新几内亚	Papua New Guinea	2		2	558	132	133
斐济	Fiji	3			32	17	
利润再投资分摊	Reinvested profit sharing				243612	343764	158196

6–29 分行业对外直接投资
Overseas Direct Investment by Sector

单位：万美元 (USD 10 000)

行业	Sector	2015	2016	2017
总计	**Total**	**1064509**	**2068424**	**875025**
农、林、牧、渔业	Farming, Forestry, Animal Husbandry and Fishery	18219	5948	1775
采矿业	Mining	19682	24942	8896
制造业	Manufacture	83138	270752	117180
电力、燃气及水的生产和供应业	Production and Supply of Electric Power, Gas and Water	4045	286	384
建筑业	Construction	17697	20117	5252
交通运输、仓储和邮政业	Transport, Storage and Postal Services	1444	13876	5431
信息传输、计算机服务和软件业	Information Transmission, Computer Services and Software	10930	65364	115229
批发和零售业	Wholesale and Retail Trades	232283	440966	110851
住宿和餐饮业	Hotels and Catering Services	2919	3225	1818
金融业	Finance	21730	5277	7862
房地产业	Real Estate	65355	140771	35394
租赁和商务服务业	Leasing and Business Services	285120	568749	260373
科学研究、技术服务和地质勘查业	Scientific Research, Technical Servicesand Geologic Prospecting	16702	21228	9207
水利、环境和公共设施管理业	Management of Water Conservancy, Environment and Public Facilities	100	1973	10122
居民服务和其他服务业	Services to Households and Other Services	31274	62931	24038
教育	Education	3349	72664	2384
卫生、社会保障和社会福利业	Health, Social Security and Social Welfare	2741	504	554
文化、体育和娱乐业	Culture, Sports and Recreation	4008	5087	81
公共管理和社会组织	Public Administration and Social Organizations	160		
利润再投资分摊	Reinvested profit sharing	243612	343764	158196

主要统计指标解释

货物进出口总额 指实际进出我国国境的货物总金额。包括对外贸易实际进出口货物，来料加工装配进出口货物，国家间、联合国及国际组织无偿援助物资和赠送品，华侨、港澳台同胞和外籍华人捐赠品，租赁期满归承租人所有的租赁货物，进料加工进出口货物，边境地方贸易及边境地区小额贸易进出口货物，中外合资企业、中外合作经营企业、外商独资经营企业进出口货物和公用物品，到、离岸价格在规定限额以上的进出口货样和广告品(无商业价值、无使用价值和免费提供出口的除外)，从保税仓库提取在中国境内销售的进口货物，以及其他进出口货物。该指标可以观察一个国家在对外贸易方面的总规模。我国规定出口货物按离岸价格统计，进口货物按到岸价格统计。

商品目的地进口额和商品货源地出口额 目的地进口额指进口货物的消费、使用或最终抵运地的实际进口额；货源地出口额指出口货物的产地或原始发货地的实际出口额。

外商投资 指我国政府、部门、企业和其他经济组织通过吸收外商直接投资以及其他方式筹措的境外现汇、技术、设备等。

利用外资的方式有：对外借款，外国（或港澳地区）企业和经济组织或个人在我国境内开办独资企业、与我国境内的企业或组织共同开办合资企业、合作经营(企业)项目或合作开发资源，以及补偿贸易、国际租赁等。

外商直接投资 是指外国投资者在我国境内通过设立外商投资企业、合伙企业、与中方投资者共同进行石油资源的合作勘探开发以及设立外国公司分支机构等方式进行投资。外国投资者可以用现金、实物、无形资产、股权等投资，还可以用从外商投资企业获得的利润进行再投资。

外商其他投资 指除对外借款和外商直接投资以外的各种利用外资的形式。包括企业在境内外股票市场公开发行的以外币计价的股票发行价总额，国际租赁进口设备的应付款，补偿贸易中外商提供的进口设备、技术、物料的价款，加工装配贸易中外商提供的进口设备、物料的价款。

实际使用外资 是指合同外资金额的实际执行数，外方投资者根据外商投资企业的合同（章程）的规定实际缴付的出资额和企业投资总额内外方投资者以自己的境外自有资金实际直接向企业提供的期限 1 年以上的中长期贷款。

对外直接投资 指我国企业、团体等(简称境内投资主体) 在国外及港澳台地区以现金、实物、无形资产等方式投资，并以控制国(境)外企业的经营管理权为核心的经济活动。对外直接投资的内涵主要体现在一经济体通过投资于另一经济体而实现其持久利益的目标。

对外承包工程 根据《对外承包工程管理条例》，对外承包工程是指中国的企业或者其他单位承包境外建设工程项目的活动。

对外劳务合作 指组织劳务人员赴其他国家或地区为国外的企业或机构工作的经营性活动。

Explanatory Notes on Main Statistical Indicators

Total Import and Export of Goods refer to the real value of commodities imported and exported across the border of China. They include the actual imports and exports through foreign trade, imported and exported goods under the processing and assembling trades and materials, supplies and gifts as aid given gratis between governments and by the United Nations and other international organizations, and contributions donated by overseas Chinese, compatriots in Hong Kong and Macao and Chinese with foreign citizenship, leasing commodities owned by tenant at the expiration of leasing period, the imported and exported commodities processed with imported materials, commodities trading in border areas, the imported and exported commodities and articles for public use of the Sino-foreign joint ventures, cooperative enterprises and ventures with sole foreign investment. Also included is import or export of samples and advertising goods for which CIF or FOB value are beyond the permitted ceiling (excluding goods of no trading or use value and free commodities for export), imported goods sold in China from bonded warehouses and other imported or exported goods. The indicator of the total imports and exports at customs can be used to observe the total size of external trade in a country. In accordance with the stipulation of the Chinese government, imports are calculated at CIF, while exports are calculated at FOB.

Import or Export Value by Location of China's Foreign Trade Managing Units refers to actual value of imports and exports carried out by corporations which have been registered by the local Customs house and are vested with right to run import export business.

Utilization of Foreign Capital refers to direct investment, commodity credits and other funds used by domistic institutions that are supplied from abroad and from Hong Kong，Macao and Taiwan。

Utilization of foreign capital takes the forms of loans from abroad, sole investment in enterprises in the boundary of China by foreign (or Hong Kong and Macao) enterprises, economic organizations or individuals, investment in Sino-foreign joint ventures, cooperative projects (enterprises), cooperative exploitation of natural resources with enterprises or organizations in China, compensation trade and international lease, etc.

Foreign Direct Investment refers to foreign investment in China through the establishment of foreign invested enterprises, cooperative exploration and development of petroleum resources with domestic investors and the establishment of branch organizations of foreign enterprises. Foreign investment can be made in forms of cash, physical investment, intangible assets and equity, in addition with reinvestment of the foreign enterprises with the profits gained from the investment.

Other Foreign Investment refers to all forms of utilization of foreign capitals other than foreign borrowings and foreign direct investment. It includes the total value of stock shares in foreign currencies issued by enterprises at domestic or foreign stock exchanges, rent payable for the imported equipment through international leasing arrangement, cost of imported equipment, technology and materials provided by foreign counterparts in compensation trade and processing and assembly trade.

Foreign capital actually used Refers to actual fulfilled amount of contracted foreign investment, this includes the actual amount paid by foreign investors, according to the contracts of foreign investment companies. This also includes the portion of foreign investment in total enterprise investment provided to enterprises in the form of mid to long term loans with a term of at least 1 year by foreign investors, using their foreign assets.

Overseas Direct Investment refers to investment made by domestic enterprises and organizations (referred to as domestic investors) in foreign countries and Hong Kong SAR, Macao SAR and Taiwan province in forms of cash, physical investment and intangible assets, and the economic activities centring on operation and management of those enterprises are under the control of domestic investors. The content of overseas direct investment mainly reflects one economic entity by investing in another economic entity to achieve its goal of lasting interest.

Overseas Contracted Projects refer to activities of contracting overseas construction projects by Chinese enterprises or any other units, which are stipulated in the Regulations on Administration of Foreign Contracted Project.

Overseas Labour Services refer to operational activities of organizing labour force to go abroad providing services to foreign enterprises or agencies.

七、能源、资源和环境

ENERGY, RESOURCES AND ENVIRONMENT

七　能源、资源和环境

简要说明

一、本篇资料反映广东自然资源状况、能源生产、能源消费、能耗水平和环境保护事业等情况。能源情况主要包括：能源生产、消费及品种构成，分行业能源消费总量，综合能源平衡，各市能源单耗，能源生产和消费弹性系数，能源加工转换效率，生活用能源消费等资料。自然资源包括土地 、气候、森林、水利、矿产资源情况。环保部分主要包括水环境、大气环境、生态环境、城市环境、农村环境、自然灾害，“三废”的排放、治理、综合利用，环境管理、环保系统自身建设情况等。

二、本篇资料由广东省统计局综合处、能源统计处根据有关资料和调查结果整理提供。

三、能源资料取自全省《地区能源平衡表》和《工业企业能源购进、消费及库存表》等。地区能源平衡表编制范围为辖区内生产和消费能源的单位，其中规模以上工业企业的能源消费根据国家统计局制发的报表制度由统计系统搜集资料逐级汇总上报；加工转换消费来源于《工业企业能源购进、消费及库存附表》；其他数据来源于有关厅 (局)、公司或企业。矿产、土地资源资料由省国土资源厅提供；海洋资料由省海洋与渔业局提供；气象资料由省气象局提供；森林资源资料由省林业厅提供；水利资料由省水利厅提供；环保事业情况由环保部门提供。

四、关于数据口径与计算的说明：

1．2010 年以后的数据已按第三次经济普查结果进行调整。

2．能源生产与消费弹性系数分别以能源生产、消费增长速度与地区生产总值增长速度相比求得。

3．能源平衡表中，进口量和出口量采用海关统计数据，电力折算标准煤系数按平均发电煤耗计算。

4．能源加工转换效率表中的电力折算标准煤系数采用当量值计算，每千瓦小时折 0.1229 千克标准煤。

7　Energy ,Resources and Environment

Brief Introduction

Ⅰ. The data in this chapter reflect the natural resource, energy production, consumption, and efficiency and environmental protection of Guangdong Province. The data on energy mainly including the energy production and consumption and their composition, the energy consumption by sector, the overall balance of energy, energy consumption per unit by city, the elasticity ratios of energy production and consumption, the efficiency of energy conversion and the consumption of energy for non-production use, etc. The data on natural resource cover land, climate, forest, water conservancy and mineral resources. The data on environmental protection mainly include water environment, atmospheric environment, ecological environment, urban environment, rural environment, natural disasters, the discharge, treatment and comprehensive utilization of waste water，waste gas and solid wastes， environment management and the improvement of environmental protection departments, etc. The data are provided by Guangdong Provincial Bureau of Environmental Protection.

Ⅱ. The data in this chapter are prepared and provided by the Division of Comprehensive Statistics of Statistics Bureau of Guangdong Province and the Division of Energy Statistics of Statistics Bureau of Guangdong Province.

Ⅲ. The data in this chapter come from the Energy Balance Sheet of the whole province and the Sheets of Energy Purchase, Consumption and Storage of Key Energy Consumption Industrial Enterprises. The coverage of the regional energy balance includes the units that produce and consume energy. Among them, the data on the energy consumption of industrial enterprises above designated size are collected by the statistical agencies in accordance with the statistical reporting scheme stipulated by the National Bureau of Statistics and tabulated and reported to the higher authorities level by level; the data on the energy processing, transformation and consumption are derived from the Sheets of Energy Purchase, Consumption and Storage of Key Energy Consumption Industrial

Enterprises; other data are provided by related government departments, companies and enterprises. The data on mineral and land resources are provided by the Land and Resources Department of Guangdong Province. The data on ocean are provided by the Oceanic and Fishery Administration of Guangdong Province. The data on meteorological phenomena are provided by the Meteorological Bureau of Guangdong Province. The data on forest are provided by the Forestry Administration of Guangdong Province. The data on water conservancy are provided by the Water Resources Department of Guangdong Province. The data on environmental protection are provided by Guangdong Provincial Bureau of Environmental Protection.

Ⅳ. Data coverage and calculation:

(1) Since 2010,data have been adjusted in accordance with the figures from the third china economics census.

(2) The elasticity ratio of energy production is calculated as the quotient of the growth rate of energy production divided by the growth rate of GDP; and the elasticity ratio of energy consumption is calculated as the quotient of the growth rate of energy consumption divided by the growth rate of GDP.

(3) In the energy balance sheet, the data on the imports and exports are data from the customs statistics.The ratio for converting electric power into the standard coal equivalent is calculated according to the average consumption of coal for generating electricity.

(4) In the table on the efficiency of energy conversion, the ratio for converting electric power into the standard coal equivalent is calculated on the basis of heat value equivalent.One kilowatt is equal to 0.1229 kg SCE.

7-1 能源主要指标
Main Indicators of Energy

项　　目	item	2015	2016	2017
一、能源生产	**Production of Energy**			
(一)一次能源生产量	Primary Energy Output			
原油 (万吨)	Crude Oil (10000tons)	1572.61	1533.15	1556.29
天然气 (亿立方米)	Natural Gas (100 million cu.m)	116.81	79.25	89.23
一次电 (亿千瓦时)	Primary Electricity (100 million kwh)	1101.12	1291.98	1204.00
(二)二次能源生产量	Secondary Energy Output			
原油加工量 (万吨)	Crude Oil Processing Capacity (10000tons)	4873.76	5018.35	5176.02
汽油 (万吨)	Gasoline (10000tons)	885.73	904.67	946.76
煤油 (万吨)	Kerosene (10000tons)	641.13	682.88	713.39
柴油 (万吨)	Diesel Oil (10000tons)	1419.41	1376.46	1370.06
燃料油 (万吨)	Fuel Oil (10000tons)	190.92	177.27	184.69
液化石油气 (万吨)	Liquefied Petroleum Gas (10000tons)	256.27	283.10	298.76
发电量 (亿千瓦时)	Power Generation (100 million kwh)	2933.78	2971.69	3332.81
二、能源消费 (万吨标准煤)	**Consumption of Energy (10000 tons of SCE)**			
能源消费总量	Total Energy Consumtion	30145.49	31240.75	32341.66
第一产业	Primary Industry	502.45	530.55	544.67
第二产业	Secondary Industry	19039.83	18958.08	19577.18
第三产业	Tertiary Industry	6238.65	6895.41	7219.81
居民消费量	Household Consumption	4364.56	4856.71	5000.00
三、节能减排 (%)	**Energy Conservation (%)**			
单位GDP能耗上升或下降(±)	Energy Consumption per Unit of GDP rises or decreases (±)	-5.71	-3.62	-3.74
规模以上工业单位工业增加值能耗上升或下降(±)	Energy Consumption per Unit of Industrial Value-added rises or decreases (±)	-10.47	-3.75	-0.01
单位GDP电耗上升或下降(±)	Electricity Consumption per Unit of GDP rises or decreases (±)	-6.10	-1.73	-1.19

7-2 能源生产总量及构成
Total Production of Energy and its Composition

项 目	Item	2000	2005	2010	2014	2015	2016	2017
能源生产总量（万吨标准煤）	**Total Energy Production (10000 tons of SCE)**	**3711.69**	**4758.79**	**4858.07**	**5594.56**	**6862.51**	**7137.96**	**7037.37**
构 成 (%)	Composition (%)	100.0	100.0	100.0	100.0	100.0	100.0	100.0
原 煤	Coal	8.0	7.2					
原 油	Crude Oil	53.6	44.1	37.8	31.8	32.8	30.7	31.6
天然气	Natural Gas	11.3	12.5	21.5	19.9	18.7	14.8	16.9
一次电力及其他能源	Primary Electricity and Other Energy	27.1	36.2	40.7	48.3	48.5	54.5	51.5

7-3 能源消费总量及构成
Total Consumption of Energy and Its Composition

年份 Year	一次能源消费量（万吨标准煤）Primary Energy Consumption (10000 tons of SCE)	构成(%) Composition(%) 合计 Total	原煤 Coal	原油 Crude Oil	天然气 Natural Gas	一次电力及其他能源 Primary Electricity and Other Energy	终端能源消费量（万吨标准煤）Final Energy Consumption (10000 tons of SCE)	构成(%) Composition(%) 合计 Total	原煤 Coal	油品 Oil Products	电力 Electricity	其他 Others
1990	3690.25	100.0	56.5	35.3		8.2	3936.44	100.0	33.6	22.4	33.0	11.0
1995	6147.61	100.0	56.4	28.5	0.2	14.9	7062.28	100.0	27.0	20.9	39.7	12.4
2000	7983.46	100.0	52.2	35.0	0.2	12.6	9080.20	100.0	17.1	22.6	45.4	14.9
2001	8169.60	100.0	52.5	34.0		13.5	9775.15	100.0	15.9	22.6	46.1	15.4
2002	9036.40	100.0	51.9	31.0		17.1	10861.68	100.0	14.5	21.6	49.2	14.7
2003	10462.09	100.0	53.5	28.6	0.2	17.7	12414.48	100.0	17.8	22.6	44.5	15.1
2004	12013.14	100.0	51.4	28.4	0.2	20.0	14487.74	100.0	11.7	20.7	52.6	15.0
2005	13086.58	100.0	52.8	26.1	0.3	20.8	17255.84	100.0	10.9	23.6	50.7	14.8
2006	15281.00	100.0	50.4	26.2	1.3	22.1	19254.03	100.0	12.5	23.7	48.7	15.1
2007	17344.10	100.0	52.0	24.2	3.5	20.3	21427.33	100.0	12.0	22.2	49.3	16.5
2008	17679.13	100.0	50.8	24.6	4.1	20.5	22671.76	100.0	13.8	21.2	48.5	16.5
2009	19235.86	100.0	46.5	27.5	5.4	20.6	23943.39	100.0	12.2	20.9	46.3	20.6
2010	21942.15	100.0	45.2	29.0	5.7	20.1	24594.92	100.0	9.7	18.8	50.4	21.1
2011	23318.44	100.0	50.2	27.0	6.4	16.4	26223.64	100.0	10.3	16.8	51.5	21.4
2012	23786.60	100.0	46.4	27.1	6.4	20.1	26763.90	100.0	9.7	16.7	52.2	21.4
2013	24930.93	100.0	46.4	27.1	6.5	20.0	27666.36	100.0	10.4	16.8	51.0	21.8
2014	25636.29	100.0	43.7	26.6	6.8	22.9	28669.57	100.0	10.2	16.6	53.5	19.7
2015	25662.31	100.0	42.3	27.3	6.4	24.0	29386.66	100.0	10.0	16.8	52.2	21.0
2016	27157.90	100.0	39.7	26.6	8.1	25.6	30729.90	100.0	9.8	14.5	52.7	23.0
2017	28728.12	100.0	39.5	25.9	8.4	26.2	31677.03	100.0	8.1	17.7	54.5	19.7

7-4 综合能源平衡表

Overall Energy Balance Sheet

单位：万吨标准煤 (10000 tons of SCE)

项 目	Item	2000	2010	2014	2015	2016	2017
可供本地区消费的能源量	**Total Energy Available for Consumption by Locality**	**9447.70**	**25445.22**	**29593.26**	**30145.49**	**31240.75**	**32341.66**
年初库存量	Stock at the Year-beginning	675.20	1347.93	1435.36	1635.41	1977.58	1820.65
一次能源生产量	Primary Energy Output	3711.69	4858.07	5594.57	6862.51	7137.95	7037.37
外省调入量	Allocation from Other Provinces	5628.27	15570.94	19278.01	20771.89	20687.86	21355.43
进口量	Imports	2757.39	8112.34	8938.27	6739.99	6352.09	16538.02
境内轮船和飞机在境外加油量	Petroleum Consumed by Chinese Airplanes and Ships Abroad		183.44	219.79	220.81	223.09	223.59
本省调出量(-)	Allocation over Other Provinces(-)	-1599.39	-1294.98	-1512.21	-2392.60	-1475.13	-10668.81
出口量(-)	Exports(-)	-980.31	-1700.12	-2390.03	-1378.80	-1503.51	-1426.81
境外轮船和飞机在境内加油量(-)	Petroleum Consumed by Foreign Airplanes and Ships in China(-)	-62.51	-275.16	-335.08	-336.16	-338.53	-339.55
年末库存量(-)	Stock at the Year-end(-)	-779.26	-1357.25	-1635.41	-1977.58	-1820.65	-2198.23
加工转换投入(-)产出(+)量	**Input Output in Processing and Transformation**	**-35.74**	**-92.50**	**-13.59**	**-0.11**	**257.60**	**76.40**
火力发电	Thermal Power						
供热	Heating		-90.80	-189.64	-128.38	-148.21	-150.91
洗选煤	Coal Washing						
炼焦	Coking	-3.85	-2.25	-9.41	-8.76	-12.92	-26.57
炼油	Petroleum Refining	-26.89	205.83	-176.10	-185.30	-76.66	-360.77
制气	Gas Production	-5.00	-1.08	-1.54	-31.76	-30.06	-28.97
回收能	Recovery of Energy	96.59	123.70	366.98	365.40	527.58	644.91
损失量	**Losses**	**331.76**	**757.80**	**910.10**	**758.72**	**768.46**	**741.03**
#运输和输配损失	Losses in Transmission	318.75	732.46	885.55	742.82	724.27	683.40
终端消费量	**End-use**	**9080.20**	**24594.92**	**28669.57**	**29386.66**	**30729.90**	**31677.03**
第一产业	Primary Industry	353.56	400.60	490.85	502.45	530.55	544.67
农、林、牧、渔业	Farming, Forestry, Animal Husbandry and Fishery	353.56	400.60	490.85	502.45	530.55	544.67
第二产业	Secondary Industry	5790.91	16452.13	18097.05	18310.07	18447.36	18912.55
工业	Industry	5693.02	15813.16	17358.86	17575.93	17707.17	18144.71
#用作原材料、燃料	As Raw Materials and Fuel	86.44	990.06	1157.69	585.31	986.53	1068.55
建筑业	Construction	97.90	638.97	738.19	734.13	740.18	767.84
第三产业	Tertiary Industry	1648.93	4749.44	6001.63	6209.59	6895.28	7219.81
交通运输仓储及邮电通信业 灌	Transport, Storage, Postal and Telecommunication Services	957.92	2332.91	3004.83	3123.41	3510.45	3607.82
批发和零售贸易业、餐饮业	Wholesale and Retail Trade and Catering	403.21	1202.83	1415.48	1445.20	1591.03	1683.23
其他	ServicesOthers	287.81	1213.70	1581.32	1640.98	1793.80	1928.75
生活消费	Residential Consumption	1286.80	2992.75	4080.05	4364.56	4856.71	5000.00
城镇	Urban Areas	818.33	1896.70	2624.22	2736.99	3084.50	3171.60
乡村	Rural Areas	468.45	1096.05	1455.83	1627.56	1772.21	1828.40
平衡差额	**Balance**						
消费量合计	**Total Energy Consumption**	**9447.70**	**25445.22**	**29593.26**	**30145.49**	**31240.75**	**32341.66**

7-5 分行业能源消费总量和原煤、电力消费量（2017年）
Consumption of Total Energy, Coal and Electricity by Sector (2017)

行业	Sector	能源消费总量（万吨标准煤）Total Energy Consumption (10000 tons of SCE)	原煤消费量（万吨）Coal Consumption (10000 tons)	电力消费量（亿千瓦小时）Electricity Consumption (100 million kwh)
消费总量	**Total**	**32341.66**	**16181.55**	**5958.97**
农、林、牧、渔业	**Farming,Forestry,Animal Husbandry and Fishery**	**544.67**	**61.15**	**99.94**
工业合计	**Industry**	**18809.34**	**16012.88**	**3815.28**
采矿业	**Mining and Quarrying**	**203.20**	**7.47**	**18.67**
煤炭开采和洗选业	Mining and Washing of Coal	0.09		
石油和天然气开采业	Extraction of Petroleum and Natural Gas	129.20		0.83
黑色金属矿采选业	Mining and Dressing of Ferrous Metal Ores	14.04	0.18	4.03
有色金属矿采选业	Mining and Dressing of Nonferrous Metal Ores	13.65	1.25	4.02
非金属矿采选业	Mining and Dressing of Nonmetal Ores	45.51	6.04	9.73
开采辅助活动	Auxiliary Minning Operations	0.44		0.03
其他采矿业	Mining and Dressing of Other Ores	0.27		0.03
制造业	**Manufacturing**	**16288.63**	**4746.25**	**3073.28**
农副食品加工业	Processing of Farm and Sideline Food	246.60	61.00	49.22
食品制造业	Manufacture of Food	154.40	24.03	33.14
酒、饮料和精制茶制造业	Manufacture of Wine, Beverage and Tea	89.73	8.70	19.04
烟草制品业	Tobacco Products	9.48	1.10	2.12
纺织业	Textile Industry	607.52	306.40	106.56
纺织服装、服饰业	Manufacture of Textile Garments, Footwear and	253.06	32.34	67.08
皮革、毛皮、羽毛(绒)及其制品业	Leather, Fur, Feather, Down and Related Products	196.93	12.56	56.82
木材加工及木、竹、藤、棕、草制品业	Timber Processing, Bamboo, Cane, Palm Fiber & Straw Products	90.81	1.15	26.25
家具制造业	Manufacture of Furniture	121.36	0.25	35.49
造纸及纸制品业	Papermaking and Paper Products	1058.15	1068.49	190.54
印刷业和记录媒介的复制	Printing and Record Medium Reproduction	135.34	2.08	37.85
文教、工美、体育和娱乐用品制造业	Manufacture of Cultural, Educational and Sports Articles	213.39	1.74	65.07
石油加工、炼焦及核燃料加工业	Petroleum Refining, Coking, and Nuclear Fuel Processing	1636.87	167.31	70.57
化学原料及化学制品制造业	Manufacture of Raw Chemical Materials and Chemical Products	1246.14	183.28	159.27
医药制造业	Manufacture of Medicines	105.13	16.73	23.52
化学纤维制造业	Manufacture of Chemical Fibers	44.94	3.60	10.67
橡胶和塑料制品业	Rubber Products	789.65	47.59	226.92
非金属矿物制品业	Nonmetal Mineral Products	3102.12	2195.51	390.41
黑色金属冶炼及压延加工业	Smelting and Pressing of Ferrous Metals	1774.83	493.16	205.28
有色金属冶炼及压延加工业	Smelting and Pressing of Nonferrous Metals	442.77	35.93	106.94
金属制品业	Metal Products	680.15	17.67	185.12
通用设备制造业	Manufacture of General-purpose Machinery	211.18	5.56	59.50
专用设备制造业	Manufacture of Special-purpose Machinery	201.43	3.16	59.88
汽车制造业	Manufacture of Automobile	301.38	0.44	87.05
铁路、船舶、航空航天和其他运输设备制造业	Manufacture of Railway ,Ship,Aeronautics and Other Transport Equipment	76.80	1.38	19.19
电气机械及器材制造业	Manufacture of Electrical Machinery and Equipment	683.10	0.80	208.28
通信设备、计算机及其他电子设备制造业	Manufacture of Communication Equipment, Computers and Other Electronic Equipment	1625.22	6.42	519.31
仪器仪表制造业	Manufacture of Instruments and Meters	78.35		24.11
其他制造业	Handicraft and Other Manufactures	44.52	46.58	10.31
废弃资源综合利用业	Recycling and Disposal of Waste	59.00	1.29	15.34
金属制品、机械和设备修理业	Manufacture of Metal Products,Machinery and Equipment Maintenance	8.30		2.43
电力、燃气及水的生产和供应业	**Production and Supply of Electric Power,Gas and Water**	**2317.51**	**11259.16**	**723.33**
电力、热力的生产和供应业	Production and Supply of Electric Power and Heat Power	2088.72	11254.46	658.62
燃气生产和供应业	Production and Supply of Gas	42.80	0.58	4.99
水的生产和供应业	Production and Supply of Water	185.99	4.12	59.72
建筑业	**Construction**	**767.84**	**4.16**	**68.89**
交通运输、仓储及邮政业	**Transport, Storage,Postal and Telecommunication Services**	**3607.82**	**4.66**	**109.46**
批发和零售贸易餐饮业	**Wholesale and Retail Trade and Catering Services**	**1683.23**	**47.97**	**333.07**
其他行业	**Others**	**1928.75**	**2.47**	**588.71**
生活消费	**Non-production Consumption**	**5000.00**	**48.26**	**943.62**

7-6 各市电力消费量

Electricity Consumption by City

单位：亿千瓦小时 (100 million kwh)

市 别	City	2000	2005	2010	2012	2013	2014	2015	2016	2017
全省总计	**Provincial Total**	**1334.58**	**2673.56**	**4060.13**	**4619.42**	**4830.13**	**5235.23**	**5310.69**	**5610.13**	**5958.97**
广 州	Guangzhou	238.78	425.67	625.90	694.13	710.69	765.85	779.32	823.57	869.59
深 圳	Shenzhen	190.35	440.21	663.55	714.01	721.48	779.93	806.68	842.09	872.15
珠 海	Zhuhai	30.82	61.58	102.26	117.47	121.73	134.32	145.37	152.90	162.67
汕 头	Shantou	43.91	87.60	136.81	154.36	160.62	174.20	178.01	190.93	200.93
佛 山	Foshan	168.84	316.29	463.08	506.95	527.06	564.13	587.84	620.82	673.82
韶 关	Shaoguan	35.81	58.72	84.06	96.67	109.28	119.14	111.31	111.80	119.48
河 源	Heyuan	9.27	23.90	51.52	58.38	65.60	74.38	78.06	83.34	86.26
梅 州	Meizhou	22.70	40.40	60.88	66.33	69.78	76.51	77.98	84.30	89.52
惠 州	Huizhou	43.53	105.22	192.46	227.36	248.44	276.41	290.62	323.41	368.35
汕 尾	Shanwei	9.35	16.87	29.73	35.19	37.74	43.80	47.05	50.37	54.96
东 莞	Dongguan	179.78	419.83	562.00	604.28	622.51	660.99	666.84	702.01	760.68
中 山	Zhongshan	54.54	123.63	186.65	206.49	217.10	237.64	245.51	259.33	279.43
江 门	Jiangmen	64.65	113.63	165.21	196.14	207.31	227.87	237.13	248.50	267.12
阳 江	Yangjiang	12.09	22.46	40.43	64.00	77.15	90.71	98.21	104.80	112.25
湛 江	Zhanjiang	24.15	49.09	78.68	93.45	98.16	109.48	116.04	153.23	181.45
茂 名	Maoming	29.98	40.11	65.80	75.12	81.94	94.77	98.40	103.93	106.94
肇 庆	Zhaoqing	24.00	48.58	105.08	131.03	142.50	156.24	152.30	159.31	168.79
清 远	Qingyuan	22.60	59.47	125.53	142.44	156.74	173.89	179.27	193.34	177.27
潮 州	Chaozhou	13.95	33.17	59.16	66.12	68.20	74.62	75.59	79.88	85.70
揭 阳	Jieyang	22.51	51.13	98.68	120.87	138.50	158.93	152.71	160.90	148.68
云 浮	Yunfu	12.14	21.55	34.89	42.43	48.93	54.85	57.81	60.61	64.16
按经济区域分	By Region									
珠 三 角	Pearl River Delta	995.29	2054.64	3066.18	3397.86	3518.83	3803.37	3911.61	4131.93	4422.61
东 翼	Eastern Region	89.72	188.77	324.38	376.55	405.06	451.55	453.34	482.09	490.27
西 翼	Western Region	66.22	111.66	184.91	232.57	257.25	294.95	312.65	361.95	400.64
山 区	Mountainous Region	102.52	204.04	356.88	406.25	450.33	498.78	504.43	533.40	536.69

注：由于各市电力消费量不包含不分区域线损，全省数不等于分市数合计。

Note: Becausee the electricity consumption by region doesn't include line losses , the sum of electricity consumption by cities is different from the provincial total.

7—7 各市单位GDP能耗增长速度

Energy Consumption per Unit of GDP by City

单位：%　　(%)

市　别	City	2009	2010	2011	2012	2013	2014	2015	2016	2017
全省总计	**Provincial Total**	**-4.27**	**-2.94**	**-3.78**	**-5.38**	**-4.55**	**-3.56**	**-5.71**	**-3.62**	**-3.74**
广　州	Guangzhou	-4.01	-4.60	-4.91	-4.94	-5.14	-3.52	-4.52	-4.96	-4.81
深　圳	Shenzhen	-2.76	-2.94	-4.39	-4.51	-5.12	-4.35	-3.26	-4.21	-4.23
珠　海	Zhuhai	-3.60	-3.67	-3.93	-4.75	-4.98	-4.12	-2.80	-3.94	-4.20
汕　头	Shantou	-3.85	-3.19	-3.44	-4.48	-3.99	-3.85	-6.81	-3.00	-5.04
佛　山	Foshan	-6.93	-4.38	-4.01	-4.53	-4.54	-4.45	-5.64	-6.63	-5.13
韶　关	Shaoguan	-4.51	-1.57	-3.68	-4.31	-4.31	-5.01	-7.95	-3.81	3.20
河　源	Heyuan	-3.65	-1.06	-3.67	-6.36	-3.67	-2.21	-4.08	-4.08	-4.15
梅　州	Meizhou	-3.90	-3.23	-4.39	-4.86	-4.51	-3.69	-5.91	-3.80	-4.80
惠　州	Huizhou	-0.95	-5.82	-3.97	-3.91	-4.35	-3.69	-7.10	-1.52	6.28
汕　尾	Shanwei	-5.60	-2.02	-3.73	-3.63	-5.69	-1.12	2.03	-3.01	-0.94
东　莞	Dongguan	-4.48	-2.02	-4.61	-4.46	-5.35	-5.88	-7.90	-4.65	-4.87
中　山	Zhongshan	-4.03	-1.50	-4.18	-3.91	-3.98	-3.81	-3.91	-3.89	-3.73
江　门	Jiangmen	-5.79	-2.30	-3.66	-5.23	-4.49	-3.02	-6.63	-4.52	-4.61
阳　江	Yangjiang	-3.56	-1.00	-3.47	-3.91	-3.97	-3.38	-4.12	7.16	5.46
湛　江	Zhanjiang	-2.76	-0.30	-3.67	-4.21	-4.04	-4.03	-2.57	38.35	8.77
茂　名	Maoming	-3.73	-4.25	-3.90	-5.16	-4.21	-2.38	-7.36	-2.82	-4.41
肇　庆	Zhaoqing	-4.80	-2.44	-3.74	-4.94	-4.03	-3.51	-4.51	-5.35	-1.97
清　远	Qingyuan	-3.82	-1.96	-3.94	-6.82	-2.81	-3.03	-7.73	-4.04	-3.93
潮　州	Chaozhou	-3.54	-3.32	-3.71	-5.55	-4.82	-3.55	-6.67	-4.07	-3.82
揭　阳	Jieyang	-3.15	-2.21	-4.22	-5.00	-4.50	-2.00	-6.35	-4.43	2.79
云　浮	Yunfu	-3.27	-1.54	-3.68	-6.95	-3.90	-3.08	-2.86	-4.76	-4.17

7-8 各市单位GDP电耗增长速度

Growth Rate of Electricity Consumption per Unit of GDP by City

单位：% (%)

市 别	City	2009	2010	2011	2012	2013	2014	2015	2016	2017
全省总计	**Provincial Total**	**-6.13**	**0.03**	**-1.46**	**-2.90**	**-3.62**	**0.59**	**-6.10**	**-1.73**	**-1.19**
广 州	Guangzhou	-6.96	-2.53	-4.74	-4.59	-8.21	-0.77	-6.13	-2.36	-1.32
深 圳	Shenzhen	-9.33	1.00	-4.69	-3.28	-8.30	-0.65	-5.01	-4.17	-4.82
珠 海	Zhuhai	-3.92	-1.21	-1.05	-2.49	-6.23	0.04	-1.61	-3.10	-2.54
汕 头	Shantou	-3.19	-0.62	-2.27	-5.87	-5.37	-0.79	-5.78	-1.33	-3.61
佛 山	Foshan	-7.23	-2.76	-5.83	-3.48	-5.07	-1.44	-3.95	-2.48	0.08
韶 关	Shaoguan	-9.88	2.44	1.45	-7.32	0.80	-0.04	-12.00	-5.49	0.96
河 源	Heyuan	2.45	3.54	1.11	-11.21	0.30	2.97	-2.96	-1.69	-1.47
梅 州	Meizhou	-2.00	-4.67	-4.25	-8.37	-5.32	1.06	-6.18	0.60	-0.52
惠 州	Huizhou	-4.56	-1.64	-4.93	-3.68	-3.82	1.15	-3.56	2.83	5.80
汕 尾	Shanwei	-6.05	-5.82	-4.61	-4.08	-4.46	6.59	-0.63	0.06	0.48
东 莞	Dongguan	-8.42	2.84	-3.40	-2.85	-6.17	-1.50	-6.54	-2.62	0.23
中 山	Zhongshan	-6.34	1.38	-5.98	-6.31	-4.42	1.35	-4.73	-1.97	1.10
江 门	Jiangmen	-7.73	1.60	0.53	-3.32	-3.71	1.96	-4.00	-2.43	-0.56
阳 江	Yangjiang	-3.92	5.66	2.24	19.28	4.50	6.41	-0.21	0.06	0.90
湛 江	Zhanjiang	-2.25	-0.12	-3.89	0.74	-6.17	1.39	-2.28	22.37	10.83
茂 名	Maoming	-3.00	-4.65	-2.99	-3.95	-6.32	4.75	-3.86	-1.38	-4.31
肇 庆	Zhaoqing	-1.12	1.74	1.33	-3.31	-2.46	-0.40	-9.92	-0.42	0.74
清 远	Qingyuan	-2.54	-2.32	-0.18	-0.10	1.74	2.82	-4.91	-0.04	-12.64
潮 州	Chaozhou	-4.89	0.85	-4.75	-6.12	-7.05	1.12	-6.44	-1.35	0.33
揭 阳	Jieyang	-2.23	-3.58	-0.34	-3.62	-1.80	3.66	-11.03	-0.87	-12.04
云 浮	Yunfu	-4.84	0.24	-2.04	-3.70	1.74	1.64	-2.85	-1.09	0.22

7—9 各市单位工业增加值能耗增长速度

Growth Rate of Energy Consumption per Unit of Industrial Value-added by City

单位：%　　(%)

市 别	City	2009	2010	2011	2012	2013	2014	2015	2016	2017
全省总计	**Provincial Total**	**-6.94**	**-6.88**	**-5.13**	**-11.18**	**-4.97**	**-9.25**	**-10.47**	**-3.75**	**-0.01**
广 州	Guangzhou	-10.52	-12.61	-10.06	-16.98	-10.89	-11.91	-13.03	-6.55	-4.85
深 圳	Shenzhen	-3.59	-3.72	-24.02	-12.68	-9.49	-8.45	-11.07	-4.98	-0.75
珠 海	Zhuhai	-5.74	-10.52	-6.61	-16.62	-9.17	-8.49	-1.88	-7.12	-6.76
汕 头	Shantou	12.65	18.74	-4.37	-22.41	5.35	-11.22	-16.00	-16.78	4.86
佛 山	Foshan	-9.37	-10.48	-8.17	-4.91	-11.45	-12.54	-13.77	-8.32	-6.36
韶 关	Shaoguan	-3.87	-2.11	-4.32	-16.04	-10.61	-12.81	-8.66	-0.49	12.52
河 源	Heyuan	61.14	-1.15	0.03	-27.94	-15.94	-19.33	-13.26	-9.65	1.44
梅 州	Meizhou	12.84	-15.33	-24.00	-18.71	-3.25	-14.92	-15.48	1.49	-23.41
惠 州	Huizhou	0.69	-16.87	0.15	-11.08	-18.18	-14.15	-12.31	-4.59	10.28
汕 尾	Shanwei	-22.70	-14.25	2.75	6.26	-30.74	-14.92	26.15	-2.24	14.78
东 莞	Dongguan	-0.26	-10.92	-6.12	-11.42	-8.45	-9.74	-10.88	-3.93	-7.95
中 山	Zhongshan	-11.70	-3.84	-8.51	-21.83	-12.34	-3.84	4.91	-1.58	-1.62
江 门	Jiangmen	-18.45	-12.91	-0.96	-15.35	-0.53	-17.45	-14.93	-10.89	-4.84
阳 江	Yangjiang	11.54	58.95	-5.11	-17.53	-16.69	-1.16	-10.30	4.58	5.45
湛 江	Zhanjiang	-4.04	-4.35	-4.94	-5.21	-7.40	-17.83	-11.45	43.40	13.09
茂 名	Maoming	-6.26	-9.91	-7.48	-20.08	-11.53	-5.04	-11.60	-6.55	-3.09
肇 庆	Zhaoqing	-14.14	-7.65	-8.44	-9.04	-9.31	-9.80	-12.94	-8.39	-0.51
清 远	Qingyuan	-11.14	-16.28	-11.77	-20.63	-0.74	-9.52	-9.16	-7.39	-0.73
潮 州	Chaozhou	-10.54	17.93	17.99	-18.92	-16.05	-21.13	-13.16	-11.45	11.53
揭 阳	Jieyang	-15.50	-15.49	-18.98	-23.59	24.31	-18.62	-15.54	-17.50	15.12
云 浮	Yunfu	-4.05	-9.70	-17.32	-25.69	-21.35	-14.19	-10.32	-7.55	-2.37

7-10 平均每天各种能源消费量

Average Daily Energy Consumption by Variety

能源品种	Energy Variety	2000	2005	2012	2013	2014	2015	2016	2017
合 计(吨标准煤)	**Total (ton of SCE)**	**248773**	**472363**	**733257**	**757982**	**785468**	**805114**	**841915**	**867864**
煤 炭 (吨)	Coal (Ton)	59590	78227	124986	122417	135491	135415	120648	102681
焦 炭 (吨)	Coke (Ton)	3973	8058	14936	16005	15286	14875	21439	25780
原 油 (吨)	Crude Oil (Ton)	250	178	437	569	580	635	642	642
燃料油 (吨)	Fuel Oil (Ton)	9248	18288	8427	8881	8481	8253	9617	9499
汽 油 (吨)	Gasoline (Ton)	8226	19330	26443	29313	30408	33601	41085	41886
煤 油 (吨)	Kerosene (Ton)	2444	4212	6661	7104	7332	7510	7998	8204
柴 油 (吨)	Diesel Oil (Ton)	18726	34920	42122	42062	42886	43303	45717	45621
液化石油气 (吨)	Liquefied Petroleum Gas(Ton)	8720	16676	13594	14698	16046	18510	19742	19183
电 力(万千瓦时)	Electricity (10000 kwh)	33978	69671	119813	124810	135908	139035	147119	157045

7-11 平均每人年生活用能源

Annual per Capita Energy Consumption of Households

能源品种	Energy Variety	2000	2005	2010	2013	2014	2015	2016	2017
合 计(千克标准煤)	**Total (kg of SCE)**	**148.90**	**227.85**	**290.97**	**350.10**	**381.88**	**404.63**	**444.59**	**451.10**
煤 炭 (千克)	Coal (kg)	9.63	10.54	6.14	6.11	6.10	6.17	6.35	6.39
汽 油 (千克)	Gasoline (kg)	4.42	14.57	36.95	45.91	45.86	49.93	61.69	62.10
煤 油 (千克)	Kerosene (kg)	0.24	0.33	0.35	0.38	0.37	0.38	0.34	0.34
柴 油 (千克)	Diesel Oil (kg)	0.57	0.98	1.39	1.75	1.74	1.77	1.89	1.90
液化石油气 (千克)	Liquefied Petroleum Gas(kg)	31.47	43.66	27.42	28.73	31.50	43.16	45.51	44.65
电 力 (千瓦时)	Electricity (kwh)	239.09	359.06	536.60	669.90	759.93	784.28	827.76	851.34

7-12 分品种生活能源年消费总量

Annual Total Energy Consumption of Households by Variety

能源品种	Energy Variety	2000	2010	2013	2014	2015	2016	2017
合　计（万吨标准煤）	**Total (10000 tons of SCE)**	**1286.80**	**2992.75**	**3722.01**	**4080.05**	**4364.56**	**4856.71**	**5000.00**
煤　炭　（万吨）	Coal (10000 tons)	83.22	63.19	64.89	65.21	66.57	69.35	70.82
汽　油　（万吨）	Gasoline (10000 tons)	38.20	380.05	487.55	489.99	538.63	673.92	688.33
煤　油　（万吨）	Kerosene (10000 tons)	2.10	3.60	3.99	4.00	4.11	3.67	3.75
柴　油　（万吨）	Diesel Oil (10000 tons)	4.90	14.30	18.55	18.64	19.10	20.68	21.11
液化石油气　（万吨）	Liquefied Petroleum Gas(10000 tons)	271.96	282.01	305.13	336.52	465.57	497.1	494.85
电　力(亿千瓦小时)	Electricity (100 million kwh)	206.62	551.92	711.37	810.84	845.96	904.25	943.62

7-13 能源加工转换效率

Efficiency of Energy Conversion

单位：%　　　　(%)

年 份 Year	火力发电 Thermal Power Generation	供 热 Heating	炼 焦 Coking	炼 油 Petroleum Refining	制 气 Gas Production
1990	31.13	79.21	93.48	99.44	
1995	31.85	80.07	90.93	99.89	86.17
2000	37.20	87.19	94.35	99.02	79.18
2001	37.21	85.09	95.23	99.12	77.90
2002	36.36	76.40	94.27	98.40	80.08
2003	40.69	71.43	82.36	98.57	78.67
2004	35.53	86.10	91.53	99.29	79.70
2005	36.22	95.99	96.66	99.53	79.18
2006	37.74	88.49	96.95	99.80	95.40
2007	38.80	70.66	99.02	99.79	97.22
2008	38.00	77.34	98.43	99.10	95.65
2009	38.69	82.15	98.31	99.58	93.47
2010	38.90	82.80	99.08	98.12	87.81
2011	38.22	79.19	98.69	98.54	89.87
2012	38.49	78.26	97.57	98.17	89.77
2013	39.66	79.57	96.01	98.48	91.00
2014	39.72	75.73	96.15	97.42	71.51
2015	40.62	84.02	97.15	97.69	57.39
2016	40.78	83.32	97.91	99.03	60.99
2017	40.79	84.41	96.56	95.78	62.77

7–14　能源生产弹性系数

Elasticity Ratio of Energy Production

年　份 Year	能源生产比上年增长（%） Growth Rate of Energy灌 Production over Preceding Year(%)	电力生产比上年增长（%） Growth Rate of Electricity Production over Preceding Year(%)	本省生产总值比上年增长（%） Growth Rate of Gross Domestic Product(GDP) over Preceding Year(%)	能源生产弹性系数 Elasticity Ratio of Energy Production	电力生产弹性系数 Elasticity Ratio of Electricity Production
1986	1.0	8.0	12.7	0.08	0.63
1990	0.3	15.3	11.6	0.02	1.32
1995	14.7	6.6	15.6	0.94	0.42
1996	43.3	10.7	11.3	3.83	0.95
1997	8.5	8.0	11.2	0.76	0.71
1998	-4.1	5.6	10.8		0.52
1999	-10.3	9.8	10.1		0.97
2000	5.8	18.7	11.5	0.50	1.63
2001	-8.2	5.9	10.5		0.56
2002	6.5	12.4	12.4	0.52	1.00
2003	12.7	17.7	14.8	0.86	1.20
2004	18.6	11.9	14.8	1.26	0.80
2005	-6.7	7.4	13.8		0.54
2006	-8.1	8.5	14.6		0.58
2007	-5.7	8.9	14.7		0.61
2008	12.5	-0.4	10.1	1.24	
2009	-0.6	-0.6	9.7		
2010	10.6	20.1	12.4	0.85	1.62
2011	-0.2	15.6	10.0		1.56
2012	5.0	-1.8	8.2	0.61	
2013	5.4	6.7	8.5	0.64	0.79
2014	4.3	0.5	7.8	0.55	0.06
2015	22.7	0.5	8.0	2.84	0.06
2016	4.0	5.7	7.5	0.53	0.76
2017	-1.4	6.4	7.5		0.85

7-15 能源消费弹性系数

Elasticity Ratio of Energy Consumption

年份 Year	能源消费比上年增长（%） Growth Rate of Energy Consumption over Preceding Year(%)	电力消费比上年增长(%) Growth Rate of Electricity Consumption over Preceding Year(%)	本省生产总值比上年增长(%) Growth Rate of Gross Domestic Product(GDP) over Preceding Year(%)	能源消费弹性系数 Elasticity Ratio of Energy Consumption	电力消费弹性系数 Elasticity Ratio of Electricity Consumption
1986	8.4	4.7	12.7	0.66	0.37
1990	4.1	14.3	11.6	0.35	1.24
1995	9.2	7.6	15.6	0.59	0.49
1996	5.5	8.9	11.3	0.48	0.79
1997	2.7	7.1	11.2	0.24	0.64
1998	5.3	7.5	10.8	0.49	0.70
1999	4.3	10.0	10.1	0.42	0.99
2000	8.2	22.9	11.5	0.71	1.99
2001	7.7	9.3	10.5	0.74	0.88
2002	11.6	15.7	12.4	0.93	1.27
2003	15.4	20.3	14.8	1.04	1.37
2004	16.1	17.5	14.8	1.09	1.18
2005	16.8	12.0	13.8	1.22	0.87
2006	11.2	12.4	14.6	0.77	0.85
2007	10.9	13.0	14.7	0.74	0.88
2008	5.3	3.3	10.1	0.52	0.32
2009	6.9	2.9	9.7	0.71	0.30
2010	8.9	12.5	12.4	0.72	1.00
2011	5.8	8.3	10.0	0.58	0.83
2012	2.3	5.0	8.2	0.28	0.61
2013	3.6	4.5	8.5	0.42	0.53
2014	3.9	8.4	7.8	0.50	1.08
2015	1.9	1.4	8.0	0.24	0.18
2016	3.6	5.6	7.5	0.48	0.75
2017	3.5	6.2	7.5	0.47	0.83

7-16 自然资源（2017年）

Natural Resources (2017)

项 目		Item		2017
一、土地资源和海洋		**Land Resources and Sea**		
土地面积	（平方公里）	Total Land Area	(sq.km)	179725.07
耕 地	（万公顷）	Cultivated Land	(10000 hectares)	259.96
林 地	（万公顷）	Afforested Land	(10000 hectares)	1001.78
园 地	（万公顷）	Plantation	(10000 hectares)	126.08
牧草地	（万公顷）	Grass Land	(10000 hectares)	32.14
海域总面积	（万平方公里）	Total Area of Sea	(10000 sq.km)	41.9
海洋滩涂面积	（万公顷）	Sea Beach Area	(10000 hectares)	20.4
海岛面积	（平方公里）	Area of Islands	(sq.km)	1592.7
大陆海岸线长度	（公里）	Length of Continental Coastline	(km)	4114.3
岛屿岸线长度	（公里）	Length of Island Coastline	(km)	2428.7
岛屿个数	（个）	Number of Islands	(unit)	1431
二、气候		**Climate**		
年平均降雨量	（毫米）	Annual Average Precipitation	(mm)	1710.7
年平均气温	（摄氏度）	Annual Average Temperature	(℃)	22.4
年日照时数	（小时）	Annual Sunshine Hours	(hour)	1757.3
三、森林		**Forest**		
活立木蓄积量	（亿立方米）	Total Standing Stock Volume	(100 million cu.m)	5.83
森林覆盖率	（%）	Forest Coverage Rate	(%)	59.08
四、水力水产		**Hydropower and Aquatic Products**		
水力资源理论蕴藏量	（万千瓦）	Theoretical Hydropower Resources	(10000 kw)	1137.2
#可开发装机容量		Developable Resources		1055.7
海水养殖可养面积	（万公顷）	Cultivatable Area in Marine Areas	(10000 hectares)	77.6
淡水可养面积	（万公顷）	Cultivatable Area in Freshwater Areas	(10000 hectares)	49.16
五、矿产		**Mineral Resources**		
煤保有资源储量	（万吨）	Ensured Reserve of Coal	(10000 tons)	59858.99
铁矿石保有资源储量	（万吨）	Ensured Reserve of Iron Ore	(10000 tons)	62943.1
硫铁矿保有资源储量	（万吨）	Ensured Reserve of Pyrite Ore	(10000 tons)	32740.3

注：1．海岛面积、岛岸线长度、岛屿个数是1994年调查数据。
2．海域总面积包括200海里专属经济区面积。
3．土地面积为2015年土地变更调查结果数据，土地资源数据未经国土资源部认可，仅供参考，最终数据以国土资源部确认的为准。

Notes: a) Data of the area of islands，length of island coastline and number of islands were obtained from surveys in 1994.
b) Total area of sea includes 200 sea miles of exclusive economic zone.
c) Data on land area are result of the land research of 2015. The land data in this table is for reference only because the data has not been examined or confirmed by Ministry of Land and Resources The final result is subject to be comfired by Ministry of Land and Resources.

7-17 各地区年平均气温

Average Temperature by Region

单位：摄氏度 (℃)

年份 Year	粤北 Northern Regions	粤东北 North Eastern Regions	粤西北 North Western Regions	粤东 Eastern Regions	粤中 Central Regions	粤西 Western Regions
1980	20.7	21.5	22.5	21.2	22.2	23.4
1985	20.2	20.9	22.0	21.1	21.6	22.6
1990	21.1	21.5	22.8	21.8	22.6	23.4
1995	20.0	20.0	22.2	21.6	22.3	23.0
1996	19.9	21.4	22.4	21.9	21.6	23.3
1997	20.4	21.3	22.7	22.1	22.0	23.7
1998	21.2	22.5	23.3	23.0	22.8	24.5
1999	20.8	21.9	22.7	22.6	22.5	24.0
2000	20.4	21.9	22.6	22.5	22.5	23.8
2001	20.5	22.0	22.5	22.7	22.6	23.8
2002	21.0	22.3	22.8	23.0	23.0	24.1
2003	20.9	21.9	22.9	22.6	23.0	24.4
2004	20.8	21.6	22.6	22.6	22.8	23.2
2005	20.5	21.6	22.5	22.3	22.8	23.0
2006	20.8	22.1	23.1	22.8	23.2	23.4
2007	21.2	22.0	23.0	22.9	23.2	23.2
2008	20.5	21.5	22.1	22.3	22.5	22.4
2009	20.6	22.3	22.9	22.6	23.0	23.3
2010	20.0	21.8	22.4	22.3	22.5	23.3
2011	19.6	21.7	22.3	22.1	21.4	22.4
2012	19.6	22.0	22.4	22.3	21.7	23.2
2013	20.0	21.2	22.7	22.6	21.5	23.0
2014	20.4	21.7	22.8	22.8	21.7	23.3
2015	20.8	22.0	23.4	23.5	22.3	24.3
2016	20.7	21.7	22.5	23.3	22.0	23.6
2017	20.8	22.0	22.6	23.5	22.1	23.7

7-18　各地区年降雨量

Annual Precipitation by Region

单位：毫米　　(mm)

年份 Year	粤北 Northern Regions	粤东北 North Eastern Regions	粤西北 North Western Regions	粤东 Eastern Regions	粤中 Central Regions	粤西 Western Regions
1980	1459.4	1461.7	1586.1	1369.1	1492.2	2274.0
1985	1360.2	1607.8	1726.9	1481.3	1706.0	2411.3
1990	1436.6	1709.0	1284.8	2236.9	1239.5	1510.2
1995	1506.9	1171.0	1766.4	1512.2	1752.4	2082.9
1996	1633.1	1361.5	1693.1	1409.0	1683.4	1222.6
1997	2045.3	1847.5	1815.3	2040.9	1997.3	2344.3
1998	1862.3	1458.2	1737.5	1593.6	1736.1	1266.4
1999	1314.3	1033.8	1318.7	1517.4	1620.4	1392.6
2000	1565.8	1850.9	1318.2	1486.7	1798.9	1762.7
2001	1689.8	1560.3	1889.2	1947.9	2678.9	2314.5
2002	1814.9	1110.3	1480.9	1409.7	1866.7	2263.3
2003	1388.2	1415.2	1251.8	1406.6	1338.7	1372.4
2004	1156.3	1251.8	1034.7	1379.7	1636.5	1068.5
2005	1772.2	1647.3	1905.2	1631.3	1986.2	1387.3
2006	1782.8	2040.2	1727.0	2507.7	2175.7	1149.8
2007	1502.3	1399.2	1252.4	1482.2	1370.3	1620.8
2008	1553.1	1300.2	2221.0	2123.6	2284.0	1865.2
2009	1275.5	1246.7	1440.4	927.9	1472.6	1849.9
2010	2104.4	1416.1	1419.6	1350.3	2353.6	1952.3
2011	1443.0	1233.1	1277.2	1027.0	1632.3	1408.5
2012	2056.3	1460.5	1919.2	1247.1	1813.9	2068.6
2013	1654.0	1930.2	1736.2	1887.2	2095.4	2084.2
2014	1517.0	1164.9	1788.2	1416.5	2234.0	1468.9
2015	2128.7	1696.3	1848.1	1446.6	2471.9	1328.9
2016	2428.9	2410.3	2132.5	2174.7	2939.7	1820.0
2017	1397.2	1396.3	1275.8	1419.0	2067.4	1760.7

7-19 各地区年日照时数

Annual Sunshine Hours by Region

单位：小时 (hour)

年份 Year	粤北 Northern Regions	粤东北 North Eastern Regions	粤西北 North Western Regions	粤东 Eastern Regions	粤中 Central Regions	粤西 Western Regions
1980	1754.1	1811.1	1945.8	1989.2	1921.8	2036.5
1985	1701.6	1926.7	1613.3	1900.6	1406.0	1868.4
1990	1613.9	1893.1	1542.8	1921.3	1648.7	1877.4
1995	1420.6	1868.7	1704.6	2038.3	1559.6	1828.3
1996	1626.5	1965.7	1796.9	2094.8	1564.7	2042.3
1997	1349.1	1490.2	1454.9	1985.8	1209.8	1895.1
1998	1578.3	1689.6	1546.1	1917.5	1469.4	1994.0
1999	1564.0	1819.7	1699.0	2237.0	1599.5	2050.7
2000	1497.2	1672.6	1714.1	2126.3	1609.2	1855.3
2001	1613.0	1884.0	1559.2	2199.8	1651.0	1794.6
2002	1506.4	1813.2	1521.7	2266.6	1566.5	1783.8
2003	1821.1	2030.1	1762.6	2341.5	1741.6	2144.5
2004	1818.5	2117.1	1640.2	2433.5	1767.4	2024.7
2005	1491.2	1736.4	1345.6	1849.5	1288.5	1784.4
2006	1487.7	1779.4	1454.8	1843.5	1328.7	1664.3
2007	1736.3	1750.6	1722.4	1961.2	1616.0	1778.7
2008	1545.0	1853.1	1638.8	1852.1	1482.2	1864.4
2009	1852.9	1962.9	1531.8	2059.8	1671.8	1981.8
2010	1631.0	1676.9	1356.5	1855.5	1484.0	1878.4
2011	1783.8	1901.1	1709.7	2077.9	1878.4	1822.3
2012	1501.0	1660.3	1361.1	1650.4	1471.2	1544.0
2013	1731.5	1827.8	1624.2	1865.8	1582.9	1811.2
2014	1886.2	1997.5	1744.5	1957.8	1613.6	1991.5
2015	1540.8	1740.4	1583.0	2010.7	1594.3	2008.1
2016	1629.2	1553.6	1466.2	1701.0	1451.8	1963.9
2017	1738.9	1831.4	1605.4	1994.6	1671.5	1891.9

7-20 各市土地面积和人口密度

Land Area and Population Density by City

市别	City	土地面积（平方公里）Land Area (sq.km)	人口密度（人/平方公里）Population Density (persons/sq.km)							
			2000	2005	2010	2013	2014	2015	2016	2017
全省合计	**Provincial Total**	**179725.07**	**486**	**511**	**581**	**592**	**597**	**604**	**612**	**621**
广州	Guangzhou	7249.27	1337	1277	1744	1783	1804	1863	1937	2000
深圳	Shenzhen	1997.47	3596	4239	5311	5323	5398	5697	5962	6272
珠海	Zhuhai	1736.46	758	839	944	922	936	943	967	1017
汕头	Shantou	2199.15	2263	2395	2400	2506	2512	2525	2537	2550
佛山	Foshan	3797.72	1400	1507	1871	1921	1936	1957	1965	2016
韶关	Shaoguan	18412.53	149	159	154	157	158	159	161	162
河源	Heyuan	15653.63	143	176	189	194	196	196	197	197
梅州	Meizhou	15864.51	240	259	267	271	273	274	275	276
惠州	Huizhou	11347.39	288	332	405	414	417	419	421	421
汕尾	Shanwei	4865.05	465	531	600	614	618	621	624	612
东莞	Dongguan	2460.08	2615	2662	3328	3381	3391	3355	3358	3391
中山	Zhongshan	1783.67	1313	1352	1735	1779	1790	1799	1811	1828
江门	Jiangmen	9506.92	414	430	467	473	475	475	478	480
阳江	Yangjiang	7955.88	278	297	304	312	314	316	318	320
湛江	Zhanjiang	13262.83	487	536	530	540	544	546	548	551
茂名	Maoming	11427.63	457	510	510	526	529	532	536	543
肇庆	Zhaoqing	14891.23	227	247	265	270	271	273	274	276
清远	Qingyuan	19035.54	164	188	193	199	201	201	202	203
潮州	Chaozhou	3146.11	780	810	862	862	865	839	841	843
揭阳	Jieyang	5265.84	999	1068	1117	1139	1146	1151	1157	1156
云浮	Yunfu	7785.11	277	301	304	312	314	316	319	322

注：1.2000、2005年数据来源于2000年广东省第五次全国人口普查公报和广东省2005年全国1%人口抽样调查公报。
2.土地面积为2017年度土地变更调查初步数据，未经自然资源部确定，最终数据以自然资源部确认为准。

Note: a) Data of 2000 and 2005 are based on the Communique of the Fifth National Population Census in Guangdong in 2000 and the Communique of 1% National Population Sample Survey in 2005.
b) Data on land area are result of the land research of 2015, provincial total area includes areas of the islands with jurisdiction.

7-21 环境保护基本情况

Basic Conditions of Environmental Protection

项　目	item	2010	2014	2015	2016	2017
水环境	**Water Environment**					
降水量 (毫米)	Precipitation (mm)	1927.1	1691.2	1875.7	2357.6	1739.2
水资源总量 (亿立方米)	Total Amount of Water Resource (100 million cu.m)	1998.8	1718.5	1933.4	2458.6	1786.6
人均水资源量 (立方米/人)	Per Capita Amount of Water Resource (cu.m/person)	1915	1608	1782	2251	1612
用水总量 (亿立方米)	Total Water Consumption (100 million cu.m)	469.0	442.5	443.1	435.0	433.5
#农业用水	Agriculture	231.3	224.3	227.0	220.5	220.3
工业用水	Industry	138.8	117.0	112.5	109.2	107
生活用水	Living	90.4	96.1	98.3	99.9	100.9
生态环境补水	Ecology	8.6	5.1	5.3	5.4	5.3
万元GDP用水量 (立方米/万元)	Water Consumption per 10000 Yuan of GDP (cu.m/10000 yuan)	103	65	61	55	48
万元工业增加值用水量 (立方米/万元)	Water Consumption per 10000 Yuan of Value-added of Industry (cu.m/10000 yuan)	65	40	37	34	30
废水排放总量 (亿吨)	Total Volume of Waste Water Discharged(100 million tons)	72.30	90.51	91.15	93.80	
#城镇生活污水	Living Waste Water	53.59	72.68	74.93	80.60	
工业废水	Industrial Waste Water	18.70	17.76	16.15	13.20	
废水中COD排放量 (万吨)	Volume of COD Discharged from Waste Water(10000 tons)	85.84	167.06	160.69	96.40	
废水中氨氮排放量 (万吨)	Volume of Ammonia and Nitrogen Discharged from Waste Water (10000 tons)	10.7	20.8	20.0	14.40	
大气环境	**Atmospheric Environment**					
工业废气排放总量 (亿立方米)	Total Volume of Industrial Waste Gas Emission (100 million cu.m)	24092	29793	30923	38846	
二氧化硫排放总量 (万吨)	Total Volume of Industrial Sulfur Dioxide Emission (10000 tons)	105.1	73.0	67.8	35.4	
#工业二氧化硫	Volume of Industrial Sulfur Dioxide Emission	98.9	69.9	64.9	33.0	
氮氧化物排放总量 (万吨)	Nitrogen Oxides (10000 tons)		112.2	99.7	84.3	
#工业氮氧化物	Industrial Nitrogen Oxides		68.3	58.8	44.9	
烟(粉)尘排放总量 (万吨)	Volume of Soot(Dust) Emission (10000 tons)		45.0	34.8	28.2	
#工业烟(粉)尘排放量	Volume of Industrial Soot(Dust) Emission		39.5	30.0	23.4	
空气质量达二级标准城市数(个)	Number of Cities Meeting Grade Ⅱ Air Quality Standard (unit)	21	6	15	14	
生态环境	**Ecological Environment**					
人均耕地面积 (亩)	Per Capita Area of Cultivated Land (mu)	0.45	0.44	0.44	0.43	0.42
累计水土流失治理面积(千公顷)	Area of Soil Erosion under Control (1000 hectares)	44.6	47.5	72.6	78.7	102.5
森林面积 (万公顷)	Forest Area (10000 hectares)	1036.28	1082.79	1086.11	1087.90	

注：1. 2014年起，空气质量达二级标准的统计标准有变。

2.2016年，环保排污数据统计口径和核算方法改变；由于2017年部分环境保护数据未经国家最后确定，数据暂时无法提供，下同。

Note:a) The scope of meeting grade Ⅱ air quality standard has been changed since 2014.

b) In 2016, the statistical coverage and accounting method of pollution discharge in environmental protection have been adjusted. Because environment statistics of year 2017 have not yet been confirmed by national authorities, the data are not able to be offered. The same applies the following table.

7-21 续表 1 continued

项　目	item	2010	2014	2015	2016	2017
森林覆盖率 (%)	Forest Coverage Rate (%)	57.00	58.69	58.88	58.98	59.08
人均森林面积 (公顷)	Per Capita Forest Area (hectare)	0.1	0.1	0.1	0.1	
活立木蓄积量 (万立方米)	Volume of Standing Forest Stock (10000 cu.m)	43936	54679	56636	57855	
森林蓄积量 (万立方米)	Stock Volume of Forest (10000 cu.m)	43190	54138	56128	57293	58300
当年营造林面积 (万公顷)	Afforested Area in Current Year (10000 hectares)	9.51	15.15	11.85	10.07	8.07
自然保护区数 (个)	Number of Natural Reserves (unit)	368	369	369	369	369
自然保护区面积 (万公顷)	Area of Natural Reserves (10000 hectares)	182.4	171.9	172.7	172.7	172.7
城市环境	**Urban Environment**					
城区面积 (平方公里)	Urban Area (sq.km)	18130.1	17036.4	16825.7	17086.3	16834.7
#建成区面积	Built-up Area	4618.07	5398.07	5633.19	5808.12	5911.05
城市建设用地面积 (平方公里)	Area of City Land Used for Construction (sq.km)	4774.76	4415.55	4958.73	5266.61	5577.44
城市供水总量 (万立方米)	Total Volume of Water Supply in Urban Areas (10000 cu.m)	806144	721646	852512	870036	896774
#生活用水量	Domestic Water Consumption	394036	448647	460359	479964	501184
城市用水普及率 (%)	Popularization Rate of Tap Water in Urban Areas (%)	98.4	97.3	98.5	98.1	97.8
城市污水排放量 (万吨)	Volume of Municipal Sewage Discharge (10000 tons)	506546	652251	671363	689202	712678
城市污水处理量 (万吨)	Volume of Municipal Sewage Disposal (10000 tons)	436041	596142	628706	647773	673323
城市污水处理厂集中处理率(%)	Rate of Municipal Sewage Disposal (%)	73.1	91.4	93.3	93.8	94.4
城市生活垃圾清运量 (万吨)	Transportation Amount of Urban Domestic Waste (10000 tons)	1398.01	2214.23	2320.33	2390.96	2644.51
城市生活垃圾无害化处理量 (万吨)	Volume of Harmless Disposal of Urban Domestic Waste (10000 tons)	1938.55	1912.70	2124.58	2363.68	2591.19
城市生活垃圾无害化处理率(%)	Rate of Harmless Disposal of Urban Domestic Waste (%)	72.1	86.4	91.6	96.2	98.0
城市燃气普及率 (%)	Popularization Rate of Gas in Urban Areas (%)	95.8	96.6	97.6	97.4	96.9
城市人均公园绿地面积(平方米)	Per Capita Urban Public Green Area (sq.m)	13.29	16.28	17.40	17.87	18.24
建成区绿化覆盖率 (%)	Green Coverage Rate in Built-up Areas (%)	41.3	41.4	41.4	42.4	43.5
城市公共交通车辆运营数(标台)	Number of Public Transportation Vehicles (Unit)		61685	62947	68965	73888
农村环境	**Rural Environment**					
农村自来水普及率 (%)	Popularization Rate of Tap Water in Rural Areas (%)	83.9	89.5	90.1	91.4	92.8
农村卫生厕所普及率 (%)	Popularization Rate of Sanitary Toilets in Rural Areas(%)	85.8	91.1	92.3	93.7	95.4
无害化卫生厕所普及率 (%)	Popularization Rate of Harmless Sanitary Toilets (%)	77.7	84.9	87.2	90.3	93.0
农村沼气池产气总量 (万立方米)	Total Output of Biogas from Rural Biogas Pools (10000 cu.m)	18724	35788	36617	35588	

7-21 续表 2 continued

项 目	item	2010	2014	2015	2016	2017
自然灾害	**Natural Disasters**					
地质灾害次数 (次)	Number of Geological Disasters (unit)	600	268	191	213	154
地质灾害直接经济损失 (万元)	Direct Economic Loss due to Geological Disasters (10000 yuan)	22732	5423	3666	4449	1186
海洋灾害发生次数 (次)	Number of Marine Disasters (time)	14	20	9	9	17
海洋灾害直接经济损失 (亿元)	Direct Economic Loss due to Marine Disasters (100 million yuan)		60.41	28.77	9.63	54.10
森林火灾次数 (次)	Number of Forest Fires (time)	59	140	273	65	302
突发环境事件 (次)	Emergent Environment Cases (time)	30	31	29	24	48
工业固体废物	**Industrial Solid Wastes**					
固体废物产生量 (万吨)	Volume of Industrial Solid Wastes Produced (10000 tons)	5455.80	5665.09	5608.60	5609.80	
固体废物排放量 (万吨)	Volume of Industrial Solid Wastes Discharged (10000 tons)	14.2	1.9	1.1	1.2	
固体废物贮存量 (万吨)	Volume of Industrial Solid Wastes Accumulated(10000 tons)	177.4	150.0	73.7	174.3	
固体废物综合利用量(万吨)	Solid Wastes Comprehensively Utilized (10000 tons)	4952.60	4893.04	5102.66	4904.20	
工业“三废”治理设施	**Facilities for Treatment of Industrial Waste**					
工业废水处理设施总数(套)	Water, Waste Gas and Solid Wastes (set)	9651	9861	9733	8248	
工业废气治理设施总数(套)	Number of Facilities for Treatment of Waste (set)	12789	22311	25673	25791	
企事业单位污染治理	**Number of Facilities for Treatment of Waste Gas**					
污染治理资金 (万元)	Pollution Treated by Enterprises and Institutions Funds for Pollution Treatment (10000 yuan)	310584	378641	356173	557434	
当年安排治理项目 (个)	Number of Projects for Pollution Treatment in Current Year (unit)	657	420	536	640	
当年竣工项目数 (个)	Number of Projects Completed in Current Year (unit)	613	503	424	537	
环境管理	**Environmental Management**					
排污费收入总额 (万元)	Total Fees for Discharging Waste in Current Year	88401	87763	74985	78255	

7–22 各市“三废”排放情况（2016年）

Statistics on Discharge of Waste Water, Waste Gas and Solid Wastes by City (2016)

市 别	City	废水排放总量（亿吨） Total Volume of Waste Water Discharged (100 million tons)	#工业废水 Industrial Waste Water	工业废气排放总量（亿立方米） Total Volume of Industrial Waste Gas Emission (100million cu.m)	工业烟(粉)尘排放总量（万吨） Volume of Industrial Soot(Dust) Emission (10000 tons)	工业固体废物产生量（万吨） Volume of Industrial Solid Wastes Produced (10000tons)	工业固体废物丢弃量（万吨） Volume of Industrial Solid Wastes Discharged (10000 tons)
广 州	Guangzhou	16.10	1.90	4122.80	0.90	498.90	
深 圳	Shenzhen	18.30	1.10	2779.50	0.20	102.60	
珠 海	Zhuhai	2.90	0.40	2332.80	1.00	245.60	
汕 头	Shantou	3.00	0.60	729.10	0.30	85.10	
佛 山	Foshan	8.30	1.40	3258.70	2.30	382.60	0.01
#顺 德	Shunde	2.90	0.50	1580.80	0.40	54.30	
韶 关	Shaoguan	1.90	0.70	3077.30	3.80	684.00	
河 源	Heyuan	1.00	0.10	444.80	0.40	147.90	
梅 州	Meizhou	1.40	0.20	1395.30	0.60	390.90	
惠 州	Huizhou	4.40	0.60	1792.70	1.50	94.20	
汕 尾	Shanwei	1.10	0.10	635.10	0.10	85.40	
东 莞	Dongguan	12.50	1.70	3642.80	1.30	457.20	0.08
中 山	Zhongshan	4.50	0.70	1561.30	0.70	105.10	0.06
江 门	Jiangmen	3.90	0.90	1310.60	1.00	212.50	
阳 江	Yangjiang	1.00	0.10	1423.60	0.70	452.10	0.96
湛 江	Zhanjiang	2.90	0.50	4400.50	1.40	546.00	0.05
茂 名	Maoming	1.40	0.30	822.80	0.60	189.20	
肇 庆	Zhaoqing	2.40	0.70	1581.50	2.70	195.60	
清 远	Qingyuan	2.20	0.30	1165.50	2.70	327.30	
潮 州	Chaozhou	1.20	0.20	631.60	0.20	84.30	
揭 阳	Jieyang	2.30	0.30	555.00	0.20	129.90	
云 浮	Yunfu	0.90	0.10	1182.80	0.80	193.30	

7-23 各市城市建设基本情况

Basic Statistics on Urban Sanitation by City

市别	City	城市污水处理率 (%) Rate of Sewage Treatment				城市生活垃圾无害化处理率 (%) Rate of Consumption Waste Treatment			
		2010	2015	2016	2017	2010	2015	2016	2017
全省	**Province Total**	**73.1**	**93.7**	**94.0**	**94.5**	**72.1**	**91.6**	**96.2**	**98.0**
广州	Guangzhou	88.1	93.2	94.3	95.0	92.0	95.2	96.1	96.5
深圳	Shenzhen	88.9	96.6	97.6	96.8	94.6	100.0	100.0	100.0
珠海	Zhuhai	84.7	95.7	96.3	96.4	92.3	100.0	100.0	100.0
汕头	Shantou	57.9	90.2	90.3	91.5	64.4	92.6	89.8	91.9
佛山	Foshan	79.7	94.4	96.7	96.4	95.6	100.0	100.0	100.0
韶关	Shaoguan	53.6	86.2	87.1	92.1	100.0	100.0	100.0	100.0
河源	Heyuan	43.0	92.9	92.5	92.6	96.5	100.0	100.0	100.0
梅州	Meizhou	33.7	88.6	96.6	96.6	100.0	100.0	100.0	100.0
惠州	Huizhou	71.5	97.6	97.0	97.2	100.0	100.0	100.0	100.0
汕尾	Shanwei	18.6	89.1	91.2	93.2		100.0	93.8	95.6
东莞	Dongguan	91.1	96.5	93.5	93.7	100.0	100.0	100.0	100.0
中山	Zhongshan	85.1	96.0	96.3	96.5	100.0	100.0	100.0	100.0
江门	Jiangmen	63.5	91.6	92.1	93.9	100.0	100.0	100.0	100.0
阳江	Yangjiang	54.6	85.5	87.9	92.4	100.0	100.0	100.0	100.0
湛江	Zhanjiang	39.6	88.5	91.1	91.1	97.4	100.0	100.0	100.0
茂名	Maoming	34.4	88.4	94.3	94.7		100.0	100.0	100.0
肇庆	Zhaoqing	70.5	85.1	89.5	94.5	83.8	100.0	100.0	100.0
清远	Qingyuan	70.4	87.6	81.5	92.8	100.0	100.0	80.6	100.0
潮州	Chaozhou	33.5	79.7	81.0	81.9	100.0	79.3	76.8	77.3
揭阳	Jieyang	20.8	89.8	78.3	82.3	90.0	95.0	96.4	97.4
云浮	Yunfu	63.7	93.1	77.9	95.6	100.0	100.0	100.0	100.0

7-23 续表 continued

市别	City	城市公共交通车辆标准运营数（标台） Number of Public Transportation Vehicles (unit)				城市人均公园绿地面积（平方米） Per Capital Area of Parks and Green Land in City (sq.m)			
		2010	2015	2016	2017	2010	2015	2016	2017
全　　省	**Province Total**		**62947**	**68965**	**73888**	**13.29**	**17.40**	**17.87**	**18.24**
广　　州	Guangzhou	10232	16179	16960	17954	11.87	21.82	22.09	22.67
深　　圳	Shenzhen	14677	17943	18899	21535	16.40	16.91	16.45	15.95
珠　　海	Zhuhai	1557	2349	2486	2580	13.70	19.50	19.70	19.80
汕　　头	Shantou	1111	1253	1740	1734	12.20	15.01	15.19	15.16
佛　　山	Foshan	3715	6783	6915	6901	10.20	14.69	13.91	16.55
韶　　关	Shaoguan	460	635	848	882	11.80	12.50	12.52	13.83
河　　源	Heyuan	294	330	388	395	12.10	12.55	12.61	12.79
梅　　州	Meizhou	238	925	1632	1861	11.80	16.70	17.00	17.10
惠　　州	Huizhou	1124	2446	2709	2878	11.10	17.75	17.85	17.88
汕　　尾	Shanwei	199	344	821	888	10.70	13.48	14.08	14.41
东　　莞	Dongguan	6129	5346	5960	6135	15.30	19.36	22.99	24.23
中　　山	Zhongshan	2151	2436	2685	2973	11.90	18.39	18.41	16.50
江　　门	Jiangmen	924	1524	1674	1785	11.00	17.75	17.78	18.34
阳　　江	Yangjiang	143	242	323	393	10.60	11.17	12.57	12.98
湛　　江	Zhanjiang	735	1167	1744	1586	12.70	13.94	13.99	14.24
茂　　名	Maoming	392	511	493	522	10.00	13.74	16.46	16.82
肇　　庆	Zhaoqing	443	814	846	758	22.70	20.73	20.39	20.11
清　　远	Qingyuan	633	778	749	765	11.30	13.03	10.00	12.69
潮　　州	Chaozhou	140	192	374	350	10.30	10.57	9.70	12.43
揭　　阳	Jieyang	377	387	403	689	12.90	8.65	12.10	14.03
云　　浮	Yunfu	176	362	329	325	12.10	12.70	19.22	17.08

注：标台营运数为不含轨道交通数。
Note: Data of track transport is not included in the number of vehicles.

主要统计指标解释

能源生产总量 指一定时期内全国（地区）一次能源生产量的总和，是观察全国（地区）能源生产水平、规模、构成和发展速度的总量指标。一次能源生产量包括原煤、原油、天然气、水电、核能及其他动力能（如风能、地热能等）发电量。不包括低热值燃料生产量、生物质能、太阳能等的利用和由一次能源加工转换而成的二次能源产量。

能源消费总量 指一定时期内全国（地区）生产和生活消费的各种能源的总和，是观察能源消费水平、构成和增长速度的总量指标，能源消费总量包括原煤和原油及其制品、天然气、电力。不包括低热值燃料、生物质能和太阳能等的利用 。能源消费总量分为三部分，即终端能源消费量、能源加工转换损失量和损失量。

(1)终端能源消费量 指一定时期内全国（地区）生产和生活消费的各种能源在扣除了用于加工转换二次能源消费量和损失量以后的数量。

(2)能源加工转换损失量 指一定时期内全国（地区）投入加工转换的各种能源数量之和与产出各种能源产品之和的差额。它是观察能源在加工转换过程中损失量变化的指标。

(3)能源损失量 指一定时期内能源在输送、分配、储存过程中发生的损失和由客观原因造成的各种损失量。不包括各种气体能源放空、放散量。

能源生产弹性系数 是研究能源生产增长速度与国民经济增长速度之间关系的指标。计算公式：

$$\text{能源生产弹性系数}=\frac{\text{能源生产总量增长速度}}{\text{国民经济增长速度}}$$

国民经济增长速度，可根据不同的目的或需要，用国民生产总值，国内生产总值等指标来计算，本资料是采用国内生产总值指标计算的。

电力生产弹性系数 是研究电力生产增长速度与国民经济增长速度之间关系的指标。一般来说，电力的发展应当快于国民经济的发展，也就是说电力应超前发展。计算公式：

$$\text{电力生产弹性系数}=\frac{\text{电力生产量增长速度}}{\text{国民经济增长速度}}$$

能源消费弹性系数 是反映能源消费增长速度与国民经济增长速度之间比例关系的指标。计算公式：

$$\text{能源消费弹性系数}=\frac{\text{能源消费量增长速度}}{\text{国民经济增长速度}}$$

电力消费弹性系数 是反映电力消费增长速度与国民经济增长速度之间比例关系的指标。计算公式：

$$\text{电力消费弹性系数}=\frac{\text{电力消费量增长速度}}{\text{国民经济增长速度}}$$

能源加工转换效率 指一定时期内能源经过加工、转换后，产出的各种能源产品的数量与同期内投入加工转换的各种能源数量的比率。它是观察能源加工转换装置和生产工艺先进与落后、管理水平高低等的重要指标。计算公式：

$$\text{能源加工转换效率}=\frac{\text{能源加工、转换产出量}}{\text{能源加工、转换投入量}}\times 100\%$$

土地资源 土地指陆地的表层部分，它主要由岩石、岩石的风化物和土壤构成。土地资源按利用类型可以分为农用地、建筑用地和未利用地。农用地包括耕地、园地、林地、牧草地和水面。建筑用地包括居民点及工矿用地、交通用地和水利设施用地。未利用地指农用地和建筑用地以外的土地，包括滩涂、荒漠、戈壁、冰川和石山等。

耕地面积 指经过开垦用以种植农作物并经常进行耕耘的土地面积。包括种有作物的土地面积、休闲地、新开荒地和抛荒未满三年的土地面积。

林业用地面积 指生长乔木、竹类、灌木、沿海红树林等林木的土地面积，包括有林地、灌木林、疏林地、未成林造林地、迹地、苗圃等。

草地面积 指牧区和农区用于放牧牲畜或割草，植被盖度在 5% 以上的草原、草坡、草山等面积。包括天然的和人工种植或改良的草地面积。

森林资源 指森林、林木、林地以及依托森林、林木、林地生存的野生动物、植物和微生物。林木指树木和竹子。森林指以乔木为主体的植物群落，是集生的乔木及与共同作用的植物、动物、微生物和土壤、气候等的总体。

活立木总蓄积量 指一定范围内土地上全部树木蓄积的总量，包括森林蓄积、疏林蓄积、散生木蓄积和四旁树蓄积。

森林覆盖率 指一个国家或地区森林面积占土地总面积的百分比。森林覆盖率是反映森林资源的丰富程度和生态平衡状况的重要指标。在计算森林覆盖率时，森林面积包括郁闭度 0.2 以上的乔木林地面积和竹林地面积，国家特别规定的灌木林地面积、农田林网以及四旁(村旁、路旁、水旁、宅旁)林木的覆盖面积。计算公式为:

$$\text{森林覆盖率}(\%)=\frac{\text{森林面积}}{\text{土地总面积}}\times 100\%$$

森林面积 指由乔木树种构成，郁闭度 0.2 以上(含 0.2)的林地或冠幅宽度 10 米以上的林带的面积，即有林地面积。森林面积包括天然起源和人工起源的针叶林面积、阔叶林面积、针阔混交林面积和竹林面积，不包括灌木林地面积和疏林地面积。

森林蓄积量 指一定森林面积上存在着的林木树干部分的总材积。它是反映一个国家或地区森林资源总规模和水平的基本指标之一，也是反映森林资源的丰富程度、衡量森林生态环境优劣的重要依据。

水资源 水在自然界中以固体、液体和气态三种聚集状态存在，分布于海洋、陆地(包括土壤)以及大气之中，通过水循环形成水资源。水资源包括经人类控制并直接可供灌溉、发电、给水、航运、养殖等用途的地表水和地下水，以及江河、湖泊、井、泉、潮汐、港湾和养殖水域等。水资源是发展国民经济不可缺少的重要自然资源。

矿产资源 矿产资源指由地质作用形成的，具有利用价值的，呈固态、液态、气态的自然资源，是社会发展的重要物质基础。

矿产基础储量 基础储量是查明矿产资源的一部分。它能满足现行采矿和生产所需的指标要求，是控制的、探明的并通过可行性或预可行性研究认为属于经济的、边界经济的部分，用未扣除设计、采矿损失的数量表表示。

矿产保有资源储量 指查明的矿产资源储量（资源储量=基础储量+资源量）扣除已开采部分损失量和加减应勘查，重算或其它原因增减量而得出的年底实有资源储量。

废水排放总量 包括生产废水和生活污水。生产废水指企、事业单位在生产、科研过程中所有排放口向外环境排放的废水量总和。生活污水指城镇居民区和企、事业单位职工集中居住区排放的污水量。

工业废水排放总量 指经过工业企业厂区所有排放口排到企业外部的工业废水量。包括外排的直接冷却水、超标排放的矿井地下水和与工业废水混排的厂区生活污水，不包括外排的间接冷却水（清污不分流的间接冷却水应计算在内）。

废气排放总量 指燃料燃烧和生产工艺过程中排放的各种废气总量,以标准状态下每年万标立方米表示。

燃料燃烧过程废气排放量 指燃煤、燃油、燃气锅炉、锻造加热炉、退火炉和其它工业炉窑在燃烧过程(燃料和物料不混合的纯加热过程)中所排废气的总量。它可以根据烟气计算公式或经验计算公式求得。

工业固体废物产生量 指工业企业在生产过程中产生的固体状、半固体状和高浓度液体状废弃物的总量，包括冶炼废渣、粉煤灰、炉渣、煤矸石、化工废渣、尾矿、放射性废渣和其它废渣等；不包括矿山开采的剥离废石和掘进废石（煤矸石和呈酸性或碱性的废石除外）。酸性或碱性废石是指采掘的废石其流经水、雨淋水 PH 值小于 4 或 PH 值大于 10. 5 者。

工业固体废物综合利用量 指已用作农业肥料、造田、生产建筑材料、筑路以及其它方式综合利用的固体废物量（包括当年利用往年的工业固体废物堆存量）。综合利用量由原产固体废物的单位统计。

Explanatory Notes on Main Statistical Indicators

Total Energy Production refers to the total production of primary energy by all energy producing enterprises in the country (region) in a given period of time. It is a comprehensive indicator of the capacity, scale, composition and development speed of energy production of the country (region). The production of primary energy includes that of coal, crude oil, natural gas, hydropower and electricity generated by nuclear energy and other means such as wind power and geothermal power. However, it excludes the production of fuel of low calorific value, bioenergy, solar energy and secondary energy converted from primary energy.

Total Domestic Energy Consumption refers to the total consumption of energy of various kinds by production sectors and households in the country (region) in a given period of time. It is a comprehensive indicator of the scale, composition and development speed of energy consumption. The total energy consumption includes that of coal, crude oil and their products, natural gas and electricity, but excludes the consumption of fuel of low calorific value, bioenergy and solar energy. Total domestic energy consumption can be divided into three parts:

(1) Final Energy Consumption: This refers to the total energy consumption by production sectors and households in the country (region) in a given period of time, excluding primary energy consumption and loss in the process of conversion into secondary energy.

(2)Loss During the Process of Energy Conversion: This refers to the total input of various kinds of energy for conversion minus the total output of various kinds of energy in the country (region) in a given period of time. It is an indicator of the loss that occurs during the process of energy conversion.

(3)Loss: This refers to the total loss of energy during the course of energy transmission, distribution and storage and the loss caused by any objective reason in a given period of time, excluding the loss of various kinds of gas due to gas discharges and stocktaking.

Elasticity Ratio of Energy Production is an indicator of the relationship between the growth rate of energy production and the growth rate of the national economy. The formula is:

$$\text{Elasticity Ratio of Energy Production} = \frac{\text{Growth Rate of Energy Production}}{\text{Growth Rate of National Economy}}$$

The average annual growth rate of the national economy can be shown by the gross national product, gross domestic product and other indicators, depending on the purposes or needs. The gross domestic product is used in the calculation of the ratio in this chapter.

Elasticity Ratio of Electricity Production is an indicator of the relationship between the growth rate of electricity production and the growth rate of the national economy. Generally speaking, the growth rate of electricity production should be higher than that of the national economy; in other words, electricity production should develop in advance of the national economy. Its formula is:

$$\text{Elasticity Ratio of Electricity Production} = \frac{\text{Growth Rate of Electricity Production}}{\text{Growth Rate of National Economy}}$$

Elasticity Ratio of Energy Consumption is an indicator of the relationship between the growth rate of energy consumption and the growth rate of the national economy. The formula is:

$$\text{Elasticity Ratio of Energy Consumption} = \frac{\text{Growth Rate of Energy Consumption}}{\text{Growth Rate of National Economy}}$$

Elasticity Ratio of Electricity Consumption is an indicator of the relationship between the growth rate of electricity consumption and the growth rate of the national economy. The formula is:

$$\text{Elasticity Ratio of Electricity Consumption} = \frac{\text{Growth Rate of Electricity Consumption}}{\text{Growth Rate of National Economy}}$$

Efficiency of Energy Processing and Conversion refers to the ratio of the total output of energy products of various kinds after processing and conversion to the total input of energy of various kinds for processing and conversion in the same reference period. It is an important indicator of the current conditions of energy processing and conversion equipment, production technique and management. The formula is:

$$\text{Efficiency of Energy Processing \& Conversion} = \frac{\text{Output of Energy after Processing \& Conversion}}{\text{Input of Energy for Processing \& Conversion}} \times 100\%$$

Land Resource **Land** refers to the surface of the earth, consisting of mainly rocks and its weathering and earth. Land resource can be classified, by its utilization, as land for agriculture, land for construction and unused land. Land for agriculture includes cultivated land, plantation, forestland, grassland and waters. Land for construction includes land for residential purpose, for manufacturing and mining, for transportation and for water conservancy projects. Unused land refers to land other than land for agriculture and construction, including beaches, deserts, Gobi, glaciers and rock mountains.

Area of Cultivated Land refers to area of land reclaimed for the regular cultivation of various farm crops, including crop-cover land, fallow, newly reclaimed land and land laid idle for less than 3 years.

Area of Afforested Land refers to land for trees, bamboos, bushes and mangrove including forest-cover land, bush-covered land, sparse forest land, land planned for forestation, slash and nurseries of young trees.

Area of Grassland refers to areas of grassland, grass-slopes and grass-covered hills with a vegetation-covering rate of over 5% that are used for animal husbandry or harvesting of grass. It includes natural, cultivated and improved grassland areas.

Forest Resource refers to forests, trees, forestland and wild animals, plants and microorganism that live on forests and trees. Trees include trees and bamboos. Forest refers to the population of clusters of trees and other plants, animals and microorganism as well as the earth and climate that have interactions with the trees.

Total Standing Stock Volume refers to the total stock volume of trees growing in land, including trees in forests, tress in sparse forests, scattered trees and trees planted by the side of villages, farm houses and along roads and rivers.

Forest Coverage Rate refers to the ratio of area of afforested land to total land area. It is a very important indicator that reflects the status of abundance of forest resource and ecosystem balance. Forest area includes the area of trees and bamboo growing with a canopy density above 0.2, the area of shrubby trees according to regulations of the government, the area of forest land inside farm land and the area of trees planted by the side of villages, farm houses and along roads and rivers. The formula for calculating forest coverage rate is as follows:

$$\text{Forest Coverage Rate (\%)} = (\text{Area of Afforested Land/Area of Total Land}) \times 100\%$$

Forest Area refers to wooded area, i.e. the area of forest where trees and bamboo grow with a canopy density above 0.2 (inclusive) or a crown width above 10 meters, including natural and planted coniferous forest, broad-leaved forest, mixed forest, and bamboo groves, but excluding shrubbery and open forest.

Stock Volume of Forest refers to total stock volume of wood growing in forest area, which shows the total size and level of forest resources of a country or a region. It is also an important indicator of the richness of forest resource and the status of forest ecological environment.

Water Resource Water exists in the nature in solid, liquid and gaseous states, is distributed in the ocean, land (including earth) and air, and constitutes water resource through circulation. Water resource includes surface water and underground water that is controlled by human beings for irrigation, power-generation, water supply, navigation and cultivation. It also includes rivers, lakes, wells, springs, tides, gulfs and water area for cultivation. Water resource as an indispensable natural resource for the development of national economy.

Mineral Resources refer to useful natural resources enriched due to geological processes, in the form of solid, liquid or gas. Minerals are important material basis for social development.

Basic Reserves of Mineral Resources Basic reserves are part of total identified mineral resources that meet present mining and production standards, which is the part of reserve controlled, proven, and found to be of economic or marginal value through feasibility assessment or pre-feasibility study. Basic reserves are indicated as a figure including designing and mining loss.

Ensured Reserves of Mineral Resources refer to the actual reserves of mineral resources at the year-end, calculated as the proven reserves of mineral resources (Reserves of Mineral Resources = Basic Reserves + Resource) minus losses in previous extraction processes, plus or minus increases or losses due to exploration, recalculation or other reasons.

Total Volume of Waste Water Discharged includes the volume of production waste water and domestic sewage Production waste water refers to the total waste water discharged in the process of production and scientific research by enterprises and institutions, through all outlets to the outside environment Domestic sewage refers to the sewage volume discharged in the urban residential areas and the residential areas of staff and workers of enterprises and institutions.

Total Volume of Industrial Waste Water Discharged refers to the volume of industrial waste water discharged, through all outlets to the outside of industrial enterprises, including direct cooling water, underground water from mines that does not meet the discharge standards, and domestic sewage mixed up with industrial waste water when discharged, but excluding indirect cooling water discharged (except unclassified discharge of indirect cooling water).

Total Volume of Waste Gas Emission refers to waste gas emitted from burning of fuels and from the production process, and is measured by 10, 000 standard cubic meters each year under normal condition.

Volume of Waste Gas Emission from Burning of Fuels refers to the total volume of waste gas emitted from burning of fuels (the pure heating process not mixed with materials), such as burning of coal, burning of oil, gas fired boiler, forging furnace, annealing furnace and other industrial furnaces It can be calculated with the gas smoke formula or an empirical formula.

Volume of Industrial Solid Wastes Produced refers to the total volume of solid, semi solid or high concentration liquid residues produced by industrial enterprises in their production process, including residues from melting, slag, powdered coal ash, gangue, chemical residues, tailings, radioactive residues and other residues, but excluding stripped or dug stones in mining (except gangue and acid or alkali waste stones, which are waste stones washed or soaked by water with a PH value smaller than 4 or larger than 10. 5).

Volume of Industrial Solid Wastes Utilized in a Comprehensive Way refers to the volume of solid wastes utilized in a comprehensive way, such as the solid wastes utilized as fertilizers, building materials, for building up fields and making roads or for other purposes (including the volume of industrial solid wastes stored up in previous years and utilized in the current year). Statistical data on utilization of industrial solid wastes are collected by solid wastes producing units.

八、财政、银行和保险

GOVERNMENT FINANCE, BANKING AND INSURANCE

八　财政、银行和保险

简要说明

一、本篇资料反映广东地方公共财政预算收支、银行、保险等方面的基本情况，金融数据均包含深圳。

二、本篇资料由广东省统计局综合处负责整理、编辑。

三、资料来源：

财政资料根据广东省财政厅提供的历年《广东省财政总决算报表》的有关项目加工整理。

银行资料由中国人民银行广州分行提供。

保险业务资料由中国保险监督管理委员会广东监管局提供。

8 Government Finance, Banking and Insurance

Brief Introduction

Ⅰ. The data in this chapter show the basic situation of local government general budgetary revenue and expenditure, banking and insurance of Guangdong Province.Data of finance of Guangdong Province include Shenzhen.

Ⅱ. The data in this chapter are prepared by the Division of Comprehensive Statistics of Statistics Bureau of Guangdong Province.

Ⅲ. Data sources:

The data on local government finance are prepared in accordance with the related tables of the Total Final Accounts of Government Finance of Guangdong provided by Guangdong Provincial Department of Finance.

The data on banking are provided by Guangzhou Branch of the People's Bank of China.

The data on insurance are provided by Guangdong Bureau of China Insurance Regulatory Commission.

8-1 地方一般公共预算收支和增长速度

Local Government General Public Budget Revenue and Expenditure and Their Growth Rates

单位：亿元 (100 million yuan)

年份 Year	地方一般公共预算收入 Local Government General Public Budget Revenue	#税收收入 Taxes	地方一般公共预算支出 Local Government General Public Budget Expenditure	收支差额 Balance	增长速度(%) Growth Rate (%) 地方一般公共预算收入 Local General Government Public Budget Revenue	增长速度(%) Growth Rate (%) 地方一般公共预算支出 Local General Government Public Budget Expenditure	地方一般公共预算收入占地区生产总值的比重(%) Percentage of Budgetary Revenue to GDP (%)
1978	41.82	25.78	28.70	13.12	17.9	42.6	22.5
1979	36.25	25.98	29.88	6.37	-13.3	4.1	17.3
1980	37.79	27.72	27.04	10.75	4.2	-9.5	15.1
1981	41.01	30.84	29.60	11.41	8.5	9.5	14.1
1982	42.23	34.72	33.34	8.89	3.0	12.6	12.4
1983	44.29	38.52	37.45	6.84	4.9	12.3	12.0
1984	49.28	43.59	47.18	2.10	11.3	26.0	10.7
1985	69.27	65.25	66.74	2.53	40.6	41.5	12.0
1986	82.41	73.29	89.55	-7.14	19.0	34.2	12.3
1987	95.88	88.65	96.59	-0.71	16.3	7.9	11.3
1988	107.57	119.17	115.20	-7.63	12.2	19.3	9.3
1989	136.87	145.02	141.16	-4.29	27.2	22.5	9.9
1990	131.02	135.62	150.69	-19.67	-4.3	6.8	8.4
1991	177.35	158.31	182.48	-5.13	35.4	21.1	9.4
1992	222.64	195.98	219.61	3.03	25.5	20.3	9.1
1993	346.56	310.78	331.27	15.29	55.7	50.8	10.0
1994	298.70	275.06	416.83	-118.13	-13.8	25.8	6.5
1995	382.34	353.64	525.63	-143.29	28.0	26.1	6.4
1996	479.45	438.25	601.23	-121.78	25.4	14.4	7.0
1997	543.95	494.76	682.66	-138.71	13.5	13.5	7.0
1998	640.75	545.62	825.61	-184.86	17.8	20.9	7.5
1999	766.19	645.28	1034.44	-268.25	19.6	25.3	8.3
2000	910.56	798.61	1069.86	-159.30	18.8	3.4	8.5
2001	1160.51	1014.72	1321.33	-160.82	27.5	23.5	9.6
2002	1201.61	1032.33	1521.08	-319.47	3.5	15.1	8.9
2003	1315.52	1109.50	1695.63	-380.11	9.5	11.5	8.3
2004	1418.51	1191.55	1852.95	-434.44	7.8	9.3	7.5
2005	1807.20	1526.97	2289.07	-481.87	27.4	23.5	8.1
2006	2179.46	1850.44	2553.34	-373.88	20.6	11.5	8.3
2007	2785.80	2415.47	3159.57	-373.77	27.8	23.7	9.0
2008	3310.32	2864.79	3778.57	-468.25	18.8	19.6	9.3
2009	3649.81	3130.61	4334.37	-684.56	10.3	14.7	9.2
2010	4517.04	3803.47	5421.54	-904.50	23.8	25.1	9.8
2011	5514.84	4548.66	6712.40	-1197.56	22.1	23.8	10.4
2012	6229.18	5073.88	7387.86	-1158.68	13.0	10.1	10.9
2013	7081.47	5767.94	8411.00	-1329.53	13.7	13.8	11.4
2014	8065.08	6510.47	9152.64	-1087.56	13.9	8.8	11.9
2015	9366.78	7377.07	12827.80	-3461.01	11.9	40.1	12.9
2016	10390.35	8098.63	13446.09	-3055.74	10.3	4.8	13.1
2017	11320.35	8871.89	15037.48	-3717.13	10.9	11.8	12.6

注：2015年起，地方公共财政预算收入和地方公共财政预算支出统一更名为地方一般公共预算收入和地方一般公共预算支出，财政收入按可比口径计算。

Note: From 2015, the name of local government budgetary revenue and local government budgetary expenditure have been changed to local public budgetary revenue and local public budgetary expenditure.Growdth rates of revenue are caculated by comparable caliber.

8-2 地方一般公共预算收支基本情况

Basic Items of General Public Budget Revenue and Expenditure

单位：亿元 (100 million yuan)

指 标	Item	2010	2012	2013	2014	2015	2016	2017
一、地方一般公共预算收入	**General Public Budget Revenue**	**4517.04**	**6229.18**	**7081.47**	**8065.08**	**9366.78**	**10390.35**	**11320.35**
税收收入	Tax Revenue	3803.47	5073.88	5767.94	6510.47	7377.07	8098.63	8871.89
#增值税	Value-added Tax	657.82	793.84	1058.85	1233.17	1339.16	2579.49	3675.43
企业所得税	Corporate Income Tax	678.75	891.03	974.68	1136.19	1303.11	1492.08	1767.83
个人所得税	Individual Income Tax	287.26	322.71	348.02	408.91	510.14	638.11	755.91
城市维护建设税	City Maintenance and Construction Tax	135.97	338.31	383.48	413.75	457.05	491.74	534.97
房产税	House Property Tax	122.44	175.42	198.63	233.89	241.00	243.97	299.46
印花税	Stamp Tax	69.93	81.16	95.57	112.00	141.41	119.47	142.29
土地增值税	Land Appriciation Tax	189.79	408.01	417.51	505.90	576.75	681.58	839.11
耕地占用税	Farm Land Occupation Tax	56.03	69.67	80.43	86.35	95.38	76.68	66.26
契税	Deed Tax	235.51	271.83	372.50	419.91	427.24	513.67	578.75
非税收入	Non-tax Revenue	713.57	1155.30	1313.53	1554.61	1989.71	2291.72	2448.46
专项收入	Special Program Receipts	97.35	202.56	233.09	255.71	598.77	863.02	873.93
行政事业性收费收入	Charge of Administrative and Units	293.43	391.62	450.10	497.67	408.19	328.30	285.37
罚没收入	Penalty Receipts	95.62	139.99	134.89	134.69	155.77	152.67	224.67
国有资本经营收入	Operation Income from State-owned Assets	90.00	120.08	123.02	60.90	62.70	54.23	39.16
国有资源(资产)有偿使用收入	Income from Use of State-owned Resources Assets	81.88	142.24	190.09	281.69	355.19	401.25	554.39
其他收入	Other Non-tax Revenue	55.29	158.80	182.34	323.95	409.09	492.26	470.94
二、地方一般公共预算支出	**General Public Budget Expenditure**	**5421.54**	**7387.86**	**8411.00**	**9152.64**	**12827.80**	**13446.09**	**15037.48**
#一般公共服务	Expenditure for General Public Services	685.39	892.62	996.45	959.44	1018.91	1147.35	1355.60
教育	Expenditure for Education	921.48	1501.22	1744.59	1808.97	2040.65	2318.47	2575.52
科学技术	Expenditure for Science and Technology	214.44	246.71	344.94	274.33	569.55	742.97	823.89
文化体育与传媒	Expenditure for Culture, Sports and Media	166.16	137.64	141.68	168.16	194.58	229.71	285.87
社会保障和就业	Expenditure for Social Safety Net and Employment Effort	469.58	611.04	746.97	797.01	1064.91	1146.31	1423.33
医疗卫生与计划生育	Expenditure for Medical and Health Care, Family Planning	304.04	505.14	569.32	777.55	918.36	1121.83	1307.56
节能环保	Expenditure for Energy Conservation and Environment Protection	239.16	235.44	307.78	259.04	322.33	297.45	433.23
城乡社区	Expenditure for Urban and Rural Community Affairs	407.64	623.28	664.77	770.11	1174.16	1515.29	2180.53
农林水	Expenditure for Agriculture, Forestry and Water Conservancy	325.02	539.56	595.28	557.59	811.90	715.44	754.40
交通运输	Expenditure for Transportation	318.17	503.57	688.04	882.86	1982.63	1014.52	848.40
其他支出	Other Expenditure	331.54	282.93	308.71	297.09	428.10	18.26	96.18

8-3 各市地方一般公共预算收支

Local Government General Budgetary Revenue and Expenditure by City

单位：亿元 (100 million yuan)

市 别	City	地方一般公共预算收入 Local Government General Budgetary Revenue								
		2000	2005	2010	2012	2013	2014	2015	2016	2017
全省合计	**Provincial Total**	**910.56**	**1807.20**	**4517.04**	**6229.18**	**7081.47**	**8065.08**	**9366.78**	**10390.35**	**11320.35**
广 州	Guangzhou	200.55	371.26	872.65	1102.40	1141.80	1243.10	1349.47	1393.64	1536.74
深 圳	Shenzhen	221.92	412.38	1106.82	1482.08	1731.26	2082.73	2726.85	3136.49	3332.13
珠 海	Zhuhai	24.23	48.97	124.53	162.60	194.20	224.31	269.96	292.37	314.38
汕 头	Shantou	18.94	29.44	72.65	96.34	112.11	123.97	131.26	137.09	150.07
佛 山	Foshan	59.53	130.85	306.05	384.08	438.21	501.19	557.55	604.50	661.58
韶 关	Shaoguan	8.63	19.93	47.81	61.48	71.78	82.01	85.23	85.05	88.71
河 源	Heyuan	2.55	8.52	25.09	37.64	48.79	60.47	67.48	68.89	71.19
梅 州	Meizhou	7.18	15.18	38.95	56.27	69.37	85.28	103.59	105.46	108.55
惠 州	Huizhou	12.94	34.72	131.23	200.88	250.17	300.75	340.02	361.30	389.08
汕 尾	Shanwei	4.16	7.09	26.23	41.09	48.15	49.23	28.83	30.78	36.77
东 莞	Dongguan	30.22	103.97	277.84	356.32	409.29	455.21	517.97	544.75	592.07
中 山	Zhongshan	17.46	54.26	139.38	201.89	225.42	251.74	287.51	295.04	312.76
江 门	Jiangmen	21.24	41.63	104.29	135.03	158.03	177.20	199.01	204.17	222.37
阳 江	Yangjiang	3.89	8.70	26.77	43.12	53.72	62.97	67.93	57.99	60.65
湛 江	Zhanjiang	12.44	24.01	66.23	92.09	105.92	114.42	121.86	112.94	135.00
茂 名	Maoming	9.08	21.26	51.95	78.12	90.36	100.37	113.92	121.43	130.14
肇 庆	Zhaoqing	10.97	20.44	76.80	103.81	120.77	139.13	143.36	91.70	94.85
清 远	Qingyuan	4.53	13.25	72.79	86.87	92.82	102.65	108.38	95.64	103.07
潮 州	Chaozhou	4.60	8.64	23.25	31.93	37.09	41.26	47.20	44.40	44.60
揭 阳	Jieyang	9.24	11.19	38.65	56.70	66.69	73.69	77.40	73.64	72.81
云 浮	Yunfu	3.65	9.33	23.54	36.76	45.76	52.87	58.70	57.42	57.49
按经济区域分	By Region									
珠 三 角	Pearl River Delta	599.06	1218.48	3139.58	4129.09	4669.16	5375.37	6391.70	6923.98	7455.96
东 翼	Eastern Region	36.94	56.38	160.78	226.07	264.04	288.15	284.69	285.92	304.25
西 翼	Western Region	25.41	53.96	144.95	213.33	250.00	277.76	303.71	292.35	325.79
山 区	Mountainous Region	26.54	66.21	208.18	279.02	328.52	383.27	423.38	412.47	429.01

8-3 续表 continued

单位：亿元 (100 million yuan)

市别	City	地方一般公共预算支出 Local Government General Budgetary Expenditure 2000	2005	2010	2012	2013	2014	2015	2016	2017
全省合计	**Provincial Total**	**1069.86**	**2289.07**	**5421.54**	**7387.86**	**8411.00**	**9152.64**	**12827.80**	**13446.09**	**15037.48**
广　州	Guangzhou	240.72	438.41	977.32	1343.65	1386.13	1436.22	1727.72	1943.75	2186.01
深　圳	Shenzhen	225.04	599.16	1266.07	1569.01	1690.83	2166.18	3521.67	4211.04	4593.80
珠　海	Zhuhai	31.14	57.77	166.41	212.20	252.03	275.90	388.77	417.16	493.89
汕　头	Shantou	27.90	50.14	121.71	172.93	191.26	213.72	280.98	295.74	331.63
佛　山	Foshan	72.48	150.85	363.35	433.96	488.40	525.01	799.93	695.85	774.96
韶　关	Shaoguan	19.94	44.55	100.24	148.04	168.32	197.18	287.07	266.95	310.75
河　源	Heyuan	16.78	37.00	94.55	134.47	169.72	210.61	268.38	293.95	282.16
梅　州	Meizhou	23.84	46.25	117.98	175.53	206.30	270.02	376.37	384.02	395.17
惠　州	Huizhou	20.14	52.41	185.44	274.08	328.29	372.97	486.07	509.08	554.01
汕　尾	Shanwei	9.99	20.05	56.51	87.99	105.31	124.85	212.95	206.88	222.60
东　莞	Dongguan	33.61	117.04	289.83	385.58	444.66	457.68	581.24	599.29	667.65
中　山	Zhongshan	19.24	56.71	145.85	215.32	237.24	261.46	355.37	367.57	455.22
江　门	Jiangmen	28.18	54.24	132.98	188.12	212.61	236.10	292.90	293.21	333.26
阳　江	Yangjiang	11.00	23.17	64.92	102.90	114.30	123.60	170.91	194.31	193.15
湛　江	Zhanjiang	27.82	57.95	153.65	218.24	265.44	279.53	412.36	381.11	442.70
茂　名	Maoming	20.67	45.28	122.49	192.27	218.59	263.24	346.78	354.57	381.41
肇　庆	Zhaoqing	20.09	40.64	127.66	176.49	200.40	241.71	267.71	248.16	271.15
清　远	Qingyuan	16.35	38.15	132.81	172.01	185.65	213.99	292.59	303.77	304.63
潮　州	Chaozhou	11.31	21.36	55.99	77.81	86.22	106.12	147.67	146.67	142.78
揭　阳	Jieyang	19.50	30.99	94.68	149.48	163.75	187.41	276.88	266.94	284.70
云　浮	Yunfu	11.18	23.87	69.28	95.15	109.08	133.14	157.42	168.50	181.49
按经济区域分	By Region									
珠三角	Pearl River Delta	690.64	1567.23	3654.91	4798.40	5240.59	5973.23	8421.36	9285.10	10329.95
东　翼	Eastern Region	68.70	122.50	328.89	488.21	546.54	632.11	918.47	916.24	981.71
西　翼	Western Region	59.49	126.40	341.06	513.42	598.33	666.37	930.04	929.99	1017.27
山　区	Mountainous Region	88.09	189.83	514.86	725.20	839.08	1024.94	1381.84	1417.18	1474.19

8-4 各市人均地方一般公共预算收入

Per Capita Local Government General Public Budget Revenue by City

单位：元 (yuan)

市 别	City	2000	2005	2010	2012	2013	2014	2015	2016	2017
全 省	**Provincial Total**	**1087.68**	**1974.59**	**4390.34**	**5904.72**	**6668.67**	**7548.74**	**8683.80**	**9511.49**	**10213.24**
广 州	Guangzhou	2061.72	3875.93	7100.70	8615.73	8862.98	9559.65	10153.45	10119.18	10768.28
深 圳	Shenzhen	3327.64	5064.37	10892.78	14105.11	16350.94	19457.70	24613.26	26937.59	27271.52
珠 海	Zhuhai	2024.57	3492.54	8025.47	10323.14	12241.05	13999.46	16621.83	17668.96	18273.96
汕 头	Shantou	409.83	596.51	1368.64	1773.45	2051.88	2253.51	2370.24	2463.21	2682.86
佛 山	Foshan	1146.57	2265.69	4349.20	5300.29	6020.44	6843.94	7544.00	8117.75	8751.43
韶 关	Shaoguan	314.70	686.57	1683.27	2150.02	2491.77	2827.09	2918.61	2889.10	2989.14
河 源	Heyuan	111.86	311.21	860.81	1256.37	1613.41	1982.27	2199.23	2238.80	2306.84
梅 州	Meizhou	188.06	370.01	924.97	1314.38	1613.10	1976.18	2391.27	2424.02	2485.40
惠 州	Huizhou	408.85	946.27	2931.87	4316.39	5337.57	6380.78	7171.79	7582.07	8146.65
汕 尾	Shanwei	170.37	255.84	893.66	1387.30	1617.23	1642.84	956.42	1016.07	1222.88
东 莞	Dongguan	503.97	1585.20	3454.53	4306.79	4928.56	5464.83	6241.63	6596.89	7131.68
中 山	Zhongshan	762.08	2231.98	4578.83	6411.82	7123.35	7908.30	8981.32	9163.25	9638.12
江 门	Jiangmen	540.87	1014.97	2365.62	3018.13	3519.54	3933.88	4407.32	4505.42	4884.25
阳 江	Yangjiang	179.12	375.62	1116.06	1754.75	2170.56	2529.40	2711.43	2301.22	2391.86
湛 江	Zhanjiang	207.35	361.18	950.34	1298.97	1483.88	1591.39	1686.16	1556.21	1852.05
茂 名	Maoming	173.63	366.48	887.70	1318.51	1508.45	1664.37	1878.43	1989.94	2111.44
肇 庆	Zhaoqing	325.95	558.68	1979.41	2616.91	3017.68	3453.32	3541.77	2251.91	2313.52
清 远	Qingyuan	143.50	372.24	1972.39	2315.36	2456.43	2697.59	2832.14	2490.43	2675.10
潮 州	Chaozhou	192.52	343.30	877.50	1186.31	1370.58	1519.18	1760.93	1679.83	1683.88
揭 阳	Jieyang	178.24	200.52	660.97	955.16	1116.16	1225.06	1280.02	1211.95	1195.61
云 浮	Yunfu	169.61	400.53	1002.33	1533.09	1889.12	2169.95	2393.45	2324.19	2306.00
按经济区域分	By Region									
珠 三 角	Pearl River Delta	1442.48	2688.72	5717.85	7284.81	8188.04	9365.92	10984.52	11663.63	12274.17
东 翼	Eastern Region	252.38	356.63	960.44	1327.14	1541.01	1672.48	1647.57	1651.32	1754.71
西 翼	Western Region	189.61	365.50	952.37	1377.88	1601.12	1768.05	1922.57	1841.10	2037.66
山 区	Mountainous Region	187.58	423.54	1300.73	1712.03	2001.04	2321.72	2550.51	2472.43	2558.61

注：本表按年中常住人口数计算。
Note: The data in this table are calculated by permanent population of the year.

8-5 各市财政收支（2017年）

单位：亿元

项　目	Item	全　省 Provincial Total	广　州 Guangzhou
一、地方一般公共预算收入	**General Public Budget Revenue of Local Governments**	**11320.35**	**1536.74**
税收收入	Tax Revenue	8871.89	1197.49
#增值税	Value-added Tax	3675.43	411.08
企业所得税	Corporate Income Tax	1767.83	191.00
个人所得税	Individual Income Tax	755.91	91.21
城市维护建设税	City Maintenance and Construction Tax	534.97	135.58
房产税	House Property Tax	299.46	89.59
土地增值税	Land Appriciation Tax	839.11	74.98
耕地占用税	Farm Land Occupation Tax	66.26	6.51
契税	Deed Tax	578.75	137.91
非税收入	Non-tax Revenue	2448.46	339.25
专项收入	Special Program Receipts	873.93	138.65
行政性收费收入	Charge of Administrative and Units	285.37	18.67
罚没收入	Penalty Receipts	224.67	24.73
国有资本经营收入	Operation Income from State-owned Assets	39.16	0.01
国有资源(资产)有偿使用收入	Income from Use of State-owned Resources Assets	554.39	56.45
其他收入	Other Non-tax Revenue	470.94	100.73
二、地方一般公共预算支出	**General Public Budget Expenditure of Local Governments**	**15037.48**	**2186.01**
#一般公共服务	Expenditure for General Public Services	1355.60	208.24
教育	Expenditure for Education	2575.52	404.33
科学技术	Expenditure for Science and Technology	823.89	171.26
文化体育与传媒	Expenditure for Culture, Sports and Media	285.87	41.20
社会保障和就业	Expenditure for Social Safety Net and Employment Effort	1423.33	236.50
医疗卫生与计划生育	Expenditure for Medical and Health Care,Family Planning	1307.56	202.35
节能环保	Expenditure for Energy Conservation and Environment Protection	433.23	26.53
城乡社区	Expenditure for Urban and Rural Community Affairs	2180.53	390.09
农林水	Expenditure for Agriculture, Forestry and Water Conservancy	754.40	73.89
交通运输	Expenditure for Transportation	848.40	68.77

Basic Conditions of Local Government General Public Budget Revenue and Expenditure by City(2017)

(100 million yuan)

深 圳 Shenzhen	珠 海 Zhuhai	汕 头 Shantou	佛 山 Foshan	韶 关 Shaoguan	河 源 Heyuan	梅 州 Meizhou	惠 州 Huizhou	汕 尾 Shanwei
3332.13	**314.38**	**150.07**	**661.58**	**88.71**	**71.19**	**108.55**	**389.08**	**36.77**
2654.89	239.06	92.67	467.63	54.10	46.75	73.56	243.37	23.23
991.28	83.35	31.97	152.16	18.75	13.20	18.96	88.00	7.80
667.85	47.42	12.28	58.83	3.30	3.28	5.61	32.13	2.39
334.33	16.05	3.64	22.19	2.06	1.36	2.43	9.79	0.77
138.56	23.41	9.72	46.49	6.81	3.56	7.11	24.06	2.04
60.94	13.85	5.84	30.89	3.09	1.99	3.80	12.31	1.02
259.32	15.28	7.08	32.89	2.63	2.91	6.06	21.79	1.91
	0.99	0.45	6.11	6.47	7.49	7.80	5.16	1.72
130.81	26.75	12.82	79.11	4.59	6.47	9.23	29.48	3.62
677.24	75.32	57.40	193.95	34.61	24.44	35.00	145.71	13.54
372.13	26.64	7.83	38.17	5.39	2.89	8.97	23.04	4.76
26.79	6.60	7.87	17.89	4.05	5.92	6.69	13.79	2.67
33.92	11.82	9.70	15.83	2.15	2.75	1.82	15.18	1.62
0.38		3.56	0.19	0.82	1.70	1.45	4.11	-0.02
155.19	12.86	7.37	53.88	17.06	4.25	13.45	17.50	1.56
88.83	17.41	21.07	67.99	5.15	6.94	2.61	72.10	2.94
4593.80	**493.89**	**331.63**	**774.96**	**310.75**	**282.16**	**395.17**	**554.01**	**222.60**
283.63	48.88	39.72	114.09	35.72	38.40	60.70	62.71	22.03
509.10	74.22	78.91	140.25	51.18	58.22	78.75	106.86	40.84
351.83	45.30	4.92	46.26	5.98	4.25	6.19	25.85	4.57
57.12	7.70	9.20	21.73	5.60	4.07	6.77	12.27	5.42
239.72	57.59	40.69	79.78	38.28	44.90	68.67	55.80	29.35
244.23	27.81	48.50	85.70	33.17	37.62	52.13	96.21	28.04
213.04	17.26	10.25	19.04	12.72	8.08	10.72	20.84	3.77
982.96	104.77	35.51	84.39	35.10	30.89	40.92	56.48	41.25
76.33	17.66	18.36	24.69	41.44	23.36	25.72	34.49	19.41
318.27	10.01	5.06	19.32	10.35	6.89	10.98	8.98	3.55

8-5 续表

单位：亿元

项 目	Item	东 莞 Dongguan	中 山 Zhongshan
一、地方一般公共预算收入	**General Public Budget Revenue of Local Governments**	**592.07**	**312.76**
税收收入	Tax Revenue	478.92	220.87
#增值税	Value-added Tax	204.79	82.40
企业所得税	Corporate Income Tax	62.19	26.72
个人所得税	Individual Income Tax	26.89	10.02
城市维护建设税	City Maintenance and Construction Tax	52.85	19.39
房产税	House Property Tax	28.03	19.09
土地增值税	Land Appriciation Tax	25.79	17.72
耕地占用税	Farm Land Occupation Tax	3.50	1.38
契税	Deed Tax	33.36	28.14
非税收入	Non-tax Revenue	113.15	91.89
专项收入	Special Program Receipts	48.64	17.84
行政性收费收入	Charge of Administrative and Units	37.72	13.76
罚没收入	Penalty Receipts	11.36	5.19
国有资本经营收入	Operation Income from State-owned Assets	0.63	
国有资源(资产)有偿使用收入	Income from Use of State-owned Resources Assets	6.94	44.55
其他收入	Other Non-tax Revenue	7.87	10.55
二、地方一般公共预算支出	**General Public Budget Expenditure of Local Governments**	**667.65**	**455.22**
#一般公共服务	Expenditure for General Public Services	64.41	23.22
教育	Expenditure for Education	147.58	66.54
科学技术	Expenditure for Science and Technology	33.96	47.60
文化体育与传媒	Expenditure for Culture, Sports and Media	21.68	9.04
社会保障和就业	Expenditure for Social Safety Net and Employment Effort	44.44	25.47
医疗卫生与计划生育	Expenditure for Medical and Health Care,Family Planning	45.64	23.89
节能环保	Expenditure for Energy Conservation and Environment Protection	27.18	15.44
城乡社区	Expenditure for Urban and Rural Community Affairs	77.63	89.88
农林水	Expenditure for Agriculture, Forestry and Water Conservancy	37.93	21.57
交通运输	Expenditure for Transportation	35.68	65.11

continued

(100 million yuan)

江门 Jiangmen	阳江 Yangjiang	湛江 Zhanjiang	茂名 Maoming	肇庆 Zhaoqing	清远 Qingyuan	潮州 Chaozhou	揭阳 Jieyang	云浮 Yunfu
222.37	**60.65**	**135.00**	**130.14**	**94.85**	**103.07**	**44.60**	**72.81**	**57.49**
156.12	38.23	75.47	80.95	68.40	71.39	30.18	46.59	34.15
55.16	12.20	29.36	28.29	23.11	24.41	10.87	19.93	9.27
17.58	3.86	6.32	4.44	6.39	8.26	2.77	4.70	2.52
5.86	1.34	3.25	1.89	2.67	2.89	1.32	1.56	3.58
15.63	3.65	9.57	11.49	6.37	6.68	3.12	6.19	2.57
10.20	2.18	3.12	2.20	2.78	2.78	2.06	1.88	1.80
13.46	4.50	6.57	12.91	8.21	7.46	1.89	2.86	3.00
1.60	2.16	1.53	3.43	2.37	1.61	1.59	0.64	3.73
20.20	3.57	9.55	10.38	10.45	12.07	2.10	3.65	4.47
66.25	22.42	59.53	49.19	26.46	31.68	14.42	26.22	23.34
14.00	3.58	8.67	8.91	5.31	5.54	2.50	5.21	2.11
9.99	6.51	6.57	13.01	5.22	7.38	3.87	6.65	4.50
6.57	4.42	34.55	5.48	3.60	3.97	2.83	3.53	1.10
13.07	0.43	0.76		1.21	0.08	0.41	2.38	2.36
16.04	5.09	4.86	19.37	9.60	4.82	1.83	3.79	6.27
6.58	2.39	4.12	2.43	1.52	9.89	2.98	4.66	7.01
333.26	**193.15**	**442.70**	**381.41**	**271.15**	**304.63**	**142.78**	**284.70**	**181.49**
39.34	18.57	34.80	32.65	32.48	35.25	13.27	27.58	25.35
73.25	33.46	96.89	116.16	58.46	68.47	35.65	66.36	37.36
11.02	1.92	3.85	1.69	5.86	4.00	1.44	1.90	3.59
7.62	3.56	6.52	9.71	6.32	6.47	3.97	6.91	3.32
53.03	25.22	69.64	65.64	34.70	37.86	19.65	42.70	25.75
37.32	27.00	62.42	49.43	37.44	38.14	21.62	43.86	27.09
4.76	1.77	6.06	10.68	3.25	4.44	2.48	7.52	2.12
21.90	14.75	17.40	17.93	14.66	26.92	13.36	16.97	7.69
20.15	23.26	54.13	28.96	23.82	36.57	11.45	28.60	16.77
9.70	17.33	20.35	9.46	11.36	9.78	2.53	12.20	7.04

8-6 历年金融机构存贷款

Deposits and Loans in All Financial Institutions

单位：亿元 (100million yuan)

年 份 Year	金融机构本外币存款余额 Deposits in Renminbi and Foreign Currencies in All Financial Institutions	#住户存款 Savings Deposit by Household	金融机构本外币贷款余额 Loans and Loans in Renminbi and Foreign Currencies in Financial Institutions	金融机构人民币存款余额 Deposits in Renminbi Currencies in Financial Institutions	#人民币住户存款 Savings Deposit by Household in Renminbi	金融机构人民币贷款余额 Loans in Renminbi Currencies in Financial Institutions
2000	19083.64	10031.68	13227.62	16919.98	8667.29	11787.14
2001	21714.85	11386.03	14472.08	19449.34	9930.12	13192.74
2002	25409.90	13372.85	16840.39	22975.88	11819.09	15314.56
2003	29640.83	15590.68	20126.24	27240.23	14061.77	18287.58
2004	33252.01	17631.07	21955.28	30869.62	16193.41	19671.52
2005	38119.91	20267.76	23261.21	35958.71	19051.35	20965.55
2006	43262.20	22677.19	25935.19	41146.58	21584.60	23617.49
2007	48955.03	23013.34	30617.27	47016.48	22242.70	27497.88
2008	56119.28	28181.18	33755.62	54309.57	27481.56	30964.62
2009	69691.46	32136.32	44510.22	67742.59	31411.40	39683.65
2010	82019.40	36965.75	51799.30	79957.97	36318.66	47191.56
2011	91590.15	41061.56	58615.27	89168.60	40405.07	53411.83
2012	105099.55	46265.58	67077.08	99934.60	45533.78	59967.26
2013	119685.15	50638.64	75664.16	114855.02	49891.35	68491.93
2014	127881.47	53215.87	84921.79	121964.85	52410.55	77889.50
2015	160388.22	55008.70	95661.12	153551.79	54238.30	89289.27
2016	179829.19	59768.75	110928.41	171024.47	58618.89	103649.79
2017	194535.75	62942.27	126031.95	184779.60	61890.08	118978.62

注：2015年前，住户存款主要为居民储蓄存款。
Note：Before 2015, the savings by households are mainly savings by residents.

8-7 金融机构本外币存贷款余额

Deposits and Loans in Renminbi and Foreign Currencies in All Financial Institutions

单位：亿元 (100million yuan)

指　　标	Item	2015	2016	2017	2017年比2016年增长(%) Growth Rate in 2017 over 2016(%)
一、各项存款	**Total Deposits**	**160388.22**	**179829.19**	**194535.75**	**8.2**
境内存款	Domestic Deposits	154559.04	174900.22	187721.95	7.3
住户存款	Deposits of Households	55008.70	59768.75	62942.27	5.3
活期存款	Demand Deposits	27350.11	31395.88	33950.96	8.1
定期及其他存款	Time & Other Deposits	27658.59	28372.87	28991.31	2.2
非金融企业存款	Deposits of Non-financial Enterprises	49345.26	63509.89	71315.62	12.3
活期存款	Demand Deposits	17169.43	22875.34	25251.72	10.4
定期及其他存款	Time & Other Deposits	32175.83	40634.55	46063.90	13.4
政府存款	Deposits of Government	26090.27	28293.70	32430.62	14.6
财政性存款	Fiscal Deposits	5635.35	5404.62	4626.73	-14.4
机关团体存款	Deposits of Government Departments &	20454.91	22889.08	27803.90	21.5
非银行业金融机构存款	Deposits of Non-banking Financial Institutions	24114.81	23327.88	21033.43	-9.8
境外存款	Overseas Deposits	5829.18	4928.98	6813.80	38.2
二、各项贷款	**Total Loans**	**95661.12**	**110928.41**	**126031.95**	**13.6**
境内贷款	Domestic Loans	93116.97	107818.07	122769.23	13.9
住户贷款	Loans to Households	33099.57	43801.57	53139.31	21.3
#短期贷款	Short-term Loans	7465.07	8165.21	10312.82	26.3
中长期贷款	Mid & Long-term Loans	25634.50	35636.36	42826.49	20.2
非金融企业及机关团体贷款	Loans to Non-financial Enterprises and Government Departments & Organizations	59872.35	63949.10	69520.06	8.7
#短期贷款	Short-term Loans	22474.01	24180.42	25521.01	5.5
中长期贷款	Mid & Long-term Loans	32407.28	33521.74	39150.23	16.8
非银行业金融机构贷款	Loans to Non-banking Financial Institutions	145.04	67.40	109.87	63.0
境外贷款	Overseas Loans	2544.16	3110.33	3262.71	4.9

注：2015年起银行资金来源项目使用新的分类。
Note: Since 2015, new categorization is applied to items of bank fund sources.

8-8 金融机构人民币存贷款余额

Deposits and Loans in Renminbi in All Financial Institutions

单位：亿元 (100 million yuan)

指 标	Item	2015	2016	2017	2017年比2016年增长(%) Growth Rate in 2017 over 2016(%)
一、各项存款	**Total Deposits**	**153551.79**	**171024.47**	**184779.60**	**8.0**
境内存款	Domestic Deposits	148231.81	167124.75	180004.67	7.7
住户存款	Deposits of Households	54238.30	58618.89	61890.08	5.6
活期存款	Demand Deposits	26874.25	30643.03	33293.12	8.7
定期及其他存款	Time & Other Deposits	27364.05	27975.86	28596.96	2.2
非金融企业存款	Deposits of Non-financial Enterprises	43998.61	57079.01	64873.97	13.7
活期存款	Demand Deposits	16138.81	21399.49	23453.99	9.6
定期及其他存款	Time & Other Deposits	27859.80	35679.52	41419.98	16.1
政府存款	Deposits of Government	26079.31	28274.38	32419.36	14.7
财政性存款	Fiscal Deposits	5635.35	5404.62	4626.73	-14.4
机关团体存款	Deposits of Government Departments & Organizations	20443.95	22869.76	27792.64	21.5
非银行业金融机构存款	Deposits of Non-banking Financial Institutions	23915.59	23152.48	20821.26	-10.1
境外存款	Overseas Deposits	5319.98	3899.72	4774.94	22.4
二、各项贷款	**Total Loans**	**89289.27**	**103649.79**	**118978.62**	**14.8**
境内贷款	Domestic Loans	88609.07	102802.86	118098.15	14.9
住户贷款	Loans to Households	33093.02	43795.17	53133.53	21.3
#短期贷款	Short-term Loans	7461.11	8161.06	10308.87	26.3
中长期贷款	Mid & Long-term Loans	25631.92	35634.11	42824.65	20.2
非金融企业及机关团体贷款	Loans to Non-financial Enterprises and Government Departments & Organizations	55371.12	58940.30	64854.76	10.0
#短期贷款	Short-term Loans	19387.33	20355.22	21824.76	7.2
中长期贷款	Mid & Long-term Loans	31131.24	32538.45	38338.34	17.8
非银行业金融机构贷款	Loans to Non-banking Financial Institutions	144.93	67.40	109.87	63.0
境外贷款	Overseas Loans	680.20	846.92	880.46	4.0

注：2015年起银行资金来源项目使用新的分类。
Note: Since 2015, new categorization is applied to items of bank fund sources.

8-9 各市中资金融机构基本情况

Basic Conditions of Chinese-funded Financial Institutions by City

市别	City	2005				2010			
		机构数(个) Number of Financial Institutions	年末从业人员(人) Number of Employed Persons at the Year-end	人民币存款(亿元) Total Deposits (100 million yuan)	人民币贷款(亿元) Total Loans (100 million yuan)	机构数(个) Number of Financial Institutions	年末从业人员(人) Number of Employed Persons at the Year-end	人民币存款(亿元) Total Deposits (100 million yuan)	人民币贷款(亿元) Total Loans (100 million yuan)
全省合计	**Provincial Total**	**15433**	**222738**	**35783.57**	**20745.27**	**14983**	**258254**	**78285.89**	**46099.26**
广　州	Guangzhou	2053	45800	11065.22	6873.34	2395	58412	22775.49	14597.74
深　圳	Shenzhen	1119	28354	8478.18	6168.03	1286	41483	20210.75	13708.16
珠　海	Zhuhai	417	6798	925.47	424.33	406	7664	2542.56	1203.85
汕　头	Shantou	655	9196	955.34	391.08	632	9476	1849.14	627.91
佛　山	Foshan	1913	21732	3770.74	2056.29	1775	25815	8293.02	4729.61
韶　关	Shaoguan	406	5153	461.78	166.55	401	5317	903.67	346.28
河　源	Heyuan	349	3759	204.20	107.99	325	3828	496.83	335.32
梅　州	Meizhou	635	7373	429.79	206.37	529	6371	835.07	330.25
惠　州	Huizhou	664	8012	781.79	367.23	650	9065	2038.58	1096.21
汕　尾	Shanwei	246	2937	140.77	57.21	217	2965	326.96	130.20
东　莞	Dongguan	1262	14985	2933.40	1500.52	1221	19395	5915.54	3302.49
中　山	Zhongshan	586	7837	1131.19	479.02	568	9017	2596.88	1324.65
江　门	Jiangmen	906	11627	1163.76	534.17	819	11194	2214.97	973.75
阳　江	Yangjiang	289	3986	245.37	99.66	268	3806	564.19	283.93
湛　江	Zhanjiang	931	10663	705.32	285.97	780	10321	1556.00	714.40
茂　名	Maoming	717	7915	521.02	225.46	612	7670	1025.39	361.30
肇　庆	Zhaoqing	551	7120	478.15	229.43	494	6874	1057.35	642.04
清　远	Qingyuan	471	5510	386.23	175.08	447	5620	986.45	510.26
潮　州	Chaozhou	304	4087	324.04	132.34	275	4187	649.81	205.91
揭　阳	Jieyang	613	6120	468.15	169.19	586	6178	963.79	400.68
云　浮	Yunfu	346	3774	213.66	96.02	297	3596	483.45	274.32
按经济区域分	By Region								
珠三角	Pearl River Delta	9642	159817	35103.66	20939.71	9614	188919	67645.13	41578.51
东　翼	Eastern Region	1762	22454	2147.42	788.51	1710	22806	3789.69	1364.70
西　翼	Western Region	1846	22857	1692.94	643.84	1660	21797	3145.59	1359.62
山　区	Mountainous Region	2156	25791	1958.72	810.10	1999	24732	3705.47	1796.43

8-9 续表 continued

市别	City	2016 机构数(个) Number of Financial Institutions	2016 年末从业人员(人) Number of Employed Persons at the Year-end	2016 人民币存款(亿元) Total Deposits (100 million yuan)	2016 人民币贷款(亿元) Total Loans (100 million yuan)	2017 机构数(个) Number of Financial Institutions	2017 年末从业人员(人) Number of Employed Persons at the Year-end	2017 人民币存款(亿元) Total Deposits (100 million yuan)	2017 人民币贷款(亿元) Total Loans (100 million yuan)
全省合计	**Provincial Total**	**16614**	**335143**	**171024.47**	**103649.79**	**16625**	**336902**	**181735.86**	**116807.03**
广州	Guangzhou	2715	87823	45937.34	28885.54	2719	89467	48290.54	32571.07
深圳	Shenzhen	1721	55739	59562.25	35165.46	1738	56733	62760.40	39940.61
珠海	Zhuhai	492	10873	5689.08	3915.61	497	10800	6442.63	4647.11
汕头	Shantou	659	11114	3076.06	1296.09	663	11172	3264.17	1518.83
佛山	Foshan	1877	32082	12789.61	8515.62	1859	31571	13561.79	9075.11
韶关	Shaoguan	418	5691	1660.40	766.59	415	5645	1743.53	859.68
河源	Heyuan	344	4571	1130.56	886.16	343	4577	1234.91	1016.10
梅州	Meizhou	575	7041	1813.05	829.33	578	7020	2008.59	982.52
惠州	Huizhou	735	12226	4544.73	3155.13	744	12190	5061.92	3798.57
汕尾	Shanwei	219	3219	739.71	350.17	217	3173	830.36	402.72
东莞	Dongguan	1375	24325	11198.43	6402.48	1377	24437	11767.06	6800.57
中山	Zhongshan	641	11684	4690.48	3238.03	636	11576	5093.24	3535.53
江门	Jiangmen	890	13116	3870.06	2367.06	892	13015	4118.06	2720.49
阳江	Yangjiang	277	4484	1122.34	825.60	277	4434	1226.74	930.88
湛江	Zhanjiang	809	12029	2834.50	1629.28	806	12139	3041.58	1858.12
茂名	Maoming	617	8281	2211.41	1005.62	616	8278	2444.04	1135.32
肇庆	Zhaoqing	549	8326	2023.09	1283.18	544	8197	2233.80	1493.79
清远	Qingyuan	473	6723	1906.06	1137.06	473	6695	2144.96	1351.60
潮州	Chaozhou	291	4482	1194.15	365.63	292	4483	1256.65	397.93
揭阳	Jieyang	623	7350	2009.05	980.65	626	7375	2094.07	1044.54
云浮	Yunfu	314	3964	1022.14	649.53	313	3925	1116.79	725.94
按经济区域分	By Region								
珠三角	Pearl River Delta	10995	256194	150305.06	92928.09	11006	257986	159329.45	104582.86
东翼	Eastern Region	1792	26165	7018.97	2992.54	1798	26203	7445.26	3364.03
西翼	Western Region	1703	24794	6168.25	3460.49	1699	24851	6712.37	3924.31
山区	Mountainous Region	2124	27990	7532.20	4268.67	2122	27862	8248.79	4935.84

注：1．本表存贷款统计口径为中资金融机构人民币存贷款。
2．机构数和年末从业人员统计范围为银行业及相关金融机构(不含人民银行、外资银行及资产管理公司)。

Notes: a) Deposits and loans in this table refer to the deposits and loans in Renminbi in domestic-funded financial institutions.
b) The number of financial institutions and the number of employed persons at the year-end refer to those in banking and related financial institutions (excluding the People's Bank of China, foreign-funded banks and assets management companies).

8-10 各市金融机构本外币存贷款

Deposits and Loans in Renminbi and Foreign Currencies in All Financial Institutions by City

单位：亿元 (100 million yuan)

市 别	City	各项存款 Total Deposits								
		2000	2005	2010	2012	2013	2014	2015	2016	2017
全省合计	**Provincial Total**	**19083.64**	**38119.91**	**82019.40**	**105099.55**	**119685.15**	**127881.47**	**160388.22**	**179829.19**	**194535.75**
广 州	Guangzhou	6200.47	11734.10	23953.96	30186.57	33838.20	35469.29	42843.67	47530.20	51369.03
深 圳	Shenzhen	3942.00	9486.76	21937.89	29662.40	33943.15	37350.50	57778.90	64407.81	69668.31
珠 海	Zhuhai	521.71	1014.08	2748.70	3449.70	4121.58	4570.67	5383.73	6124.26	6928.74
汕 头	Shantou	600.21	995.64	1873.03	2285.36	2530.16	2664.46	2857.20	3125.20	3341.60
佛 山	Foshan	2119.08	3906.93	8462.33	10167.55	11387.13	11275.63	11867.67	13281.61	14042.40
韶 关	Shaoguan	263.73	468.35	907.75	1117.81	1255.76	1394.20	1532.91	1669.70	1754.98
河 源	Heyuan	91.12	205.94	500.02	638.58	754.24	875.92	988.90	1139.26	1248.00
梅 州	Meizhou	219.47	438.71	839.63	1063.83	1245.21	1411.88	1565.28	1819.19	2014.78
惠 州	Huizhou	394.44	823.96	2090.14	2696.97	3138.79	3394.60	3836.10	4974.48	5485.55
汕 尾	Shanwei	78.19	144.45	332.70	422.71	487.35	545.74	631.03	744.28	836.84
东 莞	Dongguan	1327.79	3036.77	6077.87	7691.24	8874.91	9323.28	9968.80	11545.10	12497.97
中 山	Zhongshan	619.44	1186.76	2665.35	3469.71	4021.81	4149.69	4378.36	5031.00	5413.77
江 门	Jiangmen	805.18	1279.67	2285.75	2905.50	3335.27	3587.64	3766.81	4030.37	4271.88
阳 江	Yangjiang	142.73	248.75	575.32	729.35	816.84	910.89	1014.74	1127.45	1230.77
湛 江	Zhanjiang	408.90	716.97	1565.19	1902.35	2173.39	2430.26	2684.61	2847.29	3061.15
茂 名	Maoming	332.55	524.90	1028.67	1332.42	1571.63	1772.22	1974.75	2216.93	2452.39
肇 庆	Zhaoqing	281.64	493.23	1072.54	1355.59	1594.43	1679.26	1785.01	2041.58	2259.76
清 远	Qingyuan	213.85	393.96	995.36	1215.34	1401.35	1534.81	1699.82	1926.13	2162.89
潮 州	Chaozhou	162.70	328.97	653.27	836.51	919.35	1004.29	1076.19	1203.57	1267.02
揭 阳	Jieyang	240.07	473.60	967.03	1311.12	1529.69	1709.93	1837.87	2017.26	2107.05
云 浮	Yunfu	118.37	217.40	486.93	658.93	744.90	826.30	915.88	1026.53	1120.86
按经济区域分	By Region									
珠 三 角	Pearl River Delta	16211.75	32962.25	71294.51	91585.24	104255.28	110800.56	141609.04	158966.41	171937.41
东 翼	Eastern Region	1081.18	1942.66	3826.04	4855.70	5466.56	5924.42	6402.29	7090.31	7552.51
西 翼	Western Region	884.18	1490.63	3169.17	3964.12	4561.87	5113.37	5674.10	6191.67	6744.31
山 区	Mountainous Region	906.54	1724.37	3729.68	4694.49	5401.45	6043.11	6702.78	7580.80	8301.52

8-10 续表 continued

单位：亿元 (100 million yuan)

市 别	City	各项贷款 Total Loans 2000	2005	2010	2012	2013	2014	2015	2016	2017
全省合计	**Provincial Total**	**13227.62**	**23261.21**	**51799.30**	**67077.08**	**75664.16**	**84921.79**	**95661.12**	**110928.41**	**126031.95**
广 州	Guangzhou	4226.65	7622.20	16284.31	19936.52	22016.18	24231.71	27296.16	29669.82	34137.05
深 圳	Shenzhen	3032.13	7596.72	16808.12	21808.34	24680.07	27922.13	32449.04	40526.90	46329.33
珠 海	Zhuhai	349.20	486.72	1472.54	1920.30	2071.90	2426.24	2969.70	4098.08	4806.88
汕 头	Shantou	476.66	421.36	661.52	811.95	971.93	1072.83	1199.00	1303.90	1551.72
佛 山	Foshan	1581.90	2122.74	4868.99	6391.47	7111.31	7595.79	7950.53	8717.81	9376.97
韶 关	Shaoguan	149.23	169.68	376.06	497.90	581.38	671.16	731.84	772.51	876.77
河 源	Heyuan	62.19	108.13	338.69	472.89	573.18	699.01	801.08	888.08	1018.44
梅 州	Meizhou	147.02	206.44	331.10	454.04	547.53	635.46	736.41	830.18	984.54
惠 州	Huizhou	221.42	409.44	1225.71	1735.12	2036.92	2436.97	2701.60	3460.97	4012.86
汕 尾	Shanwei	68.74	57.21	131.12	190.83	228.54	269.61	306.14	352.70	407.80
东 莞	Dongguan	642.33	1540.48	3441.99	4446.82	4989.50	5562.36	5980.90	6545.66	6986.26
中 山	Zhongshan	382.09	498.05	1373.62	1969.07	2315.87	2644.90	2894.32	3367.09	3734.93
江 门	Jiangmen	574.26	565.45	1032.46	1467.17	1715.51	2024.51	2218.01	2469.83	2796.77
阳 江	Yangjiang	89.71	100.66	292.24	445.73	537.60	706.97	757.74	827.44	932.87
湛 江	Zhanjiang	294.70	310.03	721.00	1067.54	1227.29	1372.57	1568.76	1633.77	1869.22
茂 名	Maoming	211.96	230.93	362.40	540.64	642.08	759.50	858.33	1005.87	1146.37
肇 庆	Zhaoqing	217.44	232.13	652.01	893.63	1051.40	1172.51	1281.52	1293.43	1501.96
清 远	Qingyuan	150.82	179.13	520.62	725.87	853.65	953.48	1061.23	1152.08	1372.25
潮 州	Chaozhou	118.57	137.20	219.41	290.20	322.97	357.21	369.04	368.55	399.88
揭 阳	Jieyang	131.25	169.40	407.06	615.58	717.84	873.59	931.72	992.39	1057.63
云 浮	Yunfu	84.12	97.10	278.34	395.46	471.52	533.29	598.05	651.33	731.45
按经济区域分	By Region									
珠三角	Pearl River Delta	11227.42	21073.93	47159.74	60568.45	67988.65	76017.12	85741.78	100149.59	113683.01
东 翼	Eastern Region	795.23	785.17	1419.10	1908.56	2241.28	2573.24	2805.90	3017.55	3417.03
西 翼	Western Region	596.37	641.62	1375.65	2053.91	2406.96	2839.04	3184.82	3467.09	3948.46
山 区	Mountainous Region	593.39	760.49	1844.81	2546.16	3027.27	3492.40	3928.63	4294.18	4983.45

8-11 各市金融机构住户存款

Savings Deposit by Household in All Financial Institutions by City

单位：亿元 (100 million yuan)

市别	City	中外资金融机构本外币住户存款 Savings Deposit by Household in Renminbi and Foreign Currencies in All Financial Institutions								
		2000	2005	2010	2012	2013	2014	2015	2016	2017
全省合计	**Provincial Total**	**10031.68**	**20267.76**	**36965.75**	**46265.58**	**50638.64**	**53215.87**	**55008.70**	**59768.75**	**62942.27**
广州	Guangzhou	2683.38	5475.77	9302.33	11557.00	12496.69	12825.64	13602.38	14430.11	15032.29
深圳	Shenzhen	1391.78	3525.70	6918.19	8910.98	9690.28	10193.04	9680.24	10755.66	11159.78
珠海	Zhuhai	262.41	513.72	982.54	1234.72	1360.23	1423.01	1322.97	1457.49	1542.24
汕头	Shantou	401.88	765.26	1305.62	1549.33	1679.13	1764.78	1918.05	2093.10	2183.40
佛山	Foshan	1359.52	2465.51	4460.82	5215.16	5602.58	5806.94	6232.20	6736.22	7019.38
韶关	Shaoguan	172.46	320.00	562.11	701.41	787.84	859.52	925.18	1008.87	1086.75
河源	Heyuan	71.32	146.36	314.33	416.29	480.14	531.49	591.09	660.78	722.30
梅州	Meizhou	166.95	326.86	582.20	761.27	888.88	985.46	1061.20	1147.07	1249.65
惠州	Huizhou	276.61	548.27	1044.17	1362.56	1545.08	1651.81	1729.01	1961.99	2168.88
汕尾	Shanwei	58.89	111.83	231.32	298.38	340.35	376.34	388.93	431.35	471.84
东莞	Dongguan	753.78	1796.69	3425.89	4246.97	4517.59	4648.27	4630.69	4943.56	5160.71
中山	Zhongshan	409.23	764.69	1462.96	1771.65	1950.56	2057.33	2108.53	2309.44	2435.73
江门	Jiangmen	607.54	951.96	1516.72	1898.06	2073.97	2218.80	2270.52	2454.80	2597.46
阳江	Yangjiang	107.92	192.35	386.82	496.04	558.52	609.46	665.27	740.07	796.34
湛江	Zhanjiang	310.23	514.85	945.28	1251.64	1410.98	1520.22	1684.28	1818.28	1963.10
茂名	Maoming	251.70	413.71	752.61	986.18	1137.67	1273.71	1413.64	1532.81	1665.26
肇庆	Zhaoqing	197.68	347.39	657.31	862.12	981.92	1075.02	1160.94	1272.68	1388.91
清远	Qingyuan	152.70	279.69	593.11	744.74	840.57	927.07	1013.87	1127.16	1245.60
潮州	Chaozhou	111.07	246.32	461.35	588.53	647.49	698.39	748.54	814.54	844.81
揭阳	Jieyang	190.83	392.24	716.17	950.56	1128.99	1196.57	1251.86	1392.73	1469.54
云浮	Yunfu	93.82	168.58	343.92	462.00	519.18	573.00	609.30	680.04	738.30
按经济区域分	By Region									
珠三角	Pearl River Delta	7941.93	16389.71	29770.92	37059.20	40218.90	41899.85	42737.49	46321.96	48505.38
东翼	Eastern Region	762.66	1515.65	2714.46	3386.80	3795.95	4036.09	4307.37	4731.72	4969.59
西翼	Western Region	669.84	1120.91	2084.70	2733.86	3107.18	3403.39	3763.19	4091.16	4424.70
山区	Mountainous Region	657.25	1241.49	2395.67	3085.72	3516.61	3876.55	4200.64	4623.91	5042.60

8-11 续表 continued

单位：亿元 (100 million yuan)

市别	City	中资金融机构人民币住户存款 Savings Deposit by Household in Renminbi in Chinese-funded Financial Institutions								
		2000	2005	2010	2012	2013	2014	2015	2016	2017
全省合计	**Provincial Total**	**8667.29**	**19051.35**	**36219.15**	**44803.43**	**49287.89**	**51835.12**	**54114.45**	**58510.24**	**61756.26**
广　州	Guangzhou	2239.64	5024.69	9013.15	11174.68	12178.58	12498.70	13236.26	13939.71	14554.98
深　圳	Shenzhen	1082.43	3229.38	6717.05	8132.16	8926.10	9410.59	9429.42	10361.19	10807.45
珠　海	Zhuhai	216.08	480.87	957.58	1196.27	1331.14	1390.93	1296.96	1419.67	1506.42
汕　头	Shantou	351.40	733.50	1291.11	1528.12	1661.21	1747.76	1897.90	2066.71	2160.01
佛　山	Foshan	1216.98	2358.78	4406.34	5155.01	5548.32	5752.38	6170.92	6652.25	6938.22
韶　关	Shaoguan	165.47	313.97	559.16	698.58	784.91	856.57	921.64	1004.27	1082.60
河　源	Heyuan	69.96	145.12	313.64	415.52	479.29	530.65	590.09	659.52	721.19
梅　州	Meizhou	155.14	318.77	578.33	757.67	885.46	982.16	1057.84	1142.61	1245.59
惠　州	Huizhou	249.31	522.21	1031.63	1349.23	1533.01	1639.54	1717.05	1944.68	2151.03
汕　尾	Shanwei	54.18	108.39	229.73	296.29	337.14	373.32	385.72	428.34	468.68
东　莞	Dongguan	672.07	1728.28	3384.45	4187.68	4467.60	4598.76	4587.86	4878.75	5097.55
中　山	Zhongshan	354.65	725.06	1442.18	1747.90	1930.79	2036.77	2082.30	2277.27	2405.02
江　门	Jiangmen	483.75	851.93	1461.98	1852.48	2029.55	2173.73	2228.65	2400.89	2546.23
阳　江	Yangjiang	104.99	189.91	385.69	494.59	556.95	607.83	663.22	737.58	794.03
湛　江	Zhanjiang	298.14	505.70	940.08	1245.66	1404.49	1513.75	1675.56	1807.57	1952.70
茂　名	Maoming	247.45	410.02	750.67	984.03	1135.23	1271.20	1410.49	1528.48	1661.61
肇　庆	Zhaoqing	184.21	335.91	650.23	851.29	973.60	1066.31	1151.53	1263.09	1379.82
清　远	Qingyuan	146.27	273.86	590.26	741.99	837.35	924.16	1010.55	1122.96	1241.50
潮　州	Chaozhou	104.19	242.65	459.60	585.92	644.11	695.15	744.83	809.31	840.25
揭　阳	Jieyang	180.82	387.29	714.16	947.98	1125.55	1193.52	1247.84	1387.32	1464.85
云　浮	Yunfu	90.13	165.09	342.13	460.38	517.51	571.34	607.82	678.06	736.54
按经济区域分	By Region									
珠三角	Pearl River Delta	6699.12	15257.09	29064.60	35646.70	38918.70	40567.69	41900.94	45137.49	47386.71
东　翼	Eastern Region	690.59	1471.82	2694.60	3358.31	3768.00	4009.75	4276.29	4691.68	4933.78
西　翼	Western Region	650.58	1105.62	2076.44	2724.28	3096.67	3392.78	3749.27	4073.63	4408.34
山　区	Mountainous Region	626.97	1216.81	2383.51	3074.14	3504.52	3864.89	4187.95	4607.43	5027.42

8-12 财产保险公司主要指标
Main Indicators of Property Insurance Companies

单位：万元 (10000 yuan)

项目	Item	2014 保费收入 Premium Income	2014 赔款支出 Indemnity Expenditure	2015 保费收入 Premium Income	2015 赔款支出 Indemnity Expenditure
合计	**Total**	**8321449.51**	**4139816.65**	**9237353.31**	**4588892.60**
企业财产保险	Enterprise Property Insurance	519924.91	360518.17	533112.09	280062.76
家庭财产保险	Household Property Insurance	34679.72	5912.32	37451.72	8912.44
#投资型家财险	Of Which: Investment-Linked Household Property Insurance	907.03	160.35	2724.64	246.63
机动车辆保险	Motor Vehicle Insurance	5920909.47	3042629.14	6688160.08	3376575.15
工程保险	Project Insurance	155354.72	51913.16	137597.69	67898.19
责任保险	Liability Insurance	345735.07	131845.55	380426.73	165378.20
信用保险	Credit Insurance	244326.72	105970.24	273938.65	161012.13
保证保险	Guarantee Insurance	313287.37	39523.21	324476.39	85274.09
#机动车辆消费贷款保证保险	Of Which: Motor Vehicle Consumption Loan Guarantee Insurance	390.57	743.68	5509.87	1499.95
个人贷款抵押房屋保证保险	Personal Loan Home Mortgage Guarantee Insurance	2687.41	73.42	563.95	82.25
船舶保险	Ship Insurance	52797.89	48293.80	54291.80	28399.92
货物运输保险	Freight Transport Insurance	129688.03	62129.04	132217.10	61215.95
特殊风险保险	Peculiar Risk Insurance	154023.37	37319.12	119860.94	48307.25
农业保险	Agriculture Insurance	86325.95	38334.06	91046.05	51009.06
健康险	Health Insurance	168080.9	154281.22	190808.35	173637.74
意外伤害保险	Accident Injury Insurance	183879.81	51603.6	247881.36	61474.76
其他险	Other Property Insurance	12435.58	9544.03	26084.35	19734.95

8-12 续表 continued

单位：万元 (10000 yuan)

项目	Item	2016 保费收入 Premium Income	2016 赔款支出 Indemnity Expenditure	2017 保费收入 Premium Income	2017 赔款支出 Indemnity Expenditure
合计	**Total**	**10006161.82**	**4971007.81**	**11766073.4**	**5822812.35**
企业财产保险	Enterprise Property Insurance	548735.36	277071.52	592723.18	394575.23
家庭财产保险	Household Property Insurance	79849.26	17739.19	87644.05	30289.32
#投资型家财险	Of Which: Investment-Linked Household Property Insurance	2254.18	83.24	251.5	149.63
机动车辆保险	Motor Vehicle Insurance	7279870.86	3659744.85	8078987.55	4143180.14
工程保险	Project Insurance	136646.18	79242.61	165913.07	92557.72
责任保险	Liability Insurance	438487.65	195598.23	575456.32	244512.8
信用保险	Credit Insurance	296513.17	169933.33	393843.96	172224.79
保证保险	Guarantee Insurance	229957.59	78065.77	680411.72	110793.21
#机动车辆消费贷款保证保险	Of Which: Motor Vehicle Consumption Loan Guarantee Insurance	3874.83	702.79	2080.98	3200.84
个人贷款抵押房屋保证保险	Personal Loan Home Mortgage Guarantee Insurance	809.33	141.7	1000.38	19.12
船舶保险	Ship Insurance	50591.87	29010.13	44118.99	29943.83
货物运输保险	Freight Transport Insurance	126470.07	69025.9	129475.41	68948.93
特殊风险保险	Peculiar Risk Insurance	133438.33	49904.27	144838.71	90786.68
农业保险	Agriculture Insurance	108029.51	44272.77	129143.36	88944.57
健康险	Health Insurance	211454.94	186831.84	285034.62	217044.12
意外伤害保险	Accident Injury Insurance	339465.61	93503.98	427634.58	115055.88
其他险	Other Property Insurance	26651.4	21063.41	30847.88	23955.12

8-13 人身保险公司主要指标

Main Indicators of Life Insurance Companies

单位：亿元 (100 million yuan)

项　目	Item	2014	2015	2016	2017
保费收入	**Premium Income**	**1509.49**	**1890.64**	**2819.89**	**3127.99**
按险种分	Premium by Line of Business:				
寿险	Life Insurance	1297.09	1537.11	2038.11	2533.14
个人业务	Personal Business	1287.46	1527.41	2027.92	2527.04
新单保费	New Business Premium	632.24	846.76	1228.38	1458.80
续期保费	Renewal Premium	655.23	680.65	799.54	1068.23
团体业务	Group Business	9.62	9.70	10.19	6.10
新单保费	New Business Premium	6.67	6.88	7.72	4.45
续期保费	Renewal Premium	2.96	2.82	2.47	1.65
意外伤害险	Accident Injury Insurance	47.83	62.09	79.08	95.57
一年期以内业务	Within One-year	1.57	1.73	2.21	3.41
一年期业务	One Year	34.62	40.77	47.36	52.76
一年以上业务	Over One-year Period Business	11.64	19.59	29.50	39.40
健康险	Health Insurance	164.57	291.44	702.70	499.28
一年期以内及一年期业务	Within One Year and One-year Period Business	44.47	58.70	80.77	100.24
个人业务	Personal Business	12.32	16.55	22.15	36.21
团体业务	Group Business	32.15	42.16	58.62	64.03
一年期以上业务	Over One-year Period Business	120.10	232.74	621.94	399.04
个人业务	Personal Business	118.81	230.69	615.18	389.60
团体业务	Group Business	1.29	2.04	6.75	9.44
按新型产品分：	Premium by New Product:				
寿险保费收入合计	Total Life Insurance Premium Income	1297.09	1537.11	2038.11	2533.14
普通寿险	Ordinary Insurance	473.70	770.13	1265.91	1593.08
新单保费	New Business Premium	370.06	632.80	1019.88	1151.75
续期保费	Renewal Premium	103.64	137.33	246.04	441.33
分红寿险	Dividend Insurance	813.28	756.86	761.18	928.53
新单保费	New Business Premium	267.72	219.86	215.32	310.70
续期保费	Renewal Premium	545.56	537.01	545.85	617.83
投资连结保险	Investment Link Insurance	1.06	1.08	1.11	1.20
万能寿险	Universal Life Insurance	9.05	9.04	9.91	10.33
赔付支出	**Total Payment Expenditure**	**288.47**	**423.43**	**538.32**	**560.10**
赔款支出	Total Indemnity Expenditure	40.95	49.83	63.35	73.12
意外伤害险	Accident Injury Insurance	7.00	7.92	10.35	12.12
一年期以内业务	Within One-year Period Business	0.20	0.27	0.27	0.34
一年期业务	One-year Period Business	6.80	7.66	10.08	11.78
一年期以内及一年期健康险	Within One Year and One-year Period Health Insurance Business	33.95	41.91	53.00	61.00
个人业务	Personal Business	5.23	5.51	6.81	10.94
团体业务	Group Business	28.72	36.40	46.19	50.06
死伤医疗给付合计	Total Payment for Death, Injury and Medical Treatment	28.20	34.02	43.67	56.07
寿险	Life Insurance	14.86	16.52	18.39	20.04
个人业务	Personal Business	13.45	15.07	16.56	18.26
团体业务	Group Business	1.42	1.45	1.83	1.78
一年期以上健康险	Over One-year Period Health Insurance	13.33	17.50	25.28	36.03
个人业务	Personal Business	13.16	16.93	24.20	34.50
团体业务	Group Business	0.17	0.58	1.08	1.53
满期给付合计	Total Mature Payment	179.45	280.73	353.08	325.71
寿险	Life Insurance	179.28	280.55	352.88	325.47
个人业务	Personal Business	176.62	277.41	347.36	317.46
团体业务	Group Business	2.66	3.14	5.52	8.01
一年期以上健康险	Over One-year Period Health Insurance	0.17	0.18	0.20	0.24
个人业务	Personal Business	0.17	0.18	0.19	0.24
团体业务	Group Business			0.00	0.00
年金给付合计	Total Annuity Payment	39.87	58.85	78.22	105.19
个人业务	Personal Business	37.13	55.46	75.30	101.99
团体业务	Group Business	2.73	3.38	2.92	3.19
退保金	**Withdrawal Amount Insured**	**278.68**	**403.58**	**507.28**	**628.12**
寿险	Life Insurance	276.30	395.86	499.69	608.94
个人业务	Personal Business	273.49	393.26	493.89	604.65
团体业务	Group Business	2.81	2.60	5.80	4.29
一年期以上健康险	Over One-year Period Health Insurance	2.39	7.72	7.59	19.18

8-14 保险业务主要指标

Main Indicators of Insurance Business

指　　标	Indicators	2008	2010	2012	2013	2014	2015	2016	2017
保费收入　　（亿元）	**Premium of Insurance (100 million yuan)**	**1124.98**	**1421.68**	**1692.12**	**1902.91**	**2341.63**	**2814.37**	**3820.51**	**4304.60**
财产险	Property Insurance	292.62	429.62	571.31	660.14	796.95	879.87	945.52	1105.34
人寿险	Life Insurance	734.66	892.71	970.75	1057.87	1297.09	1537.11	2038.11	2533.14
健康险	Health Insurance	70.03	67.34	106.18	131.29	181.38	310.52	723.85	527.79
人身意外伤害险	Personal Accident Insurance	27.67	32.01	43.89	53.61	66.21	86.88	113.02	138.34
各项赔款和给付（亿元）	**Payment (100 million yuan)**	**283.17**	**318.21**	**485.01**	**619.09**	**702.45**	**882.32**	**1035.42**	**1142.38**
财产险	Property Insurance	172.04	194.77	305.45	352.65	393.39	435.38	469.07	549.07
人寿险	Life Insurance	84.88	85.58	134.51	208.35	234.01	355.92	449.50	450.70
健康险	Health Insurance	17.88	29.52	35.50	47.78	62.88	76.95	97.16	118.98
人身意外伤害险	Personal Accident Insurance	8.37	8.34	9.55	10.31	12.16	14.07	19.70	23.63
保险公司数　　（家）	**Number of Insurance Companies (unit)**	**57**	**65**	**82**	**84**	**87**	**90**	**103**	**109**
#财产保险公司	Property Insurance Companies	27	32	39	39	40	40	47	51
人身保险公司	Life Insurance Companies	30	33	43	45	47	50	56	58
#中资保险公司	Domestic Funded Insurance Companies	39	41	57	58	59	60	68	74
外资保险公司	Foreign-funded Insurance Companies	18	24	25	26	28	30	35	35
保险公司总资产（亿元）	**Total Assets of Insurance Companies(100 million yuan)**	**2182.28**	**3252.03**	**4684.92**	**5607.95**	**6957.85**	**9959.67**	**10811.14**	**12101.88**
#财产险公司	Property Insurance Companies	335.51	289.98	363.93	417.30	508.38	776.08	1017.09	1058.64
寿险公司	Life Insurance Companies	1823.48	2916.99	4113.22	4893.34	6073.89	8190.30	9472.37	10583.70
保险公司分支机构（家）	**Number of Institutions of Insurance Companies (Unit)**	**2192**	**2288**	**2425**	**2540**	**4915**	**5578**	**5815**	**6005**
从业人员数　　（万人）	**Employed Persons (person)**	**24.23**	**26.47**	**29.19**	**31.13**	**35.95**	**51.98**	**69.64**	**76.56**

注：“保险公司分支机构(家)”统计指标从2014年进行了调整，包括省级分公司、地市级分公司和中心支公司、支公司、营业部、营销服务部及电销专属机构。

Note: The number of institions of insurance companies were adjusted from 2014, including the provincial branch, municipal branch,central branch, sales department, marketing department and telemarketing exclusive agency.

8-15 分市原保险保费收入和赔付支出情况（2017年）

Premium of Primary Insurance and Payment by City (2017)

单位：亿元 (100 million yuan)

地 区	Region	原保险保费收入 Premium of Primary Insurance			赔付支出 Payment		
		小计 Sub-total	财产险业务 Property Insurance	人身险业务 Life Insurance	小计 Sub-total	财产险业务 Property Insurance	人身险业务 Life Insurance
全省合计	**Provincial Total**	**4304.60**	**1105.34**	**3199.26**	**1142.38**	**549.07**	**593.31**
广 州	Guangzhou	1127.25	255.81	871.44	269.72	128.29	141.43
深 圳	Shenzhen	1029.75	282.31	747.44	257.13	141.96	115.17
珠 海	Zhuhai	120.84	30.99	89.85	39.47	20.74	18.73
汕 头	Shantou	93.28	24.58	68.70	33.63	11.99	21.64
佛 山	Foshan	433.78	106.72	327.06	95.66	49.51	46.15
韶 关	Shaoguan	47.13	12.46	34.67	18.10	5.93	12.17
河 源	Heyuan	30.78	10.42	20.36	11.64	4.96	6.69
梅 州	Meizhou	50.06	13.71	36.35	17.75	6.23	11.53
惠 州	Huizhou	141.60	41.34	100.26	37.79	18.78	19.01
汕 尾	Shanwei	19.77	5.76	14.01	6.49	2.86	3.63
东 莞	Dongguan	468.09	120.65	347.44	106.82	56.71	50.10
中 山	Zhongshan	194.11	44.33	149.78	48.95	23.28	25.67
江 门	Jiangmen	131.64	32.49	99.15	48.84	19.18	29.66
阳 江	Yangjiang	40.11	12.60	27.51	15.19	5.98	9.22
湛 江	Zhanjiang	79.48	20.91	58.57	30.06	11.00	19.05
茂 名	Maoming	67.91	19.60	48.31	23.91	8.62	15.29
肇 庆	Zhaoqing	61.69	19.01	42.67	19.39	8.46	10.93
清 远	Qingyuan	54.73	17.04	37.69	18.44	7.96	10.49
潮 州	Chaozhou	32.92	10.17	22.75	14.21	4.87	9.34
揭 阳	Jieyang	52.52	15.82	36.70	18.19	7.90	10.28
云 浮	Yunfu	27.16	8.63	18.52	11.01	3.89	7.12

注：赔付支出不包括直保公司的分保赔付支出。
Note: The payment does not include the reinsurance payment of the direct insurance company.

主要统计指标解释

一般公共预算收入 指国家财政参与社会产品分配所取得的收入，是实现国家职能的财力保证。主要包括：

（1）各项税收：包括国内增值税、国内消费税、进口货物增值税和消费税、出口货物退增值税和消费税、营业税、企业所得税、个人所得税、资源税、城市维护建设税、房产税、印花税、城镇土地使用税、土地增值税、车船税、船舶吨税、车辆购置税、关税、耕地占用税、契税、烟叶税等。

（2）非税收入：包括专项收入、行政事业性收费、罚没收入和其他收入。财政收入按现行分税制财政体制划分为中央本级收入和地方本级收入。

一般公共预算支出 指国家财政将筹集起来的资金进行分配使用，以满足经济建设和各项事业的需要。主要包括：一般公共服务、外交、国防、公共安全、教育、科学技术、文化体育与传媒、社会保障和就业、医疗卫生与计划生育、节能环保、城乡社区、农林水、交通运输、资源勘探信息等、商业服务业等、金融、援助其他地区、国土海洋气象等、住房保障、粮油物资储备、政府债务付息等方面的支出。财政支出根据政府在经济和社会活动中的不同职权，划分为中央财政支出和地方财政支出。

信贷资金 指金融机构以信用方式集聚和分配的货币资金。金融机构信贷资金的来源有各项存款、金融债券、对国家金融机构负债、流通中现金、其他项目等；信贷自己的运用有各项贷款、有价证券及投资、黄金占款、外汇买卖、财政借款及在国家金融机构中的资产等。

存款 指企业、机关、团体或居民根据资金必须收回的原则，把货币资金存入银行或其他信用机构保管并取得一定利息的一种信用活动形式。根据存款对象或性质的不同可划分为住户存款、非金融企业存款、政府存款、非银行业金融存款等科目。它是银行信贷资金的主要来源。

贷款 指银行或其他信贷机构根据资金必须归还的原则，按一定利率，为企业、个人等提供资金的一种信用活动形式。我国银行贷款分为短期贷款、中长期贷款、融资租赁、票据融资、各项垫款、境外贷款等。

住户存款 个人客户在其他存款性公司开立账户并存入资金或货币，由其他存款性公司出具存款凭证，个人客户凭存款凭证可以支取本金或利息的存款。

保险金额 指保险人承担赔偿或者给付保险金责任的最高限额。

保费 指投保人为取得保险人在约定范围内所承担赔偿责任而支付给保险人的费用。

赔款 指保险人根据保险合同的规定，向被保险人支付的赔偿保险责任损失的金额。

给付 包括死伤医疗给付和满期给付。死伤医疗给付是指保险人根据人寿保险及长期健康保险合同的规定，因被保险人在保险期内发生保险责任范围内的保险事故支付给被保险人（或受益人）的金额。满期给付是指被保险人生存期满，保险人按人寿保险合同规定支付给被保险人的满期保险金额。

Explanatory Notes on Main Statistical Indicators

General Public Budgetary Revenue refers to income for the government finance through participating in the distribution of social products. It is the financial guarantee to ensure government functioning. The contents of government revenue include the following main items:

(1) Various tax revenues, including domestic value added tax (VAT), domestic consumption tax, VAT and consumption tax from imports, VAT and consumption tax rebate for exports, business tax, corporate income tax, individual income tax, resource tax, city maintenance and construct tax, house property tax, stamp tax, urban land use tax, land appreciation tax, tax on vehicles and boat operation, ship tonnage tax, vehicle purchase tax, tariffs, farm land occupation tax, deed tax, and tobacco leaf tax, etc.

(2) Non-tax revenue, including special program receipts, charge of administrative and institutional units, penalty receipts and others non-tax receipts.

General Public Budgetary Expenditure refers to the distribution and use of the funds which the government finance has raised, so as to meet the needs of economic construction and various undertakings. It includes the following main items: expenditure for general public services, expenditure for foreign affairs, expenditure for national defence expenditure for public security, expenditure for education, expenditure for science and technology, expenditure for culture, sport and media, expenditure for social safety net and employment effort, expenditure for medical and health care and family planning, expenditure for energy conservation and environment protection, expenditure for urban and rural community affairs, expenditure for agriculture, forestry and water conservancy, expenditure for transportation, expenditure for resource exploration and information, expenditure for affairs of commerce and services, expenditure for finance, aid to other regions, expenditure for land, ocean and weather, expenditure for housing security, expenditure for grain & oil reserves, interest payment for public debts. General public budget expenditure is divided into general public budget expenditure of central government and general public budget expenditure of local government according to the different functions of the governments played in economic and social activities.

Credit Funds refer to the monetary funds accumulated and distributed in the means of credit by the financial institutions. The sources of credit funds include various deposits, financial bonds, liabilities to international financial institutions, currency in circulation, other items. The uses of credit funds include loans, securities and investment, position for bullion purchase, foreign exchange trading, advances to treasury, and assets with international financial institutions.

Deposit is a form of credit by which enterprises, institutions, organizations or households can put money into banks and other credit institutions for safekeeping and interest earning under the principle of free withdrawal. According to different depositors, deposits are divided into household deposits, non financial enterprise deposits, government deposits, non banking financial institutions deposits. Deposits are major sources of the credit funds of banks.

Loan is a form of credit by which banks and other credit institutions provide funds at certain interest rate to enterprises and individuals in the light of the principle of unconditional repayment. Loans from Chinese banks include short-term loan, medium-term and long-term loans, financial lease, bill financing, various money advanced, foreign loans.

Savings Deposits refer to the capital which is deposited in the account opened in the reserve corporation by the individual with a deposit certificate as the proof, the principal and interest of which can be withdrew with the deposit certificate.

Amount Insured refers to the maximum that the insurant will get for the claim of the case sured.

Premium is the fee paid by the insurant to the insurer to obtain the obligation of compensation from the insurance within the agreed terms. is the compensation paid by the insurer to the insurant in accordance with the insurance contract.

Settled Claim is the compensation paid by the insurer to the insurant in accordance with the insurance contract.

Payment includes payment for death, injury or medical treatment and payment at maturity. Payment for death, injury or medical treatment refers to the money paid to the insurant (or the beneficiary) in accordance with the life or health insurance contract when the insurant encounters accidents within the insured period covered in the contract. Payment at maturity refers to the payment to the insurant in accordance with the life insurance contract at the end of the insured period.

九、价格

PRICE

九 价格

简要说明

一、本篇资料反映生产、流通、消费与投资等环节的价格变动情况。主要包括居民消费价格指数、商品零售价格指数、农业生产资料价格指数、工业生产者出厂价格指数、工业生产者购进价格指数、农产品生产者价格指数和固定资产投资价格指数。

二、本篇资料由国家统计局广东调查总队消费价格调查处和生产投资价格调查处整理提供。

三、居民消费价格指数、商品零售价格指数采用分层随机抽样调查方法编制，即在全省选择不同经济区域的市、县以及有代表性的商品和服务项目作为样本，对市场价格进行经常性调查，以样本推断总体。

四、工业生产者出厂价格指数和工业生产者购进价格指数均采用重点调查与典型调查相结合的方法统计。

五、固定资产投资价格指数采用重点调查与典型调查相结合的方法统计。

六、农产品生产者价格指数采用抽样调查和重点调查相结合的调查方法进行统计。

9 Price

Brief Introduction

Ⅰ. The data in this chapter reflect price changes in production, circulation，consumption and investment, including mainly consumer price indices, retail price indices, price indices of means of agricultural production, producer price indices for manufactured goods, producer price indices for purchased goods, producers' price indices for farm products and price indices for investment in fixed assets.

Ⅱ. The data are prepared and provided by the Division of Consumers Price Survey and the Division of Production Price Survey under Guangdong Survey Office of the National Bureau of Statistics.

Ⅲ. The data for the calculation of consumer price indices and retail price indices in the province are collected through stratified random sampling. Cities and counties distributed in different economic regions of the province are selected as sample areas, and representative commodities and services are selected as sample commodities and services. Regular surveys are conducted to collect data on market prices. The data on the population are estimated on the basis of the sample.

Ⅳ. The data for the calculation of producer price indices for manufactured goods and producer price indices for purchased goods are all collected through key-point survey combined with typical survey.

Ⅴ. The data for the calculation of price indices of investment in fixed assets are collected through key-point survey combined with typical survey.

Ⅵ. The data for the calculation of producers' price indices of farm products are collected through sampling survey combined with key-point survey.

9-1 各种价格指数

Price Indices

上年=100 (preceding year=100)

年份 Year	居民消费价格指数 Consumer Price Index	城市居民消费价格指数 Urban Household	农村居民消费价格指数 Rural Household	商品零售价格指数 Retail Price Index	工业生产者出厂价格指数 Producer Price Index for Manufactured Goods	工业生产者购进价格指数 Producer Price Index for Purchased Goods	固定资产投资价格指数 Price Index for Investment in Fixed Assets
1978		100.3		100.4			
1979		104.6		103.0			
1980		109.5		108.5			
1981		106.3		109.3			
1982		102.6		102.3			
1983		102.8		100.7			
1984	101.3	101.9	100.4	101.2			
1985	114.8	117.1	111.2	113.6			
1986	104.9	104.7	105.3	104.8			
1987	111.2	112.8	109.7	111.7			
1988	129.4	129.5	129.3	130.2			
1989	122.1	121.9	122.4	121.0			
1990	97.5	97.4	97.6	95.6			
1991	101.2	102.3	99.9	100.6			
1992	107.3	108.4	105.9	105.8			
1993	121.6	122.0	120.6	118.2			
1994	121.7	121.0	122.5	118.9			
1995	114.0	113.1	115.3	111.6			
1996	107.0	107.2	106.5	104.4			
1997	101.9	102.1	101.5	100.1	100.1	97.3	
1998	98.2	98.3	98.1	97.0	94.8	91.4	
1999	98.2	98.4	97.7	96.7	97.7	97.8	
2000	101.4	102.2	100.0	99.9	103.4	110.9	
2001	99.3	99.2	99.6	98.7	98.5	99.1	100.2
2002	98.6	98.6	98.6	98.5	96.5	96.3	99.7
2003	100.6	100.7	100.4	100.0	99.3	104.1	102.2
2004	103.0	102.6	103.7	102.9	101.7	110.6	106.4
2005	102.3	102.0	102.7	101.8	101.5	105.0	101.6
2006	101.8	101.8	101.6	101.5	101.4	103.6	100.7
2007	103.7	103.7	103.5	103.4	101.3	103.3	102.4
2008	105.6	105.5	105.8	106.0	103.1	107.9	108.6
2009	97.7	97.6	97.8	96.8	95.8	93.8	96.7
2010	103.1	103.1	103.2	103.3	103.2	107.3	103.0
2011	105.3	105.3	105.6	105.1	103.7	107.3	105.5
2012	102.8	102.8	102.9	102.2	99.5	99.5	101.5
2013	102.5	102.4	102.7	101.0	98.8	98.2	101.4
2014	102.3	102.3	102.1	101.4	98.9	98.8	101.5
2015	101.5	101.6	101.3	99.6	96.8	95.3	99.0
2016	102.3	102.4	102.0	100.8	99.4	98.0	100.3
2017	101.5	101.7	100.8	101.6	103.3	105.3	105.3

9–2 各种价格定基指数

Fixed-base Price Indices

年份 Year	居民消费价格指数(1983年为100) Consumer Price Index (1983=100)	城市居民消费价格指数(1983年为100) Urban Household (1983=100)	农村居民消费价格指数(1983年为100) Rural Household (1983=100)	商品零售价格指数(1978年为100) Retail Price Index (1978=100)	工业生产者出厂价格指数(1996年为100) Producer Price Index for Manufactured Goods (1996=100)	工业生产者购进价格指数(1996年为100) Producer Price Index for Purchased Goods (1996=100)	固定资产投资价格指数(2000年为100) Price Index for Investment in Fixed Assets (2000=100)
1978				100.0			
1979				103.0			
1980				111.8			
1981				122.0			
1982				124.9			
1983	100.0	100.0	100.0	125.7			
1984	101.3	101.9	100.4	127.2			
1985	116.3	119.3	111.6	144.5			
1986	122.0	124.9	117.6	151.5			
1987	135.7	140.9	129.0	169.2			
1988	175.5	182.5	166.8	220.3			
1989	214.3	222.5	204.1	266.6			
1990	209.0	216.7	199.2	254.8			
1991	211.5	221.7	199.0	256.4			
1992	226.9	240.3	210.7	271.3			
1993	275.9	293.1	254.2	320.6			
1994	335.8	354.7	311.3	381.3			
1995	382.8	401.2	359.0	425.6			
1996	409.6	430.1	382.3	444.3	100.0	100.0	
1997	417.4	439.1	388.1	444.7	100.1	97.3	
1998	409.9	431.6	380.7	431.4	94.9	88.9	
1999	402.5	424.7	371.9	417.1	92.7	86.9	
2000	408.1	434.1	371.9	416.7	95.9	96.4	100.0
2001	405.3	430.6	370.4	411.3	94.5	95.5	100.2
2002	399.6	424.6	365.3	405.1	91.2	92.0	99.9
2003	402.0	427.5	366.7	405.1	90.6	95.8	102.1
2004	414.1	438.6	380.3	416.9	92.1	106.0	108.6
2005	423.6	447.4	390.5	424.4	93.5	111.3	110.3
2006	431.2	455.5	396.8	430.8	94.8	115.3	111.1
2007	447.2	472.3	410.7	445.4	96.0	119.1	113.8
2008	472.2	498.3	434.5	472.2	99.0	128.4	123.6
2009	461.3	486.3	424.9	457.1	94.9	120.4	119.5
2010	475.6	501.4	438.5	472.2	97.9	129.2	123.0
2011	500.8	528.0	463.1	496.3	101.4	138.6	129.9
2012	514.8	542.8	476.5	507.2	100.9	137.9	131.8
2013	527.7	555.8	489.4	512.3	99.7	135.4	133.6
2014	539.8	568.6	499.7	519.5	98.6	134.0	135.6
2015	547.9	577.7	506.2	517.4	95.4	127.7	134.3
2016	560.5	591.6	516.3	521.5	94.8	125.1	134.7
2017	568.9	601.7	520.4	529.8	97.9	131.8	141.8

9-3 居民消费价格分类指数（2017年）

Consumer Price Indices by Category (2017)

上年=100 (preceding year=100)

项 目	Item	全省 Provincial Indices	城市 Urban Indices	农村 Rural Indices
居民消费价格总指数	**Consumer Price Index**	**101.5**	**101.7**	**100.8**
非食品烟酒价格指数	**Non food,tobacco and alcohol price index**	**102.3**	**102.3**	**102.1**
服务价格指数	**Service Price Index**	**102.6**	**102.7**	**102.1**
消费品价格指数	**Consumer Goods Price Index**	**100.9**	**101.0**	**100.1**
扣除鲜菜鲜果价格指数	**Price Index Deducting Fresh Vegetables and Fruits**	**101.8**	**101.9**	**101.2**
食品烟酒	**Foods,Tobacco and Alcohol**	**100.0**	**100.3**	**98.3**
食品	Foods	98.9	99.3	97.3
粮食	Grain	101.4	101.4	101.1
#大米	Rice	101.2	101.2	101.3
粮食制品	Grain Products	101.9	102.1	100.6
薯类	Tubers	96.8	97.7	94.1
豆类	Beans	100.6	101.0	99.2
食用油	Edible Oil	100.2	100.6	98.5
菜	Vegetables	92.4	92.7	91.0
#鲜菜	Fresh Vegetables	91.6	91.9	90.1
畜肉类	Neat of Animal	97.0	97.4	95.7
#猪肉	Pork	95.5	96.0	94.2
禽肉类	Meat of Poultris	99.6	100.3	97.4
水产品	Aquatic Products	104.3	105.0	101.7
蛋类	Eggs	97.8	98.1	96.7
奶类	Milk	99.6	99.5	100.2
干鲜瓜果类	Dried and Fresh Melons and Fruits	101.3	102.0	97.6
#鲜瓜果	Fresh Melons and Fruits	101.6	102.4	97.7
糖果糕点类	Candy and Pastry	102.0	102.1	101.6
调味品	Condiment	102.0	102.6	100.5
其他食品类	Other Foods	100.2	100.0	101.1
茶及饮料	Tea and Beverages	100.7	100.5	101.2
烟酒	Tobacco and Alcohol	101.1	101.1	100.9
烟草	Tobacco	99.9	99.7	100.5
酒类	Alcohol	103.0	103.2	102.1
在外餐饮	Outside Catering	102.4	102.5	101.9
衣着	**Clothing**	**101.5**	**101.5**	**101.4**
服装	Garments	101.5	101.5	101.9
服装材料	Garments Materials	101.8	102.0	100.9
其他衣着及配件	Other Clothing and Accessories	100.4	100.2	101.6
衣着加工服务费	Clothing Manufacturing Services	103.1	103.3	101.1
鞋类	Footwear	101.5	101.8	99.9
居住	**Residence**	**102.2**	**102.2**	**102.1**
租赁房房租	Rental Housing	101.9	102.0	100.9
住房保养维修及管理	Housing Maintenance and Management	102.9	103.2	102.0
水电燃料	Hydropower Fuel	102.9	102.7	103.9
自有住房	Own Housing	101.6	101.6	101.3

9-3 续表 continued

上年=100 (preceding year=100)

项　目	Item	全省 Provincial Indices	城市 Urban Indices	农村 Rural Indices
生活用品及服务	**Daily Necessities and Services**	**100.9**	**100.9**	**101.0**
家具及室内装饰品	Furniture and Interior Decorations	102.4	102.5	101.8
家具	Furniture	102.7	102.9	102.0
室内装饰品	Interior Decorations	99.2	99.3	98.7
家用器具	Home Appliances	98.4	98.0	100.2
家用纺织品	Home Textiles	101.9	102.2	100.4
家庭日用杂品	Household Groceries	99.6	99.5	99.8
个人护理用品	Personal-care Supply	100.6	100.7	100.0
家庭服务	Domestic Service	105.3	105.2	107.0
交通和通信	**Transportation and Communication**	**101.3**	**101.3**	**101.6**
交通	Transportation	102.7	102.6	102.9
交通工具	The Traffic Tools	98.9	99.0	98.3
交通工具用燃料	The Vehicles Fuel	108.9	108.9	108.7
交通工具使用和维修	Vehicle usage and Maintenance	100.9	100.9	100.8
交通费	Transportation	102.3	102.4	101.7
通信	Communication	99.0	98.9	99.7
通信工具	Communication Tools	95.6	95.2	98.1
通信服务	Communication Service	99.8	99.8	100.0
邮递服务	Postal service	100.5	100.5	100.8
教育文化和娱乐	**Education Culture and Entertainment**	**102.6**	**102.7**	**102.5**
教育	Education	103.8	103.9	103.4
教育用品	Education Supplies	101.3	101.1	101.9
教育服务	Education Services	104.1	104.2	103.7
文化娱乐	Cultural Entertainment	100.9	100.9	100.9
文娱耐用消费品	Recreational Consumer Goods	97.3	96.8	99.1
其他文娱用品	Other Entertainment Items	100.9	101.1	100.4
文化娱乐服务	Cultural Entertainment Service	100.8	100.8	100.5
旅游	Tourism	103.1	102.9	105.1
医疗保健	**Health Care**	**106.2**	**106.7**	**104.2**
药品及医疗器具	Medicines and Medical Instruments	105.3	105.3	105.4
中药	Traditional Chinese Medicine	106.1	105.9	106.7
西药	Western Medicines	107.6	107.9	106.6
滋补保健品	Nourishing Health Products	104.8	105.0	102.3
医疗卫生器具	Medical Appliance	100.1	100.0	100.8
保健器具	Health Care Appliances	99.9	99.9	100.0
医疗服务	Medical Services	106.9	107.8	103.6
其他用品和服务	**Other Goods and Services**	**101.7**	**101.9**	**100.7**
其他用品类	Other Products	101.2	101.3	100.7
其他服务类	Other Service Class	102.1	102.3	100.7

9-4 商品零售价格分类指数（2017年）
Retail Price Indices by Category (2017)

上年=100 (preceding year=100)

项 目	Item	全 省 Provincial Indices	城 市 Urban Indices	农 村 Rural Indices
商品零售价格指数	**Retail Price Index**	**101.6**	**101.6**	**101.5**
食品	**Foods**	**100.0**	**100.2**	**98.9**
粮食	Grain	101.3	101.4	101.0
#大米	Rice	101.2	101.2	101.3
粮食制品	Grain Products	101.4	101.5	100.7
薯类	Tubers	98.1	98.4	96.9
豆类	Beans	100.8	101.0	99.7
食用油	Edible Oil	100.5	100.8	98.8
菜	Vegetables	93.1	93.0	93.4
#鲜菜	Fresh Vegetables	92.0	92.0	92.4
畜肉类	Neat of Animal	97.5	97.7	96.1
#猪肉	Pork	95.8	96.1	94.4
禽肉类	Meat of Poultris	100.2	100.3	99.1
水产品	Aquatic Products	104.6	104.9	102.5
蛋类	Eggs	97.9	98.0	97.5
奶类	Milk	99.7	99.7	99.6
干鲜瓜果类	Dried and Fresh Melons and Fruits	101.8	102.2	99.3
#鲜瓜果	Fresh Melons and Fruits	102.4	102.8	99.3
糖果糕点类	Candy and Pastry	102.3	102.3	102.0
调味品	Condiment	102.8	103.1	101.0
其他食品类	Other Foods	100.3	100.1	102.1
在外餐饮	Dining Out	102.5	102.6	102.0
饮料、烟酒	**Beverages, Tobacco and Alcohol**	**100.9**	**100.9**	**101.1**
茶及饮料	Tea and Beverages	100.6	100.5	101.1
烟草	Tobacco	99.7	99.6	100.1
酒类	Alcohol	103.0	103.1	102.4
服装、鞋帽	**Garments, Shoes and Hats**	**101.2**	**101.2**	**101.3**
服装	Garments	101.3	101.2	101.7
鞋帽袜	Shoes, Hats and Socks	101.2	101.4	100.3
其他衣着配件	Other Clothing Accessories	100.6	100.8	99.6
纺织品	**Textiles**	**102.4**	**102.8**	**100.0**
服装材料	Clothing Material	101.7	101.9	100.5
床上用品	Bed Articles	102.6	103.2	99.7

9−4 续表 continued

上年=100 (preceding year=100)

项 目	Item	全省 Provincial Indices	城市 Urban Indices	农村 Rural Indices
家用电器及音像器材	**Household Appliances, Audio and Video Equipment**	**98.0**	**97.5**	**100.5**
家庭设备	Household Facilities	98.3	97.9	100.8
文娱用耐用消费品	Durable Consumer Goods for Cultural and Recreational Use	97.1	96.5	100.3
专业音像器材	Audio and Video Equipment	98.5	98.4	99.6
文化办公用品	**Cultural and Office Appliances**	**98.2**	**98.0**	**99.8**
日用品	**Articles for Daily Use**	**99.8**	**99.8**	**99.9**
日用百货	General Merchandise for Daily Use	99.4	99.4	99.5
厨具餐具茶具	Kitchenware, Tableware and Tea set	100.0	100.0	100.1
清洗用品	Cleaning Supplies	100.3	100.3	100.3
其他日用品	Other Articles for Daily Use	99.7	99.6	99.9
体育娱乐用品	**Sports and Recreation Articles**	**100.5**	**100.6**	**100.1**
体育户外用品	Sports Outdoor Products	100.4	100.5	100.3
娱乐用品	Recreation Articles	100.6	100.6	100.0
交通、通信用品	**Transportation and Communication Appliances**	**99.0**	**98.9**	**99.7**
交通运输机械	Transportation Machinery	100.3	100.3	100.1
通信器材	Communication Equipment	95.9	95.4	98.8
家具	**Furniture**	**102.3**	**102.3**	**102.7**
化妆品	**Cosmetics**	**100.9**	**101.0**	**100.0**
金银饰品	**Gold and Silver Jewelry**	**101.9**	**101.9**	**101.1**
中西药品及医疗保健用品	**Traditional Chinese & Western Medicines and Health Care Articles**	**106.4**	**106.5**	**106.1**
医疗卫生器具	Medical Appliance	99.6	99.4	101.3
中药	Traditional Chinese Medicine	106.4	106.2	107.4
西药	Western Medicines	109.1	109.4	107.5
保健器具及用品	Health Equipment and Supplies	104.6	104.9	101.8
书报杂志及电子出版物	**Books, Newspapers, Magazines and Electronic Publications**	**101.3**	**101.2**	**101.6**
教材及参考书	Teaching Materials and Reference Books	100.8	100.6	101.7
书报杂志	Newspapers and Magazines	102.9	102.9	102.7
计算机办公软件	Computer Office Software	99.8	99.9	98.4
燃料	**Fuels**	**110.0**	**109.9**	**110.5**
煤炭及制品	Coal and Its Products	110.0	112.6	101.2
石油及制品	Petroleum and Its Products	110.0	109.8	111.2
建筑材料及五金电料	**Building Materials and Hardware**	**101.6**	**101.6**	**101.9**
建筑装璜材料	Building Decoration Materials	102.0	102.0	102.2
五金水暖	Plumbing Hardware	100.6	100.6	100.5

9-5 各市居民消费价格分类指数（2017年）

Consumer Price Indices by Category and by City (2017)

上年=100 (preceding year=100)

市 别	City	总指数 General Index	服务价格 Service Price	食品烟酒 Foods tobacco and alcohol	食品 Foods	#粮食 Grain	食用油 Edible Oil	菜 Vegetables	畜肉类 Neat of animal	禽肉类 Meat of poultris	水产品 Aquatic Products	蛋类 Eggs
广 州	Guangzhou	102.3	103.6	101.4	100.3	100.4	100.4	93.7	98.8	102.0	104.9	97.5
深 圳	Shenzhen	101.4	101.9	100.2	98.4	101.4	99.8	89.8	97.1	99.8	104.0	97.4
珠 海	Zhuhai	100.8	100.4	100.3	99.4	105.2	100.7	96.1	93.9	99.5	103.1	97.0
汕 头	Shantou	101.5	102.2	100.6	100.7	102.0	103.0	90.7	103.0	102.0	105.7	99.5
佛 山	Foshan	101.9	104.1	99.2	98.8	101.3	99.8	94.3	96.8	96.1	107.5	99.7
韶 关	Shaoguan	101.6	103.7	99.4	98.7	100.7	103.6	94.9	93.4	101.7	104.3	100.4
河 源	Heyuan	101.1	101.0	101.0	100.5	102.2	100.4	99.8	100.1	99.8	100.8	98.1
梅 州	Meizhou	101.5	103.3	98.8	97.8	100.3	100.3	89.6	94.9	100.5	107.6	97.5
惠 州	Huizhou	101.8	103.6	100.6	100.1	103.1	100.1	94.6	97.7	104.7	105.0	101.4
汕 尾	Shanwei	100.7	101.3	100.0	99.9	97.6	99.7	94.0	99.1	100.5	106.5	96.2
东 莞	Dongguan	101.4	102.8	100.3	99.0	101.7	100.0	91.7	96.4	100.4	105.2	97.4
中 山	Zhongshan	101.6	102.9	99.7	98.0	100.3	101.0	90.0	97.2	97.0	102.2	94.1
江 门	Jiangmen	101.6	103.1	99.6	99.4	101.7	101.2	93.0	94.5	99.5	108.2	99.5
阳 江	Yangjiang	101.5	102.4	101.6	101.0	103.4	105.1	94.3	96.8	103.2	109.5	94.0
湛 江	Zhanjiang	101.3	102.1	100.2	99.0	100.7	101.5	94.1	98.0	97.7	104.0	94.4
茂 名	Maoming	101.0	102.1	99.3	97.9	101.5	102.8	94.2	92.2	96.1	104.8	93.6
肇 庆	Zhaoqing	101.6	102.6	100.1	99.6	100.0	100.6	95.0	98.2	102.5	101.9	102.9
清 远	Qingyuan	101.9	103.0	99.8	99.4	97.3	103.6	99.6	97.0	101.1	107.5	92.4
潮 州	Chaozhou	101.3	101.9	100.0	98.2	99.8	98.9	87.6	98.8	96.8	105.9	96.1
揭 阳	Jieyang	101.5	103.0	100.2	99.2	101.0	101.8	88.3	98.5	101.2	105.0	97.8
云 浮	Yunfu	101.1	101.1	99.9	99.0	100.3	103.3	93.2	97.4	100.2	101.4	98.7

9-5 续表 continued

上年=100 (preceding year=100)

市 别	City	干鲜瓜果类 Dried and Fresh Melons and Fruits	茶及饮料 Tea and Beverages	烟酒 Tobacco and Alcohol	在外餐饮 Outside catering	衣着 Clothing	居住 Residence	生活用品及服务 Daily necessities and services	交通和通信 Transpo-rtation and communi-cation	教育文化和娱乐 Education culture and enterta-inment	医疗保健 Health care	其他用品和服务 Other goods and services
广 州	Guangzhou	104.0	99.8	100.1	104.0	100.0	103.3	100.6	101.6	103.6	107.0	102.4
深 圳	Shenzhen	100.4	100.6	101.0	104.0	103.2	100.9	101.5	101.6	102.5	106.2	101.2
珠 海	Zhuhai	106.2	99.8	103.3	101.9	102.5	100.5	100.5	100.6	102.3	102.5	100.1
汕 头	Shantou	105.1	100.4	101.9	100.2	99.5	101.5	101.3	101.0	101.4	106.7	105.4
佛 山	Foshan	98.6	99.7	101.2	99.6	105.6	103.6	101.1	101.1	102.7	107.6	101.3
韶 关	Shaoguan	105.7	100.3	102.9	100.5	102.9	103.3	99.4	100.4	103.0	110.0	100.3
河 源	Heyuan	103.9	101.3	101.8	102.0	101.5	100.8	100.9	100.6	100.4	104.7	100.1
梅 州	Meizhou	100.4	100.6	101.1	100.9	100.6	104.5	100.6	101.6	102.4	107.1	100.5
惠 州	Huizhou	98.6	99.2	100.3	101.9	99.6	102.6	99.8	101.6	100.7	111.7	101.0
汕 尾	Shanwei	99.4	100.0	100.4	100.0	100.5	100.8	100.4	97.8	104.6	104.0	99.9
东 莞	Dongguan	100.4	100.2	100.1	103.3	99.2	102.1	101.8	101.0	102.7	104.0	102.5
中 山	Zhongshan	102.2	98.5	101.8	104.0	100.5	102.8	100.9	101.7	101.3	109.8	101.2
江 门	Jiangmen	106.2	103.3	99.1	99.9	99.5	101.7	100.7	101.8	103.1	113.7	100.5
阳 江	Yangjiang	102.5	97.2	100.6	104.3	98.2	99.7	101.6	103.2	103.3	103.9	99.4
湛 江	Zhanjiang	98.2	104.1	100.8	102.9	102.0	101.9	100.2	100.6	102.9	104.7	100.9
茂 名	Maoming	102.3	101.3	101.6	102.3	101.6	101.7	99.1	99.7	103.8	108.1	100.3
肇 庆	Zhaoqing	101.8	96.7	106.0	100.6	102.8	100.8	100.1	102.3	102.5	109.5	99.8
清 远	Qingyuan	98.3	98.5	98.2	102.2	106.0	103.2	101.2	100.9	101.1	108.7	102.0
潮 州	Chaozhou	102.4	108.6	101.9	103.7	99.5	101.8	102.7	101.0	102.2	106.2	101.1
揭 阳	Jieyang	104.8	99.7	100.8	103.6	102.0	102.8	100.6	101.0	102.5	105.3	99.9
云 浮	Yunfu	105.9	97.9	101.4	102.5	101.6	101.5	101.1	101.3	100.3	107.5	100.4

9-6 各市服务项目价格分类指数（2017年）

Service Price Indices by Category and by City (2017)

上年=100 (preceding year=100)

市别	City	服务价格 Service Price	#租赁房房租 Rental Housing	家庭服务 Family Services	交通费 Traffic Expense	通信服务 Communication Services	邮递服务 Postal Service	教育服务 Education Service	文化娱乐服务 Cultural and Recreational Services	旅游 Tourism	医疗服务 Medical Service	其他服务类 Other Service
广州	Guangzhou	103.6	102.8	103.3	101.4	99.4	99.7	106.4	100.4	103.2	107.1	103.3
深圳	Shenzhen	101.9	100.6	105.3	104.9	100.0	100.0	102.5	101.6	105.1	104.9	100.9
珠海	Zhuhai	100.4	100.7	99.3	99.5	100.0	102.9	102.6	100.8	105.5	102.5	100.0
汕头	Shantou	102.2	100.2	107.2	103.0	100.0	100.9	102.4	100.3	101.2	106.4	107.5
佛山	Foshan	104.1	105.6	111.8	102.2	100.0	99.9	103.7	100.1	105.5	111.7	101.1
韶关	Shaoguan	103.7	103.0	100.1	96.9	100.0	99.9	104.7	99.7	104.8	111.8	100.0
河源	Heyuan	101.0	99.8	104.8	101.5	100.0	100.0	101.4	99.9	97.6	105.9	99.8
梅州	Meizhou	103.3	103.1	99.7	103.6	100.0	102.0	102.3	104.0	105.2	109.2	100.3
惠州	Huizhou	103.6	102.9	102.8	102.5	100.0	100.6	103.0	99.8	96.1	118.6	100.3
汕尾	Shanwei	101.3	100.0	104.7	91.1	100.0	100.0	100.4	99.1	124.9	103.8	100.6
东莞	Dongguan	102.8	102.5	107.2	103.1	99.8	101.2	104.9	101.1	100.1	106.2	103.7
中山	Zhongshan	102.9	102.5	103.1	100.2	99.8	100.4	101.7	99.1	101.8	113.8	100.0
江门	Jiangmen	103.1	100.4	101.1	102.2	100.1	101.9	105.3	101.8	100.7	121.7	101.1
阳江	Yangjiang	102.4	100.0	117.4	104.3	100.0	100.0	101.7	102.0	112.5	103.3	101.1
湛江	Zhanjiang	102.1	101.5	101.7	102.0	100.0	100.0	103.8	104.3	103.0	103.7	100.8
茂名	Maoming	102.1	100.1	104.1	101.8	97.0	100.0	106.2	95.7	104.1	109.2	99.8
肇庆	Zhaoqing	102.6	100.4	103.0	102.8	100.0	103.0	104.6	100.6	100.1	108.0	100.1
清远	Qingyuan	103.0	104.6	104.4	101.9	100.0	100.1	104.4	100.8	94.8	111.4	102.1
潮州	Chaozhou	101.9	100.0	110.7	103.7	100.0	100.1	104.1	100.9	97.9	106.6	102.0
揭阳	Jieyang	103.0	101.9	104.1	103.4	100.0	100.0	102.9	100.0	104.2	106.6	100.3
云浮	Yunfu	101.1	98.4	106.2	101.5	100.0	102.7	99.5	97.8	104.7	105.6	100.1

9-7 工业生产者出厂价格指数
Producer Price Indices for Manufactured Goods

上年=100 (preceding year=100)

项 目	Item	2010	2013	2014	2015	2016	2017
工业生产者出厂价格指数	**Producer Price Index for Manufactured Goods**	**103.2**	**98.8**	**98.9**	**96.8**	**99.4**	**103.3**
按轻重工业分	**Grouped by Light and Heavy Industries**						
轻工业	Light Industry	101.7	99.6	99.9	99.3	100.7	101.9
以农产品为原料	Using Farm Products as Raw Materials	103.1	100.6	100.4	99.5	100.6	102.2
以非农产品为原料	Using Non-farm Products as Raw Materials	101.3	99.0	99.6	99.2	100.7	101.7
重工业	Heavy Industry	105.7	98.3	98.3	95.3	98.7	104.1
采 掘	Mining and Quarrying	127.9	96.3	94.7	72.0	95.9	116.8
原 料	Raw Materials	107.9	98.3	97.9	89.6	96.0	107.5
加 工	Processing	103.3	98.3	98.6	97.4	99.5	102.9
按生产生活资料分	**Grouped by Production and Living Materials**						
生产资料	Production Materials	104.1	98.3	98.4	95.1	98.6	104.5
采 掘	Mining and Quarrying	127.9	96.3	94.7	72.0	95.9	116.8
原 料	Raw Materials	108.3	98.4	97.9	89.9	95.9	107.5
加 工	Processing	102.4	98.4	98.6	97.1	99.4	103.5
生活资料	Living Materials	101.4	99.6	99.9	99.8	100.8	101.3
食 品	Food	103.3	99.8	99.5	100.1	101.4	101.9
衣 着	Clothing	101.3	101.7	101.9	101.8	101.3	101.3
一般日用品	Articles for Daily Use	102.7	99.8	100.6	99.2	101.5	101.2
耐用消费品	Durable Consumer Goods	99.9	98.6	98.8	99.3	100.0	101.0
按工业部门分	**Grouped by Industrial Sectors**						
冶金工业	Metallurgical Industry	109.1	97.0	96.4	93.4	98.9	114.6
电力工业	Power Industry	98.7	99.0	99.1	97.7	98.8	98.7
煤炭及炼焦工业	Coal and Coking Industry	107.0					
石油工业	Petroleum Industry	122.1	96.9	95.8	72.1	90.7	118.1
化学工业	Chemical Industry	105.3	98.8	99.6	96.9	98.7	104.2
机械工业	Machine Manufacturing Industry	100.2	98.6	98.8	98.6	99.7	100.6
建筑材料工业	Building Materials Industry	104.3	100.2	101.4	95.9	98.0	104.8
森林工业	Timber Industry	103.4	100.8	100.6	100.4	101.4	101.2
食品工业	Food Industry	103.7	100.9	99.2	98.0	100.1	101.4
纺织工业	Textile Industry	102.2	98.6	100.6	97.4	99.4	102.1
缝纫工业	Tailoring Industry	101.1	101.2	101.6	101.3	101.4	102.6
皮革工业	Leather Industry	101.8	103.1	102.2	102.1	101.0	99.1
造纸工业	Paper Making Industry	107.0	96.8	99.5	100.0	99.9	107.2
文教艺术用品工业	Industry for Cultural, Educational & Art Articles	100.0	99.2	99.0	99.1	102.2	101.3
其它工业	Others	106.4	99.7	101.5	99.1	103.9	101.4

9-8 各市工业生产者出厂价格指数
Producer Price Indices for Manufactured Goods by City

上年=100 (preceding year=100)

市 别	City	2005	2010	2012	2013	2014	2015	2016	2017
全 省	**Provincial Total**	**101.5**	**103.2**	**99.5**	**98.8**	**98.9**	**96.8**	**99.4**	**103.3**
广 州	Guangzhou	101.7	102.4	99.7	98.0	98.2	96.8	98.8	102.3
深 圳	Shenzhen	98.7	101.4	99.9	98.0	99.1	97.6	99.3	101.8
珠 海	Zhuhai	100.8	102.2	99.4	98.6	98.5	96.9	99.4	103.2
汕 头	Shantou	102.4	102.4	100.6	99.6	100.0	98.6	100.3	102.0
佛 山	Foshan	101.8	102.8	99.5	98.9	98.8	97.2	99.2	104.5
韶 关	Shaoguan	103.2	107.5	95.8	96.9	97.1	92.1	99.0	110.2
河 源	Heyuan	103.9	104.6	96.7	98.3	97.5	93.6	100.2	107.9
梅 州	Meizhou	101.9	103.8	99.1	98.8	99.7	95.8	99.5	103.2
惠 州	Huizhou	97.5	104.0	99.4	97.1	97.5	92.5	98.3	104.2
汕 尾	Shanwei	99.7	102.3	99.9	98.8	99.9	98.6	100.9	102.0
东 莞	Dongguan	100.4	102.6	99.8	98.9	99.0	98.2	99.9	101.7
中 山	Zhongshan	101.4	102.6	99.9	99.4	99.4	98.0	99.7	102.5
江 门	Jiangmen	102.1	103.6	99.7	99.4	99.4	97.8	99.3	103.5
阳 江	Yangjiang	103.0	103.8	99.2	98.6	98.6	95.2	99.9	106.9
湛 江	Zhanjiang	111.8	110.4	102.0	99.1	97.7	91.7	99.2	105.6
茂 名	Maoming	112.1	114.7	102.0	98.2	97.0	81.8	95.5	110.7
肇 庆	Zhaoqing	100.6	105.9	98.4	99.0	98.5	96.3	98.9	105.2
清 远	Qingyuan	103.5	108.0	97.3	98.6	99.0	94.6	97.8	107.9
潮 州	Chaozhou	102.5	101.3	102.2	100.4	100.0	97.2	99.4	101.7
揭 阳	Jieyang	101.6	102.9	99.7	99.2	99.5	97.6	100.4	104.4
云 浮	Yunfu	101.6	104.7	100.7	99.4	100.5	96.8	98.9	102.6

9-9 分行业工业生产者出厂价格指数

Producer Price Indices for Manufactured Goods by Sector

上年=100 (preceding year=100)

项　目	Item	2005	2010	2016	2017
工业生产者出厂价格指数	**Producer Price Index for Manufactured Goods**	**101.5**	**103.2**	**99.4**	**103.3**
按工业行业分	**Grouped by Industrial Sector**				
#石油和天然气开采业	Extraction of Petroleum and Natural Gas	134.3	138.9	94.2	120.8
黑色金属矿采选业	Mining and Processing of Ferrous Metal Ores	128.2	119.6	95.6	125.3
有色金属矿采选业	Mining and Processing of Non-ferrous Metal Ores	122.3	130.2	101.0	116.0
非金属矿采选业	Mining and Processing of Nonmetal Ores	102.3	105.1	99.1	102.0
农副食品加工业	Processing of Foods from Agricultural Products	103.1	107.1	99.9	102.0
食品制造业	Processing of Foodstuff	101.2	102.2	101.0	102.1
酒、饮料和精制茶制造业	Manufacture of Liquor, Beverages and Refined Tea	99.4	100.3	99.6	100.0
烟草制品业	Manufacture of Tobacco	100.7	98.9	100.3	100.0
纺织业	Textile Industry	101.6	101.3	100.3	101.6
纺织服装、服饰业	Manufacture of Texile, Wearing Apparel and Accessories	99.9	101.5	101.0	103.1
皮革、毛皮、羽毛及其制品和制鞋业	Manufacture of Leather,Fur, Feather and Related Products and Footware	101.1	101.9	101.5	98.7
木材加工及木、竹、藤、棕、草制品业	Processing of Timber, Manufacture of Wood, Bamboo, Rattan, Palm and Straw Products	100.9	104.0	99.9	101.0
家具制造业	Manufacture of Furniture	100.7	102.3	102.2	102.3
造纸和纸制品业	Manufacture of Paper and Paper Products	101.0	107.2	99.9	107.2
印刷和记录媒介复制业	Printing, Reproduction of Recording Media	99.5	101.5	100.7	100.6
文教、工美、体育和娱乐用品制造业	Manufacture of Articles for Cultrue, Education, Arts and Crafts, Sport and Entertainment Activities	101.5	99.5	104.1	100.9
石油加工、炼焦和核燃料加工业	Processing of Petroleum, Coking, Processing of Nuclear Fuel	122.7	119.6	90.8	118.9
化学原料和化学制品制造业	Manufacture of Raw Chemical Materials and Chemical Products	102.3	108.1	97.4	107.0
医药制造业	Manufacture of Medicines	101.5	102.0	102.8	102.9
化学纤维制造业	Manufacture of Chemical Fibers	104.5	120.9	95.7	107.6
橡胶和塑料制品业	Manufacture of Rubber and Plastic Products			98.9	101.8
非金属矿物制品业	Manufacture of Non-metallic Mineral Products	97.3	103.9	98.0	104.7
黑色金属冶炼和压延加工业	Smelting and Pressing of Ferrous Metals	103.3	107.9	100.7	132.0
有色金属冶炼和压延加工业	Smelting and Pressing of Nonferrous Metals	108.5	118.7	97.9	115.9
金属制品业	Manufacture of Metal Products	103.6	102.8	99.9	105.2
通用设备制造业	Manufacture of General-purpose Machinery	102.2	104.1	100.0	100.4
专用设备制造业	Manufacture of Special-purpose Machinery	100.6	98.5	99.1	102.2
汽车制造业	Manufacture of Automobiles	97.7	99.2	99.7	100.9
铁路、船舶、航空航天和其他运输设备制造业	Manufacture of Railway, Ship, Aerospace and Other Electronic Equipment			100.2	102.2
电气机械和器材制造业	Manufacture of Electrical Machinery and Equipment	102.5	102.3	99.7	103.1
计算机、通信和其他电子设备制造业	Manufacture of Communication Equipment, Computers and Other Electronic Equipment	97.1	99.0	99.8	99.4
仪器仪表制造业	Manufacture of Measuring Instruments and Machinery	100.1	99.8	100.3	100.6
其他制造业	Other Manufacturing	100.5	109.3	103.0	100.8
废弃资源综合利用业	Utilization of Waste Resources		113.4	93.1	111.7
金属制品、机械和设备修理业	Repair Service of Metal Products,Machinery and Equipment			112.6	113.1
电力、热力生产和供应业	Production and Supply of Electric Power and Heat Power	102.4	98.8	98.7	98.6
燃气生产和供应业	Production and Supply of Gas	115.9	112.1	87.2	111.8
水的生产和供应业	Production and Supply of Water	100.8	102.8	102.0	103.0

注:2016年起，由于使用新的国民经济行业分类GB/4754-2011，之前年份个别行业数据缺失或数据涵盖范围存在差异。

Note: Since 2016 indices are by the industrial classification standard of 2011's version.Datas are lost in some sub-industries and there are diffecences in the scope of datas caculated.

9-10 工业生产者购进价格指数
Producer Price Indices for Purchased Goods

上年=100 (preceding year=100)

项　目	Item	2005	2010	2013	2014	2015	2016	2017
工业生产者购进价格指数	**Producer Price Index for Purchased Goods**	**105.0**	**107.3**	**98.2**	**98.8**	**95.3**	**98.0**	**105.3**
按材料类别分	**Grouped by Type of Material**							
燃料、动力类	Fuels and Power	112.2	107.8	95.7	98.4	91.6	94.8	106.2
黑色金属材料类	Ferrous Materials	110.5	106.6	97.1	96.1	89.2	97.2	115.8
#钢材	Steel	108.5	105.9	95.8	95.9	91.2	98.1	115.8
其它	Others	114.2	107.6	99.1	96.2	85.8	95.7	115.9
有色金属材料和电线类	Nonferrous Materials and Wires	111.4	117.8	97.5	97.0	93.2	97.3	115.0
化工原料类	Chemical Materials	107.2	109.4	97.8	98.7	94.2	97.9	107.1
木材及纸浆类	Timber and Paper Pulp	102.3	107.6	99.0	99.4	99.1	99.8	108.6
建筑材料及非金属矿类	Building Materials and Nonmetal Minerals	100.6	113.6	99.2	103.5	90.7	96.0	108.2
其它工业原材料及半成品类	Other Raw Materials and Semi-finished Products	99.1	103.7	99.2	99.0	97.9	99.2	102.4
农副产品类	Farm and Products	104.8	112.9	100.0	100.9	99.0	99.6	103.6
纺织原料类	Textile Raw Materials	99.1	109.3	99.6	97.8	97.5	98.9	103.5

9-11 固定资产投资价格指数
Price Indices for Investment in Fixed Assets

上年=100 (preceding year=100)

项　目	Item	2005	2010	2013	2014	2015	2016	2017
固定资产投资价格指数	**Price Index of Investment in Fixed Assets**	**101.6**	**103.0**	**101.4**	**101.5**	**99.0**	**100.3**	**105.3**
建筑安装、装饰工程	Construction, Installation and Decoration	102.3	104.3	101.9	102.0	98.4	100.4	107.4
人工费	Manpower	104.5	109.0	108.9	107.7	106.8	105.2	105.4
材料费	Materials	101.7	103.4	99.7	100.2	95.3	98.7	108.9
钢材	Steel	100.2	103.4	96.0	96.3	89.6	97.6	117.0
木材	Timber	101.3	103.1	102.6	102.1	101.5	100.1	102.7
水泥	Cement	100.0	105.7	101.3	102.4	97.8	97.4	106.1
地方建筑材料	Local Building Materials	103.3	102.9	103.6	104.1	100.6	100.1	104.7
化工材料	Chemical Materials	106.7	106.2	101.1	100.4	96.4	97.5	102.3
电料	Electrical Materials and Appliances	105.0	101.7	100.7	101.1	100.4	100.1	102.5
其他材料	Other Materials	101.7	101.3	101.7	102.1	101.7	101.5	102.2
机械费	Machinery	101.8	102.7	103.7	102.3	101.1	101.2	102.7
设备、工器具购置	Purchase of Equipment, Tools and Instruments	98.7	99.8	99.1	99.7	99.4	99.3	100.9
其他费用	Others	102.2	101.4	101.7	101.3	101.1	100.7	101.1

9-12 农业生产资料价格分类指数
Price Indices for Means of Agricultural Production by Category

上年=100 (preceding year=100)

项　目	Item	2016	2017
农业生产资料价格指数	**Price Index of Means of Agricultural Production**	**102.0**	**100.4**
农用手工工具	Farm Handtools	103.3	104.3
饲料	Forage	99.3	95.8
混合饲料	Mixed Forage	98.6	93.2
其他饲料	Other Forage	101.8	105.0
仔畜幼禽及产品畜	Newborn Animal and Animal Products	126.2	88.2
半机械化农具	Semi-mechanized Farm Tools	100.8	100.2
机械化农具	Mechanized Farm Machinery	98.9	100.8
化学肥料	Chemical Fertilizer	99.6	102.3
氮肥	Nitrogenous Fertilizer	97.5	105.0
磷肥	Phosphate Fertilizer	102.4	102.9
钾肥	Potash Fertilizer	100.2	98.7
复合肥料	Compound Fertilizer	100.7	99.6
农药及农药器械	Pesticide and Its Appliances	100.9	102.1
化学农药	Chemical Pesticide	100.6	102.0
杀虫剂	Insecticide	100.6	101.6
杀菌剂	Bactericide	101.9	103.4
除草剂	Herbicide	99.5	101.3
生长调节剂	Growth Regulator	100.1	101.7
农药器械	Appliances for Pesticide	102.3	103.1
农机用油	Agricultural Machinery Oil	96.6	107.5
其他农用生产资料	Other Means of Agricultural Production	101.2	104.2
农用种子	Seeds for Farming	101.7	105.0
农用薄膜	Pellicle for Farming	100.3	102.4
其他农用生产资料	Other Means of Agricultural Production	99.9	102.6
农业生产服务	Services for Agricultural Production	101.0	107.4
排灌费	Expenditure of Irrigation and Drainage	100.1	101.1
机械作业费	Expenditure of Mechanical Operations	101.0	111.2
农业用电	Agricultural Use of Electricity	100.0	99.3
农业用工	Agricultural Labor	102.7	112.9

9-13 农产品生产者价格指数

Producer Price Indices for Agricultural Products

上年=100 (preceding year=100)

项 目	Item	2012	2013	2014	2015	2016	2017
农产品生产者价格指数	**Producer Price Indices of Agricultural Products**	**103.4**	**103.5**	**102.2**	**102.3**	**106.5**	**99.4**
农业产品	**Farm Products**	**106.9**	**106.3**	**102.4**	**103.2**	**107.9**	**100.9**
谷物	Cereal	106.0	100.0	103.4	106.3	98.7	100.5
#稻谷	Rice	106.0	99.9	103.5	106.4	98.7	100.5
薯类	Potato	90.3	110.5	106.1	104.0	108.6	107.6
油料	Oil-bearing Crops	104.2	99.9	101.9	105.3	102.9	98.8
豆类	Beans	102.0	107.1	107.3	100.6	104.5	96.4
糖料	Sugar Crops	75.6	93.6	99.2	99.4	110.2	114.4
未加工烟草	Raw Tobacco	122.1	108.1	99.6	103.3	101.6	99.4
蔬菜及食用菌	Vegetables & Edible Fungi	111.5	109.5	99.4	103.7	114.8	95.6
#叶菜类蔬菜	Leaf Vegetable	112.1	111.8	101.7	100.9	112.0	90.9
白菜类蔬菜	Chinese Cabbage Vegetable	108.5	113.2	98.2	103.2	124.0	90.3
芥菜类蔬菜	Mustard Vegetable	110.7	107.6	97.6	100.0	118.0	95.1
甘蓝类蔬菜	Brassica Vegetable	112.2	108.8	97.8	109.6	116.4	85.9
根茎类蔬菜	Root Vegetable	108.0	94.6	111.5	106.3	132.1	93.9
瓜菜类蔬菜	Coucurbita Vegetable	106.5	116.5	94.6	106.5	104.0	104.8
豆类蔬菜	Bean Vegetable	115.6	107.0	106.5	103.4	100.5	102.8
茄果类蔬菜	Solanaceous Vegetable	127.1	101.3	96.7	101.7	113.0	101.7
莴苣及菊苣类蔬菜	Lettuce Vegetable	118.4	115.1	93.6	102.4	122.4	94.5
葱蒜类蔬菜	Bulb Vegetable	106.5	105.0	100.7	111.7	102.2	98.9
花卉	Flowers	103.4	100.2	103.1	99.7	105.6	104.4
盆景及园艺产品	Potted Landscape and Gardening Products	101.3	95.0	104.2	96.8	102.0	94.7
水果及坚果	Fruit and Nuts	104.1	112.4	103.7	103.9	110.5	106.1
茶及饮料原料	Tea and Beveage Raw Meterials	117.3	99.7	116.7	102.7	105.5	103.7
林业产品	**Forestry Products**	**101.8**	**105.2**	**103.6**	**99.9**	**98.4**	**102.0**
育种和育苗	Seed Breeding and Seedling	104.2	107.1	106.8	96.0	97.1	93.5
木材采伐产品	Wood Logging	101.8	103.3	101.3	101.6	99.0	100.5
竹材采伐产品	Bamboo Logging	104.2	101.9	101.6	100.4	97.2	99.8
林产品	Forestry Products	92.5	110.0	105.8	100.2	99.2	117.1
饲养动物及其产品	**Farm Animal and Products**	**97.6**	**99.7**	**98.6**	**103.1**	**109.2**	**92.0**
活牲畜	Live Animals	94.2	99.1	93.9	107.0	122.5	89.1
#猪	Pig	91.2	97.2	93.5	107.0	122.5	89.1
活家禽	Live Birds	101.7	99.6	104.4	100.3	99.5	96.7
#鸡	Chicken	102.2	100.9	103.6	98.9	97.4	98.6
鸭	Duck	100.3	99.1	102.7	99.8	101.3	99.7
畜禽产品	Animal and Bird Products	103.5	105.5	102.3	98.1	96.2	87.6
#鸡蛋	Chicken Eggs	103.6	103.5	103.3	98.3	99.5	81.2
鸭蛋	Duck Eggs	103.3	109.9	99.7	97.5	88.0	103.1
渔业产品	**Fishing Products**	**104.5**	**102.8**	**105.4**	**101.1**	**104.2**	**103.9**
海水养殖产品	Marine Farm Products	104.2	100.0	101.5	103.0	105.4	104.9
#海水养殖鱼	Marine Farm Fish	99.5	94.3	100.8	101.2	103.4	104.8
海水养殖虾	Marine Farm Shrimp	101.5	97.5	109.7	102.4	103.9	103.1
海水捕捞产品	Marine Catching Products	108.5	106.6	104.1	103.5	104.0	104.7
#海水捕捞鲜鱼	Marine Catching Fish	109.6	108.1	105.2	103.4	103.6	104.3
海水捕捞虾	Marine Catching Shrimp	110.7	104.8	103.8	108.2	110.1	107.4
淡水养殖产品	Freshwater Farm Products	101.9	102.5	107.9	98.4	101.8	103.0
#养殖淡水鱼	Freshwater Fram Fish	100.3	101.6	105.0	96.5	100.9	103.2
淡水养殖虾	Freshwater Fram Shrimp	102.7	107.9	116.7	105.2	105.9	102.0
淡水捕捞产品	Freshwater Catching Products	109.7	105.2	107.7	100.1	109.9	102.8
#捕捞淡水鱼	Freshwater Catching Fish	108.7	103.0	108.4	104.7	116.8	101.7
淡水捕捞鲜虾	Freshwater Catching Shrimp	120.4	105.1	101.5	97.8	113.5	105.9

主要统计指标解释

居民消费价格指数　是度量生活消费品及服务项目价格水平随着时间而变动的相对数，反映居民家庭购买的消费品及服务项目价格水平的变动情况。该指数是宏观经济分析、决策、调控和价格总水平监测以及国民经济核算的重要指标，其按年度计算的变动率通常被用来作为反映通货膨胀(或紧缩)程度的指标。

城市居民消费价格指数　是反映城市居民家庭所购买的生活消费品和服务项目价格变动趋势和变动程度的相对数。编制该指数，可以观察和分析消费品的零售价格和服务项目价格变动对城市居民生活消费支出的影响，作为研究城市居民生活和制定工资政策的依据。

农村居民消费价格指数　是反映农村居民家庭所购买的生活消费品和服务项目价格变动趋势和变动程度的相对数。编制该指数，可以观察农村消费品的零售价格和服务项目价格变动对农村居民生活消费支出的影响，反映农村居民生活水平的实际变化情况，为分析和研究农村居民生活问题提供依据。

商品零售价格指数　是度量市场商品零售价格水平变动趋势和变动程度的相对数，反映商品在流通过程中最后一个环节的价格即工业、商业、餐饮业和其他零售企业向城乡居民、机关团体出售生活消费品和办公用品价格水平的变动趋势和变动程度。其目的在于掌握商品价格的变动趋势，为国家宏观调控和国民经济核算提供参考依据。

工业生产者出厂价格指数　是反映工业企业产品第一次出售时的出厂价格变化趋势和变动幅度的相对数（2010 年前称工业品出厂价格指数），是综合了工业企业出售给本企业以外所有单位和个人的各种产品价格指数计算取得。是反映某一时期工业生产领域价格变动情况的重要经济指标，也是制定有关经济政策和国民经济核算的重要依据。

工业生产者购进价格指数　是反映工业企业作为中间投入产品购进价格的变化趋势和变动幅度的相对数（2010 年前称原材料、燃料、动力购进价格指数）。反映工业企业作为生产投入而从物资交易市场和能源、原材料生产企业购买原材料，燃料和动力产品时，所支付的价格水平变动趋势和程度的重要指标，是扣除工业企业物质消耗成本中的价格变动影响的重要依据。

固定资产投资价格指数　是反映全社会及各类工程固定资产投资价格变动幅度和变动趋势的相对数。编制该价格指数，用以消除按现价计算的固定资产指标中的价格变动因素，真实地反映全社会及各类工程固定资产投资的规模、速度、结构和效益，为国家及各部门科学地制定、检查固定资产投资计划和进行国民经济核算提供科学的、可靠的依据。

农业生产资料价格指数　是反映一定时期内农业生产资料在流通领域最后一个环节的价格即工业、商业及其他单位和个人向农民出售农业生产资料及服务价格水平的变动趋势和程度的相对数。其编制目的是了解农业生产中物质资料及服务投入价格的变动状况，为制定经济政策提供依据。1994 年以前，农业生产资料价格指数为商品零售价格指数的一个类别，此后单独编制。

农产品生产者价格指数　是反映农产品生产者第一手(直接)出售其产品时实际获得的单位产品价格。开展农产品生产者价格调查是为了全面收集农产品生产者价格资料，客观反映农产品生产者价格水平和结构变动情况，满足农业与国民经济核算需要，为各级政府制定农业保护与农产品流通政策提供决策依据，向社会各界提供优质的农产品价格信息报务。

Explanatory Notes on Main Statistical Indicators

Consumer Price Indices measure the relative change with time in prices of consumer goods and services, reflecting the rates of change in consumer goods and services purchased by households. It is an important indicator for macroeconomic analysis, decision–making, regularization and control, supervision of general price level and national economic accounting. The annualized rates of change are generally considered as an indicator of inflation or deflation.

Consumer Price Indices of Urban Households reflect the trend and degree of changes in prices of consumer goods and services purchased by urban households and can be used to observe and analyze the impact of price changes in consumer goods and services on urban household living expenditures, thus providing the basis for policy making concerning the living cost and the wages of urban staff and workers.

Consumer Price Indices of Rural Households reflect the trend and degree of changes in prices of consumer goods and services purchased by rural households and can be used to observe and analyze the impact of change in prices of consumer goods and services on living expenditure and actual changes in the living standards of rural residents, thus providing the basis for analysis and research on the conditions of life in rural areas.

Retail Price Indices measure the relative trend and degree of changes in retail prices of commodities, reflecting the trend of changes in prices in the last link of circulation, i.e. prices of consumer goods and office appliances sold to households or organizations by enterprises of industry, commerce, catering services and other retail trades. It reflects the trend of price changes and provides a reference for macroeconomic adjustment and control as well as national economic accounting.

Producer Price Indices for Manufactured Goods reflect the trend and degree of changes in general ex-factory prices of all manufactured goods on first sale (it was referred to as Ex-factory Price Indices for Industrial Goods). It is calculated on the basis of sales of manufactured goods by an industrial enterprise to all units outside the enterprise, as well as sales of consumer goods to residents.It is an import index reflecting the price changes on the course of industrial production, and provides important data for economic policy making and national economic accounting

Producer Price Indices for Purchased Goods reflect the trend and degree of changes in prices paid by industrial enterprises when they purchase production input (it was referred to as Purchasing Price Indices of Raw Materials, Fuels and Power). They reflect changes in the level and degree of prices paid by industrial enterprises when they purchase production input such as raw materials, fuels and power from the market or from other energy or raw materials producing enterprises. These indices provide an important basis for measuring the material consumption of industrial enterprises after removing the influence of price changes.

Price Indices of Investment in Fixed Assets reflect the trend and degree of changes in prices of investment in fixed assets in various projects and in the whole country. It can be used to remove the factor of price changes in the data of investment in fixed assets calculated at current prices, to truly reflect the scale, growth rate, structure, proportion and efficiency of investment in fixed assets in various projects and in the whole country, and to provide a scientific and reliable basis for formulating the plan for investment in fixed assets and examining its fulfillment as well as for conducting national economic accounting.

Price Indices for Means of Agricultural Production reflect the trend and degree of changes in the prices of the means of agricultural production at the final stage of the circulation, or the prices at which industrial, commercial or other units sell the means of agricultural production or services to farmers. Compilation of these indices helps to understand the changes in prices of input into agricultural production and services and facilitate formulation of economic policies. Before 1994, price indices for means of agricultural production were asub-category in the retail price indices for commodities, and it has been compiled separately since 1994.

Producer Price Indices of Agricultural Products refer to the actual prices per unit of agricultural products at which the producers of the agricultural products directly sell them. The purpose of conducting the survey of producer prices of agricultural products is to comprehensively collect the data on the producer prices of agricultural products, objectively reflect the situations of the level and structural changes of the producer prices of agricultural products, meet the needs of conducting the agricultural accounts and national accounts, provide the government at different levels with the base data for making the policies of protecting agriculture and circulation of agricultural products and provide the various social circles with the high quality information on the prices of agricultural products.

十、人民生活

PEOPLE'S LIVING CONDITIONS

十 人民生活

简要说明

一、本篇资料反映广东居民生活状况，主要内容包括广东全体居民及分城乡居民家庭人口、收入与消费支出结构、住房面积和主要耐用消费品拥有量等。

二、本篇资料由国家统计局广东调查总队居民收支调查处、住户专项调查处整理提供。

三、居民调查资料采用分层、多阶段随机抽样方法抽选调查对象

四、2013 年国家统计局实行城乡住户一体化调查改革，将过去城镇与农村分别开展的调查体系，按照统一指标、统一方法、统一标准、统一调查、统一程序的原则，整合为城乡一体化住户调查新体系。由于新旧调查体系在调查范围和对象、城乡划分标准、样本抽选方法、计算和汇总方式、指标名称和口径等都发生了变化，新旧口径指标数据存在不可比因素。

五、旧调查体系的农村居民纯收入指标在新的调查体系中统一为城乡可比的可支配收入，旧调查体系中的城乡经营性收入、财产性收入与转移性收入在新的调查体系中统一为经营净收入、财产净收入与转移净收入。

六、2013 年起为新口径数据， 2013 年以前的为原调查体系的数据。

10 People's Living Conditions

Brief Introduction

Ⅰ. The data in this chapter show the basic conditions of the people’s livelihood in the urban and rural areas of Guangdong Province. The main contents include urban and rural households population, per capita income and consumption expenditure structure, housing area and possession of the major consumer goods.

Ⅱ.The data in this chapter are prepared and provided by Division of Income and Expenditure Survey and Division of Special Surveys under Guangdong Survey Office of the National Bureau of Statistics.

Ⅲ. The survey date of urban and rural residents are collected through a stratified multi-stage random sampling scheme.

Ⅳ.The National Bureau of Statistics of China started an integrated reform of household survey in 2013, including both rural and urban households. According to the principle of unified index, unified standard, unified survey, unified software, unified release, the separate urban and rural household surveys are changed to the integrated household income and expenditure survey. Because there are great difference of survey scope and object, survey methodology, sample selection, data collection methodology between the integrated and the separate household survey, the data produced by the integrated system of household survey are not comparable to those produced by the separate urban and rural household surveys prior to 2013.

Ⅴ.The net income of rural households of the old household survey are integrated to the disposal income of rural households in the new household survey since 2013. Income from properties, transfers and business of the old household survey are unified to net income from properties, transfers and business in the new household survey.

Ⅵ.Data before 2013 are produced by the old survey system , data since 2013 are new scope.

10-1 全省常住居民家庭基本情况

Basic Conditions of All Permanent Households in the Province

指标	Item	2013	2014	2015	2016	2017
调查户数 （户）	**Survey of Households (households)**	**7795**	**7825**	**7972**	**8154**	**8082**
平均每户常住人口 （人）	Average Number of per Permanent Household (person)	2.88	2.92	2.99	3.06	3.08
平均每户就业人口 （人）	Average Number of Employed Persons per Household(person)	1.67	1.69	1.74	1.76	1.77
人均住房建筑面积（平方米）	**Per Capita Housing Construction Area (square meter)**	**31.81**	**34.29**	**35.44**	**36.30**	**36.94**
人均可支配收入 （元）	**Per Capita Disposable Income (yuan)**	**23420.8**	**25684.96**	**27858.86**	**30295.80**	**33003.29**
1.工资性收入	Income of Wages and Salaries	17282.4	18439.35	19878.15	21361.90	23052.87
2.经营净收入	Net Business Income	3094.25	3458.11	3748.05	4101.77	4420.89
3.财产净收入	Net Income from Properties	1977.29	2376.20	2683.22	3096.49	3602.02
4.转移净收入	Net Income from Transfers	1066.87	1411.30	1549.43	1735.64	1927.50
可支配收入构成 （%）	**Composition of Disposable Income (%)**	**100.0**	**100.0**	**100.0**	**100.0**	**100.0**
1.工资性收入	Income of Wages and Salaries	73.8	71.8	71.4	70.5	69.9
2.经营净收入	Net Business Income	13.2	13.5	13.5	13.5	13.5
3.财产净收入	Net Income from Properties	8.4	9.3	9.6	10.2	10.8
4.转移净收入	Net Income from Transfers	4.6	5.4	5.6	5.8	5.8
人均消费支出 （元）	**Per Capita Consumption Expenditure (yuan)**	**17421.00**	**19205.50**	**20975.70**	**23448.42**	**24819.63**
1.食品烟酒	Food,Tobacco and Liquor	6097.33	6589.77	7236.65	8015.09	8317.04
2.衣着	Clothing	951.06	1014.62	1103.37	1209.90	1230.32
3.居住	Living	3962.71	4300.16	4677.06	5247.05	5790.91
4.生活用品及服务	Daily Necessities and Services	999.30	1116.53	1245.27	1401.95	1447.45
5.交通通信	Transportation and Telecommunication	2400.12	2795.14	3020.19	3296.50	3380.02
6.教育文化娱乐	Education,Culture and Entertainment	1810.95	1964.98	2117.29	2451.16	2620.37
7.医疗保健	Health Service	728.89	890.45	976.08	1144.87	1319.46
8.其他用品和服务	Other Necessities and Services	470.63	533.85	599.79	681.91	714.05
消费支出构成 （%）	**Composition of Consumption Expenditure (%)**	**100.0**	**100.0**	**100.0**	**100.0**	**100.0**
1.食品烟酒	Food,Tobacco and Liquor	35.0	34.3	34.5	34.2	33.5
2.衣着	Clothing	5.5	5.3	5.3	5.2	5.0
3.居住	Living	22.7	22.4	22.3	22.4	23.3
4.生活用品及服务	Daily Necessities and Services	5.7	5.8	5.9	6.0	5.8
5.交通通信	Transportation and Telecommunication	13.8	14.6	14.4	14.0	13.6
6.教育文化娱乐	Education,Culture and Entertainment	10.4	10.2	10.1	10.4	10.6
7.医疗保健	Health Service	4.2	4.6	4.7	4.9	5.3
8.其他用品和服务	Other Necessities and Services	2.7	2.8	2.8	2.9	2.9

10-2 按收入五等份分组的全体常住居民人均可支配收入

Per Capita Disposable Income of Provincewide Households by Income Quintile

单位：元 (yuan)

年份 Year	低收入户 (20%) Low Income Households (20%)	中等偏下户 (20%) Lower Middle Income Households (20%)	中等收入户 (20%) Middle Income Households (20%)	中等偏上户 (20%) Upper Middle Income Households (20%)	高收入户 (20%) High Income Households (20%)
2014	8217.51	15943.33	24262.68	34567.56	61108.41
2015	9061.46	17872.97	27320.78	37925.00	63045.38
2016	9544.65	19574.65	30598.48	41989.63	68599.33
2017	10534.31	20963.27	32339.36	45235.77	75774.57

10-3 全省常住居民人均主要食品消费量

Per Capita Consumption of Major Foods Provincewide

单位:千克 (Kg)

指　标	Item	2013	2014	2015	2016	2017
粮食(原粮)	**Grain(Unprocessed)**	116.06	116.91	118.31	118.12	116.80
谷物	Cereal	108.99	109.12	110.49	109.94	108.86
薯类	Tuber	1.13	1.39	1.42	1.55	1.64
豆类	Beans and the Productor	5.94	6.39	6.40	6.63	6.30
油脂类	Oil and Fats	9.41	10.39	10.18	9.57	9.23
#食用植物油	Edible Vegetable Oil	8.94	9.97	9.66	9.17	8.83
蔬菜及菜制品	Vegetable and Mushroom	90.94	96.60	98.94	98.72	100.76
#鲜菜	Fresh Vegetables	87.45	92.92	94.93	94.62	96.66
肉类	Products of Meat	33.97	35.30	36.46	36.16	36.51
#猪肉	Pork	27.82	29.04	29.70	29.07	29.07
禽类	Poultry	16.39	16.90	18.65	20.07	20.62
#鸡	Chick	10.60	10.92	12.26	13.18	13.40
水产品	Aquatic Products	19.71	20.81	22.03	21.98	22.85
#鱼类	Fresh	15.22	15.70	16.19	16.44	16.86
蛋类	Eggs	5.92	6.36	6.95	7.03	7.32
#鲜蛋	Fresh Eggs	5.49	5.99	6.55	6.65	6.89
奶及奶制品	Milk and Dairy Products	7.62	7.85	8.33	7.54	7.71
#鲜奶	Fresh Milk	4.89	4.89	4.87	4.14	4.21
干鲜瓜果类	Dried and Fresh Melons and Fruits	29.47	32.29	36.00	38.12	40.11
#鲜瓜果	Fresh Melons and Fruits	26.54	29.27	32.71	34.59	36.39
糖果糕点类	Candy Pastry	6.51	6.54	6.73	6.54	6.32
#食糖	Sugar	1.41	1.50	1.45	1.54	1.54

10-4 全省常住居民家庭平均每百户年末主要耐用消费品拥有量

Number of Major Durable Consumer Goods Owned per 100 Permanent Households

指 标		Item		2013	2014	2015	2016	2017
家用汽车	(辆)	Car	(set)	19.46	20.71	24.58	29.36	31.58
摩托车	(辆)	Motorcycle	(set)	50.22	57.61	60.75	62.78	64.24
电动助力车	(台)	Electric Bicycle	(set)	16.93	19.66	23.05	27.17	30.88
洗衣机	(台)	Washing Machine	(set)	60.62	64.06	69.28	75.09	78.18
电冰箱(柜)	(台)	Refrigerator	(set)	67.56	70.79	76.10	80.69	84.44
微波炉	(台)	Microwave Oven	(set)	31.83	32.62	33.96	36.11	38.13
彩色电视机	(台)	Color Television	(set)	97.92	102.85	104.27	104.84	106.91
空调	(台)	Air Conditioner	(set)	104.91	109.39	122.24	136.18	145.24
热水器	(台)	Water Heater	(unit)	74.33	77.31	81.98	85.23	88.72
排油烟机	(台)	Fume hood	(set)	47.19	48.68	49.98	52.67	55.35
固定电话	(部)	Telephone	(set)	48.38	55.42	51.61	45.35	43.65
移动电话	(部)	Mobile Phone	(set)	209.69	220.78	233.72	241.86	248.76
计算机	(台)	Computer	(set)	64.54	67.88	70.90	73.94	75.83
摄像机	(台)	Video Camera	(set)	4.79	5.15	4.79	4.71	
照相机	(台)	Camera	(set)	30.14	29.81	28.36	24.74	24.61
健身器材	(台)	Fitness Equipment	(set)	2.12	2.90	5.00	5.65	7.24
组合音响	(套)	Stereophonic Phonograph	(set)	16.15	17.14	15.07	13.53	

10-5 按收入五等份分组的全体常住居民家庭平均每百户主要耐用消费品年末拥有量（2017）

Grouped by Five Equal Shares of Number of Major Durable Consumer Goods Owned per100 Rural and Urban Permanent Households at Year-end (2017)

指 标		Item		低收入户 (20%) Low income families (20%)	中等偏下户 (20%) Below Average families (20%)	中等收入户 (20%) Average families (20%)	中等偏上户 (20%) Above Average families (20%)	高收入户 (20%) High income family (20%)
家用汽车	(辆)	Car	(set)	10.96	22.51	29.61	34.07	60.74
摩托车	(辆)	Motorcycle	(set)	114.16	99.69	58.32	31.20	17.90
电动助力车	(台)	Electric Bicycle	(set)	37.42	44.05	27.46	26.54	18.97
洗衣机	(台)	Washing Machine	(set)	78.26	87.38	72.85	67.18	85.23
电冰箱(柜)	(台)	Refrigerator	(set)	85.07	93.10	78.51	75.42	90.12
微波炉	(台)	Microwave Oven	(set)	24.71	35.07	35.52	38.99	56.35
彩色电视机	(台)	Color Television	(set)	117.43	118.33	97.83	89.66	111.29
空调	(台)	Air Conditioner	(set)	84.13	134.75	146.40	143.56	217.31
热水器	(台)	Water Heater	(unit)	87.74	96.84	85.01	79.90	94.12
排油烟机	(台)	Fume Hood	(set)	39.24	56.35	54.97	55.03	71.16
固定电话	(部)	Telephone	(set)	42.13	48.15	40.84	36.37	50.76
移动电话	(部)	Mobile Phone	(set)	275.27	283.12	241.96	216.60	226.89
计算机	(台)	Computer	(set)	37.83	68.44	76.37	82.84	113.64
照相机	(台)	Camera	(set)	3.47	11.53	23.78	32.38	51.87
健身器材	(台)	Fitness Equipment	(set)	1.13	3.53	6.81	7.60	17.12

10-6 全省常住居民家庭年末住房情况

Housing Condition of All Permanent Households in the Province at the Year-end

单位：% (%)

指　标	Item	2013	2014	2015	2016	2017
一、住户居住类型	**Residential type**	**100.0**	**100.0**	**100.0**	**100.0**	**100.0**
普通住宅	Ordinary Residence	83.5	85.6	87.5	87.9	89.1
集体宿舍和工棚	Dormitory and Shed	16.2	14.0	12.3	12.0	10.7
工作地住宿	Work Accommodation	0.3	0.4	0.2	0.1	0.2
二、住户居住空间样式	**Residential Space Type**	**100.0**	**100.0**	**100.0**	**100.0**	**100.0**
单栋楼房	Single building	28.8	32.3	30.6	33.9	34.9
单栋平房	Single Bungalow	10.8	11.5	10.1	8.2	8.1
四居室及以上单元房	Four Bedroom and above Apartment	4.0	3.7	4.1	4.8	5.0
三居室单元房	Tree Bedroom Apartment	17.8	17.6	17.7	18.6	18.7
二居室单元房	Two Bedroom Apartment	15.1	14.2	13.5	12.3	12.4
一居室单元房	One Bedroom Apartment	22.2	19.3	22.8	21.3	19.9
筒子楼或连片平房	Tube-shaped Apartment or Contiguous Bungalow	1.2	1.2	1.1	0.8	0.9
其他	Others	0.1	0.2	0.1	0.1	0.1
三、主要建筑材料	**Main Building Materials**	**100.0**	**100.0**	**100.0**	**100.0**	**100.0**
钢筋混凝土	Reinforced concrete	71.3	69.4	73.7	78.3	77.6
砖混材料	brick and concrete Materials	21.5	22.8	19.7	16.5	17.3
砖瓦砖木	Brick and tile	6.8	7.4	6.4	5.0	4.9
其他	Others	0.4	0.4	0.2	0.2	0.2
四、住户主要饮用水来源情况	**Main Source of Householders'drinking Water**	**100.0**	**100.0**	**100.0**	**100.0**	**100.0**
经过净化处理的自来水	Purified Tap Water	82.6	81.0	82.2	84.1	84.3
受保护的井水和泉水	Protected Well and Spring	6.5	7.7	8.2	7.6	7.4
不受保护的井水和泉水	Unprotected well and spring	4.5	4.9	4.0	3.8	3.8
桶装水	Bottled Water	5.2	5.3	4.5	3.4	3.4
其他	Others	1.2	1.1	1.1	1.1	1.1
五、住户厕所使用情况	**Household Toilet Usage**	**100.0**	**100.0**	**100.0**	**100.0**	**100.0**
本住户独用	Sole Household Use	78.8	81.1	83.7	85.5	87.2
几户合用	Several Household Share	17.8	15.7	13.8	12.7	11.3
公用厕所	Public Toilet	3.4	3.2	2.5	1.8	1.5
六、主要炊用能源状况	**Main Cooking Energy Condition**	**100.0**	**100.0**	**100.0**	**100.0**	**100.0**
柴草	Firewood	9.8	11.7	10.4	9.2	9.0
煤炭	Coal	0.5	0.2	0.1	…	0.0
罐装液化石油气	Canned Liquefied Petroleum Gas	53.4	52.7	52.4	54.6	55.1
管道液化石油气	Pipeline Liquefied Petroleum Gas	3.4	2.8	2.2	2.3	2.3
管道煤气	Pipeline Gas	1.0	0.9	0.8	0.6	0.6
管道天然气	Pipeline Natural Gas	11.0	12.3	13.8	14.5	15.2
电	Electricity	8.8	8.9	11.7	11.5	10.3
其他	Others	12.1	10.5	8.6	7.3	7.5

10−7 各市全体常住居民人均可支配收入

Per Capita Disposable Income of Urban Permanent Households by City

单位：元 (yuan)

市别	City	2014	2015	2016	2017
广州	Guangzhou	39229.1	42718.2	46667.0	50782.2
深圳	Shenzhen	40948.0	44633.3	48695.0	52938.0
珠海	Zhuhai	33234.9	36157.9	40154.1	44043.1
汕头	Shantou	17266.3	18996.0	20713.0	22521.0
佛山	Foshan	35139.8	38501.3	41940.7	45813.3
韶关	Shaoguan	16622.7	18143.1	19977.5	21865.9
河源	Heyuan	13283.1	14548.1	16077.4	17717.7
梅州	Meizhou	14893.8	16404.4	17986.6	19635.0
惠州	Huizhou	22901.6	25219.6	28061.4	31090.6
汕尾	Shanwei	15211.6	16473.5	17936.7	19325.8
东莞	Dongguan	35711.9	38650.6	41901.9	45450.6
中山	Zhongshan	32847.4	35712.2	40012.4	43553.7
江门	Jiangmen	20585.7	22364.4	24426.7	26850.6
阳江	Yangjiang	16311.2	17777.3	19513.2	21443.9
湛江	Zhanjiang	15301.8	16631.7	17934.4	19631.6
茂名	Maoming	15266.2	16847.3	18402.7	19885.2
肇庆	Zhaoqing	17333.5	18991.4	20579.8	22360.0
清远	Qingyuan	15637.0	17070.0	18859.3	20692.0
潮州	Chaozhou	15242.5	16815.6	18060.5	19429.0
揭阳	Jieyang	14953.2	16308.4	17654.1	18750.1
云浮	Yunfu	14061.3	15212.4	16517.6	17874.5
按经济区域分	By Region				
珠三角	Pearl River Delta	33642.1	36662.0	40109.1	43840.1
东翼	Eastern Region	15782.0	17274.7	18744.6	20166.7
西翼	Western Region	15448.5	16895.9	18364.5	20016.4
山区	Mountainous Region	14948.7	16344.8	17967.6	19657.1

注：按照国家统计局的统一部署，全省分市县城乡一体化住户调查工作从2013年底正式启动，从2014年开始正式对外发布分市全体常住居民人均可支配收入数据。

Note: Under the unified deployment by NBS, Guangdong province started an integrated househould survey by city and county since October 2013, inluding both urban and rural households . Since 2014 the data of per caipita disposal income and expenditures of all permannet househoulds in the province by city is realsed officially after the transitional period.

10-8 各市全体常住居民人均可支配收入来源（2017年）
Per Capita Disposable Income of Permanent Households by Sources and City (2017)

单位：元 (yuan)

地区	City	可支配收入 Disposable Income	工资性收入 Income of Wages and Salaries	经营净收入 Net Business Income	财产净收入 Net Income from Property	转移净收入 Net Income from Tranfer
广州	Guangzhou	50782.16	34244.03	3096.85	8767.49	4673.79
深圳	Shenzhen	52938.00	43906.08	6450.06	5739.34	-3157.48
珠海	Zhuhai	44043.12	32940.96	3545.37	5929.19	1627.60
汕头	Shantou	22520.95	15487.46	2755.12	1442.53	2835.84
佛山	Foshan	45813.28	29508.78	6449.21	6944.10	2911.19
韶关	Shaoguan	21865.90	12704.13	4337.03	1702.05	3122.69
河源	Heyuan	17717.70	11497.30	3519.10	519.60	2181.70
梅州	Meizhou	19635.00	11034.00	3756.70	819.40	4024.90
惠州	Huizhou	31090.60	21005.60	5842.65	2836.84	1405.55
汕尾	Shanwei	19325.80	11684.72	3530.41	655.89	3454.73
东莞	Dongguan	45450.61	34016.56	4427.79	7713.25	-706.99
中山	Zhongshan	43553.73	30003.98	5662.98	4020.13	3866.64
江门	Jiangmen	26850.60	20266.90	1952.06	2220.60	2411.04
阳江	Yangjiang	21443.90	12521.53	4591.65	1569.49	2761.22
湛江	Zhanjiang	19631.60	11359.59	4416.90	835.56	3019.57
茂名	Maoming	19885.20	11098.69	2481.34	1558.83	4746.37
肇庆	Zhaoqing	22360.01	13831.90	3705.05	1368.43	3454.62
清远	Qingyuan	20692.04	12669.15	3961.79	787.56	3273.54
潮州	Chaozhou	19429.01	11633.91	3839.22	989.25	2966.65
揭阳	Jieyang	18750.13	10385.16	4556.72	965.88	2842.38
云浮	Yunfu	17874.48	11202.77	2716.36	842.23	3113.13

10-9 各市全体常住居民人均消费支出

Per Capita Consumption Expenditure of Urban Permanent Households by City

单位：元 (yuan)

市别	City	2014	2015	2016	2017
广州	Guangzhou	30578.7	32886.7	35388.0	37496.1
深圳	Shenzhen	28852.8	32359.2	36480.6	38320.1
珠海	Zhuhai	25125.8	27199.0	30479.3	32981.4
汕头	Shantou	14562.5	16181.3	17532.6	18789.2
佛山	Foshan	24849.1	27713.1	30561.6	32648.0
韶关	Shaoguan	12221.0	13383.3	14804.1	16055.7
河源	Heyuan	9978.0	10765.2	12236.8	13580.7
梅州	Meizhou	11223.2	12394.3	13823.9	15298.6
惠州	Huizhou	16985.8	18314.9	20461.3	22968.8
汕尾	Shanwei	11596.3	12728.9	14167.0	15180.9
东莞	Dongguan	26532.4	28255.6	29905.6	31849.5
中山	Zhongshan	22013.4	23399.1	26636.9	29034.2
江门	Jiangmen	14257.7	15610.9	17281.9	19302.4
阳江	Yangjiang	13144.7	14013.9	15793.9	17217.9
湛江	Zhanjiang	11438.8	12273.8	13303.6	14513.9
茂名	Maoming	11238.7	12427.5	13480.1	14494.5
肇庆	Zhaoqing	11492.1	12554.7	13927.6	14867.7
清远	Qingyuan	11763.7	12811.9	14403.0	15580.2
潮州	Chaozhou	11899.4	12749.9	13752.1	14561.9
揭阳	Jieyang	11527.1	12440.4	13248.7	14036.1
云浮	Yunfu	10636.9	11432.2	12323.9	13383.4
按经济区域分	By Region				
珠三角	Pearl River Delta	24564.3	26780.4	29416.7	34353.0
东翼	Eastern Region	12566.6	13733.1	14856.6	15844.5
西翼	Western Region	11633.0	12608.4	13766.3	14935.3
山区	Mountainous Region	11206.9	12221.7	13614.6	14896.4

注：按照国家统计局的统一部署，广东省分市县城乡一体化住户调查工作从2013年底正式启动，从2014年开始正式对外发布分市全体常住居民人均消费支出数据。

Note: Under the unified deployment by NBS, Guangdong province started an integrated househould survey by city and county since October 2013, inluding both urban and rural households . Since 2014 the data of per caipita disposal income and expenditures of all permannet househoulds in the province by city is realsed officially after the transitional period.

10-10 城镇常住居民家庭基本情况

Basic Conditions of Urban Permanent Households

指　标	Item	2013	2014	2015	2016	2017
调查户数　（户）	**Survey of Households (household)**	**4761**	**5221**	**5453**	**5542**	**5477**
平均每户常住人口（人）	Average Number of Residents per Permanent Household (person)	2.59	2.69	2.77	2.83	2.87
平均每户就业人口（人）	Average Number of Employed Persons per Permanent Household (person)	1.54	1.59	1.63	1.66	1.67
人均住房建筑面积（平方米）	**Per Capita Housing Construction Area(sq.m)**	**30.27**	**31.88**	**32.25**	**32.74**	**33.09**
人均可支配收入　（元）	**Per Capita Disposable Income (yuan)**	**29537.29**	**32148.11**	**34757.16**	**37684.25**	**40975.14**
1.工资性收入	Income of Wages and Salaries	23031.59	24315.60	26136.85	27965.30	30087.32
2.经营净收入	Net Business Income	3117.21	3547.42	3823.19	4203.91	4560.78
3.财产净收入	Income from Properties	2762.22	3376.82	3799.54	4374.77	5077.21
4.转移净收入	Income from Transfers	626.27	908.27	997.58	1140.27	1249.83
人均消费支出　（元）	**Per Capita Consumption Expenditure (yuan)**	**21621.46**	**23611.74**	**25673.08**	**28613.33**	**30197.91**
1.食品烟酒	Food,Tobacco and Liquor	7254.04	7850.17	8533.35	9421.58	9711.65
2.衣着	Clothing	1283.22	1344.75	1453.68	1583.42	1587.10
3.居住	Living	4987.86	5291.47	5715.35	6410.37	7127.84
4.生活用品及服务	Daily Necessities and Services	1235.16	1365.10	1526.29	1721.85	1782.84
5.交通通信	Transportation and Telecommunication	3139.02	3625.42	3905.05	4198.09	4285.55
6.教育文化娱乐	Education,Culture and Entertainment	2315.55	2468.38	2671.54	3103.40	3284.28
7.医疗保健	Health Service	793.62	988.32	1096.42	1304.48	1503.56
8.其他用品和服务	Other Necessities and Services	612.98	678.14	771.41	870.14	915.10
消费支出构成　（%）	**Composition of Consumption Expenditure**	**100.0**	**100.0**	**100.0**	**100.0**	**100.0**
1.食品烟酒	Food,Tobacco and Liquor	33.6	33.2	33.2	32.9	32.2
2.衣着	Clothing	5.9	5.7	5.7	5.5	5.3
3.居住	Living	23.1	22.4	22.3	22.4	23.5
4.生活用品及服务	Daily Necessities and Services	5.7	5.8	5.9	6.0	5.9
5.交通通信	Transportation and Telecommunication	14.5	15.4	15.2	14.7	14.2
6.教育文化娱乐	Education,Culture and Entertainment	10.7	10.5	10.4	10.9	10.9
7.医疗保健	Health Service	3.7	4.2	4.3	4.6	5.0
8.其他用品和服务	Other Necessities and Services	2.8	2.8	3.0	3.0	3.0

10−11 历年城镇常住居民人均可支配收入及生活消费支出(1978−2012)
Per Capita Disposable Income and Consumption Expenditure of Urban Permanent Households (1978-2012)

年份 Year	人均可支配收入(元) Per Capita Disposable Income (yuan)	指数 Index			人均消费支出(元) Per Capita Consumption Expenditure (yuan)	指数 Index		恩格尔系数(%) Engle Coefficient (%)
		名义增长(上年为100) Nominal Growth (preceding year=100)	实际增长(上年为100) Real Growth (preceding year=100)	实际增长(1978年为100) Real Growth (1978=100)		名义增长(上年为100) Nominal Growth (preceding year=100)	实际增长(上年为100) Real Growth (preceding year=100)	
1978	412.13	101.0	96.6	100	399.96	106.3	101.5	66.6
1979	416.33	101.0	96.6	96.6	424.96	106.3	101.5	67.0
1980	472.57	113.5	103.7	100.1	485.76	114.3	104.5	65.5
1981	560.69	118.6	111.6	111.7	517.44	106.5	100.2	65.8
1982	631.45	112.6	109.8	122.7	592.08	114.4	111.5	64.2
1983	714.20	113.1	110.0	135.0	660.12	111.5	108.5	64.5
1984	818.37	114.6	112.4	151.8	744.36	112.8	110.7	63.6
1985	954.12	116.6	99.6	151.1	889.56	119.5	102.1	58.3
1986	1102.09	115.5	110.3	166.7	998.88	112.3	107.2	58.6
1987	1320.89	119.9	106.3	177.1	1215.84	121.7	107.9	56.7
1988	1583.13	119.9	92.6	163.9	1506.99	123.9	95.7	56.7
1989	2086.21	131.8	108.1	177.2	1921.05	127.5	104.6	56.5
1990	2303.15	110.4	113.3	200.8	1983.86	103.3	106.0	57.2
1991	2752.18	119.5	116.8	234.6	2388.77	120.4	117.7	53.1
1992	3476.70	126.3	116.5	273.4	2830.62	118.5	110.4	51.5
1993	4632.38	133.2	109.2	298.6	3777.43	133.4	110.3	48.9
1994	6367.08	137.4	113.6	339.2	5181.30	137.2	113.4	46.4
1995	7438.68	116.8	103.3	350.4	6253.68	120.7	106.7	48.0
1996	8157.81	109.7	102.3	358.4	6736.09	107.7	100.5	47.3
1997	8561.71	105.0	102.8	368.4	6853.48	101.7	99.7	46.0
1998	8839.68	103.2	105.0	387.0	7054.09	102.9	104.7	44.1
1999	9125.92	103.2	104.9	406.0	7517.81	106.6	108.3	40.6
2000	9761.57	107.0	104.7	424.9	8016.91	106.6	104.3	38.6
2001	10415.19	106.7	107.6	457.0	8099.63	101.0	101.8	38.1
2002	11137.20	109.1	110.6	495.7	8988.48	111.0	112.6	38.5
2003	12380.40	111.2	110.4	547.2	9636.24	107.2	106.5	37.2
2004	13627.65	110.1	107.3	587.0	10694.79	111.0	108.2	37.0
2005	14769.94	108.4	106.3	623.8	11809.87	110.4	108.2	36.1
2006	16015.58	108.4	106.5	664.3	12432.22	105.3	103.4	36.2
2007	17699.30	110.5	106.6	707.9	14336.87	115.3	111.2	35.3
2008	19732.86	111.5	105.7	748.3	15527.97	108.3	102.7	37.8
2009	21574.72	109.3	112.0	838.1	16857.51	108.6	111.3	36.9
2010	23897.80	110.8	107.5	901.0	18489.53	109.7	106.4	36.5
2011	26897.48	112.6	106.9	963.2	20251.82	109.5	104.0	36.9
2012	30226.71	112.4	109.3	1052.8	22396.35	110.6	107.6	36.9

10-12 按收入五等份分组的城镇常住居民家庭平均每人收支及构成（2017）

Per Capita of Disposal Income and Expenditure and Composition of Urban Permanent Households by Income Quintile (2017)

指标	Item	低收入户（20%）Low Income Households（20%）	中等偏下户（20%）Lower Middle Income Households（20%）	中等收入户（20%）Middle Income Households（20%）	中等偏上户（20%）Upper Middle Income Households（20%）	高收入户（20%）High Income Households（20%）
人均可支配收入（元）	**Per Capita Disposable Income (yuan)**	**17161.46**	**30134.80**	**39729.82**	**51506.77**	**82140.93**
1.工资性收入	Income of Wages and Salaries	12304.64	22522.53	31939.26	39358.29	56139.51
2.经营净收入	Net Business Income	2047.47	3276.09	3431.44	4492.72	11180.87
3.财产净收入	Net Income from Properties	1337.49	2989.24	4292.99	6359.73	12933.89
4.转移净收入	Net Income from Transfers	1471.87	1346.93	66.13	1296.03	1886.65
可支配收入构成（%）	**Composition of Disposable Income (%)**	**100.0**	**100.0**	**100.0**	**100.0**	**100.0**
1.工资性收入	Income of Wages and Salaries	71.7	74.7	80.4	76.4	68.3
2.经营净收入	Net Business Income	11.9	10.9	8.6	8.8	13.7
3.财产净收入	Net Income from Properties	7.8	9.9	10.8	12.3	15.7
4.转移净收入	Net Income from Transfers	8.6	4.5	0.2	2.5	2.3
人均消费支出（元）	**Per Capita Consumption Expenditure (yuan)**	**15080.92**	**23752.20**	**29524.76**	**36277.78**	**56279.05**
1.食品烟酒	Food,Tobacco and Liquor	5939.48	8645.98	10271.15	11403.53	14695.02
2.衣着	Clothing	623.70	1175.07	1689.44	1980.86	3104.24
3.居住	Living	3293.38	5033.82	6180.40	8416.15	15291.67
4.生活用品及服务	Daily Necessities and Services	710.83	1314.69	1794.11	2053.63	3743.81
5.交通通信	Transportation and Telecommunication	1831.99	3229.22	4034.59	5702.98	8251.05
6.教育文化娱乐	Education,Culture and Entertainment	1520.07	2474.96	3269.29	4004.81	6324.55
7.医疗保健	Health Service	846.64	1216.49	1434.20	1670.07	2778.62
8.其他用品和服务	Other Necessities and Services	314.84	661.97	851.57	1045.76	2090.10
消费支出构成（%）	**Composition of Consumption Expenditure(%)**	**100.0**	**100.0**	**100.0**	**100.0**	**100.0**
1.食品烟酒	Food,Tobacco and Liquor	39.4	36.4	34.8	31.4	26.1
2.衣着	Clothing	4.2	4.9	5.6	5.5	5.5
3.居住	Living	21.8	21.2	20.9	23.2	27.2
4.生活用品及服务	Daily Necessities and Services	4.7	5.5	6.1	5.7	6.7
5.交通通信	Transportation and Telecommunication	12.1	13.6	13.7	15.7	14.7
6.教育文化娱乐	Education,Culture and Entertainment	10.1	10.4	11.1	11.0	11.2
7.医疗保健	Health Service	5.6	5.2	4.9	4.6	4.9
8.其他用品和服务	Other Necessities and Services	2.1	2.8	2.9	2.9	3.7

10-13 全省城镇常住居民人均主要食品消费量

Per Capita Consumption of Major Foods Urban Househoulds

单位:千克 (kg)

指　　标	Item	2013	2014	2015	2016	2017
粮食(原粮)	**Grain(Unprocessed)**	**97.29**	**97.75**	**97.78**	**96.52**	**93.75**
谷物	Cereal	89.70	89.80	89.88	88.46	85.89
薯类	Tuber	1.15	1.32	1.46	1.57	1.59
豆类	Beans and the productor	6.44	6.63	6.44	6.50	6.26
油脂类	Oil and Fats	8.35	8.82	9.08	9.21	8.98
#食用植物油	Edible Vegetable Oil	8.04	8.51	8.88	8.93	8.70
蔬菜及菜制品	Vegetable and Mushroom	91.12	95.90	97.64	97.95	100.76
#鲜菜	Fresh Vegetables	87.04	91.47	92.96	93.18	96.08
肉类	Products of Meat	35.19	36.03	36.67	36.35	36.59
#猪肉	Pork	27.80	28.59	28.73	28.18	28.17
禽类	Poultry	16.25	16.45	18.01	19.15	19.28
#鸡	Chick	10.52	10.42	11.81	12.59	12.46
水产品	Aquatic Products	21.31	22.53	23.63	23.48	24.51
#鱼类	Fish	16.10	16.53	16.84	17.19	17.75
蛋类	Eggs	6.43	6.76	7.28	7.33	7.57
#鲜蛋	Fresh Eggs	5.98	6.30	6.78	6.86	7.04
奶及奶制品	Milk and Dairy Products	10.24	10.46	11.03	9.73	9.74
#鲜奶	Fresh Milk	6.80	6.70	6.62	5.55	5.55
干鲜瓜果类	Dried and Fresh Melons and Fruits	35.80	38.09	42.04	43.47	45.46
#鲜瓜果	Fresh Melons and Fruits	32.27	34.52	38.18	39.42	41.35
糖果糕点类	Candy Pastry	7.40	7.58	7.56	6.89	6.49
#食糖	Sugar	1.33	1.38	1.24	1.27	1.26

10−14 城镇常住居民平均每百户主要耐用品年末拥有量

Number of Major Durable Consumer Goods Owned per 100 Rural and Urban Permanent Households at the Year-end

项　目		Item		2013	2014	2015	2016	2017
摩托车	(辆)	Motorcycle	(set)	32.56	39.21	40.15	41.38	42.62
家用汽车	(辆)	Car	(set)	23.10	25.53	29.67	34.65	36.69
洗衣机	(台)	Washing Machine	(set)	63.44	67.57	70.91	75.32	78.08
电冰箱	(台)	Refrigerator	(set)	68.06	71.67	75.30	79.17	83.18
彩色电视机	(台)	Color Television	(set)	92.61	98.68	99.53	99.57	101.97
计算机	(台)	Computer	(set)	77.45	81.55	84.45	86.96	88.29
组合音响	(台)	Hi-fi Stereo Component System	(set)	15.99	17.63	15.42	14.06	——
摄像机	(台)	Pickup Camera	(set)	6.16	6.71	6.32	6.18	——
微波炉	(台)	Microwave Oven	(set)	36.98	38.52	39.40	41.49	43.69
空调	(台)	Air Conditioner	(set)	125.63	132.26	144.26	155.97	164.88
移动电话	(部)	Mobile Telephone	(set)	200.43	210.70	221.45	228.18	234.79

10−15 按收入五等份分组的城镇常住居民家庭平均每百户主要耐用消费品年末拥有量（2017）

Grouped by Five Equal Shares of Number of Major Durable Consumer Goods Owned per100 Rural and Urban Permanent Households at Year-end (2017)

指　标		Item		低收入户 (20%) Low income families (20%)	中等偏下户 (20%) Below Average families (20%)	中等收入户 (20%) Average families (20%)	中等偏上户 (20%) Above Average families (20%)	高收入户 (20%) High income family (20%)
家用汽车	(辆)	Car	(set)	17.93	28.75	29.81	40.22	66.65
摩托车	(辆)	Motorcycle	(set)	87.17	55.36	31.88	23.29	15.50
电动助力车	(台)	Electric Bicycle	(set)	43.20	30.13	27.98	19.97	19.31
洗衣机	(台)	Washing Machine	(set)	89.91	77.48	61.78	70.02	91.22
电冰箱(柜)	(台)	Refrigerator	(set)	91.83	82.42	70.38	74.76	96.48
微波炉	(台)	Microwave Oven	(set)	39.51	40.20	33.38	44.14	61.19
彩色电视机	(台)	Color Television	(set)	113.54	100.56	84.60	91.31	119.83
空调	(台)	Air Conditioner	(set)	138.19	157.15	130.04	160.75	238.10
热水器	(台)	Water Heater	(unit)	98.34	88.88	76.82	79.72	100.28
排油烟机	(台)	Fume Hood	(set)	64.34	61.10	49.15	57.77	77.23
固定电话	(部)	Telephone	(set)	47.94	43.66	33.73	39.48	55.06
移动电话	(部)	Mobile Phone	(set)	270.88	247.14	209.42	216.60	229.95
计算机	(台)	Computer	(set)	71.17	84.11	72.53	91.15	122.40
照相机	(台)	Camera	(set)	12.20	23.59	29.41	38.34	56.57
健身器材	(台)	Fitness Equipment	(set)	3.07	7.51	7.41	8.77	20.11

10−16 城镇常住居民家庭年末住房情况

Housing Condition of the Urban Permanent Households at the Year-end

单位：%　　(%)

指　　标	Item	2013	2014	2015	2016	2017
一、住户居住类型	**Residential Type**	**100.0**	**100.0**	**100.0**	**100.0**	**100.0**
普通住宅	Ordinary Residence	78.3	80.7	83.0	83.6	85.2
集体宿舍和工棚	Dormitory and Shed	21.3	18.9	16.8	16.2	14.6
工作地住宿	Work Accommodation	0.4	0.4	0.2	0.2	0.2
二、住户居住空间样式	**Residential Space Type**	**100.0**	**100.0**	**100.0**	**100.0**	**100.0**
单栋楼房	Single Building	18.9	22.2	17.4	19.5	20.5
单栋平房	Single Bungalow	3.2	4.4	4.3	4.2	4.2
四居室及以上单元房	Four Bedroom and Above Apartment	4.9	4.8	5.4	6.2	6.5
三居室单元房	Tree Bedroom Apartment	23.2	23.5	23.7	24.7	25.0
二居室单元房	Two Bedroom Apartment	19.9	19.0	18.0	16.4	16.5
一居室单元房	One Bedroom Apartment	29.6	25.7	30.8	28.6	26.9
筒子楼或连片平房	Tube-shaped Apartment or Contiguous Bungalow	0.3	0.4	0.4	0.4	0.3
其他	Others	…	…	…	…	0.1
三、主要建筑材料	**Main Building Materials**	**100.0**	**100.0**	**100.0**	**100.0**	**100.0**
钢筋混凝土	Reinforced Concrete	84.8	83.7	85.4	88.4	87.9
砖混材料	brick and Concrete Materials	13.1	13.7	12.0	9.4	9.8
砖瓦砖木	Brick and Tile	1.9	2.6	2.5	2.1	2.2
其他	Others	0.2	…	0.1	0.1	0.1
四、住户主要饮用水来源情况	**Main Source of Householders'drinking Water**	**100.0**	**100.0**	**100.0**	**100.0**	**100.0**
经过净化处理的自来水	Purified Tap Water	91.9	90.9	92.1	93.9	93.9
受保护的井水和泉水	Protected Well and Spring	0.7	1.0	0.9	0.8	0.7
不受保护的井水和泉水	Unprotected Well and Spring	0.3	0.6	0.7	0.6	0.6
桶装水	Bottled Water	6.9	7.2	6.1	4.4	4.5
其他	Others	0.2	0.3	0.2	0.3	0.3
五、住户厕所使用情况	**Household Toilet Usage**	**100.0**	**100.0**	**100.0**	**100.0**	**100.0**
本住户独用	Sole Household Use	75.9	78.6	81.0	82.3	84.4
几户合用	Several Household Share	22.5	19.9	17.9	16.7	14.8
公用厕所	Public Toilet	1.6	1.5	1.1	1.0	0.8
六、主要炊用能源状况	**Main Cooking Energy Condition**	**100.0**	**100.0**	**100.0**	**100.0**	**100.0**
柴草	Firewood	0.3	0.9	0.8	0.8	0.8
煤炭	Coal	0.5	0.1	0.1	…	0.0
罐装液化石油气	Canned Liquefied Petroleum Gas	53.7	54.5	53.3	54.6	55.0
管道液化石油气	Pipeline Liquefied Petroleum Gas	4.6	3.8	2.9	3.1	3.1
管道煤气	Pipeline Gas	1.3	1.1	1.0	0.9	0.8
管道天然气	Pipeline Natural Gas	14.8	16.8	18.8	19.7	20.7
电	Electricity	9.1	9.0	11.9	11.6	10.0
其他	Others	15.7	13.8	11.2	9.3	9.6

10-17 各市城镇常住居民人均可支配收入

Per Capita Disposable Income of Urban Permanent Households by City

单位：元 (yuan)

市 别	City	2014	2015	2016	2017
广 州	Guangzhou	42954.6	46734.6	50940.7	55400.5
深 圳	Shenzhen	40948.0	44633.3	48695.0	52938.0
珠 海	Zhuhai	35287.3	38322.0	42537.4	46826.4
汕 头	Shantou	21445.9	23260.1	25120.9	27175.1
佛 山	Foshan	36554.7	39756.9	43120.3	46848.5
韶 关	Shaoguan	21583.3	23504.2	25854.6	28305.9
河 源	Heyuan	18246.0	20015.8	21817.3	23779.6
梅 州	Meizhou	19845.6	21810.3	23642.4	25694.6
惠 州	Huizhou	27299.6	30056.9	33212.8	36608.3
汕 尾	Shanwei	19036.2	20616.2	22389.2	24085.5
东 莞	Dongguan	36764.0	39793.4	43096.2	46739.1
中 山	Zhongshan	34303.9	37254.0	41612.8	45295.3
江 门	Jiangmen	24976.2	27116.7	29557.2	32477.8
阳 江	Yangjiang	21239.8	23087.7	25281.0	27568.1
湛 江	Zhanjiang	21317.4	23129.4	24887.2	27119.3
茂 名	Maoming	19540.5	21396.8	23322.6	25315.4
肇 庆	Zhaoqing	21725.8	23746.3	25907.2	28276.1
清 远	Qingyuan	21093.4	22907.4	25266.9	27610.0
潮 州	Chaozhou	18854.7	20457.3	21787.1	22695.0
揭 阳	Jieyang	19635.2	21343.5	22944.2	24099.7
云 浮	Yunfu	18678.6	20154.2	21887.5	23446.0
按经济区域分	By Region				
珠 三 角	Pearl River Delta	37063.7	40284.5	43967.4	47926.9
东 翼	Eastern Region	20089.2	21798.1	23478.3	25029.1
西 翼	Western Region	20656.2	22489.3	24390.2	26542.6
山 区	Mountainous Region	20097.9	21920.5	23963.1	26084.4

注：按照国家统计局的统一部署，广东省分市县城乡一体化住户调查工作从2013年底正式启动，从2014年开始正式对外发布分市城镇常住居民人均可支配收入数据。

Note: Under the unified deployment by NBS, Guangdong province started an integrated househould survey by city and county since October 2013, inluding both urban and rural households . Since 2014 the data of per caipita disposal income of all permannet househoulds in the province by city is realsed officially after the transitional period.

10—18 各市城镇常住居民人均可支配收入来源（2017年）
Per Capita Disposable Income of Urban Permanent Households by Sources and City (2017)

单位：元 (yuan)

地 区	City	可支配收入 Disposable Income	工资性收入 Income of Wages and Salaries	经营净收入 Net Business Income	财产净收入 Net Income from Property	转移净收入 Net Income from Tranfer
广 州	Guangzhou	55400.49	37106.56	3166.26	9987.49	5140.18
深 圳	Shenzhen	52938.00	43906.08	6450.06	5739.34	-3157.48
珠 海	Zhuhai	46826.39	35141.55	3663.69	6392.33	1628.82
汕 头	Shantou	27175.06	18391.89	3339.02	2059.01	3385.14
佛 山	Foshan	46848.50	30260.50	6456.69	7147.87	2983.45
韶 关	Shaoguan	28305.90	18257.31	3679.77	2434.31	3934.52
河 源	Heyuan	23779.63	16711.11	3443.82	1004.47	2620.22
梅 州	Meizhou	25694.60	15730.30	3498.60	1625.80	4839.90
惠 州	Huizhou	36608.30	25528.70	6025.83	3695.97	1357.84
汕 尾	Shanwei	24085.50	14528.58	4066.17	1210.51	4280.23
东 莞	Dongguan	46739.09	34414.51	4718.34	8203.06	-596.82
中 山	Zhongshan	45295.35	31163.20	5933.69	4121.88	4076.58
江 门	Jiangmen	32477.80	24921.16	1901.18	2821.81	2833.65
阳 江	Yangjiang	27568.10	16825.41	4622.91	3015.22	3104.56
湛 江	Zhanjiang	27119.30	18310.80	3603.88	1835.22	3369.41
茂 名	Maoming	25315.41	16475.48	3616.29	2466.83	2756.81
肇 庆	Zhaoqing	28276.13	19439.84	2878.51	2202.71	3755.07
清 远	Qingyuan	27609.97	18013.97	3895.80	1428.11	4272.10
潮 州	Chaozhou	22695.00	13518.10	3981.45	1519.18	3676.27
揭 阳	Jieyang	24099.70	12623.26	6379.62	1831.02	3265.80
云 浮	Yunfu	23445.97	15545.90	2515.53	2021.83	3362.71

10-19 各市城镇常住居民人均消费支出

Per Capita Consumption Expenditure of Urban Permanent Households by City

单位：元 (yuan)

市　别	City	2014	2015	2016	2017
广　州	Guangzhou	33384.7	35752.5	38398.2	40636.8
深　圳	Shenzhen	28852.8	32359.2	36480.6	38320.1
珠　海	Zhuhai	26637.8	28741.5	32150.5	34734.7
汕　头	Shantou	18036.5	19352.4	20721.3	21777.6
佛　山	Foshan	26043.2	28396.4	31303.2	33451.0
韶　关	Shaoguan	15224.0	16592.5	18142.5	19630.2
河　源	Heyuan	12467.5	13430.6	15122.9	16458.2
梅　州	Meizhou	14064.3	15295.0	16835.4	18474.0
惠　州	Huizhou	20065.2	21580.8	23778.5	26423.8
汕　尾	Shanwei	14829.4	15874.5	17374.3	18497.3
东　莞	Dongguan	27071.1	29000.9	30687.7	32498.3
中　山	Zhongshan	22943.9	24326.9	27630.9	30131.5
江　门	Jiangmen	16761.5	18330.9	20459.1	22905.9
阳　江	Yangjiang	16723.2	17794.2	19757.9	21514.3
湛　江	Zhanjiang	15923.2	17092.6	18416.5	20014.0
茂　名	Maoming	13929.8	15294.9	16266.1	17511.8
肇　庆	Zhaoqing	15214.6	16361.2	17882.8	18945.0
清　远	Qingyuan	14976.3	15920.7	17795.5	19232.3
潮　州	Chaozhou	13966.8	14831.6	15861.0	16257.3
揭　阳	Jieyang	14015.2	15089.3	16060.9	16746.7
云　浮	Yunfu	12991.8	13926.6	14729.8	15920.8
按经济区域分	By Region				
珠 三 角	Pearl River Delta	27035.7	29344.6	32177.7	37684.6
东　翼	Eastern Region	15656.5	16775.1	17987.1	18847.5
西　翼	Western Region	15352.7	16571.1	17885.3	19379.9
山　区	Mountainous Region	14126.9	15234.8	16785.9	18235.0

注：按照国家统计局的统一部署，广东省分市县城乡一体化住户调查工作从2013年底正式启动，从2014年开始正式对外发布分市城镇常住居民人均消费支出数据。

Note: Under the unified deployment by NBS, Guangdong province started an integrated househould survey by city and county since October 2013, inluding both urban and rural households . Since 2014 the data of per caipita expenditures of all permannet households in the province by city is realsed officially after the transitional period.

10-20 农村常住居民家庭基本情况

Basic Conditions of Rural Permanent Households

指　标	Item	2013	2014	2015	2016	2017
调查户数　(户)	**Survey of households (household)**	**3034**	**2604**	**2602**	**2612**	**2605**
平均每户常住人口（人）	Average number of residents per Permanent Household (person)	3.71	3.54	3.60	3.69	3.65
平均每户就业人口（人）	Average Number of Employed Persons per Permanent Household (person)	2.03	1.98	2.04	2.07	2.03
人均住房建筑面积(平方米)	**Per Capita housing construction area (sq.m)**	**34.92**	**39.32**	**42.14**	**43.92**	**45.27**
人均可支配收入　(元)	**Per Capita Disposable Income (yuan)**	**11067.79**	**12245.56**	**13360.44**	**14512.15**	**15779.74**
1.工资性收入	Income of Wages and Salaries	5671.20	6220.34	6724.01	7255.30	7854.63
2.经营净收入	Net Business Income	3047.86	3272.39	3590.14	3883.59	4118.65
3.财产净收入	Income from Properties	392.04	295.53	337.01	365.76	414.81
4.转移净收入	Income from Transfers	1956.69	2457.30	2709.27	3007.50	3391.65
人均消费支出　(元)	**Per Capita Consumption Expenditure(yuan)**	**8937.76**	**10043.21**	**11103.03**	**12414.84**	**13199.62**
1.食品烟酒	Food,Tobacco and Liquor	3761.23	3968.92	4511.34	5010.47	5303.94
2.衣着	Clothing	280.23	328.15	367.13	411.96	459.47
3.居住	Living	1892.33	2238.82	2494.84	2761.88	2902.43
4.生活用品及服务	Daily Necessities and Services	522.97	599.65	654.65	718.56	722.83
5.交通通信	Transportation and Telecommunication	907.84	1068.68	1160.44	1370.48	1423.58
6.教育文化娱乐	Education,Culture and Entertainment	791.85	918.22	952.41	1057.80	1185.96
7.医疗保健	Health Service	598.17	686.95	723.15	803.88	921.72
8.其他用品和服务	Other Necessities and Services	183.15	233.82	239.09	279.81	279.70
消费支出构成　(%)	**Composition of Consumption Expenditure**	**100.0**	**100.0**	**100.0**	**100.0**	**100.0**
1.食品烟酒	Food,Tobacco and Liquor	42.1	39.5	40.6	40.4	40.2
2.衣着	Clothing	3.1	3.3	3.3	3.3	3.5
3.居住	Living	21.2	22.3	22.5	22.2	22.0
4.生活用品及服务	Daily Necessities and Services	5.9	6.0	5.9	5.8	5.5
5.交通通信	Transportation and Telecommunication	10.2	10.6	10.5	11.0	10.8
6.教育文化娱乐	Education,Culture and Entertainment	8.9	9.1	8.6	8.5	9.0
7.医疗保健	Health Service	6.7	6.8	6.5	6.5	6.9
8.其他用品和服务	Other Necessities and Services	1.9	2.4	2.2	2.3	2.1

注：2013年起为新口径数据。

Note: Since 2013, the relative data of rural households have been caculated according to the new standard.

10-21 历年农村常住居民人均收入及生活消费支出（1978-2012）

Per Capita Income and Consumption Expenditure of Rural Households (1978-2012)

年份 Year	人均纯收入（元）Per Capita Net Income (yuan)	指数 Index			人均生活消费支出（元）Per Capita Living Expenditure (yuan)	指数 Index		恩格尔系数（%）Engle Coefficient (%)
		名义增长（上年为100）Nominal Growth (Preceding year=100)	实际增长（上年为100）Real Growth (Preceding year=100)	实际增长（1978年为100）Real Growth (1978=100)		名义增长（上年为100）Nominal Growth (Preceding year=100)	实际增长（上年为100）Real Growth (Preceding year=100)	
1978	193.25	107.9		100.0	184.89	97.4		61.7
1979	222.72	115.2	113.6	113.6	205.18	111.0	110.1	59.9
1980	274.37	123.2	119.4	135.6	222.22	108.3	103.9	60.4
1981	325.37	118.6	111.4	151.1	266.05	119.7	112.1	59.3
1982	381.79	117.3	112.7	170.3	312.44	117.4	116.2	58.4
1983	395.92	103.7	107.0	182.2	328.76	105.2	106.3	60.3
1984	425.34	107.4	107.2	195.3	346.19	105.3	105.0	59.3
1985	495.31	116.5	109.8	214.5	388.00	112.1	105.7	60.4
1986	546.43	110.3	107.6	230.8	454.06	117.0	111.1	58.8
1987	662.24	121.2	111.1	256.4	545.25	120.1	109.5	57.3
1988	808.70	122.1	102.7	263.3	684.67	125.6	103.2	55.2
1989	955.02	118.1	102.0	268.6	870.59	127.2	107.3	53.7
1990	1043.03	109.2	101.6	272.9	932.63	107.1	99.7	57.7
1991	1143.06	109.6	109.4	298.5	942.40	101.1	101.2	57.4
1992	1307.65	114.4	110.4	329.6	1060.29	112.5	108.8	54.0
1993	1674.78	128.1	106.1	349.7	1391.01	131.2	106.8	52.8
1994	2181.52	130.3	103.8	363.0	1882.00	135.3	103.6	55.6
1995	2699.24	123.7	106.5	386.6	2255.01	119.8	105.3	54.5
1996	3183.46	117.9	107.6	415.9	2584.16	114.6	106.9	51.6
1997	3467.69	108.9	104.2	433.4	2617.65	101.3	100.3	52.3
1998	3527.14	101.7	103.4	448.2	2683.18	102.5	103.8	51.1
1999	3628.93	102.9	106.2	475.9	2645.94	98.6	101.7	50.7
2000	3654.48	100.7	100.9	480.2	2646.02	100.0	100.0	49.8
2001	3769.79	103.2	103.5	497.0	2703.36	102.2	102.5	49.9
2002	3911.91	103.8	105.1	522.4	2825.01	104.5	106.0	47.6
2003	4054.58	103.6	103.4	540.1	2927.35	103.6	103.4	47.9
2004	4365.87	107.7	104.0	561.8	3240.78	110.7	106.7	48.8
2005	4690.49	107.4	104.5	587.0	3707.73	114.4	111.4	48.3
2006	5079.78	108.3	106.4	624.6	3885.97	104.8	103.2	48.6
2007	5624.04	110.7	106.5	665.5	4202.32	108.1	104.5	49.7
2008	6399.77	113.8	107.6	715.8	4872.96	115.9	109.6	49.0
2009	6906.93	107.9	110.7	792.4	5019.81	103.0	105.3	48.3
2010	7890.25	114.2	110.3	874.0	5515.58	109.9	106.5	47.7
2011	9371.73	118.8	111.9	978.0	6725.55	121.9	115.5	49.1
2012	10542.84	112.5	109.3	1069.0	7458.56	110.9	107.8	49.1

注：本表数据来源于2013年之前分别开展的城镇住户调查和农村住户调查。
Note: The data shown in the table are compiled on the basis of the urban and rural househould surveys before year 2013.

10-22 按收入五等份分组的农村常住居民家庭平均每人收支及构成（2017）

Per Capita of Disposal Income and Expenditure and Composition of Rural Permanent Households by Income Quintile (2017)

指　　标	Item	低收入户 (20%) Low Income Households (20%)	中等偏下户 (20%) Lower Middle Income Households (20%)	中等收入户 (20%) Middle Income Households (20%)	中等偏上户 (20%) Upper Middle Income Households (20%)	高收入户 (20%) High Income Households (20%)
人均可支配收入（元）	**Per Capita Disposable Income (yuan)**	**6542.26**	**10961.08**	**14726.40**	**19818.07**	**32849.57**
1.工资性收入	Income of Wages and Salaries	3232.95	5528.23	8271.33	10876.52	13960.14
2.经营净收入	Net Business Income	949.98	2318.96	3167.25	4457.21	12091.72
3.财产净收入	Net Income from Properties	42.69	105.32	252.77	625.73	1362.51
4.转移净收入	Net Income from Transfers	2316.65	3008.58	3035.04	3858.60	5435.20
可支配收入构成（%）	**Composition of Disposable Income (%)**	**100.0**	**100.0**	**100.0**	**100.0**	**100.0**
1.工资性收入	Income of Wages and Salaries	49.4	50.4	56.2	54.8	42.6
2.经营净收入	Net Business Income	14.5	21.2	21.5	22.5	36.8
3.财产净收入	Net Income from Properties	0.7	1.0	1.7	3.2	4.1
4.转移净收入	Net Income from Transfers	35.4	27.4	20.6	19.5	16.5
人均消费支出　（元）	**Per Capita Consumption Expenditure(yuan)**	**8551.50**	**10970.05**	**12858.97**	**15517.20**	**20959.61**
1.食品烟酒	Food,Tobacco and Liquor	3752.09	4357.31	5131.02	6275.31	8032.62
2.衣着	Clothing	246.68	360.35	457.49	565.82	792.89
3.居住	Living	1941.51	2489.01	2850.05	3482.48	4306.07
4.生活用品及服务	Daily Necessities and Services	413.02	599.13	675.18	877.70	1237.07
5.交通通信	Transportation and Telecommunication	703.53	919.83	1286.72	1644.29	3106.07
6.教育文化娱乐	Education,Culture and Entertainment	810.19	1128.74	1273.15	1262.92	1617.59
7.医疗保健	Health Service	538.85	890.21	947.10	1024.78	1378.54
8.其他用品和服务	Other Necessities and Services	145.63	225.49	238.27	383.89	488.74
消费支出构成　（%）	**Composition of Consumption Expenditure**	**100.0**	**100.0**	**100.0**	**100.0**	**100.0**
1.食品烟酒	Food,Tobacco and Liquor	43.9	39.7	39.9	40.4	38.3
2.衣着	Clothing	2.9	3.3	3.6	3.7	3.8
3.居住	Living	22.7	22.7	22.2	22.4	20.5
4.生活用品及服务	Daily Necessities and Services	4.8	5.5	5.3	5.7	5.9
5.交通通信	Transportation and Telecommunication	8.2	8.4	10.0	10.6	14.8
6.教育文化娱乐	Education,Culture and Entertainment	9.5	10.3	9.9	8.1	7.8
7.医疗保健	Health Service	6.3	8.0	7.2	6.6	6.6
8.其他用品和服务	Other Necessities and Services	1.7	2.1	1.9	2.5	2.3

10－23 全省农村常住居民人均主要食品消费量

Per Capita Consumption of Major Foods Rural Househoulds

单位:千克 (kg)

指　　标	Item	2013	2014	2015	2016	2017
粮食(原粮)	**Grain(Unprocessed)**	**165.05**	**156.76**	**161.45**	**164.25**	**166.58**
谷物	Cereal	159.02	149.32	153.80	155.83	158.47
薯类	Tuber	1.08	1.54	1.34	1.50	1.74
豆类	Beans and the productor	4.95	5.91	6.30	6.92	6.37
油脂类	Oil and Fats	11.53	13.64	12.78	10.34	9.78
#食用植物油	Edible Vegetable Oil	10.75	13.01	12.02	9.67	9.12
蔬菜及菜制品	Vegetable and Mushroom	90.57	98.47	101.68	100.38	100.75
#鲜菜	Fresh Vegetables	88.28	95.92	99.07	97.69	97.90
肉类	Products of Meat	31.50	33.77	36.00	35.77	36.35
#猪肉	Pork	27.85	29.97	31.72	30.98	31.02
禽类	Poultry	16.66	17.83	19.99	22.05	23.50
#鸡	Chick	10.81	11.95	13.21	14.43	15.42
水产品	Aquatic Products	16.48	17.25	18.68	18.78	19.24
#鱼类	Fresh	13.45	13.98	14.83	14.83	14.95
蛋类	Eggs	4.87	5.52	6.24	6.40	6.77
#鲜蛋	Fresh Eggs	4.70	5.34	6.07	6.20	6.55
奶及奶制品	Milk and Dairy Products	2.34	2.40	2.65	2.86	3.32
#鲜奶	Fresh Milk	1.04	1.12	1.19	1.12	1.33
干鲜瓜果类	Dried and Fresh Melons and Fruits	16.68	20.24	23.28	26.69	28.55
#鲜瓜果	Fresh Melons and Fruits	14.97	18.37	21.21	24.27	25.69
糖果糕点类	Candy Pastry	4.70	4.39	4.99	5.80	5.93
#食糖	Sugar	1.58	1.77	1.90	2.12	2.12

10-24 农村常住居民平均每百户主要耐用品年末拥有量

Number of Major Durable Consumer Goods Owned per 100 Rural and Urban Permanent Households at the Year-end

项　目		Item		2013	2014	2015	2016	2017
热水器	(台)	Water Heater	(unit)	64.98	69.36	77.71	84.93	88.49
彩色电视机	(台)	Color Television	(set)	113.24	114.28	117.22	119.49	120.47
空调	(台)	Air Conditioner	(set)	45.04	46.67	62.15	81.17	91.33
洗衣机	(台)	Washing Machine	(set)	52.45	54.43	64.82	74.43	78.46
摩托车	(辆)	Motorcycle	(unit)	101.20	108.06	116.95	122.27	123.63
电冰箱	(台)	Refrigerator	(set)	66.10	68.36	78.29	84.90	87.93
固定 电话机	(部)	Fixed Telephone	(set)	54.12	60.49	55.31	46.06	42.75
移动电话	(部)	Mobile Telephone	(set)	236.45	248.41	267.18	279.89	287.12
计算机	(台)	Computer	(set)	27.23	30.40	33.93	37.73	41.61

10-25 按收入五等份分组的农村常住居民家庭平均每百户主要耐用消费品年末拥有量（2017）

Grouped by Five Equal Shares of Number of Major Durable Consumer Goods Owned per100 Rural and Urban Permanent Households at Year-end (2017)

指　标		Item		低收入户 (20%) Low income families (20%)	中等偏下户 (20%) Below Average families (20%)	中等收入户 (20%) Average families (20%)	中等偏上户 (20%) Above Average families (20%)	高收入户 (20%) High income family (20%)
家用汽车	(辆)	Car	(set)	7.66	9.68	16.52	19.45	34.52
摩托车	(辆)	Motorcycle	(set)	118.37	125.49	123.13	124.65	126.50
电动助力车	(台)	Electric Bicycle	(set)	33.05	37.20	37.74	44.20	40.34
洗衣机	(台)	Washing Machine	(set)	71.88	74.62	77.89	83.55	84.34
电冰箱(柜)	(台)	Refrigerator	(set)	81.07	82.65	88.52	91.25	96.14
微波炉	(台)	Microwave Oven	(set)	20.59	21.24	20.99	23.41	28.06
彩色电视机	(台)	Color Television	(set)	118.69	122.00	119.34	122.24	120.07
空调	(台)	Air Conditioner	(set)	57.03	72.18	87.89	110.13	129.35
热水器	(台)	Water Heater	(unit)	80.05	87.70	87.90	91.56	95.22
排油烟机	(台)	Fume Hood	(set)	24.25	31.84	41.61	41.65	47.17
固定电话	(部)	Telephone	(set)	35.63	39.99	46.56	45.55	46.01
移动电话	(部)	Mobile Phone	(set)	264.48	284.65	287.38	304.83	294.25
计算机	(台)	Computer	(set)	21.32	32.69	41.57	52.66	59.80
照相机	(台)	Camera	(set)	2.16	1.88	3.34	6.20	7.52
健身器材	(台)	Fitness Equipment	(set)	0.32	0.64	1.78	0.91	3.23

10-26 农村常住居民家庭年末住房情况

Housing Condition of the Rural Permanent Households at the Year-end

单位：% (%)

指　　标	Item	2013	2014	2015	2016	2017
一、住户居住类型	**Residential Type**	**100.0**	**100.0**	**100.0**	**100.0**	**100.0**
普通住宅	Ordinary Residence	98.4	98.9	99.8	99.8	99.6
集体宿舍和工棚	Dormitory and Shed	1.3	0.8	0.1	0.2	0.2
工作地住宿	Work Accommodation	0.3	0.3	0.1	…	0.2
二、住户居住空间样式	**Residential Space Type**	**100.0**	**100.0**	**100.0**	**100.0**	**100.0**
单栋楼房	Single Building	57.5	60.1	66.7	73.9	74.3
单栋平房	Single Bungalow	32.6	31.0	26.1	19.1	18.7
四居室及以上单元房	Four Bedroom and Above Apartment	1.5	0.6	0.9	0.8	0.8
三居室单元房	Tree Bedroom Apartment	2.3	1.7	1.2	1.5	1.5
二居室单元房	Two Bedroom Apartment	1.1	0.8	1.1	1.3	1.3
一居室单元房	One Bedroom Apartment	0.8	1.7	0.8	0.8	0.7
筒子楼或连片平房	Tube-shaped Apartment or Contiguous Bungalow	3.6	3.6	2.8	2.3	2.4
其他	Others	0.6	0.5	0.4	0.3	0.3
三、主要建筑材料	**Main Building Materials**	**100.0**	**100.0**	**100.0**	**100.0**	**100.0**
钢筋混凝土	Reinforced Concrete	32.2	30.3	41.8	50.3	49.4
砖混材料	brick and Concrete Materials	45.6	48.0	40.6	36.4	37.8
砖瓦砖木	Brick and Tile	21.0	20.8	16.9	13.0	12.5
其他	Others	1.2	0.9	0.7	0.3	0.3
四、住户主要饮用水来源情况	**Main Source of Householders'drinking Water**	**100.0**	**100.0**	**100.0**	**100.0**	**100.0**
经过净化处理的自来水	Purified Tap Water	55.9	53.7	55.2	56.9	57.7
受保护的井水和泉水	Protected Well and Spring	23.4	25.9	28.2	26.6	25.7
不受保护的井水和泉水	Unprotected Well and Spring	16.4	16.7	13.0	12.8	12.9
桶装水	Bottled Water	0.3	0.3	0.3	0.4	0.4
其他	Others	4.0	3.4	3.3	3.3	3.3
五、住户厕所使用情况	**Household Toilet Usage**	**100.0**	**100.0**	**100.0**	**100.0**	**100.0**
本住户独用	Sole Household Use	87.1	87.8	91.2	94.4	94.8
几户合用	Several Household Share	4.4	4.0	2.5	1.7	1.6
公用厕所	Public Toilet	8.5	8.2	6.3	3.9	3.6
六、主要炊用能源状况	**Main Cooking Energy Condition**	**100.0**	**100.0**	**100.0**	**100.0**	**100.0**
柴草	Firewood	37.3	41.2	36.7	32.5	31.7
煤炭	Coal	0.5	0.3	0.0	…	
罐装液化石油气	Canned Liquefied Petroleum Gas	52.6	47.8	50.0	54.6	55.3
管道液化石油气	Pipeline Liquefied Petroleum Gas	0.2		0.1	0.1	0.1
管道煤气	Pipeline Gas	0.3	0.2	0.2	0.1	0.1
管道天然气	Pipeline Natural Gas			0.1	…	0.1
电	Electricity	7.8	8.7	11.0	11.2	11.3
其他	Others	1.3	1.8	1.9	1.5	1.4

10-27 各市农村常住居民人均可支配收入

Per Capita Disposal Income of Rural Permanent Households by City

单位：元 (yuan)

市 别	City	2014	2015	2016	2017
广 州	Guangzhou	17662.8	19323.1	21448.6	23483.9
深 圳	Shenzhen				
珠 海	Zhuhai	18394.8	20510.2	22889.4	23496.4
汕 头	Shantou	11190.3	12454.8	13662.9	14904.7
佛 山	Foshan	20094.0	22063.2	24159.2	26389.6
韶 关	Shaoguan	10532.2	11606.5	12790.3	14107.6
河 源	Heyuan	9884.0	10803.2	12045.6	13300.8
梅 州	Meizhou	10785.6	11799.4	12991.2	14088.5
惠 州	Huizhou	14364.4	15829.6	17602.5	19284.3
汕 尾	Shanwei	10415.3	11290.2	12441.8	13501.3
东 莞	Dongguan	22327.1	24224.9	26526.3	29078.3
中 山	Zhongshan	22166.3	24405.1	27528.9	30012.4
江 门	Jiangmen	12746.3	13817.0	15226.3	16473.3
阳 江	Yangjiang	11488.5	12543.2	13960.5	15341.7
湛 江	Zhanjiang	11381.1	12405.4	13335.8	14484.0
茂 名	Maoming	11913.5	13224.0	14519.9	15695.2
肇 庆	Zhaoqing	12642.3	13982.4	15115.0	16430.5
清 远	Qingyuan	10600.3	11681.5	12873.0	14026.8
潮 州	Chaozhou	10551.1	11458.5	12558.5	13672.9
揭 阳	Jieyang	10145.6	11332.6	12250.6	13206.7
云 浮	Yunfu	11066.8	12007.5	13016.1	14124.4
按经济区域分	By Region				
珠 三 角	Pearl River Delta	15754.0	17296.4	19063.7	20813.5
东 翼	Eastern Region	10501.0	11607.6	12667.1	13732.9
西 翼	Western Region	11607.1	12749.0	13890.8	15081.6
山 区	Mountainous Region	10573.7	11577.2	12747.4	13924.7

注：1.按照国家统计局的统一部署，广东省分市县城乡一体化住户调查工作从2013年底正式启动，从2014年开始正式对外发布分市农村常住居民人均可支配收入数据，不再发布分市农村居民人均纯收入数据，这两项收入指标数据在调查范围、调查方法和统计口径上均有一定变化，不完全可比。

2.深圳因完全城市化，无相关数据。

Note: a)Under the unified deployment by NBS, Guangdong province started an integrated househould survey by city and county since October 2013, inluding both urban and rural households. Since 2014 the data of per caipita disposal income and expenditures of all househoulds in the province by city is realsed officially after the transitional period. The coverage, methodology and difinitions used in the integrated rural survey are differern from the survey prior to 2013, therefore the disposable income of rural permannet household of 2014 are different from the net income of rural household prior to 2013.

b)There is no data of Shenzhen city due to its totally urbanization.

10–28 各市农村常住居民人均可支配收入来源（2017年）

Per Capita Disposable Income of Rural Permanent Households by Sources and City (2017)

单位：元 (yuan)

地 区	City	可支配收入 Disposable Income	工资性收入 Income of Wages and Salaries	经营净收入 Net Business Income	财产净收入 Net Income from Property	转移净收入 Net Income from Tranfer
广 州	Guangzhou	23483.88	17324.06	2686.55	2156.29	1316.98
深 圳	Shenzhen					
珠 海	Zhuhai	23496.37	16695.67	2671.87	2510.23	1618.61
汕 头	Shantou	14904.72	10627.20	1821.17	543.52	1912.83
佛 山	Foshan	26389.63	16715.89	4421.81	3598.20	1653.74
韶 关	Shaoguan	14107.60	6108.59	5008.20	832.35	2158.46
河 源	Heyuan	13300.80	7698.47	3573.95	166.26	1862.13
梅 州	Meizhou	14088.50	6735.30	3993.00	81.20	3279.00
惠 州	Huizhou	19284.30	11327.44	5450.70	998.53	1507.65
汕 尾	Shanwei	13501.30	8171.36	2841.46	43.91	2444.57
东 莞	Dongguan	29078.28	25067.96	2306.35	2505.41	-801.44
中 山	Zhongshan	30012.41	20978.67	3571.48	3211.33	2250.93
江 门	Jiangmen	16473.30	11684.10	2045.92	1111.71	1631.57
阳 江	Yangjiang	15341.70	8233.12	4560.51	128.96	2419.12
湛 江	Zhanjiang	14484.00	6580.79	4975.82	148.31	2779.07
茂 名	Maoming	15695.19	6949.91	1605.60	858.20	6281.53
肇 庆	Zhaoqing	16430.51	8075.60	4534.82	665.44	3154.66
清 远	Qingyuan	14026.75	7519.52	4025.37	170.41	2311.45
潮 州	Chaozhou	13672.93	8313.13	3588.55	55.28	1715.96
揭 阳	Jieyang	13206.67	8065.93	2667.75	69.37	2403.61
云 浮	Yunfu	14124.43	8279.49	2851.53	48.26	2945.15

10-29 各市农村常住居民人均消费支出

Per Capita Consumption Expenditure of Rural Permanent Households by City

单位：元 (yuan)

市　别	City	2014	2015	2016	2017
广　州	Guangzhou	12867.8	14086.5	17595.1	18932.3
深　圳	Shenzhen				
珠　海	Zhuhai	14303.3	16045.9	18372.6	20038.1
汕　头	Shantou	9526.2	10798.3	12019.8	13345.6
佛　山	Foshan	13474.3	15050.3	16735.9	18262.0
韶　关	Shaoguan	8826.0	9656.6	10825.0	11810.1
河　源	Heyuan	8193.8	8939.6	10211.4	11484.1
梅　州	Meizhou	8803.0	9923.3	11164.0	12392.0
惠　州	Huizhou	11008.1	11975.2	13726.4	15576.2
汕　尾	Shanwei	7964.9	8930.5	10294.1	11122.6
东　莞	Dongguan	18504.5	19888.6	21539.4	23090.2
中　山	Zhongshan	15189.4	16595.5	19275.6	20832.6
江　门	Jiangmen	9191.1	10323.7	11584.2	12655.9
阳　江	Yangjiang	9734.1	10410.8	11977.7	12931.4
湛　江	Zhanjiang	8517.4	9180.0	9921.8	10732.6
茂　名	Maoming	9861.8	10645.3	11698.2	12481.2
肇　庆	Zhaoqing	7996.3	8934.7	9975.9	10925.6
清　远	Qingyuan	8798.3	9942.3	11233.7	12168.2
潮　州	Chaozhou	9215.2	9888.7	10825.4	11573.9
揭　阳	Jieyang	8719.5	9541.8	10376.3	11227.2
云　浮	Yunfu	8464.2	9089.7	10271.4	11169.9
按经济区域分	By Region				
珠 三 角	Pearl River Delta	11420.3	12578.0	14472.8	15836.1
东　翼	Eastern Region	8835.5	9770.2	10814.6	11758.9
西　翼	Western Region	9217.4	9928.8	10907.6	11726.9
山　区	Mountainous Region	8628.4	9550.6	10787.0	11866.5

注：1.按照国家统计局的统一部署，广东省分市县城乡一体化住户调查工作从2013年底正式启动，从2014年开始正式对外发布分市农村常住居民人均消费支出数据。

2.深圳因完全城市化，无相关数据。

Note: a)Under the unified deployment by NBS, Guangdong province started an integrated househould survey by city and county since October 2013, inluding both urban and rural households . Since 2014 the data of per caipita disposal income and expenditures of all househoulds in the province by city is realsed officially after the transitional period. The coverage, methodology and difinitions used in the integrated rural survey are differern from the survey prior to 2013, therefore the disposable income of rural permannet household of 2014 are different from the net income of rural household prior to 2013.

b)There is no data of Shenzhen city due to its totally urbanization.

10−30 常住居民人均可支配收入及生活消费支出(2013−2017)

Per Capita Disposable Income and Consumption Expenditure of Househoulds (2013-2017)

年份 Year	人均可支配收入(元) Per Capita Disposable Income (yuan)	指数 Index		人均消费支出(元) Per Capita Consumption Expenditure (yuan)	指数 Index		恩格尔系数(%) Engle Coefficient (%)
		名义增长(上年为100) Nominal Growth (Preceding year=100)	实际增长(上年为100) Real Growth (Preceding year=100)		名义增长(上年为100) Nominal Growth (Preceding year=100)	实际增长(上年为100) Real Growth (Preceding year=100)	
全体常住居民 Provincial Househould							
2013	23420.75	110.1	107.4	17421.00	108.9	106.2	35.0
2014	25684.96	109.7	107.2	19205.50	110.2	107.7	34.3
2015	27858.86	108.5	106.9	20975.70	109.2	107.6	34.5
2016	30295.80	108.7	106.3	23448.42	111.8	109.3	34.2
2017	33003.29	108.9	107.3	24819.63	105.8	104.2	33.5
城镇常住居民 Urban Household							
2013	29537.29	109.5	106.9	21621.46	107.8	105.3	33.6
2014	32148.11	108.8	106.4	23611.74	109.2	106.7	33.2
2015	34757.16	108.1	106.4	25673.08	108.7	107.0	33.2
2016	37684.25	108.4	105.9	28613.33	111.5	108.8	32.9
2017	40975.14	108.7	106.9	30197.91	105.5	103.7	32.2
农村常住居民 Rural Household							
2013	11067.79	110.7	107.8	8937.76	111.9	109.0	42.1
2014	12245.56	110.6	108.3	10043.21	112.4	110.1	39.5
2015	13360.44	109.1	107.7	11103.03	110.6	109.2	40.6
2016	14512.15	108.6	106.5	12414.84	111.8	109.6	40.4
2017	15779.74	108.7	107.8	13199.62	106.3	105.5	40.2

注：本表数据来源于自2013年起开展的城乡一体化住户收支和生活状况调查。

Notes: The data shown in the table are compiled on the basis of the integrated household income and expenditure survey ,including both urban and rural househoulds.

主要统计指标解释

一、城乡一体化住户收支与生活状况调查指标解释

从2012年四季度起，国家统计局对分别进行的城乡住户调查实施了一体化改革，规范了城乡划分范围，统一了城乡居民收入指标名称、分类和统计标准，建立了城乡统一的一体化住户调查，并据此采集全国居民有关数据。

（一）居民可支配收入

居民可支配收入指居民可用于最终消费支出和储蓄的总和，即居民可用于自由支配的收入。既包括现金收入，也包括实物收入。按照收入的来源，可支配收入包含四项，分别为：工资性收入、经营净收入、财产净收入和转移净收入。

工资性收入 指就业人员通过各种途径得到的全部劳动报酬和各种福利，包括受雇于单位或个人、从事各种自由职业、兼职和零星劳动得到的全部劳动报酬和福利。

经营净收入 指住户或住户成员从事生产经营活动所获得的净收入，是全部经营收入中扣除经营费用、生产性固定资产折旧和生产税之后得到的净收入。计算公式为：

经营净收入=经营收入-经营费用-生产性固定资产折旧-生产税

财产净收入 指住户或住户成员将其所拥有的金融资产、住房等非金融资产和自然资源交由其他机构单位、住户或个人支配而获得的回报并扣除相关的费用之后得到的净收入。财产净收入包括利息净收入、红利收入、储蓄性保险净收益、转让承包土地经营权租金净收入、出租房屋净收入、出租其他资产净收入和自有住房折算净租金等。财产净收入不包括转让资产所有权的溢价所得。

转移净收入 计算公式为：转移净收入=转移性收入-转移性支出

转移性收入 指国家、单位、社会团体对住户的各种经常性转移支付和住户之间的经常性收入转移。包括养老金或退休金、社会救济和补助、政策性生产补贴、政策性生活补贴、救灾款、经常性捐赠和赔偿、报销医疗费、住户之间的赡养收入，本住户非常住成员寄回带回的收入等。转移性收入不包括住户之间的实物馈赠。

转移性支出 指调查户对国家、单位、住户或个人的经常性或义务性转移支付。包括缴纳的税款、各项社会保障支出、赡养支出、经常性捐赠和赔偿支出以及其他经常转移支出等。

（二）居民消费支出

居民消费支出是指居民用于满足家庭日常生活消费需要的全部支出，既包括现金消费支出，也包括实物消费支出。消费支出可划分为食品烟酒、衣着、居住、生活用品及服务、交通通信、教育文化娱乐、医疗保健以及其他用品及服务八大类。

食品烟酒 指用于各种食品和烟草、酒类的支出。

衣着 指与居民穿着有关的支出，包括服装、服装材料、鞋类、其他衣类及配件、衣着相关加工服务的支出。

居住 指与居住有关的支出，包括房租、水、电、燃料、物业管理等方面的支出，也包括自有住房折算租金。

生活用品及服务 指家庭及个人的各类生活品及家庭服务。包括家具及室内装饰品、家用器具、家用纺织品、家庭日用杂品、个人用品和家庭服务。

交通通信 指用于交通和通信工具及相关的各种服务费、维修费和车辆保险等支出。

教育文化娱乐 指用于教育、文化和娱乐方面的支出。

医疗保健 指用于医疗和保健的药品、用品和服务的总费用。包括医疗器具及药品，以及医疗服务。

其他用品及服务 指无法直接归入上述各类支出的其他用品与服务支出。

二、2012 年及以前的分城镇和农村住户调查指标解释

2012 年及以前年份，中国的住户调查一直分城乡分别开展。由于分别调查，农村与城镇居民收入、支出等指标的统计口径有所不同，数据也不完全可比，城镇调查城镇居民可支配收入，农村调查农村居民纯收入。城镇居民收入与支出数据，指现金收入或现金支出，不包括实物收支；其中，计算城镇居民人均可支配收入和消费支出时，不包括自有住房折算租金，也不包括购建房支出。农村居民收入与支出数据，分为总收支和现金收支，即农村居民的总收支部分包括了自产自用的实物收支；其中，计算农村居民人均纯收入和消费支出时，也不包括自有住房折算租金，但农村居民居住消费支出中，包括了购建房支出。

为了保持历史数据的可比，本年鉴中 2012 年及以前年份的数据和指标解释仍保持了原城镇住户调查和农村住户调查方案的原貌。

（一）城镇住户调查

城镇家庭人口 指居住在一起，经济上合在一起共同生活的家庭成员。凡计算为家庭人口的成员其全部收支都包括在本家庭中。

城镇居民家庭可支配收入 指家庭成员得到可用于最终消费支出和其他非义务性支出以及储蓄的总和，即居民家庭可以用来自由支配的收入。它是家庭总收入扣除交纳的个人所得税、个人交纳的社会保障支出以及记账补贴后的收入。计算公式为：

城镇居民家庭可支配收入=家庭总收入-交纳个人所得税-个人交纳的社会保障支出-记账补贴

（二）农村住户调查

农村住户 指农村常住户。农村常住户指长期(一年以上)居住在乡镇(不包括城关镇)行政管理区域内的住户，以及长期居住在城关镇所辖行政村范围内的农村住户。户口不在本地而在本地居住一年及以上的住户也包括在本地农村常住户范围内；有本地户口，但举家外出谋生一年以上的住户，无论是否保留承包耕地都不包括在本地农村住户范围内。

农村居民家庭纯收入 指农村住户当年从各个来源得到的总收入相应地扣除所发生的费用后的收入总和。计算公式为：

农村居民家庭纯收入=总收入-家庭经营费用支出-税费支出-生产性固定资产折旧-赠送农村内部亲友

纯收入主要用于再生产投入和当年生活消费支出，也可用于储蓄和各种非义务性支出。“农民人均纯收入”是按人口平均的纯收入水平，反映的是一个地区农村居民的平均收入水平。

Explanatory Notes on Main Statistical Indicators

Ⅰ. Integrated Urban and Rural Households Survey on Income and Expenditures and Living Conditions

Since the fourth quarter of 2012, the NBS has launched its reform on the household survey programme, to form an integrated survey, instead of the two separate urban and rural household surveys. The reform regulates the division of urban and rural areas, integrates the concepts, classifications and standards, conducts the integrated household survey, and collects household data in the whole country thereafter.

1. Disposable Income of Households

Disposable Income of Households refers to the income of households for purpose of final expenditure and savings. It includes income both in cash and in kind. By sources of income, disposable income includes four categories: income from wages and salaries, net business income, net income from properties and net income from transfer.

Income from Wages and Salaries refers to remuneration of labour and salaries from all kinds of sources, including those employed by other units or individuals, freelance work, part-time jobs, and sporadic labour.

Net Business Income refers to net income earned by households and their members engaged in production and business activities. It refers to the net income of operating revenue minus operating costs, depreciation of productive fixed assets, and production tax. The formula is:

Net Business Income=Operating Revenue-Operating Costs-Depreciation of Productive Fixed Assets-Production Tax

Net Income from Properties refers to the net income received as returns by households or members of financial assets, non-financial assets such as housing, to other institutions, households or individuals, and minus relevant costs. Net income from properties includes net income of interest, bonus income, net income of saving insurance, net income of rents of transferring management right of contract land, income of renting housing, income of renting other assets, net converted rents of self-owned housing. Net income from properties do not include premium of transferring ownership of assets.

Net Income from Transfer The formula is:

Net Income from Transfer=Income from Transfers-Expenditure from Transfer

Income from Transfer refers to the regular transfer from country, institutions, social communities to households and between households. It includes old-age and retirement pension, disaster relief funds, regular donation and compensation, applying for medical fees, supporting income between households, income from non-usual-residing members of households, etc. Income from transfer do not include presents in kinds between households.

Expenditure from Transfer refers to regular or deontic transfer from households to country, institutions, households or individuals. It includes taxes paid, expenditure of all kinds of social security, supporting expenditure, regular donation and compensation and other regular transfer expenditure, etc.

2. Consumption Expenditure of Households

Consumption Expenditure of Households refers to all expenditure of households for living expenditure to satisfy family daily living. It includes expenditure in cash and in kind. It includes eight categories: food, tobacco and liquor; clothing; residence; household facilities, articles and services; transport and communications; education, cultural and recreational activities; health care and medical services, and miscellaneous goods and services.

Food, Tobacco and Liquor refers to expenditure for food, tobacco and liquor of all kinds.

Clothing refers to expenditure related to clothing, including clothes, clothing materials, footwear, other clothing and accessories, processing services related to clothing.

Residence refers to expenditure related to residence, including housing rents, water, electricity, fuel, property management, and including converted self-owned housing rents.

Household Facilities, Articles and Services refers to expenditure for family and individual articles for living purpose and family services. It includes furniture and interior decoration, home appliances, home textiles, household miscellaneous daily articles, personal articles, and family services.

Transport and Communications refers to expenditure for transport and communication and related services, maintenance and repairs, and vehicle insurance.

Education, Cultural and Recreational Activities refers to expenditure on education, cultural and recreational activities.

Health Care and Medical Services refers to expenditure on drugs, supplies and services of medical and health care. It includes medical appliances and drugs, and medical services.

Miscellaneous Goods and Services refers to expenditure of all kinds of expenditure of other articles and services that can not divided into the category above.

II. Explanatory on Inidcators before 2012

Prior to 2012, household surveys in China were conducted separately in urban and rural areas. Statistical coverage of indicators of household income and expenditure of urban and rural households were different, data were not comparable completely. Disposable income was surveyed in urban households, and net income was surveyed in rural households. Income and expenditure of urban households refer to that in cash, not including physical payments; Among which, when calculating per capita disposable income and consumption, self-owned housing conversion rental is not included, and expenditure of purchasing housing is not included either. Income and expenditure of rural households are divided into that of total and in cash, that is, total income and expenditure include self occupied physical payments; Among which, when computing per capita net income and expenditure of rural households, self-owned housing conversion rental is not included, but purchasing of housing is included in consumption expenditure of rural households.

For comparable reason, data prior to 2012 in this yearbook were still original urban households and rural households survey.

1. Urban Household Survey

Population of Urban Households refer to members of households living and sharing economically together in the urban areas. All the income and expenditure of all the members of such households are included in the income and expenditure of the household.

Disposable Income of Urban Households refers to the actual income at the disposal of members of the households which can be used for final consumption, other non-compulsory expenditure and savings. This equals to total income minus income tax, personal contribution to social security and subsidy for keeping diaries in being a sample household. The following formula is used:

Disposable Income of Urban Households= total household income - income tax - personal contribution to social security - subsidy for keeping diaries for a sampled household

2. Rural Household Survey

Rural Households refer to usual resident households in rural areas. Usual resident households in rural areas are households residing on a long term basis(for more than one year) in the areas under the administration of township governments (not including county towns), and in the areas under the administration of villages in county towns. Households residing in the current addresses for over one year with their household registration in other places are still considered as resident households of the locality. For households with their household registration in one place but all members of the households having moved away to make a living in another place for over one year, they will not be included in the rural households of the area where they are registered, irrespective of whether they still keep their contracted land.

Net Income of Rural Households refers to the total income of rural households from all sources minus all corresponding expenses. The formula for calculation is as follows:

Net income of rural households = total income - household operation expenses - taxes and fees-depreciation of fixed assets for production - gifts to rural relatives.

Net income is mainly used as input for reinvestment in production and as consumption expenditure of the year, and also used for savings and non-compulsory expenses of various forms. "Per capita net income of farmers" is the level of net income averaged by population, reflecting the average income level of rural population in a given area.

十一、农业

AGRICULTURE

十一 农业

简要说明

一、本篇资料反映广东省农业生产和农村经济的基本情况。内容主要包括农村劳动力、农业产值、主要产品产量、农业自然灾害等方面的统计资料。

二、本篇资料主要由广东省统计局农村社会经济统计处整理提供。

三、本篇资料主要来源于《广东省农林牧渔业综合统计报表制度》。农林牧渔业综合统计报表制度的统计范围包括各市县区的各种经济类型的全部农林牧渔业以及各非农行业附属的农林牧渔业生产单位。

四、根据《全国农业普查条例》，本篇资料的 1996 年部分数据以第一次全国农业普查结果为基础做了调整，2006 年部分数据以第二次全国农业普查结果为基础做了调整，2007 年及以后年份部分数据以第三次全国农业普查结果为基础做了调整。

11 Agriculture

Brief Introduction

Ⅰ.The data in this chapter show the basic conditions of agricultural production and rural economy in Guangdong Province, including mainly rural labor force, output value of agriculture, output of major products, as well as statistics on natural disasters in agriculture enterprises.

Ⅱ.The data in this chapter are mainly prepared and provided by the Division of Rural Socio-economic Statistics of Statistics Bureau of Guangdong Province.

Ⅲ.The data in this chapter mainly come from The Comprehensive Statistical Report System on Farming, Forestry, Animal Husbandry and Fishery of Guangdong Province. The statistical coverage of the statistical reporting summary scheme includes all productive units of farming, forestry, animal husbandry and fishery and units engaged in farming, forestry, animal husbandry and fishery in non-agricultural sectors with various types of ownership in cities, counties and districts of Guangdong Province.

IV. Some data of 1996 in this chapter are adjusted in accordance with the regulations of the first national agricultural census，Some data of 2006 in this chapter are adjusted in accordance with the regulations of the second national agricultural census，Some data of 2007 and subsequent years in this chapter are adjusted in accordance with the regulations of the third national agricultural census.

11-1 农业主要指标
Main Indicators of Agriculture

指标	Item	2000	2010	2014	2015	2016	2017
乡镇户数 (万户)	Number of Rural Households (10000 households)	1419.91	1686.62	1697.44	1689.97	1676.49	1677.57
乡镇人口 (万人)	Rural Population (10000 persons)	6046.62	6805.44	6901.08	6863.20	6807.01	6830.62
乡镇就业人员 (万人)	Number of Rural Employed Persons (10000 persons)	2789.89	3425.28	3542.59	3496.95	3466.41	3480.72
#农、林、牧、渔业	Farming, Forestry, Animal Husbandry and Fishery	1572.07	1468.25	1363.19	1351.83	1341.20	1342.80
按性别分	Grouped by Sex						
男	Male	1450.37	1802.67	1876.40	1854.11	1842.38	723.87
女	Female	1339.52	1622.61	1666.19	1642.84	1624.03	618.93
化肥施用量(折纯) (万吨)	Consumption of Chemical Fertilizers (100 percent equivalent,10000 tons)	176.20	233.42	234.13	238.17	241.97	237.94
#氮肥	Nitrogenous Fertilizer	95.89	94.93	90.51	90.78	93.03	90.98
磷肥	Phosphate Fertilizer	18.36	24.75	27.25	29.03	29.20	28.60
钾肥	Potash Fertilizer	35.84	46.74	46.65	47.00	47.49	46.77
农药施用量 (万吨)	Consumption of Pesticides (10000 tons)	8.47	9.10	9.24	9.23	9.60	9.46
农村用电量 (亿千瓦时)	Electricity Consumed in Rural Areas (100 million kwh)	405.45	1044.26	1314.00	1326.20	1334.89	1414.77
农业总产值 (亿元)	Gross Output Value of Agriculture (100 million yuan)	1701.18	3697.18	5053.72	5303.63	5817.55	5969.87
农业增加值 (亿元)	Value-added of Agriculture (100 million yuan)	1000.06	2254.49	3118.39	3275.05	3593.64	3712.71
农作物总播种面积 (万亩)	Total Sown Area (10000 mu)	7735.35	6394.16	6337.79	6291.83	6271.95	6341.26
粮食作物	Grain Corps	4649.83	3579.49	3346.61	3289.94	3266.67	3254.59
经济作物	Economics Corps	1093.04	959.77	1022.98	1024.33	1030.25	1057.81
其他作物	Other Corps	1847.01	1854.90	1968.21	1977.55	1975.03	2028.86
人工造林面积 (万亩)	Afforested Area in Barren Mountains (10000 mu)	25.76	142.72	199.83	177.69	150.99	121.11
主要产品产量 (万吨)	Output of Major Products (10000 tons)						
粮食	Grain	1822.33	1249.15	1229.97	1211.66	1204.22	1208.56
糖蔗	Sugarcane	1137.59	1064.09	1159.89	1093.58	1096.56	1144.14
花生	Peanuts	77.68	81.59	91.77	94.48	95.48	98.42
烟叶	Tobacco	6.21	5.00	4.61	4.52	4.40	4.26
蔬菜	Vegetables	2214.80	2551.00	2898.53	2994.70	3036.45	3177.49
水果	Fruits	643.52	1049.21	1248.18	1298.52	1331.99	1421.23
水产品	Aquatic Products	593.19	729.03	783.95	804.14	818.29	833.54
猪肉	Pork	206.85	285.14	302.86	296.31	288.24	277.96
效益指标	Efficiency Indicators						
农业中间消耗率 (%)	Farming, Forestry, Animal Husbandry and Fishery	41.2	39.0	38.3	38.9	38.2	37.8
淡水养殖水面 (元/亩)	Freshwater Aquatic Cultivation Area (yuan/mu)	3643	6930	10286	10264	11785	11092
生猪出栏率 (%)	Slaughtered Fattened Hog Rate (%)	146	156	166	172	165	172

注：表中农业总产值、农业增加值按当年价格计算，增长速度按可比价格计算。

Notes: Gross output value and value-added of agriculture in this table are calculated at current prices, whereas the growth rates are calculated at comparable prices.

11-2 各市农村基层组织情况（2017年）

Basic Conditions of Rural Grassroots Units by City (2017)

市别	City	乡镇个数（个）Number of Townships (unit)	乡镇户数（万户）Number of Rural Households (10000 households)	乡镇人口（万人）Rural Population (10000 persons)	乡镇就业人员（万人）Rural Employed Persons (10000 persons)	#农、林、牧、渔业 Farming, Forestry,Animal Husbandry and Fishery	按性别分 By Sex 男 Male	女 Female
全 省	**Provincial Total**	**1135**	**1677.57**	**6830.62**	**3480.72**	**1342.80**	**1847.60**	**1633.12**
广 州	Guangzhou	34	171.08	571.50	348.08	62.07	180.05	168.04
深 圳	Shenzhen		1.88	7.73	3.67	1.62	1.92	1.75
珠 海	Zhuhai	15	11.95	43.55	23.16	6.18	12.15	11.01
汕 头	Shantou	32	88.37	432.45	189.52	61.58	100.48	89.04
佛 山	Foshan	21	84.27	302.52	172.27	21.40	89.44	82.83
韶 关	Shaoguan	94	61.08	228.10	110.89	59.04	58.56	52.32
河 源	Heyuan	95	74.79	319.90	150.71	71.03	79.78	70.93
梅 州	Meizhou	104	85.82	327.29	182.23	79.96	93.63	88.60
惠 州	Huizhou	49	76.84	330.12	187.46	48.32	98.67	88.79
汕 尾	Shanwei	44	68.71	337.48	145.65	50.85	84.75	60.90
东 莞	Dongguan	28	56.07	190.75	98.29	5.82	52.30	45.99
中 山	Zhongshan	18	62.47	247.72	157.63	17.13	81.08	76.55
江 门	Jiangmen	61	80.66	283.93	175.17	78.94	89.59	85.58
阳 江	Yangjiang	38	64.77	250.66	129.04	47.07	70.49	58.55
湛 江	Zhanjiang	84	154.19	689.32	337.38	204.37	182.78	154.60
茂 名	Maoming	87	131.62	548.81	261.75	136.12	140.70	121.06
肇 庆	Zhaoqing	92	79.08	304.93	146.86	106.63	74.80	72.06
清 远	Qingyuan	80	80.92	329.31	168.07	95.92	88.39	79.68
潮 州	Chaozhou	41	54.00	230.45	110.87	38.48	59.31	51.56
揭 阳	Jieyang	63	126.98	609.93	251.81	80.23	139.77	112.03
云 浮	Yunfu	55	62.02	244.18	130.21	70.04	68.96	61.25
按经济区域分	By Region							
珠三角	Pearl River Delta	318	624.31	2282.74	1312.59	348.11	680.00	632.59
东 翼	Eastern Region	180	338.06	1610.32	697.84	231.14	384.31	313.54
西 翼	Western Region	209	350.58	1488.78	728.17	387.56	393.97	334.20
山 区	Mountainous Region	428	364.62	1448.78	742.11	375.99	389.33	352.79

注：乡镇个数为广东省民政厅统计年报数。

Note: The number of townships comes from the annual reports of Guangdong Provincial Department of Civil Affairs.

11-3 农业生产条件

Agricultural Production Basic Conditions

指 标	Item	2015	2016	2017
农业机械化情况	**Mechanization of Agriculture**			
农业机械总动力 (万千瓦)	Total Agricultural Machinery Power (10 000 kw)	2696.80	2390.50	2410.77
机耕面积 (千公顷)	Total Area Cultivated Using Machinery (10 000 hectares)	3741.81	3969.17	4014.05
机播面积 (千公顷)	Total Area Sown Using Machinery (1 000 hectares)	264.76	315.78	342.21
农村电气化情况	**Electrification of Rural Areas**			
农村用电量 (亿千瓦小时)	Electricity Consumed in Rural Areas (kWh)	1326.20	1334.89	1414.77
农用物资使用情况	**Use of Agricultural Materials**			
化肥施用量(折纯量) (万吨)	Consumption of Chemical Fertilizers(pure) (10 000 tons)	238.17	241.97	237.94
每亩耕地施用化肥(折纯量) (千克)	Consumption of Chemical Fertilizers per mu (pure) (kg)	60.53	61.86	61.02
农用塑料薄膜使用量 (万吨)	Plastic Agricultural Film Used (10 000 tons)	4.68	4.55	4.59
农用柴油使用量 (万吨)	Diesel Used in Agriculture (10 000 tons)	78.70	79.89	77.71
农药使用量 (万吨)	Consumption of Pesticides (10 000 tons)	9.23	9.60	9.46
农田水利情况	**Agricultural Water Conservation**			
耕地灌溉面积 (千公顷)	Irrigated Area of Cultivated Land (10 000 hectares)	1771.26	1771.71	1774.61
节水灌溉面积 (千公顷)	Water-saving Irrigated Area (10 000 hectares)	295.86	301.49	326.19
除涝面积 (千公顷)	Areas with Flood Prevention Measures (10 000 hectares)	536.53	542.68	545.54
累计水土流失治理面积 (千公顷)	Area of Soil Erosion Under Control (10 000 hectares)	1457.52	1536.17	1638.70
堤防长度 (公里)	Total Length of Dikes (10 000 km)	28326.65	28338.09	28475.36
堤防保护面积 (千公顷)	Area of Land Protected by Dikes (10 000 hectares)	1132.91	1152.54	1156.72

11-4 农业自然灾害情况

Statistics on Agriculture Covered and Affected by Natural Disasters

项 目	Item	2000	2010	2015	2016	2017
农作物受灾面积 (万亩)	Area of Farm Crops Covered by Natural Disasters(10000 mu)	948.43	916.21	1268.90	1121.25	427.70
#绝收面积	Area without Output	84.14	106.45	139.31	81.00	16.41
受灾人口 (万人)	Number of Persons Covered by Natural Disasters (10000 persons)	1801.00	1197.00	848.74	560.94	326.24
紧急转移安置人口(万人)	Number of Persons Receiving Evacuation and Re-settlement (10000 persons)	27.73	71.61	38.59	33.50	54.61
饮水困难人口 (万人)	Number of Persons Lacking Access to Clean Drinking Water (10000 persons)	23.16	1.96	7.31		
因灾死亡人口 (人)	DeathToll in Natural Disasters (person)	102	177	28	43	25
因灾伤病人口 (人)	Number of Wounded Persons in Natural Disasters (person)	14454	1121	263	59	349
倒塌房屋 (间)	Number of Broken Buildings (room)	27743	73666	9646	5984	3399
损坏房屋 (间)	Number of Damaged Buildings (room)	74052	137066	150161	14580	12492
因灾死亡大牲畜(头、只)	Number of Large Livestock Killed in Natural Disasters (head)	62417	74002	1310	4572	1464
直接经济损失 (亿元)	Volume of Direct Economic Loss (100 million yuan)	38.20	180.01	315.54	109.10	316.10

11－5 农林牧渔业总产值

Gross Output Value of Farming, Forestry, Animal Husbandry and Fishery

单位：亿元 (100 million yuan)

年份 Year	农林牧渔业总产值 Gross Output Value of Farming, Forestry, Animal Husbandry and Fishery	农业产值 Farming	林业产值 Forestry	牧业产值 Animal Husbandry	渔业产值 Fishery	农林牧渔服务业产值 Services for Farming,Forestry, Animal Husbandry and Fishery
1978	85.94	59.56	4.98	15.98	5.42	
1979	91.53	67.19	7.67	13.58	3.09	
1980	126.25	97.15	6.83	17.75	4.52	
1981	133.85	99.33	7.81	21.62	5.09	
1982	135.52	98.33	8.33	21.73	7.13	
1983	169.96	120.06	10.72	28.57	10.61	
1984	200.07	141.22	12.13	33.81	12.91	
1985	245.21	149.09	21.09	54.68	20.35	
1986	279.15	168.68	24.38	60.74	25.35	
1987	348.61	214.47	16.74	78.26	39.14	
1988	473.78	277.38	27.66	114.28	54.46	
1989	548.60	323.15	28.00	134.60	62.85	
1990	600.71	359.39	28.46	143.68	69.18	
1991	654.82	388.90	29.64	156.08	80.20	
1992	737.11	428.99	32.86	175.36	99.90	
1993	899.03	486.46	35.51	223.16	153.90	
1994	1151.38	628.17	41.07	279.98	202.16	
1995	1445.48	777.72	46.12	349.11	272.53	
1996	1577.89	825.60	49.64	398.12	304.53	
1997	1656.46	851.35	52.10	425.67	327.34	
1998	1705.44	861.97	54.65	441.61	347.21	
1999	1745.02	859.66	58.77	457.51	369.08	
2000	1701.18	807.94	59.64	450.18	383.42	
2001	1722.35	817.95	56.78	457.56	390.06	
2002	1781.06	841.77	57.09	465.91	416.29	
2003	1908.66	851.72	55.72	482.83	432.74	85.65
2004	2154.79	959.97	61.72	571.09	466.45	95.56
2005	2447.57	1109.18	66.25	638.61	523.79	109.74
2006	2536.27	1235.40	67.60	623.34	519.03	90.90
2007	2810.45	1268.70	116.96	781.97	540.58	102.24
2008	3276.02	1398.82	125.23	983.84	650.23	117.89
2009	3301.86	1442.40	139.95	939.67	657.65	122.18
2010	3697.18	1668.66	180.20	978.33	737.01	132.97
2011	4301.86	1910.21	213.71	1193.73	835.41	148.80
2012	4550.29	2060.91	228.75	1189.80	908.12	162.71
2013	4802.01	2229.64	256.99	1168.73	968.42	178.23
2014	5053.72	2357.16	289.66	1145.87	1068.00	193.03
2015	5303.63	2490.20	308.72	1195.97	1102.12	206.62
2016	5817.55	2763.79	330.04	1318.89	1179.15	225.68
2017	5969.87	2889.97	356.14	1202.30	1276.11	245.34

11-6 农林牧渔业总产值指数（1978年＝100）

Indices of Gross Output Value of Farming, Forestry, Animal Husbandry and Fishery (year of 1978=100)

1978年＝100 (year of 1978=100)

年份 Year	农林牧渔业总产值 Gross Output Value of Farming, Forestry, Animal Husbandry and Fishery	农业产值 Farming	林业产值 Forestry	牧业产值 Animal Husbandry	渔业产值 Fishery	农林牧渔服务业产值 Services for Farming,Forestry, Animal Husbandry and Fishery
1978	100.0	100.0	100.0	100.0	100.0	
1979	99.2	99.4	85.1	104.6	93.7	
1980	110.2	111.8	108.3	104.4	102.8	
1981	112.8	110.3	119.6	122.9	111.9	
1982	131.2	127.4	133.4	148.6	135.0	
1983	134.6	127.2	140.4	159.8	164.3	
1984	147.1	138.9	147.6	175.5	185.5	
1985	157.8	145.5	154.8	202.2	216.2	
1986	167.5	151.0	173.4	219.6	257.0	
1987	183.6	165.8	166.9	237.7	313.2	
1988	197.7	173.4	223.2	259.2	350.3	
1989	213.2	186.9	232.3	279.4	389.9	
1990	228.9	201.5	215.7	306.2	429.3	
1991	243.0	211.9	213.8	332.6	470.1	
1992	257.7	220.3	218.9	357.8	536.5	
1993	267.6	213.7	222.6	398.9	644.5	
1994	279.5	219.5	227.5	415.1	716.3	
1995	302.7	237.1	239.6	443.5	800.1	
1996	320.9	245.0	246.5	485.9	882.9	
1997	342.7	263.7	249.2	509.5	953.5	
1998	359.3	272.7	258.1	535.8	1033.7	
1999	379.1	286.8	271.8	563.9	1101.9	
2000	389.3	288.6	281.3	579.6	1184.5	
2001	400.1	295.6	294.0	592.7	1230.1	
2002	426.1	323.4	285.8	601.4	1310.6	
2003	438.2	331.6	277.8	614.8	1367.5	100.0
2004	457.9	350.5	287.2	625.9	1433.1	107.8
2005	479.9	362.3	295.5	660.4	1514.2	120.5
2006	499.1	375.2	280.8	680.7	1605.1	132.3
2007	515.5	385.5	289.1	701.2	1670.8	143.1
2008	536.1	392.4	289.9	750.8	1749.5	155.0
2009	562.9	414.3	310.6	779.3	1839.0	163.2
2010	586.9	434.2	324.5	803.9	1921.4	171.4
2011	609.9	458.6	351.1	795.6	2023.4	180.8
2012	632.7	476.3	373.0	811.3	2123.6	191.1
2013	647.0	490.9	393.7	796.8	2211.8	203.2
2014	666.4	512.8	413.2	788.5	2292.0	213.5
2015	687.0	534.0	437.6	785.6	2369.7	224.7
2016	707.1	554.6	467.1	777.7	2451.0	238.3
2017	730.8	580.3	490.1	771.7	2542.1	255.3

注：本表按可比价格计算。
Note: The indices are calculated at comparable prices.

11-7 农林牧渔业总产值指数（上年=100）

Indices of Gross Output Value of Farming, Forestry, Animal Husbandry and Fishery (preceding year=100)

上年=100 (preceding year=100)

年份 Year	农林牧渔业总产值 Gross Output Value of Farming, Forestry, Animal Husbandry and Fishery	农业产值 Farming	林业产值 Forestry	牧业产值 Animal Husbandry	渔业产值 Fishery	农林牧渔服务业产值 Services for Farming, Forestry,Animal Husbandry and Fishery
1979	99.2	99.4	85.1	104.6	93.7	
1980	111.1	112.5	127.3	99.8	109.7	
1981	102.4	98.7	110.4	117.6	108.9	
1982	116.3	115.5	111.5	120.9	120.6	
1983	102.6	99.9	105.2	107.6	121.7	
1984	109.3	109.2	105.1	109.8	112.9	
1985	107.3	104.8	104.9	115.2	116.5	
1986	106.1	103.8	112.0	108.6	118.9	
1987	109.6	109.8	96.3	108.2	121.9	
1988	107.7	104.6	133.7	109.0	111.8	
1989	107.8	107.8	104.1	107.8	111.3	
1990	107.4	107.8	92.9	109.6	110.1	
1991	106.2	105.1	99.1	108.6	109.5	
1992	106.0	103.9	102.4	107.6	114.1	
1993	103.8	97.0	101.7	111.5	120.1	
1994	104.4	102.7	102.2	104.1	111.1	
1995	108.3	108.0	105.3	106.8	111.7	
1996	106.0	103.3	102.9	109.6	110.3	
1997	106.8	107.6	101.1	104.8	108.0	
1998	104.8	103.4	103.6	105.2	108.4	
1999	105.5	105.2	105.3	105.2	106.6	
2000	102.7	100.6	103.5	102.8	107.5	
2001	102.8	102.4	104.5	102.2	103.8	
2002	106.5	109.4	97.2	101.5	106.5	
2003	102.8	102.5	97.2	102.2	104.3	
2004	104.5	105.7	103.4	101.8	104.8	107.8
2005	104.8	103.4	102.9	105.5	105.7	111.8
2006	104.0	103.6	95.0	103.1	106.0	109.8
2007	103.3	102.7	103.0	103.0	104.1	108.2
2008	104.0	101.8	100.3	107.1	104.7	108.3
2009	105.0	105.6	107.1	103.8	105.1	105.3
2010	104.3	104.8	104.5	103.2	104.5	105.0
2011	103.9	105.6	108.2	99.0	105.3	105.5
2012	103.7	103.9	106.3	102.0	105.0	105.7
2013	102.3	103.1	105.5	98.2	104.2	106.3
2014	103.0	104.5	105.0	99.0	103.6	105.1
2015	103.1	104.1	105.9	99.6	103.4	105.2
2016	102.9	103.9	106.8	99.0	103.4	106.1
2017	103.3	104.6	104.9	99.2	103.7	107.1

注：本表按可比价格计算。
Note: The indices are calculated at comparable prices.

11-8 各市农林牧渔业总产值（2017年）
Gross Output Value of Farming, Forestry, Animal Husbandry and Fishery by City (2017)

单位：亿元 (100 million yuan)

市别	City	农林牧渔业总产值 Gross Output Value of Farming, Forestry, Animal Husbandry and Fishery	农业产值 Farming	林业产值 Forestry	牧业产值 Animal Husbandry	渔业产值 Fishery	农林牧渔服务业产值 Services for Farming,Forestry, Animal Husbandry and Fishery
全 省	**Provincial Total**	**5969.87**	**2889.97**	**356.14**	**1202.30**	**1276.11**	**245.34**
广 州	Guangzhou	396.70	226.64	3.58	39.31	74.17	53.00
深 圳	Shenzhen	38.86	12.34	0.24	2.90	21.50	1.88
珠 海	Zhuhai	91.63	11.21	0.14	9.72	61.62	8.93
汕 头	Shantou	190.13	92.29	0.74	24.91	63.17	9.02
佛 山	Foshan	270.33	80.66	1.47	48.91	120.42	18.86
韶 关	Shaoguan	243.41	146.89	24.69	57.52	11.29	3.02
河 源	Heyuan	160.90	92.59	26.76	34.37	4.61	2.56
梅 州	Meizhou	301.99	194.79	16.02	74.79	10.17	6.21
惠 州	Huizhou	266.55	184.53	5.71	49.83	22.60	3.89
汕 尾	Shanwei	205.21	80.16	5.04	19.42	90.75	9.83
东 莞	Dongguan	35.49	26.28	0.35	1.81	5.77	1.28
中 山	Zhongshan	99.90	25.85	0.11	6.71	64.89	2.34
江 门	Jiangmen	338.00	116.66	9.69	72.56	127.85	11.24
阳 江	Yangjiang	348.54	91.66	12.49	68.27	167.13	8.98
湛 江	Zhanjiang	788.34	414.71	24.97	117.62	203.38	27.67
茂 名	Maoming	743.84	387.60	46.33	199.52	89.25	21.14
肇 庆	Zhaoqing	497.99	232.37	77.64	126.75	52.45	8.78
清 远	Qingyuan	358.84	183.70	34.37	101.73	17.83	21.20
潮 州	Chaozhou	118.72	61.90	2.35	16.90	31.32	6.25
揭 阳	Jieyang	245.25	141.89	25.53	40.75	25.60	11.49
云 浮	Yunfu	229.29	85.27	37.90	88.02	10.33	7.77
按经济区域分	By Region						
珠 三 角	Pearl River Delta	2035.45	916.54	98.93	358.49	551.28	110.21
东 翼	Eastern Region	759.30	376.24	33.67	101.97	210.84	36.58
西 翼	Western Region	1880.72	893.98	83.79	385.41	459.75	57.79
山 区	Mountainous Region	1294.43	703.25	139.75	356.43	54.24	40.76

注：本表按当年价格计算。
Note: Data in this table are calculated at current prices.

11-9 各市农林牧渔业总产值指数（2017年）
Indices of Gross Output Value of Farming, Forestry, Animal Husbandry and Fishery by City (2017)

上年=100 (preceding year=100)

市别	City	农林牧渔业总产值 Gross Output Value of Farming, Forestry, Animal Husbandry and Fishery	农业产值 Farming	林业产值 Forestry	牧业产值 Animal Husbandry	渔业产值 Fishery	农林牧渔服务业产值 Services for Farming,Forestry, Animal Husbandry and Fishery
全　省	**Provincial Total**	**103.3**	**104.6**	**104.9**	**99.2**	**103.7**	**107.1**
广　州	Guangzhou	103.7	105.7	94.4	100.2	99.0	105.4
深　圳	Shenzhen	122.7	131.4	96.9	148.5	118.2	94.5
珠　海	Zhuhai	107.3	102.7	330.9	99.3	110.4	102.0
汕　头	Shantou	103.3	104.9	92.1	99.3	103.3	101.3
佛　山	Foshan	102.1	100.5	109.6	99.6	104.2	102.9
韶　关	Shaoguan	103.7	105.5	107.2	98.6	103.1	107.1
河　源	Heyuan	103.7	105.1	104.7	99.6	101.1	106.7
梅　州	Meizhou	102.4	103.2	104.7	99.5	102.5	107.8
惠　州	Huizhou	104.0	105.6	103.8	99.3	102.1	105.3
汕　尾	Shanwei	105.5	105.7	105.2	95.0	107.9	107.6
东　莞	Dongguan	101.8	104.2	96.8	101.3	92.4	100.0
中　山	Zhongshan	97.8	82.0	184.4	98.7	106.0	101.5
江　门	Jiangmen	102.7	104.2	120.0	98.9	101.4	119.3
阳　江	Yangjiang	102.3	104.1	102.2	99.1	102.6	106.5
湛　江	Zhanjiang	103.1	104.4	101.1	99.1	102.8	108.0
茂　名	Maoming	103.4	105.7	104.7	99.1	102.7	110.5
肇　庆	Zhaoqing	103.5	104.5	104.4	99.2	108.7	112.6
清　远	Qingyuan	104.5	106.5	108.3	99.7	105.0	106.8
潮　州	Chaozhou	101.0	105.2	69.1	99.1	96.6	108.3
揭　阳	Jieyang	104.0	103.8	106.6	98.9	108.1	113.3
云　浮	Yunfu	105.2	110.6	104.2	100.7	108.6	106.4
按经济区域分	By Region						
珠三角	Pearl River Delta	103.4	104.1	105.5	99.6	104.4	106.1
东　翼	Eastern Region	103.7	104.7	102.1	98.2	104.7	107.8
西　翼	Western Region	103.1	104.9	103.2	99.1	102.7	108.7
山　区	Mountainous Region	103.8	105.7	105.8	99.7	104.4	106.9

注：本表按可比价格计算。
Note: The indices are calculated at comparable prices.

11-10 农作物播种面积
Total Sown Area of Farm Crops

单位：万亩 (10000 mu)

年份 Year	农作物总播种面积 Total Sown Area	一、粮食作物 Grain Crops	#稻谷 Rice	#薯类 Tubers	二、大豆 Soybean
1978	9962.46	7603.47	5790.39	873.02	163.71
1979	9492.62	7300.54	5691.88	845.65	185.91
1980	8954.84	6908.02	5596.10	800.67	198.18
1981	8567.83	6548.40	5450.29	767.07	199.33
1982	8539.77	6475.65	5373.51	778.51	218.52
1983	8364.03	6485.66	5406.97	780.98	197.43
1984	8313.00	6269.47	5272.01	765.51	193.21
1985	8036.82	5750.76	4815.81	730.83	175.22
1986	8037.18	5731.76	4804.77	745.48	177.59
1987	8064.78	5679.94	4750.06	743.22	174.25
1988	8063.89	5598.29	4678.26	726.61	172.60
1989	8322.71	5777.18	4768.32	743.93	173.64
1990	8507.35	5822.06	4763.67	751.70	172.44
1991	8489.09	5643.92	4596.92	746.74	163.30
1992	8231.36	5303.82	4313.79	710.56	157.48
1993	7718.41	4840.76	3944.83	681.66	160.54
1994	7807.99	4959.10	4005.47	747.93	157.12
1995	7957.19	5052.24	4052.13	775.96	155.84
1996	8156.22	5120.09	4066.33	778.70	155.04
1997	8267.25	5144.06	4055.92	772.52	149.14
1998	8310.73	5147.65	4029.10	768.09	146.06
1999	7894.24	4912.04	3836.30	697.22	144.52
2000	7735.35	4649.83	3619.05	640.15	145.46
2001	7868.21	4634.79	3638.28	661.15	132.19
2002	7207.37	4021.44	3151.22	582.81	102.14
2003	7294.58	4012.81	3144.56	578.14	114.54
2004	7211.96	4184.55	3208.50	581.55	120.60
2005	7223.06	4179.75	3206.40	579.75	125.70
2006	6573.85	3700.00	2912.90	468.40	96.90
2007	6444.51	3662.24	2895.53	448.58	85.95
2008	6410.77	3638.75	2896.11	425.09	81.17
2009	6416.17	3638.09	2900.39	404.84	73.18
2010	6394.16	3579.49	2877.21	392.65	72.66
2011	6367.10	3524.67	2847.03	372.05	63.76
2012	6372.63	3497.08	2847.31	355.91	61.87
2013	6363.36	3399.78	2774.98	339.63	58.22
2014	6337.79	3346.61	2740.15	333.84	54.53
2015	6291.83	3289.94	2707.15	319.78	51.71
2016	6271.95	3266.67	2709.05	304.07	48.47
2017	6341.26	3254.59	2708.13	300.04	46.74

注：2004年起粮食播种面积含大豆。
Note: Since 2004, the sown area of grain has included that of soybeans.

11-10 续表 continued

单位：万亩 (10000 mu)

年份 Year	三、经济作物 Economic Crops	#糖蔗 Sugarcane	#花生 Peanuts	#烟叶 Tobacco	四、其他作物 Other Crops	#蔬菜 Vegetables
1978	1277.28	258.96	486.62	69.19	918.00	
1979	1258.28	227.15	519.73	59.44	747.89	
1980	1213.98	218.57	553.24	38.62	634.66	
1981	1302.19	272.52	595.41	45.06	517.91	
1982	1327.84	331.53	588.01	48.73	517.76	
1983	1126.05	312.86	489.74	43.25	554.89	
1984	1213.32	341.02	523.56	39.06	637.00	
1985	1417.68	442.83	545.78	55.25	693.16	
1986	1334.07	405.07	560.80	41.87	793.76	
1987	1324.67	344.72	533.13	41.42	885.92	
1988	1318.08	354.90	497.82	61.39	974.92	
1989	1324.88	338.02	486.05	72.25	1047.01	
1990	1338.43	419.73	485.96	68.55	1174.42	776.00
1991	1374.36	453.90	472.15	81.93	1307.51	867.95
1992	1393.07	461.14	471.88	79.08	1376.99	946.88
1993	1295.77	353.65	499.78	73.92	1421.34	1057.02
1994	1224.21	325.62	505.35	53.15	1467.56	1147.53
1995	1185.17	320.18	499.60	44.33	1563.94	1244.96
1996	1202.15	329.28	497.42	45.10	1678.94	1348.64
1997	1211.80	334.02	499.70	55.45	1762.26	1416.62
1998	1185.21	325.59	510.83	50.30	1831.81	1484.82
1999	1071.27	261.47	468.50	42.72	1766.41	1441.85
2000	1093.04	239.60	496.61	46.64	1847.01	1515.15
2001	1088.71	215.25	511.57	53.48	2012.52	1685.69
2002	1068.46	222.66	472.49	46.27	2015.33	1692.00
2003	1055.55	198.29	488.66	44.86	2111.68	1792.29
2004	1008.72	193.45	462.20	47.42	2018.69	1720.01
2005	1001.56	188.08	464.11	47.47	2041.75	1744.08
2006	947.98	195.13	462.28	30.23	1925.87	1627.80
2007	935.16	206.37	446.50	28.62	1847.11	1570.07
2008	938.77	203.87	455.75	33.57	1833.25	1612.13
2009	950.48	203.79	459.64	34.44	1827.60	1621.20
2010	959.77	205.08	461.08	32.54	1854.90	1651.25
2011	975.22	211.58	461.80	32.31	1867.20	1662.82
2012	1003.75	219.42	466.41	31.22	1871.80	1669.40
2013	1021.41	231.18	469.80	29.99	1942.17	1736.59
2014	1022.98	225.68	470.91	28.23	1968.21	1772.00
2015	1024.33	215.36	474.87	27.42	1977.55	1782.70
2016	1030.25	214.36	471.77	26.71	1975.03	1784.79
2017	1057.81	219.36	478.65	26.11	2028.86	1840.83

注：2004年起粮食播种面积含大豆。
Note: Since 2004, the sown area of grain has included that of soybeans.

11-11 主要农产品产量

Output of Major Farm Products

单位：万吨 (10000 tons)

年份 Year	粮食作物 Grain Crops	#稻谷 Rice	#薯类 Tubers	大豆 Soybean	糖蔗 Sugarcane	花生 Peanuts	烟叶 Tobacco	蔬菜 Vegetables	茶叶 Tea	水果 Fruits
1978	1509.51	1328.56	121.04	7.99	835.42	35.17	4.73		0.92	29.40
1979	1605.36	1435.22	125.15	9.56	742.90	40.70	4.00		0.89	26.20
1980	1681.91	1523.92	123.68	11.47	834.73	50.00	2.72		1.00	29.10
1981	1521.00	1372.22	122.53	12.01	1235.50	57.39	3.68		1.13	39.20
1982	1795.72	1627.37	138.98	14.44	1496.10	61.90	4.67		1.31	46.30
1983	1817.48	1673.12	138.98	10.80	1159.83	48.08	3.41		1.45	53.00
1984	1819.33	1666.08	130.21	11.90	1454.15	53.40	3.50		1.61	73.90
1985	1604.37	1454.29	131.88	11.32	1831.40	57.07	4.89		1.75	116.28
1986	1567.00	1421.55	128.01	12.27	1622.13	60.40	3.50		2.03	185.50
1987	1701.81	1536.46	146.48	12.43	1338.60	53.50	4.05		2.28	264.10
1988	1636.70	1472.95	143.42	12.32	1538.68	51.80	5.80		2.39	277.98
1989	1817.21	1630.29	153.47	13.25	1681.34	55.38	7.15	916.88	2.35	275.83
1990	1896.29	1687.00	167.05	13.87	2093.46	57.95	7.08	976.83	2.59	328.58
1991	1873.50	1651.65	176.59	12.60	2286.38	56.11	8.46	1106.19	2.67	394.19
1992	1810.40	1602.27	170.28	13.94	2271.06	60.30	8.62	1203.54	2.87	453.62
1993	1629.11	1425.81	169.20	15.28	1603.11	66.02	7.70	1367.22	3.07	402.44
1994	1662.66	1434.04	194.68	15.44	1397.22	63.71	5.30	1509.93	3.32	401.55
1995	1803.33	1553.90	209.40	16.50	1472.21	69.98	5.04	1703.86	3.96	414.51
1996	1891.43	1626.29	210.28	17.32	1392.00	73.05	5.29	1865.10	3.62	381.17
1997	1966.75	1669.33	228.35	17.61	1629.27	74.10	7.33	1995.99	3.66	414.48
1998	1884.13	1688.53	238.28	17.32	1616.94	69.38	6.61	2011.13	3.89	453.12
1999	1935.82	1630.13	214.38	17.91	1218.30	73.31	5.80	2109.68	4.06	622.68
2000	1822.33	1528.53	199.05	18.73	1137.59	77.68	6.21	2214.80	4.21	643.52
2001	1721.55	1441.35	198.15	17.36	1073.38	79.73	6.79	2377.60	4.15	590.74
2002	1484.16	1243.46	171.02	12.67	1136.45	75.19	6.08	2442.53	4.24	698.91
2003	1488.00	1250.38	166.77	14.92	952.87	80.73	6.00	2584.20	4.14	718.59
2004	1390.00	1123.13	180.28	18.10	940.77	76.47	6.27	2557.65	4.04	787.85
2005	1394.97	1116.99	185.48	18.87	946.02	75.86	6.30	2596.02	4.45	831.69
2006	1242.42	1015.90	150.48	14.92	1025.66	76.54	4.23	2380.56	4.74	893.47
2007	1267.03	1041.38	148.04	12.64	1078.06	75.45	4.07	2316.01	4.91	934.12
2008	1210.02	994.97	136.91	12.10	1043.21	77.93	4.71	2355.51	4.88	948.32
2009	1261.99	1044.00	133.43	11.08	1062.73	79.58	4.98	2446.67	5.20	1004.99
2010	1249.15	1041.80	129.01	11.20	1064.09	81.59	5.00	2551.00	5.38	1049.21
2011	1275.73	1072.65	122.86	9.60	1111.28	83.72	5.00	2633.02	6.04	1100.20
2012	1295.69	1097.00	120.06	10.15	1164.49	86.66	5.06	2722.03	6.39	1147.12
2013	1202.48	1012.80	112.48	9.88	1218.46	89.17	4.83	2808.09	7.09	1206.39
2014	1229.97	1053.29	106.12	9.45	1159.89	91.77	4.61	2898.53	7.51	1248.18
2015	1211.66	1040.82	102.34	9.03	1093.58	94.48	4.52	2994.70	8.07	1298.52
2016	1204.22	1039.53	96.53	8.63	1096.56	95.48	4.40	3036.45	8.92	1331.99
2017	1208.56	1046.34	95.43	8.48	1144.14	98.42	4.26	3177.49	9.29	1421.23

注：2004年起粮食产量含大豆。

Note: Since 2004, the output of grain has included that of soybeans.

11-12 主要畜产品和水产品产量
Output of Major Farm Products

单位：万吨　　　　Units: (10000 tons)

年份 Year	肉类 Meat	#猪肉 Pork	牛奶 Cow Milk	水产品 Aquatic Products	淡水产品 Freshwater Aquatic Products	海水产品 Seawater Aquatic Products
1978	48.45	48.09	1.66	65.50	19.03	46.47
1979	58.96	58.30	1.90	57.44	20.73	36.71
1980	63.20	62.62	2.18	63.34	21.80	41.54
1981	69.61	69.10	2.56	64.17	24.54	39.63
1982	76.85	76.20	2.88	76.32	29.20	47.12
1983	85.24	84.50	3.16	85.61	34.03	51.58
1984	90.00	89.00	3.89	95.63	41.30	54.33
1985	128.12	97.59	4.09	109.44	50.70	58.74
1986	154.16	106.60	4.39	136.54	58.36	78.18
1987	154.15	114.12	4.55	155.36	65.19	90.17
1988	172.45	124.64	4.99	174.66	72.64	102.02
1989	181.66	132.40	5.08	189.75	76.28	113.47
1990	202.45	145.35	5.51	207.66	83.13	124.53
1991	225.08	158.01	6.03	225.31	90.20	135.11
1992	245.69	166.22	5.72	251.06	103.64	147.42
1993	271.46	173.89	5.71	280.75	122.29	158.46
1994	278.50	176.89	5.71	314.10	139.30	174.80
1995	305.06	188.75	5.49	354.34	157.13	197.21
1996	252.03	162.03	5.81	395.08	176.69	218.39
1997	275.62	176.59	6.03	520.96	190.30	330.66
1998	305.45	197.53	6.97	554.28	208.07	346.20
1999	315.86	204.40	7.77	575.95	220.58	355.37
2000	324.48	206.85	9.19	593.19	232.73	360.46
2001	333.25	213.65	10.18	609.67	242.6	367.07
2002	343.63	220.17	10.82	628.06	253.7	374.36
2003	358.50	232.77	10.55	648.55	269.34	379.21
2004	365.32	242.14	10.94	671.38	282.78	388.60
2005	384..31	256.28	11.64	695.23	297.29	397.75
2006	382.08	251.46	12.00	658.84	285.25	373.59
2007	388.60	237.41	12.17	664.34	291.22	373.12
2008	418.32	258.39	13.62	680.41	303.60	376.81
2009	436.92	268.98	14.75	702.81	315.44	376.21
2010	454.86	285.14	14.95	729.03	327.53	401.50
2011	451.65	282.93	14.95	762.53	344.31	418.22
2012	464.13	291.09	14.33	740.72	410.29	330.43
2013	459.22	295.09	14.46	765.25	419.53	345.72
2014	456.69	302.86	14.20	783.95	427.18	356.77
2015	454.71	296.31	13.61	804.14	435.15	368.99
2016	448.70	288.24	13.61	818.29	441.54	376.75
2017	444.08	277.96	13.88	833.54	451.81	381.73

11-13 主要农作物播种面积、亩产及总产量
Sown Area, Yield per Mu and Total Output of Major Farm Crops

单位：万亩、公斤、万吨 (10000 mu, kg, 10000 tons)

作物名称	Farm Crop	2010			2016			2017		
		播种面积 Sown Area	亩产 Yield per Mu	总产量 Total Output	播种面积 Sown Area	亩产 Yield per Mu	总产量 Total Output	播种面积 Sown Area	亩产 Yield per Mu	总产量 Total Output
农作物播种面积	**Total Sown Area**	**6394.16**			**6271.95**			**6341.26**		
粮食作物	**Grain Crops**	**3579.49**	**349**	**1249.15**	**3266.67**	**369**	**1204.22**	**3254.59**	**371**	**1208.56**
稻谷	Rice	2877.21	362	1041.80	2709.05	384	1039.53	2708.13	386	1046.34
早稻	Early Rice	1386.98	362	502.04	1279.22	399	510.03	1280.22	398	509.02
晚稻	Late Rice	1490.23	362	539.76	1429.83	370	529.51	1427.91	376	537.33
小麦	Wheat	1.30	191	0.25	1.34	220	0.30	0.69	213	0.15
旱粮	Upland Grain	235.67	284	66.89	203.74	291	59.22	198.99	292	58.16
#玉米	Corn	209.12	296	61.94	185.70	298	55.40	181.43	301	54.64
薯类	Tubers	392.65	329	129.01	304.07	317	96.53	300.04	318	95.43
大豆	Soybean	72.66	154	11.20	48.47	178	8.63	46.74	181	8.48
经济作物	**Economic Crops**	**959.77**			**1030.25**			**1057.81**		
甘蔗	Sugarcane and Fruit Cane	233.16	5253	1224.73	248.32	5210	1293.87	253.74	5295	1343.47
#糖蔗	Sugarcane	205.08	5189	1064.09	214.36	5115	1096.56	219.36	5216	1144.14
油料作物	Oil-bearing Crops	477.28	175	83.34	494.23	201	99.35	497.74	203	101.28
#花生	Peanuts	461.08	177	81.59	471.77	202	95.48	478.65	206	98.42
麻类	Fiber Crops	0.29	164	0.05	0.12	171	0.02	0.12	172	0.02
烟叶	Tobacco	32.54	154	5.00	26.71	165	4.40	26.11	163	4.26
木薯	Cassava	114.94	1223	140.61	101.08	1342	135.66	98.18	1367	134.20
药材	Medicinal Plants	16.92			42.74			52.33		
其他经济作物	Other Economic Crops	84.63			117.05			129.60		
其他作物	**Other Crops**	**1854.90**			**1975.03**			**2028.86**		
#蔬菜	Vegetables	1651.25	1544	2551.00	1784.79	1701	3036.45	1840.83	1726	3177.49

11-14 各市主要农作物播种面积、亩产及总产量（2017年）
Sown Area, Yield per Mu and Total Output of Major Farm Crops by City (2017)

单位：亩、公斤、吨 (mu, kg, ton)

市别	City	粮食作物 Grain Crops			#稻谷 Rice		
		播种面积 Sown Area	亩产 Yield per Mu	总产量 Total Output	播种面积 Sown Area	亩产 Yield per Mu	总产量 Total Output
全省	**Provincial Total**	**32545884**	**371**	**12085563**	**27081304**	**386**	**10463435**
广州	Guangzhou	383768	334	128173	319822	346	110524
深圳	Shenzhen	34898	259	9032	29514	254	7497
珠海	Zhuhai	58751	367	21535	53677	362	19441
汕头	Shantou	1017071	435	442704	681261	457	311623
佛山	Foshan	105839	351	37131	90131	364	32844
韶关	Shaoguan	1757716	392	688804	1528389	412	630337
河源	Heyuan	1986226	395	785370	1801884	412	743133
梅州	Meizhou	2700188	395	1067174	2388727	411	981403
惠州	Huizhou	1678936	349	586356	1310367	354	463632
汕尾	Shanwei	1193776	325	388323	1021163	337	343702
东莞	Dongguan	14600	328	4790	8437	385	3247
中山	Zhongshan	50647	338	17131	34824	367	12777
江门	Jiangmen	2665293	342	911399	2490838	347	865296
阳江	Yangjiang	1765544	344	606572	1555763	356	553806
湛江	Zhanjiang	4136215	342	1414203	3352842	356	1193386
茂名	Maoming	3783663	390	1477353	3127365	409	1280651
肇庆	Zhaoqing	2959230	388	1149607	2504228	412	1031292
清远	Qingyuan	2177828	305	664987	1780916	325	578810
潮州	Chaozhou	630387	427	269020	495331	453	224384
揭阳	Jieyang	1944861	408	794098	1215816	416	505626
云浮	Yunfu	1500447	414	621801	1290009	442	570024
按经济区域分	By Region						
珠三角	Pearl River Delta	7951962	360	2865154	6841838	372	2546550
东翼	Eastern Region	4786095	396	1894145	3413571	406	1385335
西翼	Western Region	9685422	361	3498128	8035970	377	3027843
山区	Mountainous Region	10122405	378	3828136	8789925	399	3503707

11-14 续表 1 continued

单位：亩、公斤、吨 (mu, kg, ton)

市别	City	大豆 Soybean 播种面积 Sown Area	亩产 Yield per Mu	总产量 Total Output	经济作物 Economic Crops 播种面积 Sown Area	#糖蔗 Sugarcane 播种面积 Sown Area	亩产 Yield per Mu	总产量 Total Output
全省	**Provincial Total**	**467365**	**181**	**84759**	**10578098**	**2193615**	**5216**	**11441442**
广州	Guangzhou	2946	180	530	530129			
深圳	Shenzhen				5169			
珠海	Zhuhai	605	193	117	37857	43	4998	216
汕头	Shantou	11435	202	2309	52590			
佛山	Foshan	1290	197	254	151699	5	6000	30
韶关	Shaoguan	37661	173	6511	800824	19773	5373	106233
河源	Heyuan	34721	184	6390	403983	12864	4953	63721
梅州	Meizhou	54276	170	9214	439624			
惠州	Huizhou	17611	174	3071	305239	9188	7295	67026
汕尾	Shanwei	18396	164	3008	223450	1003	5000	5015
东莞	Dongguan	1004	155	156	23024			
中山	Zhongshan	1074	158	170	61275	713	4143	2955
江门	Jiangmen	21030	181	3812	433095	17604	6493	114314
阳江	Yangjiang	50069	196	9830	427035	6514	4494	29274
湛江	Zhanjiang	27272	189	5157	3372596	1996875	5155	10294194
茂名	Maoming	37046	191	7065	986271	91727	4974	456204
肇庆	Zhaoqing	34175	178	6074	808495	5912	4994	29523
清远	Qingyuan	47086	195	9192	794723	31083	8731	271390
潮州	Chaozhou	4817	188	905	60059			
揭阳	Jieyang	46520	165	7689	167163	310	4342	1346
云浮	Yunfu	18331	180	3305	493797			
按经济区域分	By Region							
珠三角	Pearl River Delta	79735	178	14184	2355983	33466	6397	214065
东翼	Eastern Region	81168	171	13911	503262	1313	4845	6361
西翼	Western Region	114387	193	22052	4785902	2095116	5145	10779672
山区	Mountainous Region	192075	180	34612	2932951	63720	6926	441344

11-14 续表 2 continued

单位：亩、公斤、吨 (mu, kg, ton)

市 别	City	#花生 Peanuts			#烟叶 Tobacco		
		播种面积 Sown Area	亩产 Yield per Mu	总产量 Total Output	播种面积 Sown Area	亩产 Yield per Mu	总产量 Total Output
全 省	**Provincial Total**	**4786496**	**206**	**984178**	**261085**	**163**	**42616**
广 州	Guangzhou	45798	182	8352			
深 圳	Shenzhen	4319	117	505			
珠 海	Zhuhai	3105	234	725			
汕 头	Shantou	29958	177	5295			
佛 山	Foshan	12572	206	2586			
韶 关	Shaoguan	534892	230	122913	134634	164	22083
河 源	Heyuan	337456	209	70504			
梅 州	Meizhou	160109	183	29329	71844	147	10580
惠 州	Huizhou	269228	184	49575			
汕 尾	Shanwei	175355	160	28083			
东 莞	Dongguan	1004	218	219			
中 山	Zhongshan	660	232	154			
江 门	Jiangmen	150599	168	25327			
阳 江	Yangjiang	288850	155	44893	87	195	17
湛 江	Zhanjiang	843812	235	198400	7873	238	1876
茂 名	Maoming	638474	214	136583	11969	194	2321
肇 庆	Zhaoqing	354091	195	69132	20363	169	3432
清 远	Qingyuan	529618	210	110987	14237	161	2290
潮 州	Chaozhou	32816	160	5246			
揭 阳	Jieyang	117183	214	25106	49	224	11
云 浮	Yunfu	256597	196	50264	29	180	5
按经济区域分	By Region						
珠 三 角	Pearl River Delta	841377	186	156575	20363	169	3432
东 翼	Eastern Region	355312	179	63730	49	224	11
西 翼	Western Region	1771136	214	379876	19929	211	4214
山 区	Mountainous Region	1818672	211	383997	220743	158	34958

11-14 续表 3 continued

单位：亩、公斤、吨 (mu, kg, ton)

市别	City	#木薯 Cassava			其他作物 Other Crops	#蔬菜 Vegetables		
		播种面积 Sown Area	亩产 Yield per Mu	总产量 Total Output	播种面积 Sown Area	播种面积 Sown Area	亩产 Yield per Mu	总产量 Total Output
全 省	**Provincial Total**	**981816**	**1367**	**1342014**	**20288647**	**18408252**	**1726**	**31774886**
广 州	Guangzhou	838	1268	1063	2151301	2132637	1711	3647912
深 圳	Shenzhen	115	2383	274	139123	137558	1087	149544
珠 海	Zhuhai	16	638	10	131471	112104	1266	141899
汕 头	Shantou	355	3400	1209	644209	634348	2459	1559945
佛 山	Foshan	141	1215	171	571662	461345	1727	796808
韶 关	Shaoguan	13751	1649	22669	917091	708980	1593	1129617
河 源	Heyuan	33437	973	32526	556915	501202	1344	673642
梅 州	Meizhou	113944	1129	128633	1267589	967399	2115	2045674
惠 州	Huizhou	1360	1566	2130	1758488	1694694	1702	2885091
汕 尾	Shanwei	23069	2247	51846	750086	704599	1586	1117539
东 莞	Dongguan				288596	287594	1365	392431
中 山	Zhongshan				262588	244839	1625	397886
江 门	Jiangmen	33580	1604	53860	1077838	981280	1451	1424037
阳 江	Yangjiang	48293	1059	51124	775123	733812	1102	808519
湛 江	Zhanjiang	136659	1798	245775	2196677	2069470	1704	3526067
茂 名	Maoming	66115	1336	88353	1699981	1641990	1825	2996950
肇 庆	Zhaoqing	239793	1252	300130	1445927	1188795	2071	2461829
清 远	Qingyuan	118322	1195	141439	2209155	1929871	1539	2969199
潮 州	Chaozhou	4993	1446	7219	255535	218057	2221	484394
揭 阳	Jieyang	8897	1418	12616	740185	705225	2387	1683436
云 浮	Yunfu	138139	1455	200968	449108	352453	1369	482468
按经济区域分	By Region							
珠 三 角	Pearl River Delta	275842	1297	357638	7826993	7240845	1698	12297436
东 翼	Eastern Region	37314	1953	72890	2390015	2262229	2142	4845314
西 翼	Western Region	251067	1534	385252	4671781	4445272	1649	7331536
山 区	Mountainous Region	417593	1260	526235	5399857	4459906	1637	7300599

11-15 造林面积及主要林产品产量

Area of Afforestation and Output of Major Forest Products

项　目	Item	2000	2010	2014	2015	2016	2017
人工造林面积(万亩)	Artificial Afforestation Area (10000 mu)	25.76	142.72	199.83	177.69	150.99	121.11
年末实有育苗面积(万亩)	Actual Area of Seedlings Raising at the Year-end (10000 mu)	3.12	4.54	9.44	12.17	9.90	7.82
主要林产品产量	Output of Major Forest Products						
油桐籽 (吨)	Tung-oil Seeds (ton)	3817	6050	7720	7500	6904	7469
油茶籽 (吨)	Tea-oil Seeds (ton)	26268	82417	85341	149374	146833	125195
棕片 (吨)	Palm Pieces (ton)	663	2536	2579	3463	3541	3871
松脂 (万吨)	Rosin (10000 tons)	11.31	18.11	21.06	23.51	22.58	23.88
竹笋干 (吨)	Dried Bamboo Shoots (ton)	14132	30291	41602	39805	45118	57503
板栗 (吨)	Chinese Chestnuts (ton)	5440	10616	14439	21229	22556	25922
松香类产品 (万吨)	Rosin Products (10000 tons)	9.61	12.91	11.98	15.62	20.34	15.58

11-16 水产养殖面积和水产品产量

Area of Cultivation and Output of Aquatic Products

指　标	Item	2000	2010	2014	2015	2016	2017
水产品产量(万吨)	**Output of Aquatic Products(10000 tons)**	**593.19**	**729.03**	**783.95**	**804.14**	**818.29**	**833.54**
海水产品	Seawater Aquatic Products	360.45	401.50	427.18	435.15	441.54	451.81
捕捞	Catches	191.48	152.43	154.64	154.44	151.02	148.91
养殖	Artificially Cultured	168.97	249.07	272.54	280.71	290.52	302.90
淡水产品	Freshwater Aquatic Products	232.74	327.53	356.77	368.99	376.75	381.73
捕捞	Catches	13.52	12.86	12.41	12.26	12.12	12.04
养殖	Artificially Cultured	219.22	314.67	344.36	356.73	364.63	369.69
养殖面积 (万亩)	**Area of Cultivation (10000 mu)**	**846.76**	**845.12**	**733.98**	**734.88**	**721.20**	**710.66**
海水养殖	Seawater	292.33	298.89	246.28	247.76	249.30	242.53
淡水养殖	Freshwater	554.43	546.24	487.70	487.12	471.90	468.13

11-17 牲畜头数及肉类产量

Number of Livestock and Output of Meat

项 目	Item	2000	2010	2014	2015	2016	2017
牛年末存栏头数（万头）	**Number of Cattle and Buffaloes (at the year-end) (10000 heads)**	**420.64**	**175.49**	**141.87**	**132.92**	**120.12**	**120.68**
役用牛	Farming Cattle	295.20	89.62	62.06	54.61	34.25	34.80
肉用牛	Beef Cattle	121.72	80.29	73.96	72.52	79.92	79.90
奶牛	Milch Cows	3.72	5.57	5.85	5.79	5.95	5.98
牛奶产量（万吨）	**Output of Milk (10000 tons)**	**9.19**	**14.95**	**14.20**	**13.61**	**13.61**	**13.88**
山羊年末存栏只数（万只）	**Number of Goats on Hand at the Year-end (10000 heads)**	**29.33**	**50.52**	**74.21**	**83.55**	**92.82**	**93.30**
生猪年末存栏头数（万头）	**Number of Hogs at the Year-end (10000 heads)**	**2034.79**	**2332.51**	**2282.52**	**2308.54**	**2263.36**	**2132.82**
#能繁殖母猪	Number of Female Hogs with Fertility	143.75	262.65	243.77	242.52	240.22	229.43
肉猪出栏头数（万头）	**Number of Slaughtered Fattened Hogs (10000 heads)**	**2954.98**	**3863.23**	**4062.02**	**3959.62**	**3850.61**	**3712.00**
家禽年末存栏（亿只）	**Poultry at year-end (100 million heads)**	**3.89**	**4.09**	**3.74**	**3.74**	**3.79**	**3.77**
出售和自宰的家禽（亿只）	**Poultry sold or slaughtered (100 million heads)**	**9.29**	**11.75**	**10.15**	**10.48**	**10.56**	**10.87**
禽蛋产量（万吨）	**Poultry Eggs (10 000 tons)**	**33.08**	**35.54**	**35.18**	**36.40**	**36.15**	**38.50**
肉类产量（万吨）	**Output of Meat (10000 tons)**	**324.48**	**454.86**	**456.69**	**454.71**	**448.70**	**444.08**
#猪肉	Pork	206.85	285.14	302.86	296.31	288.24	277.96
牛肉	Beef	5.17	4.97	4.39	4.14	3.96	4.08
羊肉	Mutton	0.43	1.24	1.67	1.83	1.93	1.96
禽肉	Meat of Poultry	111.50	158.04	140.71	145.01	146.50	151.73
兔肉	Rabbit Meat	0.53	0.65	0.91	0.90	0.93	0.98

11-18 各市造林面积、水产品产量、牲畜头数及猪肉产量（2017年）
Area of Afforestation, Output of Aquatic Products, Number of Livestock and Output of Pork by City (2017)

市 别	City	人工造林面积（万亩）Artificial Afforestation Area (10000 mu)	水产品产量（万吨）Output of Aquatic Products (10000 tons)	#淡水养殖 Freshwater	牛年末存栏头数（万头）Number of Cattles and Buffalos at the Year-end (10000 heads)	生猪年末存栏头数（万头）Number of Hogs at the Year-end (10000 heads)	肉猪出栏头数（万头）Number of Slaughtered Fattened Hogs (10000 heads)	猪肉产量（万吨）Output of Pork (10000 tons)
全 省	**Provincial Total**	**121.11**	**833.54**	**369.69**	**120.68**	**2132.82**	**3712.00**	**277.96**
广 州	Guangzhou		44.76	31.39	1.77	34.02	76.35	5.73
深 圳	Shenzhen		8.29	0.27	0.27	3.71	7.01	0.61
珠 海	Zhuhai	0.21	30.96	20.34	0.11	23.93	31.42	2.54
汕 头	Shantou	2.66	45.88	8.51	0.88	37.95	78.33	5.75
佛 山	Foshan	0.38	64.36	63.74	0.57	66.90	129.51	9.82
韶 关	Shaoguan	12.71	7.92	7.62	4.50	138.84	222.85	16.43
河 源	Heyuan	19.11	4.18	4.03	5.43	72.03	96.40	7.32
梅 州	Meizhou	23.05	10.51	9.53	9.52	132.92	226.64	16.93
惠 州	Huizhou	0.69	16.48	8.13	6.87	78.79	140.07	10.63
汕 尾	Shanwei	20.94	55.77	4.11	4.46	28.64	58.26	4.30
东 莞	Dongguan		4.55	3.70	0.06	1.80	3.40	0.25
中 山	Zhongshan		32.29	31.53	0.05	12.80	24.59	1.69
江 门	Jiangmen	0.34	75.39	43.40	1.76	135.51	239.34	17.61
阳 江	Yangjiang	4.63	118.81	9.03	10.13	155.71	235.61	17.65
湛 江	Zhanjiang	1.91	122.17	16.90	24.31	218.27	394.38	29.50
茂 名	Maoming	5.90	89.47	28.93	15.68	357.56	679.19	51.82
肇 庆	Zhaoqing	5.79	45.43	44.93	17.96	243.21	449.60	33.90
清 远	Qingyuan	7.37	12.91	12.73	7.96	202.15	311.24	22.41
潮 州	Chaozhou	0.83	19.17	4.59	1.14	35.59	54.67	4.13
揭 阳	Jieyang	6.92	14.42	6.65	4.99	75.19	122.71	9.22
云 浮	Yunfu	6.83	9.79	9.64	2.26	77.29	130.41	9.75
按经济区域分	By Region							
珠 三 角	Pearl River Delta	7.41	322.53	247.42	29.42	600.68	1101.31	82.76
东 翼	Eastern Region	31.35	135.24	23.85	11.47	177.38	313.98	23.40
西 翼	Western Region	12.44	330.45	54.86	50.12	731.54	1309.18	98.96
山 区	Mountainous Region	69.06	45.31	43.56	29.67	623.23	987.54	72.84

11-19 茶叶、桑、水果面积及产量

Planted Area and Output of Tea, Mulberry and Fruits

指标	Item	2000	2010	2014	2015	2016	2017
茶叶年末实有面积（万亩）	Planted Area of Tea at the Year-end(10000 mu)	64.80	62.76	76.33	78.07	84.60	87.63
茶叶总产量（万吨）	Output of Tea (10000 tons)	4.21	5.38	7.51	8.07	8.92	9.29
桑地年末实有面积（万亩）	Planted Area of Mulberries at the Year-end (10000 mu)	26.89	47.73	51.71	51.25	50.36	49.64
蚕茧总产量（万吨）	Output of silkworm cocoon (10000 tons)	3.09	9.14	10.54	11.00	11.26	11.65
水果年末实有面积（万亩）	Planted Area of Fruits at the Year-end (10000 mu)	1502.35	1510.61	1457.67	1452.71	1423.98	1440.78
水果总产量（万吨）	Gross Output of Fruits (10000 tons)	643.52	1049.21	1248.18	1298.52	1331.99	1421.23
#柑桔橙年末实有面积（万亩）	Planted Area of Citruses at the Year-end (10000 mu)	123.34	326.83	303.06	296.62	276.49	273.69
柑桔橙总产量（万吨）	Output of Citruses (10000 tons)	81.06	259.34	313.84	317.53	307.77	323.18
香(大)蕉年末实有面积（万亩）	Planted Area of Bananas at the Year-end (10000 mu)	151.51	171.85	161.14	162.22	159.21	160.54
香(大)蕉总产量（万吨）	Output of Bananas (10000 tons)	235.30	334.13	345.48	357.83	373.96	395.24
菠萝年末实有面积(万亩)	Planted Area of Pineapples at the Year-end (10000 mu)	44.58	38.81	44.54	44.58	45.91	49.58
菠萝总产量（万吨）	Output of Pineapples (10000 tons)	47.53	63.21	80.61	83.76	88.01	94.53
荔枝年末实有面积(万亩)	Planted Area of Lychees at the Year-end (10000 mu)	474.83	390.99	375.34	371.82	367.91	368.08
荔枝总产量（万吨）	Output of Lychees (10000 tons)	64.75	96.53	113.97	116.18	111.55	117.47
龙眼年末实有面积(万亩)	Planted Area of Longans at the Year-end (10000 mu)	236.31	182.45	173.04	170.54	169.44	169.89
龙眼总产量（万吨）	Output of Longans (10000 tons)	34.68	58.22	72.61	76.04	78.95	83.82

11-20 各市水果面积及产量（2017年）

Planted Area and Output of Fruits by City (2017)

单位：万亩、万吨 (10000 mu，10000 tons)

市别	City	水果合计 Fruits 年末面积 Year-end Area	水果合计 Fruits 总产量 Total Output	#柑桔橙 Citrus 年末面积 Year-end Area	#柑桔橙 Citrus 总产量 Total Output	#香(大)蕉 Banana 年末面积 Year-end Area	#香(大)蕉 Banana 总产量 Total Output
全　省	**Provincial Total**	**1440.78**	**1421.23**	**273.69**	**323.18**	**160.54**	**395.24**
广　州	Guangzhou	95.86	52.81	4.82	4.46	7.98	19.34
深　圳	Shenzhen	9.52	4.13	0.58	0.66	0.24	0.28
珠　海	Zhuhai	7.98	6.23	0.22	0.18	1.36	1.95
汕　头	Shantou	17.57	23.88	1.27	2.21	2.70	4.83
佛　山	Foshan	3.14	4.30	0.19	0.65	1.34	3.03
韶　关	Shaoguan	58.72	55.77	29.22	28.90	0.47	0.45
河　源	Heyuan	52.12	38.92	12.47	9.78	1.24	1.16
梅　州	Meizhou	108.36	125.64	11.21	15.19	5.36	6.83
惠　州	Huizhou	86.27	81.80	26.75	27.49	14.07	31.93
汕　尾	Shanwei	47.75	25.98	1.47	3.38	3.25	4.03
东　莞	Dongguan	19.09	5.46	0.01	0.01	2.54	3.91
中　山	Zhongshan	4.90	8.53	0.14	0.26	1.96	5.07
江　门	Jiangmen	30.47	27.44	8.59	11.82	3.85	8.12
阳　江	Yangjiang	72.19	35.43	7.59	8.57	6.05	7.92
湛　江	Zhanjiang	134.11	245.48	6.89	6.12	40.68	119.31
茂　名	Maoming	349.08	343.45	11.48	8.93	43.76	143.90
肇　庆	Zhaoqing	109.46	154.87	77.15	122.57	9.40	13.68
清　远	Qingyuan	69.53	68.28	38.45	40.07	1.05	1.96
潮　州	Chaozhou	24.61	24.77	3.46	4.04	1.39	2.82
揭　阳	Jieyang	71.80	43.06	7.23	6.28	6.85	9.32
云　浮	Yunfu	68.24	45.03	24.52	21.63	5.03	5.44
按经济区域分	By Region						
珠三角	Pearl River Delta	366.69	345.56	118.43	168.08	42.73	87.30
东　翼	Eastern Region	161.73	117.69	13.42	15.90	14.19	20.99
西　翼	Western Region	555.38	624.35	25.96	23.62	90.50	271.12
山　区	Mountainous Region	356.98	333.63	115.87	115.57	13.14	15.83

11-20 续表 continued

单位：万亩、万吨 (10000 mu，10000 tons)

市 别	City	#菠萝 Pineapple		#荔枝 Lychee		#龙眼 Longan	
		年末面积 Year-end Area	总产量 Total Output	年末面积 Year-end Area	总产量 Total Output	年末面积 Year-end Area	总产量 Total Output
全 省	**Provincial Total**	**49.58**	**94.53**	**368.08**	**117.47**	**169.89**	**83.82**
广 州	Guangzhou	0.12	0.09	45.72	4.91	11.87	3.78
深 圳	Shenzhen	0.16	0.20	6.51	1.21	1.12	0.51
珠 海	Zhuhai	0.01	0.01	2.69	0.43	0.85	0.25
汕 头	Shantou	…	…	3.32	0.72	0.46	0.31
佛 山	Foshan	…	0.01	0.36	0.07	0.73	0.12
韶 关	Shaoguan			…	0.01	0.30	0.15
河 源	Heyuan	0.07	0.03	5.76	0.56	1.71	0.54
梅 州	Meizhou	0.23	0.13	4.96	1.91	5.16	3.02
惠 州	Huizhou	0.61	0.56	26.18	9.05	11.16	6.28
汕 尾	Shanwei	1.96	0.78	20.61	9.27	3.53	2.53
东 莞	Dongguan	…	…	13.82	0.30	1.74	0.18
中 山	Zhongshan	0.63	0.61	0.72	0.47	0.44	0.21
江 门	Jiangmen	0.05	0.04	8.76	1.87	6.09	2.16
阳 江	Yangjiang	0.09	0.06	31.08	7.35	15.62	5.41
湛 江	Zhanjiang	39.13	84.44	24.67	12.07	6.82	4.16
茂 名	Maoming	0.30	0.27	135.77	53.29	78.51	42.16
肇 庆	Zhaoqing	0.64	0.49	2.61	2.37	3.10	2.02
清 远	Qingyuan	0.01	0.01	1.95	0.71	1.22	0.65
潮 州	Chaozhou	0.52	0.64	3.22	2.04	4.58	3.69
揭 阳	Jieyang	4.89	6.01	17.44	5.85	8.16	2.73
云 浮	Yunfu	0.16	0.16	11.92	3.03	6.72	2.98
按经济区域分	By Region						
珠 三 角	Pearl River Delta	2.22	2.00	107.37	20.67	37.10	15.50
东 翼	Eastern Region	7.37	7.44	44.58	17.88	16.73	9.26
西 翼	Western Region	39.52	84.78	191.52	72.71	100.95	51.72
山 区	Mountainous Region	0.48	0.32	24.60	6.22	15.11	7.34

11-21 主要农产品产量与最高年份比较（2017年）

Output of Major Farm Products in Comparison with Peak Year (2017)

指 标	Item	2017	建国以来最高年 Peak Year since 1949		
			年份 Year	产量 Output	2017为建国以来最高年份% Percentage of 2017 to Peak Year%
粮食总产量 （万吨）	**Total Output of Grain (10000 tons)**	**1208.56**	**1997**	**1966.75**	**61.4**
#稻谷	Output of Rice	1046.34	1998	1688.53	62.0
#早稻	Early Rice	509.02	1983	862.25	59.0
晚稻	Late Rice	537.33	1998	866.51	62.0
薯类	Tubers	95.43	1998	238.28	40.1
经济作物 （万吨）	**Economic Crops (10000 tons)**				
甘蔗	Sugarcane and Fruit Canes	1343.47	1992	2376.62	56.5
#糖蔗	Sugarcane	1144.14	1992	2271.06	50.4
油料作物	Oil-bearing Crops	101.28	2016	99.35	102.0
#花生	Peanuts	98.42	2016	95.48	103.1
烟叶	Tobacco	4.26	1992	8.62	49.4
其他作物	**Other Crops**				
#蔬菜 （万吨）	Vegetables (10000 tons)	3177.49	2016	3036.45	104.6
水果 （万吨）	**Fruits (10000 tons)**	**1421.23**	**2016**	**1331.99**	**106.7**
水产品 （万吨）	**Aquatic Products (10000 tons)**	**833.54**	**2016**	**818.29**	**101.9**
生猪年末存栏量 （万头）	**Number of Hogs at the Year-end (10000 heads)**	**2132.82**	**2009**	**2455.11**	**86.9**
生猪出栏头数 （万头）	**Number of Slaughtered Fattened Hogs (10000 heads)**	**3712.00**	**2014**	**4062.02**	**91.4**
猪肉产量 （万吨）	**Output of Pork (10000 tons)**	**277.96**	**2014**	**302.86**	**91.8**
家禽年末存栏 （亿只）	**Poultry at year-end (100 million heads)**	**3.77**	**2010**	**4.09**	**92.2**
出售和自宰的家禽（亿只）	**Poultry sold or slaughtered(100 million heads)**	**10.87**	**2012**	**11.87**	**91.6**
禽肉产量 （万吨）	**Output of Poultry Meat (10 000 tons)**	**151.73**	**2012**	**161.11**	**94.2**

主要统计指标解释

农林牧渔业增加值 是指农、林、牧、渔及农林牧渔服务业在一定时期内生产货物或提供服务活动而增加的价值。它反映了农业生产经营活动的最终成果和对社会的贡献。

农业增加值的计算方法有两种：(1)生产法，是从生产角度进行计算的一种方法。即用农业总产出减去农业中间消耗求得。由于农户没有健全的核算记录，故农业增加值一般是采用生产法计算。(2)分配法，是从分配角度进行计算的一种方法。是通过农业生产单位在生产经营和劳务活动过程中形成的不含中间消耗的各种收入来计算。具体包括农业劳动者收入、福利基金、利税、固定资产折旧及大修理和其他。

农林牧渔业总产值 是以货币表现的农林牧渔业的全部产品总量和对农林牧渔业生产活动进行的各种支持性服务活动的价值。它反映一定时期内农林牧渔业生产总规模和总成果，是观察农林牧渔业生产水平和发展速度，研究农林牧渔业内部比例关系、农林牧渔业与工业、农林牧渔业与国家建设、人民生活比例关系的重要指标，同时也是计算农林牧渔业劳动生产率和农林牧渔业增加值的基础资料。

农林牧渔业总产值的计算，一般采用“产品法”，即凡有产品产量的，都按单位产品价格乘产量的办法求得每种产品产量的产值，然后相加求得各业的产值，最后各业相加求出农林牧渔业总产值。

乡镇户数 指长期（一年以上）居住在乡镇（不包括城关镇）行政管理区域内的住户，还包括居住在城关镇所辖行政村范围内的农村住户。

乡镇人口 指乡镇地区常住居民户数中的常住人口数，即经常在家或在家居住 6 个月以上，而且经济和生活与本户连成一体的人口，与乡镇户数统计范围相一致。

农作物播种面积 指农业生产经营者应在日历年度内收获的农作物在全部土地（耕地或非耕地）上的播种或移植面积。凡是本年内收获的作物，无论是本年还是上年播种，都算为当年播种面积，但不包括本年播种，下年收获的作物面积。

农作物产量 指农业生产经营者日历年度内生产的农作物数量。

Explanatory Notes on Main Statistical Indicators

Value-added of Farming, Forestry, Animal Husbandry and Fishery refers to the value-added of goods produced or services provided by farming, forestry, animal husbandry, fishery in a given period of time. It shows the final results of the activities of production and management of agriculture and its contributions to the society.

The value-added of agriculture is calculated with two approaches:

(1) Production approach is a method from the production angle, i.e. total output of agriculture minus intermediate consumption of agriculture. The value-added of agriculture is usually calculated with the production approach as no complete accounting records of the rural households are available;

(2) Distribution approach is a method from the distribution angle, i.e. various incomes from the activities of production and management of the productive units of agriculture without intermediate consumption, including incomes of the rural laborers, welfare funds, profit and tax, depreciation of fixed assets and major overhaul and others.

Gross Output Value of Agriculture refers to the total volume of products of farming, forestry, animal husbandry, and fishery and the value of various services supporting the production of farming, forestry, animal husbandry and fishery in monetary terms, which reflects the total scale and total results of farming, forestry, animal husbandry and fishery production during a given period of time. It is an important indicator to observe the production level and development speed of farming, forestry, animal husbandry and fishery, to study the internal structure of farming, forestry, animal husbandry and fishery, and to review the proportionate relationship of farming, forestry, animal husbandry and fishery to industry, to national construction and to people's life. It is also the foundation for calculating the labor productivity and value-added of farming, forestry, animal husbandry and fishery.

Generally, the gross output value of farming, forestry, animal husbandry and fishery is calculated with the production approach. Where applicable, the gross output value of each single product is obtained by multiplying the output of each product by its price. These values are then summed up to obtain the output value of each sector. The sum of output values of all sectors is the gross output value of farming, forestry, animal husbandry and fishery.

Number of Rural Households refers to the residents who live in the administrative areas of townships (not including the location of the county people's government) for a long time (including more than one year), and also include rural households living within the administrative villages under the the location of the county people's government.

Rural Population refers to the number of residents in the rural households, live in the home for more than 6 months, and their economy and life are integrated with the household。The statistical coverage are consistent with the Number of Rural Households.

Sown Area of Crops refers to area of all land (cultivated or non-cultivated area) sown or transplanted with crops that are harvested within the calendar year by agricultural producers. All crops harvested within the year are counted as sown area, regardless of being sown in this year or the previous year. Crops sown this year but will be harvested in the coming year are excluded.

Crops Output refers to total output of crops produced by agricultural producers within a calendar year.

十二、工业

INDUSTRY

十二 工业

简要说明

一、本篇主要包括如下资料：1. 全省及各地市全部工业和规模以上工业生产主要指标总量及速度。2. 规模以上工业主要产品产量。3. 全省及各地市规模以上工业主要经济效益指标。4. 规模以上工业企业按主要经济类型和企业规模分组的主要财务指标。5. 规模以上工业中高技术制造业、先进制造业主要经济指标。6. 全省工业总产值、主营业务收入、固定资产净值 50 强企业排行榜。

二、本篇资料由广东省统计局工业交通处整理提供。

三、本篇工业资料是根据国家统计局工业统计报表制度填报。2011 年定报及以前数据经各市、县统计局布置、收集、汇总整理，2011 年起通过网上直报系统收集、汇总整理。其中 1995 年度资料通过第三次全国工业普查取得，2004 年数据根据 2004 年广东省第一次全国经济普查取得，2008 年数据根据 2008 年广东省第二次全国经济普查取得。2013 年数据根据 2013 年广东省第三次全国经济普查取得。

四、规模以上工业企业的统计范围。1998 年至 2006 年为全部国有和年主营业务收入 500 万元及以上的非国有工业企业；2007 至 2010 年为年主营业务收入 500 万元及以上的工业企业（即规模以上工业企业）；从 2011 年开始，为年主营业务收入 2000 万元及以上的工业企业（即规模以上工业企业）。

五、从 2011 年年报起，工业行业分类按 2011 年《国民经济行业分类标准》划分；企业规模划分按 2011 年《统计上大中小微型企业划分办法》标准执行，增加了微型企业分组。

六、本篇规模以上工业增加值从 2011 年起按收入法公布。

12 Industry

Brief Introduction

Ⅰ. This chapter covers the following data:（1）Principal aggregate indicators and growth rates of industrial production of total industry and industry above designated size of the province and cities,（2）Output of major products of industry above designated size,（3）Main indicators on economic benefits of industry above designated size of the province and cities,（4）Main financial indicators on industry above designated size grouped by sector and scale,（5）Main economic indicators on advanced manufacturing industries and hi-tech manufacturing industries above designated size,（6）Top 50 Industrial Enterprises of the Province in terms of gross industrial output value, principal business revenue, and net value of fixed assets.

Ⅱ. The data in this chapter are prepared and provided by the Division of Industry and Transport Statistics of Statistics Bureau of Guangdong Province.

Ⅲ. The data in this chapter are compiled mainly in accordance with the industrial statistical reporting scheme stipulated by the National Bureau of Statistics. The annual data of 2011 and before 2011 are collected, tabulated and prepared by the municipal and county statistical bureaus. Since 2011, the annual data are collected, tabulated and prepared by the network reporting system. Of which the annual data of 1995 were collected in the Third National Industrial Census and the data of 2004 were collected in the First National Economic Census of Guangdong, the data of 2008 were collected in the Second National Economic Census of Guangdong, data of 2013 were collected in the Third National Economic Census of Guangdong.

Ⅳ. Industrial enterprises above designated size refers to all State-owned industrial enterprises and non-State-owned industrial enterprises with revenue from principal business over 5 million yuan from 1998 to 2006. For 2007 to 2010, the scopes of industrial statistics were all industrial enterprises with revenue from principal business over 5 million yuan, (or the industrial enterprises above designated size). Since 2011, the scope is adjusted to all industrial enterprises with revenue from principal business above 20 million yuan (i.e. industrial enterprises above designated size).

Ⅴ. Industrial sectors since 2011 in this chapter has been categorized in accordance with the 2011 Industrial Classification of the National Economy and the sizes of industrial enterprises have been categorized in accordance with the 2011 Interim Regulations on Statistical Categorization of Large, Medium , Small and Micro Industrial Enterprises. Micro industrial enterprises are added

Ⅵ. The value-added of industrial enterprises above designated size in this chapter is calculated by income approach since 2011.

12-1 工业主要指标
Main Indicators of Industry

指　　标	Item	2000	2010	2014	2015	2016	2017
全部工业	**All Industrial Enterprises**						
企业单位数　(个)	Number of Enterprises (unit)	380231	481022	531992	582813	563273	669910
工业总产值　(亿元)	Gross Industrial Output Value (100 million yuan)	16904.47	93462.97	130081.02	135308.14	144926.09	148173.99
工业增加值　(亿元)	Value-added of Industry (100 million yuan)	4518.65	21740.56	30079.24	31290.75	32650.89	35291.83
规模以上工业	**Industrial Enterprises above Designated Size**						
企业单位数　(个)	Number of Enterprises (unit)	19695	53418	41154	42134	42709	47224
亏损企业数　(个)	Number of Loss-making Enterprises	4805	6385	5224	5850	5034	5457
工业总产值　(亿元)	Gross Industrial Output Value (100 million yuan)	12480.93	85824.64	119713.04	124649.16	133768.04	135722.42
工业增加值　(亿元)	Value-added of Industry (100 million yuan)	3422.60	20338.34	28188.69	29446.21	31330.24	31349.47
工业销售产值　(亿元)	Sales Output Value of Industy(100 million yuan)	12156.19	83646.51	116336.46	121049.68	129840.69	133001.40
出口交货值　(亿元)	Export Delivery Value (100 million yuan)	4634.44	25919.08	32885.91	32035.16	32240.68	33006.63
主营业务收入　(亿元)	Main Business Revenue (100 million yuan)	12380.65	84114.85	115451.13	119157.86	129151.31	133924.37
资产总计　(亿元)	Total Assets (100 million yuan)	14370.57	62626.90	87590.27	95411.22	105604.17	115201.19
流动资产合计　(亿元)	Average Balance of Circulating Funds (100 million yuan)	6891.49	34339.97	50805.77	54715.38	61612.78	68749.03
固定资产合计　(亿元)	Average Balance of Net Value of Fixed Assets (100 million yuan)	5884.78	22407.53	25305.19	26943.69	27217.90	26540.42
负债总计　(亿元)	Total Liabilities (100 million yuan)	8272.36	35073.74	51173.28	54747.90	59318.72	64660.73
所有者权益合计(亿元)	Total Creditors' Equity (100 million yuan)	6098.21	27461.84	36149.22	40239.01	45694.31	50201.60
利润总额　(亿元)	Total Profits (100 million yuan)	564.75	6239.64	7014.99	7723.16	8383.04	8864.36
亏损企业亏损额(亿元)	Loss Value of Loss-making Enterprises (100 million yuan)	156.03	227.26	452.56	510.18	418.14	505.27
利税总额　(亿元)	Total Pre-tax Profits (100 million yuan)	1042.77	9418.42	11663.66	12375.00	13150.85	13769.27
应交增值税　(亿元)	Value-added Tax Payable (100 million yuan)	360.83	2280.56	3430.87	3284.50	3417.11	3472.77
所得税费用　(亿元)	Fee of Income Tax Payable (100 million yuan)	62.79	820.89	1082.16	1179.43	1263.40	1386.00
本年应付工资总额　(亿元)	Total Salary Payable in Current Year (100 million yuan)	676.06	5747.72	8773.60	9888.11	10761.13	11797.48
就业人员平均人数　(万人)	Average Employed Persons (10000 persons)	572.89	1568.00	1455.78	1439.33	1417.84	1403.19

注：1. 2011年起，规模以上工业统计口径从年主营业务收入500万元及以上调整为2000万元及以上，为反映可比口径速度，本表规模以上工业主要指标使用快报增速，全部工业数据含个体数据。

2. 表中全部工业增加值及增长速度是核算的年度数据，2010年及以后规模以上工业增加值按照收入法计算，与全社会工业增加值不可直接比对。2010年全部工业增加值按照第三次经济普查数据修正。

3. 2011年起，本年应付工资总额指标数据为本年应付职工薪酬；所得税费用数据2014年以前为应交所得税。

Notes: a) Since 2011,the annual principal business revenue of industrial enterprises above designated size is changed from 5 million yuan or above to 20 million yuan or above. Growth rates in this table are calculated at current price with flash statistics report in order to compare the rate. Data on all industrial enterprises include self-employed individuals.

b) The value-added and growth rates of all industries in this talbe are calculated figures of the year. The value-added of industry above designated size is calculated by income approach since 2010, and hence is not directly comparable with the value-added of all industries. All value-added of industry from 2010 have been adjusted with the third economic census.

c) Total salary payable in current year from 2011 are total employee pay payable and income tax payable are tax expenses.Data of fee of income tax payable before 2014 are income tax payable.

12-2 规模以上工业企业增加值和指数

Value-added of Industrial Enterprises above Designated Size and Their Indices

项　　目	Item	2000	2010	2015	2016	2017
工业增加值　（亿元）	**Value-added of Industry　(100 million yuan)**	**3422.60**	**20338.34**	**29446.21**	**31330.24**	**31349.47**
按经济类型分	Grouped by Ownership					
#国有控股工业	Of the Total: State-holding Industry	1035.41	3729.48	5051.87	5180.04	5465.15
国有工业	State-owned Industry	574.73	1172.21	173.46	200.96	203.07
集体工业	Collective-owned Industry	301.48	199.38	116.59	106.59	65.92
股份合作工业	Share-holding Cooperative Industry	29.15	42.23	23.10	17.52	13.10
股份制工业	Share-holding Industry	158.86	7351.85	16289.21	18170.10	18900.25
外商投资工业	Foreign-funded Industry	575.31	5200.37	5689.44	5556.86	5213.47
港澳台投资工业	Industry with Funds from Hong Kong, Macao and Taiwan	1290.47	5393.8	6545.58	6705.43	6459.57
按轻重工业分	Grouped by Light and Heavy Industries					
轻工业	Light Industry	1628.13	8038.97	11387.50	11916.13	11305.75
重工业	Heavy Industry	1794.47	12299.37	18058.71	19414.11	20043.72
按企业规模分	Grouped by Size of Enterprises					
大型企业	Large Enterprises	610.13	6579.38	13698.60	14805.94	15716.24
中型企业	Medium Enterprises	1513.26	7107.28	7864.85	8198.85	7458.51
小微型企业	Small and Micro Enterprises	1298.55	6651.68	7882.76	8325.45	8174.72
工业增加值指数(2000年=100)	**Indices of Value-added of Industry(2000=100)**	**100.0**	**592.4**	**913.2**	**974.4**	**1044.6**
按经济类型分	Grouped by Ownership					
#国有控股工业	Of the Total: State-holding Industry	100.0	354.9	502.2	527.3	537.9
国有工业	State-owned Industry	100.0	226.2	304.3	326.5	292.2
集体工业	Collective-owned Industry	100.0	81.0	110.3	110.2	113.5
股份合作工业	Share-holding Cooperative Industry	100.0	188.0	345.9	372.2	372.9
股份制工业	Share-holding Industry	100.0	4296.3	7734.8	8523.7	9239.7
外商投资工业	Foreign-funded Industry	100.0	844.5	1126.3	1154.4	1241.0
港澳台投资工业	Industry with Funds from Hong Kong, Macao and Taiwan	100.0	468.8	640.9	654.3	679.9
按轻重工业分	Grouped by Light and Heavy Industries					
轻工业	Light Industry	100.0	532.0	790.1	816.2	865.9
重工业	Heavy Industry	100.0	653.6	1032.2	1122.0	1209.5
按企业规模分	Grouped by Size of Enterprises					
大型企业	Large Enterprises	100.0	978.4	1481.0	1584.6	1705.1
中型企业	Medium Enterprises	100.0	412.9	578.4	606.1	646.8
小微型企业	Small and Micro Enterprises	100.0	637.7	1095.9	1182.4	1262.8

注：1．2011年起，规模以上工业统计口径从年主营业务收入500万元及以上调整为2000万元及以上。
2．本表工业增加值2010年以前采用生产法计算，2011年起采用收入法计算，按当年价格计算，速度为可比口径计算。
3．企业规模划分：2003年以前为一个标准，2003—2010年为一个标准，2011年起采用新的标准，并增加微型企业。

Note: a) Since 2011, the annual principal business revenue of industrial enterprises above designated size is changed from 5 million yuan or above to 20 million yuan or above.
b) Data of value-added in this table prior to 2010 are calculated with production approach and since 2011 calculated with income approach.Data of value-added of industry are calculated at current prices and the growth rates are calculated at comparable coverage.
c) Size of Industrial enterprise categorization: The standard prior to 2003 is not the same as the period from 2003 to 2010.Since 2011, New standard is adopted and micro-enterprieses is added.

12-3　历年规模以上工业增加值增长速度

Growth Rates of Industrial Enterprises above Designated Size

单位：%　　　　(%)

年份 Year	工业增加值 Gross Industrial Output Value	按轻重工分 Grouped by Light & Heavy Industry		按规模分 Grouped by Size			按经济类型分 Grouped by Ownership	
		轻工业 Light Industry	重工业 Heavy Industry	大型企业 Large Enterprises	中型企业 Medium Enterprises	小微型企业 Small and Micro Enterprises	国有控股工业 Of the Total: State-holding Industry	外商及港澳台商投资工业 Industry with Investment from Fordeign Country , Hong Kong, Macao and Taiwan
2001	15.1	12.4	18.4				4.0	14.2
2002	20.0	20.4	19.7				14.7	15.9
2003	28.4	23.4	38.5				20.8	22.2
2004	28.0	26.0	31.1	30.8	26.8	27.4	20.8	23.9
2005	24.7	20.6	25.0	23.2	21.5	28.0	6.1	16.2
2006	23.4	18.2	24.2	15.5	19.3	32.4	19.4	14.8
2007	18.2	24.2	13.2	19.2	14.2	22.1	12.6	16.9
2008	12.8	14.2	12.2	14.2	9.1	16.3	7.8	10.9
2009	8.9	7.4	10.0	11.4	-0.1	17.5	7.0	4.1
2010	16.8	16.4	17.1	15.0	13.4	22.2	12.8	14.5
2011	12.6	12.4	12.8	12.1	8.8	17.7	12.5	8.4
2012	8.4	9.2	7.9	8.1	6.0	8.8	7.3	5.7
2013	8.7	7.7	9.3	8.5	6.9	10.9	8.0	7.1
2014	8.4	7.4	9.1	8.3	7.4	9.7	6.3	5.0
2015	7.2	4.6	8.8	6.3	5.8	10.3	2.1	4.1
2016	6.7	3.3	8.7	7.0	4.8	7.9	5.0	2.3
2017	7.2	6.1	7.8	7.6	6.7	6.8	2.0	5.6

注：本表按可比口径计算。
Note: Data in this table are caculated in comparable coverage.

12-4 规模以上分行业工业增加值和增长速度

Value-added and Growth Rates of Industry above Designated Size by Sector

行　　业	Sector	工业增加值（亿元）Value-added of Industry (100 million yuan)		2017比2016增长(%) Growth Rate in 2017 over 2016 (%)
		2016	2017	
总　计	**Total**	**31330.24**	**31349.47**	**7.2**
煤炭开采和洗选业	Mining and Washing of Coal			
石油和天然气开采业	Extraction of Petroleum and Natural Gas	337.10	427.92	-2.7
黑色金属矿采选业	Mining and Dressing of Ferrous Metal Ores	38.87	22.45	5.7
有色金属矿采选业	Mining and Dressing of Nonferrous Metal Ores	27.74	36.24	-8.2
非金属矿采选业	Mining and Dressing of Nonmetal Ores	109.81	75.07	-3.3
开采辅助活动	Auxiliary Minning Operations	11.76	4.05	-3.5
其他采矿业	Mining and Dressing of Other Ores	0.86	0.29	-2.4
农副食品加工业	Processing of Farm and Sideline Food	469.70	395.15	10.3
食品制造业	Manufacture of Food	616.22	621.28	5.9
酒、饮料和精制茶制造业	Manufacture of Wine, Beverage and Refined Tea	342.65	299.55	5.0
烟草制品业	Tobacco Products	321.78	331.67	1.5
纺织业	Textile Industry	596.06	533.12	3.4
纺织服装、服饰业	Manufacture of Textile Garments, Footwear and Headgear	1012.83	960.95	0.1
皮革、毛皮、羽毛及其制品和制鞋业	Leather, Fur, Feather, Down and Related Products	682.27	605.67	0.2
木材加工和木、竹、藤、棕、草制品业	Timber Processing, Bamboo, Cane, Palm Fiber & Straw Products	208.82	177.59	2.7
家具制造业	Manufacture of Furniture	514.64	525.68	8.1
造纸和纸制品业	Papermaking and Paper Products	468.65	497.37	9.4
印刷和记录媒介复制业	Printing and Record Medium Reproduction	343.23	343.86	12.3
文教、工美、体育和娱乐用品制造业	Manufacture of Cultural, Educational,Sports and Entertainment Articles	816.92	743.67	7.0
石油加工、炼焦和核燃料加工业	Petroleum Refining, Coking and Nuclear Fuel Processing	896.26	1014.57	-3.4
化学原料和化学制品制造业	Manufacture of Raw Chemical Materials and Chemical Products	1435.48	1193.69	6.4
医药制造业	Manufacture of Medicines	494.03	502.55	10.2
化学纤维制造业	Manufacture of Chemical Fibers	33.26	37.97	7.0
橡胶和塑料制品业	Rubber and Plastic Products	1239.72	1186.54	4.8
非金属矿物制品业	Nonmetal Mineral Products	1287.34	1194.91	7.7
黑色金属冶炼和压延加工业	Smelting and Pressing of Ferrous Metals	408.65	401.79	-4.9
有色金属冶炼和压延加工业	Smelting and Pressing of Nonferrous Metals	491.29	364.88	2.4
金属制品业	Metal Products	1404.23	1374.31	7.2
通用设备制造业	Manufacture of General-purpose Machinery	868.35	900.49	8.0
专用设备制造业	Manufacture of Special-purpose Machinery	787.78	914.97	9.3
汽车制造业	Manufacture of Automobile	1612.66	1776.09	11.7
铁路、船舶、航空航天和其他运输设备制造业	Manufacture of Railway ,Ship,Aeronautics and Other Transport equipment	286.01	229.72	21.0
电气机械和器材制造业	Manufacture of Electrical Machinery and Equipment	3011.13	2969.33	10.1
计算机、通信和其他电子设备制造业	Manufacture of Communication Equipment, Computers and Other Electronic Equipment	7204.72	8122.15	12.6
仪器仪表制造业	Manufacture of Instruments and Meters	286.11	306.45	9.9
其他制造业	Other Manufactures	68.95	55.68	9.5
废弃资源综合利用业	Comprehensive Utilization of Waste	246.36	184.96	0.8
金属制品、机械和设备修理业	Manufacture of Metal Products,Machinery and Equipment Maintenance	48.05	52.34	9.1
电力、热力生产和供应业	Production and Supply of Electric Power and Heat Power	1946.61	1568.61	-4.3
燃气生产和供应业	Production and Supply of Gas	167.09	182.05	26.3
水的生产和供应业	Production and Supply of Water	186.24	213.81	2.3

注：本表工业增加值按当年价格计算，增长速度按快报可比价格计算。

Note: Data of value-added of industry in this table are calculated at current prices by income approach according to 2002 industry classification, whereas their growth rates are calculated at constant prices in accordance with flash reports.

12-5 规模以上工业企业单位数和产值
Number of Industrial Enterprises above Designated Size and Their Gross Output Values

项 目	Item	2000	2010	2015	2016	2017
工业企业单位数（个）	**Total Number of Industrial Enterprises (unit)**	**19695**	**53418**	**42134**	**42709**	**47224**
按经济类型分	Grouped by Ownership					
#国有控股工业	Of the Total: State-holding Industry	3320	1279	1056	1100	1079
国有工业	State-owned Industry	2383	567	200	201	140
集体工业	Collective-owned Industry	4158	872	212	185	160
股份合作工业	Share-holding Cooperative Industry	299	223	59	51	42
股份制工业	Share-holding Industry	1875	25490	26200	27666	32350
外商投资工业	Foreign-funded Industry	1682	5790	4374	4104	4089
港澳台投资工业	Industry with Funds from Hong Kong, Macao and Taiwan	6731	13151	9006	8561	8585
按轻重工业分	Grouped by Light and Heavy Industries					
轻工业	Light Industry	12255	29678	21746	21811	23255
重工业	Heavy Industry	7440	23740	20388	20898	23969
按企业规模分	Grouped by Size of Enterprises					
大型企业	Large Enterprises	823	524	1575	1623	1618
中型企业	Medium Enterprises	1228	6968	8880	8700	8504
小微型企业	Small and Micro Enterprises	17644	45926	31679	32386	37102
工业总产值 （亿元）	**Gross Industrial Output Value (100 million yuan)**	**12480.93**	**85824.64**	**124649.16**	**133768.04**	**135722.42**
按经济类型分	Grouped by Ownership					
#国有控股工业	Of the Total: State-holding Industry	3126.12	13166.37	17032.30	17172.18	19525.92
国有工业	State-owned Industry	1450.86	4595.82	605.34	665.85	802.95
集体工业	Collective-owned Industry	1202.49	767.03	445.29	437.76	257.22
股份合作工业	Share-holding Cooperative Industry	106.87	175.69	99.43	86.68	72.34
股份制工业	Share-holding Industry	1780.64	30626.84	66999.08	75729.59	80561.92
外商投资工业	Foreign-funded Industry	2527.06	23705.89	25952.65	25973.04	24161.44
港澳台投资工业	Industry with Funds from Hong Kong, Macao and Taiwan	4747.30	21813.34	27825.74	28269.83	27503.65
按轻重工业分	Grouped by Light and Heavy Industries					
轻工业	Light Industry	6607.84	32867.3	47604.61	50237.52	47827.76
重工业	Heavy Industry	5873.09	52957.34	77044.55	83530.51	87894.65
按企业规模分	Grouped by Size of Enterprises					
大型企业	Large Enterprises	4523.92	28306.79	55405.51	60261.43	63688.06
中型企业	Medium Enterprises	1427.65	28566.98	33097.77	34497.42	32263.16
小微型企业	Small and Micro Enterprises	6529.37	28950.88	36145.87	39009.19	39771.19

注：1．2011年起，规模以上工业统计口径从年主营业务收入500万元及以上调整为2000万元及以上。
2．企业规模划分：2003年以前为一个标准，2003—2010年为一个标准，2011年起采用新的标准，并增加微型企业.

Note: a) Since 2011, the annual principal business revenue of industrial enterprises above designated size is changed from 5 million yuan or above to 20 million yuan or above.

b) Size of Industrial enterprise categorization: The standard prior to 2003 is not the same as the period from 2003 to 2010. Since 2011, New standard is adopted and micro enterprieses is added.

12-6 全部工业总产值和指数

Gross Industrial Output Value of All Industrial Enterprises and Theirs Indices

年份 Year	绝对数（亿元） Absolute Figures (100 million yuan)			指数（1978年=100） Indices(1978=100)	
	全部工业总产值 Gross Industrial Output Value	#国有控股工业 State-holding Industry	#国有工业 State-owned Industry	全部工业总产值 Gross Industrial Output Value	#国有工业 State-owned Industry
1978	206.56		131.83	100.0	100.0
1979	221.46		142.64	107.5	106.1
1980	248.68		146.95	117.4	109.2
1981	282.95		165.53	134.5	120.3
1982	313.76		178.78	145.7	129.5
1983	356.91		204.68	163.4	144.1
1984	433.40		240.19	196.4	164.0
1985	534.72		298.42	249.6	194.0
1986	632.89		334.59	288.3	209.7
1987	878.29		427.10	384.6	255.4
1988	1318.90		594.98	519.3	316.7
1989	1647.24		714.93	603.9	335.8
1990	1902.25		765.43	707.1	366.9
1991	2524.12		973.59	909.6	442.1
1992	3479.39		1202.46	1243.0	532.5
1993	5237.37		1445.38	1731.0	552.4
1994	7273.95		1562.24	2305.9	536.8
1995	9720.54		1709.89	2880.8	539.8
1995(新规定) (New Stipulations)	8849.90		1465.82		
1996	10530.93		1544.58	3404.9	549.8
1997	12372.69		1574.39	4040.7	590.0
1998	13799.16		1453.79	4708.5	526.3
1999	15303.33	3025.68	1427.42	5385.9	487.2
2000	16904.47	3126.12	1536.50	6376.7	472.1
2001	18909.91	3309.51	1186.24	7428.9	374.8
2002	21788.71	3369.50	1217.66	8847.8	392.4
2003	27375.56	4017.54	979.19	11281.8	379.3
2004	34443.48	6039.24	1862.55	13958.7	709.5
2005	41661.74	6375.54	2068.75	16634.5	776.4
2006	51131.94	7253.17	2923.76	20137.8	1082.3
2007	62759.92	8603.94	2791.73	24399.0	1267.4
2008	74414.31	11144.50	2877.31	27636.7	1267.0
2009	75886.62	10790.11	3654.86	29405.4	1280.4
2010	93462.97	13166.37	4595.82	35110.0	1554.0
2011	103493.35	13927.70	5102.02	39358.3	1765.3
2012	105049.54	15529.16	5938.25	43490.9	1899.5
2013	119139.72	17525.16	1242.18	48796.8	2076.2
2014	130081.02	18225.94	635.82	52944.5	2153.0
2015	135308.14	17032.30	605.34	54956.4	2200.4
2016	144926.09	17172.18	665.85	58418.7	2347.8
2017	148173.99	19525.92	802.95	65078.4	2014.4

注：1．工业总产值按当年价计算，2008年根据经普结果进行调整，指数按可比价计算。
2．2000年起全部工业总产值中规模以下部分为抽样调查数。

Notes: a) Gross industrial output values are calculated at current prices, whereas their indices have been adjusted in accordance with the national economic census in 2008 and are calculated at constant prices.

b) Since 2000, data of the industrial enterprises below designated size in the gross industrial output value have been obtained from sample surveys.

12-7 规模以上工业总产值和指数

Gross Output Value of Industrial Enterprises above Designated Size and Their Indices

单位：亿元 (100 million yuan)

年份 Year	工 业 总产值 Gross Industrial Output Value	轻工业 Light Industry	重工业 Heavy Industry	#大中型工业 Large and Medium-sized Industry	指数 (1978年=100) Indices (1978=100)	轻工业 Light Industry	重工业 Heavy Industry	#大中型工业 Large and Medium-sized Industry
1978	180.73	102.32	78.41	49.34	100.0	100.0	100.0	100.0
1979	194.64	110.28	84.36	54.91	105.8	105.3	106.4	109.5
1980	212.69	128.17	84.52	56.33	115.8	127.7	100.7	103.1
1981	241.93	152.97	88.96	66.89	128.7	151.3	102.1	133.0
1982	263.02	164.17	98.85	75.37	139.9	164.2	111.2	148.5
1983	293.70	180.60	113.10	92.78	157.1	184.5	124.7	181.5
1984	359.87	223.29	136.58	110.63	188.1	226.1	142.8	209.9
1985	471.83	289.68	182.15	166.11	236.0	279.6	179.8	302.0
1986	550.49	344.70	205.79	210.27	269.5	327.7	194.7	379.7
1987	747.47	472.45	275.02	299.19	350.1	426.5	252.2	522.3
1988	1118.00	718.03	399.97	459.74	472.5	582.1	332.2	720.2
1989	1399.45	893.20	506.25	622.42	543.2	594.3	389.2	863.6
1990	1605.80	1057.02	548.78	734.35	637.6	795.5	435.8	1042.2
1991	2144.93	1371.46	773.47	1057.02	820.0	1009.7	622.1	1476.1
1992	2884.93	1796.12	1088.23	1408.48	1096.0	1331.0	854.4	1980.5
1993	4252.70	2515.77	1736.93	1891.29	1470.7	1751.6	1188.8	2412.8
1994	5565.48	3224.69	2340.79	2563.27	1819.1	2135.9	1507.6	2863.3
1995(原规定) (Original Stipulations)	7189.24	4148.78	3040.46	3227.59	2274.1	2581.8	1993.2	3519.7
1995(新规定) (New Stipulations)	6502.97	3776.94	2726.03	2824.61				
1996	7490.49	4344.25	3146.24	3470.81	2625.4	2989.5	2290.2	4253.6
1997	8442.32	4914.09	3528.23	3950.86	3045.3	3470.5	2652.8	5176.4
1998	9738.56	5765.51	3973.05	4169.16	3508.2	3866.1	3228.5	5927.0
1999	10538.17	6011.06	4527.11	4711.94	4016.9	4299.1	3861.3	7070.9
2000	12480.93	6607.84	5873.09	5951.56	4757.4	4737.6	5027.4	8590.8
2001	14035.35	7165.90	6869.44	7534.70	5637.5	5400.9	6234.0	12181.8
2002	16378.60	8161.63	8216.97	8755.02	6787.6	6313.7	7742.6	14472.0
2003	21513.46	9959.51	11553.95	14353.53	9051.9	7845.4	11063.4	19955.4
2004	29554.92	12146.01	17408.91	19799.88	12228.7	9549.6	15380.9	27054.8
2005	35942.74	14506.76	21435.97	24403.13	14652.0	11434.3	17914.1	32852.0
2006	44674.75	17148.09	27526.65	30828.93	17963.7	13549.8	21927.5	40937.6
2007	55252.86	21221.12	34031.74	37718.60	21931.9	16667.6	26370.0	49436.3
2008	65424.61	25035.86	40388.76	43866.65	25188.6	19373.2	29468.8	55765.6
2009	68275.77	26685.86	41589.91	44755.10	27430.4	20806.8	32415.7	57494.3
2010	85824.64	32867.30	52957.34	56873.77	33437.7	25200.5	39064.6	70824.4
2011	94871.68	36005.33	58866.35	67492.96	38954.9	29333.4	45549.3	79606.6
2012	95602.09	35817.39	59784.70	70178.27	43162.0	32032.1	49147.7	86134.3
2013	109673.07	41669.48	68003.59	76417.82	48686.7	36420.5	55192.9	95695.2
2014	119713.04	45756.65	73956.39	85194.40	53019.8	39953.3	59829.1	103446.5
2015	124649.16	47604.61	77044.55	88503.28	54981.5	41471.5	62042.8	106239.6
2016	133768.04	50237.52	83530.51	94758.85	58555.4	43379.2	66758.0	112826.4
2017	135722.42	47827.76	87894.65	95951.23	65582.0	47587.0	75703.6	126252.8

注：1. 工业总产值按当年价格计算，指数按可比价计算。

2. 1997年以前为乡及乡以上工业，2011年起规模以上工业统计口径从年主营业务收入500万元及以上调整为2000万元及以上。

Notes: a) Gross industrial output values are calculated at current prices, whereas their indices are calculated at constant prices.

b) Data prior to 1997 refer to the industrial enterprises at or above the township level.Since 2011, the annual principal business revenue of industrial enterprises above designated size is changed from 5 million yuan or above to 20 milliom yuan.

12-8 规模以上工业产品产量

Output of Industrial Products of Enterprises above Designated Size

产品名称		Item		2000	2010	2015	2016	2017
化学纤维	(万吨)	Chemical Fiber	(10000 tons)	45.00	44.54	58.32	58.92	51.20
#合成纤维	(万吨)	Synthetic Fiber	(10000 tons)	45.00	42.45	54.43	55.26	47.02
纱	(万吨)	Yarn	(10000 tons)	16.99	45.16	38.43	33.42	42.04
布	(亿米)	Cloth	(100 million m)	16.99	28.27	28.65	27.10	27.01
#棉布	(亿米)	Pure Cotton Cloth	(100 million m)	7.49	19.54	19.24	17.10	17.93
蚕丝	(万吨)	Silk	(10000 tons)	0.05	0.17	0.27	0.22	0.10
呢绒	(万米)	Woolen Piece Goods	(10000 m)	676.00	13.00	786.90	178.00	201.00
服装	(亿件)	Clothing	(100 million pieces)	21.99	70.26	65.85	64.24	61.60
皮革鞋靴	(亿双)	Leather Shoes and Boots	(100 million pair)	9.05	12.18	7.08	7.01	6.75
机制纸及纸板	(万吨)	Machine-made Paper and Paperboard	(10000 tons)	260.30	1434.68	2078.29	2127.52	2177.74
家用电冰箱	(万台)	Household Refrigerators	(10000 sets)	320.70	1457.76	2195.94	2135.51	1556.37
家用冷柜	(万台)	Freezers	(10000 sets)		180.14	380.87	466.90	414.35
家用洗衣机	(万台)	Household Washing Machines	(10000 sets)	244.18	467.83	747.42	762.32	749.62
家用吸尘器	(万台)	Vacuum Cleaners	(10000 sets)	251.80	2626.67	2651.32	2600.74	3170.34
家用电风扇	(万台)	Electric Fans	(10000 sets)	6759.02	14813.38	14239.15	14838.78	16028.46
家用房间空气调节器	(万台)	House Air Conditioners	(10000 sets)	697.91	5477.85	6227.86	5641.96	5374.97
家用吸排油烟机	(万台)	Smoke Absorbers	(10000 sets)	43.39	1324.67	1886.72	1859.16	1771.89
电饭锅	(万个)	Electric Rice Cookers	(10000 sets)		15207.47	29055.20	31219.32	27084.98
微波炉	(万台)	Microwave Ovens	(10000 sets)	906.51	5341.00	7642.47	9266.67	6763.16
程控交换机	(万线)	Programcontrolled Switchboards	(10000 lines)	3554.88	1602.61	1246.91	1103.12	843.28
电话单机	(万部)	Telephone Sets	(10000 sets)	7700.05	14766.80	9682.46	9294.62	6166.64
移动通信手持机(手机)	(万台)	Mobile Telephone	(10000 units)	1001.30	48626.59	84447.75	95230.18	80163.04
#智能手机	(万台)	Smart Telephone	(10000 units)			64443.20	76496.93	66462.18
传真机	(万部)	Fax Machines	(10000 sets)	109.57	176.61	161.45	174.59	225.94
微型计算机设备	(万台)	Micro-computers Equipment	(10000 units)	169.74	3581.11	3241.72	3344.93	4338.56
服务器	(万台)	Servers	(10000 units)		2.98	52.04	50.05	65.17
集成电路	(亿块)	Semiconductor Integrated Circuit	(100 million pieces)	11.76	161.01	162.65	218.83	262.51
彩色电视机	(万部)	Color TV Sets	(10000 sets)	1531.53	4494.78	7003.58	8106.36	8399.88
#智能电视	(万台)	Smart TV	(10000 sets)			3455.91	4809.22	5276.03
数字激光音、视盘机	(万台)	Laser Digital Audio,Video Disc Machine	(10000sets)	637.69	7589.01	16175.33	15119.47	13012.35
组合音响	(万部)	Hi-fi Stereo Component System	(10000 sets)	2344.58	9713.01	8447.43	7860.73	9643.17
照相机	(万架)	Cameras	(10000 sets)	3545.88	3798.93	889.44	641.94	656.59
#数码照相机	(万台)	Digital Cameras	(10000 sets)		3687.89	825.96	588.45	630.95
表	(万只)	Watches	(10000 units)	19123.23	11892.26	13979.59	14441.06	12204.00
日用玻璃制品	(万吨)	Daily Use Glassware	(10000 tons)	51.46	150.93	63.67	78.27	100.63
合成洗涤剂	(万吨)	Synthetic Detergents	(10000 tons)	26.31	224.61	476.85	480.63	315.14
精制食用植物油	(万吨)	Refined Edible Vegetablc oil	(100000tons)	7.87	244.21	512.80	451.30	488.80
成品糖	(万吨)	Refined Sugar	(10000 tons)	91.30	91.66	128.93	116.12	82.27
食用盐	(万吨)	Edible Salt	(10000 tons)			1.42	1.61	1.57
卷烟	(万箱)	Cigarettes	(10000 units)	177.30	260.69	280.60	270.82	264.73
罐头	(万吨)	Canned Food	(10000 tons)	7.11	30.18	58.81	44.61	46.90
饮料酒	(万千升)	Alcoholic Beverages (mixed weight)	(10000 kiloliter)	178.66	415.80	451.58	434.15	442.06
#白酒	(万千升)	Spirits	(10000 kiloliter)	17.88	10.27	19.29	18.88	20.65
啤酒	(万千升)	Beer	(10000 kiloliter)	158.89	401.40	424.15	405.92	412.26
乳制品	(万吨)	Dairy Products	(10000 tons)	1.29	58.12	66.43	69.13	77.29
中成药	(万吨)	Traditional Chinese Patent Medicine	(10000 tons)	6.05	19.01	24.53	23.64	24.37
化学药品原药	(万吨)	Chemical Active Pharmaceutical Ingredient	(10000 tons)	1.94	4.78	8.16	8.25	8.33

12-8 续表 continued

产品名称	Item	2000	2010	2015	2016	2017
农用氮、磷、钾化学肥料(折纯)（万吨）	Chemical Fertilizer (10000 tons)	34.65	62.15	71.47	68.62	77.06
#氮肥(折含氮100%)（万吨）	Nitrogen Fertilizer (10000 tons)	15.98	11.49			
磷肥(折五氧化二磷100%)（万吨）	Phosphate Fertilizer (10000 tons)	18.67	50.66	71.47	68.62	77.06
化学农药原药(折有效成分100%)(万吨)	Chemical Pesticide (10000 tons)	0.84	0.86	4.32	2.78	1.49
乙烯（万吨）	Ethylene (10000 tons)	54.85	203.96	215.07	241.84	248.18
合成橡胶（万吨）	Synthetic Rubber (10000 tons)	5.45	38.36	64.72	77.83	70.23
橡胶轮胎外胎（万条）	Tires (10000 pieces)	359.13	6907.25	4946.68	2907.74	2575.53
交流电动机（万千瓦）	Alternating Current Motors (10000 kw)	236.21	753.39	1070.59	1189.09	1282.42
汽车（万辆）	Motor Vehicles (10000 units)	3.94	156.29	242.23	280.25	321.06
#载货汽车（万辆）	Trucks (10000 units)	0.53	0.34	3.05	0.14	0.25
客车（万辆）	Buses (10000 units)	0.18	0.20	0.02	0.08	0.22
轿车（万辆）	Cars (10000 units)	3.22	132.67	152.30	151.17	158.82
新能源汽车（万辆）	New Energy Vehicle (10000 units)			1.89	7.08	3.07
城市轨道车辆（辆）	Urban Rail Vehicle (unit)			10	27	15
民用钢质船舶（万载重吨）	Civil Steel ship (10000ton)		177.18	161.94	256.19	351.72
摩托车整车（万辆）	Motorcycles (10000 units)	146.31	917.60	774.40	655.50	763.50
两轮脚踏自行车（万辆）	Bicycles (10000 units)	1038.00	788.75	687.77	531.00	676.64
生铁（万吨）	Pig Iron (10000 tons)	201.57	806.68	1146.33	1670.20	2024.48
粗钢（万吨）	Crude Steel (10000 tons)	286.99	1239.34	1761.74	2283.19	2890.71
成品钢材（万吨）	Rolled Steel Products (10000 tons)	406.28	2918.89	3271.01	4113.34	4213.69
十钟有色金属（万吨）	Ten Kinds of Nonferrous Metas(10000 tons)		45.31	36.56	36.14	37.96
铝材（万吨）	Aluminum (10000 tons)		496.85	537.80	558.44	538.40
汽车用发动机（万千瓦）	Automotive engines (10000 kw)		8727.56	18406.94	16833.24	19351.51
工业机器人（万套）	Industrial Robots (10000 sets)			0.79	1.15	2.07
光纤（万千米）	Optical fiber (10000km)			266.80	358.34	535.30
光缆（万芯千米）	Optical Cable (10000km)		835.99	2198.39	2221.06	2397.30
太阳能电池(光伏电池)（万千瓦）	Solar cells (photovoltaic cells) (10000kw)			192.78	137.34	167.76
水泥（万吨）	Cement (10000 tons)	5872.00	11536.67	14489.66	15078.64	15752.98
平板玻璃（万重量箱）	Plate Glass (10000 wt.cases)	632.59	7821.07	7061.90	9048.44	9146.24
硫酸(折100%)（万吨）	Sulphuric Acid (10000 tons)	138.75	236.74	279.97	244.52	242.05
纯碱（碳酸钠）（万吨）	Soda Ash (10000 tons)	24.28	40.01	62.97	31.26	33.53
烧碱(折100%)（万吨）	Caustic Soda (10000 tons)	16.43	27.62	31.25	56.36	41.95
合成氨(无水氨)（万吨）	Synthetic Ammonia (10000 tons)	23.43	6.88	0.59		

注：1. 纱包括纯棉纱、棉混纺纱、化学纤维纱，不包括棉线、代用纤维纱和手工纺纱。
2. 布包括纯棉布、棉混纺布、化学纤维布，不包括代用纤维布、手工织布。
3. 农用化肥按有效成分100%计算。
4. 成品钢材已剔除重复加工的钢材。

Notes: a) Yarn includes pure and blended cotton yarn, chemical fiber yarn, but excludes cotton thread, substitute fiber yarn and handmade yarn.
b) Cloth includes pure and blended cotton cloth,chemical fiber cloth and canvas,but excludes substitute fiber cloth,hand-woven cloth and cord fabric.
c) Output of chemical fertilizers is calculated on the basis of 100 percent effective content equivalent.
d) Output of rolled steel products excludes the steel products reprocessed.

12-9 各市规模以上工业企业单位数和工业总产值

Number and Gross Output Value of Industrial Enterprises above Designated Size by City

市别	City	工业企业单位数（个） Number of Industrial Enterprises (unit)								
		2000	2005	2010	2012	2013	2014	2015	2016	2017
广州	Guangzhou	4531	5240	6969	4373	4811	4767	4644	4660	4661
深圳	Shenzhen	1834	5214	8249	5835	6523	6355	6539	6627	7943
珠海	Zhuhai	771	992	1347	927	1054	1008	1023	1048	1163
汕头	Shantou	794	1490	2580	1880	1845	1808	1771	1846	1988
佛山	Foshan	2180	5148	7684	5950	6163	5883	5787	5671	6212
韶关	Shaoguan	406	392	559	482	556	622	628	593	536
河源	Heyuan	148	226	440	383	436	513	575	589	602
梅州	Meizhou	371	392	521	326	368	396	440	458	461
惠州	Huizhou	689	1243	1853	1430	1702	1815	1893	2140	2366
汕尾	Shanwei	94	179	452	257	251	246	238	242	237
东莞	Dongguan	1663	4504	5899	4526	5361	5377	5688	5869	7669
中山	Zhongshan	1074	3291	5063	3192	2973	2963	3045	3089	3211
江门	Jiangmen	1599	2365	3246	1851	2007	1961	2036	1998	2112
阳江	Yangjiang	250	498	596	527	569	564	571	557	542
湛江	Zhanjiang	458	578	850	695	772	789	828	833	866
茂名	Maoming	447	590	792	675	844	850	957	978	1026
肇庆	Zhaoqing	981	684	1131	1046	1086	1083	1110	1100	1163
清远	Qingyuan	304	426	813	497	514	580	611	621	644
潮州	Chaozhou	326	727	1245	768	865	871	890	885	923
揭阳	Jieyang	455	714	2525	1731	1884	1971	2030	1991	1956
云浮	Yunfu	320	264	604	460	621	732	830	914	943
按经济区域分	By Region									
珠三角	Pearl River Delta	15322	28681	41441	29130	31680	31212	31765	32202	36500
东翼	Eastern Region	1669	3110	6802	4636	4845	4896	4929	4964	5104
西翼	Western Region	1155	1666	2238	1897	2185	2203	2356	2368	2434
山区	Mountainous Region	1549	1700	2937	2148	2495	2843	3084	3175	3186

注：2011年起，规模以上工业统计口径从年主营业务收入500万元及以上调整为2000万元及以上。

Note: Since 2011, the annual principal business revenue of industrial enterprises above designated size is changed from 5 million yuan or above to 20 million yuan or above.

12-9 续表 continued

市 别	City	工业总产值（亿元） Gross Industrial Output Value (100 million yuan)								
		2000	2005	2010	2012	2013	2014	2015	2016	2017
广 州	Guangzhou	2568.57	6032.05	13831.25	14857.09	17192.88	17997.97	18424.73	18906.55	17751.17
深 圳	Shenzhen	2566.93	9867.55	18526.82	21363.05	23095.21	24777.59	25542.44	27292.29	32119.15
珠 海	Zhuhai	630.17	1569.56	2976.18	3072.56	3460.86	3702.26	3966.02	4353.38	3943.56
汕 头	Shantou	344.34	761.37	1897.57	2111.54	2481.80	2771.68	2968.80	3303.80	3517.94
佛 山	Foshan	1560.55	4780.88	14527.47	14653.96	17121.88	18796.65	19544.95	21187.32	21015.53
韶 关	Shaoguan	151.01	393.36	773.37	1000.18	1160.59	1286.70	1221.78	1237.54	1098.72
河 源	Heyuan	35.81	182.10	832.73	953.66	1140.14	1402.30	1443.02	1599.18	1345.94
梅 州	Meizhou	81.81	206.98	455.97	502.91	567.99	651.03	704.76	745.63	624.34
惠 州	Huizhou	657.83	1428.66	3905.17	5477.28	6605.29	6901.35	7044.73	7617.34	8166.93
汕 尾	Shanwei	30.08	113.45	432.42	760.63	968.72	1095.15	1166.08	1233.47	1089.04
东 莞	Dongguan	914.64	3940.11	7739.09	9492.55	11023.45	12133.71	12744.42	14692.46	17628.53
中 山	Zhongshan	532.95	2221.45	5023.63	5702.16	5673.75	6032.09	6345.28	6614.80	4916.88
江 门	Jiangmen	871.15	1453.25	3828.91	2519.47	3107.86	3625.49	3998.76	4274.38	4161.11
阳 江	Yangjiang	66.17	213.82	693.46	1197.42	1564.09	1861.94	1990.04	2050.58	1734.18
湛 江	Zhanjiang	269.10	644.27	1404.95	1717.67	2041.37	2257.33	2272.40	2564.56	2666.04
茂 名	Maoming	373.22	702.04	1360.15	1775.52	2146.12	2401.85	2328.05	2483.41	2679.24
肇 庆	Zhaoqing	392.04	321.20	1744.19	2816.44	3410.29	3863.50	4034.37	4022.12	2941.20
清 远	Qingyuan	77.51	364.34	2887.04	1334.44	1432.42	1669.76	1680.13	1813.51	1593.82
潮 州	Chaozhou	73.88	293.72	723.12	891.63	1088.31	1221.99	1325.80	1422.96	1352.55
揭 阳	Jieyang	136.46	298.82	1794.82	2828.79	3604.19	4290.68	4803.12	5131.14	4787.84
云 浮	Yunfu	146.71	153.77	466.34	573.13	785.87	972.02	1099.49	1221.61	588.72
按经济区域分	By Region									
珠 三 角	Pearl River Delta	10694.83	31614.71	72102.70	79954.57	90691.47	97830.61	101645.70	108960.64	112644.06
东 翼	Eastern Region	584.76	1467.36	4847.93	6592.59	8143.02	9379.49	10263.80	11091.37	10747.37
西 翼	Western Region	708.49	1560.13	3458.56	4690.61	5751.58	6521.12	6590.49	7098.56	7079.46
山 区	Mountainous Region	492.85	1300.55	5415.45	4364.33	5087.01	5981.82	6149.17	6617.47	5251.53

注：本表产值按当年价格计算。
Note: Data of gross industrial output value in this table are calculated at current prices.

12-10 各市规模以上工业增加值和指数

Value-added and Indices of Industry above Designated Size by City

市别	City	工业增加值(亿元) Value-add of Industry (100 million yuan)								
		2000	2005	2010	2012	2013	2014	2015	2016	2017
广　州	Guangzhou	708.40	1654.03	4073.35	3945.18	4446.93	4364.66	4535.25	4387.90	4131.02
深　圳	Shenzhen	706.85	2571.95	5015.33	5107.24	5794.50	6252.09	6426.39	7108.87	8022.73
珠　海	Zhuhai	156.16	328.74	683.98	664.93	783.68	881.04	916.94	1022.86	1139.37
汕　头	Shantou	88.56	190.30	483.20	510.21	599.23	660.49	694.62	785.21	834.13
佛　山	Foshan	401.78	1303.31	3915.12	3302.10	3872.79	4138.71	4364.33	4671.23	4335.33
韶　关	Shaoguan	50.72	108.63	219.25	264.21	310.91	326.29	309.71	334.24	307.23
河　源	Heyuan	10.66	57.78	312.36	245.41	318.41	325.36	327.57	351.00	279.18
梅　州	Meizhou	29.46	72.49	166.00	160.17	188.42	206.68	214.34	221.58	194.78
惠　州	Huizhou	129.08	315.32	881.16	1173.97	1423.20	1475.02	1617.38	1763.69	1850.49
汕　尾	Shanwei	8.74	29.17	112.34	185.74	222.14	231.47	245.10	246.70	193.32
东　莞	Dongguan	259.44	1060.49	1760.02	1978.13	2425.62	2490.84	2611.96	2968.16	3618.19
中　山	Zhongshan	136.16	551.20	1263.08	1227.06	1195.97	1209.10	1281.05	1319.96	1073.72
江　门	Jiangmen	189.49	355.10	1053.39	576.13	696.94	847.29	965.74	1065.80	991.68
阳　江	Yangjiang	21.55	66.26	184.14	294.86	390.31	429.74	452.02	408.44	366.78
湛　江	Zhanjiang	99.80	229.87	528.83	557.52	684.86	738.07	721.26	780.75	742.90
茂　名	Maoming	78.44	165.28	362.29	498.04	666.70	734.35	757.29	857.82	848.49
肇　庆	Zhaoqing	36.36	76.86	434.51	664.99	807.02	924.53	961.07	921.14	605.68
清　远	Qingyuan	21.22	90.83	686.02	290.92	320.27	392.84	396.65	439.85	398.19
潮　州	Chaozhou	20.19	69.46	194.91	241.49	301.41	329.88	352.08	377.20	318.29
揭　阳	Jieyang	39.09	77.62	512.46	685.73	878.55	974.68	1054.89	1062.21	969.08
云　浮	Yunfu	22.37	41.70	146.58	146.78	212.16	255.58	240.58	235.63	128.90
按经济区域分	By Region									
珠三角	Pearl River Delta	2723.72	8217.00	19079.95	18639.71	21446.65	22583.28	23680.10	25229.60	25768.21
东　翼	Eastern Region	156.58	366.55	1302.91	1623.17	2001.33	2196.51	2346.69	2471.32	2314.82
西　翼	Western Region	199.79	461.41	1075.26	1350.43	1741.87	1902.15	1930.57	2047.02	1958.16
山　区	Mountainous Region	134.43	371.44	1530.20	1107.49	1350.17	1506.75	1488.84	1582.30	1308.28

注：1．本表统计口径从2011年起从年主营业务收入500万元及以上调整为2000万元及以上。
　　2．本表增加值2010年及以前用生产法计算，2011年起用收入法计算。

Note:a) Since 2011, the annual principal business revenue of industrial enterprises above designated size is changed from 5 million yuan or above to 20 million yuan or above.

b) The value-added in this table in 2010 and prior to are calculated with production approach and since 2011 calculated with income approach.

12-10 续表 continued

市 别	City	指数(2000年=100) Indices (2000=100) 2000	2005	2009	2010	2012	2013	2014	2015	2016	2017
广 州	Guangzhou	100.0	223.8	391.6	455.8	566.2	623.9	674.5	723.0	770.0	797.0
深 圳	Shenzhen	100.0	391.6	635.6	723.3	873.9	957.8	1038.3	1118.2	1196.5	1307.8
珠 海	Zhuhai	100.0	229.9	360.5	426.1	523.2	581.8	647.0	709.1	750.9	830.5
汕 头	Shantou	100.0	183.0	346.9	407.9	551.1	628.3	697.4	749.7	821.7	903.9
佛 山	Foshan	100.0	312.0	713.0	851.3	1093.6	1232.5	1354.5	1461.5	1574.1	1712.6
韶 关	Shaoguan	100.0	159.8	286.3	332.4	428.4	504.7	570.3	587.4	616.8	629.1
河 源	Heyuan	100.0	460.0	1488.9	1844.7	2618.8	3071.8	3624.7	3922.0	4318.1	4456.3
梅 州	Meizhou	100.0	210.7	355.6	422.1	587.4	669.6	741.3	808.0	845.2	857.0
惠 州	Huizhou	100.0	215.2	457.3	582.5	830.5	977.4	1104.5	1215.0	1320.7	1431.6
汕 尾	Shanwei	100.0	367.4	1169.4	1541.3	2588.5	3233.0	3698.5	3972.2	4242.3	4726.0
东 莞	Dongguan	100.0	327.6	430.2	512.0	581.2	646.9	703.8	741.1	793.0	872.2
中 山	Zhongshan	100.0	494.0	869.0	1026.2	1365.5	1504.8	1655.2	1779.4	1898.6	1991.6
江 门	Jiangmen	100.0	207.7	424.5	525.1	701.1	799.9	887.9	959.0	1026.1	1128.7
阳 江	Yangjiang	100.0	266.8	530.5	705.0	1156.1	1516.7	1800.4	2038.0	2144.0	2315.5
湛 江	Zhanjiang	100.0	183.7	287.8	340.2	436.6	501.7	562.4	618.1	689.1	747.7
茂 名	Maoming	100.0	163.6	242.3	276.9	390.2	456.9	533.7	577.5	620.2	664.2
肇 庆	Zhaoqing	100.0	211.8	712.5	952.6	1464.5	1729.5	1976.9	2127.1	2205.8	2313.9
清 远	Qingyuan	100.0	353.0	1716.2	2310.0	2888.2	3136.5	3581.9	3850.6	4235.6	4371.2
潮 州	Chaozhou	100.0	321.1	663.3	796.0	1129.6	1316.0	1462.1	1576.1	1680.1	1787.6
揭 阳	Jieyang	100.0	188.3	633.4	879.7	1394.2	1726.0	1998.7	2142.6	2266.9	2334.9
云 浮	Yunfu	100.0	174.7	393.1	517.4	895.1	1127.8	1304.8	1428.8	1551.7	1629.3
按经济区域分	By Region										
珠 三 角	Pearl River Delta	100.0	205.0	343.0	399.6	480.8	522.7	566.0	606.8	647.5	697.3
东 翼	Eastern Region	100.0	208.4	430.3	532.7	757.5	873.4	988.6	1060.8	1135.1	1205.4
西 翼	Western Region	100.0	199.8	318.1	373.3	500.5	573.6	660.8	726.2	785.0	846.2
山 区	Mountainous Region	100.0	207.5	507.7	638.6	845.5	934.3	1068.8	1142.6	1230.6	1267.5

注：本表工业增加值按当年价格计算，指数按可比价格计算。

Note: Data of value-added of industry in this table are calculated at current prices, whereas their indices are calculated at constant prices.

12-11 各市规模以上工业企业单位数（2017年）

单位：个

项　目	Item	全省 Provincial Total	广州 Guangzhou
全省总计	**Provincial Total**	**47224**	**4661**
按经济类型分	Grouped by Ownership		
在总计中：国有控股工业	Of the Total:State-holding Industry	1079	264
国有工业	State-owned Industry	140	21
集体工业	Collective-owned Industry	160	16
股份合作工业	Share-holding Cooperative Industry	42	12
股份制工业	Share-holding Industry	32350	3132
外商投资工业	Foreign-funded Industry	4089	637
港澳台投资工业	Industry with Funds from Hong Kong, Macao and Taiwan	8585	751
按轻重工业分	Grouped by Light and Heavy Industries		
轻工业	Light Industry	23255	2466
重工业	Heavy Industry	23969	2195
按企业规模分	Grouped by Size of Enterprises		
大型企业	Large Enterprises	1618	179
中型企业	Medium Enterprises	8504	658
小微型企业	Small and Micro Enterprises	37102	3824
按行业分	Grouped by Sector		
煤炭开采和洗选业	Mining and Washing of Coal		
石油和天然气开采业	Extraction of Petroleum and Natural Gas	4	
黑色金属矿采选业	Mining and Dressing of Ferrous Metal Ores	28	
有色金属矿采选业	Mining and Dressing of Nonferrous Metal Ores	27	
非金属矿采选业	Mining and Dressing of Nonmetal Ores	264	3
开采辅助活动	Auxiliary Minning Operations	4	
其他采矿业	Mining and Dressing of Other Ores	2	
农副食品加工业	Processing of Farm and Sideline Food	1022	110
食品制造业	Manufacture of Food	765	133
酒、饮料和精制茶制造业	Manufacture of Wine, Beverage and Refined Tea	264	26
烟草制品业	Tobacco Products	11	1
纺织业	Textile Industry	1464	157
纺织服装、服饰业	Manufacture of Textile Garments, Footwear and Headgear	2784	408
皮革、毛皮、羽毛及其制品和制鞋业	Leather, Fur, Feather, Down and Related Products	1868	280
木材加工和木、竹、藤、棕、草制品业	Timber Processing, Bamboo, Cane, Palm Fiber & Straw Products	573	42
家具制造业	Manufacture of Furniture	1438	101
造纸和纸制品业	Papermaking and Paper Products	1150	97
印刷和记录媒介复制业	Printing and Record Medium Reproduction	956	86
文教、工美、体育和娱乐用品制造业	Manufacture of Cultural, Educational,Sports and Entertainment Articles	1708	147
石油加工、炼焦和核燃料加工业	Petroleum Refining, Coking and Nuclear Fuel Processing	91	13
化学原料和化学制品制造业	Manufacture of Raw Chemical Materials and Chemical Products	2347	394
医药制造业	Manufacture of Medicines	453	83
化学纤维制造业	Manufacture of Chemical Fibers	61	9
橡胶和塑料制品业	Rubber and Plastic Products	3811	323
非金属矿物制品业	Nonmetal Mineral Products	3119	203
黑色金属冶炼和压延加工业	Smelting and Pressing of Ferrous Metals	420	33
有色金属冶炼和压延加工业	Smelting and Pressing of Nonferrous Metals	682	51
金属制品业	Metal Products	3814	226
通用设备制造业	Manufacture of General-purpose Machinery	2028	250
专用设备制造业	Manufacture of Special-purpose Machinery	1969	200
汽车制造业	Manufacture of Automobile	833	297
铁路、船舶、航空航天和其他运输设备制造业	Manufacture of Railway ,Ship,Aeronautics and Other Transport equipment	388	72
电气机械和器材制造业	Manufacture of Electrical Machinery and Equipment	5006	339
计算机、通信和其他电子设备制造业	Manufacture of Communication Equipment, Computers and Other Electronic Equipment	5808	401
仪器仪表制造业	Manufacture of Instruments and Meters	672	52
其他制造业	Other Manufactures	297	20
废弃资源综合利用业	Comprehensive Utilization of Waste	262	7
金属制品、机械和设备修理业	Manufacture of Metal Products,Machinery and Equipment Maintenance	52	16
电力、热力生产和供应业	Production and Supply of Electric Power and Heat Power	346	32
燃气生产和供应业	Production and Supply of Gas	147	18
水的生产和供应业	Production and Supply of Water	286	31

Number of Industrial Enterprises above Designated Size by City (2017)

(unit)

深 圳 Shenzhen	珠 海 Zhuhai	汕 头 Shantou	佛 山 Foshan	韶 关 Shaoguan	河 源 Heyuan	梅 州 Meizhou	惠 州 Huizhou	汕 尾 Shanwei
7943	**1163**	**1988**	**6212**	**536**	**602**	**461**	**2366**	**237**
172	52	33	86	58	11	22	46	13
6	2	9	11	12	2	4	9	3
2	1	8	20	4	1	1	5	10
		9	10	1		1		
5489	665	1632	4629	439	421	373	1340	154
618	197	73	430	15	28	12	229	4
1819	294	142	713	55	132	37	668	53
2876	408	1599	2846	203	259	214	1160	158
5067	755	389	3366	333	343	247	1206	79
401	66	19	164	17	18	9	108	61
1605	256	473	1045	56	88	69	478	54
5937	841	1496	5003	463	496	383	1780	122
2	1							
				1	6		1	
		1		4	3	3	1	
	1	2	3	7	27	6	25	
2								
43	16	45	95	19	21	19	36	12
41	21	57	42	5	11	10	11	9
17	5	12	26	11	13	12	10	3
1		2		3		2		
57	12	196	354	9	16	6	43	11
183	40	525	240	9	27	14	71	35
103	7	19	152	4	12	5	247	7
21	8		57	26	10	5	39	4
126	10	10	335	4	7	30	125	
163	23	62	139	10	3	3	42	6
169	24	77	112	2	13	5	43	2
336	14	281	101	15	29	25	88	31
6	9		11			1	2	
188	101	89	335	121	11	10	135	6
55	22	23	40	8	12	11	15	1
4	3	3	8		2	1	2	
564	94	254	466	21	44	5	225	30
143	50	22	453	64	73	89	109	17
19	2	1	146	16	14	5	10	2
72	10	7	215	10	9	3	28	
463	58	36	808	23	23	7	126	15
407	72	37	362	18	23	11	64	1
549	76	41	291	21	13	11	51	
55	25	11	176	6	2	15	34	1
71	17	3	50		2	2	20	2
1206	153	56	794	24	44	21	216	5
2414	222	40	243	23	86	84	465	11
312	38	4	36	3	13	3	23	
83		12	14	2	9	2	13	1
3	2	31	49	2	2	10	11	3
11	4	3	2					3
22	11	12	15	35	14	18	16	10
4	8	4	6	5	6	2	2	1
28	4	10	36	5	2	5	17	8

12-11 续表

单位：个

项 目	Item	东 莞 Dongguan	中 山 Zhongshan
全省总计	**Provincial Total**	**7669**	**3211**
按经济类型分	Grouped by Ownership		
在总计中：国有控股工业	Of the Total:State-holding Industry	42	33
国有工业	State-owned Industry	2	
集体工业	Collective-owned Industry	28	13
股份合作工业	Share-holding Cooperative Industry		1
股份制工业	Share-holding Industry	4456	2155
外商投资工业	Foreign-funded Industry	1056	332
港澳台投资工业	Industry with Funds from Hong Kong, Macao and Taiwan	2083	578
按轻重工业分	Grouped by Light and Heavy Industries		
轻工业	Light Industry	3576	1935
重工业	Heavy Industry	4093	1276
按企业规模分	Grouped by Size of Enterprises		
大型企业	Large Enterprises	297	84
中型企业	Medium Enterprises	1675	525
小微型企业	Small and Micro Enterprises	5697	2602
按行业分	Grouped by Sector		
煤炭开采和洗选业	Mining and Washing of Coal		
石油和天然气开采业	Extraction of Petroleum and Natural Gas		
黑色金属矿采选业	Mining and Dressing of Ferrous Metal Ores		
有色金属矿采选业	Mining and Dressing of Nonferrous Metal Ores		
非金属矿采选业	Mining and Dressing of Nonmetal Ores	1	1
开采辅助活动	Auxiliary Minning Operations		
其他采矿业	Mining and Dressing of Other Ores		
农副食品加工业	Processing of Farm and Sideline Food	61	30
食品制造业	Manufacture of Food	49	36
酒、饮料和精制茶制造业	Manufacture of Wine, Beverage and Refined Tea	16	12
烟草制品业	Tobacco Products		
纺织业	Textile Industry	136	98
纺织服装、服饰业	Manufacture of Textile Garments, Footwear and Headgear	403	262
皮革、毛皮、羽毛及其制品和制鞋业	Leather, Fur, Feather, Down and Related Products	382	82
木材加工和木、竹、藤、棕、草制品业	Timber Processing, Bamboo, Cane, Palm Fiber & Straw Products	48	17
家具制造业	Manufacture of Furniture	380	128
造纸和纸制品业	Papermaking and Paper Products	256	95
印刷和记录媒介复制业	Printing and Record Medium Reproduction	165	59
文教、工美、体育和娱乐用品制造业	Manufacture of Cultural, Educational,Sports and Entertainment Articles	326	100
石油加工、炼焦和核燃料加工业	Petroleum Refining, Coking and Nuclear Fuel Processing	7	3
化学原料和化学制品制造业	Manufacture of Raw Chemical Materials and Chemical Products	265	142
医药制造业	Manufacture of Medicines	15	26
化学纤维制造业	Manufacture of Chemical Fibers	13	2
橡胶和塑料制品业	Rubber and Plastic Products	893	303
非金属矿物制品业	Nonmetal Mineral Products	170	92
黑色金属冶炼和压延加工业	Smelting and Pressing of Ferrous Metals	38	13
有色金属冶炼和压延加工业	Smelting and Pressing of Nonferrous Metals	90	32
金属制品业	Metal Products	598	285
通用设备制造业	Manufacture of General-purpose Machinery	380	189
专用设备制造业	Manufacture of Special-purpose Machinery	411	114
汽车制造业	Manufacture of Automobile	81	42
铁路、船舶、航空航天和其他运输设备制造业	Manufacture of Railway ,Ship,Aeronautics and Other Transport equipment	34	12
电气机械和器材制造业	Manufacture of Electrical Machinery and Equipment	846	726
计算机、通信和其他电子设备制造业	Manufacture of Communication Equipment, Computers and Other Electronic Equipment	1312	193
仪器仪表制造业	Manufacture of Instruments and Meters	128	39
其他制造业	Other Manufactures	76	34
废弃资源综合利用业	Comprehensive Utilization of Waste	4	2
金属制品、机械和设备修理业	Manufacture of Metal Products,Machinery and Equipment Maintenance	4	
电力、热力生产和供应业	Production and Supply of Electric Power and Heat Power	19	8
燃气生产和供应业	Production and Supply of Gas	24	9
水的生产和供应业	Production and Supply of Water	38	25

12-11 continued

(unit)

江 门 Jiangmen	阳 江 Yangjiang	湛 江 Zhanjiang	茂 名 Maoming	肇 庆 Zhaoqing	清 远 Qingyuan	潮 州 Chaozhou	揭 阳 Jieyang	云 浮 Yunfu
2112	**542**	**866**	**1026**	**1163**	**644**	**923**	**1956**	**943**
27	21	60	37	32	19	11	18	22
2	6	13	10	9	4	5	9	1
3	1	6	7	4	1	3	23	3
			2			6		
1333	417	719	804	835	461	612	1528	756
181	21	32	14	88	36	34	34	18
515	56	44	48	160	130	100	126	81
1094	351	508	526	419	214	684	1463	296
1018	191	358	500	744	430	239	493	647
52	11	13	7	27	29	8	40	8
317	155	93	59	210	136	188	318	46
1743	376	760	960	926	479	727	1598	889
		1						
			6	11	2			1
		5	2	2	3		1	2
18	3	16	71	28	15		6	31
		1		1				
		1						1
62	44	121	133	18	21	30	66	20
44	10	38	34	13	6	57	116	22
6	2	23	20	11	6	9	15	9
	1	1						
95	4	16	24	39	22	6	153	10
96	15	6	17	18	14	44	332	25
64	10	35	69	37	32	52	219	50
29	24	71	90	38	5	1	19	19
59	11	30	18	18	7	3	30	6
74	10	30	13	34	8	27	37	18
32	10	19	3	12	7	61	52	3
29	4	8	25	26	17	14	84	8
3		4	30	2				
140	8	27	87	105	70	25	32	56
12	5	16	29	16	7	8	33	16
6				3			5	
152	29	42	42	76	47	33	142	26
129	39	99	164	133	119	361	146	444
16	18	2	10	3	12	6	54	
29	5	4	3	43	41	10	9	11
371	204	35	34	184	24	100	149	45
71	15	7	13	58	17	8	12	13
43	8	26	11	36	13	5	31	18
36	4	4		23	14		4	3
88		2	1	2	2		7	1
232	13	115	15	38	16	11	108	28
125	6	6	28	46	25	10	48	20
2	1			7	2	3	5	1
15	2			3	1	1	6	3
3	9	14	2	41	45	3	14	5
2		4		1			2	
10	17	21	19	18	15	7	8	19
5	4	5	2	7	4	25	2	4
14	7	11	11	12	5	3	9	5

12-12 各市规模以上工业总产值（2017年）

单位：亿元

项　目	Item	全　省 Provincial Total	广　州 Guangzhou
全省总计	**Provincial Total**	**135722.42**	**17751.17**
按经济类型分	Grouped by Ownership		
在总计中：国有控股工业	Of the Total:State-holding Industry	19525.92	6238.63
国有工业	State-owned Industry	802.95	600.59
集体工业	Collective-owned Industry	257.22	21.27
股份合作工业	Share-holding Cooperative Industry	72.34	15.31
股份制工业	Share-holding Industry	80561.92	7370.21
外商投资工业	Foreign-funded Industry	24161.44	7340.05
港澳台投资工业	Industry with Funds from Hong Kong, Macao and Taiwan	27503.65	2355.54
按轻重工业分	Grouped by Light and Heavy Industries		
轻工业	Light Industry	47827.76	5180.60
重工业	Heavy Industry	87894.65	12570.57
按企业规模分	Grouped by Size of Enterprises		
大型企业	Large Enterprises	63688.06	10367.11
中型企业	Medium Enterprises	32263.16	3008.27
小微型企业	Small and Micro Enterprises	39771.19	4375.78
按行业分	Grouped by Sector		
煤炭开采和洗选业	Mining and Washing of Coal		
石油和天然气开采业	Extraction of Petroleum and Natural Gas	532.01	
黑色金属矿采选业	Mining and Dressing of Ferrous Metal Ores	65.63	
有色金属矿采选业	Mining and Dressing of Nonferrous Metal Ores	70.75	
非金属矿采选业	Mining and Dressing of Nonmetal Ores	279.08	2.38
开采辅助活动	Auxiliary Minning Operations	16.62	
其他采矿业	Mining and Dressing of Other Ores	3.86	
农副食品加工业	Processing of Farm and Sideline Food	3114.52	363.39
食品制造业	Manufacture of Food	1860.36	458.76
酒、饮料和精制茶制造业	Manufacture of Wine, Beverage and Refined Tea	1085.99	218.17
烟草制品业	Tobacco Products	438.73	202.88
纺织业	Textile Industry	2486.46	186.19
纺织服装、服饰业	Manufacture of Textile Garments, Footwear and Headgear	3843.72	289.20
皮革、毛皮、羽毛及其制品和制鞋业	Leather, Fur, Feather, Down and Related Products	2246.47	190.15
木材加工和木、竹、藤、棕、草制品业	Timber Processing, Bamboo, Cane, Palm Fiber & Straw Products	738.16	26.44
家具制造业	Manufacture of Furniture	2172.69	231.98
造纸和纸制品业	Papermaking and Paper Products	2522.10	142.43
印刷和记录媒介复制业	Printing and Record Medium Reproduction	1296.52	99.40
文教、工美、体育和娱乐用品制造业	Manufacture of Cultural, Educational,Sports and Entertainment Articles	3816.15	161.75
石油加工、炼焦和核燃料加工业	Petroleum Refining, Coking and Nuclear Fuel Processing	2553.92	510.01
化学原料和化学制品制造业	Manufacture of Raw Chemical Materials and Chemical Products	5594.37	1433.00
医药制造业	Manufacture of Medicines	1537.08	290.31
化学纤维制造业	Manufacture of Chemical Fibers	171.70	8.70
橡胶和塑料制品业	Rubber and Plastic Products	5221.83	422.50
非金属矿物制品业	Nonmetal Mineral Products	5049.66	244.65
黑色金属冶炼和压延加工业	Smelting and Pressing of Ferrous Metals	2562.42	389.95
有色金属冶炼和压延加工业	Smelting and Pressing of Nonferrous Metals	3259.21	291.49
金属制品业	Metal Products	6204.02	307.46
通用设备制造业	Manufacture of General-purpose Machinery	4150.17	612.03
专用设备制造业	Manufacture of Special-purpose Machinery	3395.32	246.99
汽车制造业	Manufacture of Automobile	7853.18	5117.04
铁路、船舶、航空航天和其他运输设备制造业	Manufacture of Railway ,Ship,Aeronautics and Other Transport equipment	1187.96	293.59
电气机械和器材制造业	Manufacture of Electrical Machinery and Equipment	12931.73	835.42
计算机、通信和其他电子设备制造业	Manufacture of Communication Equipment, Computers and Other Electronic Equipment	37301.89	2166.93
仪器仪表制造业	Manufacture of Instruments and Meters	1124.19	93.89
其他制造业	Other Manufactures	250.72	13.65
废弃资源综合利用业	Comprehensive Utilization of Waste	998.23	13.42
金属制品、机械和设备修理业	Manufacture of Metal Products,Machinery and Equipment Maintenance	177.55	71.51
电力、热力生产和供应业	Production and Supply of Electric Power and Heat Power	6369.97	1433.90
燃气生产和供应业	Production and Supply of Gas	768.72	285.27
水的生产和供应业	Production and Supply of Water	468.76	96.32

注：本表产值按当年价格计算。

Gross Output Value of Industry above Designated Size by City (2017)

(100 million yuan)

深圳 Shenzhen	珠海 Zhuhai	汕头 Shantou	佛山 Foshan	韶关 Shaoguan	河源 Heyuan	梅州 Meizhou	惠州 Huizhou	汕尾 Shanwei
32119.15	**3943.56**	**3517.94**	**21015.53**	**1098.72**	**1345.94**	**624.34**	**8166.93**	**1089.04**
3715.04	928.40	286.00	1018.72	596.29	93.62	145.28	1427.97	85.73
39.53	0.61	7.73	20.42	7.60	2.79	2.71	11.43	1.71
0.58	1.40	13.29	50.19	2.43	0.70	0.67	10.42	57.01
		14.65	34.58	0.67		0.89		
20204.43	2012.57	2792.86	13819.88	915.62	826.07	493.75	3358.86	688.11
3926.50	1215.25	244.94	2880.62	64.41	183.74	38.74	2320.64	50.66
7941.12	711.79	245.17	3539.31	105.92	320.50	68.06	2406.62	225.94
6837.30	1276.49	2597.81	9395.97	233.23	356.18	236.71	2453.21	610.05
25281.85	2667.07	920.13	11619.56	865.49	989.76	387.62	5713.72	478.99
20306.32	1745.31	460.41	6909.80	552.60	555.80	159.40	4431.41	790.72
5810.49	1035.09	1493.85	6641.47	247.26	262.28	209.09	1660.21	175.79
6002.34	1163.16	1563.68	7464.26	298.86	527.86	255.85	2075.31	122.53
247.16	109.19							
				0.27	19.44		4.18	
		4.56		29.23	3.52	4.15	0.51	
	0.43	0.45	4.32	3.95	25.93	1.71	25.66	
11.78								
237.16	87.22	109.48	357.50	15.71	33.36	14.86	96.17	23.49
57.33	53.14	57.15	228.75	3.06	27.82	10.06	8.23	12.05
172.42	14.65	11.65	254.92	7.20	22.41	6.23	64.83	5.54
63.04		8.71		64.47		78.13		
98.61	18.01	266.00	784.81	20.35	15.11	3.37	64.09	18.43
266.50	33.69	711.67	473.81	3.09	19.49	9.72	154.24	187.89
111.80	11.55	27.12	261.91	1.51	18.70	13.71	245.13	16.94
16.89	15.67		144.40	22.97	5.76	1.35	56.82	2.60
147.53	14.04	128.81	550.81	2.00	5.27	19.49	209.47	
169.62	47.67	74.31	288.79	9.05	1.97	2.32	56.18	11.18
219.43	12.55	136.76	215.31	3.81	12.46	2.00	50.40	3.30
1073.17	15.77	539.42	679.20	34.05	37.39	21.16	98.78	206.28
80.04	92.68		159.26			0.20	464.68	
298.21	298.12	185.95	951.09	77.07	10.77	4.84	649.21	6.16
275.48	146.40	52.21	114.67	14.33	20.34	7.94	25.10	0.24
5.48	33.90	1.46	39.45		0.61	1.81	4.38	
796.16	110.43	431.31	1025.74	9.90	35.80	10.99	303.22	140.78
335.54	56.87	44.51	1364.49	51.69	79.99	91.75	185.12	38.40
33.41	109.77	0.23	597.34	318.40	93.25	21.79	22.77	0.87
451.15	20.96	27.93	1246.49	96.31	6.29	9.76	35.14	
550.86	80.46	52.33	1919.03	43.45	14.08	6.79	257.18	78.68
815.41	154.68	46.57	902.26	19.94	34.74	5.53	244.39	1.00
1112.60	155.48	53.04	790.70	16.05	51.47	5.86	113.31	
750.35	96.79	42.98	897.42	4.08	0.81	28.06	221.74	38.52
345.76	22.52	2.70	130.41		1.55	0.84	22.23	0.43
2648.83	765.09	131.37	4320.50	31.80	87.25	25.00	554.88	8.41
19004.88	895.46	72.88	919.82	34.66	541.30	119.40	3531.68	202.64
505.64	68.12	5.97	119.09	11.86	18.27	3.26	21.19	
75.38		10.45	16.49	0.46	4.83	0.76	9.04	0.35
1.53	1.93	44.77	556.91	3.62	1.01	3.82	19.03	1.89
15.45	69.55	1.01	0.67					1.16
875.79	248.70	220.25	561.73	138.88	89.32	82.95	323.48	78.43
123.73	69.44	5.46	64.15	3.26	4.61	1.61	5.53	0.40
125.04	12.65	8.49	73.32	2.23	1.02	3.11	18.94	2.98

Note: Data in this table are calculated at current prices.

12-12 续表

单位：亿元

项　目	Item	东 莞 Dongguan	中 山 Zhongshan
全省总计	**Provincial Total**	**17628.53**	**4916.88**
按经济类型分	Grouped by Ownership		
在总计中：国有控股工业	Of the Total:State-holding Industry	756.73	468.81
国有工业	State-owned Industry	1.34	
集体工业	Collective-owned Industry	20.49	9.53
股份合作工业	Share-holding Cooperative Industry		0.70
股份制工业	Share-holding Industry	9983.20	2338.07
外商投资工业	Foreign-funded Industry	2932.31	1478.28
港澳台投资工业	Industry with Funds from Hong Kong, Macao and Taiwan	4661.44	1038.20
按轻重工业分	Grouped by Light and Heavy Industries		
轻工业	Light Industry	5439.65	2405.94
重工业	Heavy Industry	12188.88	2510.94
按企业规模分	Grouped by Size of Enterprises		
大型企业	Large Enterprises	9727.27	1944.01
中型企业	Medium Enterprises	3890.52	1359.56
小微型企业	Smal and Micro Enterprises	4010.73	1613.30
按行业分	Grouped by Sector		
煤炭开采和洗选业	Mining and Washing of Coal		
石油和天然气开采业	Extraction of Petroleum and Natural Gas		
黑色金属矿采选业	Mining and Dressing of Ferrous Metal Ores		
有色金属矿采选业	Mining and Dressing of Nonferrous Metal Ores		
非金属矿采选业	Mining and Dressing of Nonmetal Ores	0.29	0.48
开采辅助活动	Auxiliary Minning Operations		
其他采矿业	Mining and Dressing of Other Ores		
农副食品加工业	Processing of Farm and Sideline Food	446.30	45.81
食品制造业	Manufacture of Food	119.41	51.88
酒、饮料和精制茶制造业	Manufacture of Wine, Beverage and Refined Tea	84.33	59.24
烟草制品业	Tobacco Products		
纺织业	Textile Industry	177.81	77.91
纺织服装、服饰业	Manufacture of Textile Garments, Footwear and Headgear	470.97	186.07
皮革、毛皮、羽毛及其制品和制鞋业	Leather, Fur, Feather, Down and Related Products	336.85	82.58
木材加工和木、竹、藤、棕、草制品业	Timber Processing, Bamboo, Cane, Palm Fiber & Straw Products	34.41	16.83
家具制造业	Manufacture of Furniture	331.49	114.20
造纸和纸制品业	Papermaking and Paper Products	843.54	129.31
印刷和记录媒介复制业	Printing and Record Medium Reproduction	201.85	40.89
文教、工美、体育和娱乐用品制造业	Manufacture of Cultural, Educational,Sports and Entertainment Articles	431.21	108.60
石油加工、炼焦和核燃料加工业	Petroleum Refining, Coking and Nuclear Fuel Processing	11.56	1.74
化学原料和化学制品制造业	Manufacture of Raw Chemical Materials and Chemical Products	353.05	219.80
医药制造业	Manufacture of Medicines	24.08	113.02
化学纤维制造业	Manufacture of Chemical Fibers	13.35	0.85
橡胶和塑料制品业	Rubber and Plastic Products	849.15	289.07
非金属矿物制品业	Nonmetal Mineral Products	250.18	124.98
黑色金属冶炼和压延加工业	Smelting and Pressing of Ferrous Metals	64.85	28.16
有色金属冶炼和压延加工业	Smelting and Pressing of Nonferrous Metals	85.34	57.37
金属制品业	Metal Products	630.93	246.66
通用设备制造业	Manufacture of General-purpose Machinery	678.02	327.91
专用设备制造业	Manufacture of Special-purpose Machinery	447.08	101.06
汽车制造业	Manufacture of Automobile	204.39	165.67
铁路、船舶、航空航天和其他运输设备制造业	Manufacture of Railway ,Ship,Aeronautics and Other Transport equipment	61.55	16.98
电气机械和器材制造业	Manufacture of Electrical Machinery and Equipment	1345.47	1067.13
计算机、通信和其他电子设备制造业	Manufacture of Communication Equipment, Computers and Other Electronic Equipment	8199.80	839.88
仪器仪表制造业	Manufacture of Instruments and Meters	181.32	54.09
其他制造业	Other Manufactures	54.30	32.91
废弃资源综合利用业	Comprehensive Utilization of Waste	1.44	1.79
金属制品、机械和设备修理业	Manufacture of Metal Products,Machinery and Equipment Maintenance	2.49	
电力、热力生产和供应业	Production and Supply of Electric Power and Heat Power	604.30	276.47
燃气生产和供应业	Production and Supply of Gas	52.37	17.26
水的生产和供应业	Production and Supply of Water	35.08	20.27

12-12 continued

(100 million yuan)

江门 Jiangmen	阳江 Yangjiang	湛江 Zhanjiang	茂名 Maoming	肇庆 Zhaoqing	清远 Qingyuan	潮州 Chaozhou	揭阳 Jieyang	云浮 Yunfu
4161.11	**1734.18**	**2666.04**	**2679.24**	**2941.20**	**1593.82**	**1352.55**	**4787.84**	**588.72**
362.49	543.41	926.11	1010.58	264.51	234.73	149.00	169.34	104.53
1.22	15.41	26.38	7.40	8.07	2.80	38.52	6.43	0.27
0.94	0.20	6.90	7.40	4.33	0.36	1.78	46.85	0.47
			1.97			3.57		
2114.79	1395.43	1934.42	2362.54	1855.24	1062.15	975.11	3630.27	428.34
529.98	90.57	67.88	43.19	445.16	87.38	64.23	119.39	37.49
1465.69	134.21	582.88	110.71	494.57	436.01	132.00	425.75	102.22
2130.47	788.60	1296.16	906.27	871.30	378.67	761.12	3508.59	163.43
2030.64	945.58	1369.87	1772.97	2069.90	1215.14	591.43	1279.25	425.29
1249.98	543.38	957.07	999.84	568.70	414.02	149.51	733.88	121.51
1302.61	553.35	728.68	218.57	984.92	646.97	411.89	1496.77	125.50
1608.52	637.45	980.28	1460.83	1387.58	532.82	791.14	2557.19	341.71
		175.66						
			5.53	34.55	1.29			0.36
		2.15	3.97	14.73	2.22		3.69	2.02
13.60	1.90	10.13	106.15	51.77	5.94		12.52	11.47
		4.58		0.26				
		3.40						0.46
150.25	132.92	395.37	296.83	40.54	48.31	55.96	148.47	15.42
336.71	26.57	29.05	45.30	37.27	26.15	61.93	205.69	4.02
22.25	1.36	26.36	20.97	35.75	15.06	9.23	28.85	4.57
	2.26	19.24						
149.73	9.28	12.14	31.43	52.67	28.65	4.48	463.38	4.01
116.09	29.42	5.11	29.99	28.84	6.06	33.26	774.74	13.88
81.06	25.20	44.86	85.65	104.13	88.78	49.34	437.84	11.67
23.27	50.46	74.75	117.42	90.16	8.05	0.21	20.75	8.97
78.63	23.90	142.53	28.19	78.96	10.34	3.11	49.14	2.79
243.00	16.37	242.23	16.71	65.06	29.10	24.48	92.00	16.77
61.73	10.88	18.55	1.53	42.21	10.77	50.50	102.10	0.07
33.57	7.57	6.93	99.36	66.61	26.75	11.69	152.92	3.98
4.30		281.25	947.06	1.13				
239.83	8.66	62.10	269.67	241.04	103.78	27.58	121.25	33.21
20.69	9.98	21.34	39.76	35.48	10.88	10.15	290.21	14.46
41.03				4.26			16.44	
119.87	50.96	37.73	60.64	106.33	42.83	25.87	339.09	13.47
216.29	82.54	116.32	201.22	384.17	303.41	427.03	265.09	185.41
40.33	156.50	336.79	31.38	14.00	35.23	3.07	264.34	
80.93	230.92	14.98	3.47	150.12	256.99	149.16	14.74	29.67
459.94	476.15	60.69	39.89	475.21	27.84	100.16	341.80	34.44
107.29	19.65	14.26	10.77	70.22	41.03	15.51	20.58	8.38
93.40	13.47	47.70	19.84	55.99	7.64	3.03	50.40	10.22
117.80	3.88	8.98		101.84	29.42		14.19	9.22
253.64		0.92	0.23	0.57	15.98		17.34	0.74
441.79	22.91	276.28	18.02	63.46	48.84	13.57	194.44	31.28
302.46	6.71	2.22	31.01	157.81	74.80	53.83	108.93	34.79
1.15	7.69			11.03	1.15	1.74	18.47	0.26
12.29	3.24			2.33	1.21	1.81	10.49	0.74
2.62	37.75	24.33	0.73	129.58	114.43	4.31	30.34	2.98
0.67		1.30		5.24			8.51	
269.42	240.37	125.28	108.16	151.76	161.51	144.13	159.69	75.46
15.88	13.42	12.95	2.18	19.17	4.35	65.00	0.59	2.11
9.61	11.28	7.56	6.18	16.94	5.07	2.43	8.81	1.43

12-13 各市规模以上工业增加值（2017年）

单位：亿元

项 目	Item	全 省 Provincial Total	广 州 Guangzhou
全省总计	**Provincial Total**	**31349.47**	**4131.02**
按经济类型分	Grouped by Ownership		
在总计中：国有控股工业	Of the Total:State-holding Industry	5465.15	1472.65
国有工业	State-owned Industry	203.07	142.74
集体工业	Collective-owned Industry	65.92	11.36
股份合作工业	Share-holding Cooperative Industry	13.10	3.41
股份制工业	Share-holding Industry	18900.25	1739.28
外商投资工业	Foreign-funded Industry	5213.47	1684.54
港澳台投资工业	Industry with Funds from Hong Kong, Macao and Taiwan	6459.57	539.04
按轻重工业分	Grouped by Light and Heavy Industries		
轻工业	Light Industry	11305.75	1443.00
重工业	Heavy Industry	20043.72	2688.03
按企业规模分	Grouped by Size of Enterprises		
大型企业	Large Enterprises	15716.24	2600.95
中型企业	Medium Enterprises	7458.51	710.77
小微型企业	Small and Micro Enterprises	8174.72	819.31
按行业分	Grouped by Sector		
煤炭开采和洗选业	Mining and Washing of Coal		
石油和天然气开采业	Extraction of Petroleum and Natural Gas	427.92	
黑色金属矿采选业	Mining and Dressing of Ferrous Metal Ores	22.45	
有色金属矿采选业	Mining and Dressing of Nonferrous Metal Ores	36.24	
非金属矿采选业	Mining and Dressing of Nonmetal Ores	75.07	0.58
开采辅助活动	Auxiliary Minning Operations	4.05	
其他采矿业	Mining and Dressing of Other Ores	0.29	
农副食品加工业	Processing of Farm and Sideline Food	395.15	30.04
食品制造业	Manufacture of Food	621.28	169.67
酒、饮料和精制茶制造业	Manufacture of Wine, Beverage and Refined Tea	299.55	67.81
烟草制品业	Tobacco Products	331.67	154.32
纺织业	Textile Industry	533.12	35.14
纺织服装、服饰业	Manufacture of Textile Garments, Footwear and Headgear	960.95	96.14
皮革、毛皮、羽毛及其制品和制鞋业	Leather, Fur, Feather, Down and Related Products	605.67	60.41
木材加工和木、竹、藤、棕、草制品业	Timber Processing, Bamboo, Cane, Palm Fiber & Straw	177.59	7.89
家具制造业	Manufacture of Furniture	525.68	72.73
造纸和纸制品业	Papermaking and Paper Products	497.37	27.54
印刷和记录媒介复制业	Printing and Record Medium Reproduction	343.86	29.12
文教、工美、体育和娱乐用品制造业	Manufacture of Cultural, Educational and Sports Articles	743.67	59.51
石油加工、炼焦和核燃料加工业	Petroleum Refining, Coking and Nuclear Fuel Processing	1014.57	210.69
化学原料和化学制品制造业	Manufacture of Raw Chemical Materials and Chemical Products	1193.69	335.64
医药制造业	Manufacture of Medicines	502.55	111.72
化学纤维制造业	Manufacture of Chemical Fibers	37.97	2.02
橡胶和塑料制品业	Rubber and Plastic Products	1186.54	86.84
非金属矿物制品业	Nonmetal Mineral Products	1194.91	54.09
黑色金属冶炼和压延加工业	Smelting and Pressing of Ferrous Metals	401.79	30.99
有色金属冶炼和压延加工业	Smelting and Pressing of Nonferrous Metals	364.88	6.62
金属制品业	Metal Products	1374.31	58.17
通用设备制造业	Manufacture of General-purpose Equipment	900.49	149.20
专用设备制造业	Manufacture of Special-purpose Equipment	914.97	64.77
汽车制造业	Manufacture of Transport Equipment	1776.09	1178.58
铁路、船舶、航空航天和其他运输设备制造业	Manufacture of Railway ,Ship,Aeronautics and Other Transport equipment	229.72	45.29
电气机械和器材制造业	Manufacture of Electrical Machinery and Equipment	2969.33	159.36
计算机、通信和其他电子设备制造业	Manufacture of Communication Equipment, Computers and Other Electronic Equipment	8122.15	379.43
仪器仪表制造业	Manufacture of Instruments and Meters	306.45	29.66
其他制造业	Other Manufactures	55.68	2.11
废弃资源综合利用业	Comprehensive Utilization of Waste	184.96	5.01
金属制品、机械和设备修理业	Manufacture of Metal Products,Machinery and Equipment Maintenance	52.34	30.32
电力、热力生产和供应业	Production and Supply of Electric Power and Heat Power	1568.61	286.79
燃气生产和供应业	Production and Supply of Gas	182.05	40.51
水的生产和供应业	Production and Supply of Water	213.81	52.33

注：本表工业增加值按收入法、当年价格计算。

Value-added of Industry above Designated Size by City (2017)

(100 million yuan)

深 圳 Shenzhen	珠 海 Zhuhai	汕 头 Shantou	佛 山 Foshan	韶 关 Shaoguan	河 源 Heyuan	梅 州 Meizhou	惠 州 Huizhou	汕 尾 Shanwei
8022.73	**1139.37**	**834.13**	**4335.33**	**307.23**	**279.18**	**194.78**	**1850.49**	**193.32**
1303.98	399.74	69.46	221.28	181.32	20.20	74.04	359.65	22.97
10.13	0.20	3.43	4.07	5.35	0.35	1.39	3.95	0.82
0.20	0.12	3.40	10.75	0.74	0.10	0.16	2.58	11.12
		2.87	4.81	0.21		0.33		
5556.88	656.83	654.48	2905.08	250.31	172.28	158.51	766.73	112.49
822.67	284.60	63.88	573.60	11.72	29.60	12.46	523.75	7.42
1631.03	196.65	57.07	716.64	38.26	74.57	18.30	535.95	51.07
1431.44	462.59	625.67	2098.01	98.25	80.51	98.68	522.26	108.03
6591.29	676.78	208.46	2237.32	208.98	198.67	96.09	1328.23	85.30
5519.33	531.37	115.91	1636.30	138.05	114.88	83.08	984.16	132.41
1258.84	262.97	373.65	1365.67	101.68	61.97	55.86	401.35	41.32
1244.57	345.03	344.56	1333.36	67.50	102.33	55.84	464.97	19.59
218.62	57.46							
				0.09	7.68		1.36	
		0.99		25.34	0.98	1.35	0.36	
	0.10	0.11	1.09	0.97	3.87	0.31	11.24	
1.60								
23.76	6.19	10.91	48.71	1.82	3.76	1.49	16.02	4.10
15.45	20.18	14.92	71.97	0.68	6.48	2.02	2.08	3.30
36.52	3.59	3.29	69.40	3.64	6.28	2.52	15.59	0.85
51.84		1.70		48.99		59.64		
23.81	5.06	64.69	151.37	4.57	2.66	0.63	15.64	5.01
87.40	10.97	161.28	107.28	1.15	8.53	2.78	38.65	34.44
37.06	3.15	6.79	58.77	0.81	3.89	6.28	73.49	2.92
3.10	2.16		30.20	5.89	1.37	0.30	13.51	0.56
37.44	4.50	35.39	116.27	0.74	0.87	6.03	46.64	
34.26	6.61	17.98	57.44	2.56	0.38	0.47	10.94	1.28
68.88	4.51	35.95	38.88	1.18	2.59	0.89	12.10	0.57
131.47	5.33	131.49	74.47	16.41	10.18	3.81	29.30	35.05
34.32	88.36		27.78			0.08	117.01	
50.42	56.35	44.20	179.23	21.48	2.17	1.33	165.84	1.34
106.39	44.96	17.22	37.61	6.30	3.01	3.10	9.01	0.04
2.13	9.60	0.30	8.66		0.15	0.61	1.03	
200.33	19.29	110.76	196.46	2.25	6.34	2.28	73.51	22.45
82.19	11.06	7.29	305.19	16.69	16.01	19.54	44.96	5.34
4.74	18.68	0.04	70.22	62.23	19.52	3.28	3.80	0.20
5.56	5.29	3.83	200.36	8.74	0.54	1.02	6.01	
159.85	20.86	11.74	360.06	8.19	3.65	1.13	66.32	7.61
186.66	33.80	9.89	184.97	4.60	5.02	1.17	49.47	0.23
357.71	40.29	13.94	168.59	3.09	12.99	1.47	25.93	
103.60	22.59	11.39	217.45	0.90	0.20	8.14	54.40	4.64
93.75	3.76	0.38	21.54		0.53	0.15	5.16	0.08
530.06	320.86	27.40	1056.66	8.55	20.45	4.00	106.16	1.88
4785.28	202.29	15.83	182.91	10.26	103.23	31.72	730.46	38.45
133.31	13.88	1.39	28.47	1.91	3.68	1.19	7.67	
14.86		2.29	3.85	0.10	1.08	0.18	2.29	0.08
0.37	0.36	8.99	95.99	1.53	0.25	0.82	4.52	0.38
6.93	9.59	0.57	0.27					0.26
283.97	63.94	55.96	121.58	33.41	19.25	23.56	81.19	20.78
42.29	16.51	1.30	19.04	0.78	1.10	0.38	1.31	0.09
66.79	7.24	3.94	22.58	1.39	0.49	1.14	7.49	1.37

Note: Data of value-added of industry in this table are calculated with income approach and at current prices.

12-13 续表

单位：亿元

项　目	Item	东 莞 Dongguan	中 山 Zhongshan
全省总计	**Provincial Total**	**3618.19**	**1073.72**
按经济类型分	Grouped by Ownership		
在总计中：国有控股工业	Of the Total:State-holding Industry	150.91	74.21
国有工业	State-owned Industry	0.41	
集体工业	Collective-owned Industry	8.82	3.21
股份合作工业	Share-holding Cooperative Industry		0.16
股份制工业	Share-holding Industry	1850.60	504.74
外商投资工业	Foreign-funded Industry	613.60	269.05
港澳台投资工业	Industry with Funds from Hong Kong, Macao and Taiwan	1137.52	284.30
按轻重工业分	Grouped by Light and Heavy Industries		
轻工业	Light Industry	1331.06	580.02
重工业	Heavy Industry	2287.13	493.70
按企业规模分	Grouped by Size of Enterprises		
大型企业	Large Enterprises	1797.89	385.71
中型企业	Medium Enterprises	954.67	339.01
小微型企业	Small and Micro Enterprises	865.62	349.00
按行业分	Grouped by Sector		
煤炭开采和洗选业	Mining and Washing of Coal		
石油和天然气开采业	Extraction of Petroleum and Natural Gas		
黑色金属矿采选业	Mining and Dressing of Ferrous Metal Ores		
有色金属矿采选业	Mining and Dressing of Nonferrous Metal Ores		
非金属矿采选业	Mining and Dressing of Nonmetal Ores	0.07	0.12
开采辅助活动	Auxiliary Minning Operations		
其他采矿业	Mining and Dressing of Other Ores		
农副食品加工业	Processing of Farm and Sideline Food	35.92	5.77
食品制造业	Manufacture of Food	35.19	16.66
酒、饮料和精制茶制造业	Manufacture of Wine, Beverage and Refined Tea	20.44	21.15
烟草制品业	Tobacco Products		
纺织业	Textile Industry	47.91	16.32
纺织服装、服饰业	Manufacture of Textile Garments, Footwear and Headgear	124.36	63.61
皮革、毛皮、羽毛及其制品和制鞋业	Leather, Fur, Feather, Down and Related Products	115.02	27.06
木材加工和木、竹、藤、棕、草制品业	Timber Processing, Bamboo, Cane, Palm Fiber & Straw	8.95	3.74
家具制造业	Manufacture of Furniture	82.93	32.04
造纸和纸制品业	Papermaking and Paper Products	196.14	23.71
印刷和记录媒介复制业	Printing and Record Medium Reproduction	60.03	11.83
文教、工美、体育和娱乐用品制造业	Manufacture of Cultural, Educational and Sports Articles	116.99	40.39
石油加工、炼焦和核燃料加工业	Petroleum Refining, Coking and Nuclear Fuel Processing	4.39	0.66
化学原料和化学制品制造业	Manufacture of Raw Chemical Materials and Chemical Products	68.42	63.76
医药制造业	Manufacture of Medicines	13.34	23.50
化学纤维制造业	Manufacture of Chemical Fibers	3.35	0.17
橡胶和塑料制品业	Rubber and Plastic Products	223.01	65.00
非金属矿物制品业	Nonmetal Mineral Products	62.39	27.75
黑色金属冶炼和压延加工业	Smelting and Pressing of Ferrous Metals	13.04	3.41
有色金属冶炼和压延加工业	Smelting and Pressing of Nonferrous Metals	22.35	7.37
金属制品业	Metal Products	191.86	54.25
通用设备制造业	Manufacture of General-purpose Equipment	128.05	74.08
专用设备制造业	Manufacture of Special-purpose Equipment	132.61	24.39
汽车制造业	Manufacture of Transport Equipment	53.87	43.05
铁路、船舶、航空航天和其他运输设备制造业	Manufacture of Railway ,Ship,Aeronautics and Other Transport equipment	12.65	-4.61
电气机械和器材制造业	Manufacture of Electrical Machinery and Equipment	293.84	194.40
计算机、通信和其他电子设备制造业	Manufacture of Communication Equipment, Computers and Other Electronic Equipment	1329.08	133.00
仪器仪表制造业	Manufacture of Instruments and Meters	60.24	15.45
其他制造业	Other Manufactures	13.34	8.74
废弃资源综合利用业	Comprehensive Utilization of Waste	0.34	0.30
金属制品、机械和设备修理业	Manufacture of Metal Products,Machinery and Equipment Maintenance	0.70	
电力、热力生产和供应业	Production and Supply of Electric Power and Heat Power	121.56	55.16
燃气生产和供应业	Production and Supply of Gas	11.42	15.31
水的生产和供应业	Production and Supply of Water	14.39	6.17

12-13 continued

(100 million yuan)

江 门 Jiangmen	阳 江 Yangjiang	湛 江 Zhanjiang	茂 名 Maoming	肇 庆 Zhaoqing	清 远 Qingyuan	潮 州 Chaozhou	揭 阳 Jieyang	云 浮 Yunfu
991.68	**366.78**	**742.90**	**848.49**	**605.68**	**398.19**	**318.29**	**969.08**	**128.90**
82.29	125.32	281.70	400.77	57.15	60.79	44.51	39.96	22.26
0.22	4.51	5.43	1.56	2.03	2.10	12.10	2.18	0.10
0.21	0.02	1.28	2.51	1.15	0.16	0.53	7.37	0.12
			0.50			0.80		
439.28	296.60	398.10	762.72	374.77	239.95	218.76	750.83	91.01
114.15	11.28	10.96	8.85	101.14	17.65	17.17	25.55	9.81
426.58	32.66	316.19	27.82	95.75	137.10	35.68	84.45	22.93
547.77	161.01	251.42	236.21	173.11	95.15	189.60	732.66	39.31
443.91	205.76	491.47	612.28	432.57	303.04	128.69	236.42	89.59
372.91	126.22	303.83	396.63	129.99	104.13	43.15	172.74	26.58
276.55	124.45	210.40	56.32	214.79	177.65	118.02	320.41	32.17
342.22	116.11	228.66	395.54	260.90	116.41	157.12	475.93	70.16
		151.84						
			1.88	10.91	0.41			0.12
		1.28	1.19	1.17	0.84		2.63	0.10
3.76	0.46	3.06	33.30	8.44	1.47		0.50	5.61
		2.42		0.04				
		0.26						0.03
19.89	19.77	39.56	68.12	4.24	7.88	12.35	31.39	3.45
164.94	7.34	6.30	14.44	8.08	4.94	13.91	41.40	1.34
8.75	0.32	9.17	6.41	9.65	5.14	2.41	5.24	1.38
	0.56	14.64						
28.99	2.18	3.00	7.78	10.84	5.77	1.27	99.13	1.34
28.15	7.28	0.94	8.66	6.21	3.44	10.35	154.24	5.08
17.34	4.79	8.24	27.48	20.01	26.25	11.22	91.24	3.45
9.10	9.36	18.35	35.59	18.79	1.69	0.06	5.00	1.96
17.11	3.68	32.68	7.82	17.45	2.06	0.40	8.20	0.72
42.73	3.32	32.76	2.92	11.09	4.66	4.56	13.36	2.65
23.17	2.04	6.12	0.40	7.98	3.75	12.81	21.03	0.02
9.47	1.28	0.94	16.90	13.48	8.98	3.26	33.87	1.10
1.57		139.78	389.50	0.43				
38.18	1.72	11.77	52.94	39.00	25.57	7.02	18.35	8.95
8.58	3.48	6.81	12.60	7.86	2.99	2.70	76.31	5.04
4.96				1.54			3.45	
29.32	12.43	9.23	17.37	22.32	11.52	6.01	68.73	1.11
47.36	20.17	23.20	63.71	93.45	106.10	114.49	31.99	41.94
3.77	22.00	74.10	10.73	2.93	5.58	0.54	51.99	
9.86	13.96	1.56	0.39	19.34	44.62	3.30	1.38	2.80
105.36	99.05	15.51	10.01	93.34	5.11	21.14	72.80	8.32
29.27	5.21	3.01	3.73	13.19	10.38	3.45	3.21	1.92
23.36	3.10	9.41	4.95	12.45	1.95	0.69	11.16	2.12
30.81	0.97	3.13		26.16	11.26		2.11	2.83
44.49		0.16	0.04	0.10	3.16		2.96	0.13
97.67	4.93	72.24	5.37	11.56	7.84	3.33	38.71	4.06
66.21	1.59	0.38	8.51	34.83	22.11	21.56	19.78	5.22
0.30	1.12			2.29	0.63	0.70	4.35	0.21
1.95	1.13			0.69	0.32	0.47	2.16	0.03
0.47	6.56	5.92	0.19	28.69	12.10	0.82	10.69	0.66
0.17		0.31		0.93			2.31	
65.37	100.76	28.76	31.54	36.21	45.25	42.34	37.08	14.15
3.78	2.96	3.08	0.52	4.56	1.03	15.45	0.14	0.50
5.48	3.25	2.99	3.51	5.45	3.37	1.69	2.19	0.55

12-14 规模以上工业企业主要经济指标
Main Indicators of Industrial Enterprises above Designated Size

年份 Year	全部就业人员平均人数（万人） Annual Average Number of Employed Persons (10000 persons)	总产值（亿元） Gross Output Value of Industry (100 million yuan)	固定资产原价（亿元） Original Value of Fixed Assets (100 million yuan)	主营业务收入（亿元） Principal Business Revenue (100 million yuan)	利税总额（亿元） Total Pre-tax Profits (100 million yuan)	百元固定资产实现利税（元） Pre-tax Profits per 100 yuan of Original Value of Fixed Assets (yuan)	总资产贡献率 Ratio of Total Assets to Industrial Output Value	产值利税率（%） Ratio of Pre-tax Profits to Gross Output Value (%)	百元主营业务收入实现利税（元） Pre-tax Profits per 100 yuan of Main Business Revenue (yuan)	全员劳动生产率（元/人） Overall Labor Productivity (yuan/person)
1978	170.51	168.91	111.42		32.91	29.54		19.48		9906
1979	171.76	181.96	129.09	170.09	34.48	26.71		18.45	20.27	10594
1980	182.39	198.83	136.59	189.97	38.51	28.19		19.37	20.27	10902
1981	189.08	226.26	152.58	215.09	42.12	27.60		18.61	19.58	11966
1982	194.33	245.54	172.00	231.20	44.62	25.94		18.17	19.30	12635
1983	197.50	275.25	226.58	226.91	48.59	21.45		17.65	21.42	13937
1984	241.42	336.45	221.46	313.33	56.83	25.66		16.89	18.14	13937
1985	298.66	438.91	269.13	412.77	75.99	29.23		17.31	18.41	14696
1986	323.16	522.35	335.19	498.80	80.90	24.14		15.49	16.22	16164
1987	353.95	711.04	433.95	692.47	102.24	23.56		14.38	14.76	20089
1988	382.19	1056.47	540.37	1016.20	140.65	26.03		13.31	13.84	27643
1989	387.90	1321.33	700.66	1222.20	138.71	19.80		10.50	11.35	34064
1990	390.28	1379.98	843.88	1287.91	121.50	14.40		8.80	9.43	35359
1991	433.18	2018.62	1339.04	1875.02	188.08	14.05		9.32	10.03	46600
1992	450.99	2696.47	1485.36	2537.84	248.78	22.32		9.23	9.80	59790
1993	478.39	4085.35	2099.09	3920.98	397.40	18.93		9.73	10.14	85379
1994	537.57	5325.35	3309.63	4826.68	478.41	14.46		8.89	9.91	99063
1995	537.83	6325.19	4298.15	6195.84	445.53	10.37		7.04	7.19	117606
1996	529.13	7308.51	5066.23	6808.08	489.26	9.66		6.69	7.19	36094
1997	522.94	8201.71	5904.95	7767.79	617.90	10.46	7.54	7.53	7.95	40040
1998	548.59	9738.56	6968.36	9243.42	622.82	8.94	7.37	6.40	6.74	44553
1999	537.77	10538.17	7399.10	10208.99	778.94	10.53	7.62	7.39	7.63	50307
2000	572.89	12480.93	8005.77	12380.65	1042.77	13.03	8.86	8.35	8.42	58836
2001	578.94	14035.35	8655.82	13891.46	1139.98	13.17	8.70	8.12	8.21	67012
2002	644.39	16378.60	9550.47	16247.73	1380.24	14.45	9.17	8.43	8.50	58940
2003	741.17	21513.46	10768.77	21566.93	1850.90	17.19	10.42	8.60	8.56	77150
2004	996.44	29554.92	12713.34	28998.45	2329.79	18.33	10.52	7.90	8.03	74661
2005	1085.65	35942.74	14453.16	34781.58	2877.81	19.91	11.29	8.01	8.27	86735
2006	1203.58	44674.75	17824.33	43550.87	3907.10	21.92	12.24	8.75	8.97	97882
2007	1307.40	55252.86	19763.42	53927.94	5105.93	25.83	13.59	9.24	9.46	107880
2008	1493.38	65424.61	24529.17	63371.65	6136.69	25.02	14.32	9.38	9.68	117940
2009	1436.02	68275.77	26293.23	66117.81	6793.59	25.84	14.18	9.95	10.27	126984
2010	1568.00	85824.64	33489.49	84114.85	9418.42	28.12	15.63	10.97	11.20	129709
2011	1463.86	94871.68	33244.26	92996.88	9608.33	28.9	14.98	10.13	10.33	147987
2012	1452.16	95602.09	35983.70	93821.74	9383.63	26.08	13.94	9.82	10.00	156463
2013	1455.81	109673.07	39339.68	106361.21	11008.36	27.98	14.53	10.04	10.35	182303
2014	1455.78	119713.04	43635.95	115451.13	11663.66	26.73	13.97	9.74	10.10	193633
2015	1439.33	124649.16	48104.10	119157.86	12375.00	25.73	13.58	9.93	10.39	204582
2016	1417.84	133768.04	52729.34	129151.31	13150.85	24.94	12.98	9.83	10.18	220972
2017	1403.19	135722.42	52619.74	133924.37	13769.27	26.17	12.45	10.15	10.28	223415

注：1．利税总额包括增值税。
2．全员劳动生产率1996年后按工业增加值计算。
3．1997年以前为独立核算工业企业，1998年起统计口径改为年主营业务收入500万元及以上的规模以上工业，2011年调整为年主营业务收入2000万元及以上工业企业。

Note:a) Total pre-tax profits include value-added tax.
b) Since 1996, figures of overall labor productivity have been calculated by value-added of industry.
c) From 1998 to 2010, data are statistics of industrial enterprises above designated size with annual principal business revenue of over 5 million yuan, while data prior to 1997 are statistics of industrial enterprises with independent accounting systems. Since 2011, data are statistics of legal person industrial enterprises with annual principal business revenue of over 20 million yuan.

12-15 规模以上国有控股工业企业主要经济指标

Main Indicators of State-owned and State-holding Industrial Enterprises above Designated Size

年份 Year	全部就业人员平均人数(万人) Annual Average Number of Employed Persons (10000 persons)	总产值(亿元) Gross Output Value of Industry (100 million yuan)	固定资产原价(亿元) Original Value of Fixed Assets (100 million yuan)	主营业务收入(亿元) Principal Business Revenue (100 million yuan)	利税总额(亿元) Total Pre-tax Profits (100 million yuan)	百元固定资产实现利税(元) Pre-tax Profits per 100 yuan of Original Value of Fixed Assets (yuan)	总资产贡献率 Ratio of Total Assets to Industrial Output Value	产值利税率(%) Ratio of Pre-tax Profits to Gross Output Value (%)	百元主营业务收入实现利税(元) Pre-tax Profits per 100 yuan of Main Business Revenue (yuan)	全员劳动生产率(元/人) Overall Labor Productivity (yuan/person)
1978	120.35	122.28	96.06		26.09	27.16		21.34		10159
1979	121.97	132.30	103.51	126.87	26.89	25.96		20.31	21.18	10847
1980	126.09	136.30	107.27	127.97	28.33	25.90		20.57	22.19	10829
1981	132.60	153.54	118.82	147.85	31.18	26.24		20.31	21.09	11579
1982	139.90	165.82	131.82	158.43	33.29	25.26		20.08	21.01	11853
1983	142.18	188.09	147.53	178.04	38.18	25.88		20.30	21.45	13228
1984	143.08	222.35	162.13	205.73	44.02	27.15		19.80	21.39	15540
1985	144.14	277.87	203.80	265.05	56.34	27.64		20.28	21.26	19278
1986	150.14	312.74	235.47	305.42	59.70	25.36		19.09	19.55	20829
1987	156.48	400.55	294.46	402.63	72.44	24.60		18.09	17.99	25598
1988	162.43	555.41	328.58	545.00	91.05	27.71		16.39	16.71	34194
1989	162.85	670.95	404.50	631.61	94.11	23.26		14.93	14.90	41200
1990	163.80	713.88	488.36	689.83	84.35	17.27		11.82	12.23	43582
1991	173.85	906.72	612.24	853.62	116.26	18.99		12.82	13.62	52155
1992	171.60	1118.86	751.42	1073.94	131.24	17.47		11.73	12.22	65202
1993	153.26	1371.58	856.85	1372.66	169.40	19.77		12.35	12.34	89494
1994	152.25	1498.80	1076.47	1400.87	176.81	16.42		11.80	12.62	98443
1995	142.83	1396.35	1315.16	1499.25	160.57	12.21		11.50	10.71	97763
1996	137.50	1476.12	1599.77	1555.28	139.01	8.69		9.42	8.94	34057
1997	124.71	1505.06	1794.89	1657.79	160.92	8.97		10.69	9.71	36596
1998	102.67	1453.79	1790.91	1616.64	163.10	9.11		11.22	10.09	47019
1999	128.16	3025.68	3520.17	3153.04	376.11	10.68	8.63	12.34	11.93	72606
2000	104.39	3126.12	3513.50	3583.55	433.35	12.33	9.09	13.86	12.09	91413
2001	91.77	3236.65	3982.54	3757.95	486.46	12.21	9.53	15.03	12.94	112515
2002	83.25	3264.46	3942.57	3800.38	483.25	12.26	9.34	14.80	12.72	132894
2003	75.20	3949.03	4603.66	4717.48	623.49	13.54	10.88	15.79	13.22	191590
2004	72.53	6039.24	4913.92	6031.47	779.41	15.86	12.39	12.91	12.92	213941
2005	69.42	6375.54	5153.83	6261.70	800.26	15.53	13.03	12.55	12.78	243447
2006	60.80	7253.17	6557.86	6887.69	1213.73	18.50	14.89	16.73	17.62	391250
2007	60.86	8603.94	6702.65	8258.85	1603.72	23.92	17.68	18.63	19.41	464322
2008	77.84	11144.50	8327.10	11045.88	1676.74	20.14	15.49	15.05	15.18	430063
2009	75.33	10790.11	9249.22	10637.39	1747.60	18.89	14.73	16.20	16.43	457743
2010	78.89	13166.37	10456.03	13418.41	2398.44	22.94	17.21	18.22	17.87	518203
2011	82.98	13927.70	10891.43	13871.28	1963.69	18.03	13.54	14.10	14.16	441471
2012	82.87	15529.16	12395.46	15602.52	2172.26	17.52	14.03	13.99	13.92	515822
2013	81.67	17525.16	13124.26	17095.26	2800.64	21.34	16.57	15.98	16.38	625429
2014	79.95	18225.94	14561.95	17804.39	2810.73	19.30	15.61	15.42	15.79	645329
2015	83.23	17032.30	15949.18	16453.02	2660.82	16.68	13.53	15.62	16.17	606956
2016	82.67	17172.18	17041.31	16266.66	2889.08	16.95	13.36	16.82	17.76	626612
2017	78.17	19525.92	17858.14	19783.07	3144.43	17.61	13.04	16.10	15.89	699173

注：1998年以前为国有工业，1999年起为国有及国有控股工业，2007年起改为国有控股工业。

Note: Data prior to 1998 are statistics of state-owned industrial enterprises,data since 1999 are statistics of state-owned and state-holding industrial enterprises, and data since 2007 are statistics of state-holding industrial enterprises.

12-16 规模以上工业企业主要经济指标（2017年）

单位：亿元

项 目	Item	企业单位数（个） Number of Enterprises (unit)	工业总产值（当年价） Gross Industrial Output Value (at current prices)
全省总计	**Provincial Total**	**47224**	**135722.42**
按经济类型分	Grouped by Ownership		
在总计中：国有控股工业	Of the Total: State-holding Industry	1079	19525.92
国有工业	State-owned Industry	140	802.95
集体工业	Collective-owned Industry	160	257.22
股份合作工业	Share-holding Cooperative Industry	42	72.34
股份制工业	Share-holding Industry	32350	80561.92
外商投资工业	Foreign-funded Industry	4089	24161.44
港澳台投资工业	Industry with Funds from Hong Kong, Macao and Taiwan	8585	27503.65
按轻重工业分	Grouped by Light and Heavy Industries		
轻工业	Light Industry	23255	47827.76
重工业	Heavy Industry	23969	87894.65
按企业规模分	Grouped by Size of Enterprises		
大型企业	Large Enterprises	1618	63688.06
中型企业	Medium Enterprises	8504	32263.16
小微型企业	Small and Mciro Enterprises	37102	39771.19
按行业分	Grouped by Sector		
煤炭开采和洗选业	Mining and Washing of Coal		
石油和天然气开采业	Extraction of Petroleum and Natural Gas	4	532.01
黑色金属矿采选业	Mining and Dressing of Ferrous Metal Ores	28	65.63
有色金属矿采选业	Mining and Dressing of Nonferrous Metal Ores	27	70.75
非金属矿采选业	Mining and Dressing of Nonmetal Ores	264	279.08
开采辅助活动	Auxiliary Minning Operations	4	16.62
其他采矿业	Mining and Dressing of Other Ores	2	3.86
农副食品加工业	Processing of Farm and Sideline Food	1022	3114.52
食品制造业	Manufacture of Food	765	1860.36
酒、饮料和精制茶制造业	Manufacture of Wine, Beverage and Refined Tea	264	1085.99
烟草制品业	Tobacco Products	11	438.73
纺织业	Textile Industry	1464	2486.46
纺织服装、服饰业	Manufacture of Textile Garments, Footwear and Headgear	2784	3843.72
皮革、毛皮、羽毛及其制品和制鞋业	Leather, Fur, Feather, Down and Related Products	1868	2246.47
木材加工和木、竹、藤、棕、草制品业	Timber Processing, Bamboo, Cane, Palm Fiber & Straw Products	573	738.16
家具制造业	Manufacture of Furniture	1438	2172.69
造纸和纸制品业	Papermaking and Paper Products	1150	2522.10
印刷和记录媒介复制业	Printing and Record Medium Reproduction	956	1296.52
文教、工美、体育和娱乐用品制造业	Manufacture of Cultural, Educational,Sports and Entertainment Articles	1708	3816.15
石油加工、炼焦和核燃料加工业	Petroleum Refining, Coking and Nuclear Fuel Processing	91	2553.92
化学原料和化学制品制造业	Manufacture of Raw Chemical Materials and Chemical Products	2347	5594.37
医药制造业	Manufacture of Medicines	453	1537.08
化学纤维制造业	Manufacture of Chemical Fibers	61	171.70
橡胶和塑料制品业	Rubber and Plastic Products	3811	5221.83
非金属矿物制品业	Nonmetal Mineral Products	3119	5049.66
黑色金属冶炼和压延加工业	Smelting and Pressing of Ferrous Metals	420	2562.42
有色金属冶炼和压延加工业	Smelting and Pressing of Nonferrous Metals	682	3259.21
金属制品业	Metal Products	3814	6204.02
通用设备制造业	Manufacture of General-purpose Machinery	2028	4150.17
专用设备制造业	Manufacture of Special-purpose Machinery	1969	3395.32
汽车制造业	Manufacture of Automobile	833	7853.18
铁路、船舶、航空航天和其他运输设备制造业	Manufacture of Railway ,Ship,Aeronautics and Other Transport equipment	388	1187.96
电气机械和器材制造业	Manufacture of Electrical Machinery and Equipment	5006	12931.73
计算机、通信和其他电子设备制造业	Manufacture of Communication Equipment, Computers and Other Electronic Equipment	5808	37301.89
仪器仪表制造业	Manufacture of Instruments and Meters	672	1124.19
其他制造业	Other Manufactures	297	250.72
废弃资源综合利用业	Comprehensive Utilization of Waste	262	998.23
金属制品、机械和设备修理业	Manufacture of Metal Products,Machinery and Equipment Maintenance	52	177.55
电力、热力生产和供应业	Production and Supply of Electric Power and Heat Power	346	6369.97
燃气生产和供应业	Production and Supply of Gas	147	768.72
水的生产和供应业	Production and Supply of Water	286	468.76

Main Economic Indicators of Industrial Enterprises above Designated Size (2017)

(100 million yuan)

工业增加值 Value-added of Industry	年末资产总计 Total Assets at the Year-end	流动资产合计 Total Working Capital	固定资产合计 Toatal Fixed Assets	主营业务收入 Principal Business Revenue	主营业务成本 Cost of Principal Business	主营业务税金及附加 Tax and Extra Charges on Main Business	利润总额 Total Profits	利税总额 Total Pre-tax Profits	本年应交增值税 Value-added Tax Payable in Current Year	全部就业人员年平均人数(万人) Annual Average Number of Employed Persons (10000 persons)
31349.47	**115201.19**	**68749.03**	**26540.42**	**133924.37**	**112207.05**	**1416.39**	**8864.36**	**13769.27**	**3472.77**	**1403.19**
5465.15	25293.23	9897.36	9314.96	19783.07	16290.39	802.19	1597.99	3144.43	738.97	78.17
203.07	688.62	287.65	253.13	799.20	647.07	30.40	74.04	128.17	23.67	5.28
65.92	127.14	61.26	37.12	254.05	219.77	1.50	12.77	18.65	4.37	6.02
13.10	23.11	15.09	5.48	70.27	59.47	0.50	2.95	5.21	1.76	0.55
18900.25	72486.09	41365.93	16973.08	79919.32	66244.94	945.68	5167.42	8425.06	2301.55	723.74
5213.47	17594.47	11508.63	4145.62	23832.86	20376.08	184.78	1715.66	2431.27	528.52	219.23
6459.57	23552.09	15182.10	4822.15	26746.89	22656.10	235.85	1752.15	2553.10	562.25	423.85
11305.75	37991.23	24704.30	7261.32	47497.26	39134.68	480.28	3297.03	5030.26	1247.79	655.59
20043.72	77209.96	44044.73	19279.09	86427.11	73072.36	936.11	5567.33	8739.01	2224.98	747.60
15716.24	58666.07	34730.92	12594.48	63099.13	51810.46	856.13	4735.31	7456.35	1856.87	511.52
7458.51	27610.77	15985.74	6966.65	31435.01	26257.65	335.17	2110.04	3214.80	765.66	474.42
8174.72	28924.35	18032.38	6979.29	39390.23	34138.94	225.09	2019.01	3098.12	850.24	417.25
427.92	999.37	84.44	457.63	487.12	255.10	27.34	188.92	268.61	52.34	0.59
22.45	102.39	53.47	27.65	63.00	49.08	1.17	3.08	7.59	3.33	0.35
36.24	89.98	32.61	32.15	74.56	51.43	2.43	15.15	22.21	4.62	0.81
75.07	162.41	59.19	71.21	268.07	209.97	4.76	29.83	44.79	10.14	2.24
4.05	58.89	14.45	42.22	16.62	14.76	0.04	1.30	1.52	0.18	0.15
0.29	0.30	0.08	0.21	3.50	3.34	0.01	0.04	0.08	0.03	0.02
395.15	1912.92	1283.87	330.59	3251.38	2943.45	9.98	160.58	204.93	34.10	16.50
621.28	1344.94	786.36	317.58	1808.92	1195.80	15.82	231.01	343.93	96.96	17.60
299.55	901.21	508.33	282.85	1034.38	731.44	22.63	86.96	157.71	48.07	7.83
331.67	546.66	411.26	62.30	417.17	133.69	207.80	44.85	304.74	51.93	0.75
533.12	1402.58	805.90	407.51	2409.14	2105.17	12.27	132.08	194.68	50.18	32.74
960.95	1987.23	1290.24	480.49	3719.57	3161.69	21.67	180.32	287.47	85.18	82.93
605.67	1033.95	709.25	208.45	2220.67	1961.64	11.22	84.14	139.32	43.76	56.29
177.59	462.71	267.69	143.24	708.04	599.91	6.17	54.58	80.89	20.04	8.22
525.68	1411.92	917.07	247.97	2105.90	1782.11	11.14	128.82	196.81	56.57	35.82
497.37	2176.59	1167.09	766.42	2448.26	2119.67	10.82	155.08	234.94	68.44	21.64
343.86	1064.47	631.41	254.66	1256.60	1053.87	6.96	85.91	125.80	32.72	22.91
743.67	2449.19	1360.04	346.55	3810.17	3381.64	14.02	170.10	227.66	42.95	72.91
1014.57	1460.63	709.18	548.99	2556.87	1828.49	404.22	249.45	799.07	144.94	2.43
1193.69	4744.30	2559.56	1132.15	5592.30	4461.53	34.64	429.96	626.57	161.36	33.07
502.55	2969.57	1917.38	380.52	1449.19	862.99	12.88	296.83	388.16	78.21	13.20
37.97	193.74	92.99	49.22	168.47	142.95	0.70	14.11	18.03	3.22	1.50
1186.54	3624.25	2181.74	953.55	5087.58	4352.30	27.80	267.52	403.42	107.62	85.54
1194.91	4112.20	2196.82	1277.84	4870.35	4138.54	32.78	333.70	508.20	141.17	58.67
401.79	1855.73	591.05	903.42	2524.06	2279.38	9.17	134.04	194.79	51.55	9.16
364.88	1756.94	1129.32	394.97	3290.15	3035.52	8.41	129.51	180.58	42.53	14.90
1374.31	3781.83	2216.97	1086.98	5985.12	5208.60	30.88	332.95	504.53	140.09	83.89
900.49	3778.67	2615.14	568.20	4053.65	3384.75	19.19	282.55	394.20	91.94	49.81
914.97	3549.57	2313.98	564.04	3251.39	2513.41	20.33	296.56	401.82	84.34	47.45
1776.09	5696.38	3816.35	1163.60	7741.97	6496.90	149.26	654.40	1034.62	229.73	42.00
229.72	1278.75	873.88	237.45	1141.17	943.38	6.49	65.79	89.55	17.20	11.88
2969.33	12906.04	9054.22	1670.18	13231.14	10921.99	68.48	933.39	1350.11	347.12	168.22
8122.15	29468.02	21443.18	3812.28	36737.28	31022.01	145.30	1874.52	2831.54	808.94	341.58
306.45	1230.16	878.06	145.68	1105.46	868.96	6.30	89.30	122.99	27.33	22.70
55.68	178.82	124.94	34.95	246.44	209.84	1.37	9.60	15.44	4.45	5.54
184.96	437.95	243.27	142.81	1001.62	876.72	4.63	78.54	101.20	18.02	3.80
52.34	203.54	138.37	47.97	176.92	150.27	1.09	10.49	15.67	3.98	2.06
1568.61	11039.96	1805.82	5832.10	6326.35	5718.31	40.29	471.32	748.17	234.02	18.00
182.05	898.89	303.23	379.36	823.29	729.82	2.30	70.15	87.90	15.22	1.96
213.81	1927.55	460.85	734.47	460.53	306.63	3.63	86.94	109.04	18.24	5.54

12-17 规模以上国有控股工业企业主要经济指标（2017年）

单位：亿元

项　　目	Item	企业单位数（个）Number of Enterprises (unit)	工业总产值（当年价）Gross Industrial Output Value (at current prices)
全省总计	**Provincial Total**	**1079**	**19525.92**
按轻重工业分	Grouped by Light and Heavy Industries		
轻工业	Light Industry	359	2623.64
重工业	Heavy Industry	720	16902.28
按企业规模分	Grouped by Size of Enterprises		
大型企业	Large Enterprises	143	14859.35
中型企业	Medium Enterprises	274	2396.48
小微型企业	Small and Mciro Enterprises	662	2270.09
按行业分	Grouped by Sector		
煤炭开采和洗选业	Mining and Washing of Coal		
石油和天然气开采业	Extraction of Petroleum and Natural Gas	2	111.45
黑色金属矿采选业	Mining and Dressing of Ferrous Metal Ores	1	1.89
有色金属矿采选业	Mining and Dressing of Nonferrous Metal Ores	7	44.06
非金属矿采选业	Mining and Dressing of Nonmetal Ores	10	9.72
开采辅助活动	Auxiliary Minning Operations	2	14.40
其他采矿业	Mining and Dressing of Other Ores		
农副食品加工业	Processing of Farm and Sideline Food	55	255.82
食品制造业	Manufacture of Food	19	56.93
酒、饮料和精制茶制造业	Manufacture of Wine, Beverage and Refined Tea	20	115.15
烟草制品业	Tobacco Products	7	426.09
纺织业	Textile Industry	11	20.80
纺织服装、服饰业	Manufacture of Textile Garments, Footwear and Headgear	5	5.92
皮革、毛皮、羽毛及其制品和制鞋业	Leather, Fur, Feather, Down and Related Products	5	4.00
木材加工和木、竹、藤、棕、草制品业	Timber Processing, Bamboo, Cane, Palm Fiber & Straw Products	7	10.17
家具制造业	Manufacture of Furniture	2	3.67
造纸和纸制品业	Papermaking and Paper Products	9	81.25
印刷和记录媒介复制业	Printing and Record Medium Reproduction	22	26.30
文教、工美、体育和娱乐用品制造业	Manufacture of Cultural, Educational,Sports and Entertainment Articles	13	23.54
石油加工、炼焦和核燃料加工业	Petroleum Refining, Coking and Nuclear Fuel Processing	9	2138.49
化学原料和化学制品制造业	Manufacture of Raw Chemical Materials and Chemical Products	45	475.57
医药制造业	Manufacture of Medicines	39	240.37
化学纤维制造业	Manufacture of Chemical Fibers	1	15.88
橡胶和塑料制品业	Rubber and Plastic Products	28	89.65
非金属矿物制品业	Nonmetal Mineral Products	50	157.78
黑色金属冶炼和压延加工业	Smelting and Pressing of Ferrous Metals	21	1122.52
有色金属冶炼和压延加工业	Smelting and Pressing of Nonferrous Metals	19	627.99
金属制品业	Metal Products	38	134.62
通用设备制造业	Manufacture of General-purpose Machinery	30	150.21
专用设备制造业	Manufacture of Special-purpose Machinery	20	70.39
汽车制造业	Manufacture of Automobile	28	2432.90
铁路、船舶、航空航天和其他运输设备制造业	Manufacture of Railway ,Ship,Aeronautics and Other Transport equipment	28	265.11
电气机械和器材制造业	Manufacture of Electrical Machinery and Equipment	55	834.92
计算机、通信和其他电子设备制造业	Manufacture of Communication Equipment, Computers and Other Electronic Equipment	96	2764.76
仪器仪表制造业	Manufacture of Instruments and Meters	8	17.46
其他制造业	Other Manufactures	3	3.55
废弃资源综合利用业	Comprehensive Utilization of Waste	6	14.48
金属制品、机械和设备修理业	Manufacture of Metal Products,Machinery and Equipment Maintenance	16	71.51
电力、热力生产和供应业	Production and Supply of Electric Power and Heat Power	186	5938.85
燃气生产和供应业	Production and Supply of Gas	33	489.24
水的生产和供应业	Production and Supply of Water	123	258.52

Main Economic Indicators of State-holding Industrial Enterprises above Designated Size (2017)

(100 million yuan)

工业增加值 Value-added of Industry	年末资产总计 Total Assets at the Year-end	流动资产合计 Total Working Capital	固定资产合计 Total Fixed Assets	主营业务收入 Principal Business Revenue	主营业务成本 Cost of Principal Business	主营业务税金及附加 Tax and Other Charges on Principal Business	利润总额 Total Profits	利税总额 Total Pre-tax Profits	本年应交增值税 Value-added Tax Payable in Current Year	全部就业人员年平均人数(万人) Annual Average Number of Employed Persons (10000 persons)
5465.15	**25293.23**	**9897.36**	**9314.96**	**19783.07**	**16290.39**	**802.19**	**1597.99**	**3144.43**	**738.97**	**78.17**
1004.83	5177.09	3458.00	753.42	3551.87	2574.93	231.05	396.82	784.09	155.54	19.56
4460.32	20116.14	6439.37	8561.54	16231.19	13715.47	571.15	1201.17	2360.34	583.43	58.61
4164.15	18431.23	7197.58	6342.72	14997.25	12373.69	603.78	1202.89	2377.54	566.84	55.40
741.41	3731.56	1528.64	1470.80	2424.61	1914.17	168.25	185.88	458.76	103.81	15.00
559.59	3130.44	1171.15	1501.43	2361.20	2002.53	30.16	209.22	308.12	68.31	7.76
59.08	291.22	53.93	226.73	58.84	34.33	3.09	19.88	28.61	5.64	0.04
0.75	1.95	0.96	0.99	1.68	1.27	0.01	0.24	0.31	0.06	0.01
27.30	63.70	16.65	24.87	48.47	29.57	2.14	13.09	19.13	3.90	0.58
3.29	10.30	5.32	1.36	9.16	7.09	0.12	2.01	2.41	0.28	0.09
3.55	55.42	12.42	41.05	14.40	13.04	0.04	0.90	1.08	0.14	0.12
23.80	114.41	82.01	20.22	292.59	276.46	0.47	4.20	7.50	2.82	1.08
17.85	61.35	29.94	14.06	54.01	36.85	0.52	5.11	8.78	3.14	0.89
30.91	114.21	64.64	39.49	96.11	72.60	4.71	6.54	14.77	3.50	0.73
328.56	523.92	401.43	54.80	404.55	123.87	207.68	43.75	302.93	51.34	0.66
4.63	12.16	6.38	3.07	20.48	17.54	0.14	1.88	2.68	0.65	0.32
1.18	3.74	2.11	0.43	6.00	5.17	0.05		0.20	0.15	0.09
1.61	2.58	1.08	1.46	3.94	3.15	0.07	0.08	0.33	0.18	0.13
2.94	6.72	2.52	3.79	10.11	8.13	0.11	1.35	1.82	0.36	0.18
0.94	1.94	0.55	1.18	3.63	2.76	0.09	0.58	0.80	0.13	0.06
14.77	206.15	109.20	81.95	84.98	73.69	0.53	6.09	9.22	2.58	0.50
6.15	39.62	29.62	7.84	28.35	24.16	0.17	-1.94	-0.26	1.50	0.53
7.05	30.70	19.90	4.63	22.19	17.67	0.17	1.92	2.85	0.75	0.39
826.71	1100.50	524.85	446.16	2120.24	1468.08	392.85	212.19	741.84	136.35	1.58
125.16	652.92	190.01	231.56	474.42	383.38	4.21	68.45	86.37	13.61	1.18
91.74	577.60	347.07	48.15	235.51	127.04	2.66	45.10	65.63	17.69	2.65
5.05	22.89	10.69	9.59	14.46	9.70		4.80	4.80		0.04
19.77	185.19	80.16	75.74	98.39	82.95	0.55	2.29	4.95	1.99	1.40
44.19	214.39	98.57	61.43	158.43	123.61	1.24	19.17	27.33	6.91	1.12
178.87	1097.10	277.38	682.46	1109.76	990.79	3.37	65.92	92.92	23.63	2.01
48.91	323.44	200.10	82.70	628.19	595.71	0.90	20.13	24.21	3.18	1.06
28.10	232.39	125.20	57.43	136.24	115.88	0.96	7.22	8.56	0.32	1.33
31.62	340.31	222.60	36.47	162.81	135.14	0.87	14.20	19.10	4.01	1.65
18.78	160.17	74.44	47.56	63.94	59.80	0.37	-2.90	-1.71	0.69	1.12
512.23	1235.44	781.77	270.58	2406.54	1992.14	106.31	209.65	402.21	85.51	4.48
38.84	479.81	299.43	124.78	255.94	237.78	1.23	-8.98	-6.06	1.68	2.25
287.26	2354.13	1929.07	90.95	1685.08	1310.05	9.60	166.98	229.25	52.59	7.08
937.35	2884.22	1976.94	354.96	2263.53	1769.82	15.63	161.57	245.52	68.16	20.32
5.87	18.15	16.15	1.04	17.78	12.53	0.13	1.99	2.94	0.82	0.19
1.04	2.90	2.07	0.81	3.52	2.64	0.02	0.28	0.37	0.07	0.10
3.99	22.87	7.77	11.70	14.49	11.98	0.06	1.50	1.84	0.28	0.07
30.76	117.76	66.75	40.02	71.35	60.02	0.68	1.58	5.24	2.89	1.23
1444.05	9763.98	1394.67	5226.77	5908.39	5390.63	36.74	418.83	676.97	218.92	16.12
117.65	626.24	169.55	279.12	541.56	486.41	1.42	44.35	56.99	11.00	0.98
132.87	1340.78	263.44	607.05	253.02	176.96	2.29	37.96	52.02	11.56	3.80

12−18 规模以上集体工业企业主要经济指标（2017年）

单位：亿元

项 目	Item	企业单位数（个）Number of Enterprises (unit)	工业总产值（当年价）Gross Industrial Output Value (at current prices)
全省总计	**Provincial Total**	**160**	**257.22**
按轻重工业分	Grouped by Light and Heavy Industries		
轻工业	Light Industry	114	203.69
重工业	Heavy Industry	46	53.53
按企业规模分	Grouped by Size of Enterprises		
大型企业	Large Enterprises	5	62.21
中型企业	Medium Enterprises	24	50.67
小微型企业	Small and Mciro Enterprises	131	144.33
按行业分	Grouped by Sector		
煤炭开采和洗选业	Mining and Washing of Coal		
石油和天然气开采业	Extraction of Petroleum and Natural Gas		
黑色金属矿采选业	Mining and Dressing of Ferrous Metal Ores		
有色金属矿采选业	Mining and Dressing of Nonferrous Metal Ores		
非金属矿采选业	Mining and Dressing of Nonmetal Ores	3	3.21
开采辅助活动	Auxiliary Minning Operations		
其他采矿业	Mining and Dressing of Other Ores		
农副食品加工业	Processing of Farm and Sideline Food	8	28.99
食品制造业	Manufacture of Food	5	6.20
酒、饮料和精制茶制造业	Manufacture of Wine, Beverage and Refined Tea	1	0.29
烟草制品业	Tobacco Products		
纺织业	Textile Industry	6	21.29
纺织服装、服饰业	Manufacture of Textile Garments, Footwear and Headgear	9	50.60
皮革、毛皮、羽毛及其制品和制鞋业	Leather, Fur, Feather, Down and Related Products	9	9.59
木材加工和木、竹、藤、棕、草制品业	Timber Processing, Bamboo, Cane, Palm Fiber & Straw Products	4	10.24
家具制造业	Manufacture of Furniture	2	0.56
造纸和纸制品业	Papermaking and Paper Products	7	11.65
印刷和记录媒介复制业	Printing and Record Medium Reproduction	3	6.76
文教、工美、体育和娱乐用品制造业	Manufacture of Cultural, Educational,Sports and Entertainment Articles	9	17.30
石油加工、炼焦和核燃料加工业	Petroleum Refining, Coking and Nuclear Fuel Processing		
化学原料和化学制品制造业	Manufacture of Raw Chemical Materials and Chemical Products	6	3.93
医药制造业	Manufacture of Medicines		
化学纤维制造业	Manufacture of Chemical Fibers		
橡胶和塑料制品业	Rubber and Plastic Products	3	7.41
非金属矿物制品业	Nonmetal Mineral Products	10	11.14
黑色金属冶炼和压延加工业	Smelting and Pressing of Ferrous Metals		
有色金属冶炼和压延加工业	Smelting and Pressing of Nonferrous Metals	5	5.63
金属制品业	Metal Products	7	10.52
通用设备制造业	Manufacture of General-purpose Machinery	2	5.49
专用设备制造业	Manufacture of Special-purpose Machinery	2	2.67
汽车制造业	Manufacture of Automobile		
铁路、船舶、航空航天和其他运输设备制造业	Manufacture of Railway ,Ship,Aeronautics and Other Transport equipment	1	0.26
电气机械和器材制造业	Manufacture of Electrical Machinery and Equipment	4	4.39
计算机、通信和其他电子设备制造业	Manufacture of Communication Equipment, Computers and Other Electronic Equipment	7	13.10
仪器仪表制造业	Manufacture of Instruments and Meters	1	1.52
其他制造业	Other Manufactures	1	0.36
废弃资源综合利用业	Comprehensive Utilization of Waste		
金属制品、机械和设备修理业	Manufacture of Metal Products,Machinery and Equipment Maintenance		
电力、热力生产和供应业	Production and Supply of Electric Power and Heat Power	7	2.59
燃气生产和供应业	Production and Supply of Gas	1	1.16
水的生产和供应业	Production and Supply of Water	37	20.37

Main Economic Indicators of Collective-owned Industrial Enterprises above Designated Size (2017)

(100 million yuan)

工业增加值 Value-added of Industry	年末资产总计 Total Assets at the Year-end	流动资产合计 Total Working Capital	固定资产合计 Total Fixed Assets	主营业务收入 Principal Business Revenue	主营业务成本 Cost of Principal Business	主营业务税金及附加 Tax and Other Charges on Principal Business	利润总额 Total Profits	利税总额 Total Pre-tax Profits	本年应交增值税 Value-added Tax Payable in Current Year	全部就业人员年平均人数(万人) Annual Average Number of Employed Persons (10000 persons)
65.92	**127.14**	**61.26**	**37.12**	**254.05**	**219.77**	**1.50**	**12.77**	**18.65**	**4.37**	**6.02**
51.51	105.83	51.43	32.15	200.47	174.64	0.98	9.70	13.90	3.21	4.90
14.40	21.31	9.83	4.97	53.58	45.13	0.52	3.07	4.75	1.16	1.13
16.87	14.01	5.15	2.11	61.88	56.46	0.07	1.43	1.67	0.18	2.20
17.09	27.72	4.98	6.19	48.77	41.82	0.27	1.34	2.26	0.64	2.45
31.97	85.41	41.13	28.83	143.40	121.49	1.15	10.01	14.72	3.55	1.37
0.99	1.16	0.20	0.96	3.21	2.40	0.10	0.42	0.64	0.12	0.03
5.72	5.85	1.62	1.81	28.49	24.65	0.09	2.57	3.48	0.82	0.08
1.19	0.68	0.23	0.45	6.10	5.24	0.02	0.28	0.48	0.17	0.07
0.10	0.08	0.02	0.06	0.28	0.26		0.01	0.02	0.01	0.01
4.22	2.19	1.19	0.94	20.98	19.40	0.20	0.59	1.18	0.39	0.23
8.39	10.40	2.15	1.42	50.59	48.06	0.06	1.49	1.57	0.02	0.86
3.18	4.40	3.41	0.69	9.53	8.29	0.03	0.24	0.46	0.19	0.61
2.11	1.93	0.81	1.07	10.26	8.84	0.16	0.93	1.23	0.14	0.04
0.16	0.33	0.07	0.26	0.55	0.47		0.06	0.08	0.02	0.02
1.51	3.61	2.53	0.33	11.76	10.31	0.08	0.54	0.87	0.25	0.10
1.93	1.86	0.49	1.32	6.79	5.09	0.06	1.17	1.56	0.33	0.03
7.63	7.15	4.17	2.68	17.03	13.82	0.06	0.53	0.76	0.17	1.34
0.67	0.93	0.78	0.15	3.76	3.50	0.02	0.03	0.15	0.11	0.05
2.37	1.37	0.90	0.47	6.97	5.89	0.05	0.23	0.42	0.13	0.27
3.06	7.02	3.35	1.46	11.45	9.86	0.09	0.65	1.12	0.38	0.11
0.53	1.48	0.96	0.33	5.36	5.14	0.01	0.11	0.21	0.08	0.05
1.68	1.78	0.93	0.71	10.59	9.47	0.05	0.62	0.89	0.21	0.04
1.09	0.44	0.31	0.05	5.49	4.78	0.04	0.10	0.17	0.02	0.15
0.44	1.11	1.00	0.03	2.63	2.30	0.01	0.16	0.25	0.08	0.03
0.04	0.41	0.38	0.02	0.29	0.24		-0.01	0.01	0.01	0.01
0.74	15.95	7.18	2.24	3.17	2.76	0.03	-0.03	0.01		0.10
8.57	3.47	2.19	0.94	13.10	9.22		0.18	0.19		1.25
0.49	1.16	1.05	0.11	1.52	1.37	0.01	0.02	0.02		0.14
0.07	0.12	0.04	0.08	0.36	0.31	0.01	0.01	0.03	0.01	0.01
0.94	5.32	1.07	1.14	2.33	1.36	0.13	0.42	0.73	0.18	0.06
0.28	0.62	0.25	0.06	1.16	1.00		0.12	0.16	0.04	0.01
7.84	46.32	24.00	17.35	20.28	15.75	0.17	1.31	1.95	0.47	0.36

12-19 规模以上股份合作工业企业主要经济指标（2017年）

单位：亿元

项　　目	Item	企业单位数（个） Number of Enterprises (unit)	工业总产值（当年价） Gross Industrial Output Value (at current prices)
全省总计	**Provincial Total**	**42**	**72.34**
按轻重工业分	Grouped by Light & Heavy Industries		
轻工业	Light Industry	25	38.93
重工业	Heavy Industry	17	33.41
按企业规模分	Grouped by Size of Enterprises		
大型企业	Large Enterprises		
中型企业	Medium Enterprises	4	14.59
小微型企业	Small and Micro Enterprises	38	57.75
按行业分	Grouped by Sector		
煤炭开采和洗选业	Mining and Washing of Coal		
石油和天然气开采业	Extraction of Petroleum and Natural Gas		
黑色金属矿采选业	Mining and Dressing of Ferrous Metal Ores		
有色金属矿采选业	Mining and Dressing of Nonferrous Metal Ores		
非金属矿采选业	Mining and Dressing of Nonmetal Ores		
开采辅助活动	Auxiliary Minning Operations		
其他采矿业	Mining and Dressing of Other Ores		
农副食品加工业	Processing of Farm and Sideline Food		
食品制造业	Manufacture of Food	1	0.31
酒、饮料和精制茶制造业	Manufacture of Wine, Beverage and Refined Tea		
烟草制品业	Tobacco Products		
纺织业	Textile Industry	4	12.27
纺织服装、服饰业	Manufacture of Textile Garments, Footwear and Headgear	3	4.81
皮革、毛皮、羽毛及其制品和制鞋业	Leather, Fur, Feather, Down and Related Products	1	0.66
木材加工和木、竹、藤、棕、草制品业	Timber Processing, Bamboo, Cane, Palm Fiber & Straw Products		
家具制造业	Manufacture of Furniture		
造纸和纸制品业	Papermaking and Paper Products		
印刷和记录媒介复制业	Printing and Record Medium Reproduction	2	1.74
文教、工美、体育和娱乐用品制造业	Manufacture of Cultural, Educational,Sports and Entertainment Articles	1	0.32
石油加工、炼焦和核燃料加工业	Petroleum Refining, Coking and Nuclear Fuel Processing		
化学原料和化学制品制造业	Manufacture of Raw Chemical Materials and Chemical Products	4	9.21
医药制造业	Manufacture of Medicines		
化学纤维制造业	Manufacture of Chemical Fibers		
橡胶和塑料制品业	Rubber and Plastic Products	4	3.45
非金属矿物制品业	Nonmetal Mineral Products	4	5.25
黑色金属冶炼和压延加工业	Smelting and Pressing of Ferrous Metals		
有色金属冶炼和压延加工业	Smelting and Pressing of Nonferrous Metals	1	4.28
金属制品业	Metal Products	3	6.18
通用设备制造业	Manufacture of General-purpose Machinery	1	2.07
专用设备制造业	Manufacture of Special-purpose Machinery	1	1.42
汽车制造业	Manufacture of Automobile		
铁路、船舶、航空航天和其他运输设备制造业	Manufacture of Railway ,Ship,Aeronautics and Other Transport equipment		
电气机械和器材制造业	Manufacture of Electrical Machinery and Equipment	4	8.83
计算机、通信和其他电子设备制造业	Manufacture of Communication Equipment, Computers and Other Electronic Equipment	2	8.90
仪器仪表制造业	Manufacture of Instruments and Meters	2	0.70
其他制造业	Other Manufactures	1	0.21
废弃资源综合利用业	Comprehensive Utilization of Waste		
金属制品、机械和设备修理业	Manufacture of Metal Products,Machinery and Equipment Maintenance		
电力、热力生产和供应业	Production and Supply of Electric Power and Heat Power	1	0.55
燃气生产和供应业	Production and Supply of Gas	2	1.15
水的生产和供应业	Production and Supply of Water		

Main Economic Indicators of Share-holding Cooperative Industrial Enterprises above Designated Size (2017)

(100 million yuan)

工业增加值 Value-added of Industry	年末资产总计 Total Assets at the Year-end	流动资产合计 Total Working Capital	固定资产合计 Total Fixed Assets	主营业务收入 Principal Business Revenue	主营业务成本 Cost of Principal Business	主营业务税金及附加 Tax and Other Charges on Principal Business	利润总额 Total Profits	利税总额 Total Pre-tax Profits	本年应交增值税 Value-added Tax Payable in Current Year	全部就业人员年平均人数(万人) Annual Average Number of Employed Persons (10000 persons)
13.10	**23.11**	**15.09**	**5.48**	**70.27**	**59.47**	**0.50**	**2.95**	**5.21**	**1.76**	**0.55**
6.33	12.25	8.20	2.61	37.99	31.24	0.27	1.21	2.48	0.99	0.38
6.77	10.85	6.89	2.87	32.28	28.22	0.22	1.73	2.73	0.77	0.17
3.63	4.94	3.33	1.41	13.93	10.31	0.15	1.34	1.96	0.47	0.16
9.47	18.16	11.76	4.07	56.34	49.15	0.35	1.61	3.25	1.29	0.40
0.15	0.42	0.28	0.10	0.46	0.34		0.05	0.07	0.02	
1.45	1.99	0.94	1.03	11.88	10.86	0.10	0.41	0.63	0.12	0.09
1.25	1.13	0.71	0.33	4.73	3.76	0.06	0.15	0.37	0.16	0.05
0.17	0.26	0.25	0.01	0.66	0.60		-0.02	-0.02		0.02
0.31	0.49	0.32	0.04	1.61	1.47	0.01	0.04	0.09	0.04	0.01
0.08	0.06	0.02	0.02	0.32	0.22		0.01	0.01		0.03
1.38	7.14	5.48	0.63	9.31	5.67	0.07	0.22	0.79	0.50	0.07
0.62	0.65	0.42	0.17	3.12	2.62	0.02	0.10	0.23	0.11	0.05
1.96	5.67	3.45	1.87	4.78	3.65	0.03	0.77	1.05	0.25	0.08
0.59	0.30	0.25	0.05	4.16	3.23	0.06	0.14	0.28	0.09	0.04
1.27	0.84	0.46	0.29	5.98	5.56	0.02	0.32	0.41	0.07	0.03
0.22	0.15	0.05	0.09	2.16	2.07	0.01	0.07	0.10	0.03	0.01
0.27	0.77	0.11	0.20	1.38	1.13	0.01	0.22	0.29	0.07	0.02
0.63	0.86	0.53	0.22	8.35	7.90	0.08	0.18	0.43	0.17	0.03
2.05	0.95	0.81	0.11	8.65	8.06	0.03	0.09	0.17	0.05	0.02
0.16	0.68	0.64	0.02	0.81	0.68		0.02	0.05	0.03	0.01
0.03	0.52	0.31	0.20	0.20	0.19		-0.01		0.01	
0.24	0.16		0.06	0.55	0.35	0.01	0.18	0.23	0.04	
0.27	0.09	0.06	0.03	1.15	1.11		0.01	0.02		

12-20 规模以上股份制工业企业主要经济指标（2017年）

单位：亿元

项　　目	Item	企业单位数（个）Number of Enterprises (unit)	工业总产值（当年价）Gross Industrial Output Value (at current prices)
全省总计	**Provincial Total**	**32350**	**80561.92**
按轻重工业分	Grouped by Light and Heavy Industries		
轻工业	Light Industry	15604	27762.72
重工业	Heavy Industry	16746	52799.20
按企业规模分	Grouped by Size of Enterprises		
大型企业	Large Enterprises	673	34896.51
中型企业	Medium Enterprises	4521	17834.11
小微型企业	Small and Mciro Enterprises	27156	27831.30
按行业分	Grouped by Sector		
煤炭开采和洗选业	Mining and Washing of Coal		
石油和天然气开采业	Extraction of Petroleum and Natural Gas	1	109.19
黑色金属矿采选业	Mining and Dressing of Ferrous Metal Ores	22	36.61
有色金属矿采选业	Mining and Dressing of Nonferrous Metal Ores	22	63.27
非金属矿采选业	Mining and Dressing of Nonmetal Ores	205	216.26
开采辅助活动	Auxiliary Minning Operations	3	14.66
其他采矿业	Mining and Dressing of Other Ores	2	3.86
农副食品加工业	Processing of Farm and Sideline Food	784	2177.21
食品制造业	Manufacture of Food	536	769.32
酒、饮料和精制茶制造业	Manufacture of Wine, Beverage and Refined Tea	181	375.32
烟草制品业	Tobacco Products	11	438.73
纺织业	Textile Industry	921	1401.08
纺织服装、服饰业	Manufacture of Textile Garments, Footwear and Headgear	1974	2424.41
皮革、毛皮、羽毛及其制品和制鞋业	Leather, Fur, Feather, Down and Related Products	1154	1136.51
木材加工和木、竹、藤、棕、草制品业	Timber Processing, Bamboo, Cane, Palm Fiber & Straw Products	441	535.16
家具制造业	Manufacture of Furniture	1048	1398.04
造纸和纸制品业	Papermaking and Paper Products	767	1322.13
印刷和记录媒介复制业	Printing and Record Medium Reproduction	654	747.87
文教、工美、体育和娱乐用品制造业	Manufacture of Cultural, Educational,Sports and Entertainment Articles	949	1768.20
石油加工、炼焦和核燃料加工业	Petroleum Refining, Coking and Nuclear Fuel Processing	68	2135.63
化学原料和化学制品制造业	Manufacture of Raw Chemical Materials and Chemical Products	1653	2690.12
医药制造业	Manufacture of Medicines	337	991.69
化学纤维制造业	Manufacture of Chemical Fibers	37	79.77
橡胶和塑料制品业	Rubber and Plastic Products	2412	2796.30
非金属矿物制品业	Nonmetal Mineral Products	2411	3629.52
黑色金属冶炼和压延加工业	Smelting and Pressing of Ferrous Metals	306	1725.33
有色金属冶炼和压延加工业	Smelting and Pressing of Nonferrous Metals	484	2411.12
金属制品业	Metal Products	2646	3821.07
通用设备制造业	Manufacture of General-purpose Machinery	1425	2080.91
专用设备制造业	Manufacture of Special-purpose Machinery	1425	2204.42
汽车制造业	Manufacture of Automobile	386	1289.95
铁路、船舶、航空航天和其他运输设备制造业	Manufacture of Railway ,Ship,Aeronautics and Other Transport equipment	258	753.49
电气机械和器材制造业	Manufacture of Electrical Machinery and Equipment	3602	8842.91
计算机、通信和其他电子设备制造业	Manufacture of Communication Equipment, Computers and Other Electronic Equipment	3855	22048.33
仪器仪表制造业	Manufacture of Instruments and Meters	410	571.48
其他制造业	Other Manufactures	174	157.39
废弃资源综合利用业	Comprehensive Utilization of Waste	225	855.65
金属制品、机械和设备修理业	Manufacture of Metal Products,Machinery and Equipment Maintenance	35	51.28
电力、热力生产和供应业	Production and Supply of Electric Power and Heat Power	241	5755.41
燃气生产和供应业	Production and Supply of Gas	90	451.38
水的生产和供应业	Production and Supply of Water	195	280.96

Main Economic Indicators of Share-holding Industrial Enterprises above Designated Size (2017)

(100 million yuan)

工业增加值 Value-added of Industry	年末资产总计 Total Assets at the Year-end	流动资产合计 Total Working Capital	固定资产合计 Total Fixed Assets	主营业务收入 Principal Business Revenue	主营业务成本 Cost of Principal Business	主营业务税金及附加 Tax and Other Charges on Principal Business	利润总额 Total Profits	利税总额 Total Pre-tax Profits	本年应交增值税 Value-added Tax Payable in Current Year	全部就业人员年平均人数(万人) Annual Average Number of Employed Persons (10000 persons)
18900.25	**72486.10**	**41365.93**	**16973.07**	**79919.32**	**66244.94**	**945.68**	**5167.42**	**8425.05**	**2301.54**	**723.74**
6533.06	22750.79	14763.01	4058.56	27845.83	22929.40	361.81	1964.82	3095.59	766.49	328.62
12367.19	49735.31	26602.93	12914.51	52073.48	43315.54	583.88	3202.61	5329.46	1535.05	395.12
9300.83	36505.35	20204.78	8180.80	34996.38	27798.59	625.24	2646.24	4517.00	1240.08	208.13
3897.83	16161.69	8951.82	4023.92	17310.80	14415.44	164.00	1164.19	1776.64	446.17	228.91
5701.60	19819.05	12209.34	4768.35	27612.14	24030.91	156.44	1356.99	2131.41	615.30	286.70
57.46	285.10	50.35	226.73	56.58	32.68	3.08	19.33	27.97	5.56	0.03
13.37	88.83	51.22	16.33	35.20	27.70	0.55	1.23	3.45	1.66	0.28
31.99	78.50	29.04	28.02	67.08	45.91	2.22	14.51	21.01	4.27	0.69
57.99	133.58	48.11	58.27	208.83	163.01	3.62	23.89	35.28	7.72	1.75
3.59	55.77	12.42	41.16	14.66	13.28	0.04	0.91	1.10	0.14	0.13
0.29	0.30	0.08	0.21	3.50	3.34	0.01	0.04	0.08	0.03	0.02
278.56	1396.03	925.63	240.18	2254.41	2042.10	7.03	106.89	136.64	22.59	12.31
190.98	534.40	282.10	127.83	728.19	583.78	4.82	62.33	92.13	24.90	8.85
101.64	302.24	144.45	104.86	344.83	264.35	10.42	28.31	50.56	11.81	3.14
331.67	546.66	411.26	62.30	417.17	133.69	207.80	44.85	304.74	51.93	0.75
293.79	671.28	349.81	227.32	1355.41	1179.02	7.27	78.06	115.72	30.28	16.11
581.66	1273.79	808.42	314.49	2348.97	1977.33	13.93	127.90	200.81	58.77	43.79
281.64	427.61	300.63	84.08	1116.31	999.85	5.17	38.57	66.37	22.56	21.33
132.83	290.47	154.92	100.34	518.58	441.27	4.44	37.38	56.70	14.83	5.86
337.63	919.95	587.90	141.75	1360.45	1140.55	7.17	86.08	136.47	43.02	22.03
229.44	937.83	513.03	316.71	1289.35	1147.65	5.39	54.39	92.86	32.98	11.79
184.00	570.20	307.30	145.06	728.75	617.42	3.87	47.97	70.58	18.61	10.49
318.21	1286.74	982.24	146.97	1783.76	1563.02	6.53	88.13	116.28	21.53	24.12
801.57	1180.77	530.24	480.65	2141.48	1569.05	314.25	202.62	638.53	121.19	2.06
523.22	2300.83	1316.50	480.33	2760.92	2322.14	17.10	164.35	250.42	68.64	19.60
323.12	2184.74	1389.67	260.88	944.40	575.39	8.08	164.35	221.04	48.38	8.85
14.85	87.15	36.14	11.04	82.83	74.58	0.43	2.87	5.30	2.00	0.93
621.54	1854.05	1070.68	534.10	2747.43	2351.50	15.97	152.79	233.78	64.67	39.56
807.27	2862.72	1502.85	844.18	3481.83	2988.04	22.44	211.16	332.49	98.43	39.59
302.28	1296.63	402.77	685.24	1703.28	1514.40	6.06	106.76	151.84	39.00	6.78
252.24	1225.53	768.89	283.22	2411.33	2238.56	6.03	88.52	120.55	25.90	9.60
819.94	2191.09	1260.37	605.70	3705.21	3230.90	18.72	202.32	310.04	88.62	47.86
458.00	2064.57	1328.92	340.75	2005.96	1653.42	9.35	154.53	213.66	49.62	25.63
605.45	2461.83	1605.87	353.65	2095.44	1558.46	13.51	216.78	289.22	58.48	28.87
300.61	1307.86	837.29	227.04	1317.44	1087.04	26.71	99.45	167.65	40.72	10.69
114.69	719.53	487.18	145.83	724.09	616.56	3.44	21.50	34.22	9.25	6.76
2095.59	9506.18	6705.09	1159.18	9243.45	7477.13	48.75	733.50	1063.12	280.31	95.71
5510.24	18502.35	13526.59	1893.23	21770.25	17323.46	100.36	1217.07	1979.32	660.21	162.12
140.85	748.85	527.02	53.96	563.71	424.69	3.21	53.04	73.11	16.83	8.11
32.51	107.56	76.56	18.49	153.43	130.95	0.74	6.77	10.92	3.40	2.79
159.15	385.32	212.73	128.19	867.21	764.03	3.92	67.69	87.83	16.21	3.21
14.46	50.98	33.12	13.66	51.37	42.58	0.34	2.15	4.30	1.78	0.95
1343.99	9873.44	1363.80	5299.81	5731.99	5276.03	29.21	363.31	607.51	212.54	16.15
112.38	588.78	155.32	259.84	510.03	457.77	1.30	33.29	44.46	9.65	1.29
119.61	1186.05	269.41	511.52	274.23	192.26	2.43	41.85	57.01	12.52	3.20

12-21 规模以上“三资”工业企业主要经济指标（2017年）

单位：亿元

项目	Item	企业单位数（个） Number of Enterprises (unit)	工业总产值（当年价） Gross Industrial Output Value (at current prices)
全省总计	**Provincial Total**	**12674**	**51665.09**
按经济类型分	Grouped by Ownership		
外商投资工业	Foreign-funded Industry	4089	24161.44
港澳台投资工业	Industry with Funds from Hong Kong, Macao and Taiwan	8585	27503.65
按轻重工业分	Grouped by Light and Heavy Industries		
轻工业	Light Industry	6340	18429.70
重工业	Heavy Industry	6334	33235.39
按企业规模分	Grouped by Size of Enterprises		
大型企业	Large Enterprises	921	27978.34
中型企业	Medium Enterprises	3775	13830.56
小微型企业	Small and Micro Enterprises	7978	9856.18
按行业分	Grouped by Sector		
煤炭开采和洗选业	Mining and Washing of Coal		
石油和天然气开采业	Extraction of Petroleum and Natural Gas	3	422.82
黑色金属矿采选业	Mining and Dressing of Ferrous Metal Ores	1	8.48
有色金属矿采选业	Mining and Dressing of Nonferrous Metal Ores	1	1.76
非金属矿采选业	Mining and Dressing of Nonmetal Ores	6	4.97
开采辅助活动	Auxiliary Minning Operations	1	1.96
其他采矿业	Mining and Dressing of Other Ores		
农副食品加工业	Processing of Farm and Sideline Food	152	789.50
食品制造业	Manufacture of Food	178	1040.91
酒、饮料和精制茶制造业	Manufacture of Wine, Beverage and Refined Tea	70	698.34
烟草制品业	Tobacco Products		
纺织业	Textile Industry	410	884.95
纺织服装、服饰业	Manufacture of Textile Garments, Footwear and Headgear	698	1200.73
皮革、毛皮、羽毛及其制品和制鞋业	Leather, Fur, Feather, Down and Related Products	574	1026.83
木材加工和木、竹、藤、棕、草制品业	Timber Processing, Bamboo, Cane, Palm Fiber & Straw Products	77	156.09
家具制造业	Manufacture of Furniture	331	734.21
造纸和纸制品业	Papermaking and Paper Products	287	1086.62
印刷和记录媒介复制业	Printing and Record Medium Reproduction	224	459.36
文教、工美、体育和娱乐用品制造业	Manufacture of Cultural, Educational,Sports and Entertainment Articles	700	1949.73
石油加工、炼焦和核燃料加工业	Petroleum Refining, Coking and Nuclear Fuel Processing	22	417.93
化学原料和化学制品制造业	Manufacture of Raw Chemical Materials and Chemical Products	629	2846.10
医药制造业	Manufacture of Medicines	102	532.51
化学纤维制造业	Manufacture of Chemical Fibers	24	91.94
橡胶和塑料制品业	Rubber and Plastic Products	1211	2164.08
非金属矿物制品业	Nonmetal Mineral Products	439	1086.12
黑色金属冶炼和压延加工业	Smelting and Pressing of Ferrous Metals	88	766.24
有色金属冶炼和压延加工业	Smelting and Pressing of Nonferrous Metals	153	798.94
金属制品业	Metal Products	932	1974.94
通用设备制造业	Manufacture of General-purpose Machinery	542	2002.19
专用设备制造业	Manufacture of Special-purpose Machinery	518	1144.80
汽车制造业	Manufacture of Automobile	440	6016.14
铁路、船舶、航空航天和其他运输设备制造业	Manufacture of Railway ,Ship,Aeronautics and Other Transport equipment	117	419.28
电气机械和器材制造业	Manufacture of Electrical Machinery and Equipment	1301	3971.16
计算机、通信和其他电子设备制造业	Manufacture of Communication Equipment, Computers and Other Electronic Equipment	1891	15144.21
仪器仪表制造业	Manufacture of Instruments and Meters	257	546.83
其他制造业	Other Manufactures	116	85.91
废弃资源综合利用业	Comprehensive Utilization of Waste	21	104.92
金属制品、机械和设备修理业	Manufacture of Metal Products,Machinery and Equipment Maintenance	14	120.38
电力、热力生产和供应业	Production and Supply of Electric Power and Heat Power	71	546.09
燃气生产和供应业	Production and Supply of Gas	50	307.92
水的生产和供应业	Production and Supply of Water	23	109.21

Main Economic Indicators of Foreign-funded Industrial Enterprises above Designated Size (2017)

(100 million yuan)

工业增加值 Value-added of Industry	年末资产总计 Total Assets at the Year-end	流动资产合计 Total Working Capital	固定资产合计 Total Fixed Assets	主营业务收入 Principal Business Revenue	主营业务成本 Cost of Principal Business	主营业务税金及附加 Tax and Other Charges on Principal Business	利润总额 Total Profits	利税总额 Total Pre-tax Profits	本年应交增值税 Value-added Tax Payable in Current Year	全部就业人员年平均人数(万人) Annual Average Number of Employed Persons (10000 persons)
11673.04	**41146.56**	**26690.73**	**8967.77**	**50579.75**	**43032.19**	**420.63**	**3467.81**	**4984.36**	**1090.76**	**643.08**
5213.47	17594.47	11508.63	4145.62	23832.86	20376.08	184.78	1715.66	2431.27	528.52	219.23
6459.57	23552.09	15182.10	4822.15	26746.89	22656.10	235.85	1752.15	2553.10	562.25	423.85
4399.12	14447.55	9617.02	2869.07	18049.76	14819.15	107.12	1244.65	1803.17	448.83	303.61
7273.93	26699.01	17073.71	6098.70	32529.99	28213.04	313.50	2223.16	3181.19	641.94	339.47
6225.80	21700.00	14343.87	4230.05	27297.04	23344.37	201.06	2017.66	2818.42	597.10	297.47
3406.26	11123.65	6891.24	2822.61	13543.42	11347.74	167.95	906.71	1382.75	306.47	233.74
2040.98	8322.91	5455.62	1915.10	9739.30	8340.08	51.62	543.44	783.20	187.19	111.87
370.46	714.27	34.09	230.90	430.54	222.42	24.26	169.59	240.63	46.78	0.56
2.77	3.72	0.45	3.27	8.14	6.46	0.18	0.66	1.33	0.48	0.02
0.09	4.90	0.49	3.24	1.79	1.12	0.09	0.36	0.53	0.08	0.02
1.71	7.12	3.41	2.41	4.19	3.30	0.05	0.13	0.33	0.15	0.05
0.47	3.12	2.03	1.06	1.96	1.47		0.39	0.43	0.04	0.02
92.38	471.87	334.64	76.74	846.09	770.82	1.71	44.29	54.97	8.83	3.40
419.64	792.26	494.96	183.42	1030.13	568.52	10.63	165.63	247.26	70.94	8.26
194.94	594.49	362.27	175.94	678.17	457.55	12.06	57.92	105.93	35.94	4.58
197.01	676.26	427.45	161.51	855.70	750.79	3.42	44.45	63.68	15.79	14.37
335.34	666.86	457.80	152.66	1158.26	995.85	6.51	43.41	72.87	22.86	35.78
300.45	583.52	393.57	118.18	1022.06	888.69	5.44	42.92	68.18	19.68	32.81
33.71	157.74	107.21	35.04	143.23	119.93	1.06	13.50	18.56	3.97	1.87
179.63	474.60	321.97	99.34	705.59	607.58	3.75	40.30	56.87	12.75	13.25
248.94	1206.74	637.86	437.77	1047.82	873.75	4.46	95.64	134.05	33.48	8.94
140.90	463.63	302.48	102.35	439.55	360.11	2.51	32.63	47.04	11.83	11.63
397.78	1122.09	860.40	178.76	1929.61	1737.17	6.93	75.92	103.82	20.48	45.93
212.85	279.78	178.86	68.33	415.03	259.17	89.97	46.83	160.54	23.75	0.37
658.87	2419.18	1327.79	646.56	2773.94	2091.29	17.15	263.03	371.33	90.86	12.89
176.34	773.98	520.52	117.51	492.15	277.36	4.73	131.57	165.78	29.47	4.17
23.12	106.59	56.84	38.18	85.64	68.36	0.27	11.24	12.72	1.22	0.57
510.92	1694.81	1078.57	384.17	2087.50	1781.27	10.09	98.96	147.12	37.93	42.82
319.53	1146.43	650.87	387.11	1066.54	872.81	7.23	102.52	144.53	34.72	15.84
88.35	542.67	280.77	212.98	751.27	701.15	2.91	23.25	36.89	10.73	2.03
106.15	514.69	349.56	108.36	831.72	754.00	2.23	39.64	57.80	15.91	4.92
470.83	1446.16	903.74	411.90	1880.44	1625.49	10.21	100.73	153.65	42.49	32.56
428.13	1687.62	1272.10	220.81	1983.03	1673.95	9.53	124.72	175.44	40.85	23.24
299.78	1067.42	699.77	205.42	1111.50	916.70	6.59	76.48	107.77	24.55	18.19
1357.28	4176.85	2859.10	887.87	5879.10	4966.90	93.61	495.53	763.57	173.98	30.23
112.85	549.27	381.87	86.79	402.03	313.47	2.82	43.80	54.37	7.72	5.00
847.74	3350.04	2323.09	498.55	3874.49	3345.15	19.12	194.87	278.95	64.41	71.12
2585.65	10917.96	7882.52	1909.44	14859.18	13604.63	44.34	652.89	845.43	147.11	177.06
163.83	477.64	347.58	91.52	536.60	439.52	3.04	36.26	49.58	10.24	14.30
21.08	67.78	47.00	14.41	85.67	72.86	0.51	2.24	3.64	0.89	2.61
15.09	39.20	23.67	11.61	97.41	84.53	0.31	7.86	9.64	1.47	0.38
35.15	135.02	92.52	32.76	118.99	102.15	0.74	8.26	11.25	2.16	0.94
200.75	1068.67	410.66	487.34	529.07	391.68	10.49	103.65	131.44	17.22	1.13
67.43	307.86	146.55	119.14	303.87	263.59	0.98	36.33	42.73	5.42	0.62
55.09	433.74	115.69	64.43	111.75	60.65	0.69	39.43	43.72	3.59	0.57

12-22 规模以上私营工业企业主要经济指标（2017年）

单位：亿元

项 目	Item	企业单位数（个） Number of Enterprises (unit)	工业总产值（当年价） Gross Industrial Output Value (at current prices)
全省总计	**Provincial Total**	**19918**	**31839.51**
按轻重工业分	Grouped by Light & Heavy Industries		
轻工业	Light Industry	10007	13201.77
重工业	Heavy Industry	9911	18637.74
按企业规模分	Grouped by Size of Enterprises		
大型企业	Large Enterprises	263	7482.75
中型企业	Medium Enterprises	2495	8429.80
小微型企业	Small and Micro Enterprises	17160	15926.96
按行业分	Grouped by Sector		
煤炭开采和洗选业	Mining and Washing of Coal		
石油和天然气开采业	Extraction of Petroleum and Natural Gas		
黑色金属矿采选业	Mining and Dressing of Ferrous Metal Ores	13	33.66
有色金属矿采选业	Mining and Dressing of Nonferrous Metal Ores	8	10.09
非金属矿采选业	Mining and Dressing of Nonmetal Ores	114	129.52
开采辅助活动	Auxiliary Minning Operations	1	0.26
其他采矿业	Mining and Dressing of Other Ores		
农副食品加工业	Processing of Farm and Sideline Food	388	762.46
食品制造业	Manufacture of Food	295	357.88
酒、饮料和精制茶制造业	Manufacture of Wine, Beverage and Refined Tea	83	147.08
烟草制品业	Tobacco Products	2	8.71
纺织业	Textile Industry	635	1013.63
纺织服装、服饰业	Manufacture of Textile Garments, Footwear and Headgear	1325	1707.87
皮革、毛皮、羽毛及其制品和制鞋业	Leather, Fur, Feather, Down and Related Products	859	811.00
木材加工和木、竹、藤、棕、草制品业	Timber Processing, Bamboo, Cane, Palm Fiber & Straw Products	276	276.17
家具制造业	Manufacture of Furniture	683	746.14
造纸和纸制品业	Papermaking and Paper Products	530	647.32
印刷和记录媒介复制业	Printing and Record Medium Reproduction	433	406.74
文教、工美、体育和娱乐用品制造业	Manufacture of Cultural, Educational,Sports and Entertainment Articles	638	1160.61
石油加工、炼焦和核燃料加工业	Petroleum Refining, Coking and Nuclear Fuel Processing	19	77.26
化学原料和化学制品制造业	Manufacture of Raw Chemical Materials and Chemical Products	902	1261.69
医药制造业	Manufacture of Medicines	121	174.52
化学纤维制造业	Manufacture of Chemical Fibers	24	35.86
橡胶和塑料制品业	Rubber and Plastic Products	1559	1730.72
非金属矿物制品业	Nonmetal Mineral Products	1297	1876.61
黑色金属冶炼和压延加工业	Smelting and Pressing of Ferrous Metals	177	518.35
有色金属冶炼和压延加工业	Smelting and Pressing of Nonferrous Metals	303	989.30
金属制品业	Metal Products	1770	2418.18
通用设备制造业	Manufacture of General-purpose Machinery	920	1085.15
专用设备制造业	Manufacture of Special-purpose Machinery	882	1002.88
汽车制造业	Manufacture of Automobile	209	312.68
铁路、船舶、航空航天和其他运输设备制造业	Manufacture of Railway ,Ship,Aeronautics and Other Transport equipment	148	219.52
电气机械和器材制造业	Manufacture of Electrical Machinery and Equipment	2262	3158.68
计算机、通信和其他电子设备制造业	Manufacture of Communication Equipment, Computers and Other Electronic Equipment	2487	7915.19
仪器仪表制造业	Manufacture of Instruments and Meters	241	280.82
其他制造业	Other Manufactures	119	105.82
废弃资源综合利用业	Comprehensive Utilization of Waste	107	340.58
金属制品、机械和设备修理业	Manufacture of Metal Products,Machinery and Equipment Maintenance	15	12.87
电力、热力生产和供应业	Production and Supply of Electric Power and Heat Power	29	34.41
燃气生产和供应业	Production and Supply of Gas	18	30.95
水的生产和供应业	Production and Supply of Water	26	38.35

Main Economic Indicators of Private Industrial Enterprises above Designated Size (2017)

(100 million yuan)

工业增加值 Value-added of Industry	年末资产总计 Total Assets at the Year-end	流动资产合计 Total working Capital	固定资产合计 Total Fixed Assets	主营业务收入 Principal Business Revenue	主营业务成本 Cost of Principal Business	主营业务税金及附加 Tax and Other Charges on Principal Business	利润总额 Total Profits	利税总额 Total Pre-tax Profits	本年应交增值税 Value-added Tax Payable in Current Year	全部就业人员年平均人数(万人) Annual Average Number of Employed Persons (10000 persons)
6514.61	**21155.33**	**14043.19**	**4104.36**	**31444.49**	**26903.42**	**156.77**	**1740.32**	**2625.61**	**726.29**	**358.23**
2835.79	7705.16	5029.86	1637.60	12859.63	11065.76	70.45	687.78	1029.98	270.95	179.52
3678.82	13450.17	9013.33	2466.76	18584.86	15837.66	86.32	1052.54	1595.63	455.34	178.71
1435.79	5820.82	4114.83	773.37	7704.16	6450.36	31.77	499.97	746.61	214.35	55.56
1850.21	5999.11	3588.68	1459.93	8086.76	6766.88	43.85	550.19	774.42	179.72	122.28
3228.61	9335.41	6339.69	1871.05	15653.56	13686.17	81.16	690.16	1104.58	332.22	180.40
10.87	39.23	22.27	15.90	32.43	27.29	0.56	0.87	2.94	1.51	0.15
4.22	2.63	1.59	0.76	10.05	8.79	0.08	0.51	0.79	0.19	0.06
30.66	59.40	21.76	32.02	123.55	99.28	1.74	13.53	20.03	4.76	0.92
0.04	0.35	0.01	0.11	0.26	0.24		0.01	0.01	0.01	
111.77	576.21	387.71	100.59	775.97	688.79	3.32	45.66	58.65	9.62	5.08
80.69	168.24	89.27	43.18	348.19	293.25	1.93	23.00	34.39	9.44	3.93
36.42	94.03	39.72	32.31	140.72	114.50	2.53	10.59	16.75	3.62	1.29
1.70	18.56	8.48	4.92	8.62	6.90	0.11	0.72	1.28	0.46	0.05
213.38	454.47	224.50	160.90	992.65	869.00	5.97	54.77	83.07	22.29	10.95
413.65	792.81	536.92	189.84	1667.31	1414.03	9.74	87.90	138.05	40.27	30.67
198.07	258.88	180.14	56.69	796.94	722.35	3.63	25.10	42.94	14.16	14.09
67.02	150.26	76.13	58.83	265.68	229.79	2.40	15.27	24.73	6.99	3.29
171.74	488.82	325.73	82.09	723.87	620.61	3.48	35.42	58.68	19.74	12.15
116.70	311.90	194.21	81.02	640.87	575.64	2.81	24.71	41.18	13.63	6.89
96.14	216.37	134.10	61.09	400.48	346.90	2.06	20.35	31.18	8.75	5.87
215.83	767.37	597.26	99.29	1154.94	1015.72	4.51	53.90	72.19	13.73	16.85
20.12	77.89	19.51	29.56	98.71	90.68	0.14	4.98	5.65	0.53	0.15
247.82	880.14	492.51	219.80	1257.15	1056.00	6.66	73.07	108.45	28.65	10.20
49.37	333.59	202.32	43.92	167.91	114.29	1.51	19.27	26.75	5.95	1.86
8.63	19.94	13.99	3.51	34.79	29.81	0.20	2.08	3.11	0.83	0.56
387.33	970.35	559.88	304.32	1691.09	1445.95	10.25	101.30	148.23	36.56	24.54
403.54	1191.96	612.73	380.69	1794.50	1556.23	11.25	97.09	152.45	43.97	20.74
89.25	212.18	90.33	62.00	507.07	454.75	2.09	28.76	42.37	11.49	3.27
106.78	554.82	390.19	102.12	1008.94	927.77	3.17	39.08	54.37	12.09	5.03
522.34	1218.37	652.98	379.43	2347.66	2061.49	11.77	132.40	199.16	54.88	28.89
245.98	857.67	581.47	148.20	1033.98	850.87	4.87	77.00	108.94	27.04	14.21
262.18	961.80	694.79	148.51	947.39	736.87	6.10	72.91	107.66	28.55	15.10
75.83	246.37	157.92	49.69	298.17	247.68	1.40	21.93	30.78	7.42	4.07
33.99	170.85	123.10	26.96	214.13	187.87	1.27	6.48	11.49	3.72	2.57
625.63	2462.83	1790.44	308.33	3015.55	2569.56	14.07	153.03	227.20	59.91	41.06
1478.58	5887.58	4394.29	700.77	8103.21	6850.18	32.72	435.83	686.21	216.86	64.97
73.23	280.79	207.03	25.20	274.76	205.31	1.54	25.13	34.53	7.85	4.41
21.08	64.67	47.26	10.53	104.81	91.31	0.57	4.03	6.68	2.07	1.78
61.87	168.70	108.20	40.21	349.78	306.54	1.54	24.12	30.63	4.96	1.63
3.47	6.64	3.86	2.29	12.99	11.23	0.05	0.47	0.85	0.33	0.31
10.71	126.18	41.57	71.56	31.64	24.38	0.31	3.43	4.78	1.02	0.28
7.85	12.32	5.64	4.96	29.90	26.54	0.09	1.73	2.46	0.64	0.12
10.12	50.13	13.37	22.25	37.82	25.03	0.33	3.89	6.00	1.77	0.25

12-23 规模以上大中型工业企业主要经济指标（2017年）

单位：亿元

项目	Item	企业单位数（个）Number of Enterprises (unit)	工业总产值（当年价）Gross Industrial Output Value (at current prices)
全省总计	**Provincial Total**	**10122**	**95951.23**
按轻重工业分	Grouped by Light & Heavy Industry		
轻工业	Light Industry	5240	30544.53
重工业	Heavy Industry	4882	65406.70
按企业规模分	Grouped by Size of Enterprises		
大型企业	Large	1618	63688.06
中型企业	Medium	8504	32263.16
按行业分	Grouped by Sector		
煤炭开采和洗选业	Mining and Washing of Coal		
石油和天然气开采业	Extraction of Petroleum and Natural Gas	2	420.55
黑色金属矿采选业	Mining and Dressing of Ferrous Metal Ores	3	8.17
有色金属矿采选业	Mining and Dressing of Nonferrous Metal Ores	6	45.65
非金属矿采选业	Mining and Dressing of Nonmetal Ores	5	15.11
开采辅助活动	Auxiliary Minning Operations	2	14.40
其他采矿业	Mining and Dressing of Other Ores		
农副食品加工业	Processing of Farm and Sideline Food	147	1240.16
食品制造业	Manufacture of Food	133	1250.47
酒、饮料和精制茶制造业	Manufacture of Wine, Beverage and Refined Tea	58	830.98
烟草制品业	Tobacco Products	7	412.37
纺织业	Textile Industry	273	1319.41
纺织服装、服饰业	Manufacture of Textile Garments, Footwear and Headgear	695	2256.07
皮革、毛皮、羽毛及其制品和制鞋业	Leather, Fur, Feather, Down and Related Products	423	1107.76
木材加工和木、竹、藤、棕、草制品业	Timber Processing, Bamboo, Cane, Palm Fiber & Straw Products	58	223.90
家具制造业	Manufacture of Furniture	295	1345.85
造纸和纸制品业	Papermaking and Paper Products	173	1463.34
印刷和记录媒介复制业	Printing and Record Medium Reproduction	178	658.84
文教、工美、体育和娱乐用品制造业	Manufacture of Cultural, Educational,Sports and Entertainment Articles	632	2620.65
石油加工、炼焦和核燃料加工业	Petroleum Refining, Coking and Nuclear Fuel Processing	11	2275.20
化学原料和化学制品制造业	Manufacture of Raw Chemical Materials and Chemical Products	246	2386.93
医药制造业	Manufacture of Medicines	122	1101.29
化学纤维制造业	Manufacture of Chemical Fibers	13	115.33
橡胶和塑料制品业	Rubber and Plastic Products	701	2691.85
非金属矿物制品业	Nonmetal Mineral Products	478	2326.46
黑色金属冶炼和压延加工业	Smelting and Pressing of Ferrous Metals	67	1689.17
有色金属冶炼和压延加工业	Smelting and Pressing of Nonferrous Metals	99	1682.12
金属制品业	Metal Products	677	3107.78
通用设备制造业	Manufacture of General-purpose Machinery	360	2702.40
专用设备制造业	Manufacture of Special-purpose Machinery	364	1935.94
汽车制造业	Manufacture of Automobile	301	7134.53
铁路、船舶、航空航天和其他运输设备制造业	Manufacture of Railway ,Ship,Aeronautics and Other Transport equipment	90	870.37
电气机械和器材制造业	Manufacture of Electrical Machinery and Equipment	1202	9717.14
计算机、通信和其他电子设备制造业	Manufacture of Communication Equipment, Computers and Other Electronic Equipment	1889	33524.53
仪器仪表制造业	Manufacture of Instruments and Meters	187	702.87
其他制造业	Other Manufactures	48	96.60
废弃资源综合利用业	Comprehensive Utilization of Waste	35	497.99
金属制品、机械和设备修理业	Manufacture of Metal Products,Machinery and Equipment Maintenance	18	160.30
电力、热力生产和供应业	Production and Supply of Electric Power and Heat Power	73	5510.98
燃气生产和供应业	Production and Supply of Gas	9	220.07
水的生产和供应业	Production and Supply of Water	42	267.67

Main Economic Indicators of Large and Medium-sized Industrial Enterprises above Designated Size (2017)

(100 million yuan)

工业增加值 Value-added of Industry	年末资产总计 Total Assets at the Year-end	流动资产合计 Total Working Capital	固定资产合计 Total Fixed Assets	主营业务收入 Principal Business Revenue	主营业务成本 Cost of Principal Business	主营业务税金及附加 Tax and Extra Charges on Main Business	利润总额 Total Profits	利税总额 Total Pre-tax Profits	本年应交增值税 Value-added Tax Payable in Current Year	全部就业人员年平均人数(万人) Annual Average Number of Employed Persons (10000 persons)
23174.75	**86276.84**	**50716.65**	**19561.13**	**94534.14**	**78068.11**	**1191.30**	**6845.35**	**10671.15**	**2622.53**	**985.94**
7689.29	27322.18	17719.18	5014.71	30345.76	24251.79	377.11	2481.81	3761.58	899.09	444.92
15485.46	58954.66	32997.47	14546.42	64188.38	53816.32	814.19	4363.54	6909.56	1723.44	541.02
15716.24	58666.07	34730.92	12594.48	63099.13	51810.46	856.13	4735.31	7456.35	1856.87	511.52
7458.51	27610.77	15985.74	6966.65	31435.01	26257.65	335.17	2110.04	3214.80	765.66	474.42
368.83	708.16	30.51	230.90	428.28	220.77	24.25	169.04	239.99	46.70	0.55
3.05	40.36	20.38	8.97	8.16	4.42	0.25	0.73	1.78	0.80	0.11
27.94	67.99	21.49	25.63	49.66	30.98	1.32	13.43	18.58	3.83	0.62
7.01	31.97	13.96	6.77	14.69	10.13	0.51	1.90	3.56	1.13	0.36
3.55	55.42	12.42	41.05	14.40	13.04	0.04	0.90	1.08	0.14	0.12
149.95	964.62	676.42	141.48	1320.09	1203.26	2.89	61.99	81.78	16.73	7.90
462.83	892.46	543.49	209.56	1216.84	714.33	11.64	183.77	274.13	78.61	10.52
232.56	659.89	406.67	182.97	790.87	535.13	18.86	73.41	132.32	40.05	5.50
314.63	504.30	387.35	52.42	392.07	122.97	198.51	41.86	289.79	49.27	0.66
293.92	764.31	444.34	214.08	1267.09	1100.67	5.00	73.38	104.22	25.78	19.75
591.04	1250.59	779.68	307.15	2171.54	1810.66	12.47	113.52	181.46	55.33	55.76
323.09	633.83	422.79	133.24	1102.98	951.98	5.93	45.44	76.01	24.54	38.39
52.25	182.10	117.24	45.49	209.09	173.09	1.41	23.29	31.19	6.49	2.78
344.22	983.77	617.36	169.55	1297.74	1069.72	7.20	97.77	144.76	39.68	22.92
313.35	1490.39	702.72	618.11	1399.99	1182.96	6.25	116.58	168.18	44.82	11.50
188.08	663.68	368.15	156.76	631.29	513.89	3.59	52.61	72.57	16.24	14.65
542.91	1602.56	1185.04	247.38	2594.80	2288.35	9.22	132.70	172.48	30.06	58.12
872.48	1277.63	622.75	480.31	2219.03	1527.25	398.35	230.28	768.35	139.26	1.87
604.98	2381.17	1222.60	545.66	2328.15	1669.55	16.43	243.93	346.80	86.16	14.68
390.06	2514.75	1633.89	288.62	1045.37	585.82	9.70	256.05	327.11	61.15	9.23
25.23	116.65	66.70	39.14	114.06	95.84	0.40	11.23	14.05	2.41	1.00
649.22	2029.01	1130.40	602.91	2600.61	2191.18	15.11	156.43	222.79	50.95	52.65
639.68	2289.58	1169.58	752.38	2246.52	1866.03	14.34	193.67	281.87	73.69	33.19
282.22	1520.27	472.21	833.94	1674.73	1500.76	5.98	97.72	140.27	36.56	5.85
228.75	1000.09	526.02	300.55	1671.32	1507.42	5.21	91.83	124.15	27.07	9.40
740.18	2050.82	1130.51	648.21	2961.65	2540.88	15.39	195.31	283.71	72.65	47.47
588.18	2601.54	1771.70	367.45	2649.57	2208.57	12.36	199.93	267.38	54.71	31.37
563.38	2215.81	1401.93	367.68	1831.05	1357.11	12.39	203.82	261.56	44.92	28.64
1625.50	5030.02	3434.18	1024.21	7029.93	5887.34	145.82	606.73	966.31	212.60	35.22
176.99	985.05	669.89	187.96	833.31	669.22	4.46	56.98	72.42	10.94	8.30
2336.59	10611.73	7341.60	1360.10	10045.28	8146.49	52.82	824.23	1158.60	280.70	123.46
7409.84	26208.66	18930.88	3440.12	32963.99	27736.25	131.17	1754.41	2634.42	746.39	291.10
200.14	850.57	574.52	102.63	689.58	546.78	3.92	55.86	75.12	15.31	16.51
25.70	76.42	49.96	16.82	92.82	77.33	0.57	4.56	7.08	1.95	2.84
94.49	228.87	118.31	90.68	503.53	427.98	2.52	53.38	65.87	9.97	1.70
45.35	180.41	122.21	45.16	158.96	136.76	0.94	8.54	12.85	3.28	1.75
1244.27	8833.11	1174.75	4551.37	5492.45	5120.21	30.98	300.43	524.80	191.04	15.60
69.76	431.54	125.67	212.82	207.98	160.78	1.21	42.34	53.64	9.88	0.82
142.56	1346.75	276.38	510.92	264.68	162.21	1.92	55.32	68.11	10.74	3.08

12-24 规模以上高技术制造业主要经济指标（2017年）

单位：亿元

项　　目	Item	企业单位数（个） Number of Enterprises (unit)	工业总产值（当年价） Gross Industrial Output Value (at current prices)
高技术制造业合计	**Total**	**7604**	**42709.80**
信息化学品制造	**Manufacture of Information Chemical Products**	**41**	**132.87**
医药制造业	Manufacture of Medicines	453	1537.08
#化学药品制造	Manufacture of Chemical Medicines	122	797.05
中成药生产	Manufacture of Traditional Chinese Patent Medicines	97	313.11
生物药品制造	Manufacture of Biological and Biochemical Products	69	182.85
航空航天器及设备制造	**Manufacture of Aircraft and Spacecraft**	**19**	**329.36**
飞机制造	Manufacture of Aircraft	7	209.61
航天器制造	Manufacture of Spacecraft		
航空、航天相关设备制造	Manufacture of Aircraft and Spacecraft related products	1	0.25
其他飞行器制造	Manufacture of Air Vehicle	5	11.45
航空航天器修理	Repair of Aircraft and Spacecraft	6	108.04
电子及通信设备制造业	**Manufacture of Electronic and Communication Equipment**	**5600**	**35208.99**
通信设备制造	Manufacture of Communication Equipment	678	18755.64
#通信系统设备制造	Manufacture of Communication Transmission Equipment	209	8955.34
通信终端设备制造	Manufacture of Communication Exchange Equipment	469	9800.30
广播电视设备制造	Manufacture of Broadcasting and Television Equipment	192	422.31
雷达及配套设备制造	Manufacture of Radar Equipment	8	18.48
视听设备制造	Manufacture of Audio-visual Equipment	564	2744.52
电子器件制造	Manufacture of Electronic Parts	1022	5374.17
电子真空器件制造	Manufacture of Electronic Vacuum Devices	16	44.36
半导体分立器件制造	Manufacture of Semiconductor Discrete Devices	44	103.50
集成电路制造	Manufacture of Integrated Circuits	128	576.64
光电子器件及其他电子器件制造	Manufacture of Optical and Other Electronic Devices and Other Electronic Equipment	834	4649.67
电子元件制造	Manufacture of Electronic Parts	2096	5435.96
电子工业专用设备制造	Equipment for Electronic Industry	194	359.97
光纤、光缆制造	Optical Fiber,Cable Manufacturing	44	87.65
锂离子电池制造	Lithium Ion Battery Manufacturing	262	1160.64
其他电子设备制造	Manufacture of Electronic Devices	540	849.64
电子计算机及办公设备制造业	**Manufacture of Computers and Office Equipment**	**801**	**4290.32**
计算机整机制造	Manufacture of Complete Computers	102	1323.44
计算机零部件制造	Manufacture of Computer part Equipment	248	894.78
计算机外围设备制造	Manufacture of Computer Peripheral Equipment	263	941.61
其他计算机制造	Other computer equipment	95	541.34
办公设备制造	Manufacture of Office Equipment	93	589.15
医疗设备及仪器仪表制造业	**Manufacture of Medical Equipment, Instruments and Meters**	**690**	**1211.17**
医疗设备及器械制造	Manufacture of Medical Equipment and Appliances	247	454.69
仪器仪表制造	Manufacture of Instruments and Meters	443	756.48

Main Indicators on High-tech Manufacturingl Enterprises above Designated Size (2017)

(100 million yuan)

工业增加值 Value-added of Industry	年末资产总计 Total Assets at the Year-end	流动资产合计 Total Working Capital	固定资产 Fixed Assets	主营业务收入 Principal Business Revenue	主营业务成本 Cost of Principal Business	主营业务税金及附加 Tax and Extra Charges on Main Business	利润总额 Total Profits	利税总额 Total Pre-tax Profits	本年应交增值税 Value-added Tax Payable in Current Year	全部就业人员年平均人数(万人) Annual Average Number of Employed Persons (10000 persons)
9507.81	**36591.77**	**26308.30**	**4660.68**	**41902.42**	**34795.08**	**176.26**	**2521.74**	**3655.47**	**954.18**	**399.69**
26.92	**134.20**	**73.92**	**33.53**	**129.01**	**103.01**	**1.02**	**13.55**	**17.30**	**2.70**	**1.05**
502.55	2969.57	1917.38	380.52	1449.19	862.99	12.88	296.83	388.16	78.21	13.20
256.91	1674.30	1192.92	178.88	767.81	457.54	6.17	192.20	240.66	42.16	4.88
107.70	605.58	315.35	87.34	289.26	172.73	3.36	44.84	69.22	20.93	3.70
72.89	394.03	234.00	57.83	169.35	74.05	1.39	32.57	42.09	8.10	1.50
91.91	**262.15**	**214.76**	**20.57**	**312.69**	**200.18**	**1.92**	**50.29**	**59.20**	**6.98**	**1.77**
59.79	151.47	126.82	3.73	194.25	98.78	1.15	40.95	46.87	4.75	0.95
0.07	0.43	0.41	0.01	0.25	0.19		0.06	0.08	0.02	
2.07	5.00	4.38	0.50	11.19	8.34	0.05	0.87	1.05	0.12	0.10
29.97	105.24	83.15	16.33	107.00	92.88	0.71	8.41	11.20	2.08	0.72
7954.49	**28689.79**	**20870.50**	**3759.93**	**34623.98**	**28966.30**	**141.15**	**1853.01**	**2776.29**	**779.57**	**325.14**
4607.55	14049.16	11305.64	875.61	18642.03	15103.19	78.26	970.54	1616.58	567.12	99.65
3209.56	7599.39	5888.70	467.39	8220.93	5748.62	51.95	562.04	954.74	340.60	43.61
1397.98	6449.77	5416.94	408.22	10421.10	9354.57	26.31	408.50	661.83	226.52	56.03
83.85	325.00	220.96	40.09	397.87	343.36	1.54	16.31	25.95	8.08	6.69
4.49	41.18	27.65	1.98	20.41	15.64	0.13	1.43	1.77	0.20	0.24
371.08	2051.70	1561.57	159.76	2758.22	2466.31	11.18	133.69	184.50	39.48	26.69
1081.84	5300.07	2915.90	1400.70	5157.38	4495.70	16.29	269.31	340.91	54.77	58.31
9.18	17.81	8.95	4.04	42.83	35.53	0.16	4.52	6.10	1.42	0.30
24.78	111.14	67.74	31.19	101.60	81.91	0.51	6.82	8.99	1.67	1.56
117.29	561.72	352.31	126.25	540.87	473.65	2.00	29.68	40.82	9.07	6.44
930.58	4609.41	2486.90	1239.22	4472.08	3904.62	13.63	228.29	284.99	42.63	50.01
1310.38	4558.48	3032.67	990.87	5320.58	4591.01	25.07	310.99	422.67	85.52	100.57
80.96	327.96	271.54	23.06	338.21	276.46	1.79	21.68	29.45	5.96	4.78
16.06	109.90	77.31	11.10	107.03	95.07	0.49	4.89	7.37	1.97	0.92
206.28	1298.47	971.81	169.54	1042.30	889.07	2.74	68.82	82.32	10.75	12.70
192.01	627.86	485.44	87.22	839.96	690.49	3.67	55.34	64.80	5.71	14.60
573.46	**2967.12**	**2182.03**	**305.12**	**4187.89**	**3824.48**	**10.85**	**157.70**	**222.46**	**53.63**	**40.16**
106.39	799.71	652.07	57.30	1280.53	1223.34	1.64	31.10	49.43	16.67	5.82
137.97	581.85	457.97	61.92	862.35	787.72	2.46	16.12	28.58	9.97	12.55
131.63	659.82	447.65	109.30	928.40	848.01	3.23	30.83	40.84	6.61	11.12
94.97	473.17	335.65	27.54	529.55	457.23	1.83	38.84	55.53	14.80	5.35
102.50	452.57	288.69	49.06	587.05	508.18	1.68	40.80	48.08	5.57	5.32
358.48	**1568.93**	**1049.70**	**161.01**	**1199.66**	**838.11**	**8.44**	**150.36**	**192.07**	**33.09**	**18.36**
169.57	599.71	354.40	78.35	453.47	265.78	3.95	81.80	98.62	12.74	7.24
188.91	969.22	695.30	82.66	746.19	572.34	4.49	68.56	93.45	20.36	11.12

12-25 规模以上先进制造业主要经济指标（2017年）

单位：亿元

项　　目	Item	企业单位数（个）Number of Enterprises (unit)	工业总产值（当年价）Gross Industrial Output Value (at current prices)	工业增加值 Value-added of Industry
合　计	**Total**	**28259**	**72690.42**	**17250.14**
高端电子信息制造业	**Manufacture of Advanced Electronic Equipment and Communication Equipment**	**4296**	**31723.73**	**7331.89**
集成电路及关键元器件	Integrated Circuits and Key Components	3501	11494.41	2549.82
信息通信设备	Communication Equipment	678	18755.64	4607.55
新型显示	New-Type Displays	117	1473.68	174.53
先进装备制造业	**Manufacture of Advanced Equipment**	**5988**	**25557.46**	**7119.92**
智能制造装备	Intelligent Manufacturing Equipment	1354	2445.21	646.54
船舶与海洋工程装备	Equipment for Ships and Marine Engineering	91	330.55	60.51
节能环保装备	Equipment for Energy Conservation and Environmental Protection	794	1563.21	383.44
轨道交通设备	Equipment for Rail Transportation	21	41.48	5.45
航空装备	Equipment for Aviation	13	221.32	61.93
新能源装备	Equipment for New Energy	1112	1927.93	439.44
汽车制造	Automobiles	833	7853.18	1776.09
卫星及应用	Satellites and Applications	428	9342.00	3286.04
重要基础件	Critical Basic Components	1342	1832.57	460.47
石油化工产业	**Petrochemical Manufacturing**	**2267**	**7396.29**	**2006.32**
先进轻纺制造业	**Manufacture of Advanced Light Textiles**	**10932**	**9416.48**	**2338.53**
绿色食品饮料	Green Foods and Drinks	2099	1892.47	408.45
高附加值纺织服装	High Added-value Textile Clothing	6189	2746.14	666.24
环保多功能家具	Environmental Friendly and Multi-purpose Furniture	1438	651.81	157.71
智能节能型家电	Intelligent Energy Saving Household Appliances	1206	4126.06	1106.13
新材料制造业	**Manufacture of New Materials**	**4977**	**7163.80**	**1451.69**
高端精品钢材	High-end Fine Steel	337	1787.67	282.31
高性能复合材料及特种功能材料	High Performance Composite Materials and Special Purpose Materials	4632	5359.29	1166.70
战略前沿材料	Strategic Materials	8	16.84	2.67
生物医药及高性能医疗器械	**Manufacture of Biological Medicines and Advanced Medical Equipment**	**700**	**1593.42**	**537.70**
生物制药	Biological Medicine	453	1229.67	402.04
高性能医疗器械	Advanced Medical Equipment	247	363.76	135.66

Main Indicators on Advanced Manufacturing Enterprises above Designated Size (2017)

(100 million yuan)

年末资产总计 Total Assets at the Year-end	流动资产合计 Total Working Capital	固定资产合计 Total Fixed Assets	主营业务收入 Principal Business Revenue	主营业务成本 Cost of Principal Business	主营业务税金及附加 Tax and Extra Charges on Main Business	利润总额 Total Profits	利税总额 Total Pre-tax Profits	本年应交增值税 Value-added Tax Payable in Current Year	全部就业人员年平均人数(万人) Annual Average Number of Employed Persons (10000 persons)
60355.40	**40368.61**	**10726.65**	**71932.25**	**59302.20**	**856.76**	**4891.09**	**7682.98**	**1927.76**	**681.18**
25761.99	**18598.48**	**3497.70**	**31296.75**	**26104.66**	**129.25**	**1680.32**	**2553.55**	**741.51**	**277.80**
10498.25	6355.30	2542.79	11141.94	9646.05	44.95	616.57	816.12	152.87	170.78
14049.16	11305.64	875.61	18642.03	15103.19	78.26	970.54	1616.58	567.12	99.65
1214.57	937.54	79.30	1512.78	1355.42	6.04	93.22	120.85	21.52	7.37
22461.99	**15755.63**	**3081.11**	**24431.66**	**19114.34**	**249.15**	**1868.23**	**2887.32**	**767.23**	**212.15**
2825.07	1837.06	325.41	2349.80	1760.51	14.76	265.09	343.03	62.96	30.03
746.95	431.51	189.05	315.90	303.97	2.19	-8.79	-3.64	2.81	3.35
1525.74	1013.84	248.39	1537.40	1286.73	8.32	109.25	148.98	31.00	24.42
64.46	35.26	18.59	40.73	36.37	0.21	1.12	2.12	0.78	0.28
156.91	131.61	4.24	205.70	107.30	1.21	41.88	48.00	4.90	1.06
2150.76	1446.69	319.39	1860.73	1536.66	10.44	123.95	179.56	44.88	30.19
5696.38	3816.35	1163.60	7741.97	6496.90	149.26	654.40	1034.62	229.73	42.00
7904.19	6126.81	495.93	8595.77	6070.02	53.50	577.09	978.68	347.92	50.23
1391.54	916.50	316.51	1783.67	1515.86	9.27	104.23	155.98	42.26	30.59
5582.23	**2962.56**	**1582.20**	**7356.63**	**5771.08**	**431.98**	**622.62**	**1332.07**	**276.44**	**31.77**
7143.18	**4961.55**	**1219.87**	**9718.70**	**7948.15**	**58.62**	**714.73**	**1066.09**	**291.95**	**121.87**
1289.03	799.04	291.20	1894.56	1513.93	15.20	147.09	217.76	55.33	13.32
1418.87	887.21	351.39	2671.47	2310.09	14.50	132.89	206.06	58.46	52.87
423.58	275.12	74.39	631.77	534.63	3.34	38.65	59.04	16.97	10.75
4011.69	3000.17	502.89	4520.90	3589.50	25.57	396.10	583.22	161.19	44.94
5350.41	**2894.60**	**1676.35**	**7005.16**	**6109.15**	**33.89**	**379.32**	**559.12**	**145.48**	**83.71**
1360.89	486.78	673.74	1762.65	1593.28	6.18	93.53	135.75	36.02	5.94
3966.86	2396.91	996.73	5226.48	4501.76	27.63	285.31	422.67	109.31	77.68
22.67	10.92	5.89	16.03	14.11	0.08	0.47	0.70	0.15	0.09
2855.43	**1817.43**	**367.10**	**1522.12**	**903.01**	**13.47**	**302.90**	**389.42**	**72.76**	**16.35**
2375.65	1533.91	304.42	1159.35	690.39	10.31	237.46	310.53	62.57	10.56
479.77	283.52	62.68	362.77	212.62	3.16	65.44	78.89	10.19	5.79

12-26 规模以上工业企业主要经济效益指标（2017年）

项　　目	Item
全省总计	**Provincial Total**
按经济类型分	Grouped by Ownership
在总计中：国有控股工业	Of the Total: State-holding Industry
国有工业	State-owned Industry
集体工业	Collective-owned Industry
股份合作工业	Share-holding Cooperative Industry
股份制工业	Share-holding Industry
外商投资工业	Foreign-funded Industry
港澳台投资工业	Industry with Funds from Hong Kong, Macao and Taiwan
按轻重工业分	Grouped by Light and Heavy Industries
轻工业	Light Industry
重工业	Heavy Industry
按企业规模分	Grouped by Size of Enterprises
大型企业	Large Enterprises
中型企业	Medium Enterprises
小微型企业	Small and Micro Enterprises
按行业分	Grouped by Sector
煤炭开采和洗选业	Mining and Washing of Coal
石油和天然气开采业	Extraction of Petroleum and Natural Gas
黑色金属矿采选业	Mining and Dressing of Ferrous Metal Ores
有色金属矿采选业	Mining and Dressing of Nonferrous Metal Ores
非金属矿采选业	Mining and Dressing of Nonmetal Ores
开采辅助活动	Auxiliary Minning Operations
其他采矿业	Mining and Dressing of Other Ores
农副食品加工业	Processing of Farm and Sideline Food
食品制造业	Manufacture of Food
酒、饮料和精制茶制造业	Manufacture of Wine, Beverage and Refined Tea
烟草制品业	Tobacco Products
纺织业	Textile Industry
纺织服装、服饰业	Manufacture of Textile Garments, Footwear and Headgear
皮革、毛皮、羽毛及其制品和制鞋业	Leather, Fur, Feather, Down and Related Products
木材加工和木、竹、藤、棕、草制品业	Timber Processing, Bamboo, Cane, Palm Fiber & Straw Products
家具制造业	Manufacture of Furniture
造纸和纸制品业	Papermaking and Paper Products
印刷和记录媒介复制业	Printing and Record Medium Reproduction
文教、工美、体育和娱乐用品制造业	Manufacture of Cultural, Educational,Sports and Entertainment Articles
石油加工、炼焦和核燃料加工业	Petroleum Refining, Coking and Nuclear Fuel Processing
化学原料和化学制品制造业	Manufacture of Raw Chemical Materials and Chemical Products
医药制造业	Manufacture of Medicines
化学纤维制造业	Manufacture of Chemical Fibers
橡胶和塑料制品业	Rubber and Plastic Products
非金属矿物制品业	Nonmetal Mineral Products
黑色金属冶炼和压延加工业	Smelting and Pressing of Ferrous Metals
有色金属冶炼和压延加工业	Smelting and Pressing of Nonferrous Metals
金属制品业	Metal Products
通用设备制造业	Manufacture of General-purpose Machinery
专用设备制造业	Manufacture of Special-purpose Machinery
汽车制造业	Manufacture of Automobile
铁路、船舶、航空航天和其他运输设备制造业	Manufacture of Railway ,Ship,Aeronautics and Other Transport equipment
电气机械和器材制造业	Manufacture of Electrical Machinery and Equipment
计算机、通信和其他电子设备制造业	Manufacture of Communication Equipment, Computers and Other Electronic Equipment
仪器仪表制造业	Manufacture of Instruments and Meters
其他制造业	Other Manufactures
废弃资源综合利用业	Comprehensive Utilization of Waste
金属制品、机械和设备修理业	Manufacture of Metal Products,Machinery and Equipment Maintenance
电力、热力生产和供应业	Production and Supply of Electric Power and Heat Power
燃气生产和供应业	Production and Supply of Gas
水的生产和供应业	Production and Supply of Water

Main Indicators on Economic Benefit of Industrial Enterprises above Designated Size (2017)

总资产贡献率 (%) Ratio of Total Assets to Industrial Output Value (%)	资产负债率 (%) Assets-Liability Ratio (%)	成本费用利润率 (%) Ratio of Profits to Industrial Costs (%)	全员劳动生产率 (元/人) Overall Labor Productivity (yuan/person)	产品销售率 (%) Proportion of Products Sold (%)
12.45	**56.13**	**7.00**	**223415**	**98.00**
13.04	54.98	8.77	699173	98.05
19.45	51.24	10.24	384380	100.12
15.57	62.15	5.30	109426	99.13
22.93	49.85	4.38	236347	97.18
12.17	57.46	6.84	261146	97.89
14.21	53.19	7.60	237807	98.36
11.23	54.85	6.90	152402	97.94
13.70	54.11	7.33	172450	97.50
11.83	57.12	6.81	268108	98.27
13.04	57.51	7.96	307247	97.81
12.36	51.65	7.14	157212	97.68
11.34	57.60	5.36	195917	98.55
26.81	69.01	69.54	7257760	99.38
8.73	59.85	5.34	643628	96.19
25.84	65.25	26.06	449503	97.19
28.26	36.36	12.69	334403	97.90
2.49	26.79	8.28	271913	100.00
30.11	7.21	1.28	194313	94.91
11.64	61.45	5.13	239539	98.75
25.87	40.85	14.45	353026	96.76
18.03	52.87	9.23	382529	96.19
55.37	24.18	17.17	4450798	114.95
14.46	51.75	5.76	162834	97.43
15.05	51.52	5.10	115872	97.43
13.79	54.43	3.93	107588	98.69
18.48	50.07	8.28	216060	97.75
14.33	50.96	6.45	146747	98.14
11.56	52.41	6.60	229847	96.71
12.28	45.32	7.25	150080	97.42
10.08	58.46	4.63	101993	97.90
55.14	56.63	12.92	4183457	98.54
13.92	49.74	8.26	360920	98.07
13.84	44.16	23.79	380791	94.80
9.80	39.19	9.05	253090	98.65
11.60	52.29	5.49	138705	98.38
13.06	53.39	7.34	203660	98.23
11.92	63.54	5.49	438582	102.67
11.09	68.96	4.08	244959	99.96
13.84	52.76	5.82	163831	97.35
10.68	53.49	7.36	180774	97.92
11.70	49.58	9.82	192848	96.66
18.41	62.22	9.17	422900	99.80
7.55	61.07	5.93	193349	97.68
10.73	60.11	7.36	176514	97.09
9.82	61.56	5.25	237781	97.34
10.35	47.55	8.55	135007	98.01
9.06	54.67	4.04	100550	97.99
24.03	55.61	8.52	486260	98.72
8.64	54.72	6.22	254511	98.63
7.79	49.18	7.90	871383	99.61
10.89	55.32	8.96	928945	99.85
7.22	57.29	21.75	385746	98.22

12-27 规模以上制造业工业企业主要经济指标
Main Economic Indicators of Manufacturing Enterprises above Designated Size

项　目	Item	2000	2010	2014	2015	2016	2017
企业单位数 (个)	Number of Enterprises (unit)	18571	52102	40156	41081	41627	46116
工业总产值 (亿元)	Gross Industrial Output Value (100 million yuan)	11352.62	79504.12	110962.87	115911.71	124828.73	127147.02
工业增加值 (亿元)	Value-added of Industry (100 million yuan)	2768.88	18317.74	25265.42	26568.90	28504.15	28818.97
主营业务收入 (亿元)	Main Business Revenue (100 million yuan)	10865.66	77730.85	106839.05	110548.00	120392.32	125401.32
资产总计 (亿元)	Total Assets (100 million yuan)	11653.11	52734.31	74598.07	81676.43	90886.30	99921.43
流动资产合计 (亿元)	Total Liquid Assets (100 million yuan)		32414.52	48375.15	52178.92	58723.71	65934.89
固定资产合计 (亿元)	Total Fixed Assets (100 million yuan)		16420.14	17052.02	18383.46	19181.60	18963.43
负债总计 (亿元)	Total Liabilities (100 million yuan)	6950.47	29407.47	43747.09	47206.36	51598.88	56745.05
所有者权益合计(亿元)	Total Creditors' Equity (100 million yuan)	4576.24	23243.24	30598.23	34079.15	38725.42	42862.52
利润总额 (亿元)	Total Profits (100 million yuan)	348.92	5313.74	6110.88	6844.73	7513.00	7997.63
亏损企业亏损额(亿元)	Loss Value of Loss-making Enterprises (100 million yuan)	131.89	195.53	417.14	475.63	396.85	477.70
利税总额 (亿元)	Total Pre-tax Profits (100 million yuan)	729.92	8150.46	10276.84	11011.30	11777.24	12479.36
应交增值税 (亿元)	Value-added Tax Payable(100 million yuan)	277.66	2003.07	3048.20	2892.83	2995.94	3134.63
从业人员平均人数 (万人)	Average Employed Persons (10000 persons)	546.03	1533.72	1423.93	1406.84	1385.19	1373.54

注：本表总产值和增加值绝对数按当年价格计算，增加值2009年及以前用生产法计算，2010年起用收入法计算，2011年统计口径从年业务收入500万元及以上调整为2000万元及以上。

Note: Gross industrial output values and value-added are calculated at current prices.Value-added is calculated by production approach in 2009 and prior to and since 2010 by income approach.

12-28 各市规模以上工业企业主要经济指标（2017年）

Main Economic Indicators of Industrial Enterprises above Designated Size by City (2017)

单位：亿元 (100 million yuan)

市 别	City	主营业务收入 Main Business Revenue	主营业务成本 Cost of Principal Business	资产合计 Total Assets	负债合计 Total Liabilities	利润总额 Total Profits	利税总额 Total Pre-tax Profits	全部就业人员年平均人数(万人) Annual Average Number of Employed Persons (10000 persons)
广 州	Guangzhou	17652.65	14471.55	17608.45	8930.97	1345.76	2272.24	125.85
深 圳	Shenzhen	30821.67	24717.61	33174.65	19641.96	2101.33	3069.03	317.53
珠 海	Zhuhai	4753.60	3853.44	6305.58	3993.04	410.05	563.11	44.22
汕 头	Shantou	3424.58	2789.07	2723.85	1106.08	275.77	376.23	45.89
佛 山	Foshan	20303.16	17412.70	12676.83	6759.07	1560.76	2200.07	160.83
韶 关	Shaoguan	1097.74	902.98	1358.96	877.38	85.75	161.26	13.22
河 源	Heyuan	1297.73	1132.78	981.17	541.57	61.98	96.91	16.31
梅 州	Meizhou	598.99	467.14	853.63	396.22	33.55	103.39	10.01
惠 州	Huizhou	7971.66	7017.98	5865.22	3236.07	499.59	751.74	90.65
汕 尾	Shanwei	1059.70	982.42	656.18	336.19	25.70	43.41	19.53
东 莞	Dongguan	18240.15	15896.90	12586.92	7628.67	722.04	1179.99	270.14
中 山	Zhongshan	4831.05	4124.60	4370.73	2547.08	225.50	396.97	82.05
江 门	Jiangmen	3998.34	3318.62	3305.87	1739.19	236.98	395.97	45.97
阳 江	Yangjiang	1645.90	1416.93	1882.14	1232.71	139.13	192.56	13.91
湛 江	Zhanjiang	2536.72	2123.01	2598.04	1862.69	161.09	340.73	13.51
茂 名	Maoming	2666.24	2021.50	1299.17	522.24	313.91	614.10	15.36
肇 庆	Zhaoqing	2832.07	2461.11	1847.62	896.97	158.90	253.15	27.17
清 远	Qingyuan	1567.86	1352.02	1578.37	917.27	98.87	156.30	20.15
潮 州	Chaozhou	1314.46	1124.53	769.53	263.70	104.13	150.83	18.99
揭 阳	Jieyang	4749.18	4136.13	2127.81	896.51	275.69	403.08	42.24
云 浮	Yunfu	560.91	484.02	630.46	335.16	27.88	48.23	9.67
按经济区域分	By Region							
珠 三 角	Pearl River Delta	111404.35	93274.50	97741.87	55373.02	7260.91	11082.25	1164.40
东 翼	Eastern Region	10547.92	9032.16	6277.38	2602.47	681.30	973.55	126.65
西 翼	Western Region	6848.86	5561.44	5779.35	3617.64	614.13	1147.39	42.77
山 区	Mountainous Region	5123.24	4338.95	5402.59	3067.60	308.02	566.09	69.37

12-29 各市私营工业企业主要经济指标（2017年）

Main Economic Indicators of Private Industrial Enterprises by City (2017)

单位：亿元 (100 million yuan)

市别	City	主营业务收入 Main Business Revenue	主营业务成本 Cost of Principal Business	资产合计 Total Assets	负债合计 Total Liabilities	利润总额 Total Profits	利税总额 Total Pre-tax Profits	全部就业人员年平均人数(万人) Annual Average Number of Employed Persons (10000 persons)
广　州	Guangzhou	2313.13	1943.87	2015.08	1135.31	105.96	173.93	33.45
深　圳	Shenzhen	6314.00	5232.92	6954.93	4320.37	381.45	532.20	85.25
珠　海	Zhuhai	383.70	318.81	370.00	245.58	21.53	32.30	6.36
汕　头	Shantou	1576.64	1263.84	819.76	344.52	139.12	174.41	22.22
佛　山	Foshan	5464.39	4840.12	2772.99	1525.40	329.73	463.54	44.32
韶　关	Shaoguan	106.50	95.88	126.52	92.32	3.59	5.03	0.86
河　源	Heyuan	299.37	251.64	230.61	131.14	16.71	26.30	2.79
梅　州	Meizhou	124.72	110.34	118.36	67.06	4.02	8.14	2.41
惠　州	Huizhou	1082.21	962.01	569.79	387.96	56.87	78.34	13.21
汕　尾	Shanwei	393.73	372.32	81.48	28.47	5.82	9.04	7.89
东　莞	Dongguan	5720.27	4869.02	3479.18	2612.53	250.46	455.87	49.14
中　山	Zhongshan	1062.52	910.02	885.03	571.05	36.48	72.80	21.77
江　门	Jiangmen	774.91	680.85	495.71	328.11	28.04	52.08	10.09
阳　江	Yangjiang	531.86	471.04	238.06	108.92	36.68	53.82	6.37
湛　江	Zhanjiang	590.19	538.28	291.51	224.10	12.56	24.80	4.66
茂　名	Maoming	518.70	403.69	257.14	80.94	71.09	99.48	5.49
肇　庆	Zhaoqing	947.83	813.02	418.07	187.55	59.55	92.68	7.76
清　远	Qingyuan	239.02	214.72	213.88	160.51	7.06	13.71	2.87
潮　州	Chaozhou	447.59	373.26	216.38	81.71	38.31	54.91	8.43
揭　阳	Jieyang	2472.77	2167.20	523.01	155.40	132.20	196.37	21.41
云　浮	Yunfu	80.45	70.55	77.85	46.74	3.09	5.86	1.49
按经济区域分	By Region							
珠三角	Pearl River Delta	24062.96	20570.65	17960.78	11313.86	1270.08	1953.74	271.36
东　翼	Eastern Region	4890.72	4176.62	1640.62	610.10	315.44	434.73	59.95
西　翼	Western Region	1640.75	1413.01	786.71	413.95	120.33	178.10	16.52
山　区	Mountainous Region	850.05	743.13	767.22	497.77	34.47	59.05	10.41

12-30 各市工业企业主要经济效益指标（2017年）
Main Indicators on Economic Benefit of Industrial Enterprises by City (2017)

市 别	City	总资产贡献率 (%) Ratio of Total Assets to Industrial Output Value (%)	资产负债率 (%) Assets-Liability Ratio (%)	成本费用利润率 (%) Ratio of Profits to Industrial Costs (%)	全员劳动生产率 (元/人) Overall Labor Productivity (yuan/person)	产品销售率 (%) Proportion of Products Sold (%)
全省合计	**Provincial Total**	**12.45**	**56.13**	**7.00**	**223415**	**98.00**
广 州	Guangzhou	13.36	50.72	8.15	328260	99.23
深 圳	Shenzhen	9.67	59.21	7.13	252660	97.02
珠 海	Zhuhai	9.09	63.33	8.83	257672	99.69
汕 头	Shantou	14.48	40.61	8.75	181751	98.39
佛 山	Foshan	17.79	53.32	8.26	269555	97.99
韶 关	Shaoguan	12.91	64.56	8.28	232318	99.69
河 源	Heyuan	10.50	55.20	5.00	171128	97.59
梅 州	Meizhou	13.08	46.42	6.08	194515	100.23
惠 州	Huizhou	13.27	55.17	6.58	204131	97.00
汕 尾	Shanwei	7.09	51.23	2.48	98986	97.56
东 莞	Dongguan	9.57	60.61	4.07	133936	98.89
中 山	Zhongshan	9.60	58.28	4.83	130866	98.05
江 门	Jiangmen	12.50	52.61	6.23	215740	96.74
阳 江	Yangjiang	11.77	65.50	9.15	263712	95.69
湛 江	Zhanjiang	14.26	71.70	7.04	550070	97.11
茂 名	Maoming	48.42	40.20	14.34	552534	97.84
肇 庆	Zhaoqing	14.82	48.55	5.94	222963	97.65
清 远	Qingyuan	10.70	58.11	6.66	197638	98.28
潮 州	Chaozhou	20.28	34.27	8.62	167568	97.31
揭 阳	Jieyang	20.32	42.13	6.19	229449	99.16
云 浮	Yunfu	8.58	53.16	5.22	133319	96.51

12−30 续表 continued

市 别	City	总资产贡献率比去年增减（百分点） Percentage Gain in Ratio of Total Assets to Industrial Output Value over Preceding Year	资产负债率比去年增减（百分点） Percentage Gain in Assets-Liability Ratio over Preceding Year	成本费用利润率比去年增减（百分点） Percentage Gain in Ratio of Profits to Industrial Costs over Preceding Year	全员劳动生产率比去年增长(%) Growth in Overall Labor Productivity over Preceding Year (%)	产品销售率比去年增减（百分点） Percentage Gain in Proportion of Products Sold over Preceding Year
全省合计	**Provincial Total**	**-0.53**	**-0.04**	**0.15**	**13.30**	**0.94**
广　州	Guangzhou	-0.11	-0.78	0.79	9.40	1.36
深　圳	Shenzhen	0.06	0.59	0.26	18.00	-0.47
珠　海	Zhuhai	-0.65	1.01	-1.45	15.50	7.36
汕　头	Shantou	-0.67	0.14	-0.44	8.40	1.70
佛　山	Foshan	-0.78	-1.65	-0.21	12.50	0.80
韶　关	Shaoguan	-0.11	2.49	1.57	10.20	-0.13
河　源	Heyuan	-2.77	1.31	-0.65	6.80	0.94
梅　州	Meizhou	-2.67	-4.54	-1.60	8.40	1.43
惠　州	Huizhou	-0.77	-2.24	-0.38	7.30	0.19
汕　尾	Shanwei	-0.91	-0.10	-0.83	17.80	0.03
东　莞	Dongguan	1.52	0.33	0.63	14.50	1.22
中　山	Zhongshan	-3.98	0.45	-0.81	9.20	2.84
江　门	Jiangmen	-0.26	-1.29	0.03	16.60	2.51
阳　江	Yangjiang	-0.49	-0.98	2.11	12.20	0.77
湛　江	Zhanjiang	3.78	-2.99	3.71	20.20	0.99
茂　名	Maoming	-3.37	-1.95	-0.36	14.50	-0.11
肇　庆	Zhaoqing	-4.29	3.30	-0.25	16.90	-0.09
清　远	Qingyuan	-1.72	-2.34	-0.02	10.80	1.52
潮　州	Chaozhou	-5.41	1.93	-2.08	13.10	-0.45
揭　阳	Jieyang	-1.31	3.45	0.69	7.50	0.74
云　浮	Yunfu	-7.50	2.81	-1.39	15.20	-0.15

注：全员劳动生产率比去年增长为快报数，其他增速为年报可比口径。
Note: Growth in overall labor productivity over preceding Year is caculated by flash report，others are caculated by comparable scope.

12-31 各市规模以上国有控股工业企业主要经济效益指标（2017年）
Main Indicators on Economic Benefit of State-holding Industrial Enterprises above Designated Size by City (2017)

市别	City	总资产贡献率 (%) Ratio of Total Assets to Industrial Output Value (%)	资产负债率 (%) Assets-Liability Ratio (%)	成本费用利润率 (%) Ratio of Profits to Industrial Costs (%)	全员劳动生产率 (元/人) Overall Labor Productivity (yuan/person)	产品销售率 (%) Proportion of Products Sold (%)
全省合计	**Provincial Total**	**13.04**	**54.98**	**8.77**	**699173**	**98.05**
广州	Guangzhou	13.71	47.56	8.59	814270	99.71
深圳	Shenzhen	10.46	56.46	9.82	673261	90.55
珠海	Zhuhai	9.17	68.49	11.83	723607	105.13
汕头	Shantou	7.04	49.69	5.00	439631	99.04
佛山	Foshan	11.32	49.17	7.95	417291	99.61
韶关	Shaoguan	16.63	69.15	8.15	495143	101.31
河源	Heyuan	8.74	40.91	5.32	453462	100.28
梅州	Meizhou	27.70	42.78	8.91	993616	108.54
惠州	Huizhou	16.65	52.52	10.61	775660	98.63
汕尾	Shanwei	8.38	51.27	6.61	471398	98.82
东莞	Dongguan	6.87	57.43	3.01	316288	100.75
中山	Zhongshan	5.84	60.65	0.69	385094	97.74
江门	Jiangmen	9.03	50.36	4.99	611616	98.25
阳江	Yangjiang	8.65	74.24	12.80	826701	93.01
湛江	Zhanjiang	17.55	60.83	6.77	1149530	100.10
茂名	Maoming	64.53	46.09	15.58	2550750	99.28
肇庆	Zhaoqing	6.53	42.82	3.98	298578	100.10
清远	Qingyuan	9.46	59.08	6.51	667648	101.00
潮州	Chaozhou	13.20	33.64	8.62	701045	100.00
揭阳	Jieyang	6.24	57.73	4.03	510154	100.01
云浮	Yunfu	8.86	52.96	4.20	441111	100.15

12-32 各市按经济类型分的工业企业资产（2017年）

Total Assets of Industrial Enterprises by Ownership and by City (2017)

单位：亿元 (100 million yuan)

市 别	City	资产合计 Total Assets	#国有控股工业 State-holding Industry	集体工业 Collective-owned Industry	股份合作制工业 Share-holding Cooperative Industry	股份制工业 Share-holding Industry	外商投资工业 Foreign-funded Industry	港澳台投资工业 Industry with Funds from Hong Kong,Macao and Taiwan
广 州	Guangzhou	17608.45	7910.09	9.97	10.70	10068.83	4593.90	2481.39
深 圳	Shenzhen	33174.65	4760.25	0.19		21806.86	3496.03	7823.76
珠 海	Zhuhai	6305.58	2901.23	0.83		4236.58	1196.19	869.40
汕 头	Shantou	2723.85	428.94	4.33	3.41	2055.29	309.06	236.32
佛 山	Foshan	12676.83	1070.64	10.91	2.53	8636.98	1727.10	2088.68
韶 关	Shaoguan	1358.96	700.52	2.59	1.21	1164.19	46.43	115.24
河 源	Heyuan	981.17	107.33	1.05		632.19	98.91	242.90
梅 州	Meizhou	853.63	222.07	0.25	2.36	746.64	35.07	55.33
惠 州	Huizhou	5865.22	1478.96	4.07		2419.54	1708.24	1703.12
汕 尾	Shanwei	656.18	135.32	11.63		420.00	40.10	165.24
东 莞	Dongguan	12586.92	755.67	41.80		6867.32	1947.99	3716.94
中 山	Zhongshan	4370.73	455.03	6.33	0.21	2129.79	1251.16	957.41
江 门	Jiangmen	3305.87	416.81	0.82		1620.28	455.29	1210.95
阳 江	Yangjiang	1882.14	1097.08	0.03		1641.74	50.15	134.74
湛 江	Zhanjiang	2598.04	1133.42	15.75		1876.71	78.31	596.48
茂 名	Maoming	1299.17	531.83	2.88	0.93	1140.23	36.44	44.06
肇 庆	Zhaoqing	1847.62	343.62	4.89		1136.27	343.96	297.62
清 远	Qingyuan	1578.37	294.07	0.12		1010.26	78.47	475.06
潮 州	Chaozhou	769.53	167.94	2.84	1.77	580.76	18.10	96.84
揭 阳	Jieyang	2127.81	263.94	5.13		1825.62	37.86	135.04
云 浮	Yunfu	630.46	118.48	0.71		470.00	45.70	105.58
按经济区域分	By Region							
珠 三 角	Pearl River Delta	97741.87	20092.29	79.83	13.43	58922.46	16719.87	21149.27
东 翼	Eastern Region	6277.38	996.14	23.93	5.17	4881.68	405.12	633.44
西 翼	Western Region	5779.35	2762.33	18.65	0.93	4658.67	164.90	775.28
山 区	Mountainous Region	5402.59	1442.47	4.73	3.57	4023.29	304.58	994.10

12－33 各市规模以上大中型工业企业产值资产（2017年）

Gross Output Value and Total Assets of Large and Medium-sized Industrial Enterprises above Designated Size by City (2017)

单位：亿元 (100 million yuan)

市别	City	企业个数（个）Number of Enterprises (unit)	#大型 Large sized	工业总产值（当年价格）Gross Industrial Output Value (at current price)	#大型 Large sized	资产总计 Total Assets	#大型 Large sized
全省合计	**Provincial Total**	**10122**	**1618**	**95951.23**	**63688.06**	**86276.84**	**58666.07**
广　州	Guangzhou	837	179	13375.38	10367.11	13669.22	10544.07
深　圳	Shenzhen	2006	401	26116.81	20306.32	26605.37	20028.20
珠　海	Zhuhai	322	66	2780.40	1745.31	4769.30	3475.22
汕　头	Shantou	492	19	1954.26	460.41	1694.93	538.19
佛　山	Foshan	1209	164	13551.27	6909.80	9114.63	5154.88
韶　关	Shaoguan	73	17	799.85	552.60	919.87	542.98
河　源	Heyuan	106	18	818.08	555.80	614.07	295.47
梅　州	Meizhou	78	9	368.49	159.40	560.62	252.65
惠　州	Huizhou	586	108	6091.61	4431.41	4625.84	3479.74
汕　尾	Shanwei	115	61	966.52	790.72	553.85	354.06
东　莞	Dongguan	1972	297	13617.80	9727.27	9401.28	6166.36
中　山	Zhongshan	609	84	3303.57	1944.01	3045.66	1686.69
江　门	Jiangmen	369	52	2552.59	1249.98	2178.14	1137.62
阳　江	Yangjiang	166	11	1096.73	543.38	1584.74	1054.99
湛　江	Zhanjiang	106	13	1685.76	957.07	2076.62	1423.64
茂　名	Maoming	66	7	1218.41	999.84	627.80	455.42
肇　庆	Zhaoqing	237	27	1553.62	568.70	1069.37	550.67
清　远	Qingyuan	165	29	1061.00	414.02	1067.43	413.45
潮　州	Chaozhou	196	8	561.40	149.51	427.19	159.51
揭　阳	Jieyang	358	40	2230.65	733.88	1417.65	854.04
云　浮	Yunfu	54	8	247.01	121.51	253.25	98.20
按经济区域分	By Region						
珠三角	Pearl River Delta	8147	1378	82943.06	57249.91	74478.81	52223.46
东　翼	Eastern Region	1161	128	5712.83	2134.53	4093.63	1905.8
西　翼	Western Region	338	31	4000.90	2500.30	4289.16	2934.05
山　区	Mountainous Region	476	81	3294.43	1803.33	3415.24	1602.75

12-34 各市现代产业增加值及比重（2017年）

Value Added and Ratio of Modern Industries by City (2017)

市　别	City	先进制造业增加值（亿元）Value Added of Advanced Manufacturing Industry (100 Million yuan)	先进制造业增加值占规模以上工业比重(%) Ratio of Value Added to that of Industry (%)	高技术制造业增加值（亿元）Value Added of High-tech Industry (100 Million yuan)	高技术制造业增加值占规模以上工业比重(%) Ratio of Value Added to that of Industry (%)
全省合计	**Provincial Total**	**17250.14**	**55.0**	**9507.81**	**30.3**
广　州	Guangzhou	2456.01	59.5	564.25	13.7
深　圳	Shenzhen	5716.06	71.2	5353.06	66.7
珠　海	Zhuhai	731.96	64.2	293.35	25.7
汕　头	Shantou	283.94	34.0	46.00	5.5
佛　山	Foshan	2033.04	46.9	266.78	6.2
韶　关	Shaoguan	101.48	33.0	16.59	5.4
河　源	Heyuan	143.88	51.5	111.91	40.1
梅　州	Meizhou	54.26	27.9	35.49	18.2
惠　州	Huizhou	1195.16	64.6	811.99	43.9
汕　尾	Shanwei	78.86	40.8	38.49	19.9
东　莞	Dongguan	1920.33	53.1	1459.03	40.3
中　山	Zhongshan	485.55	45.2	173.39	16.1
江　门	Jiangmen	384.04	38.7	80.46	8.1
阳　江	Yangjiang	63.88	17.4	8.02	2.2
湛　江	Zhanjiang	320.41	43.1	7.78	1.0
茂　名	Maoming	530.31	62.5	25.83	3.0
肇　庆	Zhaoqing	179.19	29.6	51.03	8.4
清　远	Qingyuan	114.77	28.8	25.41	6.4
潮　州	Chaozhou	63.19	19.9	26.92	8.5
揭　阳	Jieyang	361.61	37.3	101.72	10.5
云　浮	Yunfu	32.20	25.0	10.32	8.0
按经济区域分	By Region				
珠 三 角	Pearl River Delta	15101.35	58.6	9053.34	35.1
东　翼	Eastern Region	787.61	34.0	213.13	9.2
西　翼	Western Region	914.60	46.7	41.62	2.1
山　区	Mountainous Region	446.58	34.1	199.71	15.3

注：本表现代产业增加值按年报收入法计算；高技术制造业增加值采用新的国家统计局高技术产业(制造业)分类(2013)。
Note: Value Added of modern industries in this table is calculated in accordance with the income method of the annual report.

12-35 全省工业总产值最大的50家工业企业（2017年）
Top 50 Industrial Enterprises of the Province in Terms of Gross Industrial Output Value (2017)

序号 Rank	企业名称	Name of Enterprises
1	华为技术有限公司	HUAWEI TECHNOLOGIES CO., LTD
2	广东电网公司	GUANGDONG POWER GRID CORPORATION
3	美的集团股份有限公司	GUANGDONG MD HOLDING CO., LTD
4	华为终端（东莞）有限公司	HUAWEI DEVICE (DONGGUAN) CO., LTD.
5	中兴通讯股份有限公司	ZTE CORPORATION
6	富泰华工业(深圳)有限公司	FUTAIHUA INDUSTRY (SHENZHEN) CO., LTD
7	东风汽车有限公司东风日产乘用车公司	DONGFENG MOTOR CO. LTD. PASSENGER VEHICLE COMPANY
8	惠州三星电子有限公司	HUIZHOU SAMSUNG ELECTRONICS CO.,LTD
9	中国石油化工股份有限公司茂名分公司	SINOPEC MAOMING COMPANY
10	广汽本田汽车有限公司	GUANGQI HONDA AUTOMOBILE CO., LTD
11	东莞市欧珀精密电子有限公司	DONGGUAN OPPO PRECISION ELECTRONIC CORP.,LTD
12	维沃通信科技有限公司	VIVO COMMUNICATION TECHNOLOGY CO., LTD
13	中国南方电网有限责任公司	CHINA SOUTHERN POWER GRID CO., LTD
14	广汽丰田汽车有限公司	GAC TOYOTA MOTOR CO.,LTD
15	深圳供电局有限公司	SHENZHEN POWER SUPPLY BUREAU CO.,LTD
16	比亚迪汽车工业有限公司	BYD AUTO INDUSTRY CO.,LTD
17	广州汽车集团乘用车有限公司	GUANGZHOU AUTOMOBILE GROUP MOTOR CO., LTD
18	广州供电局有限公司	GUANGZHOU POWER SUPPLY BUREAU CO.,LTD
19	中国石油化工股份有限公司广州分公司	SINOPEC GUANGZHOU COMPANY
20	中海油惠州石化有限公司	CNOOC HUIZHOU PETROCHEMICALS COMPANY LIMITED
21	纬创资通(中山)有限公司	WISTRON INFOCOMM (ZHONGSHAN) CORPORATION
22	深圳市裕展精密科技有限公司	SHENZHEN YUZHAN PRECISION TECHNOLOGY CO.,LTD
23	鸿富锦精密工业(深圳)有限公司	HONG FU JIN PRECISION (SHENZHEN) CO., LTD
24	广东中烟工业有限责任公司	GUANGDONG CHINA TOBACCO INDUSTRIAL CO., LTD
25	珠海格力电器股份有限公司	GREE ELECTRIC APPLIANCES, INC. OF ZHUHAI
26	乐金显示（广州）有限公司	LG DISPLAY (GUANGZHOU)CO.,LTD
27	深圳创维-RGB电子有限公司	SHENZHEN SKYWORTH-RGB ELECTRONICS CO., LTD
28	宝钢湛江钢铁有限公司	BAOSTEEL ZHANJIANG IRON & STEEL CO., LTD
29	伯恩光学（惠州）有限公司	BIEL CRYSTAL MANUFACTORY(HUIZHOU) LIMITED
30	联想信息产品(深圳)有限公司	LENOVO INFORMATION PRODUCTS (SHENZHEN)CO., LTD
31	华为机器有限公司	HUAWEI MACHINE CO., LTD
32	东风本田发动机有限公司	DONGFENG HONDA ENGINE CO., LTD
33	深圳市华星光电技术有限公司	SHENZHEN CHINA STAR OPTOELECTRONICS TECHNOLOGY CO., LTD.
34	中国石化湛江东兴石油化工有限公司	SINOPEC ZHANJIANG DONGXING PETROLEUM ENTERPRISE CO., LTD
35	中海石油（中国）有限公司深圳分公司	CNOOC (CHINA) LIMITED SHENZHEN BRANCH
36	中海壳牌石油化工有限公司	CNOOC AND SHELL PETROCHEMICALS COMPANY LIMITED
37	无限极（中国）有限公司	INFINITUS (CHINA) CO., LTD.
38	宝钢集团广东韶关钢铁有限公司	BAOWU GROUP GUANGDONG SHAOGUAN IRON & STEEL CO., LTD.
39	康美药业股份有限公司	KANGMEI PHARMACEUTICAL CO.,LTD.
40	捷普电子(广州)有限公司	JABIL CIRCUIT (GUANGZHOU) CO., LTD
41	安利（中国）日用品有限公司	AMWAY (CHINA) CO., LTD
42	东莞华贝电子科技有限公司	BAIYUN ELECTRIC GROUP CO LTD
43	东莞三星视界有限公司	SAMSUNG MOBILE DISPLAY
44	ＴＣＬ王牌电器（惠州）有限公司	TCL KING ELECTRICAL APPLIANCES(HUIZHOU) CO. LTD
45	广东广青金属科技有限公司	GUANGDONG GUANGQING METAL TECHNOLOGY CO.,LTD
46	周大福珠宝金行（深圳）有限公司	CHOW TAI FOOK JEWELLERY(SHENZHEN) CO.,LTD.
47	广州宝洁有限公司	PROCTER & GAMBLE (GUANGZHOU) CO., LTD
48	湛江晨鸣浆纸有限公司	ZHANJIANG CHENMING PULP & PAPER CO., LTD
49	玖龙纸业（东莞）有限公司	DONGGUAN NINE DRAGONS PAPER INDUSTRIES CO., LTD.
50	康佳集团股份有限公司	KONKA GROUP CO., LTD

12-36 全省主营业务收入最大的50家工业企业（2017年）

Top 50 Industrial Enterprises of the Province in Terms of Principal Business Revenue (2017)

序号 Rank	企业名称	Name of Enterprises
1	华为技术有限公司	HUAWEI TECHNOLOGIES CO., LTD
2	广东电网公司	GUANGDONG POWER GRID CORPORATION
3	华为终端（东莞）有限公司	HUAWEI DEVICE (DONGGUAN) CO., LTD.
4	美的集团股份有限公司	GUANGDONG MD HOLDING CO., LTD
5	东莞市欧珀精密电子有限公司	DONGGUAN OPPO PRECISION ELECTRONIC CORP.,LTD
6	富泰华工业(深圳)有限公司	FUTAIHUA INDUSTRY (SHENZHEN) CO., LTD
7	珠海格力电器股份有限公司	GREE ELECTRIC APPLIANCES, INC. OF ZHUHAI
8	东风汽车有限公司东风日产乘用车公司	DONGFENG MOTOR CO. LTD. PASSENGER VEHICLE COMPANY
9	维沃通信科技有限公司	VIVO COMMUNICATION TECHNOLOGY CO., LTD
10	中兴通讯股份有限公司	ZTE CORPORATION
11	惠州三星电子有限公司	HUIZHOU SAMSUNG ELECTRONICS CO.,LTD
12	广汽本田汽车有限公司	GUANGQI HONDA AUTOMOBILE CO., LTD
13	中国石油化工股份有限公司茂名分公司	SINOPEC MAOMING COMPANY
14	中国南方电网有限责任公司	CHINA SOUTHERN POWER GRID CO., LTD
15	广汽丰田汽车有限公司	GAC TOYOTA MOTOR CO.,LTD
16	深圳供电局有限公司	SHENZHEN POWER SUPPLY BUREAU CO.,LTD
17	广州汽车集团乘用车有限公司	GUANGZHOU AUTOMOBILE GROUP MOTOR CO., LTD
18	广州供电局有限公司	GUANGZHOU POWER SUPPLY BUREAU CO.,LTD
19	中国石油化工股份有限公司广州分公司	SINOPEC GUANGZHOU COMPANY
20	比亚迪汽车工业有限公司	BYD AUTO INDUSTRY CO.,LTD
21	中海油惠州石化有限公司	CNOOC HUIZHOU PETROCHEMICALS COMPANY LIMITED
22	鸿富锦精密工业(深圳)有限公司	HONG FU JIN PRECISION (SHENZHEN) CO., LTD
23	纬创资通(中山)有限公司	WISTRON INFOCOMM (ZHONGSHAN) CORPORATION
24	深圳市裕展精密科技有限公司	SHENZHEN YUZHAN PRECISION TECHNOLOGY CO.,LTD
25	广东中烟工业有限责任公司	GUANGDONG CHINA TOBACCO INDUSTRIAL CO., LTD
26	宝钢湛江钢铁有限公司	BAOSTEEL ZHANJIANG IRON & STEEL CO., LTD
27	乐金显示（广州）有限公司	LG DISPLAY (GUANGZHOU)CO.,LTD
28	康佳集团股份有限公司	KONKA GROUP CO., LTD
29	联想信息产品(深圳)有限公司	LENOVO INFORMATION PRODUCTS (SHENZHEN)CO., LTD
30	华为机器有限公司	HUAWEI MACHINE CO., LTD
31	伯恩光学（惠州）有限公司	BIEL CRYSTAL MANUFACTORY(HUIZHOU) LIMITED
32	深圳市华星光电技术有限公司	SHENZHEN CHINA STAR OPTOELECTRONICS TECHNOLOGY CO., LTD.
33	深圳创维-RGB电子有限公司	SHENZHEN SKYWORTH-RGB ELECTRONICS CO., LTD
34	中国石化湛江东兴石油化工有限公司	SINOPEC ZHANJIANG DONGXING PETROLEUM ENTERPRISE CO., LTD
35	中海石油（中国）有限公司深圳分公司	CNOOC (CHINA) LIMITED SHENZHEN BRANCH
36	东风本田发动机有限公司	DONGFENG HONDA ENGINE CO., LTD
37	宝钢集团广东韶关钢铁有限公司	BAOWU GROUP GUANGDONG SHAOGUAN IRON & STEEL CO., LTD.
38	中海壳牌石油化工有限公司	CNOOC AND SHELL PETROCHEMICALS COMPANY LIMITED
39	ＴＣＬ王牌电器（惠州）有限公司	TCL KING ELECTRICAL APPLIANCES(HUIZHOU) CO. LTD
40	中国石油天然气股份有限公司天然气销售南方分公司	SOUTH BRANCH，NATURAL GAS MARKETING COMPANY，PETROCHINA COMPANY LIMITED
41	康美药业股份有限公司	KANGMEI PHARMACEUTICAL CO.,LTD.
42	捷普电子(广州)有限公司	JABIL CIRCUIT (GUANGZHOU) CO., LTD
43	惠州比亚迪电子有限公司	HUIZHOU BYD ELECTRONICS COMPANY LIMITED
44	无限极（中国）有限公司	INFINITUS (CHINA) CO., LTD.
45	广州宝洁有限公司	PROCTER & GAMBLE (GUANGZHOU) CO., LTD
46	东莞华贝电子科技有限公司	BAIYUN ELECTRIC GROUP CO LTD
47	东莞三星视界有限公司	SAMSUNG MOBILE DISPLAY
48	周大福珠宝金行（深圳）有限公司	CHOW TAI FOOK JEWELLERY(SHENZHEN) CO.,LTD.
49	佛山群志光电有限公司	INNOLUX CORPORATION-FOSHAN
50	玖龙纸业（东莞）有限公司	DONGGUAN NINE DRAGONS PAPER INDUSTRIES CO.，LTD.

12-37 全省固定资产合计最大的50家工业企业（2017年）

Top 50 Industrial Enterprises of the Province in Terms of Net Value of Fixed Assets (2017)

序号 Rank	企业名称	Name of Enterprises
1	广东电网公司	GUANGDONG POWER GRID CORPORATION
2	中国南方电网有限责任公司	CHINA SOUTHERN POWER GRID CO., LTD
3	阳江核电有限公司	YANGJIANG NUCLEAR POWER CO., LTD.
4	宝钢湛江钢铁有限公司	BAOSTEEL ZHANJIANG IRON & STEEL CO., LTD
5	美的集团股份有限公司	GUANGDONG MD HOLDING CO., LTD
6	深圳供电局有限公司	SHENZHEN POWER SUPPLY BUREAU CO.,LTD
7	中海石油（中国）有限公司深圳分公司	CNOOC (CHINA) LIMITED SHENZHEN BRANCH
8	中海石油深海开发有限公司	CNOOC DEEPWATER DEVELOPMENT LIMITED
9	华为技术有限公司	HUAWEI TECHNOLOGIES CO., LTD
10	中海油惠州石化有限公司	CNOOC HUIZHOU PETROCHEMICALS COMPANY LIMITED
11	深圳市华星光电技术有限公司	SHENZHEN CHINA STAR OPTOELECTRONICS TECHNOLOGY CO., LTD.
12	广州市净水有限公司	GUANGZHOU SEWAGE PURIFICATION CO.,LTD
13	岭东核电有限公司	LING DONG NUCLEAR POWER CO., LTD
14	中海壳牌石油化工有限公司	CNOOC AND SHELL PETROCHEMICALS COMPANY LIMITED
15	伯恩光学（惠州）有限公司	BIEL CRYSTAL MANUFACTORY(HUIZHOU) LIMITED
16	乐金显示(中国)有限公司	LG DISPLAY (CHINA)CO.,LTD
17	湛江晨鸣浆纸有限公司	ZHANJIANG CHENMING PULP & PAPER CO., LTD
18	岭澳核电有限公司	LING'AO NUCLEAR POWER CO., LTD
19	中国石油化工股份有限公司茂名分公司	SINOPEC MAOMING COMPANY
20	比亚迪汽车工业有限公司	BYD AUTO INDUSTRY CO.,LTD
21	广州市自来水公司	GUANGZHOU WATER SUPPLY COMPANY
22	华能国际电力股份有限公司海门电厂	HUANENG HAIMEN POWER PLANT
23	广东国华粤电台山发电有限公司	GUANGDONG GUOHUA YUEDIAN TAISHAN POWER GENERATION CO.,LTD
24	玖龙纸业（东莞）有限公司	DONGGUAN NINE DRAGONS PAPER INDUSTRIES CO.，LTD.
25	中兴通讯股份有限公司	ZTE CORPORATION
26	阳西县海滨电力发展有限公司	YANGXI HARBOR ELECTRIC POWER DEVELOPMENT CO.,LTD
27	宝钢集团广东韶关钢铁有限公司	BAOWU GROUP GUANGDONG SHAOGUAN IRON & STEEL CO., LTD.
28	广东粤电靖海发电有限公司	GUANGDONG YUEDIAN JINGHAI POWER GENERATION CO., LTD
29	中国石油化工股份有限公司广州分公司	SINOPEC GUANGZHOU COMPANY
30	富泰华工业(深圳)有限公司	FUTAIHUA INDUSTRY (SHENZHEN) CO., LTD
31	鞍钢联众（广州）不锈钢有限公司	ANSHAN LIANZHONG STAINLESS STEEL CO. LTD. (GUANGZHOU)
32	天马微电子股份有限公司	TIANMA MICROELECTRONICS COMPANY, LIMITED
33	广东大唐国际潮州发电有限责任公司	GUANDDONG DATANG INTERNATIONAL CHAOZHOU POWER
34	广船国际有限公司	GUANGZHOU SHIPYARD INTERNATIONAL COMPANY LIMITED
35	广东省韶关粤江发电有限责任公司	SHAOGUAN POWER PLANT
36	亚太森博（广东）纸业有限公司	ASIA SYMBOL (GUANGDONG) PAPER CO., LTD.
37	广东省天然气管网有限公司	GUANGDONG NATURAL GAS GRID CO., LTD
38	广东汉能薄膜太阳能有限公司	GUANG DONG HANERGY THIN-FILM SOLAR CO.,LTD
39	广东红海湾发电有限公司	GUANGDONG RED BAY POWER GENERATION CO., LTD
40	华润电力（海丰）有限公司	CHINA RESOURCES POWER (HAIFENG) CO . , LTD.
41	信利半导体有限公司	TRULY SEMICONDUCTORS LTD.
42	东风汽车有限公司东风日产乘用车公司	DONGFENG MOTOR CO. LTD. PASSENGER VEHICLE COMPANY
43	广汽本田汽车有限公司	GUANGQI HONDA AUTOMOBILE CO., LTD
44	广州汽车集团乘用车有限公司	GUANGZHOU AUTOMOBILE GROUP MOTOR CO., LTD
45	深圳市燃气集团股份有限公司	SHENZHEN GAS CORPORATION LTD
46	深超光电(深圳)有限公司	CENTURY TECHNOLOGY(SHENZHEN) CO.LTD
47	深圳长城开发科技股份有限公司	SHENZHEN KAIFA TECHNOLOGY CO., LTD
48	广东中烟工业有限责任公司	GUANGDONG CHINA TOBACCO INDUSTRIAL CO., LTD
49	广汽丰田汽车有限公司	GAC TOYOTA MOTOR CO.,LTD
50	天生桥一级水电开发有限责任公司	DONGGUAN NINE DRAGONS PAPER INDUSTRIES CO.，LTD.

主要统计指标解释

工业 指从事自然资源的开采，对采掘品和农产品进行加工和再加工的物质生产部门。具体包括：(1)对自然资源的开采，如采矿、晒盐、森林采伐等（但不包括禽兽捕猎和水产捕捞）；(2)对农副产品的加工、再加工，如粮油加工、食品加工、轧花、缫丝、纺织、制革等；(3)对采掘品的加工、再加工，如炼铁、炼钢、化工生产、石油加工、机器制造、木材加工等，以及电力、自来水、煤气的生产和供应等；(4)对工业品的修理、翻新，如机器设备的修理、交通运输工具（包括小卧车）的修理等。

1984 年以前农村的村及村以下办工业归属农业，1984 年以后划归工业。

工业统计调查单位 工业统计调查单位分为两类：独立核算法人工业企业和工业生产活动单位。

(1)独立核算法人工业企业 是指从事工业生产经营活动的单位。独立核算法人工业企业应同时具备以下条件：①依法成立，有自己的名称、组织机构和场所，能够承担民事责任；②独立拥有和使用资产，承担负债，有权与其他单位签订合同；③独立核算盈亏，并能够编制资产负债表。

(2)工业生产活动单位 是指在一个场所从事一种或主要从事一种工业生产活动的经济单位。它包括独立核算工业企业按主营业务活动(即工业生产活动)划分的主营业务活动单位和非工业企业所属的工业生产活动单位（即原非独立核算工业生产单位）。工业生产活动单位，一般应同时具备以下三个条件：①具有一个场所，从事一种或主要从事一种工业活动；②单独组织工业生产、经营或业务活动；③单独核算收入和支出。

轻工业 指主要提供生活消费品和制作手工工具的工业。按其所使用的原料不同，可分为两大类：(1)以农产品为原料的轻工业，是指直接或间接以农产品为基本原料的轻工业。主要包括食品制造、饮料制造、烟草加工、纺织、缝纫、皮革和毛皮制作、造纸以及印刷等工业；(2)以非农产品为原料的轻工业，是指以工业品为原料的轻工业。主要包括文教体育用品、化学药品制造、合成纤维制造、日用化学制品、日用玻璃制品、日用金属制品、手工工具制造、医疗器械制造、文化和办公用机械制造等工业。

重工业 是指为国民经济各部门提供物质技术基础的主要生产资料的工业。按其生产性质和产品用途，可分为下列三类：(1)采掘（伐）工业，是指对自然资源的开采，包括石油开采、煤炭开采、金属矿开采、非金属矿开采和木材采伐等工业；(2)原材料工业，指向国民经济各部门提供基本材料、动力和燃料的工业。包括金属冶炼及加工、炼焦及焦炭化学、化工原料、水泥、人造板以及电力、石油和煤炭加工等工业；(3)加工工业，是指对工业原材料进行再加工制造的工业。包括装备国民经济各部门的机械设备制造工业、金属结构、水泥制品等工业，以及为农业提供的生产资料如化肥、农药等工业。

根据上述划分原则，修理业中以重工业产品为修理作业对象的划为重工业，反之划为轻工业。

工业总产值 是以货币表现的工业企业在一定时期内生产的已出售或可供出售工业产品总量，它反映一定时间内工业生产的总规模和总水平。它包括：在本企业内不再进行加工，经检验、包装入库（规定不需包装的产品除外）的成品价值，对外加工费收入，自制半成品、在产品期末期初差额价值。工业总产值采用“工厂法”计算，即以工业企业作为一个整体，按企业工业生产活动的最终成果来计算，企业内部不允许重复计算，不能把企业内部各个车间（分厂）生产的成果相加。但在企业之间、行业之间、地区之间存在着重复计算。

轻重工业总产值的划分也是按“工厂法”计算的，即一个工业企业在正常情况下生产的主要产品的性质属于轻工业，则该企业的全部总产值作为轻工业总产值；一个工业企业生产的主要产品的性质属于重工业，则该企业的全部总产值作为重工业总产值。

工业销售产值（当年价格） 是以货币形式表现的，工业企业在本年内销售的本企业生产的工业产品或提供工业性劳务价值的总价值量。工业销售产值包括的内容为：

（1）销售成品价值：指企业在报告期内实际销售（包括本期生产和非本期生产）的全部成品、半成品的总价值，即按报告期产品的实际销售数量乘以不含增值税（销项税额）的产品实际销售平均单价计算。销售成品价值中包括企业生产的自制设备及提供给本企业在建工程、其他非工业部门和生活福利部门等单位使用的成品价值，但不包括用订货者来料加工，并且只收取加工费的成品（半成品）价值。

（2）对外加工费收入：指企业在报告期内完成的对外承接的工业品加工（包括用定货者来料加工的产品）的加工费收入；对外工业品修理作业可收取的加工费收入和对内非工业部门提供的加工修理、设备安装等收入。对外加工费收入按不含增值税（销项税额）的价格计算。

对于以对外加工生产为主，对外加工费收入所占比重较大的企业，如果对外加工费收入出现跨年度支付的情况，为保证总产值生产口径计算的准确性，则应将对外加工费收入按实际情况调整，记录本年应实际收取的对外加工费收入。

出口交货值 指工业企业交给外贸部门或自营（委托）出口（包括销往香港、澳门、台湾），用外汇价格结算的产品价值，以及外商来样、来料加工、来件装配和补偿贸易等生产的产品价值。在计算出口交货值时，要把外汇价格按交易时的汇率折成人民币计算。

工业增加值 是指工业行业在报告期内以货币表现的工业生产活动的最终成果，是企业全部生产活动的总成果扣除了在生产过程中消耗或转移的物质产品和劳务价值后的余额，是企业生产过程中新增加的价值。

计算工业增加值通常采用两种方法。

一是“生产法”，即从工业生产过程中产品和劳务价值形成的角度入手，剔除生产环节中间投入的价值，从而得到新增价值的方法。公式为：

工业增加值＝工业总产值－工业中间投入＋本期应交增值税

二是“收入法”，即从工业生产过程中创造的原始收入初次分配的角度，对工业生产活动最终成果进行核算的一种方法，其计算公式为：

工业增加值＝固定资产折旧＋劳动者报酬＋生产税净额＋营业盈余

流动资产合计 资产满足以下条件之一应归为流动资产：（1）预计在一个正常营业周期中变现、出售或耗用，主要包括存货、应收账款等；（2）主要为交易目的而持有；（3）预计在资产负债表日起一年内（含一年）变现；（4）自资产负债日起一年内，交换其他资产或清偿负债的能力不受限制的现金或现金等价物。包括货币资金、应收票据、应收账款、存货等项目。来源于“资产负债表”中“流动资产合计”项目的期末余额数。

应收账款 指企业因销售商品、提供劳务等经营活动所形成的债权，包括应向客户收取的货款、增值税款和为客户代垫的运杂费等。来源于会计“资产负债表”中“应收账款”项目的期末余额数。

存货 指企业在日常活动中持有以备出售的产成品或商品、处在生产过程中的在产品、在生产过程或提供劳务过程中耗用的材料或物料等，通常包括原材料、在产品、半成品、产成品、商品以及周转材料等。来源于会计“资产负债表”中“存货”项目的期末余额数。

产成品 指企业已经完成全部生产过程并验收入库，可以按照合同规定的条件送交订货单位，或者可以作为商品对外销售的产品。来源于会计“产成品”科目的借方余额。

固定资产合计 指企业为生产商品、提供劳务、出租或经营管理而持有的，使用寿命超过一个会计年度的有形资产。包括使用期限超过一年的房屋、建筑物、机器、机械、运输工具以及其他与生产、经营有关的设备、器具、工具等。固定资产合计是时点指标，表示固定资产经过扣减折旧、减值准备等后的期末余额。执行《企业会计准则》或《小企业会计准则》的企业，来源于会计“资产负债表”中“固定资产”项目的期末余额数。

资产总计 指企业过去的交易或者事项形成的、由企业拥有或者控制的、预期会给企业带来经济利益的资源。资产一般按流动性（资产的变现或耗用时间长短）分为流动资产和非流动资产。其中流动资产可分为货币资金、交易性金融资产、应收票据、应收账款、预付款项、其他应收款、存货等；非流动资产可分为长期股权投资、固定资产、无形资产及其他非流动资产等。来源于会计“资产负债表”中“资产总计”项目的期末余额数。

负债合计 指企业过去的交易或者事项形成的，预期会导致经济利益流出企业的现时义务。负债一般按偿还期长短分为流动负债和非流动负债。来源于会计“资产负债表”中“负债合计”项目的期末余额数。

流动负债合计 负债满足下列条件之一的应归为流动负债：（1）预计在一个正常营业周期中清偿；（2）主要为交易目的而持有；（3）自资产负债表日起一年内到期应予清偿；（4）企业无权自主地将清偿推迟至

资产负债表日后一年以上。包括短期借款、应付票据、应付账款、应付职工薪酬、应交税费等项目。来源于会计“资产负债表”中“流动负债合计”项目的期末余额数。

所有者权益合计 指企业资产扣除负债后由所有者享有的剩余权益。公司的所有者权益又称股东权益。包括实收资本、资本公积、盈余公积、未分配利润等。来源于会计“资产负债表”中“所有者权益合计”项目的期末余额数。

实收资本 指企业各投资者实际投入的资本（或股本）总额，包括货币、实物、无形资产等各种形式的投入。实收资本按投资主体可分为国家资本、集体资本、法人资本、个人资本、港澳台资本和外商资本。来源于会计“资产负债表”中“所有者权益”项下“实收资本”的期末余额数。

国家资本 指有权代表国家投资的政府部门或机构、直属事业单位对企业形成的资本金。来源于会计“实收资本”科目。

集体资本 指由本企业职工等自然人集体投资或各种机构对企业进行扶持形成的集体性质的资本金。来源于会计“实收资本”科目。

法人资本 指法人以其依法可支配的资产投入企业形成的资本金。来源于会计“实收资本”科目。

个人资本 指自然人实际投入企业的资本金。来源于会计“实收资本”科目。

港澳台资本 指我国香港、澳门和台湾地区投资者实际投入企业的资本金。来源于会计“实收资本”科目。

外商资本 指外国投资者实际投入企业的资本金。来源于会计“实收资本”科目。

营业收入 指企业经营主要业务和其他业务所确认的收入总额。营业收入合计包括“主营业务收入”和“其他业务收入”。来源于会计“利润表”中“营业收入”项目的本期金额数。

主营业务收入 指企业确认的销售商品、提供劳务等主营业务的收入。来源于会计“主营业务收入”科目的期末贷方余额（结转前）。

主营业务成本 指企业经营主要业务所发生的成本总额。来源于会计“主营业务成本”科目的期末借方余额（结转前）。

销售费用 指企业在销售商品和材料、提供劳务的过程中发生的各种费用，包括保险费、包装费、展览费和广告费、商品维修费、预计产品质量保证损失、运输费、装卸费等以及为销售本企业商品而专设的销售机构（含销售网点、售后服务网点等）的职工薪酬、业务费、折旧费等经营费用。

管理费用 指企业为组织和管理企业生产经营所发生的费用，包括企业在筹建期间内发生的开办费、董事会和行政管理部门在企业经营管理中发生的，或者应当由企业统一负担的公司经费等。根据会计“利润表”中“管理费用”项目的本期金额数填报。

财务费用 指企业为筹集生产经营所需资金等而发生的筹资费用，包括企业生产经营期间发生的利息支出（减利息收入）、汇兑损失（减汇兑收益）以及相关的手续费等。根据会计“利润表”中“财务费用”项目的本期金额数填报。

利润总额 指企业在一定会计期间的经营成果，是生产经营过程中各种收入扣除各种耗费后的盈余，反映企业在报告期内实现的盈亏总额。来源于会计“利润表”中“利润总额”项目的本期金额数。

本年应交增值税 指企业按税法规定，从事货物销售或提供加工、修理修配劳务等增加货物价值的活动本期应交纳的税金。计算公式为：

本年应交增值税=销项税额－（进项税额－进项税额转出）－出口抵减内销产品应纳税额
－减免税款+出口退税

本年进项税额：指工业企业在报告期内购入货物或接受应税劳务而支付的、准予从销项税额中抵扣的增值税额。

本年销项税额：指工业企业在报告期内销售货物或提供应税劳务应收取的增值税额。

利税总额 指企业利润总额、产品销售税金及附加和应交增值税之和。

工业经济效益综合指数 是指现行综合评价工业经济效益总体水平及工业经济运行质量的指数。它是用工业产品销售率、总资产贡献率、资本保值增值率、资产负债率、流动资金周转率、成本费用利润率、全员劳动生产率等七项代表性经济效益指标，分别除以各项指标的标准值，再乘以各自的权数，加总后除以总权数求得。其计算公式为：

$$\text{工业经济效益综合指数}=\sum\left(\frac{\text{某项经济效益指标报告期数值}}{\text{该项指标标准值}}\times\text{权数}\right)\div\text{总权数}$$

上式总权数为100。

总资产贡献率 是指企业一定时期内全部资产获利能力，是企业经营业绩和管理水平的集中体现，是评价和考核企业盈利能力的核心指标。计算公式为：

$$总资产贡献率（\%）=\frac{利润总额+税金总额+利息支出}{平均资产总额}\times100\%$$

税金总额为产品销售税金及附加与应交增值税之和，平均资产总额为期初、期末资产总计的算术平均值 。

资本保值增值率 是反映企业净资产变动状况的一个重要指标，是企业发展能力的集中体现。它是指期末所有者权益总额与上年同期期末所有者权益总额的比率。计算公式为：

$$资本保值增值率（\%）=\frac{报告期期末所有者权益}{上年同期期末所有者权益}\times100\%$$

所有者权益等于资产总计减负债总计。

资产负债率 是指反映企业经营风险的大小，反映企业利用债权人提供的资金从事经营活动的能力。计算公式为：

$$资产负债率（\%）=\frac{负债总计}{资产总计}\times100\%$$

资产及负债均为报告期末数。

流动资金周转率 是指一定时期内流动资产完成的周转次数，反映投入工业企业流动资金的周转速度，一般以一年时间内周转多少次表示。计算公式为：

$$流动资产周转率（次）=\frac{主营业务收入}{流动资产平均余额}$$

成本费用利润率 是指工业企业投入生产成本及费用的经济效益，同时也反映企业降低成本所取得的经济效益。计算公式为：

$$成本费用利润率（\%）=\frac{利润总额}{成本费用总额}\times100\%$$

成本费用总额为主营业务成本和营业费用、管理费用、财务费用三项期间费用。

全员劳动生产率 是指反映企业的生产效率和劳动投入的经济效益。一般用平均每人一年创造的工业增加值表示。计算公式为：

$$全员劳动生产率（元/人）=\frac{工业增加值}{全部职工平均人数}\times100\%$$

全部职工平均人数为企业在报告期内全部从业人员的平均人数，计算公式为：

$$全部从业人员年平均人数=\frac{1至12月各月全部从业人员平均人数之和}{12}$$

或：

$$全部从业人员年平均人数=\frac{1至12月各月月初、月末全部从业人员之和}{24}$$

工业产品销售率 是指反映工业产品已实现销售的程度，是分析工业产销衔接情况、研究工业产品满足社会需求的指标。计算公式为：

$$产品销售率（\%）=\frac{现价工业销售产值}{现价工业总产值}\times100\%$$

Explanatory Notes on Main Statistical Indicators

Industry refers to the material production sector which is engaged in extraction of natural resources and processing and reprocessing of minerals and agricultural products, including (1) extraction of natural resources, such as mining, salt production, and logging (but excluding hunting and fishing); (2) processing and reprocessing of farm and sideline produces, such as rice husking, flour milling, wine making, oil pressing, cotton ginning, silk reeling, spinning and weaving, and leather making; (3) manufacture of industrial products, such as steel making, iron smelting, chemicals manufacturing, petroleum processing, machine building, timber processing; and production and supply of electricity, water and gas; (4) repair and renovation of industrial products, such as the repair of machinery and means of transport (including cars).

Prior to 1984, industrial enterprises run by villages and cooperative organizations under village were classified into agriculture. Since 1984, these enterprises have been grouped into industry.

Units of Industrial Statistics Survey These are classified into two categories: corporate industrial enterprises with independent accounting system and industrial establishments.

(1) Corporate industrial enterprises with independent accounting system refer to enterprises engaging in industrial production activities which simultaneously meet the following requirements: ①They are established legally, having their own names, organizations, location, able to take civil liability; ②They possess and use their assets independently, assume liabilities, and are entitled to sign contracts with other units; ③They are financially independent and compile their own balance sheets.

(2) Industrial establishments refer to economic units located in one single place and engaged entirely or primarily in one kind of industrial production activity, including units engaged in main business activities (industrial production activities) under industrial enterprises with independent accounting system and units engaged in industrial production activities under non-industrial enterprises (formerly industrial establishments with dependent accounting system). Industrial establishments generally meet the following requirements simultaneously: ① They have each one location and are engaged entirely or primarily in one kind of industrial activity each; ② They operate and manage their industrial production activities separately; ③ They have accounts of income and expenditure separately.

Light Industry refers to the industry that produces consumer goods and hand tools. It consists of two categories, depending on the materials used:

(1) Industries using farm products as raw materials. These are branches of light industry which directly or indirectly use farm products as basic raw materials, including the manufacture of food and beverages, tobacco processing, textile, clothing, fur and leather manufacturing, paper making, printing, etc.

(2) Industries using non-farm products as raw materials. These are branches of light industry which use manufactured goods as raw materials, including the manufacture of cultural, educational and sports articles, chemicals, synthetic fiber, chemical products for daily use, glass products for daily use, metal products for daily use, hand tools, medical apparatus and instruments, and the manufacture of cultural and clerical machinery.

Heavy Industry refers to the industry which produces capital goods and provides various sectors of the national economy with necessary material and technical basis. It consists of the following three branches according to the purpose of production or the use of products:

(1) Mining, quarrying and logging industry refers to the industry that extracts natural resources, including extraction of petroleum, coal, metal and non-metal ores, and logging.

(2) Raw materials industry refers to the industry that provides various sectors of the national economy with raw materials, fuels and power. It includes smelting and processing of metals, coking and coke chemistry, chemical materials and building materials such as cement, plywood, and power, petroleum refining and coal dressing.

(3) Manufacturing industry refers to the industry that processes raw materials. It includes machine-building industry which equips sectors of the national economy, industries of metal structure and cement products, industries producing means of agricultural production, such as chemical fertilizers and pesticides.

According to the above principle of classification, repairing trades engaged primarily in repairing products of heavy industry are classified into heavy industry, while those engaged in repairing products of light industry are classified into light industry.

Gross Industrial Output Value refers to the total volume of industrial products sold or available for sale in monetary terms during a given period, which reflects the total achievements and overall scale of industrial production during a given period. It includes the value of the finished products in the enterprises, which are not to be further processed and have been inspected, packed and put in storage (where applicable), the income from external processing and the value gain of semi-finished products at the end of the reference period over the beginning. The gross industrial output value is calculated by the factory approach, i.e. the whole industrial enterprise is regarded as the basic accounting unit in calculating the gross industrial output value. No double calculations are to be made within the same enterprise and the output value of different workshops (branch factories) should not be added. However, this approach does not exclude the possibility of double calculations between enterprises, sectors and regions.

Output value of light and heavy industries is also classified by the factory approach. Under normal conditions, if the major products of an industrial enterprise belong to light industry products, the gross output value of that enterprise is classified wholly into light industry; the same principle applies to heavy industry.

Sales Value of Industry (Current Price) refers to refers to the total value of industrial products sold or industrial services provided in monetary terms within the current year. It includes:

(1) Sales Value of Finished Products. Sale value of finished products refers to the total value of finished and semi-finished products sold within the reporting period (including those produced within and outside the period). It equals the actual sales volume of products sold within the reporting period timing the actual average sales price (excluding value added or sales tax). It includes the equipment made by the enterprise itself, as well as the finished products provided to the projects under construction, non-industrial departments and welfare department, and excludes the value of finished or semi-finished products of external processing with supplied materials that produces only processing charges.

(2) Income from External Processing: refers to income from contracted external processing of industrial products (including processing of industrial products using materials from the clients), and the income from industrial repairing work provided to other units. Income from external processing is calculated using information from the item "products sales income" in the enterprise accounting at the prices excluding value-added tax.

For an enterprise whose main business is external processing and the charges of external processing constitute a large proportion of its income, in case of cross-year payment, the income of external processing charges shall be adjusted and the actual income of external processing charges of the current year shall be recorded to ensure the accuracy of the coverage of gross industrial output.

Export Delivery Value refers to the value of the products that an industrial enterprises have delivered to export units or have exported on its own or per procurationem (including those sold to Hong Kong, Macaw and Taiwan), and the value of the products from processing and compensation trades(processing with given materials or samples, assembling supplied components). In calculating the export delivery value, the foreign exchanges shall be converted into yuan at current exchange rates.

Value-added of Industry refers to the final results of industrial production of industrial enterprises in monetary terms during the reference period. It equals to the total achievements of all industrial production minus the goods and services consumed or transferred during the industrial production of enterprises, in other terms the newly added value during the industrial production of enterprises. It is calculated by the following two approaches:

a) The production approach. The value added is calculated by taking the value of industrial intermediate input out of the final value of products and labor services that comes from industrial production. The formula used is:

Value-added of industry = gross industrial output—industrial intermediate input + value-added tax

b) The income approach. It is calculation of the final value of industrial activities by approaching the primary distribution of the primary income of industrial production. The formula used is:

Value-added of industry = depreciation of fixed assets + remuneration of laborers + net production tax+ operating surplus

Total Current Assets refer to the assets that meet one of the following requirements: (1) expected to be cashed, sold or used in a normal operation cycle, mainly including inventory and accounts receivable; (2) be owned for trading purpose mainly; (3) expected to be cashed in one year (including one year) from the day of the Balance Sheet; (4) unlimited cash or cash equivalents that can be exchanged with other assets or being capable of settling debts during one year since the day of the Balance Sheet. Included are monetary capital, notes receivable, accounts receivable and inventories. Data on this indicator can be obtained from the year-end figures of Total Current Assets in the Balance Sheet of accounting records.

Accounts Receivable refers to creditor's rights formed by business activities such as selling goods, providing labor, which include payment for goods that should be charged to the customer, value-added tax and advance freight for the clients. It comes from the ending balance of Accounts Receivable in Balance Sheet of accounting records.

Inventories refers to finished goods or commodities held in preparation for sale in enterprises' daily activities, goods in the production process, material or the physical materials consumed in the production process or in the process of providing labor, usually include raw materials, goods in the production process, semi-finished products, finished products, goods and materials in flow. It comes from the ending balance of Inventory in Balance Sheet of accounting records.

Finished Goods refers to the products that the enterprises have completed all of the production process and accepted and put in storage, and can be sent to the ordering units in accordance with the contract stipulations, or can be on sale. It comes from the debit balance of Finished Products of accounting.

Fixed Assets refers to houses, buildings machines, vehicles and other equipment, appliances and tools related to production and operation that have been used for more than one year. It also includes articles that are not major equipment of production or operation, but the value of which exceeds 2000 yuan and the service period of which exceeds 2 years. Data can be obtained from the year-end figures of Fixed Assets in the Balance Sheet of accounting records.

Total Assets refer to all resources that are owned or controlled by enterprises through previous trades or transactions with expectation of making economic profits. Classified by the degree of liquidity, total assets include current assets and non-current assets. Current assets can be classified into monetary capital, trading financial assets, notes receivable, accounts receivable, advanced payments, other receivables and inventories. Non-current assets can be divided into long-term equity investment, fixed assets, intangible assets and other non-current assets. Data on this indicator can be obtained from the year-end figures of total assets in the Balance Sheet of accounting records.

Total Liabilities refer to payable liabilities of enterprises that accumulated from previous trades or transactions with expectation of economic profits leaking out. In terms of payment, it can be divided into liquid liabilities and long-term liabilities. Data on this indicator can be obtained from the year-end figures of total liabilities in the Balance Sheet of accounting records. It comes from the debit balance of Total Liabilities in the Balance Sheet of accounting records.

Total Liquid Liabilities refer to total debt payable by enterprises within an operating cycle of one year or over one year, including short-term loans, payables and advance payments, wages payable, taxes payable and profits payable, etc. Data can be obtained from the year-end figures of Total Liquid Liabilities in the Balance Sheet of accounting records.

Creditors' Equity refers to investors' ownership of net assets of the enterprise. It is equal to the total assets of the enterprise minus its total liabilities, including the primary input from investors, capital accumulation fund, surplus accumulation fund and undistributed profit. Data can be obtained from the year-end figures of Creditors' Equity in the Balance Sheet of accounting records.

Paid-in Capital refers to the capital (or share) actually invested by the investors of an enterprise, including currency, goods, intangible assets, etc. Classified by the investing bodies, paid-in capital includes state capital, collective capital, corporate capital, individual capital, Hong Kong, Macaw and Taiwan capital and foreign capital. Data on this indicator can be obtained from the accounting subject of Paid-in Capital in the accounting record of enterprise.

State Capital refers to the investment in an enterprises made by government departments or agencies under government's jurisdiction on behalf of state. Data on this indicator can be obtained from the accounting subject of Paid-in Capital in the accounting record of enterprise.

Collective Capital refers to the collective capital contributed by work staff or other institutions to support an enterprise. Data on this indicator can be obtained from the accounting subject of Paid-in Capital in the accounting record of enterprise.

Corporate Capital refers to the investment in an enterprise made by a corporate body out of its legal disposable assets. Data on this indicator can be obtained from the accounting subject of Paid-in Capital in the accounting record of enterprise.

Individual Capital refers to the capital actually invested in an enterprise by an individual. Data on this indicator can be obtained from the accounting subject of Paid-in Capital in the accounting record of enterprise.

Hong Kong, Macaw and Taiwan Capital refers to the capital actually invested in an enterprises by investors from Hong Kong, Macaw and Taiwan. Data on this indicator can be obtained from the accounting subject of Paid-in Capital in the accounting record of enterprise.

Foreign Capital refers to the capital actually invested in an enterprise by a foreign investor. Data on this indicator can be obtained from the accounting subject of Paid-in Capital in the accounting record of enterprise.

Business Revenue refers to the revenue from the sales of products (or commodities) and from rendering of industrial services by industrial enterprises. It is classified into two categories: principal business revenue (or basic business revenue) and other business revenue (or additional business revenue). It comes from current amount of Business Revenue in income statement.

Revenue from Principal Business refers to the income confirmed of an enterprise from the principal business of selling products and providing labor services. Data on this indicator can be obtained from the year-end credit balance of Revenue from Principal Business in the accounting record of enterprise (before carryover).

Cost of Principal Business refers to the total cost occurred from the principal business of the enterprise. Data can be obtained from the year-end debit balance of Ccost of Principal Business" in the accounting record of enterprise (before carryover).

Selling Expense refers to the cost during the sale of goods and materials, providing labour services, including insurance, packing, exhibition fees and advertising fees, merchandise maintenance costs, expected product quality guarantee loss, transportation fees, handling fees, and operating expenses for the sales of the company's products such as employee compensation, business expenses, depreciation costs for dedicated sales offices (including sales outlets, after-sales service outlets, etc.).

Administrative Expense refers to the expenses for the organization and management of enterprise operating, including the start-up costs during the construction of enterprises, funds occurred during enterprises operating by board of directors and executive management in the enterprise management, or burden by enterprises. It comes from current amount of management cost in income statement.

Financial Expenses refers to cost of raising fund for enterprises to raise funds for production and operation, including interest payments (a reduction in interest income), exchange loss (less exchange gains) and related fees during the period of production. It comes from current amount of financial expenses in income statement.

Total Profits refers to the operation results in a certain accounting period, and it is the balance of various incomes minus various spendings in the course of operation, reflecting the total profits and losses of enterprises in reference period. Data are obtained from the amount of total profits in the profit statement of the accounting record of enterprise.

Value-added Tax Payable refers to the amount of the value-added tax which should be paid by the enterprises according to tax laws during the reference period of selling goods or providing such services as processing, repairing or assembling that add value to goods. The formula used is:

Value-added Tax Payable=Output Tax－(Input Tax－Input Tax Returns)－
Export Deduct Domestic Sales Goods Tax－Tax Deduction+ Export Tax Refund

Amount of Input Tax at Current Year refers to the VAT an industrial enterprise pays for purchasing goods or receiving taxable services within the reference period, which is allowed to be deducted from the amount of output tax.

Amount of Output Tax at Current Year refers to the VAT an industrial enterprise pays for selling goods or providing taxable services within the reference period.

Total Pre-Tax Profits refers to the sum of total profits, sales tax as well as additional and payable value-added taxes.

Comprehensive Index on Economic Benefit of Industry refers to the current comprehensive evaluation of the general level of economic benefit of industry and the performance of industrial economy. It is calculated by a selection of representative indicators on economic benefit divided by the standard value of each indicator respectively, multiplied by the weight of each indicator, summed and divided by total weight. The formula used is:

$$\text{Comprehensive Index on Economic Benefit of Industry} = \left(\frac{\text{Value of an Indicator on Economic Benefit in the Reference Period}}{\text{Standard Value of the Indicator}} \times \text{Weight}\right) \div \text{Total Weight where Total Weight} = 100$$

Ratio of Total Assets to Industrial Output Value refers to the profit-making capability of all assets of the enterprise. As a core indicator for the evaluation and assessment of the profit-making potential of the enterprise, it is a focused reflection of the performance and management efficiency of the enterprise. This ratio is calculated as follows:

$$\text{Ratio of Total Assets to Industrial Output Value (\%)} = \left(\frac{\text{Total Profits} + \text{Total Taxes} + \text{Interest Expenditure}}{\text{Average Assets}}\right) \times 100\% \times \left(\frac{12}{\text{cumulative number of months}}\right)$$

where Total Taxes are the sum of tax and extra charges on the sales of products and value-added tax payable; and Average Assets are the arithmetic mean of beginning assets and ending assets.

Ratio of Capital Maintenance and Appreciation is an important indicator of the changes of net assets of an enterprise and a focused reflection of the development capability of enterprises. It is the ratio of total creditors' equity at the end of the reference period to that of the same period of the previous year, calculated as follows:

$$\text{Ratio of Capital Maintenance and Appreciation (\%)} = \left(\frac{\text{Total Creditors' Equity at the End of the Reference Period}}{\text{Total Creditors' Equity of the Same Period of the Previous Year}}\right) \times 100\%$$

where Creditors' equity is equal to the total assets of the enterprise minus its total liabilities.

Assets-Liability Ratio reflects both the operation risk and the capability of the enterprise in making use of the capital from the creditors. It is calculated as follows:

$$\text{Assets-Liability Ratio(\%)} = \left(\frac{\text{Total Debts}}{\text{Total Assets}}\right) \times 100\%$$

where both assets and debts are figures at the end of the reference period.

Number of Times of Turnover of Circulating Funds refers to the number of times in which turnover of circulating funds is completed in a given period of time, which reflects the speed of the turnover of circulating funds. It is expressed as times of turnover within a year and is calculated as follows:

$$\text{Number of Times of Turnover of Circulating Funds} = \left(\frac{\text{Sales Revenue of Products}}{\text{Average Balance of Total Number of Times of Turnover of Circulating Funds}}\right) \times \left(\frac{12\%}{\text{Cumulative Number of Months}}\right)$$

Ratio of Profits to Industrial Costs refers to the ratio of profits realized in a given period to the total production costs of industrial enterprises in the same period, which also reflects the economic benefit attained by the enterprises from reduced costs. This ratio is calculated as follows:

$$\text{Ratio of Profits to Industrial Costs (\%)} = \left(\frac{\text{Total Profits}}{\text{Total Costs}}\right) \times 100\%$$

where Total costs are the sum of cost of products sold, marketing cost, management cost and financial cost.

Value-added Labor Productivity reflects the production efficiency of the enterprise and economic benefit of its labor input. It is usually expressed as the industrial value-added created by an average member of an industrial enterprise in a year. The formula used is:

$$\text{Value-added Labor Productivity (yuan/person)} = \left(\frac{\text{Value-added of Industry}}{\text{Average Number of Staff and Workers}}\right) \times \left(\frac{12}{\text{Cumulative Number of Months}}\right)$$

Average Number of Staff and Workers refers to the average number of all employed persons by an industrial enterprise within the reference period. The formula used is:

$$\text{Average Number of Staff and Workers} = \frac{\text{Sum of Average Monthly Numbers from January to December}}{12}$$

Or

$$\text{Average Number of Staff and Workers} = \frac{\text{Sum of Average Numbers at the Beginning and End of Each Month from January to December}}{24}$$

Proportion of Products Sold refers to the sales of industrial products to the gross industrial output value, and is used to analyze the linkage between production and sales and the extent to which the needs of the society are met by the supply of industrial products. It is calculated as follows:

$$\text{Proportion of Products Sold (\%)} = \left(\frac{\text{Value of Industrial Sales at Current Prices}}{\text{Gross Industrial Output Value at Current Prices}}\right) \times 100\%$$

十三、建筑业

CONSTRUCTION

十三　建筑业

简要说明

一、本篇资料反映广东省建筑业发展的基本情况。主要内容包括全省和各市建筑业企业生产经营的情况，主要指标有企业个数、就业人员数、建筑业总产值、房屋建筑面积、房屋建筑施工新开工面积、利润总额、利税总额和建筑业劳动生产率等。

二、本篇资料由广东省统计局固定资产投资统计处整理提供。

三、本篇资料是根据国家统计局制定的《建筑业统计报表制度》整理汇总的。统计范围包括：广东境内具有法人资格的独立核算建筑业企业和辖区内建筑业法人所属的产业活动单位。

四、从 2004 年开始，统计范围为具有建筑业资质的独立核算的法人建筑业企业。

13 Construction

Brief Introduction

Ⅰ. The data in this chapter show the development of the construction industry in Guangdong Province. They cover mainly the statistics of production and management of the enterprises of construction of the whole province and its cities, including the number of enterprises, the number of employed persons, gross output value of construction, floor space of buildings, value-added of construction, total profits and total pre-tax profits, Construction enterprise labor productivity, etc.

Ⅱ. The data in this chapter are prepared and provided by the Division of Investment and Construction Statistics of Statistics Bureau of Guangdong Province.

Ⅲ. The data in this chapter are collected in accordance with the Reporting Scheme of Construction Statistics stipulated by the National Bureau of Statistics. The coverage of construction statistics includes construction enterprises with legal person qualifications and independent accounting system and industrial establishments affiliated with corporate construction enterprises under the jurisdiction of Guangdong Province.

Ⅳ. The data since 2004 include all construction enterprises with legal person qualifications,construction qualifications and independent accounting system.

13-1 建筑业企业生产情况

Production Conditions of Construction Enterprises

项目	Item	2016 合计 Total of 2016	#国有及国有控股企业 State-owned and State-holding	2017 合计 Total of 2017	#国有及国有控股企业 State-owned and State-holding
企业个数 （个）	**Number of Construction Enterprises (unit)**	**5054**	**480**	**5606**	**476**
建筑业合同情况	**Contracts of Construction**				
签订的合同额 （亿元）	Value of Contracts Signed (100 million yuan)	25245.97	11531.78	30989.02	16750.22
上年结转合同额(亿元)	Value of Contracts Carried-over from the Previous Year (100 million yuan)	12288.36	6032.04	14845.74	8840.19
本年新签合同额(亿元)	Value of Newly-signed Contracts in Current Year (100 million yuan)	12957.60	5499.74	16143.28	7910.03
承包工程完成情况	**Contracted Projects Completed**				
直接从建设单位承揽工程完成产值 （亿元）	Completed Output Value of Contracted Projects Directly from Construction Units (100 million yuan)	10358.69	4077.26	12183.01	4971.41
自行完成施工产值 （亿元）	Output Value of Self-completed Projects (100 million yuan)	9366.93	3446.81	11090.36	4126.70
分包出去工程的产值 （亿元）	Output Value of Outsourcing Projects (100 million yuan)	991.76	630.45	1092.65	844.72
从建设单位以外承揽工程完成产值 （亿元）	Completed Output Value of Contracted Projects outside Construction Units (100 million yuan)	438.07	236.84	480.97	267.50
建筑业总产值 （亿元）	**Gross Output Value of Construction (100 million yuan)**	**9805.00**	**3683.65**	**11571.33**	**4394.20**
#装饰装修产值 （亿元）	Output Value of Decoration Projects (100 million yuan)	1424.09	193.14	1603.93	184.50
在外省完成的产值 （亿元）	Output Value Completed in Other Provinces (100 million yuan)	2051.36	1055.09	2196.87	1068.13
建筑工程产值 （亿元）	Output Value of Construction Projects (100 million yuan)	8344.84	3265.66	9916.33	3972.50
安装工程产值 （亿元）	Output Value of Installation Projects (100 million yuan)	1137.55	308.09	1288.13	283.49
其他产值 （亿元）	Other Output Values (100 million yuan)	322.61	109.90	366.87	138.21
竣工产值 （亿元）	**Output Value Completed (100 million yuan)**	**4755.79**	**1674.02**	**6080.98**	**2146.48**
房屋建筑施工面积 （万平方米）	**Floor Space of Buildings under Construction (10000 sq.m)**	**54358.29**	**23100.54**	**60247.20**	**25761.66**
#新开工面积 （万平方米）	Floor Space of Newly-started Buildings (10000 sq.m)	18060.46	6384.66	21644.31	7299.44
劳动人员情况	**Labor Force**				
从事建筑业活动的就业人员平均人数 （万人）	Average Number of Employed Persons in the main business activities (10000 persons)	244.36	72.09	288.42	89.89
期末就业人数 （万人）	Number of Employed Persons at the Year-end (10000 persons)	246.17	71.49	289.97	84.79
#工程技术人员 （万人）	Number of Engineering Technical Personnel (10000 persons)	29.38	8.07	33.60	10.97

13–2 建筑业企业主要指标

Main Indicators on Construction Enterprises

年份 Year	建筑业企业 单位数 (个) Number of Construction Enterprises (unit)	建筑业企业 总产值 (亿元) Gross Output Value of Construction Enterprises (100 million yuan)	建筑业企业 增加值 (亿元) Value-added of Construction Enterprises (100 million yuan)	建筑业企业 利税总额 (亿元) Total Pre-tax Profits of Construction Enterprises (100 million yuan)	建筑业企业 就业人员 (万人) Number of Employed Persons of Construction Enterprises (10000 persons)
1978	178	5.47	10.49	0.20	14.78
1979	188	6.32	9.29	0.23	16.27
1980	204	8.88	12.66	0.32	19.45
1981	224	13.44	16.74	0.49	24.29
1982	246	19.66	22.24	0.72	29.94
1983	269	24.51	26.45	0.90	36.23
1984	357	36.83	33.22	1.31	47.12
1985	462	50.45	44.01	1.54	54.47
1986	448	57.14	47.42	1.28	58.24
1987	492	65.96	56.58	1.56	59.08
1988	596	86.74	73.82	2.74	66.56
1989	646	125.65	90.07	3.62	71.88
1990	686	113.40	92.45	3.12	67.22
1991	705	137.30	107.12	4.33	67.71
1992	910	216.56	201.04	9.65	84.80
1993	1766	459.95	318.05	23.03	144.12
1994	1587	535.75	387.8	31.29	150.05
1995	1618	635.83	451.4	39.47	135.56
1996	2031	632.16	464.66	35.74	146.56
1997	2399	732.97	468.97	38.26	143.89
1998	2961	800.00	502.87	43.11	142.82
1999	3283	954.44	526.56	53.06	144.78
2000	4593	944.61	536.45	58.24	141.46
2001	3699	1179.03	564.86	84.51	147.07
2002	4019	1418.41	594.99	88.95	150.12
2003	4488	1702.87	705.81	127.48	161.48
2004	4166	1901.86	794.88	143.75	152.10
2005	4182	2200.58	866.87	164.38	166.78
2006	4172	2594.04	951.18	191.62	169.33
2007	4326	3005.32	1061.70	256.59	179.13
2008	4601	3282.55	1197.41	289.23	172.54
2009	4508	3826.83	1328.14	329.00	179.34
2010	4551	4742.09	1551.81	393.87	196.32
2011	4589	5804.21	1797.78	470.75	190.28
2012	4637	6564.37	1890.90	517.82	198.31
2013	4977	7927.13	2161.10	653.70	204.79
2014	4982	8440.29	2341.18	675.99	211.07
2015	4926	8984.86	2441.85	724.74	185.50
2016	5054	9805.00	2551.82	736.52	246.17
2017	5606	11571.33	2818.82	851.86	289.97

13-3 各市建筑业企业个数

Number of Construction Enterprises by City

单位：个 (unit)

市 别	City	2000	2005	2010	2012	2013	2014	2015	2016	2017
全省总计	**Provincial Total**	**4593**	**4182**	**4551**	**4637**	**4977**	**4982**	**4926**	**5054**	**5606**
广 州	Guangzhou	757	764	779	786	882	890	877	883	952
深 圳	Shenzhen	447	604	808	822	898	818	776	849	989
珠 海	Zhuhai	143	165	144	170	309	375	393	410	416
汕 头	Shantou	271	199	212	191	186	180	175	176	178
佛 山	Foshan	248	502	497	443	424	434	427	431	458
韶 关	Shaoguan	110	66	76	99	101	95	94	96	112
河 源	Heyuan	117	82	85	102	104	102	104	107	114
梅 州	Meizhou	154	111	146	155	153	151	151	153	163
惠 州	Huizhou	241	124	111	112	121	111	103	119	176
汕 尾	Shanwei	100	43	38	37	36	34	36	44	43
东 莞	Dongguan	183	361	444	473	502	536	540	542	624
中 山	Zhongshan	385	273	314	315	327	329	319	310	367
江 门	Jiangmen	342	156	165	158	160	162	164	171	204
阳 江	Yangjiang	122	91	95	123	117	113	113	109	115
湛 江	Zhanjiang	238	125	106	122	128	131	127	130	138
茂 名	Maoming	146	100	97	118	125	125	129	130	148
肇 庆	Zhaoqing	136	122	119	101	98	92	90	86	92
清 远	Qingyuan	136	74	80	69	72	77	88	100	110
潮 州	Chaozhou	139	90	83	80	77	73	66	59	57
揭 阳	Jieyang	121	84	107	117	112	111	111	108	110
云 浮	Yunfu	57	46	45	44	45	43	43	41	40
按经济区域分	By Region									
珠 三 角	Pearl River Delta	2882	3071	3381	3380	3721	3747	3689	3801	4278
东 翼	Eastern Region	631	416	440	425	411	398	388	387	388
西 翼	Western Region	506	316	298	363	370	369	369	369	401
山 区	Mountainous Region	574	379	432	469	475	468	480	497	539

13-4 各市建筑业企业总产值
Gross Output Value of Construction Enterprises by City

单位：亿元 (100 million yuan)

市 别	City	2000	2005	2010	2012	2013	2014	2015	2016	2017
全省总计	**Provincial Total**	**944.61**	**2200.58**	**4742.09**	**6564.37**	**7927.13**	**8440.29**	**8984.86**	**9805.00**	**11571.33**
广 州	Guangzhou	256.13	633.99	1296.19	1763.21	2216.18	2377.92	2546.94	2832.50	3234.86
深 圳	Shenzhen	153.02	545.62	1460.99	2103.05	2422.26	2217.23	2275.20	2392.11	2869.95
珠 海	Zhuhai	33.11	52.48	100.81	184.47	291.45	402.78	477.45	566.77	750.97
汕 头	Shantou	80.67	127.78	219.12	292.37	361.31	376.44	405.52	453.76	519.64
佛 山	Foshan	73.08	154.68	315.42	338.54	403.17	487.12	497.09	509.25	538.42
韶 关	Shaoguan	24.14	29.25	102.76	166.07	213.94	218.64	214.35	179.70	194.46
河 源	Heyuan	5.74	17.01	20.68	33.90	39.37	50.46	69.31	92.44	116.35
梅 州	Meizhou	15.14	54.81	125.91	169.66	185.37	216.98	241.12	267.68	302.28
惠 州	Huizhou	20.35	46.94	69.83	93.74	103.28	122.04	141.29	160.88	198.87
汕 尾	Shanwei	5.49	6.95	15.44	11.54	9.64	11.11	14.41	21.72	26.40
东 莞	Dongguan	40.45	84.35	122.06	157.57	187.90	204.21	224.59	267.22	322.58
中 山	Zhongshan	26.20	73.41	133.70	160.08	160.84	166.84	153.67	166.64	217.15
江 门	Jiangmen	47.18	56.06	119.18	173.33	203.59	212.38	225.24	240.86	284.34
阳 江	Yangjiang	18.80	32.97	66.18	81.60	115.08	124.71	120.05	103.24	111.18
湛 江	Zhanjiang	45.61	75.96	168.08	248.75	334.52	430.12	461.75	535.40	612.86
茂 名	Maoming	39.05	92.14	134.67	271.70	325.38	417.76	481.04	570.76	768.49
肇 庆	Zhaoqing	15.40	39.99	99.40	103.71	108.58	119.80	125.49	117.92	142.57
清 远	Qingyuan	11.49	20.19	52.78	64.83	73.35	96.56	101.72	110.54	132.02
潮 州	Chaozhou	12.71	18.99	25.98	30.75	34.70	40.50	43.84	44.02	44.97
揭 阳	Jieyang	12.24	21.78	75.06	91.36	107.11	114.35	133.02	134.14	143.40
云 浮	Yunfu	8.61	15.20	17.85	24.13	30.10	32.36	31.75	37.44	39.55
按经济区域分	By Region									
珠三角	Pearl River Delta	664.92	1687.53	3717.58	5077.70	6097.24	6310.31	6666.97	7254.16	8559.73
东 翼	Eastern Region	111.11	175.50	335.60	426.03	512.76	542.39	596.79	653.64	734.41
西 翼	Western Region	103.46	201.08	368.93	602.04	774.99	972.59	1062.85	1209.40	1492.53
山 区	Mountainous Region	65.12	136.47	319.98	458.59	542.14	615.00	658.26	687.80	784.66

13-5 各市建筑业企业利税总额

Total Pre-tax Profits of Construction Enterprises by City

单位：亿元 (100 million yuan)

市 别	City	2000	2005	2010	2012	2013	2014	2015	2016	2017
全省总计	**Provincial Total**	**58.24**	**164.38**	**393.87**	**517.82**	**653.70**	**675.99**	**724.74**	**736.52**	**851.86**
广 州	Guangzhou	15.17	45.42	118.16	129.12	154.74	162.11	171.85	175.16	195.66
深 圳	Shenzhen	13.79	39.76	105.09	166.61	183.80	184.30	212.92	182.78	192.42
珠 海	Zhuhai	1.43	4.16	7.44	12.31	20.35	25.84	34.12	45.20	49.36
汕 头	Shantou	4.14	9.86	17.64	22.11	28.86	30.36	32.64	36.60	47.96
佛 山	Foshan	4.70	14.31	30.47	24.65	47.72	50.13	38.40	30.70	29.14
韶 关	Shaoguan	2.00	1.57	6.66	12.35	16.95	14.16	14.55	13.18	14.44
河 源	Heyuan	0.53	1.23	2.08	3.67	5.53	7.04	10.72	13.64	16.14
梅 州	Meizhou	0.81	6.47	13.70	24.71	24.68	25.60	26.53	25.14	27.52
惠 州	Huizhou	1.02	3.63	4.96	5.56	7.53	5.32	5.44	7.31	10.12
汕 尾	Shanwei	0.58	0.58	1.43	0.77	0.58	0.83	1.29	1.73	2.77
东 莞	Dongguan	2.25	6.36	9.80	10.74	16.56	16.93	17.09	17.55	29.32
中 山	Zhongshan	1.53	6.09	13.71	13.91	14.87	14.72	11.87	14.37	15.12
江 门	Jiangmen	2.37	3.79	9.61	14.23	16.10	17.27	20.34	23.83	27.68
阳 江	Yangjiang	1.15	3.24	6.26	7.87	10.32	9.90	9.09	10.97	12.47
湛 江	Zhanjiang	1.69	3.80	10.69	14.40	16.26	22.57	23.94	28.67	39.43
茂 名	Maoming	1.82	5.97	10.01	28.34	45.53	47.33	52.94	66.36	89.97
肇 庆	Zhaoqing	0.77	2.55	6.32	6.23	8.45	8.75	7.79	7.99	11.31
清 远	Qingyuan	0.40	1.20	6.24	5.48	5.18	5.17	5.78	6.80	9.87
潮 州	Chaozhou	0.66	1.17	2.12	2.50	4.09	3.17	3.18	3.51	3.62
揭 阳	Jieyang	0.73	2.09	9.48	9.69	22.43	20.71	21.01	21.02	22.12
云 浮	Yunfu	0.70	1.13	1.98	2.55	3.19	3.77	3.26	4.01	5.44
按经济区域分	By Region									
珠 三 角	Pearl River Delta	43.03	126.06	305.57	383.36	470.12	485.38	519.81	504.89	560.11
东 翼	Eastern Region	6.11	13.70	30.68	35.08	55.95	55.08	58.12	62.86	76.47
西 翼	Western Region	4.66	13.01	26.96	50.62	72.11	79.80	85.97	106.00	141.87
山 区	Mountainous Region	4.44	11.61	30.66	48.76	55.52	55.73	60.84	62.77	73.41

13-6 各市建筑业企业利润总额

Total Profits of Construction Enterprises by City

单位：亿元 (100 million yuan)

市别	City	2000	2005	2010	2012	2013	2014	2015	2016	2017
全省总计	**Provincial Total**	**22.73**	**70.53**	**205.47**	**283.88**	**363.20**	**376.19**	**396.36**	**425.38**	**463.19**
广州	Guangzhou	5.20	18.64	65.51	70.58	87.81	90.46	96.23	106.77	106.11
深圳	Shenzhen	7.57	15.65	50.44	92.97	101.55	103.03	115.51	111.06	119.06
珠海	Zhuhai	0.37	1.98	3.47	6.45	10.12	13.83	19.05	25.97	30.31
汕头	Shantou	1.36	3.74	8.23	9.89	14.99	15.15	15.63	20.15	24.91
佛山	Foshan	2.00	6.54	19.27	14.57	27.11	36.55	24.99	19.78	16.18
韶关	Shaoguan	0.23	0.43	2.95	6.04	9.15	6.21	5.44	6.45	7.25
河源	Heyuan	0.29	0.48	0.95	2.29	3.92	4.90	7.71	9.39	10.10
梅州	Meizhou	0.21	4.56	8.44	18.70	16.23	14.84	17.08	15.09	16.80
惠州	Huizhou	0.35	1.02	1.68	2.14	3.61	1.24	2.37	3.06	3.63
汕尾	Shanwei	0.22	0.18	0.56	0.30	0.17	0.32	0.55	0.57	1.33
东莞	Dongguan	1.14	3.81	5.78	5.64	9.79	10.44	9.67	8.60	19.44
中山	Zhongshan	0.78	3.63	7.46	8.54	8.86	9.00	6.25	9.52	10.19
江门	Jiangmen	0.34	1.55	4.88	7.46	8.40	8.67	11.33	13.14	12.98
阳江	Yangjiang	0.61	1.38	3.59	4.46	5.55	5.20	4.71	5.79	5.68
湛江	Zhanjiang	0.28	1.19	3.76	5.22	6.14	8.14	8.68	9.79	12.32
茂名	Maoming	0.77	2.49	4.43	15.50	23.03	24.03	27.67	34.58	38.84
肇庆	Zhaoqing	0.09	0.65	2.51	2.22	3.96	4.28	3.26	3.70	5.61
清远	Qingyuan	0.01	0.46	3.44	2.83	2.88	2.54	3.24	3.58	4.24
潮州	Chaozhou	0.28	0.49	1.12	1.38	2.52	1.64	1.77	1.70	1.74
揭阳	Jieyang	0.26	1.22	5.90	5.18	15.55	13.45	13.46	14.26	13.86
云浮	Yunfu	0.37	0.43	1.10	1.51	1.85	2.29	1.77	2.47	2.62
按经济区域分	By Region									
珠三角	Pearl River Delta	17.84	53.48	161.00	210.59	261.22	277.49	288.67	301.58	323.51
东翼	Eastern Region	2.12	5.62	15.81	16.75	33.23	30.56	31.41	36.67	41.84
西翼	Western Region	1.66	5.06	11.78	25.18	34.72	37.37	41.05	50.16	56.84
山区	Mountainous Region	1.11	6.36	16.87	31.37	34.03	30.77	35.23	36.97	41.01

13-7 各市建筑业企业房屋建筑施工面积

Floor Space of Buildings under Construction by Construction Enterprises by City

单位：万平方米 (10000 sq.m)

市别	City	2000	2005	2010	2012	2013	2014	2015	2016	2017
全省总计	**Provincial Total**	**16333.82**	**26886.00**	**33140.39**	**42431.74**	**52397.21**	**53443.21**	**50461.59**	**54358.29**	**60247.20**
广州	Guangzhou	3161.25	5311.14	7135.48	9119.66	15055.70	16398.88	15163.70	16289.56	19323.31
深圳	Shenzhen	1999.65	4800.07	5980.34	9731.89	11502.80	7015.83	7682.65	8501.07	9240.74
珠海	Zhuhai	733.57	625.51	877.39	1004.81	1270.67	1676.35	1969.64	2307.70	1957.27
汕头	Shantou	1477.16	2176.29	2381.63	3016.58	3478.43	3856.83	4218.81	4388.16	4956.34
佛山	Foshan	1763.57	2782.45	3335.62	3240.44	3288.92	3243.14	2731.91	3104.43	3225.98
韶关	Shaoguan	362.44	424.57	781.78	1031.84	1145.51	1090.14	1063.36	1070.88	1117.79
河源	Heyuan	79.80	294.41	218.83	247.43	252.72	345.04	453.06	517.93	582.98
梅州	Meizhou	273.56	776.23	1315.80	1299.41	1340.77	1433.24	1632.23	1408.17	1870.78
惠州	Huizhou	366.05	772.13	942.90	1073.02	1410.92	1317.62	1162.39	1367.64	1274.14
汕尾	Shanwei	127.42	114.77	175.11	127.50	92.78	92.42	118.61	156.25	223.13
东莞	Dongguan	1217.56	1234.98	733.44	777.57	790.43	1102.92	1045.99	914.05	946.91
中山	Zhongshan	400.99	945.60	601.02	757.35	573.77	542.07	470.87	515.04	500.92
江门	Jiangmen	1329.02	1585.95	1640.13	1713.24	2119.12	2611.16	2457.27	2414.59	2516.28
阳江	Yangjiang	270.81	525.95	825.31	820.89	1109.02	1020.00	920.64	827.27	882.57
湛江	Zhanjiang	857.19	1399.47	1943.66	2971.01	3187.28	5988.40	3361.23	3723.52	3816.55
茂名	Maoming	734.43	1395.55	1770.78	2840.62	2933.13	3096.70	3264.79	4255.82	5195.03
肇庆	Zhaoqing	386.93	531.11	728.47	760.58	772.31	593.25	640.44	501.43	539.77
清远	Qingyuan	249.02	466.45	632.87	645.76	613.31	612.68	562.07	598.38	643.97
潮州	Chaozhou	217.15	206.67	373.12	531.09	629.79	543.70	597.67	576.46	470.33
揭阳	Jieyang	193.91	277.75	559.41	526.15	595.67	639.41	638.29	577.80	579.61
云浮	Yunfu	132.34	238.96	187.29	194.90	234.18	223.43	305.99	342.13	382.80
按经济区域分	By Region									
珠三角	Pearl River Delta	11358.59	18588.94	21974.80	28178.56	36784.63	34501.23	33324.85	35915.51	39525.32
东翼	Eastern Region	2015.64	2775.47	3489.27	4201.31	4796.66	5132.36	5573.38	5698.67	6229.40
西翼	Western Region	1862.43	3320.97	4539.75	6632.53	7229.42	10105.10	7546.67	8806.61	9894.15
山区	Mountainous Region	1097.16	2200.62	3136.57	3419.34	3586.49	3704.51	4016.70	3937.49	4598.32

13-8 各市建筑业企业房屋建筑施工新开工面积

Floor Space of Buildings Started This Year by Construction Enterprises by City

单位：万平方米 (10000 sq.m)

市别	City	2000	2005	2010	2012	2013	2014	2015	2016	2017
全省总计	**Provincial Total**	**6423.16**	**11879.41**	**14529.68**	**16118.27**	**21604.60**	**21257.33**	**15802.23**	**18060.46**	**21644.31**
广州	Guangzhou	1153.97	2313.48	2995.47	2543.37	5768.19	4487.47	3473.80	4284.00	5320.11
深圳	Shenzhen	791.59	1933.19	2443.02	3833.09	4015.85	2172.19	1833.43	2696.09	3141.98
珠海	Zhuhai	236.23	298.50	476.92	322.40	469.98	767.08	687.28	606.65	681.01
汕头	Shantou	576.48	942.72	1129.55	1073.15	1355.32	1448.64	1421.14	1278.18	1847.85
佛山	Foshan	943.98	1230.74	931.63	1127.34	1397.99	1147.02	682.05	1139.90	1526.92
韶关	Shaoguan	160.10	196.57	360.77	532.82	567.55	550.72	551.67	479.55	544.49
河源	Heyuan	40.48	151.18	126.65	108.93	146.65	197.65	283.87	294.73	398.48
梅州	Meizhou	124.38	323.52	655.48	490.15	672.79	629.71	541.14	552.65	863.42
惠州	Huizhou	185.75	380.49	444.14	279.39	480.66	322.31	325.94	420.88	379.57
汕尾	Shanwei	84.60	50.11	122.07	46.22	50.42	37.39	55.53	54.81	96.35
东莞	Dongguan		589.95	345.07	345.91	427.39	592.81	328.25	259.14	305.67
中山	Zhongshan	200.38	503.83	287.82	277.53	271.99	214.55	212.48	290.83	207.17
江门	Jiangmen	668.83	631.55	833.99	596.56	896.52	1093.60	928.62	824.94	760.05
阳江	Yangjiang	354.20	249.55	369.70	322.04	450.81	479.74	326.31	352.07	281.79
湛江	Zhanjiang	290.52	639.64	922.67	1426.14	1714.57	4390.03	1299.72	1597.82	1254.26
茂名	Maoming	138.54	600.67	848.76	1617.99	1640.95	1523.30	1614.28	1735.73	2741.81
肇庆	Zhaoqing	115.93	248.72	298.32	270.24	289.45	243.66	337.26	354.32	284.74
清远	Qingyuan	97.89	235.35	318.47	303.68	276.63	266.00	269.03	274.08	313.23
潮州	Chaozhou	99.95	96.79	134.94	118.48	161.57	125.75	98.21	54.73	97.12
揭阳	Jieyang	108.93	147.23	388.76	367.03	426.31	474.75	408.95	397.49	493.66
云浮	Yunfu	50.43	115.64	95.48	115.82	123.02	92.97	123.25	111.88	104.62
按经济区域分	By Region									
珠三角	Pearl River Delta	4296.66	8130.45	9056.38	9595.83	14018.02	11040.68	8809.12	10876.74	12607.22
东翼	Eastern Region	869.96	1236.84	1775.32	1604.88	1993.62	2086.53	1983.84	1785.22	2534.99
西翼	Western Region	783.26	1489.86	2141.14	3366.17	3806.33	6393.07	3240.31	3685.62	4277.86
山区	Mountainous Region	473.28	1022.26	1556.84	1551.39	1786.63	1737.05	1768.97	1712.88	2224.24

13-9 各市建筑业企业期末就业人员
Number of Employed Persons of Construction Enterprises at the Year-end by City

单位：万人 (10000 persons)

市 别	City	2000	2005	2010	2012	2013	2014	2015	2016	2017
全省总计	**Provincial Total**	**141.46**	**166.78**	**196.32**	**198.31**	**204.79**	**211.07**	**185.50**	**246.17**	**289.97**
广 州	Guangzhou	26.40	30.80	39.65	40.25	37.56	43.95	40.03	48.28	68.76
深 圳	Shenzhen	20.15	26.85	45.59	52.26	47.76	47.87	41.35	66.80	73.75
珠 海	Zhuhai	3.55	3.24	4.36	3.46	9.45	8.26	6.37	12.24	13.41
汕 头	Shantou	14.29	12.63	14.35	13.02	15.47	14.78	13.60	14.46	15.94
佛 山	Foshan	8.62	13.71	11.02	11.66	8.71	8.52	10.49	9.06	9.03
韶 关	Shaoguan	4.46	3.69	5.71	7.10	9.04	8.41	6.81	6.84	7.09
河 源	Heyuan	1.74	2.09	1.72	1.69	1.77	1.87	1.92	2.73	3.31
梅 州	Meizhou	3.58	7.27	9.13	7.01	7.90	7.79	6.55	6.88	8.57
惠 州	Huizhou	3.33	3.94	3.24	3.34	3.61	3.47	1.57	3.98	4.65
汕 尾	Shanwei	1.25	1.28	1.31	0.78	0.72	0.72	0.70	1.17	0.94
东 莞	Dongguan	6.65	7.78	5.73	6.35	6.40	7.97	7.58	9.35	12.98
中 山	Zhongshan	3.71	5.75	5.32	5.06	5.50	5.18	4.00	3.98	5.38
江 门	Jiangmen	10.26	10.58	8.50	7.26	6.89	7.02	6.12	6.53	7.16
阳 江	Yangjiang	3.54	4.54	5.49	5.23	6.45	5.67	4.85	5.37	5.07
湛 江	Zhanjiang	8.03	7.87	10.29	9.79	10.62	12.63	10.71	19.01	21.79
茂 名	Maoming	8.92	10.44	8.27	10.00	11.88	11.41	10.53	12.79	15.91
肇 庆	Zhaoqing	3.61	3.70	4.12	3.05	3.40	3.46	2.53	3.83	3.75
清 远	Qingyuan	2.74	2.46	3.43	2.48	3.18	3.89	2.87	4.20	4.19
潮 州	Chaozhou	2.10	2.17	1.46	1.45	1.57	2.16	1.54	1.93	1.72
揭 阳	Jieyang	2.88	3.86	5.75	5.42	5.13	4.45	3.85	5.10	4.68
云 浮	Yunfu	1.65	2.13	1.85	1.65	1.78	1.60	1.51	1.65	1.89
按经济区域分	By Region									
珠 三 角	Pearl River Delta	86.28	106.35	127.54	132.68	129.26	135.70	120.03	164.04	198.86
东 翼	Eastern Region	20.52	19.94	22.88	20.67	22.90	22.11	19.70	22.66	23.28
西 翼	Western Region	20.49	22.86	24.06	25.02	28.96	29.71	26.09	37.17	42.77
山 区	Mountainous Region	14.17	17.64	21.84	19.93	23.68	23.55	19.67	22.30	25.06

13-10 各市建筑业企业劳动生产率
Labor Productivity of Construction Enterprises by City

单位：元/人 (yuan/person)

市别	City	2000	2005	2010	2012	2013	2014	2015	2016	2017
全省总计	**Provincial Total**	**70137**	**132056**	**239595**	**345375**	**335609**	**356658**	**382570**	**401245**	**401193**
广　州	Guangzhou	91086	204454	315033	506773	542086	525416	552068	584831	508843
深　圳	Shenzhen	107549	183515	300502	350511	340574	344326	345823	355497	356148
珠　海	Zhuhai	85936	162503	228342	656863	358547	352152	385938	446465	506501
汕　头	Shantou	56057	99266	159623	253241	261516	269587	296273	323232	346526
佛　山	Foshan	86795	115051	285616	417531	492072	545077	586097	595460	606710
韶　关	Shaoguan	57743	83704	189045	328545	326916	275767	313316	279777	315880
河　源	Heyuan	33395	82741	121383	230341	239005	261644	280999	326710	353735
梅　州	Meizhou	44258	78866	141903	275983	259046	306114	327465	394734	354985
惠　州	Huizhou	60374	119974	217933	357245	332841	349105	406527	433029	446018
汕　尾	Shanwei	46496	51367	116927	170432	174520	157869	211873	201483	297909
东　莞	Dongguan	64176	108136	218052	309757	285850	275080	263489	301919	258138
中　山	Zhongshan	73597	119772	249502	380332	312868	327054	333178	414881	420283
江　门	Jiangmen	49612	64418	147038	259535	347379	294889	336038	406110	411990
阳　江	Yangjiang	59689	78360	123368	189791	230866	240397	241168	213732	223448
湛　江	Zhanjiang	57160	98452	173336	262224	311805	316124	315036	284640	299524
茂　名	Maoming	46992	90457	170522	343345	309067	359623	396918	435077	481102
肇　庆	Zhaoqing	46380	107435	257334	306971	307105	280641	385010	344260	385081
清　远	Qingyuan	42073	90596	158598	268486	250075	242105	266337	277162	340057
潮　州	Chaozhou	57817	91838	146120	261483	261170	264270	237822	195806	220225
揭　阳	Jieyang	40672	57368	131884	190814	246950	227618	242247	237181	296304
云　浮	Yunfu	49773	74640	101721	198521	190725	199710	204748	226005	216979
按经济区域分	By Region									
珠三角	Pearl River Delta	82426	156714	283028	397550	399713	400612	418380	445292	426741
东　翼	Eastern Region	53458	87357	149042	234253	255941	255566	274993	283945	322626
西　翼	Western Region	55234	90945	160692	277491	295332	319822	334707	329011	360425
山　区	Mountainous Region	47252	81395	151686	281286	272995	272680	298647	317272	331560

主要统计指标解释

建筑业总产值 是以货币表现的建筑业企业在一定时期内生产的建筑业产品和服务的总和。建筑业总产值包括三部分内容：

⑴建筑工程产值：指列入建筑工程预算内的各种工程价值。

⑵设备安装工程产值：指设备安装工程价值，但不包括设备本身的价值。

⑶其他产值：建筑业总产值中除建筑工程、安装工程以外的产值。包括房屋构筑物修理产值、非标准设备制造产值、总包企业向分包企业收取的管理费以及不能明确划分的施工活动所完成的产值。

①房屋构筑物修理产值：指房屋和构筑物的修理所完成的价值，但不包括被修理房屋构筑物的本身价值和生产设备的修理价值。

②非标准设备制造产值：指加工制造没有定型的非标准生产设备的加工费和原材料价值以及附属加工厂为本企业承建工程制作的非标准设备的价值。

竣工产值 一般是以单位工程为对象，当该工程按照设计所规定的工程内容全部完成，达到了设计规定的交工条件，经有关部门检查验收鉴定合格的单位工程价值，即为竣工产值。

房屋施工面积 指在报告期内施工的全部房屋建筑面积，它包括本期新开工的房屋面积、上期跨入本期继续施工的房屋面积、上期停缓建在本期恢复施工的房屋面积、本期竣工的房屋面积以及本期施工后又停缓建的房屋面积。

房屋新开工面积 指房地产开发企业本年新开工建设的房屋建筑面积，以单位工程为核算对象。不包括在上年开工跨入本年继续施工的房屋建筑面积和上年停缓建而在本年恢复施工的房屋建筑面积。房屋的开工应以房屋正式开始破土刨槽（地基处理或打永久桩）的日期为准。房屋新开工面积指整栋房屋的全部建筑面积，不能分割计算。

从事建筑业活动的就业人员平均人数 指建筑业企业(或单位)报告期实际拥有的、与建筑施工活动有关的人员的平均人数，包括参加本企业(或单位)建筑施工活动的非本企业(或单位)人员，但不包括企业内部社会服务性机构的人员以及由本企业支付工资但所从事的工作与本企业生产基本无关的人员。

年末就业人员中工程技术人员 指负担工程技术和工程技术管理工作，并具有工程技术工作能力的人员。

利润总额 指企业在生产经营过程中各种收入扣除各种耗费后的盈余，反映企业在报告期内实现的亏盈总额，包括营业利润、补贴收入、投资净收益和营业外收支净额。

工程结算税金及附加 指因从事建筑业生产活动，取得工程价款结算收入而按规定应该交纳的营业税、城市维护建设税等以及随同营业税金一并计算交纳的教育费附加等。

管理费用中税金 指企业按规定从管理费用中支付的各种税金,包括房产税、土地使用税、车船使用税、印花税等。

应交增值税 指按照税法规定，以销售货物、服务、无形资产、不动产或提供加工、修理修配劳务的增值额和货物进口金额为计税依据而课征的一种流转税。指按照税法规定，针对销售货物或提供加工、修理修配劳务以及进口货物实现的增值额，企业在报告期内应交纳的税金。填报本指标时，应按权责发生制核算企业本期应负担的增值税，按销项税额与进项税额之间的差额填写。如果一般纳税人企业进项税大于销项税，致使应交税金出现负数时，该项一律填零，不填负数。

应交增值税=销项税额-(进项税额-进项税额转出)-出口抵减内销产品应纳税额-减免税款+出口退税

利税总额=工程结算税金及附加+管理费用中税金+应交增值税+利润总额

建筑业全员劳动生产率=建筑业总产值÷计算建筑业劳动生产率的平均人数

Explanatory Notes on Main Statistical Indicators

Gross Output Value of Construction refers to the sum in monetary terms of construction products and services completed by construction enterprises during a given period of time. It includes:

(1) Output value of construction projects, which is the value of various projects covered by the project budgets;

(2)Output value of equipment installation projects refers to the value of the installation of equipment. It does not include the value of the equipment itself.

(3) Other output values, which are output values other than output value of construction projects and output value of installation projects, including output value of house and building repair, output value of non-standard equipment manufacture, management expenses received by overall contractor enterprises from subcontractor enterprises and output value completed in unclassified construction activities.

①Output value of house and building repair is the value created through the repairs of houses and buildings, excluding the value of houses or buildings being repaired and the value of the repair of production equipment.

②Output value of non-standard equipment manufacture is the value of non-standard production equipment with unique specifications (including raw materials and manufacturing costs), and equipment manufactured by subsidiary workshops for construction projects contracted by construction enterprises.

Output Value Completed refers to the value of unit project completed, which has come up to the designed standards for putting into use and has been checked and accepted as qualified project by related departments.

Floor Space of Buildings under Construction refers to the floor space of buildings under construction during the reference period, including newly started buildings, buildings started earlier and continued into the reference period, buildings suspended in preceding periods but resumed during the reference period, buildings completed during the reference period, and buildings started and then suspended during the reference period.

Floor Space of Buildings Started This Year refers to the total floor space area of the buildings started in the year by real estate development companies. It excludes the buildings started in previous years and continued in the year, and the buildings suspended in previous years but restarted in the year. The start of a construction is defined by the date of ground breaking or pile driving. The floor space of the building includes that of the entire building.

Average Number of Persons for Labor Productivity Calculation of the Construction Industry refers to the average number of persons actually employed in the construction enterprises (units) and engaged in related activities of construction in the reference period, including non-staff personnel engaged in the construction activities of the enterprises (units), but excluding personnel employed in social service institutions of the enterprises and those receiving remunerations therefrom but engaged in activities basically irrelevant to the production of the enterprises.

Number of Engineering Technical Personnel Employed at the Year-end refers to personnel capable of and engaged in engineering technical work and related management.

Total Profits refer to the surplus of various incomes in the production and operation of the enterprises after deducting all expenses. This reflects the total profits or losses realized by the enterprises in the reference period, including profits from operation, income from subsidies, net investment earnings and net income from activities other than operations.

Taxes and Extra Charges on Project Settlement Accounts refer to business tax, city maintenance and construction tax and extra charges for education calculated and paid with business tax, which should be borne by the enterprises obtaining project settlement incomes from the production activities of construction.

Taxes from Management Expenses refer to the taxes which should be borne by the enterprises from management expenses, including property tax, land use tax, vehicle and vessel use tax, and stamp tax.

Value added tax payable According to the tax law refers to, in order to sell goods, services, intangible assets, real estate or providing processing, repairs and replacement services appreciation and the amount of goods imported for a turnover tax assessed on profits realized from tax basis.In accordance with the provisions of the tax law, the enterprise shall pay the tax in the report period according to the value added value of goods sold or provided for processing, repair and repair services and import goods.When filling in this index, the value added tax shall be calculated according to the accrual basis of accrual basis, and the difference between the output tax and the input tax shall be filled in.If the average taxpayer enterprise enters into a tax more than the sales tax, resulting in the negative tax payable, the item will be filled to zero, and no negative value will be filled.

Value added tax payable = sales tax - (input tax - input tax) - export offset shall be tax payable - tax deduction Export tax rebate

Total Pre-tax Profits = Taxes and Extra Charges on Project Settlement Accounts + Taxes from Management Expenses + Value added tax payable + Total Profits

Overall Labor Productivity of Construction = Gross Output Value of Construction ÷ Average Number of Persons for Labor Productivity Calculation

十四、规模以上服务业

SERVICE ENTERPRISES ABOVE DESIGNATED SIZE

十四　规模以上服务业

简要说明

一、本篇资料主要反映规模以上服务业的基本情况、财务状况、从业人员及劳动报酬情况等。

二、本篇资料由广东省统计局服务业统计处整理、编辑。

三、据国家统计报表制度，2012 年规模以上服务业年报首次纳入“一套表”联网直报系统。规模以上服务业统计范围：包括交通运输、仓储和邮电业，信息传输、软件和信息技术服务业，租赁和商务服务业，科学研究和技术服务业，水利、环境和公共设施管理业，教育，卫生和社会工作，以及物业管理、房地产中介服务、自有房地产经营活动和其他房地产业等行业中年营业收入 1000 万元以上或年末就业人数 50 人以上的服务业法人企业；居民服务、修理和其他服务业，文化、体育和娱乐业等行业中年营业收入 500 万元以上或年末就业人数 50 人以上的服务业法人企业。调查方法为符合上述条件企业的全面调查。

14 Service Enterprises Above Designated Size

Brief Introduction

Ⅰ. This data in this chapter reflect the basic information, financial condition, employed persons, labor remuneration and E-commerce transactions of some service enterprises above designated size.

Ⅱ. Data of some service enterprises above designated size are prepared and edited by the Division of Service Statistics of Statistics Bureau of Guangdong Province.

Ⅲ. According to the National Statistical Reporting System, some service enterprises above designated size have been integrated into the "network reporting" system since 2012. The statistical coverage of some service enterprises above designated size all the corporative enterprises of services sector with over 50 employees by the end of the year or with annual business revenue of over 10 million yuan, including transport, storage and postal services, information transmission, software and information technology services, leasing and business services, scientific research and technical services, management of Water Conservancy, Environment and Public Facilities, education, health and social work, real estate agent services, real estate intermediary services, own real estate business activities and other real estate,etc. Also, it covers some service enterprises above designated size all the corporative enterprises of services sector with over 50 employees by the end of the year or with annual business revenue of over 5 million yuan, including households' service, repair and other services, culture, sports and entertainment services. Survey method is a comprehensive survey.

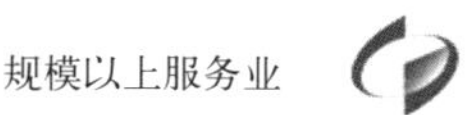

14-1 规模以上服务业企业财务指标

Main Financial Indicators of Service Enterprises above Designated Size

单位：亿元 (100 million yuan)

项　　目	Item	2016	2017	2017年比2016年增长(%) Growth Rate in 2017 Over 2016(%)
年初存货	**Inventory at Year-beginning**	**2477.48**	**2581.46**	**1.1**
期末资产负债	**Closing Balance**			
固定资产原价	Original Value of Fixed Assets	25848.18	30589.07	9.1
本年折旧	Depreciation Drawn in Current Year	1245.30	1394.63	6.0
资产总计	Total Assets	90517.32	109490.53	16.8
负债合计	Total Liabilities	45800.43	58293.71	20.2
所有者权益合计	Total Creditors'Equity	44716.88	51227.53	13.2
损益及分配	**Profits and Loss**			
营业收入	Business Revenue	19726.94	24325.18	17.6
其中：主营业务收入	Main Business Revenue	19109.50	23346.87	16.4
营业成本	Business Costs	13751.85	16843.19	18.3
其中：主营业务成本	Main Business Costs	13081.11	16071.82	18.5
营业税金及附加	Tax and Extra Charges on Business	199.86	221.57	3.5
其中：主营业务税金及附加	Tax and Extra Charges on Main Business	188.21	197.51	-1.6
销售费用	Sales Expenses	1219.14	1421.68	10.3
管理费用	Management Expenses	2472.80	2770.02	13.5
其中：税金	Taxes	41.30		
财务费用	Financial Expenses	613.28	644.75	-1.2
其中：利息收入	Interest Revenue	214.90	267.11	21.2
利息支出	Interest Expense	635.06	735.55	10.9
投资收益(损失以“-”号记)	Investment Income(loss with “-”mark)	1619.60	2120.10	29.9
营业利润	Business Profits	3104.40	4281.79	33.8
利润总额	Total Profits	3607.02	4658.61	25.5
应交所得税	Income Taxes Payable	501.98	690.93	31.2
人工成本及增值税	**Labor Cost and Value-added Tax**			
应付职工薪酬(本年贷方累计发生额)	Total Wages Payable(Credit Accumulated Amount in this year)	3810.79	4813.64	20.9
应交增值税	Value-added Tax Payable	518.69	626.77	22.7

注：增速按可比口径计算。
Note: The growdth rates are callculated on comparable coverage.

14-2 规模以上服务业企业分行业主要指标（2017年）

单位：亿元

项 目	Item	企业单位数（个） Number of Enterprises (unit)	资产总计 Total Assets at the end of the year	
			总量 Total	比2016年增长(%) Growth Rate in 2017 Over 2016(%)
全省总计	**Provincial Total**	**20386**	**109490.53**	**16.8**
按经济类型分	Grouped by Ownership			
内资企业	Domestic-funded Enterprises	18505	96259.84	17.9
#国有企业	State-owned Enterprises	468	7399.71	6.2
集体企业	Collective-owned Enterprises	590	888.98	6.4
有限责任公司	Limited Liability Corporations	7132	57013.43	21.6
私营企业	Private Enterprises	8329	11106.73	21.7
港澳台商投资企业	Enterprises with Investment from Hong Kong, Macao and Taiwan	1185	8465.19	12.1
外商投资企业	Enterprises with Foreign Investment	696	4765.49	4.7
按行业分	Grouped by Sector			
交通运输、仓储和邮政业	Transport, Storage and Postal Services	3700	30672.84	14.0
铁路运输业	Railway Transport Service	21	8287.11	7.0
#铁路旅客运输	Railway Passenger Transport	7	6999.17	5.5
铁路货物运输	Railway Freight Transport	12	189.74	1.4
道路运输业	Road Transport Services	1636	12632.85	18.4
#城市公共交通运输	Urban Public Trasport	226	6936.61	25.8
公路旅客运输	Highway Passenger Transport	212	350.43	3.8
道路货物运输	Road Freight Transport	1054	519.20	20.9
水上运输业	Waterway Transport Service	280	3470.45	18.0
#水上旅客运输	Waterway Passenger Trasport	30	135.19	-28.1
水上货物运输	Waterway Freight Transport	144	2100.46	36.7
航空运输业	Air Transport Service	34	3215.25	13.6
#航空客货运输	Air Passenger and Freight Transport	20	2805.16	13.4
管道运输业	Pipeline Transport Service	3	56.04	-5.9
装卸搬运和运输代理业	Handling and Transportation Agency	1245	1204.74	14.1
#运输代理业	Transportation Agency	1092	809.95	13.1
仓储业	Warehousing Service	345	1320.55	9.3
邮政业	Postal Service	136	485.84	22.7
#快递服务	Express Service	113	383.26	35.5
信息传输、软件和信息技术服务业	Information Transmission, Software and Information Technology Services	3320	18890.67	34.0
电信、广播电视和卫星传输服务	Telecommunications, Broadcasting Television and Satellite Transmission Services	195	4160.51	-1.2
#电信	Telecommunications	155	3862.34	-1.6
互联网和相关服务	Internet and Related Services	232	8507.71	69.9
#互联网信息服务	Internet Information Services	184	8447.41	70.3
软件和信息技术服务业	Software and Information Technology Services	2893	6222.45	27.6
#软件开发	Software Development	2022	4100.82	26.8
信息系统集成服务	Information System Integration Service	366	758.12	18.4
信息技术咨询服务	Information Technology Consulting Services	218	445.18	13.1
物业管理业	Property Management Industry	1850	2690.32	10.4
房地产中介服务业	Real Estate Agent Services	221	978.89	17.2

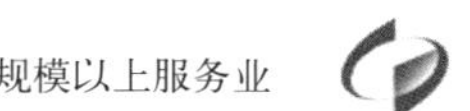

Main Indicators of Service Enterprises above Designated Size by Sector(2017)

(100 million yuan)

本年折旧 Depreciation Drawn in Current Year		营业收入 Business Revenue		营业成本 Business Costs		营业税金及附加 Tax and Extra Charges on Business		销售费用 Selling Expenses	
总量 Total	比2016年增长(%) Growth Rate in 2017 Over 2016(%)	总量 Total	比2016年增长(%) Growth Rate in 2017 Over 2016(%)	总量 Total	比2016年增长(%) Growth Rate in 2017 Over 2016(%)	总量 Total	比2016年增长(%) Growth Rate in 2017 Over 2016(%)	总量 Total	比2016年增长(%) Growth Rate in 2017 Over 2016(%)
1394.63	**6.0**	**24325.18**	**17.6**	**16843.19**	**18.3**	**221.57**	**3.5**	**1421.68**	**10.3**
1177.56	4.8	20987.61	17.7	15225.35	18.8	182.51	1.7	1160.50	12.7
128.98	-1.5	1466.74	8.0	1276.28	9.3	9.48	11.2	31.65	2.3
15.47	-13.8	170.15	2.6	80.41	0.0	3.72	-10.7	4.29	20.0
579.83	2.3	9450.40	16.0	6702.13	16.1	104.28	5.3	570.00	6.4
102.19	11.6	6242.61	29.6	4467.41	32.0	40.95	-13.7	360.48	25.2
134.93	10.2	2221.70	17.7	1019.91	14.7	20.29	-8.5	177.08	-0.6
82.14	18.0	1115.87	14.4	597.93	12.2	18.77	51.2	84.09	3.8
635.57	1.6	7174.86	15.1	6103.65	16.6	56.26	29.7	164.37	4.9
150.43	11.2	1129.27	10.6	1041.00	9.3	3.37	6.7	1.65	12.6
141.68	10.4	1107.12	10.7	1006.25	9.2	3.23	3.7	1.64	12.1
3.30	2.0	20.52	6.5	23.81	3.1	0.08	117.1	0.01	114.8
226.63	4.1	1645.52	13.1	1363.87	13.6	36.56	26.5	30.19	2.6
57.32	-41.0	348.30	-1.2	415.18	1.9	30.25	47.6	3.41	-3.1
13.78	-13.8	143.66	-2.7	122.60	1.1	1.06	11.4	1.67	-21.9
18.15	21.4	697.85	23.4	600.66	24.4	2.54	34.6	22.48	6.2
79.24	-1.9	710.38	13.3	523.99	9.8	3.24	22.9	6.58	3.4
2.63	-12.2	29.92	-46.1	18.69	-53.5	0.18	-53.2	0.93	-12.2
47.91	11.8	429.37	26.9	352.44	19.5	1.35	87.4	3.99	3.5
127.19	-6.7	1425.07	9.7	1212.00	14.5	4.12	32.8	69.14	6.5
115.25	-7.8	1305.94	9.5	1131.78	14.9	2.62	10.1	67.25	6.7
2.76	6.2	14.64	0.0	6.12	8.7	0.03	67.4		
21.30	13.6	1289.19	29.8	1144.73	30.6	2.44	38.8	30.52	14.6
9.79	20.4	1181.36	31.6	1062.46	32.0	1.78	38.8	29.22	14.5
18.11	13.6	379.72	14.9	307.40	10.1	4.34	130.3	15.44	-15.1
9.92	-45.3	581.06	17.8	504.53	31.5	2.16	13.4	10.85	12.4
5.61	53.5	422.40	26.5	359.28	29.9	0.86	10.7	10.85	12.4
406.07	11.2	7581.43	23.5	4310.82	24.7	51.94	23.6	672.17	15.7
339.91	8.0	1862.01	2.4	1150.36	2.2	8.51	10.6	207.58	7.9
326.17	8.0	1758.13	2.4	1088.16	2.4	8.11	9.8	200.76	7.9
24.56	68.4	1876.31	47.6	1093.15	54.3	17.55	34.5	132.10	28.3
23.16	69.7	1827.44	48.6	1057.61	54.7	17.41	34.7	126.82	29.0
41.59	16.6	3843.12	26.0	2067.31	27.4	25.88	21.6	332.49	16.5
23.86	17.6	2634.30	27.0	1375.82	28.9	15.82	18.6	227.08	20.2
6.49	7.1	414.75	12.1	266.34	6.3	2.10	4.7	21.09	6.3
4.77	8.3	408.29	34.5	200.85	35.0	6.18	41.7	56.07	9.3
35.75	66.3	916.32	14.1	624.33	17.6	11.45	-43.3	35.99	5.4
2.57	42.1	228.83	0.4	111.53	4.1	1.59	-64.9	49.40	-8.4

14-2 续表 1

单位：亿元

项目	Item	管理费用 Management Expenses 总量 Total	管理费用 比2016年增长(%) Growth Rate in 2017 Over 2016(%)	财务费用 Financial Expenses 总量 Total	财务费用 比2016年增长(%) Growth Rate in 2017 Over 2016(%)
全省总计	**Provincial Total**	**3142.89**	**13.5**	**644.75**	**-1.2**
按经济类型分	Grouped by Ownership				
内资企业	Domestic-funded Enterprises	2595.48	12.6	558.66	-3.6
#国有企业	State-owned Enterprises	125.37	3.3	49.78	5.0
集体企业	Collective-owned Enterprises	38.58	4.0	2.37	-17.3
有限责任公司	Limited Liability Corporations	1048.31	13.1	311.00	-3.0
私营企业	Private Enterprises	895.02	14.3	95.89	11.0
港澳台商投资企业	Enterprises with Investment from Hong Kong, Macao and Taiwan	371.90	19.8	31.05	-4.3
外商投资企业	Enterprises with Foreign Investment	175.51	13.3	55.04	36.7
按行业分	Grouped by Sector				
交通运输、仓储和邮政业	Transport, Storage and Postal Services	436.33	4.5	294.30	-11.5
铁路运输业	Railway Transport Service	35.27	-2.8	89.57	1.0
#铁路旅客运输	Railway Passenger Transport	34.06	-2.9	78.75	0.0
铁路货物运输	Railway Freight Transport	0.97	-2.9	5.43	-4.7
道路运输业	Road Transport Services	131.00	3.5	123.24	10.0
#城市公共交通运输	Urban Public Trasport	35.84	-5.8	42.44	12.6
公路旅客运输	Highway Passenger Transport	19.69	-5.7	1.46	-4.4
道路货物运输	Road Freight Transport	50.93	13.8	3.98	16.5
水上运输业	Waterway Transport Service	58.50	3.9	44.53	45.8
#水上旅客运输	Waterway Passenger Trasport	3.60	-32.6	3.21	52.5
水上货物运输	Waterway Freight Transport	31.06	10.3	30.70	107.8
航空运输业	Air Transport Service	50.03	7.0	10.47	-85.4
#航空客货运输	Air passenger and freight Transport	41.75	9.2	10.44	-85.3
管道运输业	Pipeline Transport Service	1.10	-5.7	0.58	-13.0
装卸搬运和运输代理业	Handling and Transportation Agency	77.21	7.1	11.13	-13.0
#运输代理业	Transportation Agency	65.89	8.5	6.09	-22.9
仓储业	Warehousing Service	28.79	3.8	12.89	-10.2
邮政业	Postal Service	54.42	7.6	1.88	10.9
#快递服务	Express Service	40.56	15.7	1.68	7.1
信息传输、软件和信息技术服务业	Information Transmission, Software and Information Technology Services	1130.12	22.3	-95.51	58.7
电信、广播电视和卫星传输服务	Telecommunications, Broadcasting Television and Satellite Transmission Services	103.83	0.7	-17.53	-6.9
#电信	Teleccommunications	85.43	-1.0	-17.37	-7.1
互联网和相关服务	Internet and Related Services	252.36	49.8	-80.01	103.4
#互联网信息服务	Internet Information Services	247.02	51.3	-80.22	101.4
软件和信息技术服务业	Software and Information Technology Services	773.94	18.7	2.03	-200.7
#软件开发	Software Development	555.27	19.4	-1.06	-44.5
信息系统集成服务	Information System Integration Service	75.51	30.0	1.06	45.5
信息技术咨询服务	Information Technology Consulting services	55.07	16.6	-0.18	-81.8
物业管理业	Property Management Industry	158.37	6.2	24.04	18.1
房地产中介服务业	Real Estate Agent Services	49.95	13.5	3.66	250.1

14-2 1 continued

(100 million yuan)

利润总额 Total Profits		应交所得税 Income Taxes Payable		应付职工薪酬 Total Wages Payable		应交增值税 Value-added Taxes Payable		就业人员平均人数（万人） Average number of employed persons (10000 persons)
总量 Total	比2016年增长(%) Growth Rate in 2017 Over 2016(%)	总量 Total	比2016年增长(%) Growth Rate in 2017 Over 2016(%)	总量 Total	比2016年增长(%) Growth Rate in 2017 Over 2016(%)	总量 Total	比2016年增长(%) Growth Rate in 2017 Over 2016(%)	
4658.61	**25.5**	**690.93**	**31.2**	**4813.64**	**20.9**	**626.77**	**22.7**	**437.95**
3591.72	24.2	544.94	37.1	4075.03	21.5	550.38	21.0	393.44
62.59	-20.1	13.59	-18.9	476.77	28.3	50.78	2.8	36.13
47.38	4.3	3.21	0.1	37.84	5.6	4.27	90.6	7.05
1748.64	16.1	290.62	16.3	1791.82	18.3	257.70	11.6	165.55
619.95	55.6	88.65	18.3	921.62	25.1	164.75	61.9	124.34
754.96	36.0	96.99	16.8	472.09	22.5	47.15	46.4	25.88
311.93	18.0	49.00	6.6	266.51	10.8	29.23	21.6	18.63
658.66	44.8	129.02	23.0	1398.93	19.2	139.56	5.0	112.10
-41.28		6.52	-29.3	346.21	42.0	45.25	-6.1	22.47
-23.00		6.51	-29.4	341.86	42.4	45.12	-6.1	22.10
-9.29		0.01	-47.1	2.21	4.9	0.13	0.2	0.19
278.43	51.8	42.86	13.3	383.60	8.6	35.32	30.8	43.29
68.83	328.3	1.82	-17.1	212.36	6.7	3.66	7.3	20.10
10.60	-16.3	2.21	-20.2	40.92	1.8	4.06	3.9	6.52
25.27	33.1	6.24	24.4	80.32	17.0	14.63	39.4	11.41
128.92	26.2	24.23	43.1	109.84	11.2	6.56	-6.3	6.46
18.97	108.3	4.99	72.2	6.56	-32.3	0.62	-17.5	0.54
31.32	12.3	6.07	47.2	56.59	22.8	2.99	-24.3	2.79
126.34	32.7	26.12	16.7	300.64	23.9	27.22	-2.2	12.61
96.95	34.9	19.02	18.3	260.26	25.8	25.95	2.1	9.99
6.84	-4.6	1.74	-4.4	0.63	8.7	0.17	-8.8	0.03
44.08	90.9	8.53	24.1	108.63	23.4	10.04	24.8	12.51
26.84	131.8	5.87	24.7	83.84	27.9	7.95	26.6	9.36
88.47	141.9	14.54	169.0	33.99	10.4	5.78	31.8	4.23
26.86	-61.0	4.48	1.2	115.39	-0.3	9.21	-10.2	10.51
35.11	-8.5	4.48	3.3	65.89	9.0	8.27	-14.0	7.04
1782.27	16.9	253.89	28.7	1140.78	26.6	226.86	15.6	66.62
486.07	-5.9	103.26	20.1	232.79	9.2	58.22	-16.9	13.41
465.58	-6.5	102.24	20.1	204.83	9.7	56.60	-17.2	11.58
498.24	40.3	64.89	37.8	203.31	48.8	27.21	131.2	6.39
495.34	39.5	64.37	38.0	196.83	50.4	24.42	130.8	5.80
797.95	22.2	85.74	33.6	704.68	27.7	141.43	23.5	46.81
571.71	19.3	51.93	26.1	465.25	24.5	107.30	21.4	27.74
59.74	-6.8	7.01	10.2	68.16	18.7	13.44	23.1	5.18
107.74	66.0	17.34	65.7	93.28	62.8	8.54	82.3	7.23
112.67	-0.9	28.60	52.4	329.82	11.5	33.65	95.0	51.93
25.24	-8.0	5.36	-5.9	99.06	-0.8	10.77	42.9	9.82

14-2 续表 2

单位：亿元

项　　目	Item	企业单位数(个) Number of Enterprises (unit)	资产总计 Total Assets at the end of the year 总量 Total	比2016年增长(%) Growth Rate in 2017 Over 2016(%)
租赁和商务服务业	Leasing and Business Services	5391	40967.05	14.5
租赁业	Leasing	230	1453.10	27.3
#机械设备租赁	Machinery Equipment Leasing	217	1443.77	27.4
商务服务业	Business Services	5161	39513.95	14.1
#企业管理服务	Enterprise Management Service	1813	32302.96	12.1
咨询与调查	Consultation and Investigation	760	2936.19	25.2
广告业	Advertising	621	638.48	1.4
旅行社及相关服务	Travel Agency and Related Services	460	200.13	14.2
科学研究和技术服务业	Scientific Research and Technical Services	2349	4789.51	10.8
研究和试验发展	Research and Experimental Development	314	1156.52	16.1
#工程和技术研究和试验发展	Engineering and Technology Research and Experimental Development	233	765.86	5.7
专业技术服务业	Professional Technical Services	1780	3241.51	17.5
科技推广和应用服务业	Services of Science and Technology Exchanges and Promotion	255	391.47	-31.0
水利环境和公共设施管理业	Management of Water Conservancy, Environment and Public Facilities	401	1736.39	2.8
水利管理业	Management of Water Conservancy	15	15.54	1.6
生态保护和环境治理业	Ecological Protection and Environmental Treatment	104	785.18	0.0
#生态保护	Ecological Protection	4	5.37	-9.5
环境治理业	Environmental Treatment	100	779.81	0.1
公共设施管理业	Management of Public Facilities	282	935.67	5.3
居民服务、修理和其他服务业	Households' service, Repair and Other Services	783	248.97	11.7
居民服务业	Services to Households	191	80.12	19.9
机动车、电子产品和日用产品修理业	Motor Vehicle, Electronic Products and Consumer Products repair	257	70.49	-0.5
#汽车、摩托车修理与维护	Automobile, Motorcycle Repair and Maintenance	154	28.78	5.9
其他服务业	Other Services	335	98.35	15.4
教育	Education	659	471.22	13.0
#中等教育	Secondary Education	135	109.90	3.9
高等教育	Higher Education	19	163.22	24.6
卫生和社会工作	Health and Social Work	333	270.87	11.1
卫生	Health	320	267.36	11.0
#医院	Hospital	238	217.57	8.7
社区医疗与卫生院	Community Medical and Health Center	9	1.48	18.5
社会工作	Social Work	13	3.51	23.2
文化、体育和娱乐业	Culture, Sports and Entertainment	699	1937.38	8.3
新闻和出版业	News and Publication	79	271.98	1.2
#出版业	Publication	76	265.49	8.6
广播、电视、电影和影视录音制作业	Production of Radio, Television, Film and Video Recording	278	1028.38	5.1
文化艺术业	Culture and Arts	84	43.41	20.7
体育	Sports	120	260.37	11.1
娱乐业	Entertainment	138	333.24	22.7

14-2 2 continued

(100 million yuan)

本年折旧 Depreciation Drawn in Current Year		营业收入 Business Revenue		营业成本 Business Costs		营业税金及附加 Tax and Extra Charges on Business		销售费用 Selling Expenses	
总量 Total	比2016年增长(%) Growth Rate in 2017 Over 2016(%)	总量 Total	比2016年增长(%) Growth Rate in 2017 Over 2016(%)	总量 Total	比2016年增长(%) Growth Rate in 2017 Over 2016(%)	总量 Total	比2016年增长(%) Growth Rate in 2017 Over 2016(%)	总量 Total	比2016年增长(%) Growth Rate in 2017 Over 2016(%)
159.93	2.5	4329.36	16.3	2949.17	17.1	53.19	-2.2	261.12	5.9
18.57	8.8	149.63	26.0	97.41	20.7	0.74	6.3	6.13	12.0
18.30	8.3	145.04	25.0	94.70	19.5	0.72	11.2	5.45	9.1
141.37	1.8	4179.73	16.0	2851.77	17.0	52.45	-2.3	255.00	5.7
105.55	0.0	1212.96	11.2	655.84	11.0	35.90	3.6	45.21	9.2
6.83	18.5	494.36	20.5	239.96	27.6	2.63	-12.1	72.24	1.9
2.81	-15.4	519.96	5.8	421.05	4.2	4.15	21.9	31.49	6.7
1.93	-0.2	639.22	10.2	589.71	9.6	0.66	-51.8	25.95	4.0
53.56	27.6	2183.99	16.6	1545.34	16.0	12.75	-10.4	99.91	16.3
11.30	14.7	341.00	11.0	223.38	7.6	2.02	14.5	19.96	55.4
8.16	16.5	266.01	11.2	180.21	9.1	1.52	4.1	11.92	80.1
36.11	35.5	1709.85	17.4	1237.92	17.3	9.96	-15.2	71.71	7.2
6.15	12.1	133.14	22.2	84.05	21.0	0.78	7.7	8.24	34.6
16.50	3.3	324.04	29.2	203.95	16.0	10.67	75.7	7.21	10.9
0.37	-15.7	7.77	14.8	5.82	21.7	0.05	-28.7	0.06	12.6
4.62	11.4	62.66	18.4	42.82	15.9	0.48	7.8	1.62	5.5
0.30	-5.8	3.99	2.4	1.83	2.5	0.03	-13.9	0.59	-7.7
4.32	12.8	58.67	19.7	41.00	16.6	0.45	9.6	1.04	14.8
11.52	1.1	253.61	32.7	155.31	15.8	10.14	82.4	5.53	12.5
4.73	13.4	251.24	19.1	169.56	17.7	1.63	-51.6	28.46	20.3
1.47	1.3	58.27	21.5	32.83	15.8	0.31	-64.2	9.83	9.4
1.18	17.7	77.26	17.1	52.91	16.8	0.48	-15.9	9.87	30.3
0.50	-2.0	32.23	17.3	23.40	22.0	0.19	-10.5	4.49	55.1
2.08	21.1	115.70	19.2	83.82	19.1	0.84	-56.4	8.75	23.5
16.36	-9.1	249.74	15.7	162.27	17.7	0.92	-48.8	14.63	14.5
5.40	-25.3	53.22	13.2	41.59	14.0	0.02	-81.3	0.10	-16.2
3.99	-5.7	40.99	13.2	22.75	8.9	0.10	33.7	0.06	-19.0
9.02	-15.3	264.85	18.8	179.52	17.5	0.24	81.0	27.82	34.3
8.91	-15.6	261.93	18.7	178.24	17.5	0.24	81.3	27.34	35.5
7.38	-22.9	219.75	18.1	153.63	17.5	0.19	130.1	18.25	39.3
0.04	-5.2	1.56	17.2	0.93	3.1	0.00	33.3	0.31	25.5
0.10	15.4	2.93	22.3	1.28	16.9	0.00	-81.8	0.48	-9.8
22.44	0.0	445.14	3.5	314.27	9.3	7.80	-14.8	46.04	-14.2
2.93	-38.9	89.88	0.2	65.93	-0.9	1.32	3.9	6.77	-17.0
2.93	-39.0	89.41	0.2	65.76	-1.0	1.31	4.0	6.77	-17.0
9.23	47.2	192.73	7.8	140.18	11.3	3.03	2.0	17.65	-30.8
0.32	-29.5	27.20	44.1	18.86	50.1	0.14	-12.2	2.23	35.0
4.13	-6.7	58.21	15.0	50.67	21.7	1.96	16.2	7.01	-12.0
5.84	-10.2	77.11	-16.5	38.62	-5.4	1.34	-56.2	12.37	19.2

14-2 续表 3

单位：亿元

项　目	item	管理费用 Management Expenses 总量 Total	管理费用 比2016年增长(%) Growth Rate in 2017 Over 2016(%)	财务费用 Financial Expenses 总量 Total	财务费用 比2016年增长(%) Growth Rate in 2017 Over 2016(%)
租赁和商务服务业	Leasing and Business Services	685.19	8.5	290.03	11.8
租赁业	Leasing	20.04	16.4	10.53	18.8
#机械设备租赁	Machinery Equipment Leasing	19.30	17.0	10.55	18.7
商务服务业	Business Services	665.15	8.3	279.51	11.6
#企业管理服务	Enterprise Management Service	323.24	11.2	249.60	12.3
咨询与调查	Consultation and Investigation	123.70	-4.6	17.08	-0.3
广告业	Advertising	36.93	6.7	0.88	-40.3
旅行社及相关服务	Travel Agency and Related Services	17.54	-3.5	0.91	0.9
科学研究和技术服务业	Scientific Research and Technical Services	330.92	15.5	31.23	30.3
研究和试验发展	Research and Experimental Development	62.69	2.6	8.83	15.2
#工程和技术研究和试验发展	Engineering and Technology Research and Experimental Development	39.90	6.3	7.14	22.4
专业技术服务业	Professional Technical Services	239.34	19.5	20.15	38.8
科技推广和应用服务业	Services of Science and Technology Exchanges and Promotion	28.89	14.6	2.25	25.4
水利环境和公共设施管理业	Management of Water Conservancy, Environment and Public Facilities	32.67	17.6	8.81	-17.8
水利管理业	Management of Water Conservancy	0.92	-1.3	0.19	29.0
生态保护和环境治理业	Ecological Protection and Environmental Treatment	7.29	17.7	0.99	-3.5
#生态保护	Ecological Protection	0.37	-6.2	-0.03	-154.4
环境治理业	Environmental Treatment	6.92	19.4	1.02	5.2
公共设施管理业	Management of Public Facilities	24.46	18.5	7.63	-20.0
居民服务、修理和其他服务业	Households' service, Repair and Other Services	37.55	13.8	1.57	36.6
居民服务业	Services to Households	10.71	23.5	0.41	46.7
机动车、电子产品和日用产品修理业	Motor Vehicle, Electronic Products and Consumer Products repair	10.24	3.3	0.53	45.3
#汽车、摩托车修理与维护	Automobile, Motorcycle Repair and	4.89	-3.3	0.06	-76.4
其他服务业	Other Services	16.61	15.2	0.63	24.6
教育	Education	63.57	16.6	2.14	-21.4
#中等教育	Secondary Education	12.98	8.5	0.68	48.7
高等教育	Higher Education	10.47	9.0	0.42	-22.6
卫生和社会工作	Health and Social Work	44.69	12.8	1.94	0.9
卫生	Health	43.88	12.8	1.93	0.7
#医院	Hospital	36.93	13.0	1.83	10.2
社区医疗与卫生院	Community Medical and Health Center	0.25	5.2	…	-32.2
社会工作	Social Work	0.82	11.4	0.01	47.6
文化、体育和娱乐业	Culture, Sports and Entertainment	68.74	7.6	9.69	-1.4
新闻和出版业	News and Publication	15.87	4.6	-0.19	233.3
#出版业	Publication	15.79	4.5	-0.06	39.3
广播、电视、电影和影视录音制作业	Production of Radio, Television, Film and Video Recording	21.17	9.2	3.07	1.8
文化艺术业	Culture and Arts	5.72	18.8	0.01	-65.0
体育	Sports	14.23	0.5	1.89	-2.2
娱乐业	Entertainment	11.76	13.3	4.91	-0.1

14-2 3 continued

(100 million yuan)

利润总额 Total Profits		应交所得税 Income Taxes Payable		应付职工薪酬 Total Wages Payable		应交增值税 Value-added Tax Payable		就业人员平均人数(万人) Average Number of Employed Persons (10000 persons)
总量 Total	比2016年增长(%) Growth Rate in 2017 Over 2016(%)	总量 Total	比2016年增长(%) Growth Rate in 2017 Over 2016(%)	总量 Total	比2016年增长(%) Growth Rate in 2017 Over 2016(%)	总量 Total	比2016年增长(%) Growth Rate in 2017 Over 2016(%)	
1533.47	34.9	190.53	59.6	860.43	27.6	97.55	43.8	101.08
16.16	33.4	4.94	-45.9	19.91	19.4	3.73	12.5	2.29
15.62	32.3	4.78	-46.7	19.18	20.1	3.59	11.4	2.21
1517.31	34.9	185.59	68.4	840.52	27.8	93.83	45.4	98.79
1162.67	36.0	135.52	137.5	244.46	36.8	31.02	51.2	20.32
133.33	39.3	9.57	-47.4	168.38	16.7	15.13	16.8	14.78
27.78	-11.2	7.44	18.3	44.86	26.0	6.85	8.9	3.27
5.30	1643.3	2.09	65.0	24.81	16.8	3.52	160.2	3.62
266.87	32.8	37.83	19.7	504.42	18.6	64.91	28.4	35.36
48.88	42.1	6.90	41.7	66.62	21.7	7.19	9.4	4.04
35.88	1.9	5.29	38.4	48.63	22.3	5.81	5.4	2.90
200.70	33.2	28.36	18.9	410.57	18.2	53.90	30.0	28.89
17.29	9.2	2.57	-10.9	27.23	17.4	3.82	50.2	2.43
76.69	154.3	15.56	106.8	48.10	12.7	12.67	55.4	7.77
1.00	7.2	0.17	1.9	1.65	16.6	0.28	21.7	0.14
11.56	27.6	1.54	4.7	8.47	16.8	3.17	62.9	0.77
1.25	21.9	0.32	34.6	0.96	10.7	0.05	8.4	0.09
10.31	28.3	1.22	-1.1	7.51	17.7	3.13	64.1	0.68
64.13	218.1	13.85	135.4	37.98	11.6	9.22	54.2	6.86
13.66	21.1	3.68	16.6	94.02	19.4	9.21	37.0	19.99
4.42	43.4	1.25	27.1	14.89	24.0	1.37	98.9	2.49
3.58	-13.2	1.29	12.3	17.47	16.1	3.19	-8.3	2.28
-0.75		0.44	-2.5	6.66	22.3	1.22	-33.9	0.98
5.67	38.9	1.14	11.4	61.66	19.3	4.64	81.9	15.22
12.36	-1.3	3.19	17.6	99.83	19.5	3.58	114.5	11.20
-0.21		0.36	7.0	25.66	16.4	0.15	351.3	2.92
7.94	43.8	0.33	78.3	12.98	11.1	0.11	184.4	1.11
12.44	18.7	3.95	20.6	75.35	22.9	0.29	112.9	7.91
12.04	15.8	3.85	18.1	74.17	23.0	0.24	76.8	7.70
10.59	18.9	3.37	21.4	62.15	24.4	0.12	75.9	6.29
0.03		…	175.0	0.57	19.3			0.08
0.40	366.6	0.10	473.7	1.19	17.5	0.05		0.21
27.83	-38.4	7.76	-32.7	110.50	14.3	12.52	9.8	8.98
8.44	-65.2	0.63	-86.2	29.09	1.6	2.07	-6.9	1.80
7.82	-5.2	0.55	61.4	28.97	1.4	2.06	6.7	1.79
18.33	46.2	2.57	-11.7	23.93	13.3	5.01	1.2	2.34
3.29	45.9	0.62	8.7	6.32	34.1	0.79	50.4	0.52
-10.58		0.96	42.9	34.42	20.9	1.84	69.1	2.06
8.34	-56.3	2.98	6.0	16.74	21.8	2.80	7.3	2.27

14-3 各市规模以上服务业企业主要指标（2017年）

单位：亿元

市别	City	企业单位数(个) Number of Enterprises (unit)	资产总计 Total Assets at the end of the year		本年折旧 Depreciation Drawn in Current Year	
			总量 Total	比2016年增长(%) Growth Rate in 2017 Over 2016(%)	总量 Total	比2016年增长(%) Growth Rate in 2017 Over 2016(%)
广　州	Guangzhou	7414	46765.33	12.7	605.45	11.8
深　圳	Shenzhen	6371	47028.12	24.2	329.09	-6.5
珠　海	Zhuhai	828	3413.11	7.1	35.85	8.7
汕　头	Shantou	293	629.77	18.6	19.29	2.5
佛　山	Foshan	1057	2273.97	6.9	97.34	3.5
韶　关	Shaoguan	199	206.85	2.6	8.01	15.0
河　源	Heyuan	88	139.41	12.2	7.09	9.8
梅　州	Meizhou	52	123.21	0.9	9.33	6.5
惠　州	Huizhou	439	1464.21	6.4	31.11	-0.6
汕　尾	Shanwei	83	164.77	33.8	7.21	11.5
东　莞	Dongguan	1563	3997.13	12.5	98.46	-1.2
中　山	Zhongshan	611	1255.59	6.8	38.78	110.1
江　门	Jiangmen	286	385.97	5.2	17.73	3.2
阳　江	Yangjiang	73	84.63	2.6	10.82	160.7
湛　江	Zhanjiang	362	597.88	2.8	32.49	45.7
茂　名	Maoming	218	215.43	14.2	11.29	-5.5
肇　庆	Zhaoqing	124	277.69	43.8	9.53	4.8
清　远	Qingyuan	154	252.99	11.6	8.78	-34.9
潮　州	Chaozhou	51	65.07	-5.2	6.23	-2.6
揭　阳	Jieyang	77	71.25	3.4	4.65	-35.7
云　浮	Yunfu	43	78.10	2.8	6.08	-2.7
按经济区域分	By Region					
珠三角	Pearl River Delta	18693	106861.14	17.0	1263.35	5.6
东　翼	Eastern Region	504	930.87	17.6	37.38	-3.9
西　翼	Western Region	653	897.95	5.3	54.60	42.2
山　区	Mountainous Region	536	800.57	6.6	39.30	-6.3

Main Indicators of Service Enterprises above Designated Size by City (2017)

(100 million yuan)

营业收入 Business Revenue		营业成本 Business Costs		营业税金及附加 Tax and Extra Charges on Business		销售费用 Selling Expenses	
总量 Total	比2016年增长(%) Growth Rate in 2017 Over 2016(%)	总量 Total	比2016年增长(%) Growth Rate in 2017 Over 2016(%)	总量 Total	比2016年增长(%) Growth Rate in 2017 Over 2016(%)	总量 Total	比2016年增长(%) Growth Rate in 2017 Over 2016(%)
9813.31	16.8	7398.23	17.4	75.17	8.0	564.94	12.2
10103.02	20.8	6641.78	22.5	111.12	5.7	578.42	6.7
697.15	16.6	446.17	8.4	6.54	-11.1	37.11	20.1
220.02	16.8	150.32	15.8	1.45	11.6	20.01	11.5
729.62	9.6	480.65	13.1	5.42	-16.4	47.36	11.8
83.78	14.4	68.97	15.7	0.50	-28.1	4.35	25.8
37.53	11.4	29.82	5.4	0.31	0.9	3.19	14.5
45.29	5.2	33.14	4.9	0.24	-18.5	3.78	24.1
294.00	11.6	205.95	13.2	1.94	-19.8	13.65	0.4
46.53	14.9	38.27	14.9	0.26	-7.9	2.80	8.7
1169.13	13.1	585.32	11.4	9.45	-7.0	70.77	19.5
294.44	9.7	201.24	10.4	3.47	7.4	23.18	11.3
152.61	5.2	103.80	4.6	1.36	-42.6	10.97	19.8
52.80	13.0	38.77	16.9	0.27	9.2	3.51	15.2
191.02	17.1	135.14	16.8	1.40	-0.6	9.55	6.2
114.76	8.5	84.65	10.8	0.89	-6.9	7.03	3.1
78.22	8.5	57.03	7.3	0.51	6.9	5.25	13.6
81.65	17.1	58.60	16.3	0.51	-26.1	4.43	10.3
37.79	14.2	27.26	7.3	0.20	31.2	3.32	24.0
50.24	7.0	34.80	12.1	0.28	17.6	5.81	17.1
32.26	6.3	23.28	10.7	0.29	47.5	2.25	12.1
23331.50	17.8	16120.17	18.5	214.98	3.7	1351.64	10.2
354.59	14.8	250.65	14.2	2.18	11.0	31.94	13.4
358.58	13.6	258.57	14.8	2.56	-2.0	20.10	6.6
280.51	12.2	213.80	12.0	1.85	-15.3	18.00	17.5

14−3 续表

单位：亿元

市别	City	管理费用 Management Expenses 总量 Total	比2016年增长(%) Growth Rate in 2017 Over 2016(%)	财务费用 Financial Expenses 总量 Total	比2016年增长(%) Growth Rate in 2017 Over 2016(%)	利润总额 Total Profits 总量 Total	比2016年增长(%) Growth Rate in 2017 Over 2016(%)
广　州	Guangzhou	1083.40	12.8	317.10	-4.1	1235.17	15.6
深　圳	Shenzhen	1427.11	14.6	203.98	2.1	2609.20	34.0
珠　海	Zhuhai	116.25	23.4	30.16	18.0	151.07	100.2
汕　头	Shantou	21.62	9.5	4.50	13.9	28.50	24.5
佛　山	Foshan	88.46	13.8	22.14	13.6	118.73	-6.7
韶　关	Shaoguan	8.48	8.3	0.51	30.1	1.98	-4.2
河　源	Heyuan	4.00	-2.4	0.59	19.1	-0.30	
梅　州	Meizhou	5.07	6.7	3.01	-1.8	1.15	-30.0
惠　州	Huizhou	30.33	8.1	20.60	-6.4	89.38	34.7
汕　尾	Shanwei	4.78	6.5	2.35	193.4	-0.38	
东　莞	Dongguan	226.17	11.1	19.23	-20.9	296.38	6.8
中　山	Zhongshan	41.73	8.7	5.48	19.8	44.92	9.1
江　门	Jiangmen	15.22	-10.6	3.67	-26.3	20.17	5.1
阳　江	Yangjiang	5.92	9.7	0.53	33.2	4.63	-20.5
湛　江	Zhanjiang	22.70	4.7	4.00	-2.3	23.67	33.4
茂　名	Maoming	10.62	2.4	1.02	15.5	11.69	-11.9
肇　庆	Zhaoqing	9.16	-1.3	1.63	-29.7	6.78	-2.8
清　远	Qingyuan	11.47	37.0	3.14	-5.2	3.88	-18.9
潮　州	Chaozhou	2.93	11.3	0.45	-25.2	4.69	94.9
揭　阳	Jieyang	3.65	-5.1	0.05	48.4	5.09	-29.6
云　浮	Yunfu	3.82	11.5	0.62	17.5	2.22	-41.3
按经济区域分	By Region						
珠三角	Pearl River Delta	3037.83	13.6	623.99	-1.5	4571.80	26.0
东　翼	Eastern Region	32.98	7.4	7.34	36.5	37.89	12.6
西　翼	Western Region	39.24	4.8	5.55	3.3	39.99	8.6
山　区	Mountainous Region	32.84	15.3	7.87	1.0	8.93	-27.2

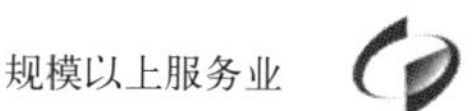

14-3 continued

(100 million yuan)

应交所得税 Income Taxes Payable		应付职工薪酬 Total Wages Payable		应交增值税 Value-added Tax Payable		就业人员平均人数(万人) Average Number of Employed Persons (10000 persons)
总量 Total	比2016年增长(%) Growth Rate in 2017 Over 2016(%)	总量 Total	比2016年增长(%) Growth Rate in 2017 Over 2016(%)	总量 Total	比2016年增长(%) Growth Rate in 2017 Over 2016(%)	
231.29	30.6	2016.45	24.0	251.76	21.8	163.55
342.05	40.7	1987.75	20.4	247.94	23.3	167.45
22.18	66.0	143.80	17.3	19.90	34.8	14.11
4.26	-3.3	39.08	14.1	3.53	-1.9	5.12
15.35	-8.4	128.84	11.2	20.20	21.3	17.83
0.70	18.7	13.94	14.1	2.00	37.7	2.31
0.25	-10.6	9.03	9.7	0.86	-12.9	1.52
0.88	-0.7	9.34	13.1	1.00	-29.6	0.98
9.19	-12.6	45.97	11.7	7.27	31.4	6.71
0.47	-37.1	12.27	16.4	0.72	-41.2	1.42
35.31	11.2	194.09	24.6	43.04	39.1	27.10
7.45	13.8	63.50	9.7	8.26	8.5	8.89
4.64	1.1	29.28	7.9	4.38	19.0	4.29
1.16	2.4	8.65	-5.5	0.90	16.5	1.37
6.46	39.5	42.85	12.1	5.12	-4.5	5.40
2.90	-6.8	18.19	9.0	3.33	4.7	2.99
2.09	-5.2	14.26	17.2	1.70	6.0	1.92
1.89	25.0	16.17	6.9	2.39	16.2	2.44
0.39	-17.0	5.11	4.5	0.70	37.5	0.68
1.25	-28.2	8.14	11.8	1.02	-6.1	1.00
0.77	-25.9	6.92	13.1	0.74	7.6	0.86
669.54	32.3	4623.94	21.4	604.46	23.7	411.86
6.37	-13.5	64.59	13.4	5.97	-7.0	8.23
10.53	18.6	69.70	8.7	9.35	0.4	9.75
4.49	4.2	55.41	10.9	6.99	5.8	8.11

主要统计指标解释

从事服务业活动从业人员平均人数 指报告期内平均拥有的从事服务业活动的人员数。按“谁用工，谁统计”的原则实施统计，包括参加企业服务业活动的正式人员，劳务派遣人员和临时聘用人员。不包括在本企业领取工资、股息、红利未参加服务业活动的人员。

Explanatory Notes on Main Statistical Indicators

The average number of persons engaged in service activities refers to the average number of persons engaged in the service industry activities within the reporting period, according to the statistics principle of "who labor, who statistics", including the formal staff, labor dispatch personnel and temporary staff who participate in the activities of the service industry enterprises. And the people receiving wages, dividends, bonus from the enterprise but not participating in the service industry activities are not included.

十五、运输和邮电

TRANSPORTATION, POSTAL AND TELECOMMUNICATION SERVICES

十五　运输和邮电

简要说明

一、本篇资料反映广东运输和邮电通信业发展的基本状况。

交通运输业资料主要包括：运输线路里程、运输设备拥有量、货物运输量和旅客运输量、港口设备和吞吐量、航站吞吐量等。

邮电通信业资料主要包括：邮电通信主要工具及设备情况，主要邮电业务完成情况，邮电通信发展水平等。

二、资料调查范围和统计单位

1. 铁路资料：包括国家铁路、地方铁路和合资铁路运营情况，不含军用铁路及由厂矿企事业单位自建的铁路专用线和专用铁道。2017 年起，铁路客运量和货运量按发送量计算。

2. 公路、水路、港口资料：(1)公路和水路线路里程为年末通车和通航里程数。公路里程、桥梁、渡口统计从 2006 年起包括农村公路。(2)民用汽车拥有量，根据公安交通管理局所属车管部门登记注册的车辆资料整理；(3)民用运输船舶拥有量，不含渔船、水上施工作业船，根据水上航运管理部门登记注册的船舶资料整理；(4)公路、水路客货运输量资料，包括在广东公路水路运输管理部门注册登记或审批备案的、从事营业性公路、水路客、货运输的营业性运输工具(包括个体联户)所完成的运输量。此部分数据 2005 年之前由统计局收集整理，2005 年起改由省交通运输厅通过抽样调查方法负责收集整理。2009 年，交通运输部统一部署更换调查方法收集整理。2014-2015 年，按交通运输部要求，公路水路客货运输量采用经济调查结果进行推算。2016 年，公路水路客货运输量采用 2015 年专项调查结果进行推算。每次更换调查方法，均会导致公路水路客货运输量数据与以往不可比。(5)港口设备及吞吐量，根据各地港务管理部门注册的港口企业和从事港口生产活动单位的资料整理。

3. 管道运输资料：包括输原油、输成品油、输天然气、输其他气体的管线长度、输送能力及完成的运输量。数据主要来源于中国石油天然气集团公司和中国石油化工集团公司所属的本地各管道运输单位。

4. 民航运输资料：统计对象为在广东境内注册、从事民用航空运输飞行和通用飞行的航空运输企业和民用航空机场，不包括在境内运输飞行的国内其他航空公司及外国航空公司。统计范围为各航空公司从事国内运输、港澳台运输、国际运输的定期航班航线条数及里程、运输量及期末飞机在册架数、民用航空机场航班起降架次和客货吞吐量等。

5. 邮电通信资料：包括全省电信和邮政运营企业为社会公众提供的各类电信和邮政服务，不含专用网业务资料。资料主要来源于省通信管理局、邮政管理局以及邮政、电信、移动、联通等运营单位。2017 年起，电信业务总量按 2015 年不变价格计算。

三、本篇资料由广东省统计局服务业统计处整理、编辑。资料主要来源于省内民航、铁路、公路、水运、港口、公安、邮政、通信等行业主管部门以及各有关单位。

15 Transportation,Postal and Telecommunication Services

Brief Introduction

Ⅰ. The data in this chapter cover mainly the basic conditions of the development of transport, postal and telecommunication services in Guangdong Province.

The data on transport cover mainly the route length of five means of transportation, the possession of transport equipment, the freight and passenger traffic the possession of port equipment and the volume of freight handled in ports, the passenger and freight throughput of airports, etc.

The data on postal and telecommunication services cover mainly major means and equipment of post and telecommunications, achievements of main businesses of postal and telecommunication services, and the level of development of postal and telecommunication services, etc.

Ⅱ. Coverage and Statistical Units

1.Data on railway transportation: including the operation and management of the national, local and joint-venture railways, but excluding the railways for military purpose, lines built by factories, mines, enterprises and institutions for exclusive use, and special railways. Starting from 2017, passenger traffic and freight traffic by railway are calculated according to the amount of traffic sent.

2. Data on highways, waterways and ports: (1) The length of highways and waterways refer to the length open to traffic or navigation at the end of the year. The Statistical of leng of highways,bridges,ferries from 2006 include rural highway. (2) The data on the possession of civil motor vehicles are compiled according to registration data of vehicles at the divisions of vehicle management under the traffic management departments of public security authorities. (3) The data on the possession of civil vessels exclusive of fishing boats and engineering ships over water are compiled according to registration data of vessels at the authorities of navigation and port management. (4) The data on the volume of transportation by highways and waterways, including all enterprises, institutions, and individuals (or individual partnerships) registered in Guangdong for passenger and freight transportation by highways and waterways, were collected and prepared by the Bureau of Statistics before 2005. Since 2005, the data were collected and prepared by the Department of Transport of Guangdong through sample survey. Since 2009, the data are collected and prepared in accordance with the new survey method stipulated by the Ministry of Transport. Since 2015, the data are prepared according to the third economic census of Guangdong Province. Since the new survey method has new criteria for survey target and urban-rural division, the data are not comparable with those of the previous years. (5) The data on possession of port equipment and production capacity and handling capacity of ports are compiled according to registration data of port enterprises and production units at local port authorities.

3. Data on pipeline transport: The data on pipeline transport cover the length, transport capacity and the volume transported of pipelines of petroleum (crude oil), petroleum products, natural gas and other gases. The data are mainly provided by enterprises engaged in the pipeline transport subordinate to the China National Petroleum Corporation and China Petrochemical Corporation.

4. Data on civil aviation transport: Data on civil aviation transport include air transport enterprises and civil airports registered for civil aviation transport and general aviation, excluding other domestic aviation companies and foreign aviation companies engaged in air transport within Chinese territory. The statistics cover regular flights of domestic transport, transport between the mainland of China and Hong Kong, Macao and Taiwan, and international transport managed by various aviation companies, concerning the number of lines, length, transport volume, number of registered aircrafts at the end of the reference period, sorties at civil airports, and volumes of passenger and freight handled at civil airports.

5. Data on post and telecommunications: Data in this category include telecommunications and postal services rendered to the public by telecommunications and postal enterprises of the whole province, but exclude services provided through dedicated networks. Statistics are mainly provided by Guangdong Communications Administration and corresponding enterprises, including China Post, China Telecom, China Mobile, China Unicom, China TieTong, and China Netcom. Since 2017, the business volume of telecommunication services has been calculated at prices constant with 2015 prices.

Ⅲ. The data in this chapter are prepared and compiled by the Division of Service Industry Statistics of Statistics Bureau of Guangdong Province. Raw data are mainly provided by authorities and related enterprises and institutions within the province of civil aviation, railways, highways, waterways, ports, public securities, and post and telecommunications.

15-1 运输邮电主要指标

Main Indicators on Transport, Postal and Telecommunication Services

指标	Item	2000	2010	2016	2017	2017 比 2016增长% Growth Rate in 2017 over 2016 (%)
铁路营业里程 (公里)	Length of Railways in Operation (km)	1942	2297	4265	4307	1.0
公路通车里程 (公里)	Length of Highways (km)	102606	190144	218085	219580	0.7
内河通航里程 (公里)	Length of Navigable Inland Waterways (km)	13696	13596	12150	12108	-0.3
民航航线里程 (万公里)	Length of Civil Aviation Routes (10000 km)	50.03	180.74	255.23	280.44	9.9
管道输油(气)里程 (公里)	Length of Petroleum and Gas Pipelines (km)	1535.57	6033.62	8553.51	8765.34	2.5
港口码头泊位 (个)	Number of Berths in Coastal Ports (unit)	3191	3082	2998	2886	-3.7
#万吨级泊位	Berths at 10000 Ton Class	126	245	304	309	1.6
码头泊位长度 (米)	Length of Quay Line (m)	180238	252762	270132	267722	-0.9
公路桥梁 (座)	Number of Highway Bridges (unit)	19668	42330	46485	47794	2.8
#永久式	Permanent	19656	42233	46398	47702	2.8
民用汽车 (万辆)	Number of Civil Motor Vehicles (10000 units)	172.91	783.50	1675.50	1894.94	13.1
机动船舶数 (艘)	Number of Motor Vessels (unit)	21733	8793	8579	8274	-3.6
吨位数 (万净载重吨)	Tonnage (10000 dead weight ton)	526.88	1140.71	2144.80	2280.29	6.3
民用运输飞机 (架)	Number of Civil Aircrafts (unit)	106	441	651	688	5.7
长途电话交换机容量 (万路端)	Capacity of Automatic Long-distance Telephone Exchanges (10000 lines)	70.34	269.11	58.11	50.17	-13.7
本地交换设备容量 (万门)	Capacity of Local Telephone Exchanges (10000 lines)	1939.45	5383.59	1505.62	815.33	-45.8
移动电话交换机容量 (万户)	Capacity of Mobile Telephone Exchanges (10000 subscribers)	1825.40	14766.90	21982.30	23037.51	4.8
本地电话用户 (万户)	Subscribers of Local Fixed Telephones (10000 subscribers)	1414.94	3169.14	2609.71	2406.09	-7.8
移动电话用户 (万户)	Subscribers of Mobile Telephones (10000 subscribers)	1357.26	9710.09	14348.96	14798.85	3.1
客运量 (万人)	Passenger Traffic (10000 persons)	164791	467049	144262	148549	5.6
旅客周转量 (亿人公里)	Passenger-kilometers (100 million passenger-km)	1218.59	3342.23	3842.58	4140.29	7.6
货运量 (万吨)	Freight Traffic (10000 tons)	119216	205034	377645	400601	6.9
货物周转量 (亿吨公里)	Freight Ton-kilometers (100 million ton-km)	3064.51	5933.88	22032.27	28192.23	28.0
港口货物吞吐量 (万吨)	Volume of Freight Handled in Ports (10000 tons)	31649	122258	179924	198015	10.1
港口旅客吞吐量 (万人)	Volume of Passengers Handled in Ports(10000 persons)	1670.32	2483.21	3434.94	3659.63	6.5
航站旅客吞吐量 (万人)	Volume of Passengers Handled at Airports (10000 persons)	2142.84	7188.64	11439.71	12940.22	13.1
邮电业务总量 (亿元)	Business Volume of Postal and Telecommunication Services (100 million yuan)	757.22	4832.94	6892.41	6107.19	58.0
邮政 (亿元)	Postal Service (100 million yuan)	50.40	118.57	1886.25	2526.29	33.9
通信 (亿元)	Telecommunication Service (100 million yuan)	706.82	4714.37	5006.16	3580.90	81.0

注：1．邮电业务总量1989—2000年按1990年价格计算，2011年起按2010年不变价格计算，从2017年起电信业务总量按2015年不变价格计算。增长速度按可比价格计算。

2．2017年起，铁路客运量和货运量改为按发送量计算，客运量货运量数据与往年不可比。增长速度按可比口径计算。

Note: a) Business volume of postal services have been calculated at 2010 constant prices Since 2011.Business volume of postal services was calculated with 1990 constant prices.Starting from 2017, business volume of telecommunication services have been calculated with 2015 constant prices. Growth rate is calculated with comparable prices.

b) Since 2017, passenger and cargo traffic by rail have been calculated according traffic sent, as such, data of cargo and passenger traffic by rail is incomparable with previous years. Growth rate is calculated with a comparable prices.

15-2 全社会旅客运输量

Total Passenger Traffic

年份 Year	客运量(万人) Passenger Traffic (10000 persons) 合计 Total	铁路 Railways	公路 Highways	水路 Waterways	民航 Civil Aviation	旅客周转量（亿人公里） Passenger-kilometers (100 million passenger-km) 合计 Total	铁路 Railways	公路 Highways	水路 Waterways	民航 Civil Aviation
1985	49848	3357	41826	4427	238	270.23	50.41	178.27	20.46	21.09
1986	126890	3742	113561	9295	292	450.35	56.70	346.81	19.82	27.02
1987	158715	4129	144684	9557	345	796.86	66.98	678.04	21.20	30.64
1988	218915	4828	204278	9420	389	402.34	82.53	261.18	22.43	36.20
1989	66727	4882	58110	3377	358	447.62	84.38	309.25	20.50	33.49
1990	78046	4467	70681	2428	470	453.21	82.56	307.40	19.68	43.57
1991	83460	5004	75570	2317	569	526.66	102.11	348.85	20.89	54.81
1992	93678	6243	83128	3503	804	624.55	131.99	385.76	25.75	81.05
1993	95468	6835	84708	3078	847	696.92	161.04	422.88	25.60	87.40
1994	125036	6920	111447	5636	1033	929.48	164.11	619.52	33.21	112.64
1995	130998	6283	118406	5146	1163	936.29	163.11	613.07	31.13	128.98
1996	128831	5593	117815	4232	1191	938.65	153.86	626.60	20.65	137.54
1997	123649	6201	113259	3032	1157	957.20	177.61	616.48	17.21	145.90
1998	132462	6743	121795	2729	1195	994.84	194.16	630.65	13.87	156.16
1999	148636	7553	137324	2605	1154	1082.14	212.13	700.74	13.62	155.65
2000	164791	12165	148945	2363	1318	1218.59	241.51	780.74	11.65	184.69
2001	178676	12783	161967	2382	1544	1342.12	252.37	858.86	11.40	219.49
2002	188657	13310	171191	2347	1809	1490.34	273.19	945.16	11.31	260.68
2003	191202	12935	174288	2208	1771	1505.83	267.14	983.67	11.41	243.61
2004	202414	15142	183012	1827	2433	1738.21	308.38	1076.06	10.17	343.60
2005	212104	16106	189881	2062	4055	2122.14	327.74	1190.73	9.54	594.13
2005(调整) (adjusted)	161357	16106	139158	2038	4055	2043.23	327.74	1111.57	9.79	594.13
2006	197314	15109	175567	2073	4565	2245.37	347.60	1212.76	12.14	672.87
2007	211215	16762	186835	2071	5548	2626.71	387.61	1410.72	10.98	817.40
2007(调整) (adjusted)	206504	12050	186835	2071	5548	2626.71	387.61	1410.72	10.98	817.40
2008	238375	13739	216902	1902	5832	2844.79	420.12	1566.73	9.80	848.14
2008(调整) (adjusted)	484161	13739	462997	1593	5832	2551.92	420.12	1276.12	7.54	848.14
2009	428705	13394	406704	1873	6734	2853.30	407.72	1470.06	7.06	968.46
2010	467049	14956	442224	2241	7628	3342.23	456.46	1736.34	8.36	1141.07
2011	522095	17902	493618	2594	7981	3851.84	505.16	2082.68	9.63	1254.37
2012	586299	18528	556510	2725	8535	4372.06	514.88	2470.11	10.01	1377.06
2013	636816	20459	604934	2426	8997	4852.41	565.91	2776.08	10.23	1500.19
2013(调整) (adjusted)	175109	20459	143406	2247	8997	3538.10	565.91	1462.82	9.18	1500.19
2014	193363	23744	157234	2613	9771	3967.28	670.78	1629.79	10.67	1656.05
2015	207345	26536	168028	2728	10054	4335.79	747.05	1769.61	10.50	1808.63
2015(调整) (adjusted)	137368	26536	98050	2728	10054	3601.12	747.05	1034.94	10.50	1808.63
2016	144262	28954	102094	2648	10566	3842.58	793.44	1079.80	10.34	1959.00
2017	148549	28476	105919	2733	11420	4140.29	872.08	1129.53	10.85	2127.82

15-3 旅客运输量指数

Indices of Passenger Traffic

上年=100 (preceding year=100)

年份 Year	客运量 Passenger Traffic					旅客周转量 Passenger-kilometers				
	合计 Total	铁路 Railways	公路 Highways	水路 Waterways	民航 Civil Aviation	合计 Total	铁路 Railways	公路 Highways	水路 Waterways	民航 Civil Aviation
1978	107.9	105.6	109.0	104.8	144.8	110.4	112.8	109.8	102.3	151.9
1979	114.9	115.5	116.0	109.2	144.2	123.5	129.1	119.8	117.1	165.2
1980	117.3	101.0	125.2	97.7	118.6	121.2	120.4	128.0	109.3	97.4
1981	107.4	100.0	110.0	99.1	125.1	110.9	109.0	112.2	106.0	121.0
1982	119.7	95.7	126.6	99.9	122.4	111.8	102.6	117.1	102.4	125.4
1983	107.2	107.2	108.6	96.4	89.6	111.9	117.8	114.0	99.7	94.6
1984	119.7	109.2	124.4	87.3	142.9	125.6	115.3	130.4	98.3	183.2
1985	109.2	112.6	109.1	103.6	131.6	118.1	121.3	116.1	101.0	148.7
1986	90.0	102.8	88.2	91.7	125.2	95.0	106.7	86.0	91.4	130.8
1987	125.1	110.3	127.4	102.8	118.2	176.9	118.1	195.5	107.0	113.4
1988	137.9	116.9	141.2	98.6	112.8	50.5	123.2	38.5	105.8	118.1
1989	30.5	101.1	28.4	35.8	92.0	111.3	102.2	118.4	91.4	92.5
1990	117.0	91.5	121.6	71.9	131.3	101.2	97.8	99.4	96.0	130.1
1991	106.9	112.0	106.9	95.4	121.1	116.2	123.7	113.5	106.1	125.8
1992	112.2	124.8	110.0	151.2	141.3	118.6	129.3	110.6	123.3	147.9
1993	101.9	109.5	101.9	87.9	105.3	111.6	122.0	109.6	99.4	107.8
1994	131.0	101.2	131.6	183.1	122.0	133.4	101.9	146.5	129.7	128.9
1995	104.8	90.8	106.2	91.3	112.6	100.7	99.4	99.0	93.7	114.5
1996	98.3	89.0	99.5	82.2	102.4	100.3	94.3	102.2	66.3	106.6
1997	96.0	110.9	96.1	71.6	97.1	102.0	115.4	98.4	83.3	106.1
1998	107.1	108.7	107.5	90.0	103.3	103.9	109.3	102.3	80.6	107.0
1999	112.2	112.0	112.8	95.5	96.6	108.8	109.3	111.1	98.2	99.7
2000	108.4	111.9	108.5	90.7	114.2	112.6	113.8	111.4	85.5	118.7
2001	108.4	105.1	108.7	100.8	117.1	110.1	104.5	110.0	97.9	118.8
2002	105.6	104.1	105.7	98.5	117.2	111.0	108.2	110.0	99.2	118.8
2003	101.3	97.2	101.8	94.1	97.9	101.0	97.8	104.1	100.9	93.5
2004	105.9	117.1	105.0	82.7	137.4	115.4	115.4	109.4	89.1	141.0
2005	104.8	106.4	103.8	112.9	166.7	122.1	106.3	110.7	93.8	172.9
2006	122.3	93.8	126.2	101.7	112.6	109.9	106.1	109.1	124.0	113.3
2007	107.0	110.9	106.4	99.9	121.5	117.0	111.5	116.3	90.4	121.5
2008	115.4	114.0	116.1	91.8	105.1	108.3	108.4	111.1	89.3	103.8
2009	88.5	97.5	87.8	117.6	115.4	111.8	97.0	115.2	93.6	114.2
2010	108.9	111.7	108.7	119.6	113.3	117.1	112.0	118.1	118.4	117.8
2011	111.8	119.7	111.6	115.8	104.6	115.2	110.7	119.9	115.2	109.9
2012	112.3	103.5	112.7	105.1	106.9	113.5	101.9	118.6	103.9	109.8
2013	108.6	110.4	108.7	89.0	105.4	111.0	109.9	112.4	102.2	108.9
2014	110.5	116.1	109.6	116.2	108.6	112.1	118.5	111.4	116.2	110.4
2015	107.2	111.8	106.9	104.4	102.9	109.3	111.4	108.6	98.4	109.2
2016	105.0	109.1	104.1	97.1	105.1	106.7	106.2	104.3	98.5	108.3
2017	105.6	112.1	103.7	103.2	108.1	107.6	109.4	104.6	104.9	108.6

15-4 各市客运量

Passenger Traffic by City

单位：万人 (10000 persons)

市　别	City	2005	2010	2011	2013	2013 (调整) (adjusted)	2014	2015	2015 (调整) (adjusted)	2016	2017
总　计	**Total**	**161357**	**467049**	**522095**	**636816**	**175109**	**193363**	**207345**	**137368**	**144262**	**148549**
广　州	Guangzhou	22583	47872	51186	70891	70891	78762	85170	22859	23879	25482
深　圳	Shenzhen	9500	151404	163376	195998	6387	6831	7040	6509	6039	6467
珠　海	Zhuhai	4874	19078	22547	28642	3314	3726	4017	3684	3708	3393
汕　头	Shantou	1991	2539	2925	3794	1821	1766	1642	1582	1555	1604
佛　山	Foshan	11472	25166	34881	49146	5168	5768	5387	5203	5307	5268
韶　关	Shaoguan	2280	10200	11878	17144	4223	5032	5515	4891	5166	5291
河　源	Heyuan	1969	3294	3878	5575	2406	2922	3257	2876	3223	3527
梅　州	Meizhou	3550	4399	5055	6415	2420	2627	2859	2557	2705	2856
惠　州	Huizhou	5049	12763	13008	16673	5939	6411	6799	6157	6422	6617
汕　尾	Shanwei	3800	7250	9524	12636	1116	1171	1237	1123	1196	1371
东　莞	Dongguan	30951	77446	80337	78113	5638	5555	5071	4961	4874	4342
中　山	Zhongshan	9200	13258	21083	33903	1985	2256	1822	1896	1599	1518
江　门	Jiangmen	8249	18096	19052	20102	10162	9546	10272	9239	9742	9606
阳　江	Yangjiang	1585	4111	4285	4315	1521	1571	1586	1472	1519	1549
湛　江	Zhanjiang	6413	12745	13892	15643	6508	7764	9026	7926	8660	9429
茂　名	Maoming	5079	6830	7427	8672	4954	5664	6367	5611	5977	6515
肇　庆	Zhaoqing	4436	6388	7322	7674	3089	3114	3119	2905	3039	3042
清　远	Qingyuan	1959	9874	11061	14354	2271	2668	3088	2714	2823	2997
潮　州	Chaozhou	733	2056	2717	3762	1757	1987	2255	1983	2240	2377
揭　阳	Jieyang	3014	4789	5380	6216	1836	1944	2041	1856	2074	2221
云　浮	Yunfu	2509	4907	5398	7693	2246	2762	3188	2775	2994	3179
不分地区	Unclassified	20161	22584	25883	29456	29456	33516	36589	36589	39520	39897
按经济区域分	By Region										
珠三角	Pearl River Delta	126475	394055	438675	530597	142030	155484	165285	100001	104130	105632
东　翼	Eastern Region	9538	16634	20546	26408	6529	6869	7175	6544	7065	7573
西　翼	Western Region	13077	23686	25604	28630	12983	14999	16979	15009	16156	17494
山　区	Mountainous Region	12267	32674	37270	51181	13567	16011	17907	15814	16911	17850

注：分市数据仅含公路和水路运输，铁路和民航运输在“不分地区”反映。下表同。

Note: Data by city only include the figures of highway and waterway transportation, whereas data of railway and civil aviation transportation are reflected in the category “Unclassified by Region”. The same applies to the following table.

15-5　各市旅客周转量

Passenger-kilometers by City

单位：亿人公里　　(100 million passenger-km)

市　别	City	2005	2010	2012	2013	2013 (调整) (adjusted)	2014	2015	2015 (调整) (adjusted)	2016	2017
总　计	**Total**	**2043.23**	**3342.23**	**4372.06**	**4852.41**	**3538.10**	**3967.28**	**4335.79**	**3601.12**	**3842.58**	**4140.29**
广　州	Guangzhou	193.24	461.34	607.61	698.67	698.66	793.50	861.08	229.50	241.60	258.07
深　圳	Shenzhen	71.42	242.13	320.76	357.20	129.70	137.85	144.31	130.41	118.59	125.76
珠　海	Zhuhai	41.69	68.90	81.40	80.42	57.76	63.45	69.18	61.62	60.94	53.77
汕　头	Shantou	21.08	51.67	73.48	84.87	26.30	24.24	22.45	21.53	20.98	22.30
佛　山	Foshan	50.94	82.76	117.54	125.27	51.40	60.09	59.31	55.15	63.49	66.67
韶　关	Shaoguan	14.17	40.41	63.12	70.74	21.42	26.04	28.55	25.21	26.64	27.31
河　源	Heyuan	36.97	38.18	53.41	63.91	27.39	33.49	38.44	33.23	37.02	41.05
梅　州	Meizhou	41.73	51.79	78.66	88.14	33.35	35.46	39.52	34.69	37.03	39.44
惠　州	Huizhou	35.97	49.46	116.48	124.59	46.60	51.90	57.43	50.46	53.26	55.60
汕　尾	Shanwei	26.90	52.98	93.34	106.96	10.77	12.39	14.05	12.22	13.34	15.68
东　莞	Dongguan	158.53	129.07	156.88	155.99	86.71	85.46	81.55	77.13	77.32	68.14
中　山	Zhongshan	48.84	88.99	216.61	277.03	11.61	14.15	21.77	16.54	18.90	24.05
江　门	Jiangmen	60.30	58.99	64.46	67.31	61.65	59.61	64.71	57.36	60.62	61.10
阳　江	Yangjiang	26.29	21.80	30.03	31.14	10.58	10.91	11.01	10.12	10.32	10.53
湛　江	Zhanjiang	62.10	82.45	103.00	114.06	65.33	80.23	95.49	81.17	88.30	96.14
茂　名	Maoming	64.83	61.47	80.05	87.22	43.80	50.87	59.23	50.75	55.05	60.93
肇　庆	Zhaoqing	25.40	33.22	41.85	42.72	14.67	14.68	14.71	13.58	13.79	13.88
清　远	Qingyuan	35.45	38.68	51.19	57.68	17.04	20.51	24.08	20.67	21.82	23.51
潮　州	Chaozhou	19.37	23.93	38.84	43.13	21.30	24.24	27.53	23.87	27.02	29.28
揭　阳	Jieyang	67.53	37.28	53.20	60.70	19.82	21.12	22.22	20.03	22.28	23.87
云　浮	Yunfu	18.62	29.21	38.21	48.55	16.15	20.29	23.49	20.19	21.82	23.30
不分地区	Unclassified	921.87	1597.53	1891.94	2066.10	2066.10	2326.82	2555.68	2555.68	2752.44	2999.90
按经济区域分	By Region										
珠 三 角	Pearl River Delta	1608.20	2812.37	3615.53	3995.29	3224.87	3607.50	3929.73	3247.43	3460.96	3726.96
东　翼	Eastern Region	134.87	165.86	258.86	295.67	78.19	81.98	86.25	77.66	83.62	91.14
西　翼	Western Region	153.23	165.72	213.08	232.43	119.70	142.01	165.73	142.03	153.67	167.60
山　区	Mountainous Region	146.93	198.27	284.59	329.02	115.35	135.79	154.08	133.99	144.33	154.60

15-6 全社会货物运输量

Total Freight Traffic

年份 Year	货运量(万吨) Freight Traffic (10000 tons)						货物周转量(亿吨公里) Freight Ton-kilometers (100 million ton-km)					
	合计 Total	铁路 Railways	公路 Highways	水路 Waterways	民航 Civil Aviation	管道 Pipelines	合计 Total	铁路 Railways	公路 Highways	水路 Waterways	民航 Civil Aviation	管道 Pipelines
1985	58726	3000	42813	12045	4	864	1767.86	102.29	156.45	1503.47	0.38	5.27
1986	65078	4269	49030	10831	4	944	1845.33	130.02	127.28	1581.60	0.45	5.98
1987	74571	4493	57393	11664	5	1016	1982.59	142.56	179.41	1653.81	0.54	6.27
1988	79811	4504	57717	16583	6	1001	2209.11	151.55	216.22	1834.41	0.67	6.26
1989	85054	4888	63254	15820	6	1086	2419.57	168.39	301.16	1942.79	0.71	6.52
1990	85809	4803	63709	16198	8	1091	2598.88	179.54	346.27	2065.69	0.90	6.48
1991	94136	5347	69784	17718	10	1277	3181.83	206.18	386.49	2580.79	1.06	7.31
1992	113119	6089	84181	21346	12	1491	3560.59	239.34	583.36	2727.97	1.41	8.51
1993	125273	6595	87567	29660	14	1437	3797.09	261.91	428.17	3097.19	1.70	8.12
1994	119901	6971	81361	30165	20	1384	4326.09	280.31	443.54	3592.35	2.39	7.50
1995	111063	7634	68884	32952	21	1572	4642.91	290.78	352.45	3990.19	2.75	6.74
1996	95598	8138	60131	25699	24	1606	3761.09	294.12	327.81	3129.27	3.27	6.62
1997	99763	8430	62728	26873	25	1707	3837.78	294.45	341.08	3185.26	3.99	13.00
1998	101933	8288	65682	25669	28	2266	3453.92	290.65	371.08	2750.19	4.90	37.10
1999	106334	8150	70626	24857	31	2670	2980.69	282.68	426.70	2223.75	5.45	42.11
2000	119216	15172	75365	25696	31	2952	3064.51	295.97	472.49	2247.86	6.45	41.74
2001	131621	15435	86555	26434	35	3162	3221.47	296.79	522.89	2350.73	7.54	43.52
2002	137032	14790	92736	26263	42	3201	3229.39	277.87	576.35	2323.27	9.94	41.96
2003	143964	15375	97806	27412	42	3329	3666.83	285.02	614.01	2719.83	11.76	36.21
2004	156094	19495	102843	29783	49	3924	4148.54	341.26	657.49	3091.39	13.22	45.18
2005	158470	18647	105581	30179	73	3989	4359.97	319.68	781.41	3195.85	17.45	45.58
2005(调整) (adjusted)	133992	18647	84861	26422	73	3989	3917.43	319.68	646.55	2888.17	17.45	45.58
2006	145911	16170	97461	27503	79	4698	4162.77	333.12	742.67	2964.89	18.70	103.39
2007	165426	16480	112611	30893	87	5355	4430.93	337.31	906.84	3043.53	20.14	123.11
2007(调整) (adjusted)	160455	11285	112611	30893	87	5578	4489.69	337.31	906.84	3043.53	20.14	181.87
2008	176279	11545	126068	32318	85	6263	4520.12	344.96	1064.55	2878.85	18.38	213.38
2008(调整) (adjusted)	153256	11545	101428	33935	85	6263	4591.22	344.96	1225.30	2853.92	18.38	148.66
2009	179722	11254	125433	36623	90	6322	4942.83	309.55	1518.43	2937.94	18.83	158.08
2010	205034	12170	142389	43092	116	7267	5933.88	329.49	1753.40	3642.22	32.98	175.79
2011	234978	12034	166567	48856	118	7403	7113.29	322.25	2150.04	4427.64	37.00	176.36
2012	266359	12002	189034	57737	128	7458	9780.56	306.04	2434.95	6820.29	42.40	176.89
2013	305833	12042	217630	68378	131	7652	12495.93	301.55	2875.68	9104.57	44.20	169.94
2013(调整) (adjusted)	328138	12042	239462	68851	131	7652	12212.56	301.55	2668.03	9028.84	44.20	169.94
2014	353732	11143	257135	77220	144	8090	15020.92	274.81	3113.84	11407.80	51.05	173.42
2015	376434	10072	279983	78093	149	8137	15130.59	253.90	3454.99	11190.91	56.47	174.33
2015(调整) (adjusted)	349832	10072	255993	75481	149	8137	14667.43	253.90	3108.81	11073.92	56.47	174.33
2016	377645	10135	272826	85633	160	8891	22032.27	254.41	3381.92	18160.35	61.85	173.74
2017	400601	7254	288904	94871	166	9407	28192.23	261.97	3636.89	24011.92	68.73	212.71

15-7 货物运输量指数

Indices of Freight Traffic

上年=100 (preceding year=100)

年份 Year	货运量 Freight Traffic 合计 Total	铁路 Railways	公路 Highways	水路 Waterways	民航 Civil Aviation	管道 Pipelines	货物周转量 Freight Ton-kilometers 合计 Total	铁路 Railways	公路 Highways	水路 Waterways	民航 Civil Aviation	管道 Pipelines
1978	96.3	109.2	74.9	104.5	126.6		110.9	110.9	93.0	111.1	140.0	
1979	92.1	103.5	88.9	87.2	100.0	197.2	138.4	103.5	96.6	141.9	142.9	192.9
1980	101.4	93.8	85.3	111.3	151.0	151.4	98.2	99.1	90.7	98.1	100.0	596.3
1981	92.2	84.8	87.0	93.1	102.6	165.3	84.3	92.7	93.8	83.5	100.0	280.7
1982	104.6	107.8	98.1	105.7	125.8	105.7	104.9	105.4	105.3	104.9	130.0	103.8
1983	100.4	104.9	92.4	100.5	118.5	108.7	110.1	108.8	87.6	110.3	123.1	109.8
1984	100.0	108.6	92.6	98.4	133.8	105.3	98.8	112.2	84.7	97.9	162.5	101.9
1985	177.1	105.5	225.5	115.1	133.3	101.2	109.2	111.8	206.5	104.0	146.2	100.4
1986	110.8	142.3	114.5	89.9	100.0	109.3	104.4	127.1	81.4	105.2	118.4	113.5
1987	114.6	105.2	117.1	107.7	125.0	107.6	107.4	109.6	141.0	104.6	120.0	104.8
1988	107.0	100.2	100.6	142.2	120.0	98.5	111.4	106.3	120.5	110.9	124.1	99.8
1989	106.6	108.5	109.6	95.4	100.0	108.5	109.5	111.1	139.3	105.9	106.0	104.2
1990	100.9	98.3	100.7	102.4	133.3	100.5	107.4	106.6	115.0	106.3	126.8	99.4
1991	109.7	111.3	109.5	109.4	125.0	117.0	122.4	114.8	111.6	124.9	117.8	112.8
1992	120.2	113.9	120.6	120.5	120.0	116.8	111.9	116.1	150.9	105.7	133.0	116.4
1993	110.7	108.3	104.0	138.9	116.7	96.4	106.6	109.4	73.4	113.5	120.6	95.4
1994	95.7	105.7	92.9	101.7	142.9	96.3	113.9	107.0	103.6	116.0	140.6	92.4
1995	92.6	109.5	84.7	109.2	105.0	113.6	107.3	103.7	79.5	111.1	115.1	89.9
1996	86.1	106.6	87.3	78.0	114.3	102.2	81.0	101.1	93.0	78.4	118.9	98.2
1997	104.4	103.6	104.3	104.6	104.2	106.3	102.0	100.1	104.0	101.8	122.0	196.4
1998	102.2	98.3	104.7	95.5	112.0	132.7	90.0	98.7	108.8	86.3	122.8	285.4
1999	104.3	98.3	107.5	96.8	110.7	117.8	86.3	97.3	115.0	80.9	111.2	113.5
2000	106.0	106.0	106.7	103.4	100.0	110.6	102.8	104.7	110.7	101.1	118.3	99.1
2001	110.4	101.7	114.8	102.9	112.9	107.1	105.1	100.3	110.7	104.6	116.9	104.3
2002	104.1	95.8	107.1	99.4	120.0	101.2	100.2	93.6	110.2	98.8	131.8	96.4
2003	105.1	104.0	105.5	104.4	100.0	104.0	113.5	102.6	106.5	117.1	118.3	86.3
2004	108.4	126.8	105.1	108.6	116.7	117.9	113.1	119.7	107.1	113.7	112.4	124.8
2005	101.5	95.7	102.7	101.3	149.0	101.7	105.1	93.7	118.8	103.4	132.0	100.9
2006	108.9	86.7	114.8	104.1	108.1	117.8	106.3	104.2	114.9	102.7	107.2	226.8
2007	113.4	101.9	115.5	112.3	110.5	114.0	106.4	101.3	122.1	102.7	107.7	119.1
2008	109.9	102.3	111.9	104.6	97.1	112.3	100.7	102.3	117.4	94.6	91.3	117.3
2009	117.3	97.5	123.7	107.9	106.8	101.0	107.7	89.7	123.9	102.9	102.4	106.3
2010	114.1	108.1	113.5	117.7	128.1	114.9	120.1	106.4	115.5	124.0	175.1	111.2
2011	114.6	98.9	117.0	113.4	102.4	101.9	119.9	97.8	122.6	121.6	112.2	100.3
2012	111.5	99.7	113.5	109.1	107.9	100.7	116.0	95.0	113.3	119.5	114.6	100.3
2013	114.8	100.3	115.1	118.4	102.7	102.6	127.8	98.5	118.1	133.5	104.2	96.1
2014	107.8	92.5	107.4	112.2	110.0	105.7	123.0	91.1	116.7	126.3	115.5	102.0
2015	106.4	90.4	108.9	101.1	102.9	100.6	100.7	92.4	111.0	98.1	110.6	100.5
2016	108.0	100.6	106.6	113.4	107.6	109.3	150.2	100.2	108.8	164.0	109.5	99.7
2017	106.9	101.3	105.9	110.8	103.7	105.8	128.0	104.3	107.5	132.2	111.1	122.4

15-8 各市货运量

Freight Traffic by City

单位：万吨 (10000 tons)

市别	City	2005	2010	2012	2013	2013 (调整) (adjusted)	2014	2015	2015 (调整) (adjusted)	2016	2017
总计	**Total**	**133992**	**205034**	**266359**	**305833**	**328138**	**353732**	**376434**	**349832**	**377645**	**400601**
广州	Guangzhou	28026	51335	67678	82052	93804	90208	94303	89662	103083	114595
深圳	Shenzhen	7837	25706	28217	29226	27055	29183	32331	30814	30999	32100
珠海	Zhuhai	2225	7038	7581	8457	9862	10874	11626	10528	10869	11471
汕头	Shantou	1703	3087	4078	4628	5349	6055	6469	5766	6150	6403
佛山	Foshan	17354	19153	24757	27206	27206	28756	29428	27880	29372	30997
韶关	Shaoguan	3251	6364	9738	12184	13916	17291	19024	16925	18397	19442
河源	Heyuan	986	2244	3296	3995	4789	5755	6509	5519	6203	6702
梅州	Meizhou	3751	4092	5608	6325	6325	7159	7820	7227	7913	8356
惠州	Huizhou	4786	11104	17111	19063	17821	21545	23435	21711	23455	24693
汕尾	Shanwei	1106	1232	1765	1934	2310	2432	2536	2344	2515	2722
东莞	Dongguan	5127	9312	11191	12863	14690	15375	15923	15386	15593	16725
中山	Zhongshan	5985	7820	14770	16719	16719	18864	17963	18076	18336	17656
江门	Jiangmen	5626	7458	8996	9999	11292	13926	15407	13177	14046	14975
阳江	Yangjiang	417	1752	4173	7672	7372	10340	11385	10038	9975	10013
湛江	Zhanjiang	5016	6808	9530	10590	12391	14157	16528	14690	16023	17559
茂名	Maoming	4388	4365	6157	7123	8451	8860	9895	8808	9653	10520
肇庆	Zhaoqing	3689	2869	3681	4472	5226	6382	7303	6200	6626	7171
清远	Qingyuan	3200	7155	9238	10363	12048	13989	15267	13460	14568	15866
潮州	Chaozhou	1310	2339	3541	3944	3944	4413	4928	4476	5053	5482
揭阳	Jieyang	2213	1945	2559	2784	3333	3547	3898	3468	3795	4092
云浮	Yunfu	3286	2303	3106	4410	4410	5244	6099	5318	5835	6236
不分地区	Unclassified	22710	19553	19588	19825	19825	19377	18358	18358	19186	16826
按经济区域分	By Region										
珠三角	Pearl River Delta	103365	161348	203570	229882	243500	254491	266078	251791	271565	287210
东翼	Eastern Region	6332	8603	11943	13290	14936	16447	17831	16055	17513	18699
西翼	Western Region	9821	12925	19860	25385	28214	33357	37808	33535	35651	38091
山区	Mountainous Region	14474	22158	30986	37277	41488	49438	54719	48450	52916	56602

注：分市数据仅含公路和水路运输，铁路、民航和管道运输在“不分地区”反映。下表同。

Note: Data by city only include the figures of highway and waterway transportation, whereas data of railway, civil aviation and pipeline transportation are reflected in the category “Unclassified by Region”. The same applies to the following table.

15-9 各市货物周转量

Freight Ton-kilometers by City

单位：亿吨公里 (100 million ton-km)

市别	City	2005	2010	2012	2013	2013 (调整) (adjusted)	2014	2015	2015 (调整) (adjusted)	2016	2017
总计	**Total**	**3917.43**	**5933.88**	**9780.56**	**12495.93**	**12212.56**	**15020.92**	**15130.59**	**14667.43**	**22032.27**	**28192.23**
广州	Guangzhou	2431.16	2032.86	4570.28	6563.75	6527.54	8396.58	8225.53	8144.78	15348.54	21173.71
深圳	Shenzhen	317.28	1627.56	1969.89	2090.03	1986.97	2374.25	2241.11	2254.79	2232.10	2286.82
珠海	Zhuhai	84.89	168.12	115.17	133.39	135.31	155.75	167.01	158.97	149.38	155.57
汕头	Shantou	38.41	101.79	161.12	183.93	185.99	186.80	170.80	161.86	138.68	147.81
佛山	Foshan	182.11	152.08	215.99	240.72	221.95	252.45	266.40	246.36	271.81	299.24
韶关	Shaoguan	26.97	118.91	206.87	255.05	262.45	330.35	359.42	309.17	340.47	360.51
河源	Heyuan	8.48	34.02	50.39	60.47	63.21	76.60	87.46	73.81	82.64	90.02
梅州	Meizhou	45.95	73.69	115.02	133.26	133.26	157.63	177.60	154.25	168.34	182.46
惠州	Huizhou	40.29	152.97	287.86	336.30	297.99	390.28	476.75	396.19	436.43	462.92
汕尾	Shanwei	8.60	13.44	22.97	26.07	22.25	25.77	29.30	26.87	29.67	31.92
东莞	Dongguan	32.94	109.03	296.71	432.27	435.39	448.01	508.71	504.85	455.23	483.62
中山	Zhongshan	43.03	64.81	122.05	146.55	146.55	171.06	167.46	160.72	164.95	156.77
江门	Jiangmen	70.96	112.55	115.29	135.07	138.32	168.24	182.29	158.49	169.24	186.62
阳江	Yangjiang	2.98	39.93	95.35	152.64	139.95	183.83	195.05	183.47	166.15	101.15
湛江	Zhanjiang	57.47	177.54	301.27	388.21	321.69	406.03	469.13	432.04	473.27	528.66
茂名	Maoming	23.78	92.42	140.43	162.06	167.27	190.25	211.71	190.14	214.80	238.97
肇庆	Zhaoqing	24.87	38.56	50.73	60.39	53.07	65.15	76.11	67.47	71.06	76.11
清远	Qingyuan	29.37	118.19	158.39	179.57	186.52	223.74	262.28	218.53	238.45	261.90
潮州	Chaozhou	25.27	103.37	163.68	175.63	175.63	201.64	234.40	215.51	254.40	276.26
揭阳	Jieyang	22.64	26.93	42.34	51.18	53.41	65.10	77.53	63.74	69.84	75.16
云浮	Yunfu	17.26	36.83	53.44	73.72	42.13	52.13	59.85	60.72	66.81	72.59
不分地区	Unclassified	382.72	538.26	525.33	515.69	515.69	499.28	484.69	484.70	490.00	543.42
按经济区域分	By Region										
珠三角	Pearl River Delta	3610.25	4996.80	8269.29	10654.14	10458.78	12921.04	12796.07	12577.32	19788.74	25824.80
东翼	Eastern Region	94.92	245.54	390.11	436.81	437.29	479.31	512.03	467.98	492.60	531.16
西翼	Western Region	84.22	309.90	537.05	702.91	628.92	780.11	875.89	805.65	854.23	868.78
山区	Mountainous Region	128.04	381.64	584.11	702.07	687.57	840.45	946.61	816.48	896.71	967.49

15-10 运输工具和线路拥有量
Number of Means of Transport and Length of Transport Routes

项目		Item		2000	2010	2014	2015	2016	2017
铁路		**Railways**							
铁路机车	（台）	Number of Locomotives	(unit)	538	448	354	350	424	342
铁路营业里程	（公里）	Length of Railways in Operation	(km)	1942	2297	3818	3859	4265	4307
中央铁路		National Railways		694	629	629	629	629	629
地方铁路		Local Railways		1248	1668	3189	3230	3636	3678
公路		**Highways**							
公路通车里程	（公里）	Length of Highways	(km)	102606	190144	212094	216023	218085	219580
民用汽车	（万辆）	Civil Motor Vehicles	(10000 units)	172.91	783.50	1332.94	1472.33	1675.50	1894.94
载客汽车	（万辆）	Passenger Vehicles	(10000 units)	85.34	629.30	1144.18	1290.57	1485.65	1691.96
	（万客位）	Passenger Vehicle Seats	(10000 seats)	796.92	4148.85	6832.82	7572.21	8612.19	9719.63
私人轿车	（万辆）	Private Vehicles	(10000 units)	25.39	380.46	722.23	820.12	940.03	1054.56
载货汽车	（万辆）	Freight Vehicles	(10000 units)	84.38	147.53	181.81	174.90	183.02	196.00
	（万吨位）	Tonnage of Freight Vehicles	(10000 tonnages)	351.75	268.23	357.46	354.81	383.77	424.65
水运		**Waterways**							
内河通航里程	（公里）	Length of Navigable Inland Waterways	(km)	13696	13596	12150	12150	12150	12108
机动船	（艘）	Number of Motor Vessels	(unit)	21733	8793	8709	8716	8579	8274
	（万净载重吨位）	Tonnage of Motor Vessels	(1000 dead weight tonnage)	526.88	1140.71	2728.05	2703.55	2144.80	2280.29
	（客位）	Number of Motor Vessel Seats	(seat)	149004	65960	83020	80219	83815	82419
	（总功率万千瓦）	Total Power	(10000 kws)		420.54	677.39	688.33	622.23	625.78
驳　船	（艘）	Number of Barges	(unit)	1076	23	19	19	18	16
	（净载重吨位）	Tonnage of Barges	(dead weight tonnage)	274836	29318	33717	28220	26758	26108
民航		**Civil Aviation**							
民用航空航线条数	（条）	Number of Civil Aviation Routes	(line)	329	815	930	963	1021	1064
民用航空航线里程	（万公里）	Length of Civil Aviation Routes	(10000 kms)	50.03	180.74	228.58	237.29	255.23	280.44
民用运输飞机	（架）	Number of Civil Aircrafts	(unit)	106	441	581	625	651	688
管道		**Pipelines**							
条　数	（条）	Number of Pipelines	(line)	45	105	107	116	119	134
输油(气)里程	（公里）	Length of Petroleum and Gas Pipelines	(km)	1535.57	6033.62	5404.26	6500.90	8553.51	8765.34

15-11 各市民用汽车拥有量（2017年）
Possession of Civil Vehicles by City (2017)

单位：辆 (unit)

市别	City	民用汽车总计 Total	载客汽车 Passenger Vehicles	#轿车 Sedan Cars	按车型分 By Vehicle Type 大型 Large	中型 Medium	小型 Small	微型 Minibuses
总计	**Total**	**18949381**	**16919605**	**11189807**	**174730**	**64906**	**16600894**	**79075**
广州	Guangzhou	2399158	2069713	1302334	37729	13795	2005998	12191
深圳	Shenzhen	3214434	2827106	1846850	44571	12223	2757290	13022
珠海	Zhuhai	549458	504921	343328	7935	1749	495224	13
汕头	Shantou	643728	566742	394378	4195	1627	556948	3972
佛山	Foshan	2281402	2080795	1385337	12160	5809	2052343	10483
韶关	Shaoguan	310586	278683	180984	2300	1417	273630	1336
河源	Heyuan	306480	271768	180751	2173	1244	267439	912
梅州	Meizhou	425884	368804	258135	3131	1136	362417	2120
惠州	Huizhou	1040908	968341	659193	8033	2011	954492	3805
汕尾	Shanwei	175973	161341	109659	2613	558	157419	751
东莞	Dongguan	2627618	2449663	1575156	17277	4694	2422122	5570
中山	Zhongshan	969335	856783	561492	5394	1869	844370	5150
江门	Jiangmen	699776	619844	429568	3889	2000	610352	3603
阳江	Yangjiang	313340	276751	206376	1418	590	273404	1339
湛江	Zhanjiang	467240	408301	289787	4609	1793	400400	1499
茂名	Maoming	510046	449104	322595	3084	2089	440969	2962
肇庆	Zhaoqing	490052	424407	268359	3256	1529	418217	1405
清远	Qingyuan	532145	469438	295942	3063	1822	462730	1823
潮州	Chaozhou	290022	257673	174178	992	432	252421	3828
揭阳	Jieyang	423699	370685	251752	3464	1153	364115	1953
云浮	Yunfu	242736	210435	144960	1429	1167	206504	1335
不分地区	Unclassified	35361	28307	8693	2015	4199	22090	3
按经济区域分	By Region							
珠三角	Pearl River Delta	14307502	12829880	8380310	142259	49878	12582498	55245
东翼	Eastern Region	1533422	1356441	929967	11264	3770	1330903	10504
西翼	Western Region	1290626	1134156	818758	9111	4472	1114773	5800
山区	Mountainous Region	1817831	1599128	1060772	12096	6786	1572720	7526

15-11 续表 continued

单位：辆 (unit)

市别	City	载货汽车 Freight Vehicles	按车型分 By Vehicle Type 重型 Heavy	中型 Medium	轻型 Light	微型 Mini Trucks	其他汽车 Others
总计	**Total**	**1959958**	**332542**	**118061**	**1484872**	**24483**	**69818**
广州	Guangzhou	317911	58770	22026	232277	4838	11534
深圳	Shenzhen	372024	91887	19397	260345	395	15304
珠海	Zhuhai	42808	7635	1417	33750	6	1729
汕头	Shantou	75731	7396	2727	58853	6755	1255
佛山	Foshan	195343	27039	12986	154380	938	5264
韶关	Shaoguan	30778	5110	724	24677	267	1125
河源	Heyuan	31004	4029	2228	24433	314	3708
梅州	Meizhou	55144	7437	2159	44870	678	1936
惠州	Huizhou	69510	10175	3612	55376	347	3057
汕尾	Shanwei	13764	2276	1764	9464	260	868
东莞	Dongguan	172735	27440	13844	131021	430	5220
中山	Zhongshan	110113	10198	5645	93764	506	2439
江门	Jiangmen	78317	10134	4824	62601	758	1615
阳江	Yangjiang	35276	5482	2263	27187	344	1313
湛江	Zhanjiang	56886	9873	5507	41140	366	2053
茂名	Maoming	58666	11460	3204	42925	1077	2276
肇庆	Zhaoqing	64381	11342	4899	48070	70	1264
清远	Qingyuan	60908	13945	3344	43404	215	1799
潮州	Chaozhou	30069	1887	1139	25364	1679	2280
揭阳	Jieyang	51515	4637	3228	42570	1080	1499
云浮	Yunfu	31458	4359	938	23002	3159	843
不分地区	Unclassified	5617	31	186	5399	1	1437
按经济区域分	By Region						
珠三角	Pearl River Delta	1428759	254651	88836	1076983	8289	48863
东翼	Eastern Region	171079	16196	8858	136251	9774	5902
西翼	Western Region	150828	26815	10974	111252	1787	5642
山区	Mountainous Region	209292	34880	9393	160386	4633	9411

15−12 各市私人汽车拥有量（2017年）

Possession of Private Vehicles by City (2017)

单位：辆 (unit)

市别	City	汽车总计 Total	载客汽车 Passenger Vehicles	#轿车 Sedan Cars	载货汽车 Freight Vehicles	其它汽车 Others
总计	**Total**	**16796443**	**15606481**	**10545590**	**1160972**	**28990**
广州	Guangzhou	1912613	1773298	1150945	135335	3980
深圳	Shenzhen	2622439	2526389	1699158	92030	4020
珠海	Zhuhai	484092	456913	319597	26602	577
汕头	Shantou	599323	542814	383434	56080	429
佛山	Foshan	2098604	1960583	1324393	136003	2018
韶关	Shaoguan	283670	261461	173066	21797	412
河源	Heyuan	281497	252677	170439	25824	2996
梅州	Meizhou	401012	352702	250902	47133	1177
惠州	Huizhou	964774	915178	632896	48354	1242
汕尾	Shanwei	158720	147170	102532	10982	568
东莞	Dongguan	2395586	2290070	1493074	103729	1787
中山	Zhongshan	892281	809461	537052	81944	876
江门	Jiangmen	639601	584734	414224	54317	550
阳江	Yangjiang	296196	265673	200826	29874	649
湛江	Zhanjiang	431473	384625	279321	45492	1356
茂名	Maoming	481521	432510	314953	47270	1741
肇庆	Zhaoqing	458192	404437	261425	53055	700
清远	Qingyuan	493866	444162	284064	48812	892
潮州	Chaozhou	274886	248786	170565	24718	1382
揭阳	Jieyang	399537	353707	243305	44686	1144
云浮	Yunfu	226560	199131	139419	26935	494
按经济区域分	By Region					
珠三角	Pearl River Delta	12468182	11721063	7832764	731369	15750
东翼	Eastern Region	1432466	1292477	899836	136466	3523
西翼	Western Region	1209190	1082808	795100	122636	3746
山区	Mountainous Region	1686605	1510133	1017890	170501	5971

15-13 各市公路基本情况（2017年）

Basic Conditions of Highways by City (2017)

单位：公里 (km)

市别	City	通车里程 Length of Highways	按等级分 By Class		按路面分 By Pavement			桥梁 Bridges	
			等级路 Expres-sways and Class I to IV Highways	等外路 Highways below Class IV	有铺装路面 Paved Highways	简易铺装路面 Simply-paved Highways	未铺装路面 Unpaved Highways	座 Number (unit)	米 Span (meter)
总计	**Total**	**219580**	**206461**	**13119**	**155849**	**7602**	**56129**	**47794**	**3846964**
广州	Guangzhou	9311	8624	687	8552	75	685	3167	564595
深圳	Shenzhen	1634	1634		1634			815	117772
珠海	Zhuhai	1453	1427	26	1301	24	128	475	122514
汕头	Shantou	3903	3893	10	3011	11	881	1139	92947
佛山	Foshan	5366	5366		5366			2422	450896
韶关	Shaoguan	16633	16595	38	11982	155	4496	2403	172600
河源	Heyuan	16018	15313	705	11122	70	4827	3560	158585
梅州	Meizhou	17898	16637	1261	14085	8	3804	3937	211981
惠州	Huizhou	13823	13805	18	10122	118	3582	3189	194044
汕尾	Shanwei	5582	5355	227	3945	76	1560	1356	61044
东莞	Dongguan	5262	5179	83	5218	10	35	1452	249110
中山	Zhongshan	2665	2621	44	2562	6	96	1230	182974
江门	Jiangmen	10166	8349	1817	6911	64	3191	2708	190086
阳江	Yangjiang	10459	9860	600	6054	2198	2207	2318	97612
湛江	Zhanjiang	22252	16301	5952	11860	1410	8982	2315	94704
茂名	Maoming	17603	16812	791	10249	228	7126	3984	136318
肇庆	Zhaoqing	14439	14435	4	11380	222	2837	2540	193990
清远	Qingyuan	24816	24689	127	14700	2825	7291	3918	237592
潮州	Chaozhou	5274	5209	65	4194	2	1078	1019	43925
揭阳	Jieyang	7323	7226	97	5299	2	2022	2057	125576
云浮	Yunfu	7701	7132	568	6302	100	1299	1790	148100
按经济区域分	By Region								
珠三角	Pearl River Delta	64119	61441	2678	53045	519	10555	17998	2265980
东翼	Eastern Region	22081	21682	400	16449	91	5541	5571	323492
西翼	Western Region	50315	42972	7343	28164	3836	18316	8617	328634
山区	Mountainous Region	83065	80367	2699	58191	3157	21717	15608	928858

15-14 公路通车里程和桥梁数

Length of Highways and Number of Bridges

项 目	Item	2000	2010	2013	2014	2015	2016	2017
通车里程 （公里）	**Length of Highways (km)**	**102606**	**190144**	**202915**	**212094**	**216023**	**218085**	**219580**
按等级分	By Class							
等级路	Expressways and Class Ⅰ to Ⅳ Highways	93695	170144	186357	197131	201456	204614	206461
高速公路	Expressways	1186	4839	5703	6266	7021	7683	8347
一 级	First Class	5391	10126	10621	10787	10936	11332	11628
二 级	Second Class	13397	19082	19125	19233	19213	19200	19210
三 级	Third Class	9156	16089	17364	17840	18662	18838	18978
四 级	Fourth Class	64565	120008	133544	143005	145624	147561	148299
等外公路	Highways below Class Ⅳ	8911	19999	16558	14963	14567	13471	13119
按路面分	By Pavement							
有铺装路面	Paved Highways		123784	139115	143953	147976	153063	155849
简易铺装路面	Simply-paved Highways		5721	4972	9837	9418	8443	7602
未铺装路面	Unpaved Highways		60638	58828	58304	58629	56579	56129
桥 梁 （座）	**Number of Bridges (unit)**	**19668**	**42330**	**45501**	**45196**	**45589**	**46485**	**47794**
（米）	Span of Bridges (m)	819770	2340261	3019570	3137439	3205460	3487336	3846964
#永久式 （座）	Number of Permanent Bridges (unit)	19656	42233	45417	45110	45501	46398	47702
（米）	Span of Permanent Bridges (m)	819502	2337490	3017251	3134981	3202958	3484884	3844398
半永久式 （座）	Number of Semi-permanent Bridges (unit)	12	52	42	46	48	47	52
（米）	Span of Semi-permanent Bridges (m)	268	1391	1020	1222	1266	1216	1330
渡 口 （个）	**Number of Ferries (unit)**	**33**	**71**	**80**	**80**	**79**	**80**	**78**

15-15 输油(气)管道长度和运输量

Length and Traffic of Petroleum and Gas Pipelines

项 目	Item	2000	2010	2013	2014	2015	2016	2017
总 计	**Total**							
条 数 （条）	Number of Pipelines (line)	45	105	107	107	116	119	134
输送里程 （公里）	Length of Pipelines (km)	1535.57	6033.62	6470.39	5404.26	6500.90	8553.51	8765.34
输油(气)量 （万吨）	Pipeline Traffic (10000 tons)	2952	7267	7652	8090	8137	8891	9407
输油(气)周转量(万吨公里)	Ton-kilometers (10000 ton-km)	417432	1757891	1699404	1734197	1743309	1737378	2127126
原油管道	**Crude Oil Pipelines**							
条 数 （条）	Number of Pipelines (line)	7	17	42	25	25	25	38
输送里程 （公里）	Length of Pipelines (km)	352.67	634.18	906.18	615.53	595.38	595.38	658.34
输油量 （万吨）	Pipeline Traffic (10000 tons)	1912	3364	3919	3807	4474	5267	4896
输油周转量 （万吨公里）	Ton-kilometers (10000 ton-km)	189623	352764	365214	390996	382146	397318	413774
成品油管道	**Refined Oil Pipelines**							
条 数 （条）	Number of Pipelines (line)	27	62	35	53	53	54	55
输送里程 （公里）	Length of Pipelines (km)	211.00	3925.88	4091.06	4144.67	4283.67	6347.66	6497.66
输油量 （万吨）	Pipeline Traffic (10000 tons)	663	3015	3036	3645	3431	3382	3689
输油周转量 （万吨公里）	Ton-kilometers (10000 ton-km)	13250	1153210	1178405	1219624	1247144	1234102	1601061
其他管道	**Other Pipelines**							
条 数 （条）	Number of Pipelines (line)	11	26	30	29	38	40	41
输送里程 （公里）	Length of Pipelines (km)	971.90	1473.56	1473.15	644.06	1621.85	1610.47	1609.34
输气量 （万吨）	Pipeline Traffic (10000 tons)	377	887	697	637	233	242	822
输气周转量 （万吨公里）	Ton-kilometers(10000 ton-km)	214559	251917	155784	123577	114020	105958	112291

15-16 民航航站吞吐量
Throughput of Civil Aviation Airports

年份 Year	合计 Total			进港 In-port			出港 Out-port		
	架次（万次）Sorties (10000 sorties)	旅客（万人）Passenger Traffic (10000 persons)	货物（万吨）Freight Traffic (10000 tons)	架次（万次）Sorties (10000 sorties)	旅客（万人）Passenger Traffic (10000 persons)	货物（万吨）Freight Traffic (10000 tons)	架次（万次）Sorties (10000 sorties)	旅客（万人）Passenger Traffic (10000 persons)	货物（万吨）Freight Traffic (10000 tons)
1980	1.60	161	2.90	0.80	81	1.40	0.80	80	1.50
1985	4.00	318	6.20	2.00	160	3.00	2.00	158	3.20
1990	6.20	687	13.50	3.10	343	5.90	3.10	344	7.60
1995	17.70	1963	39.50	8.80	963	14.10	8.90	1000	25.40
1996	18.20	2025	45.60	9.10	993	15.90	9.10	1032	29.70
1997	19.00	1981	49.00	9.50	974	16.70	9.50	1007	32.30
1998	20.80	2010	55.80	10.40	986	20.80	10.40	1024	35.00
1999	22.20	1929	63.70	11.10	942	25.60	11.10	987	38.10
2000	23.60	2143	73.00	11.80	1044	30.90	11.80	1099	42.10
2001	25.10	2344	81.00	12.50	1136	33.90	12.60	1208	47.10
2002	28.00	2731	95.70	14.00	1340	40.40	14.00	1391	55.30
2003	28.10	2751	82.40	14.10	1351	34.90	14.00	1400	47.50
2004	34.70	3661	115.80	17.30	1801	50.80	17.40	1860	65.00
2005	38.40	4100	133.00	19.20	2023	58.60	19.20	2077	74.40
2006	42.36	4599	151.13	21.18	2262	64.40	21.18	2337	86.70
2007	46.61	5407	133.20	23.30	2614	53.00	23.31	2793	80.20
2008	49.33	5738	130.47	24.60	2756	52.70	24.60	2982	77.78
2009	54.20	6462	158.50	27.10	3150	65.30	27.10	3312	93.20
2010	58.56	7189	198.40	29.30	3533	83.00	29.30	3655	115.50
2011	61.18	7768	203.96	30.59	3837	84.56	30.59	3931	119.40
2012	65.60	8283	213.59	32.79	4090	86.81	32.81	4193	126.78
2013	70.83	9124	226.75	35.41	4502	91.96	35.42	4622	134.79
2014	76.90	9924	246.27	38.45	4877	99.93	38.45	5047	146.34
2015	79.90	10494	260.26	39.95	5170	108.06	39.96	5324	152.20
2016	85.65	11440	284.36	42.82	5642	118.26	42.83	5798	166.10
2017	94.30	12940	301.27	47.15	6408	125.95	47.15	6532	175.32

15-17 港口泊位及吞吐量

Berth and Throughput of Coastal Ports

项　　目	Item	2000	2010	2014	2015	2016	2017
码头泊位合计　　（个）	**Number of Berths　　(unit)**	**3191**	**3082**	**3111**	**3093**	**2998**	**2886**
沿海港口	**Coastal Ports**	**1373**	**1884**	**1993**	**2005**	**1988**	**1912**
#广州港	Guangzhou Port	141	633	579	584	553	553
湛江港	Zhanjiang Port	41	184	177	174	175	132
汕头港	Shantou Port	28	91	92	92	92	92
深圳港	Shenzhen Port	121	172	153	156	152	155
内河港口	**Ports of Inland Rivers**	**1818**	**1198**	**1118**	**1088**	**1010**	**974**
万吨级码头泊位合计　（个）	**Berths at 10000 Ton Class　　(unit)**	**126**	**245**	**281**	**291**	**304**	**309**
沿海港口	**Coastal Ports**	**126**	**245**	**281**	**291**	**304**	**309**
#广州港	Guangzhou Port	32	62	71	74	76	76
湛江港	Zhanjiang Port	24	31	32	33	35	36
汕头港	Shantou Port	6	18	19	19	19	19
深圳港	Shenzhen Port	34	69	67	67	72	74
内河港口	**Ports of Inland Rivers**						
码头泊位长度　　（米）	**Length of Quay Line　　(m)**	**180238**	**252762**	**265783**	**266828**	**270132**	**267722**
沿海港口	**Coastal Ports**	**105193**	**176753**	**194738**	**200025**	**208999**	**208430**
#广州港	Guangzhou Port	13496	51673	50654	51722	54507	54507
湛江港	Zhanjiang Port	6635	17458	17243	18419	18494	17388
汕头港	Shantou Port	3152	9715	9898	9898	9898	9898
深圳港	Shenzhen Port	17150	31377	30231	30627	31922	32800
内河港口	**Ports of Inland Rivers**	**75045**	**76009**	**71045**	**66803**	**61133**	**59292**
货物吞吐量合计　　（万吨）	**Total Volume of Freight Handled　　(10000 tons)**	**31649**	**122258**	**165455**	**171109**	**179924**	**198015**
沿海港口	**Coastal Ports**	**25495**	**105300**	**137631**	**142059**	**149026**	**164408**
#广州港	Guangzhou Port	11128	42526	48217	50053	52254	57003
湛江港	Zhanjiang Port	2038	13638	20238	22036	25612	28209
汕头港	Shantou Port	1284	3509	5161	5181	4985	4890
深圳港	Shenzhen Port	4224	22097	22324	21706	21410	24136
内河港口	**Ports of Inland Rivers**	**6154**	**16958**	**27824**	**29050**	**30898**	**33607**
集装箱吞吐量合计(万TEU)	**Total Volume of Containers Handled (10000 TEUS)**	**862.68**	**4360.14**	**5325.93**	**5512.12**	**5728.03**	**6226.65**
沿海港口	**Coastal Ports**	**655.15**	**3867.77**	**4752.08**	**4914.73**	**5094.14**	**5504.13**
#广州港	Guangzhou Port	142.98	1270.00	1638.86	1739.66	1866.18	2016.97
湛江港	Zhanjiang Port	7.48	32.01	58.08	60.12	72.36	90.33
汕头港	Shantou Port	11.44	93.50	130.30	117.86	124.02	129.92
深圳港	Shenzhen Port	395.84	2250.96	2403.73	2420.45	2397.94	2520.87
内河港口	**Ports of Inland Rivers**	**207.53**	**492.37**	**573.85**	**597.38**	**633.89**	**722.52**
旅客吞吐量合计　　（万人）	**Total Volume of Passengers Handled(10000 persons)**	**1670.32**	**2483.21**	**3346.87**	**3432.96**	**3434.94**	**3659.63**
沿海港口	**Coastal Ports**	**1330.81**	**2109.39**	**2842.60**	**2867.17**	**2855.10**	**3061.33**
#广州港	Guangzhou Port	15.00	79.01	71.07	61.32	87.34	92.19
湛江港	Zhanjiang Port	29.60	1051.41	1303.18	1299.79	1328.63	1466.06
汕头港	Shantou Port	5.50					
深圳港	Shenzhen Port	203.36	333.88	568.55	586.52	576.72	613.26
内河港口	**Ports of Inland Rivers**	**339.51**	**373.82**	**504.27**	**565.79**	**579.84**	**598.31**

15-18 各市港口货物吞吐量
Freight Throughput of Ports by City

单位：万吨 (10000 tons)

市别	City	2000	2005	2010	2012	2013	2014	2015	2016	2017
总计	**Total**	**31649**	**70926**	**122258**	**140776**	**156373**	**165455**	**171109**	**179924**	**198015**
广州	Guangzhou	12455	27283	42526	45125	47200	50008	52096	54437	59012
深圳	Shenzhen	5697	15351	22098	22807	23398	22324	21706	21410	24136
珠海	Zhuhai	1770	3557	6056	7745	10023	10703	11209	11779	13586
汕头	Shantou	1284	1736	3509	5253	5038	5161	5181	4985	4890
佛山	Foshan	2033	3951	5410	4563	5474	5907	6147	6610	7967
韶关	Shaoguan	131	118	40	82	53	58	62	45	54
河源	Heyuan	45	49							16
梅州	Meizhou	145	306	132	128	125	124	114	110	102
惠州	Huizhou	825	1515	4673	5257	8045	6486	7013	7657	7214
汕尾	Shanwei	25	107	489	772	628	646	858	896	1155
东莞	Dongguan	746	2280	5657	9228	11187	12900	13149	14584	15714
中山	Zhongshan	635	2072	4798	5153	6876	7845	7319	6789	8044
江门	Jiangmen	879	2438	4965	6211	6737	7352	7525	7923	8267
阳江	Yangjiang	68	222	799	1605	2055	1748	2139	2337	2734
湛江	Zhanjiang	2688	6620	13638	17092	18006	20238	22036	25612	28209
茂名	Maoming	1104	1360	2284	2390	2370	2654	2685	2560	2491
肇庆	Zhaoqing	189	520	1597	2729	2954	3033	2945	3261	3973
清远	Qingyuan	193	461	639	729	1008	2513	2927	3152	3910
潮州	Chaozhou	60	80	635	951	1051	1136	1144	854	1153
揭阳	Jieyang	266	248	1290	1601	2510	2709	2851	2695	2968
云浮	Yunfu	411	654	1023	1355	1635	1909	2002	2228	2419
按经济区域分	By Region									
珠三角	Pearl River Delta	25229	58966	97779	108818	121895	126558	129108	134450	147914
东翼	Eastern Region	1635	2171	5924	8577	9226	9653	10035	9430	10166
西翼	Western Region	3860	8202	16721	21087	22431	24640	26860	30509	33434
山区	Mountainous Region	925	1588	1834	2294	2821	4604	5106	5535	6501

15−19 各市城市公共交通情况（2017年）

Basic Statistics on Public Transportation in Cities by City (2017)

市别	City	公共汽电车 Public Bus and Trolly Bus				出租汽车 Taxi	
		运营车辆(辆) Number of Vehicles under Operation (unit)	运营线路条数(条) Number of operating lines	运营线路长度(公里) Length under Operation (Km)	客运量(万人) Passenger Traffic (10000 persons)	运营车辆(辆) Number of Vehicles in Operation (unit)	客运量(万人) Passangers Transported (10000 persons)
总计	**Total**	**65772**	**5467**	**105909**	**656993**	**68477**	**152964**
广州	Guangzhou	14852	1223	17433	238504	22279	60676
深圳	Shenzhen	17430	992	20895	165425	18379	37080
珠海	Zhuhai	2081	307	4130	32212	3627	6319
汕头	Shantou	1695	128	3049	10904	836	1478
佛山	Foshan	6920	638	15797	60465	3962	6496
韶关	Shaoguan	839	93	1703	6339	599	1580
河源	Heyuan	403	50	706	4195	706	2422
梅州	Meizhou	2163	104	3533	4299	783	1959
惠州	Huizhou	2746	206	5596	23773	1896	4941
汕尾	Shanwei	968	66	1198	2392	613	580
东莞	Dongguan	5553	453	8385	38036	5980	17461
中山	Zhongshan	2808	208	3803	20503	1700	1643
江门	Jiangmen	1682	312	5314	13142	944	1728
阳江	Yangjiang	404	42	813	4483	294	336
湛江	Zhanjiang	1570	148	2912	8799	1611	2909
茂名	Maoming	543	89	1783	4139	516	864
肇庆	Zhaoqing	940	124	2847	8627	1044	1664
清远	Qingyuan	794	140	2836	6967	705	1237
潮州	Chaozhou	349	32	924	1230	915	391
揭阳	Jieyang	698	38	733	1226	749	670
云浮	Yunfu	334	74	1521	1333	339	533
按经济区域分	By Region						
珠三角	Pearl River Delta	55012	4463	84199	600687	59811	138007
东翼	Eastern Region	3710	264	5904	15752	3113	3119
西翼	Western Region	2517	279	5507	17420	2421	4108
山区	Mountainous Region	4533	461	10299	23134	3132	7730

15-19 续表 continued

市别	City	轨道交通 Subway, Light Rail and Streetcar				客运轮渡 Passanger Ferryboat	
		运营车数（辆）Number of Vehicles under Operation (unit)	运营线路条数(条) Number of operating lines	运营线路长度（公里）Length under Operation (km)	客运量（万人）Passangers Transported (10000 persons)	运营船舶（艘）Number of Vehicles under Operation (unit)	客运量（万人）Passangers Transported (10000 persons)
总　计	**Total**	**4837**	**25**	**742**	**450141**	**66**	**2004**
广　州	Guangzhou	2408	14	398	280561	52	1713
深　圳	Shenzhen	2284	9	298	165602		
珠　海	Zhuhai	25	1	8	104		
汕　头	Shantou					5	210
佛　山	Foshan					5	68
韶　关	Shaoguan						
河　源	Heyuan						
梅　州	Meizhou						
惠　州	Huizhou						
汕　尾	Shanwei						
东　莞	Dongguan	120	1	38	3874		
中　山	Zhongshan						
江　门	Jiangmen						
阳　江	Yangjiang						
湛　江	Zhanjiang					4	13
茂　名	Maoming						
肇　庆	Zhaoqing						
清　远	Qingyuan						
潮　州	Chaozhou						
揭　阳	Jieyang						
云　浮	Yunfu						
按经济区域分	By Region						
珠三角	Pearl River Delta	4837	25	742	450141	57	1782
东　翼	Eastern Region					5	210
西　翼	Western Region					4	13
山　区	Mountainous Region						

15-20 邮电业务总量和指数

Business Volume of Postal and Telecommunication Services and Their Indices

年份 Year	邮电业务总量(亿元) Business Volume of Postal and Telecommunication Services (100million yuan)			指数(上年=100) Indices (preceding year=100)		
	合计 Total	邮政 Postal Services	电信 Telecommunication Services	合计 Total	邮政 Postal Services	电信 Telecommunication Services
1978	0.90			103.4		
1979	0.96			106.7		
1980	1.05			109.4		
1981	1.15			109.5		
1982	1.17			101.7		
1983	1.31			112.0		
1984	1.56			119.1		
1985	2.05			131.4		
1986	2.54			123.9		
1987	3.49			137.4		
1988	5.11			146.4		
1989	10.33	0.75	9.58	135.9	90.4	141.5
1990	26.30	3.91	22.39	254.6	521.3	233.7
1991	38.89	4.60	34.29	147.9	117.6	153.1
1992	57.06	5.59	51.47	146.7	121.5	150.1
1993	94.25	7.10	87.15	165.2	127.0	169.3
1994	142.78	8.32	134.46	151.5	117.2	154.3
1995	204.93	9.63	202.60	143.5	115.7	150.7
1996	265.56	10.92	254.64	129.6	113.4	125.7
1997	330.38	11.44	318.94	124.4	104.8	125.3
1998	418.18	15.20	402.98	126.6	132.9	126.3
1999	542.65	19.72	522.93	129.8	129.8	129.8
2000	757.22	50.40	706.82	139.5	255.5	135.2
2001	782.67	42.13	740.54	129.9	105.1	131.7
2002	917.87	48.36	869.51	117.3	114.8	117.4
2003	1202.52	54.33	1148.19	131.0	112.3	132.1
2004	1781.78	55.12	1726.66	148.2	101.5	150.4
2005	2121.94	59.82	2062.12	119.1	108.5	119.4
2006	2540.54	69.48	2471.06	119.7	116.1	119.8
2007	3070.55	77.30	2993.25	120.9	111.3	121.1
2008	3564.85	87.97	3476.88	116.1	113.8	116.2
2009	3938.15	101.16	3837.00	110.5	115.0	110.4
2010	4832.94	118.57	4714.37	122.7	117.2	124.4
2011	1918.01	291.36	1626.65	116.4	129.9	114.3
2012	2174.67	395.18	1779.49	113.4	135.6	109.4
2013	2507.99	592.00	1915.99	115.3	149.8	107.7
2013(调整) (adjusted)	2820.42	592.00	2228.42	115.3	149.8	107.7
2014	3394.39	859.81	2534.58	120.4	145.2	113.7
2015	4397.09	1228.75	3168.34	129.5	142.9	125.0
2016	6892.41	1886.25	5006.16	156.7	153.5	158.0
2016(调整) (adjusted)	3864.37	1886.25	1978.12			
2017	6107.19	2526.29	3580.90	158.0	133.9	181.0

注：1. 邮电业务总量1988年及以前按1980年不变价格计算，1989—2000年按1990年不变价格计算，2001—2010年按2000年不变价格计算，2011—2016年起按2010年不变价格计算,2017年起，电信业务总量按2015年不变价格计算，邮政业务总量仍按2010年不变价格计算。指数按可比价格计算。

2. 统计范围是辖区内全社会所有从事电信运营企业和国家邮政企业,以及获得快递业务经营许可的快递服务企业。

Notes: a) The business volume of postal and telecommunication services in and before 1988 was calculated at 1980 constant prices,that from 1989 to 2000 was calculated at 1990 constant prices, that from 2001 to 2010 was calculated at 2000 constant prices, and that from 2011 on was calculated at 2010 constant prices.

b) The statistical coverages of business volume of postal and Telecommunication services are all telecom enter prises, the national postal enterprises and express mail enterprises with express license.

15-21 各市邮电业务总量

Business Volume of Postal and Telecommunication Services by City

单位：亿元 (100 million yuan)

市别	City	2000	2010	2012	2013	2014	2015	2016	2017
总计	**Total**	**757.22**	**4832.94**	**2174.67**	**2507.99**	**3394.39**	**4397.09**	**6892.41**	**6107.19**
广州	Guangzhou	168.26	1051.65	495.88	568.74	838.40	1092.94	1628.28	1544.90
深圳	Shenzhen	154.20	1031.26	463.95	598.10	798.22	1069.43	1718.69	1659.20
珠海	Zhuhai	22.31	137.61	49.11	54.39	72.14	91.22	139.69	108.48
汕头	Shantou	36.61	173.81	68.82	75.39	102.98	134.46	222.30	198.12
佛山	Foshan	66.29	428.72	148.78	165.35	222.89	282.87	450.29	360.64
韶关	Shaoguan	11.11	69.58	25.59	27.49	36.08	45.17	73.53	51.96
河源	Heyuan	6.26	46.33	23.75	26.36	33.64	41.85	68.82	50.99
梅州	Meizhou	12.87	52.48	43.17	46.72	54.58	68.43	103.70	67.78
惠州	Huizhou	27.19	201.02	80.05	86.44	118.40	146.50	245.43	203.73
汕尾	Shanwei	11.10	48.01	20.73	23.05	30.74	38.05	64.36	47.46
东莞	Dongguan	74.05	674.09	250.47	254.73	359.56	475.59	756.06	694.35
中山	Zhongshan	30.10	194.98	80.22	87.33	123.85	156.64	256.33	211.28
江门	Jiangmen	32.02	135.08	56.64	60.07	82.96	102.06	167.13	128.86
阳江	Yangjiang	8.60	50.67	25.25	28.09	36.11	45.30	75.12	54.18
湛江	Zhanjiang	19.38	116.85	68.72	76.45	99.03	122.72	206.05	146.05
茂名	Maoming	13.21	87.27	48.50	53.53	68.39	86.71	145.31	107.57
肇庆	Zhaoqing	13.22	95.05	37.48	41.13	55.66	69.81	115.19	84.18
清远	Qingyuan	9.96	56.06	33.50	36.86	48.46	61.24	104.62	78.23
潮州	Chaozhou	12.78	54.52	24.70	27.26	36.50	46.13	77.82	62.34
揭阳	Jieyang	20.81	94.01	41.29	45.36	66.89	96.30	202.40	202.66
云浮	Yunfu	6.89	33.91	20.34	21.53	29.34	37.69	60.51	42.72
不分地区	Unclassified			67.74	103.62	79.57	85.99	10.80	1.50
按经济区域分	By Region								
珠三角	Pearl River Delta	587.64	3949.45	1730.31	2019.89	2751.65	3573.05	5487.87	4997.13
东翼	Eastern Region	81.31	370.35	155.53	171.07	237.12	314.94	566.87	510.58
西翼	Western Region	41.19	254.79	142.47	158.07	203.52	254.72	426.48	307.80
山区	Mountainous Region	47.09	258.35	146.36	158.96	202.11	254.38	411.19	291.68

15-22 各市邮电业务情况（2017年）
Conditions of Postal and Telecommunication Services by City (2017)

市别	City	业务总量（亿元）Business Volume of Postal and Telecommunication Services (100million yuan)	#电信 Business Volume of Telecommunications	函件（万件）Number of Letters (10000 pcs)	报刊累计数（万份）Newspaper and Magazine Issue (10000 copies)	快递（万件）Pieces of Express Mail Services (10000 pcs)	移动电话用户（万户）Subscribers of Mobile Telephones (10000 subscribers)	本地电话用户（万户）Subscribers of Local Fixed Telephones (10000 subscribers)
总计	**Total**	**6107.19**	**3580.90**	**66587.51**	**79099.21**	**1013468.00**	**14798.85**	**2406.09**
广州	Guangzhou	1544.90	724.48	18645.18	15656.63	393320.21	2705.26	437.50
深圳	Shenzhen	1659.20	743.74	22133.94	9498.65	259509.66	2679.31	478.22
珠海	Zhuhai	108.48	89.37	5387.02	2161.60	7271.52	332.46	61.79
汕头	Shantou	198.12	117.34	369.65	2798.29	39982.35	539.47	105.92
佛山	Foshan	360.64	276.36	158.36	2097.76	39016.62	1167.43	220.45
韶关	Shaoguan	51.96	46.16	66.93	3848.32	1512.57	246.18	40.93
河源	Heyuan	50.99	46.49	508.07	2844.10	1608.78	216.24	36.98
梅州	Meizhou	67.78	57.70	271.02	4185.90	3261.80	319.13	45.56
惠州	Huizhou	203.73	161.84	13.11	842.58	20259.28	611.51	100.14
汕尾	Shanwei	47.46	39.76	9429.38	3901.38	3243.84	198.17	34.77
东莞	Dongguan	694.35	429.69	993.78	2501.67	122485.76	1827.36	246.13
中山	Zhongshan	211.28	148.16	1839.29	4130.81	31194.62	605.71	92.63
江门	Jiangmen	128.86	109.23	4672.76	7560.27	7755.92	562.20	105.14
阳江	Yangjiang	54.18	43.43	491.17	1513.32	3667.24	214.18	40.42
湛江	Zhanjiang	146.05	130.70	292.30	2947.08	3997.62	570.22	55.90
茂名	Maoming	107.57	96.95	370.26	3016.78	2467.89	433.33	55.01
肇庆	Zhaoqing	84.18	75.22	202.88	2111.02	3193.37	337.16	59.52
清远	Qingyuan	78.23	71.01	305.28	3374.42	2561.80	327.77	32.23
潮州	Chaozhou	62.34	44.82	268.90	1494.43	7963.53	229.65	52.99
揭阳	Jieyang	202.66	88.75	48.16	1317.08	58330.25	487.88	70.49
云浮	Yunfu	42.72	38.19	120.07	1297.12	863.38	188.21	33.39
不分地区	Unclassified	1.50	1.50					
按经济区域分	By Region							
珠三角	Pearl River Delta	4997.13	2759.59	54046.32	46560.99	884006.96	10828.40	1801.51
东翼	Eastern Region	510.58	290.68	10116.09	9511.18	109519.97	1455.18	264.17
西翼	Western Region	307.80	271.08	1153.73	7477.18	10132.74	1217.73	151.33
山区	Mountainous Region	291.68	259.55	1271.37	15549.86	9808.32	1297.54	189.09

15-23 邮政通信业基本情况
Basic Conditions of Postal and Telecommunication Services

项　目	Item	2000	2010	2014	2015	2016	2017
邮路长度 (公里)	Length of Postal Routes (km)	180724	137740	122537	137945	155466	214889
农村投递路线 (公里)	Length of Rural Delivery Routes (km)	185223	214877	224371	231858	234641	411663
长途光缆线路长度 (公里)	Length of Long-distance Optical Cable Routes (km)		46289	50650	52662	50545	55188
长途电话交换机容量 (万路端)	Capacity of Long-distance Telephone Exchanges (10000 lines)	70.34	269.11	66.34	63.30	58.11	50.17
本地交换设备容量 (万门)	Capacity of Local Telephone Exchanges (10000 lines)	1939.45	5383.59	3167.62	2810.28	1505.62	815.33
移动电话交换机容量(万户)	Capacity of Mobile Telephone Exchanges (10000 subscribers)	1825.40	14766.90	21418.10	22025.80	21982.30	23037.51
本地电话用户 (万户)	Number of Subscribers of Local Telephones (10000 subscribers)	1414.94	3169.14	2949.46	2807.11	2609.71	2406.09
移动电话用户 (万户)	Number of Mobile Telephones Subscribers (10000 subscribers)	1357.26	9710.09	14943.37	15009.75	14348.96	14798.85
互联网宽带接入用户(万户)	Broadband Subscribers of Internet (10000 subscribers)	216.41	1523.22	2243.87	2285.19	2850.60	3288.15
函件 (万件)	Number of Letters (10000 pcs)	106603	76204	69568	64547	70410	66588
快递 (万件)	Pieces of Express Mail Services (10000 pcs)	1328	59108	335556	501335	767242	1013468
报刊累计数 (万份)	Newspaper and Magazine Circulation (10000 copies)	107755	87895	93826	91159	83405	79099
全省平均每人每年发函件数 (件)	Annual Number of Per Capita Letter Mailed (pcs)	13.80	8.31	6.54	5.95	6.49	6.06
全省平均每百人每年订报刊数 (份)	Annual Average Number of Newspapers and Magazines Subscribed per 100 Persons(copies)	15.10	8.21	8.94	8.40	6.25	4.99
本地电话普及率 (户/百人)	Popularization Rate of Local Telephones (subscribers/100 persons)	18.40	30.38	27.51	25.87	23.73	21.54
移动电话普及率 (户/百人)	Popularization Rate of Mobile Telephones (subscribers/100 persons)	17.61	93.09	139.35	138.35	130.46	132.48

注：表中互联网宽带接入用户数2015年及以前年份数据口径为(固定)互联网用户数。
Note: Data of Broadband Subscribers of Internet in 2015 and prior years referred to Number of (fixed)Internet Subscribers.

主要统计指标解释

铁路营业里程 又称营业长度(包括正式营业和临时营业里程)，指办理客货运输业务的铁路正线总长度。凡是全线或部分建成双线及以上的线路，以第一线的实际长度计算；复线、站线、段管线、岔线和特殊用途线以及不计算运费的联络线都不计算营业里程。该指标可以反映铁路运输业基础设施的发展水平，也是计算客货周转量、运输密度和机车车辆运用效率等指标的基础资料。

公路通车里程 指在一定时期内实际达到《公路工程技术标准 JTJ01-88》规定的等级公路，并经公路主管部门正式验收交付使用的公路里程数。包括大中城市的郊区公路以及通过小城镇街道部分的公路里程和桥梁、渡口的长度，不包括大中城市的街道、厂矿、林区生产用道和农业生产用道的里程。两条或多条公路共同经由同一路段，只计算一次，不得重复计算里程长度。该指标可以反映公路建设的发展规模，也是计算运输网密度等指标的基础资料。

内河航道里程 也称内河通航里程，指在一定时期内，能通航运输船舶及排筏的天然河流、湖泊水库、运河及通航渠道的长度。包括全年季节性通航累计三个月以上的航道，不包括仅供零散流放竹、木排的河道。该指标可以反映内河水运网的规模、水平和发展情况。

民用航空航线里程 指民航运输定期班机飞行的航线长度的总和。航线长度按机场之间的距离计算，通常有两种计算方法：一是将每条航线长度相加称为重复计算航线里程；一是将两线或两条以上航线经过同一区段里程，只计算一次航线长度称为不重复计算航线里程。一般常用的是后者，该指标可以确切反映民航运输网的规模，是表明民航事业为国民经济服务和方便人民生活程度的主要指标。

输油(气)管道里程 指油品(或天然气)的实际输送距离，一般按输油(气)管道的单线长度计算。若包括复线和备用线长度则称为输油(气)管道延展长度，是指管道铺设的实际长度。我们通常使用的是不包括复线的“输油(气)管道里程”，该指标可以反映管道运输的发展规模和水平。

货(客)运量 指在一定时期内，各种运输工具实际运送的货物(旅客)数量。该指标是反映运输业为国民经济和人民生活服务的数量指标，也是制定和检查运输生产计划、研究运输发展规模和速度的重要指标。货运按吨计算，客运按人计算。货物不论运输距离长短、货物类别，均按实际重量统计。旅客不论行程远近或票价多少，均按一人一次客运量统计；半价票、小孩票也按一人统计。

货物(旅客)周转量 指在一定时期内，由各种运输工具运送的货物(旅客)数量与其相应运输距离的乘积之总和。该指标可以反映运输业生产的总成果，也是编制和检查运输生产计划，计算运输效率、劳动生产率以及核算运输单位成本的主要基础资料。计算货物(旅客)周转量通常按发出站与到达站之间的最短距离，也就是计费距离计算。计算公式为：

货物（旅客）周转量=Σ（货物（旅客）运输量×运输距离）

港口货物吞吐量 指经水运进出港区范围，并经过装卸的货物数量，包括邮件及办理托运手续的行李、包裹以及补给运输船舶的燃料、物料和淡水。货物吞吐量按货物流向分为进口、出口吞吐量，按货物交流性质分为外贸货物吞吐量和国内贸易货物吞吐量。货物吞吐量的货类构成及其流向，是衡量港口生产能力大小的重要指标。

民用汽车 指报告期末，在公安交通管理部门按照《机动车注册登记工作规范》，已注册登记领有民用车辆牌照的全部汽车数量。汽车统计的主要分类：根据汽车结构分为载客汽车、载货汽车及其他汽车；根据汽车所有者不同分为个人(私人)汽车、单位汽车；根据汽车的使用性质分为营运汽车、非营运汽车；根据汽车大小规格不同载客汽车分为大型、中型、小型和微型，载货汽车分为重型、中型、轻型和微型。

机动船 又称自航船，指装有各种发动机推进装置，以机械动力行驶的船舶。

驳船 指本身无动力装置，或只设简易动力装置，依靠拖船或推船带动的平底船。

船舶净载重量 指报告期末所拥有船舶的总载重量减去燃（物）料、淡水、粮食及供应品、人员及其行李等的重量及船舶常数后，能够装载货物的实际重量。

沿海港口 指位于海沿岸，具有一定设施和条件，供船舶停靠、旅客上下、货物装卸、生活物料供应等作业的港口。

内河港口　指位于江、河、湖沿岸，具有一定设施和条件，供船舶停靠、旅客上下、货物装卸、生活物料供应等作业的港口。

民用航空航线条数　民用航空航线指出于商业的目的，运输飞机从地球表面一点(起飞)飞到另一点(终点)的航行线路。应同时具备三个条件：一是有运输飞机定期飞行，二是有足以保证运输飞机飞行和起降所需要的机场及地面设施，三是经过批准并在一个航季中正常执行。计算条数时，来回程计为一条。分为国内航线、国际航线和地区航线。

民航运输飞机　从事公共航空运输的民用飞机。分为大中型飞机和小型飞机，大中型飞机指 100 座及以上的运输飞机，小型飞机指 100 座以下的运输飞机。

城市公共交通　指城市中供公众乘用的、经济方便的各种交通方式的总称。包括公共汽车、电车、轨道交通（地铁、轻轨、有轨电车、磁悬浮、索道、缆车等）、出租汽车、公共轮渡等客运交通设施。

运营线路网长度　指公共交通线路所通过的运营线路净长度。计算公式：运营线路网长度=运营线路总长度－Σ重复的线路长度

运营线路总长度　指全部运营线路长度之和。计算公式：运营线路长度=Σ各条运营线路长度=Σ〔1/2（上行起点至终点里程+下行起点至终点里程+上下行终点掉头里程〕。单向行驶的环行线路长度等于起点至终点里程与终点下客站至起点里程之和的一半，不包括折返、试车、联络线等非运营线路。

运营车辆数　指城市中用于公共交通运营业务的全部车辆数。地铁和轻轨在统计时一自然节为一辆。出租汽车指已经领取出租汽车专用牌照的运营车辆，包括技术完好的、在修的、长期行驶的以及拟报废尚未经上级机关批准的车辆。

轮渡运营船舶数　指用于城市客渡运营业务的全部船舶数。不含旅游客轮（长途旅游、市内供游人游览江、河、湖泊的船只）。

城市公共交通客运总量　指报告期内城市公共交通各种运输方式运送乘客的总人次。

邮电业务总量　指以价值量形式表现的邮电通信企业为社会提供各类邮电通信服务的总数量。邮电业务量按专业分类包括函件、包件、汇票、报刊发行、邮政快件、特快专递、邮政储蓄、集邮、公众电报、用户电报、传真、长途电话、出租电路、无线寻呼、移动电话、分组交换数据通信、出租代维等。计算方法为各类产品乘以相应的平均单价(不变价)之和，再加上出租电路和设备、代用户维护电话交换机和线路等的服务收入。该指标综合反映了一定时期邮电业务发展的总成果，是研究邮电业务量构成和发展趋势的重要指标。计算公式为：

邮电业务总量=Σ（各类邮电业务量×不变单价）+出租代维及其他业务收入

=邮政业务总量+通信业务总量

移动电话用户　指通过移动电话交换机进入移动电话网、占用移动电话号码的各类电话用户。包括签约用户和智能网预付费用户。一个移动电话号码统计为一户。

本地电话用户　指接入本地电信运营商固定电话网上的电话用户。包括：住宅用户、单位用户、公用电话用户等。按电话用户位置又分为城市电话用户和乡村电话用户。按通信手段又分为固定电话用户和无线市话用户。1997 年以前，“城市（内）电话用户”是指接入县城及县以上城市的电话网上的电话用户；“乡（农）村电话用户”是指接入县邮电局农话台及县以下农村电话交换点，以县城为中心(除市话用户外)联通县、乡(镇)、行政村、村民小组的用户。从 1997 年起，电话用户数分组调整为以用户所在区域划分为“城市电话用户”和“乡村电话用户”，与过去的按市内电话和农村电话划分方法不同。

城市电话用户　指直辖市、省辖市、地级市、县级市的市区、市郊区及县城(包括县人民政府所在地的县城关区或行政建制相当于县人民政府所在地的镇)范围内接入局用交换机的电话用户数，包括分布在农村地区的独立工矿区、林区、驻军等电话用户数。

乡村电话用户　指按行政区划属于城市范围以外的乡(镇)、村的电话用户数。

国际互联网用户　包括互联网窄带拨号用户和互联网宽带接入用户。互联网窄带拨号用户又分为互联网注册拨号用户、互联网主叫电话记费用户、互联网上网卡用户等几种。互联网注册拨号用户指由基础电信运营商用户提供的，使用固定帐号上网的一种方式，由用户到运营商的营业厅或业务代理商处申请办理，获得拨号上网帐号及密码，用户根据该帐号及密码拨叫上网特服号，通过认证获得动态 IP 地址接入宽带互联网。互联网主叫电话记费用户指用户不需要到运营商的营业厅或业务代理商处申请办理，只需要拨打某一运营商已经开通的主叫特服号码即可上网，上网费用随主叫电话收取。互联网上网卡用户指使用上网卡

上的帐号和密码认证，通过 PSTN、N-ISDN 等方式接入宽带互联网的用户。互联网宽带接入用户指采用分组交换网、DDN 网、帧中继/ATM 网以及模拟专线、数字专线等方式，不经过基础电信运营商的宽带 IP 城域网，直接接入宽带互联网节点的用户，不含 XDSL、专线和 LAN 专线用户。

长途电话交换机容量 指用于接入长途电话网的电话交换机设备的额定容量，包括国际电话交换机容量。

本地交换设备容量 指安装在电信运营企业内用于接续本地固定电话的电话交换机容量，包括现用和备用的人工或自动交换机的全部容量。包括局用交换机容量、接入网设备容量（含无线市话）和用户交换机容量。

移动电话交换机容量 指移动电话交换机根据一定话务模型和交换机处理能力计算出来的最大同时服务用户的数量。

Explanatory Notes on Main Statistical Indicators

Length of Railways in Operation refers to the total length of the trunk line under passenger and freight transportation (including both regular operations and temporary operations). In the case of wholly or partially double- or multi-track railways, calculation is based on the actual length of the first track, regardless of other tracks, station sidings, tracks under the charge of stations, branch lines, special-purpose lines and non-payable connecting lines. The length of railways in operation is an important indicator of the development of infrastructure for railway transport, as well as the foundation for the calculation of passenger-kilometers and freight ton-kilometers, traffic density and utilization efficiency of locomotives and carriages.

Length of Highways refers to the length of highways built in conformity with the grades specified by the Technical Standards JTJ01-88 for Highway Engineering, formally checked and accepted by highway authorities and put into use. The length of highways includes that of suburban highways at large and medium-sized cities and highways passing through streets at small cities and towns, as well as the span of bridges and ferries. However, it does not include the length of streets in large and medium-sized cities and highways built for production purposes at factories, mines, forest areas and agricultural areas. If two or more highways share the same segment, the length of the shared segment is only calculated for once and no duplication is allowed. The length of highways is an important indicator of the scale of development of highway construction, as well as the foundation for the calculation of transport network density and other indicators.

Length of Navigable Inland Waterways refers to the length of natural rivers, lakes, reservoirs, canals, and ditches open to navigation during a given period, which enables the transport by ships and rafts. This includes channels open to seasonal navigation for an accumulative period of over 3 months in a year, but excludes river courses used exclusively for wood or bamboo rafts on an irregular basis. This indicator reflects the scale, level and development situation of the inland waterway network.

Length of Civil Aviation Routes refers to the length of all routes for regular civil aviation flights. Calculation of route lengths is based on the distance between airports, usually in either of the following ways: duplicated calculation of route lengths, which directly sums up the length of every single air route; or singular calculation of route lengths, which calculates the same segments of aviation routes shared by two or more routes only once. In general practice, the latter is used, as it can precisely reflect the size of the civil aviation network and indicate the extent to which civil aviation serves the national economy and the needs of the people.

Length of Petroleum and Gas Pipelines refers to the actual transport distance of oil or gas products, generally calculated as the length of single pipelines. Inclusion of double pipelines and alternate pipeline in the calculation is termed the extension length of petroleum and gas pipelines, which indicates the actual length of the pipelines built. In general practice, the "Length of Petroleum and Gas Pipelines" exclusive of double pipelines is used, which reflects the scale and degree of development in pipeline transport.

Freight (Passenger) Traffic refers to the volume of freight (passengers) transported with various means. This indicator provides a quantitative measure of how the transport industry serves the national economy and the needs of the people, as well as an important reference for drafting and checking production plans in the transport industry and for studying the scale and speed of development in the transport industry. Freight transport is calculated in tons and passenger traffic is calculated in the number of persons. Freight transport is calculated in the actual weight of goods regardless of traveling distances and types of freight; while passenger traffic is calculated as the number of individuals traveling once, regardless of traveling distances, ticket prices, whether the passengers are traveling with half-price tickets or child tickets.

Freight Ton-kilometers (Passenger-kilometers) refer to the sum of the products of the volume of transported cargo (passengers) multiplied by the transport distance. These are important indicators of the total achievements of the transport industry, as well as the major foundation for drafting and checking production plans in the transport industry and for calculating the efficiency, labor productivity and the cost of transport enterprises. Normally, the shortest distance between the departure station and the destination station (i.e. the payable distance) is the basis to calculate the freight ton-kilometers and passenger-kilometers on. These indicators are calculated as follows:

Freight Ton-kilometers (Passenger-kilometers) = Σ (Freight (Passenger) Traffic ×Transport Distance)

Volume of Freight Handled in Ports refers to the volume of cargo passing in and out of the harbor area that undergoes the loading and unloading processes, including mails, checked baggage and bales, as well as fuel, material and fresh water supplies to ships. The volume of freight handled may be classified by direction of flow as import volume and export volume, or by nature of cargo as volume of freight for domestic trade and volume of freight for foreign trade. The classification of volume of freight handled and its direction of flow are important indicators of the production capacity of ports.

Possession of Civil Motor Vehicles refers to the total number of vehicles that are registered at transport management offices under the public security authorities and provided with civil vehicle licenses and tags according to the Work Standard for Motor Vehicles Registration at the end of the reference period. Major categories of vehicle are: passenger vehicles, freight vehicles and other vehicles in terms of structure; private vehicles and organization-owned vehicles in terms of ownership; commercial vehicles and non-commercial vehicles in terms of use; large, medium, small and mini passenger vehicles, and heavy, medium, light and mini trucks in terms of size.

Motor Vessels refer to vessels installed with power units and propelled by mechanical power. It is also known as self-propelled vessels.

Barges refer to flat-bottomed vessels driven by drawers or propellers. It has no power units or has only simple power units.

Dead Weight Tonnage of Vessels refers to the actual tonnage all the vessels within the reference period are capable of carrying. It equals the tonnage of all the vessels minus that of fuel, material and fresh water, foods, supplies, persons and luggages on vessels.

Coastal Seaports refer to seaports located alongside the coasts that have the right facilities and conditions for vessel mooning, passenger boarding and alighting, cargo loading and disloading, and supply of daily life materials.

Inland Ports refer to ports located along rivers and lakes that have the right facilities and conditions for vessel mooning, passenger boarding and alighting, cargo loading and disloading, and supply of daily life materials.

Number of Civil Aviation Routes refers to the number of all routes of commercial civil aviation flights from one point of the earth to another. Civil aviation routes shall meet three conditions. First, there shall be regular flights. Second, there shall be adequate airport and ground facilities to ensure the flight, takeoff and landing. Third, the flights are approved and carried out normally during the flight season. Singular calculation is used in calculating the number of routes. Civil aviation routes are divided into domestic routes, international routes and regional routes.

Civil Aviation Aircraft refer to aircraft used in public civil aero transport. They are divided into large and medium-sized aircraft and small-sized aircraft. The former refer to those with 100 seats and above, and the latter refer to those with less than 100 seats.

Urban Public Transportation refers to all the economical transport taken by the public in cities. It includes buse, trolley bus, rail transport (subway, light rail, streetcar, magnetically levitated trains, cableway, telpher, etc.), taxi, ferry boast, etc.

Length of Public Transportation Network refers to the net length covered by the public transportation routes. The following formula is used:

Length of Public Transportation Network=Length of Public Transportation under Operation - ΣLength of Repeated Routes

Length of Public Transportation under Operation refers to the sum of all public transportation routes under operation. The following formula is used:

Length of Public Transportation under Operation= -Σ(1/2 (length from starting station to terminal of forward trip+length from terminal to beginning station of backward trip+length of take-turning of both trips)

Number of Vehicles under Operation refers to the total number of vehicles under operation in public transportation in cities. For subway and light rail, each compartment is calculated as one unit. Taxi refers to all those with special operation license, including those in good condition, under maintenance, in long-term operation and with pending approval for writing-off.

Number of Ferry Boats refer to the total number of boats for ferry operation., excluding the long-distance or intra-city cruiser.

Total Passenger Traffic in Cities refers to the total number of persons transported by public transportation in cities.

Business Volume of Postal and Telecommunication Services refers to the total amount of postal and telecommunication services, expressed in value terms, provided by postal and telecommunication enterprises for the society. Postal and telecommunication services can be classified as letters, parcels, remittance, delivery of newspapers and magazines, fast mail service, express mail service, savings deposits, stamps for collection, public and individual telegraph service, facsimiles, long-distance telephone service, leasing of telephone lines, urban paging service, mobile telephone service, data communication through packet networks, network elements lease and maintenance, etc. To calculate the volume, the business volume of each product is multiplied by its average unit price (at constant prices), summed, and added to income from other services such as leasing of telephone lines and equipment, maintenance of telephone switchboards and lines on behalf of customers. This indicator reflects the overall achievements of postal and telecommunication services during a given period, and is an important reference for studying the composition of business volume and the development trend of postal and telecommunication services. This volume is calculated as follows:

Business Volume of Postal and Telecommunication Services = Σ(Business Volume of Each Product × Constant Unit Price) + Income from Leasing, Maintenance, and Other Services = Business Volume of Postal Services + Business Volume of Telecommunication Services

Mobile Telephone Subscribers refer to persons who own mobile telephone numbers and are connected with the mobile telephone communication network through mobile telephone switchboards, including contracted subscribers and pre-paid subscribers for intelligent network. One mobile telephone number is calculated as one subscriber.

Local Telephone Subscribers refer to subscribers that are connected to the local telecommunication service provider through fix line network, including household subscribers, institutional subscribers and public telephones. They are also classified as urban subscribers and rural subscribers according to locations, or fixed-line subscribers and wireless subscribers according to the means of telecommunication. Before 1997, urban subscribers referred to those connected to urban telephone networks in county towns and cities, while rural subscribers referred to those connected to rural telephone stations at or below the county level, clustered around the county town (excluding urban subscribers), and further connected to the county, towns and townships, administrative villages and villagers' groups. Since 1997, the classification of telephone subscribers into urban telephone subscribers and rural telephone subscribers was modified on the basis of geographical location of the subscribers, which is different from the previous distinction between urban telephones and rural telephones.

Urban Telephone Subscribers refer to the number of telephone subscribers located at municipalities under the jurisdiction of the central government, cities under the jurisdiction of provinces, cities at prefecture level, downtown and suburb of cities at county level and county towns (including county towns where the county governments are located, and towns where the governments of other administrative regions at county level are located), that are connected to the public line telephone network, including the number of telephone subscribers in independent mining areas, forest areas, and military zones located in rural areas.

Rural Telephone Subscribers refer to telephone subscribers located at townships, towns and villages outside the range of cities according to administrative jurisdiction.

Number of Internet Subscribers include both narrow-band dial-up users and broad-band access users of the internet. Narrow-band dial-up users are further classified into registered dial-up users, pay-per-calling users, and pre-pay card users. Registered dial-up service enables internet access through fixed accounts provided by basic telecommunication operators. Users of this service apply to the operators or their agents for accounts and passwords, with which they dial special numbers for internet connection and acquire dynamic IP addresses through authentification to gain access to the broad-band internet. Pay-per-calling service implies that instead of applying to the operators or their agents, users only need to dial a certain operator’s special numbers to gain access to the internet and pay internet fees together with their calling fees. Pre-pay card users refer to those connected to the broad-band internet through PSTN and N-ISDN networks with accounts and passwords provided by the pre-pay cards. Broad-band access users (exclusive of XDSL and LAN users) refer to users directly connected to broad-band internet nodes through packet networks, DDN networks, frame relay/ATM networks, and special analog or digital lines, bypassing the broad-band IP MAN provided by basic telecommunication operators.

Capacity of Long Distance Telephone Exchanges refers to the rated capacity of telephone exchanges connected to long distance telephone networks, including capacity of international telephone exchanges.

Capacity of Local Telephone Exchanges refers to the capacity of telephone exchanges installed in the offices of telecommunication service providers for communication between fixed telephones. It includes the capacity of both manual and automatic exchanges in use and for stand-by purpose. It consists of the capacity of office telephone exchanges, access network equipment(including wireless city call) and subscriber exchanges.

Capacity of Mobile Telephone Exchanges refers to the maximum number of subscribers that can be served simultaneously, calculated according to a certain calling model and the handling capacity of the mobile telephone exchanges.

十六、批发和零售业

WHOLESALE AND RETAIL TRADES

十六　批发零售业

简要说明

一、本篇资料反映包括批发零售业商品流通情况、社会消费品零售总额等。

二、本篇资料主要根据国家统计局《批发和零售业统计报表制度》进行搜集和加工整理。资料中限额以上批发和零售业采用全面调查的方法自下而上逐级综合汇总而得，限额以下企业及个体户资料采用抽样调查方法推算而得。

三、各表的调查范围：

限额以上批发和零售业统计限额标准：批发业年主营业务收入2000万元及以上；零售业年主营业务收入500万元及以上。

商品购、销、存总额表为各种经济类型的限额以上和限额以下批发零售业法人及产业活动单位和个体户。

社会消费品零售总额表为各种经济类型的法人及产业活动单位、个体户对城乡居民和社会集团的零售。

四、本篇资料由广东省统计局贸易外经处整理提供。

16 Wholesale and Retail Trades

Brief Introduction

Ⅰ. The date in this chapter show the development of Guangdong's domestic market，including mainly the circulation of commodities in the wholesale and retail trades and the total retail sales of consumer goods，etc.

Ⅱ. The data are collected and processed in accordance with the Statistical Reporting Scheme on Wholesale and Retail Trades stipulated by the National Bureau of Statistics. Data on basic conditions for all corporate enterprises of wholesale, retail above the designated size are collected through comprehensive reporting systems and data are reported level by level in a bottom-up manner. Data on small-size enterprises and individual enterprises below the designated size are collected through sample surveys.

Ⅲ. The statistical coverage in this chapter comes as follows:

Criteria for wholesale and retail sale trades above designated size is defined as follows：wholesale trade with annual principal business sales of 20 million yuan or above, retail sale trade with annual principal business sales of 5 million yuan or above.

The table of total purchases，sales and inventory include corporate units, establishments and individuals of various types of ownership both above and below designated size by category of commodities.

The table of total retail sales of consumer goods includes the retail sales of corporate units, establishments and individuals of various types of ownership to urban and rural residents and institutions.

Ⅳ. The data in this chapter are prepared and provided by the Division of Trade and External Economic Relations Statistics of　Statistics Bureau of Guangdong Province.

16-1 批发零售业主要指标
Main Indicators on Domestic Trade

指　标	Item	2000	2010	2014	2015	2016	2017
社会消费品零售总额（亿元）	**Total Retail Sales of Consumer Goods (100 million yuan)**	**4379.81**	**17458.44**	**28471.15**	**31517.56**	**34739.00**	**38200.07**
按消费形态分							
商品零售	Retail Sales			25634.59	28278.73	31242.41	34519.74
餐饮收入	Catering Income			2836.56	3238.83	3496.59	3680.33
按城乡分	By Urban and Rural Area						
城镇	Urban Areas	3290.33	14896.98	24939.92	27610.44	30418.16	33423.74
乡村	Rural Areas	1089.48	2561.46	3531.23	3907.12	4320.84	4776.33
批发零售业商品销售总额（亿元）	**Total Sales in Wholesale and Retail Trades (100 million yuan)**	**10316.88**	**47217.39**	**106900.75**	**115442.98**	**127092.00**	**142828.38**
批发额	Wholesale Value	6691.51	31727.96	81430.22	87415.19	95929.77	108398.35
零售额	Retail Value	3625.37	15489.43	25470.53	28027.79	31162.23	34430.03
按行业分	By Sector						
批发业销售额	Sales in Wholesale Trade	7053.14	30173.58	82875.98	89258.24	97952.99	110882.22
批发额	Wholesale Value	6247.11	28849.48	78943.69	84796.41	92989.40	105174.57
零售额	Retail Value	806.03	1324.10	3932.29	4461.83	4963.59	5707.65
零售业销售额	Sales in Retail Trade	3263.74	17043.81	24024.77	26184.74	29139.01	31946.16
批发额	Wholesale Value	444.40	2878.48	2486.53	2618.78	2940.37	3223.78
零售额	Retail Value	2819.34	14165.33	21538.23	23565.96	26198.64	28722.38
按规模分	By Size						
限额以上销售额	Sales above Designated Size	4922.10	30316.84	72282.30	66166.10	74045.02	86478.92
批发额	Wholesale Value	4036.15	24600.85	60351.79	53553.50	60245.99	71916.10
零售额	Retail Value	885.95	5715.99	11930.51	12612.60	13799.03	14562.82
限额以下销售额	Sales below Designated Size	5394.78	16900.55	34618.45	49276.88	53046.98	56349.46
批发额	Wholesale Value	2655.36	7127.11	21078.43	33861.69	35683.78	36482.25
零售额	Retail Value	2739.42	9773.44	13540.02	15415.19	17363.20	19867.21
限额以上连锁总店数（个）	**Number of General Chain Stores above Designated Size (unit)**		**206**	**387**	**386**	**385**	**388**
限额以上连锁门店数（个）	**Number of Branch Chain Stores above Designated Size (unit)**		**23096**	**28305**	**25903**	**31922**	**31913**
限额以上连锁店销售总额（亿元）	**Total Sales of Chain Stores above Designated Size (100 million yuan)**		**3502.08**	**5597.23**	**5241.15**	**5356.58**	**3699.70**
#零售额	Retail Value		2980.36	4563.17	4420.51	4604.38	3171.36
亿元以上商品交易市场成交额（亿元）	**Transaction Value of Commodity Markets above 100 Million Yuan (100 million yuan)**		**4828.13**	**5657.02**	**5576.63**	**5512.94**	**5462.94**

16–2 按行业及城乡分社会消费品零售总额

Total Retail Sales of Consumer Goods by Sector and by Urban and Rural Area

单位：亿元 (100 million yuan)

年份 Year	社会消费品零售总额 Total Retail Sales of Consumer Goods	按行业分 By Sector		按城乡分 By Urban and Rural Area	
		#批发零售业 Wholesale and Retail Trades	#住宿餐饮业 Hotels and Catering Services	城镇 Urban Areas	乡村 Rural Areas
1978	79.86	66.92	5.39	38.42	41.44
1979	92.69	76.76	6.09	43.25	49.44
1980	117.67	94.52	7.30	66.72	50.95
1981	142.38	114.56	8.85	71.19	71.19
1982	164.23	131.86	10.19	82.77	81.46
1983	183.62	144.88	11.58	97.32	86.30
1984	226.13	170.06	16.04	131.61	94.52
1985	289.23	209.38	26.74	178.45	110.78
1986	327.02	235.59	28.68	172.67	154.35
1987	405.19	294.17	37.83	214.34	190.85
1988	568.07	414.30	50.79	306.19	261.88
1989	636.15	451.24	65.69	345.43	290.72
1990	667.36	463.92	71.11	457.34	210.02
1991	786.64	535.40	87.87	531.57	255.07
1992	1109.55	951.21	128.60	809.96	299.59
1993	1518.31	1309.60	168.75	1137.80	380.51
1994	1991.33	1705.13	234.42	1511.03	480.30
1995	2478.35	2121.16	300.24	1864.90	613.45
1996	2772.83	2358.28	356.23	2093.18	679.65
1997	3139.32	2653.90	409.95	2362.67	776.65
1998	3567.01	2962.27	505.56	2688.64	878.37
1999	3932.44	3268.96	569.18	2960.30	972.14
2000	4379.81	3625.37	655.94	3290.33	1089.48
2001	4856.65	3996.92	751.32	3638.52	1218.13
2002	5392.64	4443.64	843.82	4044.52	1348.12
2003	6029.86	5021.81	897.26	4540.94	1488.92
2004	6852.03	5734.94	953.84	5177.13	1674.90
2005	7915.51	6773.37	1016.63	5967.71	1947.80
2006	9194.29	7944.17	1155.39	6913.19	2281.10
2007	10731.28	9373.42	1298.31	8064.08	2667.20
2008	12986.60	11423.07	1498.91	9754.30	3232.30
2009	14891.78	13228.45	1656.30	11278.66	3613.12
2010	17458.44	15565.04	1893.40	14896.98	2561.46
2011	20297.52	18110.21	2187.31	17399.70	2897.82
2012	22677.11	20231.14	2445.97	19767.95	2909.16
2013	25453.93	22728.10	2725.83	22283.48	3170.46
2014	28471.15	25518.70	2952.45	24939.92	3531.23
2015	31517.56	28285.78	3231.78	27610.44	3907.12
2016	34739.00			30418.16	4320.84
2017	38200.07			33423.74	4776.33

注：本表1992—2004年数据根据广东省第一次全国经济普查资料进行了调整，2005—2008年数据根据广东省第二次全国经济普查资料进行了调整，2009—2013年数据根据广东省第三次全国经济普查资料进行了调整。

Note: Data of 1992 to 2004 in this table have been adjusted in accordance with the figures from the first national economic census of Guangdong Province，Data of 2005 to 2008 in this table have been adjusted in accordance with the figures from the second national economic census of Guangdong Province，Data of 2009 to 2013 in this table have been adjusted in accordance with the figures from the third national economic census of Guangdong Province.

16-3 各市社会消费品零售总额（2017年）
Total Retail Sales of Consumer Goods by City (2017)

单位：亿元 (100 million yuan)

市别	City	社会消费品零售总额 Total Retail Sales of Consumer Goods	按消费形态分 By Sector		按城乡分 By Urban and Rural Area	
			商品零售 Retail Sales	餐饮收入 Catering Income	城镇 Urban Area	乡村 Rural Area
广州	Guangzhou	9402.59	8325.05	1077.54	9147.44	255.15
深圳	Shenzhen	6016.19	5335.28	680.91	6016.19	
珠海	Zhuhai	1128.18	997.93	130.25	1096.56	31.62
汕头	Shantou	1683.16	1589.52	93.64	1231.26	451.90
佛山	Foshan	3320.43	2989.14	331.29	2637.32	683.11
韶关	Shaoguan	687.39	623.73	63.66	597.92	89.47
河源	Heyuan	585.57	544.86	40.71	448.33	137.24
梅州	Meizhou	677.63	631.93	45.70	500.66	176.97
惠州	Huizhou	1363.46	1247.03	116.43	1099.53	263.93
汕尾	Shanwei	572.62	510.72	61.90	420.38	152.24
东莞	Dongguan	2687.88	2515.70	172.18	2363.37	324.51
中山	Zhongshan	1309.89	1191.92	117.97	1194.12	115.77
江门	Jiangmen	1279.63	1159.55	120.08	971.34	308.29
阳江	Yangjiang	689.90	617.40	72.50	534.41	155.49
湛江	Zhanjiang	1578.08	1400.06	178.02	1280.69	297.39
茂名	Maoming	1457.00	1332.33	124.67	989.06	467.94
肇庆	Zhaoqing	809.93	748.19	61.74	575.37	234.56
清远	Qingyuan	683.84	630.01	53.83	532.08	151.76
潮州	Chaozhou	544.05	499.43	44.62	462.44	81.61
揭阳	Jieyang	1080.96	1035.66	45.30	779.80	301.16
云浮	Yunfu	381.60	359.19	22.41	297.74	83.86
按经济区域分	By Region					
珠三角	Pearl River Delta	27318.18	24509.79	2808.39	25101.24	2216.94
东翼	Eastern Region	3880.79	3635.33	245.46	2893.88	986.91
西翼	Western Region	3724.98	3349.79	375.19	2804.16	920.82
山区	Mountainous Region	3016.03	2789.72	226.31	2376.73	639.30

16-4 各市社会消费品零售总额

Total Retail Sales of Consumer Goods by City

单位：亿元 (100 million yuan)

市别	City	2000	2005	2010	2012	2013	2014	2015	2016	2017
广州	Guangzhou	1121.13	1905.84	4500.28	5977.27	6426.91	7144.45	7987.96	8706.49	9402.59
深圳	Shenzhen	735.02	1441.61	3000.76	4008.78	4500.46	4919.00	5017.84	5512.76	6016.19
珠海	Zhuhai	121.17	220.19	486.03	635.20	720.52	815.71	915.20	1016.13	1128.18
汕头	Shantou	218.99	345.23	830.41	1029.82	1056.81	1186.04	1349.34	1515.19	1683.16
佛山	Foshan	337.55	650.18	1687.13	2019.50	2122.63	2400.58	2705.22	3017.76	3320.43
韶关	Shaoguan	85.40	141.67	329.78	409.59	471.11	522.68	580.79	638.21	687.39
河源	Heyuan	37.12	73.02	163.07	209.37	381.02	435.01	482.99	537.44	585.57
梅州	Meizhou	67.28	131.85	319.05	403.5	450.18	499.97	559.50	619.77	677.63
惠州	Huizhou	126.48	252.01	582.53	754.15	857.91	968.70	1070.72	1227.88	1363.46
汕尾	Shanwei	69.84	130.45	352.06	424.32	398.72	440.11	489.61	533.11	572.62
东莞	Dongguan	235.16	506.29	1108.06	1354.58	1786.66	1942.29	2184.70	2470.78	2687.88
中山	Zhongshan	141.81	277.08	648.11	809.33	890.55	981.80	1086.74	1205.84	1309.89
江门	Jiangmen	177.03	310.44	655.86	807.21	831.85	923.35	1034.30	1159.06	1279.63
阳江	Yangjiang	86.46	159.22	370.58	467.01	481.98	531.90	584.46	634.83	689.90
湛江	Zhanjiang	156.59	269.98	679.79	861.33	1010.70	1162.10	1308.95	1432.96	1578.08
茂名	Maoming	158.11	287.96	704.97	902.20	983.13	1093.90	1214.38	1339.88	1457.00
肇庆	Zhaoqing	77.31	142.99	332.89	433.39	493.12	559.90	648.36	731.98	809.93
清远	Qingyuan	72.27	130.03	370.50	459.63	466.45	520.28	571.50	626.80	683.84
潮州	Chaozhou	60.57	103.32	245.47	317.04	354.71	395.86	444.15	495.61	544.05
揭阳	Jieyang	82.38	144.76	446.62	521.05	657.66	759.02	872.42	978.42	1080.96
云浮	Yunfu	31.30	59.71	136.97	180.31	224.73	268.49	304.71	345.22	381.60
按经济区域分	By Region									
珠三角	Pearl River Delta	3204.99	5878.70	12613.24	16552.69	18630.61	20655.78	22651.04	25048.68	27318.18
东翼	Eastern Region	450.38	745.58	1818.56	2258.56	2467.90	2781.03	3155.52	3522.33	3880.79
西翼	Western Region	418.44	738.78	1702.90	2197.78	2475.81	2787.90	3107.79	3407.67	3724.98
山区	Mountainous Region	306.00	552.45	1279.96	1668.08	1993.49	2246.43	2499.49	2767.44	3016.03

16-5 批发零售业商品销售总额
Total Sales of Commodities in Wholesale and Retail Trades

单位：亿元 (100 million yuan)

项目	Item	2000	2010	2015	2016	2017
合计	**Total**	**10316.88**	**47217.39**	**115442.98**	**127092.00**	**142828.38**
按行业分组	By sector					
批发业	Wholesale Trade	7053.14	30173.58	89258.24	97952.99	110882.22
零售业	Retail Trade	3263.74	17043.81	26184.74	29139.01	31946.16
按规模分组	By Size of Enterprises					
限额以上企业和个体户	**Enterprises above Designated Size and Individuals**	**4922.10**	**30316.84**	**66166.10**	**74045.02**	**86478.91**
食品、饮料、烟酒类	Food, Beverages, Tobacco and Liquor	843.07	2635.17	7097.34	7537.89	7680.56
粮油类	Grain and Edible Oil	17.02	366.51	1134.22	1457.42	1337.15
肉禽蛋类	Meat, Poultry and Eggs	110.80	230.13	703.26	823.50	841.83
饮料类	Beverages	24.27	192.76	1046.10	774.62	822.27
烟酒类	Tobacco and Liquor	464.74	1175.56	1939.10	2021.58	2102.40
其它食品类	Other Food	226.24	670.21	2274.66	2460.77	2576.91
服装鞋帽、针纺织品类	Garments,Footwear,Headgear,Knitwear and Textiles	437.67	1869.06	5244.01	5120.19	3995.48
服装类	Garments	277.69	1133.19	3451.73	3182.00	2426.09
鞋帽类	Footwear and Headgear	49.29	206.49	689.94	696.01	715.12
针、纺织品类	Knitwear and Textiles	110.69	529.38	1102.34	1242.18	854.28
化妆品类	Cosmetics	20.12	138.83	401.67	409.68	447.51
金银珠宝类	Gold, Silver and Jewelry	26.10	221.13	1280.64	1462.81	1635.40
日用品类	Daily-use Articles	206.22	762.55	2347.19	2623.51	2745.68
#洗涤用品类	Detergents	22.54	232.11			
儿童玩具类	Toys for Children	15.33	32.61	96.89	91.32	94.65
五金、电料类	Hardware and Electrical Appliances	50.65	266.24	761.81	854.67	956.58
体育、娱乐用品类	Sports and Recreational Articles	22.79	153.92	168.46	208.32	214.89
书报杂志类	Newspapers and Magazines	43.41	77.67	161.28	174.24	135.01
电子出版物及音像制品类	E-journals and Video Products	6.67	23.12	29.96	32.00	25.70
家用电器和音像器材类	Household Appliances and Video Appliances	329.32	1221.85	2459.14	2204.93	2629.84
中西药品类	Traditional Chinese and Western Medicines	275.71	1248.10	2957.35	3331.35	3530.23
#西药	Western Medicines	170.09	848.37	1939.97	2211.95	2343.70
中草药及中成药	Traditional Chinese Medicines	70.92	256.71	659.07	681.13	713.07
文化办公用品类	Articles for Cultural and Office Use	55.91	637.27	3586.88	3579.56	4038.35
家具类	Furniture	31.98	189.07	542.19	596.35	515.06
通讯器材类	Communication Appliances	70.47	719.27	3176.14	3858.88	5030.08
煤炭及制品类	Coal and Related Products	82.94	1144.17	1293.35	1002.98	1354.38
木材及制品类	Timber and Related Products	10.08	60.20	163.68	201.47	241.45
石油及制品类	Petroleum and Related Products	1176.36	7779.83	7792.01	8739.15	11587.29
化工材料及制品类	Chemical Materials and Products	172.79	1566.66	3952.91	4117.36	5190.73
金属材料类	Metal Materials	324.60	4380.16	8268.17	9240.29	13110.77
建筑及装潢材料类	Construction and Decoration Materials	36.43	432.07	1171.45	1292.86	1530.39
机电产品及设备类	Mechanical and Electrical Products and Equipment	119.99	1235.24	2888.60	3163.79	3790.97
汽车类	Motor Vehicles	213.08	2773.14	6494.43	8648.68	9774.17
种子饲料类	Seeds and Feedstuff	22.64	53.57	208.81	279.16	343.87
棉麻类	Cotton and Hemp	6.52	20.81	93.09	51.13	73.59
其它类	Others	336.58	707.74	3625.54	5313.77	5900.93
限额以下企业和个体户	**Enterprises below Designated Size and Individuals**	**5394.78**	**16900.55**	**49276.88**	**53046.98**	**56349.47**

16-6 批发零售业商品批发额

Total Wholesale Value of Commodities in Wholesale and Retail Trades

单位：亿元 (100 million yuan)

项 目	Item	2000	2010	2015	2016	2017
合 计	**Total**	**6691.51**	**31727.96**	**87415.19**	**95929.77**	**108398.35**
按行业分组	By sector					
批发业	Wholesale Trade	6247.11	28849.48	84796.41	92989.40	105174.57
零售业	Retail Trade	444.40	2878.48	2618.78	2940.37	3223.78
按规模分组	By Size of Enterprises					
限额以上企业和个体户	**Enterprises above Designated Size and Individuals**	**4036.15**	**24600.85**	**53553.50**	**60245.99**	**71916.00**
食品、饮料、烟酒类	Food, Beverages, Tobacco and Liquor	677.15	2067.13	5863.76	6146.13	6307.54
粮油类	Grain and Edible Oil	6.87	279.88	928.33	1218.81	1132.92
肉禽蛋类	Meat, Poultry and Eggs	94.01	168.66	536.39	634.51	669.71
饮料类	Beverages	13.88	134.29	907.60	619.26	666.33
烟酒类	Tobacco and Liquor	418.34	1065.75	1737.72	1788.96	1876.40
其它食品类	Other Food	144.05	418.55	1753.72	1884.59	1962.18
服装鞋帽、针纺织品类	Garments,Footwear,Headgear,Knitwear and Textiles	344.17	1385.88	3993.25	3833.40	2793.04
服装类	Garments	210.88	786.06	2606.88	2311.06	1615.20
鞋帽类	Footwear and Headgear	35.16	117.36	415.44	419.86	436.83
针、纺织品类	Knitwear and Textiles	98.13	482.46	970.93	1102.48	741.02
化妆品类	Cosmetics	5.45	56.22	228.49	226.70	255.95
金银珠宝类	Gold, Silver and Jewelry	12.37	151.49	1045.36	1212.58	1365.97
日用品类	Daily-use Articles	147.50	569.53	1760.89	1955.68	2037.13
#洗涤用品类	Detergents	11.35	166.98			
儿童玩具类	Toys for Children	12.05	19.52	61.29	60.42	66.48
五金、电料类	Hardware and Electrical Appliances	44.79	241.86	635.55	706.54	819.81
体育、娱乐用品类	Sports and Recreational Articles	15.68	131.35	97.62	122.45	121.62
书报杂志类	Newspapers and Magazines	29.11	50.89	109.76	122.38	84.24
电子出版物及音像制品类	E-journals and Video Products	2.42	16.38	14.56	17.02	12.85
家用电器和音像器材类	Household Appliances and Video Appliances	255.61	790.44	1742.73	1432.98	1777.70
中西药品类	Traditional Chinese and Western Medicines	217.40	957.64	2349.21	2638.41	2757.47
#西药	Western Medicines	136.84	651.83	1524.78	1738.34	1813.19
中草药及中成药	Traditional Chinese Medicines	55.80	216.34	571.22	596.39	615.63
文化办公用品类	Articles for Cultural and Office Use	41.13	570.14	3229.34	3177.67	3564.44
家具类	Furniture	23.41	156.89	392.91	415.40	322.65
通讯器材类	Communication Appliances	65.29	639.96	2731.33	3353.94	4419.17
煤炭及制品类	Coal and Related Products	82.62	1137.75	1264.48	973.49	1349.19
木材及制品类	Timber and Related Products	9.73	60.20	163.68	201.47	241.45
石油及制品类	Petroleum and Related Products	1043.57	6488.12	5822.76	6794.15	9511.78
化工材料及制品类	Chemical Materials and Products	169.88	1566.66	3952.91	4117.36	5190.73
金属材料类	Metal Materials	322.33	4380.16	8268.17	9240.29	13110.77
建筑及装潢材料类	Construction and Decoration Materials	33.07	392.48	1021.24	1122.89	1356.37
机电产品及设备类	Mechanical and Electrical Products and Equipment	102.51	1200.20	2741.70	3012.12	3644.81
汽车类	Motor Vehicles	100.37	920.60	2720.82	4338.16	5164.40
种子饲料类	Seeds and Feedstuff	22.64	53.57	208.81	279.16	343.87
棉麻类	Cotton and Hemp	6.52	20.81	92.93	51.02	73.52
其它类	Others	261.43	594.50	3101.24	4754.60	5289.53
限额以下企业和个体户	**Enterprises below Designated Size and Individuals**	**2655.36**	**7127.11**	**33861.69**	**35683.78**	**36482.35**

 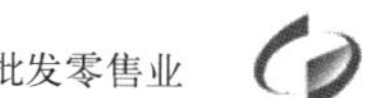

16—7 批发零售业商品零售额

Total Retail Value of Commodities in Wholesale and Retail Trades

单位：亿元 (100 million yuan)

项　目	Item	2000	2010	2015	2016	2017
合　计	**Total**	**3625.37**	**15489.43**	**28027.79**	**31162.23**	**34430.03**
按行业分组	By sector					
批发业	Wholesale Trade	806.03	1324.10	4461.83	4963.59	5707.65
零售业	Retail Trade	2819.34	14165.33	23565.96	26198.64	28722.38
按规模分组	By Size of Enterprises					
限额以上企业和个体户	**Enterprises above Designated Size and Individuals**	**885.95**	**5715.99**	**12612.60**	**13799.03**	**14562.91**
食品、饮料、烟酒类	Food, Beverages, Tobacco and Liquor	165.92	568.04	1233.58	1391.76	1373.02
粮油类	Grain and Edible Oil	10.15	86.63	205.89	238.61	204.23
肉禽蛋类	Meat, Poultry and Eggs	16.79	61.47	166.87	188.99	172.12
饮料类	Beverages	10.39	58.47	138.50	155.36	155.94
烟酒类	Tobacco and Liquor	46.40	109.81	201.38	232.62	226.00
其它食品类	Other Food	82.19	251.66	520.94	576.18	614.73
服装鞋帽、针纺织品类	Garments,Footwear,Headgear,Knitwear and Textiles	93.50	483.18	1250.76	1286.79	1202.44
服装类	Garments	66.81	347.13	844.85	870.94	810.89
鞋帽类	Footwear and Headgear	14.13	89.13	274.50	276.15	278.29
针、纺织品类	Knitwear and Textiles	12.56	46.92	131.41	139.70	113.26
化妆品类	Cosmetics	14.67	82.61	173.18	182.98	191.56
金银珠宝类	Gold, Silver and Jewelry	13.73	69.64	235.28	250.23	269.43
日用品类	Daily-use Articles	58.72	193.02	586.30	667.83	708.55
#洗涤用品类	Detergents	11.19	65.13			
儿童玩具类	Toys for Children	3.28	13.09	35.60	30.90	28.17
五金、电料类	Hardware and Electrical Appliances	5.86	24.38	126.26	148.13	136.77
体育、娱乐用品类	Sports and Recreational Articles	7.11	22.57	70.84	85.87	93.27
书报杂志类	Newspapers and Magazines	14.30	26.78	51.52	51.86	50.77
电子出版物及音像制品类	E-journals and Video Products	4.25	6.74	15.40	14.98	12.85
家用电器和音像器材类	Household Appliances and Video Appliances	73.71	431.41	716.41	771.95	852.14
中西药品类	Traditional Chinese and Western Medicines	58.31	290.46	608.14	692.94	772.76
#西药	Western Medicines	33.25	196.54	415.19	473.61	530.51
中草药及中成药	Traditional Chinese Medicines	15.12	40.37	87.85	84.74	97.44
文化办公用品类	Articles for Cultural and Office Use	14.78	67.13	357.54	401.89	473.91
家具类	Furniture	8.57	32.18	149.28	180.95	192.41
通讯器材类	Communication Appliances	5.18	79.31	444.81	504.94	610.91
煤炭及制品类	Coal and Related Products	0.32	6.42	28.87	29.49	5.19
木材及制品类	Timber and Related Products	0.35				
石油及制品类	Petroleum and Related Products	132.79	1291.71	1969.25	1945.00	2075.51
化工材料及制品类	Chemical Materials and Products	2.91				
金属材料类	Metal Materials	2.27				
建筑及装潢材料类	Construction and Decoration Materials	3.36	39.59	150.21	169.97	174.02
机电产品及设备类	Mechanical and Electrical Products and Equipment	17.48	35.04	146.90	151.67	146.16
汽车类	Motor Vehicles	112.71	1852.54	3773.61	4310.52	4609.77
种子饲料类	Seeds and Feedstuff					
棉麻类	Cotton and Hemp			0.16	0.11	0.07
其它类	Others	75.15	113.24	524.30	559.17	611.40
限额以下企业和个体户	**Enterprises below Designated Size and Individuals**	**2739.42**	**9773.44**	**15415.19**	**17363.20**	**19867.12**

16-8 各市批发零售业商品销售总额

Total Sales of Enterprises in Wholesale and Retail Trades by City

单位：亿元 (100 million yuan)

市别	City	2016			2017		
		销售总额 Total Sales	批发额 Wholesale Trade	零售额 Retail Trade	销售总额 Total Sales	批发额 Wholesale Trade	零售额 Retail Trade
广　州	Guangzhou	55972.75	48373.07	7599.68	62164.66	53905.31	8259.35
深　圳	Shenzhen	24860.15	19988.08	4872.07	31486.79	26151.51	5335.28
珠　海	Zhuhai	4915.82	4013.92	901.90	5657.00	4659.07	997.93
汕　头	Shantou	2917.30	1488.73	1428.57	3352.24	1762.95	1589.29
佛　山	Foshan	10201.78	7503.77	2698.01	11885.64	8898.77	2986.87
韶　关	Shaoguan	985.57	408.93	576.64	1115.32	491.58	623.74
河　源	Heyuan	590.88	95.25	495.63	639.31	94.45	544.86
梅　州	Meizhou	779.59	204.98	574.61	834.47	203.11	631.36
惠　州	Huizhou	2022.24	906.51	1115.73	2301.25	1056.80	1244.45
汕　尾	Shanwei	591.20	115.50	475.70	637.49	126.82	510.67
东　莞	Dongguan	6192.34	3883.37	2308.97	6921.09	4410.09	2511.00
中　山	Zhongshan	2587.73	1492.74	1094.99	2787.30	1595.63	1191.67
江　门	Jiangmen	1901.29	856.21	1045.08	2098.71	939.92	1158.79
阳　江	Yangjiang	759.44	187.62	571.82	812.12	194.72	617.40
湛　江	Zhanjiang	2987.59	1717.51	1270.08	3180.60	1780.75	1399.85
茂　名	Maoming	2810.18	1587.22	1222.96	3041.61	1709.58	1332.03
肇　庆	Zhaoqing	1314.59	656.04	658.55	1384.44	654.85	729.59
清　远	Qingyuan	878.43	301.49	576.94	990.03	360.02	630.01
潮　州	Chaozhou	906.20	452.45	453.75	936.80	437.36	499.44
揭　阳	Jieyang	2044.58	1106.87	937.71	2270.21	1234.52	1035.69
云　浮	Yunfu	644.03	329.63	314.40	670.13	322.04	348.09
按经济区域分	By Region						
珠三角	Pearl River Delta	109968.69	87673.71	22294.98	126686.88	102271.95	24414.93
东　翼	Eastern Region	6459.28	3163.55	3295.73	7196.74	3561.65	3635.09
西　翼	Western Region	6557.21	3492.35	3064.86	7034.33	3685.05	3349.28
山　区	Mountainous Region	3878.50	1340.28	2538.22	4249.26	1471.20	2778.06

16－9 限额以上批发企业商品购、销、存总额（2017年）

Total Purchases, Sales and Inventory of Enterprises above Designated Size in Wholesale Trade (2017)

单位：亿元 (100 million yuan)

项目	Item	企业单位数（个）Number of Enterprises (unit)	购进总额 Total Purchases	#进口 Imports	商品销售总额 Total Sales of Commodities
批发业合计	**Total Wholesale Trade**	**18598**	**66862.81**	**6471.95**	**69515.19**
#国有控股	State-owned and State-controlled Enterprises	895	19765.10	1143.73	20035.28
按登记注册类型分组	By Status of Registration				
内资企业	Domestic-funded Enterprises	17161	60138.53	5661.75	61951.09
国有企业	State-owned Enterprises	239	563.10	14.99	643.69
集体企业	Collective-owned Enterprises	58	37.57		41.29
股份合作企业	Share-holding Cooperative Enterprises	19	13.14	0.83	14.08
联营企业	Joint-operation Enterprises	8	7.37		9.27
国有联营企业	State-owned Joint-operation Enterprises	2	2.37		3.77
集体联营企业	Collective Joint-operation Enterprises	2	3.16		3.38
国有与集体联营企业	State-collective Joint-operation Enterprises	1	0.62		0.74
其他联营企业	Other Joint-operation Enterprises	3	1.22		1.38
有限责任公司	Limited Liability Corporations	6194	33682.16	3117.83	34653.92
国有独资企业	State Sole Investment Enterprises	153	5880.91	64.64	6130.15
其他有限责任公司	Other Limited Liability Companies	6041	27801.25	3053.19	28523.77
股份有限公司	Share-holding Corporations Ltd.	344	5242.11	386.80	4665.26
私营企业	Private Enterprises	10249	20555.89	2140.92	21876.69
私营独资企业	Private Sole Investment Enterprises	36	20.44	0.08	22.91
私营合伙企业	Private Partnership Enterprises	5	1.50		1.61
私营有限责任公司	Private Limited Liability Corporations	9969	19893.52	2120.12	21167.54
私营股份有限公司	Private Share-holding Corporations Ltd.	239	640.43	20.72	684.63
其他企业	Other Enterprises	50	37.19	0.38	46.89
港、澳、台商投资企业	Enterprises with Investment from Hong Kong, Macao and Taiwan	937	3042.14	409.70	3459.23
合资经营企业	Joint Ventures	107	535.26	27.25	594.08
合作经营企业	Cooperative Enterprises	7	19.83		21.97
独资经营企业	Sole Investment Enterprises	778	2427.62	371.50	2760.84
投资股份有限公司	Share-holding Corporations Ltd.	28	38.48	7.79	55.28
其他港、澳、台商投资企业	Others	17	20.95	3.16	27.06
外商投资企业	Enterprises with Foreign Investment	500	3682.14	400.50	4104.87
中外合资经营企业	Sino-foreign Joint Ventures	72	1011.04	105.17	1255.50
中外合作经营企业	Sino-foreign Cooperative Enterprises	6	19.76	8.09	21.77
外资企业	Foreign-funded Enterprises	384	2265.66	284.88	2422.93
外商投资股份有限公司	Share-holding Corporations Ltd.	14	238.86	0.48	247.87
其他外商投资企业	Others	24	146.82	1.88	156.80
按国民经济行业分组	By Economic Sector				
农、林、牧、渔产品批发	Wholesale of Farm and Livestock Products	359	1052.09	133.32	1133.41
食品、饮料及烟草制品批发业	Wholesale of Food, Beverages and Tobacco Products	1754	4733.61	256.33	5752.36
#米、面制品及食用油批发业	Wholesale of Rice, Flour Products and Edible Oil	247	571.84	67.66	587.60
烟草制品批发业	Wholesale of Tobacco Products	46	1140.75	5.35	1544.57
纺织、服装及日用品批发业	Wholesale of Textiles, Garments and Daily-use Products	2671	4268.68	141.26	4904.79
#服装批发业	Wholesale of Garments	532	655.31	19.05	793.70
家用视听设备批发	Wholesale of Household Audio-visual Equipments	169	589.07	5.87	633.16
日用家电批发	Wholesale of Household Appliances	291	567.11	16.69	611.54
文化、体育用品及器材批发业	Wholesale of Cultural and Sports Articles and Appliances	830	2197.98	91.77	2426.98
医药及医疗器材批发业	Wholesale of Medicines and Medical Appliances and Chemical Products	1437	4392.77	1456.23	3571.85
矿产品、建材及化工产品批发	Wholesale of Mineral Products, Building Materials	6354	32525.69	1884.98	32792.38
#煤炭及制品批发业	Wholesale of Coal and Related Products	249	1311.44	96.08	1374.38
石油及制品批发业	Wholesale of Petroleum and Related Products	757	10058.00	1172.82	9458.04
金属及金属矿批发业	Wholesale of Metal and Related Products	1746	12264.43	156.01	12586.11
建材批发业	Wholesale of Building Materials	1003	2717.49	97.57	2863.60
化肥批发业	Wholesale of Chemical Fertilizers	109	137.73	8.96	147.60
机械设备、五金交电及电子产品批发业	Wholesale of Machinery, Hardware, Electric and Electronic Products	3889	13711.15	1699.83	14694.20
#汽车及零配件批发	Wholesale of Motor Vehicles and Parts	377	4404.91	116.19	4810.36
计算机、软件及辅助设备批发业	Wholesale of Computers, Software and Assistant Equipments	360	970.92	97.42	1033.75
贸易经纪与代理	Trade Broker and Agency	658	3129.52	706.26	3291.26
其他批发业	Other Wholesale Trades	646	851.32	101.97	947.96

16-9 续表 continued

单位：亿元 (100 million yuan)

项目	Item	批发额 Wholesale Trade	#出口 Exports	零售额 Retail Trade	年末库存总额 Inventory at the Year-end
批发业合计	**Total Wholesale Trade**	**67309.71**	**4515.47**	**2205.48**	**4083.74**
#国有控股	State-owned and State-controlled Enterprises	19484.21	635.57	551.07	776.51
按登记注册类型分组	By Status of Registration				
内资企业	Domestic-funded Enterprises	60033.24	4198.39	1917.85	3506.77
国有企业	State-owned Enterprises	626.24	25.55	17.45	88.60
集体企业	Collective-owned Enterprises	35.81	3.03	5.48	3.25
股份合作企业	Share-holding Cooperative Enterprises	13.52		0.56	0.78
联营企业	Joint-operation Enterprises	9.05		0.22	0.79
国有联营企业	State-owned Joint-operation Enterprises	3.55		0.22	0.47
集体联营企业	Collective Joint-operation Enterprises	3.38			0.05
国有与集体联营企业	State-collective Joint-operation Enterprises	0.74			0.03
其他联营企业	Other Joint-operation Enterprises	1.38			0.24
有限责任公司	Limited Liability Corporations	33827.35	1606.12	826.57	1643.52
国有独资企业	State Sole Investment Enterprises	6067.90	120.35	62.25	229.94
其他有限责任公司	Other Limited Liability Companies	27759.45	1485.77	764.32	1413.58
股份有限公司	Share-holding Corporations Ltd.	4234.87	554.81	430.39	266.53
私营企业	Private Enterprises	21243.63	2008.63	633.06	1502.68
私营独资企业	Private Sole Investment Enterprises	19.96	0.33	2.95	1.29
私营合伙企业	Private Partnership Enterprises	1.53		0.08	0.13
私营有限责任公司	Private Limited Liability Corporations	20551.04	1968.12	616.50	1444.37
私营股份有限公司	Private Share-holding Corporations Ltd.	671.10	40.18	13.53	56.89
其他企业	Other Enterprises	42.77	0.25	4.12	0.62
港、澳、台商投资企业	Enterprises with Investment from Hong Kong, Macao and Taiwan	3234.02	114.50	225.21	324.70
合资经营企业	Joint Ventures	562.87	5.48	31.21	39.39
合作经营企业	Cooperative Enterprises	21.29	9.75	0.68	0.81
独资经营企业	Sole Investment Enterprises	2573.91	98.77	186.93	275.52
投资股份有限公司	Share-holding Corporations Ltd.	51.18	0.47	4.10	7.94
其他港、澳、台商投资企业	Others	24.77	0.03	2.29	1.04
外商投资企业	Enterprises with Foreign Investment	4042.45	202.58	62.42	252.27
中外合资经营企业	Sino-foreign Joint Ventures	1234.36	37.17	21.14	70.77
中外合作经营企业	Sino-foreign Cooperative Enterprises	21.75	0.01	0.02	0.77
外资企业	Foreign-funded Enterprises	2383.03	163.91	39.90	171.76
外商投资股份有限公司	Share-holding Corporations Ltd.	247.21	0.75	0.66	7.56
其他外商投资企业	Others	156.10	0.74	0.70	1.41
按国民经济行业分组	By Economic Sector				
农、林、牧、渔产品批发	Wholesale of Farm and Livestock Products	1107.33	28.15	26.08	103.21
食品、饮料及烟草制品批发业	Wholesale of Food, Beverages and Tobacco Products	5602.32	130.79	150.04	481.29
#米、面制品及食用油批发业	Wholesale of Rice, Flour Products and Edible Oil	544.48	1.10	43.12	212.19
烟草制品批发业	Wholesale of Tobacco Products	1540.58	1.89	3.99	48.44
纺织、服装及日用品批发业	Wholesale of Textiles, Garments and Daily-use Products	4585.68	1126.14	319.11	413.42
#服装批发业	Wholesale of Garments	706.56	240.97	87.14	82.93
家用视听设备批发	Wholesale of Household Audio-visual Equipments	620.28	54.76	12.88	31.82
日用家电批发	Wholesale of Household Appliances	592.34	48.82	19.20	79.47
文化、体育用品及器材批发业	Wholesale of Cultural and Sports Articles and Appliances	2332.60	73.64	94.38	520.40
医药及医疗器材批发业	Wholesale of Medicines and Medical Appliances and Chemical Products	3456.36	41.93	115.49	311.94
矿产品、建材及化工产品批发	Wholesale of Mineral Products, Building Materials	31981.96	736.78	810.42	1198.36
#煤炭及制品批发业	Wholesale of Coal and Related Products	1328.47	2.65	45.91	61.77
石油及制品批发业	Wholesale of Petroleum and Related Products	9017.73	344.54	440.31	353.06
金属及金属矿批发业	Wholesale of Metal and Related Products	12424.38	94.22	161.73	316.29
建材批发业	Wholesale of Building Materials	2821.97	160.81	41.63	111.95
化肥批发业	Wholesale of Chemical Fertilizers	142.19	0.84	5.41	14.17
机械设备、五金交电及电子产品批发业	Wholesale of Machinery, Hardware, Electric and Electronic Products	14212.23	1435.49	481.97	860.94
#汽车及零配件批发	Wholesale of Motor Vehicles and Parts	4669.01	53.22	141.35	59.58
计算机、软件及辅助设备批发业	Wholesale of Computers, Software and Assistant Equipments	993.09	115.52	40.66	79.89
贸易经纪与代理	Trade Broker and Agency	3154.11	824.23	137.15	117.68
其他批发业	Other Wholesale Trades	877.12	118.32	70.84	76.50

16−10 限额以上零售企业商品购、销、存总额（2017年）
Total Purchases, Sales and Inventory of Enterprises above Designated Size in Retail Trade (2017)

单位：亿元 (100 million yuan)

项目	Item	企业单位数(个) Number of Enterprises (unit)	购进总额 Total Purchases	#进口 Imports	商品销售总额 Total Sales of Commodities
零售业合计	**Total Retail Trade**	**8797**	**10751.31**	**408.71**	**12940.99**
#国有控股	State-owned and State-controlled Enterprises	459	1470.12	42.22	2226.79
按登记注册类型分组	By Status of Registration				
内资企业	Domestic-funded Enterprises	8376	8109.20	320.81	9956.11
国有企业	State-owned Enterprises	98	78.44		82.19
集体企业	Collective-owned Enterprises	179	76.80	0.01	88.01
股份合作企业	Share-holding Cooperative Enterprises	28	5.47		6.21
联营企业	Joint-operation Enterprises	25	20.63		25.40
国有联营企业	State-owned Joint-operation Enterprises	5	2.24		4.62
集体联营企业	Collective Joint-operation Enterprises	8	12.94		13.72
国有与集体联营企业	State-collective Joint-operation Enterprises	4	1.32		1.69
其他联营企业	Other Joint-operation Enterprises	8	4.13		5.37
有限责任公司	Limited Liability Corporations	3791	4599.65	218.59	5376.00
国有独资企业	State Sole Investment Enterprises	53	106.43	25.66	138.90
其他有限责任公司	Other Limited Liability Companies	3738	4493.22	192.93	5237.10
股份有限公司	Share-holding Corporations Ltd.	191	455.43	1.94	1125.23
私营企业	Private Enterprises	3999	2854.67	100.27	3232.42
私营独资企业	Private Sole Investment Enterprises	402	88.74		100.15
私营合伙企业	Private Partnership Enterprises	32	5.99		6.47
私营有限责任公司	Private Limited Liability Corporations	3475	2696.70	94.01	3038.98
私营股份有限公司	Private Share-holding Corporations Ltd.	90	63.24	6.26	86.82
其他企业	Other Enterprises	65	18.11		20.65
港、澳、台商投资企业	Enterprises with Investment from Hong Kong, Macao and Taiwan	251	909.47	62.40	1054.57
合资经营企业	Joint Ventures	46	369.46	15.05	435.34
合作经营企业	Cooperative Enterprises	14	12.98		17.11
独资经营企业	Sole Investment Enterprises	184	495.02	47.35	567.69
投资股份有限公司	Share-holding Corporations Ltd.	5	30.48		31.57
其他港澳台投资企业	Others	2	1.53		2.86
外商投资企业	Enterprises with Foreign Investment	170	1732.64	25.50	1930.31
中外合资经营企业	Sino-foreign Joint Ventures	53	580.18	11.07	713.86
中外合作经营企业	Sino-foreign Cooperative Enterprises	6	41.32	0.67	48.37
外资企业	Foreign-funded Enterprises	92	386.22	11.27	450.07
外商投资股份有限公司	Share-holding Corporations Ltd.	7	11.18		20.78
其他外商投资企业	Other Foreign Enterprises	12	713.74	2.49	697.23
按国民经济行业分组	By Economic Sector				
综合零售业	Comprehensive Retail Trade	778	1663.02	9.71	1870.46
#百货零售	Retail of General Merchandise	364	792.36	9.09	915.90
超级市场零售	Retail in Supermarkets	319	783.50	0.61	850.05
食品、饮料及烟草制品专门零售业	Retail of Food, Beverages and Tobacco Products	549	282.56	11.18	439.89
纺织、服装及日用品专门零售业	Retail of Textiles, Garments and Daily-use Products	623	409.30	14.01	630.23
#服装零售	Retail of Garments	277	192.28	7.05	340.71
文化、体育用品及器材专门零售业	Retail of Cultural and Sports Articles and Appliances	380	155.10	0.51	188.78
#体育用品及器材零售	Retail of Sports Articles and Appliances	20	11.51	0.38	17.99
图书、报刊零售	Retail of Books	135	60.04		65.58
医药及医疗器材专门零售业	Retail of Medicines and Medical Appliances	404	406.40	0.75	485.45
#西药零售	Retail of Western Medicines	273	344.42	0.02	389.54
中药零售	Retail of Traditional Chinese Medicines	59	19.04	0.08	26.94
汽车、摩托车、燃料及零配件零售业	Retail of Motor Vehicles, Motorcycles and Parts	3836	5467.28	341.26	6658.82
#汽车新车零售	Retail of Motor Vehicles	2550	4445.18	333.06	4718.41
机动车燃油零售	Retail of Motor Vehicle Fuels	907	874.03	1.11	1773.60
家用电器及电子产品专门零售业	Retail of Household Appliances and Electronic Products	984	800.45	6.82	892.19
#家用视听设备零售	Retail of Household Audio-visual Equipments	73	140.89	0.03	149.13
日用家电零售	Retail of Household Appliances	362	390.07	2.69	415.03
计算机、软件及辅助设备零售业	Retail of Computers, Software and Assistant Equipments	294	72.28	0.91	86.25
通讯设备零售	Retail of Communication Equipments	117	132.43	0.77	145.93
五金、家具及室内装修材料专门零售业	Retail of Hardware, Furniture and Interior Decoration Materials	649	237.43	2.76	283.54
货摊、无店铺及其他零售业	Stall,Non-shop and Other Retails	594	1329.77	21.71	1491.63

16−10 续表 continued

单位：亿元 (100 million yuan)

项 目	Item	批发额 Wholesale Trade	#出口 Exports	零售额 Retail Trade	年末库存总额 Inventory at the Year-end
零售业合计	**Total Retail Trade**	**1495.71**	**12.92**	**11445.28**	**1378.67**
#国有控股	State-owned and State-controlled Enterprises	406.02		1820.77	170.59
按登记注册类型分组	By Status of Registration				
内资企业	Domestic-funded Enterprises	1328.50	9.01	8627.61	1067.59
国有企业	State-owned Enterprises	16.98		65.21	12.92
集体企业	Collective-owned Enterprises	16.29		71.72	4.88
股份合作企业	Share-holding Cooperative Enterprises	1.66		4.55	0.40
联营企业	Joint-operation Enterprises	9.64		15.76	0.65
国有联营企业	State-owned Joint-operation Enterprises	0.06		4.56	0.14
集体联营企业	Collective Joint-operation Enterprises	9.54		4.18	0.21
国有与集体联营企业	State-collective Joint-operation Enterprises			1.69	0.05
其他联营企业	Other Joint-operation Enterprises	0.04		5.33	0.25
有限责任公司	Limited Liability Corporations	634.39	3.13	4741.61	567.96
国有独资企业	State Sole Investment Enterprises	25.62		113.28	15.84
其他有限责任公司	Other Limited Liability Companies	608.77	3.13	4628.33	552.12
股份有限公司	Share-holding Corporations Ltd.	226.70	0.08	898.53	119.69
私营企业	Private Enterprises	420.99	5.80	2811.43	360.16
私营独资企业	Private Sole Investment Enterprises	8.39		91.76	4.73
私营合伙企业	Private Partnership Enterprises	0.56		5.91	0.28
私营有限责任公司	Private Limited Liability Corporations	394.26	5.72	2644.72	342.54
私营股份有限公司	Private Share-holding Corporations Ltd.	17.78	0.08	69.04	12.61
其他企业	Other Enterprises	1.85		18.80	0.93
港、澳、台商投资企业	Enterprises with Investment from Hong Kong, Macao and Taiwan	70.41	3.64	984.16	207.61
合资经营企业	Joint Ventures	23.29	0.46	412.05	92.11
合作经营企业	Cooperative Enterprises	0.27		16.84	1.08
独资经营企业	Sole Investment Enterprises	46.85	3.18	520.84	112.36
投资股份有限公司	Share-holding Corporations Ltd.			31.57	1.73
其他港澳台投资企业	Others			2.86	0.33
外商投资企业	Enterprises with Foreign Investment	96.80	0.27	1833.51	103.47
中外合资经营企业	Sino-foreign Joint Ventures	75.56	0.02	638.30	41.99
中外合作经营企业	Sino-foreign Cooperative Enterprises	0.82		47.55	5.35
外资企业	Foreign-funded Enterprises	16.51	0.25	433.56	46.84
外商投资股份有限公司	Share-holding Corporations Ltd.	3.16		17.62	3.60
其他外商投资企业	Other Foreign Enterprises	0.75		696.48	5.69
按国民经济行业分组	By Economic Sector				
综合零售业	Comprehensive Retail Trade	119.53	0.01	1750.93	198.17
#百货零售	Retail of General Merchandise	10.52	0.01	905.38	118.67
超级市场零售	Retail in Supermarkets	104.15		745.90	67.08
食品、饮料及烟草制品专门零售业	Retail of Food, Beverages and Tobacco Products	75.80	0.91	364.09	47.95
纺织、服装及日用品专门零售业	Retail of Textiles, Garments and Daily-use Products	106.79	3.40	523.44	156.24
#服装零售	Retail of Garments	51.28	1.52	289.43	86.28
文化、体育用品及器材专门零售业	Retail of Cultural and Sports Articles and Appliances	48.55	0.58	140.23	42.86
#体育用品及器材零售	Retail of Sports Articles and Appliances	1.14		16.85	1.55
图书零售	Retail of Books	16.89		48.69	15.53
医药及医疗器材专门零售业	Retail of Medicines and Medical Appliances	161.59		323.86	75.33
#西药零售	Retail of Western Medicines	110.16		279.38	65.28
中药零售	Retail of Traditional Chinese Medicines	5.16		21.78	4.28
汽车、摩托车、燃料及零配件零售业	Retail of Motor Vehicles, Motorcycles and Parts	598.87	5.15	6059.95	600.99
#汽车新车零售	Retail of Motor Vehicles	294.68	4.68	4423.73	525.22
机动车燃油零售	Retail of Motor Vehicle Fuels	278.40		1495.20	47.64
家用电器及电子产品专门零售业	Retail of Household Appliances and Electronic Products	173.36	0.05	718.83	163.94
#家用视听设备零售	Retail of Household Audio-visual Equipments	7.94		141.19	7.04
日用家电零售	Retail of Household Appliances	63.81		351.22	123.44
计算机、软件及辅助设备零售业	Retail of Computers, Software and Assistant Equipments	22.52		63.73	6.05
通讯设备零售	Retail of Communication Equipments	59.07	0.01	86.86	19.55
五金、家具及室内装修材料专门零售业	Retail of Hardware, Furniture and Interior Decoration Materials	65.02	0.44	218.52	26.90
货摊、无店铺及其他零售业	Stall,Non-shop and Other Retails	146.20	2.38	1345.43	66.29

16－11 各市限额以上批发零售企业商品购、销、存总额（2017年）

Total Purchases, Sales and Inventory of Enterprises above Designated Size in Wholesale and Retail Trades by City (2017)

单位：万元 (10000 yuan)

市别	City	商品购进总额 Total Purchases	#进口 Imports	商品销售总额 Total Sales	批发额 Wholesale Trade	#出口 Exports	零售额 Retail Trade	年末库存总额 Inventory at the Year-end
合　计	**Total**	**776141134**	**68806518**	**824561864**	**688054287**	**45283944**	**136507577**	**54624089**
批发业	**Wholesale Trade**	**668628075**	**64719463**	**695151944**	**673097144**	**45154697**	**22054800**	**40837418**
广　州	Guangzhou	251155979	12179582	257610432	252045535	8353735	5564897	12268819
深　圳	Shenzhen	206275267	27990615	219601143	210771775	17125540	8829368	14694455
珠　海	Zhuhai	24183400	5775282	25633270	24850137	2768086	783133	1931023
汕　头	Shantou	12374673	874873	13809364	13047295	397749	762069	1797166
佛　山	Foshan	77887827	13770752	70954583	69300140	5869050	1654443	3649406
韶　关	Shaoguan	4497572	12569	5079276	4766630	37307	312646	181798
河　源	Heyuan	554125	10596	691023	685612	32062	5411	41354
梅　州	Meizhou	1041170	601	1268695	1244272	31668	24423	60875
惠　州	Huizhou	4998751	31362	5990747	5538152	257282	452595	332425
汕　尾	Shanwei	478060	3098	588260	581632		6628	35874
东　莞	Dongguan	36176450	2619520	38979088	37774642	4692550	1204446	2996308
中　山	Zhongshan	8992760	388758	9620051	9478074	2869552	141977	672291
江　门	Jiangmen	7505768	455909	8193021	7926240	2121617	266781	400691
阳　江	Yangjiang	916601	3693	1264608	1216790	250239	47818	63668
湛　江	Zhanjiang	6312156	88038	7231417	7022903	111811	208514	394878
茂　名	Maoming	13575344	105902	14573048	14402887	2566	170161	613096
肇　庆	Zhaoqing	1375393	328464	1743137	1522884	119283	220253	121387
清　远	Qingyuan	2850074	4889	3061561	2580750	34859	480811	184475
潮　州	Chaozhou	775003	14564	1014815	934246	12607	80569	44677
揭　阳	Jieyang	5245424	5435	6208695	5380066	67134	828629	198091
云　浮	Yunfu	1456278	54961	2035710	2026482		9228	154661
零售业	**Retail Trade**	**107513059**	**4087055**	**129409920**	**14957143**	**129247**	**114452777**	**13786671**
广　州	Guangzhou	30946655	1144668	36615500	4456547	45957	32158953	2861091
深　圳	Shenzhen	26496170	1513831	30418827	3941420	38714	26477407	5670026
珠　海	Zhuhai	2875470	136924	3719853	918246	5233	2801607	355594
汕　头	Shantou	3090821	39937	3334850	443605		2891245	326251
佛　山	Foshan	8333382	173747	9176222	1357204	26105	7819018	1406161
韶　关	Shaoguan	808661		936389	18992		917397	95223
河　源	Heyuan	719292	13734	1208598	118272		1090326	85120
梅　州	Meizhou	812102	20816	1287884	89932		1197952	144272
惠　州	Huizhou	3871100	100468	5419384	747590	1759	4671794	270965
汕　尾	Shanwei	270729		422057	55208		366849	30537
东　莞	Dongguan	10474464	572291	12434886	362684	5626	12072202	877402
中　山	Zhongshan	4567562	126225	6382583	210722	157	6171861	481339
江　门	Jiangmen	3083503	18411	3637627	282355	1248	3355272	274237
阳　江	Yangjiang	477423		896814	98172		798642	54000
湛　江	Zhanjiang	1539337	14416	2304545	374968		1929577	168966
茂　名	Maoming	1285640	8223	2125014	333669		1791345	250145
肇　庆	Zhaoqing	2460545	155059	2720723	270407	334	2450316	127889
清　远	Qingyuan	954231	27050	1031443	43442	2749	988001	92379
潮　州	Chaozhou	524576	14261	667540	41170		626370	47055
揭　阳	Jieyang	3306346	1039	3781059	686708	1365	3094351	95305
云　浮	Yunfu	615050	5955	888122	105830		782292	72714

16－12 限额以上批发零售业个体户商品购、销、存总额（2017年）
Total Purchases, Sales and Inventory of Enterprises above Designated Size in Wholesale and Retail Trade Individuals(2017)

单位：万元 (10000 yuan)

项 目	Item	单位数（个）Number of Enterprises (unit)	购进总额 Total Purchases	商品销售总额 Total Sales of Commodities
合计	**Total**	**3778**	**17314348**	**20630295**
批发业	**Wholesale Trade**	**1479**	**12301990**	**14776265**
农、林、牧、渔产品批发业	Wholesale of Farm and Livestock Products	9	68494	76476
食品、饮料及烟草制品批发业	Wholesale of Food, Beverages and Tobacco Products	362	3077287	3476348
纺织、服装及家庭用品批发业	Wholesale of Textiles, Garments and Household Products	563	4127264	5225002
纺织品、针织品及原料批发	Wholesale of Textiles,Knitwear and Raw Material	9	86742	96916
服装批发	Wholesale of Garments	248	1009681	1818709
灯具、装饰物品批发	Wholesale of Lamps and Lanterns,Decorative Items	130	1672304	1824250
文化、体育用品及器材批发业	Wholesale of Cultural and Sports Articles and Appliances	124	2620202	3230561
首饰、工艺品及收藏品批发	Wholesale of Jewelry,Art Work and Collector	121	2602374	3210610
医药及医疗器材批发业	Wholesale of Medicines and Medical Appliances and Chemical Products	54	540194	598576
中药批发	Wholesale of Traditional Chinese Medicine	54	540194	598576
矿产品、建材及化工产品批发	Wholesale of Mineral Products, Building Materials	42	284127	341763
机械设备、五金产品及电子产品批发业	Wholesale of Machinery, Hardware, Electric and Electronic Products	318	1540778	1778545
电气设备批发	Wholesale of Electric Apparatus	95	245578	267279
计算机、软件及辅助设备批发	Wholesale of Computers, Software and Assistant Equipments	50	286384	372052
通讯设备批发	Wholesale of Communications Equipments	19	38646	43088
其他批发业	Other Wholesale Trades	7	43644	48994
零售业	**Retail Trade**	**2299**	**5012358**	**5854030**
综合零售业	Comprehensive Retail Trade	329	325924	398826
百货零售	Retail of General Merchandise	181	155737	190755
超级市场零售	Retail in Supermarkets	91	106771	129241
食品、饮料及烟草制品专门零售业	Retail of Food, Beverages and Tobacco Products	323	326062	435459
纺织、服装及日用品专门零售业	Retail of Textiles, Garments and Daily-use Products	272	1284990	1446808
纺织品及针织品零售	Retail of Textiles and Knitwear	30	35285	49234
服装零售	Retail of Garments	36	38220	47449
鞋帽零售	Retail of Footwear and Headgear	48	498365	564999
文化、体育用品及器材专门零售业	Retail of Cultural and Sports Articles and	260	1281368	1395538
珠宝首饰零售	Retail of Bijouterie	58	54879	71222
工艺美术品及收藏品零售	Retail of Art Work and Collector	161	1150237	1236247
医药及医疗器材专门零售业	Retail of Medicines and Medical Appliances	38	44725	59705
西药零售	Retail of Western Medicines	38	44725	59705
汽车、摩托车、零配件和燃料及其他动力销售	Retail of Motor Vehicles, Motorcycles and Parts	76	92232	110527
家用电器及电子产品专门零售业	Retail of Household Appliances and and Electronic Products	498	938139	1125999
计算机、软件及辅助设备零售	Retail of Computers, Software and Assistant Equipments	241	520436	636376
通信设备零售	Retail of Communication Equipments	82	168768	189130
五金、家具及室内装修材料专门	Retail of Hardware, Furniture and Interior	468	668569	817296
货摊、无店铺及其他零售业	Stall,Non-shop and Other Retails	35	50349	63872

16−12 续表 continued

单位：万元 (10000 yuan)

项 目	Item	批发额 Wholesale Trade	零售额 Retail Trade	年末库存总额 Inventory at the Year-end
合计	**Total**	**14070099**	**6560196**	**573742**
批发业	**Wholesale Trade**	**13951055**	**825210**	**278726**
农、林、牧、渔产品批发业	Wholesale of Farm and Livestock Products	72393	4083	341
食品、饮料及烟草制品批发业	Wholesale of Food, Beverages and Tobacco Products	3309269	167079	106242
纺织、服装及家庭用品批发业	Wholesale of Textiles, Garments and Household Products	5027486	197516	73125
纺织品、针织品及原料批发	Wholesale of Textiles,Knitwear and Raw Material	96328	588	1165
服装批发	Wholesale of Garments	1650269	168440	50535
灯具、装饰物品批发	Wholesale of Lamps and Lanterns,Decorative Items	1809584	14666	11919
文化、体育用品及器材批发业	Wholesale of Cultural and Sports Articles and Appliances	3070569	159992	42559
首饰、工艺品及收藏品批发	Wholesale of Jewelry,Art Work and Collector	3052398	158212	42521
医药及医疗器材批发业	Wholesale of Medicines and Medical Appliances and Chemical Products	596981	1595	25165
中药批发	Wholesale of Traditional Chinese Medicine	596981	1595	25165
矿产品、建材及化工产品批发	Wholesale of Mineral Products, Building Materials	332550	9213	5797
机械设备、五金产品及电子产品批发业	Wholesale of Machinery, Hardware, Electric and Electronic Products	1501839	276706	25275
电气设备批发	Wholesale of Electric Apparatus	204514	62765	902
计算机、软件及辅助设备批发	Wholesale of Computers, Software and Assistant Equipments	287766	84286	4728
通讯设备批发	Wholesale of Communications Equipments	33066	10022	178
其他批发业	Other Wholesale Trades	39968	9026	222
零售业	**Retail Trade**	**119044**	**5734986**	**295016**
综合零售业	Comprehensive Retail Trade	9496	389330	33655
百货零售	Retail of General Merchandise	3743	187012	13215
超级市场零售	Retail in Supermarkets	2997	126244	14162
食品、饮料及烟草制品专门零售业	Retail of Food, Beverages and Tobacco Products	12332	423127	18151
纺织、服装及日用品专门零售业	Retail of Textiles, Garments and Daily-use Products	4363	1442445	30303
纺织品及针织品零售	Retail of Textiles and Knitwear	26	49208	2377
服装零售	Retail of Garments	1922	45527	3716
鞋帽零售	Retail of Footwear and Headgear		564999	4946
文化、体育用品及器材专门零售业	Retail of Cultural and Sports Articles and	10622	1384916	43394
珠宝首饰零售	Retail of Bijouterie	9389	61833	5998
工艺美术品及收藏品零售	Retail of Art Work and Collector		1236247	30125
医药及医疗器材专门零售业	Retail of Medicines and Medical Appliances	2339	57366	3092
西药零售	Retail of Western Medicines	2339	57366	3092
汽车、摩托车、零配件和燃料及其他动力销售	Retail of Motor Vehicles, Motorcycles and Parts	4750	105777	6039
家用电器及电子产品专门零售业	Retail of Household Appliances and and Electronic Products	53763	1072236	90418
计算机、软件及辅助设备零售	Retail of Computers, Software and Assistant Equipments	22372	614004	51385
通信设备零售	Retail of Communication Equipments	7342	181788	16908
五金、家具及室内装修材料专门	Retail of Hardware, Furniture and Interior	21369	795927	67119
货摊、无店铺及其他零售业	Stall,Non-shop and Other Retails	10	63862	2845

16-13 限额以上连锁批发零售业经营情况（2017年）

Business of Chain Stores above Designated Size in Wholesale and Retail Trade (2017)

项目	Item	连锁总店数(个) Number of General Chain Stores (unit)	销售总额(万元) Total Sales Revenue (10000 yuan)	#零售额(万元) Retail Sales (10000 yuan)	营业面积(平方米) Operational Area (sq.m)
批发零售业合计	**Wholesale and Retail Trade**	**308**	**34087635**	**29035083**	**14543990**
按注册登记类型分	By Status of Registration				
内资企业	Domestic-funded Enterprises	250	23374451	19268220	9184074
国有企业	State-owned Enterprises	13	4422174	2648825	980062
集体企业	Collective-owned Enterprises	3	50262	48460	14651
股份合作企业	Share-holding Cooperative Enterprises	1	33159		7124
联营企业	Joint-operation Enterprises	1	73674	73674	21706
有限责任公司	Limited Liability Corporations	127	8869558	8081055	3521749
股份有限公司	Share-holding Corporations Ltd.	27	7141621	6316663	3196738
私营企业	Private Enterprises	78	2784003	2099543	1442044
其他企业	Other Enterprises				
港、澳、台商投资企业	Enterprises with Investment from Hong Kong, Macao and Taiwan	33	4211905	3983244	2380593
合资经营企业(港或澳、台资)	Joint Ventures	7	2660028	2491065	1399482
合作经营企业(港或澳、台资)	Cooperative Enterprises	3	53166	53166	6337
港、澳、台商独资经营企业	Sole Investment Enterprises	22	1444310	1384612	947623
港、澳、台商投资股份有限公司	Share-holding Corporations Ltd.	1	54401	54401	27151
外商投资企业	Enterprises with Foreign Investment	25	6501279	5783619	2979323
中外合资经营企业	Sino-foreign Joint Ventures	13	1999953	1989241	1132179
中外合作经营企业	Sino-foreign Cooperative Enterprises	3	904854	904854	748800
外资企业	Foreign-funded Enterprises	9	3596472	2889524	1098344
其他外商投资	Others				
按零售业态分	By Type of Operation				
便利店	Convenience Store	8	512611	482602	148467
超市	Supermarket	34	1401211	1397833	1243670
大型超市	HyperMarket	18	5376098	4667815	3392450
百货商店	Department Store	14	4167572	3875056	2524221
专业店	Specialty Store	158	19227613	15596179	6249616
专卖店	Franchised Store	53	1834658	1728524	601192
家居建材店	Building Material Store	1	28965	17509	11670
其他	Others	22	1538907	1269565	372704

16-13 续表 continued

项 目	Item	从业人数(人) Number of Employed Persons (person)	连锁门店数(个) Number of Branch Chain Stores (unit)	直营店(个) Under Direct Management (unit)	加盟店(个) Through License Arrangement (unit)
批发零售业合计	**Retail Trade**	**232614**	**27542**	**16452**	**11090**
按注册登记类型分	By Status of Registration				
内资企业	Domestic-funded Enterprises	146989	22889	12485	10404
国有企业	State-owned Enterprises	13734	803	755	48
集体企业	Collective-owned Enterprises	1735	138	46	92
股份合作企业	Share-holding Cooperative Enterprises	156	29	29	
联营企业	Joint-operation Enterprises	739	188	146	42
有限责任公司	Limited Liability Corporations	62351	9203	6103	3100
股份有限公司	Share-holding Corporations Ltd.	25933	4609	2378	2231
私营企业	Private Enterprises	42341	7919	3028	4891
其他企业	Other Enterprises				
港、澳、台商投资企业	Enterprises with Investment from Hong Kong, Macao and Taiwan	33970	3485	2835	650
合资经营企业(港或澳、台资)	Joint Ventures	18473	1676	1488	188
合作经营企业(港或澳、台资)	Cooperative Enterprises	661	69	69	
港、澳、台商独资经营企业	Sole Investment Enterprises	13768	1509	1047	462
港、澳、台商投资股份有限公司	Share-holding Corporations Ltd.	1068	231	231	
外商投资企业	Enterprises with Foreign Investment	51655	1168	1132	36
中外合资经营企业	Sino-foreign Joint Ventures	13303	550	538	12
中外合作经营企业	Sino-foreign Cooperative Enterprises	11505	422	398	24
外资企业	Foreign-funded Enterprises	26847	196	196	
其他外商投资	Others				
按零售业态分	By Type of Operation				
便利店	Convenience Store	9456	2042	1303	739
超市	Supermarket	21656	772	750	22
大型超市	HyperMarket	51190	349	320	29
百货商店	Department Store	22621	879	876	3
专业店	Specialty Store	74997	8679	7789	890
专卖店	Franchised Store	24217	6769	3556	3213
家居建材店	Building Material Store	399	10	10	
其他	Others	28078	8042	1848	6194

16-14 亿元以上商品交易市场成交额

Turnover of Commodity Exchange Markets with Transaction Value over 100 Million Yuan

单位：亿元 (100 million yuan)

项　目	Item	2005	2010	2013	2014	2015	2016	2017
合　计	**Total**	**1948.95**	**4828.13**	**5418.15**	**5657.02**	**5576.63**	**5512.94**	**5462.94**
食品、饮料、烟酒类	Food, Beverages, Tobacco and Liquor	853.12	1591.87	1844.52	1852.12	1933.27	2115.67	2126.71
#粮油类	Grain and Edible Oil	136.45	192.61	172.69	167.86	172.99	185.05	179.75
服装鞋帽、针、纺织品类	Garments,Footwear,Headgear,Knitwear and Textiles	457.60	1028.01	1086.16	1273.99	1294.61	1248.43	1198.29
化妆品类	Cosmetics	8.18	15.69	19.17	15.50	18.67	17.56	17.18
金银珠宝类	Gold, Silver and Jewelry	1.14	47.17	26.92	25.33	21.98	20.73	19.55
日用品类	Daily-use Articles	42.93	209.48	271.20	293.60	197.15	197.96	190.93
五金、电料类	Hardware and Electrical Appliances	19.07	121.51	143.03	125.43	191.98	167.75	169.30
体育、娱乐用品类	Sports and Recreational Articles	5.09	7.44	13.15	10.38	10.09	11.90	13.97
书报杂志类	Newspapers and Magazines	2.37	4.75	3.20	2.70	2.64	2.13	2.01
电子出版物及音像制品类	E-journals and Video Products	2.22	5.84	7.50	11.06	11.52	8.40	6.40
家用电器和音像器材类	Household Appliances and Video Appliances	15.20	33.88	28.59	22.11	19.31	23.03	21.41
中西药品类	Traditional Chinese and Western Medicines	13.24	12.49	13.92	12.31	16.39	18.14	18.59
#中草药及中成药类	Chinese Herbal Medicines and Chinese Patent Medicines	12.52	11.76	13.09	11.49	13.49	14.41	14.78
文化办公用品类	Articles for Cultural and Office Use	62.63	66.35	56.68	48.10	57.66	37.15	36.09
家具类	Furniture	3.03	9.05	8.27	8.50	8.28	8.15	8.70
通讯器材类	Communication Appliances	2.24	52.00	62.99	40.92	38.80	38.27	40.18
煤炭及制品类	Coal and Related Products					0.17		0.01
木材及制品类	Timber and Related Products	34.84	45.27	107.74	102.06	70.78	45.70	54.95
化工材料及制品类	Chemical Materials and Products	5.11	388.17	401.25	442.70	431.15	406.58	394.10
金属材料类	Metal Materials	82.11	485.52	562.23	558.53	418.28	326.51	256.49
建筑及装潢材料类	Construction and Decoration Materials	43.93	73.64	87.02	101.91	110.99	113.19	173.71
机电产品及设备类	Mechanical and Electrical Products and Equipments	17.68	28.11	35.30	46.55	47.40	51.52	62.04
汽车类	Motor Vehicles	175.68	531.59	513.61	520.61	555.89	553.99	557.73
种子饲料类	Seeds and Feedstuff		0.07	0.10	0.09	0.08	0.10	0.10
其他类	Others	101.54	70.23	125.60	142.52	119.54	100.08	94.50

16-15 限额以上批发零售企业财务状况（2017年）

Financial Indicators of Enterprises above Designated Size in Wholesale and Retail Trades Services (2017)

单位：万元 (10000 yuan)

项目	Item	批发零售业合计 Wholesale and Retail Trades	批发业 Wholesale Trade	零售业 Retail Trade
企业数 (个)	Number of Enterprises (unit)	27344	18561	8783
年初存货	Inventory at the Year-beginning	43535387	34449349	9086038
流动资产合计	Circulating Assets	295259306	240562830	54696476
#存货	Inventory	46463800	36547156	9916644
固定资产原价	Original Value of Fixed Assets	23922122	16557102	7365020
累计折旧	Accumulated Depreciation	10180461	6805382	3375079
#本年折旧	Depreciation Drawn in Current Year	1512762	954817	557945
资产合计	Total Assets	358678812	291030031	67648781
负债合计	Total Liabilities	264485042	220629365	43855677
所有者权益合计	Total Creditors' Equity	94193770	70400666	23793104
实收资本	Paid-up Capital	49749247	39547579	10201668
#国家资本	State Capital	7119243	5420484	1698759
集体资本	Collective Capital	799685	622724	176961
法人资本	Legal Person Capital	24628260	19800054	4828206
个人资本	Personal Capital	92628078	7255696	2012382
港澳台资本	Capital from Hong Kong, Macao and Taiwan	5049057	4151872	897185
外商资本	Foreign Capital	2884924	2296749	588175
营业收入	Business Revenue	735621036	618787899	116833137
#主营业务收入	Main Business Revenue	730047575	615583720	114463855
营业成本	Business Costs	678383310	579559475	98823835
#主营业务成本	Main Business Costs	675675603	577575741	98099862
营业税金及附加	Tax and Extra Charges on Business	2863142	2416044	447098
#主营业务税金及附加	Tax and Extra Charges on Main Business	2824677	2392984	431693
其它业务利润	Profits from Other Businesses	2528558	1362605	1165953
销售费用	Marketing Expenses	26482828	16729326	9753502
管理费用	Management Expenses	12768562	9275559	3493003
财务费用	Financial Expenses	2542491	2065605	476886
#利息支出	Interests	724947	640596	84351
营业利润	Business Profits	14403971	10177426	4226545
营业外收入	Non-operating Revenue	926459	708146	218313
利润总额	Total Profits	15216133	10662453	4553680
应交所得税	Income Taxes Payable	2930364	2186175	744189
本年应付职工薪酬	Total Wages Payable in Current Year	12316040	7863817	4452223
本年应交增值税	Value-added Tax Payable in Current Year	7778017	5456314	2321703

16-16 限额以上批发企业财务状况（2017年）

单位:万元

项　　目	Item	企业数(个) Number of Enterprises	年初库存 Beginning Inventory	流动资产合计 Circulating Assets
批发业合计	**Total Wholesale Trade**	**18561**	**34449349**	**240562830**
#国有及国有控股	State-owned and State-controlled Enterprises	896	6999701	48128025
按登记注册类型分	By Status of Registration			
内资企业	Domestic-funded Enterprises	17124	24558264	209921849
国有企业	State-owned Enterprises	239	913275	2618644
集体企业	Collective-owned Enterprises	58	19345	121827
股份合作企业	Share-holding Cooperative Enterprises	19	5020	54236
联营企业	Joint-operation Enterprises	8	9191	32820
国有联营企业	State-owned Joint-operation Enterprises	2	4938	21603
集体联营企业	Collective Joint-operation Enterprises	2	1973	2667
国有与集体联营企业	State-collective Joint-operation Enterprises	1	255	126
其他联营企业	Other Joint-operation Enterprises	3	2025	8424
有限责任公司	Limited Liability Corporations	6181	11298005	102929350
国有独资企业	State Sole Investment Enterprises	153	1741700	10697889
其他有限责任公司	Other Limited Liability Companies	6028	9556305	92231461
股份有限公司	Share-holding Corporations Ltd.	345	2394502	21847095
私营企业	Private Enterprises	10224	9913347	82261074
私营独资企业	Private Sole Investment Enterprises	36	5479	64554
私营合伙企业	Private Partnership Enterprises	5	837	3554
私营有限责任公司	Private Limited Liability Corporations	9946	9501978	79956086
私营股份有限公司	Private Share-holding Corporations Ltd.	237	405053	2236880
其他企业	Other Enterprises	50	5579	56803
港、澳、台商投资企业	Enterprises with Investment from Hong Kong, Macao and Taiwan	937	7970925	17573451
合资经营企业	Joint Ventures	107	342840	2212951
合作经营企业	Cooperative Enterprises	7	8291	66540
独资经营企业	Sole Investment Enterprises	778	7559738	14595879
投资股份有限公司	Share-holding Corporations Ltd.	28	52808	341743
其它港澳台商投资企业	Others	17	7248	356338
外商投资企业	Enterprises with Foreign Investment	500	1920160	13067530
中外合资经营企业	Sino-foreign Joint Ventures	72	649181	3571075
中外合作经营企业	Sino-foreign Cooperative Enterprises	6	5844	50477
外资企业	Foreign-funded Enterprises	384	1176449	8836956
外商投资股份有限公司	Share-holding Corporations Ltd.	14	60304	215768
其它外商投资企业	Others	24	28382	393254
按国民经济行业分	By Economic Sector			
农林牧产品批发业	Wholesale of Farm and Livestock Products	358	806294	3502593
食品、饮料及烟草制品批发业	Wholesale of Food, Beverages and Tobacco Products	1751	4507258	19881377
#米、面制品及食用油批发业	Wholesale of Rice, Flour Products and Edible Oil	245	1344744	2923161
烟草制品批发业	Wholesale of Tobacco Products	46	436614	3111817
纺织、服装及日用品批发业	Wholesale of Textiles, Garments and Daily-use Products	2668	7784949	21985980
#服装批发业	Wholesale of Garments	532	776511	4377346
家用视听设备批发	Wholesale of Household Audio-visual Equipments	169	4786785	2252846
日用家电批发	Wholesale of Household Appliances	291	636121	3385475
文化、体育用品及器材批发业	Wholesale of Cultural and Sports Articles and Appliances	828	3471052	12188914
医药及医疗器材批发业	Wholesale of Medicines and Medical Appliances	1437	2518409	15479455
矿产品、建材及化工产品批发	Wholesale of Mineral Products, Building Materials and Chemical Products	6339	8536089	87522275
#煤炭及制品批发业	Wholesale of Coal and Related Products	247	592546	3837333
石油及制品批发业	Wholesale of Petroleum and Related Products	753	2948736	21569453
金属及金属矿批发业	Wholesale of Metal and Related Products	1746	2291058	32259890
建材批发业	Wholesale of Building Materials	998	862576	12790903
化肥批发业	Wholesale of Chemical Fertilizers	109	123827	599199
机械设备、五金交电及电子产品批发业	Wholesale of Machinery, Hardware, Electric and Electronic Products	3882	5560481	54681320
汽车零配件批发业	Wholesale of Motor Vehicles and Parts	377	580078	10662985
计算机、软件及辅助设备批发业	Wholesale of Computers, Software and Assistant Equipments	359	598972	4167117
贸易经纪与代理	Trade Broker and Agency	653	774631	20689276
其他批发业	Other Wholesale Trades	645	490186	4631640

Financial Indicators of Enterprises above Designated Size in Wholesale Trade (2017)

(10000 yuan)

固定资产原价 Original Value of Fixed Assets	累计折旧 Accumulated Depreciation	本年折旧 Depreciation Drawn in Current Year	资产合计 Total Assets	负债合计 Total Liabilities	所有者权益合计 Total Creditors' Equity	实收资本 Paid-up Capital	营业收入 Business Revenue	主营业务收入 Main Business Revenue	营业成本 Business Costs
16557102	**6805382**	**954817**	**291030031**	**220629365**	**70400666**	**39547579**	**618787899**	**615583720**	**579559475**
7599323	3295330	347089	65645121	43001906	22643215	10371636	175469817	174735784	164580458
14558884	5933870	822313	252130309	193444987	58685322	31512961	551801480	549643296	519051101
403467	172560	17555	4514232	2392582	2121650	1592402	5957090	5902789	5262672
27562	11063	875	164339	95829	68510	21214	392089	389768	357612
8481	4741	323	60915	41659	19256	6528	126089	124699	115396
3550	2137	492	34888	12426	22462	5326	84763	84606	76059
2820	1799	249	22719	4030	18689	1960	32128	31971	25559
583	243	243	3566	3455	111	207	33841	33841	32084
2	2		126	-40	166	150	6287	6287	6248
145	93		8477	4981	3496	3009	12507	12507	12168
6322307	2428828	363695	121649846	96525660	25124186	13608212	306151367	305037290	287523066
2243976	818771	97900	14292836	9307850	4984986	2026178	53167181	53114733	50509171
4078331	1610057	265795	107357010	87217810	20139200	11582034	252984186	251922557	237013895
4045172	1901219	165472	33019838	19223632	13796206	4956790	42658900	42311619	39927724
3725385	1407319	272602	92579987	75113988	17465999	11303410	195963180	195325191	185427272
7353	1871	409	83194	47302	35892	11180	216135	216135	169882
419	234	37	4160	2986	1174	681	14784	14784	13684
3555628	1351013	262800	89789770	73356265	16433505	10833936	189636494	189011905	179576711
161985	54201	9356	2702863	1707435	995428	457613	6095767	6082367	5666995
22960	6003	1299	106264	39211	67053	19079	468002	467334	361300
935892	396099	58503	21988357	15345036	6643321	4787603	31113333	30699497	27412376
197174	75112	8745	2715701	2146439	569262	350065	5225889	5169244	4801649
11838	4237	481	87361	56903	30458	15281	205295	205295	184474
679818	290633	45743	18041326	12434937	5606389	4179224	24896027	24606858	21872122
21656	7284	1819	395723	281716	114007	63154	488274	481858	362578
25406	18833	1715	748246	425041	323205	179879	297848	236242	191553
1062326	475413	74001	16911365	11839342	5072023	3247015	35873086	35240927	33095998
449519	186758	23361	4867743	3473205	1394538	961638	9899505	9869566	9213153
2204	1599	105	51127	40673	10454	5630	202395	202395	197236
450554	210319	35545	10947771	7821589	3126182	2050780	21962758	21426613	20036242
138183	68729	14119	503674	196122	307552	185686	2226900	2167478	2120923
21866	8008	871	541050	307753	233297	43281	1581528	1574875	1528444
529649	158962	20956	6408810	2856399	3552411	2860971	10530998	10484815	9983654
2257411	920499	132511	25980472	16247324	9733148	3057823	50944797	50594812	43451491
366571	112573	19155	4010579	2895734	1114845	294496	5659700	5624843	5343082
424601	217404	17973	3551257	818250	2733007	60537	13321706	13308270	9936446
1085058	491334	83867	26376955	20025197	6351758	3173528	44616377	44376912	39276270
238884	110799	17451	5182101	3749078	1433023	670203	7320196	7260147	6226772
44379	16231	3295	2363360	2035505	327855	240376	5591983	5549899	5251768
120802	52615	15114	4602311	3690108	912203	373332	5409283	5392752	4984390
577467	212414	35679	14090259	10207933	3882326	2994658	21832366	21340768	19770489
783619	302725	62747	18324351	12844856	5479495	2463040	31689618	31499994	27970631
8782587	3782145	414982	108051336	83283706	24767630	15961606	288741907	287900264	280275003
641609	211266	23179	4703510	3849475	854035	754703	12109222	12049475	11596162
5694646	2528636	253675	30030022	19770459	10259563	6606315	83909032	83530983	81251780
1299509	551202	67962	37785180	33220503	4564677	3346854	109659425	109498000	108152376
370988	147820	24085	16371590	12156977	4214613	2309721	25705611	25558095	24373572
42345	15939	2106	718967	538661	180306	98411	1357145	1354806	1268024
1888140	728764	170800	63131127	50395148	12735979	6749092	131733434	130951049	121824457
318555	99215	49425	12214396	10459853	1754543	1149353	41368023	41209545	37350028
101948	42199	7739	4433777	3359783	1073994	594246	9239960	9201582	8623823
403161	107184	18573	22951696	20249230	2702466	1626518	30054907	29859158	29190897
250010	101355	14702	5715025	4519572	1195453	660343	8643495	8575948	7816583

16−16 续表

单位:万元

项　目	Item	主营业务成本 Main Business Costs	营业税金及附加 Tax and Extra Charges on Business	主营业务税金及附加 Tax and Extra Charges on Main Business
批发业合计	**Total Wholesale Trade**	**577575741**	**2416044**	**2392984**
#国有及国有控股	State-owned and State-controlled Enterprises	163954191	1790220	1777877
按登记注册类型分	By Status of Registration			
内资企业	Domestic-funded Enterprises	517434873	2257770	2236480
国有企业	State-owned Enterprises	5220509	287850	286025
集体企业	Collective-owned Enterprises	357290	1195	1058
股份合作企业	Share-holding Cooperative Enterprises	114951	369	366
联营企业	Joint-operation Enterprises	74826	527	527
国有联营企业	State-owned Joint-operation Enterprises	25453	179	179
集体联营企业	Collective Joint-operation Enterprises	30957	343	343
国有与集体联营企业	State-collective Joint-operation Enterprises	6248	2	2
其他联营企业	Other Joint-operation Enterprises	12168	3	3
有限责任公司	Limited Liability Corporations	286737926	1626911	1613724
国有独资企业	State Sole Investment Enterprises	50468836	454274	451995
其他有限责任公司	Other Limited Liability Companies	236269090	1172637	1161729
股份有限公司	Share-holding Corporations Ltd.	39593867	125461	123400
私营企业	Private Enterprises	184974533	212793	208717
私营独资企业	Private Sole Investment Enterprises	169882	2933	2919
私营合伙企业	Private Partnership Enterprises	13684	28	28
私营有限责任公司	Private Limited Liability Corporations	179129790	201704	197690
私营股份有限公司	Private Share-holding Corporations Ltd.	5661177	8128	8080
其他企业	Other Enterprises	360971	2664	2663
港、澳、台商投资企业	Enterprises with Investment from Hong Kong, Macao and Taiwan	27188208	112333	111115
合资经营企业	Joint Ventures	4754730	25343	24993
合作经营企业	Cooperative Enterprises	184474	266	266
独资经营企业	Sole Investment Enterprises	21702487	83429	82600
投资股份有限公司	Share-holding Corporations Ltd.	362059	2027	2001
其它港澳台商投资企业	Others	184458	1268	1255
外商投资企业	Enterprises with Foreign Investment	32952660	45941	45389
中外合资经营企业	Sino-foreign Joint Ventures	9189639	11540	11319
中外合作经营企业	Sino-foreign Cooperative Enterprises	195228	245	205
外资企业	Foreign-funded Enterprises	19974961	30970	30800
外商投资股份有限公司	Share-holding Corporations Ltd.	2065974	1938	1842
其它外商投资企业	Others	1526858	1248	1223
按国民经济行业分	By Economic Sector			
农林牧产品批发业	Wholesale of Farm and Livestock Products	9922843	7358	6224
食品、饮料及烟草制品批发业	Wholesale of Food, Beverages and Tobacco Products	43196072	1655332	1652822
#米、面制品及食用油批发业	Wholesale of Rice, Flour Products and Edible Oil	5315489	7214	6732
烟草制品批发业	Wholesale of Tobacco Products	9928571	1567687	1567271
纺织、服装及日用品批发业	Wholesale of Textiles, Garments and Daily-use Products	39101517	115906	114193
#服装批发业	Wholesale of Garments	6174625	39592	39132
家用视听设备批发	Wholesale of Household Audio-visual Equipments	5219385	7710	7674
日用家电批发	Wholesale of Household Appliances	4974714	8256	8162
文化、体育用品及器材批发业	Wholesale of Cultural and Sports Articles and Appliances	19646931	62106	60642
医药及医疗器材批发业	Wholesale of Medicines and Medical Appliances	27950142	77916	76194
矿产品、建材及化工产品批发	Wholesale of Mineral Products, Building Materials and Chemical Products	279501453	243851	232583
#煤炭及制品批发业	Wholesale of Coal and Related Products	11564041	15437	15261
石油及制品批发业	Wholesale of Petroleum and Related Products	80928211	62080	58381
金属及金属矿批发业	Wholesale of Metal and Related Products	107931581	58316	54798
建材批发业	Wholesale of Building Materials	24277602	39723	39105
化肥批发业	Wholesale of Chemical Fertilizers	1267505	2185	2178
机械设备、五金交电及电子产品批发业	Wholesale of Machinery, Hardware, Electric and Electronic Products	121426169	209176	207333
汽车零配件批发业	Wholesale of Motor Vehicles and Parts	37222484	97185	96960
计算机、软件及辅助设备批发业	Wholesale of Computers, Software and Assistant Equipments	8612520	14799	14611
贸易经纪与代理	Trade Broker and Agency	29068342	15659	15141
其他批发业	Other Wholesale Trades	7762272	28740	27852

16-16 continued

(10000 yuan)

其他业务利润 Profits from Other Businesses	销售费用 Marketing Expenses	管理费用 Manag-ement Expenses	财务费用 Financial Expenses	营业利润 Business Profits	营业外收入 Non-operating revenue	利润总额 Total Profits	应交所得税 Income Taxes Payable	本年应付职工薪酬 Staff Salary Payable in Current Year	本年应交增值税 Value-added Tax Payable in Current Year
1362605	**16729326**	**9275559**	**2065605**	**10177426**	**708146**	**10662453**	**2186175**	**7863817**	**5456314**
114826	3810022	1314106	276872	4203496	242738	4364210	1017658	1793403	1756415
735809	13505068	7454619	1966594	8646439	578005	9047401	1820089	5988721	4721596
11183	159767	166896	40649	60420	99604	141472	23137	150484	130936
1104	11312	8398	874	12679	820	12547	786	8170	2654
1235	3574	4310	442	2032	109	2024	437	3765	1218
52	1662	2026	104	4441	62	4189	995	2982	1384
51	1032	1543	-38	3910	56	3958	993	2783	1205
	464	298	136	518		222		50	132
	32	4		1	2	2		24	19
1	134	181	6	12	4	7	2	125	28
349652	7550569	3194897	821646	5720967	262954	5782533	1312997	2660157	2840996
16912	736651	235062	35905	1286664	31489	1304819	282416	287590	392622
332740	6813918	2959835	785741	4434303	231465	4477714	1030581	2372567	2448374
47511	1057703	694016	254089	919569	52771	1181742	103768	676400	306210
325057	4703358	3363551	847597	1856629	161655	1853434	372890	2479710	1432422
3	13162	11203	1382	17703	76	17739	2106	4053	2246
	339	388	19	326	1	326	29	314	206
317867	4527698	3227272	822946	1691181	150257	1707352	342945	2376826	1379005
7187	162159	124688	23250	147419	11321	128017	27810	98517	50965
15	17123	20525	1193	69702	30	69460	5079	7053	5776
61555	1869386	927225	18251	770650	62741	796018	192357	1003505	493598
8210	175014	112857	6559	99058	14720	102990	22676	112537	64524
25	12746	2787	680	4980	170	5280	638	4746	2772
49556	1587783	765710	-367	619810	46329	641359	165588	843449	401770
3536	75804	36430	29	10923	1475	10580	3056	35214	17741
228	18039	9441	11350	35879	47	35809	399	7559	6791
565241	1354872	893715	80760	760337	67400	819034	173729	871591	241120
10049	261135	118299	61103	353138	8873	358308	67372	292827	53396
433	3327	2469	-101	1203	48	1250	471	2409	580
550925	985058	740934	18862	389368	53860	440587	85041	547744	167301
935	78411	20439	1176	3480	3932	4938	17523	11981	14560
2899	26941	11574	-280	13148	687	13951	3322	16630	5283
7460	157362	147037	64032	195127	50616	221208	20928	105688	30296
95129	2480062	1444076	105089	2160165	177822	2282865	425366	1610151	951206
8800	204689	91067	60823	36906	96818	129718	13280	74143	17217
34630	211237	381238	-57665	1306776	3794	1271605	286675	459634	549887
59612	2778135	1421359	107700	962284	109062	1236519	206532	1322604	634076
9607	568785	307278	9126	162405	31041	182659	40794	300990	149045
3671	172416	93792	3266	66068	7046	71464	15827	61455	35425
5851	185035	119439	23261	88369	5107	73349	13201	167435	48863
348151	991778	508060	97409	409350	33499	426066	102383	513746	214432
63398	1845652	889034	151350	940087	26308	939381	175413	728651	537962
166834	3233515	1903756	870545	2766347	155644	2766759	597360	1579350	1694944
2732	243250	58794	73838	128848	13852	128204	25346	49421	74633
41224	926578	404543	230008	1267065	57096	1230013	289277	579063	532539
71860	516963	424659	315652	291292	38922	321110	97911	322650	502340
15111	505365	372087	105079	386554	17621	421016	72350	207854	252862
549	36509	24633	10159	20738	3637	23959	3217	20993	3043
596843	4667799	2471768	370174	2538972	128861	2551359	606241	1714140	1169808
30101	2344669	201774	-7793	1560827	8676	1559459	377113	180759	535483
12505	210950	239842	20113	111660	7712	118959	34412	194379	74915
11892	247441	282434	258159	48271	15612	80102	23736	137486	139650
13286	327582	208035	41147	156823	10722	158194	28216	152001	83940

16-17 限额以上零售企业财务状况（2017年）

单位:万元

项目	Item	企业数（个）Number of Enterprises (unit)	年初库存 Beginning Inventory	流动资产合计 Circulating Assets
零售业合计	**Total Retail Trade**	**8783**	**9086038**	**54696476**
#国有及国有控股	State-owned and State-controlled Enterprises	456	974327	15451162
按登记注册类型分	By Status of Registration			
内资企业	Domestic-funded Enterprises	8364	7470331	44020943
国有企业	State-owned Enterprises	98	111290	1015954
集体企业	Collective-owned Enterprises	179	31846	180828
股份合作企业	Share-holding Cooperative Enterprises	29	3874	16507
联营企业	Joint-operation Enterprises	25	12114	67986
国有联营企业	State-owned Joint-operation Enterprises	5	1359	22033
集体联营企业	Collective Joint-operation Enterprises	8	6861	25825
国有与集体联营企业	State-collective Joint-operation Enterprises	4	969	7270
其他联营企业	Other Joint-operation Enterprises	8	2925	12858
有限责任公司	Limited Liability Corporations	3785	3976909	21157171
国有独资企业	State Sole Investment Enterprises	53	161917	551215
其他有限责任公司	Other Limited Liability Companies	3732	3814992	20605956
股份有限公司	Share-holding Corporations Ltd.	190	436566	9522330
私营企业	Private Enterprises	3993	2890091	12034339
私营独资企业	Private Sole Investment Enterprises	402	46035	163648
私营合伙企业	Private Partnership Enterprises	32	2573	17063
私营有限责任公司	Private Limited Liability Corporations	3470	2766833	11460974
私营股份有限公司	Private Share-holding Corporations Ltd.	89	74650	392654
其他企业	Other Enterprises	65	7641	25828
港、澳、台商投资企业	Enterprises with Investment from Hong Kong, Macao and Taiwan	250	843535	5601840
合资经营企业	Joint Ventures	45	303194	2896119
合作经营企业	Cooperative Enterprises	14	7982	69543
独资经营企业	Sole Investment Enterprises	184	510351	2539858
投资股份有限公司	Share-holding Corporations Ltd.	5	18220	79382
其他港澳台商投资企业	Others	2	3788	16938
外商投资企业	Enterprises with Foreign Investment	169	772172	5073693
中外合资经营企业	Sino-foreign Joint Ventures	52	302901	1543545
中外合作经营企业	Sino-foreign Cooperative Enterprises	6	41375	282652
外资企业	Foreign-funded Enterprises	92	341406	1453235
外商投资股份有限公司	Share-holding Corporations Ltd.	7	29757	115570
其它外商投资企业	Others	12	56733	1678691
按国民经济行业分	By Economic Sector			
综合零售业	Comprehensive Retail	778	1122921	7572236
#百货零售业	Retail of General Merchandise	363	387627	5230627
超级市场零售业	Retail in Supermarkets	319	671488	2108755
食品、饮料及烟草制品专门零售业	Retail of Food, Beverages and Tobacco Products	547	421767	2457388
纺织、服装及日用品专门零售业	Retail of Textiles, Garments and Daily-use Products	623	1424197	4029461
#服装零售业	Retail of Garments	277	823134	2431084
文化、体育用品及器材专门零售业	Retail of Cultural and Sports Articles and Appliances	379	335628	1109110
#体育用品及器材零售	Retail of Sports Articles and Appliances	20	16480	77977
图书零售业	Retail of Books	135	100644	383369
医药及医疗器材专门零售业	Retail of Medicines and Medical Appliances	403	497260	2046753
#西药零售	Retail of Western Medicines	273	419341	1518620
中药零售	Retail of Traditional Chinese Medicines	59	40155	118960
汽车、摩托车、燃料及零配件专门零售业	Retail of Motor Vehicles, Motorcycles and Parts	3829	3955411	28278806
#汽车新车零售	Retail of Motor Vehicles	2549	3300067	14049322
机动车燃料零售业	Retail of Motor Vehicle Fuels	903	328823	13485135
家用电器及电子产品专门零售业	Retail of Household Appliances and Electronic Products	984	621924	3677860
#家用视听设备零售	Retail of Household Audio-visual Equipments	73	50576	351151
日用家电零售	Retail of Household Appliances	362	377738	1833792
计算机、软件及辅助设备零售业	Retail of Computers, Software and Assistant Equipments	294	53459	399716
通讯设备零售业	Retail of Communication Equipments	117	81354	544970
五金、家具及室内装修材料专门零售业	Retail of Hardware, Furniture and Interior Decoration Materials	648	152296	1301059
货摊、无店铺及其他零售业	Stall,Non-shop and Other Retails	592	554634	4223803

Financial Indicators of Enterprises above Designated Size in Retail Trade (2017)

(10000 yuan)

固定资产原价 Original Value of Fixed Assets	累计折旧 Accumulated Depreciation	本年折旧 Depreciation Drawn in Current Year	资产合计 Total Assets	负债合计 Total Liabilities	所有者权益合计 Total Creditors' Equity	实收资本 Paid-up Capital	营业收入 Business Revenue	主营业务收入 Main Business Revenue	营业成本 Business Costs
7365020	**3375079**	**557945**	**67648781**	**43855677**	**23793104**	**10201668**	**116833137**	**114463855**	**98823835**
1754121	825117	77352	19370881	9734615	9636266	2044399	19706610	19322192	16847469
5289009	2303318	361982	53060174	34556415	18503759	7509414	90084942	88342934	77648610
198492	97658	8056	1341304	592190	749114	89893	771305	752724	644239
49595	24103	1958	226661	125522	101139	27137	816843	813662	703057
3071	1490	85	18577	9818	8759	2521	55506	55498	44540
12102	8881	916	73467	49184	24283	9992	237418	237218	208971
5168	3642	368	23559	22581	978	5099	41668	41668	33972
2111	1572	378	27025	12863	14162	3067	133117	133079	124639
1497	1180	33	8098	4524	3574	362	14496	14478	10929
3326	2487	137	14785	9216	5569	1464	48137	47993	39431
2716185	1150108	200379	25605604	17965772	7639832	3476992	48779533	47982265	42205541
105001	48846	4443	983206	284347	698859	286851	1333536	1288495	1106028
2611184	1101262	195936	24622398	17681425	6940973	3190141	47445997	46693770	41099513
888157	416274	38720	11565487	5003809	6561678	1053840	9662768	9388860	8185555
1410151	600991	111341	14190955	10793358	3397597	2840993	29560582	28911941	25501261
65456	23236	3874	234064	130165	103899	58922	960189	959404	760803
9136	3368	563	26200	11560	14640	8812	63042	62936	51193
1261200	552123	103393	13434768	10399411	3035357	2690680	27756355	27120023	24119428
74359	22264	3511	495923	252222	243701	82579	780996	769578	569837
11256	3813	527	38119	16762	21357	8046	200987	200766	155446
876673	431529	88257	8088978	4767160	3321818	1457223	9410879	9018781	7174064
315977	163950	30597	4761944	2416404	2345540	515478	3788551	3622309	2765499
13752	10043	515	74798	37616	37182	39095	155199	152248	115804
482117	230649	55299	3068489	2146294	922195	879945	5156205	4937383	4017987
13022	5437	1846	119227	95136	24091	17655	283862	279779	256528
51805	21450		64520	71710	-7190	5050	27062	27062	18246
1199338	640232	107706	6499629	4532102	1967527	1235031	17337316	17102140	14001161
420792	196242	17906	2282234	940838	1341396	530231	6351725	6307098	4741231
89992	57652	3288	343086	295292	47794	66928	484360	438690	339488
528841	297486	53664	1904088	1491850	412238	523426	4080592	3948262	3153893
21248	7160	990	148573	97863	50710	12073	187975	181899	103589
138465	81692	31858	1821648	1706259	115389	102373	6232664	6226191	5662960
2136706	1101503	141599	11889291	7552529	4336762	2077713	17034253	16300768	13489969
1031930	513453	70101	8313047	4791959	3521088	1105659	8112979	7701096	6251378
1026084	550120	64315	3239313	2440663	798650	848475	7963764	7670937	6479153
295997	120714	24135	3250606	1580342	1670264	547351	4037676	3998790	2473221
339601	141733	44286	4839017	3099533	1739484	981777	5533255	5466606	3513105
165739	71788	21766	3017487	1722770	1294717	482141	2968458	2920965	1618619
285012	134139	15378	1547545	841772	705773	340846	1772619	1714721	1325871
36764	17986	4325	103900	77427	26473	48073	161204	152056	113663
210929	98480	9036	709713	377389	332324	144803	660522	640220	488475
167029	66009	13589	2385851	1616950	768901	328010	4360541	4305705	3375350
126123	52065	10570	1782035	1263702	518333	234067	3518672	3466334	2838950
9845	4252	712	145929	107937	37992	17476	239671	238211	172851
3213559	1424761	227121	33196425	21157646	12038779	4024787	60110585	59084251	54374259
1928809	792259	162821	17081390	12888619	4192771	2851919	43191718	42437168	39829913
1179868	584203	57388	15255540	7582981	7672559	1047957	15397398	15139009	13199845
293103	110804	14962	4232791	3251657	981134	581647	7864345	7593579	6739052
17465	8534	1038	403817	272560	131257	63462	1302710	1287388	1199849
159110	54968	5667	2057440	1677431	380009	175384	3435472	3380021	2981946
26297	12073	2805	429061	251656	177405	117892	810578	799466	670239
39931	17545	3081	659644	533392	126252	76800	1340212	1320090	1196573
199289	59855	23138	1619084	1162881	456203	309516	2649967	2640441	2159347
434724	215561	53737	4688171	3592367	1095804	1010021	13469896	13358994	11373661

16-17 续表

单位：万元

项　　目	Item	主营业务成本 Main Business Costs	营业税金及附加 Tax and Extra Charges on Business	主营业务税金及附加 Tax and Extra Charges on Main Business
零售业合计	**Total Retail Trade**	**98099862**	**447098**	**431693**
#国有及国有控股	State-owned and State-controlled Enterprises	16626185	65241	59534
按登记注册类型分	By Status of Registration			
内资企业	Domestic-funded Enterprises	76992188	345555	332378
国有企业	State-owned Enterprises	599357	5412	4655
集体企业	Collective-owned Enterprises	701216	4924	4875
股份合作企业	Share-holding Cooperative Enterprises	44540	155	152
联营企业	Joint-operation Enterprises	208842	1237	1228
国有联营企业	State-owned Joint-operation Enterprises	33972	174	174
集体联营企业	Collective Joint-operation Enterprises	124639	822	813
国有与集体联营企业	State-collective Joint-operation Enterprises	10916	77	77
其他联营企业	Other Joint-operation Enterprises	39315	164	164
有限责任公司	Limited Liability Corporations	41948095	166849	161278
国有独资企业	State Sole Investment Enterprises	1090688	3761	2841
其他有限责任公司	Other Limited Liability Companies	40857407	163088	158437
股份有限公司	Share-holding Corporations Ltd.	8040589	36745	34856
私营企业	Private Enterprises	25294368	126568	121671
私营独资企业	Private Sole Investment Enterprises	758037	22588	21229
私营合伙企业	Private Partnership Enterprises	51193	521	521
私营有限责任公司	Private Limited Liability Corporations	23922534	99096	95676
私营股份有限公司	Private Share-holding Corporations Ltd.	562604	4363	4245
其他企业	Other Enterprises	155181	3665	3663
港、澳、台商投资企业	Enterprises with Investment from Hong Kong, Macao and Taiwan	7134508	39038	37207
合资经营企业	Joint Ventures	2741849	15961	14438
合作经营企业	Cooperative Enterprises	115687	712	710
独资经营企业	Sole Investment Enterprises	4002574	20641	20335
投资股份有限公司	Share-holding Corporations Ltd.	256152	860	860
其他港澳台商投资企业	Others	18246	864	864
外商投资企业	Enterprises with Foreign Investment	13973166	62505	62108
中外合资经营企业	Sino-foreign Joint Ventures	4721372	38130	37901
中外合作经营企业	Sino-foreign Cooperative Enterprises	339488	1374	1374
外资企业	Foreign-funded Enterprises	3145948	13664	13498
外商投资股份有限公司	Share-holding Corporations Ltd.	103406	1371	1370
其它外商投资企业	Others	5662952	7966	7965
按国民经济行业分	By Economic Sector			
综合零售业	Comprehensive Retail	13435648	75583	71182
#百货零售业	Retail of General Merchandise	6217055	47984	45471
超级市场零售业	Retail in Supermarkets	6461498	22825	20976
食品、饮料及烟草制品专门零售业	Retail of Food, Beverages and Tobacco Products	2457574	39735	39224
纺织、服装及日用品专门零售业	Retail of Textiles, Garments and Daily-use Products	3494722	39666	39538
#服装零售业	Retail of Garments	1604389	25374	25259
文化、体育用品及器材专门零售业	Retail of Cultural and Sports Articles and Appliances	1301235	21360	20100
#体育用品及器材零售	Retail of Sports Articles and Appliances	113607	795	762
图书零售业	Retail of Books	484792	3474	2637
医药及医疗器材专门零售业	Retail of Medicines and Medical Appliances	3358332	21483	19687
#西药零售	Retail of Western Medicines	2824026	15099	13311
中药零售	Retail of Traditional Chinese Medicines	172188	982	974
汽车、摩托车、燃料及零配件专门零售业	Retail of Motor Vehicles, Motorcycles and Parts	53906350	165098	158423
#汽车新车零售	Retail of Motor Vehicles	39580281	104155	100643
机动车燃料零售业	Retail of Motor Vehicle Fuels	12987754	54693	51620
家用电器及电子产品专门零售业	Retail of Household Appliances and Electronic Products	6696567	24640	24253
#家用视听设备零售	Retail of Household Audio-visual Equipments	1193725	2683	2682
日用家电零售	Retail of Household Appliances	2970301	13463	13312
计算机、软件及辅助设备零售业	Retail of Computers, Software and Assistant Equipments	662928	3040	2880
通讯设备零售业	Retail of Communication Equipments	1194643	3019	2957
五金、家具及室内装修材料专门零售业	Retail of Hardware, Furniture and Interior Decoration Materials	2153772	23749	23656
货摊、无店铺及其他零售业	Stall,Non-shop and Other Retails	11295662	35784	35630

16-17 continued

(10000 yuan)

其它业务利润 Profits from Other Businesses	销售费用 Marketing Expenses	管理费用 Manag-ement Expenses	财务费用 Financial Expenses	营业利润 Business Profits	营业外收入 Non-operating revenue	利润总额 Total Profits	应交所得税 Income Taxes Payable	本年应付职工薪酬 Staff Salary Payable in Current Year	本年应交增值税 Value-added Tax Payable in Current Year
1165953	**9753502**	**3493003**	**476886**	**4226545**	**218313**	**4553680**	**744189**	**4452223**	**2321703**
138544	1312935	358869	40930	1302521	33813	1320269	141413	708481	290237
679911	6205860	2767346	429064	2929616	161684	3111584	499489	3218135	1556348
4341	43977	40931	2617	73904	6337	75803	3419	40545	9712
444	37233	24150	2499	41893	1139	40811	8684	22416	15087
68	2809	2020	105	1671	8	1704	356	2180	1038
64	6291	4695	420	15875	52	15851	3831	17008	4405
	1395	1407	64	4658	48	4695	1310	12296	1146
64	2817	1999	289	2616	2	2576	500	2846	1249
	695	268	3	2525		2522	554	623	580
	1384	1021	64	6076	2	6058	1467	1243	1430
364099	3397463	1285887	227203	1626411	78997	1711299	306149	1620058	773165
9487	67481	28569	-3512	150778	5281	153074	32099	36661	14026
354612	3329982	1257318	230715	1475633	73716	1558225	274050	1583397	759139
71717	681838	206365	14582	552757	11368	560210	44408	343184	190913
238768	2024891	1194144	179560	597705	63756	687310	131185	1166740	558108
19585	51310	43272	8963	75706	436	75692	4148	24504	16108
11	3035	3250	246	4803	2	4690	535	1824	1494
218174	1859621	1105105	165016	467510	60995	554027	114189	1080756	504145
998	110925	42517	5335	49686	2323	52901	12313	59656	36361
410	11358	9154	2078	19400	27	18596	1457	6004	3920
213447	1356078	398368	21914	475996	24557	473870	111647	632020	271120
105471	617619	162832	6628	262978	9314	265649	58859	298604	83944
3198	14802	5293	-155	18892	58	18850	4871	7348	3761
99883	706084	222137	12619	188450	14825	182358	46453	321803	180969
3708	15871	3719	-467	7102	36	7032	1464	3580	1677
1187	1702	4387	3289	-1426	324	-19		685	769
272595	2191564	327289	25908	820933	32072	968226	133053	602068	494235
69510	940048	142287	17909	577173	20419	588157	75166	215015	330180
45670	95367	14191	239	33214	423	33374	3589	31945	11940
148766	589312	139386	8910	164077	5152	293639	49810	236780	80312
4149	46227	14212	229	21425	1000	22386	763	25935	13371
4500	520610	17213	-1379	25044	5078	30670	3725	92393	58432
574698	2453748	538938	63226	570954	60754	596194	157248	1069976	302618
337142	1178893	240672	17535	475578	17118	474047	122326	483374	143884
215187	1129001	249859	41967	98996	39892	120433	33308	521522	125224
7624	821112	196270	-1347	607040	23737	623068	76869	186748	204542
41283	1229416	422245	25556	283238	17714	273055	60738	586941	234780
23903	845252	252077	17669	194892	11838	176248	39529	380200	152137
17429	199498	132591	7499	99229	9333	105914	16154	128863	26543
840	31149	16414	719	-1039	68	-888	245	8388	3538
11036	67029	65257	2368	45839	6557	50885	3040	71600	5976
38421	565264	190638	19923	191887	8078	210327	52352	331654	141565
34645	439595	136710	16325	76147	5481	109401	27805	272083	84049
2503	38973	17722	971	8814	514	8340	3434	20676	6083
415730	2273605	1192458	290934	1937745	63280	2054820	289214	1438591	1103532
366213	1491383	922880	249134	707014	49421	812580	172422	1090742	804742
45354	704575	224324	30671	1195382	6597	1199416	110161	290049	250752
41105	576561	380264	37058	118172	16421	131223	21167	284849	119552
5387	74288	20387	2504	2314	1077	3005	1881	28934	14856
17784	314677	89438	11808	30266	5769	36069	4418	121425	46339
1827	55057	58931	3663	20965	3310	23594	2250	64177	24794
15681	70933	40418	12820	15407	4139	19951	2614	34802	10859
10568	181690	140392	10831	138778	2352	271341	17683	93828	48466
19095	1452608	299207	23206	279502	16644	287738	52764	330773	140105

16-18 各市限额以上批发零售企业财务状况（2017年）

单位：万元

市 别	City	企业数（个）Number of Enterprises (unit)	年初库存 Beginning Inventory	流动资产合计 Circulating Assets	固定资产原价 Original Value of Fixed Assets	累计折旧 Accumulated Depreciation
批发零售业合计	**Total Wholesale and Retail Trades**	**27344**	**43535387**	**295259306**	**23922122**	**10180461**
批发业	**Wholesale Trade**	**18561**	**34449349**	**240562830**	**16557102**	**6805382**
广 州	Guangzhou	4921	10260041	67331540	6772374	2879315
深 圳	Shenzhen	5104	16071973	108501483	4135273	1749062
珠 海	Zhuhai	634	1001167	11943990	404778	148821
汕 头	Shantou	528	695063	3771671	460804	171852
佛 山	Foshan	2443	2322722	15404451	873017	375897
韶 关	Shaoguan	221	122786	979088	174192	65304
河 源	Heyuan	44	23806	185765	22149	9068
梅 州	Meizhou	62	57513	368378	67038	24813
惠 州	Huizhou	318	210524	1817427	261048	84779
汕 尾	Shanwei	31	29009	158792	16478	5885
东 莞	Dongguan	1588	1455078	12441158	1440560	501954
中 山	Zhongshan	543	543616	3705181	206440	84706
江 门	Jiangmen	458	314511	2506496	256141	114093
阳 江	Yangjiang	117	83626	315492	100094	44971
湛 江	Zhanjiang	331	278949	3732829	427532	193041
茂 名	Maoming	586	325810	2885659	149512	53436
肇 庆	Zhaoqing	103	112510	589728	46832	22427
清 远	Qingyuan	77	175457	1508753	129923	51324
潮 州	Chaozhou	38	44443	250670	71260	35992
揭 阳	Jieyang	361	146121	1517391	247239	63633
云 浮	Yunfu	53	174624	646888	294418	125009
零售业	**Retail Trade**	**8783**	**9086038**	**54696476**	**7365020**	**3375079**
广 州	Guangzhou	1640	2113797	15678528	1760650	875305
深 圳	Shenzhen	1118	3178427	14305640	1619300	798203
珠 海	Zhuhai	294	268433	2164634	251959	109348
汕 头	Shantou	356	174070	729922	188501	66093
佛 山	Foshan	624	694039	2864328	620599	257183
韶 关	Shaoguan	261	83572	308307	78432	31329
河 源	Heyuan	219	74193	834883	101593	40670
梅 州	Meizhou	114	100265	850885	125629	52104
惠 州	Huizhou	376	300424	2091148	360572	134691
汕 尾	Shanwei	71	23855	197914	46106	20479
东 莞	Dongguan	634	804558	5496854	637508	306164
中 山	Zhongshan	523	382070	2357860	308736	150290
江 门	Jiangmen	386	206051	1701596	241942	117661
阳 江	Yangjiang	105	45866	615745	82057	41412
湛 江	Zhanjiang	354	144463	1356313	206154	79053
茂 名	Maoming	315	110931	443822	169760	62522
肇 庆	Zhaoqing	194	111020	1279014	172251	76610
清 远	Qingyuan	191	92614	298542	59078	24420
潮 州	Chaozhou	102	36457	142171	50333	26689
揭 阳	Jieyang	608	77806	551960	173633	65346
云 浮	Yunfu	298	63127	426410	110227	39507

Financial Indicators of Enterprises above Designated Size in Wholesale and Retail Trades by City (2017)

(10000 yuan)

#本年折旧 Depreciation Drawn in Current Year	资产合计 Total Assets	负债合计 Total Liabilities	所有者权益合计 Total Creditors' Equity	实收资本 Paid-up Capital	营业收入 Business Revenue	主营业务收入 Main Business Revenue	营业成本 Business Costs
1512762	**358678812**	**264485042**	**94193770**	**49749247**	**735621036**	**730047575**	**678383310**
954817	**291030031**	**220629365**	**70400666**	**39547579**	**618787899**	**615583720**	**579559475**
392385	82251332	60736610	21514722	11854558	224817740	223570205	210121893
268681	130503270	102608052	27895218	16470175	197959927	196650181	186890225
30988	14226160	9642023	4584137	1961991	23744352	23624599	22300820
13455	4583914	2797054	1786860	910441	12736134	12729836	11772929
49860	17496983	14505383	2991600	1823278	63180891	63100229	60625828
9914	1218987	819065	399922	122002	4424716	4405585	3992086
1343	222162	103102	119060	32924	613137	612748	486827
3023	466600	267446	199154	65901	1155274	1151629	950122
12133	2999221	1775749	1223472	930924	5443334	5424057	4818283
1023	175101	87968	87133	17991	522095	522050	403724
64859	14995039	11839906	3155133	1721756	34639905	34462511	32145962
10171	4012503	3458399	554104	410336	8698280	8675845	8068653
12945	2943141	2321280	621861	371661	7447189	7434442	6939194
5471	420999	269494	151505	45586	1216545	1215309	1046884
20734	5514546	3927306	1587240	1743677	6454701	6405374	6082476
8292	3137457	2372309	765148	241979	12653663	12582167	12035724
2660	652171	496512	155659	72398	1548743	1546666	1346594
5561	1793975	1016891	777084	159289	2672845	2627079	2456089
4137	358668	307496	51172	45134	884756	882157	771223
14294	2105911	997143	1108768	391185	5992122	5991640	4656506
22888	951891	280177	671714	154393	1981550	1969411	1647433
557945	**67648781**	**43855677**	**23793104**	**10201668**	**116833137**	**114463855**	**98823835**
162702	18585156	13707580	4877576	2216990	32349843	31785536	27599945
125350	18986499	11774606	7211893	3596667	27773883	27001132	22401983
14983	2678837	1490783	1188054	388065	3398183	3341040	2787374
10768	957425	588977	368448	212435	3071411	3043544	2769759
43939	3636124	2766137	869987	587589	8500975	8370357	7477462
4821	403572	264747	138825	90841	835955	821184	723563
6401	960942	589434	371508	84430	1051346	1042332	939839
8220	1016506	533172	483334	350599	1112349	1033094	954073
38126	2567005	1547977	1019028	275075	4750033	4656711	4243558
1680	289948	158084	131864	53408	411659	400143	355681
35892	6193785	4089049	2104736	578770	11289025	11044000	10163660
25547	2826202	1405689	1420513	336874	5650236	5561229	4140844
16981	2042212	1228018	814194	288548	3278009	3221983	2946637
3285	696332	394402	301930	288140	854208	835729	739978
12890	1634366	939047	695319	171505	2077623	2034356	1779075
8637	659046	416940	242106	132592	1861582	1837150	1664828
10344	1488266	856146	632120	97172	2449030	2347438	2118598
5381	380424	296304	84120	119081	930569	917141	826774
2881	195722	131753	63969	65933	621580	616110	569437
9181	827394	348165	479229	174957	3760722	3754809	2918617
9936	623018	328667	294351	91997	804916	798837	702150

16-18 续表

单位:万元

市 别	City	主营业务成本 Main Business Costs	营业税金及附加 Tax and Extra Charges on Business	主营业务税金及附加 Tax and Extra Charges on Main Business	其它业务利润 Profits from Other Businesses	销售费用 Marketing Expenses
批发零售业合计	**Total Wholesale and Retail Trades**	**675675603**	**2863142**	**2824677**	**2528558**	**26482828**
批发业	**Wholesale Trade**	**577575741**	**2416044**	**2392984**	**1362605**	**16729326**
广 州	Guangzhou	209381725	560641	548513	540188	7365363
深 圳	Shenzhen	186112439	441758	437685	625775	4832465
珠 海	Zhuhai	22219701	64900	63653	19448	618408
汕 头	Shantou	11738376	127064	126784	2988	260475
佛 山	Foshan	60570121	157341	155971	29188	1088201
韶 关	Shaoguan	3974865	51169	51014	8807	137009
河 源	Heyuan	486709	46736	46736	32632	19500
梅 州	Meizhou	948125	60970	60960	171	44873
惠 州	Huizhou	4805298	79578	78541	9413	172932
汕 尾	Shanwei	403724	44067	44067	584	19244
东 莞	Dongguan	32087439	154069	153495	48069	872155
中 山	Zhongshan	8061571	60457	59997	12933	294800
江 门	Jiangmen	6931750	74578	74550	8370	246693
阳 江	Yangjiang	1046273	29682	29680	828	41197
湛 江	Zhanjiang	6005827	62245	60994	8510	123770
茂 名	Maoming	11969969	53829	53782	7153	142266
肇 庆	Zhaoqing	1345450	53108	53077	1969	47300
清 远	Qingyuan	2429050	52847	52799	3522	83545
潮 州	Chaozhou	770383	41454	41438	486	20738
揭 阳	Jieyang	4652979	167497	167237	866	275450
云 浮	Yunfu	1633967	32054	32011	705	22942
零售业	**Retail Trade**	**98099862**	**447098**	**431693**	**1165953**	**9753502**
广 州	Guangzhou	27500968	102949	98557	391828	2879440
深 圳	Shenzhen	22247641	94843	93388	368088	3118706
珠 海	Zhuhai	2756802	12167	11989	26723	247252
汕 头	Shantou	2766266	18052	18012	20659	109279
佛 山	Foshan	7422013	23014	21649	85250	521513
韶 关	Shaoguan	716556	2676	2500	6706	57314
河 源	Heyuan	936398	3992	3771	3341	52767
梅 州	Meizhou	944399	3055	2939	3549	61825
惠 州	Huizhou	4161151	13488	13247	33047	263966
汕 尾	Shanwei	352476	856	811	4121	43594
东 莞	Dongguan	10094068	22652	21723	89974	600976
中 山	Zhongshan	4111732	34222	33780	48881	839054
江 门	Jiangmen	2920806	10150	9746	32396	202194
阳 江	Yangjiang	726712	2611	1446	3158	45448
湛 江	Zhanjiang	1740190	7849	7401	9072	131994
茂 名	Maoming	1650368	7543	7345	8251	68282
肇 庆	Zhaoqing	2050950	8340	7451	7632	181563
清 远	Qingyuan	820923	2151	2148	8048	60048
潮 州	Chaozhou	568858	1869	1765	5089	25654
揭 阳	Jieyang	2910670	71127	68656	5518	190081
云 浮	Yunfu	699915	3492	3369	4622	52552

16-18 continued

(10000 yuan)

管理费用 Management Expenses	财务费用 Financial Expenses	营业利润 Business Profits	营业外收入 Non-operating revenue	利润总额 Total Profits	应交所得税 Income Taxes Payable	本年应付职工薪酬 Staff Salary Payable in Current Year	本年应交增值税 Value-added Tax Payable in Current Year
12768562	**2542491**	**14403971**	**926459**	**15216133**	**2930364**	**12316040**	**7778017**
9275559	**2065605**	**10177426**	**708146**	**10662453**	**2186175**	**7863817**	**5456314**
2748964	390754	4216082	266618	4563210	1036817	2635316	2221992
3348461	1066531	2074737	212386	2171362	496718	3084300	1507822
295513	115080	411201	36904	442832	91258	298044	178333
185275	38615	336714	17848	309920	48731	135221	119965
702161	142080	512279	48311	564112	101675	344136	292946
70500	6196	168283	5690	172336	26124	73771	68911
22459	1014	38255	732	38653	9421	21831	19918
37741	2767	63756	1802	59206	2974	39705	30937
92091	13556	268916	4707	234051	27491	88738	60281
19003	22	36038	112	35224	9701	14508	17075
852893	109187	480799	44042	493235	80948	400267	302621
136847	19045	152476	18394	166804	39953	158271	176672
93320	30222	21759	13459	32884	9962	109029	72956
30102	3112	66100	821	65615	6535	34815	16044
94943	73438	-2479	15290	-2484	20217	78137	54759
79141	20493	324934	8826	335043	67193	72923	75352
40060	4583	55620	2248	56735	12323	37722	27859
34625	1213	74007	5925	76637	9622	59927	36186
19139	2328	59124	365	34339	9192	21122	18965
307101	24508	562052	925	556391	73179	72060	143257
65220	861	256773	2741	256348	6141	83974	13463
3493003	**476886**	**4226545**	**218313**	**4553680**	**744189**	**4452223**	**2321703**
900283	101634	891686	48627	911876	168726	1280651	592033
1082788	122721	1073287	75440	1272004	260150	1433558	687157
125275	12628	221564	8817	223363	51318	140866	82357
60944	9378	96076	2233	80417	11995	60588	37492
249312	58010	185597	13823	194119	40778	246092	123398
31243	5031	16065	1659	16699	3130	40136	13726
33537	6411	15011	814	23629	1175	33059	18522
31806	7104	55773	1437	55932	1295	36033	36805
95697	16323	143473	3611	144776	26334	136506	74834
12420	1435	-2066	154	-1773	432	15170	6899
200480	58291	251109	24646	312944	52737	304821	132148
156739	9056	530186	16565	539468	64982	198605	232943
66505	11099	53198	3489	58265	8966	99344	69109
12200	3735	50838	240	51743	1803	20252	21317
47859	5470	108982	2807	110658	4238	96696	24086
63790	7855	54914	1647	78383	4200	64865	30048
93034	4901	42383	5328	47952	6698	81061	29877
29210	5128	10061	3101	12740	3813	35922	16728
8937	1520	15009	246	14045	1461	13990	5395
171030	25753	387949	2084	379116	27838	69170	74242
19914	3403	25450	1545	27324	2120	44838	12587

主要统计指标解释

社会消费品零售总额 指各种经济类型的批发零售业、住宿餐饮业和其他行业的企业（单位）或个体户，售予城乡居民用于生活消费和社会集团用于公共消费的商品金额的总和。

批发零售业商品购进总额 指从本企业以外的单位和个人购进（包括从国外直接进口）作为转卖或加工后转卖的商品金额。本指标由“从生产者购进额”、“从批发零售业购进额”、“进口额”和“其他购进”组成。 这个指标反映批发零售企业从国内、国外市场上购进商品的总量。

批发零售业商品销售总额 指售予本企业以外的单位和个人的商品金额（包括对国（境）外直接出口及售给本单位消费用的商品）。本指标由“对生产经营单位批发额”、“对批发零售业批发额”、“出口额”和“对居民和社会集团商品零售额”项目组成。这个指标反映批发零售业在国内市场上销售商品以及出口商品的总量。

批发 指除零售以外的一切商品销售活动。包括对生产经营单位批发、对批发零售业批发和出口。

对生产经营单位批发 指售给国民经济和社会各部门作为生产或经营使用的商品。

零售 指出售城乡居民用于生活消费商品和社会集团直接用于公用消费商品的活动。

批发零售业年末库存总额 指批发零售企业已取得所有权的全部商品。这个指标反映批发零售贸易企业的商品库存情况，对市场商品供应的保证程度。

批发零售业住宿餐饮业法人单位 指各种经济类型独立核算法人批发零售企业、住宿餐饮企业的单位个数。法人单位应同时具备以下条件：1. 依法成立，有自己的名称、组织机构和场所，能够独立承担民事责任；2. 独立拥有和使用资产，承担负债，有权与其他单位签订合同；3. 独立核算盈亏，并能够编制资产负债表。

批发业 是指从工农业生产者或从商品流通企业单位和个体户购进商品，转卖给工业、农业、建筑业、运输邮电业、住宿餐饮业、服务业等生产经营单位作为生产经营用，以及将商品转卖给其他批发企业或零售企业的商品流通企业(单位)和个体户。

零售业 是指从工农业生产者、批发业或居民购进商品，转卖给城乡居民作为生活消费和售给社会集团作为公共消费的商品流通企业(单位)和个体户。

Explanatory Notes on Main Statistical Indicators

Total Retail Sales of Consumer Goods refer to the sum of retail sales of consumer goods sold by enterprises (establishments) or individuals in wholesale, retail trade, accommodations, catering services and other industries of various types of ownership to urban and rural households for living consumption and to social institutions for public consumption.

Total Purchases of Commodities by Wholesale and Retail Trades refer to the purchases of commodities from other establishments or individuals (including direct import from abroad) for the purpose of reselling, either with or without further processing of the commodities purchased This indicator includes the purchases from producers, the purchases from wholesale and retail trades, imports and other purchases It is used to show the total value of purchases of commodities by wholesale and retail establishments from domestic and overseas markets.

Total Sales of Commodities by Wholesale and Retail Trades refer to the value of commodities sold to other establishments and individuals (including direct export and commodities sold to the sellers themselves for consumption). This indicator includes the value of wholesale to production and operation units, the value of wholesale to wholesale and retail trades, exports and retail sales to urban and rural households and social institutions It is an indicator of the total value of sales of commodities at domestic markets and export.

Wholesale refers to all selling activities of commodities except retail trade, including wholesale to production and operation units, wholesale to wholesale and retail trades and export.

Wholesale to Production and Operation Units refers to commodities sold to departments of national economy and social departments for their production and operation.

Retail Sale refers to the selling of commodities to urban and rural households for living consumption and to social institutions for direct public consumption.

Total Inventory of Wholesale and Retail Trades at the Year-end refers to the total commodities possessed by wholesale and retail enterprises, which reflects the commodity stock level of various wholesale and retail enterprises and the potential for market supply.

Corporate Units in Wholesale and Retail Trades, Accommodations and Catering Services refer to the number of corporate enterprises of various types of ownership in the wholesale and retail trades, accommodations and catering services with independent accounting systems An enterprise can be called a corporate enterprise only when it simultaneously meets the following requirements:(1)It is established according to law, with its own name, organization and location for business operation, as well as the capability to independently assume civil responsibility (2)It owns and uses its assets independently, assumes liabilities and is entitled to sign contracts with other units (3)It has an independent accounting system and is able to compile balance sheets.

Wholesale Trade refers to the commodity circulation enterprises (establishments) and individuals which purchase commodities from producers in industry and agriculture or from commodity circulation enterprises and individuals for the purpose of reselling them to establishments in industry, agriculture, construction, transportation, postal and telecommunications services, accommodations and catering services and other services for their production and operation as well as reselling them to other wholesale or retail enterprises.

Retail Trade refers to the commodity circulation enterprises (establishments) and individuals which purchase commodities from producers in industry and agriculture, wholesale trade or residents for the purpose of reselling them to urban and rural households for living consumption and to social institutions for public consumption.

十七、住宿餐饮业和旅游

HOTELS，CATERING SERVICES AND TOURISM

十七 住宿餐饮业和旅游

简要说明

一、本篇资料主要反映住宿和餐饮业的基本情况、经营情况和旅游产业的发展情况。主要内容包括：限额以上住宿和餐饮业基本情况、经营情况、财务情况；连锁餐饮业经营情况；经广东口岸入境游客人数（港澳台和外国人）、城市接待国内外旅游人数、旅行社组织接待人数、以及旅游收入等基本情况。

二、本篇资料来源

本篇资料中住宿和餐饮业主要根据国家统计局《住宿和餐饮业统计报表制度》进行搜集和加工整理；旅游资料主要由广东省旅游局提供。入境游客人数由广州、深圳、珠海、汕头出入境边防检查站，武警广东省边防总队所报资料汇总而得。

三、本篇资料的统计范围

限额以上住宿和餐饮业的企业、个体户；餐饮连锁集团；旅行社、星级饭店和旅游者。住宿业年主营业务收入 200 万元及以上；餐饮业年主营业务收入 200 万元及以上。

四、本篇的调查方法

限额以上住宿和餐饮业资料采用全面调查的方法自下而上逐级综合汇总而得，限额以下企业及个体户资料采用抽样调查方法推算而得。旅游部门基本情况、住宿设施接待人数、旅行社接待人数由各基层企业上报汇总，城市接待旅游人数、国内外旅游收入根据抽样调查资料测算。

五、本篇资料由广东省统计局贸易外经处整理、编辑。

17 Hotels,Catering Services and Tourism

Brief Introduction

Ⅰ. Data in this chapter reflect the development of hotel and catering services and tourism in China. They mainly include: the basic conditions, operating and financial status of hotel and catering services above the designated size; the operating status of chain catering services; number of international tourists entering China through ports in Guangdong (including foreigners, Chinese compatriots from Hong Kong, Macao and Taiwan), number of domestic and international tourists received by cities, number of tourists received by travel agencies, and earnings from tourism, etc.

Ⅱ. Data sources :

The data are collected and processed in accordance with the Statistical Reporting Scheme on Accommodations and Catering Services stipulated by the National Bureau of Statistics. The data in this chapter are provided by Guangdong Provincial Tourism Administration. Number of international tourists entering China through ports in Guangdong is a summary of data provided by the frontier inspection posts of Guangzhou, Shenzhen, Zhuhai, and Shantou, as well as the Guangdong Provincial Command of the Chinese People's Armed Police Force.

Ⅲ. The statistical coverage in this chapter comes as follows:

Data in this chapter cover the enterprises of hotel and catering services above the designated size, self-employed households of hotel and catering services; chain catering services, travel agencies, star-rated hotels and tourists; hotels with annual turnover of 2 million yuan or above, and catering services with annual turnover of 2 million yuan or above.

Ⅳ. The statistical coverage in this chapter comes as follows:

Data on basic conditions for all corporate enterprises of accommodations and catering services above the designated size are collected through comprehensive reporting systems and data are reported level by level in a bottom-up manner. Data on small-size enterprises and individual enterprises below the designated size are collected through sample surveys. Basic statistics on tourist agencies, the number of tourists received by lodging facilities, and the number of tourists received by travel agencies are summaries of reports from various enterprises, whereas the number of tourists received by cities and earnings from domestic and international tourism are estimates from sample surveys.

V. The data in this chapter are prepared and edited by the Division of Trade and External Economic Relations Statistics of Statistics Bureau of Guangdong Province.

17-1 住宿、餐饮业、旅游主要指标
Main Indicators on Hotels, Catering Services and Tourism

指标	Item	2000	2010	2013	2014	2015	2016	2017
限额以上住宿餐饮业营业额（亿元）	**Business Revenue from Hotels and Catering Services above Designated Size (100 million yuan)**		**901.95**	**1443.67**	**1505.74**	**1600.72**	**1564.69**	**1499.70**
#客房收入	Revenue from Accommodations		189.48	277.16	316.78	326.56	327.15	330.91
餐费收入	Revenue from Restaurants		645.66	1069.14	1078.63	1153.00	1110.15	1026.89
商品销售收入	Revenue from Sales of Commodities		15.17	21.30	25.77	30.78	32.26	45.03
旅行社数（个）	**Number of Travel Agencies (unit)**	**504**	**1292**	**1810**	**1984**	**2150**	**2345**	**2639**
旅行社从业人员（人）	**Engaged Persons of Travel Agencies (person)**		**37841**	**52418**	**55853**	**62779**	**65348**	**66522**
星级宾馆(酒店)数(个)	**Number of Star-rated Hotels (unit)**	**750**	**1209**	**1083**	**1012**	**960**	**861**	**771**
接待过夜旅游者人数（万人次）	**Number of Tourists Staying Overnight Received (10000 person-times)**	**7662.95**	**21283.05**	**30151.01**	**32761.25**	**36225.18**	**39718.47**	**44385.26**
入境旅游者	Inbound Tourists	1198.94	3141.09	3397.88	3355.45	3445.36	3518.38	3645.50
外国人	Foreigners	212.85	732.25	760.49	775.19	781.83	824.93	861.54
港澳同胞	Chinese Compatriots from Hong Kong and Macao	813.84	2091.07	2352.15	2301.17	2382.48	2418.00	2501.83
台湾同胞	Chinese Compatriots from Taiwan	172.25	316.74	285.24	279.09	281.05	275.45	282.13
国内旅游者	Domestic Tourists	6464.01	18141.96	26753.13	29405.80	32779.82	36200.09	40739.76
旅行社组织接待人数（万人）	**Number of Visitors Received by Travel Agencies (10000 persons)**	**653.41**	**2409.36**	**2604.98**	**2336.49**	**2498.08**	**2701.52**	**2820.40**
入境游客	Overseas Visitor Arrivals	264.22	448.74	406.84	348.46	341.33	371.59	394.14
国内游客	Domestic Visitors	389.19	1960.62	2198.14	1988.03	2156.75	2329.93	2426.26
团体出境旅游人数（万人）	**Number of Outbound Visitors in Group Tours (10000 persons)**	**116.20**	**426.52**	**774.18**	**860.54**	**899.53**	**1021.24**	**988.54**
港澳游	Visits to Hong Kong and Macao	86.07	276.74	462.74	498.48	467.56	456.74	434.48
其他	Others	30.13	149.78	311.44	362.06	431.97	564.50	554.06
旅游收入（亿元）	**Earnings from Tourism(100 million yuan)**	**1149.95**	**3809.44**	**6716.69**	**7850.56**	**9080.76**	**10433.81**	**11994.79**
旅游外汇收入	Foreign Exchange Earnings	340.08	844.85	1008.05	1049.31	1104.16	1233.51	1327.65
国内旅游收入	Domestic Tourism Earnings	809.87	2964.59	5708.64	6801.25	7976.60	9200.30	10667.14

注：2000年香港同胞包括澳门同胞。
Note: In 2000, data of Chinese compatriots from Hong Kong include those from Macao.

17−2　限额以上住宿业经营情况（2017年）

Business of Hotels above Designated Size (2017)

单位：万元　　　　(10000 yuan)

项　目	Item	企业(单位)数(个) Number of Enterprises (unit)	营业额合计 Business Revenue	#客房收入 Revenue from Hotels	#餐费收入 Revenue from Restaurants	#商品销售收入 Revenue from Sales of Commodities
住宿业合计	**Total Accommodations**	**2578**	**5817279**	**3031575**	**1827513**	**145905**
#国有及国有控股	State-owned and State-controlled Enterprises	219	948243	476896	308325	8335
按登记注册类型分组	By Status of Registration					
内资企业	Domestic-funded Enterprises	2015	4436262	2251713	1397922	99239
国有企业	State-owned Enterprises	100	323272	149809	111399	3962
集体企业	Collective-owned Enterprises	29	23482	9318	8846	437
股份合作企业	Share-holding Cooperative Enterprises	4	1968	1189	746	32
联营企业	Joint-operation Enterprises	2	2610	2031	150	313
国有联营企业	State-owned Joint-operation Enterprises	1	2414	1952	150	313
集体联营企业	Collective Joint-operation Enterprises	1	196	79		
国有与集体联营企业	State-collective Joint-operation Enterprises					
其他联营企业	Other Joint-operation Enterprises					
有限责任公司	Limited Liability Corporations	821	2450538	1154155	782572	67710
国有独资企业	State Sole Investment Enterprises	39	217585	104888	79821	1351
其他有限责任公司	Other Limited Liability Companies	782	2232953	1049267	702751	66359
股份有限公司	Share-holding Corporations Ltd.	47	135767	66881	41901	1911
私营企业	Private Enterprises	977	1464404	849200	440895	24657
私营独资企业	Private Sole Investment Enterprises	144	114457	72649	27552	3609
私营合伙企业	Private Partnership Enterprises	32	31315	13671	12864	296
私营有限责任公司	Private Limited Liability Corporations	771	1273874	741106	383642	19949
私营股份有限公司	Private Share-holding Corporations Ltd.	30	44758	21774	16837	803
其他企业	Other Enterprises	35	34221	19130	11413	217
港、澳、台商投资企业	Enterprises with Investment from Hong Kong,Macao and Taiwan	141	693851	329972	255732	33075
合资经营企业	Joint Ventures	53	208563	92030	77790	9835
合作经营企业	Cooperative Enterprises	23	156219	77466	58102	8716
独资经营企业	Sole Investment Enterprises	57	317912	153472	118337	12326
投资股份有限公司	Share-holding Corporations Ltd.	6	10486	6644	1262	2187
其他港澳台投资企业	Others	2	671	360	241	11
外商投资企业	Enterprises with Foreign Investment	69	473314	272451	145403	8733
中外合资经营企业	Sino-foreign Joint Ventures	23	145868	92069	42202	974
中外合作经营企业	Sino-foreign Cooperative Enterprises	14	72096	25852	28093	4560
外资企业	Foreign-funded Enterprises	26	212001	135271	52442	2842
外商投资股份有限公司	Share-holding Corporations Ltd.	3	630	568	60	
其他外商投资企业	Others	3	42719	18691	22606	357
个体工商户	Self-employed Individuals	353	213852	177439	28456	4858
按国民经济行业分组	By Economic Sector					
旅游饭店	Tourist Hotels	1433	4712101	2233832	1629524	128479
一般旅馆	General Hotels	1002	955994	688777	170477	14810
其它住宿服务	Others	143	149184	108966	27512	2616

17-3 限额以上餐饮业经营情况（2017年）

Business of Catering Services Enterprises above Designated Size (2017)

单位：万元 (10000 yuan)

项 目	Item	企业(单位)数(个) Number of Enterprises (unit)	营业额 Business Revenue	#客房收入 Revenue from Hotels	#餐费收入 Revenue from Restaurants	#商品销售收入 Revenue from Sales of Commodities
餐饮业合计	**Total Catering Services**	**5604**	**9179752**	**277534**	**8441402**	**304400**
#国有及国有控股	State-owned and State-controlled Enterprises	43	267912	22648	189182	32131
按登记注册类型分	By Status of Registration					
内资企业	Domestic-funded Enterprises	2796	4693307	244201	4115798	203069
国有企业	State-owned Enterprises	23	58584	13129	39931	395
集体企业	Collective-owned Enterprises	28	53170	14036	31491	1893
股份合作企业	Share-holding Cooperative Enterprises	26	38459		38455	4
联营企业	Joint-operation Enterprises	1	2254	1070	1144	40
国有联营企业	State-owned Joint-operation Enterprises					
集体联营企业	Collective Joint-operation Enterprises					
国有与集体联营企业	State-collective Joint-operation Enterprises					
其他联营企业	Other Joint-operation Enterprises	1	2254	1070	1144	40
有限责任公司	Limited Liability Corporations	722	1714110	97238	1493212	71756
国有独资企业	State Sole Investment Enterprises	5	28945	1043	17929	3732
其他有限责任公司	Other Limited Liability Companies	717	1685165	96195	1475283	68024
股份有限公司	Share-holding Corporations Ltd.	31	117968	1916	86694	27220
私营企业	Private Enterprises	1894	2653232	114287	2372965	101085
私营独资企业	Private Sole Investment Enterprises	488	432624	14389	406352	9635
私营合伙企业	Private Partnership Enterprises	75	78533	1005	74997	1671
私营有限责任公司	Private Limited Liability Corporations	1291	2098698	89456	1858923	89044
私营股份有限公司	Private Share-holding Corporations Ltd.	40	43377	9437	32693	735
其他企业	Other Enterprises	71	55530	2525	51906	676
港、澳、台商投资企业	Enterprises with Investment from Hong Kong, Macao and Taiwan	213	1333568	12209	1259834	54761
合资经营企业	Joint Ventures	34	84979	1131	75572	7832
合作经营企业	Cooperative Enterprises	10	91019	5211	83025	1798
独资经营企业	Sole Investment Enterprises	166	1146780	5867	1090720	44861
投资股份有限公司	Share-holding Corporations Ltd.	3	10790		10517	270
外商投资企业	Enterprises with Foreign Investment	69	1596570	3870	1551003	29819
中外合资经营企业	Sino-foreign Joint Ventures	14	417198	1425	412301	57
中外合作经营企业	Sino-foreign Cooperative Enterprises	3	5494	1860	2357	242
外资企业	Foreign-funded Enterprises	41	1122628	51	1105966	9307
外商投资股份有限公司	Share-holding Corporations Ltd.	4	25257	534	4386	20213
其他外商投资企业	Others	7	25993		25993	
个体工商户	Self-employed Individuals	2526	1556307	17254	1514767	16751
按国民经济行业分	By Economic Sector					
正餐服务业	Restaurant Service	5161	5902468	273233	5371465	132310
快餐服务业	Fast Food Service	208	2327219	21	2290312	22791
饮料及冷饮服务业	Beverage and Cold Drink Service	58	432629	200	374671	55561
其他餐饮服务业	Other Services	177	517436	4080	404954	93738

17-4 各市限额以上住宿餐饮业经营情况（2017年）
Business of Enterprises above Designated Size of Hotels and Catering Services by City (2017)

单位：万元 (10000 yuan)

市别	Item	企业(单位)数(个) Number of Enterprises (unit)	营业额 Business Revenue	#客房收入 Revenue from Hotels	#餐费收入 Revenue from Restaurants	#商品销售收入 Revenue from Sales of Commodities
合　计	**Total**	**8182**	**14997031**	**3309109**	**10268915**	**450305**
住宿业	**Accommodation**	**2578**	**5817279**	**3031575**	**1827513**	**145905**
广　州	Guangzhou	534	1331257	761230	351543	16455
深　圳	Shenzhen	385	1350004	806574	396452	8728
珠　海	Zhuhai	143	668766	271264	162196	38161
汕　头	Shantou	98	122865	65557	40773	2132
佛　山	Foshan	158	337578	135600	133963	13032
韶　关	Shaoguan	84	95555	51271	34257	2321
河　源	Heyuan	62	73899	39968	25255	3593
梅　州	Meizhou	51	70965	28883	30028	4081
惠　州	Huizhou	135	294863	151083	104530	13199
汕　尾	Shanwei	29	26214	16069	8770	213
东　莞	Dongguan	177	423350	175337	190112	4719
中　山	Zhongshan	123	182847	80032	73877	2058
江　门	Jiangmen	125	173525	76799	59074	7875
阳　江	Yangjiang	38	31332	25773	4751	87
湛　江	Zhanjiang	86	113431	51887	49965	2577
茂　名	Maoming	73	73209	51681	14720	1369
肇　庆	Zhaoqing	73	85435	50930	27279	3080
清　远	Qingyuan	58	110070	56256	37110	1653
潮　州	Chaozhou	32	21538	12781	6323	180
揭　阳	Jieyang	48	186616	95757	63611	19055
云　浮	Yunfu	66	43960	26843	12924	1337
餐饮业	**Catering Service**	**5604**	**9179752**	**277534**	**8441402**	**304400**
广　州	Guangzhou	1205	3158152	46151	2961814	102341
深　圳	Shenzhen	772	2591359	49679	2402311	86681
珠　海	Zhuhai	331	263217	2251	254992	3984
汕　头	Shantou	124	107496	834	105970	321
佛　山	Foshan	310	464100	22854	425219	9010
韶　关	Shaoguan	101	56982	9168	46023	570
河　源	Heyuan	120	69080	7141	57714	3394
梅　州	Meizhou	57	37571	6334	29993	1036
惠　州	Huizhou	218	203656	23321	161590	6987
汕　尾	Shanwei	54	38397	2556	34344	221
东　莞	Dongguan	391	579173	7374	512654	52582
中　山	Zhongshan	285	284119	440	281620	237
江　门	Jiangmen	310	207771	4425	200151	945
阳　江	Yangjiang	188	158704	7999	147727	837
湛　江	Zhanjiang	290	254680	16775	229771	6435
茂　名	Maoming	250	188966	9699	176672	1755
肇　庆	Zhaoqing	194	144083	6731	129210	4674
清　远	Qingyuan	71	50448	7061	41862	718
潮　州	Chaozhou	102	60103	1743	54137	2413
揭　阳	Jieyang	82	211981	41750	142904	17865
云　浮	Yunfu	149	49714	3248	44724	1394

17-5 限额以上连锁住宿餐饮业经营情况（2017年）
Business of Chain Stores above Designated Size in Hotels and Catering Services (2017)

项　　目	Item	连锁总店数(个) Number of General Chain Stores (unit)	营业收入(万元) Total Business Revenue (10000 yuan)	#零售额(万元) Retail Sales (10000 yuan)	营业面积(平方米) Operational Area (sq.m)
住宿餐饮业合计	**Catering Service**	**80**	**2909330**	**2678552**	**1358646**
按注册登记类型分	By Status of Registration				
内资企业	Domestic-funded Enterprises	46	712307	622426	373612
国有企业	State-owned Enterprises	2	26086	22548	4344
集体企业	Collective-owned Enterprises	1	11635	10577	12000
股份合作企业	Cooperative Enterprises	1	714	714	1040
有限责任公司	Limited Liability Corporations	14	323149	305536	157593
股份有限公司	Share-holding Enterprises	3	144803	96775	71731
私营企业	Private Enterprises	25	205920	186276	126904
其他企业	Other Enterprises				
港、澳、台商投资企业	Enterprises with Investment from Hong Kong, Macao and Taiwan	19	784878	670824	227371
合资经营企业(港或澳、台资)	Joint Ventures	2	26073	26073	14757
合作经营企业(港或澳、台资)	Cooperative Enterprises	1	25160	25160	17000
港、澳、台商独资经营企业	Sole Investment Enterprises	16	733645	619591	195614
港、澳、台商投资股份有限公司	Share-holding Corporations Ltd.				
外商投资企业	Enterprises with Foreign Investment	15	1412145	1385302	757663
中外合资经营企业	Sino-foreign Joint Ventures	3	416104	389261	190714
中外合作经营企业	Sino-foreign Cooperative Enterprises				
外资企业	Foreign-funded Enterprises	11	993110	993110	566259
其他外商投资企业	Others	1	2931	2931	690
按行业分	By Sector				
旅游饭店	Tour Hotel	5	194741	3651	10526
一般旅馆	General Hotel	8	38783	845	2379
正餐服务	Restaurant	25	351895	350734	221676
快餐服务	Fast Food	34	2029165	2028576	1043923
咖啡馆服务	Cafe Service	6	293249	293249	79310
其他餐饮及冷饮服务	Other dining and beverage service	2	1497	1497	832

17−5 续表 continued

项　目	Item	就业人数(人) Number of Employed Persons (person)	连锁门店数(个) Number of Branch Chain Stores (unit)	直营店(个) Under Direct Management (unit)	加盟店(个) Through License Arrangement (unit)
住宿餐饮业合计	**Catering Service**	**114896**	**4371**	**4315**	**56**
按注册登记类型分	By Status of Registration				
内资企业	Domestic-funded Enterprises	32666	1349	1339	10
国有企业	State-owned Enterprises	810	58	58	
集体企业	Collective-owned Enterprises	560	3	3	
股份合作企业	Share-holding Cooperative Enterprises	38	2	2	
有限责任公司	Limited Liability Corporations	15044	667	664	3
股份有限公司	Share-holding Corporations Ltd.	6118	62	55	7
私营企业	Private Enterprises	10096	557	557	
其他企业	Other Enterprises				
港、澳、台商投资企业	Enterprises with Investment from Hong Kong, Macao and Taiwan	28095	1034	988	46
合资经营企业　(港或澳、台资)	Joint Ventures	797	25	25	
合作经营企业　(港或澳、台资)	Cooperative Enterprises	583	4	4	
港、澳、台商独资经营企业	Sole Investment Enterprises	26715	1005	959	46
港、澳、台商投资股份有限公司	Share-holding Corporations Ltd.				
外商投资企业	Enterprises with Foreign Investment	54135	1988	1988	
中外合资经营企业	Sino-foreign Joint Ventures	10538	416	416	
中外合作经营企业	Sino-foreign Cooperative Enterprises				
外资企业	Foreign-funded Enterprises	43319	1545	1545	
其他外商投资企业	Others	278	27	27	
按行业分	By Sector				
旅游饭店	Tourist Hotel	4690	111	105	6
一般旅馆	General Hotel	1223	102	102	
正餐服务	Restaurant	13789	310	309	1
快餐服务	Fast Food	86818	3026	2984	42
咖啡馆服务	Cafe Service	8296	812	808	4
其他餐饮及冷饮服务	Other dining and beverage service	80	10	7	3

17-6 限额以上住宿餐饮企业财务状况（2017年）

Financial Indicators of Enterprises above Designated Size in Hotels and Catering Services (2017)

单位：万元 (10000 yuan)

项　目	Item	住宿和餐饮业合计 Total Hotels and Catering Services	住宿业 Hotels Services	餐饮业 Catering Services
企业数（个）	Number of Enterprises (unit)	5284	2217	3067
年初存货	Inventory at the Year-beginning	582956	393276	189680
流动资产合计	Circulating Assets	10610427	7639694	2970733
#存货	Inventory	627645	464406	163239
固定资产原价	Original Value of Fixed Assets	12545959	10242107	2303852
累计折旧	Accumulated Depreciation	5834521	4729946	1104575
#本年折旧	Depreciation Drawn in Current Year	571616	440494	131122
资产合计	Total Assets	22723734	17222908	5500826
负债合计	Total Liabilities	18362609	14573284	3789325
所有者权益合计	Total Creditors' Equity	4361125	2649624	1711501
实收资本	Paid-up Capital	8843164	7628836	1214328
#国家资本	State Capital	891457	845517	45940
集体资本	Collective Capital	66770	54703	12067
法人资本	Legal Person Capital	2449891	1997983	451908
个人资本	Personal Capital	3958939	3598404	360535
港澳台资本	Capital from Hong Kong, Macao and Taiwan	1024707	788586	236121
外商资本	Foreign Capital	451400	343643	107757
营业收入	Business Revenue	12667801	5387450	7280351
#主营业务收入	Main Business Revenue	12558408	5316190	7242218
营业成本	Business Costs	5786748	2193393	3593355
#主营业务成本	Main Business Costs	5711692	2152191	3559501
营业税金及附加	Tax and Extra Charges on Business	129434	77751	51683
#主营业务税金及附加	Tax and Extra Charges on Main Business	125026	74797	50229
其它业务利润	Profits from Other Businesses	81417	44680	36737
销售费用	Marketing Expenses	3956971	1510147	2446824
管理费用	Management Expenses	2163527	1351839	811688
财务费用	Financial Expenses	299380	253563	45817
#利息支出	Interests	207751	188964	18787
营业利润	Business Profits	396665	46985	349680
营业外收入	Non-operating Revenue	83250	51655	31595
利润总额	Total Profits	463524	78089	385435
应交所得税	Income Taxes Payable	156455	57350	99105
本年应付职工薪酬	Total Wages Payable in Current Year	2899668	1345328	1554340

17-7 限额以上住宿企业财务状况（2017年）

单位：万元

项　目	Item	企业数（个）Number of Enterprises (unit)	年初库存 Beginning Inventory	流动资产合计 Circulating Assets	固定资产原价 Original Value of Fixed Assets
住宿业合计	**Total Hotels**	**2217**	**393276**	**7639694**	**10242107**
#国有及国有控股	State-owned and State-controlled Enterprises	217	33608	984902	2028734
按登记注册类型分	By Status of Registration				
内资企业	Domestic-funded Enterprises	2008	167476	5552839	7235527
国有企业	State-owned Enterprises	100	8333	277526	606909
集体企业	Collective-owned Enterprises	29	516	13928	43462
股份合作企业	Share-holding Cooperative Enterprises	4	163	645	5629
联营企业	Joint-operation Enterprises	2	210	6505	808
国有联营企业	State-owned Joint-operation Enterprises	1	207	6435	619
集体联营企业	Collective Joint-operation Enterprises	1	3	70	189
国有与集体联营企业	State-collective Joint-operation Enterprises				
其他联营企业	Other Joint-operation Enterprises				
有限责任公司	Limited Liability Corporations	818	87471	3553314	4519700
国有独资企业	State Sole Investment Enterprises	38	3814	302177	552505
其他有限责任公司	Other Limited Liability Companies	780	83657	3251137	3967195
股份有限公司	Share-holding Corporations Ltd.	47	11902	285735	240858
私营企业	Private Enterprises	973	57851	1401800	1782726
私营独资企业	Private Sole Investment Enterprises	143	2112	66313	116304
私营合伙企业	Private Partnership Enterprises	32	745	23109	39059
私营有限责任公司	Private Limited Liability Corporations	768	54268	1278743	1558547
私营股份有限公司	Private Share-holding Corporations Ltd.	30	726	33635	68816
其他企业	Other Enterprises	35	1030	13386	35435
港、澳、台商投资企业	Enterprises with Investment from Hong Kong, Macao and Taiwan	140	220168	1129115	1863305
合资经营企业	Joint Ventures	52	4749	290810	544008
合作经营企业	Cooperative Enterprises	23	3002	156687	415018
独资经营企业	Sole Investment Enterprises	57	211943	657659	899057
投资股份有限公司	Share-holding Corporations Ltd.	6	456	23895	5004
其他港澳台商投资企业	Others	2	18	64	218
外商投资企业	Enterprises with Foreign Investment	69	5632	957740	1143275
中外合资经营企业	Sino-foreign Joint Ventures	23	2095	367772	432849
中外合作经营企业	Sino-foreign Cooperative Enterprises	14	1402	87751	174434
外资企业	Foreign-funded Enterprises	26	1733	497554	531891
外商投资股份有限公司	Share-holding Corporations Ltd.	3		164	3761
其它外商投资企业	Others	3	402	4499	340
按国民经济行业分	By Economic Sector				
旅游饭店	Tourist Hotels	1346	373799	6435857	9116620
一般旅馆	General Hotels	797	17863	1038170	1007708
其它住宿服务	Others	74	1614	165667	117779
按控股情况分组	By Holdings				
国有控股	State Holdings	217	33608	984902	2028734
集体控股	Collective Holdings	47	871	32278	88676
私人控股	Private Holdings	1420	109827	3409690	4266086
港澳台商控股	Hongkong,Macaw and Taiwan Holdings	117	218429	1173524	1572711
外商控股	Foreign Holdings	43	2413	671822	655612
其他	Others	373	28128	1367478	1630288
按星级分组	By sStar Rating				
五星	Five Star	128	220617	2502256	3033067
四星	Four Star	208	24854	1040711	1208947
三星	Three Star	347	16739	523968	692583
二星	Two Star	60	1005	52999	79691
一星	One Star	8	28	2978	9814
其他	Others	1466	130033	3516782	5218005

Financial Indicators of Hotels above Designated Size (2017)

(10000 yuan)

累计折旧 Accumulated Depreciation	本年折旧 Depreciation Drawn in Current Year	资产合计 Total Assets	负债合计 Total Liabilities	所有者权益合计 Total Creditors' Equity	实收资本 Paid-up Capital	营业收入 Business Revenue	主营业务收入 Main Business Revenue	营业成本 Business Costs
4729946	**440494**	**17222908**	**14573284**	**2649624**	**7628836**	**5387450**	**5316190**	**2193393**
1035916	64262	2857353	1364289	1493064	1026462	910065	893699	328925
3102145	348669	12887529	11019735	1867794	5905971	4265479	4204742	1741984
338827	20333	764119	403733	360386	196926	305028	299174	96366
30689	1029	38682	49133	-10451	15320	22753	21384	9790
4154	268	3701	3974	-273	702	1876	1876	421
585	78	10212	1372	8840	8000	2298	2298	140
585	78	8217	922	7295	6000	2102	2102	135
		1995	450	1545	2000	196	196	5
1733803	224774	8313241	7359124	954117	1742344	2364870	2329788	1003822
263421	19257	794219	435939	358280	272195	216640	213775	99986
1470382	205517	7519022	6923185	595837	1470149	2148230	2116013	903836
145061	9321	665199	256318	408881	217626	130230	129754	46669
828661	90041	3057608	2932244	125364	3702742	1404494	1387650	564477
52656	4365	160256	93074	67182	67646	111470	111232	59840
16381	1385	52031	43538	8493	10044	30033	29083	13557
733506	76545	2737671	2712553	25118	3596706	1219492	1204023	468558
26118	7746	107650	83079	24571	28346	43499	43312	22522
20365	2825	34767	13837	20930	22311	33930	32818	20299
1041357	58551	2561640	2055325	506315	1147825	663767	658580	271625
342290	17803	706648	668789	37859	253075	204893	203115	87250
204672	17124	445962	290704	155258	242373	149684	149092	67726
491611	23163	1367965	1056453	311512	605617	298558	295956	110835
2734	442	40807	38972	1835	46660	9980	9765	5699
50	19	258	407	-149	100	652	652	115
586444	33274	1773739	1498224	275515	575040	458204	452868	179784
155785	12138	721119	776404	-55285	120888	142337	140326	37981
128202	2944	172445	242844	-70399	113994	68801	67971	19024
300969	18098	868311	542647	325664	331172	203785	201290	97993
1481	87	2902	788	2114	3284	605	605	195
7	7	8962	-64459	73421	5702	42676	42676	24591
4221264	386659	14930547	12860291	2070256	6914944	4473040	4411696	1758459
454396	48376	2024097	1507267	516830	649420	808423	798996	390098
54286	5459	268264	205726	62538	64472	105987	105498	44836
1035916	64262	2857353	1364289	1493064	1026462	910065	893699	328925
58528	2492	87885	85228	2657	33176	45267	41891	22852
1615567	219695	7850229	7434656	415573	4425601	2640615	2612473	1172802
911247	43406	2360944	1951699	409245	1041716	576486	572664	216529
384477	21984	1098016	778765	319251	400111	268400	263909	113237
724211	88655	2968481	2958647	9834	701770	946617	931554	339048
1663145	87732	5292936	4011652	1281284	1488869	1338723	1325060	422118
623459	36880	2215400	1948357	267043	572988	716383	706075	286127
404964	26005	1028286	692958	335328	402299	556003	546083	221741
57066	4883	99983	82870	17113	55450	56780	55058	25795
3944	516	9439	7784	1655	2241	4890	4731	2261
1977368	284478	8576864	7829663	747201	5106989	2714671	2679183	1235351

17-7 续表

单位：万元

项 目	Item	主营业务成本 Main Business Costs	营业税金及附加 Tax and Extra Charges on Business	主营业务税金及附加 Tax and Extra Charges on Main Business
住宿业合计	**Total Hotels**	**2152191**	**77751**	**74797**
#国有及国有控股	State-owned and State-controlled Enterprises	318111	18750	17296
按登记注册类型分	By Status of Registration			
内资企业	Domestic-funded Enterprises	1707020	60545	58050
国有企业	State-owned Enterprises	95640	5354	4906
集体企业	Collective-owned Enterprises	9502	389	311
股份合作企业	Share-holding Cooperative Enterprises	421	22	22
联营企业	Joint-operation Enterprises	140	22	22
国有联营企业	State-owned Joint-operation Enterprises	135	20	20
集体联营企业	Collective Joint-operation Enterprises	5	2	2
国有与集体联营企业	State-collective Joint-operation Enterprises			
其他联营企业	Other Joint-operation Enterprises			
有限责任公司	Limited Liability Corporations	975588	34144	32526
国有独资企业	State Sole Investment Enterprises	95812	3794	3047
其他有限责任公司	Other Limited Liability Companies	879776	30350	29479
股份有限公司	Share-holding Corporations Ltd.	46524	2424	2419
私营企业	Private Enterprises	559690	17580	17269
私营独资企业	Private Sole Investment Enterprises	59442	2065	1967
私营合伙企业	Private Partnership Enterprises	13347	624	605
私营有限责任公司	Private Limited Liability Corporations	464730	14389	14201
私营股份有限公司	Private Share-holding Corporations Ltd.	22171	502	496
其他企业	Other Enterprises	19515	610	575
港、澳、台商投资企业	Enterprises with Investment from Hong Kong, Macao and Taiwan	269712	10062	9972
合资经营企业	Joint Ventures	85668	2651	2641
合作经营企业	Cooperative Enterprises	67722	2049	1983
独资经营企业	Sole Investment Enterprises	110508	5159	5145
投资股份有限公司	Share-holding Corporations Ltd.	5699	178	178
其他港澳台商投资企业	Others	115	25	25
外商投资企业	Enterprises with Foreign Investment	175459	7144	6775
中外合资经营企业	Sino-foreign Joint Ventures	36475	2865	2608
中外合作经营企业	Sino-foreign Cooperative Enterprises	19024	835	745
外资企业	Foreign-funded Enterprises	95174	3312	3312
外商投资股份有限公司	Share-holding Corporations Ltd.	195	32	32
其它外商投资企业	Others	24591	100	78
按国民经济行业分	By Economic Sector			
旅游饭店	Tourist Hotels	1727106	66729	64100
一般旅馆	Ordinary Hotels	382511	9499	9192
其它住宿服务	Others	42574	1523	1505
按控股情况分组	By Holdings			
国有控股	State Holdings	318111	18750	17296
集体控股	Collective Holdings	21066	640	534
私人控股	Private Holdings	1155708	33030	32248
港澳台商控股	Hongkong,Macaw and Taiwan Holdings	215948	8701	8620
外商控股	Foreign Holdings	108913	4422	4205
其他	Others	332445	12208	11894
按星级分组	By Star Rating			
五星	Five Star	418686	19766	19314
四星	Four Star	274824	12433	11380
三星	Three Star	216541	6935	6788
二星	Two Star	24184	704	640
一星	One Star	2164	90	90
其他	Others	1215792	37823	36585

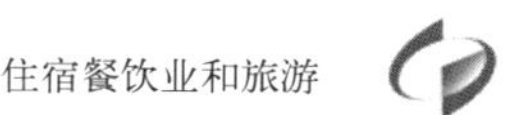

17-7 continued

(10000 yuan)

其它业务利润 Profits from Other Businesses	销售费用 Marketing Expenses	管理费用 Management Expenses	财务费用 Financial Expenses	营业利润 Business Profits	营业外收入 Non-operating revenue	利润总额 Total Profits	应交所得税 Income Taxes Payable	本年应付职工薪酬 Staff Salary Payable in Current Year
44680	**1510147**	**1351839**	**253563**	**46985**	**51655**	**78089**	**57350**	**1345328**
5245	266565	256353	16232	55541	15634	66091	18950	299229
33731	1222012	1056203	235217	-9054	43913	17191	38544	1084606
4387	100750	97187	4803	10157	12705	22533	4200	113064
479	7458	5795	586	-1273	227	190	130	6926
	983	913	7	-471	1	-475	10	763
	1866	75	10	185	2	228	59	774
	1708	41	10	187	2	230	59	678
	158	34		-2		-2		96
12057	632269	573526	165124	-31653	25930	-24603	20020	583045
29	55284	51657	147	7226	916	6807	3160	74923
12028	576985	521869	164977	-38879	25014	-31410	16860	508122
82	38866	35410	3941	22696	1165	22278	2536	36988
16882	434862	337779	60552	-10812	3816	-5418	11444	336917
4053	21706	14637	2583	10761	117	11075	2728	23412
	8075	6456	1023	299	91	285	129	7527
12621	394542	308594	56078	-22672	3246	-18256	7951	296135
208	10539	8092	868	800	362	1478	636	9843
-156	4958	5518	194	2117	67	2458	145	6129
3589	159628	179104	11870	34947	6578	40309	10798	155528
923	55891	48236	11765	-136	900	913	1474	49328
2167	31611	39079	4684	7202	2902	9582	3222	35781
496	70303	87865	-4606	29228	2573	31035	6097	67009
3	1446	3778	24	-1353	198	-1212	5	3079
	377	146	3	6	5	-9		331
7360	128507	116532	6476	21092	1164	20589	8008	105194
335	59522	53593	3156	-14662	502	-14564	2511	31333
6309	27092	19897	199	2111	251	1996	806	16883
716	39200	38890	2837	22408	411	21922	4674	45351
	72	544	2	-238		-238	1	169
	2621	3608	282	11473		11473	16	11458
33902	1264892	1136047	228579	60183	43931	83205	50090	1128844
8878	215022	188681	20470	-13446	6087	-6790	6355	190286
1900	30233	27111	4514	248	1637	1674	905	26198
5245	266565	256353	16232	55541	15634	66091	18950	299229
595	12844	9852	945	-2104	557	-251	253	11814
23584	695405	626117	175286	-52764	25108	-34208	15157	625174
3591	154386	158160	4109	37599	3768	40219	10237	132700
737	60023	63352	4378	23531	535	23048	4916	54732
10928	320924	238005	52613	-14818	6053	-16810	7837	221679
8640	365237	387617	57530	111840	7227	113173	22338	318346
6039	217016	170329	44460	-7445	3409	2489	5541	185819
6930	185811	119238	10379	18093	11837	26923	8892	155421
220	14540	10627	482	4681	145	4716	1148	13365
	818	1570	111	63	1	126	98	1337
22851	726725	662458	140601	-80247	29036	-69338	19333	671040

17-8 限额以上餐饮企业财务状况（2017年）

单位：万元

项　目	Item	企业数（个） Number of Enterprises (unit)	年初库存 Beginning Inventory	流动资产合计 Circulating Assets	固定资产原价 Original Value of Fixed Assets
餐饮业合计	**Total Catering Services**	**3067**	**189680**	**2970733**	**2303852**
#国有及国有控股	State-owned and State-controlled Enterprises	43	5175	191832	216655
按登记注册类型分	By Status of Registration				
内资企业	Domestic-funded Enterprises	2785	142508	2083082	1566866
国有企业	State-owned Enterprises	23	1871	26371	75635
集体企业	Collective-owned Enterprises	27	875	21858	9748
股份合作企业	Share-holding Cooperative Enterprises	26	4209	6437	2817
联营企业	Joint-operation Enterprises	1		4316	
国有联营企业	State-owned Joint-operation Enterprises				
集体联营企业	Collective Joint-operation Enterprises				
国有与集体联营企业	State-collective Joint-operation Enterprises				
其他联营企业	Other Joint-operation Enterprises	1		4316	
有限责任公司	Limited Liability Corporations	720	42227	964121	797771
国有独资企业	State Sole Investment Enterprises	5	481	12998	8724
其他有限责任公司	Other Limited Liability Companies	715	41746	951123	789047
股份有限公司	Share-holding Corporations Ltd.	31	1741	126387	23673
私营企业	Private Enterprises	1886	90443	925745	638917
私营独资企业	Private Sole Investment Enterprises	485	7548	80096	124017
私营合伙企业	Private Partnership Enterprises	75	25997	17815	18059
私营有限责任公司	Private Limited Liability Corporations	1287	56398	812474	479944
私营股份有限公司	Private Share-holding Corporations Ltd.	39	500	15360	16897
其他企业	Other Enterprises	71	1142	7847	18305
港、澳、台商投资企业	Enterprises with Investment from Hong Kong,Macao and Taiwan	213	28919	700885	407107
合资经营企业	Joint Ventures	34	2560	41090	36677
合作经营企业	Cooperative Enterprises	10	4326	27472	20963
独资经营企业	Sole Investment Enterprises	166	21788	626997	341875
投资股份有限公司	Share-holding Corporations Ltd.	3	245	5326	7592
外商投资企业	Enterprises with Foreign Investment	69	18253	186766	329879
中外合资经营企业	Sino-foreign Joint Ventures	14	4543	40986	143252
中外合作经营企业	Sino-foreign Cooperative Enterprises	3		9276	516
外资企业	Foreign-funded Enterprises	41	9567	122074	181198
外商投资股份有限公司	Share-holding Corporations Ltd.	4	916	8151	3611
其它外商投资企业	Others	7	3227	6279	1302
按国民经济行业分	By Economic Sector				
正餐服务业	Dinner Service	2744	149559	2150158	1687952
快餐服务业	Fast Food Service	136	25215	472433	514713
饮料及冷饮服务业	Beverage and Cold Drink Service	44	6146	169332	49977
餐饮配送及外卖送餐服务	Food and Beverage Distribution and Takeout Service	90	5015	116408	22178
其他餐饮服务业	Other Services	53	3745	62402	29032
按控股情况分组	By Holdings				
国有控股	State Holdings	43	5175	191832	216655
集体控股	Collective Holdings	41	3035	42603	22430
私人控股	Private Holdings	2405	117098	1515553	1087770
港澳台商控股	Hongkong,Macaw and Taiwan Holdings	209	28546	700267	393195
外商控股	Foreign Holdings	58	17695	170410	327385
其他	Others	311	18131	350068	256417

Financial Indicators of Catering Services Enterprises above Designated Size (2017)

(10000 yuan)

累计折旧 Accumulated Depreciation	本年折旧 Depreciation Drawn in Current Year	资产合计 Total Assets	负债合计 Total Liabilities	所有者权益合计 Total Creditors' Equity	实收资本 Paid-up Capital	营业收入 Business Revenue	主营业务收入 Main Business Revenue	营业成本 Business Costs
1104575	**131122**	**5500826**	**3789325**	**1711501**	**1214328**	**7280351**	**7242218**	**3593355**
101389	11785	390179	245021	145158	68144	254255	249360	152438
680414	97324	3730583	2916017	814566	783213	4505005	4479379	2461645
50714	4616	71621	39829	31792	10500	58706	56236	32380
7382	325	29529	14641	14888	6320	51657	51605	35107
2099	161	9462	8125	1337	721	36773	36773	21898
		10426	8573	1853	138	2254	2254	1130
		10426	8573	1853	138	2254	2254	1130
299378	42054	1816252	1499333	316919	294727	1643508	1632693	885707
4794	3562	17609	4069	13540	2960	26833	26741	22630
294584	38492	1798643	1495264	303379	291767	1616675	1605952	863077
11700	1016	200144	51308	148836	45431	107711	105511	53030
301525	48237	1572158	1287768	284390	419550	2550348	2540377	1399066
49001	6164	175171	98518	76653	59486	416618	415815	263587
8825	862	28874	13521	15353	19342	75101	75039	42276
238648	39804	1334748	1148771	185977	327429	2016187	2007148	1069196
5051	1407	33365	26958	6407	13293	42442	42375	24007
7616	915	20991	6440	14551	5826	54048	53930	33327
236438	21351	1168370	586900	581470	276086	1263725	1255060	453004
20828	1510	67567	35075	32492	37670	77188	77179	35645
15649	902	37727	40290	-2563	17507	84623	84623	53090
196823	18545	1051369	506911	544458	212490	1091796	1083143	359241
3138	394	11707	4624	7083	8419	10118	10115	5028
187723	12447	601873	286408	315465	155029	1511621	1507779	678706
81100	5038	169498	38042	131456	30182	394400	394215	134201
86	2	12443	4483	7960	8264	5481	5481	3880
104767	7340	392057	212690	179367	111125	1064346	1060793	504950
1424	5	10354	12508	-2154	2613	22064	21960	16275
346	62	17521	18685	-1164	2845	25330	25330	19400
784374	103467	3804308	2976976	827332	928060	4225373	4201413	2164838
271153	20318	1157743	565211	592532	211851	2176913	2166204	980801
22951	4557	272180	86530	185650	21032	404862	404667	127975
13746	414	177765	116707	61058	30632	315567	314347	238753
12351	2366	88830	43901	44929	22753	157636	155587	80988
101389	11785	390179	245021	145158	68144	254255	249360	152438
13450	1586	70310	33444	36866	19315	133344	132915	78642
474625	69738	2658141	2174373	483768	590328	3596847	3581999	1977673
226060	20719	1160402	582616	577786	272978	1227719	1219054	432816
186969	12174	578542	275500	303042	143758	1481022	1477334	660191
102082	15120	643252	478371	164881	119805	587164	581556	291595

17-8 续表

单位：万元

项　目	Item	主营业务成本 Main Business Costs	营业税金及附加 Tax and Extra Charges on Business	主营业务税金及附加 Tax and Extra Charges on Main Business
餐饮业合计	**Total Catering Services**	**3559501**	**51683**	**50229**
#国有及国有控股	State-owned and State-controlled Enterprises	151240	2680	2530
按登记注册类型分	By Status of Registration			
内资企业	Domestic-funded Enterprises	2450429	40539	39185
国有企业	State-owned Enterprises	31921	1193	1067
集体企业	Collective-owned Enterprises	35107	583	581
股份合作企业	Share-holding Cooperative Enterprises	21898	201	201
联营企业	Joint-operation Enterprises	1130	35	9
国有联营企业	State-owned Joint-operation Enterprises			
集体联营企业	Collective Joint-operation Enterprises			
国有与集体联营企业	State-collective Joint-operation Enterprises			
其他联营企业	Other Joint-operation Enterprises	1130	35	9
有限责任公司	Limited Liability Corporations	880351	11056	10281
国有独资企业	State Sole Investment Enterprises	22630	257	257
其他有限责任公司	Other Limited Liability Companies	857721	10799	10024
股份有限公司	Share-holding Corporations Ltd.	52952	892	892
私营企业	Private Enterprises	1394030	24874	24458
私营独资企业	Private Sole Investment Enterprises	262916	8930	8712
私营合伙企业	Private Partnership Enterprises	42237	950	950
私营有限责任公司	Private Limited Liability Corporations	1065623	14179	13981
私营股份有限公司	Private Share-holding Corporations Ltd.	23254	815	815
其他企业	Other Enterprises	33040	1705	1696
港、澳、台商投资企业	Enterprises with Investment from Hong Kong,Macao and Taiwan	449928	3814	3738
合资经营企业	Joint Ventures	35375	336	332
合作经营企业	Cooperative Enterprises	53090	593	593
独资经营企业	Sole Investment Enterprises	356435	2859	2787
投资股份有限公司	Share-holding Corporations Ltd.	5028	26	26
外商投资企业	Enterprises with Foreign Investment	659144	7330	7306
中外合资经营企业	Sino-foreign Joint Ventures	133576	237	213
中外合作经营企业	Sino-foreign Cooperative Enterprises	3880	57	57
外资企业	Foreign-funded Enterprises	486927	6794	6794
外商投资股份有限公司	Share-holding Corporations Ltd.	15381	116	116
其它外商投资企业	Others	19380	126	126
按国民经济行业分	By Economic Sector			
正餐服务业	Dinner Service	2152973	39080	38252
快餐服务业	Fast Food Service	961257	9519	8924
饮料及冷饮服务业	Beverage and Cold Drink Service	126961	660	660
餐饮配送及外卖送餐服务	Food and Beverage Distribution and Takeout Service	237434	1384	1373
其他餐饮服务业	Other Services	80876	1040	1020
按控股情况分组	By Holdings			
国有控股	State Holdings	151240	2680	2530
集体控股	Collective Holdings	78479	974	964
私人控股	Private Holdings	1970265	33394	32317
港澳台商控股	Hongkong,Macaw and Taiwan Holdings	429740	3473	3399
外商控股	Foreign Holdings	641274	7170	7170
其他	Others	288503	3992	3849

17-8 continued

(10000 yuan)

其它业务利润 Profits from Other Businesses	销售费用 Marketing Expenses	管理费用 Management Expenses	财务费用 Financial Expenses	营业利润 Business Profits	营业外收入 Non-operating revenue	利润总额 Total Profits	应交所得税 Income Taxes Payable	本年应付职工薪酬 Staff Salary Payable in Current Year
36737	**2446824**	**811688**	**45817**	**349680**	**31595**	**385435**	**99105**	**1554340**
2700	52636	32379	1963	31614	1436	34759	3336	76725
24193	1267957	590104	44610	125059	22176	158840	40739	973946
552	12022	11115	163	-1142	632	1562	795	17754
23	8501	2958	46	4461	54	4483	1069	7284
	9818	3371	273	1212	97	1142	413	5795
	454	372	24	239		239	60	299
	454	372	24	239		239	60	299
4484	488145	203552	22762	35347	4551	60855	14422	386547
92	1149	2050	58	690	471	1114	-203	19194
4392	486996	201502	22704	34657	4080	59741	14625	367353
2260	32913	12567	-793	30926	346	30454	2295	26580
16498	706167	350653	21383	51253	16459	57202	21332	518813
415	70874	45390	2645	25416	381	24864	4976	69296
524	19159	9209	310	3221	47	2626	795	14230
15072	607079	289803	17982	20793	15948	29128	15236	425982
487	9055	6251	446	1823	83	584	325	9305
376	9937	5516	752	2763	37	2903	353	10874
9664	581744	100631	1054	127221	5573	129224	34873	246499
14	26056	12420	227	2485	229	3430	1100	18416
	20722	6346	90	635	54	246	914	17769
9647	531796	80793	726	123289	5273	124723	32853	207631
3	3170	1072	11	812	17	825	6	2683
2880	597123	120953	153	97400	3846	97371	23493	333895
-21	206812	15823	589	37159	396	33262	7643	83687
	553	716	55	220		225	17	767
2631	381943	98820	-483	60950	3440	64934	15221	243966
	3029	3870	-29	-303	7	-331	611	3099
270	4786	1724	21	-626	3	-719	1	2376
23426	1328399	559299	42807	113704	18497	150731	42687	944169
12922	856820	180515	3139	141292	6903	140259	32798	449578
61	176712	25572	-1361	75346	1066	75033	19452	78208
300	38632	25532	1030	10974	4514	10896	2147	57845
28	46261	20770	202	8364	615	8516	2021	24540
2700	52636	32379	1963	31614	1436	34759	3336	76725
228	33519	11502	366	8516	201	8874	2318	26914
19290	1001575	475389	34591	79262	18673	91408	30453	744695
9920	573219	95722	1051	125309	5542	127356	34204	234597
2609	587924	119272	82	95936	3816	96062	23261	329453
1990	197951	77424	7764	9043	1927	26976	5533	141956

17–9 各市限额以上住宿和餐饮企业财务状况（2017年）

单位：万元

市 别	City	企业数（个）Number of Enterprises (unit)	年初库存 Beginning Inventory	流动资产合计 Circulating Assets	固定资产原价 Original Value of Fixed Assets	累计折旧 Accumulated Depreciation
住宿餐饮业合计	**Total Hotels and Catering Services**	**5284**	**582956**	**10610427**	**12545959**	**5834521**
住宿业	**Hotels**	**2217**	**393276**	**7639694**	**10242107**	**4729946**
广 州	Guangzhou	518	28306	1648141	2324120	1197715
深 圳	Shenzhen	332	22182	2346018	2020080	993680
珠 海	Zhuhai	128	156156	914700	1763772	606373
汕 头	Shantou	98	3420	99483	296606	138613
佛 山	Foshan	158	42674	404080	507119	260575
韶 关	Shaoguan	83	10413	106593	126162	54906
河 源	Heyuan	50	12990	49608	104486	45207
梅 州	Meizhou	38	4040	102657	154155	54574
惠 州	Huizhou	120	38912	322155	409189	181284
汕 尾	Shanwei	24	866	18074	72633	22815
东 莞	Dongguan	172	41911	507944	981822	557218
中 山	Zhongshan	121	3390	160144	373280	134244
江 门	Jiangmen	71	7522	222354	294061	149131
阳 江	Yangjiang	13	249	42840	24283	13195
湛 江	Zhanjiang	51	4344	142194	180908	55564
茂 名	Maoming	37	2593	116764	53785	16748
肇 庆	Zhaoqing	45	917	138374	129163	53852
清 远	Qingyuan	52	8462	206041	254273	112770
潮 州	Chaozhou	26	452	10895	37050	18884
揭 阳	Jieyang	45	933	34858	78120	44369
云 浮	Yunfu	35	2544	45777	57040	18229
餐饮业	**Catering Services**	**3067**	**189680**	**2970733**	**2303852**	**1104575**
广 州	Guangzhou	870	57971	905032	721373	382317
深 圳	Shenzhen	581	54115	1101413	565669	302672
珠 海	Zhuhai	115	3735	65716	23827	14257
汕 头	Shantou	73	1431	12304	9848	6132
佛 山	Foshan	290	7635	161584	181833	89610
韶 关	Shaoguan	95	2435	31914	64334	13811
河 源	Heyuan	38	874	35237	32875	15538
梅 州	Meizhou	15	708	7890	28815	10475
惠 州	Huizhou	108	2148	64943	73083	38098
汕 尾	Shanwei	26	867	21369	12262	5913
东 莞	Dongguan	215	34257	221745	106459	61581
中 山	Zhongshan	201	8447	81049	38415	20922
江 门	Jiangmen	83	1552	27291	46889	17434
阳 江	Yangjiang	51	1590	25026	27551	12617
湛 江	Zhanjiang	72	4056	46854	169532	50084
茂 名	Maoming	75	1076	38396	41023	9463
肇 庆	Zhaoqing	34	1437	45300	45034	11132
清 远	Qingyuan	21	1143	28635	46414	15532
潮 州	Chaozhou	30	1019	2943	16028	3519
揭 阳	Jieyang	51	1338	35924	37522	16838
云 浮	Yunfu	23	1846	10168	15066	6630

Financial Indicators of Enterprises above Designated Size of Hotels and Catering Services by City (2017)

(10000 yuan)

#本年折旧 Depreciation Drawn in Current Year	资产合计 Total Assets	负债合计 Total Liabilities	所有者权益合计 Total Creditors' Equity	实收资本 Paid-up Capital	营业收入 Business Revenue	主营业务收入 Main Business Revenue	营业成本 Business Costs
571616	**22723734**	**18362609**	**4361125**	**8843164**	**12667801**	**12558408**	**5786748**
440494	**17222908**	**14573284**	**2649624**	**7628836**	**5387450**	**5316190**	**2193393**
85389	3840572	2759916	1080656	1173061	1247901	1228265	435992
63672	4080146	3086274	993872	4060214	1287077	1266887	437624
90728	2823551	2719582	103969	555162	626748	622511	340259
7757	326740	255899	70841	170304	118161	117295	49260
27817	825292	616984	208308	281351	330462	326621	143502
6311	253273	219162	34111	66887	92044	91328	40533
4638	131740	90552	41188	43011	64870	64723	24023
13552	247935	189357	58578	67346	55933	55759	23440
39644	750734	673103	77631	170860	277448	276962	133960
2443	85397	36039	49358	69640	22709	22660	9571
33287	1124851	1413758	-288907	251023	404896	398548	142563
13695	523259	454688	68571	232793	171267	168232	59590
15267	444101	383846	60255	155842	141541	134875	56063
282	55932	41409	14523	18335	11880	11588	5881
5469	427535	421290	6245	48614	101651	99853	47911
5495	195743	187465	8278	24678	41064	40177	19164
5553	238921	253134	-14213	57736	57270	56753	27455
11759	434506	498315	-63809	76330	103233	102287	41570
1375	84566	73860	10706	20959	16629	16342	7893
3156	157943	91601	66342	63509	181768	181752	133445
3205	170171	107050	63121	21181	32898	32772	13694
131122	**5500826**	**3789325**	**1711501**	**1214328**	**7280351**	**7242218**	**3593355**
39878	1787742	1171435	616307	368590	2736445	2726818	1235419
30442	1650999	1123582	527417	352047	2411032	2398169	1110452
692	132718	112090	20628	27531	134201	133315	69849
647	21479	15988	5491	6080	65615	65486	42101
12340	346935	281209	65726	73909	428130	423747	244490
2937	110554	65180	45374	19372	53473	53270	30495
1272	61925	45829	16096	10612	27986	27967	15298
2131	29529	20702	8827	21192	11260	11260	5953
8635	132119	108213	23906	55918	140221	136908	72227
594	32595	18772	13823	14575	20532	20390	11716
5631	335991	150680	185311	96231	443503	442551	281786
2110	130263	112596	17667	26339	229637	229483	124741
6385	81653	38932	42721	22844	96583	93046	47368
937	44178	29977	14201	8995	58799	58777	35533
8437	198402	216552	-18150	27737	98005	97386	54970
2150	73573	50335	23238	14064	51294	50404	30938
589	92481	71071	21410	11655	33726	33528	18628
2794	85622	114226	-28604	11881	26159	26065	10720
333	67341	14410	52931	4836	15830	15750	11576
1490	64233	17486	46747	37012	183991	183990	130520
698	20494	10060	10434	2908	13929	13908	8575

17-9 续表

单位：万元

市 别	City	主营业务成本 Main Business Costs	营业税金及附加 Tax and Extra Charges on Business	主营业务税金及附加 Tax and Extra Charges on Main Business	其它业务利润 Profits from Other Businesses
住宿餐饮业合计	**Total Hotels and Catering Services**	**5711692**	**129434**	**125026**	**81417**
住宿业	**Hotels**	**2152191**	**77751**	**74797**	**44680**
广 州	Guangzhou	424354	20238	18933	10144
深 圳	Shenzhen	428076	14537	13871	8000
珠 海	Zhuhai	337674	10147	10003	7093
汕 头	Shantou	48998	2758	2616	841
佛 山	Foshan	139317	5307	5202	1166
韶 关	Shaoguan	40210	1769	1733	430
河 源	Heyuan	23593	1607	1554	
梅 州	Meizhou	23420	594	591	510
惠 州	Huizhou	129856	5486	5420	1370
汕 尾	Shanwei	9547	519	498	31
东 莞	Dongguan	141200	3912	3866	8896
中 山	Zhongshan	57610	1239	1238	1091
江 门	Jiangmen	54215	2187	2186	2683
阳 江	Yangjiang	5873	234	234	99
湛 江	Zhanjiang	47234	1654	1590	-46
茂 名	Maoming	19023	787	784	39
肇 庆	Zhaoqing	27239	776	774	151
清 远	Qingyuan	39984	1124	987	873
潮 州	Chaozhou	7696	400	389	805
揭 阳	Jieyang	133439	1877	1829	34
云 浮	Yunfu	13633	599	499	470
餐饮业	**Catering Services**	**3559501**	**51683**	**50229**	**36737**
广 州	Guangzhou	1231327	15530	15248	8543
深 圳	Shenzhen	1086361	11514	10804	15620
珠 海	Zhuhai	69635	821	797	410
汕 头	Shantou	40739	1246	1228	12
佛 山	Foshan	243398	3317	3117	679
韶 关	Shaoguan	30482	1566	1529	92
河 源	Heyuan	15235	533	507	374
梅 州	Meizhou	5953	255	208	
惠 州	Huizhou	70864	1413	1410	576
汕 尾	Shanwei	11716	477	477	358
东 莞	Dongguan	281317	2013	1996	4245
中 山	Zhongshan	124732	1554	1538	106
江 门	Jiangmen	47351	909	902	3513
阳 江	Yangjiang	35471	1206	1206	47
湛 江	Zhanjiang	54612	1661	1640	930
茂 名	Maoming	30847	1013	996	986
肇 庆	Zhaoqing	18628	392	370	178
清 远	Qingyuan	10719	443	443	-34
潮 州	Chaozhou	11550	354	350	102
揭 阳	Jieyang	130233	5139	5137	
云 浮	Yunfu	8331	327	326	

17-9 continued

(10000 yuan)

销售费用 Marketing Expenses	管理费用 Management Expenses	财务费用 Financial Expenses	营业利润 Business Profits	营业外收入 Non-operating revenue	利润总额 Total Profits	应交所得税 Income Taxes Payable	本年应付职工薪酬 Staff Salary Payable in Current Year
3956971	**2163527**	**299380**	**396665**	**83250**	**463524**	**156455**	**2899668**
1510147	**1351839**	**253563**	**46985**	**51655**	**78089**	**57350**	**1345328**
389054	354577	47515	32667	6797	36343	20018	361623
351641	348173	59110	86061	14182	102421	22243	309113
119524	125321	45402	-8136	16572	-11814	2792	163758
33836	28152	4812	-350	698	-1798	933	25025
107564	82231	8233	-13308	2862	-11491	3893	73762
24088	21187	3660	637	519	972	402	23686
19121	15463	1844	2958	71	2801	697	15735
18697	20186	2920	-9515	141	-9146	380	17209
65137	55573	13659	3340	507	8267	-752	56192
7552	5674	134	-780	17	-470	305	6529
141592	111513	16861	-21960	1798	-17413	2126	109894
70610	43920	4993	-6335	528	-5923	706	49628
46584	37475	8703	-9190	1279	-8236	464	33690
3359	2406	451	-393	4	-391	32	4027
30678	18590	8939	-4550	57	860	844	23342
12040	7881	4473	-3280	3247	-1177	189	10547
14233	13680	7805	-6579	558	-5454	264	11880
27767	36612	8306	-12187	1223	-13312	418	23730
5685	5833	587	-3752	505	-3369	140	3176
10877	9449	2962	23150	31	16600	875	12616
10508	7543	2194	-1513	59	-181	381	10166
2446824	**811688**	**45817**	**349680**	**31595**	**385435**	**99105**	**1554340**
1021619	296985	9831	170221	10284	189738	44798	608599
906728	261677	12231	110429	11022	123343	33603	533406
43159	17716	1858	1508	504	1907	1052	39085
11957	6001	298	3870	28	3155	718	8330
111540	54718	4788	7645	1105	10738	3709	74115
8869	9063	569	3080	147	2910	863	11031
6001	3948	1460	779	397	493	174	5433
2290	3003	188	-433	251	-365	31	3099
40485	18837	2706	5021	287	4916	1225	30054
4960	2929	36	516	30	348	103	9541
99204	48626	-645	15300	4950	15091	4158	83514
79272	20226	1217	2686	729	3143	2981	55155
31328	13369	348	3412	57	3895	1609	19316
12388	6140	552	2980	54	2340	422	13783
22441	16396	2631	-103	107	651	829	18935
9457	6132	923	2830	39	2688	590	11666
9392	5280	1682	-1516	436	-1236	132	8462
9690	7386	2862	-4827	1111	-3540	230	6427
1011	1464	62	1363		1361	123	2670
12115	10309	1884	24605		23530	1747	8013
2918	1483	336	314	57	329	8	3706

17-10 各市住宿餐饮业营业收入

Business of Enterprises above Designated Size of Hotels and Catering Services by City

单位：万元 (10000 yuan)

市别	Item	2016 住宿业 Hotels Service	2016 餐饮业 Catering Service	2017 住宿业 Hotels Service	2017 餐饮业 Catering Service
广州	Guangzhou	2397397	11129106	2519192	11744697
深圳	Shenzhen	1367863	6436965	1499126	6822078
珠海	Zhuhai	676946	959254	747613	1042979
汕头	Shantou	164545	843513	189116	867061
佛山	Foshan	417387	3435921	462847	3504661
韶关	Shaoguan	127074	601240	135956	633397
河源	Heyuan	186052	246287	213393	266221
梅州	Meizhou	133904	377864	153510	404309
惠州	Huizhou	395346	946948	544707	875470
汕尾	Shanwei	77044	594541	87890	619433
东莞	Dongguan	490708	1435008	549295	1512508
中山	Zhongshan	264104	1065704	266477	1124704
江门	Jiangmen	252917	1092399	264103	1143964
阳江	Yangjiang	123992	593472	130339	672226
湛江	Zhanjiang	193134	1601041	222566	1699389
茂名	Maoming	291520	1176028	299931	1253299
肇庆	Zhaoqing	138807	805030	152106	850617
清远	Qingyuan	172849	472967	197583	490804
潮州	Chaozhou	35498	429462	38262	465009
揭阳	Jieyang	207671	449867	240061	492286
云浮	Yunfu	69910	292401	81272	308472
按经济区域分	By Region				
珠三角	Pearl River Delta	6401475	27306335	7005466	28621678
东翼	Eastern Region	484758	2317383	555329	2443789
西翼	Western Region	608646	3370541	652836	3624914
山区	Mountainous Region	689789	1990759	781714	2103203

17-11 旅游部门基本情况

Basic Statistics on Tourism-related Agencies

指 标	Item	2000	2010	2013	2014	2015	2016	2017
宾馆(酒店) (家)	Number of Hotels (unit)	2655	9179	15367	15926	16440	16693	16255
按星级分：五星	By Star Rating: Five Star	19	94	115	119	117	110	108
四星	Four Star	61	194	187	184	178	162	153
三星	Three Star	283	661	629	589	566	498	438
二星	Two Star	339	246	144	115	107	87	68
一星	One Star	48	14	7	5	4	4	4
未评星级	Unrated	1905	7970	14285	14914	15468	15832	15484
宾馆(酒店)接待能力	Reception Capability of Hotels							
客房 (间)	Number of Guest Rooms (unit)	202277	565582	884942	931516	982628	983102	988204
床位 (张)	Number of Beds (unit)	401718	938389	1361127	1481397	1535288	1542226	1426209
客房出租率 (%)	Room Occupancy (%)	58.0	59.9	56.5	58.4	61.5	58.8	60.8
旅行社 (家)	Number of Travel Agencies(unit)	504	1292	1810	1984	2150	2345	2639

17-12 城市接待外国游客人数

Number of Foreign Visitors Received by Cities

单位：人次 (person-time)

国 别	Country	1995	2000	2010	2012	2013	2014	2015	2016	2017
总计	**Total**	**1173919**	**2128501**	**7322478**	**7745127**	**7604935**	**7751868**	**7818342**	**8249290**	**8615437**
日本	Japan	288978	413833	1077329	1156694	1120847	1007828	892362	1015426	930498
韩国	Republic of Korea	25172	71841	418115	419950	454828	481319	474549	577584	593965
菲律宾	Philippines	10312	20793	47184	56831	75391	76742	59613	67626	79288
新加坡	Singapore	60760	93762	284832	304594	338151	308000	285197	313165	338751
泰国	Thailand	51185	48341	134313	139158	167255	169965	147501	185529	229957
印度尼西亚	Indonesia	40583	63159	158879	198305	219302	198852	118720	147674	159217
马来西亚	Malaysia	70639	110384	421556	432150	494279	423202	351926	395384	423748
美国	United States	129238	196362	645783	664836	645703	633574	710768	754468	804071
加拿大	Canada	24908	35968	133138	115997	129464	123185	133020	167033	177629
英国	United Kingdom	41020	59123	138353	146587	169879	171919	146989	164223	180888
法国	France	29728	43578	119850	132017	156752	153625	148791	152930	164166
德国	Germany	32864	44707	118332	127784	139769	136736	142266	156765	158395
意大利	Italy	19187	19792	86454	89949	95340	72853	78488	104559	101512
俄罗斯	Russia	1937	10407	58568	82878	121327	128209	84489	102985	113862
澳大利亚	Australia	28789	34595	149780	137042	162316	156491	138169	165342	196612
新西兰	New Zealand	4133	5835	24119	26866	31130	30341	30740	34613	43334
其他	Others	314486	856021	3305893	3513489	3083202	3479027	3874754	3743984	3919544

17−13 各市旅游宾馆(酒店)住宿设施（2017年）

Lodging Facilities of Tourist Hotels by City (2017)

市别	City	宾馆(酒店)(个) Number of Hotels (unit)	五星级 Five Star	四星级 Four Star	三星级 Three Star	二星级 Two Star	一星级 One Star	客房(间) Number of Rooms (unit)	床位(张) Number of Beds (unit)	客房出租率(%) Room Occupancy (%)
全省合计	**Total**	**771**	**108**	**153**	**438**	**68**	**4**	**1017297**	**1470180**	**60.8**
广州	Guangzhou	168	22	34	95	17		207350	308952	65.7
深圳	Shenzhen	108	24	23	47	14		102601	155532	69.4
珠海	Zhuhai	66	8	8	47	3		51242	74415	60.6
汕头	Shantou	29	3	5	18	2	1	36533	50012	52.2
佛山	Foshan	46	10	15	20	1		29093	43971	57.0
韶关	Shaoguan	56	1	4	45	5	1	33994	56865	55.2
河源	Heyuan	20	1	2	12	5		27856	44771	60.9
梅州	Meizhou	34	2	5	26	1		30692	52676	62.5
惠州	Huizhou	31	5	8	18			46857	7200	53.9
汕尾	Shanwei	14	1	2	11			16572	25304	
东莞	Dongguan	33	14	12	6	1		110229	141531	59.2
中山	Zhongshan	21	2	4	12	2	1	40775	58867	49.5
江门	Jiangmen	15	5	1	9			46250	70056	67.2
阳江	Yangjiang	21	3	2	16			37670	70839	58.5
湛江	Zhanjiang	27	3	7	13	4		45089	70288	60.1
茂名	Maoming	8	1	2	5			30500	47700	65.3
肇庆	Zhaoqing	21	1	1	12	6	1	36510	54355	67.8
清远	Qingyuan	18	1	3	12	2		42169	69686	56.3
潮州	Chaozhou	13		6	4	3		7751	11492	49.4
揭阳	Jieyang	10	1	5	4			21520	29892	50.2
云浮	Yunfu	12		4	6	2		16044	25776	50.4
按经济区域分	By Region									
珠三角	Pearl River Delta	509	91	106	266	44	2	670907	914879	
东翼	Eastern Region	66	5	18	37	5	1	82376	116700	
西翼	Western Region	56	7	11	34	4		113259	188827	
山区	Mountainous Region	140	5	18	101	15	1	150755	249774	

注：本表星级宾馆(酒店)指2010年底止已得到国家旅游局或广东省旅游局批准的，不包已报未批部分。

Note: Star-rated hotels in this table refer to those approved by the National Tourism Administration or Guangdong Provincial Tourism Administration by the end of 2010, excluding hotels under examination.

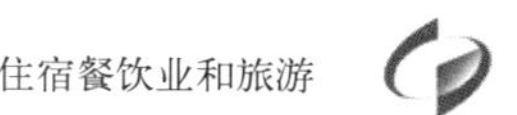

17-14 各市接待过夜旅游者人数

Number of Overnight Tourists by City

单位：万人次 (10000 person-times)

市别	City	2016 合计 Total	2016 入境游客 Overseas Tourist Arrivals	2016 国内游客 Domestic Tourists	2017 合计 Total	2017 入境游客 Overseas Tourist Arrivals	2017 国内游客 Domestic Tourists
全省合计	**Provincial Total**	**39718.47**	**3518.38**	**36200.09**	**44385.26**	**3645.50**	**40739.76**
广　州	Guangzhou	5941.22	862.52	5078.70	6272.28	897.13	5375.15
深　圳	Shenzhen	5695.72	1171.19	4524.53	6011.78	1203.40	4808.38
珠　海	Zhuhai	2226.41	317.23	1909.18	2288.62	318.25	1970.37
汕　头	Shantou	1628.97	24.40	1604.57	1879.67	29.10	1850.57
佛　山	Foshan	1351.05	139.76	1211.29	1497.81	146.09	1351.72
韶　关	Shaoguan	1430.19	4.43	1425.76	1650.21	4.09	1646.12
河　源	Heyuan	1258.15	8.04	1250.11	1548.46	7.65	1540.81
梅　州	Meizhou	1750.58	29.28	1721.30	2000.66	34.43	1966.23
惠　州	Huizhou	2032.92	227.52	1805.40	2477.87	238.93	2238.94
汕　尾	Shanwei	789.57	4.93	784.64	845.12	5.92	839.20
东　莞	Dongguan	2007.67	253.44	1754.23	2161.48	254.26	1907.22
中　山	Zhongshan	1117.81	62.17	1055.64	1333.52	66.11	1267.41
江　门	Jiangmen	2000.56	222.70	1777.86	2258.95	229.39	2029.56
阳　江	Yangjiang	1176.25	6.98	1169.27	1317.50	7.02	1310.48
湛　江	Zhanjiang	1942.33	30.10	1912.23	2231.46	37.20	2194.26
茂　名	Maoming	843.35	3.85	839.50	1096.32	4.45	1091.87
肇　庆	Zhaoqing	1236.66	51.51	1185.15	1327.72	49.89	1277.83
清　远	Qingyuan	1095.42	16.83	1078.59	1192.11	17.39	1174.72
潮　州	Chaozhou	1077.23	61.33	1015.90	1534.60	71.80	1462.80
揭　阳	Jieyang	1681.22	3.39	1677.83	1933.91	5.49	1928.42
云　浮	Yunfu	1435.19	16.78	1418.41	1525.21	17.51	1507.70
按经济区域分	By Region						
珠三角	Pearl River Delta	23610.02	3308.04	20301.98	25630.03	3403.45	22226.58
东　翼	Eastern Region	5176.99	94.05	5082.94	6193.30	112.31	6080.99
西　翼	Western Regicn	3961.93	40.93	3921.00	4645.28	48.67	4596.61
山　区	Mountainous Region	6969.53	75.36	6894.17	7916.65	81.07	7835.58

17–15 各市旅行社组团出境游人数（2017年）

Number of Outbound Visitors in Group Tours by City (2017)

单位：人 (person)

市别	City	合计 Total	香港 Hong Kong	澳门 Macao	其它 Others
全省合计	**Provincial Total**	**9885391**	**2798968**	**1545783**	**5540640**
广州	Guangzhou	2863054	388994	652593	1821467
深圳	Shenzhen	4410507	1679749	349990	2380768
珠海	Zhuhai	482660	152610	87827	242223
汕头	Shantou	59134	6504	8793	43837
佛山	Foshan	1355477	383370	254234	717873
韶关	Shaoguan	6281	234	392	5655
河源	Heyuan	725	20	12	693
梅州	Meizhou	4565	454	1009	3102
惠州	Huizhou	49354	22011	9300	18043
汕尾	Shanwei	869	201	84	584
东莞	Dongguan	153945	31496	22637	99812
中山	Zhongshan	228258	85888	21685	120685
江门	Jiangmen	162565	28318	84800	49447
阳江	Yangjiang	2536	177	72	2287
湛江	Zhanjiang	15416	1573	333	13510
茂名	Maoming	14254	1226	2756	10272
肇庆	Zhaoqing	46298	7408	37547	1343
清远	Qingyuan	18252	7363	10539	350
潮州	Chaozhou	8051	1139	1088	5824
揭阳	Jieyang	1553	125	81	1347
云浮	Yunfu	1637	108	11	1518
按经济区域分	By Region				
珠三角	Pearl River Delta	9752118	2779844	1520613	5451661
东翼	Eastern Region	69607	7969	10046	51592
西翼	Western Region	32206	2976	3161	26069
山区	Mountainous Region	31460	8179	11963	11318

17－16　各市旅游业收入

Tourism Earnings by City

单位：亿元　　(100 million yuan)

市　别	City	收入合计 Total Earnings		旅游外汇收入 Foreign Exchange Earnings		国内旅游收入 Domestic Tourism Earnings	
		2016	2017	2016	2017	2016	2017
全省合计	**Provincial Total**	**10433.81**	**11994.79**	**1233.51**	**1327.65**	**9200.30**	**10667.14**
广　州	Guangzhou	3217.05	3614.21	416.47	426.32	2800.58	3187.89
深　圳	Shenzhen	1368.67	1485.45	313.86	336.64	1054.81	1148.81
珠　海	Zhuhai	317.08	367.70	69.37	81.70	247.71	286.00
汕　头	Shantou	353.82	445.35	7.70	10.76	346.12	434.59
佛　山	Foshan	624.72	710.84	95.91	102.27	528.81	608.57
韶　关	Shaoguan	324.93	390.13	1.61	1.63	323.32	388.50
河　源	Heyuan	237.76	272.86	1.13	1.06	236.63	271.80
梅　州	Meizhou	376.76	445.18	8.95	10.43	367.81	434.75
惠　州	Huizhou	364.14	439.28	61.51	65.48	302.63	373.80
汕　尾	Shanwei	121.86	130.23	1.79	2.42	120.07	127.81
东　莞	Dongguan	445.40	488.90	103.17	107.75	342.23	381.15
中　山	Zhongshan	247.00	287.40	18.06	23.85	228.94	263.55
江　门	Jiangmen	409.90	492.53	72.59	87.13	337.31	405.40
阳　江	Yangjiang	214.06	267.61	2.79	2.87	211.27	264.74
湛　江	Zhanjiang	349.91	421.43	5.65	7.27	344.26	414.16
茂　名	Maoming	242.32	328.33	0.96	1.47	241.36	326.86
肇　庆	Zhaoqing	285.75	308.28	21.74	23.59	264.01	284.69
清　远	Qingyuan	269.72	314.50	10.73	11.27	258.99	303.23
潮　州	Chaozhou	181.26	234.76	15.31	19.02	165.95	215.74
揭　阳	Jieyang	248.41	292.21	1.01	1.31	247.40	290.90
云　浮	Yunfu	233.29	257.61	3.20	3.41	230.09	254.20
按经济区域分	By Region						
珠 三 角	Pearl River Delta	7279.71	8194.59	1172.68	1254.73	6107.03	6939.86
东　翼	Eastern Region	905.35	1102.55	25.81	33.51	879.54	1069.04
西　翼	Western Region	806.29	1017.37	9.40	11.61	796.89	1005.76
山　区	Mountainous Region	1442.46	1680.28	25.62	27.80	1416.84	1652.48

17–17　国际旅游外汇收入

Foreign Exchange Earnings from International Tourism

单位：万美元　　(USD 10000)

指　标	Item	2000	2010	2012	2013	2014	2015	2016	2017
全省总计	**Provincial Total**	**411221**	**1243154**	**1562257**	**1627808**	**1707588**	**1788466**	**1857713**	**1966330**
商品性收入	**Commodity Earnings**	**87837**	**300843**	**373379**	**418347**	**467879**	**491471**	**553601**	**644956**
商品销售收入	Shopping	40834	203877	226527	284866	326149	346426	388264	452256
饮食销售收入	Food and Beverage	47003	96966	146852	133480	141730	145045	165337	192700
劳务性收入	**Service Earnings**	**323384**	**942311**	**1188877**	**1209461**	**1239709**	**1296996**	**1304112**	**1321374**
景区游览费	Sightseeing	14804	44754	62490	56973	81964	54727	61305	60956
宿费	Accommodation	59216	159124	221840	208359	225402	224810	247077	287084
长途交通费	Long Distance Transportation	173535	493532	640525	579499	628392	708590	626050	601697
民航	Civil Aviation	113086	361758	499922	421602	461049	425834	364112	350007
铁路	Railway	43589	44754	59366	61857	59766	55800	61305	58990
轮船	Waterway	6991	45997	34370	35812	34152	183139	144902	139609
汽车	Highway	9869	41024	46868	60229	73426	43817	55732	53091
市内交通费	Local Transportation	7813	26106	28121	35812	30737	36306	40870	43259
邮政电讯费	Postal and Communication Services	9458	19890	21872	161153	22199	27006	37154	35394
文化娱乐费	Cultural and Recreational Services	37010	94480	112482	29301	136607	85131	102732	112081
其他	Others	21548	104425	101547	138364	114408	160425	188923	180903

17–18 各市国际旅游外汇收入

Foreign Exchange Earnings from International Tourism by City

单位：万美元 (USD 10000)

市 别	City	2000	2005	2009	2010	2012	2013	2014	2015	2016	2017
全 省	**Provincial Total**	**411221**	**639739**	**1002813**	**1243154**	**1562257**	**1627808**	**1707588**	**1788466**	**1857713**	**1966330**
广 州	Guangzhou	150580	229400	362396	468858	514458	516884	547522	569601	627215	631422
深 圳	Shenzhen	141669	200869	276026	318058	432882	453102	456559	496837	472673	498586
珠 海	Zhuhai	39395	70148	102670	122339	95045	83767	92105	96263	104473	121001
汕 头	Shantou	11705	5950	4910	5016	5175	5431	7046	8927	11601	15930
佛 山	Foshan	15973	34485	65194	72896	120984	126984	133448	137548	144446	151468
韶 关	Shaoguan	351	2782	2112	10309	3110	3730	4475	2848	2429	2408
河 源	Heyuan	798	850	1267	1389	926	1097	1100	1420	1701	1574
梅 州	Meizhou	1487	1975	2624	2962	4086	4204	5509	10321	13484	15443
惠 州	Huizhou	5333	16549	40107	50168	67786	77039	85652	88494	92637	96975
汕 尾	Shanwei	387	455	511	1175	1418	1180	1768	2538	2697	3581
东 莞	Dongguan	7618	28189	51756	67592	126924	144981	157493	157743	155377	159582
中 山	Zhongshan	14692	21027	20434	27591	21979	23891	48135	29843	27197	35327
江 门	Jiangmen	8295	10521	40891	47657	69917	79768	84318	96887	109324	129040
阳 江	Yangjiang	230	852	1412	1876	2226	2008	2550	3729	4203	4252
湛 江	Zhanjiang	1004	1483	2237	2716	4816	5845	6540	7305	8512	10761
茂 名	Maoming	169	676	981	1198	1315	1395	1556	1739	1442	2178
肇 庆	Zhaoqing	6264	4718	8089	12440	48689	55441	28046	32231	32744	34946
清 远	Qingyuan	834	2051	4511	11062	14417	13579	14395	15608	16152	16691
潮 州	Chaozhou	3071	5264	11072	13207	21303	21770	22208	22296	23060	28167
揭 阳	Jieyang	701	587	1481	2150	1768	2110	2990	1820	1522	1942
云 浮	Yunfu	665	907	2132	2499	3033	3602	4173	4468	4824	5056
按经济区域分	By Region										
珠三角	Pearl River Delta	389819	615907	967563	1187597	1498663	1561857	1633278	1705447	1766086	1858347
东 翼	Eastern Region	15864	12256	17974	21547	29664	30491	34011	35581	38880	49620
西 翼	Western Region	1403	3012	4629	5790	8357	9248	10647	12773	14157	17191
山 区	Mountainous Region	4135	8564	12647	28220	25573	26212	29653	34665	38590	41172

注：本表数为广东省旅游局抽样调查测算数。
Note: Data in this table are obtained from the sample surveys of Guangdong Provincial Tourism Administration.

主要统计指标解释

住宿业 是指为顾客提供临时住宿服务的企业(单位)和个体户。

餐饮业 是指从事食品的烹饪、调制并直接售给居民和社会集团的企业(单位)和个体户。

入境旅游人数 指来我国参观、访问、旅行、探亲、访友、休养 、考察、参加会议和从事经济、科技、文化、教育、体育、宗教等活动的外国人、华侨、港澳台同胞的人数。不包括外国在我国的常驻机构，如使领馆、通讯社、企业办事处的工作人员；来我国常驻的外国专家、留学生以及在岸逗留不过夜人员。

国际旅游外汇收入 指入境旅游的外国人、华侨、港澳台同胞在中国大陆旅游过程中发生的一切旅游支出，对于国家来说就是国际旅游外汇收入。

Explanatory Notes on Main Statistical Indicators

Hotel Services refers to the enterprises (establishments) and individuals engaged in providing temporary accommodation to customers.

Catering Services refer to the enterprises (establishments) and individuals engaged in food cooking, seasoning and selling food directly to households and social institutions.

Number of Overseas Visitor Arrivals refers to the number of foreigners, overseas Chinese, Chinese compatriots from Hong Kong, Macao and Taiwan coming to China for sight-seeing, visits, tours, family reunions, gatherings of friends, recuperation, inspection, conferences and other activities in the nature of business, science and technology, culture, education, sports, and religion. The statistics excludes representatives and employees of resident institutions of foreign countries in China such as embassies, consulates, news agencies and offices of foreign companies and organizations, as well as long-term foreign experts or students residing in China, and persons in transition without staying overnight in China.

Foreign Exchange Earnings from International Tourism refer to the total expenditures of foreigners, overseas Chinese, Chinese compatriots from Hong Kong, Macao and Taiwan during their stay in the mainland of China, or earnings of foreign exchange from international tourism in terms of national economy.

十八、教育和科技

EDUCATION AND TECHNOLOGY

十八　教育和科技

简要说明

一、本篇资料主要反映广东教育、科学技术活动基本情况。

二、本篇资料主要包括：

1. 高、中、初等教育，幼儿教育和各种类型的各级成人教育，指标主要包括各级各类的学校数、在校生数、招生数、毕业生数、教职工数和专任教师数等。

2. 科技成果奖励和技术市场情况，专利申请受理量和批准量，研究与开发机构基本情况，高校研究与发展人员及经费，科协系统科技活动情况等数据。

三、本篇资料由广东省统计局社会和科技统计处负责整理、编辑。

四、统计资料来源：

教育统计资料根据广东省教育厅、广东省人力资源和社会保障厅提供的统计年报加工整理。科技统计资料根据广东省科技厅、广东省人力资源和社会保障厅、广东省教育厅、广东省科协等部门提供的统计年报加工整理。

18 Education and Technology

Brief Introduction

Ⅰ. The data in this chapter show the basic conditions on the development Guangdong's education, science and technology.

Ⅱ. The data in this chapter mainly include:

(1) The data on tertiary, secondary, primary, and kindergarten education and various types of adult education at all levels, including the number of schools, the number of students enrolled, the number of new enrollments, the number of graduates, the number of staff and workers, and the number of full-time teachers of various levels and categories.

(2) The data on scientific and technological achievements and prizes, conditions of technological markets, numbers of patent applications accepted and granted, basic conditions of R&D institutions, R&D personnel and funds in universities and colleges, and scientific and technological activities of associations of science and technology, etc.

Ⅲ. The data are prepared and edited by the Division of Social, Scientific and Technological Statistics of Statistics Bureau of Guangdong Province.

Ⅳ. Data sources:

Data on education are processed and prepared in accordance with the annual statistical reports provided by Guangdong Provincial Department of Education and Guangdong Provincial Department of Human Resources and Social Security. Data on science and technology are processed and prepared in accordance with the annual statistical reports provided by Guangdong Provincial Department of Science and Technology, Guangdong Provincial Department of Human Resources and Social Security，Guangdong Provincial Department of Education, Guangdong Provincial Department of Personnel and Guangdong Provincial Association of Science and Technology.

18-1 教育、科技主要指标
Main Indicators on Education, Science and Technology

指　　标	Item	2000	2010	2014	2015	2016	2017
在校学生数　(万人)	Number of Total Enrollment　(10000 persons)						
普通本专科	Regular Institutions of Higher Education	29.95	142.66	179.42	185.64	189.29	192.58
成人本专科	Institutions of Higher Education for Adults	20.14	46.40	62.69	66.45	65.20	65.31
中等学校	Secondary Schools	541.72	939.23	781.25	736.79	705.05	700.12
#普通中学	Regular Secondary Schools	460.69	709.05	590.77	560.72	545.22	545.37
高等教育毛入学率(%)	Gross Enrollment Rate of High Education　(%)	11.35	28.00	31.88	33.00	35.10	38.71
高中毛入学率　(%)	Gross Enrollment Rate of Senior Secondary Schools　(%)	38.70	86.20	95.90	95.70	96.00	96.48
小学毕业生升学率(%)	Percentage of Graduates of Primary School Entering Junior Secondary School　(%)	96.15	95.50	96.15	95.90	95.90	96.04
学龄儿童入学率　(%)	Percentage of School-age Children Enrolled　(%)	99.70	99.95	99.99	99.98	100.00	99.99
每万人口普通高校在校学生数　(人)	Number of Students Enrolled in Regular Institutions of Higher Education per 10000 Population　(person)	41.19	148.02	167.31	171.11	172.10	175.09
科技研究机构数　(个)	Number of R&D Institutions　(unit)		4452	5333	8164	14311	23318
研究与实验发展(R&D)人员　(万人)	Number of R&D Personnel　(10000 persons)		44.66	67.52	68.02	73.52	87.99
R&D人员全时当量　(万人年)	Full-time Equivalent of (R&D Personnel　(10 000 man-year)	7.11	36.47	50.66	50.17	51.56	56.53
研究与实验发展(R&D)经费内部支出(亿元)	R&D Expenditure Internal Expernditure　(100 million yuan)	107.12	808.75	1605.45	1798.17	2035.14	2343.63
#基础研究	Basic Research		16.72	42.41	54.21	86.02	109.42
应用研究	Applied Research		37.32	126.5	165	164.5	215.6
试验发展	Experimental Development		754.70	1436.53	1478.96	1784.62	2018.61
#政府资金	Government Funds	101.38	65.76	116.66	145.85	186.60	240.40
企业资金	Enterprises Funds	86.44	708.93	1445.72	1606.21	1795.78	2047.59
R&D经费支出占地区生产总值比例　(%)	Percentage of Research and Development Expenditure in Provincial GDP　(%)	0.99	1.74	2.33	2.43	2.52	2.61
研究与实验发展(R&D)课题（项目)数　(个)	Number of R&D Programs/Projects　(item)		72747	108109	112680	135652	170214
省级及以上科技奖励成果　(项)	Number of Achievements in Science and Technology Awarded by Provincial-level and Higher Agencies(item)	289	296	295	269	272	284
专利申请受理量　(件)	Number of Patent Applications Accepted　(piece)	21123	152907	278351	355939	505667	627819
#发明专利	Inventions	1760	40866	75148	103941	155581	182639
专利申请批准量　(件)	Number of Patent Applications Granted　(piece)	15799	119346	179953	241176	259032	332648
#发明专利	Inventions	261	13691	22276	33477	38626	45740
技术合同成交额(亿元)	Transaction Value of Technological Contracts　(100 million yuan)	48.21	242.5	543.14	663.53	789.68	949.48

注：1．2000年起报纸出版统计不包校报、院报。
2．全省小学毕业生升学率，按照教育部统一口径，根据教育统计报表，当年本省初中招生数除以小学毕业生数计算，不考虑学生跨省流动。
3．R&D经费支出占地区生产总值比例指标历史数据，已根据修订后的地区生产总值数据进行调整。

Note: a) Since 2000, the number of newspaper published does not include that of college or institute newspaper.
b) According to the Ministry of Eduucation,the percentage of graduates of primary schools entering junior secondary schools is calculated as the number of new enrollments of local junior secondary schools divided by the number of graduates from local primary schools and the trans-provincial flow of students are without consideration.
c) Historical statistics on ratio of expenditure on R&D to GDP have been adjusted according to amended GDP statistics.

18-2 各级各类学校在校学生数

Number of Total Enrollment by Level and Type of School

单位：万人 (10000 persons)

年份 Year	高等学校 Institutions of Higher Education	中等学校 Secondary Schools			小学 Primary Schools
		中等职业教育学校 Vocational Secondary Schools	技工学校 Technical Schools	普通中学 Regular Secondary Schools	
1978	3.07	3.64		313.32	743.02
1979	3.79	4.51	0.71	268.73	743.81
1980	4.10	6.28	1.61	252.11	748.86
1981	4.47	6.12	1.39	218.71	734.78
1982	4.09	6.51	0.99	200.19	723.03
1983	4.56	9.96	0.92	199.59	705.34
1984	5.47	12.99	1.01	220.69	692.73
1985	6.99	18.01	1.45	236.45	671.25
1986	7.83	28.22	1.45	249.93	670.62
1987	8.63	34.26	2.63	252.60	677.37
1988	9.72	37.63	3.40	244.23	688.72
1989	10.04	42.09	3.93	235.73	715.15
1990	9.59	45.27	5.22	234.03	747.29
1991	9.27	44.74	5.63	238.28	788.93
1992	9.74	46.29	6.58	255.02	808.98
1993	11.70	50.24	7.68	277.19	832.14
1994	13.75	55.89	9.57	307.38	862.21
1995	15.18	66.67	11.10	339.46	883.19
1996	16.40	67.30	12.28	373.19	897.64
1997	17.47	72.70	13.29	400.85	911.34
1998	18.50	70.50	14.50	423.61	918.02
1999	22.08	69.50	23.00	443.91	920.96
2000	29.95	65.57	14.46	460.69	929.93
2001	38.19	62.00	16.67	489.70	952.98
2002	46.78	61.20	17.82	513.40	979.61
2003	58.78	63.08	23.90	545.91	1025.37
2004	72.69	65.54	28.11	580.86	1049.62
2005	87.47	71.02	32.81	611.69	1067.03
2006	100.86	80.84	38.16	639.29	1056.99
2007	111.97	90.76	45.81	655.38	1017.62
2008	121.64	100.08	53.54	679.65	956.47
2009	133.41	120.46	64.11	696.11	887.65
2010	142.66	154.78	75.56	709.05	848.55
2011	152.73	152.05	85.13	699.47	822.06
2012	161.68	149.57	88.52	668.40	808.24
2013	170.99	140.89	87.62	625.24	807.94
2014	179.42	128.22	62.26	590.77	831.91
2015	185.64	117.21	58.86	560.72	868.88
2016	189.29	106.57	53.26	545.22	905.22
2017	192.58	99.39	55.37	545.37	941.96

注：1. 高等学校人数指普通本、专科人数，下同。
2. 1986年后中等职业教育学校包括普通中专、成人中专、职业高中，1986年前缺成人中专数据。

Notes: a) Number of students in institutions of higher education refers to the number of students in regular universities with full undergraduate courses and colleges with specialized courses. The same applies to the following tables.
b) Since 1986, vocational secondary schools have included regular specialized secondary schools, specialized secondary schools for adults and vocational senior secondary schools. Prior to 1986, no data of specialized secondary schools for adults are available.

18-3 各级各类学校情况

Statistics on Various Levels and Types of Schools

项　目	Item	2000	2010	2014	2015	2016	2017
高等学校	**Institutions of Higher Education**						
学校数　(所)	Number of Schools (unit)	52	131	141	143	149	151
毕业生数　(万人)	Number of Graduates (10000 persons)	5.00	33.42	44.09	47.69	48.94	51.12
本科	Universities with Full Undergraduate Courses	2.40	15.29	21.14	22.41	23.36	24.56
专科	Colleges with Specialized Courses	2.60	18.13	22.95	25.28	25.58	26.57
招生数　(万人)	Number of New Enrollments (10000 persons)	12.08	44.02	54.51	56.15	54.98	57.08
本科	Universities with Full Undergraduate Courses	5.01	21.7	26.72	27.54	28.04	28.56
专科	Colleges with Specialized Courses	7.07	22.31	27.79	28.61	26.94	28.52
在校学生数(万人)	Number of Enrolled Students (10000 persons)	29.95	142.66	179.42	185.64	189.29	192.58
本科	Universities with Full Undergraduate Courses	15.03	77.86	99.82	104.08	107.68	110.58
专科	Colleges with Specialized Courses	14.92	64.8	79.60	81.56	81.61	82.00
教职工数　(万人)	Number of Teachers and Staff (10000 persons)	4.68	11.4	13.52	13.99	14.29	14.81
#专任教师	Full-time Teachers	2.04	7.86	9.52	9.89	10.12	10.44
中等职业教育	**Vocational Secondary Schools**						
学校数　(所)	Number of Schools (unit)	658	566	495	481	468	459
毕业生数　(万人)	Number of Graduates (10000 persons)	21.54	33.17	45.70	41.73	38.92	34.23
招生数　(万人)	Number of New Enrollment (10000 persons)	21.10	74.13	41.70	39.54	35.19	32.23
在校学生数(万人)	Number of Total Enrollment (10000 persons)	65.57	154.78	128.22	117.21	106.57	99.39
教职工数　(万人)	Number of Teachers and Staff (10000 persons)	5.70	5.86	5.81	5.78	5.75	5.81
#专任教师	Full-time Teachers	3.70	4.35	4.52	4.50	4.48	4.52
技工学校	**Technical Schools**						
学校数　(所)	Number of Schools (unit)	186	246	243	163	166	162
毕业生数　(万人)	Number of Graduates (10000 persons)	4.28	12.80	14.22	14.46	16.14	14.65
招生数　(万人)	Number of New Enrollments (10000 persons)	5.84	28.2	20.25	19.94	18.63	18.88
在校学生数(万人)	Number of Total Enrollment (10000 persons)	15.46	75.56	62.26	58.86	53.26	55.37
教职工数　(万人)	Number of Teachers and Staff (10000 persons)	1.07	2.78	2.87	2.94	2.92	3.04
#专任教师	Full-time Teachers	0.68	1.98	2.08	2.10	2.16	2.26
普通中学	**Regular Secondary Schools**						
学校数　(所)	Number of Schools (unit)	3964	4334	4399	4434	4510	4566
毕业生数　(万人)	Number of Graduates (10000 persons)	131.82	210.23	211.17	201.96	191.65	179.12
招生数　(万人)	Number of New Enrollments (10000 persons)	171.16	241.96	189.24	182.89	186.14	187.82
在校学生数(万人)	Number of Total Enrollment (10000 persons)	460.69	709.05	590.77	560.72	545.22	545.37
教职工数　(万人)	Number of Teachers and Staff (10000 persons)	27.57	44.53	47.36	47.54	47.85	48.48
#专任教师	Full-time Teachers	22.86	39.15	42.69	42.67	42.74	43.13

注：普通高等学校数包含独立学院数。

Note: The number of regular schools (institutions) of higher education includes independent colleges.

18-3 续表 continued

项 目	Item	2000	2010	2014	2015	2016	2017
小学	**Primary Schools**						
学校数 (万所)	Number of Schools (10000 units)	2.42	1.68	1.07	1.01	1.02	1.03
毕业生数 (万人)	Number of Graduates (10000 persons)	148.48	174.19	124.35	121.49	127.04	131.91
招生数 (万人)	Number of New Enrollments (10000 persons)	155.73	135.92	153.67	165.80	171.18	174.37
在校学生数 (万人)	Number of Students Enrolled (10000 persons)	929.93	848.55	831.91	868.88	905.22	941.96
教职工数 (万人)	Number of Teachers and Staff (10000 persons)	42.08	48.78	49.77	51.44	53.60	56.04
#专任教师	Full-time Teachers	36.41	43.07	45.44	46.86	48.66	50.78
学龄儿童	**School-age Children**						
学龄儿童总数 (万人)	Total number (10000 persons)	905.39	801.82	795.74	836.09	874.14	895.63
已入学学龄儿童数(万人)	Primary School Enrollment number (10000 persons)	902.65	801.45	795.63	835.93	874.14	895.58
学龄儿童入学率 (%)	Enrollment Rate (%)	99.70	99.95	99.99	99.98	100.00	99.99
小学毕业生	**Primary School Graduates**						
小学毕业生人数 (万人)	Number of Graduates (10000 persons)	148.48	174.19	124.35	121.49	127.04	131.91
已升学人数 (万人)	Number of Students Entering into Junior Secondary Schools (10000 persons)	142.77	166.37	119.56	116.45	121.81	126.67
小学毕业生升学率 (%)	Promotion Rate from Primary Schools to Junior Secondary Schools (%)	96.15	95.51	96.15	95.85	95.88	96.04
幼儿园	**Kindergartens**						
幼儿园数 (所)	Number of Kindergartens (unit)	12027	11161	15416	16368	17288	18048
在园幼儿数 (万人)	Number of Children in Kindergartens(10000 persons)	214.18	227.23	379.34	402.28	421.67	441.41
教职工数 (万人)	Number of Teachers and Staff (10000 persons)	12.91	23.68	38.80	43.62	46.94	51.51
#专任教师	Full-time Teachers	8.36	13.63	21.38	24.07	25.65	28.17
特殊教育学校	**Special Schools**						
特殊教育学校数 (所)	Number of Schools (unit)	61	75	104	116	127	133
招生数 (人)	Number of New Enrollments (persons)	2000	3666	5300	7303	6853	8893
在校学生数 (人)	Number of Total Enrollment (persons)	27507	26064	28285	36048	37756	44084

注：1. 2003年起中等职业教育学校包括：普通中等专业学校、成人中等专业学校、职业高中数据。
2. 特殊教育学校是指独立设置招收盲哑和智残儿童，以及其他特殊需要的儿童、青少年进行普通或职业初、中等教育的教学机构。

Notes: a) Since 2003 , vocational secondary schools have included regular specialized secondary schools , specialized secondary schools for adults and vocational senior secondary schools.

b) Special schools refer to separate institutions providing regular or vocational primary and secondary education for blinded, dumb or mentally-retarded children, or other children and adolescents in need of special care in education.

18-4 研究生教育情况

Statistics on Postgraduate Education

项　目	Item	2000	2010	2013	2014	2015	2016	2017
培养单位数（个）	**Number of Institutions of Postgraduate Education (unit)**	**26**	**31**	**27**	**28**	**28**	**28**	**28**
高等学校	Institutions of Higher Education	18	23	24	25	25	25	25
科研单位	Research Institutions	8	8	3	3	3	3	3
招生数　（人）	**Number of New Enrollments (person)**	**5672**	**25798**	**28798**	**29769**	**30650**	**32393**	**38832**
攻读博士学位	For Doctor Degree	1053	3307	3375	3559	3540	3742	3997
高等学校	Institutions of Higher Education	1001	3117	3368	3551	3532	3734	3989
科研单位	Research Institutions	52	190	7	8	8	8	8
攻读硕士学位	For Master Degree	4619	22491	25423	26210	27110	28651	34835
高等学校	Institutions of Higher Education	4510	22135	25342	26134	27018	28555	34732
科研单位	Research Institutions	109	356	81	76	92	96	103
在校学生数（人）	**Number of Enrolled Students (person)**	**13023**	**72455**	**83788**	**86568**	**89404**	**92875**	**102912**
攻读博士学位	For Doctor Degree	2558	12341	13691	14169	14474	14990	15686
高等学校	Institutions of Higher Education	2445	11706	13659	14136	14443	14958	15658
科研单位	Research Institutions	113	635	32	33	31	32	28
攻读硕士学位	For Master Degree	10405	60114	70097	72399	74930	77885	87226
高等学校	Institutions of Higher Education	10161	59159	69863	72164	74682	77614	86929
科研单位	Research Institutions	244	955	234	235	248	271	297
毕业生数　（人）	**Number of Graduates (person)**	**2182**	**17862**	**23983**	**25538**	**26174**	**27155**	**27148**
攻读博士学位	For Doctor Degree	417	2436	2739	2837	2947	2947	3055
高等学校	Institutions of Higher Education	387	2288	2732	2830	2937	2940	3047
科研单位	Research Institutions	30	148	7	7	10	7	8
攻读硕士学位	For Master Degree	1765	15426	21244	22701	23227	24208	24093
高等学校	Institutions of Higher Education	1692	15158	21170	22627	23151	24134	24018
科研单位	Research Institutions	73	268	74	74	76	74	75

注：2014年起中国科学院大学下辖广州化学研究所、南海海洋研究所、华南植物研究所、广州能源研究所和广州地球化学研究所的教育事业报表统一归口中国科学院大学管理，并调整2013年起数据，从2013年起研究生数据均不含以上培养研究生单位数据。

Notes: Since 2014, Guangzhou Institute of Chemistry、South China Sea Institute of Oceanography、South China Institute of Botany、Guangzhou Institute of Energy and the Guangzhou Institute of Geochemistry's education statistics are under the centralized to the University of Chinese Academy of Sciences and since 2013 data has been adjusted and the number of sutdents has excluded the number of students in these institutions.

18-5 各级各类成人教育在校学生数

Number of Total Enrollment by Level and Type of Adult School

单位：人　　(person)

项　目	Item	2000	2010	2013	2014	2015	2016	2017
成人高等教育	**Higher Education for Adults**	**201410**	**463987**	**534376**	**626927**	**664495**	**651963**	**653103**
成人高等学校	Institutions of Higher Education for Adults	84057	22025	16803	16055	17556	18905	29546
广播电视大学	Radio and TV Universities	34242	10980	9196	8799	10256	13326	23925
职工高等学校	Schools of Higher Education for Staff and Workers	17147	6344	5498	5166	5411	5579	5621
管理干部学院	Colleges for Management Cadres	20142	4398					
教育学院	Teachers' Colleges	12526	303	2109	2090	1889		
普通高校附设	Departments Run by Institutions of Higher Education	117353	441962	517573	610872	646939	633058	623557
函授部	Correspondence Divisions	51028	173761	185880	235440	281334	319929	319662
夜大学	Evening Universities	43063	265713	331693	375432	365605	312884	
成人脱产班	Full-time Courses for Adults	23262	2488				245	
成人中等教育	**Secondary Education for Adults**		**29105**	**20951**	**13774**			
成人中专学校	Specialized Secondary Schools for Adults		27327	19732	11743	7341	4682	4156
成人中学	Secondary Schools for Adults	44006	5358	1219	2031			

18-6 高等学校情况（2017年）
Statistics on Institutions of Higher Education (2017)

项目	Item	学校数（所）Number of Schools (unit)	毕业生数（人）Number of Graduates (person)	招生数（人）Number of New Enrollments (person)	在校学生数（人）Number of Total Enrollment (person)	教职工数（人）Number of Teachers and Staff (person)	#专任教师 Full-time Teachers
总　计	**Total**	**151**	**511222**	**570775**	**1925775**	**148059**	**104381**
#女性	Female		277133	294567	1013351	72020	49838
按隶属关系分	**Grouped by Relation of Leadership**	**151**	**511222**	**570775**	**1925775**	**148059**	**104381**
中央属	Under Central Government	5	21847	24015	94194	14828	9335
地方属	Under Local Government	146	489375	546760	1831581	133231	95046
按学校类别分	**Grouped by Type of Institution**	**151**	**511222**	**570775**	**1925775**	**148059**	**104381**
综合大学	University	71	245624	275246	907551	68527	47930
理工院校	Science and Engineering College	33	124723	140331	451021	31277	22871
农业院校	Agriculture College	3	20204	21659	88905	6578	4996
医药院校	Medicine College	10	23458	27340	96682	11215	8448
师范院校	Teacher Education College	7	27556	28017	104952	10725	6305
语文院校	Language and Literature College	2	6817	7134	29037	2946	1929
财经院校	Economics and Finance College	13	51217	56783	203023	11492	8916
政法院校	Politics and Law College	3	2520	3186	10641	1288	601
体育院校	Physical Culture College	3	3180	3644	11536	1378	767
艺术院校	Art College	6	5923	7435	22427	2633	1618
其他	Others						
总计中：职业技术学院	Vocational Technological College	87	236154	270045	762334	51222	36948

18-7 中等学校情况（2017年）
Statistics on Secondary Schools (2017)

项目	Item	学校数（所）Number of Schools (unit)	毕业生数（人）Number of Graduates (person)	招生数（人）Number of New Enrollments (person)	在校学生数（人）Number of Total Enrollment (person)	教职工数（人）Number of Teachers and Staff (person)	#专任教师 Full-time Teachers
中等职业教育	**Vocational Secondary Education**	**459**	**342297**	**322267**	**993850**	**58112**	**45197**
调整后中等职业学校	Vocational Secondary Schools after Adjustment	278	217549	209340	649273	35065	26485
普通中专	General Secondary Schools	59	47399	42102	129989	7120	5132
成人中等专业学校	Specialized Secondary Schools for Adults	6	1948	1443	4156	281	248
职业高中学校	Vocational Senior Secondary Schools	116	67067	61776	187955	14543	12476
其他机构	Other Institutions	39	6798	6250	17765	1103	856
附设中职班	Affiliated Vocational Class	19	1536	1356	4712		
技工学校	**Technical Schools**	**162**	**146514**	**188840**	**553727**	**30362**	**22610**
普通中学	**Regular Secondary Schools**	**4566**	**1791237**	**1878201**	**5453670**	**484846**	**431256**
#高中	Senior Schools	1030	676686	611384	1892669		151435

注：2011年起增加附设中职班。其他机构和附设中职班不计学校数。普通中专包括中等技术学校和中等师范学校。

Note: Since 2011, the item of Affiliated Vocational Class is added. The number of schools of other institutions and affiliated secondary vocational classes is not included in the total number schools of vocational secondary education. The general secondary schools include the secondary technical schools and secondary normal schools.

18-8 各市普通中学情况（2017年）

Statistics on Regular Secondary Schools by City (2017)

市别	City	学校数(所) Number of Schools (unit)	毕业生数(人) Number of Graduates (person)	高中 Senior Secondary Schools	初中 Junior Secondary Schools	招生数(人) Number of New Enrollments (person)
广州	Guangzhou	518	160974	58392	102582	176496
深圳	Shenzhen	368	119643	39367	80276	152395
珠海	Zhuhai	74	27283	9204	18079	32461
汕头	Shantou	304	123119	50482	72637	122195
佛山	Foshan	200	98012	37336	60676	116372
韶关	Shaoguan	151	50503	20054	30449	52714
河源	Heyuan	191	58457	22272	36185	62897
梅州	Meizhou	230	81171	35677	45494	78064
惠州	Huizhou	263	85641	30311	55330	103325
汕尾	Shanwei	169	63182	24349	38833	57277
东莞	Dongguan	234	85796	26274	59522	115754
中山	Zhongshan	103	46645	15766	30879	54698
江门	Jiangmen	189	67118	25008	42110	73248
阳江	Yangjiang	113	40929	16116	24813	45240
湛江	Zhanjiang	308	157600	62027	95573	135202
茂名	Maoming	261	162675	65727	96948	145078
肇庆	Zhaoqing	180	80633	28281	52352	76005
清远	Qingyuan	181	62334	23166	39168	68179
潮州	Chaozhou	139	46772	20243	26529	44255
揭阳	Jieyang	289	128760	49800	78960	119961
云浮	Yunfu	101	43990	16834	27156	46385
按经济区域分	By Region					
珠三角	Pearl River Delta	2129	771745	269939	501806	900754
东翼	Eastern Region	901	361833	144874	216959	343688
西翼	Western Region	682	361204	143870	217334	325520
山区	Mountainous Region	854	296455	118003	178452	308239

18−8 续表 continued

市 别	City	在校学生数 (人) Number of Total Enrollment (person)	高中 Senior Secondary Schools	初中 Junior Secondary Schools	教职工数 (人) Number of Teachers and Staff (person)	#专任教师 Full-time Teachers
广 州	Guangzhou	509427	170676	338751	59568	51181
深 圳	Shenzhen	417641	127099	290542	62164	51013
珠 海	Zhuhai	90237	29991	60246	9401	8187
汕 头	Shantou	359791	140639	219152	36731	31631
佛 山	Foshan	327678	116913	210765	29912	26261
韶 关	Shaoguan	154534	52754	101780	15751	14431
河 源	Heyuan	178416	60983	117433	20511	18469
梅 州	Meizhou	232262	89626	142636	26079	23903
惠 州	Huizhou	287517	90562	196955	29447	25660
汕 尾	Shanwei	177354	62544	114810	18254	16293
东 莞	Dongguan	310169	81052	229117	36347	29705
中 山	Zhongshan	154456	47212	107244	17051	14730
江 门	Jiangmen	210114	75599	134515	19808	17903
阳 江	Yangjiang	129769	44955	84814	15453	13603
湛 江	Zhanjiang	411677	153396	258281	39726	36959
茂 名	Maoming	449748	172257	277491	39700	37364
肇 庆	Zhaoqing	228705	75326	153379	21711	19824
清 远	Qingyuan	196431	67981	128450	19329	17149
潮 州	Chaozhou	131203	51911	79292	13600	12318
揭 阳	Jieyang	363287	135635	227652	35619	31562
云 浮	Yunfu	133254	45558	87696	12081	11246
按经济区域分	By Region					
珠 三 角	Pearl River Delta	2535944	814430	1721514	285409	244464
东 翼	Eastern Region	1031635	390729	640906	104204	91804
西 翼	Western Region	991194	370608	620586	94879	87926
山 区	Mountainous Region	894897	316902	577995	93751	85198

注：本表2016年普通中学教职工、专任教师数包含初级中学、九年、十二年一贯制学校、职业初中、完全中学、高级中学。

Note: The data of teachers and staff and of full-time teachers of regular secondary schools include junior middle and high schools,the nine-year primary-secondary schools, technical secondary school, combined junior and senior high school and senior high school.

18-9 各市中等职业教育基本情况（2017年）

Basic Statistics on Vocational Secondary Education by City (2017)

市别	City	学校数（所）Number of Schools (unit)	毕业生数（人）Number of Graduates (person)	招生数（人）Number of New Enrollments (person)	在校学生数（人）Number of Total Enrollment (person)	教职工数（人）Number of Teachers and Staff (person)	#专任教师 Full-time Teachers
广州	Guangzhou	83	73208	63027	196796	11609	8044
深圳	Shenzhen	15	12205	13005	39234	3447	2636
珠海	Zhuhai	8	6907	5906	20117	1163	952
汕头	Shantou	21	13479	14604	58701	2208	1699
佛山	Foshan	35	23099	20946	66878	4809	3960
韶关	Shaoguan	16	6621	9719	25339	1971	1617
河源	Heyuan	13	7327	7547	21896	1413	1107
梅州	Meizhou	27	12908	9760	29074	1930	1555
惠州	Huizhou	25	18338	19143	53284	3219	2404
汕尾	Shanwei	12	3857	4126	11289	878	757
东莞	Dongguan	21	16441	20703	57964	4042	2755
中山	Zhongshan	11	7407	8173	23133	1837	1559
江门	Jiangmen	19	14520	12938	40419	2390	2166
阳江	Yangjiang	5	4622	4942	14399	730	584
湛江	Zhanjiang	54	23003	21656	65433	3707	2741
茂名	Maoming	21	17432	21172	51168	2937	2551
肇庆	Zhaoqing	18	19449	18335	55274	3270	2582
清远	Qingyuan	13	10971	11145	30935	1865	1613
潮州	Chaozhou	10	4227	3075	9472	924	766
揭阳	Jieyang	18	37903	24271	100097	2510	2090
云浮	Yunfu	14	8373	8074	22948	1253	1059
按经济区域分	By Region						
珠三角	Pearl River Delta	235	191574	182176	553099	35786	27058
东翼	Eastern Region	61	59466	46076	179559	6520	5312
西翼	Western Region	80	45057	47770	131000	7374	5876
山区	Mountainous Region	83	46200	46245	130192	8432	6951

18-10 各市小学情况（2017年）
Statistics on Primary Schools by City (2017)

市别	City	学校数（所）Number of Schools (unit)	毕业生数（人）Number of Graduates (person)	升学率（%）Percentage of Graduates of Primary Schools Entering Junior Secondary Schools (%)	招生数（人）Number of New Enrollments (person)	在校学生数（人）Number of Total Enrollment (person)	教职工数（人）Number of Teachers and Staff (person)	#专任教师 Full-time Teachers
广州	Guangzhou	961	139815	95.75	191092	1004695	48709	44749
深圳	Shenzhen	342	119948	99.85	181516	964510	31098	27795
珠海	Zhuhai	122	22605	88.39	29876	162238	7321	6900
汕头	Shantou	745	77935	99.69	92085	526460	23537	22254
佛山	Foshan	409	77585	100.00	105318	543598	26873	24895
韶关	Shaoguan	196	35498	100.00	44973	236257	12307	11980
河源	Heyuan	343	40948	100.00	50569	299994	16933	15907
梅州	Meizhou	452	49125	99.34	60806	341593	19185	18365
惠州	Huizhou	463	75052	99.69	102481	556985	22649	21122
汕尾	Shanwei	470	38407	99.97	45441	255489	15653	14094
东莞	Dongguan	329	103106	100.00	142485	765120	28428	23067
中山	Zhongshan	207	41466	100.00	55626	297389	12600	11346
江门	Jiangmen	319	48067	99.69	58859	322934	14700	13974
阳江	Yangjiang	147	31048	99.84	43892	233790	11593	11152
湛江	Zhanjiang	802	88278	98.55	120170	633240	36152	33908
茂名	Maoming	1385	91514	97.05	115751	620850	33769	32617
肇庆	Zhaoqing	221	53513	100.00	67796	369217	18376	17652
清远	Qingyuan	330	45100	100.00	68151	343170	17508	16619
潮州	Chaozhou	615	29969	95.79	33029	199304	10579	9662
揭阳	Jieyang	1232	78904	98.08	89769	510277	29587	27364
云浮	Yunfu	168	31223	99.18	43972	232471	13833	13234
按经济区域分	By Region							
珠三角	Pearl River Delta	3373	681157	98.66	935049	4986686	210754	191500
东翼	Eastern Region	3062	225215	98.65	260324	1491530	79356	73374
西翼	Western Region	2334	210840	98.09	279813	1487880	81514	77677
山区	Mountainous Region	1489	201894	99.74	268471	1453485	79766	76105

注：1. 各地市小学毕业生升学率，由于跨地市流动学生较多，如按教育部口径计算将与实际差异较大，因此采用各地填报的小学升上本地及外地高一级学校(包括普通初中、职业初中等)就读的学生数除以小学毕业生进行计算。

2. 2011年起小学教职工、专任教师数包含小学、教学点，不含九年一贯制和十二年一贯制学校小学部的教职工和专任教师数。

Note: a) Due to the large number of mobile students,the percentage of graduates of primary schools entering junior secondary schools by city would be greatlly different from the real situation if calculated as the method by the Ministry of Education. Thus the percentage of graduates of primary schools entering junior secondary schools by city in this table is calculated as the number of new enrollments of local junior and outside secondary Schools(ordinary secondary schools and professional secondary schools are incluede) from local primary school divided by the umber of graduates from local primary schools

b) Since 2011,the data of of the number of teachers and staff and of full-time teachers include primary schools and sub-campuses, but exclude the primary education section of the nine-year and twelve-year primary-secondary schools.

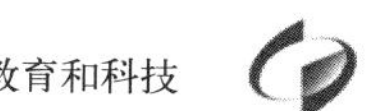

18－11 各市学龄儿童入学情况

Statistics on School-age Children Enrolled in Schools by City

市别	City	2016 学龄儿童人数(人) Number of School-age Children (person)	2016 已入学人数(人) Number of School-age Children Enrolled in Schools (person)	2016 入学率(%) Enrollment Rate (%)	2017 学龄儿童人数(人) Number of School-age Children (person)	2017 已入学人数(人) Number of School-age Children Enrolled in Schools (person)	2017 入学率(%) Enrollment Rate (%)
广州	Guangzhou	951820	951820	100.0	988961	988960	100.0
深圳	Shenzhen	895907	895907	100.0	951889	951889	100.0
珠海	Zhuhai	149204	149204	100.0	156703	156129	99.6
汕头	Shantou	491608	491608	100.0	506336	506336	100.0
佛山	Foshan	503181	503181	100.0	534917	534917	100.0
韶关	Shaoguan	218660	218660	100.0	229765	229765	100.0
河源	Heyuan	256122	256122	100.0	247430	247430	100.0
梅州	Meizhou	319463	319463	100.0	287730	287730	100.0
惠州	Huizhou	528535	528535	100.0	556046	556046	100.0
汕尾	Shanwei	247000	247000	100.0	251470	251470	100.0
东莞	Dongguan	717244	717244	100.0	748010	748010	100.0
中山	Zhongshan	278020	278020	100.0	292309	292309	100.0
江门	Jiangmen	297149	297149	100.0	308256	308256	100.0
阳江	Yangjiang	217579	217579	100.0	226301	226301	100.0
湛江	Zhanjiang	583505	583505	100.0	615305	615305	100.0
茂名	Maoming	598560	598560	100.0	562560	562560	100.0
肇庆	Zhaoqing	329586	329586	100.0	307322	307322	100.0
清远	Qingyuan	302394	302394	100.0	325687	325687	100.0
潮州	Chaozhou	182471	182471	100.0	185041	185041	100.0
揭阳	Jieyang	465989	465989	100.0	480824	480824	100.0
云浮	Yunfu	207432	207432	100.0	193467	193467	100.0
按经济区域分	By Region						
珠三角	Pearl River Delta	4650646	4650646	100.0	4844413	4843838	100.0
东翼	Eastern Region	1387068	1387068	100.0	1423671	1423671	100.0
西翼	Western Region	1399644	1399644	100.0	1404166	1404166	100.0
山区	Mountainous Region	1304071	1304071	100.0	1284079	1284079	100.0

18-12 研究与试验发展(R&D)基本情况

Basic Statistics on Research and Development (R&D)

指 标	Item	2010	2013	2014	2015	2016	2017
研究机构数 （个）	**Number of R&D Institutions (units)**	**4452**	**5030**	**5333**	**8164**	**14311**	**23318**
科学研究与技术开发机构	Scientific Research and Technological Development Institutions	186	186	189	189	202	199
全日制普通高等学校	Full-time Regular Institutions of Higher Education	450	652	704	850	1123	1369
工业企业	Industiral Enterprises	3309	3700	3930	6553	11834	20030
其他	Others	507	492	510	572	1152	1720
研究与试验发展(R&D)活动人员 （人）	**Number of R&D Personnel (persons)**	**446579**	**652405**	**675206**	**680237**	**735188**	**879854**
科学研究与技术开发机构	Scientific Research and Technological Development Institutions	9488	14868	15897	15739	17452	17635
全日制普通高等学校	Full-time Regular Institutions of Higher Education	33865	44051	47540	57346	57048	63332
工业企业	Industrial Enterprises	359476	530551	544906	534293	585089	696385
其他	Others	43750	62935	66863	72859	75599	102502
研究与试验发展(R&D)经费内部支出 （亿元）	**Internal Expenditure on R&D (100 million yuan)**	**808.75**	**1443.45**	**1605.45**	**1798.17**	**2035.14**	**2343.63**
科学研究与技术开发机构	Scientific Research and Technological Development Institutions	21.35	44.80	53.64	63.98	73.74	83.84
全日制普通高等学校	Full-time Regular Institutions of Higher Education	28.58	45.83	49.82	62.97	108.08	137.53
工业企业	Industrial Enterprises	703.68	1237.48	1375.29	1520.55	1676.27	1865.03
其他	Others	55.14	115.35	126.70	150.67	177.05	257.23
研究与试验发展(R&D)活动课题(项目)数 （个）	**Number of R&D Programs/Projects (item)**	**72747**	**107639**	**108109**	**112680**	**135652**	**170214**
科学研究与技术开发机构	Scientific Research and Technological Development Institutions	3499	5047	5412	6712	7163	8034
全日制普通高等学校	Full-time Regular Institutions of Higher Education	35749	50119	53138	61677	70697	79050
工业企业	Industrial Enterprises	28423	46948	42941	37375	50740	73439
其他	Others	5076	5525	6618	6916	7052	9691

18−13 公有经济企业、事业单位专业技术人员年末人数

Number of Professional and Technical Personnel in State-owned Enterprises and Institutions at the Year-end

单位：人 (person)

年 份 Year	专业技术人员 Professional and Technical Personnel	#工程技术人员 Engineering	#农业技术人员 Agriculture	#科学技术人员 Scientific Research	#卫生技术人员 Health Care	#教学人员 Teaching
1978	211149	48836	16017	7852	53068	80287
1979	211117	48641	16975	7277	53155	79748
1980	291939	56144	18176	7356	61445	86192
1981	303892	60071	19017	6763	63536	97109
1982	328455	70699	19431	7822	69056	102178
1983	547038	85327	21636	5744	74183	109210
1984	579740	89348	22505	5573	79806	120016
1985	642542	102506	23030	6431	86174	133013
1986	656380	108210	23854	6368	89545	313009
1987	664085	118601	23553	6231	93553	333245
1988	674085	119167	19478	4904	85092	313419
1989	810130	137803	20644	5986	90751	364965
1990	838403	145535	21194	5731	92912	379894
1991	814651	140906	13050	4810	93141	398276
1992	883821	149916	13749	4566	104334	412681
1993	957725	163440	14246	4388	117959	434036
1994	1017804	174960	14670	4118	128079	460702
1995	1077848	180530	15219	4425	134586	511418
1996	1167583	186156	15449	4610	147155	573934
1997	1223897	191954	15779	4443	156889	613121
1998	1262343	190486	15703	4413	165721	649873
1999	1291078	184304	15660	4585	171461	677110
2000	1297804	180223	15083	4705	175521	696005
2001	1285708	168354	14151	4467	181703	710967
2002	1274140	160458	13386	4425	184192	721719
2003	1264983	135621	12575	4918	202548	734721
2004	1374679	149214	17321	5253	238886	774022
2005	1399042	146411	17407	5434	248547	791255
2006	1375416	137802	16999	5163	246679	805397
2007	1391934	140828	17311	5711	246480	824462
2008	1419852	144941	16701	5745	260940	837059
2009	1462861	153563	15805	5984	268796	856665
2010	1458044	149724	14084	4551	259131	885446
2011	1448011	151700	13475	5260	253992	879621
2012	1459018	151998	12256	5021	264976	861104
2013	1455605	139807	12538	3813	269147	888962
2014	1493095	155964	12772	5850	283499	888862
2015	1449255	139817	16076	6139	288384	928348
2016	1486082	151883	16681	7340	308402	893189
2017	1551010	169994	13161	10992	306208	897089

注：本表未包中央单位专业技术人员数。
Note:Data in this table do not include professional and technical personnel from the central units stationed in Guangdong.

18–14 高层次人才情况

Statistics on High-level Talents

单位：人 (person)

项 目	Item	2000	2010	2013	2014	2015	2016	2017
享受国家津贴新增人数	Number of Persons Granted State Allowances	164	137		161		172	
高级职称批准人数	Number of Persons with Senior Professional Titles	6111	19031	22000	13997	16581	21532	24336
博士后招收人数	Number of Persons in Working Stations for Post-doctoral Research	163	560	746	893	1297	1596	1851
博士生情况	Status of Doctorate Students							
招生数	Number of New Enrollments	1053	3307	3375	3559	3540	3742	3997
在校生	Number of Enrolled Students	2558	12341	14691	14169	14474	14990	15686
毕业生	Number of Graduates	417	2436	2739	2837	2947	2947	3055

注：享受国家津贴的人数从2003年起逢双年评比一次。
Note: The number of persons granted state allowances has been appraised every double-digital year since 2003.

18–15 各类技术合同签订情况

Statistics on Technical Contracts Signed by Type

项 目	Item	2000	2005	2010	2014	2015	2016	2017
技术合同项目数（项）	**Number of Technical Contracts (item)**	**5464**	**14432**	**17558**	**19150**	**17344**	**17480**	**17423**
技术开发合同	Technical Development Contracts	921	5983	11629	14662	13786	13484	13065
技术咨询合同	Technical Consultation Contracts	572	1279	1649	980	430	476	389
技术转让合同	Technical Transfer Contracts	297	639	868	1028	1242	1277	1405
技术服务合同	Technical Service Contracts	3674	6531	3412	2480	1886	2243	2564
技术合同金额（万元）	**Value of Technical Contracts (10000 yuan)**	**482104**	**1124740**	**2425045**	**5431388**	**6635253**	**7896802**	**9494790**
技术开发合同	Technical Development Contracts	142107	571458	1961788	2567383	2359626	2773111	5277277
技术咨询合同	Technical Consultation Contracts	12530	31696	48539	28058	17050	13005	8617
技术转让合同	Technical Transfer Contracts	110279	288881	344264	1626221	2923722	3453327	2619466
技术服务合同	Technical Service Contracts	217188	232705	70454	1209726	1334855	1657360	1589429

18-16 科技成果项数

Number of Achievements for Scientific and Technological Research

单位：项 (item)

项目	Item	2000	2010	2012	2013	2014	2015	2016	2017
国家级科技奖励成果	**National Prizes for Scientific and Technological Research Achievements**	**24**	**36**	**26**	**28**	**46**	**32**	**33**	**38**
国际合作奖	National Coperation Prize					1			
国家发明奖	National Invention Prize		2	5	10	12	5	6	10
国家自然科学奖	National Prize for Natural Sciences		1	3	4	2	5	4	
国家科技进步奖	National Prize for Progress in Science and Technology	24	33	18	14	31	22	23	28
省级重大科技成果	**Major Provincial Scientific and Technological Achievements**			**1799**	**1809**	**1748**	**2133**	**1963**	**2511**
基础理论成果	Achievements in Fundamental Theory			72	67	55	126	140	204
应用技术成果	Achievements in Applied Technology			1691	1713	1656	1990	1805	2258
软科学成果	Achievements in Soft Sciences			36	29	37	17	18	49
省级科技奖励成果	**Provincial Prizes for Scientific and Technological Achievements**	**265**	**260**	**280**	**262**	**249**	**237**	**239**	**246**
省科技进步奖	Provincial Prize for Progress in Science and Technology	265	260	280	262	249	237	239	246
农业方面	Agriculture	46	31	45	43	33	31	27	31
工业方面	Industry	113	145	138	132	129	148	138	122
医药卫生方面	Medicine and Health Care	72	65	53	58	42	42	35	36
其他	Others	34	19	44	29	45	16	39	57

注：省级重大科技成果为全社会口径。
Note: Data of major provincial scientific and technological achievements are the whole society caliber.

18-17 县级政府部门属研究与开发机构基本情况

Basic Statistics on Research and Development Institutions under Government Departments at County Level

项目	Item	2000	2010	2012	2013	2014	2015	2016	2017
机构数 （个）	Number of Institutions (unit)	183	143	133	131	128	124	117	116
职工总数 （人）	Number of Staff and Workers(person)	4379	2798	2433	2362	2241	2054	1838	1797
科技活动人员(人)	Scientists and Engineers (person)		1390	1250	1270	1259	1119	1032	1044
经费收入 （万元）	Funds (10000 yuan)	13409	16592	24435	23708	24550	27162	21539	27094
#来自政府的经费	Government Funds	5426	9605	12543	11937	15024	17467	16218	20596

18-18 县级以上政府部门属研究与开发机构基本情况

Basic Statistics on Research and Development Institutions under Government Departments at and above County Level

项 目	Item	2000	2010	2014	2015	2016	2017
总 计	**Total**						
机构数 (个)	Number of Institutions (unit)	296	181	184	184	197	194
职工总数 (人)	Number of Staff and Workers (person)	24926	16922	22233	22582	22848	23649
科技活动人员 (人)	Scientists and Engineers		12819	17873	17929	17883	19036
经费收入 (万元)	Funds (10000 yuan)	358844	665228	1225429	1450489	1496107	1511226
#政府拨款	Government Appropriations	98386	332815	653052	781376	865137	899445
经费支出 (万元)	Expenditures (10000 yuan)	330098	674994	1168470	1363744	1418833.9	1502586.7
科技经费支出(万元)	Expenditures on Purchase of Assets(10000 yuan)		408216	790769	962263	1039841	1179112
自然科学及技术领域	**Natural Sciences and Technology**						
机构数 (个)	Number of Institutions (unit)	263	156	158	158	169	166
职工总数 (人)	Number of Staff and Workers (person)	23623	15601	20616	21011	21143	21932
科技活动人员 (人)	Scientists and Engineers		11738	16557	16675	16438	17573
经费收入 (万元)	Funds (10000 yuan)	345582	626119	1165667	1375436	1415095	1423930
#政府拨款	Government Appropriations	89595	306735	614819	728278	806310	835030
经费支出 (万元)	Expenditures (10000 yuan)	317219	634843	1110131	1297806	1346255	1415204
科技经费支出(万元)	Expenditures on Purchase of Assets(10000 yuan)		378555	749993	919010	986612	1112910
社会及人文科学领域	**Social Sciences and Humanities**						
机构数 (个)	Number of Institutions (unit)	16	10	10	10	12	12
职工总数 (人)	Number of Staff and Workers (person)	780	645	631	675	779	774
科技活动人员 (人)	Scientists and Engineers		567	560	616	718	713
经费收入 (万元)	Funds (10000 yuan)	6906	18906	25406	32129	42192	45090
#政府拨款	Government Appropriations	5908	14003	22518	26643	36846	39459
经费支出 (万元)	Expenditures (10000 yuan)	6897	17585	25973	30830	35818	45692
科技经费支出(万元)	Expenditures on Purchase of Assets(10000 yuan)		14334	19933	23636	28517	35449
科技情报和文献机构	**Scientific-Technological Information and Literature Institutions**						
机构数 (个)	Number of Institutions (unit)	17	15	16	16	16	16
职工总数 (人)	Number of Staff and Workers (person)	523	676	986	896	926	943
科技活动人员 (人)	Scientists and Engineers		514	756	638	727	750
经费收入 (万元)	Funds (10000 yuan)	6356	20203	34356	42923	38820	42206
#政府拨款	Government Appropriations	2883	12078	15715	26455	21981	24956
经费支出 (万元)	Expenditures (10000 yuan)	5982	22566	32367	35108	36760	41692
科技经费支出(万元)	Expenditures on Purchase of Assets(10000 yuan)		15327	20843	19618	24713	30753

18-19 各市县级及以上政府部门属研究与开发机构基本情况

Basic Statistics on Research and Development Institutions under Government Departments at and above County Level by City

市别	City	2016 机构数（个）Number of Institutions (unit)	就业人员（人）Number of Employed Persons (person)	#科技活动人员（人）R&D Personnel (person)	经费收入（万元）Funds (10000 yuan)	#政府拨款 Government Appropr-iations	经费支出（万元）Expenditures (10000 yuan)	科技经费支出（万元）R&D Expenditure (100 million yuan)
全省合计	**Provincial Total**	**314**	**24686**	**18915**	**1517646**	**881354**	**1440434**	**1053151**
广州	Guangzhou	104	17578	13756	1309924	720685	1256675	913734
深圳	Shenzhen	6	1946	1435	70301	47623	68050	56489
珠海	Zhuhai	7	291	220	17018	15146	7665	6010
汕头	Shantou	11	456	342	8048	6262	6892	3919
佛山	Foshan	4	138	104	7250	5390	7095	5353
韶关	Shaoguan	17	316	253	7780	5759	7582	5806
河源	Heyuan	16	264	135	2188	1996	2465	1870
梅州	Meizhou	15	340	270	7527	7074	6378	5166
惠州	Huizhou	22	381	296	10520	9394	9549	7882
汕尾	Shanwei	6	99	47	893	874	891	549
东莞	Dongguan	8	460	339	16966	12871	15335	9769
中山	Zhongshan	3	105	80	4560	2987	4545	2183
江门	Jiangmen	9	184	135	4782	3694	4412	3146
阳江	Yangjiang	3	85	71	1246	1099	1628	854
湛江	Zhanjiang	22	980	694	32204	26696	25168	18702
茂名	Maoming	16	311	209	4728	3989	4952	3467
肇庆	Zhaoqing	15	179	146	3600	3380	2981	2292
清远	Qingyuan	11	71	46	1245	1119	1047	620
潮州	Chaozhou	4	119	94	1787	1651	1676	1205
揭阳	Jieyang	10	320	206	4010	2979	4246	3488
云浮	Yunfu	5	63	37	1071	689	1204	645

18−19 续表 continued

市别	City	2017 机构数(个) Number of Institutions (unit)	就业人员(人) Number of Employed Persons (person)	#科技活动人员(人) R&D Personnel (person)	经费收入(万元) Funds (10000 yuan)	#政府拨款 Government Appropr-iations	经费支出(万元) Expenditures (10000 yuan)	科技经费支出(万元) R&D Expenditure (100 million yuan)
全省合计	**Provincial Total**	**310**	**25446**	**20080**	**1538320**	**920041**	**1529061**	**1195459**
广　州	Guangzhou	102	18247	15148	1301240	728273	1309595	1024444
深　圳	Shenzhen	6	2069	1206	89910	68626	84633	71124
珠　海	Zhuhai	7	355	270	20674	19520	10750	8732
汕　头	Shantou	11	433	330	8522	6649	7659	4620
佛　山	Foshan	4	141	109	6473	6129	6374	5577
韶　关	Shaoguan	17	307	250	9101	6967	9530	6890
河　源	Heyuan	15	240	124	2328	2175	2387	1804
梅　州	Meizhou	15	332	269	6459	5936	6665	5520
惠　州	Huizhou	22	383	305	13026	12335	12309	10507
汕　尾	Shanwei	6	90	47	1354	1347	1350	903
东　莞	Dongguan	8	479	343	14627	10127	14342	8945
中　山	Zhongshan	3	103	81	4901	3096	4901	2235
江　门	Jiangmen	9	182	135	4677	3682	4520	3359
阳　江	Yangjiang	3	86	55	1243	1153	1337	756
湛　江	Zhanjiang	21	969	682	33727	27315	33993	26970
茂　名	Maoming	16	293	207	5863	4669	5515	3834
肇　庆	Zhaoqing	15	173	137	4042	3722	3434	2174
清　远	Qingyuan	11	73	48	1435	1208	1170	628
潮　州	Chaozhou	4	111	86	1865	1749	1857	1272
揭　阳	Jieyang	10	317	212	5186	4314	5074	4200
云　浮	Yunfu	5	63	36	1666	1049	1668	966

注：本表统计范围不含已转制的科研机构。

Note: The statistical coverage of this table excludes scientific research institutions which have undergone changes in ownership and/or mode of operation.

18-20 三种专利申请量与授权量
Three Types of Patent Application and Granted

单位：件 (item)

年份 Year	申请量 Number of Patent Applications	发明 Inventions	实用新型 Utility Models	外观设计 Designs	授权量 Number of Patent Applic-ations Granted	发明 Inventions	实用新型 Utility Models	外观设计 Designs
1990	1948	231	1001	716	889	40	571	278
1995	7729	463	2367	4899	4611	57	1446	3108
2000	21123	1760	6033	13330	15799	261	4797	10741
2001	27596	2549	8144	16903	18259	301	5246	12712
2002	34339	3806	9972	20561	22760	351	6396	16013
2003	43186	6181	12985	24020	29235	953	7921	20361
2004	52201	8093	14682	29426	31446	1941	9307	20198
2005	72220	12887	18951	40382	36894	1876	11017	24001
2006	90886	21351	23886	45649	43516	2441	15644	25431
2007	102449	26692	25389	50368	56451	3714	21636	31101
2008	103883	28099	28883	46901	62031	7604	25072	29355
2009	125673	32247	39027	54399	83621	11355	27438	44828
2010	152907	40866	47706	64335	119346	13691	43901	61754
2011	196275	52012	67336	76927	128415	18242	51402	58771
2012	229514	60448	78731	90335	153598	22153	65946	65499
2013	264265	68990	93592	101683	170430	20084	77503	72843
2014	278351	75148	96136	107067	179953	22276	83202	74475
2015	355939	103941	135717	116281	241176	33477	105254	102445
2016	505667	155581	203609	146477	259032	38626	118157	102249
2017	627819	182639	283560	161620	332648	45740	169017	117891

注：2017年起，专利申请量统计口径调整为国家知识产权局受理的按规定缴足申请费、符合进入初步审查阶段条件的专利申请数量，2017年前，该口径数据称为专利申请受理量。

Note: Starting from 2017, the statistic for the number of patent applications accepted only includes patents that have passed initial review conditions and paid application fees as stipulated by the State Intellectual Property Office. Data before 2017 of this coverage were named as number of patent applications. auepted.

18-21 分市全社会研究与试验发展经费（2017年）
Researoh and Developmant Expenditure by City (2017)

单位：万元 (10000yuan)

市别	City	总计 Total	科研机构 R&D Institutions	高校 Institutions of Higher Education	企业 Enterprises	其他 others
全省	**Provincial Total**	**23436283.0**	**838421.1**	**1375323.5**	**20830074.3**	**392464.3**
广州	Guangzhou	5324084.6	710653.8	1005404.7	3423979.0	184047.1
深圳	Shenzhen	9769376.8	66316.5	184696.6	9405625.1	112738.6
珠海	Zhuhai	671525.5	2839.4	6274.5	659713.9	2697.7
汕头	Shantou	193145.9	414.9	26299.6	164554.0	1877.4
佛山	Foshan	2231550.8	1830.1	26205.9	2196471.1	7043.7
韶关	Shaoguan	145406.2	2101.1	3315.6	135785.9	4203.6
河源	Heyuan	33578.8		624.7	32381.3	572.8
梅州	Meizhou	31602.0	685.6	2834.6	27253.9	827.9
惠州	Huizhou	839794.5	2208.6	8676.3	818494.2	10415.4
汕尾	Shanwei	62461.0	3000.0	679.6	58284.9	496.5
东莞	Dongguan	1881418.7	10299.2	53886.2	1769344.1	47889.2
中山	Zhongshan	791708.4	11267.8	1659.6	774407.9	4373.1
江门	Jiangmen	514318.8	574.3	15215.6	492576.0	5952.9
阳江	Yangjiang	101043.1	2110.5	230.0	97661.8	1040.8
湛江	Zhanjiang	108881.4	6613.7	19526.1	79582.9	3158.7
茂名	Maoming	177681.2	543.8	8676.0	167161.2	1300.2
肇庆	Zhaoqing	242265.3	3184.1	3943.8	234760.5	376.9
清远	Qingyuan	70722.7		275.4	70154.7	292.6
潮州	Chaozhou	72027.8	2126.8	6612.6	62701.8	586.6
揭阳	Jieyang	133302.0	650.9	174.7	131837.4	639.0
云浮	Yunfu	40387.5	11000.0	111.2	27342.7	1933.6

18−22 规模以上工业企业的科技活动基本情况

Basic Statistics on Science and Technology Activities of Industrial Enterprises above Designated size

指　　标		2015	2016	2017
企业基本情况	**Statistics on Industrial Enterprises**			
有R&D活动企业数 (个)	Number of Enterprises with R&D Activities (unit)	8113	10928	16793
有R&D活动企业所占比重 (%)	Percentage of Enterprises with R&D Activities (%)	19.3	25.6	35.6
R&D活动情况	**Statistics on R&D Activities**			
R&D人员全时当量 (万人年)	Full-time Equivalent of R&D Personnel (10 000 man-years)	41.10	42.40	45.70
R&D经费支出 (亿元)	Expenditure on R&D (100 million yuan)	1520.50	1676.30	1865.00
R&D经费支出与主营业务收入之比 (%)	Percentage of Expenditure on R&D to Sales Revenue (%)	1.28	1.30	1.39
R&D项目数 (项)	R&D Projects (item)	37375	50740	73439
R&D项目经费支出 (亿元)	Expenditure on R&D Projects (100 million yuan)	1456.50	1632.50	1862.50
企业办R&D机构情况	**Statistics on R&D Institutions**			
机构数 (个)	Number of R&D Institutions (units)	6553	11834	20030
机构人员数 (万人)	R&D Personnel (10 000 persons)	47.80	67.50	91.10
机构经费支出 (亿元)	Expenditure on R&D (100 million yuan)	1433.80	1993.60	2630.20
新产品开发及生产情况	Statistics on New Products Development and Production			
新产品开发项目数 (个)	Number of New Products (unit)	43456	66843	103149
新产品开发经费支出 (亿元)	Expenditure on New Products Development (100 million yuan)	1831.00	2309.70	2828.60
新产品销售收入 (亿元)	Sales Revenue of New Products (100 million yuan)	22642.50	28671.40	34863.00
#新产品出口	Export	7484.10	9231.60	11051.70
专利情况	**Statistics on Patents**			
专利申请数 (件)	Number of Patent Applications (piece)	106038	145448	199293
#发明专利	Inventions	51672	68168	86724
有效发明专利数 (件)	Number of Inventions in Force (piece)	177047	236918	289238
技术获取和技术改造情况	**Statistics on Technology Acquisition and Technology Reconstruction**			
引进国外技术经费支出 (亿元)	Expenditure for Acquisition of Foreign Technology(100 million yuan)	87.30	131.60	94.60
引进技术消化吸收经费支出(亿元)	Expenditure for Assimilation of Technology (100 million yuan)	5.20	4.80	3.90
购买国内技术经费支出 (亿元)	Expenditure for Purchase of Domestic Technology (100 million yuan)	40.90	62.60	44.40
技术改造经费支出 (亿元)	Expenditure for Technical Renovation (100 million yuan)	172.00	205.00	314.10

18-23 规上工业企业研究与发展经费内部支出
Internal Expenditures of Industrial Enterprises Above Designated Size

单位：亿元 (100 million yuan)

指　　标	Item	2015	2016	2017
总　计	**Totals**	**1520.55**	**1676.27**	**1865.03**
按登记注册类型分	**By Status of Registration**			
内资企业	Domestic Funded	1060.73	1192.94	1384.47
国有企业	State-owned Enterprises	1.47	1.73	4.93
集体企业	Collective-owned Enterprises	0.42	0.52	0.29
股份合作企业	Cooperative Enterprises	0.51	0.35	0.47
联营企业	Joint Ownership Enterprises	0.06	0.09	0.14
有限责任公司	Limited Liability Enterprises	548.66	641.50	719.75
#国有独资	State Sole Funded Corporations	22.13	16.51	22.11
股份有限公司	Share-holding Corporations Limited	271.97	238.97	274.00
私营企业	Private Enterprises	235.09	309.33	384.60
其他企业	Other Enterprises	2.55	0.45	0.30
港、澳、台商投资企业	Enterprises with Funds from Hong Kong,Macao, and Taiwan	258.92	260.26	263.35
外商投资企业	Foreign Funded Enterprises	200.90	223.07	217.21
按企业规模分	**By Size of Enterprises**			
大型企业	Large Enterprises	976.03	1041.04	1129.06
中型企业	Medium-sized Enterprises	311.52	340.42	359.72
小微型企业	Small Enterprises	233.00	294.82	376.25
按行业分	**By Industry**			
采矿业	**Mining**	**5.70**	**3.54**	**2.98**
煤炭开采和洗选业	Mining and Washing of Coal			
石油和天然气开采业	Extraction Petroleum and Natural Gas	3.42	2.05	0.98
黑色金属矿采选业	Mining and Processing of Ferrous Metal Ores	0.25	0.32	0.44
有色金属矿采选业	Mining and Processing of Non-ferrous Metal Ores	0.10	0.15	0.20
非金属矿采选业	Mining and Processing of Non-metal Ores	1.18	0.96	1.35
开采辅助活动	Support Activities for Mining	0.75	0.05	0.02
其他采矿业	Mining of Other Ores			
制造业	**Manufacturing**	**1495.03**	**1655.00**	**1837.27**
农副食品加工业	Processing of Food from Agricultural Products	20.10	13.23	22.37
食品制造业	Manufacture of Foods	9.77	14.36	19.22
酒、饮料和精制茶制造业	Manufacture of Liquor, Beverages and Refined Tea	4.32	5.96	8.18
烟草制品业	Manufacture of Tobacco	1.87	2.77	1.96
纺织业	Manufacture of Textile	10.86	10.66	14.63
纺织服装、服饰业	Manufacture of Textile, Wearing Apparel, and Accessories	6.20	6.76	11.95

18-23 续表 continued

单位：亿元 (100 million yuan)

指 标	Item	2015	2016	2017
皮革、毛皮、羽毛及其制品和制鞋业	Manufacture of Leather, Fur, Feather and Related Products and Footwear	5.45	6.56	8.76
木材加工和木、竹、藤、棕、草制品业	Processing of Timber, Manufacture of Wood,Bamboo, Rattan, Palm and Straw Products	2.18	3.04	3.91
家具制造业	Manufacture of Furniture	9.37	10.15	17.16
造纸和纸制品业	Manufacture of Paper and Paper Products	17.75	14.88	22.75
印刷和记录媒介复制业	Printing and Reproduction of Recording Media	7.76	8.15	9.77
文教、工美、体育和娱乐用品制造业	Manufacture of Articles for Culture, Education, Arts and Crafts, Sport and Entertainment Activities	10.70	12.18	18.12
石油加工、炼焦和核燃料加工业	Processing of Petroleum, Coking and Processing of Nuclear Fuel	5.30	5.61	6.00
化学原料和化学制品制造业	Manufacture of Raw Chemical Materials and Chemical Products	73.06	66.71	60.01
医药制造业	Manufacture of Medicines	38.67	35.52	28.71
化学纤维制造业	Manufacture of Chemical Fibers	1.00	1.41	1.54
橡胶和塑料制品业	Manufacture of Rubber and Plastics Products	34.51	43.58	49.35
非金属矿物制品业	Manufacture of Non-metallic Mineral Products	35.49	36.51	40.20
黑色金属冶炼和压延加工业	Smelting and Pressing of Ferrous Metals	12.92	13.90	19.73
有色金属冶炼和压延加工业	Smelting and Pressing of Non-ferrous Metals	15.59	20.68	30.29
金属制品业	Manufacture of Metal Products	36.73	41.57	53.49
通用设备制造业	Manufacture of General Purpose Machinery	54.24	62.88	64.13
专用设备制造业	Manufacture of Special Purpose Machinery	52.53	56.02	63.53
汽车制造业	Manufacture of Automobiles	64.23	82.16	89.25
铁路、船舶、航空航天和其他运输设备制造业	Manufacture of Railway, Ship, Aerospace and Other Transport Equipment	14.44	33.26	21.31
电气机械和器材制造业	Manufacture of Electrical Machinery and Apparatus	193.50	201.60	234.46
计算机、通信和其他电子设备制造业	Manufacture of Computers, Communication and Other Electronic Equipment	728.77	816.38	883.10
仪器仪表制造业	Manufacture of Measuring Instruments and Machinery	20.71	21.64	26.04
其他制造业	Other Manufacture	2.59	2.12	2.77
废弃资源综合利用业	Utilization of Waste Resources	1.62	2.23	2.38
金属制品、机械和设备修理业	Repair Service of Metal Products, Machinery and Equipment	2.78	2.51	2.19
电力、热力、燃气及水生产和供应业	**Production and Supply of Electric Power, Heat Power, and Water**	**19.82**	**17.73**	**24.78**
电力、热力生产和供应业	Production and Supply of Electric Power and Heat Power	16.40	13.10	18.94
燃气生产和供应业	Production and Supply of Gas	1.49	2.52	2.61
水的生产和供应业	Production and Supply of Water	1.93	2.10	3.22

18-24 分市规模以上工业企业R&D活动人员和经费

R&D Personnel and Expenditure of Industrial Enterprises by City

市别	City	R&D活动人员(人) Number of R&D Personnel (person)			R&D经费内部支出(亿元) Internal Expenditure on R&D(100 million yuan)		
		2015	2016	2017	2015	2016	2017
全　省	**Provincial Total**	**534293**	**585089**	**696385**	**1520.55**	**1676.27**	**1865.03**
广　州	Guangzhou	82594	80509	97894	212.26	231.77	254.86
深　圳	Shenzhen	174953	202684	232421	672.65	760.03	841.10
珠　海	Zhuhai	16229	16737	23152	43.40	49.05	59.09
汕　头	Shantou	7698	7697	9863	11.20	12.71	15.43
佛　山	Foshan	68198	74427	96072	192.99	194.88	216.02
韶　关	Shaoguan	5280	6146	5173	11.49	12.52	13.27
河　源	Heyuan	1285	1473	2123	2.41	2.48	3.24
梅　州	Meizhou	1369	1962	2214	2.25	2.50	2.72
惠　州	Huizhou	24376	34929	43255	59.72	67.69	80.31
汕　尾	Shanwei	2958	2314	2584	5.03	5.97	5.83
东　莞	Dongguan	59469	64963	73644	126.79	143.40	161.42
中　山	Zhongshan	38488	38970	45301	69.24	74.79	76.60
江　门	Jiangmen	17584	17120	22902	38.74	40.28	48.45
阳　江	Yangjiang	1898	1692	1788	8.40	9.22	9.76
湛　江	Zhanjiang	2611	3053	3136	7.18	6.59	7.82
茂　名	Maoming	5011	5004	6580	13.31	15.31	16.56
肇　庆	Zhaoqing	11513	12100	11611	19.22	21.44	23.42
清　远	Qingyuan	3823	3684	4987	5.79	5.33	7.01
潮　州	Chaozhou	3281	3634	4161	5.11	5.86	6.27
揭　阳	Jieyang	4166	4018	5697	10.82	11.82	13.18
云　浮	Yunfu	1509	1973	1827	2.56	2.63	2.67
按经济区域分	By Region						
珠三角	Pearl River Delta	493404	542439	646252	1435.00	1583.33	1761.26
东　翼	Eastern Region	18103	17663	22305	32.16	36.36	40.71
西　翼	Western Region	9520	9749	11504	28.89	31.12	34.14
山　区	Mountainous Region	13266	15238	16324	24.50	25.46	28.92

注：本表统计范围是规模以上工业企业。
Note: Data in this table refer to industrial enterprises above designated size.

18-25 分市规模以上工业企业新产品产出情况
Production of New Products by Industrial Enterprises by City

单位：万元 (10000 yuan)

市别	City	2016 新产品产值 Output Value of New Products	2016 新产品销售收入 Sales Revenue of New Products	2016 #出口 Exports	2017 新产品产值 Output Value of New Products	2017 新产品销售收入 Sales Revenue of New Products	2017 #出口 Exports
全　省	**Provincial Total**	**292303980**	**286714109**	**92315817**	**354665099**	**348630305**	**110517202**
广　州	Guangzhou	39893409	39041841	4652496	43889275	44303351	6009414
深　圳	Shenzhen	104986925	101883636	45264597	128017918	121387080	53227890
珠　海	Zhuhai	14411329	13436491	3090715	13026788	12313080	3253289
汕　头	Shantou	2278937	2277269	507538	3042690	3089577	709664
佛　山	Foshan	30277451	29610947	7628060	36353427	37385382	8464774
韶　关	Shaoguan	1032645	977769	123876	1200187	1441597	182340
河　源	Heyuan	827974	856880	183342	1216052	1356639	204632
梅　州	Meizhou	579548	472972	60101	736352	749902	131713
惠　州	Huizhou	21032772	20968536	7828346	25321299	25932921	10804489
汕　尾	Shanwei	2199452	2205393	855234	2493538	2489798	634058
东　莞	Dongguan	45756078	46427486	16506231	64091704	63927517	18840166
中　山	Zhongshan	8753863	8304444	2552042	10961804	10491736	3410823
江　门	Jiangmen	7510552	7324623	1820957	10356739	10042840	2514720
阳　江	Yangjiang	142536	141441	34106	438004	507185	52503
湛　江	Zhanjiang	849170	857233	130625	2506012	1934747	635293
茂　名	Maoming	878466	880226	84129	1048053	1003952	211568
肇　庆	Zhaoqing	6103902	6318725	266280	3473428	3492148	237379
清　远	Qingyuan	1978686	1949502	303479	2865384	2914125	379198
潮　州	Chaozhou	775506	771247	265381	1026399	1288881	319932
揭　阳	Jieyang	1837100	1807952	91139	2323032	2294953	178153
云　浮	Yunfu	197681	199495	67144	277017	282895	115202
按经济区域分	By Region						
珠三角	Pearl River Delta	278726280	273316730	89609725	335492381	329276055	106762945
东　翼	Eastern Region	7090995	7061861	1719292	8885659	9163209	1841807
西　翼	Western Region	1870171	1878901	248860	3992068	3445884	899365
山　区	Mountainous Region	4616534	4456618	737941	6294991	6745157	1013085

注：本表统计范围是规模以上工业企业。
Note: Data in this table refer to industrial enterprises above designated size.

18−26 科协机构及活动情况

Statistics on Associations for Science and Technology and Their Activities

项 目	Item	2000	2010	2014	2015	2016	2017
科协机构 （个）	**Number of Associations for Science and Technology (unit)**	**357**	**1026**	**143**	**142**	**142**	**141**
省科协	Provincial Associations	1	1	1	1	1	1
市科协	City Associations	21	21	21	21	21	21
县(市、区)科协	County (County-level City, District) Associations	123	121	121	120	120	119
厂矿科协	Factory and Mine Associations	212	883				
各级学会及农技协 （个）	**Number of Learned Societies and Research Societies at Various Levels (unit)**	**3780**	**2371**	**3767**	**3777**	**3762**	**2973**
省级学会	Provincial Learned Societies	146	151	150	151	151	151
市级学会	City Learned Societies	734	780	796	838	938	910
县级学会	County Learned Societies			1431	1428	1308	903
农村专业技术协会	Rural Specialized Technological Societies	2900	1440	1390	1360	1365	1009
各级学会及农技协会员（人）	**Number of Members of Learned Societies and Rural Specialized Technological Societies at Various Levels (person)**	**704094**	**393734**	**592276**	**710402**	**726938**	**706533**
省级学会会员	Members of Provincial Learned Societies	203861	265046	469411	581796	590870	597177
#学会从业人员	Personnel in Learned Societies		574	908	909	1054	1028
农村专业技术协会会员	Members of Rural Specialized Technological Societies	223687	128688	122865	128606	135014	109356
科协活动开展情况	**Activities of Associations for Science and Technology**						
举办各类学术交流会(次)	Number of Academic Meetings Held	4769	677	1419	1466	1630	1241
举办科技科普展览 （次）	Number of Scientific and Technological Popularization Exhibitions Lectures (time)	2258	3582	1298	1561	2031	1156
青少年科技竞赛 （次）	Number of Scientific and Technological Competitions for Adolescents (time)	1286	407	307	327	388	412
参加科协各类活动人次 （人次）	**Number of Participants in Activities Organized by Associations for Science and Technology (person-time)**	**8367629**	**11164480**	**7467949**	**8641510**	**15867372**	**6868126**
参加各类学术交流会	Number of Participants in Academic Meetings	505235	295009	251609	335713	341086	444377
参加各类科技培训	Number of Participants in Training Programs	654742	251993	349654	325922	318969	141444
参加各类科普活动	Number of Participants in Scientific and Technological Popularization Activities	7207652	10617478	6866686	7979875	15207317	6282305
主办科技期刊 （种）	**Publications of Academic Journals and Scientific and Technological Popularization Readings (kind)**	**582**	**611**	**72**	**110**	**41**	**66**
科技期刊总印数 （万册、万份）	Number of Academic Journals and Scientific and Technological Popularization Readings Issued (10000 copies)	562	513	340	303	54	85

注：1．2013年，科协机构数不包括厂矿科协。
2．2013年起，主办科技期刊只统计在新闻出版机构注册登记，有正式刊号或内部准印证并由本单位直接主办、负责编辑的期刊。
3．各类科技培训统计口径变更为实用技术培训。

Note: a) In 2013, factory and mice associations are not included in number of associations for science and technology.
b) From 2013,publications of academic journals and scientific and technological popularization readings refer only to those with official numbrs registered by press and publicaton or those with internal permit directly edited by the unit
c) The scope of participants in training programs has been changed to operative technology training.

主要统计指标解释

普通高等学校 指按照国家规定的设置标准和审批程序批准举办，通过国家统一招生考试，收高中毕业生为主要培养对象，实施高等教育的全日制大学、独立设置的学院和高等专科学校，高等职业学校和其他机构。

成人高等学校 指按照国家有关规定审批、招收通过全国成人高教统一招生考试的具有高中毕业或同等学历的在职从业人员利用脱产、半脱产、业余或函授等多种形式对其实施高等学历教育，培养高等教育专科或本科毕业水平的专门人才，修业年限、课程设置和总学时的数按高等学历教育要求付诸实施的学校。包括广播电视大学、职工高等学校、农民高等学校、管理干部学院、教育学院、独立设置的函授学院等。

小学学龄儿童入学率 指调查范围内已入小学学习的学龄儿童占校内外学龄儿童总数（包括弱智儿童在内，但不包括盲聋哑儿童）的比重。

研究与试验发展(R&D) 指在科学技术领域，为增加知识总量，以及运用这些知识去创造新的应用进行的系统的创造性的活动，包括基础研究、应用研究、试验发展三类活动。国际上通常采用 R&D 活动的规模和强度指标反映一国的科技实力和核心竞争力。

基础研究 指为了获得关于现象和可观察事实的基本原理的新知识(揭示客观事物的本质、运动规律，获得新发现、新学说)而进行的实验性或理论性研究，它不以任何专门或特定的应用或使用为目的。其成果以科学论文和科学著作为主要形式。用来反映知识的原始创新能力。

应用研究 指为获得新知识而进行的创造性研究，主要针对某一特定的目的或目标。应用研究是为了确定基础研究成果可能的用途，或是为达到预定的目标探索应采取的新方法(原理性)或新途径。其成果形式以科学论文、专著、原理性模型或发明专利为主。用来反映对基础研究成果应用途径的探索。

试验发展 指利用从基础研究、应用研究和实际经验所获得的现有知识，为产生新的产品、材料和装置，建立新的工艺、系统和服务，以及对已产生和建立的上述各项作实质性的改进而进行的系统性工作。其成果形式主要是专利、专有技术、具有新产品基本特征的产品原型或具有新装置基本特征的原始样机等。在社会科学领域，试验发展是指把通过基础研究、应用研究获得的知识转变成可以实施的计划(包括为进行检验和评估实施示范项目)的过程。人文科学领域没有对应的试验发展活动。主要反映将科研成果转化为技术和产品的能力，是科技推动经济社会发展的物化成果。

R&D 人员 指参与研究与试验发展项目研究、管理和辅助工作的人员，包括项目(课题)组人员，企业科技行政管理人员和直接为项目(课题)活动提供服务的辅助人员。反映投入从事拥有自主知识产权的研究开发活动的人力规模。

R&D 人员全时当量 指全时人员数加非全时人员按工作量折算为全时人员数的总和。例如：有两个全时人员和三个非全时人员(工作时间分别为 20%、30%和 70%)，则全时当量为 2+0.2+0.3+0.7=3.2 人年。为国际上比较科技人力投入而制定的可比指标。

R&D 经费支出合计 指调查单位用于内部开展 R&D 活动（基础研究、应用研究和试验发展）的实际支出。包括用于 R&D 项目（课题）活动的直接支出，以及间接用于 R&D 活动的管理费、服务费、与 R&D 有关的基本建设支出以及外协加工费等。不包括生产性活动支出、归还贷款支出以及与外单位合作或委托外单位进行 R&D 活动而转拨给对方的经费支出。

R&D 经费支出中政府资金 指 R&D 经费内部支出中来自各级政府部门的各类资金，包括财政科学技术拨款、科学基金、教育等部门事业费以及政府部门预算外资金的实际支出。

R&D 经费支出中企业资金 指 R&D 经费内部支出中来自本企业的自有资金和接受其他企业委托而获得的经费，以及科研院所、高校等事业单位从企业获得的资金的实际支出。

R&D 项目（课题）数 指在当年立项并开展研究工作、以前年份立项仍继续进行研究的研发项目（课题）数，包括当年完成和年内研究工作已告失败的研发项目（课题），但不包括委托外单位进行的研发项目（课题）数。

新产品销售收入 指报告期企业销售新产品实现的销售收入。新产品是指采用新技术原理、新设计构思研制、生产的全新产品，或在结构、材质、工艺等某一方面比原有产品有明显改进，从而显著提高了产品性能或扩大了使用功能的产品。既包括经政府有关部门认定并在有效期内的新产品，也包括企业自行研制开发，未经政府有关部门认定，从投产之日起一年之内的新产品。

专利 是专利权的简称，是对发明人的发明创造经审查合格后，由专利局依据专利法授予发明人和设计人对该项发明创造享有的专有权。包括发明、实用新型和外观设计。反映拥有自主知识产权的科技和设计成果情况。

发明（专利） 指对产品、方法或者其改进所提出的新的技术方案。是国际通行的反映拥有自主知识产权技术的核心指标。

实用新型（专利） 指对产品的形状、构造或者其结合所提出的适于实用的新的技术方案。反映具有一定技术含量的技术成果情况。

外观设计（专利） 指对产品的形状、图案、色彩或者其结合所作出的富有美感并适于工业上应用的新设计。反映拥有自主知识产权的外观设计成果情况。

Explanatory Notes on Main Statistical Indicators

Regular Institutions of Higher Education refer to educational establishments set up according to government standards and evaluation and approval procedures, mainly enrolling graduates from senior secondary schools through uniform national matriculation examinations and providing higher education. Such institutions include full-time universities, independent colleges, technical colleges, professional colleges, and other institutions.

Institutions of Higher Learning for Adults refer to educational establishments approved according to relevant government rules, enrolling staff and workers with senior secondary or equivalent education through uniform national matriculation examinations, and providing them with regular higher education in various forms such as full-time, part-time, spare-time and correspondence courses in accordance with requirements of regular higher education in years of education, curricula, and total learning hours, so that they meet the standards for graduation of universities or junior colleges Institutions of higher learning for adults include radio and TV universities, colleges for staff and workers, colleges for farmers, colleges for management cadres, teachers' colleges, and independent correspondence colleges.

Enrollment Rate of Primary School-age Children refers to the proportion of school-age children enrolled at primary schools in the total number of school-age children both in and outside schools (including retarded children, but excluding blind, deaf and dumb children).

Research and Development (R&D) refers to systematic and creative activities in the field of science and technology aiming at increasing the knowledge and using the knowledge for new application. R&D includes 3 categories of activities: basic research, applied research and experiments and development. The scale and intensity of R&D are widely used internationally to reflect the strength of S&T and the core competitiveness of a country in the world.

Basic Research refers to empirical or theoretical research aiming at obtaining new knowledge on the fundamental principles regarding phenomena or observable facts to reveal the intrinsic nature and underlying laws and to acquire new discoveries or new theories. Basic research takes no specific or designated application as the aim of the research. Results of basic research are mainly released or disseminated in the form of scientific papers or monographs. This indicator reflects the innovation capacity for original knowledge.

Applied Research refers to creative research aiming at obtaining new knowledge on a specific objective or target. Purpose of the applied research is to identify the possible uses of results from basic research, or to explore new (fundamental) methods or new approaches. Results of applied research are expressed in the form of scientific papers, monographs, fundamental models or invention patents. This indicator reflects the exploration of ways to apply the results of basic research.

Experiments and Development refer to systematic activities aiming at using the knowledge from basic and applied researches or from practical experience to develop new products, materials and equipment, to establish new production process, systems and services, or to make substantial improvement on the existing products, process or services. Results of experiment and development activities are embodied in patents, exclusive technology, and monotype of new products or equipment. In social sciences, experiment and development activities refer to the process of converting the knowledge from basic or applied researches into feasible programmes (including conduct of demonstration projects for assessment and evaluation). There are no experiment and development activities in the science of humanities. This indicator reflects the capability of transferring the results of S&T into technique and products, and measures the realization of S&T in spearheading the economic and social development.

R & D Personnel refer to persons engaged in research, management and supporting activities of R & D, including persons in the project teams, persons engaged in the management of S&T activities of enterprises and supporting staff providing direct service to the research projects. This indicator reflects the size of personnel engaged in R&D activities with independent intellectual property.

Full-time Equivalent of R&D Personnel refers to the sum of the full-time persons and the full-time equivalent of part-time persons converted by workload. For instance, if there are 2 full-time persons and 3 part-time workers (20%, 30% and 70% of working hours respectively on R&D activities), the full-time equivalent are 2+0.2+0.3+0.7=3.2 person-years. This is an internationally comparable indicator of S&T manpower input.

Total Expenditure of Funds on R&D refers to the real expenditure of surveyed units on their own R&D activities (basic research, applied research, experiments and development) including direct expenditure on R&D activities, indirect expenditure of management and services on R&D activities, expenditure on capital construction and material processing by others. Excluding the expenditure on production activities, return of loan, and fees transferred to cooperated or entrusted agencies on R&D activities.

Expenditure of Government Funds on R&D refers to the expenditure of funds on R&D activities from government agencies at different levels, including appropriate funds on science and technology from financial departments, scientific funds, operating expenses from education departments and the real expenditure of extra budgetary funds from government agencies.

Expenditure of Funds of Enterprises on R&D refers to the expenditure of funds on R&D activities from self-raised funds of enterprises and funds from other enterprises through entrustment, and the expenditure of funds of institutions, such as institution of scientific research and universities, from enterprises.

Number of R&D Projects (subjects) refers to the number of R&D projects (subjects) set up and implemented at the reference year, and the number of R&D projects (subjects) set up in former years and under implementation, including the projects (subjects) finished and failed at the reference year, excluding the projects (subjects) implemented by others through entrustment.

Sales Income of New Products refers to the sales income of new products of the enterprises at the reference period. New products refer to products developed and produced with new technologies and designs or improved in structure, material, process or other aspects so that their performance are improved or their functions expanded. New products include those affirmed by government authorities in their validity period and also those developed by enterprises without the affirmation of government authorities within one year after they are put into production.

Patent is an abbreviation for the patent right and refers to the exclusive right of ownership by the inventors or designers for the creation or inventions, given from the patent offices after due process of assessment and approval in accordance with the Patent Law. Patents are granted for inventions, utility models and designs. This indicator reflects the achievements of S&T and design with independent intellectual property.

Patented Inventions refer to new technical proposals to the products or methods or their modifications. This is universal core indicator reflecting the technologies with independent intellectual property.

Patented Utility Models refer to the practical and new technical proposals on the shape and structure of the product or the combination of both. This indicator reflects the condition of technological results with certain technical content.

Designs refer to the aesthetics and industrially applicable new designs for the shape, pattern and colour of the product, or their combinations. This indicator reflects the appearance design achievements with independent intellectual property.

十九、文化与体育

CULTURE AND SPORTS

十九　文化与体育

简要说明

一、本篇资料主要反映文化事业和体育的基本情况。

二、本篇资料主要包括：

1. 文化艺术、文物、图书馆、新闻出版、广播、电影、电视等文化事业的机构、人员及业务活动开展情况等。

2. 体育系统职工人数、群众体育活动开展情况及运动竞技成绩等。

三、本篇资料由广东省统计局社会和科技统计处负责整理、编辑。

四、统计资料来源：

文化、体育统计资料根据广东省文化厅、广东省新闻出版广电局、广东省体育局及广东省档案局等有关部门提供的统计年报加工整理。

19 Culture and Sports

Brief Introduction

Ⅰ. The data in this chapter show the basic conditions on the development Guangdong's cultural undertakings. as well as Sports.

Ⅱ. The data in this chapter mainly include:

(1) The data on institutions, personnel and business activities of culture and arts, cultural relics, libraries, news and publication, radio, film and television, etc.

(2) the number of staff and workers in sports departments，mass sports and athletics sports，etc.

Ⅲ. The data are prepared and edited by the Division of Social, Scientific and Technological Statistics of Statistics Bureau of Guangdong Province.

Ⅳ. Data sources:

The data on culture and sport are processed and prepared in accordance with the annual statistical reports provided by Guangdong Provincial Department of Culture, Guangdong Provincial Administration of Press, Publication, Radio, Film and Television, Guangdong Provincial Bureau of Sports, Guangdong Provincial Bureau of Archives and the related departments.

19-1 文化、体育主要指标
Main Indicators on Culture and Education

指标	Item	2000	2010	2015	2016	2017
电影放映单位 (个)	Number of Film Projection Units (unit)	1626	1306	1793	1974	2237
艺术表演团体 (个)	Number of Art Performance Troupes (unit)	138	133	72	72	74
文化馆 (个)	Number of Cultural Centers (unit)	118	129	146	146	146
公共图书馆 (个)	Number of Public Libraries (unit)	125	133	140	142	143
公共图书馆藏量 (万册、件)	Holdings of Public Libraries (10000 volumes)	2330	4615	7008	7900	8708
博物馆（含美术馆） (个)	Number of Museums (including arts museum) (unit)	131	169	193	192	197
博物馆藏品数(含美术馆)(万件)	Holdings of Museums (including arts museum) (10000 pieces)	49.09	84.46	101.83	101.27	106.81
档案馆 (个)	Number of Archives (unit)	161	205	217	192	192
利用档案 (万卷次)	Archives Utilized (10000 volume-times)	36.32	301.00	495.00	560.00	510.00
图书出版量 (万册)	Number of Books Published (10000 copies)	26978	23134	31287	31195	30197
杂志出版量 (万册)	Number of Magazines Published (10000 copies)	26299	21201	14458	12270	11428
报纸出版量 (亿份)	Number of Newspapers Published(100 million copies)	34.63	45.59	32.77	29.88	27.47
广播电台 (座)	Number of Radio Stations (unit)	106	22	22	22	22
电视台 (座)	Number of TV Stations (unit)	67	24	24	24	24
广播综合人口覆盖率 (%)	Overall Population Coverage Rate of Radio (%)	96.0	98.0	99.9	99.9	99.9
电视综合人口覆盖率 (%)	Overall Population Coverage Rate of Television (%)	96.4	98.0	99.9	99.9	99.9
举办全民健身活动次数 (次)	Number of National Body-building Activities Held (time)		9477	5000	5350	4680

注：1．由于统计口径出现变化，已对2012年全省公共图书馆藏量数进行了调整。

2．由于文化部门改制，2012年起只统计事业单位和省直企业中的文化部门艺术表演团体。自2013年起，艺术表演团体口径进行调整，分为公有制艺术表演团体(事业)和公有制艺术表演团体(企业)。

Note: a)Data of 2012 of holdings of public libraries have been adjusted due to the change of coverage.

b)Due to institutional restructuring of cultural departments, the data of art performance troupes since 2012 only covers those of institutional organizations and directly under provincial jurisdiction.The coverage of art performance troupes has been adjusted to include public ownership art performance troupes(Institution) and public ownershipart performance troupes(Enterprises).

19-2 文化艺术、文物事业机构数

Number of Institutions of Culture, Arts and Cultural Relics

单位：个 (unit)

年份 Year	电影放映单位 Film Projection Units	艺术表演团体 Arts Performance Troupes	文化馆 Cultural Centers	公共图书馆 Public Libraries	博物馆 Museums	档案馆 Archives
1978	6346	172	124	76	30	
1980	7375	195	113	97	26	
1985	6037	171	123	117	106	
1990	4024	130	113	103	106	138
1991	4041	122	110	104	107	147
1992	3917	125	113	108	108	150
1993	3974	126	115	110	108	148
1994	3750	132	116	111	111	156
1995	3668	134	115	114	113	155
1996	3670	136	115	115	114	157
1997	3463	138	117	119	117	157
1998	3621	139	117	120	122	157
1999	2938	140	117	121	128	162
2000	1626	138	118	125	131	161
2001	1794	139	118	129	140	175
2002	904	141	120	131	140	185
2003	840	144	117	129	144	185
2004	684	140	119	128	143	185
2005	720	139	117	129	146	185
2006	1542	138	120	129	147	186
2007	1844	128	122	130	153	186
2008	1450	130	121	132	152	188
2009	1265	127	128	133	160	197
2010	1392	133	129	133	169	205
2011	1357	100	134	134	161	209
2012	1419	61	137	137	168	209
2013	1506	75	147	137	191	214
2014	1673	72	147	138	192	218
2015	1793	72	146	140	193	217
2016	1974	72	146	142	192	192
2017	2237	74	146	143	197	192

注：由于全国文化文物统计制度统计口径的改变，2009年以后博物馆包含美术馆，其他年份博物馆不含美术馆。

Note: Due to the change in statistical coverage in national culture and cultural relics survey, the number of museums after 2009 includes arts museum, and that of other years does not include arts museum.

19−3 文化部门艺术表演团体演出基本情况（2017年）
Basic Statistics on Performances of Art Troupes under(of) Cultural Departments (2017)

项　目	Item	剧团数（个）Number of Troupes (unit)	国内演出场次（万场）Number of Domestic Performances (10000 shows)	#到农村演出 Shows in Rural Areas	国内演出观众人次(万人次) Number of Domestic Spectators (10000 person-times)
合　计	**Total**	**390**	**4.12**	**2.85**	**2350.15**
公有制艺术表演团体(事业)	Public Ownership Arts Performance Troupes (Institution)	42	0.57	0.39	633.09
国有	State-owned	42	0.57	0.39	633.09
集体	Collective-owned				
其他	Others				
公有制艺术表演团体(企业)	Public Ownership Arts Performance Troupes (Enterprises)	32	0.44	0.18	391.83
国有	State-owned	28	0.41	0.15	345.35
集体	Collective-owned				
其他	Others	4	0.03	0.03	46.47
按剧种分	**By Type of Art Performance Troupe**				
#话剧、儿童剧、滑稽剧类	Modern Drama, Children Drama, Farce Drama	64	0.51	0.26	222.99
歌舞、音乐类	Dance, Music	80	0.60	0.30	389.30
京剧、昆曲类	Beijing Opera, Kunqu Opera	3	0.01	…	7.25
地方戏曲类	Local Opera	157	2.24	2.00	1425.72
杂技、魔术、马戏类	Magic, Acrobatics, Circus	5	0.04	0.02	51.20
曲艺类	Chinese Folk Art	21	0.19	0.07	78.94
乌兰牧骑	Nei Monggol Cultural Troupe Mounted on Horseback				
综合性艺术表演团体	Comprehensive Art Troupes	60	0.54	0.19	174.74

19-4 文化、文物机构及人员数（2017年）
Number of Institutions and Personnel in Culture and Cultural Relics (2017)

项 目	Item	合计 Total		文化部门 Cultural Departments		其他部门 Others	
		机构数（个） Number of Institutions (unit)	人数（人） Number of Personnel (person)	机构数（个） Number of Institutions (unit)	人数（人） Number of Personnel (person)	机构数（个） Number of Institutions (unit)	人数（人） Number of Personnel (person)
总 计	**Total**	**24111**	**269593**	**2553**	**34533**	**21558**	**235060**
文化合计	**Culture**	**23833**	**264920**	**2289**	**30021**	**21544**	**234899**
艺术事业	Arts	473	14932	112	5507	361	9425
图书馆事业	Libraries	143	4450	143	4450		
群众文化事业	Mass Culture	1756	11972	1756	11972		
艺术教育业	Art Education	4	771	4	771		
文化市场经营机构(不含非公有制艺术表演团体)	Cultural Market Operating Units	21126	218373			21126	218373
文艺科研	Scientific Research on Arts	7	97	7	97		
艺术展览创作机构	Art Exhibition Creative Agency	14	342	14	342		
文化行政主管部门	Administrative Department	151	4752	151	4752		
其他文化机构	Other Agencies	159	9231	102	2130	57	7101
文物合计	**Cultural Relics**	**278**	**4673**	**264**	**4512**	**14**	**161**
文物科研机构	Institutions for Cultural Relics	4	179	4	179		
文物保护管理机构	Agencies of Cultural Relics Preservation	34	305	32	305	2	
博物馆	Museums	184	3651	172	3490	12	161
文物商店	Cultural Relics Stores	3	67	3	67		
其他文物机构	Other Agencies	53	471	53	471		

19-5 公共图书馆、群众文化事业机构及人员数（2017年）
Number of Institutions and Personnel in Public Libraries and Mass Culture (2017)

项 目	Item	合计 Total		文化部门 Cultural Departments		其他部门 Others	
		机构数（个） Number of Institutions (unit)	人数（人） Number of Personnel (person)	机构数（个） Number of Institutions (unit)	人数（人） Number of Personnel (person)	机构数（个） Number of Institutions (unit)	人数（人） Number of Personnel (person)
图书馆事业	**Libraries**	**143**	**4450**	**143**	**4450**		
#少儿图书馆	Children's Libraries	5	220	5	220		
群众文化事业	**Mass Culture**	**1756**	**11972**	**1756**	**11972**		
群众艺术馆、文化馆	Mass Art Centers	146	2415	146	2415		
文化站	Cultural Stations	1610	9557	1610	9557		

19-6 各市文化、文物事业机构数（2017年）

Number of Institutions in Culture and Cultural Relics by City (2017)

单位：个 (unit)

市 别	City	艺术表演团体 Art Troupes	文化馆 Cultural Centers	公共图书馆 Public Libraries	博物馆(含美术馆) Museums (including art museums)	档案馆 Archives
全 省	**Provincial Total**					
广 州	Guangzhou	7	12	13	29	14
深 圳	Shenzhen	2	8	11	20	10
珠 海	Zhuhai	3	4	3	3	6
汕 头	Shantou	6	8	9	7	10
佛 山	Foshan	2	7	6	17	7
韶 关	Shaoguan	2	11	10	9	12
河 源	Heyuan	4	7	7	8	8
梅 州	Meizhou	6	9	10	10	15
惠 州	Huizhou	1	6	5	7	8
汕 尾	Shanwei	4	6	4	5	6
东 莞	Dongguan		1	1	7	3
中 山	Zhongshan		1	1	6	3
江 门	Jiangmen	2	8	7	11	11
阳 江	Yangjiang	1	5	5	4	7
湛 江	Zhanjiang	8	11	9	9	13
茂 名	Maoming	4	6	6	6	7
肇 庆	Zhaoqing	2	9	9	8	11
清 远	Qingyuan	2	10	10	11	10
潮 州	Chaozhou	2	4	4	6	5
揭 阳	Jieyang	5	6	6	6	6
云 浮	Yunfu	1	6	6	5	6
省直属单位	Units Directly under Provincial Government	10	1	1	3	14
按经济区域分	By Region					
珠 三 角	Pearl River Delta	19	56	56	108	73
东 翼	Eastern Region	17	24	23	24	27
西 翼	Western Region	13	22	20	19	27
山 区	Mountainous Region	15	43	43	43	51

注：1.自2013年起，艺术表演团体分为公有制艺术表演团体(事业)和公有制艺术表演团体(企业)。
2.各区域不包省直单位部分。

Note: a) The coverage of art performance troupes has been adjusted to include public ownership art performance troupes(Institution) and public ownershipart performance troupes(Enterprises) since 2013.
b) By Region does not incluce agenies directly under provincial jurisdiction.

19-7 各市文化、文物事业机构的人员数（2017年）

Number of Personnel in Culture and Cultural Relics by City (2017)

单位：人 (person)

市 别	City	艺术表演团体 Art Troupes	文化馆 Cultural Centers	公共图书馆 Public Libraries	博物馆(含美术馆) Museums (including art museums)	档案馆 Archives
全 省	**Provincial Total**					
广 州	Guangzhou	775	218	675	709	187
深 圳	Shenzhen	227	247	1240	449	82
珠 海	Zhuhai	50	96	107	58	45
汕 头	Shantou	190	120	120	80	71
佛 山	Foshan	112	163	350	451	83
韶 关	Shaoguan	70	182	106	105	102
河 源	Heyuan	187	90	84	107	54
梅 州	Meizhou	163	139	138	117	105
惠 州	Huizhou	88	115	134	158	68
汕 尾	Shanwei	213	56	52	58	26
东 莞	Dongguan		78	180	342	26
中 山	Zhongshan		38	58	112	29
江 门	Jiangmen	73	94	111	159	108
阳 江	Yangjiang	46	57	73	119	72
湛 江	Zhanjiang	335	108	93	144	108
茂 名	Maoming	84	74	147	63	82
肇 庆	Zhaoqing	101	122	158	147	70
清 远	Qingyuan	65	111	99	112	84
潮 州	Chaozhou	110	68	44	79	31
揭 阳	Jieyang	253	111	117	70	42
云 浮	Yunfu	6	82	67	55	56
省直属单位	Units Directly under Provincial Government	1198	46	297	273	183
按经济区域分	By Region					
珠 三 角	Pearl River Delta	1426	1171	3013	2585	698
东 翼	Eastern Region	766	355	333	287	170
西 翼	Western Region	465	239	313	326	262
山 区	Mountainous Region	491	604	494	496	401

注：1.2012年起，分市数只统计事业单位的文化部门艺术表演团体。
　　2.各区域不包省直单位部分。

Note: a)Since 2012, number of art troupes by city only covers data of art troupes of institutional organizations.
　　b)"By Region" does not include agencies directly under provincial jurisdiction.

19−8 图书、杂志、报纸出版数量

Number of Books, Magazines and Newspapers Published

项 目	Item	2000	2010	2014	2015	2016	2017
图书出版	**Books Published**						
种数 (种)	Number of Publications (kind)	4374	6354	9495	10089	10840	9867
总印数 (万册)	Total Printed Copies(10000 copies)	26978	23134	29867	31287	31195	30197
总印张数(千印张)	Total Printed Sheets (1000 sheets)	1482942	1597301	2326580	2434970	2419143	2316790
杂志出版	**Magazines Published**						
种数 (种)	Number of Publications (kind)	337	380	381	382	381	381
总印数 (万册)	Total Printed Copies(10000 copies)	26299	21201	15520	14458	12270	11428
总印张数(千印张)	Total Printed Sheets (1000 sheets)	919514	1251752	917005	844427	663517	607564
报纸出版	**Newspapers Published**						
种数 (种)	Number of Publications (kind)	101	100	101	100	99	99
总印数 (万份)	Total Printed Copies(10000 copies)	346268	455912	389869	327660	298845	274721
总印张数(千印张)	Total Printed Sheets (1000 sheets)	17669099	43788152	31458182	20081573	16595386	14274199

注：2000年开始报纸出版统计不包含校报、院报。
Note: Since 2000, the number of newspaper published does not include that of college or institute newspaper.

19−9 图书出版情况（2017年）

Statistics on Books Published (2017)

门 类	Category	本版图书种数(种) Number of Publications (kind)	#新出 New Public-ations	总印数(万册) Total Printed Copies (10000 copies)	总印张数(千印张) Total Printed Sheets (1000 sheets)
合 计	**Total**	**9867**	**5031**	**30197**	**2316790**
马克思主义、列宁主义、毛泽东思想	Marxism, Leninism and Mao Zedong Thought	16	7	5	465
哲学	Philosophy	165	121	94	12604
社会科学总论	General Social Sciences	102	66	36	6261
政治、法律	Politics and Law	234	146	331	32447
经济	Economy	12	7	11	1580
军事	Military Affairs	590	400	224	33066
文化、科学、教育、体育	Culture, Science, Education and Sports	5146	1701	27235	2004657
语言、文字	Language, Philology	233	135	87	11992
文学	Literature	1215	940	1055	108045
艺术	Arts	633	490	438	31663
历史、地理	History and Geography	484	357	252	26909
自然科学总论	General Natural Sciences	12	5	2	193
数理科学、化学	Mathematics, Physics and Chemistry	64	24	12	1835
天文学、地理科学	Astronomy and Geology	25	23	12	875
生物科学	Biological Science	63	50	60	2598
医药、卫生	Medicine and Health Care	267	172	138	15052
农业科学	Agricultural Science	52	37	25	1752
工业技术	Industrial Technology	337	175	88	11931
交通运输	Transportation	39	18	34	3490
环境科学	Environmental Science	2	2	3	151
航空、航天	Aeronautics and Aerospace	32	24	20	1409
综合性图书	General Books	144	131	36	7814

注：本表图书种数、总印数和总印张不包含非“中国标准书号”部分。
Notes: Total Printed Copies and Total Printed Sheets does not include publications without “China International Standard Book Number”.

19－10　杂志出版情况（2017年）
Statistics on Magazines Published (2017)

项　目	Item	种数（种）Number of Publications (kind)	平均期印数（万册）Average Printed Copies per Issue (10000 copies)	总印数（万册）Total Printed Copies (10000 copies)	总印张数（千印张）Total Printed Sheets (1000 sheets)
合　计	**Total**	**381**	**594**	**11428**	**607564**
综　合	General	27	24	331	20892
哲学、社会科学	Philosophy, Social Sciences	95	273	5582	296966
自然科学、技术	Natural Sciences, Technology	181	219	4015	199548
文化、教育	Culture, Education	47	60	1233	67464
文学、艺术	Literature, Arts	31	19	267	22694

19－11　报纸出版情况（2017年）
Statistics on Newspapers Published (2017)

项　目	Item	种数(种) Number of Publications (kind)	平均期印数(万册) Average Printed Copies per Issue (10000 copies)	总印数(万册) Total Printed Copies (10000 copies)	总印张数(千印张) Total Printed Sheets (1000 sheets)
合　计	**Total**	**99**	**1073**	**274299**	**14268079**
按类型分	**By Type**				
综合报	General Newspapers	66	921	250812	13072477
专业报	Specialized Newspapers	33	152	23487	1195602
按范围分	**By Region**				
省　级	Provincial-level Newspapers	32	475	124602	6867751
市　级	City-level Newspapers	67	598	149698	7400328

注：报纸出版情况统计表中，不含校报、院报数据。
Note: The number of newspaper does not include that of college or institute newspaper.

19-12 广播、电视事业发展情况

Statistics on Radio and Television Stations

项 目	Item	2000	2010	2013	2014	2015	2016	2017
广播电台 (座)	Number of Radio Stations	106	22	22	22	22	22	22
中波广播发射台和转播台 (座)	Number of Medium Wave Radio Transmission Stations and Relaying Stations	10	21	27	27	27	27	27
电视台 (座)	Number of Television Stations	67	24	24	24	24	24	24
1000瓦及以上电视发射台和转播台 (座)	Number of Television Transmission and Relaying Stations at 1000 W and above	49	83	83	83	83	83	83
县、市广播电视台(座)	Number of Radio and Television Stations in Counties and Cities	83	79	79	79	79	79	79
有线广播电视用户 (万户)	Number of Subscribers to Cable Radio and Television (10000 subscribers)		1701.53	1980.27	2161.86	2089.00	2017.00	1798.00
数字电视用户 (万户)	Number of Subscribers to Digital Television (10000 subscribers)		950.45	1571.11	1971.21	1622.10	1755.90	1691.70

注：1000瓦及以上电视发射台和转播台，从2006年起改为100瓦以上(含100瓦)电视发射台和转播台。

Note: Television transmission and relaying stations at 1000 W and above since 2006 have been replaced by television transmission and relaying stations at 100W and above.

19-13 广播电台宣传基本情况（2017年）

Basic Statistics on Radio Stations (2017)

项 目	Item	广播电台 (座) Number of Radio Stations (unit)	节目套数 (套) Number of Programs (unit)	平均每日播音时间 (小时) Average Daily Broadcasting Hours (hour)	#自办节目时间 Self-produced Programs	#新闻节目 News Programs	#专题节目 Special Subject Programs	#文艺节目 Programs of Entertainment
合 计	**Total**	**22**	**131**	**2145**	**1599**	**420**	**414**	**364**
省 级	Provincial Level	1	9	202	199	25	69	35
市 级	City Level	21	53	986	834	157	197	141
县 级	County Level		69	958	566	237	148	189

19-14 电视台宣传基本情况（2017年）

Basic Statistics on Television Stations (2017)

项目	Item	电视台（座） Television Stations (unit)	节目套数（套） Number of Programs (unit)	平均每日播出音时间(小时) Average Daily Broadcasting Hours (hour)	#自办节目时间 Self-produced Programs	#新闻节目 News Programs	#专题节目 Special Subject Programs	#文艺节目 Entertainment Programs
合计	**Total**	**24**	**154**	**2201**	**729**	**342**	**311**	**115**
省级	Provincial Level	2	13	265	116	36	33	7
市级	City Level	22	65	1083	440	155	196	52
县级	County Level		76	853	172	151	82	56

19-15 各市广播、电视事业机构数（2017年）

Number of Institutions of Radio and Television by City (2017)

单位：座 (unit)

市别	City	广播电台 Number of Radio Stations	中波广播发射台和转播台 Number of Medium Wave Radio Transmission Stations and Relaying Stations	电视台 Number of Television Stations	100瓦及以上电视发射台和转播台 Number of Television Transmission and Relaying Stations at 100 W and above	县、市广播电视台 Number of Radio and Television Stations in Counties and Cities
广州	Guangzhou	1	2	1	3	7
深圳	Shenzhen	1	2	2	2	3
珠海	Zhuhai	1		1	1	2
汕头	Shantou	1	1	1	6	
韶关	Shaoguan	1	1	1	8	8
河源	Heyuan	1		1	2	5
梅州	Meizhou	1	1	1	8	7
惠州	Huizhou	1	1	1	6	4
汕尾	Shanwei	1		1	2	3
东莞	Dongguan	1		1	1	
中山	Zhongshan	1		1	1	
江门	Jiangmen	1		1	6	5
佛山	Foshan	1		1		
阳江	Yangjiang	1		1	3	3
湛江	Zhanjiang	1	1	1	5	5
茂名	Maoming	1	1	1	4	4
肇庆	Zhaoqing	1		1	3	6
清远	Qingyuan	1		1	5	7
潮州	Chaozhou	1		1	1	2
揭阳	Jieyang	1		1	5	4
云浮	Yunfu	1		1	5	4
省直属单位	Units Directly under Provincial Government	1	17	2	6	

19-16 体育事业情况

Statistics on Sports

指　标	Item	2010	2014	2015	2016	2017
体育系统年末职工人数　（人）	**Number of Staff and Workers in Sports Departments at the Year-end (person)**	**9405**	**7377**	**10620**	**10226**	**10304**
运动员	Athletes	1036	1152	1649	1429	1593
专职教练员	Full-time Coaches	1094	1455	1485	1430	1445
专职文化教师	Full-time Teachers for Literacy Classes	918	751	907	942	924
科技人员	Scientific and Technological Personnel	113	84	114	89	102
医务人员	Medical Personnel	97	59	60	112	122
管理人员	Administrative Personnel	3328	2499	4401	4243	4203
其他人员	Others	2819	1377	2004	1981	1915
体育比赛成绩	**Achievements in Sports Tournament**					
破世界纪录　（项）	Number of World Records Chalked Up (item)	1	3	1	2	1
获世界冠军　（人次）	Number of World Championships Won (unit)	27	17	27	19	21
破亚洲纪录　（项）	Number of Asian Records Chalked Up (item)	2	2	4	1	1
破全国纪录　（项次）	Number of National Records Chalked Up (item-time)	5	5	5	4	3
获得全国冠军　（项次）	Number of National Championships Won (item-time)	132	138	124	111	148
体育活动开展情况	**Sports Meets and Activities**					
举办全民健身活动次数(次)	Number of National Body-building Activities Held (time)	9477	4886	5000	5350	4680

注：2009—2012年口径为正式运动员，2013年口径除正式运动员外，还包含集训、实训、职业过渡期运动员。

Note: The number of athletes from 2009 to 2012 refers to formal athletes only.Since 2013, the number of athletes includes trainer athletes and occupation transition athletes besides formal athletes.

主要统计指标解释

文化事业机构 指从事专业文化工作和为专业文化工作服务的独立建制的单独核算的单位。不包括这些单位另外举办独立核算的其他机构和各部门的业余文化组织。

艺术表演团体 指由文化部门主办或者实行行业管理（经文化行政部门审批并领取营业性演出许可证），专门从事表演艺术等活动的各类专业艺术表演团体，含民间职业剧团（不包括群众业余文艺表演团体）。

电影放映单位 指具有放映机器设备、固定或不固定的放映场所与专职或兼职的放映技术人员，经有关部门登记批准，经常为一定的观众对象放映电影的机构。包括经批准对外开放进行营业，并与电影发行放映管理机构分帐的专用放映单位和军委系统租片单位。

艺术表演观众人数(人次) 指售票、包场等有演出收入的场次和政府采纳的公益性演出场次及参加汇演、 等无演出收入的公开演出场次，不包括彩排审查和内部观摩演出的观看人次数。

Explanatory Notes on Main Statistical Indicators

Cultural Institutions refer to units which have their own organizational system and independent accounting system and specialize in or serve cultural development. They exclude other establishments with independent accounting system run by these cultural institutions and amateur cultural groups established by various departments.

Arts Performance Troupes refer to the various professional performing arts groups, which sponsored by the cultural sectors or guided by the cultural society (approved by the cultural administration authority, or registered and permitted with the relative certificate), including non-governmental troupes. The mass amateur arts performance troupes are not included.

Film Projection Units refer to units with film projection equipment, full or part-time projectionists, permanent or non-permanent cinemas, approved by and registered with related administrative departments to show films regularly for certain groups of audience, including film projection units which have been approved to give commercial shows and share profits with administrative agencies of film circulation and projection, as well as film renting units of the military system.

Number of Spectators at Art Performance (person-time) refers to the number of attendants at commercial shows, completely booked shows or free shows given in minority national areas, excluding the number of spectators at rehearsals for examination and internal shows for study.

二十、卫生、社会福利、社会保障和其他

PUBLIC HEALTH, SOCIAL WELFARE, SOCIAL INSURANCE AND OTHERS

二十 卫生、社会福利、社会保障和其他

简要说明

一、本篇资料主要反映广东卫生、社会福利、社会保险、安全生产及其他事业的发展情况。

二、本篇资料由广东省统计局社会科技统计处负责整理、编辑。

三、卫生部分主要包括卫生事业机构、床位及人员数等，资料由广东省卫计委提供。

四、社会福利部分主要包括各种社会福利事业情况、城乡基层社会保障情况、婚姻登记状况等，资料由广东省民政厅提供。

五、社会保险部分主要包括城乡基本养老保险、失业保险、城乡基本医疗保险等基金征缴收入和参保人数，资料由广东省人力资源和社会保障厅提供。

六、亿元生产总值安全生产事故死亡率数据由广东省安全生产监督管理局提供。

七、其他部分主要包括司法工作开展情况和交通、火灾事故发生情况等，资料由广东省司法厅 、广东省公安厅提供。

20 Public Health,Social Welfare,Social Insurance and Others

Brief Introduction

Ⅰ. The data in this chapter mainly show the development of Guangdong's public health，social welfare，social security, safe production and other undertakings.

Ⅱ. The data are prepared by the Division of Social，Scientific and Technological Statistics of Statistics Bureau of Guangdong Province.

Ⅲ. The data on public health mainly include the number of health institutions， hospital beds and personnel，etc. The data are provided by Health Department of Guangdong Province.

Ⅳ. The data on social welfare mainly include the social welfare services，grassroots social security in urban and rural areas and marriage registration status，etc. The data are provided by Guangdong Provincial Department of Civil Affairs.

Ⅴ.The data on social security mainly include the statistics on basic pension insurance for urban and rural residents, the unemployment insurance, the amount collected and percentage of collection and the number of persons participating in urban and rural basic medical care insurance.The data is provided by Guangdong Provincial Department of Human Resources and Social Security.

VI. The rate of death from work safety accidents per 100 million yuan of GDP is provided by Guangdong Provincial Bureau of Work Safety.

Ⅶ. Other data mainly include judicial conditions and basic statistics on traffic and fire accidents，etc. The data are provided by Guangdong Provincial Department of Justice and Guangdong Provincial Department of Public Security.

20-1 卫生、社会福利和其他主要指标

Main Indicators of Sports, Public Health, Social Welfare, Environmental Protection and Others

指　标	Item	2000	2010	2015	2016	2017
医疗卫生机构数（个）	Number of Health Care Institutions (unit)	8984	44880	48367	49124	49926
#医院、卫生院	Hospitals	2426	2444	2539	2581	2666
医疗卫生机构床位数（万张）	Number of Beds in Health Care Institutions (10000 units)	16.81	30.01	43.57	46.52	49.21
#医院、卫生院床位	Hospital Beds	15.72	27.71	40.07	42.84	45.30
卫生技术人员数（万人）	Number of Medical Technical Personnel (10000 persons)	26.50	45.55	62.00	66.75	70.99
#执业(助理)医生	Doctors	11.12	17.51	22.94	24.41	25.89
平均每千人口有卫生机构床位数（张）	Number of Beds in health Institutions per 1000 Population (bed)	1.94	2.87	4.02	4.23	4.41
平均每千人口有卫生技术人员数（人）	Number of Medical Technical Personnel per 1000 Population (person)	3.07	4.36	5.71	6.07	6.36
#执业(助理)医生	Doctors	1.29	1.68	2.11	2.22	2.32
优抚收养性单位收养人数(人次)	Number of Persons Adopted by Special Care Units (person)	1785	3179	3389	3410	3745
社会救济总人数（万人）	Number of Persons Receiving Relief Funds (10000 persons)	154.70	288.00	227.25	209.75	210.08
登记结婚件数（对）	Registered Marriages (couple)	562118	857146	840411	786123	758123
离婚总数（对）	Registered Divorces (couple)	47521	127048	193360	211858	220343
执业律师人数（人）	Number of Full-time Lawyers (person)	7292	20228	29633	32380	35045
公证人员数（人）	Number of Notarial Personnel (person)	1380	1694	2190	2208	2309
人民调解委员会调解人员数(人)	Number of Mediators of People's Mediation Committees (person)	250117	190775	181205	178052	181441
亿元生产总值生产安全事故死亡率	Rate of Death from Work Safety Accidents per 100 Million Yuan of Gross Regional Product	1.08	0.15	0.09	0.05	0.04
交通事故发生数（起）	Number of Traffic Accidents (unit)	66072	30480	24672	24876	24138
交通事故损失折款（万元）	Losses from Traffic Accidents Converted into Cash (10000 yuan)	27526	8051	6784	7414	10553
火灾事故发生数（起）	Number of Fire Accidents (unit)	8622	6065	17992	16923	16501
火灾事故损失折款（万元）	Losses from Fire Accidents Converted into Cash (10000 yuan)	10065	17500	37857	40838	28017

注：2010年起医疗卫生机构、人员数总数含村卫生室数，千人口数据分母为常住人口。

Note: Since 2010,Data of village clinics was included in the total number of health care institutons and their personnel. The population of per 1000 persons used in this table are resident population.

20-2 医疗卫生机构、床位及人员数

Number of Health Care Institutions, Beds and Personnel

年份 Year	机构 (个) Health Institutions (unit)	#医院及卫生院 Hospitals	床位 (张) Beds (bed)	#医院及卫生院床位 Hospital Beds	卫生工作人员 (人) Medical Personnel (person)	#卫生技术人员 Medical Technical Personnel
1978	6949	1968	90645	84120	159583	126606
1979	7304	1974	91955	85144	171703	136568
1980	7649	1988	92506	84999	181480	144537
1981	8045	2002	94794	87010	191370	151971
1982	8331	2014	97441	88688	202162	160710
1983	8443	2037	100042	90851	208506	166543
1984	8525	2042	103231	93770	213193	170495
1985	8479	1853	107702	98231	220593	175337
1986	8713	1860	110022	99632	225526	180045
1987	8705	1880	114773	104932	230444	184126
1988	8820	1906	119328	109280	234807	187307
1989	8948	1886	122055	111816	240581	192147
1990	8989	1885	124015	114056	244039	194771
1991	9032	1906	129774	119079	249717	199051
1992	8989	1943	135527	124835	257043	205110
1993	8572	1968	139812	129317	267432	211874
1994	8720	2231	144865	134334	277398	220153
1995	8848	2267	148825	137756	288715	229894
1996	8921	2319	151553	141221	196108	237623
1997	8942	2348	155313	144496	305562	245862
1998	8805	2373	158351	147604	313737	252213
1999	8699	2415	162398	151367	320432	258591
2000	8984	2426	168143	157164	327065	264990
2001	8638	2444	172735	162197	330418	268347
2002	15500	2415	180791	165498	323294	262633
2003	15409	2410	188543	172981	336175	273620
2004	15744	2391	200056	183107	348203	283351
2005	16318	2428	209741	192551	364520	297334
2006	16953	2433	221886	204071	408972	332829
2007	16490	2435	234179	216951	452080	360674
2008	15821	2428	250497	231583	479462	383876
2009	16238	2442	271972	250364	513997	413444
2010	44880	2444	300083	277126	593503	455524
2011	45935	2411	325038	298070	627347	486356
2012	46556	2437	355274	324744	664825	520243
2013	47855	2447	378367	346478	710288	555498
2014	48087	2482	405707	372637	734345	584356
2015	48367	2539	435666	400745	771034	620004
2016	49124	2581	465228	428423	821880	667525
2017	49926	2666	492113	453022	866925	709894

注：从2002年开始，机构数中包含个体诊所机构数；从2010年开始机构、人员总计中含村卫生室数。

Note: Since 2002, the number of institutions has included the number of individual clinics;since 2010,number of village clinics was included in health care institutions.

20-3 医疗卫生机构、床位和人员数（2017年）

Number of Health Care Institutions, Beds and Personnel (2017)

机构类别	Type of Institution	机构（个） Number of Institutions (unit)	床位数（张） Beds (bed)	人员数（人） Personnel (person)	#卫生技术人员 Medical Technical Personnel	#执业(助理)医师 Certified (Assistant) Doctors
医疗卫生机构数	**Health Care Institutions**	**49926**	**492113**	**866925**	**709894**	**258889**
医　院	Hospitals	1464	393449	524319	437542	140970
卫生院	Health Centers	1202	59573	92491	79040	31495
疗养院	Sanatoriums	17	786	1154	730	291
社区卫生服务中心	Community Health Service Centers	1098	8727	45718	39539	17186
社区卫生服务站	Community Health Service Stations	1445	1	7978	7419	3200
门诊部、诊所、卫生所等	Outpatient Departments and Clinics	16867	296	77621	71134	37139
#诊所	Outpatient Departments	10780	37	31864	30752	17847
卫生所(医务室)	Clinics (Medical Stations)	2999	12	9383	9060	4812
急救中心(站)	Emergency Centers (Stations)	23		571	290	57
采供血机构	Blood Taking and Supply Agencies	42		2639	1949	280
妇幼保健机构	Maternity and Child Care Centers	128	23126	47418	39846	12287
专科疾病防治院(所、站)	Specialized Prevention and Treatment Stations	130	6155	9067	6990	2799
疾病预防控制机构	Disease Prevention and Control Centers (Antiepidemic Stations)	123		10588	7874	4148
卫生监督所	Sanitation Supervision Stations	202		4938	3656	
卫生监督检验(监测、检测)所(站)	Sanitation Supervision Quarantine Stations	1		3		
医学科学研究机构	Research Institutions of Medical Science	11		209	38	18
医学在职培训机构	On-the-job Medical Training Institutions	11		542	199	52
健康教育所(站、中心)	Health Education Stations (Centers)	31		305	138	70
村卫生室	Rural Medical Stations	26459		33059	9008	7112
其他卫生机构	Other Health Agencies	672		8305	4502	1785

注：总数中含村卫生室数。

Note: Number of village clinics was included in health care institutions

20-4 各市医疗卫生机构、床位和人员数（2017年）

Number of Health Care Institutions, Beds and Personnel by City (2017)

市别	City	机构（个）Number of Institutions (unit)	#医院 Hospitals	床位数（张）Beds (bed)	#医院床位 Hospital Beds	卫生工作人员（人）Medical Personnel (person)	#卫生技术人员 Medical Technical Personnel	执业(助理)医师（人）Certified Doctors (person)
全省总计	**Provincial Total**	**49926**	**1464**	**492113**	**393449**	**866925**	**709894**	**258889**
广　州	Guangzhou	4058	243	90222	81747	175714	145045	49747
深　圳	Shenzhen	4049	136	39777	36798	104351	85256	33293
珠　海	Zhuhai	742	43	9394	8335	20128	16962	6427
汕　头	Shantou	1435	44	18075	15343	28269	23537	9741
佛　山	Foshan	1715	110	35273	32646	60078	51314	18134
韶　关	Shaoguan	2119	54	17125	12546	25525	20619	7387
河　源	Heyuan	2062	52	14538	7922	20869	16625	5742
梅　州	Meizhou	3198	42	17789	11811	29796	24122	9548
惠　州	Huizhou	2725	72	22589	15550	39408	32953	12582
汕　尾	Shanwei	1705	33	9241	6339	15770	11802	5153
东　莞	Dongguan	2446	97	29866	29046	60197	50600	17506
中　山	Zhongshan	806	59	15256	15140	26505	22904	8115
江　门	Jiangmen	1608	44	22774	16605	34531	28885	9859
阳　江	Yangjiang	1843	51	13208	10119	19877	15590	5201
湛　江	Zhanjiang	3400	103	35091	25338	48239	38232	12810
茂　名	Maoming	4061	71	33579	20383	41792	33652	13362
肇　庆	Zhaoqing	3079	54	16612	12678	30949	23844	7620
清　远	Qingyuan	2393	57	16710	11005	26035	21392	7493
潮　州	Chaozhou	2322	27	6710	4568	13551	10127	4600
揭　阳	Jieyang	2858	50	18332	12871	28993	23470	10172
云　浮	Yunfu	1302	22	9952	6659	16348	12963	4397
按经济区域分	By Region							
珠三角	Pearl River Delta	21228	858	281763	248545	551861	457763	163283
东　翼	Eastern Region	8320	154	52358	39121	86583	68936	29666
西　翼	Western Region	9304	225	81878	55840	109908	87474	31373
山　区	Mountainous Region	11074	227	76114	49943	118573	95721	34567

注：机构、人员数含村卫生室数。
Note: Number of village clinics was included in health care institutions

20−5 各类医疗卫生机构、床位和人员数

Number of Health Institutions, Beds and Personnel by Type

指　　标	Item	2000	2010	2013	2014	2015	2016	2017
医疗卫生机构数(个)	**Number of Institutions (unit)**	**8984**	**44880**	**47855**	**48087**	**48367**	**49124**	**49926**
#医院	Hospitals	746	1088	1222	1260	1323	1380	1464
卫生院	Health Centers	1680	1356	1225	1222	1216	1201	1202
门诊部、诊所、卫生所 (所)	Clinics, Health Stations and Community Health	5710	11056	11989	12766	14068	15380	16867
专科疾病防治院(所、站)	Specialized Disease Prevention &Treatment Institution	158	147	141	136	131	135	130
疾病预防控制机构	Sanitation and Anti-epidemic Institutions	171	134	137	137	137	137	135
妇幼保健机构	Maternity and Child Care Centers	31	126	128	130	130	129	128
医学科学研究机构	Research Institutions of Medical Science	20	18	17	17	17	17	11
村卫生室	Rural Medical Stations		28339	28767	28162	27178	26886	26459
床位数 (张)	**Number of Beds (unit)**	**168143**	**300083**	**378367**	**405707**	**435666**	**465228**	**492113**
人员数 (人)	**Number of Personnel (person)**	**327065**	**593503**	**710288**	**734345**	**771034**	**821880**	**866925**
卫生技术人员	Medical Technical Personnel	264990	455524	555498	584356	620004	667525	709894
#执业(助理)医生	Doctors	111172	175100	211061	217376	229389	244139	258889
注册护士	Nurses	83198	168043	217874	233570	254430	284223	308158
其他技术人员	Other Technical Personnel	8910	54491	56529	51959	50033	51403	68969
管理人员	Administrative Personnel	24320	29541	30250	29156	30638	31386	32312
工勤人员	Logistics Personnel	28845	53947	68011	68874	70359	71566	73744

注：从2002年开始，机构数中包含个体诊所机构数；门诊部(所)含门诊部、诊所、卫生所、医务室、护理站等；妇幼保健院归入妇幼保健机构统计；医生指执业(助理)医师。2008年起，门诊部(所)含护理站，不含社区卫生服务站(纳入其他卫生机构)。2010年起机构、人员数含村卫生室数。

Note: Since 2002, the number of institutions has included the number of individual clinics, covered in the category of outpatient departments (clinics); maternity and child care centers have been included in the number of maternity and child care institutions; doctors have referred to certified (assistant) doctors; and Since 2008, clinics include nurse stations, but exclude community health stations, which is listed as Other Healthcare Institutions. Since 2010,Number of village clinics was included in health care institutions

20−6 各市社会保险基金征缴收入(2017年)

Amount Collected of Security Insurance (2017)

单位：万元 (10000 yuan)

市别	City	城镇职工基本养老保险基金征缴收入 Amount Collected of Basic Retirement Security Program	城乡居民基本养老保险基金征缴收入 Amount Collected of Basic Retirement Security Program	城镇职工基本医疗保险基金征缴收入 Amount Collected of Basic Health Care Program	城乡居民基本医疗保险基金征缴收入 Amount Collected of Basic Health Care Program	失业保险基金征缴收入 Amount Collected of Unemployment Insurance	工伤保险基金征缴收入 Amount Collected of Industrial Accident Insurance	生育保险基金征缴收入 Amount Collected of Child-bearing Insurance
合计	**Total**	**31432847**	**398325**	**11323654**	**4049411**	**995465**	**645154**	**826427**
广州	Guangzhou	5370892	76430	3622412	309958	205514	96548	308146
深圳	Shenzhen	9406328	645	2723083	267829	388746	176615	218406
珠海	Zhuhai	1039517	7300	435465		36386	14724	
汕头	Shantou	440743	18991	139678	271261	19215	9322	20494
佛山	Foshan	2627195	14543	1057474		51131	59475	62600
韶关	Shaoguan	280554	19822	186568	149851	9658	10945	5960
河源	Heyuan	252628	10534	97287	195038	6735	4832	5811
梅州	Meizhou	382557	12285	133478	273783	7630	6963	6039
惠州	Huizhou	1106323	17862	393135	176158	31242	30919	173
汕尾	Shanwei	133759	9296	46897	153788	3967	3592	2911
东莞	Dongguan	3593552		815285		106815	117675	90720
中山	Zhongshan	1446309	10	379174		46410	25867	40373
江门	Jiangmen	808377	21711	378573	187714	18799	13893	10656
阳江	Yangjiang	187928	11238	81353	158791	4710	5671	8464
湛江	Zhanjiang	419980	25214	214211	432665	10071	10361	10867
茂名	Maoming	327724	18546	154546	405035	11647	8481	7151
肇庆	Zhaoqing	353225	17283	139880	219309	10177	11266	7145
清远	Qingyuan	337877	80867	159219	210935	13292	10009	7174
潮州	Chaozhou	180120	6854	61165	144653	4329	3515	4570
揭阳	Jieyang	360549	17185	39930	333714	5096	2001	1949
云浮	Yunfu	203212	11708	64841	158931	3894	5063	6816
省直	Directly under Provincial Government	2173496					17415	2
按经济区域分	By Region							
珠三角	Pearl River Delta	25751719	155785	9944481	1160967	895221	546983	738218
东翼	Eastern Region	1115171	52326	287670	903416	32608	18430	29924
西翼	Western Region	935632	54999	450110	996491	26427	24513	26482
山区	Mountainous Region	1456828	135215	641392	988537	41209	37813	31801

注：各区域不包省直单位部分。
Note: “By Region” does not include agencies directly under provincial jurisdiction.

20-7 各市社会保险参保人数（2017年）

Number of Persons Participating in Social Insurance by City (2017)

单位：万人 (10000 persons)

市别	City	城乡基本养老保险参保人数 Number of Persons Participating in Basic Retirement Security Program	失业保险参保人数 Number of Persons Participating in Unemployment Insurance	城乡基本医疗保险参保人数 Number of Persons Participating in Basic Health Care Program	工伤保险参保人数 Number of Persons Participating in Industrial Accident Insurance	生育保险参保人数 Number of Persons Participating in Child-bearing Insurance
合计	**Total**	**8399.40**	**3163.67**	**10365.07**	**3402.03**	**3300.89**
广州	Guangzhou	1322.02	540.80	1161.68	579.31	518.92
深圳	Shenzhen	1134.32	1089.49	1396.11	1100.68	1160.57
珠海	Zhuhai	130.94	98.18	175.11	99.80	99.92
汕头	Shantou	376.10	79.99	502.27	78.25	58.08
佛山	Foshan	584.09	244.84	517.74	246.05	245.29
韶关	Shaoguan	172.50	29.80	294.16	38.85	28.42
河源	Heyuan	210.13	29.39	323.50	32.40	26.74
梅州	Meizhou	277.18	29.92	470.98	42.56	30.52
惠州	Huizhou	348.88	125.24	431.20	148.17	155.08
汕尾	Shanwei	200.78	21.02	306.15	21.21	21.95
东莞	Dongguan	694.49	404.01	566.09	430.55	466.15
中山	Zhongshan	247.40	143.24	266.98	155.22	148.85
江门	Jiangmen	382.77	81.81	388.81	93.33	85.69
阳江	Yangjiang	180.94	16.52	268.05	28.01	20.13
湛江	Zhanjiang	379.33	42.46	715.03	44.41	47.41
茂名	Maoming	371.22	27.82	641.33	34.26	30.45
肇庆	Zhaoqing	240.45	45.02	408.52	47.12	43.00
清远	Qingyuan	277.17	37.65	403.06	42.88	38.70
潮州	Chaozhou	158.99	34.15	264.37	34.18	33.26
揭阳	Jieyang	344.91	24.00	589.45	21.29	21.69
云浮	Yunfu	166.13	18.33	274.50	19.44	20.08
省直	Directly under Provincial Government	198.68			64.04	
按经济区域分	By Region					
珠三角	Pearl River Delta	5085.34	2772.62	5312.23	2900.23	2923.46
东翼	Eastern Region	1080.78	159.17	1662.23	154.93	134.98
西翼	Western Region	931.49	86.80	1624.41	106.69	97.99
山区	Mountainous Region	1103.10	145.09	1766.20	176.14	144.46

注：1)各区域不包省直单位部分。
2)2012年8月起，新型社会农村养老保险和城镇居民社会养老保险制度全覆盖工作全面启动，合并为城乡居民社会养老保险。

Note: a) "By Region" does not include agencies directly under provincial jurisdiction.
b) Since August 2012,system of new old-age insurance and urban basice pension insurance have started completely, and called basic pension insurance for urban and rural residents as total.

20−8 优抚、社会救济和福利事业情况

Statistics on Preferential Treatment and Resettlement, Social Relief and Welfare

项 目	Item	2010	2013	2014	2015	2016	2017
优抚事业	**Preferential Treatment and Resettlement**						
优抚收养性事业单位数（个）	Number of Institutions for Preferential Treatment and Resettlement (unit)	81	79	71	57	55	56
编制登记	Registered with State Office for Public Sector Reform	57	50	48	46	43	41
工商登记	Registered with Industry and Commerce Administration						
民政登记	Registered with Civil Affairs Administration	21	6	5			
未登记	Unregistered	3	23	18	11	12	15
优抚收养性单位收养人数（人次）	Number of Persons Adopted byPreferential Treatment and Resettlement Institutions (person-time)	3179	3647	3734	3389	3410	3745
编制登记	Registered with State Office for Public Sector Reform	2896	3271	3392	3296	3353	3681
工商登记	Registered with Industry and Commerce Administration						
民政登记	Registered with Civil Affairs Administration	177	22	10			
未登记	Unregistered	106	354	332	93	57	64
优抚事业费用 （万元）	Expenses onPreferential Treatment and Resettlement (10000 yuan)	181099	314419	340071	378681	445492	476108
民政部门支出	Expenses by Civil Administration Departments	181099	314419	340071	378681	445492	476108
社会救济	**Social Relief**						
社会救济总人数 （万人）	Total Number under Social Relief (10000 persons)	288.00	249.04	231.15	227.25	209.75	210.08
#农村传统救济对象人数	Number of People Receiving Traditional Social Relief in Rural Areas	31.40	17.51	9.47	12.95		
城乡居民最低生活保障人数（万人）	Number of Urban and Rural Residents Receiving Minimum Income Relief (10000 persons)	224.70	197.21	190.36	183.30	170.60	169.62
城镇	Urban Areas	40.70	33.99	31.60	29.69	25.46	22.85
农村	Rural Areas	184.00	163.22	158.76	153.60	145.14	146.77
城乡居民最低生活保障家庭户数 （万户）	Number of Urban and Rural Households Receiving Minimum Income Relief (10000 households)	91.80	88.29	87.43	86.39	73.92	69.86
城镇	Urban Areas	17.30	16.14	15.68	15.19	13.25	11.92
农村	Rural Areas	74.50	72.15	71.75	71.20	60.67	57.94
城乡居民最低生活保障金支出 （万元）	Expenditures on Minimum Income Relief for Urban and Rural Residents (10000 yuan)	244490	470565	532682	553022	617139	643068
城镇	Urban Areas	79665	130450	154579	159530	177732	166329
农村	Rural Areas	164825	340114	378103	393493	439407	476739

20-8 续表 continued

项目	Item	2000	2010	2013	2014	2015	2016	2017
社会福利 (亿元)	Expenses on Social Welfare (100 million yuan)			30.84	34.92	40.89	55.33	80.64
社会救助(不含优抚对象医疗补助) (亿元)	Expenses on Social Relief(Medical Aid for Special-care Recipient not included (100 million yuan)			72.15	86.07	94.79	109.61	129.05
自然灾害救济费 (万元)	Relief Funds for Natural Calamities (10000 yuan)	8456	45995	68784	51646	51051	37414	27057
社会福利	**Social Welfare**							
提供住宿的社会服务机构 (个)	Number of Social Welfare Institutions with Accomodations (unit)	2086	2514	1913	1637	1588	1643	1734
编制登记	Registered with State Office for Scopsr		256	429	1045	1282	1339	1366
工商登记	Registered with Industry and Commerce Administration		27	30	30	48	56	67
民政登记	Registered with Civil Affairs Administration		1791	566	262	220	222	256
未登记	Unregistered		440	888	300	38	26	45
提供住宿的社会服务机构年末在院人数 (人)	Number of People Taken in by Social Welfare Institutions with Accomodations at the year-end (person)		92224	89894	91941	92043	92085	96139
编制登记	Registered with State Office for Scopsr		26402	32786	55991	61360	59041	58847
工商登记	Registered with Industry and Commerce Administration		3188	3780	4058	8481	10696	12074
民政登记	Registered with Civil Affairs Administration		51516	35088	24649	20525	21904	23244
未登记	Unregistered		11118	18240	7243	1677	444	1974
社会福利企业单位 (个)	Number of Social Welfare Enterprises (unit)	517	172	154	147	134	103	
安排"四残"人员就业数 (人)	Number of "Four Kinds of Disabled Persons" Arranged for Employment (person)	8165	4818	5987	5689	5310	3650	
编制登记	Registered with State Office for Scopsr		75	139	129	125	121	
工商登记	Registered with Industry and Commerce Administration		4743	5848	5560	5185	3529	
城乡基层社会保障	**Urban and Rural Social Security**							
城镇社区服务设施数(个)	Number of Urban Community Service Facilities (unit)	4983	15960	45233	55374	57108	66677	68919
社区服务指导中心	Community Service Guidance Centers			31	35	29	28	18
社区服务中心	Community Service Centers		1366	2492	2741	2893	1843	2108
社区服务站	Community Service Stations		1632	12381	12992	13284	20097	21793
社区养老机构和设施	Communtiry Nursing Facilities and Insitution				363	621	1768	2732
社区互助型养老设施	Communtiry Mutual Aid Nursing Facilities						74	307
其他社区服务设施	Other Communtiry Service Facilities		12962	30329	39243	40281	42867	41961

注：1.2013年起，社会福利收养性事业单位数和社会福利收养性事业单位收养人数指标分别修改为提供住宿的社会服务机构数和提供住宿的社会服务机构年末在院人数。

2.未登记注册机构包含一个机构多块牌子的机构。

Note: a)Since 2013，the indicator of number of social welfare institutions and number of people taken in by social welfare institutions are amended as the indicator of social welfare institutions with accomodations and number of people taken in by social welfare institutions with accomodations at year-end respectively.

b) Unregistered Institutions include one organization with a few brands.

20-9 婚姻登记情况

Statistics on Marriage Registration

项目	Item	2000	2010	2014	2015	2016	2017
登记结婚件数 （对）	**Marriage Registration number (couple)**	**562118**	**857146**	**891457**	**840411**	**786123**	**758123**
登记结婚人数 （人）	**Nmber of Persons Registered (person)**	**1124236**	**1714292**	**1782914**	**1680822**	**1572246**	**1516246**
按居住地分类	By Place of Residence						
内地居民登记结婚件数 （对）	Mainland Residents Marriage Registration Number (couple)	550388	850448	883056	832694	777990	750392
内地居民登记结婚人数 （人）	Number of mainland residents registered (person)	1100776	1700896	1764438	1665442	1556826	1500502
涉外及华侨、港澳台居民登记结婚件数(对)	Marriage Registration Number with Foreigners, Overseas Chinese and Citizens of HongKong, Macao and Taiwan (couple)	11730	6698	8401	7717	8133	7731
内地居民 （人）	Mainland Residents (person)	11608	6676	8329	7676	8077	7648
#女性 （人）	Female (person)	9676	5241	5977	5324	5368	4619
香港居民 （人）	Hongkong Residents (person)	5247	1552	2630	2436	2802	2682
澳门居民 （人）	Macao Residents (person)		765	948	827	809	677
台湾居民 （人）	Taiwan Residents (person)	1409	770	887	840	780	695
华侨 （人）	Overseas Chinese (person)	1848	1069	1825	1526	1272	873
外国人 （人）	Foreigners (person)	3348	2564	2183	2129	2526	2887
按婚前状况分类	By pre marital status						
初婚人数 （人）	Number of First Marriages (person)		1583025	1620113	1501835	1365312	1304060
再婚人数 （人）	Number of Remarriages (person)		131267	162801	178987	206934	212186
#女性 （人）	Female (person)		57536	76146	85208	99589	106202
恢复结婚件数 （对）	Resumption of Marriages (couple)		12764	19607	27356	33170	35137
按年龄分类	By age						
#20～24 （人）	20～24 (person)		549611	550911	490868	431319	396826
25～29 （人）	25～29 (person)		703191	758750	718631	655385	638100
30～34 （人）	30～34 (person)		237064	241158	230655	228708	225529
35～39 （人）	35～39 (person)		105735	91820	90905	99803	98622
40以上 （人）	above 40 (person)		118691	140275	149763	157031	157169
离婚总数 （对）	**Total Number of Divorce (couple)**	**47521**	**127048**	**177945**	**193360**	**211858**	**220343**
民政离婚登记 （对）	Registered Divorce (couple)	19786	100759	151645	167544	186406	193846
内地居民登记离婚(对)	Nmber of Mainland Residents Registered Divorces (couple)	19537	99536	150151	166142	185025	192514
涉外及华侨、港澳台居民登记离婚 （对）	Divorce from Foreigners,Overseas Chinese and Citizens of Hong Kong, Macao and Taiwan (couple)	249	1223	1494	1402	1381	1332
#外国人 （人）	Foreigners (person)		397	264	290	403	408
法院调解离婚 （对）	Divorces through Law Court Mediation(couple)	15973	17644	16183	15268	14492	14963
法院判决离婚 （对）	Divorces through Law Court Judgment (couple)	11762	8645	10117	10548	10960	11534

20−10 律师、公证、基层司法基本情况

Basic Statistics on Lawyers, Notarization, Grassroots Judicial Work

项　目	Item	2000	2014	2015	2016	2017
律师工作	**Lawyers**					
律师事务所 (个)	Number of Law Offices (unit)	822	2346	2550	2768	2788
执业律师 (人)	Number of Full-time Lawyers (person)	7292	27208	29633	32380	35045
担任常年法律顾问 (家)	Number of Units as Permanent Legal Advisors (unit)	15759	48868	59664	64339	70687
民事代理 (件)	Agent of Civil Cases (case)	29769	185879	225385	237622	715338
非诉讼法律事务 (件)	Agent of Non-litigious Legal Affairs (case)	50795	126852	174951	204550	165275
刑事辩护 (件)	Defender of Criminal Cases (case)	13364	28467	30739	41003	63511
解答法律询问 (件)	Agent of Legal Advisory Services (case)	101104	362947	385600	406954	314830
公证工作	**Notarization**					
公证处 (个)	Number of Notary Offices (unit)	146	145	146	147	147
公证人员 (人)	Number of Notarial Personnel (person)	1380	2198	2190	2208	2309
办结公证总数 (件)	Number of Notarized Documents (case)	1189475	1343775	1525912	1603887	1609296
国内公证	Domestic Notary		865093	1044876	1163173	1219559
涉外及港澳台民事经济公证	Foreign-related and Hong Kong, Macao and Taiwan Related Civil Economic Notarization	489049	478676	481036	440714	389737
基层司法工作	**Grassroots Judicial Work**					
法律服务所 (个)	Number of Law Service Offices (unit)	1916	1191	1078	1019	1017
法律服务所人员 (人)	Number of Personnel Working in Law Service Offices (person)	5992	2353	2086	1966	1856
担任法律顾问 (家)	Number of Units with Legal Advisors	28723	8362	6474	5132	2738
民事诉讼代理 (件)	Agent of Civil Cases (case)	16668	5385	5078	5904	8041
非诉讼代理 (件)	Agent of Non-litigious Legal Affairs (case)	66132	13681	8122	9616	21805
避免、挽回经济损失 (万元)	Avoiding and Retrieving Economic Losses (10000 yuan)	139935	46963	39372	44275	
人民调解委员会 (个)	Number of People's Mediation Committees (unit)	29548	33541	33592	33274	33750
调解人员 (人)	Number of Mediators (person)	250117	176764	181205	178052	181441
调解纠纷总数 (件)	Number of Disputes Mediated (case)	136598	331104	326174	323552	361079

注：司法部2012年对公证统计表格进行了修改，不再区分国内民事公证和国内经济公证，统称为国内公证。

Note: Because the Justice Department modified the form of notarization tables in 2012,the items of “domestic civil case notarization” and “domestic economic notary” are both referred to as “the domestic notary”.

20-11 交通事故发生情况（2017年）

Statistics on Traffic Accidents (2017)

项 目	Item	合计 Total	按道路横断面位置分 By Cross-section Location of Roads				按事故发生道路类型分 By Type of Roads Where Accidents Occurs			
			机动车道 Roads for Motored Vehicles	非机动车道 Roads for Non-motored Vehicles	混合道 Mixed Roads	其他道 Others	高速公路 Express Highways	等级公路 Classified Highways	城市道路 Urban Roads	其他路 Others
发生 （起）	Number of Traffic Accidents (case)	24138	185346	669	4329	859	771	8827	10488	4114
死亡 （人）	Number of Deaths (person)	5459	4297	119	831	214	470	2413	1723	854
受伤 （人）	Number of Injuries (person)	24680	18610	706	4720	749	972	9532	10201	4078
损失折款 （万元 ）	Losses Converted into Cash (10000 yuan)	10553	9393	85	809	286	5141	1805	2742	885
平均每起事故损失 （元）	Average Loss per Traffic Accident (yuan)	4372	5120	1274	1868	3326	66674	2045	2614	2151

注：1．等级公路分为一至四级公路和等外公路；
2．城市道路包括城市快速路和一般城市道路；
3．其他路包括单位小区自建路、公共停车场、公共广场、乡道、村道、田间地头、农垦区等区域。

Notes: a) Classified highways refer to highways of Class I to IV and Unclassified Highway.
b) Urban roads include express roads and normal roads in urban areas.
c) Other roads include roads within residential neighborhoods, public parking lots, squares, country roads, village roads, farm roads and reclaimed areas.

20-12 火灾事故发生情况（2017年）

Statistics on Fire Accidents (2017)

项 目	Item	合计 Total	特大 Extraordinarily Serious Accidents	重大 Serious Accidents	较大 Relatively Serious Accidents	一般 Ordinary Accidents
发生 （起）	Number of Traffic Accidents (case)	16501			8	16493
死亡 （人）	Number of Deaths (person)	109			34	75
受伤 （人）	Number of Injuries (person)	64			7	57
损失折款 （万元 ）	Losses Converted into Cash(10000 yuan)	28017			262	27755
平均每起事故损失(元)	Average Loss per Traffic Accident(yuan)	16979			327500	16828

20-13 各市亿元生产总值生产安全事故死亡率

Rate of Death from Work Safety Accidents per 100 Million Yuan of Gross Domestic Product by City

单位：%　　(%)

市别	City	2000	2005	2010	2011	2012	2013	2014	2015	2016	2017
全省	**Provincial Rate**	**1.08**	**0.51**	**0.15**	**0.13**	**0.11**	**0.10**	**0.09**	**0.09**	**0.05**	**0.04**
广州	Guangzhou	0.77	0.37	0.10	0.08	0.07	0.06	0.06	0.05	0.03	0.02
深圳	Shenzhen	0.32	0.23	0.07	0.05	0.04	0.04	0.03	0.03	0.02	0.01
珠海	Zhuhai	0.56	0.33	0.11	0.09	0.09	0.08	0.07	0.06	0.04	0.03
汕头	Shantou		0.53	0.18	0.15	0.15	0.13	0.11	0.11	0.04	0.04
佛山	Foshan	1.15	0.42	0.13	0.11	0.10	0.07	0.06	0.06	0.03	0.03
韶关	Shaoguan		1.18	0.36	0.28	0.26	0.22	0.20	0.17	0.12	0.11
河源	Heyuan		0.90	0.26	0.22	0.20	0.18	0.17	0.14	0.09	0.10
梅州	Meizhou		1.58	0.29	0.23	0.22	0.21	0.18	0.18	0.06	0.05
惠州	Huizhou	1.51	0.91	0.20	0.16	0.13	0.11	0.10	0.10	0.07	0.06
汕尾	Shanwei	2.01	1.15	0.30	0.25	0.19	0.23	0.20	0.19	0.14	0.17
东莞	Dongguan	1.21	0.44	0.14	0.11	0.10	0.10	0.09	0.08	0.05	0.04
中山	Zhongshan	1.64	0.60	0.19	0.15	0.13	0.12	0.11	0.11	0.07	0.05
江门	Jiangmen	1.46	0.74	0.26	0.22	0.20	0.20	0.17	0.16	0.08	0.06
阳江	Yangjiang	1.82	0.87	0.28	0.21	0.18	0.16	0.14	0.14	0.12	0.09
湛江	Zhanjiang	0.86	0.43	0.17	0.14	0.11	0.11	0.09	0.09	0.07	0.06
茂名	Maoming		0.48	0.19	0.15	0.12	0.12	0.11	0.10	0.04	0.03
肇庆	Zhaoqing	1.91	0.80	0.24	0.18	0.16	0.15	0.13	0.13	0.09	0.06
清远	Qingyuan		1.19	0.20	0.17	0.22	0.18	0.15	0.16	0.20	0.19
潮州	Chaozhou	0.98	0.56	0.17	0.13	0.13	0.11	0.16	0.16	0.07	0.05
揭阳	Jieyang	1.27	0.79	0.21	0.16	0.13	0.11	0.11	0.10	0.04	0.04
云浮	Yunfu	1.38	2.14	0.38	0.24	0.22	0.20	0.20	0.17	0.16	0.14

注：1. 2005—2016年全省生产安全事故包括工矿商贸、道路交通、火灾、铁路路外、水上交通及渔业船舶 死亡人数；各市生产安全事故包括工矿商贸、道路交通、火灾事故死亡人数。
2. 2016年国家安全监管总局开展生产安全事故统计改革，调整了生产安全事故统计范围。

Note: 1.Work safery accidents from 2005 to 2016 of the Province include the number of deaths related to industry, mining, traffic、 fire,railway, water traffic and fishing boats accidents, and work safety accidents of each city include the number of deaths related to mining, traffic and fire accidents.
2. Due to the statistics reform of production safety accident conducted byState Administration of Work Safety in 2016, the statistical coverage of production safety acciden has been adjusted.

主要统计指标解释

卫生技术人员 指卫生事业机构支付工资的全部固定职工和合同制职工，现任职务为卫生技术工作的专业人员。包括中医师、西医师、中西医结合高级医师、护师、中药师、西药师、检验师、其他技师、中医士、西医士、护士、助产士、中药剂士、西药剂士、检验士、其他技士、其他中医、护理员、中药剂员、西药剂员、检验员，其他初级卫生技术人员。

医生 指经卫生部门审查合格，具有执业资格的医疗专业人员。

提供住宿的社会服务活动机构 根据《2014 年社会服务业统计制度》，提供住宿的社会服务活动机构包括：为老年人与残疾人提供收留抚养服务的机构、为智障与精神病人提供收留抚养服务的机构、为儿童提供收留抚养和救助服务机构以及其他提供住宿的服务机构。

律师 指受聘参加法律顾问处工作，提任法律顾问、刑（民）事代理人、刑事辩护人，办理非诉讼事件、解答法律询问，代写法律事务文书等主要从事律师事务的司法人员。

公证人员 指在国家公证机关依法办理公证事务的司法人员。包括公证员、助理公证员和在公证处工作的其他人员。

调解人员 在人民调解委员会担负调解民间一般民事纠纷和轻微违法行为所引起的纠纷的工作人员。包括调解委员会的委员和调解小组的调解员。

亿元生产总值生产安全事故死亡率 指一定时期内，每生产亿元生产总值，因各类生产安全事故造成的死亡人数。

Explanatory Notes on Main Statistical Indicators

Medical Technical Personnel refer to all permanent and contract medical staff and workers employed by medical institutions, including doctors of Chinese and Western medicine, senior doctors who integrate traditional Chinese therapeutics with Western therapeutics in practice, senior nurses, pharmacists of Chinese and Western medicine, laboratory specialists, other specialists, paramedics of Chinese and Western medicine, nurses, midwives, druggists in Chinese and Western medicine, laboratory technicians, other technicians, other practitioners of Chinese medicine, nursing attendants, pharmacological workers of Chinese and Western medicine, laboratory workers, and other primary medical personnel.

Doctors refer to qualified medical professionals approved to practice by public health departments.

Social Welfare Institutions with Accomodations In accordance with Statistical System of Social Service in 2014, Social Welfare Institutions with Accomodations includes: Institutions taking care of old people and handicapped people, institutions taking care of retarded people and mental patients, institutions adopting and salving children and other social welfare institutions with accomodations. That is, from 1995 to 2012 the caliber is Number of Social Welfare Institutions (unit); since 2013, due to the change of system in Ministry of Civil Affairs, the caliber changes to Social Welfare Institutions with Accomodations .

Lawyers refer to legal workers who are employed by legal counseling firms to act as legal advisers, agents in criminal or civil lawsuits, or defenders in criminal lawsuits, or to handle non litigious legal affairs, to advise on matters of law or to write legal papers for others.

Notary Personnel refer to judicial workers of the state notary offices handling notarization work according to law They include notaries, assistant notaries, and other people working for notary offices.

Mediators refer to workers on people’s mediation committees responsible for mediating in civil disputes and cases of slight infraction of the law They include members of the mediation committees and mediators of mediation groups.

Rate of Death from Work Safety Accidents per 100 Million Yuan of Gross Domestic Product refers to the number of deaths due to various work safety accidents in the production process of every 100 million yuan of gross domestic product within a certain period.

二十一、区域经济主要指标

MAJOR ECONOMIC REGIONS

二十一　区域主要经济指标

简要说明

一、本篇主要反映广东境内主要区域社会经济发展的基本情况，内容主要包括：珠江三角洲、广州和深圳、东西两翼、山区县以及少数民族县等经济区域的主要统计指标数据。

二、本篇资料分别由广东省统计局各有关专业处整理提供，综合处负责编辑。

三、本篇资料根据国家统计局制定的各有关专业统计报表制度填报汇总而成。

四、本篇各项指标数据为各经济区域汇总数，由于各市生产总值等指标汇总数不等于全省数，因此仅适合反映该地区发展变化情况。

21 Major Economic Regions

Brief Introduction

Ⅰ. The data in this chapter mainly reflect the basic conditions of social and economic development of main economic regions in Guangdong, including the main indicators on the cities of the Pearl River Delta, Guangzhou and Shenzhen, the East and West Wings, counties in mountainous areas and minority counties.

Ⅱ. The data in this chapter are prepared and provided by the related specialized divisions and compiled by the Division of Comprehensive Statistics of Statistics Bureau of Guangdong Province.

Ⅲ. The data in this chapter are tabulated and reported in accordance with the various statistical reporting schemes stipulated by the National Bureau of Statistics.

Ⅳ. The indicators in this chapter are overall figures of various economic regions that only reflect the status of development of the corresponding regions, as the provincial total is not equal to the sum of indicators of various cities, such as gross domestic product.

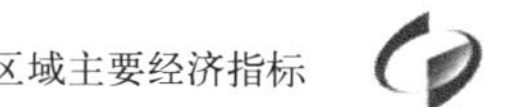

21−1 区域主要经济指标
Main Indicators on Regional Economies

指标	Item	2016 珠江三角洲 Pearl River Delta	2016 东翼 East Wing	2016 西翼 West Wing	2016 山区 Mountainous Areas
土地面积 (平方公里)	Land Area (sq.km.)	54764	15475	32646	76751
年末常住人口 (万人)	Permanent Population at the Year-end (10000 persons)	5998.49	1735.58	1592.46	1672.47
#城镇人口 (万人)	Urban Population (10000 persons)	5089.64	1041.61	679.69	800.35
年末就业人员 (万人)	Employed Persons at the Year-end (10000 persons)	3926.93	759.87	755.29	837.13
地区生产总值 (亿元)	Gross Domestic Product (100 million yuan)	69070.26	5873.83	6474.39	5172.26
第一产业	Primary Industry	1153.92	446.68	1119.28	779.88
第二产业	Secondary Industry	29692.80	3066.98	2584.25	1942.37
第三产业	Tertiary Industry	38223.54	2360.17	2770.85	2450.01
人均生产总值 (元)	Per Capita GDP (yuan)	116351	33924	40773	31004
地区生产总值指数(上年=100)	Index of Gross Domestic Product (preceding year=100)	108.3	107.4	107.2	107.3
第一产业	Primary Industry	102.2	103.2	102.8	103.1
第二产业	Secondary Industry	107.1	105.7	106.9	105.7
第三产业	Tertiary Industry	109.4	110.7	109.3	110.1
人均生产总值指数(上年=100)	Index of Per Capita Gross Domestic Product (preceding year=100)	106.1	107.2	106.6	106.8
规模以上工业增加值 (亿元)	Value-added of Industry above Designated Size (100 million yuan)	25229.60	2471.32	2047.02	1582.30
固定资产投资总额 (亿元)	Investment in Fixed Assets (100 million yuan)	22321.24	4172.14	3298.27	3217.21
#房地产开发投资	Investment in Real Estate Development	8601.16	478.40	434.43	793.80
社会消费品零售总额 (亿元)	Total Retail Sales of Consumer Goods(100 million yuan)	25048.68	3522.33	3407.67	2767.44
出口总额 (亿美元)	Total Exports (USD 100 million)	5650.87	172.28	58.29	104.20
进口总额 (亿美元)	Total Imports (USD 100 million)	3450.88	46.26	24.52	45.56
实际外商直接投资 (亿美元)	Foreign Direct Investment Actually Utilized (USD 100 million)	225.90	2.00	2.07	3.53
地方一般公共预算收入(亿元)	Local Public Budgetary Revenue (100 million yuan)	6923.98	285.92	292.35	412.47
地方一般公共预算支出(亿元)	Local Public Budgetary Expenditure (100 million yuan)	9285.10	916.24	929.99	1417.18
金融机构本外币存款 (亿元)	Deposits in Renminbi and Foreign Currencies in All Financial Institutions (100 million yuan)	158966.41	7090.31	6191.67	7580.80
#本外币住户存款	Savings Deposits by Resident	46321.96	4731.72	4091.16	4623.91
金融机构本外币贷款 (亿元)	Loans in Renminbi and Foreign Currencies in All Financial Institutions (100 million yuan)	100149.59	3017.55	3467.09	4294.17
常住居民人均可支配收入(元)	Per Capita Annual Disposable Income of Permanent Residents	40109.1	18744.6	18364.5	17967.6
城镇居民人均可支配收入(元)	Per Capita Annual Disposable Income of Permanent Urban Residents (yuan)	43967.4	23478.3	24390.2	23963.1
农村常住居民人均可支配收入 (元)	Per Capita Annual Net Income of Permanent Rural Residents (yuan)	19063.7	12667.1	13890.8	12747.4

21－1 续表 continued

指标	Item	2017 珠江三角洲 Pearl River Delta	东翼 East Wing	西翼 West Wing	山区 Mountainous Areas
土地面积 (平方公里)	Land Area (sq.km.)	54770	15476	32646	76751
年末常住人口 (万人)	Permanent Population at the Year-end (10000 persons)	6150.54	1732.26	1605.20	1681.00
#城镇人口 (万人)	Urban Population (10000 persons)	5245.70	1040.57	698.66	816.54
年末就业人员 (万人)	Employed Persons at the Year-end (10000 persons)	3981.41	759.62	757.79	841.96
地区生产总值 (亿元)	Gross Domestic Product (100 million yuan)	75710.14	6202.54	7022.40	5539.75
第一产业	Primary Industry	1181.53	455.36	1172.86	800.36
第二产业	Secondary Industry	31542.82	3115.66	2674.70	1973.38
第三产业	Tertiary Industry	42985.80	2631.53	3174.84	2766.01
人均生产总值 (元)	Per Capita GDP (yuan)	124564	35844	43922	33039
地区生产总值指数 (上年=100)	Index of Gross Domestic Product (preceding year=100)	107.9	107.2	107.0	105.6
第一产业	Primary Industry	103.1	104.8	103.2	104.3
第二产业	Secondary Industry	107.4	105.9	106.0	101.5
第三产业	Tertiary Industry	108.4	109.4	109.4	109.3
人均生产总值指数 (上年=100)	Index of Per Capita Gross Domestic Product (preceding year=100)	105.4	107.3	106.3	105.0
规模以上工业增加值 (亿元)	Value-added of Industry above Designated Size (100 million yuan)	25768.21	2314.82	1958.16	1308.28
固定资产投资总额 (亿元)	Investment in Fixed Assets (100 million yuan)	25463.54	4844.08	3597.47	3572.87
#房地产开发投资	Investment in Real Estate Development	9827.78	623.49	630.77	993.66
社会消费品零售总额 (亿元)	Total Amount of Retail Sales of Consumer Goods (100 million yuan)	27318.18	3880.79	3724.98	3016.03
出口总额 (亿美元)	Total Exports (USD 100 million)	5902.41	165.34	63.22	97.76
进口总额 (亿美元)	Total Imports (USD 100 million)	3709.89	45.85	29.01	53.31
实际外商直接投资 (亿美元)	Foreign Direct Investment Actually Utilized (USD 100 million)	218.11	5.08	2.02	3.86
地方一般公共预算收入 (亿元)	Local Public Budgetary Revenue (100 million yuan)	7455.96	304.25	325.79	429.01
地方一般公共预算支出 (亿元)	Local Public Budgetary Expenditure (100 million yuan)	10329.95	981.71	1017.27	1474.19
金融机构本外币存款 (亿元)	Deposits in Renminbi and Foreign Currencies in All Financial Institutions (100 million yuan)	171937.41	7552.51	6744.31	8301.52
#本外币住户存款	Savings Deposits by Resident	48505.38	4969.59	4424.7	5042.6
金融机构本外币贷款 (亿元)	Loans in Renminbi and Foreign Currencies in All Financial Institutions (100 million yuan)	113683.01	3417.03	3948.46	4983.45
常住居民人均可支配收入 (元)	Annual Disposable Income of Permanent Residents	43840.1	20166.7	20016.4	19657.1
城镇常住居民人均可支配收入 (元)	Per Capita Annual Income of Permanent Urban Residents (yuan)	47926.9	25029.1	26542.6	26084.4
农村常住居民人均可支配收入 (元)	Per Capita Annual DisposableIncome of Permanent Rural Residents (yuan)	20813.5	13732.9	15081.6	13924.7

注：1. 珠江三角洲包括：广州、深圳、珠海、佛山、江门、东莞、中山、惠州和肇庆。东翼指汕头、汕尾、潮州和揭阳。西翼指湛江、茂名和阳江。山区指韶关、河源、梅州、清远和云浮。

2. 本表地区生产总值、工业增加值绝对数按当年价格计算，增长速度按可比价格计算，下表同。

Notes: a) The pearl river delta include Guangzhou, Shenzhen, Zhuhai, Foshan, Jiangmen, Dongguan, Zhongshan, Huizhou and Zhaoqing. The East Wing includes Shantou, Shanwei, Chaozhou and Jieyang. The West Wing includes Zhanjiang, Maoming and Yangjiang.The mountainous areas include Shaoguan, Heyuan, Meizhou, Qingyuan and Yunfu.

b) The figures in value terms on GDP and value-added of industry are calculated at current prices, whereas the growth rates are calculated at comparable prices.The same applies to the following tables.

21-2 区域主要经济指标占全省比重

Percentage of Main Regional Economic Indicators to the Provincial Total

单位：% (%)

指标	Item	2016 珠江三角洲占全省比重 Percentage of Pearl River Delta to the Whole Province	东翼占全省比重 Percentage of East Wing to the Whole Province	西翼占全省比重 Percentage of West Wing to the Whole Province	山区占全省比重 Percentage of Mountainous Areas to the Whole Province
土地面积	Land Area	30.5	8.6	18.2	42.7
年末常住人口	Permanent Population at the Year-end	54.5	15.8	14.5	15.2
#城镇人口	Urban Population	66.9	13.7	8.9	10.5
年末就业人员	Employed Persons at the Year-end	62.5	12.1	12.0	13.3
地区生产总值	Gross Domestic Product	79.7	6.8	7.5	6.0
第一产业	Primary Industry	33.0	12.7	32.0	22.3
第二产业	Secondary Industry	79.7	8.2	6.9	5.2
第三产业	Tertiary Industry	83.4	5.2	6.1	5.3
规模以上工业增加值	Value-added of Industry above Designated Size	80.5	7.9	6.5	5.1
固定资产投资总额	Investment in Fixed Assets	67.6	12.6	10.0	9.7
#房地产开发投资	Investment in Real Estate Development	83.4	4.6	4.2	7.7
社会消费品零售总额	Total Retail Sales of Consumer Goods	72.1	10.1	9.8	8.0
出口总额	Total Exports	94.4	2.9	1.0	1.7
进口总额	Total Imports	96.7	1.3	0.7	1.3
实际外商直接投资	Foreign Direct Investment Actually Utilized	96.7	0.9	0.9	1.5
地方一般公共预算收入	Local Public Budgetary Revenue	87.5	3.6	3.7	5.2
地方一般公共预算支出	Local Public Budgetary Expenditure	74.0	7.3	7.4	11.3
金融机构本外币存款	Deposits in Renminbi and Foreign Currencies in All Financial Institutions	88.4	4.0	3.4	4.2
#本外币住户存款	Savings Deposits by Resident	77.5	7.9	6.8	7.7
金融机构本外币贷款	Loans in Renminbi and Foreign Currencies in All Financial Institutions	90.3	2.7	3.1	3.9

21-2 续表 continued

单位：% (%)

指 标	Item	2017 珠江三角洲占全省比重 Percentage of Pearl River Delta to the Whole Province	东翼占全省比重 Percentage of East Wing to the Whole Province	西翼占全省比重 Percentage of West Wing to the Whole Province	山区占全省比重 Percentage of Mountainous Areas to the Whole Province
土地面积	Land Area	30.5	8.6	18.2	42.7
年末常住人口	Permanent Population at the Year-end	55.1	15.5	14.4	15.1
#城镇人口	Urban Population	67.2	13.3	9.0	10.5
年末就业人员	Employed Persons at the Year-end	62.8	12.0	12.0	13.2
地区生产总值	Gross Domestic Product	80.1	6.6	7.4	5.9
第一产业	Primary Industry	32.7	12.6	32.5	22.2
第二产业	Secondary Industry	80.3	7.9	6.8	5.0
第三产业	Tertiary Industry	83.4	5.1	6.1	5.4
规模以上工业增加值	Value-added of Industry above Designated Size	82.2	7.4	6.2	4.2
固定资产投资总额	Investment in Fixed Assets	67.9	12.9	9.6	9.5
#房地产开发投资	Investment in Real Estate Development	81.4	5.2	5.2	8.2
社会消费品零售总额	Total Retail Sales of Consumer Goods	72.0	10.2	9.8	8.0
出口总额	Total Exports	94.8	2.6	1.0	1.6
进口总额	Total Imports	96.7	1.2	0.7	1.4
实际外商直接投资	Foreign Direct Investment Actually Utilized	95.2	2.2	0.9	1.7
地方一般公共预算收入	Local Public Budgetary Revenue	87.6	3.6	3.8	5.0
地方一般公共预算支出	Local Public Budgetary Expenditure	74.8	7.1	7.4	10.7
金融机构本外币存款	Deposits in Renminbi and Foreign Currencies in All Financial Institutions	88.4	3.9	3.5	4.3
#本外币住户存款	Savings Deposits by Resident	77.1	7.9	7.0	8.0
金融机构本外币贷款	Loans in Renminbi and Foreign Currencies in All Financial Institutions	90.2	2.7	3.1	4.0

注：各指标在计算分区域占全省比重时，分母为21个市相加的合计数。

Notes: While calaulating the percentage of each indicator of Pearl River Delta, East Wing, West Wing and Mountainous Areas to the whole province, the denominator is the sum of 21 cities.

21-3 珠江三角洲主要经济指标
Main Economic Indicators of the Pearl River Delta Economic Zone

年份 Year	年末常住人口(万人) Permanent Population at the Year-end (10000 persons)	#城镇人口 Urban Population	年末户籍总人口(万人) Total Population with Residence Registration at the Year-end (10000 persons)	年末就业人员(万人) Employed Persons at the Year-end (10000 persons)	#城镇单位就业人员 Employed Persons in Urban Areas
1990	2369.93	1696.63	2371.57		
1995	3292.03		2372.76		
2000	4289.78	2981.23	2563.60	1902.93	495.46
2001	4376.10		2595.24	1947.10	480.97
2002	4414.68		2595.24	2034.09	498.78
2003	4463.55		2660.46	2250.43	523.34
2004	4516.50		2714.08	2492.27	570.64
2005	4547.14	3516.06	2763.32	2822.60	636.10
2006	4735.47	3771.33	2821.27	2963.93	675.38
2007	4930.68	3919.89	2872.47	3107.38	718.88
2008	5138.48	4119.52	2920.82	3232.88	724.38
2009	5361.72	4375.17	2967.02	3412.10	767.05
2010	5616.39	4645.88	3024.57	3572.01	823.67
2011	5646.51	4687.17	3073.87	3630.21	927.40
2012	5689.64	4770.19	3105.01	3638.83	969.59
2013	5715.19	4802.55	3156.02	3784.09	1552.80
2014	5763.38	4848.41	3207.94	3845.25	1555.45
2015	5874.27	4969.10	3265.69	3871.26	1532.73
2016	5998.49	5089.64	3350.52	3926.93	1547.13
2017	6150.54	5245.70	3475.10	3981.41	1560.00

注：2006—2009年年末常住人口根据2010年第六次全国人口普查快速汇总数进行平滑调整，城镇人口也作了相应的调整。

Note: The year-end populations from 2006 to 2009 have been adjusted in accordance with the fast sum figure obtained from the 6th National Population Census and the same applied to urban population.

21-3 续表 1 continued

年份 Year	地区生产总值(亿元) Gross Domestic Product (100 million yuan)	第一产业 Primary Industry	第二产业 Secondary Industry	第三产业 Tertiary Industry	人均生产总值(元) Per Capita Gross Domestic Product(yuan)
1990	1006.88	153.78	441.65	411.45	4295
1995	4077.74	346.94	1984.48	1746.32	12681
2000	8471.28	460.17	4044.38	3966.73	20398
2001	9622.41	478.19	4544.01	4600.21	22208
2002	11030.18	499.42	5185.23	5345.53	25095
2003	13041.47	514.54	6321.58	6205.35	29379
2004	15615.63	560.41	7748.57	7306.65	34778
2005	18440.37	557.96	9392.60	8489.80	40691
2006	21901.00	567.69	11301.58	10031.73	47187
2007	26021.88	631.40	13215.60	12174.88	53841
2008	30267.12	721.65	15182.53	14362.94	60118
2009	32656.62	717.86	15784.12	16154.63	62202
2010	38377.06	797.94	18761.56	18817.56	69916
2011	44401.55	904.55	21551.16	21945.84	78846
2012	48593.96	958.57	22795.18	24840.21	85793
2013	54197.64	984.03	24904.27	28309.35	95110
2014	58640.12	1030.07	26839.16	30770.89	102173
2015	63381.85	1073.87	28135.99	34171.99	108929
2016	69070.26	1153.92	29692.80	38223.54	116351
2017	75710.14	1181.53	31542.82	42985.80	124564

21-3 续表 2 continued

年份 Year	地区生产总值指数(上年=100) Index of Gross Domestic Product (preceding year=100)	第一产业 Primary Industry	第二产业 Secondary Industry	第三产业 Tertiary Industry	人均生产总值指数(上年=100) Index of Per Capita Gross Domestic Product(preceding year=100)
1990	117.5	107.2	119.9	119.0	115.2
1995	120.4	108.2	122.4	120.0	112.9
2000	113.9	104.3	114.6	114.0	107.4
2001	113.4	104.7	113.7	114.1	108.7
2002	114.4	105.9	115.5	114.1	112.8
2003	116.9	101.8	121.9	113.3	115.7
2004	117.0	103.2	120.6	114.3	115.7
2005	115.7	103.5	118.3	113.7	114.7
2006	116.9	98.8	118.9	115.8	114.1
2007	116.3	100.6	116.1	117.5	111.7
2008	112.9	103.5	112.0	114.3	108.4
2009	109.7	104.0	109.3	110.3	105.2
2010	112.2	104.2	114.2	110.4	107.3
2011	110.1	103.9	110.5	109.8	107.3
2012	108.2	103.3	106.8	109.7	107.5
2013	109.3	101.8	107.6	111.3	108.7
2014	107.8	102.9	107.6	108.2	107.1
2015	108.6	102.8	107.5	109.8	107.1
2016	108.3	102.2	107.1	109.4	106.1
2017	107.9	103.7	107.4	108.4	105.4

21-3 续表 3 continued

年份 Year	公路通车里程(公里) Total Length of Highways in Operation (km)	货运量(万吨) Freight Traffic (10000 tons)	邮电业务总量(亿元) Total Business Volume of Postal and Telecommunication Services (100 million yuan)	本地电话年末用户(万户) Number of Subscribers of Local Telephones at the Year-end (10000 subscribers)	移动电话年末用户 (万户) Number of Subscribers of Mobile Telephones at the Year-end (10000 subscribers)	固定资产投资额(亿元) Investment in Fixed Assets (100 million yuan)	#房地产开发投资 Investment in Real Estate Development
1990						264.34	
1995	20323		152.60			1515.82	
2000	29029		587.64			2364.71	
2001	29792		614.33	1069.79	1867.67	2612.88	
2002	30354		728.24	1253.95	2508.32	2945.74	
2003	30919		967.45	1663.32	3118.25	3749.51	
2004	31582		1446.30	1915.25	4502.45	4515.27	
2005	32312	103365	1738.94	2355.10	5317.71	5328.37	
2006	52139	113275	2068.19	2559.62	5497.75	5964.60	
2007	53106	122408	2348.22	2651.33	6075.36	6909.74	
2008	53418	120916	2754.77	2529.77	6463.22	7829.03	
2009	54261	142733	2983.47	2400.25	6867.61	9603.55	2583.17
2010	55848	161348	3949.45	2269.84	7457.64	11355.80	3118.66
2011	56380	182281	1544.39	2284.31	8285.85	12366.76	4022.87
2012	58590	203570	1730.31	2295.29	9573.16	13974.24	4483.67
2013	59555	243500	2019.89	2288.94	11228.38	16030.78	5362.75
2014	61548	254491	2751.65	2195.47	11318.90	17542.28	6293.55
2015	63054	266078	3573.05	2086.68	11437.39	20048.69	7075.57
2016	63631	271565	5487.87	1954.24	10933.74	22321.24	8601.16
2017	64119	287210	4997.13	1801.51	10828.40	25463.54	9827.78

21-3 续表 4 continued

年份 Year	社会消费品零售总额(亿元) Total Retail Sales of Consumer Goods (100 million yuan)	出口总额(亿美元) Total Exports (USD 100 million)	进口总额(亿美元) Total Imports (USD 100 million)	实际外商直接投资额(亿美元) Foreign Direct Investment Actually Utilized (USD 100 million)	地方一般公共预算收入(亿元) Local Public General Budgetary Revenue (100 million yuan)	地方一般公共预算支出(亿元) Local Public Genera lBudgetary Expenditure (100 million yuan)
1990	424.35	222.21	196.77	12.36	97.98	80.03
1995	1694.60	513.31	429.29	79.47	275.26	322.81
2000	3204.99	847.77	743.15	103.87	599.06	690.64
2001	3581.35	908.29	776.32	114.96	749.65	832.94
2002	3996.23	1126.08	992.57	116.17	772.97	976.78
2003	4497.21	1450.56	1262.47	137.41	867.88	1113.18
2004	5106.86	1824.44	1596.44	90.16	930.99	1234.13
2005	5878.70	2273.18	1837.58	113.34	1218.48	1567.23
2006	6810.19	2887.45	2181.97	130.86	1460.77	1714.73
2007	7919.89	3540.85	2560.28	151.88	1882.01	2145.82
2008	9539.76	3872.08	2697.61	169.21	2248.16	2550.77
2009	10834.73	3417.77	2430.46	175.08	2522.29	2882.33
2010	12613.24	4318.02	3195.01	183.47	3139.58	3654.91
2011	14575.57	5064.89	3678.00	195.29	3674.70	4444.97
2012	16552.69	5477.09	3956.56	215.53	4129.09	4798.40
2013	18630.61	6070.93	4403.38	230.62	4669.16	5240.59
2014	20655.78	6137.68	4153.86	248.61	5375.37	5973.23
2015	22651.04	6087.57	3664.49	256.24	6391.70	8421.36
2016	25048.68	5650.87	3450.88	225.90	6923.98	9285.10
2017	27318.18	5902.41	3709.89	218.11	7455.96	10329.95

21-3 续表 5 continued

年份 Year	金融机构本外币存款(亿元) Deposits in Renminbi and Foreign Currencies in All Financial Institutions (100 million yuan)	#本外币住户存款(亿元) Savings Deposits by Urban and Rural Residents (100 million yuan)	金融机构本外币贷款(亿元) Loans in Renminbi and Foreign Currencies in All Financial Institutions (100 million yuan)	常住居民人均可支配收入(元) Annual Disposable Income of Permanent Residents (yuan)	城镇居民人均可支配收入(元) Per Capita Annual Disposable Income of Permanent Urban Residents (yuan)	农村常住居民人均可支配收入(元) Per Capita Annual Disposable Income of Permanent Rural Residents (yuan)
1990						
1995						
2000	16211.75	7941.54	11227.42			
2001	18562.11	9064.31	12447.65			
2002	21881.50	10734.65	14689.30			
2003	25574.00	12553.20	17772.73			
2004	28704.24	14193.04	19642.60			
2005	32962.25	16389.71	21073.93			
2006	37367.68	18306.14	23613.32			
2007	42555.31	18485.09	27982.87			
2008	48512.14	22711.25	31044.80			
2009	60618.78	25914.62	40608.44			
2010	71294.51	29770.92	47159.74			
2011	79575.13	33015.57	53133.57			
2012	91585.24	37059.20	60568.45			
2013	104255.28	40218.90	67988.65			
2014	110800.56	41899.85	76017.12	33642.1	37063.7	15754.0
2015	141609.04	42737.49	85741.78	36662.0	40284.5	17296.4
2016	158966.41	46321.96	100149.59	40109.1	43967.4	19063.7
2017	171937.41	48505.38	113683.01	43840.1	47926.9	20813.5

注：珠江三角洲包括广州、深圳、珠海、佛山、江门、东莞、中山、惠州、肇庆九市。

Notes: The Pearl River Delta Economic Zone covers the areas of 13 cities and counties (districts), including Guangzhou, Shenzhen, Zhuhai, Foshan, Jiangmen, Dongguan, Zhongshan, urban districts of Huizhou, Huidong County, Boluo County, urban districts of Zhaoqing, Gaoyao County-level City and Sihui County-level City. The data on banking refer to the sum of the nine cities in the Pearl River Delta, including Guangzhou, Shenzhen, Zhuhai, Foshan, Jiangmen, Dongguan, Zhongshan, Huizhou and Zhaoqing.

21-4 珠江三角洲工业企业主要指标（2017年）

单位：亿元

项　目	Item	企业单位数（个）Number of Enterprises (unit)	#亏损企业 Loss-making Enterprises
总　计	**Total**	**36500**	**4602**
按经济类型分	Grouped by Ownership		
在总计中：国有控股经济	Of the Total: State-controlled Economy	754	128
国有经济	State-owned Economy	62	13
集体经济	Collective-owned Economy	92	10
股份合作经济	Share-holding Cooperative Economy	23	3
股份制经济	Share-holding Economy	24034	2642
外商投资经济	Economy with Foreign Investment	3768	625
港澳台投资经济	Economy with Investment from Hong Kong, Macao and Taiwan	7581	1261
按轻重工业分	Grouped by Light and Heavy Industry		
轻工业	Light Industry	16780	2240
重工业	Heavy Industry	19720	2362
按企业规模分	Grouped by Size of Enterprise		
大型企业	Large	1378	97
中型企业	Medium	6769	801
小微型企业	Small and Micro	28353	3704
按行业分	Grouped by Sector		
煤炭开采和洗选业	Mining and Washing of Coal		
石油和天然气开采业	Extraction of Petroleum and Natural Gas	3	
黑色金属矿采选业	Mining and Dressing of Ferrous Metal Ores	12	
有色金属矿采选业	Mining and Dressing of Nonferrous Metal Ores	3	
非金属矿采选业	Mining and Dressing of Nonmetal Ores	80	5
开采辅助活动	Auxiliary Minning Operations	3	
其他采矿业	Mining and Dressing of Other Ores		
农副食品加工业	Processing of Farm and Sideline Food	471	67
食品制造业	Manufacture of Food	390	61
酒、饮料和精制茶制造业	Manufacture of Beverage	129	21
烟草制品业	Tobacco Products	2	
纺织业	Textile Industry	991	119
纺织服装、服饰业	Manufacture of Textile Garments, Footwear and Headgear	1721	262
皮革、毛皮、羽毛及其制品和制鞋业	Leather, Fur, Feather, Down and Related Products	1354	177
木材加工和木、竹、藤、棕、草制品业	Timber Processing, Bamboo, Cane, Palm Fiber & Straw Products	299	29
家具制造业	Manufacture of Furniture	1282	143
造纸和纸制品业	Papermaking and Paper Products	923	92
印刷和记录媒介复制业	Printing and Record Medium Reproduction	702	89
文教、工美、体育和娱乐用品制造业	Manufacture of Cultural, Educational and Sports Articles	1167	208
石油加工、炼焦和核燃料加工业	Petroleum Refining, Coking and Nuclear Fuel Processing	56	5
化学原料和化学制品制造业	Manufacture of Raw Chemical Materials and Chemical Products	1805	184
医药制造业	Manufacture of Medicines	284	22
化学纤维制造业	Manufacture of Chemical Fibers	50	4
橡胶和塑料制品业	Plastic Products	3096	338
非金属矿物制品业	Nonmetal Mineral Products	1482	161
黑色金属冶炼和压延加工业	Smelting and Pressing of Ferrous Metals	280	36
有色金属冶炼和压延加工业	Smelting and Pressing of Nonferrous Metals	570	54
金属制品业	Metal Products	3119	339
通用设备制造业	Manufacture of General-purpose Machinery	1853	164
专用设备制造业	Manufacture of Special-purpose Machinery	1771	202
汽车制造业	Manufacture of Automobile	769	84
铁路、船舶、航空航天和其他运输设备制造业	Manufacture of Railway ,Ship,Aeronautics and Other Transport equipment	366	82
电气机械和器材制造业	Manufacture of Electrical Machinery and Equipment	4550	589
计算机、通信和其他电子设备制造业	Manufacture of Communication Equipment, Computers and Other Electronic Equipment	5421	870
仪器仪表制造业	Manufacture of Instruments and Meters	637	97
其他制造业	Other Manufactures	258	31
废弃资源综合利用业	Comprehensive Utilization of Waste	122	14
金属制品、机械和设备修理业	Manufacture of Metal Products,Machinery and Equipment Maintenance	40	5
电力、热力生产和供应业	Production and Supply of Electric Power and Heat Power	151	21
燃气生产和供应业	Production and Supply of Gas	83	9
水的生产和供应业	Production and Supply of Water	205	18

注：本表统计范围为年主营业务收入2000万元及以上的工业法人企业。

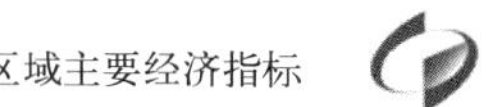

Main Indicators of Industrial Enterprises of the Pearl River Delta (2017)

(100 million yuan)

工业总产值（当年价）Gross Industrial Output Value (at current prices)	工业增加值（收入法）Value-added of Industry (by production approach)	年末资产总计 Total Assets at the Year-end	#产成品 Finished Products	流动资产合计 Total Current Asserts	固定资产合计 Net Value of Fixed Assets	年末负债合计 Total Liabilities at the Year-end
112644.06	**25768.21**	**97741.87**	**4431.26**	**61254.58**	**19795.76**	**55373.02**
15181.30	4121.85	20092.29	502.51	8564.83	6360.26	10806.79
683.19	163.74	513.76	20.29	222.49	186.44	280.25
119.15	38.41	79.83	1.07	43.53	21.74	52.96
50.59	8.38	13.43	1.05	9.53	2.32	7.81
63057.25	14794.20	58922.46	2662.38	35671.49	11427.05	34279.91
23068.80	4987.12	16719.87	706.07	11059.26	3816.00	8895.10
24614.28	5563.47	21149.27	1029.88	14072.05	4234.49	11673.28
35990.94	8589.25	31281.11	1670.42	21006.74	5280.20	17419.45
76653.12	17178.96	66460.75	2760.84	40247.84	14515.56	37953.57
57249.91	13958.61	52223.46	2139.83	32369.66	9893.88	30012.17
25693.15	5784.62	22255.34	1045.83	13539.23	4938.50	11558.59
29701.00	6024.98	23263.06	1245.59	15345.68	4963.38	13802.26
356.35	276.08	600.43	1.50	72.36	457.23	290.75
38.73	12.27	26.29	0.80	5.22	20.73	10.01
15.24	1.53	4.00	0.25	1.63	0.75	1.17
98.93	25.41	49.40	2.60	21.09	19.24	24.29
12.04	1.64	56.17	0.01	12.98	41.11	13.05
1824.34	190.54	1043.09	47.48	696.48	168.41	600.02
1351.48	504.22	1064.21	47.28	646.60	246.72	445.32
926.56	252.91	758.17	19.67	448.25	227.36	410.88
265.92	206.15	314.57	8.24	245.14	33.20	67.80
1609.82	335.08	1039.30	57.62	621.79	253.64	549.12
2019.41	562.78	1340.66	108.26	974.28	197.93	744.04
1425.16	412.31	786.72	63.66	564.30	128.11	449.61
424.89	97.46	305.97	13.86	192.41	82.17	151.18
1757.11	427.10	1184.72	58.75	783.93	210.53	624.42
1985.61	410.46	1754.27	56.40	987.00	557.34	906.23
943.78	256.50	841.56	27.91	520.53	196.92	405.41
2668.67	480.40	1962.10	353.04	1617.92	203.65	1256.89
1325.41	485.22	1023.91	18.06	487.58	393.33	634.03
4683.34	996.85	4021.05	148.39	2282.84	917.28	2013.38
1045.23	362.96	2007.20	81.74	1221.66	256.01	855.04
151.39	33.46	176.81	6.49	82.59	45.74	68.53
4022.47	916.07	3060.67	148.24	1958.62	668.24	1669.44
3162.28	728.45	2633.46	140.57	1516.64	724.47	1469.71
1300.57	151.59	739.06	46.93	392.25	267.94	469.44
2418.99	282.75	1302.27	205.26	843.86	289.49	903.55
4927.73	1110.05	3267.08	134.20	2004.77	829.59	1763.78
3912.21	848.67	3619.37	177.13	2511.88	530.42	1939.26
3116.61	850.10	3275.84	155.51	2156.85	500.59	1634.93
7673.04	1730.52	5552.43	161.39	3724.77	1128.34	3452.39
1147.24	222.12	1250.62	35.68	855.69	229.86	764.37
12042.56	2770.57	12204.67	528.69	8703.03	1512.64	7403.68
36018.71	7843.50	28543.19	1459.34	20929.45	3514.34	17685.84
1055.51	291.28	1205.86	62.08	863.67	137.77	574.45
216.39	47.83	153.78	9.27	110.24	26.92	86.40
728.25	136.05	271.57	10.32	140.06	106.12	137.66
165.57	48.90	193.06	4.25	133.21	45.15	109.60
4745.55	1115.77	7617.00	28.70	1255.15	3619.42	3363.05
652.79	154.72	762.83	1.09	267.53	337.82	416.94
408.18	187.92	1728.50	0.59	400.31	669.26	1007.37

Notes: The statistical coverage of industry refers to the legal person industrial enterprises with annual main business revenue over 20 million yuan.

21-4 续表

单位：亿元

项 目	Item	年末所有者权益合计 Total Creditors' Equity at the Year-end
总 计	**Total**	**42125.06**
按经济类型分	Grouped by Ownership	
在总计中：国有控股经济	Of the Total: State-controlled Economy	9274.30
国有经济	State-owned Economy	229.12
集体经济	Collective-owned Economy	26.26
股份合作经济	Share-holding Cooperative Economy	5.45
股份制经济	Share-holding Economy	24509.60
外商投资经济	Economy with Foreign Investment	7782.36
港澳台投资经济	Economy with Investment from Hong Kong, Macao and Taiwan	9424.40
按轻重工业分	Grouped by Light and Heavy Industry	
轻工业	Light Industry	13741.29
重工业	Heavy Industry	28383.77
按企业规模分	Grouped by Size of Enterprise	
大型企业	Large	22201.01
中型企业	Medium	10680.61
小微型企业	Small and Micro	9243.44
按行业分	Grouped by Sector	
煤炭开采和洗选业	Mining and Washing of Coal	
石油和天然气开采业	Extraction of Petroleum and Natural Gas	309.68
黑色金属矿采选业	Mining and Dressing of Ferrous Metal Ores	16.28
有色金属矿采选业	Mining and Dressing of Nonferrous Metal Ores	2.84
非金属矿采选业	Mining and Dressing of Nonmetal Ores	24.03
开采辅助活动	Auxiliary Minning Operations	43.12
其他采矿业	Mining and Dressing of Other Ores	
农副食品加工业	Processing of Farm and Sideline Food	437.72
食品制造业	Manufacture of Food	618.44
酒、饮料和精制茶制造业	Manufacture of Beverage	345.95
烟草制品业	Tobacco Products	246.77
纺织业	Textile Industry	483.25
纺织服装、服饰业	Manufacture of Textile Garments, Footwear and Headgear	584.84
皮革、毛皮、羽毛及其制品和制鞋业	Leather, Fur, Feather, Down and Related Products	327.07
木材加工和木、竹、藤、棕、草制品业	Timber Processing, Bamboo, Cane, Palm Fiber & Straw Products	153.00
家具制造业	Manufacture of Furniture	550.00
造纸和纸制品业	Papermaking and Paper Products	836.40
印刷和记录媒介复制业	Printing and Record Medium Reproduction	433.86
文教、工美、体育和娱乐用品制造业	Manufacture of Cultural, Educational and Sports Articles	700.18
石油加工、炼焦和核燃料加工业	Petroleum Refining, Coking and Nuclear Fuel Processing	389.81
化学原料和化学制品制造业	Manufacture of Raw Chemical Materials and Chemical Products	1998.73
医药制造业	Manufacture of Medicines	1152.17
化学纤维制造业	Manufacture of Chemical Fibers	75.86
橡胶和塑料制品业	Plastic Products	1383.34
非金属矿物制品业	Nonmetal Mineral Products	1147.87
黑色金属冶炼和压延加工业	Smelting and Pressing of Ferrous Metals	266.19
有色金属冶炼和压延加工业	Smelting and Pressing of Nonferrous Metals	395.74
金属制品业	Metal Products	1477.47
通用设备制造业	Manufacture of General-purpose Machinery	1672.63
专用设备制造业	Manufacture of Special-purpose Machinery	1638.22
汽车制造业	Manufacture of Automobile	2091.75
铁路、船舶、航空航天和其他运输设备制造业	Manufacture of Railway ,Ship,Aeronautics and Other Transport equipment	484.75
电气机械和器材制造业	Manufacture of Electrical Machinery and Equipment	4790.16
计算机、通信和其他电子设备制造业	Manufacture of Communication Equipment, Computers and Other Electronic Equipment	10818.47
仪器仪表制造业	Manufacture of Instruments and Meters	628.17
其他制造业	Other Manufactures	65.96
废弃资源综合利用业	Comprehensive Utilization of Waste	133.16
金属制品、机械和设备修理业	Manufacture of Metal Products,Machinery and Equipment Maintenance	83.39
电力、热力生产和供应业	Production and Supply of Electric Power and Heat Power	4249.59
燃气生产和供应业	Production and Supply of Gas	346.90
水的生产和供应业	Production and Supply of Water	721.28

21-4 continued

(100 million yuan)

主营业务收入 Principal Business Revenue	主营业务税金及附加 Tax and Extra Charges on Principal Business	利润总额 Total Profits	#亏损总额 Total Losses	利税总额 Total Pretax Profits	本年应交增值税 Value-added Tax Payable in Current Year	全部从业人员年平均人数（万人） Annual Average Number of Employed Persons (10000 persons)
111404.35	**951.10**	**7260.91**	**451.90**	**11082.25**	**2858.20**	**1164.40**
15471.64	461.11	1251.67	64.71	2269.10	553.13	62.88
682.02	29.69	67.97	1.80	116.67	18.96	2.90
118.10	0.51	6.55	0.17	9.21	2.14	3.75
48.95	0.32	1.54	0.03	3.01	1.15	0.23
62834.16	600.17	3974.65	234.26	6424.15	1842.36	562.52
22753.42	179.78	1657.51	100.78	2343.60	504.04	205.83
23945.05	134.61	1502.12	114.36	2105.82	466.43	378.90
36009.58	331.41	2534.64	129.93	3852.87	982.28	499.99
75394.77	619.69	4726.27	321.97	7229.38	1875.92	664.41
56763.99	620.64	4220.47	80.11	6491.30	1644.55	456.57
25013.36	188.88	1645.03	186.25	2413.72	576.48	383.34
29627.01	141.58	1395.41	185.54	2177.22	637.16	324.49
314.76	17.86	123.19		177.36	36.31	0.34
37.17	0.74	2.22		4.98	2.02	0.18
19.08	0.06	0.69		0.83	0.09	0.07
93.65	2.12	7.15	0.31	11.91	2.64	0.55
12.04	0.01	0.50		0.56	0.05	0.06
1960.73	3.09	92.29	4.82	109.57	14.01	6.88
1327.06	12.57	194.50	5.17	290.39	83.26	12.26
880.83	19.75	78.54	3.54	141.28	42.95	6.08
253.61	131.62	27.38		191.16	32.00	0.36
1550.75	6.93	83.23	4.85	122.48	32.19	20.90
1920.17	10.62	75.38	8.73	136.64	50.41	52.97
1414.06	7.22	48.50	7.16	83.63	27.71	42.69
412.67	2.84	32.88	0.76	46.36	10.59	4.40
1714.93	9.08	109.32	4.52	162.30	43.64	31.50
1946.64	8.29	126.81	3.68	195.28	59.64	18.01
914.73	4.90	55.60	6.88	83.62	22.93	18.52
2695.46	7.99	95.95	8.61	132.78	28.30	48.86
1323.20	156.35	108.43	3.89	340.25	75.46	1.40
4703.09	29.09	361.93	16.47	527.95	136.47	26.13
982.00	9.51	220.89	2.98	290.91	60.31	9.76
149.06	0.56	12.39	0.20	15.54	2.58	1.18
3915.29	18.16	181.05	26.20	283.40	83.72	69.56
3068.91	17.26	190.84	10.28	290.20	81.71	34.84
1260.46	4.60	50.18	7.02	74.56	19.77	4.55
2491.79	6.55	106.86	3.89	145.05	31.52	11.99
4743.04	23.70	254.86	19.05	388.29	109.14	68.71
3829.57	18.02	266.33	14.07	371.31	86.50	47.02
2991.79	18.42	279.86	24.36	377.10	78.24	44.06
7555.33	148.23	641.07	24.66	1015.72	225.23	39.29
1105.50	5.94	63.46	16.93	85.98	16.51	11.55
12382.46	63.11	898.14	36.11	1294.71	332.50	157.75
35491.87	139.91	1802.18	162.92	2727.38	782.97	324.70
1037.76	6.02	84.82	9.26	117.01	26.11	21.47
212.42	1.10	7.89	0.77	12.87	3.86	4.86
725.94	3.21	66.92	0.32	85.16	15.02	2.11
164.54	1.04	9.55	1.43	14.30	3.61	1.78
4690.05	29.71	356.00	6.69	555.19	168.50	11.68
710.33	1.93	61.20	4.63	76.83	13.47	1.40
401.64	2.99	81.93	0.75	101.42	16.29	3.98

21-5 广州、深圳主要经济指标（2017年）

Main Economic Indicators of Guangzhou and Shenzhen (2017)

指标	Item	合计 Total	广州市 Guangzhou	深圳市 Shenzhen
土地面积 (平方公里)	Land Area (sq.km)	9246.74	7249.27	1997.47
年末常住人口 (万人)	Permanent Population at the Year-end (10000 persons)	2702.67	1449.84	1252.83
#城镇人口	Urban Population	2498.43	1248.89	1249.54
年末户籍总人口 (万人)	Total Population with Residence Registration at the Year-end (10000 persons)	1343.71	897.97	445.74
年末就业人员 (万人)	Employed Persons at the Year-end (10000 persons)	1805.62	862.33	943.29
#城镇单位就业人员	Employed Persons in Urban Areas	792.96	329.17	463.79
地区生产总值 (亿元)	Gross Domestic Product (100 million yuan)	43993.21	21503.15	22490.06
第一产业	Primary Industry	240.02	220.45	19.57
第二产业	Secondary Industry	15329.11	6011.01	9318.10
第三产业	Tertiary Industry	28424.08	15271.69	13152.39
人均生产总值 (元)	Per Capita Gross Domestic Product (yuan)	165861	150678	183544
地区生产总值指数(上年=100)	Index of Gross Domestic Product (preceding year=100)	107.9	107.0	108.8
第一产业	Primary Industry	103.8	102.2	127.0
第二产业	Secondary Industry	107.2	104.6	109.2
第三产业	Tertiary Industry	108.3	108.2	108.4
人均生产总值指数(上年=100)	Index of Per Capita Gross Domestic Product (preceding year=100)	103.6	103.2	103.9
公路通车里程 (公里)	Total Length of Highways in Operation (km)	10945	9311	1634
民用汽车拥有量 (万辆)	Number of Civil Vehicles Owned (100 million unit)	561.36	239.92	321.44
私人汽车拥有量	Number of Private Vehicles Owned	453.51	191.26	262.24
邮电业务总量 (亿元) (按2010年不变价计算)	Total Business Volume of Postal and Telecommunication Services (calculated at 2010 constant Prices) (100 million yuan)	3204.10	1544.90	1659.20
本地电话年末用户 (万户)	Number of Subscribers of Local Telephones at the Year-end (10000 subscribers)	915.71	437.50	478.22
#城市	Subscribers in Urban Areas			
移动电话年末用户 (万户)	Number of Subscribers of Mobile Telephones at the Year-end (10000 subscribers)	5384.58	2705.26	2679.31
固定资产投资额 (亿元)	Investment in Fixed Assets (100 million yuan)	11067.15	5919.83	5147.32
#项目投资 (亿元)	Urban (100 million yuan)	6228.40	3216.94	3011.46
房地产开发投资 (亿元)	Investment in Real Estate Development (100 million yuan)	4838.75	2702.89	2135.86
社会消费品零售总额 (亿元)	Total Retail Sales of Consumer Good (100 million yuan)	15418.78	9402.59	6016.19
出口总额 (亿美元)	Total Exports (USD 100 million)	3296.79	853.20	2443.59
进口总额 (亿美元)	Total Imports (USD 100 million)	2277.17	579.30	1697.87
实际外商直接投资额(亿美元)	Foreign Direct Investment Actually Utilized (USD 100 million)	136.90	62.89	74.01
地方一般公共预算收入(亿元)	Local Public Budgetary Revenue (100 million yuan)	4868.87	1536.74	3332.13
地方一般公共预算支出(亿元)	Local Public Budgetary Expenditure (100 million yuan)	6779.81	2186.01	4593.80
金融机构本外币存款 (亿元)	Deposits in Renminbi and Foreign Currencies in All Financial Institutions (100 million yuan)	121037.34	51369.03	69668.31
#本外币住户存款	Savings Deposits by Residents	26192.07	15032.29	11159.78
金融机构本外币贷款 (亿元)	Loans in Renminbi and Foreign Currencies in All Financial Institutions (100 million yuan)	80466.38	34137.05	46329.33
常住居民可支配收入 (元)	Annual Disposable Income of Permanent Residents		50782.2	52938.0
城镇居民人均可支配收入(元)	Per Capita Annual Disposable Income of Permanent Urban Residents (yuan)		55400.5	52938.0
农村常住居民人均可支配收入 (元)	Per Capita Annual Net Income of Permanent Rural Residents(yuan)		23483.9	

21-6 粤东西北主要经济指标

Main Economic Indicators of the East and West and Mountainous Area

年份 Year	年末常住人口(万人) Permanent Population at the Year-end (10000 persons)	#城镇人口 Urban Population	年末户籍总人口(万人) Total Population with Residence Registration at the Year-end (10000 persons)	年末就业人员(万人) Employed Persons at the Year-end (10000 persons)	#城镇单位就业人员 Employed Persons in Urban Areas
2000	4235.41	1787.22	4934.94	2252.12	274.48
2001	4357.08		4970.09	2279.71	262.55
2002	4427.40		5024.37	2313.42	254.28
2003	4499.14		5062.96	2145.51	255.45
2004	4594.16		5090.66	2187.27	257.74
2005	4646.85	2098.62	5136.32	2198.33	266.15
2006	4706.60	2191.04	5227.44	2213.08	277.04
2007	4728.84	2202.07	5283.58	2234.13	280.72
2008	4755.00	2216.23	5346.26	2239.35	281.78
2009	4768.46	2256.19	5398.98	2276.52	287.98
2010	4824.55	2262.47	5496.98	2298.47	294.85
2011	4858.50	2298.91	5563.33	2330.53	310.82
2012	4904.36	2369.88	5530.87	2921.01	334.39
2013	4928.81	2409.84	5603.44	2333.59	403.50
2014	4960.61	2443.91	5678.95	2337.98	407.20
2015	4974.73	2485.25	5742.67	2348.04	404.70
2016	5000.51	2521.65	5814.38	2352.29	410.44
2017	5018.46	2555.77	5841.81	2359.37	403.10

注：2006—2009年年末常住人口根据2010年第六次全国人口普查快速汇总数进行平滑调整，城镇人口也作了相应的调整。

Note: The year-end populations from 2006 to 2009 have been adjusted in accordance with the fast sum figure obtained from the 6th National Population Census and the same applied to urban population.

21-6 续表 1 continued

年份 Year	地区生产总值(亿元) Gross Domestic Product (100 million yuan)	第一产业 Primary Industry	第二产业 Secondary Industry	第三产业 Tertiary Industry	人均生产总值(元) Per Capita Gross Domestic Product(yuan)
2000	2775.18	726.47	1054.10	994.61	6579
2001	2967.84	745.05	1141.98	1080.80	6908
2002	3181.57	778.07	1224.68	1178.82	7244
2003	3550.67	818.69	1426.03	1305.94	7955
2004	4082.32	897.96	1681.55	1502.81	8979
2005	4640.29	901.99	1989.52	1748.77	10043
2006	5464.89	958.16	2523.24	1983.49	11685
2007	6465.64	1063.15	3058.40	2344.10	13705
2008	7630.76	1233.49	3624.04	2773.24	16092
2009	8173.59	1281.66	3689.32	3202.60	17165
2010	9631.52	1461.25	4395.31	3774.96	20080
2011	11355.73	1698.70	5161.15	4495.88	23455
2012	12590.21	1842.36	5671.65	5076.20	25810
2013	14058.28	1916.89	6446.27	5695.13	28613
2014	15333.54	2018.70	7127.56	6187.28	31010
2015	16255.10	2145.60	7294.55	6814.96	32722
2016	17520.48	2345.85	7593.61	7581.02	35128
2017	18764.69	2428.58	7763.74	8572.37	37484

21-6 续表 2 continued

年份 Year	地区生产总值指数(上年=100) Index of Gross Domestic Product (preceding year=100)	第一产业 Primary Industry	第二产业 Secondary Industry	第三产业 Tertiary Industry	人均生产总值指数(上年=100) Index of Per Capita Gross Domestic Product(preceding year=100)
2000	108.2	105.3	108.1	110.4	107.4
2001	106.4	104.8	105.6	108.5	104.5
2002	108.5	105.4	109.3	109.9	106.1
2003	110.8	104.4	114.8	111.1	109.1
2004	112.3	104.8	115.8	113.3	110.2
2005	113.7	103.6	117.8	115.3	111.9
2006	115.3	104.7	121.3	114.0	113.9
2007	115.5	103.6	119.5	116.2	114.4
2008	111.5	104.2	111.7	114.4	111.0
2009	110.7	105.5	109.8	113.8	110.2
2010	113.8	105.0	116.1	114.3	113.0
2011	111.1	104.5	112.5	112.0	110.0
2012	109.8	104.8	111.8	109.2	108.9
2013	110.3	103.3	112.1	110.6	109.6
2014	109.2	103.6	111.4	108.2	108.5
2015	108.0	103.6	107.6	109.9	107.5
2016	107.3	103.0	106.1	110.0	106.9
2017	106.6	103.8	104.8	109.3	106.2

21-6 续表 3 continued

年份 Year	公路通车里程(公里) Total Length of Highways in Operation (km)	货运量(万吨) Freight Traffic (10000 tons)	邮电业务总量(亿元) Total Business Volume of Postal and Telecommunication Services (100 million yuan)	本地电话年末用户(万户) Number of Subscribers of Local Telephones at the Year-end (10000 subscribers)	移动电话年末用户 (万户) Number of Subscribers of Mobile Telephones at the Year-end (10000 subscribers)	固定资产投资额(亿元) Investment in Fixed Assets (100 million yuan)	#房地产开发投资 Investment in Real Estate Development
2000	69133		169.58	549.37		532.72	73.33
2001	70449	48307	168.33	641.30	543.26	616.30	80.39
2002	73076	50111	189.63	730.86	706.06	773.80	95.52
2003	74106	52616	236.67	848.28	888.71	957.97	99.40
2004	74690	54202	333.87	1210.00	1317.44	1210.44	112.74
2005	77369	30627	383.01	1083.96	1448.30	1538.49	142.70
2006	124739	32636	472.35	1073.86	1620.17	1909.86	179.68
2007	128900	38046	722.32	1091.75	1766.69	2401.76	281.61
2008	129736	42258	810.08	1043.60	1932.03	2919.84	370.54
2009	130699	36989	954.68	966.38	2071.24	3749.59	378.15
2010	134296	43686	883.49	899.35	2252.45	4757.39	541.04
2011	134345	52697	373.62	862.85	2507.03	4477.07	787.04
2012	136354	62789	444.36	840.51	2894.83	5333.28	869.12
2013	143359	75952	488.10	810.96	3477.68	6797.87	1126.85
2014	150546	101477	642.75	753.98	3624.47	8385.82	1344.90
2015	152969	110358	824.04	720.43	3572.36	9982.51	1462.90
2016	154454	106080	1404.54	655.48	3415.21	10687.62	1706.63
2017	155461	113392	1110.06	604.59	3970.45	12014.42	2247.92

21-6 续表 4 continued

年份 Year	社会消费品零售总额(亿元) Total Retail Sales of Consumer Goods (100 million yuan)	出口总额(亿美元) Total Exports (USD 100 million)	进口总额(亿美元) Total Imports (USD 100 million)	实际外商直接投资额(亿美元) Foreign Direct Investment Actually Utilized (USD 100 million)	地方一般公共预算收入(亿元) Local Public General Budgetary Revenue (100 million yuan)	地方一般公共预算支出(亿元) Local Public Genera lBudgetary Expenditure (100 million yuan)
2000	1174.82	71.42	38.72	13.70	88.89	216.28
2001	1275.3	45.92	34.34	14.14	101.53	239.76
2002	1396.41	58.5	33.77	15.68	108.83	300.61
2003	1532.65	77.92	44.27	19.14	121.96	348.73
2004	1745.17	91.26	59.17	9.96	133.47	386.45
2005	2036.81	108.53	60.74	10.30	176.54	438.76
2006	2384.1	132.04	70.27	14.25	219.70	538.75
2007	2811.39	151.53	87.68	19.38	278.37	673.46
2008	3446.84	169.8	95.43	22.24	338.91	801.64
2009	4057.05	171.79	91.17	20.27	400.35	965.51
2010	4801.42	213.89	122.04	19.14	513.91	1184.81
2011	5671.15	253.04	137.41	22.70	619.29	1464.85
2012	6124.42	263.49	142.32	19.96	718.42	1726.82
2013	6937.20	292.71	151.20	18.90	842.56	1983.95
2014	7815.36	323.19	151.11	20.10	949.18	2323.42
2015	8762.80	347.12	128.79	12.51	1011.79	3230.36
2016	9697.44	334.77	116.33	7.59	990.73	3263.41
2017	10621.80	326.32	128.17	10.95	1059.05	3473.17

21-6 续表 5 continued

年份 Year	金融机构本外币存款(亿元) Deposits in Renminbi and Foreign Currencies in All Financial Institutions (100 million yuan)	#本外币住户存款(亿元) Savings Deposits by Urban and Rural Residents (100 million yuan)	金融机构本外币贷款(亿元) Loans in Renminbi and Foreign Currencies in All Financial Institutions (100 million yuan)	常住居民人均可支配收入(元) Annual Disposable Income of Permanent Residents (yuan)	城镇居民人均可支配收入(元) Per Capita Annual Disposable Income of Permanent Urban Residents (yuan)	农村常住居民人均可支配收入(元) Per Capita Annual Disposable Income of Permanent Rural Residents (yuan)
2000	2871.90	2089.75	1984.98			
2001	3149.51	2321.72	2011.43			
2002	3511.40	2638.20	2134.33			
2003	4066.83	3037.48	2353.51			
2004	4547.77	3438.04	2312.68			
2005	5157.66	3878.05	2187.28			
2006	5894.51	4371.05	2321.86			
2007	6399.72	4528.21	2634.39			
2008	7607.15	5469.95	2791.07			
2009	9072.69	6221.71	3901.78			
2010	10724.89	7194.83	4639.56			
2011	12015.02	8045.99	5481.70			
2012	13514.31	9206.38	6508.63			
2013	15429.88	10419.74	7675.51			
2014	17080.90	11316.03	8904.68			
2015	18779.17	12271.21	9919.34	16843.9	22018.2	12019.1
2016	20862.78	13446.79	10778.82	18364.5	23871.9	13147.1
2017	22598.34	14436.89	12348.94	19948.4	25767.5	14297.8

注：粤东西北地区包括汕头、汕尾、潮州、揭阳、湛江、茂名、阳江、韶关、河源、梅州、清远和云浮12市。

Note：East and West Wings and Mountainous areas in Guangdong include Shantou, Shanwei, Chaozhou, Jieyang, Zhanjiang, Maoming, Yangjiang, Shaoguan,Heyuan,Meizhou，Qingyuan and Yunfu.

21-7 东翼主要经济指标

Main Economic Indicators of the East Wing

指 标	Item	2016	2017	2017比2016增长% Growth Rate in 2017 over 2016
土地面积 (平方公里)	Land Area (sq.km)	15475	15476	
年末常住人口 (万人)	Permanent Population at the Year-end (10000 persons)	1735.58	1732.26	-0.2
#城镇人口	Urban Population	1041.61	1040.57	-0.1
年末户籍总人口 (万人)	Total Population with Residence Registration at the Year-end (10000 persons)	1892.23	1906.99	0.8
年末就业人员 (万人)	Employed Persons at the Year-end (10000 persons)	759.87	759.62	-0.03
#城镇单位就业人员	Employed Persons in Urban Areas	142.72	137.57	-3.61
地区生产总值 (亿元)	Gross Domestic Product (100 million yuan)	5873.83	6202.54	7.2
第一产业	Primary Industry	446.68	455.36	4.8
第二产业	Secondary Industry	3066.98	3115.66	5.9
第三产业	Tertiary Industry	2360.17	2631.53	9.4
人均生产总值 (元)	Per Capita Gross Domestic Product (yuan)	33924	35844	7.3
地区生产总值指数（上年=100）	Index of Gross Domestic Product (preceding year=100)	107.4	107.2	7.2
第一产业	Primary Industry	103.2	104.8	4.8
第二产业	Secondary Industry	105.7	105.9	5.9
第三产业	Tertiary Industry	110.7	109.4	9.4
人均生产总值指数（上年=100）	Index of Per Capita Gross Domestic Product (preceding year=100)	107.2	107.3	7.3
公路通车里程 (公里)	Total Length of Highways in Operation (km)	21919	22081	0.7
邮电业务总量 (亿元)（按2010年不变价计算）	Total Business Volume of Postal and Telecommunication Services (calculated at 2010 constant Prices) (100 million yuan)	566.87	510.58	66.2
本地电话年末用户 (万户)	Number of Subscribers of Local Telephones at the Year-end (10000 subscribers)	281.50	264.17	-6.2
移动电话年末用户 (万户)	Number of Subscribers of Mobile Telephones at the Year-end (10000 subscribers)	1336.81	1455.18	8.9
固定资产投资额 (亿元)	Investment in Fixed Assets (100 million yuan)	4172.14	4844.08	16.1
#房地产开发投资 (亿元)	Investment in Real Estate Development (100 million yuan)	478.40	623.49	30.3
社会消费品零售总额 (亿元)	Total Retail Sales of Consumer Goods (100 million yuan)	3522.33	3880.79	10.3
出口总额 (亿美元)	Total Exports (USD 100 million)	172.28	165.34	-4.0
进口总额 (亿美元)	Total Imports (USD 100 million)	46.26	45.86	-0.9
实际外商直接投资额 (亿美元)	Foreign Direct Investment Actually Utilized (USD 100 million)	2.00	5.08	153.5
地方一般公共预算收入 (亿元)	Local Public Budgetary Revenue (100 million yuan)	285.92	304.25	6.4
地方一般公共预算支出 (亿元)	Local Public Budgetary Expenditure (100 million yuan)	916.24	981.71	7.1
金融机构本外币存款 (亿元)	Deposits in Renminbi and Foreign Currencies in All Financial Institutions (100 million yuan)	7090.31	7552.51	6.5
#住户存款	Savings Deposits by Residents	4731.72	4969.59	5.0
金融机构本外币贷款 (亿元)	Loans in Renminbi and Foreign Currencies in All Financial Institutions (100 million yuan)	3017.55	3417.03	13.2
常住居民人均可支配收入 (元)	Annual Disposable Income of Permanent Residents	18744.6	20166.7	7.6
城镇常住居民人均可支配收入 (元)	Per Capita Annual Income of Permanent Urban Residents (yuan)	23478.3	25029.1	6.6
农村常住居民人均可支配收入 (元)	Per Capita Annual DisposableIncome of Permanent Rural Residents (yuan)	12667.1	13732.9	8.4

21-8 西翼主要经济指标

Main Economic Indicators of the West Wing

指 标	Item	2016	2017	2017比2016增长% Growth Rate in 2017 over 2016
土地面积 (平方公里)	Land Area (sq.km)	32646	32646	
年末常住人口 (万人)	Permanent Population at the Year-end (10000 persons)	1592.46	1605.20	0.8
#城镇人口	Urban Population	679.69	698.66	2.8
年末户籍总人口 (万人)	Total Population with Residence Registration at the Year-end (10000 persons)	1929.72	1939.84	0.5
年末就业人员 (万人)	Employed Persons at the Year-end (10000 persons)	755.29	757.79	0.3
#城镇单位就业人员	Employed Persons in Urban Areas	123.03	123.96	0.8
地区生产总值 (亿元)	Gross Domestic Product (100 million yuan)	6474.39	7022.40	7.0
第一产业	Primary Industry	1119.28	1172.86	3.2
第二产业	Secondary Industry	2584.25	2674.70	6.0
第三产业	Tertiary Industry	2770.85	3174.84	9.4
人均生产总值 (元)	Per Capita Gross Domestic Product (yuan)	40773	43922	6.3
地区生产总值指数 (上年=100)	Index of Gross Domestic Product (preceding year=100)	107.2	107.0	7.0
第一产业	Primary Industry	102.8	103.2	3.2
第二产业	Secondary Industry	106.9	106.0	6.0
第三产业	Tertiary Industry	109.3	109.4	9.4
人均生产总值指数 (上年=100)	Index of Per Capita Gross Domestic Product (preceding year=100)	106.6	106.3	6.3
公路通车里程 (公里)	Total Length of Highways in Operation (km)	50081	50315	0.5
邮电业务总量 (亿元) (按2010年不变价计算)	Total Business Volume of Postal and Telecommunication Services (calculated at 2010 constant Prices) (100 million yuan)	426.48	307.80	63.0
本地电话年末用户 (万户)	Number of Subscribers of Local Telephones at the Year-end (10000 subscribers)	165.36	151.33	-8.5
移动电话年末用户 (万户)	Number of Subscribers of Mobile Telephones at the Year-end (10000 subscribers)	1002.54	1217.73	21.5
固定资产投资额 (亿元)	Investment in Fixed Assets (100 million yuan)	3298.27	3597.47	9.1
#房地产开发投资 (亿元)	Investment in Real Estate Development (100 million yuan)	434.43	630.77	45.2
社会消费品零售总额 (亿元)	Total Retail Sales of Consumer Goods (100 million yuan)	3407.67	3724.98	9.3
出口总额 (亿美元)	Total Exports (USD 100 million)	58.29	63.22	8.5
进口总额 (亿美元)	Total Imports (USD 100 million)	24.52	29.01	18.3
实际外商直接投资额 (亿美元)	Foreign Direct Investment Actually Utilized (USD 100 million)	2.07	2.02	-2.5
地方一般公共预算收入 (亿元)	Local Public Budgetary Revenue (100 million yuan)	292.35	325.79	11.4
地方一般公共预算支出 (亿元)	Local Public Budgetary Expenditure (100 million yuan)	929.99	1017.27	9.4
金融机构本外币存款 (亿元)	Deposits in Renminbi and Foreign Currencies in All Financial Institutions (100 million yuan)	6191.67	6744.31	8.9
#本外币住户存款	Savings Deposits by Residents	4091.16	4424.70	8.2
金融机构本外币贷款 (亿元)	Loans in Renminbi and Foreign Currencies in All Financial Institutions (100 million yuan)	3467.09	3948.46	13.9
常住居民人均可支配收入 (元)	Annual Disposable Income of Permanent Residents	18364.5	20016.4	9.0
城镇常住居民人均可支配收入 (元)	Per Capita Annual Income of Permanent Urban Residents (yuan)	24390.2	26542.6	8.8
农村常住居民人均可支配收入 (元)	Per Capita Annual DisposableIncome of Permanent Rural Residents (yuan)	13890.8	15081.6	8.6

21-9 山区主要经济指标

Main Economic Indicators of Mountainous Areas

指　　标	Item	2016	2017	2017比2016增长% Growth Rate in 2017 over 2016
土地面积 (平方公里)	Land Area (sq.km)	76751	76751	
年末常住人口 (万人)	Permanent Population at the Year-end (10000 persons)	1672.47	1681.00	0.5
#城镇人口	Urban Population	800.35	816.55	2.0
年末户籍总人口 (万人)	Total Population with Residence Registration at the Year-end (10000 persons)	1992.43	1994.98	0.1
年末就业人员 (万人)	Employed Persons at the Year-end (10000 persons)	837.13	841.96	0.6
#城镇单位就业人员	Employed Persons in Urban Areas	144.70	141.56	-2.2
地区生产总值 (亿元)	Gross Domestic Product (100 million yuan)	5172.26	5539.75	5.6
第一产业	Primary Industry	779.88	800.36	4.3
第二产业	Secondary Industry	1942.37	1973.38	1.5
第三产业	Tertiary Industry	2450.01	2766.01	9.3
人均生产总值 (元)	Per Capita Gross Domestic Product (yuan)	31004	33039	5.0
地区生产总值指数 (上年=100)	Index of Gross Domestic Product (preceding year=100)	107.3	105.6	5.6
第一产业	Primary Industry	103.1	104.3	4.3
第二产业	Secondary Industry	105.7	101.5	1.5
第三产业	Tertiary Industry	110.1	109.3	9.3
人均生产总值指数 (上年=100)	Index of Per Capita Gross Domestic Product (preceding year=100)	106.8	105.0	5.0
公路通车里程 (公里)	Total Length of Highways in Operation (km)	82454	83065	0.7
邮电业务总量 (亿元) (按2010年不变价计算)	Total Business Volume of Postal and Telecommunication Services (calculated at 2010 constant Prices) (100 million yuan)	411.19	291.68	65.0
本地电话年末用户 (万户)	Number of Subscribers of Local Telephones at the Year-end (10000 subscribers)	208.61	189.09	-9.4
移动电话年末用户 (万户)	Number of Subscribers of Mobile Telephones at the Year-end (10000 subscribers)	1075.86	1297.54	20.6
固定资产投资额 (亿元)	Investment in Fixed Assets (100 million yuan)	3217.21	3572.87	11.1
#房地产开发投资 (亿元)	Investment in Real Estate Development (100 million yuan)	793.80	993.66	25.2
社会消费品零售总额 (亿元)	Total Retail Sales of Consumer Goods (100 million yuan)	2767.44	3016.03	9.0
出口总额 (亿美元)	Total Exports (USD 100 million)	104.20	97.76	-6.2
进口总额 (亿美元)	Total Imports (USD 100 million)	45.56	53.31	17.0
实际外商直接投资额 (亿美元)	Foreign Direct Investment Actually Utilized (USD 100 million)	3.53	3.86	9.5
地方一般公共预算收入 (亿元)	Local Public Budgetary Revenue (100 million yuan)	412.47	429.01	4.0
地方一般公共预算支出 (亿元)	Local Public Budgetary Expenditure (100 million yuan)	1417.18	1474.19	4.0
金融机构本外币存款 (亿元)	Deposits in Renminbi and Foreign Currencies in All Financial Institutions (100 million yuan)	7580.80	8301.52	9.5
#本外币住户存款	Savings Deposits by Residents	4623.91	5042.60	9.1
金融机构本外币贷款 (亿元)	Loans in Renminbi and Foreign Currencies in All Financial Institution	4294.17	4983.45	16.1
常住居民人均可支配收入 (元)	Annual Disposable Income of Permanent Residents	17967.6	19657.1	9.4
城镇常住居民人均可支配收入 (元)	Per Capita Annual Income of Permanent Urban Residents (yuan)	23963.1	26084.4	8.9
农村常住居民人均可支配收入 (元)	Per Capita Annual DisposableIncome of Permanent Rural Residents (yuan)	12747.4	13924.7	9.2

21-10 山区县(市、区)主要经济指标

Main Economic Indicators of Counties (County-level Cities and Districts) in Mountainous Areas

指 标	Item	2016	2017	2017比2016增长% Growth Rate in 2017 over 2016
年末户籍总人口 (万人)	Total Population with Residence Registration at the Year-end (10000 persons)	3466.13	3474.80	0.3
年末就业人员 (万人)	Employed Persons at the Year-end (10000 persons)	1537.05	1546.17	0.6
地区生产总值 (亿元)	Gross Domestic Product (100 million yuan)	9324.37	9830.66	5.7
第一产业	Primary Industry	1506.13	1553.76	4.2
第二产业	Secondary Industry	3853.87	3766.06	3.1
第三产业	Tertiary Industry	3964.38	4510.84	8.9
人均生产总值 (元)	Per Capita Gross Domestic Product (yuan)	32904	34540	5.2
地区生产总值指数(上年=100)	Index of Gross Domestic Product (preceding year=100)	107.2	105.7	5.7
第一产业	Primary Industry	103.9	104.2	4.2
第二产业	Secondary Industry	106.8	103.1	3.1
第三产业	Tertiary Industry	109.0	108.9	8.9
人均生产总值指数(上年=100)	Index of Per Capita Gross Domestic Product(preceding year=100)	106.9	105.2	5.2
固定资产投资额 (亿元)	Investment in Fixed Assets (100 million yuan)	5461.26	6018.60	10.2
#房地产开发投资 (亿元)	Investment in Real Estate Development (100 million yuan)	919.93	1130.11	22.8
社会消费品零售总额 (亿元)	Total Retail Sales of Consumer Goods (100 million yuan)	4297.54	4713.53	9.7
出口总额 (亿美元)	Total Exports (USD 100 million)	125.20	148.68	18.8
地方一般公共预算收入(亿元)	Local Public Budgetary Revenue (100 million yuan)	437.75	453.80	3.7
地方一般公共预算支出(亿元)	Local Public Budgetary Expenditure (100 million yuan)	1753.91	1876.05	7.0

注：50个山区县(市、区)包括:从化区、南澳县、曲江区、乐昌市、南雄市、仁化县、始兴县、翁源县、新丰县、乳源县、东源县、和平县、龙川县、紫金县、连平县、梅江区、兴宁市、梅县区、平远县、蕉岭县、大埔县、丰顺县、五华县、惠东县、龙门县、海丰县、陆河县、阳春市、信宜市、高州市、高要区、广宁县、德庆县、封开县、怀集县、英德市、连州市、佛冈县、清新区、连山县、连南县、阳山县、饶平县、潮安区、普宁市、揭西县、罗定市、新兴县、郁南县、云安区。

Notes: Counties(county-level cities and districts)in mountainous areas total 50, including Conghua District, Nan'ao County,Qujiang District,Nanxiong City, Lechang City,Renhua County, Shixing County, Wengyuan County, Xinfeng County, Ruyuan County, Dongyuan County, Heping County, Longchuan County, Zijin County, Lianping County, Meijiang District, Xingning City,Meixian County, Pingyuan County,Jiaoling County,Dabu County,Fengshun County,Wuhua County,Huidong County,Longmen County,Haifeng County,Luhe County,Yangchun City,Xinyi City,Gaozhou City, Gaoyao City, Guangning County,Deqing County, Fengkai County, Huaiji County,Yingde City, Lianzhou City, Fogang County, Qingxin County,Lianshan County, Liannan County,Yangshan County, Raoping County, Chao'an District, Puning City, Jiexi County, Luoding City, Xinxing County, Yunan County, and Yun'an District.

21-11 少数民族县主要经济指标（2017年）
Main Economic Indicators of Minority Counties（2017）

指　　标	Item	合计 Total	乳源县 Ruyuan County	连山县 Lianshan County	连南县 Liannan County
土地面积（平方公里）	Land Area (sq.km)	4758	2299	1218	1241
年末户籍总人口（万人）	Total Population with Residence Registration at the Year-end (10000 persons)	52.51	22.66	12.34	17.51
少数民族人口（万人）	Population of Minority Nationalities (10000 persons)	20.49	2.65	7.96	9.88
年末就业人员（万人）	Employed Persons at the Year-end (10000 persons)	22.40	9.63	4.86	7.91
地区生产总值（亿元）	Gross Domestic Product (100 million yuan)	158.19	82.65	31.45	44.08
第一产业	Primary Industry	23.42	6.57	7.90	8.95
第二产业	Secondary Industry	59.02	39.82	8.30	10.91
第三产业	Tertiary Industry	75.75	36.26	15.26	24.23
人均生产总值（元）	Per Capita Gross Domestic Product (yuan)	38085	44295	33351	32788
地区生产总值指数（上年=100）	Index of Gross Domestic Product (preceding year=100)	109.6	100.1	104.0	105.9
第一产业	Primary Industry	103.8	109.5	103.4	105.4
第二产业	Secondary Industry	108.2	87.3	91.3	100.9
第三产业	Tertiary Industry	112.4	103.0	110.6	109.9
人均生产总值指数（上年=100）	Index of Per Capita Gross Domestic Product (preceding year=100)	103.6	108.6	99.7	103.6
公路通车里程（公里）	Total Length of Highways in Operation (km)	4857	2044	1069	1744
本地电话年末用户（户）	Number of Subscribers of Local Telephones at the Year-end (subscriber)	40589	24100	6404	10085
#乡村	Subscribers in Rural Areas	18482	13351	1626	3505
移动电话年末用户（户）	Number of Subscribers of Mobile Telephones at the Year-end (subscriber)	344566	153500	82811	108255
固定资产投资额（亿元）	Investment in Fixed Assets (100 million yuan)	92	75	6	11
#房地产开发投资（亿元）	Investment in Real Estate Development (100 million yuan)	6	4	1	1
社会消费品零售总额（亿元）	Total Retail Sales of Consumer Goods (100 million yuan)	40.18	24.24	6.78	9.16
地方一般公共预算收入（亿元）	Local Public Budgetary Revenue (100 million yuan)	7.88	5.63	1.00	1.25
地方一般公共预算支出（亿元）	Local Public Budgetary Expenditure (100 million yuan)	53.34	26.88	10.22	16.26
城镇单位在岗职工年平均工资(元)	Annual Average Wage of Staff and Workers (yuan)	68733	64601	75712	71870
农村常住居民人均可支配收入(元)	Per Capita Net Income of Rural Permanent Households (yuan)		13001	12005	12049
普通中学（所）	Number of Regular Secondary Schools (unit)	28	8	9	11
在校学生数（人）	Number of Students Enrolled in Regular Secondary Schools (person)	21312	9491	4384	7437
小学（所）	Number of Primary Schools (unit)	54	13	10	31
在校学生数（人）	Number of Students Enrolled in Primary Schools (person)	38786	16437	8692	13657

二十二、县（市、区）主要经济指标

COUNTIES AND DISTRICTS UNDER CITY ADMINISTRATION

二十二　县（市、区）主要经济指标

简要说明

一、本篇资料反映广东县(市、区)经济发展基本情况，主要包括：各县(市)区的地区生产总值、工农业总产值、主要农产品产量、固定资产投资、消费品零售总额、就业人员和工资水平、财政收支等内容。

二、本篇资料由广东省统计局各有关专业处整理提供，综合处负责编辑。

三、本篇资料依据国家统计局制定的各有关专业年度报表制度填报汇总而成。

四、本篇各县(市、区)生产总值、产值、财政类指标数据汇总数不等于全省数。

22 Counties and Districts Under City Administration

Brief Introduction

Ⅰ. The data in this chapter show the basic conditions of the economic development of counties and districts under city administration in Guangdong Province, mainly including gross domestic product, gross output value of industry and agriculture, output of major farm products, investment in fixed assets, total retail sales of consumer goods, number and wages of fully employed staff and workers, local government budgetary revenue and expenditure etc.

Ⅱ. The data in this chapter are prepared and provided by the related specialized divisions and compiled by the Division of Comprehensive Statistics of Statistics Bureau of Guangdong Province.

Ⅲ. The data in this chapter are compiled on the basis of data in accordance with related specialized annual report schemes formulated by the National Bureau of Statistics.

Ⅳ. The tabulated data on gross domestic product, output value and government finance of the counties and districts in this chapter do not sum up to the provincial total.

22−1 各县(市、区)地区生产总值
Gross Domestic Product by County (County-level City and District)

县(市、区)	County (County-level City and District)	地区生产总值(万元) Gross Domestic Product(10000 yuan) 2016	2017	指数(上年=100) Index (preceding year=100) 2016	2017
广州市	Guangzhou				
越秀区	Yuexiu District	29213258	31544843	107.5	106.1
海珠区	Haizhu District	15697877	17379262	108.0	107.5
荔湾区	Liwan District	10872190	11592657	106.3	105.1
天河区	Tianhe District	38470573	42856173	109.0	109.6
白云区	Baiyun District	16451114	18154721	107.5	105.8
黄埔区	Huangpu District	30178184	32422306	105.7	106.6
花都区	Panyu District	11854815	12899249	108.4	108.6
番禺区	Huadu District	17759172	19722430	108.2	107.9
南沙区	Nansha District	12986982	13787250	113.7	110.4
从化区	Conghua District	3766338	4001046	107.6	104.5
增城区	Zengcheng District	10571173	10671579	108.4	100.7
深圳市	Shenzhen				
福田区	Futian District	35745612	38205692	108.7	108.2
罗湖区	Luohu District	19762459	21616969	109.1	108.4
盐田区	Yantian District	5402693	5859975	108.8	108.6
南山区	Nanshan District	39784758	46177993	109.3	109.1
宝安区	Baoan District	38132793	43054385	109.0	109.3
龙岗区	Longgang District	37815179	42023904	109.7	109.5
龙华区	Longhua District	18845820	21394243	108.1	108.8
坪山区	Pingshan District	5307729	6079395	113.1	112.1
珠海市	Zhuhai				
香洲区	Xiangzhou District	14888863	17564229	109.2	110.6
金湾区	Jinwan District	4652700	5627033	107.0	111.4
斗门区	Doumen District	3128634	3560533	106.4	110.8
汕头市	Shantou				
金平区	Jinping District	4296001	4830897	109.1	110.0
龙湖区	Longhu District	3110593	3573549	108.8	110.1
澄海区	Chenghai District	4254975	4783764	109.8	109.7
濠江区	Haojiang District	886388	1042286	108.2	111.7
潮阳区	Chaoyang District	3702305	4127918	106.3	108.6
潮南区	Chaonan District	3509173	3923002	109.7	108.9
南澳县	Nanao County	200985	224091	106.0	106.1
佛山市	Foshan				
禅城区	Chancheng District	16049205	17224961	107.9	107.8
南海区	Nanhai District	24434657	26678921	108.0	108.4
顺德区	Shunde District	28432244	30159062	108.2	108.3
高明区	Gaoming District	7665106	8413139	107.9	108.2
三水区	Sanshui District	10984623	11509091	108.4	108.5
韶关市	Shaoguan				
浈江区	Zhengjiang District	2113964	2288424	105.5	106.1
武江区	Wujiang District	2133838	2302093	105.4	106.1
曲江区	Qujiang District	1502152	1792694	107.9	113.0
乐昌市	Lechang City	1065367	1146562	106.4	105.0
南雄市	Nanxiong City	1025312	1086427	107.4	105.2
仁化县	Renhua County	986804	1089933	107.6	103.3
始兴县	Shixing County	698122	758146	107.6	106.9
翁源县	Wengyuan County	844190	917651	107.5	106.2
新丰县	Xinfeng County	636303	695173	108.3	107.7
乳源县	Ruyuan County	713727	826542	109.8	109.6

注：2016年起，海丰县不包含深圳市、汕尾市合作区地区生产总值数据。
Notes: Since 2016, GDP of Shenzhen-Shanwei Cooperation Zone is not inclueded in Shenzhen and Shanwei city.

22-1 续表 1 continued

县(市、区)	County (County-level City and District)	地区生产总值(万元) Gross Domestic Product(10000 yuan) 2016	2017	指数(上年=100) Index(preceding year=100) 2016	2017
河源市	Heyuan				
源城区	Urban District	3418677	3790678	107.6	104.8
东源县	Dongyuan County	1034512	1185454	107.6	106.8
和平县	Heping County	927462	1025906	106.9	105.7
龙川县	Longchuan County	1295328	1442858	106.4	106.9
紫金县	Zijin County	1165397	1268130	105.3	103.6
连平县	Lianping County	694721	748573	102.1	102.5
梅州市	Meizhou				
梅江区	Meijiang District	2168512	2313703	104.8	106.4
梅县区	Meixian District	1832813	1877635	107.9	105.3
兴宁市	Xingning City	1620855	1691850	106.2	105.8
平远县	Pingyuan County	751586	800917	108.6	106.3
蕉岭县	Jiaoling County	719913	772462	106.1	107.5
大埔县	Dabu County	791823	804731	109.4	107.4
丰顺县	Fengshun County	1009572	1031116	107.5	103.5
五华县	Wuhua County	1371003	1461838	108.9	106.4
惠州市	Huizhou				
惠城区	Huicheng District	12546084	13395199	106.1	104.6
惠阳区	Huiyang District	8684212	10683064	107.2	110.3
惠东县	Huidong County	6031854	6203838	112.5	108.0
博罗县	Boluo County	6200949	6400087	111.8	107.0
龙门县	Longmen County	1793149	1638583	112.0	86.4
汕尾市	Shanwei				
市城区	Urban District	1867784	1848563	107.4	96.6
陆丰市	Lufeng City	2454105	2688242	106.4	108.2
海丰县	Haifeng County	2415407	2671387	107.3	108.5
陆河县	Luhe County	523675	585943	111.3	108.5
东莞市	Dongguan	69370818	75820879	108.0	108.1
中山市	Zhongshan	32486835	34303130	107.6	106.6
江门市	Jiangmen			100.0	100.0
蓬江区	Pengjiang District	6041689	6487523	108.5	107.2
江海区	Jianghai District	1611204	1729000	107.8	109.0
新会区	Xinhui District	5446796	5976240	106.5	108.5
台山市	Taishan City	3576773	3978596	107.6	108.0
开平市	Kaiping City	3127968	3415674	107.1	107.5
鹤山市	Heshan City	2891604	3189488	108.2	108.8
恩平市	Enping City	1639329	1811135	107.1	108.2
阳江市	Yangjiang				
江城区	Jiangcheng District	2827989	2859266	106.5	106.2
阳东区	Yangdong District	2745304	2804750	106.5	106.3
阳春市	Yangchun City	3619454	3793330	104.7	105.9
阳西县	Yangxi County	2126155	2226542	106.8	105.9

22-1 续表 2 continued

县(市、区)	County (County-level City and District)	地区生产总值(万元) Gross Domestic Product(10000 yuan) 2016	2017	指数(上年=100) Index(preceding year=100) 2016	2017
湛江市	Zhanjiang				
赤坎区	Chikan District	2876807	3096907	107.4	106.6
霞山区	Xiashan District	3895803	4268999	107.1	105.1
麻章区	Mazhang District	1309540	1512160	111.7	110.1
坡头区	Potou District	2437433	2608901	107.2	103.4
雷州市	Leizhou City	2713894	2872707	107.0	104.0
廉江市	Lianjiang County	4649143	5062932	111.9	106.1
吴川市	Wuchuan City	2471486	2696818	110.1	107.8
遂溪县	Suixi County	2787065	2974640	106.9	106.2
徐闻县	Xuwen County	1533104	1721028	105.4	107.5
茂名市	Maoming				
茂南区	Maonan District	2432395	3055659	109.0	107.5
电白区	Dianbai District	5854977	6136922	108.1	108.0
信宜市	Xinyi City	4082084	4525097	108.0	109.0
高州市	Gaozhou City	5046301	5661186	109.0	109.6
化州市	Huazhou City	4411234	4874707	106.9	108.1
肇庆市	Zhaoqing				
端州区	Tuanzhou District	2085882	1979778	105.5	104.0
鼎湖区	Dinghu District	1055782	1084415	106.0	107.8
高要区	Gaoyao District	3949323	4004384	98.9	103.6
四会市	Sihui City	5816966	5285746	105.3	105.3
广宁县	Guangning County	1443654	1466467	106.2	105.8
德庆县	Deqing County	1292882	1336772	105.7	106.2
封开县	Fengkai County	1435841	1507757	104.2	102.0
怀集县	Huaiji County	2280630	2233556	104.5	107.0
清远市	Qingyuan				
清城区	Qingcheng District	4867144	5044678	107.2	104.3
清新区	Qingxin District	2586322	2710246	107.6	104.5
英德市	Yingde City	2542658	2720263	108.0	105.5
连州市	Lianzhou City	1372353	1460655	105.9	104.9
佛冈县	Fogang County	1176864	1296021	108.4	104.7
阳山县	Yangshan County	965270	969474	103.8	103.0
连山县	Lianshan County	309710	314503	102.9	100.1
连南县	Liannan County	425728	440830	107.8	104.0
潮州市	Chaozhou				
湘桥区	Xiangqiao District	2055704	2169036	107.2	106.6
潮安区	Chaoan District	5944927	5876479	107.3	107.2
饶平县	Raoping County	2415064	2505596	106.8	106.8
揭阳市	Jieyang			100.0	100.0
榕城区	Rongcheng District	4946738	5113303	106.6	104.7
揭东区	Jiedong District	4266927	4290403	107.0	104.8
普宁市	Puning City	6321272	6702453	106.3	105.2
揭西县	Jiexi County	2290312	2360996	106.3	104.7
惠来县	Huilai County	2524941	2645134	105.7	104.5
云浮市	Yunfu				
云城区	Yuncheng District	1019574	1101488	109.0	103.9
云安区	Yuanan District	782570	822645	108.5	104.1
罗定市	Luoding City	1943528	2043062	108.4	104.5
新兴县	Xinxing County	2431262	2455389	108.2	101.8
郁南县	Yunan County	998855	1036227	107.9	102.9

22−2　各县(市、区)三次产业地区生产总值

Gross Domestic Product by County (County-level City and District)

单位：万元　　(10000 yuan)

县(市、区)	County (County-level City and District)	第一产业 Primary Industry 2016	2017	第二产业 Secondary Industry 2016	2017	第三产业 Tertiary Industry 2016	2017
广州市	Guangzhou						
越秀区	Yuexiu District			541072	581654	28672186	30963189
海珠区	Haizhu District	7597	6335	2035359	2473571	13654921	14899356
荔湾区	Liwan District	47852	48068	2314367	2704368	8509971	8840221
天河区	Tianhe District	3924	2969	3858919	3405869	34607730	39447335
白云区	Baiyun District	283260	278883	3243881	3121162	12923973	14754676
黄埔区	Huangpu District	59252	55928	19057928	19544876	11061004	12821502
花都区	Panyu District	292180	339006	6461152	6736282	5101483	5823961
番禺区	Huadu District	277733	273202	6445232	7418599	11036207	12030629
南沙区	Nansha District	490387	525398	8431132	8277076	4065463	4984776
从化区	Conghua District	217394	216929	1693336	1671272	1855608	2112845
增城区	Zengcheng District	480737	457799	5047035	4175350	5043401	6038430
深圳市	Shenzhen						
福田区	Futian District	18766	17809	2270533	2171179	33456313	36016704
罗湖区	Luohu District	10501	9894	772410	828707	18979548	20778368
盐田区	Yantian District	807	899	848428	879351	4553458	4979725
南山区	Nanshan District	6171	17048	18760392	20783129	21018195	25377816
宝安区	Baoan District	24850	26002	20571920	23518385	17536023	19509998
龙岗区	Longgang District	11385	16997	25453877	28187227	12349917	13819680
龙华区	Longhua District	2528	2705	10776541	12321771	8066751	9069767
坪山区	Pingshan District	7832	8528	3652412	4219754	1647485	1851113
珠海市	Zhuhai						
香洲区	Xiangzhou District	26203	29388	6040075	6871723	8822585	10663118
金湾区	Jinwan District	68808	75854	3465822	4107003	1118070	1444176
斗门区	Doumen District	356533	383000	1639540	1893132	1132561	1284401
汕头市	Shantou						
金平区	Jinping District	32672	30571	1530292	1668270	2733037	3132056
龙湖区	Longhu District	72177	66810	1251143	1360984	1787273	2145755
澄海区	Chenghai District	319377	328397	2378834	2673807	1556764	1781560
濠江区	Haojiang District	77911	81516	570193	637580	238284	323190
潮阳区	Chaoyang District	233640	241602	2402261	2636760	1066404	1249556
潮南区	Chaonan District	201953	200886	2106602	2372549	1200618	1349567
南澳县	Nanao County	70662	78607	54292	59444	76031	86040
佛山市	Foshan						
禅城区	Chancheng District	3055	2667	7529884	7488358	8516267	9733936
南海区	Nanhai District	451510	447007	14377634	14850837	9605513	11381077
顺德区	Shunde District	451051	440186	16540028	16969464	11441165	12749412
高明区	Gaoming District	161139	160459	6055510	6448444	1448457	1804236
三水区	Sanshui District	275711	286155	8327556	8489350	2381356	2733586
韶关市	Shaoguan						
浈江区	Zhengjiang District	61637	62240	327605	355643	1724722	1870542
武江区	Wujiang District	57219	57193	902359	951626	1174260	1293273
曲江区	Qujiang District	131190	132316	815211	1039168	555751	621210
乐昌市	Lechang City	210437	217145	205288	208275	649641	721142
南雄市	Nanxiong City	255166	259954	218599	209784	551548	616689
仁化县	Renhua County	165386	173073	361428	425857	459989	491002
始兴县	Shixing County	175726	183313	210962	224287	311434	350547
翁源县	Wengyuan County	205671	220114	199171	215294	439347	482243
新丰县	Xinfeng County	104663	108202	213351	232345	318289	354626
乳源县	Ruyuan County	65206	65750	337912	398150	310609	362642

22-2 续表 1 continued

单位：万元 (10000 yuan)

县(市、区)	County (County-level City and District)	第一产业 Primary Industry 2016	2017	第二产业 Secondary Industry 2016	2017	第三产业 Tertiary Industry 2016	2017
河源市	Heyuan						
源城区	Urban District	27370	27558	1891734	2074447	1499573	1688672
东源县	Dongyuan County	173342	172622	415676	389947	445493	622886
和平县	Heping County	164000	167588	341632	369484	421830	488833
龙川县	Longchuan County	250455	252012	319723	381892	725150	808954
紫金县	Zijin County	255242	260744	324771	354417	585384	652970
连平县	Lianping County	130620	144023	192967	195033	371134	409516
梅州市	Meizhou						
梅江区	Meijiang District	91204	89463	1093909	1125634	983399	1098606
梅县区	Meixian District	438019	439564	690863	671724	703931	766347
兴宁市	Xingning City	413849	413116	395732	351378	811274	927356
平远县	Pingyuan County	110638	114050	272471	255077	368477	431790
蕉岭县	Jiaoling County	113022	114556	218177	227839	388714	430067
大埔县	Dabu County	197045	200220	242069	225155	352709	379356
丰顺县	Fengshun County	214138	214720	425348	405264	370086	411132
五华县	Wuhua County	290992	290532	370165	338676	709846	832630
惠州市	Huizhou						
惠城区	Huicheng District	266441	264398	6527835	6487575	5751808	6643226
惠阳区	Huiyang District	182728	178803	5750817	7201323	2750668	3302938
惠东县	Huidong County	416177	441767	2874446	2578590	2741232	3183481
博罗县	Boluo County	535764	520083	3393305	3396840	2271880	2483164
龙门县	Longmen County	228247	250610	821805	575778	743098	812195
汕尾市	Shanwei						
市城区	Urban District	195939	221524	920407	797800	751438	829239
陆丰市	Lufeng City	516993	548143	1054848	1184174	882264	955925
海丰县	Haifeng County	283650	302806	1039739	1184521	1092018	1184060
陆河县	Luhe County	116289	105455	83228	121289	324158	359199
东莞市	Dongguan	227590	228500	32683016	36632267	36460212	38960113
中山市	Zhongshan	609314	556391	17298470	17249686	14579051	16497053
江门市	Jiangmen						
蓬江区	Pengjiang District	65854	45348	2788704	2639466	3187131	3802709
江海区	Jianghai District	49623	43572	989545	1048257	572036	637171
新会区	Xinhui District	374146	392540	3124763	3376662	1947887	2207038
台山市	Taishan City	615505	649235	1881575	2117329	1079693	1212032
开平市	Kaiping City	290535	298190	1540049	1658345	1297384	1459139
鹤山市	Heshan City	221447	203270	1525749	1663087	1144408	1323131
恩平市	Enping City	176157	187775	550206	569004	912966	1054356
阳江市	Yangjiang						
江城区	Jiangcheng District	215738	225808	1222019	1189348	1390232	1444110
阳东区	Yangdong District	463814	489155	1457204	1436149	824285	879446
阳春市	Yangchun City	606889	603595	1177555	1209819	1835009	1979916
阳西县	Yangxi County	520208	539531	764330	755001	841617	932010

22-2 续表 2 continued

单位：万元 (10000 yuan)

县(市、区)	County (County-level City and District)	第一产业 Primary Industry 2016	2017	第二产业 Secondary Industry 2016	2017	第三产业 Tertiary Industry 2016	2017
湛江市	Zhanjiang						
赤坎区	Chikan District	15759	15575	476883	513652	2384165	2567680
霞山区	Xiashan District	21011	21849	1791715	1816227	2083077	2430922
麻章区	Mazhang District	210276	233941	816201	932562	283063	345657
坡头区	Potou District	171853	166872	1797017	1790619	468562	651410
雷州市	Leizhou City	1010778	1103989	329429	289841	1373687	1478878
廉江市	Lianjiang County	970780	985707	2094157	2372761	1584207	1704464
吴川市	Wuchuan City	283084	288039	1083099	1218400	1105304	1190378
遂溪县	Suixi County	1003295	1070753	788193	821873	995577	1082014
徐闻县	Xuwen County	709283	777642	109195	125897	714626	817489
茂名市	Maoming						
茂南区	Maonan District	225954	277206	951954	1070117	1254487	1708336
电白区	Dianbai District	1227279	1209491	2361082	2438181	2266616	2489250
信宜市	Xinyi City	940550	978255	1303804	1323075	1837730	2223767
高州市	Gaozhou City	1146926	1209224	1604352	1870641	2295023	2581321
化州市	Huazhou City	952179	1016617	1379879	1563958	2079176	2294132
肇庆市	Zhaoqing						
端州区	Tuanzhou District	3168	2337	862297	502805	1220417	1474637
鼎湖区	Dinghu District	156927	144814	570836	583982	328019	355618
高要区	Gaoyao District	730208	749705	2205148	1709391	1013967	1545287
四会市	Sihui City	519958	508859	3596086	2449153	1700922	2327733
广宁县	Guangning County	358763	386221	545872	455049	539019	625197
德庆县	Deqing County	264638	279338	510033	409460	518211	647974
封开县	Fengkai County	409099	435324	490469	487584	536273	584850
怀集县	Huaiji County	709734	747368	591642	412454	979254	1073735
清远市	Qingyuan						
清城区	Qingcheng District	235182	229557	2207830	1899581	2424132	2915540
清新区	Qingxin District	410607	417138	1016023	953573	1159692	1339535
英德市	Yingde City	494241	520398	844113	885400	1204304	1314465
连州市	Lianzhou City	352449	359742	307029	323115	712874	777798
佛冈县	Fogang County	129445	137347	545365	584417	502054	574257
阳山县	Yangshan County	345440	343027	192491	189271	427339	437176
连山县	Lianshan County	74004	78995	92056	82950	143650	152558
连南县	Liannan County	88728	89479	110668	109056	226332	242295
潮州市	Chaozhou						
湘桥区	Xiangqiao District	39312	40381	926105	853228	1090286	1275428
潮安区	Chaoan District	192346	178938	3670081	3393959	2082500	2303582
饶平县	Raoping County	449097	442921	1010694	964084	955273	1098591
揭阳市	Jieyang						
榕城区	Rongcheng District	122939	116107	2947924	2934910	1875875	2062287
揭东区	Jiedong District	325745	329325	2801600	2685583	1139582	1275495
普宁市	Puning City	307079	312324	4153511	4274291	1860682	2115838
揭西县	Jiexi County	328506	330447	1259059	1258485	702747	772064
惠来县	Huilai County	457542	469481	1455286	1490099	612113	685554
云浮市	Yunfu						
云城区	Yuncheng District	110755	117949	486557	462307	422262	521232
云安区	Yuanan District	109291	120736	460904	448285	212375	253624
罗定市	Luoding City	404289	450891	767125	755394	772114	836777
新兴县	Xinxing County	520195	527331	950610	787705	960457	1140353
郁南县	Yunan County	200346	209583	297818	337581	500691	489063

22-3 各县(市、区)三次产业地区生产总值指数

Gross Domestic Product by County (County-level City and District)

上年=100 (preceding year=100)

县(市、区)	County (County-level City and District)	第一产业 Primary Industry		第二产业 Secondary Industry		第三产业 Tertiary Industry	
		2016	2017	2016	2017	2016	2017
广州市	Guangzhou						
越秀区	Yuexiu District			97.5	100.3	107.7	106.2
海珠区	Haizhu District	77.1	75.2	106.8	139.2	108.3	102.5
荔湾区	Liwan District	106.6	106.6	100.3	104.4	108.0	105.3
天河区	Tianhe District	89.3	88.3	104.7	103.3	109.7	110.4
白云区	Baiyun District	100.7	100.6	104.5	105.7	108.6	106.0
黄埔区	Huangpu District	100.0	100.0	102.4	105.4	112.6	109.0
花都区	Panyu District	112.1	117.7	110.3	110.0	105.5	106.0
番禺区	Huadu District	95.7	95.1	111.7	113.1	106.6	105.2
南沙区	Nansha District	103.6	103.6	109.0	108.4	128.5	116.2
从化区	Conghua District	101.7	95.5	106.8	103.4	109.1	106.5
增城区	Zengcheng District	98.7	100.5	104.4	93.2	114.2	109.1
深圳市	Shenzhen						
福田区	Futian District	73.3	90.9	106.9	104.9	108.9	108.4
罗湖区	Luohu District	189.2	87.8	105.5	102.5	109.3	108.6
盐田区	Yantian District	182.8	112.4	105.8	103.1	109.4	109.6
南山区	Nanshan District	57.3	272.7	104.8	107.3	114.7	111.0
宝安区	Baoan District	130.4	101.5	109.2	109.9	108.8	108.6
龙岗区	Longgang District	110.1	149.5	110.9	110.3	107.6	107.8
龙华区	Longhua District	53.2	100.6	105.2	109.9	112.4	107.2
坪山区	Pingshan District	115.0	111.7	118.4	113.4	101.8	108.7
珠海市	Zhuhai						
香洲区	Xiangzhou District	83.1	107.3	107.6	110.3	110.5	110.9
金湾区	Jinwan District	105.9	107.6	108.5	110.2	102.5	115.5
斗门区	Doumen District	91.9	109.1	107.1	114.9	111.0	105.3
汕头市	Shantou						
金平区	Jinping District	102.1	98.2	110.6	106.2	108.4	112.4
龙湖区	Longhu District	102.8	96.0	107.1	109.2	110.4	111.3
澄海区	Chenghai District	103.0	105.2	109.7	110.0	111.6	110.2
濠江区	Haojiang District	101.3	102.1	108.7	109.8	109.7	119.6
潮阳区	Chaoyang District	105.3	103.5	105.9	109.6	107.6	107.5
潮南区	Chaonan District	102.3	102.7	111.5	110.3	107.7	107.3
南澳县	Nanao County	102.0	104.5	104.0	105.9	109.9	107.7
佛山市	Foshan						
禅城区	Chancheng District	113.6	89.9	106.2	105.8	109.3	109.6
南海区	Nanhai District	100.6	102.0	107.0	108.4	110.0	108.8
顺德区	Shunde District	101.9	101.3	107.4	108.8	109.6	107.7
高明区	Gaoming District	104.0	102.9	107.5	107.9	110.0	110.1
三水区	Sanshui District	104.5	103.0	107.9	108.9	110.5	107.5
韶关市	Shaoguan						
浈江区	Zhengjiang District	103.8	103.7	91.8	104.6	108.7	106.5
武江区	Wujiang District	102.3	103.2	102.4	103.6	108.1	108.1
曲江区	Qujiang District	102.0	104.0	108.5	116.6	108.5	109.8
乐昌市	Lechang City	104.2	103.9	96.1	95.2	110.9	108.5
南雄市	Nanxiong City	103.1	104.1	105.2	95.3	110.2	109.5
仁化县	Renhua County	104.1	105.9	99.8	102.9	116.1	102.7
始兴县	Shixing County	105.1	104.8	106.4	105.3	109.9	109.0
翁源县	Wengyuan County	104.3	104.9	100.2	104.4	112.7	107.6
新丰县	Xinfeng County	107.4	105.0	103.6	105.0	112.0	110.5
乳源县	Ruyuan County	104.5	103.8	110.7	108.2	110.0	112.4

22-3 续表 1 continued

上年=100 (preceding year=100)

县(市、区)	County (County-level City and District)	第一产业 Primary Industry 2016	2017	第二产业 Secondary Industry 2016	2017	第三产业 Tertiary Industry 2016	2017
河源市	Heyuan						
源城区	Urban District	97.8	105.4	107.7	102.3	107.7	108.2
东源县	Dongyuan County	101.6	102.8	107.9	87.0	109.7	128.5
和平县	Heping County	105.6	104.4	101.7	101.0	112.5	110.5
龙川县	Longchuan County	101.5	102.7	98.2	111.2	113.0	106.4
紫金县	Zijin County	101.5	104.3	96.3	100.8	113.7	105.1
连平县	Lianping County	104.2	108.8	89.0	94.3	110.7	104.9
梅州市	Meizhou						
梅江区	Meijiang District	102.3	102.3	103.6	103.3	106.4	110.2
梅县区	Meixian District	102.1	102.1	108.7	103.9	110.8	108.4
兴宁市	Xingning City	103.1	103.1	106.2	101.0	107.8	109.6
平远县	Pingyuan County	102.4	102.4	110.4	104.9	109.2	108.7
蕉岭县	Jiaoling County	102.4	102.4	108.9	106.8	105.6	109.3
大埔县	Dabu County	103.8	103.8	114.8	107.1	108.8	109.4
丰顺县	Fengshun County	103.4	103.4	105.6	99.3	112.7	108.7
五华县	Wuhua County	102.6	102.6	111.3	106.1	110.3	108.0
惠州市	Huizhou						
惠城区	Huicheng District	103.3	104.5	104.4	99.5	108.4	110.6
惠阳区	Huiyang District	102.7	103.2	107.1	109.6	107.8	112.3
惠东县	Huidong County	106.1	105.5	115.8	105.1	110.1	111.6
博罗县	Boluo County	103.4	98.9	115.9	106.5	107.8	109.4
龙门县	Longmen County	105.9	107.8	115.7	67.0	109.6	103.8
汕尾市	Shanwei						
市城区	Urban District	99.2	104.0	106.2	84.9	111.5	110.5
陆丰市	Lufeng City	103.5	104.6	105.9	110.9	108.8	106.7
海丰县	Haifeng County	103.3	107.8	107.7	110.8	108.0	106.4
陆河县	Luhe County	104.4	103.0	126.7	114.3	108.8	108.2
东莞市	Dongguan	106.0	102.1	108.6	110.7	107.6	105.7
中山市	Zhongshan	98.8	93.6	106.2	104.8	109.8	109.3
江门市	Jiangmen						
蓬江区	Pengjiang District	93.0	71.3	108.2	98.5	109.1	115.8
江海区	Jianghai District	103.3	89.4	108.0	111.2	107.8	106.6
新会区	Xinhui District	103.1	103.4	104.9	110.1	110.1	106.7
台山市	Taishan City	105.0	103.8	108.3	108.8	107.8	108.7
开平市	Kaiping City	104.3	106.0	107.1	107.6	107.7	107.7
鹤山市	Heshan City	105.0	96.4	106.5	109.0	111.3	110.7
恩平市	Enping City	103.3	105.9	104.5	108.0	109.7	108.7
阳江市	Yangjiang	100.0	100.0	100.0	100.0	100.0	100.0
江城区	Jiangcheng District	104.0	102.4	102.2	106.1	111.8	106.7
阳东区	Yangdong District	103.1	103.5	103.8	106.9	114.6	106.6
阳春市	Yangchun City	93.4	101.4	102.0	106.0	111.2	107.3
阳西县	Yangxi County	103.3	102.8	107.4	107.7	108.4	105.9

22-3 续表 2 continued

上年=100 (preceding year=100)

县(市、区)	County (County-level City and District)	第一产业 Primary Industry 2016	第一产业 Primary Industry 2017	第二产业 Secondary Industry 2016	第二产业 Secondary Industry 2017	第三产业 Tertiary Industry 2016	第三产业 Tertiary Industry 2017
湛江市	Zhanjiang						
赤坎区	Chikan District	89.4	97.9	94.7	106.5	110.5	106.6
霞山区	Xiashan District	86.7	98.7	110.4	95.5	104.5	114.0
麻章区	Mazhang District	113.7	105.5	113.6	108.6	105.3	118.2
坡头区	Potou District	104.5	96.7	105.9	99.9	113.5	118.8
雷州市	Leizhou City	104.7	105.3	100.0	99.4	110.9	104.5
廉江市	Lianjiang County	107.3	103.0	115.0	107.9	110.8	105.8
吴川市	Wuchuan City	106.7	102.0	114.1	106.1	107.2	111.1
遂溪县	Suixi County	104.0	104.3	104.7	105.4	112.0	108.8
徐闻县	Xuwen County	100.7	106.7	93.6	108.9	112.8	108.0
茂名市	Maoming						
茂南区	Maonan District	100.3	102.5	109.5	105.5	110.1	109.8
电白区	Dianbai District	104.2	105.1	109.0	108.4	109.1	108.8
信宜市	Xinyi City	103.1	104.7	109.1	109.0	109.6	111.0
高州市	Gaozhou City	103.8	105.9	110.7	113.6	110.3	108.6
化州市	Huazhou City	104.2	106.1	106.8	110.8	108.1	107.1
肇庆市	Zhaoqing						
端州区	Tuanzhou District	69.3	80.9	104.6	101.7	106.2	105.6
鼎湖区	Dinghu District	100.1	97.5	104.7	110.3	111.6	108.1
高要区	Gaoyao District	101.4	103.4	95.0	98.2	106.0	114.9
四会市	Sihui City	99.3	99.3	105.0	105.0	107.6	107.6
广宁县	Guangning County	104.3	105.6	111.7	106.1	102.4	105.7
德庆县	Deqing County	103.9	103.9	105.7	107.7	106.6	105.9
封开县	Fengkai County	103.9	105.7	106.7	102.4	102.1	98.7
怀集县	Huaiji County	105.5	105.4	103.2	109.7	104.8	106.1
清远市	Qingyuan						
清城区	Qingcheng District	102.8	101.0	106.0	93.0	108.8	115.2
清新区	Qingxin District	104.6	103.2	111.4	92.3	105.4	116.2
英德市	Yingde City	102.2	106.7	114.9	104.8	105.6	105.6
连州市	Lianzhou City	106.2	106.0	110.3	101.2	104.0	106.0
佛冈县	Fogang County	104.3	108.3	111.1	99.3	106.3	110.1
阳山县	Yangshan County	103.7	103.1	104.7	96.7	103.5	106.0
连山县	Lianshan County	109.6	105.1	103.1	87.3	99.5	106.5
连南县	Liannan County	106.2	103.4	95.1	91.3	116.5	110.6
潮州市	Chaozhou						
湘桥区	Xiangqiao District	101.8	104.7	107.1	104.6	107.6	108.4
潮安区	Chaoan District	104.0	101.8	106.6	105.6	109.0	110.6
饶平县	Raoping County	112.9	102.0	103.1	106.6	108.2	109.3
揭阳市	Jieyang	100.0	100.0	100.0	100.0	100.0	100.0
榕城区	Rongcheng District	103.5	96.8	105.3	102.1	109.1	109.3
揭东区	Jiedong District	104.4	105.8	105.8	102.3	111.0	111.3
普宁市	Puning City	104.4	104.2	106.2	103.6	106.7	108.9
揭西县	Jiexi County	104.5	103.7	105.7	103.7	108.2	106.7
惠来县	Huilai County	103.4	103.0	105.0	103.3	109.1	108.4
云浮市	Yunfu						
云城区	Yuncheng District	102.3	106.2	109.4	95.9	110.3	113.0
云安区	Yuanan District	102.2	104.7	109.1	98.1	111.0	117.1
罗定市	Luoding City	104.5	105.1	109.7	98.8	109.2	110.2
新兴县	Xinxing County	102.0	102.8	109.2	91.2	110.7	112.9
郁南县	Yunan County	101.6	101.4	88.4	113.8	128.8	96.7

22-4 各县(市、区)人均地区生产总值及指数

Per Capita Gross Domestic Product and Growth Rates by County (County-level City and District)

县(市、区)	County (County-level City and District)	绝对数（元） Absolute Figure (yuan)		指数(上年=100) Index(Preceding year=100)	
		2016	2017	2016	2017
广州市	Guangzhou				
越秀区	Yuexiu District	252056	271365	106.8	105.8
海珠区	Haizhu District	96555	105297	106.7	105.9
荔湾区	Liwan District	117741	123655	104.4	103.5
天河区	Tianhe District	242197	257479	104.8	104.6
白云区	Baiyun District	67904	72412	104.1	102.2
黄埔区	Huangpu District	304646	298328	94.9	97.2
花都区	Panyu District	114495	121097	104.2	105.6
番禺区	Huadu District	111511	117381	102.3	102.3
南沙区	Nansha District	193374	195232	109.3	105.0
从化区	Conghua District	59755	62644	106.3	103.1
增城区	Zengcheng District	93319	91070	104.8	97.4
深圳市	Shenzhen				
福田区	Futian District	242977	249474	103.4	103.9
罗湖区	Luohu District	199661	212849	106.3	105.6
盐田区	Yantian District	241353	252749	106.4	104.8
南山区	Nanshan District	300546	332108	100.2	103.8
宝安区	Baoan District	109382	117576	103.7	104.0
龙岗区	Longgang District	169093	178457	105.4	104.0
龙华区	Longhua District	123139	135703	104.1	105.6
坪山区	Pingshan District	138946	145457	101.8	102.4
珠海市	Zhuhai				
香洲区	Xiangzhou District	155335	176118	107.1	106.3
金湾区	Jinwan District	177178	205968	105.2	107.1
斗门区	Doumen District	72155	79149	104.6	106.8
汕头市	Shantou				
金平区	Jinping District	51394	57572	108.6	109.6
龙湖区	Longhu District	56153	64169	108.3	109.5
澄海区	Chenghai District	51629	57785	109.3	109.2
濠江区	Haojiang District	32075	37506	107.7	111.1
潮阳区	Chaoyang District	22040	24441	105.8	108.0
潮南区	Chaonan District	26317	29260	109.2	108.3
南澳县	Nanao County	32365	35970	105.5	105.8
佛山市	Foshan				
禅城区	Chancheng District	142343	150082	106.6	105.9
南海区	Nanhai District	90216	97035	107.2	106.8
顺德区	Shunde District	111938	116914	107.4	106.6
高明区	Gaoming District	177845	193028	107.5	107.0
三水区	Sanshui District	171715	177843	108.0	107.2
韶关市	Shaoguan				
浈江区	Zhengjiang District	51991	55911	104.7	105.4
武江区	Wujiang District	68667	73257	104.4	104.9
曲江区	Qujiang District	47597	56330	107.1	112.0
乐昌市	Lechang City	25796	27558	105.6	104.3
南雄市	Nanxiong City	30925	32518	106.5	104.4
仁化县	Renhua County	47386	51951	106.8	102.5
始兴县	Shixing County	32707	35238	106.9	106.0
翁源县	Wengyuan County	24462	26396	106.6	105.4
新丰县	Xinfeng County	29651	32110	107.4	106.8
乳源县	Ruyuan County	38601	44295	108.9	108.6

22−4 续表 1 continued

县(市、区)	County (County-level City and District)	绝对数（元） Absolute Figure (yuan)		指数(上年=100) Index(Preceding year=100)	
		2016	2017	2016	2017
河源市	Heyuan				
源城区	Urban District	70408	77614	107.2	104.2
东源县	Dongyuan County	22543	25754	107.3	106.4
和平县	Heping County	23760	26215	106.6	105.5
龙川县	Longchuan County	17872	19867	106.1	106.7
紫金县	Zijin County	17489	18990	105.0	103.4
连平县	Lianping County	19776	21269	101.9	102.3
梅州市	Meizhou				
梅江区	Meijiang District	51564	54795	104.4	105.9
梅县区	Meixian District	33906	34611	107.5	104.9
兴宁市	Xingning City	16411	17068	105.8	105.4
平远县	Pingyuan County	32085	34111	108.3	106.0
蕉岭县	Jiaoling County	34225	36601	105.7	107.1
大埔县	Dabu County	20707	20989	109.0	107.1
丰顺县	Fengshun County	20551	20894	106.9	103.0
五华县	Wuhua County	12650	13426	108.4	105.9
惠州市	Huizhou				
惠城区	Huicheng District	76475	81504	105.6	104.5
惠阳区	Huiyang District	107979	131971	106.3	109.6
惠东县	Huidong County	64609	66369	112.0	107.8
博罗县	Boluo County	57969	59778	111.4	106.9
龙门县	Longmen County	56531	51585	111.7	86.2
汕尾市	Shanwei				
市城区	Urban District	44802	44112	106.9	96.1
陆丰市	Lufeng City	17583	19178	105.8	107.7
海丰县	Haifeng County	32143	35483	106.9	108.3
陆河县	Luhe County	18125	20170	110.8	108.0
东莞市	Dongguan	84007	91329	108.6	107.5
中山市	Zhongshan	100897	105711	107.0	105.8
江门市	Jiangmen				
蓬江区	Pengjiang District	81760	86929	107.8	106.1
江海区	Jianghai District	61344	64939	106.8	107.5
新会区	Xinhui District	62932	68831	106.1	108.1
台山市	Taishan City	37621	41810	107.5	107.9
开平市	Kaiping City	44146	48095	106.8	107.3
鹤山市	Heshan City	57390	62959	107.8	108.2
恩平市	Enping City	32689	35960	106.6	107.7
阳江市	Yangjiang				
江城区	Jiangcheng District	51942	52191	105.9	105.5
阳东区	Yangdong District	59765	60683	105.9	105.7
阳春市	Yangchun City	41163	42872	104.1	105.3
阳西县	Yangxi County	45460	47308	106.2	105.2

22-4 续表 2 continued

县(市、区)	County (County-level City and District)	绝对数（元） Absolute Figure (yuan) 2016	2017	指数(上年=100) Index(Preceding year=100) 2016	2017
湛江市	Zhanjiang				
赤坎区	Chikan District	91139	97559	106.9	106.0
霞山区	Xiashan District	76982	83926	106.7	104.5
麻章区	Mazhang District	48117	55301	109.8	109.6
坡头区	Potou District	70065	74632	106.8	102.9
雷州市	Leizhou City	18339	19332	106.5	103.6
廉江市	Lianjiang County	31114	33741	110.4	105.7
吴川市	Wuchuan City	25674	27897	108.8	107.3
遂溪县	Suixi County	30297	32202	106.3	105.8
徐闻县	Xuwen County	21215	23716	105.7	107.0
茂名市	Maoming				
茂南区	Maonan District	51509	50359	108.7	106.3
电白区	Dianbai District	35137	39793	107.8	107.7
信宜市	Xinyi City	42018	45847	107.0	107.3
高州市	Gaozhou City	37062	41141	108.3	108.5
化州市	Huazhou City	35232	38476	106.1	106.8
肇庆市	Zhaoqing				
端州区	Tuanzhou District	105241	98870	104.9	102.9
鼎湖区	Dinghu District	61347	62287	105.4	106.6
高要区	Gaoyao District	50461	50891	98.3	103.0
四会市	Sihui City	100945	90836	105.4	104.3
广宁县	Guangning County	32941	33268	105.5	105.2
德庆县	Deqing County	36626	37634	105.1	105.5
封开县	Fengkai County	34923	36468	103.5	101.4
怀集县	Huaiji County	27047	26367	103.8	106.5
清远市	Qingyuan				
清城区	Qingcheng District	57726	59626	106.8	103.9
清新区	Qingxin District	35644	37229	107.2	104.2
英德市	Yingde City	25997	27724	107.6	105.2
连州市	Lianzhou City	35958	38157	108.6	104.6
佛冈县	Fogang County	37426	41078	108.0	104.4
阳山县	Yangshan County	26134	26156	103.5	102.6
连山县	Lianshan County	32965	33351	102.5	99.7
连南县	Liannan County	31771	32788	107.5	103.6
潮州市	Chaozhou				
湘桥区	Xiangqiao District	36385	38211	109.9	109.6
潮安区	Chaoan District	47316	49480	108.6	108.5
饶平县	Raoping County	27765	28680	108.5	106.6
揭阳市	Jieyang				
榕城区	Rongcheng District	50377	51909	106.0	104.4
揭东区	Jiedong District	43444	43467	106.2	104.4
普宁市	Puning City	29829	31630	106.0	105.2
揭西县	Jiexi County	26758	27511	105.5	104.4
惠来县	Huilai County	22214	23190	105.3	104.1
云浮市	Yunfu				
云城区	Yuncheng District	27482	29424	102.0	103.0
云安区	Yuanan District	27716	28875	107.7	103.2
罗定市	Luoding City	20200	21043	109.9	103.6
新兴县	Xinxing County	54348	54281	107.6	100.7
郁南县	Yunan County	24551	25240	107.2	101.9

注：本表中，绝对数按当年价格计算，指数按可比价格计算。
Note: In this table, the absolute figure are calculated at current prices,and the index are calculated at comparable prices.

22-5 各县(市、区)工、农业总产值

Gross Output Value of Industry and Agriculture by County (County-level City and District)

单位：万元 (10000 yuan)

县(市、区)	County (County-level City and District)	工业总产值 Gross Output Value of Industry		农业总产值 Gross Output Value of Agriculture	
		2016	2017	2016	2017
广州市	Guangzhou				
越秀区	Yuexiu District	372823	375458		
海珠区	Haizhu District	1789708	3099475	13959	9906
荔湾区	Liwan District	3535698	3919609	73724	73718
天河区	Tianhe District	7989646	8106284	48927	48503
白云区	Baiyun District	8651867	7374388	537175	541009
黄埔区	Huangpu District	72820203	73917371	127640	123949
番禺区	Panyu District	19693349	19302761	475287	467371
花都区	Huadu District	21361538	23272371	526534	600058
南沙区	Nansha District	30666985	23073774	793517	833414
从化区	Conghua District	6935329	3196248	401301	416389
增城区	Zengcheng District	15248333	11873923	874722	852647
深圳市	Shenzhen				
福田区	Futian District	9922858	10217941	41295	45757
罗湖区	Luohu District	9397116	10015650	15386	23634
盐田区	Yantian District	6625540	5332964	1472	2196
南山区	Nanshan District	49622037	56390511	26452	28722
宝安区	Baoan District	112051185	89909149	52125	54410
龙岗区	Longgang District	85304208	85721918	38496	39964
龙华区	Longhua District		46996169		5140
坪山区	Pingshan District		16147263		17179
珠海市	Zhuhai				
香洲区	Xiangzhou District	19887186	16894888	63044	79218
金湾区	Jinwan District	15347825	15705239	112882	140140
斗门区	Doumen District	8298761	6835481	656828	710493
汕头市	Shantou				
金平区	Jinping District	5370723	5803550	52114	51610
龙湖区	Longhu District	4314435	4599196	132403	127870
澄海区	Chenghai District	6983350	7522463	595368	623347
濠江区	Haojiang District	1387874	1683949	110815	116868
潮阳区	Chaoyang District	8619231	8584036	483926	488890
潮南区	Chaonan District	6336118	6965707	297735	296681
南澳县	Nanao County	26305	20540	178509	195994
佛山市	Foshan				
禅城区	Chancheng District	26717265	22913911	5622	5120
南海区	Nanhai District	57008330	58788600	823496	822607
顺德区	Shunde District	67458467	66138624	896182	879292
高明区	Gaoming District	28807088	29857798	345666	340849
三水区	Sanshui District	31882094	32456394	655419	655425
韶关市	Shaoguan				
浈江区	Zhengjiang District	753177	876265	110331	109972
武江区	Wujiang District	2113575	2116935	98224	96784
曲江区	Qujiang District	2918779	4081171	228439	226567
乐昌市	Lechang City	551024	319160	351043	357569
南雄市	Nanxiong City	1616281	334234	435121	436751
仁化县	Renhua County	803330	801470	273846	282555
始兴县	Shixing County	891885	459600	288808	296705
翁源县	Wengyuan County	872629	415892	327458	346583
新丰县	Xinfeng County	920906	476778	167967	171631
乳源县	Ruyuan County	933792	1105649	106708	106247

22-5 续表 1 continued

单位：万元 (10000 yuan)

县(市、区)	County (County-level City and District)	工业总产值 Gross Output Value of Industry 2016	2017	农业总产值 Gross Output Value of Agriculture 2016	2017
河源市	Heyuan				
源城区	Urban District	8448470	8346544	49143	48429
东源县	Dongyuan County	1688911	1355383	279144	280527
和平县	Heping County	1839111	1190002	259494	264262
龙川县	Longchuan County	1164270	1005964	387608	388939
紫金县	Zijin County	1484442	1132828	395988	407545
连平县	Lianping County	1366637	428646	201438	219299
梅州市	Meizhou				
梅江区	Meijiang District	1842982	2015823	155149	151166
梅县区	Meixian District	1808780	1465289	702890	703769
兴宁市	Xingning City	632604	406177	669024	664485
平远县	Pingyuan County	560440	501879	183943	187593
蕉岭县	Jiaoling County	454821	515691	190720	191438
大埔县	Dabu County	454062	449819	315272	319581
丰顺县	Fengshun County	1019192	650517	367605	367291
五华县	Wuhua County	683407	238191	504896	501214
惠州市	Huizhou				
惠城区	Huicheng District	30678564	34391780	434640	428681
惠阳区	Huiyang District	21128282	25943173	285577	279320
惠东县	Huidong County	7946085	6132504	673503	713414
博罗县	Boluo County	14112431	13891892	891733	857160
龙门县	Longmen County	2308062	1309908	356607	390601
汕尾市	Shanwei				
市城区	Urban District	4330899	3957404	393036	436947
陆丰市	Lufeng City	3477972	3254345	872993	920552
海丰县	Haifeng County	4003765	3190723	607229	518221
陆河县	Luhe County	522016	487941	174412	176338
东莞市	Dongguan	146924605	176285285	354657	354888
中山市	Zhongshan	66147981	49168795	1018519	998984
江门市	Jiangmen				
蓬江区	Pengjiang District	11781788	11303944	139953	94672
江海区	Jianghai District	3900461	4592063	88723	76993
新会区	Xinhui District	9398000	10187870	668293	707831
台山市	Taishan City	5998782	5410527	1106876	1176072
开平市	Kaiping City	5310360	4323472	569740	581899
鹤山市	Heshan City	4916019	4432097	421344	381178
恩平市	Enping City	1438370	1361148	312811	340258
阳江市	Yangjiang				
江城区	Jiangcheng District	8574845	8027174	740401	787899
阳东区	Yangdong District	5647687	3890572	781306	815865
阳春市	Yangchun City	4223082	3568976	1040695	1027555
阳西县	Yangxi County	2060231	1855078	820182	861983

22-5 续表 2 continued

单位：万元 (10000 yuan)

县(市、区)	County (County-level City and District)	工业总产值 Gross Output Value of Industry 2016	工业总产值 Gross Output Value of Industry 2017	农业总产值 Gross Output Value of Agriculture 2016	农业总产值 Gross Output Value of Agriculture 2017
湛江市	Zhanjiang				
赤坎区	Chikan District	966141	971997	24706	24073
霞山区	Xiashan District	5796543	5753509	32852	34181
麻章区	Mazhang District	4255512	6864809	763140	740633
坡头区	Potou District	2334742	2373006	284355	273754
雷州市	Leizhou City	846467	516749	1597253	1736697
廉江市	Lianjiang County	7047198	5919987	1598722	1642825
吴川市	Wuchuan City	2246992	2556445	496403	505052
遂溪县	Suixi County	1994078	1525425	1615134	1712831
徐闻县	Xuwen County	157897	178463	1106425	1212324
茂名市	Maoming				
茂南区	Maonan District	10657334	12262112	392969	478310
电白区	Dianbai District	5603652	5623237	2022283	1969770
信宜市	Xinyi City	2754790	2586118	1447774	1494024
高州市	Gaozhou City	3085293	3451794	1811876	1896289
化州市	Huazhou City	2733080	2869159	1519334	1599935
肇庆市	Zhaoqing				
端州区	Tuanzhou District	4772241	3807676	5239	4035
鼎湖区	Dinghu District	2560930	1898301	304931	284894
高要区	Gaoyao District	9552401	6802086	1158183	1178764
四会市	Sihui City	15697994	10883335	842176	805103
广宁县	Guangning County	2040834	1755576	495202	533509
德庆县	Deqing County	2623176	2170822	410199	433242
封开县	Fengkai County	1467402	1136534	637429	675200
怀集县	Huaiji County	1506175	957680	1005339	1053377
清远市	Qingyuan				
清城区	Qingcheng District	8783507	8073405	428206	417195
清新区	Qingxin District	3373143	2835818	659984	666578
英德市	Yingde City	3068088	2262533	868531	904691
连州市	Lianzhou City	535214	624967	569790	575253
佛冈县	Fogang County	1977932	1964209	202451	210569
阳山县	Yangshan County	189786	146022	548133	537365
连山县	Lianshan County	82667	6627	117722	119277
连南县	Liannan County	124787	24579	133835	134675
潮州市	Chaozhou				
湘桥区	Xiangqiao District	3014330	3331119	95555	103467
潮安区	Chaoan District	8498688	7828603	285693	290564
饶平县	Raoping County	2716576	2365756	772787	795814
揭阳市	Jieyang				
榕城区	Rongcheng District	12426265	12550042	198637	190097
揭东区	Jiedong District	12234080	11044086	497522	502617
普宁市	Puning City	17512603	16264298	498880	512521
揭西县	Jiexi County	2359797	2195859	526749	541799
惠来县	Huilai County	6778699	5824077	676922	700127
云浮市	Yunfu				
云城区	Yuncheng District	2722079	1830062	176834	185167
云安区	Yuanan District	2018966	747331	170471	179592
罗定市	Luoding City	1676262	1244745	622424	652720
新兴县	Xinxing County	4437614	1318234	905692	914100
郁南县	Yunan County	1361173	746833	317556	328550

注：本表按当年价格计算。
Note: The data in this table are calculated at current prices.

22-6 各县(市、区)粮食产量

Output of Grain by County (County-level City and District)

单位：吨 (ton)

县(市、区)	County (County-level City and District)	粮食 Grain			
				#稻谷 Rice	
		2016	2017	2016	2017
广州市	Guangzhou				
越秀区	Yuexiu District				
海珠区	Haizhu District				
荔湾区	Liwan District				
天河区	Tianhe District				
白云区	Baiyun District	12485	1175	10672	181
黄埔区	Huangpu District	5255	4311	4921	4045
番禺区	Panyu District	1854	1397	346	294
花都区	Huadu District	25260	10536	18111	5581
南沙区	Nansha District	7974	5081	3713	2705
从化区	Conghua District	61469	61830	59513	59602
增城区	Zengcheng District	79767	43843	74901	38116
深圳市	Shenzhen				
福田区	Futian District				
罗湖区	Luohu District	6	5		
盐田区	Yantian District	1	1		
南山区	Nanshan District				
宝安区	Baoan District	97	103	44	42
龙岗区	Longgang District	99	111	14	13
龙华区	Longhua District				
坪山区	Pingshan District				
珠海市	Zhuhai				
香洲区	Xiangzhou District	264	193	102	80
金湾区	Jinwan District	1619	1307	266	202
斗门区	Doumen District	22862	20035	21907	19159
汕头市	Shantou				
金平区	Jinping District	9754	9812	9407	9502
龙湖区	Longhu District	18160	18320	13975	14057
澄海区	Chenghai District	86183	82923	70303	67295
濠江区	Haojiang District	14408	14332	7685	7743
潮阳区	Chaoyang District	165859	165032	115076	112199
潮南区	Chaonan District	150121	148696	98299	98633
南澳县	Nanao County	3640	3589	2244	2194
佛山市	Foshan				
禅城区	Chancheng District				
南海区	Nanhai District	1429	1134	784	744
顺德区	Shunde District	577	97		
高明区	Gaoming District	32168	31247	30340	30224
三水区	Sanshui District	3790	4653	2495	1876
韶关市	Shaoguan				
浈江区	Zhengjiang District	18660	18524	17304	17277
武江区	Wujiang District	21774	22242	20873	21274
曲江区	Qujiang District	68403	68481	66074	65915
乐昌市	Lechang City	82544	85781	67624	70056
南雄市	Nanxiong City	180651	181752	166881	167826
仁化县	Renhua County	66362	66713	61615	61752
始兴县	Shixing County	64253	65231	61672	62601
翁源县	Wengyuan County	86465	88488	82442	84310
新丰县	Xinfeng County	46708	47984	41891	42852
乳源县	Ruyuan County	42830	43608	36389	36474

22-6 续表 1 continued

单位：吨 (ton)

县(市、区)	County (County-level City and District)	粮食 Grain			
		2016	2017	#稻谷 Rice	
				2016	2017
河源市	Heyuan				
源城区	Urban District	10353	10817	9621	10109
东源县	Dongyuan County	141882	146738	135121	139856
和平县	Heping County	110487	114580	101909	106191
龙川县	Longchuan County	230585	232666	220790	222560
紫金县	Zijin County	184320	193409	174566	183581
连平县	Lianping County	84880	87160	78648	80836
梅州市	Meizhou				
梅江区	Meijiang District	18592	18728	17068	17160
梅县区	Meixian District	169714	169426	157875	158173
兴宁市	Xingning City	284062	285133	262848	264727
平远县	Pingyuan County	74283	75269	61337	61613
蕉岭县	Jiaoling County	56560	56658	54357	54151
大埔县	Dabu County	33907	33977	29685	29821
丰顺县	Fengshun County	113458	114396	96257	97011
五华县	Wuhua County	310562	313587	296748	298747
惠州市	Huizhou				
惠城区	Huicheng District	91234	101798	63202	73613
惠阳区	Huiyang District	39481	41470	30627	32573
惠东县	Huidong County	193477	192832	148711	146846
博罗县	Boluo County	147577	145592	113127	111759
龙门县	Longmen County	97661	104664	91808	98842
汕尾市	Shanwei				
市城区	Urban District	21634	22345	19249	20096
陆丰市	Lufeng City	164636	166281	136817	139208
海丰县	Haifeng County	152743	149264	144203	141921
陆河县	Luhe County	48595	50433	40738	42477
东莞市	Dongguan	4806	4790	3130	3247
中山市	Zhongshan	17137	17131	12374	12777
江门市	Jiangmen				
蓬江区	Pengjiang District	2095	2034	1652	1585
江海区	Jianghai District	236	249	114	117
新会区	Xinhui District	141711	141085	125033	123404
台山市	Taishan City	359248	362184	350565	353656
开平市	Kaiping City	211443	216295	199976	205192
鹤山市	Heshan City	53698	56184	51028	53204
恩平市	Enping City	131773	133368	126287	128138
阳江市	Yangjiang				
江城区	Jiangcheng District	81916	82029	77244	78233
阳东区	Yangdong District	130685	133653	119551	121735
阳春市	Yangchun City	261793	265273	235046	236985
阳西县	Yangxi County	123586	125617	115357	116853

22-6 续表 2 continued

单位：吨 (ton)

县(市、区)	County (County-level City and District)	粮食 Grain 2016	粮食 Grain 2017	#稻谷 Rice 2016	#稻谷 Rice 2017
湛江市	Zhanjiang				
赤坎区	Chikan District	2883	2840	2573	2552
霞山区	Xiashan District	7813	7784	7143	7276
麻章区	Mazhang District	83769	86163	69921	73496
坡头区	Potou District	63190	66342	52871	56154
雷州市	Leizhou City	341258	338047	312835	310364
廉江市	Lianjiang County	397261	395271	338451	338777
吴川市	Wuchuan City	154373	159050	139126	144294
遂溪县	Suixi County	216662	226340	175012	185008
徐闻县	Xuwen County	126824	132365	71069	75465
茂名市	Maoming				
茂南区	Maonan District	100364	130389	86687	112357
电白区	Dianbai District	317130	298590	267287	251201
信宜市	Xinyi City	328177	326110	244965	247667
高州市	Gaozhou City	391266	393373	374559	377832
化州市	Huazhou City	327046	328891	288646	291594
肇庆市	Zhaoqing				
端州区	Tuanzhou District	504	276	503	276
鼎湖区	Dinghu District	40911	38624	34784	33579
高要区	Gaoyao District	235775	234437	208052	207957
四会市	Sihui City	116049	115975	91369	90961
广宁县	Guangning County	154220	155808	140399	142115
德庆县	Deqing County	127741	128660	117260	119439
封开县	Fengkai County	201535	204367	183595	186010
怀集县	Huaiji County	272027	271460	252065	250955
清远市	Qingyuan				
清城区	Qingcheng District	70882	63501	69709	61283
清新区	Qingxin District	144125	117077	134941	110387
英德市	Yingde City	147507	181785	132489	159898
连州市	Lianzhou City	82889	103797	66577	88072
佛冈县	Fogang County	51410	52315	50647	49327
阳山县	Yangshan County	101926	84322	65482	59107
连山县	Lianshan County	37970	35104	37171	32038
连南县	Liannan County	36694	27086	22797	18698
潮州市	Chaozhou				
湘桥区	Xiangqiao District	22352	21546	18651	18188
潮安区	Chaoan District	92792	94041	73170	72261
饶平县	Raoping County	149487	153433	131459	133935
揭阳市	Jieyang				
榕城区	Rongcheng District	71462	70938	54940	54787
揭东区	Jiedong District	178072	176224	110390	110724
普宁市	Puning City	198957	198640	128446	129500
揭西县	Jiexi County	167882	169836	109858	111939
惠来县	Huilai County	180678	178460	96948	98676
云浮市	Yunfu				
云城区	Yuncheng District	46208	47684	42308	43639
云安区	Yuanan District	66604	66842	53321	54218
罗定市	Luoding City	244104	244917	228127	229358
新兴县	Xinxing County	129262	133094	123857	127648
郁南县	Yunan County	129562	129264	114336	115161

注：本表按当年价格计算。
Note: The data in this table are calculated at current prices.

22-7 各县(市、区)糖蔗、水果和蔬菜产量

Output of Sugarcane,Fruits and Vegetable by County (County-level City and District)

单位：吨 (ton)

县(市、区)	County (County-level City and District)	糖蔗 Sugarcane		水果 Fruits		蔬菜 Vegetable	
		2016	2017	2016	2017	2016	2017
广州市	Guangzhou						
越秀区	Yuexiu District						
海珠区	Haizhu District			5470	6090	14382	11007
荔湾区	Liwan District					4319	3967
天河区	Tianhe District			212	262	11375	9419
白云区	Baiyun District			6804	6142	717943	758619
黄埔区	Huangpu District	220		11504	10911	72755	70473
番禺区	Panyu District			14247	12918	182351	160969
花都区	Huadu District	4665		20772	20754	329815	448271
南沙区	Nansha District			167708	190340	614246	652883
从化区	Conghua District			103328	121057	345783	308114
增城区	Zengcheng District			164723	159605	1251077	1224190
深圳市	Shenzhen						
福田区	Futian District					483	
罗湖区	Luohu District			3	597	2266	187
盐田区	Yantian District			7	12		
南山区	Nanshan District			9970	9068	184	178
宝安区	Baoan District			463	1147	52895	67599
龙岗区	Longgang District			1861	3583	26595	11888
龙华区	Longhua District						9698
坪山区	Pingshan District				620		29673
珠海市	Zhuhai						
香洲区	Xiangzhou District	102	28	2306	2439	7980	8535
金湾区	Jinwan District			39679	39405	44447	47540
斗门区	Doumen District	693	189	22822	20418	80240	85824
汕头市	Shantou						
金平区	Jinping District			493	501	45167	46636
龙湖区	Longhu District			224	224	180495	178394
澄海区	Chenghai District			83333	84025	608413	625743
濠江区	Haojiang District			424	652	54095	58735
潮阳区	Chaoyang District			86585	123136	321464	323997
潮南区	Chaonan District			24383	26284	304344	315061
南澳县	Nanao County			3714	3976	11347	11380
佛山市	Foshan						
禅城区	Chancheng District			252		4411	3077
南海区	Nanhai District			929	2144	309117	302442
顺德区	Shunde District		30	8272	8674	97368	98684
高明区	Gaoming District			12150	12350	133392	137654
三水区	Sanshui District			18923	19835	254380	254952
韶关市	Shaoguan						
浈江区	Zhengjiang District	298		19424	20894	57858	61297
武江区	Wujiang District			10441	10729	73523	77951
曲江区	Qujiang District			31299	34828	95769	99332
乐昌市	Lechang City	917	953	137707	144197	199948	208280
南雄市	Nanxiong City			35722	41129	159820	170664
仁化县	Renhua County			87826	114253	74907	78472
始兴县	Shixing County			75922	81126	111167	124561
翁源县	Wengyuan County	102341	104598	66144	69768	114639	119540
新丰县	Xinfeng County	720	682	31327	32916	132848	145505
乳源县	Ruyuan County			7401	7815	41568	44015

22−7 续表 1 continued

单位：吨 (ton)

县(市、区)	County (County-level City and District)	糖蔗 Sugarcane 2016	糖蔗 Sugarcane 2017	水果 Fruits 2016	水果 Fruits 2017	蔬菜 Vegetable 2016	蔬菜 Vegetable 2017
河源市	Heyuan						
源城区	Urban District	823	823	4001	4236	33567	35804
东源县	Dongyuan County	28757	29532	30456	31905	97494	101652
和平县	Heping County			42124	46524	115263	120745
龙川县	Longchuan County			69519	71016	123244	129252
紫金县	Zijin County	24747	33366	124530	129756	179285	191987
连平县	Lianping County			93274	105759	87860	94200
梅州市	Meizhou						
梅江区	Meijiang District			33186	34535	101364	107023
梅县区	Meixian District			627861	644324	415092	429436
兴宁市	Xingning City			139703	147001	615026	657915
平远县	Pingyuan County			81777	79389	59323	59195
蕉岭县	Jiaoling County			36482	37436	92446	94823
大埔县	Dabu County			171172	180508	162003	168627
丰顺县	Fengshun County			58014	59682	192147	200595
五华县	Wuhua County			69651	73527	311913	328061
惠州市	Huizhou						
惠城区	Huicheng District	7649	2510	38971	40712	491045	508389
惠阳区	Huiyang District	168		34309	36938	432597	457880
惠东县	Huidong County	644	649	89219	97230	693347	733927
博罗县	Boluo County	51944	59067	176587	192087	863740	906059
龙门县	Longmen County	4581	4801	416706	451053	257867	278836
汕尾市	Shanwei						
市城区	Urban District			9872	10433	60868	62185
陆丰市	Lufeng City			89132	88218	529729	551932
海丰县	Haifeng County	5000	5015	81997	66741	408740	416580
陆河县	Luhe County			92281	94426	79049	86842
东莞市	Dongguan			55081	54583	400016	392431
中山市	Zhongshan	3212	2955	91243	85284	433930	397886
江门市	Jiangmen						
蓬江区	Pengjiang District			2107	2129	61314	61458
江海区	Jianghai District			4067	5927	46633	40711
新会区	Xinhui District	35599	40600	94956	105307	150051	148399
台山市	Taishan City	51856	54711	46434	48960	401224	417180
开平市	Kaiping City	12791	1262	48327	46751	298083	325778
鹤山市	Heshan City			11900	12289	252168	256850
恩平市	Enping City	15741	17741	49683	53017	161105	173660
阳江市	Yangjiang						
江城区	Jiangcheng District			9526	9949	90706	90791
阳东区	Yangdong District	19262	11853	57163	59691	176679	181132
阳春市	Yangchun City	17972	17421	229459	245314	343670	354305
阳西县	Yangxi County			34327	39360	176321	182291

22−7 续表 2 continued

单位：吨 (ton)

县(市、区)	County (County-level City and District)	糖蔗 Sugarcane 2016	2017	水果 Fruits 2016	2017	蔬菜 Vegetable 2016	2017
湛江市	Zhanjiang						
赤坎区	Chikan District	860	860	282	287	17848	18769
霞山区	Xiashan District	4200	2148	269	273	13802	13863
麻章区	Mazhang District	356275	377157	89087	82905	84695	88988
坡头区	Potou District	18480	14909	23487	24034	81980	86721
雷州市	Leizhou City	3939432	4161505	636953	669391	752574	791714
廉江市	Lianjiang County	390535	370184	381159	411365	826774	867370
吴川市	Wuchuan City	33113	33665	70442	73571	126704	133621
遂溪县	Suixi County	3943401	4131759	221329	234877	738586	763487
徐闻县	Xuwen County	1122403	1202007	925173	958076	707298	761534
茂名市	Maoming						
茂南区	Maonan District	14287	12791	20328	39577	238707	333134
电白区	Dianbai District	4245	4322	362078	378580	872551	823739
信宜市	Xinyi City			841343	905892	416365	448881
高州市	Gaozhou City	10014	10451	1382016	1482838	753255	784210
化州市	Huazhou City	418972	428640	572615	627567	579427	606986
肇庆市	Zhaoqing						
端州区	Tuanzhou District			171	145	7336	7220
鼎湖区	Dinghu District			26376	25020	118477	117441
高要区	Gaoyao District			191703	199159	905407	938579
四会市	Sihui City			111192	103959	222928	228560
广宁县	Guangning County			154805	169975	193860	212858
德庆县	Deqing County			317990	336278	199996	214036
封开县	Fengkai County	34861	29343	351934	376660	262228	284516
怀集县	Huaiji County	1805	180	276802	337474	419728	458619
清远市	Qingyuan						
清城区	Qingcheng District	6705	6082	22027	31267	205747	223785
清新区	Qingxin District	5070	5328	225534	245887	446247	491834
英德市	Yingde City	259681	259681	61299	64487	645396	690579
连州市	Lianzhou City			105007	112813	644959	676833
佛冈县	Fogang County			93778	94725	147983	154196
阳山县	Yangshan County	270	299	74274	81180	484359	529114
连山县	Lianshan County			29198	31578	91523	97444
连南县	Liannan County			17737	20836	96676	105413
潮州市	Chaozhou						
湘桥区	Xiangqiao District			75566	76946	62227	65568
潮安区	Chaoan District			45076	46527	154912	160945
饶平县	Raoping County	7432		116890	124200	252043	257881
揭阳市	Jieyang						
榕城区	Rongcheng District			34805	34716	160796	166520
揭东区	Jiedong District	2878	1346	34517	35306	487475	522572
普宁市	Puning City			161312	173258	314805	334177
揭西县	Jiexi County			70022	74368	270386	293329
惠来县	Huilai County			106127	112989	357100	366838
云浮市	Yunfu						
云城区	Yuncheng District			36340	37202	20848	21063
云安区	Yuanan District			68094	70104	48786	50416
罗定市	Luoding City			69368	70718	111615	112802
新兴县	Xinxing County			91248	96809	245494	262086
郁南县	Yunan County			164320	175447	34509	36102

22-8 各县(市、区)猪肉产量、禽肉产量和水产品产量
Output of Pork , Output of Meat of Poultry and Output of Aquatic Products by County (County-level City and District)

单位：万吨 (10000 tons)

县(市、区)	County (County-level City and District)	猪肉产量 Output of Pork		禽肉产量 Output of Meat of Poultry		水产品产量 Output of Aquatic Products	
		2016	2017	2016	2017	2016	2017
广州市	Guangzhou						
越秀区	Yuexiu District						
海珠区	Haizhu District					0.10	0.10
荔湾区	Liwan District					0.08	0.04
天河区	Tianhe District					0.04	0.03
白云区	Baiyun District	0.53	0.56	1.95	2.03	3.25	2.97
黄埔区	Huangpu District	1.01	1.13	0.23	0.25	0.62	0.54
番禺区	Panyu District	0.02	0.03	0.86	1.17	14.14	14.93
花都区	Huadu District	1.93	1.39	2.17	1.42	6.86	7.09
南沙区	Nansha District	0.85	0.99	0.75	0.91	14.13	13.24
从化区	Conghua District	1.46	1.50	0.52	0.65	0.88	0.76
增城区	Zengcheng District	0.14	0.14	1.15	1.47	4.98	5.06
深圳市	Shenzhen						
福田区	Futian District						
罗湖区	Luohu District					0.58	0.33
盐田区	Yantian District						
南山区	Nanshan District					0.32	0.29
宝安区	Baoan District	0.02		0.01	0.01	0.03	
龙岗区	Longgang District	0.22	0.21	0.01	0.02	0.52	0.36
龙华区	Longhua District						
坪山区	Pingshan District						
珠海市	Zhuhai						
香洲区	Xiangzhou District	0.01	0.01	0.21	0.21	2.73	3.66
金湾区	Jinwan District	0.43	0.45	0.08	0.08	4.00	4.00
斗门区	Doumen District	2.20	2.08	0.68	0.70	23.17	23.30
汕头市	Shantou						
金平区	Jinping District	0.39	0.29	0.17	0.18	1.59	1.63
龙湖区	Longhu District	0.78	0.77	0.67	0.52	1.08	1.13
澄海区	Chenghai District	1.32	1.38	1.76	2.31	7.97	8.20
濠江区	Haojiang District	0.17	0.19	0.10	0.07	4.47	4.60
潮阳区	Chaoyang District	1.74	1.44	0.77	0.58	9.33	9.65
潮南区	Chaonan District	1.38	1.49	0.29	0.27	2.55	2.51
南澳县	Nanao County	0.18	0.19	0.06	0.03	17.94	18.17
佛山市	Foshan						
禅城区	Chancheng District					0.31	0.32
南海区	Nanhai District	0.82	0.74	0.86	0.86	18.68	19.34
顺德区	Shunde District	1.26	1.22	0.46	0.42	24.93	25.59
高明区	Gaoming District	3.32	3.12	2.06	2.22	6.28	6.41
三水区	Sanshui District	4.78	4.75	6.31	6.52	12.30	12.71
韶关市	Shaoguan						
浈江区	Zhengjiang District	0.95	0.90	0.24	0.16	0.92	0.96
武江区	Wujiang District	0.92	0.88	0.15	0.25	0.29	0.30
曲江区	Qujiang District	2.54	2.47	0.44	0.45	1.48	1.53
乐昌市	Lechang City	2.85	2.73	0.33	0.07	0.50	0.51
南雄市	Nanxiong City	3.87	3.73	1.27	0.40	1.62	1.68
仁化县	Renhua County	1.76	1.72	0.60	0.51	0.90	0.93
始兴县	Shixing County	1.34	1.29	0.54	1.30	0.59	0.61
翁源县	Wengyuan County	1.17	1.15	0.54	0.55	0.73	0.75
新丰县	Xinfeng County	0.86	0.83	0.30	0.30	0.39	0.37
乳源县	Ruyuan County	0.76	0.74	0.07	0.64	0.27	0.29

22-8 续表 1 continued

单位：万吨 (10000 tons)

县(市、区)	County (County-level City and District)	猪肉产量 Output of Pork 2016	2017	禽肉产量 Output of Meat of Poultry 2016	2017	水产品产量 Output of Aquatic Products 2016	2017
河源市	Heyuan						
源城区	Urban District	0.46	0.41	0.44	0.45	0.11	0.12
东源县	Dongyuan County	1.38	1.35	1.09	1.13	0.87	0.88
和平县	Heping County	1.39	1.34	1.09	1.14	0.36	0.39
龙川县	Longchuan County	2.06	1.97	0.75	0.78	1.30	1.31
紫金县	Zijin County	1.40	1.36	1.36	1.40	0.92	0.93
连平县	Lianping County	0.90	0.88	0.46	0.47	0.53	0.54
梅州市	Meizhou						
梅江区	Meijiang District	1.41	1.28	0.58	0.59	0.73	0.76
梅县区	Meixian District	2.59	2.55	1.40	1.45	2.71	2.82
兴宁市	Xingning City	3.93	3.76	1.61	1.67	1.61	1.69
平远县	Pingyuan County	1.05	1.01	0.28	0.29	0.90	0.90
蕉岭县	Jiaoling County	1.65	1.60	0.48	0.51	0.57	0.60
大埔县	Dabu County	1.40	1.37	0.85	0.89	0.68	0.67
丰顺县	Fengshun County	1.71	1.65	2.91	3.00	1.40	1.41
五华县	Wuhua County	3.81	3.70	1.11	1.15	1.69	1.69
惠州市	Huizhou						
惠城区	Huicheng District	2.09	2.39	1.16	1.19	3.19	3.27
惠阳区	Huiyang District	0.42	0.41	0.82	0.87	3.26	3.26
惠东县	Huidong County	2.26	2.57	1.21	1.24	6.43	6.42
博罗县	Boluo County	5.77	4.74	3.50	3.63	2.75	2.88
龙门县	Longmen County	0.48	0.52	0.54	0.56	0.63	0.64
汕尾市	Shanwei						
市城区	Urban District	0.48	0.43	0.22	0.22	22.24	22.72
陆丰市	Lufeng City	2.51	2.25	1.38	1.40	22.80	23.25
海丰县	Haifeng County	0.91	0.77	0.70	0.64	13.94	9.75
陆河县	Luhe County	0.95	0.85	0.33	0.30	0.43	0.37
东莞市	Dongguan	0.26	0.25	0.38	0.40	5.02	4.55
中山市	Zhongshan	1.76	1.69	0.79	0.82	32.60	32.29
江门市	Jiangmen						
蓬江区	Pengjiang District	2.15	0.41	0.25	0.24	1.65	1.70
江海区	Jianghai District	0.59	0.30	0.03	0.03	2.21	2.26
新会区	Xinhui District	2.62	2.88	2.45	2.59	17.11	17.45
台山市	Taishan City	1.78	2.71	1.40	1.37	37.84	38.66
开平市	Kaiping City	3.76	4.23	3.54	3.71	4.91	5.05
鹤山市	Heshan City	5.65	4.74	0.91	0.98	5.80	5.69
恩平市	Enping City	1.71	2.32	0.85	0.84	4.48	4.59
阳江市	Yangjiang						
江城区	Jiangcheng District	1.85	1.77	0.37	0.37	36.66	37.67
阳东区	Yangdong District	4.24	4.06	1.09	1.09	29.41	29.21
阳春市	Yangchun City	8.91	8.64	1.93	2.02	3.85	3.26
阳西县	Yangxi County	3.31	3.18	1.11	1.17	46.80	48.14

22-8 续表 2 continued

单位：万吨 (10000 tons)

县(市、区)	County (County-level City and District)	猪肉产量 Output of Pork 2016	猪肉产量 Output of Pork 2017	禽肉产量 Output of Meat of Poultry 2016	禽肉产量 Output of Meat of Poultry 2017	水产品产量 Output of Aquatic Products 2016	水产品产量 Output of Aquatic Products 2017
湛江市	Zhanjiang						
赤坎区	Chikan District	0.05		0.01	0.01	0.57	0.59
霞山区	Xiashan District			0.06	0.06	1.66	1.64
麻章区	Mazhang District	1.97	1.81	0.74	0.77	20.49	20.00
坡头区	Potou District	2.49	2.26	0.44	0.46	8.03	8.06
雷州市	Leizhou City	3.44	3.34	1.60	1.66	17.48	20.16
廉江市	Lianjiang County	10.77	10.53	2.66	2.75	18.31	17.56
吴川市	Wuchuan City	3.09	2.99	2.18	2.25	8.95	8.89
遂溪县	Suixi County	7.07	6.92	3.55	3.68	37.43	37.62
徐闻县	Xuwen County	1.71	1.64	0.66	0.68	7.34	7.71
茂名市	Maoming						
茂南区	Maonan District	4.56	5.32	3.02	3.43	3.04	3.40
电白区	Dianbai District	13.65	12.32	3.39	3.21	63.34	64.37
信宜市	Xinyi City	9.01	8.75	7.41	7.71	2.91	2.99
高州市	Gaozhou City	13.35	12.73	4.53	4.63	7.01	7.37
化州市	Huazhou City	13.17	12.69	2.56	2.67	10.83	11.85
肇庆市	Zhaoqing						
端州区	Tuanzhou District	0.03	0.02			0.06	0.03
鼎湖区	Dinghu District	4.57	4.51	0.78	0.74	4.30	4.34
高要区	Gaoyao District	7.01	6.63	2.77	2.81	16.66	18.34
四会市	Sihui City	11.59	11.02	2.48	2.55	13.51	14.43
广宁县	Guangning County	1.84	1.76	1.18	1.18	0.71	0.78
德庆县	Deqing County	0.94	1.06	1.08	1.14	1.81	1.86
封开县	Fengkai County	1.69	1.70	1.38	1.39	3.64	3.89
怀集县	Huaiji County	7.49	7.21	2.30	2.58	2.97	3.18
清远市	Qingyuan						
清城区	Qingcheng District	2.03	1.98	5.46	5.38	3.95	4.17
清新区	Qingxin District	4.21	4.17	3.25	3.34	3.26	3.39
英德市	Yingde City	3.94	3.86	1.09	1.19	2.89	2.99
连州市	Lianzhou City	5.17	4.84	0.53	0.61	0.69	0.73
佛冈县	Fogang County	1.08	1.03	0.38	0.42	0.71	0.75
阳山县	Yangshan County	5.49	5.27	1.23	1.33	0.49	0.51
连山县	Lianshan County	0.82	0.79	0.21	0.26	0.19	0.20
连南县	Liannan County	0.49	0.46	0.31	0.36	0.16	0.17
潮州市	Chaozhou						
湘桥区	Xiangqiao District	0.25	0.26	0.25	0.31	0.53	0.58
潮安区	Chaoan District	1.12	1.10	0.69	0.72	1.85	1.88
饶平县	Raoping County	2.91	2.77	1.54	1.54	15.98	16.70
揭阳市	Jieyang						
榕城区	Rongcheng District	0.85	0.76	0.41	0.41	1.55	1.37
揭东区	Jiedong District	1.35	1.36	0.82	0.82	1.68	1.71
普宁市	Puning City	2.76	2.64	0.72	0.74	0.89	0.90
揭西县	Jiexi County	2.75	2.74	1.52	1.62	1.98	2.04
惠来县	Huilai County	1.85	1.72	1.30	1.35	8.44	8.47
云浮市	Yunfu						
云城区	Yuncheng District	1.50	1.41	1.37	1.42	1.02	1.04
云安区	Yuanan District	0.80	0.73	0.32	0.33	0.95	0.97
罗定市	Luoding City	1.68	1.55	1.79	1.86	3.54	3.63
新兴县	Xinxing County	5.47	5.40	10.88	11.27	2.93	3.01
郁南县	Yunan County	0.67	0.67	1.72	1.78	1.10	1.13

22-9 各县(市、区)固定资产投资

Investment in Fixed Assets by County (County-level City and District)

单位：万元 (10000 yuan)

县(市、区)	County (County-level City and District)	投资完成额 Completed Investment 2016	投资完成额 Completed Investment 2017	#房地产开发投资 Investment in Real Estate Development 2016	#房地产开发投资 Investment in Real Estate Development 2017
广州市	Guangzhou				
越秀区	Yuexiu District	3376473	2688803	736265	642737
海珠区	Haizhu District	6412438	6558705	1564319	1048135
荔湾区	Liwan District	3401508	1793758	2723826	1251775
天河区	Tianhe District	5466613	5344873	2999505	3069882
白云区	Baiyun District	4895715	5493279	1055184	1383378
黄埔区	Huangpu District	8565504	11011895	3997123	4637900
番禺区	Panyu District	6043599	6361786	2738869	3536865
花都区	Huadu District	3181520	3508049	2476236	1991814
南沙区	Nansha District	8131492	7449292	2883217	3914988
从化区	Conghua District	2300773	2090527	1218527	1199527
增城区	Zengcheng District	5260225	6897349	3015478	4351934
深圳市	Shenzhen				
福田区	Futian District	3000289	3745056	1805677	2394047
罗湖区	Luohu District	1843702	2289818	929097	987984
盐田区	Yantian District	1225743	1486533	416716	471006
南山区	Nanshan District	8879664	10967612	3503488	4579379
宝安区	Baoan District	14477957	11886199	6183224	3716282
龙岗区	Longgang District	11354283	10243457	4727007	4498093
龙华区	Longhua District		6182721		3316984
坪山区	Pingshan District		3776637		1344845
珠海市	Zhuhai				
香洲区	Xiangzhou District	8304911	10001860	4434895	4148399
金湾区	Jinwan District	3791525	4463353	998781	1433528
斗门区	Doumen District	1801109	2155001	976639	1079231
汕头市	Shantou				
金平区	Jinping District	2858108	3685109	384444	390448
龙湖区	Longhu District	2232870	2880441	1336816	1728771
澄海区	Chenghai District	1547365	1984541	357561	337457
濠江区	Haojiang District	1350191	1830150	431100	681765
潮阳区	Chaoyang District	3695795	4585766	286414	277944
潮南区	Chaonan District	3229341	4032780	147372	106721
南澳县	Nanao County	155016	191521	120139	86616
佛山市	Foshan				
禅城区	Chancheng District	6000010	7064744	3296561	3361678
南海区	Nanhai District	10782942	13156163	4829718	6027059
顺德区	Shunde District	7648520	9717642	3115488	3547010
高明区	Gaoming District	4015222	4753013	346998	626524
三水区	Sanshui District	6673699	7966357	710904	977627
韶关市	Shaoguan				
浈江区	Zhengjiang District	772472	625451	229583	229621
武江区	Wujiang District	1112935	1154367	654721	798490
曲江区	Qujiang District	561713	591337	98790	116736
乐昌市	Lechang City	371640	450286	105172	146924
南雄市	Nanxiong City	1155318	819337	109149	139285
仁化县	Renhua County	637496	674556	51008	76968
始兴县	Shixing County	667118	703708	56911	145150
翁源县	Wengyuan County	694675	727740	62930	103682
新丰县	Xinfeng County	377827	427292	40062	97640
乳源县	Ruyuan County	669742	754119	60030	42833

22-9 续表 1 continued

单位：万元 (10000 yuan)

县(市、区)	County (County-level City and District)	投资完成额 Completed Investment		#房地产开发投资 Investment in Real Estate Development	
		2016	2017	2016	2017
河源市	Heyuan				
源城区	Urban District	2425983	2661438	1048306	1186392
东源县	Dongyuan County	917610	1154626	158018	214015
和平县	Heping County	720087	903449	84379	127898
龙川县	Longchuan County	977989	1456752	326616	449406
紫金县	Zijin County	819096	891665	114918	210640
连平县	Lianping County	662143	716740	25003	50986
梅州市	Meizhou				
梅江区	Meijiang District	1912604	1452537	582961	605359
梅县区	Meixian District	1397562	1871717	478561	478229
兴宁市	Xingning City	544096	832637	210992	295292
平远县	Pingyuan County	395660	550483	72748	160733
蕉岭县	Jiaoling County	388164	530095	50693	93835
大埔县	Dabu County	587974	780177	131432	164939
丰顺县	Fengshun County	531668	731094	148769	238000
五华县	Wuhua County	745876	1318933	49173	144022
惠州市	Huizhou				
惠城区	Huicheng District	4680952	5188926	2150231	2388433
惠阳区	Huiyang District	6445224	6587063	2628208	3500132
惠东县	Huidong County	3825399	4591059	1423089	1332027
博罗县	Boluo County	3426605	4080025	617119	955725
龙门县	Longmen County	2018876	1901695	657677	665632
汕尾市	Shanwei				
市城区	Urban District	768379	1192135	214082	487863
陆丰市	Lufeng City	2095005	2388146	61419	115989
海丰县	Haifeng County	3262116	2896104	248748	221908
陆河县	Luhe County	398987	216885	43407	38397
东莞市	Dongguan	15574580	17128291	6427591	7021544
中山市	Zhongshan	11490146	12484816	5435851	6239748
江门市	Jiangmen				
蓬江区	Pengjiang District	3170486	3704140	1162912	1218454
江海区	Jianghai District	1104125	1279270	477759	554033
新会区	Xinhui District	2878280	3413481	529351	967646
台山市	Taishan City	2220515	2620502	479992	616453
开平市	Kaiping City	2550744	2985515	313103	432368
鹤山市	Heshan City	1821502	2121486	385609	511839
恩平市	Enping City	1263189	1471900	187441	204770
阳江市	Yangjiang				
江城区	Jiangcheng District	1515675	1785943	673248	763263
阳东区	Yangdong District	1604009	1438532	55711	144626
阳春市	Yangchun City	1077066	1203453	132097	273745
阳西县	Yangxi County	842405	974187	152756	267002

22-9 续表 2 continued

单位：万元 (10000 yuan)

县(市、区)	County (County-level City and District)	投资完成额 Completed Investment 2016	2017	#房地产开发投资 Investment in Real Estate Development 2016	2017
湛江市	Zhanjiang				
赤坎区	Chikan District	888306	1007585	590362	731836
霞山区	Xiashan District	1031376	1167628	348008	605041
麻章区	Mazhang District	669510	673527	48464	126470
坡头区	Potou District	924949	1119597	203439	184563
雷州市	Leizhou City	758501	896016	32260	18812
廉江市	Lianjiang County	4705143	4914593	288269	563280
吴川市	Wuchuan City	1977419	2380856	186651	351090
遂溪县	Suixi County	1746564	1980193	39244	62460
徐闻县	Xuwen County	370050	497540	60475	58790
茂名市	Maoming				
茂南区	Maonan District	2671278	3023680	297035	559977
电白区	Dianbai District	3858306	4209357	397161	446151
信宜市	Xinyi City	2285827	2519849	143957	211571
高州市	Gaozhou City	2268857	2619470	122608	261166
化州市	Huazhou City	1543328	1784932	137663	203285
肇庆市	Zhaoqing				
端州区	Tuanzhou District	1858812	1994177	533296	573586
鼎湖区	Dinghu District	1025921	1346898	124005	281233
高要区	Gaoyao District	2667275	2895082	103385	407889
四会市	Sihui City	4642430	5065304	358768	477144
广宁县	Guangning County	653700	712536	104669	116260
德庆县	Deqing County	1064063	1163020	19509	27669
封开县	Fengkai County	898402	760474	55272	7475
怀集县	Huaiji County	926836	1038056	153063	189137
清远市	Qingyuan				
清城区	Qingcheng District	2900823	3091510	1415431	1764832
清新区	Qingxin District	733019	844609	201401	248917
英德市	Yingde City	1383342	1420726	277745	338593
连州市	Lianzhou City	399612	446667	118710	126096
佛冈县	Fogang County	352275	437783	189909	167641
阳山县	Yangshan County	209699	250132	55423	96668
连山县	Lianshan County	51362	55734	1100	8996
连南县	Liannan County	101043	108196	15489	11498
潮州市	Chaozhou				
湘桥区	Xiangqiao District	1408822	1421836	441978	452120
潮安区	Chaoan District	1922568	2112601	95915	131715
饶平县	Raoping County	758731	973326	79568	84239
揭阳市	Jieyang				
榕城区	Rongcheng District	4175318	4901015	234255	540035
揭东区	Jiedong District	2922440	3372343	86343	65512
普宁市	Puning City	4226814	4687212	104222	347762
揭西县	Jiexi County	1114585	1274897	80068	43183
惠来县	Huilai County	2281319	2437605	30170	96418
云浮市	Yunfu				
云城区	Yuncheng District	1537860	1548498	296504	301881
云安区	Yuanan District	631149	713128	55898	34611
罗定市	Luoding City	1171453	1380906	143911	224168
新兴县	Xinxing County	1402016	1556164	160713	209658
郁南县	Yunan County	660144	784934	54791	85729

注：部分地市由于不分区项目、开发区项目，各区相加小于合计。
Note: Due to the projects that can't be classified by region and the development zone projects, the sum of the counties are less than the city.

22-10 各县(市、区)社会消费品零售总额

Total Retail Sales of Consumer Goods by County (County-level City and District)

单位：万元 (10000 yuan)

县(市、区)	County (County-level City and District)	社会消费品零售总额 Total Retail Sales of Consumer Goods		#商品零售 Retail Sales	
		2016	2017	2016	2017
广州市	Guangzhou				
越秀区	Yuexiu District	12452920	13380663	11184836	12095819
海珠区	Haizhu District	8661482	9812942	7188646	8412432
荔湾区	Liwan District	7897560	8389103	7128219	7542837
天河区	Tianhe District	18183526	17940728	16749634	16468015
白云区	Baiyun District	11136775	12133628	9903455	10897867
黄埔区	Huangpu District	6119839	8216592	5820060	7915237
番禺区	Panyu District	11430371	12293478	9434030	10324205
花都区	Huadu District	4417397	4812798	3764399	4152761
南沙区	Nansha District	1971566	2148041	1368393	1533985
从化区	Conghua District	1423508	1530137	1146868	1241753
增城区	Zengcheng District	3369932	3367798	2648540	2665602
深圳市	Shenzhen				
福田区	Futian District	16651168	18175067	14750200	16118020
罗湖区	Luohu District	11524697	12567821	10208988	11145400
盐田区	Yantian District	710891	773912	629733	686321
南山区	Nanshan District	7371059	8038715	6529547	7128896
宝安区	Baoan District	10895135	8993704	9651299	7975800
龙岗区	Longgang District	7974606	7930087	7064190	7032563
龙华区	Longhua District		2878048		2552312
坪山区	Pingshan District		776437		688560
珠海市	Zhuhai				
香洲区	Xiangzhou District	8456938	9359097	7568260	8450897
金湾区	Jinwan District	489572	561390	405600	443325
斗门区	Doumen District	1214771	1361277	1075178	1085045
汕头市	Shantou				
金平区	Jinping District	5183706	5773971	4953106	5529778
龙湖区	Longhu District	2901818	3238381	2756144	3075636
澄海区	Chenghai District	1629432	1808774	1552073	1724690
濠江区	Haojiang District	412705	453151	390347	426154
潮阳区	Chaoyang District	2450317	2709658	2260409	2513347
潮南区	Chaonan District	2353557	2603210	2185916	2415294
南澳县	Nanao County	220411	244452	189968	210315
佛山市	Foshan				
禅城区	Chancheng District	7472943	8310850	6996301	7801765
南海区	Nanhai District	9678825	10612982	8479105	9367753
顺德区	Shunde District	9754522	10700701	8758133	9677433
高明区	Gaoming District	1176486	1285899	1016201	1114806
三水区	Sanshui District	2094869	2293880	1753876	1929672
韶关市	Shaoguan				
浈江区	Zhengjiang District	2214588	2368445	2003539	2138931
武江区	Wujiang District	1114499	1202081	1016097	1088470
曲江区	Qujiang District	627234	678355	572663	611635
乐昌市	Lechang City	612726	664174	570255	616225
南雄市	Nanxiong City	507258	548843	461477	491765
仁化县	Renhua County	304816	328726	273770	291765
始兴县	Shixing County	189685	206225	173854	187791
翁源县	Wengyuan County	343568	369777	326538	349074
新丰县	Xinfeng County	242986	264821	229742	246086
乳源县	Ruyuan County	224741	242448	203511	215570

22-10 续表 1 continued

单位：万元 (10000 yuan)

县(市、区)	County (County-level City and District)	社会消费品零售总额 Total Retail Sales of Consumer Goods 2016	2017	#商品零售 Retail Sales 2016	2017
河源市	Heyuan				
源城区	Urban District	1555024	1701689	1441371	1593243
东源县	Dongyuan County	698164	770448	648571	715990
和平县	Heping County	591627	600198	543551	540890
龙川县	Longchuan County	1033572	1138354	968511	1067752
紫金县	Zijin County	927417	1022606	860613	949266
连平县	Lianping County	568610	622360	531129	581420
梅州市	Meizhou				
梅江区	Meijiang District	1309541	1426321	1244066	1358694
梅县区	Meixian District	1420073	1538772	1252866	1354504
兴宁市	Xingning City	956230	1058602	921236	1016659
平远县	Pingyuan County	251612	275738	231417	254215
蕉岭县	Jiaoling County	371887	408090	348125	383059
大埔县	Dabu County	490979	537370	450905	493033
丰顺县	Fengshun County	492697	550875	458746	515562
五华县	Wuhua County	904661	980533	864379	943553
惠州市	Huizhou				
惠城区	Huicheng District	5756123	6354006	5283715	5960962
惠阳区	Huiyang District	1772389	1980700	1607083	1802099
惠东县	Huidong County	2474784	2786600	2243240	2540228
博罗县	Boluo County	1688550	1868415	1582884	1753491
龙门县	Longmen County	586959	644914	479047	526716
汕尾市	Shanwei				
市城区	Urban District	1124308	1183230	988276	1036941
陆丰市	Lufeng City	1758508	1893950	1608530	1725266
海丰县	Haifeng County	2102587	2276259	1824199	1997167
陆河县	Luhe County	345651	372789	323485	347832
东莞市	Dongguan	24707782	26878849	23114703	25156970
中山市	Zhongshan	12058435	13098884	10952834	11919229
江门市	Jiangmen				
蓬江区	Pengjiang District	2461272	2719687	2337891	2598367
江海区	Jianghai District	430621	498739	394338	461286
新会区	Xinhui District	2371641	2612277	2170078	2395517
台山市	Taishan City	2078858	2286884	1857299	2049375
开平市	Kaiping City	1740949	1918335	1548378	1711911
鹤山市	Heshan City	1617662	1782841	1358032	1507144
恩平市	Enping City	889636	977572	789841	871955
阳江市	Yangjiang				
江城区	Jiangcheng District	2835869	3076540	2567053	2810681
阳东区	Yangdong District	699612	767039	610490	661127
阳春市	Yangchun City	2218254	2408338	2061083	2190162
阳西县	Yangxi County	594613	647092	481212	512047

22-10 续表 2 continued

单位：万元 (10000 yuan)

县(市、区)	County (County-level City and District)	社会消费品零售总额 Total Retail Sales of Consumer Goods 2016	2017	#商品零售 Retail Sales 2016	2017
湛江市	Zhanjiang				
赤坎区	Chikan District	3564348	3949229	3232425	3600851
霞山区	Xiashan District	3605678	3999758	3271819	3630184
麻章区	Mazhang District	612734	682474	545263	610066
坡头区	Potou District	385327	423622	330274	364194
雷州市	Leizhou City	1438751	1546108	1243159	1336020
廉江市	Lianjiang County	1746148	1941952	1502031	1646052
吴川市	Wuchuan City	1125699	1255349	986560	1094434
遂溪县	Suixi County	1033932	1130256	904571	987886
徐闻县	Xuwen County	816953	852054	703394	730878
茂名市	Maoming				
茂南区	Maonan District	4916278	5190300	4491134	4757859
电白区	Dianbai District	2510586	2804110	2323253	2607317
信宜市	Xinyi City	2045086	2254552	1881137	2062761
高州市	Gaozhou City	2042284	2246201	1843792	2030443
化州市	Huazhou City	1884537	2074835	1703637	1864912
肇庆市	Zhaoqing				
端州区	Tuanzhou District	3114560	3483858	2813458	3253368
鼎湖区	Dinghu District	293390	324313	241623	281102
高要区	Gaoyao District	835882	915683	716515	818634
四会市	Sihui City	1220845	1347538	1155603	1300785
广宁县	Guangning County	459561	503867	419600	465923
德庆县	Deqing County	434764	478124	384130	431418
封开县	Fengkai County	345291	377184	298049	328024
怀集县	Huaiji County	615531	668756	542152	602673
清远市	Qingyuan				
清城区	Qingcheng District	3000858	3264717	2884321	3156109
清新区	Qingxin District	645192	714547	575539	637009
英德市	Yingde City	1214886	1332147	1122352	1226277
连州市	Lianzhou City	484046	520323	404279	434890
佛冈县	Fogang County	406893	444333	343535	365429
阳山县	Yangshan County	369623	403010	312133	339688
连山县	Lianshan County	62356	67770	53216	57895
连南县	Liannan County	84136	91591	76534	82820
潮州市	Chaozhou				
湘桥区	Xiangqiao District	1420413	1533595	1344996	1462068
潮安区	Chaoan District	2478647	2738429	2232206	2467268
饶平县	Raoping County	1057081	1168523	963039	1064995
揭阳市	Jieyang				
榕城区	Rongcheng District	2140347	2361276	2070341	2286575
揭东区	Jiedong District	1907107	2103876	1835300	2065372
普宁市	Puning City	3290268	3653098	3216635	3573526
揭西县	Jiexi County	1257518	1385345	1181170	1274765
惠来县	Huilai County	1188964	1306014	1111040	1156356
云浮市	Yunfu				
云城区	Yuncheng District	1048061	1141301	978140	1095909
云安区	Yuanan District	180166	200663	161370	191288
罗定市	Luoding City	985614	1106687	919354	1059259
新兴县	Xinxing County	652220	721231	566526	654464
郁南县	Yunan County	586118	646107	520352	591011

注：本表按当年价格计算。
Note: The data in this table are calculated at current prices.

22-11 各县(市、区)年末就业人员和城镇单位就业人员
Number of Fully Employed Staff and Workers by County (County-Level City and District)

单位：人 (person)

县(市、区)	County (County-level City and District)	就业人员 Employed Persons 2016	就业人员 Employed Persons 2017	#城镇单位就业人员 Number of Fully Employed Staff and Workers 2016	#城镇单位就业人员 Number of Fully Employed Staff and Workers 2017
广州市	Guangzhou				
越秀区	Yuexiu District	897516	897889	544120	531434
海珠区	Haizhu District	646670	657222	289123	272996
荔湾区	Liwan District	343169	346261	148488	152707
天河区	Tianhe District	1057315	1162029	645934	697349
白云区	Baiyun District	1167551	1239787	332341	327616
黄埔区	Huangpu District	786420	794302	505809	508473
番禺区	Panyu District	1134721	1153538	249267	248341
花都区	Huadu District	752003	752755	163122	174467
南沙区	Nansha District	459126	493835	163655	188218
从化区	Conghua District	408821	416121	78092	70366
增城区	Zengcheng District	699268	709539	132389	119729
深圳市	Shenzhen				
福田区	Futian District		1735641	1033582	924085
罗湖区	Luohu District		752775	426728	375424
盐田区	Yantian District		133828	67076	63795
南山区	Nanshan District		1335999	727431	800966
宝安区	Baoan District		2604625	1466506	1071478
龙岗区	Longgang District		1467674	841002	718022
龙华区	Longhua District		1114120		524199
坪山区	Pingshan District		261079		157843
珠海市	Zhuhai				
香洲区	Xiangzhou District			480614	489356
金湾区	Jinwan District			133972	147561
斗门区	Doumen District			116645	125062
汕头市	Shantou				
金平区	Jinping District	370820	371802	140544	143464
龙湖区	Longhu District	221713	222828	139612	142704
澄海区	Chenghai District	467552	468657	76336	89895
濠江区	Haojiang District	111143	112409	40144	45826
潮阳区	Chaoyang District	619492	621105	97853	104677
潮南区	Chaonan District	508234	508314	48964	51835
南澳县	Nanao County	29179	29247	5096	4738
佛山市	Foshan				
禅城区	Chancheng District	627275	629588	249717	233238
南海区	Nanhai District	1592749	1596094	466657	474560
顺德区	Shunde District	1517236	1476329	730735	678054
高明区	Gaoming District	272885	273277	154973	113758
三水区	Sanshui District	377996	379795	115146	152008
韶关市	Shaoguan				
浈江区	Zhengjiang District	181540	181910	66114	62600
武江区	Wujiang District	165156	166015	81053	82786
曲江区	Qujiang District	145697	146721	37402	35093
乐昌市	Lechang City	194173	194188	21307	20883
南雄市	Nanxiong City	182637	182669	30648	23830
仁化县	Renhua County	108948	109002	18188	18514
始兴县	Shixing County	109104	109329	23937	22225
翁源县	Wengyuan County	164629	163614	22063	21016
新丰县	Xinfeng County	96634	96970	16695	16244
乳源县	Ruyuan County	96243	96258	17752	16800

22-11 续表 1 continued

单位：人 (person)

县(市、区)	County (County-level City and District)	就业人员 Employed Persons 2016	2017	#城镇单位就业人员 Number of Fully Employed Staff and Workers 2016	2017
河源市	Heyuan				
源城区	Urban District	275098	290702	142418	144774
东源县	Dongyuan County	193074	194256	23838	25057
和平县	Heping County	175747	175857	26202	27750
龙川县	Longchuan County	299118	301488	40729	39050
紫金县	Zijin County	291225	296374	30035	29016
连平县	Lianping County	149892	151514	15763	15385
梅州市	Meizhou				
梅江区	Meijiang District	194854	202607	74542	79001
梅县区	Meixian District	263255	268869	37811	36583
兴宁市	Xingning City	520086	520656	54772	50743
平远县	Pingyuan County	121016	120022	15549	14281
蕉岭县	Jiaoling County	116189	123874	15357	16186
大埔县	Dabu County	204441	204465	18845	19655
丰顺县	Fengshun County	246777	246850	28909	31592
五华县	Wuhua County	476789	478128	43420	43261
惠州市	Huizhou				
惠城区	Huicheng District	588242	595307	201552	204835
惠阳区	Huiyang District	367971	386108	166400	185504
惠东县	Huidong County	572654	572393	65455	64054
博罗县	Boluo County	635442	635081	157673	161500
龙门县	Longmen County	171816	174415	25542	25642
汕尾市	Shanwei				
市城区	Urban District	236606	225992	91536	81399
陆丰市	Lufeng City	518298	516881	71693	67764
海丰县	Haifeng County	356320	355122	62397	42871
陆河县	Luhe County	99771	104083	11938	11987
东莞市	Dongguan	6539724	6603923	2312387	2423988
中山市	Zhongshan	2130132	2121813	809462	778995
江门市	Jiangmen				
蓬江区	Pengjiang District	403160	420099	177004	168640
江海区	Jianghai District	145061	148031	57124	56832
新会区	Xinhui District	464130	466986	98411	95667
台山市	Taishan City	530840	531383	71039	66575
开平市	Kaiping City	408744	411988	81403	80871
鹤山市	Heshan City	275512	275288	70087	68065
恩平市	Enping City	213220	195619	40287	30477
阳江市	Yangjiang				
江城区	Jiangcheng District	226191	227214	81085	84598
阳东区	Yangdong District	255491	255434	50520	45086
阳春市	Yangchun City	446204	446977	60745	58937
阳西县	Yangxi County	258138	258308	43561	41725

22−11 续表 2 continued

单位：人 (person)

县(市、区)	County (County-level City and District)	就业人员 Employed Persons 2016	2017	#城镇单位就业人员 Number of Fully Employed Staff and Workers 2016	2017
湛江市	Zhanjiang				
赤坎区	Chikan District	143680	143750	57824	57350
霞山区	Xiashan District	238365	236613	98181	95660
麻章区	Mazhang District	158276	158876	28021	20625
坡头区	Potou District	184732	187467	22829	22923
雷州市	Leizhou City	700300	713803	54451	53470
廉江市	Lianjiang County	592016	597725	82418	82448
吴川市	Wuchuan City	466599	463588	74970	71780
遂溪县	Suixi County	466050	453573	38177	37442
徐闻县	Xuwen County	367185	367228	35134	32928
茂名市	Maoming				
茂南区	Maonan District	402616	457557	133876	140609
电白区	Dianbai District	761622	704549	104429	120742
信宜市	Xinyi City	446701	451795	64775	66164
高州市	Gaozhou City	638715	644850	76671	74919
化州市	Huazhou City	575558	581883	84889	91148
肇庆市	Zhaoqing				
端州区	Tuanzhou District	232446	231436	129513	122938
鼎湖区	Dinghu District	100757	102896	21107	22400
高要区	Gaoyao District	479904	480817	63933	55466
四会市	Sihui City	356747	358531	110909	98550
广宁县	Guangning County	245735	245890	19796	18617
德庆县	Deqing County	192740	194206	23217	21389
封开县	Fengkai County	205008	206602	23191	22504
怀集县	Huaiji County	389791	392684	31804	31007
清远市	Qingyuan				
清城区	Qingcheng District	421107	447284	133203	141210
清新区	Qingxin District	347033	303184	61885	59486
英德市	Yingde City	566231	581351	45194	45557
连州市	Lianzhou City	231614	232263	21641	20670
佛冈县	Fogang County	165405	166206	30590	29159
阳山县	Yangshan County	198735	196193	18049	17506
连山县	Lianshan County	48420	48594	6107	5879
连南县	Liannan County	78915	79122	8875	9519
潮州市	Chaozhou				
湘桥区	Xiangqiao District	234396	234179	80661	77650
潮安区	Chaoan District	548506	551025	88695	87071
饶平县	Raoping County	462646	461882	32349	32125
揭阳市	Jieyang				
榕城区	Rongcheng District	439093	440115	89290	84673
揭东区	Jiedong District	515616	516699	73333	65177
普宁市	Puning City	910941	906713	165587	146310
揭西县	Jiexi County	473526	475724	35832	35408
惠来县	Huilai County	410540	410189	49320	47040
云浮市	Yunfu				
云城区	Yuncheng District	157109	157485	28901	29929
云安区	Yuanan District	144537	144549	15588	14033
罗定市	Luoding City	536898	537993	59975	54443
新兴县	Xinxing County	246743	246855	65562	51673
郁南县	Yunan County	234440	234459	26955	23490

注：本表按当年价格计算。
Note: The data in this table are calculated at current prices.

22−12 各县(市、区)城镇单位就业人员工资总额及平均工资
Total Wages and Average Wage of Fully Employed Staff and Workers by County (County-level City and District)

县(市、区)	County (County-level City and District)	工资总额（万元） Total Wages (10000yuan)		平均工资（元） AverageWage (yuan)	
		2016	2017	2016	2017
广州市	Guangzhou				
越秀区	Yuexiu District	4510073	5007410	84338	92964
海珠区	Haizhu District	2551392	2799851	89429	103175
荔湾区	Liwan District	1331154	1473714	89245	96938
天河区	Tianhe District	6788189	7861222	106579	114940
白云区	Baiyun District	3126473	3427683	94281	105155
黄埔区	Huangpu District	4618265	5030496	90137	98916
番禺区	Panyu District	1836191	2009542	72167	80208
花都区	Huadu District	1140064	1315382	70477	77376
南沙区	Nansha District	1217973	1537035	75110	81511
从化区	Conghua District	469149	483992	60809	68814
增城区	Zengcheng District	949057	1037606	71721	86674
深圳市	Shenzhen				
福田区	Futian District	9855035	10382710	96493	114957
罗湖区	Luohu District	4296534	4262460	101620	114072
盐田区	Yantian District	603024	633398	86117	96534
南山区	Nanshan District	8618965	10172822	119774	128508
宝安区	Baoan District	10060637	7857706	66896	72448
龙岗区	Longgang District	7611092	7580532	89609	103942
龙华区	Longhua District		3787171		72855
坪山区	Pingshan District		1155326		74827
珠海市	Zhuhai				
香洲区	Xiangzhou District	3786022	4134903	79762	85159
金湾区	Jinwan District	917236	1074467	68086	73141
斗门区	Doumen District	715488	854959	60352	69801
汕头市	Shantou				
金平区	Jinping District	728945	825027	52442	57923
龙湖区	Longhu District	799150	932610	58739	65353
澄海区	Chenghai District	441415	584563	58342	65355
濠江区	Haojiang District	265878	320231	66948	77581
潮阳区	Chaoyang District	482291	493772	49118	48767
潮南区	Chaonan District	283430	297228	57630	58852
南澳县	Nanao County	31044	31080	61121	65336
佛山市	Foshan				
禅城区	Chancheng District	1872809	19025115	74902	81254
南海区	Nanhai District	3091592	34239250	65823	71749
顺德区	Shunde District	5067584	50159984	69033	74150
高明区	Gaoming District	848615	6962233	55341	61789
三水区	Sanshui District	670548	8981969	58135	59736
韶关市	Shaoguan				
浈江区	Zhengjiang District	458723	452325	68864	72713
武江区	Wujiang District	516221	559422	64295	67174
曲江区	Qujiang District	253495	268567	67390	75375
乐昌市	Lechang City	107625		51119	
南雄市	Nanxiong City	158939		52781	
仁化县	Renhua County	98643		53751	
始兴县	Shixing County	121102		50457	
翁源县	Wengyuan County	109476		54199	
新丰县	Xinfeng County	81046		49000	
乳源县	Ruyuan County	100616		58569	

22-12 续表 1 continued

县(市、区)	County (County-level City and District)	工资总额（万元） Total Wages (10000yuan)		平均工资（元） AverageWage (yuan)	
		2016	2017	2016	2017
河源市	Heyuan				
源城区	Urban District	830769	883213	57668	62198
东源县	Dongyuan County	122307	146191	52110	58528
和平县	Heping County	143405	158422	53245	58323
龙川县	Longchuan County	224096	237082	56032	61650
紫金县	Zijin County	159387	169104	53854	59855
连平县	Lianping County	81249	87967	51939	57691
梅州市	Meizhou				
梅江区	Meijiang District	533890	624814	72057	79837
梅县区	Meixian District	246942	261985	66218	73282
兴宁市	Xingning City	246422	255959	45915	50332
平远县	Pingyuan County	81412	86458	52425	60851
蕉岭县	Jiaoling County	89604	110219	59593	68480
大埔县	Dabu County	117737	134751	62549	68496
丰顺县	Fengshun County	174731	203576	61484	64607
五华县	Wuhua County	206162	235309	47547	54388
惠州市	Huizhou				
惠城区	Huicheng District	1460922	3085041	72059	72522
惠阳区	Huiyang District	989723	2186280	60346	71498
惠东县	Huidong County	371925	421727	57209	66876
博罗县	Boluo County	974616	1058969	60738	65505
龙门县	Longmen County	135534	150413	54011	58481
汕尾市	Shanwei				
市城区	Urban District	539117	497238	57766	59052
陆丰市	Lufeng City	345731	356666	50985	55411
海丰县	Haifeng County	328130	243805	53805	57151
陆河县	Luhe County	50315	56634	42492	45483
东莞市	Dongguan	13405375	15103237	57537	61373
中山市	Zhongshan	5310662	5304012	64697	67728
江门市	Jiangmen				
蓬江区	Pengjiang District	1262760	1236594	71669	74357
江海区	Jianghai District	336512	358804	58585	62863
新会区	Xinhui District	590465	649252	59875	67420
台山市	Taishan City	352582	386910	50209	57813
开平市	Kaiping City	447659	461609	56088	58055
鹤山市	Heshan City	379059	403054	53454	58608
恩平市	Enping City	173475	171871	49562	57394
阳江市	Yangjiang				
江城区	Jiangcheng District	448128	505094	58159	63512
阳东区	Yangdong District	261752	257225	52610	57674
阳春市	Yangchun City	305818	327591	51397	56795
阳西县	Yangxi County	210100	229851	49641	52665

22-12 续表 2 continued

县(市、区)	County (County-level City and District)	工资总额（万元） Total Wages (10000yuan) 2016	2017	平均工资（元） AverageWage (yuan) 2016	2017
湛江市	Zhanjiang				
赤坎区	Chikan District	394945	4339205	68470	75968
霞山区	Xiashan District	607066	6646123	62795	69583
麻章区	Mazhang District	136389	1274432	49123	63335
坡头区	Potou District	203079	2060257	86727	90255
雷州市	Leizhou City	207511	2190809	36722	40524
廉江市	Lianjiang County	416893	4573963	50974	56147
吴川市	Wuchuan City	340056	3297608	45952	51180
遂溪县	Suixi County	182407	1917100	48596	52528
徐闻县	Xuwen County	160193	1674679	45551	50814
茂名市	Maoming				
茂南区	Maonan District	849405	980684	63384	70292
电白区	Dianbai District	479192	606883	48728	51337
信宜市	Xinyi City	340497	365482	53458	55698
高州市	Gaozhou City	436773	489353	57056	65542
化州市	Huazhou City	433748	478144	52794	53752
肇庆市	Zhaoqing				
端州区	Tuanzhou District	823545	890887	64009	72332
鼎湖区	Dinghu District	121880	136321	55205	59835
高要区	Gaoyao District	428198	364845	67129	66251
四会市	Sihui City	623537	610532	56453	62095
广宁县	Guangning County	102675	107166	50915	56819
德庆县	Deqing County	103106	114099	43387	53407
封开县	Fengkai County	112131	118188	48655	52763
怀集县	Huaiji County	177440	180894	56026	58768
清远市	Qingyuan				
清城区	Qingcheng District	887939	1015204	68551	72528
清新区	Qingxin District	377244	392975	60456	65651
英德市	Yingde City	319874	376046	70205	82412
连州市	Lianzhou City	136975	152623	63224	73838
佛冈县	Fogang County	182794	195765	62185	67313
阳山县	Yangshan County	121786	110293	66148	62859
连山县	Lianshan County	37903	43403	62321	74219
连南县	Liannan County	60340	64253	68288	71258
潮州市	Chaozhou				
湘桥区	Xiangqiao District	502534	487243	58446	60691
潮安区	Chaoan District	445517	511363	49979	59340
饶平县	Raoping County	145590	151189	44931	47272
揭阳市	Jieyang				
榕城区	Rongcheng District	486475	505080	54722	59419
揭东区	Jiedong District	343638	319510	46227	49217
普宁市	Puning City	817028	725905	49170	49451
揭西县	Jiexi County	151918	153178	42480	43371
惠来县	Huilai County	198298	202053	40348	42955
云浮市	Yunfu				
云城区	Yuncheng District	149865	168825	52455	55202
云安区	Yuanan District	66279	88243	42741	63603
罗定市	Luoding City	305919	305165	51010	57300
新兴县	Xinxing County	336172	333942	52122	65161
郁南县	Yunan County	136201	129970	50779	55000

注：本表按当年价格计算。
Note: The data in this table are calculated at current prices.

22-13 各县(市、区)财政收支

Local Government Budgetary Revenue and Expenditure by County (County-level City and District)

单位：万元 (10000yuan)

县(市、区)	County (County-level City and District)	地方一般公共预算收入 Local Government Gernal Public Budget Revenue		地方一般公共预算支出 Local Government Gernal Public Budget Expenditure	
		2016	2017	2016	2017
广州市	Guangzhou				
越秀区	Yuexiu District	519197	543695	994319	1211130
海珠区	Haizhu District	499941	510094	934978	1034181
荔湾区	Liwan District	457448	463309	814835	898646
天河区	Tianhe District	659556	700381	1102089	1380855
白云区	Baiyun District	554143	560222	1056562	1372462
黄埔区	Huangpu District	1412121	1603154	1706816	2305375
番禺区	Panyu District	818151	800602	1230819	1198250
花都区	Huadu District	714556	975503	1027977	1334467
南沙区	Nansha District	691834	706608	1395151	1500500
从化区	Conghua District	245383	269187	580468	833980
增城区	Zengcheng District	730006	834038	1123429	1473522
深圳市	Shenzhen				
福田区	Futian District	1471267	1637062	2291063	2055398
罗湖区	Luohu District	938218	976259	1695761	2780283
盐田区	Yantian District	323957	336725	678758	682924
南山区	Nanshan District	1863735	2378174	2739555	2806726
宝安区	Baoan District	3814192	2853879	6836632	5637835
龙岗区	Longgang District	2994090	2608966	5102788	4306525
龙华区	Longhua District		1207981		2673273
坪山区	Pingshan District		454656		1380415
珠海市	Zhuhai				
香洲区	Xiangzhou District	359138	368143	496921	583633
金湾区	Jinwan District	213890	235054	296961	510807
斗门区	Doumen District	249638	262401	364233	411926
汕头市	Shantou				
金平区	Jinping District	100213	110022	267134	273370
龙湖区	Longhu District	150079	162318	243193	272257
澄海区	Chenghai District	199566	210510	375073	425452
濠江区	Haojiang District	57333	65850	144401	167511
潮阳区	Chaoyang District	195321	198857	642838	671819
潮南区	Chaonan District	124871	127547	518324	495013
南澳县	Nanao County	21858	23119	86657	141804
佛山市	Foshan				
禅城区	Chancheng District	768579	874484	870151	1142637
南海区	Nanhai District	2033426	2248715	2126311	2278122
顺德区	Shunde District	2018964	2229893	1918286	2246913
高明区	Gaoming District	320917	363672	346823	413853
三水区	Sanshui District	483266	543813	520344	594717
韶关市	Shaoguan				
浈江区	Zhengjiang District	32889	27318	109281	136931
武江区	Wujiang District	37776	38942	96290	120120
曲江区	Qujiang District	80715	85018	165410	218076
乐昌市	Lechang City	53010	59099	271326	322126
南雄市	Nanxiong City	58157	61168	264567	313861
仁化县	Renhua County	62767	53833	226293	207417
始兴县	Shixing County	38721	40023	159555	200849
翁源县	Wengyuan County	39774	42372	220422	271273
新丰县	Xinfeng County	30985	33030	160959	183464
乳源县	Ruyuan County	52071	56301	223451	268575

22-13 续表 1 continued

单位：万元 (10000yuan)

县(市、区)	County (County-level City and District)	地方一般公共预算收入 Local Government Gernal Public Budget Revenue		地方一般公共预算支出 Local Government Gernal Public Budget Expenditure	
		2016	2017	2016	2017
河源市	Heyuan				
源城区	Urban District	103918	105349	245869	216311
东源县	Dongyuan County	83063	88127	393239	405454
和平县	Heping County	52214	56413	345901	371840
龙川县	Longchuan County	63279	67129	514986	562538
紫金县	Zijin County	65277	69250	435347	406273
连平县	Lianping County	66760	66770	322544	285820
梅州市	Meizhou				
梅江区	Meijiang District	70293	73090	181448	204632
梅县区	Meixian District	218830	197317	511097	515465
兴宁市	Xingning City	110386	114809	608741	620180
平远县	Pingyuan County	73804	81386	230951	238637
蕉岭县	Jiaoling County	79950	87978	220543	239970
大埔县	Dabu County	96011	97028	355377	359029
丰顺县	Fengshun County	84372	92103	440441	411685
五华县	Wuhua County	69018	81618	587550	673818
惠州市	Huizhou				
惠城区	Huicheng District	389151	423893	563026	606330
惠阳区	Huiyang District	448427	483288	575852	607893
惠东县	Huidong County	367751	379443	704916	730992
博罗县	Boluo County	406323	441089	769806	800729
龙门县	Longmen County	80908	93448	291877	302858
汕尾市	Shanwei				
市城区	Urban District	33024	49993	155179	188575
陆丰市	Lufeng City	60685	67399	626181	702914
海丰县	Haifeng County	73359	76864	568965	526133
陆河县	Luhe County	26550	29753	215865	256561
东莞市	Dongguan	5447543	5920682	5992899	6676462
中山市	Zhongshan	2950382	3127571	3675692	4552228
江门市	Jiangmen				
蓬江区	Pengjiang District	240889	260385	305910	338932
江海区	Jianghai District	102545	120163	158817	147833
新会区	Xinhui District	469201	519135	640185	737191
台山市	Taishan City	243258	266888	452823	504934
开平市	Kaiping City	219510	233348	341451	364704
鹤山市	Heshan City	249661	273888	299092	395802
恩平市	Enping City	100338	105083	243958	269555
阳江市	Yangjiang				
江城区	Jiangcheng District	40149	40143	186983	172476
阳东区	Yangdong District	107081	120607	342019	300807
阳春市	Yangchun City	103842	112807	470303	528747
阳西县	Yangxi County	66173	68798	242451	291308

22-13 续表 2 continued

单位：万元 (10000yuan)

县(市、区)	County (County-level City and District)	地方一般公共预算收入 Local Government Gernal Public Budget Revenue		地方一般公共预算支出 Local Government Gernal Public Budget Expenditure	
		2016	2017	2016	2017
湛江市	Zhanjiang				
赤坎区	Chikan District	40248	35292	99840	94370
霞山区	Xiashan District	73699	81069	147455	147843
麻章区	Mazhang District	40791	43323	111070	116433
坡头区	Potou District	51937	47277	134833	140281
雷州市	Leizhou City	50255	44909	606067	658737
廉江市	Lianjiang County	113048	116928	613928	643086
吴川市	Wuchuan City	66889	67454	366065	476564
遂溪县	Suixi County	67277	69316	388142	420123
徐闻县	Xuwen County	45338	44469	309373	371445
茂名市	Maoming				
茂南区	Maonan District	61543	66606	231371	276571
电白区	Dianbai District	232899	232652	826593	780735
信宜市	Xinyi City	93196	101133	548070	582169
高州市	Gaozhou City	172115	173831	718854	720050
化州市	Huazhou City	112757	118650	530772	575744
肇庆市	Zhaoqing				
端州区	Tuanzhou District	97796	90536	181598	210073
鼎湖区	Dinghu District	62964	67071	129139	123328
高要区	Gaoyao District	148248	135275	281382	310376
四会市	Sihui City	125024	138172	268361	337299
广宁县	Guangning County	42528	44527	242959	234987
德庆县	Deqing County	53903	53687	189080	215115
封开县	Fengkai County	35913	42982	216371	223758
怀集县	Huaiji County	49439	52831	328439	390228
清远市	Qingyuan				
清城区	Qingcheng District	132991	154750	393693	386875
清新区	Qingxin District	126318	132887	355956	418757
英德市	Yingde City	156791	164227	586231	625620
连州市	Lianzhou City	62275	62852	234245	260494
佛冈县	Fogang County	84413	90259	221038	255691
阳山县	Yangshan County	41065	44033	234157	216715
连山县	Lianshan County	12259	10010	178100	102201
连南县	Liannan County	14807	12471	156006	162565
潮州市	Chaozhou				
湘桥区	Xiangqiao District	44295	38878	137402	138670
潮安区	Chaoan District	113771	120106	431285	413466
饶平县	Raoping County	80194	76769	427537	452545
揭阳市	Jieyang				
榕城区	Rongcheng District	72930	77802	155279	176806
揭东区	Jiedong District	112951	111284	414447	448605
普宁市	Puning City	201701	212252	804684	807821
揭西县	Jiexi County	43048	46048	386988	403741
惠来县	Huilai County	57671	51290	390558	424844
云浮市	Yunfu				
云城区	Yuncheng District	52287	49993	151221	172468
云安区	Yuanan District	35297	30619	133931	147451
罗定市	Luoding City	115684	124961	472007	524824
新兴县	Xinxing County	168285	175233	397352	454609
郁南县	Yunan County	57125	42538	235229	235240

附录

APPENDIX

附　录

简要说明

一、本篇资料包括部分省市社会经济主要指标、中国香港特别行政区、中国澳门特别行政区、中国台湾省主要统计指标及国际主要统计指标。

二、附录 A、附录 B、附录 C 资料来源于国家统计局编辑、中国统计出版社出版的《中国统计年鉴》和《中国统计摘要》。附录 D 资料来源于国家统计局编辑、中国统计出版社出版的《国际统计年鉴——2016》。

三、一些国际组织及其组成成员：

经济合作与发展组织（经合组织，OECD），成员国有 35 个：澳大利亚、奥地利、比利时、加拿大、智利、捷克、丹麦、爱沙尼亚、芬兰、法国、德国、希腊、匈牙利、冰岛、爱尔兰、以色列、意大利、日本、韩国、拉脱维亚、卢森堡、墨西哥、荷兰、新西兰、挪威、波兰、葡萄牙、斯洛伐克、斯洛文尼亚、西班牙、瑞典、瑞士、土耳其、英国、美国。

欧洲联盟（欧盟，EU），成员国有 28 个：法国、德国、意大利、荷兰、比利时、卢森堡、丹麦、爱尔兰、英国、希腊、西班牙、葡萄牙、奥地利、芬兰、瑞典、塞浦路斯、捷克、爱沙尼亚、匈牙利、拉脱维亚、立陶宛、马耳他、波兰、斯洛伐克、斯洛文尼亚、保加利亚、罗马尼亚和克罗地亚。

欧洲货币联盟（欧元区，Euro Area），成员国有 19 个：德国、比利时、奥地利、荷兰、法国、意大利、西班牙、葡萄牙、卢森堡、爱尔兰、芬兰、希腊、斯洛文尼亚、塞浦路斯、马耳他、斯洛伐克、爱沙尼亚、拉脱维亚和立陶宛。

东南亚国家联盟（东盟，ASEAN），成员国有 10 个：菲律宾、马来西亚、泰国、新加坡、印度尼西亚、文莱（1984 年）、越南（1995 年）、缅甸（1997 年）、老挝（1997 年）和柬埔寨（1999 年）。

北美自由贸易区（NAFTA）：成立于 1994 年 1 月 1 日，成员国有 3 个，加拿大、墨西哥和美国。

西方七国（G7）：包括美国、日本、英国、德国、法国、意大利和加拿大。

四、一些国家(含地区)分类含义：

按收入分组国家：按照世界银行 2016 年分组标准，高收入国家指按图表集法计算的人均国民总收入 12236 美元及以上的国家，中等偏上收入国家指人均国民总收入 3956 美元至 12235 美元的国家，中等偏下收入国家指人均国民总收入 1006 美元至 3955 美元的国家，低收入国家指人均国民总收入 1005 美元及以下的国家。

发达国家与发展中国家：联合国统计司对“发达国家”及“发展中国家”没有一个明确的划分标准。通常是把亚洲的日本、北美的加拿大和美国、大洋洲的澳大利亚和新西兰、欧洲（除前南斯拉夫、东欧、独联体外）都列入发达国家。在国际贸易统计中，南部非洲关税联盟和以色列被认为是发达地区和国家；前南斯拉夫为发展中国家，东欧国家和在欧洲的独联体国家既不是发达国家，也不是发展中国家。

国际货币基金组织指出“发达经济体”包括 39 个国家或地区：澳大利亚、奥地利、比利时、加拿大、塞浦路斯、捷克、丹麦、爱沙尼亚、芬兰、法国、德国、希腊、中国香港、冰岛、爱尔兰、以色列、意大利、日本、韩国、拉脱维亚、立陶宛、卢森堡、中国澳门、马耳他、荷兰、新西兰、挪威、葡萄牙、波多黎各、圣马力诺、新加坡、斯洛伐克、斯洛文尼亚、西班牙、瑞典、瑞士、中国台湾、英国及美国。其他为新兴市场及发展中经济体。

五、2017 年各省市资料中，除广东为正式年报数外，其余各省市资料均为快速年报数。

六、本篇资料由广东省统计局综合处负责整理、编辑。

Appendix

Brief Introduction

I. The data in this chapter include main social and economic indicators of some provinces and municipalities,main statistical indicators of Hong Kong and Macao Special Administrative Regions and Taiwan Province of the People's Republic of China, as well as main international statistical indicators.

II. Data in Appendices A, B, C come from China Statistical Yearbook and China Statistical Abstract compiled by National Bureau of Statistics and published by China Statistics Press. Data in Appendix D come from International Statistical Yearbook compiled by National Bureau of Statistics and published by China Statistics Press.

III. International organizations and their members included are as follows:

Organization for Economic Co-operation and Development (OECD), has 35 members, i.e., Australia, Austria, Belgium, Canada, Chile, Czech, Denmark, Estonia, Finland, France, Germany, Greece, Hungary, Iceland, Ireland, Israel, Italy, Japan, Korea, Latvia, Luxembourg, Mexico, Netherlands, New Zealand, Norway, Poland, Portugal, Slovak, Slovenia, Spain, Sweden, Switzerland, Turkey, United Kingdom, United States.

European Union (EU), it expanded to 28 members, i.e., France, Germany, Italy, Netherlands, Belgium, Luxembourg, Denmark, Ireland, United Kingdom, Greece, Spain, Portugal, Austria, Finland, Sweden, Cyprus, the Czech Republic, Estonia, Hungary, Latvia, Lithuania, Malta, Poland, Slovakia and Slovenia, Bulgaria, Romania and Croatia.

European Monetary Union (Euro Area), it has 19 members and member countries are Germany, Belgium, Austria, Netherlands, France, Italy, Spain, Portugal, Luxembourg, Ireland, Finland, Greece, Slovenia, Cyprus, Malta, Slovak, Estonia, Latvia and Lithuania.

Association of South East Asian Countries (ASEAN), it has 10 members, i.e., the Philippines, Malaysia, Thailand, Singapore, Indonesia, Brunei Darussalam (1984), Viet Nam (1995), Myanmar (1997), Lao People's Democratic Republic (1997) and Cambodia (1999).

North American Free Trade Area(NAFTA), was founded on January 1, 1994, with members unchanged hitherto, i.e., Canada, Mexico and the United States.

Group 7, includes the United States, Japan, the United Kingdom, Germany, France, Italy and Canada.

IV. Countries (territories) are classified as follows:

Countries by Income Group According to the criteria by the World Bank, countries and territories (referred to as economies) are classified into high income (higher than \$12236), higher middle income (between \$3956 and \$12235), lower middle income (between \$1006 and \$3955) and low income (\$1005 and below) groups by their per capita GNI (calculated by Atlas method)in the year 2016.

Developed and Developing Countries There is no established convention for the designation of "developed" and "developing" countries or areas in the United Nations system. In common practice, Japan in Asia, Canada and the United States in northern America, Australia and New Zealand in Oceania, and Europe are considered "developed" regions or areas. In international trade statistics, the Southern African Customs Union is also treated as a developed region and Israelas a developed country; countries emerging from the former Yugoslavia are treated as developing countries; and countries of eastern Europe and of the Commonwealth of Independent States in Europe are not included under either developed or developing regions.

Advanced economies in International Monetary Fund (IMF) are composed of 39 countries: Australia, Austria, Belgium, Canada, Cyprus, Czech Republic, Denmark, Estonia, Finland, France, Germany, Greece, Hong Kong SAR, Iceland, Ireland, Israel, Italy, Japan, Korea, Latvia, Lithuania, Luxembourg, Macao, China, Malta, Netherlands, New Zealand, Norway, Portugal,Puerto Rico, San Marino, Singapore, Slovak Republic, Slovenia, Spain, Sweden, Switzerland, Taiwan Province of China, United Kingdom, and United States. Others are emerging market and developing economies.V. Among the data of various provinces and municipalities in 2017, all come from flash annual reports except the data of Guangdong, which come from formal annual reports.

VI. The data in this chapter are prepared and compiled by the Division of Comprehensive Statistics of Guangdong Provincial Bureau of Statistics.

附录A-1 人口及地区生产总值（2017年）
Population and Gross Domestic Product (2017)

地 区	Province or Municipality	年末常住人口(万人) Year-end Permanent Population (10000 persons)	年末城镇人口比重(%) Proportion of Urban Population (%)	地区生产总值(亿元) Gross Domestic Product (100 million yuan)	第一产业 Primary Industry	第二产业 Secondary Industry	第三产业 Tertiary Industry	地区生产总值比上年增长(%) Increase by (%)	人均地区生产总值(元) Per Capita GDP (yuan)	人均地区生产总值比上年增长(%) Increase by(%)
全 国	**National Total**	**139008**	**58.52**	**827121.7**	**65467.6**	**334622.6**	**427031.5**	**6.9**	**59660**	**6.3**
北 京	Beijing	2171	86.50	28000.4	120.5	5310.6	22569.3	6.7	128927	6.7
天 津	Tianjing	1557	82.93	18595.4	218.3	7590.4	10786.7	3.6	119238	3.3
河 北	Hebei	7520	55.01	35964.0	3507.9	17416.5	15039.7	6.7	47985	6.0
山 西	Shanxi	3702	57.34	14973.5	777.9	6181.8	8013.9	7.0	40557	6.4
内蒙古	Nei Monggol	2529	62.02	16103.2	1647.2	6408.6	8047.4	4.0	63786	3.6
辽 宁	Liaoning	4369	67.49	23942.0	2182.1	9397.8	12362.1	4.2	54745	4.3
吉 林	Jilin	2717	56.65	15288.9	1429.2	7012.9	6846.9	5.3	56102	6.0
黑龙江	Heilongjiang	3789	59.40	16199.9	2968.8	4289.7	8941.4	6.4	42699	6.7
上 海	ShangHai	2418	87.70	30133.9	99.0	9251.4	20783.5	6.9	124571	6.8
江 苏	Jiangsu	8029	68.76	85900.9	4076.7	38654.9	43169.4	7.2	107189	6.8
浙 江	Zhejiang	5657	68.00	51768.3	2017.4	22471.5	27279.3	7.8	92057	6.6
安 徽	Anhui	6255	53.49	27518.7	2611.7	13486.6	11420.4	8.5	44206	7.6
福 建	Fujian	3911	64.80	32298.3	2442.4	15770.3	14085.5	8.1	82976	7.1
江 西	Jiangxi	4622	54.60	20818.5	1953.9	9972.1	8892.6	8.9	45187	8.2
山 东	Shandong	10006	60.58	72678.2	4876.7	32925.1	34876.3	7.4	72851	6.5
河 南	Henan	9559	50.16	44988.2	4339.5	21450.0	19198.7	7.8	47130	7.3
湖 北	Hubei	5902	59.30	36523.0	3759.7	16259.9	16503.4	7.8	61972	7.3
湖 南	Hunan	6860	54.62	34590.6	3690.0	14145.5	16755.1	8.0	50563	7.4
广 东	Guangdong	11169	69.85	89705.2	3611.4	38008.1	48085.7	7.5	80932	6.0
广 西	Guangxi	4885	49.21	20396.3	2906.9	9297.8	8191.5	7.3	41955	6.3
海 南	Hainan	926	58.04	4462.5	979.3	997.1	2486.1	7.0	48430	6.1
重 庆	Chongqing	3075	64.08	19500.3	1339.6	8596.6	9564.0	9.3	63689	8.3
四 川	Sichuan	8302	50.79	36980.2	4282.8	14294.0	18403.4	8.1	44651	7.5
贵 州	Guizhou	3580	46.02	13540.8	2020.8	5439.6	6080.4	10.2	37956	9.4
云 南	Yunnan	4801	46.69	16531.3	2310.7	6387.5	7833.1	9.5	34545	8.8
西 藏	Tibet	337	30.89	1310.6	122.8	514.5	673.3	10.0	39259	7.9
陕 西	Shanxi	3835	56.79	21898.8	1739.5	10895.4	9264.0	8.0	57266	7.3
甘 肃	Gansu	2626	46.39	7677.0	1063.6	2562.7	4050.8	3.6	29326	3.0
青 海	Qinghai	598	53.07	2642.8	238.4	1180.4	1224.0	7.3	44348	6.4
宁 夏	Ningxia	682	57.98	3453.9	261.1	1580.5	1612.3	7.8	50917	6.7
新 疆	Xinjiang	2445	49.38	10920.1	1691.6	4292.0	4936.5	7.6	45099	5.8

注：地区生产总值为初步核算数。
Note: GDP is the preliminary calculated number.

附录A-2 固定资产投资完成额（2017年）

Investment in Fixed Assets (2017年)

地 区	Province or Municipality	固定资产投资（含农户）(亿元) Investment in Fixed Assets (including farmers) (100 million yuan)	固定资产投资（不含农户）(亿元) Investment in Fixed Assets (excluding farmers) (100 million yuan)	#房地产开发 Real Estate Development	商品房销售额(亿元) Total Sales of Commercial Housing (100 million yuan)	#住宅 Residential Builidings	房屋竣工面积(万平方米) Completion of Commercial Housing Area (10000 sq.m)	商品房销售面积(万平方米) Floor Sapce of Commercial Buildings Sold (10000 sq.m)
全 国	**National Total**	**641238.4**	**631683.96**	**109798.5**	**133701.3**	**110239.5**	**101486**	**169408**
北 京	Beijing	8370.4	8307.33	3692.5	2796.0	2077.0	1467	870
天 津	Tianjing	11288.9	11274.69	2233.4	2272.3	2032.9	2023	1482
河 北	Hebei	33406.8	33012.23	4823.9	4628.4	3925.4	3416	6426
山 西	Shanxi	6040.5	5722.16	1166.3	1357.5	1225.9	1970	2416
内蒙古	Nei Monggol	14013.2	13827.85	889.7	956.8	731.7	1714	2068
辽 宁	Liaoning	6676.7	6444.75	2289.7	2771.7	2452.2	2788	4148
吉 林	Jilin	13283.9	13130.90	910.1	1135.2	920.8	1479	1885
黑龙江	Heilongjiang	11292.0	11079.65	815.6	1459.7	1134.5	1651	2256
上 海	ShangHai	7246.6	7240.95	3856.5	4026.7	3336.1	3388	1692
江 苏	Jiangsu	53277.0	53000.21	9629.1	13066.9	11325.8	9582	14211
浙 江	Zhejiang	31696.0	31125.99	8226.8	12340.0	10300.3	6884	9600
安 徽	Anhui	29275.1	28816.37	5612.5	5865.8	4878.6	4748	9201
福 建	Fujian	26416.3	26110.34	4794.2	5705.2	4202.0	4267	5854
江 西	Jiangxi	22085.3	21770.43	2014.0	3592.5	2879.7	1854	5842
山 东	Shandong	55202.7	54236.03	6637.2	8097.0	6891.7	8429	12813
河 南	Henan	44496.9	43890.36	7090.2	7129.4	5897.7	6202	13314
湖 北	Hubei	32282.4	31872.57	4574.9	6258.9	5380.3	3220	8155
湖 南	Hunan	31959.2	31328.08	3426.1	4460.7	3570.8	4084	8532
广 东	Guangdong	37761.7	37403.91	12075.7	18792.8	15437.9	8196	15959
广 西	Guangxi	20499.1	19908.27	2683.5	3016.6	2635.7	1856	5171
海 南	Hainan	4244.4	4125.40	2053.1	2713.7	2473.2	1267	2293
重 庆	Chongqing	17537.0	17440.57	3980.1	4557.9	3601.6	5056	6711
四 川	Sichuan	31902.1	31235.89	5149.9	6757.1	5173.6	5621	10869
贵 州	Guizhou	15503.9	15288.01	2201.0	2240.8	1623.4	1172	4697
云 南	Yunnan	18936.0	18474.89	2786.3	2561.2	1973.7	2420	4327
西 藏	Tibet	1975.6	1975.60	40.4	35.3	25.2	44	53
陕 西	Shanxi	23819.4	23468.21	3102.0	2661.1	2215.2	2392	3890
甘 肃	Gansu	5827.8	5696.35	944.5	890.3	738.2	848	1560
青 海	Qinghai	3883.6	3819.86	408.6	296.5	211.7	441	494
宁 夏	Ningxia	3728.4	3640.12	652.8	464.1	369.3	1329	1021
新 疆	Xinjiang	12089.1	11795.64	1037.9	793.4	597.5	1680	1598

注：各地固定资产投资不含跨省投资。
Note: Trans-provincial investments are not included in the investment in fixed assets of various province.

附录A−3　居民人均收入与支出(2017年)

Per Capita Income and Expenditure (2017)

单位：元　　(yuan)

地　区	Province or Municipality	全体居民 All residents		城镇常住居民 Urban resident		农村常住居民 Rural resident	
		人均可支配收入 Per Capita Disposable	人均消费支出 Per Capita Consumption Expenditure	人均可支配收入 Per Capita Disposable Income	人均消费支出 Per Capita Consumption Expenditure	人均可支配收入 Per Capita Disposable Income	人均消费支出 Per Capita Consumption Expenditure
全　国	**National Total**	**25973.8**	**18322.1**	**36396.2**	**24445.0**	**13432.4**	**10954.5**
北　京	Beijing	57229.8	37425.3	62406.3	40346.3	24240.5	18810.5
天　津	Tianjing	37022.3	27841.4	40277.5	30283.6	21753.7	16385.9
河　北	Hebei	21484.1	15437.0	30547.8	20600.3	12880.9	10535.9
山　西	Shanxi	20420.0	13664.4	29131.8	18404.0	10787.5	8424.0
内蒙古	Nei Monggol	26212.2	18945.5	35670.0	23637.8	12584.3	12184.4
辽　宁	Liaoning	27835.4	20463.4	34993.4	25379.4	13746.8	10787.3
吉　林	Jilin	21368.3	15631.9	28318.7	20051.2	12950.4	10279.4
黑龙江	Heilongjiang	21205.8	15577.5	27446.0	19269.8	12664.8	10523.9
上　海	ShangHai	58988.0	39791.9	62595.7	42304.3	27825.0	18089.8
江　苏	Jiangsu	35024.1	23468.6	43621.8	27726.3	19158.0	15611.5
浙　江	Zhejiang	42045.7	27079.1	51260.7	31924.2	24955.8	18093.4
安　徽	Anhui	21863.3	15751.7	31640.3	20740.2	12758.2	11106.1
福　建	Fujian	30047.7	21249.3	39001.4	25980.5	16334.8	14003.4
江　西	Jiangxi	22031.4	14459.0	31198.1	19244.5	13241.8	9870.4
山　东	Shandong	26929.9	17280.7	36789.4	23072.1	15117.5	10342.1
河　南	Henan	20170.0	13729.6	29557.9	19422.3	12719.2	9211.5
湖　北	Hubei	23757.2	16937.6	31889.4	21275.6	13812.1	11632.5
湖　南	Hunan	23102.7	17160.4	33947.9	23162.6	12935.8	11533.6
广　东	Guangdong	33003.3	24819.6	40975.1	30197.9	15779.7	13199.6
广　西	Guangxi	19904.8	13423.7	30502.1	18348.6	11325.5	9436.6
海　南	Hainan	22553.2	15402.7	30817.4	20371.9	12901.8	9599.4
重　庆	Chongqing	24153.0	17898.1	32193.2	22759.2	12637.9	10936.1
四　川	Sichuan	20579.8	16179.9	30726.9	21990.6	12226.9	11396.7
贵　州	Guizhou	16703.6	12969.6	29079.8	20347.8	8869.1	8299.0
云　南	Yunnan	18348.3	12658.1	30995.9	19559.7	9862.2	8027.3
西　藏	Tibet	15457.3	10320.1	30671.1	21087.5	10330.2	6691.5
陕　西	Shanxi	20635.2	14899.7	30810.3	20388.2	10264.5	9305.6
甘　肃	Gansu	16011.0	13120.1	27763.4	20659.4	8076.1	8029.7
青　海	Qinghai	19001.0	15503.1	29168.9	21473.0	9462.3	9902.7
宁　夏	Ningxia	20561.7	15350.3	29472.3	20219.5	10737.9	9982.1
新　疆	Xinjiang	19975.1	15087.3	30774.8	22796.9	11045.3	8712.6

附录A-4 居民消费价格指数(2017年)

Consumer Price Indices (2017)

上年=100

(Preceding Year=100)

地 区	Province or Municipality	居民消费价格指数 Consumer Price Index	食品烟酒 Foods, Tobacco and Liquor	衣 着 Clothing	居 住 Residence	生活用品及服务 Daily Necessities and Services	交通和通信 Transportation and Communication	教育文化和娱乐 Education, Culture and Recreation	医疗保健 Health Care	其他用品和服务 Other Articles and Services
全 国	**National Total**	**101.6**	**99.6**	**101.3**	**102.6**	**101.1**	**101.1**	**102.4**	**106.0**	**102.4**
北 京	Beijing	101.9	100.5	97.8	103.8	100.6	100.3	102.3	107.4	102.7
天 津	Tianjing	102.1	100.3	100.2	101.4	100.8	100.1	103.2	115.4	101.5
河 北	Hebei	101.7	99.3	101.4	103.0	100.8	100.4	101.6	106.9	110.1
山 西	Shanxi	101.1	98.9	100.9	101.4	100.2	101.0	101.8	107.5	102.3
内蒙古	Nei Monggol	101.7	99.8	101.3	101.7	100.7	101.4	101.0	110.0	101.2
辽 宁	Liaoning	101.4	99.4	101.2	101.3	100.8	100.1	103.5	107.5	101.8
吉 林	Jilin	101.6	98.9	101.3	100.9	101.2	101.5	102.0	110.9	101.6
黑龙江	Heilongjiang	101.3	98.6	100.7	101.7	100.3	99.5	103.6	110.4	101.5
上 海	ShangHai	101.7	101.2	100.5	101.7	101.5	100.7	100.9	106.6	102.6
江 苏	Jiangsu	101.7	100.4	102.3	102.8	103.1	101.8	102.0	101.5	102.4
浙 江	Zhejiang	102.1	100.3	101.9	105.1	100.7	101.3	102.7	102.3	101.1
安 徽	Anhui	101.2	98.9	101.8	102.7	101.4	100.4	103.3	103.9	101.5
福 建	Fujian	101.2	99.0	100.6	102.4	101.2	100.9	102.3	103.0	107.4
江 西	Jiangxi	102.0	99.3	102.1	103.4	101.2	101.9	102.5	109.0	102.6
山 东	Shandong	101.5	99.6	101.1	102.6	100.9	101.1	102.8	105.4	101.8
河 南	Henan	101.4	98.4	101.3	103.6	101.5	100.2	102.7	106.3	102.7
湖 北	Hubei	101.5	99.4	100.8	102.0	100.6	101.0	101.7	110.6	101.6
湖 南	Hunan	101.4	99.3	101.0	103.5	100.7	101.9	101.5	105.0	101.1
广 东	Guangdong	101.5	100.0	101.5	102.2	100.9	101.3	102.6	106.2	101.7
广 西	Guangxi	101.6	99.7	101.9	102.4	100.9	102.0	102.1	106.1	101.6
海 南	Hainan	102.8	100.1	98.8	106.0	100.3	102.0	104.4	111.1	103.1
重 庆	Chongqing	101.0	98.2	102.8	101.9	100.7	101.5	103.3	104.2	100.8
四 川	Sichuan	101.4	98.6	102.5	102.4	101.2	101.6	104.1	104.2	103.7
贵 州	Guizhou	100.9	100.0	100.1	101.5	101.0	101.9	101.3	101.8	101.0
云 南	Yunnan	100.9	100.4	100.2	100.8	100.1	101.3	101.1	104.3	101.6
西 藏	Tibet	101.6	102.0	102.3	101.6	100.6	100.8	101.1	102.7	100.4
陕 西	Shanxi	101.6	99.4	101.4	102.2	101.1	101.4	102.0	108.6	101.4
甘 肃	Gansu	101.4	100.1	100.8	102.5	100.6	101.1	101.7	105.2	100.9
青 海	Qinghai	101.5	99.9	100.9	102.9	100.7	101.0	100.8	105.9	101.7
宁 夏	Ningxia	101.6	99.5	101.2	102.3	101.9	102.7	102.3	104.8	102.4
新 疆	Xinjiang	102.2	102.1	101.3	100.4	101.5	100.8	102.7	109.6	101.0

附录A-5 农林牧渔业总产值和增速（2017年）

Gross Output Value of Farming,Forestry,Animal Husbandry and Fishery and Growth Rate (2017)

地　区	Province or Municipality	农林牧渔业总产值（亿元）Gross Output Value of Farming, Forestry, Animal Husbandry and Fishery (100 million yuan)	#农业 Farming	#林业 Forestry	#畜牧业 Animal Husbandry	#渔业 Fishery	农林牧渔业总产值比上年增长(%) Growth Rate in Gross Output Value of Farming, Forestry ,Animal Husbandry and Fishery (%)
全　国	**National Total**	**114653.1**	**61720.2**	**4987.1**	**30242.8**	**12320.1**	**3.9**
北　京	Beijing	308.3	129.8	58.8	101.4	9.6	-6.9
天　津	Tianjing	471.9	247.8	9.0	119.9	83.1	0.5
河　北	Hebei	6142.5	3491.7	160.9	1899.4	215.0	4.1
山　西	Shanxi	1519.7	983.4	108.2	325.9	9.6	3.0
内蒙古	Nei Monggol	2822.4	1383.2	99.9	1261.0	31.3	3.4
辽　宁	Liaoning	4398.5	1861.1	140.3	1505.8	705.2	3.0
吉　林	Jilin	2618.9	1174.7	101.6	1205.2	44.9	3.1
黑龙江	Heilongjiang	5680.3	3324.8	236.3	1852.0	135.2	5.4
上　海	ShangHai	261.6	141.2	14.9	40.9	53.3	-7.4
江　苏	Jiangsu	7210.4	3805.0	136.7	1167.0	1623.4	2.3
浙　江	Zhejiang	3212.5	1559.4	170.2	351.8	1052.9	2.3
安　徽	Anhui	4727.5	2333.6	319.1	1285.7	524.3	4.1
福　建	Fujian	4302.5	1810.1	326.4	669.5	1347.9	3.7
江　西	Jiangxi	3187.6	1501.4	338.7	720.1	506.9	4.4
山　东	Shandong	9298.2	4602.8	165.1	2399.7	1536.0	4.0
河　南	Henan	7913.4	4812.5	128.9	2425.8	141.9	4.6
湖　北	Hubei	6560.2	3094.0	213.1	1652.4	1088.7	5.0
湖　南	Hunan	6269.5	3408.6	325.0	1713.5	439.6	4.0
广　东	Guangdong	5969.9	2890.0	356.1	1202.3	1276.1	3.3
广　西	Guangxi	4742.8	2545.5	346.5	1136.3	500.5	4.3
海　南	Hainan	1528.2	727.0	110.3	244.7	385.2	3.8
重　庆	Chongqing	2009.4	1193.7	85.2	601.4	94.8	3.7
四　川	Sichuan	6963.8	4016.0	239.1	2326.7	239.1	3.7
贵　州	Guizhou	3389.8	2043.0	228.8	885.8	70.0	6.6
云　南	Yunnan	3808.8	2034.0	381.5	1153.4	108.2	6.0
西　藏	Tibet	178.2	78.4	2.9	92.2	0.3	4.4
陕　西	Shanxi	3070.5	2119.4	96.9	664.0	27.5	4.6
甘　肃	Gansu	1907.7	1377.2	31.6	315.3	2.1	5.2
青　海	Qinghai	364.1	162.4	9.0	183.0	3.4	4.8
宁　夏	Ningxia	513.9	320.0	9.7	141.1	18.6	4.5
新　疆	Xinjiang	3054.9	2206.1	54.3	685.3	23.2	1.6

注：本表绝对数按当年价格计算，增速按可比价格计算。

Note: the figures in this table are calculated at current prices, the growth rate is calculated at comparable prices.

附录A-6 主要农产品产量（2017年）

Output of Major Agricultural Products (2017)

单位：万吨 (10000 tons)

地 区	Province or Municipality	粮食 Grain	油料 Oil-bearing	糖料 Sugarcane	肉类 Meat	蔬菜 Vegetable	水果 Fruits
全 国	**National Total**	**61793.0**			**8588.1**		
北 京	Beijing	41.1			26.4		
天 津	Tianjing	212.0			37.4		
河 北	Hebei	3508.0			463.7		
山 西	Shanxi	1299.9			82.5		
内蒙古	Nei Monggol	2768.4			267.7		
辽 宁	Liaoning	2136.7			440.5		
吉 林	Jilin	3720.0			265.5		
黑龙江	Heilongjiang	6018.8			242.4		
上 海	ShangHai	89.2			11.6		
江 苏	Jiangsu	3539.8			343.2		
浙 江	Zhejiang	768.6			104.4		
安 徽	Anhui	3476.0			404.3		
福 建	Fujian	665.4			232.7		
江 西	Jiangxi	2127.1			335.2		
山 东	Shandong	4723.2			795.6		
河 南	Henan	5973.4			705.3		
湖 北	Hubei	2599.7			429.4		
湖 南	Hunan	2984.0			543.9		
广 东	Guangdong	1208.6		1144.1	444.1	3177.5	1421.2
广 西	Guangxi	1467.7			415.4		
海 南	Hainan	168.9			79.5		
重 庆	Chongqing	1167.2			208.1		
四 川	Sichuan	3498.4			666.0		
贵 州	Guizhou	1178.6			207.6		
云 南	Yunnan	1929.5			388.1		
西 藏	Tibet	105.1			32.8		
陕 西	Shanxi	1216.2			111.8		
甘 肃	Gansu	1128.3			100.6		
青 海	Qinghai	100.7			38.5		
宁 夏	Ningxia	368.2			32.2		
新 疆	Xinjiang	1447.6			163.2		

注：1.水果产量含瓜果产量。
2.因与农业普查数据衔接工作尚未完成，除粮食以外，其他种植业数据暂时无法提供。

Note:a)The output of fruits includes melons in this table.
b)Due to the data are not adjusted according to the agricultural census, other planting data except for grain are temporarily unable to be provided

附录A-7 规模以上工业企业主要经济指标（2017年）

Main Economic Indicators of Industrial Enterprises above Designated Size (2017)

单位：亿元 (100 million yuan)

地　区	Province or Municipality	主营业务收入 Main Business Revenue	主营业务成本 Main Business Cost	利润总额 Total Profit	应收账款 Accounts Receivable	产成品 Finished Goods	资产总计 Total Asstes
全　国	**National Total**	**1164623.8**	**988959.2**	**75187.1**	**134778.0**	**41886.1**	**1122881.5**
北　京	Beijing	20354.9	16885.4	1992.5	4327.7	908.1	45496.4
天　津	Tianjing	17019.6	14452.8	1096.0	2961.3	958.4	21936.3
河　北	Hebei	51900.5	45323.7	3118.7	3673.6	1565.9	46882.9
山　西	Shanxi	17725.3	14278.8	1024.5	2641.5	772.2	35766.7
内蒙古	Nei Monggol	13638.2	10560.8	1409.1	1841.7	571.5	30101.4
辽　宁	Liaoning	22480.2	18749.3	1001.4	3809.8	1332.6	35348.3
吉　林	Jilin	23162.3	19651.5	1129.2	1551.8	812.1	19657.0
黑龙江	Heilongjiang	10158.7	8409.9	474.7	1308.9	420.3	14816.8
上　海	ShangHai	37426.8	29997.9	3210.9	7270.4	1592.1	41414.1
江　苏	Jiangsu	154899.9	132624.2	10359.7	20767.4	5144.3	119408.8
浙　江	Zhejiang	67081.0	56126.7	4569.8	11976.2	3439.4	72966.0
安　徽	Anhui	43408.1	37691.3	2285.3	4921.4	1455.4	35510.3
福　建	Fujian	48004.3	41444.8	3208.6	4465.3	1568.8	33952.1
江　西	Jiangxi	35585.1	30947.2	2475.7	2518.0	937.0	22909.3
山　东	Shandong	142660.2	124816.3	8327.6	9334.4	4846.0	108692.9
河　南	Henan	80605.7	70581.7	5272.4	6050.2	1663.7	61143.2
湖　北	Hubei	43531.2	37066.9	2470.6	4525.2	1557.5	38363.5
湖　南	Hunan	39463.9	33019.3	1930.9	3413.3	968.7	27071.0
广　东	Guangdong	133924.4	112207.1	8864.4	20726.2	5273.8	115201.2
广　西	Guangxi	24170.3	20653.8	1559.3	1599.2	832.2	17158.7
海　南	Hainan	1831.5	1428.7	110.4	208.5	62.3	2890.2
重　庆	Chongqing	21333.2	18068.5	1498.4	2719.4	724.0	19135.6
四　川	Sichuan	42423.4	35723.5	2610.6	4538.5	1368.5	42378.5
贵　州	Guizhou	11085.7	8826.3	873.1	1041.4	361.0	14936.2
云　南	Yunnan	12058.0	9537.2	772.0	1201.3	592.7	20399.8
西　藏	Tibet	207.3	154.9	25.2	29.5	10.0	1360.6
陕　西	Shanxi	22375.0	17757.9	2185.7	2336.0	871.0	30269.8
甘　肃	Gansu	8487.6	7314.1	246.9	763.5	432.6	12240.3
青　海	Qinghai	2094.8	1710.9	73.2	341.0	111.4	6458.8
宁　夏	Ningxia	4083.6	3422.8	152.1	682.2	275.1	9425.7
新　疆	Xinjiang	9768.8	7703.6	736.8	1233.3	457.7	20372.1

注：本表为快报数。
Note:The data in this table come from flash annual report.

附录A-8　主要工业产品产量(2017年)

Output of Major Industrial Products (2017)

地 区	Province or Municipality	发电量 (亿千瓦小时) Generating Capacity (billion kilowatt hours)	生 铁 (万吨) Pig Iron (ten thousand tons)	钢 材 (万吨) Steels (ten thousand tons)	水 泥 (万吨) Cement (ten thousand tons)	农用化肥 (万吨) Agricultural Chemical Fertilizer (ten thousand tons)	汽 车 (万辆) Car (10000 vehicles)	家 用 电冰箱 (万台) Household Refrigerators (10000 sets)	微型计算机设备 (万台) Micro-computers Equipment (10000 units)
全 国	**National Total**	**64951.4**	**71075.9**	**104958.8**	**233679.1**	**6184.3**	**2901.8**	**8548.4**	**30678.4**
北 京	Beijing	388.4		179.0	374.4		197.0		742.4
天 津	Tianjing	611.0	1637.8	4374.0	418.6	13.6	83.3	53.5	
河 北	Hebei	2817.1	17997.3	24551.1	9125.5	223.8	100.9		
山 西	Shanxi	2823.9	3951.9	4335.4	3760.3	373.9	9.3		
内蒙古	Nei Monggol	4435.9	1550.4	2002.7	3073.9	438.3	3.1		
辽 宁	Liaoning	1829.3	6121.9	6393.0	3795.2	46.0	94.8	146.0	0.8
吉 林	Jilin	800.3	906.5	1028.0	2715.2	68.8	276.9		
黑龙江	Heilongjiang	917.3	438.8	410.6	2452.7	52.8	12.2		0.6
上 海	ShangHai	859.3	1447.7	2056.0	417.7	1.9	291.3	54.7	2487.3
江 苏	Jiangsu	4914.7	7132.0	12295.4	17357.3	163.9	119.9	895.0	5617.1
浙 江	Zhejiang	3312.3	855.5	3148.2	11285.0	19.7	74.0	647.3	186.4
安 徽	Anhui	2456.3	2265.4	3143.9	13435.9	233.6	115.8	3256.8	1876.8
福 建	Fujian	2200.7	937.9	2725.7	8479.4	24.1	27.9		998.4
江 西	Jiangxi	1128.8	2143.2	2524.4	8984.6	23.3	56.6	112.1	
山 东	Shandong	5162.7	6561.7	9209.8	15318.2	427.9	91.6	821.4	22.9
河 南	Henan	2739.6	2702.6	4036.0	15042.0	470.5	46.5	196.8	9.3
湖 北	Hubei	2615.5	2401.3	3609.9	11118.6	851.0	266.6	473.7	1279.8
湖 南	Hunan	1434.7	1789.9	2210.2	11985.0	90.3	51.9		32.5
广 东	Guangdong	4503.4	2024.5	4213.7	15753.0	77.1	321.1	1556.4	4338.6
广 西	Guangxi	1401.1	1310.6	3270.7	12540.6	89.2	245.2		2.6
海 南	Hainan	299.3		1.1	2213.3	60.5	4.0		
重 庆	Chongqing	728.1	384.1	917.3	6376.8	150.4	251.6	132.2	6619.8
四 川	Sichuan	3480.4	1899.7	2491.2	13823.8	425.7	83.2	83.2	6981.7
贵 州	Guizhou	1899.1	343.7	495.7	11363.3	567.3	0.3	125.9	23.4
云 南	Yunnan	2955.1	1322.1	1607.4	11528.2	299.2	14.3		17.9
西 藏	Tibet	55.7		0.1	642.1				
陕 西	Shanxi	1814.0	1137.1	1377.6	7940.3	150.0	61.6		
甘 肃	Gansu	1349.1	456.2	702.3	4021.4	25.1	1.9		
青 海	Qinghai	626.6	102.4	127.1	1462.6	463.4			
宁 夏	Ningxia	1380.9	192.0	221.8	2188.2	46.2			
新 疆	Xinjiang	3010.8	1061.9	1299.6	4581.0	306.4	2.1		

附录A-9 建筑业主要指标（2017年）
Indicators of Construction Industry (2017)

地 区	Province or Municipality	企业个数（个） Number of Enterprises (unit)	从事建筑业活动的从业人员平均人数（万人） Number of Employed Persons of Construciton Enterprises (10000 persons)	建筑业总产值（亿元） Gross Output Value of Construction Enterprises (100 million yuan)	房屋建筑施工面积（万平方米） Construction Area of housing Construction (10000 square meters)	房屋建筑面积竣工面积（万平方米） Completion Area of Housing Construction (10000 square meters)	按建筑业总产值计算的劳动生产率（元/人） Labor Productivity Calculated by Gross Output Value of Construction Industry (yuan/person)
全 国	**National Total**	**88059**	**6157.6**	**213954.0**	**1317195.4**	**419074.1**	**347462**
北 京	Beijing	2683	172.6	9736.7	65290.1	9844.4	564242
天 津	Tianjing	1563	95.2	4262.4	15231.2	3218.4	447862
河 北	Hebei	2522	150.8	5656.0	34565.9	9835.9	374964
山 西	Shanxi	2538	104.0	3566.6	15861.8	3552.6	342956
内蒙古	Nei Monggol	886	35.9	1122.2	5453.9	2031.5	312871
辽 宁	Liaoning	5186	111.4	3687.9	16509.0	5320.6	331181
吉 林	Jilin	2323	62.3	2219.0	9336.2	3834.3	356333
黑龙江	Heilongjiang	1614	59.9	1560.1	4768.7	2127.0	260553
上 海	ShangHai	2554	120.7	6426.4	41197.5	8066.5	532485
江 苏	Jiangsu	8640	894.9	27956.0	232034.2	75454.3	312391
浙 江	Zhejiang	6230	787.3	27235.8	205855.0	66565.3	345959
安 徽	Anhui	3111	175.7	6829.4	42711.3	14980.0	388727
福 建	Fujian	4029	382.8	9993.7	65711.8	16895.0	261053
江 西	Jiangxi	2372	228.8	6166.8	30726.8	15042.2	269589
山 东	Shandong	6717	349.2	11477.8	77332.7	23344.4	328732
河 南	Henan	5757	284.1	10085.5	55688.8	20226.0	355054
湖 北	Hubei	3690	264.5	13391.2	79247.7	30836.9	506235
湖 南	Hunan	2280	267.6	8422.9	54603.9	19840.3	314788
广 东	Guangdong	5606	288.4	11571.3	60247.2	16678.4	401193
广 西	Guangxi	1235	139.4	4210.1	25598.0	8438.6	302120
海 南	Hainan	152	8.1	322.8	2060.5	562.5	398207
重 庆	Chongqing	2707	239.3	7608.0	33210.8	13448.2	317907
四 川	Sichuan	4501	395.1	11400.3	58278.7	21648.3	288517
贵 州	Guizhou	1029	80.1	2933.0	18041.2	4714.1	366276
云 南	Yunnan	2656	150.5	4726.4	17318.1	7451.8	313996
西 藏	Tibet	231	4.7	147.9	352.7	153.8	312188
陕 西	Shanxi	2388	152.6	6227.5	26977.3	6981.6	408219
甘 肃	Gansu	1363	62.3	1825.4	9777.6	3031.5	292893
青 海	Qinghai	363	14.3	406.8	861.2	338.7	284554
宁 夏	Ningxia	681	22.6	549.2	2569.4	791.8	243009
新 疆	Xinjiang	1156	78.0	2428.1	9910.6	3810.2	311477

注：本表为具有资质等级的施工总承包、专业承包建筑业企业(不含劳务分包建筑业企业)数据。

Note: Data in this table refer to construction enterprises with qualification grade of main contractor and professional contractors(not including labor subcontracting construction enterprises)

附录A−10　客运量和旅客周转量（2017年）

Passenger Traffic and Passenger-kilometers (2017)

地 区	Province or Municipality	客运量（万人）Passenger Traffic (10000 Persons)	铁路 Railways	公路 Highways	水运 Waterways	旅客周转量（亿人公里）Passenger-kilometers (100 million kilometers)	铁路 Railways	公路 Highways	水运 Waterways
全　国	**National Total**	**1848620.1**	**308379.3**	**1456784.3**	**28300.3**	**32812.8**	**13456.9**	**9765.2**	**77.7**
北　京	Beijing	58871.0	13930.8	44940.1		253.2	153.8	99.4	
天　津	Tianjing	17440.2	4792.0	12538.0	110.2	266.9	193.9	72.8	0.2
河　北	Hebei	50022.5	11526.9	38494.0	1.7	1282.8	1042.7	239.9	0.1
山　西	Shanxi	25155.1	7664.3	17333.0	157.8	373.8	223.3	150.4	0.1
内蒙古	Nei Monggol	14867.0	5446.0	9421.0		362.7	220.0	142.7	
辽　宁	Liaoning	72482.6	14265.6	57665.0	552.0	939.8	634.9	298.9	6.1
吉　林	Jilin	32989.1	7662.8	25203.0	123.3	425.4	262.2	163.0	0.2
黑龙江	Heilongjiang	34669.5	10411.5	23917.0	341.0	452.0	274.6	177.1	0.4
上　海	ShangHai	15484.9	11616.7	3420.0	448.3	224.8	107.3	116.7	0.8
江　苏	Jiangsu	126782.7	19785.5	104566.0	2431.2	1515.3	765.2	746.9	3.2
浙　江	Zhejiang	104496.7	20114.1	80099.0	4283.6	1096.0	658.2	431.6	6.3
安　徽	Anhui	69105.2	11487.2	57365.0	253.0	1153.7	746.2	407.1	0.4
福　建	Fujian	51133.7	11624.2	37584.8	1924.6	604.2	373.6	227.8	2.8
江　西	Jiangxi	62997.2	10223.7	52506.0	267.5	1000.3	722.7	277.3	0.3
山　东	Shandong	65299.4	14151.5	49111.0	2036.9	1247.3	754.1	481.0	12.1
河　南	Henan	114350.8	15252.3	98753.0	345.5	1761.7	1024.5	736.6	0.6
湖　北	Hubei	103143.8	15747.2	86772.0	624.6	1278.1	791.8	482.3	4.1
湖　南	Hunan	114936.5	12872.3	100390.2	1674.0	1500.5	970.5	526.6	3.5
广　东	Guangdong	148549.0	28476.0	105919.0	2733.0	4140.3	872.1	1129.5	10.9
广　西	Guangxi	48578.3	9838.4	38083.0	656.9	778.3	404.6	370.4	3.3
海　南	Hainan	14659.9	2673.9	10107.0	1879.0	129.3	47.9	77.5	3.8
重　庆	Chongqing	60521.9	6349.3	53307.0	865.6	496.3	201.1	289.5	5.7
四　川	Sichuan	109093.0	12630.9	94098.0	2364.1	881.5	358.0	521.3	2.2
贵　州	Guizhou	91803.3	5796.5	83809.0	2197.9	720.1	249.5	463.9	6.7
云　南	Yunnan	44621.5	4753.5	38569.0	1299.0	453.4	142.2	308.3	2.9
西　藏	Tibet	1319.2	320.2	999.0		44.8	18.1	26.7	
陕　西	Shanxi	67880.4	8907.9	58579.5	393.0	760.9	471.0	289.2	0.7
甘　肃	Gansu	42637.6	4467.5	38079.7	90.4	619.6	371.7	247.8	0.2
青　海	Qinghai	6273.8	1134.5	5069.7	69.7	136.8	87.0	49.8	0.1
宁　夏	Ningxia	7345.5	650.4	6518.0	177.1	99.2	43.3	55.8	0.1
新　疆	Xinjiang	27083.4	3515.4	23568.0		428.5	271.0	157.6	
不分地区	Not Classified by Region	55156.1				9513.0			

注：不分地区合计为民航完成数。
Notes: The total passenger-kilometers not classified by rigion refers to that completed by civil aviation.

附录A－11　货运量和货物周转量(2017年)

Freight Traffic and Freight Ton_Kilometers (2017)

地　区	Province or Municipality	货运量 (万吨) Freight volume (10000 tons)	铁路 Railways	公路 Highways	水运 Waterways	货物周转量 (亿吨公里) Turnover of goods (100 million tons)	铁路 Railways	公路 Highways	水运 Waterways
全　国	**National Total**	**4804850.4**	**368864.8**	**3686857.6**	**667846.0**	**197372.4**	**26962.2**	**66771.5**	**98611.2**
北　京	Beijing	20110.0	736.4	19373.7		958.4	799.2	159.2	
天　津	Tianjing	51800.5	8735.8	34720.0	8344.7	2169.5	480.5	398.0	1291.1
河　北	Hebei	228853.7	17100.3	207340.3	4413.2	13381.6	4278.4	7899.3	1203.9
山　西	Shanxi	189516.1	74615.9	114880.0	20.2	4185.0	2426.3	1758.7	0.1
内蒙古	Nei Monggol	213317.8	65834.8	147483.0		5146.8	2382.3	2764.5	
辽　宁	Liaoning	216135.4	17740.4	184273.0	14122.0	12757.2	1089.7	3058.6	8608.9
吉　林	Jilin	49903.2	5097.0	44728.0	78.2	1634.7	482.9	1151.6	0.2
黑龙江	Heilongjiang	56398.2	11161.1	44127.0	1110.1	1657.7	737.2	913.5	7.1
上　海	ShangHai	96850.1	487.9	39743.0	56619.2	24998.7	10.1	297.9	24690.7
江　苏	Jiangsu	220532.3	5949.3	128915.0	85668.0	9057.6	297.5	2377.9	6382.2
浙　江	Zhejiang	242504.1	4071.0	151920.1	86513.1	10106.2	215.8	1821.2	8069.2
安　徽	Anhui	403425.8	8939.8	280471.0	114015.0	11429.8	747.0	5179.7	5503.1
福　建	Fujian	132227.3	3175.4	95598.8	33453.1	6779.8	135.9	1214.0	5429.8
江　西	Jiangxi	154437.3	4871.1	138074.0	11492.2	4217.3	532.5	3433.0	251.9
山　东	Shandong	327006.5	22295.2	288052.0	16659.3	9719.5	1310.8	6650.2	1758.4
河　南	Henan	230113.7	10086.9	207066.0	12960.7	8228.7	1966.6	5341.7	920.5
湖　北	Hubei	188107.1	4252.7	147711.0	36143.4	6344.8	814.1	2741.9	2788.8
湖　南	Hunan	225551.1	4185.4	198805.8	22559.9	4300.7	813.1	2990.5	497.1
广　东	Guangdong	400601.0	7254.0	288904.0	94871.0	28192.2	262.0	3636.9	24011.9
广　西	Guangxi	174641.7	6634.3	139602.0	28405.4	4613.3	709.7	2456.7	1447.0
海　南	Hainan	21351.3	963.0	11223.0	9165.3	864.3	15.1	78.6	770.6
重　庆	Chongqing	115536.1	2011.6	95019.0	18505.5	3374.3	179.7	1069.0	2125.7
四　川	Sichuan	172922.1	6982.1	158190.0	7750.1	2696.2	763.8	1676.8	255.6
贵　州	Guizhou	96242.1	5279.1	89298.0	1665.0	1656.5	602.8	1008.6	45.1
云　南	Yunnan	129298.2	4567.7	124064.0	666.5	1825.0	448.4	1360.4	16.2
西　藏	Tibet	2203.4	55.7	2147.7		136.3	30.5	105.8	
陕　西	Shanxi	163079.1	39162.1	123721.0	196.0	3760.6	1641.8	2118.2	0.7
甘　肃	Gansu	66203.8	6052.2	60117.0	34.6	2439.7	1390.7	1048.9	0.1
青　海	Qinghai	17923.0	3051.7	14871.3		519.5	266.0	253.4	
宁　夏	Ningxia	38187.3	6528.3	31659.0		753.7	253.6	500.2	
新　疆	Xinjiang	84395.1	9635.1	74760.0		2176.4	869.7	1306.7	
不分地区	Not Classified by Region	83695.9			2414.0	7563.0			2535.6

注：不分地区合计中包括管道运输企业、民航运输企业、中国远洋海运集团有限公司下属海外公司完成量。货运量和货物周转量的全国总计等于分省数与不分地区数据之和。

Notes: The Freight Traffic and freight ton-kilometers not clssifed by region refer to pipelins ,civil aviation and that completed by companies aboroad under the China Ocean Shipping(Group)Company.The Freight Traffic and freight ton-kilometers is equal to the sum of the provinces and the not classified by region .

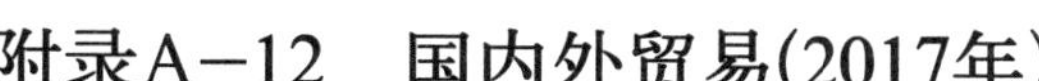

附录A-12 国内外贸易(2017年)

Retail Trades and Foreign Trades (2017)

地 区	Province or Municipality	社会消费品零售总额(亿元) Total Retail Sales of Social Consumer Goods (100 million yuan)	进出口总额(亿美元) Total Import and Export Volume (100 million dollars)	出口 Export	进口 Import	进出口总额(亿元) Total Import and Export Volume (100 million yuan)	出口 Export	进口 Import
全 国	**National Total**	**366261.6**	**41045.0**	**22635.2**	**18409.8**	**277923.0**	**153320.6**	**124602.4**
北 京	Beijing	11575.4	3237.2	585.0	2652.2	21923.8	3962.5	17961.3
天 津	Tianjing	5729.7	1129.4	435.6	693.8	7646.8	2952.3	4694.5
河 北	Hebei	15907.6	498.1	313.6	184.5	3375.8	2126.2	1249.6
山 西	Shanxi	6918.1	171.7	102.0	69.8	1161.9	690.3	471.5
内蒙古	Nei Monggol	7160.2	139.0	49.4	89.6	942.4	334.8	607.6
辽 宁	Liaoning	13807.2	994.5	449.0	545.5	6739.2	3043.5	3695.7
吉 林	Jilin	7855.8	185.4	44.3	141.1	1254.6	299.9	954.7
黑龙江	Heilongjiang	9099.2	188.1	51.4	136.7	1272.3	348.2	924.1
上 海	ShangHai	11830.3	4761.2	1936.8	2824.4	32237.8	13120.3	19117.5
江 苏	Jiangsu	31737.4	5911.2	3633.0	2278.2	40020.8	24607.2	15413.6
浙 江	Zhejiang	24308.5	3779.0	2868.9	910.0	25604.2	19445.9	6158.2
安 徽	Anhui	11192.6	536.4	304.8	231.5	3631.6	2065.2	1566.4
福 建	Fujian	13013.0	1710.3	1049.3	661.0	11590.8	7114.1	4476.7
江 西	Jiangxi	7448.1	444.7	326.9	117.8	3020.0	2222.6	797.5
山 东	Shandong	33649.0	2630.6	1471.0	1159.5	17823.9	9965.4	7858.5
河 南	Henan	19666.8	776.1	470.3	305.8	5232.8	3171.8	2061.0
湖 北	Hubei	17394.1	463.1	305.0	158.1	3134.3	2064.1	1070.2
湖 南	Hunan	14854.9	360.4	231.8	128.7	2434.6	1565.8	868.8
广 东	Guangdong	38200.1	10066.8	6228.7	3838.1	68168.9	42192.9	25976.0
广 西	Guangxi	7813.0	572.1	274.6	297.5	3866.3	1855.2	2011.1
海 南	Hainan	1618.8	103.7	43.7	60.0	702.4	295.7	406.7
重 庆	Chongqing	8067.7	666.0	426.0	240.0	4508.2	2883.7	1624.5
四 川	Sichuan	17480.5	681.2	375.5	305.7	4605.9	2538.5	2067.4
贵 州	Guizhou	4154.0	81.6	57.9	23.7	551.1	391.3	159.9
云 南	Yunnan	6423.1	235.1	115.4	119.7	1586.4	779.3	807.1
西 藏	Tibet	523.3	8.7	4.4	4.3	58.9	29.5	29.3
陕 西	Shanxi	8236.4	401.4	245.6	155.9	2715.2	1660.0	1055.1
甘 肃	Gansu	3426.6	50.6	18.3	32.2	341.7	123.8	218.0
青 海	Qinghai	839.0	6.6	4.2	2.3	44.4	28.7	15.7
宁 夏	Ningxia	930.4	50.4	36.5	13.9	341.3	247.7	93.6
新 疆	Xinjiang	3044.6	206.6	177.3	29.3	1398.4	1200.4	198.0

附录B-1 中国香港特别行政区主要社会经济指标
Main Statistical Indicators of Hong Kong Special Administrative Region

指 标	Item	2000	2010	2016	2017
本地生产总值	**Gross Domestic Product (GDP)**				
按2015年环比物量计算①	At 2015 Link Ratios①				
本地生产总值年增长率 (%)	Annual Growth Rate (%)	7.7	6.8	2.1	3.8
本地生产总值 (亿港元)	GDP (HKD 100 million)	13915	20740	24495	25432
人均本地生产总值 (港元)	Per Capita GDP (HKD)	208780	295264	333879	344060
按当年价格计算	At Current Prices				
本地生产总值年增长率 (%)	Annual Growth Rate (%)	4.0	7.1	3.9	6.9
本地生产总值 (亿港元)	GDP (HKD 100 million)	13375	17763	24907	26626
人均本地生产总值 (港元)	Per Capita GDP (HKD)	200675	252887	339490	360220
人口及生命统计	**Population and Vital Events**				
年中人口 (万人)	Mid-year Population (10000 persons)	666.5	702.4	733.7	739.2
粗出生率 (‰)	Crude Birth Rate (‰)	8.1	12.6	8.3	7.7
粗死亡率 (‰)	Crude Death Rate (‰)	5.1	6.0	6.4	6.3
劳动、就业⑥	**Labor and Employment⑥**				
劳动人口 (万人)	Labor Force (10000 persons)	337.4	363.1	392.0	394.7
劳动人口参与率 (%)		61.4	59.6	61.1	61.1
失业率 (%)	Unemployment Rate (%)	4.9	4.3	3.4	3.1
政府收支、货币、金融(亿港元)	**Public Accounts, Money and Finance(HKD 100 million)**				
政府收入总额②	Total Government Revenue ②	2251	3765	5731	6124
政府支出总额②	Total Government Expenditure ②	2329	3014	4621	4744
货币供应量M3	Money Supply M3	36928	71563	125513	138038
居民消费物价指数 (2014年10月至2015年9月=100)	**Consumer Price Index** (Oct. 2014 to Sep. 2015 = 100)				
综合消费物价指数	Composite Consumer Price Index	78.4	81.8	103.0	104.5
工业生产	**Industrial Production**				
工业生产指数③(2008年=100)	Index of Industrial Production③ (2008=100)		95.0	92.7	93.1
工业电力消费量 (万亿焦耳)	Industrial Electricity Consumption (terajoules)	17769	11080	11252	11196
工业煤气消费量 (万亿焦耳)	Industrial Gas Consumption (terajoules)	982	917	1477	1569
运输、旅游	**Transport and Tourism**				
进出香港的货物					
总卸下 (万吨)		13035	17282	16669	19086
总装上 (万吨)		8692	12882	11647	11777
集装箱吞吐量④ (万标准集装箱单位)	Volume of Containers Handled④ (10000 TEUs)	1810	2370	1981	2077
访港旅客⑤ (万人次)	Visitor Arrivals ⑤ (10000 person-times)	1306	3603	5665	5847
酒店入住率 (%)	Hotel Room Occupancy Rate (%)	83	87	87	89
对外商品贸易	**External Merchandise Trade**				
港产品出口 (亿港元)	Domestic Exports (HKD 100 million)	1810	695	429	435
转口 (亿港元)	Re-exports (HKD 100 million)	13917	29615	35454	38324
进口 (亿港元)	Imports (HKD 100 million)	16580	33648	40084	43570
教育	**Education**				
小学学生人数 (人)	Student Enrolment in Primary Schools (person)	493979	331112	349008	362049
中学学生人数 (人)	Student Enrolment in Secondary Schools (person)	466710	452581	339437	332030

注：本表数据由香港特别行政区政府统计处提供，国家统计局整理编辑。
①以环比物量计算的本地生产总值及其组成部分的参照年为2015年。
②财政年度数字。指当年4月1日至第二年3月31日。
③自2005年统计年度开始，所有工业生产指数均按《香港标准行业分类2.0版》编制。
④1998年起，采用一系列新的集装箱吞吐量数字，与1998年以前的数字不可比。
⑤1996年及以后的数字包括澳门访港的非澳门居民旅客人数。
⑥统计数字在编制过程中涉及应用人口数字。数字已就2016年中期人口统计的结果而作出了修订。2016年中期人口统计的结果提供了一个基准，用作修订自2011年人口普查以来编制的人口数字。

Notes: Data in this table are provided by the Census and Statistics Department of the Government of Hong Kong Special Administrative Region, and further prepared and edited by the National Bureau of Statistics.
①The chain volume measures of GDP and its components have been re-referenced by 2015.
②Figures are as at end of the financial year. Financial year is from 1 April to 31 March of the next year,unless otherwise specified.
③Since 2005, all indices of industrial production are compiled based on the Hong Kong Standard Industrial Classification (HSIC) Version 2.0.
④Since 1998,new figures of container throughput are adopted,and therefore not comparable with the previous years.
⑤Figures of 1996 and after include arrival of non-Macao residents via Macao.
⑥Figures of popultaion are involved in the process of compiling data. The data of mid-year population since 2011 has been adjusted on the base of the mid-year population in 2016.

附录B-2　中国澳门特别行政区主要社会经济指标
Main Statistical Indicators of Macao Special Administrative Region

指　标	Item	2000	2010	2016	2017
本地生产总值①	**Gross Domestic Product①**	**(GDP)**			
以2015年环比物量计算	At 2015 Link Ratios				
本地生产总值实际增长率（支出法） (%)	Real Growth Rate of GDP by Expenditure	5.7	25.3	-0.9	9.1
本地生产总值 (亿澳门元)	GDP (100 million MOP)	1084.4	3163.7	3590.9	3917.5
人均本地生产总值(万澳门元)	Per Capita GDP (10000 MOP)	25.2	58.9	55.6	60.4
按当年价格计算	At Current Prices				
本地生产总值名义增长率（支出法） (%)	Nominal Growth Rate of GDP by Expenditure	4.0	31.3	…	11.6
本地生产总值 (亿澳门元)	GDP (100 million MOP)	539.4	2250.5	3622.7	4042.0
人均本地生产总值(万澳门元)	Per Capita GDP (10000 MOP)	12.5	41.9	56.1	62.3
人口及生命统计	**Population and Vital Events**				
年中人口 (万人)	Mid-year Estimates of Population (10000 persons)	43.1	53.7	65.3	64.8
出生率 (‰)	Crude Birth Rate (‰)	8.9	9.5	11.0	10.1
死亡率 (‰)	Crude Death Rate (‰)	3.1	3.3	3.4	3.3
劳动、就业②	**Labor②**				
劳动人口 (万人)	Labor Force (10000 persons)	20.9	32.4	39.7	38.7
失业率 (%)	Unemployment Rate (%)	6.8	2.8	1.9	2.0
对外商品贸易	**External Trade**				
出口 (亿澳门元)	Exports (100 million MOP)	203.8	69.6	100.5	112.8
本地产品出口 (亿澳门元)	Domestic Exports (100 million MOP)	170.8	23.9	19.6	17.9
转口 (亿澳门元)	Re-exports (100 million MOP)	33.0	45.7	80.8	95.0
进口 (亿澳门元)	Imports (100 million MOP)	181.0	441.2	713.5	758.5
工业生产	**Industrial Production**				
工业电力消耗量 (亿千瓦小时)	Industrial Electricity Consumption (100 million kwh)	1.5	1.5	1.6	1.6
运输、旅游	**Transport and Tourism**				
进出澳门货运车辆数目②(万辆)	Lorries Entering and Departing Macao②(10000 times)	45.4	35.8	36.3	34.5
访澳旅客③ (万人次)	Visitor Arrivals③ (10000 person-times)	916.2	2496.5	3095.0	3261.1
酒店入住率 (%)	Hotel Room Occupancy Rate (%)	58	80	83	87
政府收支、货币、金融	**Government Accounts, Money and Finance**				
政府总收入① (亿澳门元)	Total Government Revenue① (100 million MOP)	153.4	884.9	1105.0	1180.7
政府总开支① (亿澳门元)	Total Government Expenditure① (100 million MOP)	150.2	383.9	826.3	776.9
货币供应（广义货币供应量M2） (亿澳门元)	Money Supply (M2) (100 million MOP)	849.2	2430.5	5324.8	5914.9
消费价格指数	**Consumer Price Index**				
(2013年10月至2014年9月=100)	(Oct.2013 to Sep.2014= 100)				
综合消费价格指数	Composite Consumer Price Index	64.82	80.50	108.23	109.56
教育④	**Education**				
小学生 (人)	Students in Primary Education (person)	45474	23785	28438	30169
中学生 (人)	Students in Secondary Education (person)	38156	37224	27473	26608
高等教育学生 (人)	Students in Higher Education (person)	8358	25539	32750	33098

注：本表数据由澳门特别行政区政府统计暨普查局提供，国家统计局整理编辑。

①数字在日后得到更多资料时会作出修订。

②自2000年开始包括进出关闸及路(氹)城边检站的数字。而自2007年开始亦包括进出跨境工业区边检站的数字。

③自2008年开始，访澳旅客不包括外地雇员及学生等。

④不包括特殊教育学生。第n年的学生人数是指n/n+1学年年底学生人数。2007/2008学年起不包括回归教育学生人数；2010/2011学年起为注册学生人数。

Notes: Data in this table are provided by the Statistics and Census Services of the Government of Macao Special Administrative Region, and further prepared and edited by the National Bureau of Statistics.

① Figures of are subject to revision as more data become available.

②Starting from 2000,data include the figures via inspection stations.Starting from 2007,data include those via inspection stations of the cross-border industrial zone.are also included.

③Starting from 2008,foreign employees and students are not included in Macao Visitor arrivals.

④Special education students are not included.The number of students in year n refers to the number of students at the end of the n/n+1 academic year. The number of students returning to education will not be included from the 2007/2008 academic year.Starting from the 2010/2011 academic year, statistics only include registered students.

附录C　中国台湾省主要社会经济指标

Main Statistical Indicators of Taiwan Province

指　　标	Item	2000	2010	2016	2017
国民经济核算	**National Accounts**				
本地居民生产总值(新台币亿元)	Gross National Product (NT$ 100 million)	104908	145489	176824	178744
本地生产总值　(新台币亿元)	Gross Domestic Product (NT$ 100 million)	103513	141192	171521	174447
经济增长率 (%)	Economic Growth Rate (%)	6.4	10.6	1.4	2.9
人均本地居民生产总值	Per Capita Gross National Product				
新台币元	NT$	472889	628706	751934	758903
美元	USD	15142	19864	23258	24936
居民储蓄总额（新台币亿元）	Gross Deposits (NT$ 100 million)	31055	48218	60667	60200
储蓄率 (%)	Deposit Rate	29.6	33.1	34.3	33.7
人口	**Population**				
户籍登记人口数① (万人)	Year-end Population① (10000 persons)	2228	2316	2354	2357
人口自然增加率 (‰)	Natural Population Growth Rate (‰)	8.08	0.91	1.53	0.96
人口密度 (人/平方公里)	Population Density (persons/sq.km)	616	640	650	651
劳动、就业	**Labor and Employment**				
劳动力人口 (万人)	Labor Force (10000 persons)	978	1107	1173	1180
失业率 (%)	Unemployment Rate (%)	3.0	5.2	3.9	3.8
工业	**Industry**				
工业生产指数 (2011年＝100)	Index of Industrial Production (2011=100)	61.9	95.8	106.5	109.6
制造业生产指数 (2011年=100)	Index of Industrial Production (2011=100)	59.2	95.5	107.4	111.4
对外贸易	**Foreign Trade**				
贸易额 (亿美元)	Total Value of Imports and Exports (USD 100 million)				
出口	Exports	1520	2780	2803	3172
进口	Imports	1407	2563	2306	2593
运输、旅游	**Transportation and Tourism**				
铁路	Railways	4.6	7.8	10.9	11.2
公路	Highways	11.0	11.1	12.2	12.4
航空 (万人)	Airway (10000 persons)	2633	2543	3664	3667
高速公路通行车辆数③(万辆次)	Vehicles for Motorway Transportation③(10000 unit-times)	45381	55506	579103	591902
每百人机动车辆数① (辆)	Vehicles per 100 Persons① (unit)	76.4	93.8	91.4	92.1
港埠货物装卸量 (万收费吨)	Inward and Outward Movements Cargo (10000 tons)	56695	65540	73356	72550
观光 (万人次)	Tourism (10000 person-times)				
出岛旅客	Outbound Tourists	733	942	1459	1565
来台湾旅客	Inbound Tourists	262	557	1069	1074
财政、金融	**Public Accounts and Finance**				
赋税实征净额② (新台币亿元)	Revenue② (NT$ 100 million)	19298	16222	22241	22512
货币供应量M2① (新台币亿元)	Money Supply M2① (NT$ 100 million)	188978	309544	413018	427702
年增长率 (%)	Average Annual Growth Rate (%)	6.5	5.5	3.6	3.6
存款① (新台币亿元)	Deposits① (NT$ 100 million)	193087	310063	407174	420940
物价年涨跌率 (%)	**Price Indices Annual Growth Rate (%)**				
批发	Wholesale Trade Price	1.82	5.46	-2.98	0.90
消费者	Consumer Price	1.25	0.96	1.39	0.62

注：①年底数。
②为年度资料。
③从2013年12月30日起，国道高速公路由计次收费改为计程电子收费。

Notes: ① Year-end data.
② Annual data, of which year of 2000 refers to the second half year of 1999 and year of 2000.
③Since 30th December 2013, toll for national highway has been charged for mileage instead of charged by the number of times.

附录D-1 部分国家和地区主要经济指标（2016年）

Main Economic Indicators of Some Countries and Territories (2016)

国家和地区	Country or Territory	国内生产总 值（亿美元）Gross Domestic Product (USD 100 million)	人均国民总收入（美元）Per Capita Gross National Income (USD)	国内生产总值增长率（%）Growth Rate of GDP (%)	对GDP增长贡献率(%) Contribution Share in GDP Growth (%)		
					第一产业 Primary Industry	第二产业 Secondary Industry	第三产业 Tertiary Industry
世　界	World	756416	10302	2.4			
高收入国家	High Income Countries	484076	41046	1.7			
经合组织高收入国家	OECD High Income Countries						
中等收入国家	Middle Income Countries	268358	4909	3.9			
中等偏下收入国家	Lower Middle Income Countries	62522	2079	5.1			
中等偏上收入国家	Upper Middle Income Countries	205708	8210	3.5			
中低收入国家	Low and Middle Income Countries	271907	4451	3.9			
低收入国家	Low Income Countries	4055	612	4.1			
最不发达地区	Most Underdeveloped Countries	9403	950	4.2			
中　国	China	111991	8260	6.7	3.9	42.7	53.4
巴　西	Brazil	17962	8840	-3.6	13.6	28.5	57.9
加拿大	Canada	15298	43660	1.5	3.4	-24.8	121.4
法　国	France	24655	38950	1.2	-17.6	6.1	111.5
德　国	Germany	34668	43660	1.9	0.1	29.5	70.4
印　度	India	22635	1680	7.1	11.4	26.6	62.1
印度尼西亚	Indonesia	9323	3400	5.0	9.6	36.0	54.4
意大利	Italy	18500	31590	0.9	-2.1	36.1	65.9
日　本	Japan	49394	38000	1.0	-10.9①	21.6①	89.3①
韩　国	Korea, Rep.	14112	27600	2.8	-2.4	48.0	54.4
马来西亚	Malaysia	2964	9850	4.2	-10.7	37.1	73.5
墨西哥	Mexico	10460	9040	2.3	5.8	-0.4	94.6
俄罗斯	Russia	12832	9720	-0.2	-54.7	17.6	137.1
新加坡	Singapore	2970	51880	2.0		43.8	56.2
泰　国	Thailand	4068	5640	3.2	1.3	23.4	75.4
英　国	United Kingdom	26189	42390	1.8	-1.5	6.8	94.7
美　国	United States of America	185691	56180	1.6	1.3①	17.1①	81.6①

注：①2015年数据。
Note:①Data refer to 2015.

附录D-1 续表 continued

国家和地区	Country or Territory	GDP产业构成 (%) Structure of GDP by Production Approach (%) 农业增加值占GDP比重 Agriculture	工业增加值占GDP比重 Industry	服务业增加值占GDP比重 Service Industry	能源生产量(2014年，万吨标准油) Energy Production (2014, 10000 tons of SOE)	能源最终消费量(2014年，万吨标准油) Total Energy Consumption (2014, 10000 tons of SOE)	货物进出口贸易总额(亿美元) Total Merchandise Imports and Exports (USD 100 million)	货物出口总额(亿美元) Merchandise Exports (USD 100 million)	货物进口总额(亿美元) Merchandise Imports (USD 100 million)
世界	World	3.8①	27.1①	69.0①	1380544	942469	321800	159550	162250
高收入国家	High Income Countries	1.4①	24.4①	74.2①					
经合组织高收入国家	OECD High Income Countries								
中等收入国家	Middle Income Countries	9.2	32.9	57.8					
中等偏下收入国家	Lower Middle Income Countries	16.6	29.6	53.2					
中等偏上收入国家	Upper Middle Income Countries	7.0	33.9	59.2					
中低收入国家	Low and Middle Income Countries	9.5	32.8	57.6					
低收入国家	Low Income Countries	29.7	22.2	48.1					
最不发达地区	Most Underdeveloped Countries	26.0	24.3	49.7					
中国	China	8.6	39.8	51.6	259311	198783	36856	20982	15874
巴西	Brazil	5.5	21.2	73.3	26725	23211	3288	1853	1435
加拿大	Canada	1.8②	28.8②	69.3②	46999	20040	8067	3901	4166
法国	France	1.5	19.4	79.2	13713	14765	10743	5013	5730
德国	Germany	0.6	30.5	68.9	11975	21632	23945	13396	10549
印度	India	17.4	28.8	53.8	54181	55574	6231	2640	3591
印度尼西亚	Indonesia	13.5	39.3	43.7	45800	16526	2801	1445	1357
意大利	Italy	2.1	24.1	73.8	3669	11657	8660	4615	4044
日本	Japan	1.1①	28.9①	70.0①	2659	29554	12519	6449	6069
韩国	Korea, Rep.	2.2	38.6	59.2	4911	17029	9016	4954	4062
马来西亚	Malaysia	8.6	35.7	55.7	9464	5329	3578	1894	1684
墨西哥	Mexico	3.8	32.7	63.5	20827	11826	7714	3739	3975
俄罗斯	Russia	4.7	32.4	62.8	130568	45450	4732	2818	1914
新加坡	Singapore		26.2	73.8	65	1735	6127	3298	2829
泰国	Thailand	8.3	35.8	55.8	7874	9588	4100	2153	1947
英国	United Kingdom	0.6	19.2	80.2	10824	12292	10452	4094	6358
美国	United States of America	1.1①	20.0①	78.9①	201198	153763	37060	14546	22514

注：①2015年数据。②2013年数据。
Note:①Data refer to 2015.②Data refer to 2013.

附录D-2 部分国家和地区国内生产总值
Gross Domestic Product of Some Countries and Territories

单位：亿美元 (USD 100 million)

国家和地区	Country or Territory	1990	2000	2005	2010	2015	2016
世界总计	**World**	**225798**	**335432**	**473856**	**659062**	**746064**	**756416**
低收入国家	Low Income Countries	963	1133	1599	2900	4016	4055
中等收入国家	Middle Income Countries	35840	58515	96589	204315	268145	268358
中等偏下收入国家	Lower Middle Income Countries	9140	13348	21851	46599	60347	62522
中等偏上收入国家	Upper Middle Income Countries	26680	45167	74737	157722	207738	205708
中、低收入国家	Low and Middle Income Countries	36585	59397	97713	206621	271674	271907
高收入国家	High Income Countries	188965	275715	375586	451878	474095	484076
经合组织成员国	OECD Countries	182625	261511	356089	424986		
非经合组织高收入国家	Non-OECD High Income Countries	13277	18586	28356	49061		
中国	China	3609	12113	22860	61006	110647	111991
中国香港	Hong Kong, China	769	1717	1816	2286	3094	3209
中国澳门	Macao, China	32	67	121	281	454	448
阿根廷	Argentina	1414	2842	1987	4236	5847	5459
澳大利亚	Australia	3114	4154	6938	11429	13454	12046
孟加拉国	Bangladesh	316	534	694	1153	1951	2214
白俄罗斯	Belarus	217	127	302	572	565	474
巴西	Brazil	4620	6554	8916	22089	18037	17962
保加利亚	Bulgaria	206	131	298	506	502	524
加拿大	Canada	5939	7423	11694	16135	15528	15298
捷克	Czech Republic	403	615	1360	2070	1852	1929
埃及	Egypt	431	998	897	2189	3327	3363
法国	France	12753	13684	22037	26468	24336	24655
德国	Germany	17650	19500	28614	34171	33636	34668
印度	India	3167	4621	8089	16566	21118	22635
印度尼西亚	Indonesia	1061	1650	2859	7551	8613	9323
伊朗	Iran	1248	1096	2198	4678	3934	
以色列	Israel	525	1324	1428	2338	2994	3187
意大利	Italy	11773	11418	18527	21251	18249	18500
日本	Japan	31400	48875	47554	57001	43831	49394
哈萨克斯坦	Kazakhstan	269	183	571	1480	1844	1337
韩国	Korea, Rep.	2793	5616	8981	10945	13828	14112
马来西亚	Malaysia	440	938	1435	2550	2963	2964
墨西哥	Mexico	2627	6836	8663	10511	11510	10460
蒙古	Mongolia	26	11	25	72	117	112
荷兰	Netherlands	3143	4128	6785	8364	7503	7708
新西兰	New Zealand	455	526	1147	1466	1756	1850
尼日利亚	Nigeria	308	464	1122	3691	4811	4051
巴基斯坦	Pakistan	400	740	1095	1774	2710	2837
菲律宾	Philippines	443	810	1031	1996	2928	3049
波兰	Poland	660	1719	3061	4793	4773	4695
罗马尼亚	Romania	390	374	997	1680	1775	1867
俄罗斯	Russia	5168	2597	7640	15249	13659	12832
新加坡	Singapore	362	958	1274	2364	2968	2970
南非	South Africa	1156	1364	2578	3753	3174	2948
西班牙	Spain	5351	5954	11573	14316	11930	12321
斯里兰卡	Sri Lanka	80	163	244	567	806	813
泰国	Thailand	853	1264	1893	3411	3992	4068
土耳其	Turkey	1507	2730	5014	7719	8594	8577
乌克兰	Ukraine	815	313	861	1360	910	933
英国	United Kingdom	10932	16354	25081	24297	28611	26189
美国	United States of America	59796	102848	130937	149644	180366	185691
委内瑞拉	Venezuela	470	1171	1455	3932		
越南	Viet Nam	65	336	576	1159	1932	2026

附录D-3 部分国家和地区国内生产总值增长率

Growth Rates of GDP of Some Countries and Territories

单位：% (%)

国家和地区	Country or Territory	1990	2000	2005	2010	2015	2016
世　界	**World**	**3.0**	**4.4**	**3.9**	**4.3**	**2.7**	**2.4**
高收入国家	High Income Countries	3.3	4.1	2.7	2.9	2.2	1.7
经合组织高收入国家	OECD High Income Countries	3.0	3.9	2.6	2.8		
非经合组织高收入国家	Non-OECD High Income Countries	1.4	6.3	6.6	5.7		
中等收入国家	Middle Income Countries	2.1	5.6	7.1	7.5	3.8	3.9
中等偏下收入国家	Lower Middle Income Countries	3.7	4.4	6.8	7.3	5.4	5.1
中等偏上收入国家	Upper Middle Income Countries	1.7	6.0	7.2	7.6	3.3	3.5
中低收入国家	Low and Middle Income Countries	2.1	5.6	7.1	7.5	3.8	3.9
低收入国家	Low Income Countries	0.4	1.8	6.1	6.7	4.6	4.1
最不发达地区	Most Underdeveloped Countries	0.5	4.3	8.4	6.0	3.9	4.2
中　国	China	3.9	8.5	11.4	10.6	6.9	6.7
中国香港	Hong Kong, China	3.8	7.7	7.4	6.8	2.4	2.1
阿根廷	Argentina	-2.4	-0.8	8.9	10.1	2.7	-2.3
澳大利亚	Australia	3.5	3.9	3.2	2.0	2.4	2.8
孟加拉国	Bangladesh	5.6	5.3	6.5	5.6	6.6	7.1
白俄罗斯	Belarus		5.8	9.4	7.8	-3.8	-2.7
巴　西	Brazil	-3.1	4.1	3.2	7.5	-3.8	-3.6
保加利亚	Bulgaria	-9.1	5.0	7.2	0.1	3.6	3.4
加拿大	Canada	0.2	5.2	3.2	3.1	0.9	1.5
捷　克	Czech Republi		4.3	6.4	2.3	4.5	2.4
埃　及	Egypt	5.7	5.4	4.5	5.2	4.4	4.3
法　国	France	2.9	3.9	1.6	2.0	1.1	1.2
德　国	Germany	5.3	3.0	0.7	4.1	1.7	1.9
印　度	India	5.5	3.8	9.3	10.3	8.0	7.1
印度尼西亚	Indonesia	7.2	4.9	5.7	6.2	4.9	5.0
伊　朗	Iran	13.6	5.9	4.2	6.6	-1.5	
以色列	Israel	6.8	8.9	4.4	5.5	2.5	4.0
意大利	Italy	2.0	3.7	1.0	1.7	0.8	0.9
日　本	Japan	5.6	2.8	1.7	4.2	1.2	1.0
哈萨克斯坦	Kazakhstan		9.8	9.7	7.3	1.2	1.0
韩　国	Korea，Rep.	9.8	8.9	3.9	6.5	2.8	2.8
马来西亚	Malaysia	9.0	8.9	5.3	7.0	5.0	4.2
墨西哥	Mexico	5.1	5.3	3.0	5.1	2.6	2.3
蒙　古	Mongolia	-3.2	1.2	7.3	6.4	2.4	1.0
缅　甸	Myanmar	2.8	13.8	13.6	9.6	7.3	6.5
荷　兰	Netherlands	4.2	4.2	2.2	1.4	2.0	2.1
新西兰	New Zealand	0.2	2.9	3.3	1.5	2.4	4.0
尼日利亚	Nigeria	12.8	5.3	3.5	7.8	2.7	-1.5
巴基斯坦	Pakistan	4.5	4.3	7.7	1.6	4.7	5.7
菲律宾	Philippines	3.0	4.4	4.8	7.6	6.1	6.9
波　兰	Poland		4.6	3.5	3.6	3.8	2.7
罗马尼亚	Romania	-5.6	2.4	4.2	-0.8	3.9	4.8
俄罗斯	Russia	-3.0	10.0	6.4	4.5	-2.8	-0.2
新加坡	Singapore	10.0	8.9	7.5	15.2	1.9	2.0
南　非	South Africa	-0.3	4.2	5.3	3.0	1.3	0.3
西班牙	Spain	3.8	5.3	3.7	0.0	3.2	3.2
斯里兰卡	Sri Lanka	6.4	6.0	6.2	8.0	4.8	4.4
泰　国	Thailand	11.2	4.5	4.2	7.5	2.9	3.2
土耳其	Turkey	9.3	6.6	9.0	8.5	6.1	2.9
乌克兰	Ukraine	-6.3	5.9	2.7	4.2	-9.8	2.3
英　国	United Kingdom	0.7	3.8	3.0	1.9	2.2	1.8
美　国	United States of America	1.9	4.1	3.4	2.5	2.6	1.6
委内瑞拉	Venezuela	6.5	3.7	10.3	-1.5	-5.7	
越　南	Viet Nam	5.1	6.8	7.6	6.4	6.7	6.2

附录D-4 部分国家和地区人均国民总收入

Per Capita Gross National Income of Some Countries and Territories

单位：美元 (USD)

国家和地区	Country or Territory	1990	2000	2005	2010	2015	2016
世界总计	**World**	**4192**	**5441**	**7343**	**9383**	**10582**	**10302**
低收入国家	Low Income Countries	293	230	304	501	623	612
中等收入国家	Middle Income Countries	834	1166	1852	3624	5012	4909
中等偏下收入国家	Lower Middle Income Countries	490	554	848	1531	2068	2079
中等偏上收入国家	Upper Middle Income Countries	1146	1789	2927	5966	8424	8210
中、低收入国家	Low and Middle Income Countries	792	1086	1705	3314	4550	4451
高收入国家	High Income Countries	18619	25619	34844	39868	42046	41046
非经合组织成员国	Non-OECD Countries	8502	6073	8650	14835		
经合组织成员国	OECD Countries	19434	26658	35970	41073		
中　国	China	330	930	1760	4340	7940	8260
中国香港	Hong Kong, China	12660	26930	28890	33620	41100	43240
阿根廷	Argentina	3170	7440	4600	9170	12430	11960
澳大利亚	Australia	17220	21110	30340	46560	60330	54420
孟加拉国	Bangladesh	310	420	530	780	1190	1330
白俄罗斯	Belarus		1380	2820	6080	6720	5600
巴　西	Brazil	2710	3840	3940	9610	10080	8840
保加利亚	Bulgaria	2260	1660	3800	6910	7480	7470
加拿大	Canada	20420	22520	34120	44370	47250	43660
捷　克	Czech Republic		6320	12380	19210	18150	17570
埃　及	Egypt	750	1420	1210	2330	3360	3460
法　国	France	20660	25150	36000	43790	40530	38950
德　国	Germany	21340	26210	35880	44790	45780	43660
印　度	India	390	450	700	1220	1600	1680
印度尼西亚	Indonesia	610	560	1220	2520	3440	3400
伊　朗	Iran	2560	1760	2890	5990		
以色列	Israel	10860	18800	21220	29620	35780	36190
意大利	Italy	18610	21820	32390	37690	32870	31590
日　本	Japan	27560	34980	40560	43440	38780	38000
哈萨克斯坦	Kazakhstan		1260	2950	7440	11390	8710
韩　国	Korea, Rep.	6480	10750	17790	21260	27250	27600
马来西亚	Malaysia	2370	3420	5280	8240	10440	9850
墨西哥	Mexico	2750	5750	7810	8940	9830	9040
蒙　古	Mongolia	1430	470	900	2000	3850	3550
荷　兰	Netherlands	20060	28560	42390	53530	48850	46310
新西兰	New Zealand	13640	14070	25430	29680	40020	39070
尼日利亚	Nigeria	290	270	670	1470	2870	2450
巴基斯坦	Pakistan	420	490	730	1080	1430	1510
菲律宾	Philippines	720	1220	1520	2730	3520	3580
波　兰	Poland		4690	7340	12730	13300	12680
罗马尼亚	Romania	1710	1720	3930	8590	9520	9470
俄罗斯	Russia		1710	4450	9980	11660	9720
新加坡	Singapore	11450	23670	28370	44790	52740	51880
南　非	South Africa	3390	3140	5020	6220	6090	5480
西班牙	Spain	12220	15900	25930	32130	28370	27520
斯里兰卡	Sri Lanka	470	880	1220	2430	3750	3780
泰　国	Thailand	1490	1990	2790	4580	5690	5640
土耳其	Turkey	2300	4200	6760	10430	12000	11180
乌克兰	Ukraine	1610	700	1540	2990	2650	2310
英　国	United Kingdom	17270	27400	42770	41390	43700	42390
美　国	United States of America	24150	36070	46340	48950	56070	56180
委内瑞拉	Venezuela	2560	4070	4910	11570		
越　南	Viet Nam	130	400	680	1270	1990	2050

附录D-5 部分国家和地区人均国内生产总值增长率

Growth Rates of Per Capita GDP of Some Countries and Territories

单位：% (%)

国家和地区	Country or Territory	1990	2000	2005	2010	2015	2016
世　　界	**World**	**1.2**	**3.0**	**2.6**	**3.1**	**1.5**	**1.2**
低收入国家	Low Income Countries	-2.3	-0.9	3.2	3.8	1.8	1.4
中等收入国家	Middle Income Countries	0.4	4.4	5.8	6.3	2.7	2.7
中等偏下收入国家	Lower Middle Income Countries	1.9	2.5	5.0	5.7	3.9	3.6
中等偏上收入国家	Upper Middle Income Countries	0.2	5.2	6.4	6.8	2.6	2.7
中、低收入国家	Low and Middle Income Countries	0.3	4.2	5.7	6.1	2.5	2.5
高收入国家	High Income Countries	2.4	3.3	2.0	2.3	1.6	1.1
非经合组织成员国	Non-OECD Countries	0.4	5.8	5.9	4.8		
经合组织成员国	OECD Countries	2.3	3.3	2.0	2.3		
中　　国	China	2.4	7.6	10.7	10.1	6.4	6.1
中国香港	Hong Kong, China	3.5	6.7	6.9	6.0	1.5	1.5
中国澳门	Macao, China	4.6	4.1	5.6	22.6	-23.1	-3.9
阿 根 廷	Argentina	-3.8	-1.9	7.7	9.0	1.6	-3.3
澳大利亚	Australia	2.0	2.6	1.9	0.4	1.0	1.3
孟加拉国	Bangladesh	3.1	3.3	5.0	4.4	5.4	6.0
白俄罗斯	Belarus		6.1	10.2	8.0	-4.0	-2.8
巴　　西	Brazil	-4.8	2.6	2.0	6.5	-4.6	-4.4
保加利亚	Bulgaria	-7.5	5.5	8.1	0.7	4.3	4.2
加 拿 大	Canada	-1.3	4.3	2.2	1.9	0.1	0.2
捷　　克	Czech Republic		4.6	6.3	2.0	4.3	2.3
埃　　及	Egypt	3.2	3.5	2.6	3.1	2.2	2.2
法　　国	France	2.3	3.2	0.9	1.5	0.6	0.8
德　　国	Germany	4.4	2.8	0.8	4.2	0.8	0.7
印　　度	India	3.4	2.0	7.6	8.8	6.8	5.9
印度尼西亚	Indonesia	7.1	3.5	4.3	4.8	3.7	3.8
伊　　朗	Iran	10.7	4.1	3.0	5.3	-2.7	
以 色 列	Israel	3.6	6.1	2.6	3.6	0.5	2.0
意 大 利	Italy	1.9	3.7	0.5	1.4	0.9	1.1
日　　本	Japan	5.2	2.1	1.7	4.2	1.3	1.1
哈萨克斯坦	Kazakhstan		10.1	8.7	5.8	-0.3	-0.4
韩　　国	Korea, Rep.	8.2	7.9	3.7	6.0	2.3	2.4
马来西亚	Malaysia	6.0	6.4	3.3	5.1	3.3	2.7
墨 西 哥	Mexico	3.0	3.7	1.6	3.5	1.3	1.0
蒙　　古	Mongolia	-5.1	0.3	6.0	4.6	0.5	-0.7
缅　　甸	Myanmar	1.3	12.4	12.6	8.9	6.3	5.5
新 西 兰	New Zealand	-0.8	2.2	2.1	0.4	0.5	1.8
尼日利亚	Nigeria	9.9	2.7	0.8	5.0		-4.1
巴基斯坦	Pakistan	1.5	1.9	5.5	-0.5	2.6	3.7
菲 律 宾	Philippines	0.5	2.2	2.8	5.9	4.4	5.3
波　　兰	Poland		5.4	3.5	3.9	3.9	2.8
罗马尼亚	Romania	-5.8	2.5	4.8	-0.2	4.4	5.4
俄罗斯	Russia	-3.4	10.5	6.8	4.5	-3.0	-0.4
新 加 坡	Singapore	5.9	7.0	5.0	13.2	0.7	0.7
南　　非	South Africa	-2.3	1.7	3.9	1.6	-0.3	-1.3
西 班 牙	Spain	3.6	4.4	2.0	-0.5	3.3	3.2
斯里兰卡	Sri Lanka	4.9	5.3	5.5	7.2	3.9	3.2
泰　　国	Thailand	9.7	3.3	3.5	7.0	2.6	2.9
土 耳 其	Turkey	7.4	5.2	7.6	7.0	4.4	1.3
乌 克 兰	Ukraine	-6.6	7.0	3.5	4.6	-9.4	2.7
英　　国	United Kingdom	0.3	3.4	2.3	1.1	1.4	1.0
美　　国	United States of America	0.8	2.9	2.4	1.7	1.9	0.9
委内瑞拉	Venezuela	3.9	1.8	8.4	-3.0	-7.0	
越　　南	Viet Nam	3.1	5.4	6.3	5.3	5.5	5.1

主要统计指标解释

国民总收入 国内生产总值减去生产税和进口税净额，减去支付给国外的雇员报酬和财产收入，加来自国外的雇员报酬和财产收入（即国内生产总值减去支付给非常住单位的初次收入，加上收到的非常住单位的初次收入）。按市场价格计算国民总收入的另一种方法是各部门所有初次收入的总和。国民总收入即国民生产总值，国民生产总值是以往国民核算中使用的概念。

按购买力平价计算的人均国民总收入 根据购买力平价计算的人均国民总收入。购买力平价国民总收入是用购买力平价比率、以国际元计算的国民总收入。国民总收入中一国际元的购买力等于美国一美元购买力。

香港居民消费价格指数 《香港统计年刊》中称为“消费物价指数”。香港特别行政区政府统计处编制不同的居民消费价格指数数列，以反映消费价格变动对不同开支范围的住户的影响。甲类、乙类及丙类消费价格指数分别根据较低、中等及较高开支范围的住户消费模式编制而成。而综合消费价格指数是根据上述住户的整体开支模式而编制，反映消费价格转变对全体住户的影响。

Explanatory Notes on Main Statistical Indicators

Gross National Income is gross domestic product (GDP) minus net taxes on production and imports, minus remuneration and property income for employees abroad, plus the corresponding items from employees abroad (in other words, GDP minus primary incomes payable to non- resident units plus primary incomes receivable from non-resident units). An alternative approach to measuring GNI at market prices is the sum of gross primary incomes from all sectors. Gross national income is identical to gross national product (GNP), as previously used in national accounts.

Per Capita GNI in PPP is per capita GNI based on purchasing power parity (PPP). PPP GNI is gross national income (GNI) converted to international dollars using purchasing power parity rates. An international dollar has the same purchasing power over GNI as a U.S. dollar has in the United States of America.

Consumer Price Index by Residents in Hong Kong refers to a series of consumer price indices reflected in Hong Kong Annual Digest of Statistics. The series of consumer price indices (CPIs) are compiled by the Census and Statistics Department of Hong Kong Special Administrative Region to reflect the impact of consumer price changes on households in different expenditure ranges. The CPI(A), CPI(B) and CPI(C) are compiled based on the expenditure patterns of households in the relatively low, medium and relatively high expenditure ranges. By aggregating the expenditure patterns of all households covered by the above three indices, a composite CPI is also compiled to reflect the impact of consumer price changes on the household sector as a whole.

中国统计出版社最新图书简目

(仅供参考,以实际出版为准)

统计资料

中国统计年鉴　中国统计摘要　中国第三产业统计年鉴
中国第三次全国农业普查综合资料　国际统计年鉴　金砖国家联合统计手册
中国-东盟国家统计手册　中国农村统计年鉴　中国县域统计年鉴
中国农产品价格调查年鉴　中国城市统计年鉴　中国价格统计年鉴
中国贸易外经统计年鉴　中国零售和餐饮连锁企业统计年鉴　中国商品交易市场统计年鉴
大中型批发零售和住宿餐饮企业统计年鉴　中国住户调查年鉴　中国工业统计年鉴
中国环境统计年鉴　中国能源统计年鉴　中国建筑业统计年鉴
中国房地产统计年鉴　中国固定资产投资统计年鉴　中国对外直接投资统计公报
中国人口和就业统计年鉴　中国劳动统计年鉴　中国社会统计年鉴
中国科技统计年鉴　中国高技术产业统计年鉴　全国企业创新调查年鉴
中国文化及相关产业统计年鉴　2018年时间利用调查资料　中国妇女儿童状况统计资料
中国基本单位统计年鉴　中国教育统计年鉴　中国教育经费统计年鉴
中国民族统计年鉴　中国残疾人事业统计年鉴

省级综合统计年鉴系列

北京 天津 河北 山西 内蒙古 辽宁 吉林 黑龙江 上海 江苏 浙江 安徽 福建 江西 山东 河南 湖北 湖南 广东 广西 海南 重庆 四川 贵州 云南 西藏 陕西 甘肃 青海 宁夏 新疆 新疆生产建设兵团

市(县)级综合统计年鉴系列

滨海新区 石家庄 唐山 邯郸 保定 沧州 邢台 廊坊 承德 衡水 秦皇岛 张家口 太原 大同 阳泉 长治 晋城 朔州 晋中 运城 忻州 临汾 吕梁 呼和浩特 呼和浩特新城区 鄂尔多斯 包头 沈阳 大连 长春 吉林 延吉 四平 通化 松原 哈尔滨 齐齐哈尔 黑龙江垦区 上海浦东新区 南京 无锡 徐州 常州 苏州 南通 连云港 淮安 盐城 扬州 镇江 泰州 宿迁 江阴 丹阳 海门 杭州 宁波 温州 嘉兴 湖州 绍兴 金华 衢州 舟山 台州 丽水 合肥 安庆 马鞍山 福州 厦门 宁德 漳州 龙岩 南昌 九江 上饶 新余 抚州 萍乡 赣州 吉安 景德镇 济南 青岛 潍坊 枣庄 日照 滕州 郑州 洛阳 平顶山 三门峡 商丘 信阳 济源 汝州 武汉 十堰 荆州 宜昌 荆门 咸宁 长沙 广州 深圳 惠州 东莞 汕尾 南宁 柳州 桂林 梧州 来宾 河池 防城港 海口 三亚 成都 贵阳 黔南 毕节 昆明 西安 咸阳 延安 宝鸡 安康 铜川 汉中 榆林 兰州 庆阳 银川 乌鲁木齐 兵团一师 兵团十师

调查年鉴系列

天津 内蒙古 上海 浙江 福建 河南 湖北 湖南 广东 广西 重庆 四川 云南 甘肃 宁夏

统计方法应用/实用手册

实用SAS统计分析教程　Python数据分析基础　统计公文知识问答　领导干部统计知识问答
乡镇统计人员岗位知识培训系列教材：辅助调查员岗位基础知识　乡镇统计人员岗位基础知识
县级统计人员岗位知识培训系列教材：Excel在统计工作中的应用　简明统计分析
地市级统计人员岗位知识培训系列教材：统计报告与演示　中国国民经济核算体系（2016）基础知识
全国统计专业技术资格考试系列考试用书：统计业务知识（第四版）　统计业务知识学习指导与习题
全国统计专业技术资格考试系列考试用书：统计相关知识（第四版）　统计相关知识学习指导与习题

统计通俗读物/统计科普图书

我国20个统计指标的历史变迁　联合国工业发展组织：2016年工业发展报告
中国古代统计发展史　理解国民账户

重点图书

波澜壮阔四十年　砥砺奋进铸就辉煌——改革开放40年与时俱进的中国统计
新编英汉汉英统计大词典　中国国民经济核算体系2016　国民经济行业分类注释
挑大学选专业2019—考研择校指南　挑大学选专业2019—高考志愿填报指南　中华医学统计百科全书